HIPPOCRENE PR

MW01006135

ITALIAN

ENGLISH-ITALIAN
ITALIAN-ENGLISH

HIPPOCRENE PRACTICAL DICTIONARY

ITALIAN

ENGLISH-ITALIAN
ITALIAN-ENGLISH

PETER F. ROSS

HIPPOCRENE BOOKS, INC.
New York

Revised Hippocrene Edition with larger type, 1995.
Second printing of large type edition, 1999.
First Hippocrene Edition, 1983.

©Laurence Urdang Associates, 1982.

Glossary of Menu Terms and special American usage entries ©Hippocrene Books, 1983.

ISBN 0-7818-0354-3

For information, address:
HIPPOCRENE BOOKS, INC.
171 Madison Avenue
New York, NY 10016
Printed in the United States of America.

Abbreviations/Abbreviazioni

adj adjective
admin administration
adv adverb
aero aeronautics
agg aggettivc
agric agriculture, agricoltura
anat anatomy, anatomia
arch architecture, architettura
art article, articolo
astrol astrology, astrologia
astron astronomy, astronomia
auto automobilismo
aux auxiliary
avv avverbio
biol biology, biologia
bot botany, botanica
chem chemistry
chim chimica
coll colloquial
comm commerce, commercio
cong congiunzione
conj conjunction
derog derogatory
dir diritto
econ economics, economia
elec electricity
elett elettricità
f feminine, femminile
fam familiar, familiare
ferr ferrovia
fig figurato
filos filosofia
fis fisica
foto fotografia
gastr gastronomia
geog geography, geografia

geol geology, geologia
geom geometry, geometria
gramm grammar, grammatica
impol impolite
inter interiezione
interj interjection
invar invariable, invariabile
m masculine, maschile
mar marina
mat matematica
math mathematics
mec mechanical, meccanica
med medicine, medicina
mil military, militare
n noun
naut nautical
phone telephone
phot photography
pl plural, plurale
pol politics, politica
prep preposition, preposizione
pron pronoun, pronome
psic psicologia, psichiatria
psych psychology, psychiatry
rail railways
rel religion, religione
s sostantivo
sing singular, singolare
spreg spregiativo
tec tecnologia
tech technical
TV television, televisione
v verb, verbo
V vide (see, vedi)
volg volgare
zool zoology, zoologia

Italian pronunciation

As wide variations exist between pronunciations in different parts of Italy, we have favoured the standard accepted in the north as this is rapidly gaining general acceptance.

a sano ['sano]
ɛ bene ['bɛne]
e festa ['festa]
i tinto ['tinto]
ɔ brodo ['brɔdo]
o mondo ['mondo]
u fune ['fune]
b bene ['bɛne]
d dito ['dito]
f fine ['fine]
g gallo ['gallo]
j lezione [le'tsjone]
k capo ['kapo]
l legge ['leddʒe]
m mago ['mago]

n nitido ['nitido]
p pulce ['pultʃe]
r rete ['rete]
s sabbia ['sabbja]
t tanto ['tanto]
v via ['via]
w quando ['kwando]
z viso ['vizo]
dz zucchero ['dzukkero]
ts anzi ['antsi]
ʃ sciame ['ʃame]
tʃ cibo ['tʃibo]
dʒ gentile [dʒen'tile]
ʎ figlio ['fiʎo]
ɲ ragno ['raɲo]
ŋ smoking ['zmɔkiŋ]

The symbol ' indicates that the following syllable should be stressed.

Pronuncia inglese

a hat [hat]
e bell [bell]
i big [big]
o dot [dot]
ʌ bun [bʌn]
u book [buk]
ə alone [ə'loun]
aː card [kaːd]
əː word [wəːd]
iː team [tiːm]
oː torn [toːn]
uː spoon [spuːn]
ai die [dai]
ei ray [rei]
oi toy [toi]
au how [hau]
ou road [roud]
eə lair [leə]
iə fear [fiə]
uə poor [puə]
b back [bak]
d dull [dʌl]
f find [faind]

g gaze [geiz]
h hop [hop]
j yell [jel]
k cat [kat]
l life [laif]
m mouse [maus]
n night [nait]
p pick [pik]
r rose [rouz]
s sit [sit]
t toe [tou]
v vest [vest]
w week [wiːk]
z zoo [zuː]
θ think [θiŋk]
ð those [ðouz]
ʃ shoe [ʃuː]
ʒ treasure ['treʒə]
tʃ chalk [tʃoːk]
dʒ jump [dʒʌmp]
ŋ sing [siŋ]

Il simbolo ' precede la sillaba che ha l'accento tonico principale.
Il simbolo , precede la sillaba che ha l'accento tonico secondario.

Guide to the dictionary

Irregular plural forms are shown at the headword and in the text. The following categories of Italian plural forms are considered regular:

albero	alberi
viale	viali
chiesa	chiese
amica	amiche
lunga	lunghe
città	città
tesi	tesi

In addition, masculine Italian words ending in -a are considered regular if they form their plural in -i. Masculine words ending in -co and -go form their plurals in -chi and -ghi unless the word is of more than two syllables and the -co or -go preceded by a vowel, in which case the plural is formed in -ci and -gi. Exceptions to this rule are considered irregular.

Irregular verbs listed in the verb tables are marked with an asterisk in the headword list. Compounds are not listed in the verb tables.

Adverbs are shown only if their formation is irregular. English adverbs are considered regular if they are formed by adding -*ly* or -*ally* to the adjective. Italian adverbs are considered regular if they are formed by adding -*mente* to the feminine form of the adjective.

Guida all'uso del vocabolario

I plurali irregolari dei sostantivi sono indicati sia sotto la voce di partenza sia nel testo stesso. Le seguenti categorie vengono considerate di formazione regolare in inglese:

cat	cats
glass	glasses
fly	flies
half	halves
wife	wives

I verbi irregolari nell'apposita tavola sono contraddistinti con un asterisco nella lista delle voci di partenza. Non sono compresi nella tavola i verbi composti.

Gli avverbi sono indicati con voci proprie solo quando si tratta di formazioni irregolari. Vengono considerati regolari in inglese gli avverbi formati con l'aggiunta di -*ly* o di -*ally* all'aggettivo. Vengono considerati regolari in italiano gli avverbi formati mediante l'aggiunta di -*mente* al femminile dell'aggettivo.

Italian irregular verbs

Infinitive	Present	Past Absolute	Future	Past Participle
addurre	adduco	addussi	addurrò	addotto
affiggere	affiggo	affissi	affiggerò	affisso
affliggere	affliggo	afflissi	affliggerò	afflitto
alludere	alludo	allusi	alluderò	alluso
andare	vado	andai	andrò	andato
annettere	annetto	annessi	annetterò	annesso
apparire	appaio	apparvi	apparirò	apparso
appendere	appendo	appesi	appenderò	appeso
aprire	apro	aprii	aprirò	aperto
ardere	ardo	arsi	ardirò	arso
assistere	assisto	assistetti	assisterò	assistito
assolvere	assolvo	assolsi	assolverò	assolto
assumere	assumo	assunsi	assumerò	assunto
avere	ho	ebbi	avrò	avuto
bere	bevo	bevvi	berrò	bevuto
cadere	cado	caddi	cadrò	caduto
cogliere	colgo	colsi	coglierò	colto
comprimere	comprimo	compressi	comprimerò	compresso
concedere	concedo	concedetti	concederò	concesso
conoscere	conosco	conobbi	conoscerò	conosciuto
correre	corro	corsi	correrò	corso
crescere	cresco	crebbi	crescerò	cresciuto
cuocere	cuocio	cossi	cuocerò	cotto
dare	do	diedi	darò	dato
dire	dico	dissi	dirò	detto
dirigere	dirigo	diressi	dirigerò	diretto
discutere	discuto	discussi	discuterò	discusso
dissuadere	dissuado	dissuasi	dissuaderò	dissuaso
distinguere	distinguo	distinsi	distinguerò	distinto
dolere	dolgo	dolsi	dorrò	doluto
dovere	debbo	dovetti	dovrò	dovuto
emergere	emergo	emersi	emergerò	emerso
erigere	erigo	eressi	erigerò	eretto
esigere	esigo	esigetti	esigerò	esatto
espellere	espello	espulsi	espellerò	espulso
esplodere	esplodo	esplosi	esploderò	esploso
essere	sono	fui	sarò	stato

Infinitive	Present	Past Absolute	Future	Past Participle
estinguere	estinguo	estinsi	estinguerò	estinto
evadere	evado	evasi	evaderò	evaso
fare	faccio	feci	farò	fatto
flettere	fletto	flessi	fletterò	flesso
fondere	fondo	fusi	fonderò	fuso
friggere	friggo	frissi	friggerò	fritto
giacere	giaccio	giacqui	giacerò	giaciuto
godere	godo	godetti	godrò	goduto
incutere	incuto	incussi	incuterò	incusso
infliggere	infliggo	inflissi	infliggerò	inflitto
invadere	invado	invasi	invaderò	invaso
leggere	leggo	lessi	leggerò	letto
mettere	metto	misi	metterò	messo
mordere	mordo	morsi	morderò	morso
morire	muoio	morii	morirò	morto
muovere	muovo	mossi	muoverò	mosso
nascere	nasco	nacqui	nascerò	nato
nascondere	nascondo	nascosi	nasconderò	nascosto
nuocere	nuoccio	nocqui	nuocerò	nociuto
offrire	offro	offersi	offrirò	offerto
parere	paio	parvi	parrò	parso
perdere	perdo	perdetti	perderò	perso
persuadere	persuado	persuasi	persuaderò	persuaso
piacere	piaccio	piacque	piacerò	piaciuto
porgere	porgo	porsi	porgerò	porto
porre	pongo	posi	porrò	posto
potere	posso	potei	potrò	potuto
proteggere	proteggo	protessi	proteggerò	protetto
redimere	redimo	redensi	redimerò	redento
redigere	redigo	redassi	redigerò	redatto
reggere	reggo	ressi	reggerò	retto
rifulgere	rifulgo	rifulsi	rifulgerò	rifulso
rimanere	rimango	rimasi	rimarrò	rimasto
rispondere	rispondo	risposi	risponderò	risposto
rodere	rodo	rosi	roderò	roso
rompere	rompo	ruppi	romperò	rotto
sapere	so	seppi	saprò	saputo
scegliere	scelgo	scelsi	sceglierò	scelto
scindere	scindo	scissi	scinderò	scisso

Infinitive	Present	Past Absolute	Future	Past Participle
sciogliere	sciolgo	sciolsi	scioglierò	sciolto
scoprire	scopro	scoprii	scoprirò	scoperto
scorgere	scorgo	scorsi	scorgerò	scorto
scrivere	scrivo	scrissi	scriverò	scritto
scuotere	scuoto	scossi	scuoterò	scosso
sedere	siedo	sedetti	sederò	seduto
solere	soglio	solei	solerò	solito
sommergere	sommergo	sommersi	sommergerò	sommerso
sorgere	sorgo	sorsi	sorgerò	sorto
spandere	spando	spansi	spanderò	spanto
spargere	spargo	sparsi	spargerò	sparso
spegnere	spengo	spensi	spegnerò	spento
stare	sto	stetti	starò	stato
stringere	stringo	strinsi	stringerò	stretto
struggere	struggo	strussi	struggerò	strutto
svellere	svello	svelsi	svellerò	svelto
tacere	taccio	tacqui	tacerò	taciuto
tenere	tengo	tenni	terrò	tenuto
togliere	tolgo	tolsi	toglierò	tolto
torcere	torco	torsi	torcerò	torto
trarre	traggo	trassi	trarrò	tratto
udire	odo	udii	udirò	udito
ungere	ungo	unsi	ungerò	unto
uscire	esco	uscii	uscirò	uscito
valere	valgo	valsi	varrò	valso
vedere	vedo	vidi	vedrò	visto
venire	vengo	venni	verrò	venuto
vincere	vinco	vinsi	vincerò	vinto
vivere	vivo	vissi	vivrò	vissuto
volere	voglio	volli	vorrò	voluto
volgere	volgo	volsi	volgerò	volto

For verbs ending in:

-cedere see concedere
-durre see addurre
-endere see appendere
-figgere see affiggere
-idere or -udere see alludere

-nettere see annettere
-ngere (except stringere) see ungere
-parire see apparire
-primere see comprimere
-sistere see assistere

Verbi inglesi irregolari

Infinito	Preterito	Participo Passato	Infinito	Preterito	Participo Passato
abide	abode	abode	deal	dealt	dealt
arise	arose	arisen	dig	dug	dug
awake	awoke	awoken	do	did	done
be	was	been	draw	drew	drawn
bear	bore	borne	dream	dreamed	dreamed
		or born		or dreamt	or dreamt
beat	beat	beaten	drink	drank	drunk
become	became	become	drive	drove	driven
begin	began	begun	dwell	dwelt	dwelt
behold	beheld	beheld	eat	ate	eaten
bend	bent	bent	fall	fell	fallen
bet	bet	bet	feed	fed	fed
beware			feel	felt	felt
bid	bid	bidden	fight	fought	fought
		or bid	find	found	found
bind	bound	bound	flee	fled	fled
bite	bit	bitten	fling	flung	flung
bleed	bled	bled	fly	flew	flown
blow	blew	blown	forbid	forbade	forbidden
break	broke	broken	forget	forgot	forgotten
breed	bred	bred	forgive	forgave	forgiven
bring	brought	brought	forsake	forsook	forsaken
build	built	built	freeze	froze	frozen
burn	burnt	burnt	get	got	got
	or burned	or burned	give	gave	given
burst	burst	burst	go	went	gone
buy	bought	bought	grind	ground	ground
can	could		grow	grew	grown
cast	cast	cast	hang	hung	hung
catch	caught	caught		or hanged	or hanged
choose	chose	chosen	have	had	had
cling	clung	clung	hear	heard	heard
come	came	come	hide	hid	hidden
cost	cost	cost	hit	hit	hit
creep	crept	crept	hold	held	held
cut	cut	cut	hurt	hurt	hurt

Infinito	Preterito	Participo Passato	Infinito	Preterito	Participo Passato
keep	kept	kept	say	said	said
kneel	knelt	knelt	see	saw	seen
knit	knitted	knitted	seek	sought	sought
	or knit	or knit	sell	sold	sold
know	knew	known	send	sent	sent
lay	laid	laid	set	set	set
lead	led	led	sew	sewed	sewn
lean	leant	leant			or sewed
	or leaned	or leaned	shake	shook	shaken
leap	leapt	leapt	shear	sheared	sheared
	or leaped	or leaped			or shorn
learn	learnt	learnt	shed	shed	shed
	or learned	or learned	shine	shone	shone
leave	left	left	shoe	shod	shod
lend	lent	lent	shoot	shot	shot
let	let	let	show	showed	shown
lie	lay	lain	shrink	shrank	shrunk
light	lit	lit	shut	shut	shut
	or lighted	or lighted	sing	sang	sung
lose	lost	lost	sink	sank	sunk
make	made	made	sit	sat	sat
may	might		sleep	slept	slept
mean	meant	meant	slide	slid	slid
meet	met	met	sling	slung	slung
mow	mowed	mown	slink	slunk	slunk
must			slit	slit	slit
ought			smell	smelt	smelt
pay	paid	paid		or smelled	or smelled
put	put	put	sow	sowed	sown
quit	quitted	quitted			or sowed
	or quit	or quit	speak	spoke	spoken
read	read	read	speed	sped	sped
rid	rid	rid		or speeded	or speeded
ride	rode	ridden	spell	spelt	spelt
ring	rang	rung		or spelled	or spelled
rise	rose	risen	spend	spent	spent
run	ran	run	spill	spilt	spilt
saw	sawed	sawn		or spilled	or spilled
		or sawed	spin	spun	spun

Infinito	Preterito	Participo Passato	Infinito	Preterito	Participo Passato
spit	spat	spat	swim	swam	swum
split	split	split	swing	swung	swung
spread	spread	spread	take	took	taken
spring	sprang	sprung	teach	taught	taught
stand	stood	stood	tear	tore	torn
steal	stole	stolen	tell	told	told
stick	stuck	stuck	think	thought	thought
sting	stung	stung	throw	threw	thrown
stink	stank	stunk	thrust	thrust	thrust
	or stunk		tread	trod	trodden
stride	strode	stridden	wake	woke	woken
strike	struck	struck	wear	wore	worn
string	strung	strung	weave	wove	woven
strive	strove	striven	weep	wept	wept
swear	swore	sworn	win	won	won
sweep	swept	swept	wind	wound	wound
swell	swelled	swollen	wring	wrung	wrung
		or swelled	write	wrote	written

Glossary of menu terms

Italy is a happy place to eat. Waiters, food store owners, hostesses all urge you to have something good to eat. Italian cuisine is based on the food that is available locally, and it is, therefore, seasonal. A good look at a market will give you an idea of what is most abundent and freshest.

There are three main meals and any number of informal snacks in Italy. **Prima colazione** (breakfast) is usually only coffee and bread for Italians. If you want a more substantial meal, try a café at midmorning, or better yet, shop in a food store or open market the night before. **Colazione** (or **pranzo**) is lunch and **cena** is dinner. These two meals are much alike; choose to have your major meal at whichever time is convenient. (If you plan to have two large meals, include some vigorous sightseeing or sports; you will have consumed a lot of food.)

Traditionally each of the regions of Italy (Tuscany, Latium, Venezia, Apulia, etc.) had its own distinctive cuisine, employing its own particular crops, cheeses, and wines, quite different from that of other regions. Modern standardization is having its effects here as elsewhere, but you will still find dishes on local menus which are not found any place else. Only some of the more famous of these regional specialties could be included here.

The title **ristorante** is used for the larger, more elegant — and more expensive — eating establishments. For every **ristorante**, there are many **trattorie** (singular: **trattoria**), where one might eat in plainer surroundings, and much more cheaply, food at least as good as that in a **ristorante**. In recent years **trattorie** have been disappearing, but a good one is still worth looking for.

Italian eating establishments usually list all or most of the following categories on their menus: **antipasta** (hors d'oeuvre), **minestre** (soups), **pasta** (spaghetti, etc.), **pesce** (seafood), **carne** (meats), **contorni** (vegetables), **insalata** (salads), **uova** (egg dishes), **formaggi** (cheeses), **frutta** (fruits), **dolci** (desserts). A very special Italian meal might include an item from every category, but the waiter **(cameriere)** of today knows that the tourist is not so ambitious.

Most Italian restaurants offer a fixed-price meal (**prezzo fisso,** abbreviation p.f.), a full-course dinner, no substitutions allowed. If you order from the full menu, you may find some dishes marked **piatti del giorno** or **pronti.** These are ready to serve. Others will be **piatti da farsi,** dishes which have to be made up. This may take a far amount of time.

You must ask for the check **(conto);** it is not brought automatically. Law now requires that you be given a legible itemized bill. There will be a fixed percentage added for service **(servizio),** but your waiter will still expect a modest tip in addition.

Antipasti (Hors d'Oeuvre)

Italian hors d'oeuvre may range from a single dish to a wide selection of appetizers. A typical antipasto might include cold cuts: **salami** there are a number of regional varieties, Genovese, Milanese, etc; **prosciutto** thin sliced uncooked ham; **mortadella** similar to U.S. bologna but with more fat; **coppa** pork sausage fish: **acciughe** anchovies; **tonno** tuna; **sardine** sardines

vegetables done as salads: **fagioli** beans; **carciofi** artichokes; **peperoni** peppers (sweet); **peperoncini** small pickled peppers

pickles: **funghi sott'olio** pickled mushrooms; **caponata** eggplant in sweet and sour sauce

hardcooked eggs: **uova sode coi tonno** eggs stuffed with tuna; **uova sode coi spinachi** eggs stuffed with spinach

Dishes which may be served separately or as part of an antipasto:

prosciutto e melone sliced ham with honeydew melon

prosciutto e fichi sliced ham with figs

crostini di acciughe anchovies on toast

crostini alla napoletana toast with anchovies, cheese, and tomatoes

crostini alla fiorentina chicken livers on toast

mozzarella in carozza fried cheese sandwiches

Minestre (Soups)

Soups are as important a part of the Italian menu as pasta (and the two are never taken at the same meal; generally lunch is accompanied by some form of pasta, dinner by soup). Most soups are either **brodo**, broth of chicken, meat, fish, or vegetables, either plain or with pasta **(pastina in brodo)**; or **minestrone** (literally "big soup," combinations of several fresh or dried vegetables). All are served with generous helpings of grated cheese **(parmigiana, romana).** Every region has its own particular version of **minestrone**, e.g. **minestrone alla Genovese, alla Milanese,** etc.; and the vegetables used will vary according to what is in season. Other famous soups:

zuppa di pesce Italian equivalent of bouillabaisse, a stew of mixed fish and shellfish (the combination varies according to the area)

zuppa di cozze mussel soup

minestra di pasta e fagioli bean and pasta soup

stracciatella broth with egg strands

zuppa pavese poached egg in broth with toast

Pasta

Pasta is a mainstay of the Italian menu but **not** the principal dish Americans often make of it. Nor is it just spaghetti and macaroni; there are literally hundreds of different sizes and shapes of dried pasta made of the semolina flour in common use in Italy. For example, **vermicelli** (finer than spaghetti); **rigatoni** (ridged tubes); **ziti** (smaller tubes); **linguine** (flat narrow strips); **tagliatelle** (broader than **linguine**); **lasagne** (very broad); **farfalle** (butterfly-shaped bows, used in soups); and many, many more. Also, the same pasta is often called by another name in different regions: what is called **tagliatelle** in Bologna is **fettucine** in Rome. In general, **pasta asciutte** ("dry pasta," even when served swimming in sauce) is distinguished from **pasta in brodo,** soup with some variety of pasta in it.

Pasta with sauces:

al burro dressed with butter

aglio e olio with olive oil and lightly fried garlic

alla Bolognese with rich meat sauce

alle cozze with mussels

alla carbonara with a sauce of bacon and lightly cooked egg

al pesto (Genovese) with a sauce of fresh basil, pine nuts, and cheese pounded to paste (a specialty of Genoa)

Pasta stuffed and baked (usually served as main dishes):

cannelloni tubes of pasta stuffed with meat or cheese and baked in sauce

lasagne layers of flat pasta baked with cheese and tomato sauce

lasagne verde lasagne made with spinach kneaded into the dough giving it a pale green color

gnocchi dumplings made of semolina, potato, or corn meal baked with butter, cheese, or other sauce

ravioli pasta dumplings stuffed with meat, cheese, or various vegetables, served plain or with sauce

Riso (Rice)

Northern Italy is rice country, and there the distinctive rise dish, **risotto,** may take the place of the pasta course on the menu.

risotto alla Milanese rice cooked in chicken stock and wine sauce with a touch of saffron

risotto alla Piemontese rice in a meat sauce with cheese

risotto alla marinara rice cooked in fish stock with shrimp and mussels

risi e bisi risotto with green peas (a specialty of Venice)

arancini "oranges": rice balls stuffed with meat, cheese, and tomato sauce and deep-fried (a specialty of Sicily)

Polenta

Italians don't eat corn on the cob, but they are fond of this corn-meal dish. To call it "corn-meal mush" may discourage those unfamiliar with what the Italian do with it. Every region has its own special way of cooking **polenta,** and it is served with a variety of sauces, meats, and cheeses. Be sure to try it.

Pesce (Fish)

Italian waters are rich in fish, but it is difficult to give the tourist an idea of what is available, for the varieties are so different and names and even types of fish vary from region to region. For example, **cozze** is a common word for mussel, but in Genoa mussels are called **muscoli;** in Venice they are called **peoci,** etc. Some common names are:

acciughe anchovies; **anguille** eels (small); **calamare** squid; **calamaretti** baby squid; **capitone** eels (large); **cozze** mussels; **merluzzo** cod; **sardine** sardines; **scampi** shrimp; **scungilli** conch; **spigola** bream; **tonno** tunny; **triglie** mullet; **trote** trout

Fish is usually cooked by grilling **(alla griglia),** frying **(fritti)** or roasting **(arrosto),** whole (including the head), or in slices.

Some common fish sauces:

alla marinara sailor style with tomato and herbs

alla pizzaiola tomato sauce

alla Napoletana lemon juice, oil, and herbs

alla Siciliana capers, olives, and herbs

Baccalà is a popular stew of dried cod with tomatoes and herbs.

Carni e Pollame (Meats and Fowl)

Meat, in Italy, almost invariably means veal **(vitello)** — so much so that menus normally carry the seemingly contradictory item **bistecca di vitello** — literally, "veal beefsteak." Some areas offer excellent dishes of lamb **(agnello)** and pork **(maiale).**

Similarly, fowl mainly means chicken **(pollo);** but turkey **(tachino)** is quite common, and game birds like pheasant **(fagiano)** are excellent when avialable.

Veal is very commonly served in the form of **scallope** (or **scaloppini),** thin slices fried with various sauces: **scallope al Marsala,** wine sauce; **alla piccata,** lemon juice; **alla Bolognese,** topped with cheese.

saltimbocca a Roman specialty, is veal scallops topped with thin slices of ham and cheese, and cooked with sage

costolette breaded veal cutlets; **alla Milanese,** lightly fried and served with lemon wedges; **alla Modenese,** baked in wine and tomato sauce; **alla Parmeggiana,** baked with tomatoes and cheese

arrosto di vitello veal roast

vitello tonnato pot roast of veal in tuna sauce

arista fiorentina pork roast Florentine style
bistecca alla fiorentina grilled steak (usually cooked well done on the outside and rare on the inside)
bistecca alla pizzaiola fried steak with sauce of tomato and herbs
costoletto di agnello piccante lamb chops fried with herbs and dressed with lemon juice
abbacchio al forno roast leg of lamb
ossobucchi alla Milanese veal shanks with marrow cooked in wine
stufato rich beef stew (meat may vary) with wine and herbs
fritto misto deep-fried pieces of organ meats (liver, heart, brains, etc)
fegato alla Veneziana liver and onions
rognoni trifolati kidneys cooked with anchovies and lemon juice
cervelli fritti calf brains sliced, breaded, and fried
regalo cocks' combs in wine sauce
pollo alla cacciatore chicken stewed with wine, tomatoes, mushrooms, and herbs
pollo alla diavola chicken covered with red pepper flakes and cooked in a light wine sauce
pollo alla Romana chicken stewed with tomatoes, peppers, wine, and herbs
petti di pollo alla Bolognese chicken breasts topped with ham and cheese
petti di pollo al Marsala chicken breasts cooked in wine
fegato di pollo alla salvia chicken livers cooked with sage

Contorni (di verdure) (Vegetables)

In Italian restaurants, while some vegetables may be served with the meat, it is common for vegetables to be eaten as a separate course, often before the main dish. Cooking is usually simple: green vegetables are blanched or steamed briefly and served with olive oil and lemon. Eggplant, tomatoes, and peppers are often stuffed with meat or vegetable mixtures and various spices.

carciofi artichokes (Italian artichokes are usually smaller and tenderer than the American kind and eaten whole)
melanzane eggplant
zucchine zucchini
peperoni sweet peppers
finocchi fennel (rather like celery with an anise flavor)
piselli peas
spinaci spinach
pomidori tomatoes
patate potatoes; **patate fritte** — "French-fried" potatotes
funghi mushrooms
cavalfiore cauliflower
legumi beans
sedani celery
cipolle onions
broccoli broccoli
asparago asparagus
carota carrots

Insalate (Salads)

Salads are an important part of the Italian meal, and may appear as part of the antipasto, as an accompaniment to the main dish, or as a separate course after the meat. Most are very simple with vinegar (or lemon juice) and oil dressing. Restaurants usually set the table with cruets of vinegar and oil so that the diner may make his own dressing. Many of the vegetables listed as hot dishes under **contorni** may also be served cold as salad.
insalata verde green salad, lettuce and other available greens
insalata de pomidori tomato salad
insalata di broccoli broccoli salad (fresh or cooked)
insalata di melanzane eggplant salad
insalata di finocchi fennel salad
fagiolini al tonno salad of green beans and tuna
insalata Nizzarda salad Nicoise: lettuce, tomatoes, green beans, peppers, olives, and anchovies in vinegar and oil.

Uova (Egg Dishes)

Eggs are never served for breakfast in Italy (though a homesick tourist may sometimes coax a dish of scrambled eggs from a sympathetic cook with the phrase **uova strapazzate**). But they are often fare for lunch or a light supper.

uova al tegamino fried eggs served in the cooking pan

frittata the Italian omelet; unlike the French variety, it is turned and browned on both sides, cooked right through; often served with chopped meats, vegetables, fish, as : **frittata coi carcioff** artichoke omelet; **frittata con tonno** omelet with tuna; **frittata con zucchine** omelet with zucchini; **frittata con spinachi** spinach omelet; **uova al piatto coi pomidori** eggs poached in tomato sauce; **uova al piatto coi fegatini** eggs with chicken livers.

Formaggi (Cheeses)

Italy produces many excellent cheeses, and they are an indispensable element in the Italian cuisine. Many are also delicious for eating and form a separate course in the Italian dinner, between the main dish and dessert. Some common eating cheeses:

gorgonzola a blue veined cheese, similar to Roquefort but richer and stronger flavored

bel paese a mild, smooth cheese, excellent for eating and cooking

Parmigiano Parmesan, always served grated with pasta and main dishes, also served for eating

pecorino sheeps' milk cheese, widely used for eating fresh; for grating when aged

provolone a sweet eating cheese when fresh; acquires a sharp flavor when aged and is used for cooking

mozzarella a fresh cheese, rather like cottage cheese; used for cooking and eating

ricotta a creamy fresh cheese eaten and used in desserts

Frutte (Fruits)

It is not unusual for an Italian meal to end with cheese and fruit rather than a formal dessert. Fruits are usually served raw and peeled at the table (an Italian never touches his fruit except with knife and fork; this seems difficult to the uninitiate but can be learned).

mele apples
Arancie oranges
pesche peaches
banane bananas
fragole strawberries
ciliege cherries
pera pears
fichi figs
melone melon
macedonia de frutta mixed fruit salad

Dolci (Desserts)

zabaglione (or zabaione) custard-flavored with Marsala wine
montebianco puréed chestnuts flavored with Marsala and topped with whipped cream
cassata rich cheese cake flavored with liqueurs (a specialty of Sicily)
dolce al rhum rum cake
pan di spagna sponge cake
budino di ricotta ricotta cheese pudding
gelata, spumone ice cream
granite fruit ices

Bevande (Drinks)

Italian restaurants do not usually serve cocktails; the Italian preference is for an aperitif **(aperitivo),** of which there are many. **Vermouth bianco** is probably the most popular. With the meal, it is usually a safe bet to take one of the local wines — every region has its own vintages, and they often have a remarkable affinity for the local dishes. Some wines which are available country-wide are:
Asti spumante the Italian champagne
Bardo a robust full-bodied red **(rosso)**
Valpolicella a light red
Soave one of the best whites (bianco)

Chianti real Chianti is a revelation if you have encountered only imitations
Orvieto a superb white: either dry (secco) or semi-sweet (abboccato)
Est! Est! Est! a white famous since the Middle Ages
Frascati the classic white wine of Rome
Capri and **Ischia** the Neapolitan islands produce good dry reds and whites
Lacrima Christi the famous dessert wine from Mount Vesuvius
Marsala (dolce) the dessert wine of Sicily

Coffee. Most Italians like to end their meal with the strong sweet **espresso**. **Cappuccino** is strong coffee with milk. **Caffelatte** is coffee and milk half-and-half. Tea **(te)** is usually available. Nowadays, you can usually order milk with your meal **(bicchiere di latte)** without causing a major sensation. Italians often drink bottled mineral water **(acqua minerale)** with their meal in preference to wine. Many varieties are available nationally.

English—Italiano

A

a, an [ə, ən] *art* un, uno *m*; una *f*.
aback [ə'bak] *adv* be taken aback essere colto di sorpresa.
abandon [ə'bandən] *v* abbandonare. *n* abbandono *m*.
abashed [ə'baʃt] *adj* confuso.
abate [ə'beit] *v* diminuire. **abatement** *n* diminuzione *f*.
abattoir ['abətwaɪ] *n* macello *m*.
abbey ['abi] *n* abbazia *f*. **abbess** *n* badessa *f*. **abbot** *n* abate *m*.
abbreviate [ə'briɪvieit] *v* abbreviare. **abbreviation** *n* abbreviazione *f*.
abdicate ['abdikeit] *v* abdicare. **abdication** *n* abdicazione *f*.
abdomen ['abdəmən] *n* addome *m*. **abdominal** *adj* addominale.
abduct [əb'dʌkt] *v* rapire. **abduction** *n* rapimento *m*.
aberration [abə'reiʃən] *n* aberrazione *f*. **aberrant** *adj* aberrante.
abet [ə'bet] *v* favoreggiare. **aid and abet** farsi complice di.
abeyance [ə'beiəns] *n* sospensione *f*. **in abeyance** in sospeso.
abhor [əb'hoɪ] *v* aborrire. **abhorrence** *n* aborrimento *m*. **abhorrent** *adj* aborrevole, odioso.
*abide [ə'baid] *v* (*wait*) aspettare; (*tolerate*) soffrire. **abide by** sostenere, restar fedele a.
ability [ə'biləti] *n* abilità *f*. **to the best of one's ability** come meglio potrà.
abject [,abdʒekt] *adj* abietto.
ablaze [ə'bleiz] *adj* in fiamme, risplendente.
able ['eibl] *adj* capace; (*talented*) abile. **able-bodied** *adj* robusto. **be able** potere, essere in grado di.

abnormal [ab'noɪml] *adj* anormale. **abnormality** *n* anormalità *f*.
aboard [ə'boɪd] *adv, prep* a bordo (di). **all aboard!** tutti a bordo! **go aboard** imbarcarsi.
abode [ə'boud] *V* **abide**. *n* dimora *f*.
abolish [ə'boliʃ] *v* abolire. **abolition** *n* abolizione *f*.
abominable [ə'bominəbl] *adj* abominevole. **abominate** *v* detestare. **abomination** *n* abominazione *f*.
aborigine [abə'ridʒini] *n* indigeno *m*.
abortion [ə'boɪʃən] *n* aborto *m*. **abort** *v* abortire.
abound [ə'baund] *v* abbondare.
about [ə'baut] *adv* (*around*) intorno; (*nearly*) verso, presso; circa; (*concerning*) su. *prep* di, su; intorno a. **be about to** stare per.
above [ə'bʌv] *adv* in alto, di sopra. *prep* sopra, al di sopra di; (*number*) più di; (*rank*) superiore a. **above all** sopratutto. **above-mentioned** *adj* suddetto. **from above** dall'alto.
abrasion [ə'breiʒən] *n* abrasione *f*. **abrasive** *adj* abrasivo.
abreast [ə'brest] *adv* **keep abreast of** or **with** tenersi al corrente di. **two abreast** due per due.
abridge [ə'bridʒ] *v* abbreviare. **abridgement** *n* abbreviazione *f*.
abroad [ə'broɪd] *adv* all'estero.
abrupt [ə'brʌpt] *adj* brusco.
abscess ['abses] *n* ascesso *m*.
abscond [əb'skond] *v* rendersi latitante.
absent ['absənt] *adj* assente. **absent-minded** *adj* distratto. *v* **absent oneself** assentarsi. **absence** *n* assenza *f*. **absentee** *n* assente *m*. **absenteeism** *n* assenteismo *m*.
absolute ['absəluɪt] *adj* assoluto. **absolutely** *adv* assolutamente, perfettamente. **absolutism** *n* assolutismo *m*.

absolve [əb'zolv] v assolvere. **absolution** n assoluzione f.

absorb [əb'zoɪb] v assorbire. **be absorbed in** essere concentrato in. **absorbent** adj assorbente. **absorbing** adj (coll) molto interessante. **absorption** n assorbimento m.

abstain [əb'stein] v astenersi. **abstention** n astensione f.

abstemious [əb'stiɪmiəs] adj astemio.

abstinence ['abstinəns] n astinenza f.

abstract ['abstrakt; v ab'strakt] adj astratto. v astrarre. **abstractedly** adv distrattamente. **abstraction** n astrazione f.

absurd [əb'səɪd] adj assurdo, ridicolo. **absurdity** n assurdità f.

abundance [ə'bʌndəns] n abbondanza f. **abundant** adj abbondante.

abuse [ə'bjuɪs; v ə'bjuɪz] n abuso m; insulto m. v abusare di, maltrattare; insultare, oltraggiare. **abusive** adj offensivo; abusivo.

abyss [ə'bis] n abisso m. **abysmal** adj abissale; profondo.

academy [ə'kadəmi] n accademia f. **academic** n, adj accademico, -a.

accede [ak'siɪd] v accedere.

accelerate [ək'seləreit] v accelerare. **acceleration** n accelerazione f. **accelerator** n acceleratore m.

accent ['aksənt] n accento m. v accentuare; (gramm) accentare.

accept [ək'sept] v accettare, accogliere. **acceptable** adj (agreeable) gradevole; accettabile. **acceptance** n accettazione f.

access ['akses] n accesso m. **accessible** adj accessibile.

accessory [ək'sesəri] n accessorio m; (law) complice m, f. adj accessorio.

accident ['aksidənt] n accidente m, infortunio m. **by accident** per caso. **accidental** adj fortuito.

acclaim [ə'kleim] v acclamare. n also **acclamation** acclamazione f.

acclimatize [ə'klaimətaiz] v acclimatare.

accolade ['akəleid] n abbraccio m.

accommodate [ə'komədeit] v accomodare; (lodge) ospitare; (provide) provvedere (di). **accommodating** adj cortese, conciliante. **accommodation** n (housing) alloggio m; (hotel) posto m.

accompany [ə'kʌmpəni] v accompagnare. **accompaniment** n accompagnamento m. **accompanist** n accompagnatore, -trice m, f.

accomplice [ə'kʌmplis] n complice m, f.

accomplish [ə'kʌmpliʃ] v compiere, realizzare. **accomplished** adj (talented) compito. **accomplishment** n effettuazione f; talento m.

accord [ə'kɔɪd] v concedere, accordare. n accordo m. **of one's own accord** spontaneamente. **in accordance with** in conformità con. **accordingly** adv pertanto, quindi, di conseguenza. **according to** secondo.

accordion [ə'kɔɪdiən] n fisarmonica f.

accost [ə'kost] v rivolgersi a.

account [ə'kaunt] n (report) relazione f, versione f; (status) importanza f; (bank) conto m. **by all accounts** a quanto si dice. **on no account** a nessuna condizione. **on one's own account** per propria iniziativa. v **account for** spiegare la ragione di, giustificare. **accountant** n contabile m, f, ragioniere m.

accrue [ə'kruɪ] v accrescere.

accumulate [ə'kjuɪmjuleit] v accumulare. **accumulation** n ammasso m, accumulamento m.

accurate ['akjurət] adj accurato, preciso. **accuracy** n accuratezza f, precisione f.

accuse [ə'kjuɪz] v accusare, incolpare. **the accused** n l'imputato, -a m, f. **accusation** n accusa f.

accustom [ə'kʌstəm] v abituare.

ace [eis] n asso m. **within an ace of** a un dito di.

ache [eik] n dolore m. v far male, dolere.

achieve [ə'tʃiɪv] v concludere, ottenere, compiere. **achievement** n compimento m, successo m.

acid ['asid] nm, adj acido.

acknowledge [ək'nolidʒ] v riconoscere, ammettere. **acknowledge receipt of** accusare ricevuta di. **acknowledgement** n riconoscimento m; ricevuta f.

acne ['akni] n acne m.

acorn ['eikɔɪn] n ghianda f.

acoustic [ə'kuɪstik] adj acustico. **acoustics** pl n acustica f sing.

acquaint [ə'kweint] v avvertire, mettere al corrente. **acquaintance** n (knowledge) conoscenza f; (person) conoscente m, f. **become acquainted with** (person) fare la conoscenza di; (thing) informarsi su.

acquiesce [akwi'es] v acconsentire tacitamente. **acquiescence** n acquiescenza f. **acquiescent** adj acquiescente.

acquire [ə'kwaiə] v acquisire, acquistare.
acquisition [akwi'ziʃən] n acquisto m;
acquisizione f. acquisitive adj avido di
guadagno.
acquit [ə'kwit] v esonerare. acquit oneself
comportarsi. acquittal n (law) assoluzione f.
acrid ['akrid] adj acre, pungente.
acrimony ['akriməni] n acrimonia f. acrimonious adj acrimonioso, astioso.
acrobat ['akrəbat] n acrobata m, f. acrobatic adj acrobatico. acrobatics pl n
acrobazie f pl.
across [ə'kros] adv per traverso; (crossword) orizzontali. prep al di là di,
attraverso.
acrylic [ə'krilik] adj acrilico.
act [akt] v agire; (theatre) recitare;
(behave) comportarsi. act as fungere da.
act for agire per conto di. n (deed) azione
f; (theatre) atto m; (law) decreto m. actor
n attore m. actress n attrice f.
action ['akʃən] n azione f; (law) processo
m; (mil) combattimento m. out of action
fuori uso.
active ['aktiv] adj attivo, energico. activate v attivare. activist n attivista m.
activity n attività f.
actual ['aktʃuəl] adj effettivo, reale. actually adv effettivamente.
actuate ['aktjueit] v mettere in atto or
moto.
acupuncture ['akjupʌŋktʃə] n acupuntura
f.
acute [ə'kjuit] adj acuto, perspicace.
adamant ['adəmənt] adj inflessibile.
Adam's apple [adəm'zapl] n pomo
d'Adamo m.
adapt [ə'dapt] v adattare, modificare.
adaptability n adattibilità f. adaptable adj
adattabile. adaptation n adattamento m.
adapter n (theatre) riduttore m; (elec)
raccordo m.
add [ad] v aggiungere. add to aumentare.
add up fare la somma di, sommare. addition n addizione f. additional adj supplementare.
addendum [ə'dendəm] n aggiunta f.
adder ['adə] n vipera f.
addict ['adikt; v ə'dikt] n (drug) drogato,
-a m, f, tossicomane m, f. be addicted to
essere abituato or dedito a. addiction n
dedizione f; tossicomania f.
additive ['aditiv] n aggiunta f.

address [ə'dres] v (letter) indirizzare;
(meeting, etc.) rivolgere la parola a, fare
un discorso a. address oneself to mettersi
a. n (speech) discorso m; (letter) indirizzo
m, recapito m. addressee n destinatario
m.
adenoids ['adənoidz] pl n adenoidi f pl.
adept [ə'dept] nm, adj esperto.
adequate ['adikwət] adj sufficiente,
adeguato.
adhere [əd'hiə] v aderire, attaccarsi. adhesion n adesione f. adhesive nm, adj
adesivo.
adherent [əd'hiərənt] n partigiano m,
seguace m.
adjacent [ə'dʒeisənt] adj adiacente, contiguo.
adjective ['adʒiktiv] n aggettivo m.
adjoin [ə'dʒoin] v confinare (con). adjoining adj adiacente.
adjourn [ə'dʒɜin] v aggiornare, rinviare.
adjournment n rinvio m.
adjudicate [ə'dʒuidikeit] v aggiudicare.
adjudicator n arbitro m.
adjust [ə'dʒʌst] v regolare, mettere a punto. adjustment n adattamento m, rettifica
f.
ad-lib ['ad'lib] v improvvisare.
administer [əd'ministə] v amministrare;
(med) somministrare. administration n
amministrazione f. administrative adj
amministrativo. administrator n
amministratore, -trice m, f.
admiral ['admərəl] n ammiraglio m.
admire [əd'maiə] v ammirare. admirable
adj ammirevole. admiration n ammirazione f. admiringly adv con meraviglia.
admit [əd'mit] v ammettere; concedere;
confessare. admissible adj ammissibile.
admission n ammissione f. admittance n
ingresso m, entrata f.
adolescence [adə'lesns] n adolescenza f.
adolescent n(m+f), adj adolescente.
adopt [ə'dopt] v adottare. adopted adj
(child) adottivo. adoption n adozione f.
adore [ə'doi] v adorare. adoration n
adorazione f.
adorn [ə'doin] v abbellire, guarnire.
adornment n ornamento m.
adrenaline [ə'drenəlin] n adrenalina f.
adrift [ə'drift] adv alla deriva.
adroit [ə'droit] adj abile, destro.
adulation [adju'leiʃən] n adulazione f.
adult ['adʌlt] n, adj adulto, -a.

adulterate [ə'dʌltəreit] *v* adulterare; (*wine*) sofisticare.
adultery [ə'dʌltəri] *n* adulterio *m*. **adulterer** *n* adultero, -a *m, f*.
advance [əd'vɑːns] *v* avanzare, progredire, anticipare. *n* avanzamento *m*; (*mil*) marcia in avanti *f*; (*cash*) anticipo *m*. **book in advance** prenotare.
advantage [əd'vɑːntidʒ] *n* vantaggio *m*, beneficio *m*. **take advantage of** approfittare di. **advantageous** *adj* vantaggioso.
advent ['advənt] *n* avvento *m*.
adventure [əd'ventʃə] *n* avventura *f*, impresa rischiosa *f*. **adventurer** *n* avventuriero *m*. **adventurous** *adj* avventuroso.
adverb ['advəːb] *n* avverbio *m*.
adversary ['advəsəri] *n* avversario, -a *m, f*.
adverse ['advəːs] *adj* avverso. **adversity** *n* avversità *f*.
advertise ['advətaiz] *v* annunziare, fare pubblicità a. **advertisement** *n* annunzio *m*, inserzione *f*. **advertising** *n* pubblicità *f*.
advise [əd'vaiz] *v* consigliare, raccomandare. **ill-advised** *adj* imprudente, inopportuno. **well-advised** *adj* saggio.
advice *n* consiglio *m*, suggerimento *m*.
advisable *adj* opportuno, consigliabile.
adviser *n* consulente *m, f*. **advisory** *adj* consultivo.
advocate ['advəkeit] *v* sostenere.
aerial ['eəriəl] *adj* aereo. *n* antenna *f*.
aerodynamics [eərədai'namiks] *n* aerodinamica *f*.
aeronautics [eərə'nɔːtiks] *n* aeronautica *f*.
aeroplane ['eərəplein] *n* aereo *m*.
aerosol ['eərəsol] *n* aerosol *m*.
aesthetic [iːs'θetik] *adj* estetico. **aesthetics** *n* estetica *f*.
affair [ə'feə] *n* affare *m*. **have an affair** avere una relazione intima.
affect[1] [ə'fekt] *v* (*influence*) colpire, toccare.
affect[2] [ə'fekt] *v* (*pretend*) fingere, simulare.
affection [ə'fekʃən] *n* affetto *m*, affezione *f*. **affectionate** *adj* affezionato.
affiliate [ə'filieit] *v* affiliare. **affiliation** *n* affiliazione *f*.
affinity [ə'finəti] *n* affinità *f*.
affirm [ə'fəːm] *v* affermare, confermare. **affirmation** *n* affermazione *f*, conferma *f*. **affirmative** *adj* affermativo.
affix [ə'fiks] *v* affiggere.

afflict [ə'flikt] *v* affliggere, angosciare. **affliction** *n* afflissione *f*, dolore *m*.
affluent ['afluənt] *adj* ricco, opulento. **affluence** *n* affluenza *f*, ricchezza *f*.
afford [ə'fɔːd] *v* avere i mezzi per; (*produce*) dare, offrire; (*allow oneself to*) permettersi di.
affront [ə'frʌnt] *n* affronto *m*, offesa *f*. *v* insultare, offendere.
afloat [ə'flout] *adv* a galla.
afoot [ə'fut] *adv* a piedi; (*fig*) in atto.
aforesaid [ə'fɔːsed] *adj* suddetto, soprannominato.
afraid [ə'freid] *adj* impaurito, pauroso, spaventato. **be afraid of** temere, aver paura di.
afresh [ə'freʃ] *adv* da capo, nuovamente.
Africa ['afrikə] *n* Africa *f*. **African** *n, adj* africano, -a.
aft [ɑːft] *adv* a poppa.
after ['ɑːftə] *prep* dopo, in seguito a. *adv* dopo, poi. *conj* dopo che. **after all** dopo tutto, insomma. **afterwards** *adv* dopo, poi.
afternoon [ˌɑːftə'nuːn] *n* pomeriggio *m*, dopo pranzo *m*. **good afternoon!** buona sera!
aftershave ['ɑːftəʃeiv] *n* dopobarba *m invar*.
again [ə'gen] *adv* di nuovo, ancora. **again and again** ripetutamente. **never again** mai più.
against [ə'genst] *prep* contro, in opposizione a.
age [eidʒ] *n* età *f*; era *f*. **of age** maggiorenne. **old age** vecchiaia *f*. **under age** minorenne. *v* invecchiare. **aged** *adj* vecchio; (*seasoned*) invecchiato.
agency ['eidʒənsi] *n* agenzia *f*, rappresentanza *f*.
agenda [ə'dʒendə] *n* ordine del giorno *m*.
agent ['eidʒənt] *n* agente *m, f*; rappresentante *m, f*.
aggravate ['agrəveit] *v* aggravare; (*coll*) irritare. **aggravation** *n* aggravamento *m*; (*coll*) irritazione *f*.
aggregate ['agrigət] *nm, adj* aggregato.
aggression [ə'greʃən] *n* aggressione *f*.
aggressive *adj* aggressivo. **aggressor** *n* aggressore *m*.
aghast [ə'gɑːst] *adj* stupefatto, atterrito.
agile ['adʒail] *adj* agile. **agility** *n* agilità *f*.
agitate ['adʒiteit] *v* agitare, turbare. **agitation** *n* agitazione *f*. **agitator** *n* agitatore, -trice *m, f*.

agnostic [ag'nostik] *n*, *adj* agnostico, -a.
agnosticism *n* agnosticismo *m*.
ago [ə'gou] *adv* fa.
agog [ə'gog] *adj* bramoso.
agony ['agəni] *n* agonia *f*, angoscia *f*. **be in agony** soffrire dolori atroci.
agree [ə'griː] *v* essere *or* andare d'accordo, convenire, accordarsi. **agreeable** *adj* piacevole, simpatico. **agreement** *n* accordo *m*, patto *m*, contratto *m*.
agriculture ['agrikʌltʃə] *n* agricoltura *f*. **agricultural** *adj* agricolo.
aground [ə'graund] *adv* arenato. **run aground** incagliarsi.
ahead [ə'hed] *adv* (in) avanti.
aid [eid] *v* aiutare, sovvenire, soccorrere. *n* aiuto *m*, sussidio *m*. **first aid** pronto soccorso *m*. **in aid of** a favore di.
aim [eim] *v* puntare, prendere di mira; aspirare. *n* mira *f*; (*purpose*) scopo *m*, proposito *m*.
air [eə] *n* aria *f*; (*bearing*) aspetto *m*, contegno *m*. *v* ventilare.
airbed ['eəbed] *n* materassimo pneumatico *m*.
airborne ['eəbɔɪn] *adj* aerotrasportato.
air-conditioned *adj* ad aria condizionata.
aircraft ['eəkraift] *n* aereo *m*. **aircraft-carrier** *n* portaerei *m invar*.
airfield ['eəfiɪld] *n* campo d'aviazione *m*.
air force *n* aviazione *f*.
air-hostess *n* assistente di volo *f*, hostess *f invar*.
air lift *n* ponte aereo *m*.
airline ['eəlain] *n* linea aerea *f*.
airmail ['eəmeil] *n* posta aerea *f*.
airport ['eəpɔɪt] *n* aeroporto *m*.
air-raid *n* incursione aerea *f*. **air-raid shelter** rifugio contraereo *m*.
airtight ['eətait] *adj* ermetico, impenetrabile all'aria.
airy ['eəri] *adj* arioso, ben ventilato.
aisle [ail] *n* navata *f*.
ajar [ə'dʒaɪ] *adj* socchiuso.
akin [ə'kin] *adj* simile, parente.
alabaster ['aləbaɪstə] *n* alabastro *m*.
alarm [ə'laɪm] *n* allarme *m*. **alarm clock** sveglia *f*. *v* allarmare.
alas [ə'las] *interj* purtroppo!
Albania [al'beinjə] *n* Albania *f*. **Albanian** *n*(*m*+*f*), *adj* albanese.
albatross ['albətros] *n* albatro *m*.
albino [al'biːnou] *n*, *adj* albino -a.
album ['albəm] *n* album *m*.

alchemy ['alkəmi] *n* alchimia *f*. **alchemist** *n* alchimista *m*, *f*.
alcohol ['alkəhol] *n* alcool *m*.
alcoholic [alkə'holik] *adj* alcoolico. *n* alcoolizzato, -a *m*, *f*. **alcoholism** *n* alcoolismo *m*.
alcove ['alkouv] *n* nicchia *f*.
alderman ['ɔɪldəmən] *n* assessore municipale *m*.
ale [eil] *n* birra *f*.
alert [ə'lɔɪt] *adj* vigilante. *v* avvertire. **be on the alert** stare all'erta.
algebra ['aldʒibrə] *n* algebra *f*.
alias ['eiliəs] *adv* altrimenti detto.
alibi ['alibai] *n* alibi *m invar*.
alien ['eiliən] *n*, *adj* straniero, -a, forestiero, -a. **alienate** *v* alienare. **alienation** *n* alienazione *f*.
alight[1] [ə'lait] *v* scendere, smontare.
alight[2] [ə'lait] *adj* acceso, illuminato.
align [ə'lain] *v* allineare.
alike [ə'laik] *adj* simile, somigliante. *adv* ugualmente. **be alike** assomigliarsi.
alimentary canal [ali'mentəri] *adj* alimentare.
alimony ['aliməni] *n* alimenti *m pl*.
alive [ə'laiv] *adj* vivo, vivente. **alive to** sensibile a.
alkaline ['alkəlain] *adj* alcalino.
all [ɔɪl] *adj* tutto. *adv* completamente. *n* tutti *m pl*, tutte *f pl*. **all right!** va bene! **All Saints' Day** Ognissanti *m*. **All Souls' Day** giorno dei morti *m*. **all the same** con tutto ciò. **not at all** niente affatto.
allay [ə'lei] *v* calmare.
allege [ə'ledʒ] *v* allegare, asserire. **alleged** *adj* sedicente.
allegiance [ə'liːdʒəns] *n* obbedienza *f*, fedeltà *f*.
allegory ['aligəri] *n* allegoria *f*.
allergy ['alədʒi] *n* allergia *f*. **allergic** *adj* allergico.
alleviate [ə'liːvieit] *v* alleviare, attenuare.
alley ['ali] *n* vicolo *m*.
alliance [ə'laiəns] *n* alleanza *f*, patto *m*.
alligator ['aligeitə] *n* alligatore *m*.
alliteration [əlitə'reifən] *n* allitterazione *f*.
allocate ['aləkeit] *v* assegnare, collocare. **allocation** *n* assegnamento *m*.
allot [ə'lot] *v* assegnare. **allotment** *n* (*land*) lotto *m*, pezzo di terreno *m*; (*portion*) parte assegnata *f*.
allow [ə'lau] *v* permettere, concedere. **allow for** tener conto di. **allow me!**

permetta! **allowance** *h* (*grant*) assegno *m*; (*reduction*) sconto *m*.
alloy ['aloi; *v* ə'loi] *n* lega *f*. *v* legare, amalgamare.
allude [ə'luːd] *v* riferirsi (a), alludere (a).
allusion *n* allusione *f*, riferimento *m*.
allure [ə'ljuə] *n* fascino *m*. *v* affascinare.
alluring *adj* seducente.
ally ['alai; *v* ə'lai] *n* alleato, -a *m*, *f*. *v* alleare.
almanac ['oɪlmənak] *n* almanacco *m*.
almighty [oɪl'maiti] *adj* onnipotente. **the Almighty** *n* il Padreterno *m*.
almond ['aɪmənd] *n* (*nut*) mandorla *f*; (*tree*) mandorlo *m*.
almost ['oɪlmoust] *adv* quasi.
alms [aɪmz] *pl n* elemosina *f sing*. **give alms** fare l'elemosina. **almshouse** *n* ospizio dei poveri *m*.
aloft [ə'loft] *adv* in alto.
alone [ə'loun] *adj* solo. *adv* solo, da solo; (*only*) solamente. **leave alone** lasciar stare.
along [ə'loŋ] *prep* lungo. **along with** insieme a. **come along!** su! avanti! **alongside** *prep* accanto a.
aloof [ə'luːf] *adj* riservato, freddo. *adv* a distanza.
aloud [ə'laud] *adv* ad alta voce.
alphabet ['alfəbit] *n* alfabeto *m*.
Alps [alps] *pl n* **the Alps** le Alpi *f pl*. **alpine** *adj* alpino.
already [oɪl'redi] *adv* già.
also ['oɪlsou] *adv* anche, pure, inoltre.
altar ['oɪltə] *n* altare *m*. **altarpiece** *n* pala d'altare *f*. **high altar** altare maggiore *m*.
alter ['oɪltə] *v* alterare, cambiare, alterarsi. **alteration** *n* cambiamento *m*, mutamento *m*.
alternate ['oɪltəneit; *adj* oɪl'təɪnət] *v* alternare, alternarsi, ·succedersi. *adj* alterno. **alternation** *n* alternazione *f*, successione reciproca *f*.
alternative [oɪl'təɪnətiv] *adj* alternativo. *n* alternativa *f*.
although [oɪl'ðou] *conj* sebbene, benché.
altitude ['altitjuɪd] *n* altezza *f*, altitudine *f*; (*aircraft*) quota *f*.
altogether [oɪltə'geðə] *adv* complessivamente, nell'insieme.
altruistic [altru'istik] *adj* altruistico. **altruism** *n* altruismo *m*. **altruist** *n* altruista *m*, *f*.
aluminium [alju'miniəm] *n* alluminio *m*.

always ['oɪlweiz] *adv* sempre.
am [am] *V* **be.**
amalgamate [ə'malgəmeit] *v* amalgamare. **amalgam** *n* amalgama *m*.
amass [ə'mas] *v* accumulare.
amateur ['amətə] *n* dilettante *m*, *f*. **amateurish** *adj* da dilettante.
amaze [ə'meiz] *v* stupire, meravigliare. **amazement** *n* stupore *m*, meraviglia *f*. **amazing** *adj* straordinario, stupendo.
ambassador [am'basədə] *n* ambasciatore, -trice *m*, *f*.
amber ['ambə] *n* ambra *f*.
ambidextrous [ambi'dekstrəs] *adj* ambidestro.
ambiguous [am'bigjuəs] *adj* ambiguo. **ambition** [am'biʃən] *n* ambizione *f*. **ambitious** *adj* ambizioso.
ambivalent [am'bivələnt] *adj* ambivalente.
amble ['ambl] *v* camminare lentamente.
ambulance ['ambjuləns] *n* ambulanza *f*.
ambush ['ambuʃ] *n* imboscata *f*, agguato *m*. *v* tendere un agguato.
ameliorate [ə'miːliəreit] *v* migliorare.
amenable [ə'miːnəbl] *adj* trattabile, suscettibile.
amend [ə'mend] *v* emendare, correggere. **amendment** *n* emendamento *m*, correzione *f*. **make amends** fare ammenda.
amenity [ə'miːnəti] *n* amenità *f*. **amenities** *pl n* comodità *f pl*.
America [ə'merikə] *n* America *f*. **American** *n*, *adj* americano, -a.
amethyst ['aməθist] *n* ametista *f*.
amiable ['eimiəbl] *adj* gentile, amabile.
amicable ['amikəbl] *adj* amichevole.
amid [ə'mid] *prep* fra, tra, in mezzo a.
amiss [ə'mis] *adv* **take amiss** aversene a male.
ammonia [ə'mouniə] *n* ammoniaca *f*.
ammunition [amju'niʃən] *n* munizioni *f pl*.
amnesia [am'niːziə] *n* amnesia *f*.
amnesty ['amnəsti] *n* amnistia *f*.
amoeba [ə'miːbə] *n* ameba *f*.
among [ə'mʌŋ] *prep* fra, tra, in mezzo a.
amoral [ei'morəl] *adj* amorale.
amorous ['amərəs] *adj* amoroso.
amorphous [ə'moɪfəs] *adj* amorfo.
amount [ə'maunt] *n* quantità *f*, importo *m*, somma *f*. *v* ammontare, equivalere.
ampere ['ampeə] *n* ampere *m invar*.
amphetamine [am'fetəmiɪn] *n* amfetamina *f*, anfetamina *f*.

amphibian [am'fibiən] *nm, adj* anfibio.
amphitheatre ['amfiθiətə] *n* anfiteatro *m*.
ample ['ampl] *adj* ampio, abbondante.
amplify ['amplifai] *v* amplificare, ampliare. **amplification** *n* amplificazione *f.* **amplifier** *n* amplificatore *m*.
amputate ['ampjuteit] *v* amputare. **amputation** *n* amputazione *f.*
amuse [ə'mjuɪz] *v* divertire, dilettare. **amusement** *n* divertimento *m*, svago *m*. **amusing** *adj* divertente, buffo.
anachronism [ə'nakrənizəm] *n* anacronismo *m*.
anaemia [ə'niːmiə] *n* anemia *f.* **anaemic** *adj* anemico.
anaesthetic [anəs'θetik] *nm, adj* anestetico. **anaesthesia** *n* anestesia *f.* **anaesthetist** *n* anestesista *m, f.* **anaesthetize** *v* anestetizzare.
anagram ['anəgram] *n* anagramma *m*.
anal ['einl] *adj* anale.
analogy [ə'nalədʒi] *n* analogia *f.* **analogous** *adj* analogo (*m pl* -ghi).
analysis [ən'aləsis] *n, pl* -ses analisi *f.* **analyse** *v* analizzare. **analyst** *n* analista *m, f.* **analytical** *adj* analitico.
anarchy ['anəki] *n* anarchia *f.* **anarchic** *adj* anarchico. **anarchist** *n* anarchico, -a *m, f.*
anathema [ə'naθəmə] *n* anatema *f.*
anatomy [ə'natəmi] *n* anatomia *f.* **anatomical** *adj* anatomico. **anatomist** *n* anatomista *m, f.*
ancestor ['ansestə] *n* antenato *m*. **ancestral** *adj* avito. **ancestry** *n* stirpe *f*, lignaggio *m*.
anchor ['aŋkə] *n* ancora *f. v* ancorare.
anchovy ['antʃəvi] *n* acciuga *f.*
ancient ['einʃənt] *adj* antico (*m pl* -chi), anziano.
ancillary [an'siləri] *adj* ausiliario, sussidiario.
and [and] *conj* e, ed.
anecdote ['anikdout] *n* aneddoto *m*.
anemone [ə'neməni] *n* anemone *m*.
anew [ə'njuɪ] *adv* da capo, di nuovo.
angel ['eindʒəl] *n* angelo *m*. **angelic** *adj* angelico.
anger ['aŋgə] *n* rabbia *f*, stizza *f*, ira *f. v* far arrabbiare.
angina [an'dʒainə] *n* (*med*) angina *f.*
angle ['aŋgl] *n* (*corner*) angolo *m*; (*viewpoint*) punto di vista *m*.
angling ['aŋgliŋ] *n* pesca all'amo *f.* **angler** *n* pescatore *m*.

angry ['aŋgri] *adj* arrabbiato, stizzito.
anguish ['aŋgwiʃ] *n* angoscia *f*, tormento *m. v* angosciare, tormentare.
angular ['aŋgjulə] *adj* angolare.
animal ['animəl] *n* animale *m*, bestia *f. adj* animale.
animate ['animət; *v* 'animeit] *adj* animato, vivente. *v* animare. **animated** *adj* vivace. **animation** *n* animazione *f.*
animosity [ani'mosəti] *n* animosità *f.*
aniseed ['anisiɪd] *n* anice *m*.
ankle ['aŋkl] *n* caviglia *f.*
annals ['anlz] *pl n* annali *m pl.*
annex [ə'neks; *n* 'aneks] *v* annettere. *n* annesso *m*; (*hotel*) dipendenza *f.* **annexation** *n* annessione *f.*
annihilate [ə'naiəleit] *v* annientare. **annihilation** *n* annientamento *m*.
anniversary [ani'vəisəri] *nm, adj* anniversario.
annotate ['anəteit] *v* annotare.
announce [ə'nauns] *v* annunciare, rendere noto. **announcement** *n* annuncio *m*. **announcer** *n* annunciatore, -trice *m, f.*
annoy [ə'noi] *v* dar noia a, disturbare, seccare. **annoyance** *n* fastidio *m*, noia *f.* **annoying** *adj* seccante, fastidioso.
annual ['anjuəl] *adj* annuale, annuo. *n* (*book*) annuario *m*; (*plant*) pianta annuale *f.* **annually** *adv* annualmente.
annuity [ə'njuɪəti] *n* annualità *f.* **life annuity** *n* vitalizio *m*.
annul [ə'nʌl] *v* annullare. **annulment** *n* annullamento *m*.
●**Annunciation** [ə,nʌnsi'eiʃn] *n* (*rel*) Annunziazione *f.*
anode ['anoud] *n* anodo *m*.
anomaly [ə'noməli] *n* anomalia *f.* **anomalous** *adj* anomalo, irregolare.
anonymous [ə'noniməs] *adj* anonimo.
anorak ['anərak] *n* giacca a vento *f.*
another [ə'nʌðə] *adj, pron* un altro. **one another** l'un l'altro.
answer ['ainsə] *v* rispondere (a). **answer for** rispondere di. *n* risposta *f.*
ant [ant] *n* formica *f.* **ant-hill** *n* formicaio *m*.
antagonize [an'tagənaiz] *v* provocare l'ostilità (di). **antagonism** *n* antagonismo *m*. **antagonist** *n* antagonista *m, f.*
antecedent [anti'siɪdənt] *adj* antecedente. **antecedents** *pl n* precedenti *m pl*; (*forbears*) antenati *m pl.*

antelope 8

antelope ['antəloup] *n* antilope *f*.
antenatal [anti'neitl] *adj* prenatale.
antenna [an'tenə] *n* antenna *f*.
anthem ['anθəm] *n* inno *m*.
anthology [an'θolədʒi] *n* antologia *f*.
anthropology [anθrə'polədʒi] *n* antropologia *f*. anthropologist *n* antropologo, -a *m, f*.
anti-aircraft [anti'eəkraift] *adj* contraereo.
antibiotic [antibai'otik] *nm, adj* antibiotico.
antibody ['anti,bodi] *n* anticorpo *m*.
anticipate [an'tisipeit] *v* anticipare, prevenire. in anticipation in anticipo.
anticlimax [anti'klaimaks] *n* conclusione banale *f*.
anticlockwise [anti'klokwaiz] *adj, adv* in senso antiorario.
antics ['antiks] *pl n* buffoneria *f sing*.
anticyclone [anti'saikloun] *n* anticiclone *m*.
antidote ['antidout] *n* antidoto *m*.
antifreeze ['antifriiz] *n* antigelo *m*.
antipathy [an'tipəθi] *n* antipatia *f*.
antique [an'tiik] *adj* antico (*m pl* -chi). *n* oggetto antico *m*. antique dealer *n* antiquario *m*. antiquity *n* antichità *f*.
anti-Semitic [antisə'mitik] *n* antisemita *m, f*. anti-Semitism *n* antisemitismo *m*.
antiseptic [anti'septik] *nm, adj* antisettico.
antisocial [anti'souʃəl] *adj* antisociale.
anti-tank [anti'taŋk] *adj* anticarro.
antithesis [an'tiθəsis] *n, pl* -ses antitesi *f*.
antler ['antlə] *n* corno *m*.
antonym ['antənim] *n* antonimo *m*.
anus ['einəs] *n* ano *m*.
anvil ['anvil] *n* incudine *f*.
anxious ['aŋkʃəs] *adj* ansioso, preoccupato. anxiety *n* ansia *f*, ansietà *f*.
any ['eni] *adj* del, della, etc.; qualche *invar*; alcuno. *pron* alcuno, nessuno, ne. anybody *or* anyone *pron* qualcuno, alcuno; chiunque. anyhow *or* anyway *adv* in ogni caso, tuttavia; ad ogni modo. anything *pron* qualcosa, qualche cosa; (*everything*) qualunque cosa. anywhere *adv* in qualunque luogo, in alcun luogo; (*everywhere*) dovunque.
apart [ə'pait] *adv* a parte, in disparte. come apart disfarsi. tell apart distinguere l'uno dall'altro.
apartment [ə'paitmənt] *n* appartamento *m*, alloggio *m*.
apathy ['apəθi] *n* apatia *f*. apathetic *adj* apatico.

ape [eip] *n* scimmia *f*. *v* scimmiottare, imitare.
aperitif [əperi'tiif] *n* aperitivo *m*.
aperture ['apətjuə] *n* apertura *f*.
apex ['eipeks] *n* vertice *m*, apice *m*.
aphid ['eifid] *n* afide *m*.
aphrodisiac [afrə'diziak] *n* afrodisiaco *m*.
apiece [ə'piis] *adv* a testa, per ciascuno, per uno.
apology [ə'polədʒi] *n* scusa *f*, giustificazione *f*. apologetic *adj* apologetico. apologize *v* chiedere scusa, scusarsi.
apoplexy ['apəpleksi] *n* apoplessia *f*. apoplectic *adj* apoplettico. apoplectic fit colpo apoplettico *m*.
apostle [ə'posl] *n* apostolo *m*.
apostrophe [ə'postrəfi] *n* (*punctuation*) apostrofo *m*; (*speech*) apostrofe *f*.
appal [ə'poil] *v* inorridire, sgomentare. appalling *adj* terribile, spaventoso.
apparatus [apə'reitəs] *n* apparecchio *m*, apparato *m*.
apparent [ə'parənt] *adj* apparente, evidente, manifesto.
apparition [apə'riʃən] *n* visione *f*, fantasma *m*.
appeal [ə'piil] *n* appello *m*. *v* appellarsi, fare appello; (*law*) ricorrere in appello. appealing *adj* attraente, commovente.
appear [ə'piə] *v* apparire, sembrare, parere. appearance *n* apparenza *f*, aspetto *m*. put in an appearance fare atto di presenza.
appease [ə'piiz] *v* calmare, pacificare. appeasement *n* pacificazione *f*.
appendix [ə'pendiks] *n* appendice *m*. appendicitis *n* appendicite *f*.
appetite ['apitait] *n* appetito *m*. appetizing *adj* gustoso, succolento.
applaud [ə'ploid] *v* applaudire. applause *n* applauso *m*.
apple ['apl] *n* (*fruit*) mela *f*; (*tree*) melo *m*.
apply [ə'plai] *v* rivolgersi, fare domanda; (*refer*) riferirsi; (*use*) applicare. apply oneself to dedicarsi a. appliance *n* apparecchio *m*, strumento *m*. applicable *adj* applicabile, idoneo. applicant *n* candidato *m*. application *n* domanda *f*, richiesta *f*. application form modulo di richiesta *m*.
appoint [ə'point] *v* nominare; (*arrange*) fissare. appointment *n* (*engagement*) appuntamento *m*; (*post*) nomina *f*.

apportion [ə'pɔɪʃən] v distribuire.
appraisal [ə'preizl] n valutazione f.
appraise v stimare, valutare.
appreciate [ə'priːʃieit] v (esteem) apprezzare, stimare; (be aware of) rendersi conto di; (increase in value) aumentare di valore. **appreciable** adj apprezzabile, sensibile. **appreciation** n apprezzamento m, stima f.
apprehend [apri'hend] v cogliere, arrestare. **apprehension** n arresto m; (worry) timore m. **apprehensive** adj timoroso, preoccupato.
apprentice [ə'prentis] n apprendista m, f. **apprenticeship** n tirocinio m, apprendistato m.
approach [ə'proutʃ] v avvicinare; (come near) avvicinarsi (a). n avvicinamento m, accesso m.
appropriate [ə'proupriət; v ə'prouprieit] adj adatto, opportuno. v impadronirsi di.
approve [ə'pruɪv] v approvare, dare il benestare. **approval** n approvazione f, benestare m. **on approval** in visione, in esame. **approved** adj approvato, convalidato, riconosciuto.
approximate [ə'prɔksimeit; adj ə'prɔksimət] v approssimare. adj approssimativo. **approximately** adv approssimativamente, all'incirca, su per giù.
apricot ['eiprikɔt] n (fruit) albicocca f; (tree) albicocco m.
April ['eiprəl] n aprile m.
apron ['eiprən] n grembiule m, grembiale m.
apt [apt] adj atto, adatto.
aptitude ['aptitjuɪd] n abilità f, attitudine f.
aqualung ['akwəlʌŋ] n autorespiratore m.
aquarium [ə'kweəriəm] n acquario m.
Aquarius [ə'kweəriəs] n Acquario m.
aquatic [ə'kwatik] adj acquatico.
aqueduct ['akwidʌkt] n acquedotto m.
Arab ['arəb] n, adj arabo, -a. **Arabia** n Arabia f. **Arabic** n (language) arabo m.
arable ['arəbl] adj arabile.
arbitrary ['aɪbitrəri] adj arbitrario.
arbitrate ['aɪbitreit] v arbitrare. **arbitration** n arbitraggio m.
arc [aɪk] n arco m. **arc lamp** lampada ad arco f.
arcade [aɪ'keid] n portico m, galleria f.
arch¹ [aɪtʃ] n arco m, volta f. v curvare, arcuare.

arch² [aɪtʃ] adj (chief) arci-.
archaeology [aɪki'ɔlədʒi] n archeologia f. **archaeologist** n archeologo, -a m, f.
archaic [aɪ'keiik] adj arcaico.
archbishop [aɪtʃ'biʃəp] n arcivescovo m. **archduke** [aɪtʃ'djuɪk] n arciduca m.
archery ['aɪtʃəri] n tiro all'arco m. **archer** n arciere m.
archetype ['aɪkitaip] n archetipo m.
archipelago [aɪki'peləgou] n arcipelago (pl -ghi) m.
architect ['aɪkitekt] n architetto, -a m, f. **architecture** n architettura f.
archives ['aɪkaivz] pl n archivio m sing.
arctic ['aɪktik] adj artico.
ardent ['aɪdənt] adj ardente, appassionato.
ardour ['aɪdə] n ardore m, fervore m.
arduous ['aɪdjuəs] adj arduo, difficile.
are [aɪ] V be.
area ['eəriə] n area f, superficie f, zona f.
arena [ə'riɪnə] n arena f.
argue ['aɪgjuɪ] v argomentare, discutere, disputare. **arguable** adj discutibile. **argument** n argomento m, discussione f. **argumentative** adj polemico.
arid ['arid] adj arido.
Aries ['eəriɪz] n Ariete m.
***arise** [ə'raiz] v alzarsi, sorgere.
arisen [ə'rizn] V arise.
aristocracy [ari'stokrəsi] n aristocrazia f. **aristocrat** n aristocratico, -a m, f. **aristocratic** adj aristocratico.
arithmetic [ə'riθmətik] n aritmetica f.
ark [aɪk] n arca f. **Noah's Ark** arca di Noè f.
arm¹ [aɪm] n (limb) braccio m (pl -a f). **armchair** n poltrona f. **arm in arm** a braccetto. **armpit** n ascella f. **within arm's reach** a portata di mano.
arm² [aɪm] n (weapon) arma (pl -i) f. **bear arms** essere sotto le armi. **be up in arms against** essere in rivolta contro. **coat of arms** stemma m. v armare.
armistice ['aɪmistis] n armistizio m.
armour ['aɪmə] n armatura f, corazza f. **armourer** n armiere m. **armour-plated** adj corazzato. **armoury** n arsenale m.
army ['aɪmi] n esercito m, armata f.
aroma [ə'roumə] n aroma m.
arose [ə'rouz] V arise.
around [ə'raund] prep attorno a, intorno a. adv intorno. **all around** tutto intorno.
arouse [ə'rauz] v destare, eccitare.

arrange [ə'reindʒ] *v* accomodare, ordinare; *(music)* adattare; *(meeting, etc.)* organizzare; *(put in order)* sistemare. **arrangement** *n* combinazione *f*; accomodamento *m*; adattamento *m*. **come to an arrangement** mettersi d'accordo.

array [ə'rei] *n* schieramento *m*; mostra imponente *f*. *v* ornare, schierare.

arrears [ə'riəz] *pl n* arretrati *m pl*. **be in arrears** avere degli arretrati.

arrest [ə'rest] *n* arresto. **under arrest** in stato d'arresto. *v* arrestare, sospendere.

arrive [ə'raiv] *v* arrivare, giungere. **arrival** *n* arrivo *m*; *(person)* arrivato, -a *m, f*.

arrogant ['arəgənt] *adj* arrogante. **arrogance** *n* arroganza *f*.

arrow ['arou] *n* freccia *f*.

arse [ais] *n* *(vulgar)* culo *m*.

arsenal ['aisənl] *n* arsenale *m*.

arsenic ['aisnik] *n* arsenico *m*.

arson ['aisn] *n* incendio doloso *m*.

art [ait] *n* arte *f*. **art gallery** galleria d'arte *f*, pinacoteca *f*. **artful** *adj* astuto.

artefact ['aitifakt] *n* artefatto *m*.

artery ['aitəri] *n* arteria *f*.

arthritis [ai'θraitis] *n* artrite *f*.

artichoke ['aititʃouk] *n* carciofo *m*.

article ['aitikl] *n* articolo *m*; oggetto *m*.

articulate [ai'tikjuleit; *adj* ai'tikjulət] *v* articolare. *adj* articolato, distinto.

artifice ['aitifis] *n* artifizio *m*, astuzia *f*.

artificial [aiti'fiʃəl] *adj* artificiale, finto. **artificiality** *n* artificiosità *f*.

artillery [ai'tiləri] *n* artiglieria *f*.

artisan [aiti'zan] *n* artigiano, -a *m, f*.

artist ['aitist] *n* artista *m, f*. **artistic** *adj* artistico.

as [az] *adv* come, quanto. *conj* come; *(while)* mentre; *(because)* poiché, siccome. **as ... as** così ... come, tanto ... quanto. *prep* da. **as far as** *(distance)* sino a. **as for** *or* **to** per quanto riguarda. **as if** come se. **as long as** finché, purché. **as much** altrettanto. **as soon as** (non) appena. **as well** anche. **as well as** *(in addition to)* oltre a.

asbestos [az'bestos] *n* asbesto *m*, amianto *m*.

ascend [ə'send] *v* salire, ascendere. **ascendancy** *n* ascendente *m*. **ascension** *n* ascensione *f*. **ascent** *n* ascesa *f*, salita *f*.

ascertain [asə'tein] *v* accertarsi di, verificare.

ascetic [ə'setik] *adj* ascetico. *n* asceta *m, f*.

ash¹ [aʃ] *n* *(cinder)* cenere *f*. **ashen** *adj* cinereo. **ashtray** *n* portacenere *m*.

ash² [aʃ] *n* *(tree)* frassino *m*.

ashamed [ə'ʃeimd] *adj* vergognoso. **be ashamed of** vergognarsi di.

ashore [ə'ʃoi] *adv* a terra, sulla riva.

Ash Wednesday *n* mercoledì delle Ceneri *m*.

Asia ['eiʃə] *n* Asia *f*. **Asian** *n, adj* asiatico, -a.

aside [ə'said] *adv* da parte, a parte, in disparte. *n* *(theatre)* parole dette a parte *f pl*.

ask [aisk] *v* domandare, chiedere. **ask about** informarsi di *or* su. **ask after** chiedere notizie di.

askew [ə'skjui] *adv* di traverso.

asleep [ə'sliip] *adj* addormentato. **fall asleep** addormentarsi.

asparagus [ə'sparəgəs] *n* asparago *m*.

aspect ['aspekt] *n* aspetto *m*, apparenza *f*.

asphalt ['asfalt] *n* asfalto *m*.

asphyxiate [əs'fiksieit]

aspire [ə'spaiə] *v* ambire. **aspiration** *n* ambizione *f*.

aspirin ['aspərin] *n* aspirina *f*.

ass [as] *n* asino *m*, somaro *m*.

assail [ə'seil] *v* assalire, aggredire. **assailant** *n* aggressore *m*.

assassinate [ə'sasineit] *v* assassinare. **assassin** *n* assassino, -a *m, f*. **assassination** *n* assassinio *m*.

assault [ə'soilt] *n* assalto *m*, attacco *m*. *v* assalire, attaccare.

assemble [ə'sembl] *v* riunire, riunirsi; *(put together)* montare. **assembly** *n* assemblea *f*, riunione *f*. **assembly line** catena di montaggio *f*.

assent [ə'sent] *v* assentire, approvare. *n* assenso *m*, consenso *m*.

assert [ə'soit] *v* asserire, sostenere. **assert oneself** farsi valere, imporsi. **assertion** *n* asserzione *f*, rivendicazione *f*.

assess [ə'ses] *v* valutare, stimare. **assessment** *n* valutazione *f*, imposizione di tassa *f*. **assessor** *n* assessore *m*, agente del fisco *m*.

asset ['aset] *n* bene *m*. **assets** *pl n* attività *f pl*.

assiduous [ə'sidjuəs] *adj* assiduo.

assign [ə'sain] *v* assegnare; *(law)* delegare. **assignee** *n* mandatario *m*. **assignment** *n* assegnazione *f*, attribuzione *f*.

assimilate [ə'simileit] v assimilare. **assimilation** n assimilazione f.
assist [ə'sist] v assistere, aiutare. **assistance** n assistenza f, soccorso m. **assistant** n assistente m, f, aiutante m, f; (shop) commesso, -a m, f.
associate [ə'sousieit; n ə'sousiət] v associare, associarsi. **associate with** frequentare. n socio, -a m, f, collega m, f. **association** n associazione f, società f; (club) circolo m.
assorted [ə'sɔɪtid] adj assortito. **assortment** n assortimento m.
assume [ə'sjuɪm] v assumere; presumere. **assumption** n assunzione f, supposizione f. **assuming that** supposto che.
assure [ə'ʃuə] v assicurare. **assurance** n assicurazione f, certezza f, promessa f.
asterisk ['astərisk] n asterisco m.
asthma ['asmə] n asma m.
astonish [ə'stoniʃ] v stupire, meravigliare. **astonishing** adj sbalorditivo, sorprendente. **astonishment** n sorpresa f, stupore m.
astound [ə'staund] v stupefare, stupire. **astounding** adj stupefacente, sbalorditivo.
astray [ə'strei] adv fuori strada. **go astray** smarrirsi. **lead astray** sviare, traviare.
astride [ə'straid] adv a cavalcioni.
astringent [ə'strindʒənt] adj astringente.
astrology [ə'strolədʒi] n astrologia f. **astrologer** n astrologo, -a m, f.
astronaut ['astrənɔit] n astronauta m, f.
astronomy [ə'stronəmi] n astronomia f. **astronomer** n astronomo, -a m, f. **astronomic(al)** adj astronomico.
astute [ə'stjuɪt] adj astuto, furbo.
asunder [ə'sʌndə] adv a pezzi.
asylum [ə'sailəm] n ricovero m, rifugio m; (for the insane) manicomio m.
at [at] prep a, in, da.
ate [et] V eat.
atheism ['eiθiizəm] n ateismo m. **atheist** n ateo, -a m, f.
Athens ['aθinz] n Atene f. **Athenian** n(m+f), adj ateniese.
athlete ['aθliɪt] n atleta m, f. **athletic** adj atletico. **athletics** n atletica f.
Atlantic [ət'lantik] nm, adj atlantico.
atlas ['atləs] n atlante m.
atmosphere ['atməsfiə] n atmosfera f; ambiente m. **atmospheric** adj atmosferico. **atmospherics** pl n disturbi atmosferici m pl.

atom ['atəm] n atomo m. **atomic** adj atomico.
atone [ə'toun] v espiare, fare ammenda. **atonement** n espiazione f.
atrocious [ə'trouʃəs] adj atroce, terribile. **atrocity** n atrocità f.
attach [ə'tatʃ] v attaccare, attribuire. **become attached to** affezionarsi a. **attachment** n (friendship) affezione f; (law) sequestro m; (tech) accessorio m.
attaché [ə'taʃei] n addetto m. **attaché case** n valigetta rigida f, borsa per documenti f.
attack [ə'tak] v attaccare, assalire. n attacco m; offensiva f; (med) accesso. **attacker** n aggressore m.
attain [ə'tein] v ottenere, raggiungere. **attainment** n raggiungimento m, conseguimento m. **attainments** pl n coltura f sing.
attempt [ə'tempt] v tentare, provare. n tentativo m, prova f; (crime) attentato m.
attend [ə'tend] v (wait on) servire, accompagnare; (listen) prestar attenzione; (be present at) assistere. **attendance** n presenza f; servizio m. **attendant** n inserviente m, f; sorvegliante m, f, assistente m, f.
attention [ə'tenʃən] n attenzione f, cura f. **pay attention** far attenzione, stare attento. **attentive** adj attento, sollecito, premuroso.
attic ['atik] n attico m, soffitta f.
attire [ə'taiə] n abbigliamento m. v vestire.
attitude ['atitjuɪd] n atteggiamento m, posa f.
attorney [ə'təɪni] n procuratore m. **power of attorney** procura f.
attract [ə'trakt] v attrarre, attirare; affascinare. **attraction** n attrazione f; fascino m. **attractive** adj attraente; affascinante.
attribute ['atribjuɪt; v ə'tribjuɪt] n attributo m, qualità f. v attribuire, ascrivere. **attribution** n attribuzione f.
attrition [ə'triʃən] n attrito m.
atypical [ei'tipikl] adj atipico.
aubergine ['oubəʒiɪn] n melanzana f.
auburn ['ɔɪbən] adj invar color rame.
auction ['ɔɪkʃən] n asta f. v vendere all'asta. **auctioneer** n venditore all'asta m, banditore m.
audacious [ɔɪ'deiʃəs] adj audace, intrepido. **audacity** n temerità f.

audible ['ɔɪdəbl] *adj* udibile. **audibility** *n* udibilità *f.*

audience ['ɔɪdjəns] *n* pubblico *m*; *(assembly of spectators)* uditorio *m*; *(formal interview)* udienza *f.*

audiovisual [ɔɪdiou'viʒuəl] *adj* audiovisivo.

audit ['ɔɪdit] *n* controllo *m*, verifica dei conti *f*, revisione *f. v* rivedere, verificare i conti. **auditor** *n* revisore di conti *m*; sindaco *m.*

audition [ɔɪ'diʃən] *n* audizione *f. v* ascoltare in audizione.

auditorium [ɔɪdi'tɔɪriəm] *n* sala per concerti *f*, auditorio *m.*

augment [ɔɪg'ment] *v* aumentare, crescere.

August ['ɔɪgəst] *n* agosto *m.*

aunt [aɪnt] *n* zia *f.*

au pair [ou 'peə] *n* ragazza alla pari *f.*

aura ['ɔɪrə] *n* aura *f.*

auspicious [ɔɪ'spiʃəs] *adj* propizio, di buon augurio.

austere [ɔɪ'stiə] *adj* austero. **austerity** *n* austerità *f.*

Australia [o'streiljə] *n* Australia *f.* **Australian** *n*, *adj* australiano, -a.

Austria ['ostriə] *n* Austria *f.* **Austrian** *n*, *adj* austriaco, -a.

authentic [ɔɪ'θentik] *adj* autentico. **authenticate** *v* convalidare. **authenticity** *n* autenticità *f.*

author ['ɔɪθə] *n* autore, -trice *m*, *f.*

authority [ɔɪ'θɔɪəti] *n* autorità *f*; *(influence)* ascendente *m*; *(accepted source)* fonte autorevole *f.* **on good authority** da fonte autorevole. **authoritative** *adj* autorevole. **authoritarian** *adj* autoritario.

authorize ['ɔɪθəraiz] *v* autorizzare. **authorization** *n* autorizzazione *f.*

autobiography [ɔɪtoubai'ogrəfi] *n* autobiografia *f.* **autobiographical** *adj* autobiografico.

autocratic [ɔɪtou'kratik] *adj* autocratico.

autograph ['ɔɪtəgraɪf] *n* autografo *m. v* autografare.

automatic [ɔɪtə'matik] *adj* automatico. **automation** *n* automazione *f.*

automobile ['ɔɪtəməbiɪl] *n* automobile *f*; *(fam)* macchina *f.*

autonomous [ɔɪ'tonəməs] *adj* autonomo.

autopsy ['ɔɪtopsi] *n* autopsia *f.*

autumn ['ɔɪtəm] *n* autunno *m.* **autumnal** *adj* autunnale.

auxiliary [ɔɪg'ziljəri] *n*, *adj* ausiliario, -a.

avail [ə'veil] *v* servire, giovare a. **avail oneself of** servirsi di. *n* vantaggio *m.* **be of no avail** non servire a nulla.

available [ə'veiləbl] *adj* disponibile, libero; *(to hand)* sotto mano. **availability** *n* disponibilità *f.*

avalanche ['avəlainʃ] *n* valanga *f.*

avarice ['avəris] *n* avarizia *f.* **avaricious** *adj* avaro.

avenge [ə'vendʒ] *v* vendicare, vendicarsi. **avenger** *n* vendicatore, -trice *m*, *f.*

avenue ['avinjuɪ] *n* viale *m.*

average ['avəridʒ] *n* media *f.* **on average** in media. *adj* medio. *v* fare la media.

aversion [ə'vəɪʃən] *n* avversione *f*, antipatia *f.* **not be averse to** non aver nulla in contrario a.

avert [ə'vəɪt] *n* *(turn away)* distogliere; *(ward off)* allontanare; *(prevent)* prevenire.

aviary ['eiviəri] *n* uccelliera *f.*

aviation [eivi'eiʃən] *n* aviazione *f.*

avid ['avid] *adj* avido.

avocado [avə'kaɪdou] *n* pera avocado *f.*

avoid [ə'void] *v* evitare, schivare. **avoidance** *n* fuga *f*; l'evitare *m.*

await [ə'weit] *v* aspettare, attendere.

***awake** [ə'weik] *adj* sveglio. *v* svegliare, svegliarsi. **awaken** *v* risvegliare, risvegliarsi. **awakening** *n* risveglio *m.*

award [ə'wɔɪd] *n* premio *m*; *(honour)* onorificenza *f. v* aggiudicare, premiare, conferire.

aware [ə'weə] *adj* consapevole, conscio. **be aware of** sapere, rendersi conto di. **awareness** *n* consapevolezza *f*, sensibilità *f.*

away [ə'wei] *adv* lontano, via; *(absent)* fuori.

awe [ɔɪ] *n* timore reverenziale *m.* **awestruck** *adj* in preda a timore. **awe-inspiring** *adj* che incute rispetto.

awful ['ɔɪful] *adj* terribile, spaventoso. **awfully** *adv* terribilmente; *(coll)* molto.

awkward ['ɔɪkwəd] *adj* goffo, sgraziato.

awl [ɔɪl] *n* lesina *f.*

awning ['ɔɪniŋ] *n* tenda *f.*

awoke [ə'wouk] *V* awake.

awoken [ə'woukn] *V* awake.

axe [aks] *n* ascia *f*, scure *f.*

axiom ['aksiəm] *n* assioma *f.*

axis ['aksis] *n* asse *m.*

axle ['aksl] *n* asse *m*; perno *m.*

B

babble ['babl] *v* balbettare, ciarlare. *n* balbettio *m*.
baby ['beibi] *n* bimbo, -a *m*, *f*, bebè *m*.
babysitter *n* babysitter *m*,*f invar*. **babyish** *adj* bambinesco.
bachelor ['batʃələ] *n* scapolo *m*. **Bachelor of Arts/Science** *n* laureato, -a in lettere/scienze *m*, *f*.
back [bak] *n* (*anat*) dorso *m*, schiena *f*; (*chair*) schienale *m*; (*reverse*) rovescio *m*. **back to front** a rovescio. *adv* dietro, indietro, di ritorno. *v* appoggiare, sostenere; (*bet on*) scommettere su, puntare su. **back out** ritirarsi.
*backbite ['bakbait] *v* calunniare, sparlare di.
backbone ['bakboun] *n* spina dorsale *f*.
backdate [ˌbak'deit] *v* retrodatare.
backfire [ˌbak'faiə] *v* far ritorno di fiamma; (*coll*) andare all'aria.
background ['bakgraund] *n* sfondo *m*; (*milieu*) ambiente *m*.
backhand ['bakhand] *n* rovescio *m*.
backlash ['baklaʃ] *n* contraccolpo *m*.
backlog ['baklog] *n* arretrati *m pl*.
back pay *n* arretrati di paga *m pl*.
backside ['baksaid] *n* sedere *m*.
*backslide ['bakslaid] *v* ricadere nell'errore.
backstage ['baksteidʒ] *adv* dietro le quinte.
backstroke ['bakstrouk] *n* nuoto sul dorso *m*.
backward ['bakwəd] *adj* tardivo, arretrato.
backwards ['bakwədz] *adv* indietro, all'indietro.
backwater ['bakwoitə] *n* (*pool*) acqua stagnante *f*; (*place*) posto dove non succede mai nulla *m*.
bacon ['beikən] *n* pancetta *f*.
bacteria [bak'tiəriə] *pl n* batteri *m pl*.
bad [bad] *adj* cattivo, malvagio, dannoso, brutto; (*serious*) grave. **bad language** parolacce *f pl*. **feel bad** sentirsi male. **go bad** andare a male. **badly** *adv* male, malamente; (*seriously*) gravemente.
badge [badʒ] *n* distintivo *m*, emblema *m*.
badger ['badʒə] *n* tasso *m*. *v* molestare.
baffle ['bafl] *v* sconcertare, confondere.
baffling *adj* sconcertante.

bag [bag] *n* sacco *m*, borsa *f*, borsetta *f*. *v* insaccare; (*coll*) impadronirsi di, prendere.
bail¹ [beil] *n* (*law*) cauzione *f*, garanzia *f*. **grant bail** concedere libertà provvisoria (su cauzione). **stand bail for** rendersi garante per. *v* dar garanzia per, prestar cauzione a. **bail out** ottenere libertà provvisoria (su cauzione) per.
bail² *or* **bale** [beil] *v* **bail out** (*flooded boat*) aggottare; (*from aircraft*) lanciarsi.
bailiff ['beilif] *n* (*law*) funzionario incaricato a fare sequestri *m*; (*of estate*) fattore *m*.
bait [beit] *n* (*fishing*) esca *f*; (*lure*) lusinga *f*. *v* adescare; (*annoy*) tormentare.
bake [beik] *v* cuocere al forno. **baker** *n* fornaio panettiere *m*. **bakery** *n* panificio *m*. **baking powder** lievito minerale *m*, bicarbonato *m*. **baking tin** teglia *f*.
balance ['baləns] *n* equilibrio *m*, armonia *f*; (*scales*) bilancia *f*; (*comm*) bilancio *m*. **balance of payments** bilancia dei pagamenti *f*. *v* bilanciare, equilibrare; (*comm*) fare il bilancio.
balcony ['balkəni] *n* balcone *m*; (*theatre*) balconata *f*.
bald [boild] *adj* calvo; (*naked*) nudo, disadorno. **baldness** *n* calvizie *f invar*.
bale¹ [beil] *n* balla *f*. *v* imballare.
bale² *V* **bail²**.
baleful ['beilful] *adj* maligno, distruttivo.
ball¹ [boil] *n* palla *f*; (*inflatable*) pallone *m*; (*sphere*) sfera *f*. **ball-bearings** *pl n* cuscinetti a sfere *m pl*. **ball-point pen** penna a sfera *f*.
ball² [boil] *n* (*dance*) ballo *m*. **ballroom** *n* sala da ballo *f*.
ballad ['baləd] *n* ballata *f*; (*music*) canzone popolare *f*.
ballast ['baləst] *n* zavorra *f*. *v* zavorrare.
ballet ['balei] *n* balletto *m*. **ballet dancer** ballerino, -a *m*, *f*.
ballistic [bə'listik] *adj* balistico. **ballistic missile** proiettile balistico *m*.
balloon [bə'luin] *n* pallone *m*, aerostato *m*; (*toy*) palloncino *m*. **balloonist** *n* aeronauta *m*.
ballot ['balət] *n* votazione *f*, scrutinio *m*; (*paper*) scheda *f*. *v* ballottare, votare segretamente. **ballot-box** *n* urna elettorale *f*.

bamboo [bam'buː] *n* bambù *m*.
ban [ban] *n* proibizione *f*, bando *m*, interdizione *f*. *v* proibire, interdire.
banal [bə'naːl] *adj* banale.
banana [bə'naːnə] *n* (*fruit*) banana *f*; (*tree*) banano *m*.
band[1] [band] *n* (*troop*) banda *f*, schiera *f*; (*music*) banda *f*, orchestrina *f*. **bandstand** *n* palco per banda *m*. *v* **band together** legare insieme.
band[2] [band] *n* (*strip*) striscia *f*, fascia *f*.
bandage ['bandidʒ] *n* benda *f*, fascia *f*. *v* bendare, fasciare.
bandit ['bandit] *n* bandito *m*.
bandy ['bandi] *adj* storto, curvo. **bandy-legged** *adj* a gambe storte. *v* **bandy words** scambiare parole.
bang [baŋ] *n* colpo *m*, botta *f*. *v* sbattere.
bangle ['baŋgl] *n* braccialetto *m*.
banish ['baniʃ] *v* bandire, esiliare. **banishment** *n* bando *m*, esilio *m*.
banister ['banistə] *n* ringhiera *f*.
banjo ['bandʒou] *n* banjo *m invar*.
bank[1] [baŋk] *n* (*edge*) sponda *f*; (*river*) riva *f*. *v* arginare.
bank[2] [baŋk] *n* banca *f*, banco *m*. **bank account** conto in banca *m*. **bank holiday** festa legale *f*. **bank manager** direttore di banca *m*. *v* depositare in banca. **bank on** contare su.
bankrupt ['baŋkrʌpt] *adj* fallito. *v* far fallire. **bankruptcy** *n* fallimento *m*.
banner ['banə] *n* stendardo *m*, insegna *f*.
banquet ['baŋkwit] *n* banchetto *m*.
banter ['bantə] *v* canzonare, prendere in giro. *n* presa in giro *f*.
baptize [bap'taiz] *v* battezzare. **baptism** *n* battesimo *m*. **baptismal** *adj* battesimale. **Baptist** *n* battista *m*.
bar [baː] *n* (*metal*) sbarra *f*, stanga *f*; (*line*) striscia *f*; (*chocolate*) tavoletta *f*; (*law*) ordine degli avvocati *m*; barriera *f*; (*drinks*) bar *m invar*; (*music*) battuta *f*. **barmaid** *n* cameriera al banco *f*, barista *f*. **barman** *n* barista *m*. *v* proibire, impedire, escludere. *prep* eccetto, tranne.
barbarian [baː'beəriən] *n*, *adj* barbaro, -a.
barbecue ['baːbikjuː] *n* arrosto all'aperto *m*. *v* arrostire all'aperto.
barb [baːb] *n* spina *f*. **barbed** *adj* pungente. **barbed wire** filo spinato *m*.
barber ['baːbə] *n* barbiere *m*, parrucchiere *m*.
barbiturate [baː'bitjurət] *n* barbiturato *m*.

bare [beə] *adj* (*without covering*) scoperto; (*simple*) semplice; (*naked*, *unadorned*) nudo; (*just sufficient*) appena sufficiente. *v* denudare, rivelare. **barefoot** *adj*, *adv* scalzo, a piedi scalzi. **barely** *adv* appena.
bargain ['baːgin] *n* (*transaction*) affare *m*; (*offer*) occasione *f*. **into the bargain** per giunta, in più. *v* contrattare, mercanteggiare.
barge [baːdʒ] *n* barcone *m*, chiatta *f*. *v* **barge in** intervenire a sproposito, irrompere. **barge into** imbattersi per caso.
baritone ['baritoun] *n* baritono *m*.
bark[1] [baːk] *n* (*dog*) latrato *m*. *v* abbaiare, latrare.
bark[2] [baːk] *n* (*tree*) scorza *f*, corteccia *f*.
barley ['baːli] *n* orzo *m*. **barley sugar** zucchero d'orzo *m*. **barley water** tisana d'orzo *f*.
barn [baːn] *n* granaio *m*.
barometer [bə'romitə] *n* barometro *m*.
baron ['barən] *n* barone *m*. **baroness** *n* baronessa *f*. **baronet** *n* baronetto *m*.
baroque [bə'rok] *nm*, *adj* barocco.
barracks ['baraks] *pl n* caserma *f sing*.
barrage ['baraːʒ] *n* sbarramento *m*.
barrel ['barəl] *n* (*cask*) barile *m*, botte *f*; (*gun*, *etc.*) canna *f*. **barrel organ** organetto *m*.
barren ['barən] *adj* sterile, infecondo.
barricade [bari'keid] *n* barricata *f*. *v* barricare.
barrier ['bariə] *n* barriera *f*.
barrister ['baristə] *n* avvocato *m*.
barrow ['barou] *n* carretta *f*; (*archaeol*) tumulo *m*.
barter ['baːtə] *v* barattare. *n* baratto *m*.
base[1] [beis] *v* fondare, basare. *n* base *f*, fondamento *m*. **baseless** *adj* infondato.
base[2] [beis] *adj* vile, basso. **baseness** *n* bassezza *f*.
basement ['beismənt] *n* sottosuolo *m*.
bash [baʃ] *n* colpo violento *m*. *v* colpire violentemente.
bashful ['baʃful] *adj* timido, vergognoso.
basic ['beisik] *adj* fondamentale; (*chem*) basico.
basil ['bazl] *n* basilico *m*.
basin ['beisin] *n* bacino *m*, catino *m*; (*wash-basin*) lavabo *m*.
basis ['beisis] *n*, *pl* -**ses** base *f*, fondamento *m*.
bask [bask] *v* crogiolarsi.

basket ['baɪskɪt] n cesto m, paniere m.
basketball n pallacanestro f.
Basle [baɪl] n Basilea f.
bas-relief ['basriˌliːf] n bassorilievo m.
bass¹ [beis] n basso m.
bass² [bas] n (sea) branzino m, spigola f; (freshwater) pesce persico m.
bassoon [bə'suːn] n fagotto m.
bastard ['baɪstəd] n, adj bastardo, -a.
baste [beist] v (cookery) arrosolare; (sewing) imbastire; (beat) bastonare.
bastion ['bastjən] n bastione m.
bat¹ [bat] n (cricket, baseball) mazza f; (table tennis) racchetta f. v battere.
bat² [bat] n (zool) pipistrello m. blind as a bat cieco come una talpa.
batch [batʃ] n lotto m, partita f; (bread) infornata f.
bath [baɪθ] n bagno m. v fare un bagno; lavare. bathchair n carrozzella per invalidi f. bathmat n stuoia da bagno f. bathrobe n accappatoio m. bathroom n stanza da bagno f.
bathe [beið] v bagnare, fare un or il bagno. bather n bagnante m, f. bathing cap cuffia da bagno f. bathing costume costume da bagno m. bathing trunks calzoncini da bagno m pl.
baton ['batn] n (mil) bastone m; (music) bacchetta f.
battalion [bə'taljən] n battaglione m.
batter¹ ['batə] v percuotere, colpire con violenza. battering ram (mil) ariete m.
batter² ['batə] n (cookery) pastella f.
battery ['batəri] n batteria f, pila f.
battle ['batl] n battaglia f, combattimento m. battlefield n campo di battaglia m. battleship n nave da battaglia f. v combattere, lottare.
bawdy ['boɪdi] adj licenzioso.
bawl [boɪl] v urlare, gridare.
bay¹ [bei] n (geog) baia f, golfo m, insenatura f.
bay² [bei] v (cry) abbaiare. n latrato m. at bay a bada.
bay³ [bei] n (tree) lauro m.
bayonet ['beiənit] n baionetta f.
bay window n finestra sporgente f.
*be [biː] v essere, esistere; (remain) stare.
beach [biːtʃ] n spiaggia f, lido m.
beacon ['biːkən] n faro m; (fire) falò m.
bead [biːd] n grano m; (liquid) goccia f.
beagle ['biːgl] n cane da caccia m.
beak [biːk] n becco m, rostro m.
beaker ['biːkə] n coppa f.

beam [biːm] n (wood) trave f; (light) raggio m; (radio) segnale m; (smile) sorriso m. v irradiare; (smile) sorridere.
bean [biːn] n fava f, fagiolo m; (coffee) chicco m. French bean fagiolino m. full of beans energico.
*bear¹ [beə] v (carry) portare; (support weight) reggere; (tolerate) soffrire, sopportare; (give birth to) dare alla luce. bear oneself comportarsi. bear with aver pazienza con. bearable adj sopportabile. bearer n portatore, -trice m, f.
bear² [beə] n orso, -a m, f.
beard [biəd] n barba f. v sfidare. bearded adj barbuto. beardless adj imberbe.
bearing ['beəriŋ] n condotta f, contegno m; (aircraft) rilevamento m; (mech) cuscinetto m. bearings pl n orientamento m sing, senso di direzione m sing. lose one's bearings disorientarsi.
beast [biːst] n bestia f, animale m. beastly adj bestiale; (coll) veramente cattivo.
*beat [biːt] v battere; (hit) bastonare; (heart) palpitare; (defeat) sconfiggere; (eggs, etc.) sbattere. n battito m, palpito m; (music) battuta f; (police) ronda f. beating n bastonata f, sconfitta f.
beaten ['biːtn] V beat.
beauty ['bjuːti] n bellezza f. beautiful adj bello. beautify v abbellire.
beaver ['biːvə] n castoro m.
became [bi'keim] V become.
because [bi'koz] conj perché, poiché. because of a causa di.
beckon ['bekən] v chiamare con un cenno.
*become [bi'kʌm] v diventare, divenire. becoming adj che sta bene; (suitable) conveniente.
bed [bed] n letto m; (sea) fondo m; (coal) giacimento m; (flowers) aiuola f. bedbug n cimice m. bedroom n camera da letto f. bedside n capezzale m. bedsitter n camera studio f. bedspread n copriletto m. double bed letto matrimoniale m. go to bed andare a letto. twin beds letti gemelli m pl. bedding n (sheets) lenzuola f pl; (covers) coperte f pl.
bedevil [bi'devl] v vessare.
bedlam ['bedləm] n confusione f.
bedraggled [bi'dragld] adj fradicio, inzaccherato.
bee [biː] n ape f. beehive n alveare m. bee-keeper n apicoltore m.

beech [biːtʃ] *n* faggio *m*.
beef [biːf] *n* manzo *m*. **beefsteak** *n* bistecca *f*.
been [biːn] *V* be.
beer [biə] *n* birra *f*.
beetle ['biːtl] *n* scarabeo *m*. **black beetle** scarafaggio *m*.
beetroot ['biːtruːt] *n* barbabietola *f*.
before [bi'fɔː] *adv* prima, già. *prep* prima di, davanti a. *conj* prima che. **beforehand** *adv* in anticipo.
befriend [bi'frend] *v* sostenere, mostrarsi amico a.
beg [beg] *v* implorare, pregare; (*for alms*) chiedere l'elemosina. **beggar** *n* mendicante *m, f*.
began [bi'gan] *V* **begin**.
***begin** [bi'gin] *v* cominciare, iniziare. **to begin with** anzitutto. **beginner** *n* principiante *m, f*. **beginning** *n* principio *m*, inizio *m*.
begrudge [bi'grʌdʒ] *v* invidiare.
begun [bi'gʌn] *V* **begin**.
behalf [bi'haːf] *n* **on behalf of** a nome di.
behave [bi'heiv] *v* comportarsi. **behaviour** *n* condotta *f*, comportamento *m*.
behead [bi'hed] *v* decapitare.
beheld [bi'held] *V* **behold**.
behind [bi'haind] *adv* dietro, indietro; (*late*) in ritardo. *prep* dietro a *or* di, dopo. **behindhand** *adv* in arretrato, in ritardo. *n* (*coll*) sedere *m*.
***behold** [bi'hould] *v* vedere. **beholder** *n* osservatore, -trice *m, f*.
beige [beiʒ] *adj* beige *invar*.
being ['biːiŋ] *n* essere *m*, creatura *f*. **for the time being** per il momento.
belated [bi'leitid] *adj* tardivo.
belch [beltʃ] *v* ruttare. *n* rutto *m*.
belfry ['belfri] *n* campanile *m*.
Belgium ['beldʒəm] *n* Belgio *m*. **Belgian** *n*(*m+f*), *adj* belga (*m pl* -gi).
believe [bi'liːv] *v* credere, pensare, aver fede in. **make believe** *v* far finta. **belief** *n*, *pl* -s fede *f*, credenza *f*, opinione *f*. **believable** *adj* credibile. **believer** *n* credente *m, f*, fedele *m, f*.
bell [bel] *n* campana *f*; (*door*) campanello *m*. **bellringer** *n* campanaro *m*. **bell-tower** *n* campanile *m*.
belligerent [bi'lidʒərənt] *adj* belligerente.
bellow ['belou] *v* urlare, muggire.
bellows ['belouz] *pl n* soffietto *m sing*, mantice *m sing*.

belly ['beli] *n* pancia *f*, ventre *m*.
belong [bi'loŋ] *v* appartenere, spettare, far parte (di). **belongings** *pl n* roba *f sing*, effetti personali *m pl*.
beloved [bi'lʌvid] *n, adj* amato, -a.
below [bi'lou] *adv* sotto, di sotto, giù. *prep* sotto, al di sotto di, inferiore a.
belt [belt] *n* cintura *f*; (*mech*) cinghia *f*; (*zone*) fascia *f*. *v* (*coll: hit*) picchiare; (*coll: rush*) precipitarsi.
bench [bentʃ] *n* (*workshop*) banco *m*; (*long seat*) panchina *f*, panca *f*; (*law*) magistratura *f*.
***bend** [bend] *v* piegare, curvare. *n* curva *f*, svolta *f*.
beneath [bi'niːθ] *adv* giù, abbasso. *prep* sotto, al di sotto di.
benefactor ['benəfaktə] *n* benefattore, -trice *m, f*. **benefaction** *n* beneficenza *f*.
benefit ['benəfit] *n* beneficio *m*, vantaggio *m*, utilità *f*. *v* giovare a, far bene a, approfittare. **beneficial** *adj* vantaggioso, utile. **beneficiary** *n, adj* beneficiario, -a.
benevolent [bi'nevələnt] *adj* benevolo, caritatevole. **benevolence** *n* benevolenza *f*.
benign [bi'nain] *adj* benevolo; (*med*) benigno.
bent [bent] *V* **bend**. *adj* curvato; (*determined*) risoluto; (*dishonest*) corrotto. *n* tendenza *f*.
bequeath [bi'kwiːð] *v* lasciare per testamento. **bequest** *n* lascito *m*.
bereaved [bi'riːvd] **be bereaved** essere in lutto. **bereavement** *n* lutto *m*.
beret ['berei] *n* beretto *m*.
berry ['beri] *n* bacca *f*, chicco *m*.
berserk [bə'səːk] *adv* **go berserk** montare su tutte le furie.
berth [bəːθ] *n* (*sleeping*) cuccetta *f*; (*naut*) posto d'ormeggio *m*. **give a wide berth to** evitare. *v* ancorare.
beside [bi'said] *prep* accanto a, presso, vicino a. **be beside oneself** essere fuori di sè. **besides** *adv* d'altronde, inoltre, per di più.
besiege [bi'siːdʒ] *v* assediare.
best [best] *adj* il migliore. *adv* meglio. **as best one can** come meglio si può, il meglio possibile. **come off best** avere la meglio. **do one's best** fare del proprio meglio. **the best** il meglio. **to the best of my knowledge** per quanto ne sappia.
bestial ['bestjəl] *adj* bestiale.

bestow [bi'stou] *v* conferire, dare.
bet [bet] *n* scommessa *f. v* scommettere.
betray [bi'tɪei] *v* tradire, svelare. **betrayal** *n* tradimento *m.*
better ['betə] *adj* meglio, migliore. *adv* meglio, in modo migliore. *v* migliorare. **all the better** tanto meglio. **be** *or* **feel better** star meglio. **get the better of** aver la meglio su.
between [bi'twiɪn] *adv* in mezzo. *prep* tra, fra, in mezzo a.
beverage ['bevəridʒ] *n* bevanda *f*, bibita *f.*
***beware** [bi'weə] *v* guardarsi da, stare attento a. **beware of the dog!** attenti al cane!
bewilder [bi'wildə] *v* sconcertare, confondere. **bewildered** *adj* sconcertato, perplesso. **bewildering** *adj* sconcertante. **bewilderment** *n* disorientamento *m.*
beyond [bi'jond] *adv* oltre, più in là. *prep* oltre, al di là di.
bias ['baiəs] *n* inclinazione *f*, pregiudizio *m*, preconcetto *m.* **on the bias** (*tailoring*) per sbieco. **biased** *adj* prevenuto.
bib [bib] *n* bavaglino *m.*
Bible ['baibl] *n* bibbia *f.* **biblical** *adj* biblico.
bibliography [bibli'ogrəfi] *n* bibliografia *f.* **bibliographer** *n* bibliografo, -a *m, f.* **bibliographical** *adj* bibliografico.
biceps ['baiseps] *n* bicipite *m.*
bicker ['bikə] *v* litigare, bisticciare. **bickering** *n* bisticciarsi *m invar.*
bicycle ['baisikl] *n* bicicletta *f.*
***bid** [bid] *n* offerta *f*; (*cards*) dichiarazione *f. v* (*order*) comandare; (*auction*) offrire; (*cards*) dichiarare. **bidder** *n* offerente *m, f*; dichiaratore, -trice *m, f.* **bidding** *n* ordine *m*; dichiarazione *f.*
bide [baid] *v* **bide one's time** aspettare il momento propizio.
bidet ['biɪdei] *n* bidè *m.*
biennial [bai'eniəl] *adj* biennale.
bifocals [bai'foukəlz] *pl n* lenti bifocali *f pl.*
big [big] *adj* grande, grosso, importante.
bigamy ['bigəmi] *n* bigamia *f.* **bigamist** *n* bigamo *m.* **bigamous** *adj* bigamo.
bigot ['bigət] *n* bigotto *m*, fanatico, -a *m, f.* **bigoted** *adj* bigotto, fanatico. **bigotry** *n* bigotteria *f*, fanatismo *m.*
bikini [bi'kiɪni] *n* bikini *m invar.*
bilateral [bai'latərəl] *adj* bilaterale.
bilingual [bai'liŋwəl] *adj* bilingue.

bilious ['biljəs] *adj* (*med*) biliare; (*irritable*) collerico; (*sickly*) nauseante. **bile** *n* bile *f.* **biliousness** *n* travaso di bile *m.*
bill[1] [bil] *n* (*hotel, restaurant*) conto *m*; (*shop, invoice*) fattura *f*; (*pol*) progetto di legge *m*, atto *m*; (*poster*) affisso *m*; (*theatre*) cartellone *m.* **bill of fare** menù *m. v* fatturare; (*poster*) affiggere; (*theatre*) mettere in programma.
bill[2] [bil] *n* (*beak*) becco *m*, rostro *m.*
billiards ['biljədz] *n* biliardo *m.*
billion ['biljən] *n* (10^{12}) bilione *m*, mille miliardi *m pl*; (10^9) miliardo *m.*
billow ['bilou] *n* onda *f*; (*smoke*) ondata *f. v* (*sail*) gonfiarsi; (*smoke*) emanare.
bin [bin] *n* recipiente *m*; (*dustbin*) pattumiera *f.*
binary ['bainəri] *adj* binario.
***bind** [baind] *v* legare, attaccare; (*book*) rilegare; (*force*) costringere. *n* (*slang*) scocciatura *f.*
binding ['baindiŋ] *n* legatura *f*, legame *m*; (*book*) rilegatura *f. adj* impegnativo, obbligatorio.
binoculars [bi'nokjuləz] *pl n* binocolo *m sing.*
biography [bai'ogrəfi] *n* biografia *f.* **biographer** *n* biografo, -a *m, f.* **biographical** *adj* biografico.
biology [bai'olədʒi] *n* biologia *f.* **biological** *adj* biologico. **biologist** *n* biologo, -a *m, f.*
birch [bəɪtʃ] *n* betulla *f.*
bird [bəɪd] *n* uccello *m.* **bird's-eye view** veduta a volo d'uccello *f.*
birth [bəɪθ] *n* nascita *f*; origine *f*; discendenza *f.* **birth certificate** atto di nascita *m.* **birth control** controllo delle nascite *m.* **birthday** *n* compleanno *m.* **birthmark** *n* voglia *f.* **birthplace** *n* luogo di nascita *m.* **birth rate** natalità *f*, indice demografico *m.* **give birth to** mettere al mondo, dare alla luce.
biscuit ['biskit] *n* biscotto *m.*
bishop ['biʃəp] *n* (*church*) vescovo *m*; (*chess*) alfiere *m.*
bison ['baisən] *n* bisonte *m.*
bit[1] [bit] *V* bite. *n* (*horse*) morso *m*; (*drill*) punta *f*, morsa *f.*
bit[2] [bit] *n* (*morsel*) boccone *m*; (*small piece*) pezzo *m*, pezzetto *m.* **bit by bit** poco a poco. **do one's bit** fare la propria parte. **wait a bit!** aspetta un po'!
bitch [bitʃ] *n* cagna *f*; (*slang*) antipatica *f.* **bitchy** *adj* malvagio.

*bite [bait] *n* morso *m*; (*insect*) puntura *f*; (*fish*) l'abboccare *m*; (*food*) boccone *m*. *v* mordere, addentare. **biting** *adj* pungente, mordente.
bitten ['bitn] *V* bite.
bitter ['bitə] *adj* amaro, aspro, accanito. **bitter-sweet** *adj* agrodolce. **to the bitter end** ad oltranza. **bitterness** *n* amarezza *f*, rancore *m*.
bizarre [bi'zɑ:] *adj* bizzarro, strano.
black ['blak] *adj* nero. **things look black** le cose si mettono male. *n* (*colour*) nero *m*; (*person*) negro, -a *m*, *f*. **blacken** *v* annerire.
blackberry ['blakbəri] *n* (*fruit*) mora *f*; (*bush*) rovo *m*.
blackbird ['blakbə:d] *n* merlo *m*.
blackboard ['blakbɔ:d] *n* lavagna *f*.
blackcurrant [,blak'kʌrənt] *n* ribes nero *m* invar.
blackhead ['blakhed] *n* comedone *m*.
blackleg ['blakleg] *n* crumiro *m*.
blackmail ['blakmeil] *n* ricatto *m*. *v* ricattare. **blackmailer** *n* ricattatore, -trice *m*, *f*.
black market *n* borsa nera *f*.
blackout ['blakaut] *n* oscuramento *m*; (*med*) svenimento *m*.
blacksmith ['blaksmiθ] *n* fabbro *m*.
blackshirt ['blakʃə:t] *n* camicia nera *f*.
bladder ['bladə] *n* vescica *f*.
blade [bleid] *n* lama *f*; (*oar, propeller*) pala *f*; (*grass*) filo d'erba *m*.
blame [bleim] *n* biasimo *m*, responsabilità *f*. *v* biasimare, incolpare, rimproverare. **blameless** *adj* innocente.
blanch [blɑ:ntʃ] *v* (*cookery*) sbollentare; (*go pale*) impallidire.
bland [bland] *adj* blando.
blank [blaŋk] *adj* vuoto, in bianco; (*puzzled*) perplesso. *n* spazio vuoto *m*; (*cartridge*) cartuccia a salve *f*. **point blank** a bruciapelo.
blanket ['blaŋkit] *n* coperta *f*. *v* ricoprire.
blare [bleə] *v* squillare, sonare con tutta forza. *n* (*trumpet*) squillo *m*; (*loud noise*) chiasso *m*.
blaspheme [blas'fi:m] *v* bestemmiare. **blasphemous** *adj* blasfemo, empio. **blasphemy** *n* bestemmia *f*.
blast [blɑ:st] *n* (*wind*) raffica *f*; esplosione *f*. *v* far esplodere, far saltare. **blast-furnace** *n* altoforno (*pl* altiforni) *m*.
blatant ['bleitənt] *adj* vistoso, evidente.
blaze [bleiz] *n* (*flame*) fiamma *f*; (*sudden*

outburst of *fire*) vampata *f*. *v* ardere, divampare. **blazer** *n* giacca sportiva *f*.
bleach [bli:tʃ] *v* scolorire, candeggiare. *n* candeggina *f*.
bleak [bli:k] *adj* (*desolate*) triste; (*dreary*) squallido; (*depressing*) deprimente.
bleat [bli:t] *v* belare.
bled [bled] *V* bleed.
*bleed [bli:d] *v* sanguinare, perder sangue. **bleeding** *n* emoraggia *f*, perdita di sangue *f*.
blemish ['blemiʃ] *n* difetto *m*, imperfezione *f*. *v* sfigurare, macchiare.
blend [blend] *v* mescolare, combinare. *n* miscela intima *f*.
bless [bles] *v* benedire. **be blessed with** godere di, essere dotato di. **bless you!** salute! **blessing** *n* benedizione *f*.
blew [blu:] *V* blow².
blind [blaind] *adj* cieco. **blind drunk** ubriaco fradicio. **blind spot** punto cieco *m*. **turn a blind eye to** chiudere gli occhi davanti a. **blindness** *n* cecità *f*. *v* accecare, ingannare. *n* (*window*) tendina *f*, persiana *f*; (*pretence*) finzione *f*.
blindfold ['blaindfould] *n* benda (agli occhi) *f*. *v* bendare gli occhi.
blink [bliŋk] *v* battere le palpebre; (*wink*) ammiccare.
bliss [blis] *n* beatitudine *f*. **blissful** *adj* beato.
blister ['blistə] *n* bolla *f*, vescica *f*. *v* far venire vesciche; coprirsi di vesciche.
blizzard ['blizəd] *n* tormenta *f*, bufèra *f*.
blob [blob] *n* macchia *f*.
bloc [blok] *n* blocco *m*.
block [blok] *v* bloccare, sbarrare. *n* blocco *m*, ceppo *m*; (*large building*) palazzo *m*; (*obstacle*) ostacolo *m*. **block letter** stampatello *m*; (*capital*) maiuscola *f*.
blockade [blo'keid] *n* blocco *m*, assedio *m*. *v* bloccare.
bloke [blouk] *n* (*coll*) tipo *m*.
blond [blond] *adj* biondo. **blonde** *n* bionda *f*.
blood [blʌd] *n* sangue *m*; (*descent*) stirpe *f*. **blood clot** coagulo di sangue *m*. **bloodcurdling** *adj* raccapricciante. **blood group** gruppo sanguigno *m*. **bloodhound** *n* segugio *m*. **blood poisoning** setticemia *f*. **blood pressure** pressione sanguigna *f*. **bloodshed** *n* carneficina *f*. **bloodshot** *adj* arrossato. **bloodthirsty** *adj* assetato di sangue. **bloody** *adj* macchiato di sangue; (*slang*) maledetto.

bloom [bluːm] *v* fiorire. *n* fiore *m*, fioritura *f*.
blot [blot] *n* macchia *f*, sgorbio *m*. *v* macchiare. **blot out** cancellare. **blotting paper** carta assorbente *f*.
blouse [blauz] *n* blusa *f*, camicetta *f*.
blow¹ [blou] *n* colpo *m*; (*fist*) pugno *m*; (*stick*) bastonata *f*. **come to blows** venire alle mani.
*blow² [blou] *v* soffiare; (*trumpet*, *etc*.) suonare. **blow away** spazzar via. **blow one's nose** soffiarsi il naso. **blow out** spegnere. **blow up** (*explode*) far saltare; (*inflate*) gonfiare.
blown [bloun] *V* **blow²**.
blubber ['blʌbə] *n* (*whale*) grasso di balene *m*. *v* (*weep*) piangere singhiozzando.
blue [bluː] *nm*, *adj* azzurro; (*pale*) celeste; (*dark*) blu. **bluebell** *n* giacinto selvatico *m*. **blueprint** *n* progetto *m*.
bluff [blʌf] *v* ingannare; (*cards*) bluffare. *n* vanteria infondata *f*; (*poker*) bluff *m* *invar*.
blunder [blʌndə] *n* errore *m*, papera *f*. *v* commettere un errore.
blunt [blʌnt] *adj* (*not sharp*) ottuso, spuntato; (*frank*) brusco. *v* smussare, ottundere.
blur [bləː] *v* rendere confuso, oscurare. *n* offuscamento *m*, macchia *f*.
blush [blʌʃ] *v* arrossire. *n* rossore *m*.
boar [boː] *n* cinghiale *m*.
board [boːd] *v* (*ship*, *etc*.) abbordare, imbarcarsi. *n* (*wood*) asse *m*, tavola *f*; (*food*) vitto *m*; (*examiners*) commissione *f*. **board of directors** consiglio d'amministrazione *m*. **full board** pensione completa *f*. **half board** mezza pensione *f*. **on board** a bordo. **boarding house** pensione *f*. **boarding school** collegio *m*.
boast [boust] *n* vanto *m*. *v* vantare. **boastful** *adj* millantatore, vanaglorioso.
boat [bout] *n* barca *f*, battello *m*. **boat race** gara di canottaggio *f*. **boating** *n* canottaggio *m*.
bob [bob] *v* **bob up** (*come to surface*) venire a galla. **bob up and down** muoversi in su e in giù.
bobbin ['bobin] *n* bobina *f*.
bodice ['bodis] *n* busto *m*, liseuse *f*.
body ['bodi] *n* corpo *m*; entità *f*; gruppo *m*; (*corpse*) cadavere *m*; (*organization*) ente *m*. **bodyguard** *n* guardia del corpo *f*.

bog [bog] *n* palude *f*, pantano *m*.
bogus ['bougəs] *adj* falso.
bohemian [bə'hiːmiən] *adj* da artista.
boil¹ [boil] *v* bollire, far bollire, lessare. **boiler** *n* caldaia *f*. **boiler suit** tuta *f*. **boiling point** punto d'ebollizione *m*.
boil² [boil] *n* (*swelling*) foruncolo *m*.
boisterous ['boistərəs] *adj* chiassoso, impetuoso.
bold [bould] *adj* audace, ardito, sfacciato. **boldness** *n* audacia *f*, coraggio *m*.
bolster ['boulstə] *n* capezzale *m*, cuscino *m*. *v* **bolster up** sostenere.
bolt [boult] *n* (*for nut*) bullone *m*; (*door*) catenaccio *m*; (*arrow*) freccia *f*. *v* (*bar*) sprangare; (*run away*) scappare. **a bolt from the blue** un fulmine a ciel sereno. **bolt upright** diritto come un fuso.
bomb [bom] *n* bomba *f*. *v* bombardare. **bombing** *n* bombardamento *m*.
bond [bond] *n* (*tie*) legame *m*, vincolo *m*; (*agreement*) impegno *m*; (*comm*) titolo *m*; (*law*) cauzione *f*. **bonded warehouse** magazzino doganale *m*. **bondage** *n* schiavitù *f*.
bone [boun] *n* osso *m* (*pl* -a *f*). *v* disossare. **bony** *adj* ossuto.
bonfire ['bonfaiə] *n* falò *m*.
bonnet ['bonit] *n* (*hat*) cappellino *m*; (*car*) cofano *m*.
bonus ['bounəs] *n* gratifica *f*, premio *m*.
booby trap ['buːbi] *n* mina nascosta *f*, trappola esplosiva *f*; (*pitfall*) trabocchetto *m*.
book [buk] *n* libro *m*. *v* (*reserve*) prenotare.
bookcase ['bukkeis] *n* scaffale *m*.
booking ['bukiŋ] *n* prenotazione *f*.
bookkeeping ['buk‚kiːpiŋ] *n* contabilità *f*. **bookkeeper** *n* contabile *m*, *f*.
booklet ['buklit] *n* opuscolo *m*.
bookmaker ['bukmeikə] *n* bookmaker *m* *invar*, allibratore *m*.
bookmark ['bukmaːk] *n* segnalibro *m*.
bookseller ['buksələ] *n* libraio *m*.
bookshop ['bukʃop] *n* libreria *f*.
bookstall ['bukstoːl] *n* edicola *f*.
boom [buːm] *v* (*noise*) rimbombare, tuonare; (*econ*) essere in gran voga. *n* rimbombo *m*, tuono *m*; (*econ*) boom *m* *invar*.
boorish ['buəriʃ] *adj* grossolano.
boost [buːst] *n* pressione *f*, spinta *f*. *v* aumentare, spingere.

boot

boot [buːt] *n* (*shoe*) stivale *m*; (*car*) portabagagli *m*.

booth [buːð] *n* baracca *f*, cabina *f*.

booze [buːz] (*coll*) *n* bevanda alcoolica *f*. *v* ubriacarsi, sbronzarsi.

border ['boːdə] *n* orlo *m*, limite *m*, frontiera *f*. *v* (*embroidery*) orlare; (*geog*) confinare (con). **borderline case** caso limite *m*.

bore¹ [boː] *n* (*hole*) buco *m*, foro *m*; (*gun*) calibro *m*. *v* forare, trapanare; (*mech*) alesare.

bore² [boː] *v* (*weary*) seccare, annoiare. *n* (*person*) seccatore, -trice *m*, *f*; (*matter*) seccatura *f*; noia *f*.

bore³ [boː] *V* **bear¹**.

born [boːn] *adj* nato. **be born** nascere.

borne [boːn] *V* **bear¹**.

borough ['bʌrə] *n* comune *m*, borgo *m*.

borrow ['borou] *v* prendere a prestito, farsi prestare.

bosom ['buzəm] *n* petto *m*, seno *m*.

boss [bos] *n* capo *m*, direttore *m*. *v* comandare. **bossy** *adj* prepotente.

botany ['botəni] *n* botanica *f*. **botanical** *adj* botanico. **botanist** *n* botanico, -a *m*, *f*.

both [bouθ] *adj*, *pron* ambedue, entrambi, tutti e due.

bother ['boðə] *n* seccatura *f*, noia *f*. *v* seccare, preoccuparsi.

bottle ['botl] *n* bottiglia *f*. *v* imbottigliare. **bottleneck** *n* ingorgo *m*. **bottle-opener** *n* apribottiglie *m* *invar*.

bottom ['botəm] *n* fondo *m*. *adj* ultimo, inferiore. **bottomless** *adj* senza fondo.

bough [bau] *n* ramo *m*.

bought [boːt] *V* **buy**.

boulder ['bouldə] *n* macigno *m*, masso roccioso *m*.

bounce [bauns] *v* (*far*) rimbalzare. *n* balzo *m*, rimbalzo *m*.

bound¹ [baund] *v* saltare, rimbalzare. *n* salto *m*, balzo *m*. **by leaps and bounds** a passi da gigante.

bound² [baund] *n* confine *m*, restrizione *f*. *v* porre limiti a, confinare. **boundary** *n* limite *m*, frontiera *f*. **boundless** *adj* illimitato.

bound³ [baund] *adj* **bound for** diretto per, con destinazione per.

bound⁴ [baund] *V* **bind**.

bouquet [buːkei] *n* mazzo *m*.

bourgeois ['buəʒwaː] *n*(*m*+*f*), *adj* borghese.

bout [baut] *n* periodo d'attività *m*; (*illness*) attacco *m*; (*match*) ripresa *f*.

bow¹ [bau] *n* (*greeting*) saluto *m*; (*bend*) inchino *m*. *v* inchinarsi, salutare, chinare.

bow² [bou] *n* (*archery*) arco *m*; (*violin, etc.*) archetto *m*; (*ribbon*) fiocco *m*. **bow-legged** *adj* dalle gambe storte. **bow-tie** *n* cravatta a farfalla *f*.

bow³ [bau] *n* (*naut*) prua *f*, prora *f*.

bowels ['bauəlz] *pl n* viscere *f pl*.

bowl¹ [boul] *n* (*basin*) scodella *f*, bacino *m*.

bowl² [boul] *n* (*ball*) boccia *f*. *v* far rotolare, servire la palla. **bowls** *n* gioco delle bocce *m*. **bowler** *n* (*hat*) bombetta *f*.

box¹ [boks] *n* scatola *f*, cassetta *f*; (*theatre*) palco *m*. **box number** casella postale *f*. **box office** botteghino *m*.

box² [boks] *v* fare a pugni, fare del pugilato, fare la boxe. **boxing** *n* pugilato *m*, boxe *f*.

Boxing Day *n* giorno di San Stefano *m*.

boy [boi] *n* ragazzo *m*. **boyhood** *n* fanciullezza *f*. **boyish** *adj* da ragazzo.

boycott ['boikot] *n* boicottaggio *m*. *v* boicottare.

bra [braː] *n* reggipetto *m*, reggiseno *m*.

brace [breis] *v* fortificare, rinvigorire. *n* sostegno; (*tool*) trapano *m*; (*pair*) coppia *f*. **braces** *pl n* bretelle *f pl*.

bracelet ['breislit] *n* braccialetto *m*.

bracken ['brakən] *n* felce *f*.

bracket ['brakit] *n* mensola *f*, braccio *m*; (*printing*) parentesi *f invar*. **put in brackets** mettere fra parentesi. **bracket together** accoppiare.

brag [brag] *v* vantarsi. **braggart** *n* fanfarone *m*.

brain [brein] *n* cervello *m*. **brainwashing** *n* lavaggio del cervello *m*. **brainwave** *n* idea geniale *f*. **brainy** *adj* intelligente.

braise [breiz] *v* brasare, cuocere a stufato.

brake [breik] *n* freno *m*. *v* frenare, serrare il freno.

bramble ['brambl] *n* (*bush*) rovo *m*; (*fruit*) mora *f*.

bran [bran] *n* crusca *f*.

branch [braːntʃ] *n* ramo *m*; (*office*) succursale *f*. **branch off** biforcarsi. **branch out** estendersi.

brand [brand] *n* (*trademark*) marchio *m*; (*grade, make*) marca *f*; (*marking*) marchio *m*, stigma *m*; (*burning wood*) tizzone *m*. **brand-new** *adj* nuovo di zecca,

nuovo fiammante. *v* marchiare, stigmatizzare.
brandish ['brandiʃ] *v* brandire.
brandy ['brandi] *n* cognac *m*, acquavite *f*.
brass [braɪs] *n* ottone *m*. **brassy** *adj* d'ottone; (*impudent*) sfacciato.
brassiere ['brasiə] *V* **bra**.
brave [breiv] *adj* prode, coraggioso, ardito. *v* sfidare, affrontare. **bravery** *n* audacia *f*, coraggio *m*.
brawl [brɔɪl] *n* rissa *f*, zuffa *f*. *v* rissare, azzuffarsi.
brawn [brɔɪn] *n* (*strength*) forza muscolare *f*; (*meat*) testina *f*.
brazen ['breɪzn] *adj* sfacciato, impudente; (*brass*) di ottone.
breach [briɪtʃ] *n* violazione *f*, rottura *f*; (*mil*) breccia *f*. *v* far una breccia in, rompere.
bread [bred] *n* pane *m*. **breadcrumbs** *pl n* briciole di pane *f pl*.
breadth [bredθ] *n* larghezza *f*, ampiezza *f*; (*cloth*) altezza *f*.
*****break** [breik] *n* rottura *f*, frattura *f*; interruzione *f*, pausa *f*; (*chance*) opportunità *f*. *v* rompere, spezzare, infrangere; (*record*) battere. **at breakneck speed** a rompicollo. **break away** fuggire, distaccarsi. **break off** mandare a monte. **break out** (*war*) scoppiare. **breakthrough** *n* scoperta *f*, innovazione *f*. **breakable** *adj* fragile. **breakage** *n* rottura *f*.
breakdown ['breikdaun] *n* crollo *m*; (*car*) panna *f*; (*nerves*) esaurimento nervoso *m*. *v* **break down** demolire; analizzare; (*car*) avere una panna; (*nerves*) avere un esaurimento nervoso.
breakfast ['brekfəst] *n* prima colazione *f*.
breast [brest] *n* petto *m*, seno *m*. **breastbone** *n* sterno *m*. **breast-stroke** *n* nuoto a rana *m*.
breath [breθ] *n* respiro *m*, fiato *m*, soffio *m*. **breathless** *adj* ansimante. **breathtaking** *adj* sorprendente.
breathalyser ['breθəlaizə] *n* analizzatore del fiato *m*.
breathe [briɪð] *v* respirare, prender fiato; (*sigh*) sospirare. **breathing** *n* respirazione *f*.
bred [bred] *V* **breed**.
*****breed** [briɪd] *v* generare, allevare. *n* razza *f*, stirpe *f*. **breeding** *n* (*animals*) allevamento *m*; (*manners*) educazione *f*.
breeze [briɪz] *n* brezza *f*. **breezily** *adj* con disinvoltura.

brew [bruɪ] *v* (*beer*) far fermentare; (*tea*) preparare; (*storm*) essere nell'aria. *n* miscela *f*. **brewer** *n* birraio *m*. **brewery** *n* birreria *f*.
bribe [braib] *v* corrompere, allettare. *n* dono a scopo di corruzione *m*; (*coll*) bustarella *f*. **bribery** *n* corruzione *f*.
brick [brik] *n* mattone *m*. **bricklayer** *n* muratore *m*. **drop a brick** fare una gaffe.
bride [braid] *n* sposa *f*, sposina *f*. **bridal** *adj* nuziale. **bridegroom** *n* sposo *m*. **bridesmaid** *n* damigella d'onore della sposa *f*.
bridge[1] [bridʒ] *n* ponte *m*. *v* congiungere. **bridge a gap** colmare una lacuna.
bridge[2] [bridʒ] *n* (*cards*) bridge *m*.
bridle ['braidl] *n* briglia *f*, freno *m*. *v* risentirsi. **bridle-path** *n* sentiero percorribile a cavallo *m*.
brief [briɪf] *adj* breve. *n* riassunto *m*; istruzioni *m pl*; lettera *f*. *v* riassumere per sommi capi; (*law*) affidare una causa. **brief-case** *n* borsa *f*.
brigade [bri'geid] *n* brigata *f*.
bright [brait] *adj* lucido, risplendente; (*lively*) vivace; (*clever*) intelligente. **brighten** *v* rendere più brillante, illuminare. **brightness** *n* luminosità *f*, splendore *m*.
brilliant ['briljənt] *adj* brillante.
brim [brim] *n* orlo *m*, bordo *m*; (*hat*) falda *f*. **brimful** *adj* colmo.
brine [brain] *n* acqua salata *f*.
*****bring** [briŋ] *v* portare, condurre. **bring about** causare. **bring back** riportare; restituire. **bring up** educare; vomitare.
brink [briŋk] *n* orlo *m*.
brisk [brisk] *adj* vivace, arzillo.
bristle ['brisl] *n* (*human*) pelo duro *m*; (*animal*) setola *f*. *v* rizzarsi.
Britain ['britn] *n* Gran Bretagna *f*. **British** *adj* britannico. **Briton** *n* britannico, -a *m*, *f*.
brittle ['britl] *adj* fragile.
broach [broutʃ] *v* (*subject*) intavolare un discorso su.
broad [brɔɪd] *adj* (*wide*) largo, ampio; (*overall*) generale. **broad bean** fava *f*. **broad-minded** *adj* di larghe vedute. **broaden** *v* allargare.
*****broadcast** ['brɔɪdkaɪst] *v* trasmettere alla radio. *adj* radiodiffuso. *n* trasmissione radio *f*.

broccoli ['brokǝli] *n* broccolo *m.*
brochure ['brouʃuǝ] *n* opuscolo *m.*
broke [brouk] *V* **break.** *adj* (*coll*) al verde, rovinato.
broken ['broukn] *V* **break.**
broker ['broukǝ] *n* agente *m*, commissionario *m*, sensale *m.*
bronchitis [broŋ'kaitis] *n* bronchite *f.*
bronze [bronz] *n* bronzo *m. v* abbronzare.
brooch [broutʃ] *n* spilla *f.*
brood [bruɪd] *n* covata *f*, figliolanza *f. v* covare; (*think*) meditare.
brook [bruk] *n* ruscello *m. v* ammettere.
broom [bruɪm] *n* (*brush*) scopa *f*; (*plant*) ginestra *f.*
broth [broθ] *n* brodo *m.*
brothel ['broθl] *n* bordello *m.*
brother ['brʌðǝ] *n* fratello *m.* **brother-in-law** *n* cognato *m.* **brotherhood** *n* fratellanza *f*, fraternità *f.* **brotherly** *adj* fraterno.
brought [broɪt] *V* **bring.**
brow [brau] *n* fronte *f*; (*hill*) cima *f.* **browbeat** *v* intimidire.
brown [braun] *nm, adj* bruno, marrone, castano. *v* abbrunire, abbronzare; (*cooking*) rosolare.
browse [brauz] *v* brucare, scartabellare.
bruise [bruɪz] *v* ammaccare, intaccare. *n* livido *m*, contusione *f.* **bruised** *adj* (*person*) contuso; (*fruit*) ammaccato.
brunette [bruɪ'net] *nf, adj* bruna, brunetta.
brush [brʌʃ] *n* spazzola *f*; spazzolino *m*; (*paint*) pennello *m*; (*encounter*) scontro *m. v* spazzolare. **brush against** sfiorare. **brush aside** ignorare. **brush up** (*revise*) ripassare.
brusque [brusk] *adj* brusco.
Brussels ['brʌsǝlz] *n* Brusselle *f.* **Brussels sprouts** cavoli di Brusselle *m pl.*
brute [bruɪt] *nm, adj* bruto. **brutal** *adj* brutale.
bubble ['bʌbl] *n* bolla *f. v* formar bolle, gorgogliare.
buck [bʌk] *n* maschio *m*; (*deer*) daino *m.* **buck-tooth** *n* dente sporgente *m.* **pass the buck** scaricare la responsabilità. *v* **buck up** (*rear up*) impennarsi; (*coll: cheer up*) rallegrarsi.
bucket ['bʌkit] *n* secchio *m*, secchia *f.*
buckle ['bʌkl] *n* fibbia *f*, fermaglio *m. v* affibbiare.
bud [bʌd] *n* bocciolo *m*, gemma *f. v*

germogliare, sbocciare. **nip in the bud** troncare sul nascere.
budge [bʌdʒ] *v* scostarsi.
budget ['bʌdʒit] *n* bilancio preventivo *m. v* fare un bilancio preventivo.
buffalo ['bʌfǝlou] *n* bufalo, -a *m, f.*
buffer ['bʌfǝ] *n* (*trains*) respingente *m.* **buffer state** stato cuscinetto *m.*
buffet¹ ['bʌfit] *v* (*hit*) schiaffeggiare. *n* schiaffo *m.*
buffet² ['bufei] *n* (*cafeteria*) buffet *m*, caffè ristoratore *m*; (*sideboard*) credenza *f.* **cold buffet** cibi freddi *m pl.*
bug [bʌg] *n* cimice *f*; (*coll*) piccolo insetto *m.*
bugger ['bʌgǝ] (*impol*) *n* sodomita *m*; (*fellow*) tizio *m*; (*derog*) brutto ceffo *m. v* inculare. **bugger off** *v* svignarsela. **bugger off!** va a quel paese! va al diavolo! **buggery** *n* sodomia *f*, pederastia *f.*
bugle ['bjuɪgl] *n* tromba *f.*
***build** [bild] *v* costruire, fabbricare. *n* corporatura *f.* **building** *n* edificio *m*, costruzione *f.* **building society** *n* società immobiliare *f*, credito edilizio *m.*
built [bilt] *V* **build.**
bulb [bʌlb] *n* (*plant*) bulbo *m*; (*light*) lampadina *f.*
Bulgaria [bʌl'geǝriǝ] *n* Bulgaria *f.* **Bulgarian** *n, adj* bulgaro, -a.
bulge [bʌldʒ] *n* protuberanza *f*, gonfiore *m. v* gonfiarsi, sporgere.
bulk [bʌlk] *n* massa *f*, volume *m.* **the bulk** la maggior parte *f.* **bulky** *adj* massiccio, voluminoso.
bull [bul] *n* toro *m*; (*papal*) bolla *f.* **bulldog** *n* mastino *m.* **bulldozer** *n* livellatrice *f.* **bullfight** *n* corrida *f.* **bull's eye** centro (del bersaglio) *m.*
bullet ['bulit] *n* pallottola *f.* **bullet-proof** *adj* blindato, corazzato.
bulletin ['bulǝtin] *n* bollettino *m.*
bullion ['buliǝn] *n* lingotto (di metallo prezioso) *m.*
bully ['buli] *n* prepotente *m. v* tiranneggiare, maltrattare.
bum [bʌm] (*coll*) *n* sedere *m. adj* scadente. *v* **bum around** vagabondare.
bump [bʌmp] *v* urtare. *n* protuberanza *f*, bernoccolo *m.* **bump into** (*collide*) andare a sbattere contro; (*meet*) incontrare per caso. **bumpy** *adj* irregolare.
bumper ['bʌmpǝ] *n* (*mot*) paraurti *m. adj* abbondante.

bun [bʌn] n (cake) focaccia f; (hair) crocchia f.

bunch [bʌntʃ] n fascio m, mazzo m, gruppo m; (grapes) grappolo d'uva m. v riunire, raggruppare.

bundle ['bʌndl] n fagotto m, involto m. v mettere insieme alla rinfusa, fare un involto di, affastellare.

bungalow ['bʌŋgəlou] n bungalow m, villino ad un piano m.

bungle ['bʌŋgl] v sciupare, lavorar male. n lavoro malfatto m. **bungler** n confusionario m, guastamestieri m.

bunion ['bʌnjən] n protuberanza callosa f.

bunk [bʌŋk] n cuccetta f.

bunker ['bʌŋkə] n (coal) carbonaia f; (mil) ricovero militare seminterrato m; (golf) ostacolo m.

buoy [boi] n gavitello m, boa f. **buoyancy** n galleggiabilità f. **buoyant** adj galleggiante.

burden ['bəɪdn] n peso m, onere m. v caricare, tassare.

bureau ['bjuərou] n (desk) scrittoio m; (office) ufficio m.

bureaucracy [bju'rokrəsi] n burocrazia f. **bureaucrat** n burocrate m, f. **bureaucratic** adj burocratico.

burglar ['bəɪglə] n scassinatore m, ladro m. **burgle** v scassinare, svaligiare.

***burn** [bəɪn] v bruciare, scottare, risplendere. **burn down** incendiare. n ustione f, scottatura f. **burner** n bruciatore m, becco a gas m.

burnt [bəɪnt] V **burn**.

burrow ['bʌrou] n tana f, covo m. v farsi una tana, scavare.

***burst** [bəɪst] n scoppio m, raffica f. v scoppiare, esplodere.

bury ['beri] v seppellire, sotterrare. **burial** n sepoltura f.

bus [bʌs] n autobus m invar. **bus station** capolinea (pl capilinea) m. **bus stop** fermata dell'autobus f.

bush [buʃ] n (shrub) cespuglio m; (woodland) macchia f. **bushy** adj folto.

business ['biznis] n affare m, mestiere m. **business-like** adj metodico. **businessman** n uomo d'affari m.

bust[1] [bʌst] n (anat) busto m, petto m.

bust[2] [bʌst] adj (coll: bankrupt) rovinato. v rovinare.

bustle ['bʌsl] n trambusto m, agitazione f. v agitarsi, affacendarsi.

busy ['bizi] adj occupato, attivo, indaffarato. **busybody** n ficcanaso m. v **busy** oneself with occuparsi di.

but [bʌt] conj ma. adv (only) solo, soltanto. prep (except) eccetto, tranne.

butane ['bjuɪtein] n butano m.

butcher [butʃə] n macellaio m. **butcher's shop** macelleria f. v macellare, massacrare. **butchery** n strage f, massacro m.

butler ['bʌtlə] n maggiordomo m.

butt[1] [bʌt] n (gun) calcio m, impugnatura f; (cigarette) mozzicone m.

butt[2] [bʌt] n (laughing-stock) bersaglio m, zimbello m.

butt[3] [bʌt] n (hit) cornata f, cozzo m. v cozzare, urtare con la testa. **butt in** interrompere, intromettersi.

butter ['bʌtə] n burro m. v imburrare.

buttercup ['bʌtəkʌp] n ranuncolo m.

butterfly ['bʌtəflai] n farfalla f.

buttocks ['bʌtəks] pl n natiche f pl.

button ['bʌtn] n bottone m. **buttonhole** n occhiello m, asola f. v attaccare un bottone. **button up** abbottonare.

buttress ['bʌtris] n sostegno m, sperone m. v sostenere.

***buy** [bai] v acquistare, comprare. n acquisto m. **buyer** n compratore m.

buzz [bʌz] n ronzio m; (phone) telefonata f. v ronzare; telefonare.

by [bai] adv vicino. prep da, con, a, di, per, entro. **by and large** generalmente parlando. **by the way** a proposito. **by-law** n legge locale f. **bypass** n circonvallazione f; deviazione stradale f. **by-product** n prodotto secondario m. **bystander** n astante m, f. **byword** n detto m.

C

cab [kab] n tassì m.

cabaret ['kabərei] n caffè concerto m, cabaret m invar.

cabbage ['kabidʒ] n cavolo m.

cabin ['kabin] n cabina f, capanna f.

cabinet ['kabinit] n (furniture) armadietto m; (pol) gabinetto m; (cocktails) bar m invar. **cabinet-maker** n ebanista m.

cable ['keibl] n cavo m; telegramma m. v telegrafare. **cable-car** n funivia f.

cackle ['kakl] v (hens) schiamazzare; (people) chiacchierare. n schiamazzo m, chiacchiera f.

cactus ['kaktəs] *n* cactus *m*.
caddie ['kadi] *n* (*golf*) caddie *m*.
cadence ['keidəns] *n* cadenza *f*.
cadet [kə'det] *n* cadetto *m*.
café ['kafei] *n* caffè *m*.
cafeteria [kafə'tiəriə] *n* bar-ristorante *m*.
caffeine ['kafiːn] *n* caffeina *f*.
cage [keidʒ] *n* gabbia *f*. *v* ingabbiare.
cagey *adj* cauto.
cake [keik] *n* (*sweet*) torta *f*, focaccia *f*, dolce *m*; (*soap*) saponetta *f*, pezzo di sapone *m*. *v* incrostarsi.
calamine ['kaləmain] *n* calamina *f*.
calamity [kə'laməti] *n* calamità *f*, disgrazia *f*.
calcium ['kalsiəm] *n* calcio *m*.
calculate ['kalkjuleit] *v* calcolare. **calculation** *n* calcolo *m*. **calculator** *n* calcolatore *m*, macchina calcolatrice *f*.
calendar ['kaləndə] *n* calendario *m*.
calf¹ [kaɪf] *n* (*animal*) vitello, -a *m*, *f*.
calf² [kaɪf] *n* (*leg*) polpaccio *m*.
calibre ['kalibə] *n* calibro *m*, qualità *f*.
call [koɪl] *n* chiamata *f*, appello *m*, grido *m*, visita *f*. **call-box** *n* cabina telefonica *f*. **call-girl** *n* ragazza squillo *f*. *v* chiamare. **call off** annullare. **call on** visitare. **call up** telefonare; (*mil*) richiamare sotto le armi. **calling** *n* vocazione *f*.
callous ['kaləs] *adj* insensibile. *n* insensibilità *f*.
calm [kaɪm] *adj* calmo. *v* calmare. **calm down** calmarsi. *n* calma *f*.
calorie ['kaləri] *n* caloria *f*.
came [keim] *V* **come**.
camel ['kaməl] *n* cammello *m*.
camera ['kamərə] *n* macchina fotografica *f*. (*film/television*) **cameraman** *n* operatore (cinematografico/televisivo) *m*.
camouflage ['kaməflaɪʒ] *v* mimetizzazione *f*, mascheramento *m*. *v* mimetizzare, mascherare.
camp [kamp] *n* campo *m*, accampamento *m*. **camp-bed** *n* branda *f*. **campsite** *n* campeggio *m*. *v* accamparsi, campeggiare.
campaign [kam'pein] *n* campagna *f*. *v* fare una campagna.
campus ['kampəs] *n* campo universitario *m*.
camshaft ['kamʃaɪft] *n* albero a camme *or* eccentrici *m*.
*can¹ [kan] *v* (*be able*) potere, essere in grado di; (*know how*) sapere.

can² [kan] *n* scatola *f*, recipiente *m*. **can-opener** *n* apriscatole *m* *invar*. *v* mettere in scatola.
Canada ['kanədə] *n* Canadà *m*. **Canadian** *n*(*m+f*), *adj* canadese.
canal [kə'nal] *n* canale *m*.
canary [kə'neəri] *n* canarino *m*.
cancel ['kansəl] *v* annullare, disdire. **cancellation** *n* annullamento *m*.
cancer ['kansə] *n* cancro *m*. **Cancer** *n* Cancro *m*.
candid ['kandid] *adj* candido, sincero.
candidate ['kandidət] *n* candidato, -a *m*, *f*.
candle ['kandl] *n* candela *f*; (*church*) cero *m*. **candlelight** *n* lume di candela *m*. **candlestick** *n* candeliere *m*.
candour ['kandə] *n* franchezza *f*.
candy ['kandi] *n* (*US*) caramella *f*. **candied** *adj* candito.
cane [kein] *n* canna *f*, bastone *m*; (*school*) verga *f*. *v* bastonare.
canine ['keinain] *adj* canino.
canister ['kanistə] *n* latta *f*.
cannabis ['kanəbis] *n* hascisc *m*.
cannibal ['kanibəl] *n* cannibale *m*. **cannibalism** *n* cannibalismo *m*.
cannon ['kanən] *n* cannone *m*. **cannonball** *n* palla di cannone *f*.
canoe [kə'nuɪ] *n* canoa *f*.
canon ['kanən] *n* canone *m*, criterio *m*; (*church dignitary*) canonico *m*. **canonical** *adj* canonico. **canonize** *v* canonizzare.
canopy ['kanəpi] *n* baldacchino *m*.
canteen [kan'tiɪn] *n* (*dining place*) mensa *f*; (*cutlery*) posateria *f*.
canter ['kantə] *n* piccolo galoppo *m*. *v* andare al piccolo galoppo.
canvas ['kanvəs] *n* tela *f*; (*sails*) velatura *f*.
canvass ['kanvəs] *v* (*orders, votes*) sollecitare. **canvasser** *n* sollecitatore, -trice *m*, *f*.
canyon ['kanjən] *n* burrone *m*.
cap [kap] *n* (*hat*) berretto *m*; (*bathing*) cuffia *f*; (*mech*) coperchio *m*, cappello *m*. *v* coprire; sorpassare.
capable ['keipəbl] *adj* capace. **capability** *n* capacità *f*.
capacity [kə'pasəti] *n* capacità *f*, abilità *f*. **in the capacity of** nella qualità di.
cape¹ [keip] *n* (*cloak*) mantellina *f*.
cape² [keip] *n* (*geog*) capo *m*, promontorio *m*.

25

caper¹ ['keipə] n (bot) cappero m.
caper² ['keipə] n capriola f.
capillary [kə'piləri] adj capillare. n vaso capillare m.
capital ['kapitl] n capitale f; (arch) capitello m; (letter) maiuscola f. adj capitale. **capitalism** n capitalismo m. **capitalist** n(m+f), adj capitalista. **capitalize** v capitalizzare.
Capitol ['kapitl] n Campidoglio m.
capitulate [kə'pitjuleit] v capitolare. **capitulation** n resa f.
capricious [kə'priʃəs] adj capriccioso.
Capricorn ['kaprikoɪn] n Capricorno m.
capsicum ['kapsikəm] n peperone m.
capsize [kap'saiz] v capovolgere, capovolgersi.
capsule ['kapsjuɪl] n capsula f.
captain ['kaptin] n (chief) capo m; (army, team) capitano m; (navy) capitano di vascello m; comandante m. v comandare.
caption ['kapʃən] n didascalia f.
captive ['kaptiv] n, adj prigioniero, -a; schiavo, -a. **captivate** v cattivare. **captivity** n cattività f, prigionia f.
capture ['kaptʃə] v catturare. n cattura f. **captor** n catturatore m.
car [kaɪ] n macchina f, automobile f. **car park** parcheggio m. **go by car** andare in macchina.
carafe [kə'raf] n caraffa f.
carat ['karət] n carato m.
caravan ['karəvan] n (vehicle) roulotte (pl -s) f; (travelling group) carovana f.
caraway ['karəwei] n cumino m.
carbohydrate [kaɪbə'haidreit] n carboidrato m.
carbon ['kaɪbən] n carbonio m. **carbon paper** carta carbone f.
carbuncle ['kaɪbʌŋkl] n carbonchio m, pustola f.
carburettor ['kaɪbjuretə] n carburatore m.
carcass ['kaɪkəs] n carcassa f.
card [kaɪd] n carta f; (greetings, etc.) cartolina f; (playing) carta da gioco; (visiting) biglietto da visita m; (index) scheda f.
cardboard ['kaɪdboɪd] n cartone m, cartoncino m.
cardiac ['kaɪdiak] adj cardiaco. **cardiac arrest** arresto cardiaco m.
cardigan ['kaɪdigən] n golf m, giacca f.
cardinal ['kaɪdənl] nm, adj cardinale.

care [keə] v curare; preoccuparsi; interessarsi. n cura f, premura f; ansietà f; responsabilità f. **carefree** adj spensierato. **care of** presso. **caretaker** n custode m, f. **care-worn** adj preoccupato. **careful** adj attento; (thorough) curato. **careless** adj disattento, trascurato. **carelessness** n trascuratezza f.
career [kə'riə] n carriera f.
caress [kə'res] n carezza f. v accarezzare.
cargo ['kaɪgou] n carico (pl -chi) m.
caricature ['karikətjuə] n caricatura f. v mettere in caricatura. **caricaturist** n caricaturista m, f.
carnage ['kaɪnidʒ] n strage f.
carnal ['kaɪnl] adj carnale, sensuale.
carnation [kaɪ'neiʃən] n garofano m.
carnival ['kaɪnivəl] n carnevale m.
carnivorous [kaɪ'nivərəs] adj carnivoro. **carnivore** n carnivoro m.
carol ['karəl] n cantico m. **Christmas carol** cantico di Natale m.
carpenter ['kaɪpəntə] n falegname m. **carpentry** n falegnameria f, ebanisteria f.
carpet ['kaɪpit] n tappeto m, moquette f.
carriage ['karidʒ] n (vehicle) carrozza f, vettura f; (bearing) portamento m; (railway) vagone m.
carrier ['kariə] n portatore, -trice m, f; (comm) trasportatore m; (med) vettore m. **carrier bag** sacchetto per acquisti m. **carrier pigeon** piccione viaggiatore m.
carrot ['karət] n carota f.
carry ['kari] v portare, trasportare. **carrycot** n culla portabile f. **carry on** proseguire, gestire. **carry out** eseguire, realizzare. **carry over** riportare.
cart [kaɪt] n carro m, carretta f. **cartload** n carrettata f. **turn cartwheels** fare la ruota. v **cart off** portar via.
cartilage ['kaɪtəlidʒ] n cartilagine f.
cartography [kaɪ'togrəfi] n cartografia f. **cartographer** n cartografo, -a m, f.
carton ['kaɪtən] n scatola di cartone f; (cigarettes) stecca f.
cartoon [kaɪ'tuɪn] n (drawing) cartone m; (film) cartone animato m; caricatura f. **cartoonist** n disegnatore, -trice m, f; caricaturista m, f.
cartridge ['kaɪtridʒ] n cartuccia f.
carve [kaɪv] v (meat) tagliare, trinciare; (art) scolpire, intagliare. **carving** n intaglio m. **carving knife** trinciante m.
cascade [kas'keid] n cascata f. v scrosciare.

case¹ [keis] n (*matter*) caso m, fatto m, questione f; cosa f; (*law*) causa f, processo m. **in any case** ad ogni modo. **in case** qualora. **in most cases** in genere. **in that case** allora.

case² [keis] n (*box*) scatola f; (*luggage*) valigia f; (*glasses, pens*) astuccio f.

cash [kaʃ] v incassare, riscuotere. n denaro m; contanti m pl. **cash desk** cassa f. **cash payment** pagamento in contanti m. **petty cash** spese varie f pl.

cashier¹ [ka'ʃiə] n cassiere, -a m, f.

cashier² [ka'ʃiə] v destituire.

cashmere [kaʃ'miə] n cachemire m invar.

casing ['keisiŋ] n copertura f, rivestimento m.

casino [kə'siːnou] n casinò m.

casket ['kaɪskit] n cofanetto m; (*coffin*) cassa da morto f.

casserole ['kasəroul] n casseruola f. v cucinare in umido.

cassette [kə'set] n cassetta f.

cassock ['kasək] n tonaca f.

*cast [kaɪst] n (*throw*) lancio m, getto m; (*mould*) forma f, calco m; (*metal*) fusione f; (*theatre*) complesso m, insieme degli attori m; (*plaster*) ingessatura f. v lanciare, gettare; (*metal*) fondere; (*theatre*) dare la parte. **cast away** gettar via. **cast iron** ghisa f. **cast-off** adj abbandonato.

caste [kaɪst] n casta f.

castle ['kaɪsl] n castello m.

castor ['kaɪstə] n (*furniture*) rotella al piede di mobili f; (*condiments*) ampolliera f. **castor oil** olio di ricino m. **castor sugar** zucchero semolato m.

castrate [kə'streit] v castrare. **castration** n castratura f.

casual ['kaʒuəl] adj casuale, fortuito, disinvolto.

casualty ['kaʒuəlti] n vittima f; (*accident*) incidente m; (*hospital*) pronto soccorso m.

cat [kat] n gatto, -a m, f. **cat's eye** catarifrangente m. **catty** adj malevolo.

catalogue ['katəlog] n catalogo (*pl* -ghi) m, elenco m. v elencare.

catalyst ['katəlist] n catalizzatore m. **catalysis** n, *pl* -ses catalisi f.

catamaran [katəmə'ran] n catamarano m.

catapult ['katəpʌlt] n catapulta f, fionda f. v scagliare.

cataract ['katərakt] n cateratta f.

catarrh [kə'taɪ] n catarro m.

catastrophe [kə'tastrəfi] n catastrofe f. **catastrophic** adj catastrofico.

*catch [katʃ] n preda f, cattura f; (*door*) spranga f; (*fish*) retata f. v prendere, acchiappare; (*fish*) pescare. **catch-phrase** n frase fatta f. **catch up with** raggiungere. **catchword** n slogan m. **catching** adj (*med*) contagioso, infettivo.

category ['katəgəri] n categoria f. **categorical** adj categorico.

cater ['keitə] v provvedere cibo. **cater for** provvedere a. **caterer** n approvvigionatore, -trice m, f. **catering** n approvvigionamento m.

caterpillar ['katəpilə] n bruco m.

cathedral [kə'θiːdrəl] n cattedrale f.

catheter ['kaθətə] n catetere m.

cathode ['kaθoud] n catodo m.

catholic ['kaθəlik] n, adj cattolico, -a. **catholicism** n cattolicesimo m.

catkin ['katkin] n gattino m.

cattle ['katl] n bestiame m.

caught [kɔɪt] V **catch**.

cauliflower ['koliflauə] n cavolfiore m.

cause [kɔɪz] n causa f, ragione f, motivo m. v causare, provocare, suscitare.

causeway ['kɔɪzwei] n strada rialzata f; (*main highway*) strada maestra f.

caustic ['kɔɪstik] adj caustico.

caution ['kɔɪʃən] n cautela f, circospezione f; (*law*) diffida f, ammonimento m. v ammonire, mettere in guardia. **cautious** adj cauto, prudente.

cavalry ['kavəlri] n cavalleria f.

cave [keiv] n caverna f, grotta f.

caviar ['kaviaɪ] n caviale m.

cavity ['kavəti] n cavità f, buco m.

cease [siɪs] v cessare, smettere. **cease-fire** n tregua f, cessate il fuoco m invar. **ceaseless** adj continuo, incessante.

cedar ['siɪdə] n cedro m.

ceiling ['siɪliŋ] n soffitto m.

celebrate ['seləbreit] v celebrare, festeggiare, far festa. **celebration** n festa f, commemorazione f. **celebrity** n celebrità f.

celery ['seləri] n sedano m.

celestial [sə'lestiəl] adj celestiale, celeste.

celibate ['selibət] n, adj celibe m. **celibacy** n celibato m.

cell [sel] n (*room*) cella f; (*biol*) cellula f; (*elec*) pila f.

cellar ['selə] n cantina f, sottosuolo m.

cello ['tʃelou] *n* violoncello *m*. **cellist** *n* violoncellista *m*, *f*.

cellular ['seljulə] *adj* cellulare.

cement [sə'ment] *n* cemento *m*. *v* cementare, consolidare.

cemetery ['semətri] *n* cimitero *m*, camposanto *m*.

censor ['sensə] *n* censore *m*. *v* censurare. **censorious** *adj* ipercritico. **censorship** *n* censura *f*.

censure ['senʃə] *n* censura *f*.

census ['sensəs] *n* censimento *m*.

cent [sent] *n* centesimo *m*, soldo *m*.

centenary [sen'tiɪnəri] *nm, adj* centenario.

centigrade ['sentigreid] *adj* centigrado.

centimetre ['sentimiːtə] *n* centimetro *m*.

centipede ['sentipiɪd] *n* millepiedi *m invar*.

centre ['sentə] *n* centro *m*. *v* centrare, accentrare. **central** *adj* centrale. **central heating** riscaldamento centrale *m*. **centralization** *n* centralizzazione *f*. **centralize** *v* centralizzare.

centrifugal [sen'trifjugəl] *adj* centrifugo (*m pl* -ghi). **centrifuge** *n* centrifuga *f*.

century ['sentʃuri] *n* secolo *m*.

ceramic [sə'ramik] *adj* ceramico. **ceramics** *n* ceramica *f*.

cereal ['siəriəl] *nm, adj* cereale.

cerebral ['serəbrəl] *adj* cerebrale.

ceremony ['serəməni] *n* cerimonia *f*, funzione *f*. **stand on ceremony** far complimenti. **ceremonial** *adj* solenne, rituale. **ceremonious** *adj* formalista, cerimonioso.

certain ['səɪtn] *adj* certo, sicuro. **certainly** *adv* certo, certamente, senza dubbio. **certainty** *n* certezza *f*, sicurezza *f*.

certificate [sə'tifikət] *n* certificato *m*, atto *m*, diploma *m*. **certify** *v* certificare, attestare, vidimare; (*declare insane*) classificare come pazzo.

cervix ['səɪviks] *n* cervice *f*.

cesspool ['sespuɪl] *n* cloaca *f*.

chafe [tʃeif] *v* irritarsi.

chaffinch ['tʃafintʃ] *n* fringuello *m*.

chain [tʃein] *n* catena *f*. **chain-smoke** *v* fumare ininterrottamente. **chain store** magazzino a catena *m*. *v* incatenare.

chair [tʃeə] *n* sedia *f*, seggio *m*; (*university*) cattedra *f*. **chairlift** *n* seggiovia *f*. **chairman** *n* presidente *m*. *v* presiedere.

chalk [tʃoɪk] *n* gesso *m*. **chalky** *adj* gessoso; pallido.

challenge ['tʃalindʒ] *n* sfida *f*, provocazione *f*. *v* sfidare, opporsi a, provocare. **challenging** *adj* stimolante, provocatorio.

chamber ['tʃeimbə] *n* camera *f*. **chambermaid** *n* cameriera *f*. **chamber music** musica da camera *f*.

chameleon [kə'miːliən] *n* camaleonte *m*.

chamois ['ʃamwaɪ] *n* camoscio *m*; (*leather*) pelle di camoscio *f*.

champagne [ʃam'pein] *n* champagne *m*.

champion ['tʃampiən] *n* campione, -essa *m*, *f*. **championship** *n* campionato *m*. *v* difendere, sostenere.

chance [tʃaɪns] *n* caso *m*, fortuna *f*, opportunità *f*, rischio *m*. **by chance** per caso. *v* (*risk*) arrischiare; (*happen*) capitare. *adj* fortuito.

chancellor [tʃaɪnsələ] *n* cancelliere *m*; (*university*) rettore titolare *m*.

chandelier [ʃandə'liə] *n* lampadario *m*.

change [tʃeindʒ] *n* cambio *m*, mutamento *m*; (*money*) resto *m*, spiccioli *m pl*. *v* cambiare, mutare, cambiarsi. **changeable** *adj* variabile, mutevole. **changeability** *n* variabilità *f*. **changeless** *adj* immutevole, costante.

channel ['tʃanl] *n* canale *m*. **English Channel** Manica *f*. *v* incanalare.

chant [tʃaɪnt] *n* canto *m*, salmodia *f*. *v* cantare, salmodiare.

chaos ['keios] *n* caos *m*.

chap¹ [tʃap] *v* screpolare, screpolarsi. *n* fessura *f*.

chap² [tʃap] *n* (*fellow*) tipo *m*, tizio *m*.

chapel ['tʃapəl] *n* cappella *f*.

chaperon ['ʃapəroun] *n* chaperon *m*. *v* accompagnare.

chaplain ['tʃaplin] *n* cappellano *m*.

chapter ['tʃaptə] *n* capitolo *m*.

char¹ [tʃaɪ] *v* carbonizzare, bruciare.

char² [tʃaɪ] *v* fare i lavori di casa. **charwoman** *n* donna di servizio *f*, donna a mezzo servizio *f*.

character ['karəktə] *n* carattere *m*, indole *f*, qualità *f*; (*acting*) personaggio *m*. **characterization** *n* caratterizzazione *f*. **characterize** *v* caratterizzare.

characteristic [ˌkarəktə'ristik] *adj* caratteristico. *n* caratteristica *f*.

charcoal ['tʃaɪkoul] *n* carbone di legna *m*.

charge [tʃaɪdʒ] *n* spesa *f*, costo *m*; cura *f*, custodia *f*; (*law*) accusa *f*; (*mil*) carica *f*. **free of charge** gratis, gratuito. **in charge**

addetto, incaricato. **take charge of** incaricarsi di. *v* addebitare; caricare. **chargeable** *adj* addebitabile.
charity ['tʃarəti] *n* carità *f*, elemosina *f*. **charitable** *adj* caritatevole.
charm [tʃaɪm] *n* fascino *m*, incantesimo *m*; (*trinket*) portafortuna *m invar*. *v* affascinare, incantare. **charming** *adj* incantevole, affascinante.
chart [tʃaɪt] *n* mappa *f*, diagramma *m*, grafico *m*, quadro *m*. *v* tracciare un diagramma *or* grafico di.
charter ['tʃaɪtə] *n* carta *f*, documento *m*; (*flight*) volo charter *m*. *v* (*document*) istituire; (*hire*) noleggiare. **chartered accountant** ragioniere diplomato *m*.
chase [tʃeis] *n* caccia *f*, inseguimento *m*. *v* cacciare, inseguire; (*jewellery*) incastonare; (*metal*) cesellare.
chasm ['kazəm] *n* abisso *m*.
chassis ['ʃasi] *n* telaio *m*.
chaste [tʃeist] *adj* casto, austero. **chastity** *n* castità *f*, purezza *f*.
chastise [tʃas'taiz] *v* castigare, punire. **chastisement** *n* castigo (*pl* -ghi) *m*, punizione *f*.
chat [tʃat] *n* chiacchiera *f*, chiacchierata *f*. *v* chiacchierare.
chatter ['tʃatə] *v* chiacchierare; (*teeth*) battere. *n* chiacchiera *f*.
chauffeur ['ʃoufə] *n* autista *m*, *f*.
chauvinism ['ʃouvinizəm] *n* sciovinismo *m*. **chauvinist** *n*(*m* + *f*), *adj* sciovinista.
cheap [tʃiɪp] *adj* economico, a buon mercato, poco caro; (*derog*) spregevole. **cheapen** *v* abbassare il prezzo di, screditare.
cheat [tʃiɪt] *n* imbroglione, -a *m*, *f*, truffatore, -trice *m*, *f*; (*cards*) baro, -a *m*, *f*. *v* imbrogliare, truffare; barare. **cheating** *n* imbroglio *m*, truffa *f*.
check [tʃek] *n* controllo *m*, pausa *f*, ostacolo *m*; (*chess*) scacco *m*. *v* controllare, verificare, fermare; (*chess*) dare scacco. **check in** registrare all'arrivo. **check up on** informarsi su.
check [tʃek] *n* assegno *m*. **check book** *n*. libretto d' assegni *m*.
cheek [tʃiɪk] *n* guancia *f*; (*insolence*) faccia tosta *f*. **cheeky** *adj* sfacciato, sfrontato.
cheer [tʃiə] *n* (*shout*) applauso *m*; (*mood*) allegria *f*, buonumore *m*. **cheerio!** *interj* ciao! arrivederci! *v* applaudire. **cheer up**

rallegrare, rallegrarsi. **cheerful** *adj* allegro, di buonumore. **cheerless** *adj* triste.
cheese [tʃiɪz] *n* formaggio *m*. **cheesecloth** *n* garza *f*. **cheese-paring** *adj* tirchio.
chef [ʃef] *n* capocuoco (*pl* -chi) *m*.
chemical ['kemikl] *n* prodotto chimico *m*. *adj* chimico.
chemistry ['kemistri] *n* chimica *f*. **chemist** *n* chimico, -a *m*, *f*, farmacista *m*, *f*. **chemist's shop** farmacia *f*.
cherish ['tʃeriʃ] *v* tener caro, nutrire, amare.
cherry ['tʃeri] *n* (*fruit*) ciliegia *f*; (*tree*) ciliegio *m*.
chess [tʃes] *n* scacchi *m pl*. **chessboard** *n* scacchiera *f*.
chest [tʃest] *n* cassa *f*; (*anat*) petto *m*, torace *m*. **chest of drawers** cassettone *m*.
chestnut ['tʃesnʌt] *n* (*fruit*) castagna *f*; (*tree*) castagno *m*. *adj* castano.
chew [tʃuɪ] *v* masticare. **chew over** meditare. **chewing-gum** *n* chewing gum *m invar*, gomma da masticare *f*.
chicken ['tʃikin] *n* pollo *m*; (*chick*) pulcino *m*. **chicken-coop** *n* pollaio *m*. **chicken-pox** *n* varicella *f*.
chicory ['tʃikəri] *n* cicoria *f*, indivia *f*.
chick-pea ['tʃik,piɪ] *n* cece *m*.
chide [tʃaid] *v* sgridare.
chief [tʃiɪf] *nm*, *pl* -s, *adj* capo, principale.
chilblain ['tʃilblein] *n* gelone *m*.
child [tʃaild] *n*, *pl* **children** bambino, -a *m*, *f*; ragazzo, -a *m*, *f*; (*offspring*) figlio, -a *m*, *f*. **childbirth** *n* parto *m*. **childhood** *n* infanzia *f*. **childish** *adj* puerile, infantile. **childlike** *adj* da bambino, semplice, innocente.
chill [tʃil] *v* raffreddare, agghiacciare. *adj* freddo, gelido. *n* freddo *m*, brivido *m*; (*illness*) raffreddore *m*. **catch a chill** buscarsi un raffreddore. **take the chill off** intiepidire. **chilly** *adj* freddo, fresco, freddoloso.
chilli ['tʃili] *n* peperone *m*, pepe rosso *m*.
chime [tʃaim] *v* suonare, scampanare. *n* scampanio *m*, rintocco *m*.
chimney ['tʃimni] *n* camino *m*, caminetto *m*. **chimney-pot** *n* ciminiera *f*, fumaiolo *m*. **chimney-sweep** *n* spazzacamino *m*.
chimpanzee [tʃimpən'ziɪ] *n* scimpanzè *m*.
chin [tʃin] *n* mento *m*. **chin-strap** *n* sottogola *m invar*.
china ['tʃainə] *n* porcellana *f*, ceramica *f*. **china clay** caolino *m*.

China ['tʃainə] n Cina f. **Chinese** n(m+f), adj cinese.

chink¹ [tʃiŋk] n (fissure) fessura f, crepa f.

chink² [tʃiŋk] n (sound) tintinnio m. v tintinnare.

chip [tʃip] n scheggia f, frammento m, truciolo m; (gambling) cip (pl -s) m, gettone m. **chips** pl n (cookery) patatine fritte f pl. v scheggiare. **chip in** intervenire; (contribute money) contribuire.

chiropodist [ki'ropədist] n pedicure m, f invar.

chirp [tʃəɪp] v cinguettare, pigolare. n cinguettio m, pigolio m. **chirpy** adj allegro.

chisel ['tʃizl] n cesello m, bulino m. v cesellare.

chivalry ['ʃivəlri] n galanteria f. **chivalrous** adj galante.

chive [tʃaiv] n erba cipollina f.

chlorine ['kloɪriɪn] n cloro m.

chlorophyll ['klorəfil] n clorofilla f.

chocolate ['tʃokələt] n cioccolato m, cioccolatino m; (drink) cioccolata f. adj cioccolato invar.

choice [tʃois] n scelta f, assortimento m. adj scelto, di prima qualità.

choir ['kwaiə] n coro m.

choke [tʃouk] v soffocare, strozzare. n (motor) valvola dell'aria f, diffusore m.

cholera ['kolərə] n colera m.

***choose** [tʃuɪz] v scegliere, eleggere, preferire.

chop¹ [tʃop] n (meat) braciola f; (blow) colpo m. v (split) spaccare; (mince) tagliuzzare, tritare. **chop down** abbattere. **chopper** n accetta f. **chopping-block** n tagliere m. **choppy sea** maretta f.

chop² [tʃop] v **chop and change** fare e disfare. **chop logic** cavillare.

chops [tʃops] pl n mascelle f pl. **lick one's chops** leccarsi i baffi.

chord [koɪd] n corda f, accordo m.

chore [tʃoɪ] n (task) lavoro m, compito m. **household chores** lavori domestici m pl.

choreography [kori'ogrəfi] n coreografia f. **choreographer** n coreografo, -a m, f.

chorus ['koɪrəs] n coro m. **choral** adj corale. **chorister** n corista m, f.

chose [tʃouz] V **choose**.

chosen ['tʃouzn] V **choose**.

Christ [kraist] n Cristo m.

christen ['krisn] v battezzare; (name) chiamare. **christening** n battesimo m.

Christian ['kristʃən] n, adj cristiano, -a. **Christian Democrat** democriziano, -a m, f. **Christian name** nome di battesimo m. **Christendom** n cristianesimo m. **Christianity** n cristianità f.

Christmas ['krisməs] n Natale m. adj di Natale; natalizio.

chromatic [krə'matik] adj cromatico.

chromium ['kroumiəm] n cromo m. **chromium-plate** v cromare. **chromium-plating** n cromatura f.

chromosome ['krouməsoum] n cromosoma m.

chronic ['kronik] adj cronico.

chronicle ['kronikl] n cronaca f. v narrare, fare la cronaca di.

chronological [kronə'lodʒikəl] adj cronologico.

chrysalis ['krisəlis] n crisalide f.

chrysanthemum [kri'sanθəməm] n crisantemo m.

chubby ['tʃʌbi] adj paffuto, grassoccio.

chuck [tʃʌk] v gettare, buttare. **chuck out** buttar fuori.

chuckle ['tʃʌkl] v ridacchiare, ridere di soppiatto.

chunk [tʃʌŋk] n grosso pezzo m; (food) fetta f.

church [tʃəɪtʃ] n chiesa f. **church-goer** n praticante m, f. **churchyard** n cimitero m, camposanto m.

churlish ['tʃəɪliʃ] adj burbero.

churn [tʃəɪn] n zangola f. v agitare, sbattere.

chute [ʃuɪt] n (slide) scivolo m; (waterfall) cascata f.

cider ['saidə] n sidro m.

cigar [si'gaɪ] n sigaro m.

cigarette [sigə'ret] n sigaretta f. **cigarette-end** n mozzicone m. **cigarette-lighter** n accendino m.

cinder ['sində] n tizzone m, cenere f. **burnt to a cinder** carbonizzato.

cine camera ['sini] n macchina da presa f.

cinema ['sinəmə] n cinema m.

cinnamon ['sinəmən] n cannella f.

circle ['səɪkl] n cerchio m, circolo m; (theatre) galleria f; (environment) cerchia f, ambiente m. v girare attorno a, accerchiare; (aeroplane) volteggiare. **circular** adj circolare. n volantino m. **circulate** v circolare, mettere in circolazione, girare. **circulation** n (movement) circolazione f; (distribution) tiratura f.

circuit ['sɜːkit] n circuito m, giro m.
circumcise ['sɜːkəmsaiz] v circoncidere.
circumcision n circoncisione f.
circumference [sɜːˈkʌmfərəns] n circonferenza f.
circumscribe ['sɜːkəmskraib] v circoscrivere.
circumstance ['sɜːkəmstans] n circostanza f, condizione f. circumstantial adj particolareggiato. circumstantial evidence prove indiziarie indirette f pl.
circus ['sɜːkəs] n circo m; (convergence of streets) largo m.
cistern ['sistən] n cisterna f, serbatoio m.
cite [sait] v citare. citation n citazione f; (mil) encomio m.
citizen ['sitizn] n cittadino, -a m, f. citizenship n cittadinanza f.
citrus fruits ['sitrəs] pl n agrumi m pl.
city ['siti] n città f; (business centre) centro degli affari m. city hall municipio m.
civic ['sivik] adj civico, municipale.
civil ['sivl] adj civile; (polite) cortese, educato. civil engineer ingegnere civile m. civil engineering ingegneria civile f. civil servant funzionario, -a statale m, f. Civil Service amministrazione dello Stato f. civil war guerra civile f.
civilian [səˈviljən] n(m+f), adj civile, borghese. in civilian clothes in borghese.
civilization [ˌsivilaiˈzeifən] n civiltà f, civilizzazione f. civilize v civilizzare, incivilire. civilized adj civilizzato.
clad [klad] adj vestito.
claim [kleim] n (right) diritto m; (title) titolo m; (complaint) reclamo m; (insurance) rivendicazione f; asserzione f. v chiedere, esigere; rivendicare; asserire.
clairvoyant [kleəˈvoiənt] n chiaroveggente m, f.
clam [klam] n vongola f.
clamber ['klambə] v arrampicarsi.
clammy ['klami] adj viscido.
clamour ['klamə] n clamore m, schiamazzo m. v strepitare, vociferare. clamorous adj clamoroso, strepitoso.
clamp [klamp] n morsa f, morsetto m. v tener fermo, stringere. clamp down on far smettere.
clan [klan] n tribù f, famiglia f. clannish adj imbevuto di spirito di parte.
clandestine [klanˈdestin] adj clandestino.
clang [klaŋ] n suono metallico m, strepito m. v strepitare.

clap [klap] n (blow, noise) colpo m, scoppio m; applauso m, battimano m. v applaudire. clap hands battere le mani. clap into prison sbattere in prigione. clapper n (bell) battaglio m. claptrap n sproloquio m.
claret ['klarət] n chiaretto m.
clarify ['klarəfai] v chiarire, raffinare.
clarinet [klarəˈnet] n clarinetto m. clarinettist n clarinettista m, f.
clash [klaʃ] n (noise) strepito m; (collision) urto m; (conflict) scontro m, contrasto m; (colours, sounds) stonatura f. v urtare, urtarsi; scontrarsi; stonare.
clasp [klɑːsp] n (device) fermaglio m; (grasp) stretta f; (embrace) abbraccio m. clasp-knife n coltello a serramanico m. v agganciare, stringere, abbracciare.
class [klɑːs] n classe f, categoria f, qualità f. class-mate n compagno, -a di classe m, f. classroom n aula f. v also classify classificare. classy adj di classe.
classic ['klasik] nm, adj classico.
clatter ['klatə] n fracasso m. v far fracasso.
clause [klɔːz] n clausola f, proposizione f, articolo m.
claustrophobia [klɔːstrəˈfoubiə] n claustrofobia f. claustrophobic adj claustrofobico.
claw [klɔː] n artiglio m; (tool) raffio m. v (seize) aggraffare; (scratch) graffiare.
clay [klei] n argilla f, creta f.
clean [kliːn] adj pulito, nitido. clean-shaven adj sbarbato. make a clean breast confessare tutto. v pulire; (remove stains) smacchiare. cleanliness n pulizia f, nettezza f.
cleanse [klenz] v pulire, depurare.
clear [kliə] adj chiaro, limpido; ovvio; libero. keep clear of tenersi lontano da. v chiarire, chiarificare; (empty) vuotare; (overcome) superare; (law) assolvere; (comm) sdoganare. clear away portar via; (table) sparecchiare. clear off andarsene. clear up chiarire, mettere in chiaro; (weather) rasserenarsi; (tidy) rassettare.
clearance n (customs) sdoganamento m; (sale) liquidazione f; (distance) gioco m.
clearing n (land) radura f; (bank) clearing m; (emptying) sgombro m.
clef [klef] n chiave f.
clench [klentʃ] v stringere. with clenched fists a pugni stretti.

clergy ['klɜɪdʒi] *n* clero *m*. **clergyman** *n* ecclesiastico *m*, pastore *m*, prete *m*.

clerical ['klerɪkəl] *adj* (*church*) clericale; (*office*) d'ufficio, impiegatizio. **clerical error** *n* errore materiale *m*, errore di trascrizione *m*.

clerk [klaɪk] *n* impiegato, -a *m*, *f*; commesso, -a *m*, *f*.

clever ['klevə] *adj* abile, ingegnoso, bravo. **cleverness** *n* abilità *f*, ingegnosità *f*, intelligenza *f*.

cliché ['kliːʃei] *n* espressione stereotipata *f*, frase fatta *f*.

click [klik] *n* scatto *m*, schiocco *m*. *v* scattare, schioccare.

client ['klaɪənt] *n* cliente *m*, *f*.

cliff [klif] *n* scoglio *m*.

climate ['klaɪmət] *n* clima *m*.

climax ['klaɪmaks] *n* apice *m*, apogeo *m*.

climb [klaim] *v* scalare, salire, arrampicarsi. *n* scalata *f*, salita *f*. **climb down** scendere; (*withdraw*) tirarsi indietro. **climb over** scavalcare.

***cling** [kliŋ] *v* aggrapparsi, aderire.

clinic ['klinik] *n* clinica *f*, ambulatorio *m*. **clinical** *adj* clinico.

clip¹ [klip] *n* (*cut*) taglio *m*; (*slap*) scappellotto *m*. *v* tagliare, tosare. **clip the wings of** tarpare le ali a.

clip² [klip] *n* (*fastener*) fermaglio *m*, graffa *f*.

clipper ['klipə] *n* (*boat*) clipper *m*, goletta *f*.

clitoris ['klitəris] *n* clitoride *f*.

cloak [klouk] *n* (*garment*) mantello *m*, cappa *f*; (*mask*) maschera *f*; (*pretext*) pretesto *m*, scusa *f*. *v* (*conceal*) celare. **cloak and dagger** cappa e spada. **cloakroom** *n* guardaroba *m*.

clock [klok] *n* orologio *m*. **clockmaker** *n* orologiaio *m*. **clockwork** *n* meccanismo d'orologeria *m*. **clockwise** *adv* in senso orario.

clog [klog] *n* (*shoe*) zoccolo *m*. *v* intasare.

cloister ['klɔɪstə] *n* chiostro *m*. *v* rinchiudere in convento.

close¹ [klouz] *v* chiudere, concludere. **close down** (*shop*) chiudere bottega. **close ranks** serrare le file. *n* (*end*) fine *f*.

close² [klous] *n* (*place*) recinto *m*. *adj* vicino, stretto; intimo. **close by** vicino.

closet ['klozit] *n* gabinetto *m*, studio *m*. *v* rinchiudere.

clot [klot] *n* grumo *m*, coagulo *m*; (*coll*) scemo, -a *m*, *f*. *v* raggrumare, coagulare,

coagularsi, rapprendersi. **clotted cream** panna rappresa *f*.

cloth [kloθ] *n* panno *m*, stoffa *f*, tessuto *m*; (*for dishes*) strofinaccio *m*.

clothe [klouð] *v* vestire, abbigliare; (*dress*) vestirsi. **clothes** *pl n* vestiti *m pl*, abiti *m pl*, indumenti *m pl*. **clothes line** corda per il bucato *f*. **clothes peg** molletta *f*. **clothing** *n* vestiario *m*, abbigliamento *m*.

cloud [klaud] *n* nuvola *f*. **cloudburst** *n* acquazzone *m*. *v* annuvolare; (*obscure*) offuscare. **cloud over** annuvolarsi. **cloudy** *adj* nuvoloso; (*liquid*) torbido.

clove¹ [klouv] *n* (*plant*) garofano *m*; (*spice*) chiodo di garofano *m*.

clove² [klouv] *n* (*part of bulb*) spicchio *m*.

clover ['klouvə] *n* trifoglio *m*.

clown [klaun] *n* pagliaccio *m*, buffone, -a *m*, *f*. *v* fare il pagliaccio. **clownery** *n* pagliacciata *f*. **clownish** *adj* pagliaccesco.

club [klʌb] *n* (*stick*) mazza *f*, randello *m*; (*golf*) bastone da golf *m*; (*social*) circolo *m*, club *m*; (*cards*) fiore *m*. *v* picchiare, bastonare. **club together** associarsi, riunirsi.

clue [kluɪ] *n* indizio *m*, chiave *f*.

clump [klʌmp] *n* gruppo *m*, cespo *m*.

clumsy ['klʌmzi] *adj* maldestro, goffo. **clumsiness** *n* goffaggine *f*, malaccortezza *f*.

clung [klʌŋ] *V* **cling**.

cluster ['klʌstə] *n* gruppo *m*; (*bunch*) grappolo *m*.

clutch [klʌtʃ] *n* presa *f*; (*mot*) frizione *f*. **fall into the clutches of** cadere nelle grinfie di. *v* afferrare, aggrapparsi a.

clutter ['klʌtə] *n* ingombro *m*, confusione *f*. *v* ingombrare.

coach [koutʃ] *n* carrozza *f*; (*bus*) corriera *f*, torpedone *m*; (*tutor*) ripetitore, -trice *m*, *f*; (*sport*) allenatore, -trice *m*, *f*. **coachbuilder** *n* carrozziere *m*. **coachwork** *n* carrozzeria *f*. *v* (*teach*) dare lezioni private; (*sport*) allenare.

coagulate [kou'agjuleit] *v* coagulare, coagularsi, accagliarsi. **coagulant** *n* coagulante *m*.

coal [koul] *n* carbone *m*. **coal-tar** *n* catrame *m*. **coalmine** *n* miniera di carbone *f*.

coalition [kouə'liʃən] *n* coalizione *f*.

coarse [koɪs] *adj* (*rude*) grossolano, rozzo; (*rough*) ruvido. **coarseness** *n* volgarità *f*, ruvidezza *f*.

coast [koust] *n* costa *f*, litorale *m*. *v* (*cycling*) scendere a ruota libera; (*motoring*) andare in folle. **coastal** *adj* costiero.
coat [kout] *n* soprabito *m*, cappotto *m*; (*jacket*) giacca *f*; (*animal*) pelame *m*, pelliccia *f*; (*paint*) mano *f*. **coat-hanger** *n* attaccapanni *m*. **coat-of-arms** *n* stemma *m*. **coating** *n* rivestimento *m*. *v* coprire, rivestire.
coax [kouks] *v* blandire, lusingare.
cobbler ['koblə] *n* ciabattino *m*, calzolaio *m*.
cobra ['koubrə] *n* cobra *m*.
cobweb ['kobweb] *n* ragnatela *f*.
cocaine [kə'kein] *n* cocaina *f*.
cock¹ [kok] *n* (*male bird*) uccello maschio *m*; (*chicken*) gallo *m*; (*tap*) rubinetto *m*; (*gun*) cane *m*; (*vulgar*) cazzo *m*. **cocky** *adj* impertinente, pieno di sè.
cock² [kok] *v* (*gun*) armare; (*ears*) drizzare. **cock a snook** fare marameo.
cockle ['kokl] *n* cardio *m*. **cockle-shell** *n* conchiglia *f*.
cockpit ['kokpit] *n* (*plane*) carlinga *f*, cabina di guida *f*; (*naval*) cassero *m*.
cockroach ['kokroutʃ] *n* scarafaggio *m*.
cocktail ['kokteil] *n* cocktail *m*.
cocoa ['koukou] *n* cacao *m*.
coconut ['koukənʌt] *n* noce di cocco *f*.
cocoon [kə'kuin] *n* bozzolo *m*.
cod [kod] *n* merluzzo *m*. **cod-liver oil** olio di fegato di merluzzo *m*.
code [koud] *n* cifrario *m*, codice *m*.
codeine ['koudiin] *n* codeina *f*.
coeducation [kouedju'keiʃən] *n* scuola mista *f*.
coerce [kou'əis] *v* costringere, forzare.
coexist [kouig'zist] *v* coesistere. **coexistence** *n* coesistenza *f*.
coffee ['kofi] *n* caffè *m*. **coffee bean** chicco di caffè *m*. **coffee pot** caffettiera *f*.
coffin ['kofin] *n* cassa da morto *f*, bara *f*, feretro *m*.
cog [kog] *n* dente *m*.
cohabit [kou'habit] *v* coabitare.
coherent [kou'hiərənt] *adj* coerente. **cohesion** *n* coesione *f*.
coil [koil] *n* rotolo *m*, bobina *f*. *v* avvolgere, attorcigliare, ravvolgere.
coin [koin] *n* moneta *f*.
coincide [kouin'said] *v* coincidere. **coincidence** *n* coincidenza *f*.
colander ['koləndə] *n* colabrodo *m*, colino *m*.

cold [kould] *adj* freddo, gelido; (*unfriendly*) riservato. **be cold** (*person*) aver freddo; (*weather*) far freddo. *n* freddo *m*; (*illness*) raffreddore *m*. **catch a cold** prendere un raffreddore, raffreddarsi. **have a cold** essere raffreddato.
colic ['kolik] *n* colica *f*.
collaborate [kə'labəreit] *v* collaborare. **collaboration** *n* collaborazione *f*. **collaborator** *n* collaboratore, -trice *m, f*.
collapse [ke'laps] *v* crollare, afflosciarsi. *n* crollo *m*, collasso *m*, rovina *f*.
collar ['kolə] *n* colletto *m*, bavero *m*; (*animal*) collare *m*; (*mech*) manicotto *m*. *v* afferrare per il collo; (*take possession*) appropriarsi di.
colleague ['koliig] *n* collega (*m pl* -ghi) *m, f*.
collect [kə'lekt] *v* raccogliere, riunire; (*take delivery*) prendere in consegna, ricuperare; (*make collection of*) far collezione di; (*meet*) radunarsi. **collect call** *n* (*US*) chiamata rovesciata *f*. **collected** *adj* calmo, padrone di sè. **collection** *n* collezione *f*, raccolta *f*; (*charity*) colletta *f*. **collective** *adj* collettivo. **collector** *n* collezionista *m, f*.
college ['kolidʒ] *n* collegio *m*, istituto *m*, università *f*.
collide [kə'laid] *v* scontrarsi, investire. **collision** *n* urto *m*, scontro *m*, investimento *m*.
colloid ['koloid] *n* colloide *m*.
colloquial [kə'loukwiəl] *adj* familiare. **colloquialism** *n* espressione familiare *f*.
colon ['koulon] *n* (*biol*) colon *m invar*; (*gramm*) due punti *m*.
colonel ['kəinl] *n* colonnello *m*.
colonnade [kolə'neid] *n* colonnata *f*, portico *m*.
colony ['koləni] *n* colonia *f*. **colonial** *n*, *adj* coloniale. **colonize** *v* colonizzare.
colossal [kə'losəl] *adj* colossale, enorme.
colour ['kʌlə] *n* colore *m*, tinta *f*. **colour bar** discriminazione razziale *f*. **colour-blind** *adj* daltonico. *v* colorare, tingere, colorire. **coloured** *adj* colorato, colorito, a colori; (*person*) di colore. **colourful** *adj* pittoresco, a tinte vivaci. **colouring** *n* colorito *m*.
colt [koult] *n* puledro *m*.
column ['koləm] *n* colonna *f*; (*newspaper*) rubrica *f*, cronaca *f*. **columnist** *n* cronista *m. f*, giornalista *m, f*.

coma ['koumə] n coma m invar.
comb [koum] n pettine m; (horse) striglia f; (birds) cresta f. v pettinare, strigliare. **comb one's hair** pettinarsi.
combat ['kombat] n combattimento m, lotta f. v combattere, lottare. **combatant** n combattente m, f.
combine [kəm'bain; n 'kombain] v combinare, unire, abbinare, combinarsi. n associazione f, consorzio m. **combine-harvester** n mietitrebbiatrice f. **combination** n combinazione f.
combustion [kəm'bʌstʃən] n combustione f. **internal combustion engine** motore a combustione interna m.
***come** [kʌm] v venire, arrivare, giungere. **come about** accadere. **come across** incontrare per caso, trovare per caso. **come in** entrare. **come into force** entrare in vigore. **come off** (succeed) riuscire. **come to blows** venire alle mani. **come to light** venire alla luce. **come up** salire; (to the surface) venire a galla.
comedy ['komədi] n commedia f. **comedian** n commediante m, f, comico, -a m, f.
comet ['komit] n cometa f.
comfort ['kʌmfət] n agio m, conforto m, consolazione f, agiatezza f. v consolare, confortare.
comic ['komik] n comico, -a m, f; (periodical) giornaletto a fumetti m. adj comico. **comic opera** opera buffa f. **comic strip** fumetto m. **comical** adj comico.
comma ['komə] n virgola f. **in inverted commas** fra virgolette.
command [kə'maind] n comando m, ordine m. v comandare; (mil) ordinare, avere il comando di. **commander** n comandante m, capo m. **commanding position** posizione dominante f. **commandment** n comandamento m, precetto m.
commandeer [komən'diə] v requisire.
commando [kə'maindou] n truppe d'assalto f pl, commando m invar.
commemorate [kə'meməreit] v commemorare. **commemoration** n commemorazione f.
commence [kə'mens] v cominciare, iniziare. **commencement** n inizio m, principio m.
commend [kə'mend] v raccomandare, lodare. **commendable** adj lodevole, encomiabile. **commendation** n lode f, encomio m.

comment ['koment] n commento m, osservazione f, rilievo m. v commentare, fare delle osservazioni. **commentary** n commentario m, cronaca f. **commentator** n commentatore, -trice m, f; cronista m, f; radiocronista m, f.
commerce ['koməis] n commercio m, scambi m pl. **commercial** adj commerciale.
commiserate [kə'mizəreit] v commiserare, compiangere.
commission [kə'miʃən] n commissione f, delegazione f; (authority) incarico m; (comm) provvigione f; (mil) brevetto da ufficiale m. v incaricare, dare una carica; nominare ufficiale; (ship) armare. **commissionaire** n portiere m. **commissioned officer** ufficiale m. **non-commissioned officer** sottufficiale m. **commissioner** commissario m.
commit [kə'mit] v commettere; affidare, rimettere. **commit oneself** impegnarsi. **commit to memory** imparare a memoria. **commitment** n impegno m. **committed** adj impegnato.
committee [kə'miti] n comitato m, commissione f.
commodity [kə'modəti] n merce f, derrata f.
common ['komən] adj comune, ordinario, volgare. n parco demaniale m. **commonplace** adj ordinario, banale. **common sense** buonsenso m.
commotion [kə'mouʃən] n agitazione f, confusione f.
commune¹ [kə'mjuin] v intrattenersi, discutere.
commune² ['komjuin] n comune m, comunità f. **communal** adj comunale, in comune.
communicate [kə'mjuinikeit] v comunicare, informare, trasmettere. **communicate with** essere in comunicazione con.
communication n comunicazione f, informazione f, rapporto m.
communion [kə'mjuinjən] n comunione f.
communism ['komjunizəm] n comunismo m. **communist** n(m+f), adj comunista.
community [kə'mjuinəti] n comunità f.
commute [kə'mjuit] v commutare; (travel) fare il pendolare. **commuter** n pendolare m, f.
compact¹ [kəm'pakt; n 'kompakt] adj compatto, serrato. n (powder) portacipria m invar.

compact[2] ['kompakt] *n* (*agreement*) patto *m*, accordo *m*.

companion [kəm'panjən] *n* compagno, -a *m*, *f*. **companionship** *n* compagnia *f*, cameratismo *m*, amicizia *f*.

company ['kʌmpəni] *n* compagnia *f*, comitiva *f*; (*comm*) ditta *f*, società *f*; (*ship*) equipaggio *m*. **in the company of** accompagnato da. **part company with** separarsi da.

compare [kəm'peə] *v* paragonare, confrontare, essere paragonabile a. **comparable** *adj* paragonabile, comparabile. **comparative** *adj* comparativo, relativo. **compared with** rispetto a, di fronte a. **comparison** *n* confronto *m*, paragone *m*.

compartment [kəm'paitmənt] *n* compartimento *m*, casella *f*; (*railway*) scompartimento *m*.

compass ['kʌmpəs] *n* bussola *f*. **compasses** *pl n* compasso *m sing*. *v* cingere, circondare.

compassion [kəm'paʃən] *n* compassione *f*, pietà *f*, misericordia *f*. **compassionate** *adj* misericordioso, pieno di compassione.

compatible [kəm'patəbl] *adj* compatibile. **compatibility** *n* compatibilità *f*.

compel [kəm'pel] *v* costringere, obbligare, forzare. **compel respect** farsi rispettare. **compelling** *adj* irresistibile.

compensate ['kompənseit] *v* compensare, ricompensare, indennizzare. **compensation** *n* compenso *m*, ricompensa *f*; (*comm*) compensazione *f*.

compete [kəm'piit] *v* concorrere, fare concorrenza a, gareggiare. **competition** *n* (*contest*) gara *f*; (*rivalry*) concorrenza *f*; (*exam*) concorso *m*. **competitive** *adj* competitivo. **competitor** *n* concorrente *m*, *f*; rivale *m*, *f*.

competent ['kompətənt] *adj* competente, capace. **competence** *n* competenza *f*, capacità *f*.

compile [kəm'pail] *v* compilare. **compilation** *n* compilazione *f*.

complacent [kəm'pleisnt] *adj* soddisfatto di sè.

complain [kəm'plein] *v* lamentarsi, lagnarsi. **complaint** *n* (*discontent*) lamentela *f*; (*merchandise*) reclamo *m*; (*illness*) malattia *f*.

complement ['kompləmənt] *n* complemento *m*. *v* completare, fare da complemento a. **complementary** *adj* complementare.

complete [kəm'pliit] *adj* completo, intero. *v* completare, finire. **completion** *n* fine *f*, compimento *m*.

complex ['kompleks] *nm*, *adj* complesso.

complexion [kəm'plekʃən] *n* (*skin*) colorito *m*; (*nature*) aspetto *m*.

complicate ['komplikeit] *v* complicare. **complicated** *adj* complicato, complesso. **complication** *n* difficoltà *f*.

complicity [kəm'plisəti] *n* complicità *f*.

compliment ['kompləmənt] *n* complimento *m*. *v* congratularsi con. **complimentary** *adj* (*flattering*) lusinghiero; (*free*) di favore.

comply [kəm'plai] *v* ubbidire, acconsentire. **in compliance with** conforme a.

component [kəm'pounənt] *nm*, *adj* componente.

compose [kəm'pouz] *v* comporre. **composed** *adj* calmo. **composer** *n* compositore, -trice *m*, *f*. **composite** *adj* composto, misto. **composition** *n* composizione *f*.

compost ['kompost] *n* concime *m*.

composure [kəm'pouʒə] *n* compostezza *f*, calma *f*.

compound[1] [kəm'paund; *n* 'kompaund] *v* (*compose*) comporre; (*mix*) mescolare; (*settle*) regolare. *n* composto *m*, miscela *f*. *adj* composto.

compound[2] ['kompaund] *n* (*enclosure*) campo *m*, accampamento *m*.

comprehend [kompri'hend] *v* comprendere, capire. **comprehensible** *adj* comprensibile. **comprehension** *n* comprensione *f*. **comprehensive** *adj* comprensivo, esauriente.

compress [kəm'pres; *n* 'kompres] *v* comprimere. *n* compressa *f*. **compression** *n* compressione *f*.

comprise [kəm'praiz] *v* includere.

compromise ['komprəmaiz] *n* compromesso *m*. *v* giungere a un compromesso; (*endanger*) compromettere. **compromising** *adj* comprometente, imbarazzante.

compulsion [kəm'pʌlʃən] *n* costrizione *f*, obbligo *m*. **compulsive** *adj* coercitivo. **compulsory** *adj* obbligatorio.

compunction [kəm'pʌŋkʃən] *n* rimorso *m*.

computer [kəm'pjuitə] *n* computer (*pl* -s) *m*, elaboratore elettronico *m*.

comrade ['komrid] *n* compagno, -a *m*, *f*; camerata *m*, *f*. **comradeship** *n* cameratismo *m*.

concave [kon'keiv] *adj* concavo.
conceal [kən'siːl] *v* celare, nascondere.
concede [kən'siːd] *v* concedere, ammettere, riconoscere.
conceit [kən'siːt] *n* vanità *f*, presunzione *f*. conceited *adj* vanitoso, presuntuoso.
conceive [kən'siːv] *v* concepire; immaginare. conceivable *adj* concepibile, immaginabile.
concentrate ['konsəntreit] *v* concentrare. *n* concentrato *m*. concentration *n* concentrazione *f*. concentration camp campo di concentramento *m*.
concentric [kən'sentrik] *adj* concentrico.
concept ['konsept] *n* concetto *m*, nozione *f*.
conception [kən'sepʃən] *n* concezione *f*, idea *f*.
concern [kən'səːn] *n* (care) sollecitudine *f*, preoccupazione *f*; (business) affare *m*, faccenda *f*; interesse *m*; (firm) azienda *f*, ditta *f*. *v* riguardare, toccare. concerned *adj* in questione; (anxious) preoccupato. concerning *prep* riguardo a, in merito a, inerente a.
concert ['konsət] *n* concerto *m*. concerted *adj* predisposto, stabilito d'accordo con altri.
concertina [konsə'tiːna] *n* fisarmonica *f*.
concerto [kən'tʃəːtou] *n* concerto *m*.
concession [kən'seʃən] *n* concessione *f*.
conciliate [kən'silieit] *v* conciliare. conciliation *n* conciliazione *f*. conciliatory *adj* conciliatorio.
concise [kən'sais] *adj* conciso, breve.
conclude [kən'kluːd] *v* concludere, dedurre. conclusion *n* conclusione *f*, fine *f*. in conclusion *adv* in fine, insomma. conclusive *adj* conclusivo.
concoct [kən'kokt] *v* (contrive) inventare. concoction *n* intruglio *m*, pasticcio *m*.
concrete ['koŋkriːt] *adj* concreto. *n* calcestruzzo *m*, cemento *m*. concrete mixer betoniera *f*. reinforced concrete cemento armato *m*. *v* cementare, rivestire di calcestruzzo.
concussion [kən'kʌʃən] *n* commozione cerebrale *f*.
condemn [kən'dem] *v* condannare. condemnation *n* condanna *f*.
condense [kən'dens] *v* condensare. condensation *n* condensazione *f*.
condescend [kondi'send] *v* degnarsi. condescending *adj* condiscendente. condescension *n* condiscendenza *f*.

condition [kən'diʃən] *n* condizione *f*. *v* condizionare. conditional *adj* condizionale.
condolence [kən'douləns] *n* condoglianza *f*. express condolences fare le condoglianze.
condom ['kondom] *n* preservativo *m*.
condone [kən'doun] *v* perdonare.
conducive [kən'djuːsiv] *adj* contribuente.
conduct [kən'dʌkt; *n* 'kondʌkt] *v* condurre; (music) dirigere. conduct oneself comportarsi. *n* condotta *f*, comportamento *m*.
conductor [kən'dʌktə] *n* (transport) bigliettario, -a *m*, *f*; (music) direttore d'orchestra *m*; (physics) conduttore *m*.
cone [koun] *n* cono *m*; (fir) pigna *f*.
confectioner [kən'fekʃənə] *n* pasticciere, -a *m*, *f*. confectioner's shop *n* pasticceria *f*.
confederate [kən'fedərət] *adj* confederato, alleato. *v* confederarsi, allearsi.
confer [kən'fəː] *v* conferire, consultarsi. conference *n* conferenza *f*. conferment *n* conferimento *m*.
confess [kən'fes] *v* confessare, ammettere; (rel) confessarsi. confession *n* confessione *f*, professione *f*. confessor *n* confessore *m*.
confetti [kən'feti] *n* coriandoli *m pl*.
confide [kən'faid] *v* confidare. confidant, -e *n* confidente *m*, *f*. confidence *n* fiducia *f*; sicurezza di sè *f*. have confidence in aver fiducia in. in confidence in confidenza. confident *adj* fiducioso, sicuro. confidential *adj* riservato.
confine [kən'fain] *n* confine *m*. *v* relegare; (to barracks) consegnare. be confined (childbirth) partorire. confinement *n* imprigionamento *m*, segregazione *f*; (childbirth) parto *m*.
confirm [kən'fəːm] *v* confermare; (statement) ribadire; (rel) cresimare; (law) omologare. confirmation *n* conferma *f*; (law) ratifica *f*; (rel) confermazione *f*, cresima *f*. confirmed *adj* confermato; (belief) convinto, impenitente.
confiscate ['konfiskeit] *v* confiscare.
conflict ['konflikt; *v* kən'flikt] *n* conflitto *m*, lotta *f*, contrasto *m*. *v* conflict with essere in disaccordo *or* contrasto con. conflicting *adj* (evidence) contraddittorio; (interests) contrastante.

conform [kən'fɔːm] v conformare, adattarsi. **conformist** n conformista m, f. **conformity** n conformità f. **in conformity with** conforme a, conformemente a.

confound [kən'faund] v sconcertare, sconvolgere.

confront [kən'frʌnt] v affrontare; (law) mettere a confronto. **confrontation** n confronto m.

confuse [kən'fjuːz] v confondere, sconcertare, disorientare, scambiare. **confusing** adj sconcertante, che rende perplesso. **confusion** n confusione f, disordine m.

congeal [kən'dʒiːl] v (freeze) congelare, congelarsi; coagulare, coagularsi.

congenial [kən'dʒiːniəl] adj congeniale.

congenital [kən'dʒenitl] adj congenito, innato.

congested [kən'dʒestid] adj congestionato. **congestion** n congestione f.

conglomeration [kən,glɔmə'reiʃən] n conglomerazione f.

congratulate [kən'gratjuleit] v congratularsi con, felicitare, felicitarsi con. **congratulation** n felicitazione f. **congratulations!** interj auguri!

congregate ['kɔŋgrigeit] v congregare, riunirsi. **congregation** n (rel) comunità f, adunanza dei fedeli f.

congress ['kɔŋgres] n congresso m.

conical ['kɔnikəl] adj conico.

conifer ['kɔnifə] n conifera f.

conjecture [kən'dʒektʃə] v supporre. n supposizione f.

conjugal ['kɔndʒugəl] adj coniugale.

conjugate ['kɔndʒugeit] v coniugare. **conjugation** n coniugazione f.

conjunction [kən'dʒʌŋkʃən] n congiunzione f.

conjunctivitis [kən,dʒʌŋkti'vaitis] n congiuntivite f.

conjure ['kʌndʒə; (invoke) kən'dʒuə] v fare giochi di prestigio; (invoke) scongiurare. **conjure up** evocare. **conjurer** n prestigiatore, -trice m, f. **conjuring trick** gioco di prestigio m.

connect [kə'nekt] v connettere, congiungere; associare; (trains) far coincidenza. **connection** n connessione f, rapporto m; coincidenza f. **in connection with** in merito a.

connoisseur [kɔnə'sɔː] n intenditore, -trice m, f.

connotation [kɔnə'teiʃən] n significato implicito m.

conquer ['kɔŋkə] v conquistare, vincere. **conqueror** n conquistatore, -trice m, f; vincitore, -trice m, f. **conquest** n conquista f, vittoria f.

conscience ['kɔnʃəns] n coscienza f. **conscientious** [kɔnʃi'enʃəs] adj coscienzioso, diligente. **conscientious objector** obiettore di coscienza m.

conscious ['kɔnʃəs] adj conscio, cosciente; (deliberate) intenzionale. **consciousness** n coscienza f.

conscript ['kɔnskript] v chiamare alle armi, arruolare. n soldato di leva m. **conscription** n leva f.

consecrate ['kɔnsikreit] v consacrare. **consecration** n consacrazione f.

consecutive [kən'sekjutiv] adj consecutivo.

consensus [kən'sensəs] n consenso m, assenso m.

consent [kən'sent] v consentire, acconsentire. n consenso m, benestare m, accordo m.

consequence ['kɔnsikwəns] n conseguenza f, effetto m, importanza f. **consequently** adv di conseguenza, quindi, perciò.

conserve [kən'sɔːv] v conservare, preservare. n conserva f. **conservation** n preservazione f. **conservative** adj conservativo, cauto; (pol) conservatore. **conservatoire** n (music) conservatorio m. **conservatory** n serra f.

consider [kən'sidə] v considerare, giudicare, ritenere, pensare. **considerable** adj notevole. **considerate** adj sollecito, riguardoso. **consideration** n considerazione f, riflessione f; (feeling, regard) riguardo m, sollecitudine f, delicatezza f.

consign [kən'sain] v consegnare, affidare. **consignee** n destinatario, -a m, f. **consignor** n mittente m, f. **consignment** n spedizione f, invio m; (goods) partita di merce f.

consist [kən'sist] v consistere (in), essere composto. **consistency** n consistenza f. **consistent** adj regolare, costante, coerente.

console¹ [kən'soul] v confortare. **consolation** n consolazione f, conforto m.

console² ['kɔnsoul] n (arch) mensola f; (furniture) mobile m; (tech) quadro di comando m.

consolidate [kən'solideit] v consolidare.
consolidation n consolidazione f.
consommé [kən'somei] n brodo m.
consonant ['konsənənt] n consonante f.
consortium [kən'soɪtiəm] n consorzio m.
conspicuous [kən'spikjuəs] adj cospicuo, evidente.
conspire [kən'spaiə] v complottare. conspiracy n complotto m, congiura f.
constable ['kʌnstəbl] n vigile m, poliziotto m.
constant ['konstənt] adj costante, invariabile. n costante f.
constellation [konstə'leiʃən] n costellazione f.
constipation [konsti'peiʃən] n stitichezza f. constipated adj stitico.
constitute ['konstitjuɪt] v costituire, creare. constituent nf, adj costituente.
constituency n collegio elettorale m. constitution n costituzione f; statuto m; (health) salute f.
constraint [kən'streint] n (restriction) costrizione f; (embarrassment) imbarazzo m.
constrict [kən'strikt] v stringere, restringere, comprimere. constriction n restringimento m; (tight feeling) oppressione f.
construct [kən'strʌkt] v costruire. construction n costruzione f; (building) edificio m; (meaning) senso m. constructive adj costruttivo, positivo.
consul ['konsəl] n console. consulate n consolato m.
consult [kən'sʌlt] v consultare; (consider) tener conto di. consultant n consulente m, f, esperto, -a m, f. consultation n consultazione f; (med) consulta f. consulting room (med) studio m.
consume [kən'sjuɪm] v consumare. consumer n consumatore, -trice m, f. consumer goods generi di consumo m pl.
contact ['kontakt] n contatto m; (acquaintance) conoscenza f. v mettere in contatto con, mettersi in contatto. contact lens n lente a contatto f.
contagious [kən'teidʒəs] adj contagioso.
contain [kən'tein] v contenere, includere. container n recipiente m.
contaminate [kən'tamineit] v contaminare, inquinare. contamination n contaminazione f; inquinamento m.
contemplate ['kontəmpleit] v contemplare, meditare; (intend to) proporsi,

aver intenzione di. contemplation n contemplazione f.
contemporary [kən'tempərəri] n, adj contemporaneo, -a; coetaneo, -a.
contempt [kən'tempt] n disprezzo m. contempt of court oltraggio alla corte m. contemptible adj spregevole. contemptuous adj sprezzante, altezzoso.
contend [kən'tend] v contendere, sostenere, affermare. bone of contention pomo della discordia m.
content¹ ['kontent] n contenuto m.
content² [kən'tent] adj contento, soddisfatto. v accontentare.
contest ['kontest; v kən'test] n gara f, lotta f. v contestare, impugnare.
context ['kontekst] n contesto m.
continent ['kontinənt] nm, adj continente. continental adj continentale.
contingency [kən'tindʒənsi] n contingenza f.
continue [kən'tinjuɪ] v continuare, proseguire. continual or continuous adj continuo, ininterrotto. continuation n seguito m. continuity n continuità f; (film) sceneggiatura f.
contort [kən'toɪt] v contorcere. contortion n contorcimento m. contortionist n contorsionista m, f.
contour ['kontuə] n contorno m. contour map/line carta/curva ipsometrica f.
contraband ['kontrəband] n contrabbando m.
contraception [kontrə'sepʃən] n pratiche antifecondative f pl. contraceptive nm, adj anticoncezionale, anticoncettivo, antifecondativo.
contract ['kontrakt; v kən'trakt] n patto m, accordo m, contratto m. v (draw together) contrarre, restringere; (acquire, take on) contrarre; (enter into) contrattare. contraction n contrazione f.
contradict [kontrə'dikt] v contraddire, smentire. contradiction n contraddizione f, smentita f.
contralto [kən'traltou] n contralto m.
contraption [kən'trapʃən] n congegno m, aggeggio m.
contrary ['kontrəri] nm, adj contrario, opposto. contrary to contrariamente a. on the contrary al contrario, anzi.
contrast ['kontraist; v kən'traist] n contrasto m, antitesi f invar. v contrastare, confrontare, mettere in contrasto.

contravene [kontrə'viːn] *v* contravvenire a.
contribute [kən'tribjut] *v* contribuire. **contributor** *n* contributore, -trice *m*, *f*; (*writer*) collaboratore, -trice *m*, *f*. **contribution** *n* contributo *m*; (*writing*) articolo *m*.
contrive [kən'traiv] *v* riuscire a, escogitare.
control [kən'troul] *v* controllare, dominare. *n* controllo *m*, autorità *f*. **controls** *pl n* comandi *m pl*. **remote control** controllo a distanza *m*, telecontrollo *m*.
controversy [kən'trovəsi] *n* controversia *f*. **controversial** *adj* controverso.
convalesce [konvə'les] *v* rimettersi in salute. **convalescence** *n* convalescenza *f*. **convalescent home** convalescenziario *m*.
convector [kən'vektə] *nm*, *adj* convettore.
convenience [kən'viːnjəns] *n* comodo *m*, comodità *f*, convenienza *f*. **at the earliest convenience** alla prima occasione. **public convenience** gabinetto pubblico *m*. **convenient** *adj* conveniente, comodo.
convent ['konvənt] *n* convento *m*.
convention [kən'venʃən] *n* convenzione *f*; (*meeting*) adunata *f*; (*agreement*) accordo *m*. **convene** *v* convocare, adunare. **conventional** *adj* convenzionale.
converge [kən'vəɪdʒ] *v* convergere.
converse [kən'vəɪs; *n*, *adj* 'konvəɪs] *v* conversare. *nm*, *adj* contrario, opposto. **conversation** *n* conversazione *f*.
convert [kən'vəɪt; *n* 'konvəɪt] *v* convertire, trasformare. *n* convertito, -a *m*, *f*. **convertible** *n* (*car*) auto decapottabile *f*.
convex ['konveks] *adj* convesso.
convey [kən'vei] *v* trasportare; (*impart*) esprimere. **conveyance** *n* mezzo di trasporto *m*; (*law*) atto di cessione *f*. **conveyor belt** nastro trasportatore *m*.
convict [kən'vikt; *n* 'konvikt] *v* condannare. *n* carcerato, -a *m*, *f*; prigioniero, -a *m*, *f*.
conviction [kən'vikʃən] *n* (*sentence*) condanna *f*; persuasione *f*, convinzione *f*.
convince [kən'vins] *v* convincere, persuadere.
convivial [kən'viviəl] *adj* allegro.
convoy ['konvoi] *n* convoglio *m*, scorta *f*. *v* convogliare, scortare.
convulsion [kən'vʌlʃən] *n* convulsione *f*. *v* **be convulsed (with laughter)** contorcersi (dalle risa).
cook [kuk] *n* cuoco, -a *m*, *f*. *v* cuocere, cucinare, far la cucina. **cook the books** falsificare i registri. **cooker** *n* fornello *m*.
cookery *or* **cooking** *n* cucina *f*, arte culinaria *f*.
cool [kuːl] *adj* fresco, calmo. *v* rinfrescare, raffreddare. **cooler** *n* refrigerante *m*; (*slang*) gattabuia *f*.
coop [kuːp] *n* stia *f*. *v* **coop up** stipare, pigiarsi.
cooperate [kou'opəreit] *v* cooperare. **cooperation** *n* cooperazione *f*, collaborazione *f*. **cooperative** *adj* cooperativo. **cooperator** *n* collaboratore, -trice *m*, *f*.
coordinate [kou'oɪdineit] *v* coordinare. *n* coordinata *f*. *adj* coordinato. **coordination** *n* coordinazione *f*.
cop [kop] *n* (*slang*) poliziotto *m*. *v* pescare. **cop it** prenderle.
cope[1] [koup] *v* riuscire a. **cope with** far fronte a.
cope[2] [koup] *n* cappa *f*.
Copenhagen [koupən'heigən] *n* Copenhagen *f*.
copious ['koupiəs] *adj* abbondante.
copper[1] ['kopə] *n* rame *m*. *adj* color rame.
copper[2] ['kopə] *n* (*slang*) poliziotto *m*.
copulate ['kopjuːleit] *v* accoppiarsi. **copulation** *n* accoppiamento *m*, copulazione *f*.
copy ['kopi] *v* copiare; ricopiare, riprodurre; imitare. *n* copia *f*, trascrizione *f*, imitazione *f*; (*book*) esemplare *m*. **copyright** *n* diritti d'autore *m pl*.
coral ['korəl] *n* corallo *m*.
cord [koɪd] *n* corda *f*; (*string*) spago *m*; (*elec*) filo *m*, cavo *m*.
cordial ['koɪdiəl] *adj* cordiale, caloroso.
cordon ['koɪdn] *n* cordone *m*. **cordon off** fare cordone intorno a, isolare.
corduroy ['koɪdəroi] *n* fustagno *m*.
core [koɪ] *n* centro *m*; (*fruit*) torsolo *m*; (*mech*) anima *f*.
cork [koɪk] *n* (*bark*) sughero *m*; (*stopper*) tappo *m*, turacciolo *m*. **corkscrew** *n* cavatappi *m invar*. *v* turare. **corked** *adj* (*wine*) che sa di turacciolo.
corn[1] [koɪn] *n* (*grain*) grano *m*; (*wheat*) frumento *m*; (*maize*) mais *m invar*, granturco *m*. **cornflour** *n* farina finissima di granturco *f*. **corny** *adj* banale.
corn[2] [koɪn] *n* (*toe*) callo *m*.
corner ['koɪnə] *n* angolo *m*; (*football*) corner *m invar*, calcio d'angolo *m*. *v* (*prevent escape*) mettere alle strette; (*stock*) accaparrare; (*drive*) fare una curva.

cornet ['kɔɪnit] n (*music*) cornetta f; (*ice-cream*) cono m.

coronary ['kɔrənəri] adj coronario. **coronary thrombosis** trombosi coronaria f.

coronation [kɔrə'neiʃən] n incoronazione f.

corporal[1] ['kɔɪpərəl] adj (*bodily*) corporale; (*material*) corporeo.

corporal[2] ['kɔɪpərəl] n caporale, -a m, f.

corporation [ˌkɔɪpə'reiʃən] n corporazione f, ente m.

corps [kɔɪ] n corpo m.

corpse [kɔɪps] n cadavere m.

correct [kə'rekt] v correggere. adj corretto, giusto, esatto. **correction** n correzione f, rettifica f.

correlate ['kɔrəleit] v mettere in correlazione. **correlated** adj correlativo. **correlation** n correlazione f.

correspond [kɔrə'spond] v corrispondere, equivalere; (*letters*) essere in corrispondenza, scambiare lettere. **correspondence** n corrispondenza f, scambio di lettere m. **correspondent** n corrispondente m, f. **corresponding** adj corrispondente.

corridor ['kɔridɔɪ] n corridoio m.

corrode [kə'roud] v corrodere, corrodersi. **corrosion** n corrosione f. **corrosive** adj corrosivo.

corrupt [kə'rʌpt] v corrompere. adj corrotto. **corruption** n corruzione f.

corset ['kɔɪsit] n busto m; (*orthopaedic*) corsetto m.

Corsica ['kɔɪsikə] n Corsica f. **Corsican** n, adj corso, -a.

cosh [kɔʃ] n randello m.

cosmetic [koz'metik] nm, adj cosmetico. **cosmetics** pl n prodotti di bellezza m pl.

cosmic ['kozmik] adj cosmico. **cosmonaut** n cosmonauta m, f.

cosmopolitan [kozmə'politən] nm, adj cosmopolitano.

***cost** [kost] n costo m, prezzo m. v costare. **costly** adj costoso, caro.

costume ['kostjuɪm] n costume m, abito m; (*suit*) tailleur m.

cosy ['kouzi] adj comodo, intimo, accogliente.

cot [kot] n lettino m, culla f.

cottage ['kotidʒ] n villino m, casetta f.

cotton ['kotn] n cotone m. **cotton-wool** n bambagia f, ovatta f; (*med*) cotone idrofilo m.

couch [kautʃ] n divano m, canapè m.

cough [kof] n tosse f. **cough mixture** sciroppo per la tosse m. v tossire.

could [kud] V **can**[1]

council ['kaunsəl] n consiglio m; (*rel*) concilio m. **councillor** n consigliere m, membro del consiglio m.

counsel ['kaunsəl] n (*advice*) consiglio m; (*lawyer*) avvocato m. v raccomandare, consigliare. **counsellor** n consigliere, -a m, f; (*consultant*) consulente m, f.

count[1] [kaunt] v contare, includere. **count on** contare su, fare affidamento su. n conto m, calcolo m; (*law*) capo d'accusa m.

count[2] [kaunt] n conte m. **countess** n contessa f.

countenance ['kauntinəns] n espressione f. v tollerare.

counter[1] ['kauntə] n (*token*) gettone m; (*table top*) banco m; (*device*) calcolatore m.

counter[2] ['kauntə] v opporsi a, controbattere. adj contrario, opposto.

counteract [kauntə'rakt] v neutralizzare, invalidare, mandare a vuoto.

counter-attack n contrattacco m. v contrattaccare.

counterfeit ['kauntəfit] adj falsificato, falso. v falsificare.

counterfoil ['kauntəˌfoil] n matrice f, figlia f.

counterpart ['kauntəˌpaɪt] n contropartita f, complemento m.

country ['kʌntri] n (*countryside*) campagna f; (*state*) paese m; (*homeland*) patria f.

county ['kaunti] n provincia f, regione f.

coup [kuɪ] n **coup de grace** colpo di grazia m. **coup d'état** colpo di stato m.

couple ['kʌpl] n coppia f, paio m (pl -a f). v accoppiare, abbinare.

coupon ['kuɪpon] n tagliando m, scontrino m.

courage ['kʌridʒ] n coraggio m. **courageous** adj coraggioso.

courgette [kuə'ʒet] n zucchina f, zucchino m.

courier ['kuriə] n accompagnatore, -trice m, f; messaggero, -a m, f.

course [kɔɪs] n corso m, percorso m, linea f; (*food*) piatto m; (*aircraft*) rotta f. **in due course** a tempo debito. **in the course of** durante, nel corso di. **of course** naturalmente, beninteso.

court [kɔɪt] *n* corte *f*; (*law*) tribunale *m*; (*tennis*) campo *m*. **court-martial** *n* corte marziale *f*. **courtyard** *n* cortile *m*. *v* corteggiare, far la corte a.

courteous ['kɔɪtiəs] *adj* cortese, gentile. **courtesy** *n* cortesia *f*, gentilezza *f*.

cousin ['kʌzn] *n* cugino, -a *m*, *f*.

cove [kouv] *n* insenatura *f*.

cover ['kʌvə] *n* coperta *f*, copertura *f*; (*shelter*) riparo *m*; (*book*) copertina *f*. *v* coprire, ricoprire; (*travel*) percorrere; (*journalism*) riferire. **covering** *n* copertura *f*. **covering letter** lettera d'accompagnamento *f*.

cow [kau] *n* vacca *f*, mucca *f*. *v* intimidire.

coward ['kauəd] *n* vigliacco, -a *m*, *f*; vile *m*, *f*. **cowardly** *adj* vigliacco, vile. **cowardice** *n* vigliaccheria *f*.

cower ['kauə] *v* accovacciarsi, rannicchiarsi.

cowl [kaul] *n* (*chimney*) comignolo *m*; (*hood*) cappa *f*; (*car*) cofano *m*.

coy [koi] *adj* ritroso, timido.

crab [krab] *n* granchio *m*.

crack [krak] *n* (*opening*) screpolatura *f*, fessura *f*; (*whip*) schiocco *m*; (*rifle*) scoppio *m*; (*noise*) schianto *m*. **have a crack at** provare a fare. *v* spaccare, schioccare, screpolare.

cracker ['krakə] *n* (*biscuit*) cracker (*pl* -s) *m*, gallettina *f*; (*firework*) mortaretto *m*.

crackle ['krakl] *v* crepitare, scricchiolare. *n* crepitio *m*, scricchiolio *m*.

cradle ['kreidl] *n* culla *f*. *v* cullare.

craft [kraɪft] *n* mestiere *m*, professione *f*; (*cunning*) astuzia *f*; (*boat*) imbarcazione *f*. **crafty** *adj* astuto.

cram [kram] *v* ficcare, cacciare.

cramp [kramp] *n* (*med*) crampo *m*. *v* paralizzare, bloccare.

cranberry ['kranbəri] *n* mirtillo rosso *m*.

crane [krein] *n* gru *f invar*. *v* **crane one's neck** allungare il collo.

crank [kraŋk] *n* (*mech*) gomito *m*, manovella *f*; eccentrico, -a *m*, *f*. *v* **crank up** avviare.

crap [krap] *n* (*vulgar*) merda *f*; (*impol*: *nonsense*) scemenze *f pl*, stupidaggini *f pl*. *v* (*vulgar*) cacare.

crash [kraʃ] *n* (*collision*) scontro *m*; (*noise*) fracasso *m*; (*collapse*) crollo *m*; (*aircraft*) caduta *f*. **crash-helmet** *n* casco paraurti *m*. **crash-landing** *n* atterraggio di

fortuna *m*. *v* (*clash*) scontrarsi; fracassare; crollare; precipitare.

crate [kreit] *n* cassa *f*. *v* imballare.

crater ['kreitə] *n* cratere *m*.

crave [kreiv] *v* ambire, bramare. **craving** *n* smania *f*, brama *f*.

crawl [krɔɪl] *v* trascinarsi, strisciare. *n* (*swimming*) crawl *m invar*.

crayfish ['kreifiʃ] *n* gambero (di˙fiume) *m*.

crayon ['kreiən] *n* pastello *m*, matita colorata *f*.

craze [kreiz] *n* mania *f*, pazzia *f*. **crazy** *adj* pazzo, matto. **drive crazy** far impazzire.

creak [kriɪk] *v* cigolare, scricchiolare. *n* cigolio *m*, scricchiolio *m*.

cream [kriɪm] *n* panna *f*, crema *f*. *v* scremare. **creamy** *adj* cremoso; (*soft*) morbido.

crease [kriɪs] *n* piega *f*, grinza *f*. *v* sgualcirsi, raggrinzarsi. **creased** *adj* raggrinzato; (*clothes*) sgualcito.

create [kri'eit] *v* creare, provocare. **creation** *n* creazione *f*. **creative** *adj* creativo, originale. **creativity** *n* potenza creativa *f*, originalità *f*. **creator** *n* creatore, -trice *m*, *f*. **creature** *n* creatura *f*.

credentials [kri'denʃəlz] *pl n* credenziali *f pl*.

credible ['kredəbl] *adj* credibile. **credibility** *n* credibilità *f*.

credit ['kredit] *n* credito *m*; (*trustworthyness*) fiducia *f*; considerazione *f*; (*bank*) attivo *m*. **credit balance** saldo attivo *m*. **credit card** carta di credito *f*. *v* (*comm*) accreditare; (*have faith in*) credere, prestar fede a; (*ascribe*) attribuire. **creditable** *adj* degno di lode, che fa onore. **creditor** *n* creditore, -trice *m*, *f*.

credulous ['kredjuləs] *adj* credulo, ingenuo.

creed [kriɪd] *n* credo *m*, professione di fede *f*.

***creep** [kriɪp] *v* strisciare, insinuarsi; (*plants*) arrampicarsi. **creeper** *n* (*plant*) pianta rampicante *f*. **creepy** *adj* che dà i brividi.

cremate [kri'meit] *v* cremare. **cremation** *n* cremazione *f*. **crematorium** *n* crematorio *m*.

crept [krept] *V* **creep**.

crescent ['kresnt] *n* mezzaluna *f*.

cress [kres] *n* crescione *m*. **mustard and cress** crescione inglese *m*, agretto *m*. **watercress** *n* crescione d'acqua *m*.

crest [krest] *n* cresta *f*, ciuffo *m*; (*heraldry, helmet*) cimiero *m*. **crestfallen** *adj* mortificato.

crevice ['krevis] *n* crepa *f*, fessura *f*.

crew [kruː] *n* equipaggio *m*, squadra *f*.

crib [krib] *n* (*rel*) presepio *m*; (*bed*) lettino *m*; (*manger*) mangiatoia *f*; (*coll*) bigino *m*. *v* plagiare.

cricket¹ ['krikit] *n* (*insect*) grillo *m*.

cricket² ['krikit] *n* (*sport*) cricket *m*.

crime [kraim] *n* delitto *m*, reato *m*. **criminal** *n*(*m*+*f*), *adj* criminale.

crimson ['krimzn] *adj* cremisi.

cringe [krindʒ] *v* comportarsi in modo servile.

crinkle ['kriŋkl] *n* grinza *f*. *v* raggrinzare.

cripple ['kripl] *n* storpio, -a *m*, *f*; invalido, -a *m*, *f*. *v* storpiare, mutilare, paralizzare.

crisis ['kraisis] *n*, *pl* -ses crisi *f invar*.

crisp [krisp] *adj* (*lively*) nitido; (*bracing*) invigorante; (*firm, fresh*) fresco; (*brittle*) croccante; (*crinkled*) crespo. **crisps** *pl n* patatine fritte croccanti *f pl*.

criterion [krai'tiəriən] *n*, *pl* -ria criterio *m*.

criticize ['kriti,saiz] *v* criticare, esprimere un giudizio su. **critic** *n* critico *m*. **critical** *adj* critico. **criticism** *n* critica *f*; (*philosophy*) criticismo *m*. **critique** *n* saggio critico *m*.

croak [krouk] *v* gracchiare, gracidare; (*grumble*) brontolare. *n* gracchiare *m*, gracchio *m*, gracidio *m*.

crochet ['krouʃei] *v* lavorare all'uncinetto.

crockery ['krokəri] *n* vasellame *m*, stoviglie *f pl*.

crocodile ['krokə,dail] *n* coccodrillo *m*.

crocus ['kroukəs] *n* croco *m*.

crook [kruk] *n* (*hook*) uncino *m*; (*bishop's*) pastorale *m*; (*shepherd's*) bastone da pastore *m*; (*criminal*) truffatore, -trice *m*, *f*. *v* piegare, curvare.

crooked ['krukid] *adj* (*bent*) piegato, storto; disonesto.

crop [krop] *n* (*produce*) raccolto *m*; (*riding*) frusta *f*; (*gullet*) gozzo *m*. *v* (*clip hair*) tagliar corto; (*trees*) mozzare; (*cut grain, etc.*) mietere. **come a cropper** far fiasco.

croquet ['kroukei] *n* croquet *m invar*.

cross [kros] *n* croce *f*. *adj* arrabbiato. **be cross** arrabbiarsi. *v* incrociare; (*street, etc.*) attraversare; (*threshold*) varcare; (*cheque*) sbarrare; (*annoy*) ostacolare. **cross oneself** segnarsi. **cross one's mind**

venire in mente a uno. **cross out** cancellare. **cross-examine** *v* sottoporre a interrogatorio. **cross-examination** *n* interrogatorio *m*. **cross-eyed** *adj* strabico. **crossfire** *n* fuoco incrociato *m* **cross-legged** *adj* a gambe accavallate. **cross-reference** *n* richiamo *m*. **crossroads** *n* crocevia *m*, incrocio *m*. **crossword** *n* cruciverba *m invar*, parole incrociate *f pl*. **crossing** *n* traversata *f*.

crotchet ['krotʃit] *n* (*music*) semiminima *f*; (*hook*) uncinetto *m*. **crotchety** *adj* irritabile.

crouch [krautʃ] *v* ranicchiarsi.

crow¹ [krou] *n* (*bird*) corvo *m*, cornacchia *f*. **as the crow flies** in linea diretta. **crow's nest** coffa *f*. **crow's foot** ruga *f*, zampa di gallina *f*.

crow² [krou] *v* cantare, esultare; (*boast*) vantarsi, trionfare.

crowd [kraud] *n* folla *f*, massa *f*, compagnia *f*. *v* affollare, ammassare. **crowded** *adj* affollato, stipato, pieno zeppo.

crown [kraun] *n* corona *f*; (*hat*) cocuzzolo *m*; (*head*) calotta *f*; (*road*) colmo *m*. **crown-prince** *n* principe ereditario *m*. *v* incoronare; (*reward*) ricompensare; (*tooth*) mettere una corona a. **to crown it all** come se non bastasse.

crucial ['kruːʃəl] *adj* decisivo, critico.

crucify ['kruːsi,fai] *v* crocifiggere, mettere in croce; tormentare, mortificare. **crucifix** *n* crocifisso *m*. **crucifixion** *n* crocifissione *f*.

crude [kruːd] *adj* (*rough, vulgar*) grossolano, rozzo, volgare; (*unrefined*) grezzo.

cruel ['kruːəl] *adj* crudele. **be cruel to** maltrattare. **cruelty** *n* crudeltà *f*.

cruise [kruːz] *n* crociera *f*. **go on a cruise** fare una crociera.

crumb [krʌm] *n* briciola *f*.

crumble ['krʌmbl] *v* sgretolare; (*collapse*) crollare. **crumbly** *adj* friabile.

crumple ['krʌmpl] *v* sgualcire, sgualcirsi; (*collapse*) sfasciarsi, accasciarsi.

crunch [krʌntʃ] *v* sgretolare, sgranocchiare. *n* scricchiolio *m*; (*critical point*) momento di crisi *m*.

crusade [kruː'seid] *n* crociata *f*. **crusader** *n* crociato *m*.

crush [krʌʃ] *v* schiacciare, frantumare; (*destroy*) annientare. *n* calca *f*, ressa *f*. **have a crush on** prendersi una cotta per. **crusher** *n* frantoio *m*.

crust [krʌst] *n* crosta *f*, corteccia *f*. **crusty** *adj* crostoso; (*surly*) burbero.

crutch [krʌtʃ] *n* gruccia *f*, stampella *f*.

crux [krʌks] *n* the crux of the matter il nodo della questione *m*.

cry [krai] *n* urlo *m*, strillo *m*, lamento *m*. *v* urlare, gridare; (*weep*) piangere.

crypt [kript] *n* cripta *f*. **cryptic** *adj* ambiguo, misterioso.

crystal ['kristl] *n* cristallo *m*. **crystallization** *n* cristallizzazione *f*. **crystallize** *v* cristallizzare.

cub [kʌb] *n* cucciolo *m*.

cube [kjuɪb] *n* cubo *m*. *v* elevare al cubo. **cubic** *adj* cubico.

cubicle ['kjuɪbikl] *n* stanzino *m*; (*changing-room*) spogliatoio *m*.

cuckold ['kʌkould] *n* cornuto *m*. *v* fare le corna a.

cuckoo ['kukuɪ] *n* cuculo *m*, cucù *m*.

cucumber [kju'kʌmbə] *n* cetriolo *m*.

cuddle ['kʌdl] *v* coccolare, abbracciare teneramente. *n* abbraccio tenero *m*.

cue[1] [kjuɪ] *n* (*theatre*) battuta d'entrata *f*; (*hint*) spunto *m*.

cue[2] [kjuɪ] *n* (*billiards*) stecca *f*.

cuff[1] [kʌf] *n* (*shirt*) polsino *m*. **cuff-links** *pl n* gemelli *m pl*.

cuff[2] [kʌf] *n* (*hit*) schiaffo *m*, sberla *f*. *v* schiaffeggiare.

culinary ['kʌlinəri] *adj* culinario, gastronomico.

culminate ['kʌlmiˌneit] *v* concludersi. **culmination** *n* culmine *m*.

culprit ['kʌlprit] *n* colpevole *m*, *f*.

cult [kʌlt] *n* culto *m*.

cultivate ['kʌltiˌveit] *v* coltivare. **cultivation** *n* coltivazione *f*, coltura *f*.

culture ['kʌltʃə] *n* cultura *f*; (*land, plants*) coltura *f*. **cultural** *adj* culturale. **cultured** *adj* colto.

cumbersome ['kʌmbəsəm] *adj* ingombrante.

cunning ['kʌniŋ] *adj* scaltro, astuto. *n* astuzia *f*, scaltrezza *f*.

cup [kʌp] *n* tazza *f*; (*sport*) coppa *f*.

cupboard ['kʌbəd] *n* armadio *m*, credenza *f*. **cupboard love** amore interessato *m*.

curate ['kjuərət] *n* curato *m*, parroco *m*.

curator [kjuə'reitə] *n* direttore, -trice di museo *m*, *f*; curatore, -trice *m*, *f*.

curb [kəɪb] *v* frenare.

curdle ['kəɪdl] *v* cagliare, cagliarsi; (*blood*) gelare.

cure [kjuə] *n* cura *f*, rimedio *m*. *v* sanare,

guarire; (*food*) conservare; (*salt*) salare; (*smoke*) affumicare.

curfew ['kəɪfjuɪ] *n* coprifuoco *m*.

curious ['kjuəriəs] *adj* (*odd*) strano, curioso, insolito; (*inquisitive*) curioso.

curl [kəɪl] *n* ricciolo *m*. *v* arricciare, arrotolare; (*lip*) torcere. **curl up** rannicchiarsi; (*animal*) accucciarsi. **curler** *n* bigodino *m*.

currant ['kʌrənt] *n* ribes *m invar*; (*dried*) uva passa *f*, uvetta *f*.

currency ['kʌrənsi] *n* decorrenza *f*; (*money*) valuta *f*, moneta legale *f*.

current ['kʌrənt] *n* corrente *f*. *adj* corrente, comune.

curry ['kʌri] *n* curry *m invar*. *v* **curry favour** ingraziarsi.

curse [kəɪs] *n* (*oath*) bestemmia *f*; (*evil*) maledizione *f*. *v* bestemmiare, maledire. **be cursed with** essere afflitto da.

curt [kəɪt] *adj* brusco.

curtail [kəɪ'teil] *v* limitare, ridurre.

curtain ['kəɪtn] *n* cortina *f*; (*cloth*) tenda *f*, tendina *f*; (*theatre*) sipario *m*.

curtsy ['kəɪtsi] *n* inchino *m*. *v* inchinarsi.

curve [kəɪv] *n* curva *f*, svolta *f*. *v* curvare, svoltare.

cushion ['kuʃən] *n* cuscino *m*; (*billiards*) sponda *f*. *v* smorzare, assorbire.

custody ['kʌstədi] *n* custodia *f*, guardia *f*. **take into custody** arrestare. **custodian** *n* guardiano *m*, custode *m*, *f*.

custom ['kʌstəm] *n* costume *m*, usanza *f*, abitudine *f*. **customs** *n* dogana *f*. **customs officer** doganiere, -a *m*, *f*. **customary** *adj* abituale, solito. **customer** *n* cliente *m*, *f*.

*****cut** [kʌt] *n* taglio *m*, incisione *f*; (*wound*) ferita *f*. *v* tagliare, incidere; (*wound*) ferire; (*cards*) alzare le carte. **cut down** ridurre; (*fell*) abbattere. **cut off** tagliar via; (*suspend*) sospendere. **cut out** ritagliare; omettere; (*elec*) interrompere. **cut it out!** piantala! **cut price** prezzo ridotto *m*. **cut-throat** *adj* spietato.

cute [kjuɪt] *adj* grazioso, ingegnoso.

cutlery ['kʌtləri] *n* posate *f pl*, posateria *f*; (*knives*) coltelleria *f*.

cutlet ['kʌtlit] *n* costoletta *f*, cotoletta *f*.

cutting ['kʌtiŋ] *adj* tagliente. *n* (*newspaper*) ritaglio *m*; (*plant*) margotta *f*; (*railway*) trincea *f*.

cycle ['saikl] *n* ciclo *m*, periodo *m*; (*bicycle*) bicicletta *f*. *v* andare in bicicletta. **cyclic** *adj* ciclico. **cycling** *n* ciclismo *m*. **cyclist** *n* ciclista *m*, *f*.

cyclone ['saikloun] *n* ciclone *m*.
cylinder ['silində] *n* cilindro *m*; (*revolver*) tamburo *m*; (*printing*) rullo *m*; (*gas*) bombola *f*.
cymbal ['simbəl] *n* cembalo *m*.
cynic ['sinik] *n* cinico, -a *m, f*. **cynical** *adj* cinico. **cynicism** *n* cinismo *m*.
cypress ['saiprəs] *n* cipresso *m*.
Cyprus ['saiprəs] *n* Cipro *m*. **Cypriot** *n*(*m*+*f*), *adj* cipriota.
cyst [sist] *n* cisti *f*.
Czechoslovakia [ˌtʃekəslə'vakiə] *n* Cecoslovacchia *f*. **Czech** *n, adj* ceco, -a, cecoslovacco, -a.

D

dab [dab] *v* toccare leggermente; applicare. *n* (*small quantity*) tocco *m*; (*light blow*) colpetto *m*.
dabble ['dabl] *v* (*dip, paddle*) guazzare. **dabble in** dilettarsi a; fare da dilettante.
dad [dad] *n* babbo *m*, papà *m*.
daffodil ['dafədil] *n* narciso *m*.
daft [daːft] *adj* scemo, sciocco.
dagger ['dagə] *n* pugnale *m*, stiletto *m*. **be at daggers drawn** essere ai ferri corti.
daily ['deili] *adj* giornaliero, quotidiano. *n* giornale *m*; (*maid*) domestica a giornata *f*. *adv* ogni giorno, quotidianamente.
dainty ['deinti] *adj* delicato, squisito.
dairy ['deəri] *n* latteria *f*. **dairy produce** latticini *m pl*.
daisy ['deizi] *n* margherita *f*.
dam [dam] *n* diga *f*, argine *m*. *v* sbarrare, arginare.
damage ['damidʒ] *n* danno *m*, guasto *m*; (*law*) indennizzo *m*. *v* danneggiare, guastare, nuocere. **damaging** *adj* dannoso.
damn [dam] *v* dannare, maledire. *interj* maledizione! *n* (*negligible amount*) bel niente *m*.
damp [damp] *adj* umido, madido. *n* umido *m*. *v* also **dampen** (*moisten*) inumidire; (*dull*) smorzare, deprimere. **damper** *n* (*furnace*) valvola di tiraggio *f*; (*elec*) smorzatore *m*; (*music*) sordina *f*.
damson ['damzən] *n* (*fruit*) susina selvatica *f*; (*tree*) susino selvatico *m*.
dance [daːns] *n* danza *f*, ballo *m*. *v* danzare, ballare. **dancer** *n* danzatore, -trice *m, f*; ballerino, -a *m, f*.
dandelion ['dandiˌlaiən] *n* dente di leone *m*.
dandruff ['dandrəf] *n* forfora *f*.
danger ['deindʒə] *n* pericolo *m*. **dangerous** *adj* pericoloso.
dangle ['daŋgl] *v* (far) ciondolare *or* dondolare.
Danish ['deiniʃ] *nm, adj* danese. **Dane** *n* danese *m, f*.
dare [deə] *v* (*be bold*) osare; (*challenge*) sfidare. **I dare say** suppongo; probabilmente; (*not deny*) non nego.
daring ['deəriŋ] *adj* audace. *n* audacia *f*.
dark [daːk] *n also* **darkness** buio *m*, oscurità *f*. *adj* buio, oscuro, cupo. **darken** *v* scurire, offuscare, rabbuiarsi.
darling ['daːliŋ] *n* tesoro *m*, gioia *f*, favorito, -a *m, f*. *adj* carissimo, amatissimo.
darn [daːn] *v* rammendare. *n* rammendo *m*, rammendatura *f*.
dart [daːt] *n* dardo *m*, freccia *f*. *v* (*move swiftly*) balzare, slanciarsi, precipitarsi; (*throw*) lanciare.
dash [daʃ] *v* buttare, urtare; (*spoil*) frustrare; (*rush*) scappare. *n* spruzzo *m*; (*rush*) slancio *m*; (*drink*) goccio *m*; (*pinch*) pizzico *m*; (*printing*) lineetta *f*. **dashboard** *n* cruscotto *m*.
data ['deitə] *pl n* dati *m pl*, elementi *m pl*. **data processing** elaborazione di dati *f*.
date¹ [deit] *n* (*calendar*) data *f*; (*appointment*) appuntamento *m*. *v* datare, fare appuntamento con. **date from** risalire a. **out of date** fuori moda, antiquato. **up to date** aggiornato.
date² [deit] *n* (*fruit*) dattero *m*.
daughter ['doːtə] *n* figlia *f*, figliola *f*. **daughter-in-law** *n* nuora *f*.
daunt [doːnt] *v* intimidire.
dawdle ['doːdl] *v* sprecar tempo, bighellonare. **dawdler** *n* fannullone, -a *m, f*; bighellone, -a *m, f*.
dawn [doːn] *n* alba *f*, aurora *f*; (*beginning*) inizio *m*. *v* albeggiare; (*appear*) apparire, manifestarsi.
day [dei] *n* giorno *m*, giornata *f*. **by day** di giorno. **daybreak** *n* alba *f*, spuntar del giorno *m*. **daylight** *n* luce del giorno *f*. **every other day** un giorno sì e uno no. **the day before yesterday** ieri l'altro. **the day after tomorrow** dopodomani.
daydream ['deidriːm] *v* sognare ad occhi aperti; fantasticare. *n* sogno ad occhi aperti *m*, fantasticheria *f*.

daze [deiz] v stordire, sbalordire. n stupore m.

dazzle ['dazl] v abbagliare.

dead [ded] adj morto, defunto; (coll: absolute) assoluto, completo. **dead drunk** ubriaco fradicio. **deadline** n scadenza f. **deadlock** n punto morto m; incaglio m. **dead slow** a passo d'uomo. **deaden** v attutire. **deadly** adj mortale.

deaf [def] adj sordo. **turn a deaf ear** fare orecchi da mercante. **deaf-mute** n sordomuto, -a m, f. **deafen** v rendere sordo, intontire. **deafness** n sordità f.

*deal [diːl] v (cards) dare le carte. **deal in** commerciare in. **deal with** occuparsi di; (things) trattare di; (people) avere rapporti con. n (business) affare m; (agreement) accordo m; (amount) quantità f. **dealer** n commerciante m, f; (retail) dettagliante m, f; (wholesale) grossista m, f.

dealt [delt] V deal.

dean [diːn] n (university) preside di facoltà m, f; (rel) decano m.

dear [diə] adj caro. **oh dear!** ahimè! Dio mio!

death [deθ] n morte f. **death certificate** certificato di morte m. **death duties** tassa di successione f sing. **death warrant** sentenza di morte f. **deathly** adj, adv mortale; cadaverico.

debase [di'beis] v degradare, svalutare.

debate [di'beit] v dibattere, discutere. n dibattito m, discussione f.

debit ['debit] n debito m; (accounts) dare m. v addebitare.

debris ['deibriː] n detrito m, macerie f pl.

debt [det] n debito m; (obligation) obbligo m. **debt collector** n esattore, -trice m, f. **debtor** n debitore, -trice m, f.

decade ['dekeid] n decennio m.

decadent ['dekədənt] adj decadente.

decant [di'kant] v travasare. **decanter** n caraffa f.

decay [di'kei] v deperire, putrefare, putrefarsi, andare in rovina; (teeth) cariare. n sfacelo m, rovina f, deperimento m.

deceased [di'siːst] n, adj defunto, -a. **decease** n decesso m.

deceit [di'siːt] n inganno m, truffa f. **deceitful** adj falso, perfido.

deceive [di'siːv] v ingannare, imbrogliare, illudersi.

December [di'sembə] n dicembre m.

decent ['diːsənt] adj (proper) decente; (fitting) decoroso; (fair) discreto; (respectable) bravo. **decency** n decenza f, decoro m.

deceptive [di'septiv] adj ingannevole, illusorio. **deception** n inganno m, imbroglio m.

decibel ['desiˌbel] n decibel m invar.

decentralization [diːˌsentrəlaiˈzeiʃn] n decentramento m.

decide [di'said] v decidere, decidersi. **decided** adj deciso, risoluto.

deciduous [di'sidjuəs] adj deciduo.

decimal ['desiməl] nm, adj decimale.

decipher [di'saifə] v decifrare.

decision [di'siʒən] n decisione f. **decisive** adj decisivo.

deck [dek] n (naut) ponte m, coperta f; (cards) mazzo m. v ornare. **deck-chair** n sedia a sdraio f.

declare [di'kleə] v dichiarare, proclamare. **declaration** n dichiarazione f, proclama m.

decline [di'klain] v (refuse) rifiutare; (gramm) declinare; (deteriorate) deperire. n (gradual loss) declino m; deterioramento m; decadenza f.

decompose [ˌdiːkəm'pouz] v decomporre. **decomposition** n decomposizione f putrefazione f.

decorate ['dekəˌreit] v decorare, ornare; (house) verniciare. **decoration** n decorazione f, ornamento m. **decorator** n (interior) arredatore, -trice m, f; (building) decoratore, -trice m, f, pittore, -trice m, f. **decorous** adj decoroso. **decorum** n decoro m.

decoy ['diːkoi] n richiamo m, uccello da richiamo m, esca f; (person) adescatore, -trice m, f.

decrease [di'kriːs] v diminuire. n diminuzione f, ribasso m.

decree [di'kriː] n decreto m, ordinanza f. v decretare.

decrepit [di'krepit] adj decrepito.

dedicate ['dediˌkeit] v dedicare. **dedication** n dedicazione f; (book) dedica f.

deduce [di'djuːs] v dedurre, inferire. **deduction** n (inference) deduzione f.

deduct [di'dʌkt] v dedurre, sottrarre. **deduction** n (subtraction) sottrazione f.

deed [diːd] n fatto m, azione f; (law) atto notarile m, strumento m; (undertaking) impresa f. **good deed** buona azione f.

deep [diːp] *adj* profondo, alto; (*colour*) scuro, cupo. **deep-rooted** *or* **deep-seated** *adj* radicato. **deepen** *v* approfondire.
deep-freeze *v* surgelare. *n* congelatore *m*, freezer *m invar*.
deer [diə] *n* (*roe*) capriolo *m*; (*fallow*) daino *m*.
deface [di'feis] *v* sfregiare, mutilare.
defamatory [di'famətəri] *adj* diffamatorio. **defamation** *n* diffamazione *f*, calunnia *f*.
default [di'fɔːlt] *v* rendersi contumace. *n* **by default** in contumacia. **in default of** in difetto di.
defeat [di'fiːt] *n* sconfitta *f*, disfatta *f*. *v* sconfiggere. **defeatism** *n* disfattismo *m*. **defeatist** *n* disfattista *m, f*.
defect[1] ['diːfekt] *n* difetto *m*, mancanza *f*. **defective** *adj* difettoso, imperfetto; (*gramm*) difettivo.
defect[2] [di'fekt] *v* disertare. **defection** *n* diserzione *f*, defezione *f*.
defend [di'fend] *v* difendere, proteggere. **defence** *n* difesa *f*. **defenceless** *adj* indifeso, senza difesa. **defendant** *n* imputato, -a *m, f*. **defender** *n* difensore *m*.
defensive [di'fensiv] *adj* difensivo. *n* difensiva *f*. **be on the defensive** stare sulla difesa.
defer[1] [di'fəː] *v* (*put off*) rimandare, rinviare.
defer[2] [di'fəː] *v* (*yield to*) sottoporsi. **deferential** *adj* rispettoso, deferente.
deficient [di'fiʃənt] *adj* deficiente, incompleto, insufficiente. **deficiency** *n* deficienza *f*, mancanza *f*, carenza *f*.
deficit ['defisit] *n* deficit *m invar*, disavanzo *m*.
define [di'fain] *v* definire, precisare. **definition** *n* definizione *f*.
definite ['definit] *adj* definito, determinato, preciso.
deflate [di'fleit] *v* sgonfiare; (*comm*) deflazionare. **deflation** *n* sgonfiamento *m*, deflazione *f*.
deflect [di'flekt] *v* deviare. **deflection** *n* deviazione *f*.
deform [di'fɔːm] *v* deformare. **deformity** *or* **deformation** *n* deformazione *f*.
defraud [di'frɔːd] *v* frodare, defraudare.
defray [di'frei] *v* **defray expenses** rimborsare le spese.
defrost [diː'frɔst] *v* scongelare.
deft [deft] *adj* destro, lesto. **deftness** *n* destrezza *f*, agilità *f*.

defunct [di'fʌŋkt] *adj* defunto.
defy [di'fai] *v* sfidare, provocare. **defiance** *n* (*resistance*) sfida *f*; dispetto *m*. **in defiance of** a dispetto di. **defiant** *adj* ribelle, ricalcitrante.
degenerate [di'dʒenərit; *v* di'dʒenəreit] *adj* degenerato, perverso. *v* degenerare. **degeneracy** *or* **degeneration** *n* degenerazione *f*.
degrade [di'greid] *v* degradare. **degrading** *adj* degradante.
degree [di'griː] *n* grado *m*; (*diploma*) titolo di studio *m*, laurea *f*.
dehydrate [diː'haidreit] *v* disidratare. **dehydration** *n* disidratazione *f*.
de-icer [diː'aisə] *n* dispositivo antighiaccio *m*.
deign [dein] *v* degnarsi.
deity ['diːəti] *n* divinità *f*, deità *f*.
dejected [di'dʒektid] *adj* avvilito, abbattuto.
delay [di'lei] *n* ritardo *m*, indugio *m*. *v* ritardare, differire.
delegate ['deləgit; *v* 'deləgeit] *n* delegato, -a *m, f*. *v* delegare, autorizzare. **delegation** *n* delegazione *f*.
delete [di'liːt] *v* espungere. **deletion** *n* cancellatura *f*, espunzione *f*.
deliberate [di'libərət; *v* di'libəreit] *adj* (*intentional*) voluto; (*unhurried*) misurato; (*carefully considered*) ponderato. *v* deliberare, riflettere. **deliberation** *n* riflessione *f*, deliberazione *f*.
delicate ['delikət] *adj* delicato, fine; (*sensitive*) sensibile. **delicacy** *n* delicatezza *f*; sensibilità *f*; (*food*) leccornia *f*.
delicious [di'liʃəs] *adj* delizioso; (*food*) squisito.
delight [di'lait] *n* delizia *f*, diletto *m*. *v* dilettare. **delight in** rallegrarsi di. **delighted** *adj* ben lieto. **delightful** *adj* delizioso, incantevole, simpaticissimo.
delinquency [di'liŋkwənsi] *n* delinquenza *f*. **delinquent** *n*(*m*+*f*), *adj* delinquente.
delirious [di'liriəs] *adj* (*feverish*) delirante; (*wildly excited*) ebbro.
deliver [di'livə] *v* (*hand over*) recapitare, consegnare; (*set free*) liberare; (*save*) salvare; (*speech*) pronunciare. **deliverance** *n* liberazione *f*. **delivery** *n* consegna *f*; (*birth*) parto *m*; (*diction*) dizione *f*.
delta ['deltə] *n* delta *m*.
delude [di'luːd] *v* deludere, deludersi. **delusion** *n* delusione *f*.

deluge ['deljuɪdʒ] *n* diluvio *m. v* diluviare.
delve [delv] *v* (*dig*) scavare; (*research*) far ricerche.
demand [di'maɪnd] *v* esigere, pretendere. *n* pretesa *f*, richiesta *f*. **in demand** ricercato. **on demand** su richiesta. **demanding** *adj* esigente.
demented [di'mentid] *adj* demente, impazzito.
democracy [di'mokrəsi] *n* democrazia *f*.
democrat *n* democratico, -a *m, f*. **democratic** *adj* democratico.
demolish [di'moliʃ] *v* demolire, abbattere. **demolition** *n* demolizione *f*.
demon ['diɪmən] *n* demonio *m*, diavolo *m*.
demonstrate ['demən,streit] *v* dimostrare. **demonstrable** *adj* dimostrabile. **demonstration** *n* dimostrazione *f*; (*proof*) prova *f*; (*meeting*) manifestazione *f*. **demonstrative** *adj* dimostrativo; (*feeling*) espansivo.
demoralize [di'morə,laiz] *v* demoralizzare, scoraggiare.
demure [di'mjuə] *adj* modesto, schivo.
den [den] *n* tana *f*.
denial [di'naiəl] *n* (*contradiction*) smentita *f*; (*negation*) diniego *m*; (*refusal*) rifiuto *m*.
denim ['denim] *n* tela pesante *f*.
Denmark ['denmaɪk] *n* Danimarca *f*.
denomination [di,nomi'neiʃən] *n* denominazione *f*; (*belief*) setta *f*, religione *f*; (*money*) taglio *m*. **denominator** *n* denominatore *m*.
denote [di'nout] *v* denotare, indicare.
denounce [di'nauns] *v* denunciare; (*openly accuse*) inveire contro.
dense [dens] *adj* denso, fitto. **density** *n* densità *f*.
dent [dent] *n* tacca *f*, ammaccatura *f*. *v* intaccare, ammaccare.
dental ['dentl] *adj* dentale; (*of dentistry*) dentistico.
dentist ['dentist] *n* dentista *m, f*. **dentistry** *n* odontoiatria *f*.
denture ['dentʃə] *n* dentiera *f*.
denude [di'njuɪd] *v* denudare, privare.
denunciation [dinʌnsi'eiʃən] *n* denuncia *f*.
deny [di'nai] *v* negare, smentire. **deny oneself** privarsi di, fare a meno di.
deodorant [diɪ'oudərənt] *nm, adj* deodorante.
depart [di'paɪt] *v* (*leave*) partire; (*diverge*) deviare. **departure** *n* partenza *f*, deviazione *f*.

department [di'paɪtmənt] *n* reparto *m*. **department store** grande magazzino *m*.
depend [di'pend] *v* dipendere, fare assegnamento. **depend on** dipendere da, fare assegnamento su. **dependable** *adj* fidato. **dependence** *n* dipendenza *f*. **dependent** *n(m+f)*, *adj* dipendente.
depict [di'pikt] *v* rappresentare, descrivere.
deplete [di'pliɪt] *v* esaurire, vuotare.
deplore [di'plor] *v* biasimare, disapprovare. **deplorable** *adj* riprensibile, biasimevole.
deport [di'poɪt] *v* deportare, espellere. **deportation** *n* deportazione *f*, espulsione *f*.
depose [di'pouz] *v* (*dismiss*) deporre; (*witness*) testimoniare. **deposition** *n* deposizione *f*, testimonianza *f*.
deposit [di'pozit] *v* depositare, posare. *n* deposito *m*; (*security*) cauzione *f*, pegno *m*. **deposit account** conto vincolato *m*.
depot ['depou] *n* deposito *m*, magazzino *m*, parco *m*.
deprave [di'preiv] *v* corrompere, depravare.
depreciate [di'priɪʃi,eit] *v* deprezzare; (*money*) svalutare; (*belittle*) screditare, denigrare. **depreciation** *n* deprezzamento *m*, svalutazione *f*; discredito *m*, denigrazione *f*.
depress [di'pres] *v* deprimere. **depressed** *adj* depresso, abbattuto; (*market*) basso. **depressing** *adj* deprimente, triste. **depression** *n* depressione *f*; (*comm*) crisi *f invar*.
deprive [di'praiv] *v* privare. **deprivation** *n* privazione *f*.
depth [depθ] *n* profondità *f*, altezza *f*. **be out of one's depth** non essere all'altezza.
deputy ['depjuti] *n* delegato *m*, deputato *m*. **deputation** *n* deputazione *f*.
derail [di'reil] *v* uscire dalle rotaie, deragliare. **derailment** *n* deragliamento *m*.
derelict ['derilikt] *adj* derelitto, abbandonato.
deride [di'raid] *v* deridere, schernire. **derision** *n* derisione *f*, scherno *m*. **derisive** *or* **derisory** *adj* irrisorio, derisivo.
derive [di'raiv] *v* derivare, provenire. **derivation** *n* derivazione *f*, provenienza *f*, origine *f*.
derogatory [di'rogətəri] *adj* sprezzante, diffamante.

descend [di'send] v scendere; (*come from*) derivare, discendere. **descent** n discesa f; (*ancestry*) discendenza f, lignaggio m. **descendant** n discendente m, f.

describe [di'skraib] v descrivere. **description** n descrizione f.

desert[1] ['dezət] n deserto m.

desert[2] [di'zəit] v disertare, abbandonare. **deserter** n disertore m. **desertion** n diserzione f, abbandono m.

desert[3] [di'zəit] n **get one's just deserts** ricevere quel che si merita.

deserve [di'zəiv] v meritare, essere degno di.

design [di'zain] v (*plan*) progettare; (*intend*) destinare. n disegno m, progetto m; (*intention*) proposito m. **have designs on** avere delle mire su. **designer** n progettista m, f, modellista m, f.

designate ['dezig,neit] v designare. adj designato.

desire [di'zaiə] v desiderare, bramare. n (*wish*) desiderio m; (*craving*) brama f; passione f. **desirable** adj desiderabile.

desk [desk] n scrivania f; (*school*) banco m; (*cash*) cassa f.

desolate ['desələt] adj desolato; (*barren*) deserto; (*lonely*) solitario; (*sad*) afflitto, rattristato.

despair [di'speə] n disperazione f. v disperare.

desperate ['despərət] adj disperato; (*hopeless*) senza speranza. **desperation** n disperazione f.

despise [di'spaiz] v disprezzare.

despite [di'spait] prep malgrado.

despondent [di'spondənt] adj accasciato, depresso.

despot ['despot] n despota m, f.

dessert [di'zəit] n dessert m invar.

destine ['destin] v destinare. **destination** n destinazione f, recapito m. **destiny** n destino m, sorte f.

destitute ['destitjuit] adj indigente.

destroy [di'stroi] v distruggere. **destruction** n distruzione f.

detach [di'tatʃ] v staccare, distaccare. **detached** adj staccato; (*house*) isolato; (*aloof*) distaccato; (*objective*) obiettivo. **detachment** n distacco m; (*army*) distaccamento m; indifferenza f; obiettività f.

detail ['diiteil] n particolare m, dettaglio m. v dettagliare, descrivere minutamente.

detain [di'tein] v detenere; (*delay*) trattenere. **detainee** n detenuto, -a m, f; carcerato, -a m, f.

detect [di'tekt] v scoprire, individuare. **detection** n scoperta f. **detective** n detective m invar, investigatore, -trice m, f. **detective novel** romanzo poliziesco m, romanzo giallo m.

détente [dei'tãint] n distensione f.

detention [di'tenʃən] n detenzione f.

deter [di'təi] v dissuadere, scoraggiare. **deterrent** n deterrente m.

detergent [di'təidʒənt] nm, adj detergente, detersivo.

deteriorate [di'tiəriə,reit] v deteriorare, peggiorare. **deterioration** n deterioramento m, peggioramento m.

determine [di'təimin] v determinare, stabilire; decidere. **determination** n determinazione f, risolutezza f. **determined** adj determinato, risoluto.

detest [di'test] v detestare, odiare. **detestable** adj detestabile, odioso.

detonate ['detə,neit] v detonare, esplodere. **detonation** n detonazione f, esplosione f. **detonator** n detonatore m.

detour ['diituə] n deviazione f.

detract [di'trakt] v detrarre.

detriment ['detrimənt] n **to the detriment of** a scapito di.

deuce [djuis] n (*cards*) due m; (*tennis*) quaranta pari.

devalue [dii'valjui] v svalutare. **devaluation** n svalutazione f.

devastate ['devə,steit] v devastare, rovinare. **devastating** adj devastatore; (*highly effective*) schiacciante.

develop [di'veləp] v sviluppare; elaborare; (*land*) usare come terreno da costruzione. **develop into** diventare. **developer** n (*phot*) sviluppatore m; (*land*) persona che apporta migliorie f. **development** n sviluppo m; evoluzione f; (*land*) valorizzazione di terreno f.

deviate ['diivi,əit] v deviare. **deviation** n deviazione f.

device [di'vais] n (*contrivance*) congegno m; (*crafty scheme*) schema m, espediente m; (*heraldry*) motto m, divisa f.

devil ['devl] n diavolo m, demonio m. **devilish** adj diabolico, infernale.

devious ['diiviəs] adj indiretto, tortuoso.

devise [di'vaiz] v escogitare, progettare.

devoid [di'void] adj privo.

devolution [,diivə'luiʃən] n devoluzione f.

devote [di'vout] *v* dedicare, consacrare. **devoted** *adj* devoto, affezionato. **devotion** *n* devozione *f*; (*prayer*) preghiere *f pl*.
devour [di'vauə] *v* divorare.
devout [di'vaut] *adj* devoto, pio, fervente.
dew [dju:] *n* rugiada *f*.
dextrous ['dekstrəs] *adj* destro, abile. **dexterity** *n* destrezza *f*.
diabetes [ˌdiəə'bi:ti:z] *n* diabete *m*. **diabetic** *nm, adj* diabetico.
diagnose [ˌdiəəg'nouz] *v* fare la diagnosi. **diagnosis** *n, pl* -ses diagnosi *f*. **diagnostic** *adj* diagnostico.
diagonal [dai'agənəl] *nf, adj* diagonale.
diagram ['daiəˌgram] *n* diagramma *m*.
dial ['daiəl] *n* (*watch*) quadrante *m*; (*telephone*) disco combinatore *m*. *v* (*number*) comporre.
dialect ['diəəlekt] *n* dialetto *m*.
dialogue ['daiəlog] *n* dialogo (*pl* -ghi) *m*.
diameter [dai'amitə] *n* diametro *m*.
diamond ['daiəmənd] *n* diamante *m*. **diamonds** *pl n* (*cards*) quadri *m pl*.
diaper ['daiəpə] *n* (*US*) pannolino (per neonati) *m*.
diaphragm ['daiəˌfram] *n* diaframma *m*.
diarrhoea [ˌdaiə'riə] *n* diarrea *f*.
diary ['daiəri] *n* diario *m*, agenda *f*.
dice [dais] *n* dado *m*.
dictate [dik'teit] *v* dettare, imporre. *n* (*order*) comando *m*; (*rule*) regola *f*. **dictation** *n* dettato *m*. **dictator** *n* dittatore *m*. **dictatorial** *adj* dittatorio, dittatoriale. **dictatorship** *n* dittatura *f*.
dictionary ['dikʃənəri] *n* dizionario *m*, vocabolario *m*.
did [did] *V* **do**.
die [dai] *v* morire. **die away** scomparire. **die down** spegnersi lentamente.
diehard ['daihaid] *n*(*m+f*), *adj* tradizionalista, intransigente.
diesel ['di:zəl] *n* **diesel engine** motore diesel *m*. **diesel oil** gasolio *m*, nafta *f*.
diet ['daiət] *n* dieta *f*; (*food*) alimentazione *f*, vitto *m*. **be on a diet** stare a dieta, stare *or* essere a regime. **dietary** *adj* dietetico.
differ ['difə] *v* essere diverso, differire; (*disagree*) dissentire. **difference** *n* differenza *f*. **different** *adj* differente, diverso.
difficult ['difikəlt] *adj* difficile; (*troublesome, tricky*) difficoltoso. **difficulty** *n* difficoltà *f*.
diffident ['difidənt] *adj* timido.

*dig [dig] *v* scavare; (*agric*) vangare. *n* (*archaeol*) scavi *m pl*.
digest [dai'dʒest; *n* 'daidʒest] *v* digerire, assimilare. *n* sommario *m*, selezione *f*. **digestible** *adj* digeribile. **digestion** *n* digestione *f*.
digit ['didʒit] *n* (*figure*) numero semplice *m*, cifra *f*; (*finger, toe*) dito *m*. **digital** *adj* digitale.
dignified ['digniˌfaid] *adj* dignitoso, nobile.
dignity ['dignəti] *n* dignità *f*.
digress [dai'gres] *v* digredire, deviare. **digression** *n* digressione *f*.
digs [digz] *pl n* alloggio *m sing*.
dilapidated [di'lapiˌdeitid] *adj* decrepito.
dilate [dai'leit] *v* dilatare.
dilemma [di'lemə] *n* dilemma *m*.
diligent ['dilidʒent] *adj* diligente, assiduo.
dilute [dai'lu:t] *v* diluire, allungare. *adj* diluito.
dim [dim] *v* attenuare, affievolire. *adj* fioco, tenue; (*stupid*) poco intelligente.
dimension [di'menʃən] *n* dimensione *f*.
diminish [di'miniʃ] *v* diminuire, ridurre.
diminutive [di'minjutiv] *adj* diminutivo, minuscolo.
dimple ['dimpl] *n* fossetta *f*.
din [din] *n* fracasso *m*, baccano *m*.
dine [dain] *v* pranzare. **dining car** vagone ristorante *m*. **dining room** sala da pranzo *f*.
dinghy ['diŋgi] *n* barca *f*.
dingy ['dindʒi] *adj* squallido.
dinner ['dinə] *n* pranzo *m*, cena *f*.
dinosaur ['dainəˌsoi] *n* dinosauro *m*.
diocese ['daiəsis] *n* diocesi *f invar*.
dip [dip] *v* abbassare, tuffare, immergere. *n* immersione *f*; (*swim*) nuotata *f*; inclinazione *f*.
diphthong ['difθoŋ] *n* dittongo *m*.
diploma [di'ploumə] *n* diploma *m*.
diplomacy [di'plouməsi] *n* diplomazia *f*. **diplomat** *n* diplomatico *m*. **diplomatic** *adj* diplomatico.
dipstick ['dipstik] *n* asta di livello *f*.
dire [daiə] *adj* **dire need** bisogno urgente *m*. **dire straits** miseria squallida *f sing*.
direct [di'rekt] *adj* diretto, immediato; sincero. *v* dirigere, amministrare. **direction** *n* direzione *f*; (*management*) amministrazione; (*address*) indirizzo *m*; (*stage*) didascalia *f*. **director** *n* (*comm*) amministratore, -trice *m, f*; (*theatre*)

regista *m, f.* **directory** *n* annuario *m*, guida *f*; (*phone*) elenco telefonico *m*.

dirt [dəɪt] *n* sporcizia *f*. **dirty** *adj* sporco, sudicio. **dirty word** parolaccia *f*.

disability [disə'biləti] *n* incapacità *f*, inabilità *f*. **disabled** *nm, adj* invalido, mutilato.

disadvantage [ˌdisəd'vaɪntidʒ] *n* svantaggio *m*.

disagree [ˌdisə'griɪ] *v* non andar d'accordo, non essere d'accordo. **disagree with** (*food*) far male a. **disagreeable** *adj* sgradevole, antipatico. **disagreement** *n* disaccordo *m*, dissenso *m*.

disappear [ˌdisə'piə] *v* sparire, scomparire. **disappearance** *n* scomparsa *f*.

disappoint [ˌdisə'point] *v* deludere. **disappointed** *adj* deluso, scontento. **disappointment** *n* delusione *f*.

disapprove [ˌdisə'pruɪv] *v* disapprovare, riprovare. **disapproval** *n* disapprovazione *f*.

disarm [dis'aɪm] *v* disarmare. **disarmament** *n* disarmo *m*.

disaster [di'zaɪstə] *n* disastro *m*, disgrazia *f*; calamità *f*. **disastrous** *adj* disastroso.

disband [dis'band] *v* sbandare, sciogliere, congedare.

disc *or US* **disk** [disk] *n* disco *m*.

discard [dis'kaɪd] *v* scartare.

discern [di'səɪn] *v* discernere, scorgere, **discerning** *adj* avveduto, accorto. **discernment** *n* discernimento *m*, giudizio *m*.

discharge [dis'tʃaɪdʒ] *v* scaricare; (*dismiss*) licenziare; (*law*) assolvere; (*radiation*) emettere; (*med*) suppurare; (*a duty*) adempiere; (*a debt*) saldare. *n* scarico *m*; licenziamento *m*; assoluzione *f*; emissione *f*; suppurazione *f*; (*elec*) scarica *f*.

disciple [di'saipl] *n* discepolo, -a *m, f*.

discipline ['disiplin] *n* disciplina *f*. *v* disciplinare. **disciplinary** *adj* disciplinare.

disclaim [dis'kleim] *v* ripudiare, sconfessare, smentire. **disclaimer** *n* ripudio *m*, smentita *f*; denunzia di un contratto *f*.

disclose [dis'klouz] *v* svelare, rivelare. **disclosure** *n* rivelazione *f*.

discolour [dis'kʌlə] *v* scolorire, sbiadire.

discomfort [dis'kʌmfət] *n* disagio *m*. *v* mettere a disagio.

disconcert [diskən'səɪt] *v* sconcertare. **disconcerting** *adj* sconcertante.

disconnect [diskə'nekt] *v* sconnettere; (*mech*) disinnestare

disconsolate [dis'konsələt] *adj* sconsolato, desolato.

discontinue [diskən'tinjuɪ] *v* sospendere, interrompere, terminare.

discord ['diskoɪd] *n* discordia *f*, dissenso *m*; (*music*) dissonanza *f*, disarmonia *f*. **discordant** *adj* discorde; (*noise*) discordante; dissonante.

discotheque ['diskətek] *n* discoteca *f*.

discount ['diskaunt] *v* (*disregard*) non badare a. *n* sconto *m*, ribasso *m*.

discourage [dis'kʌridʒ] *v* scoraggiare. **discouragement** *n* scoraggiamento *m*. **discouraging** *adj* scoraggiante.

discover [dis'kʌvə] *v* scoprire. **discovery** *n* scoperta *f*.

discredit [dis'kredit] *v* screditare, mettere in dubbio.

discreet [di'skriɪt] *adj* discreto, riservato. **discretion** *n* discrezione *f*; prudenza *f*; (*judgment*) giudizio *m*. **discretionary** *adj* discrezionale.

discrepancy [di'skrepənsi] *n* divario *m*, disaccordo *m*.

discrete [di'skriɪt] *adj* separato, distinto, discreto.

discriminate [di'skrimiˌneit] *v* discriminare, differenziare. **discriminating** *adj* penetrante, giudizioso. **discrimination** *n* discriminazione *f*, distinzione *f*.

discus ['diskəs] *n* disco *m*.

discuss [di'skʌs] *v* discutere, dibattere. **discussion** *n* discussione *f*, dibattimento *m*.

disease [di'ziːz] *n* malattia *f*. **diseased** *adj* malato, ammalato.

disembark [disim'baɪk] *v* sbarcare.

disengage [disin'geidʒ] *v* disimpegnare, liberare; (*mech*) disinnestare. **disengaged** *adj* libero.

disfigure [dis'figə] *v* sfigurare, deturpare.

disgrace [dis'greis] *n* disonore *m*, vergogna *f*, scandalo *m*, ignominia *f*. *v* disonorare, screditare. **disgraceful** *adj* vergognoso.

disgruntled [dis'grʌntld] *adj* di cattivo umore, scontento.

disguise [dis'gaiz] *v* camuffare, mascherare. *n* maschera *f*, travestimento *m*.

disgust [dis'gʌst] *n* disgusto *m*, ribrezzo *m*, schifo *m*. *v* disgustare, far schifo, nauseare. **disgusting** *adj* disgustoso, schifoso.

dish [diʃ] *n* piatto *m*. **dishcloth** *n*

strofinaccio per i piatti *m*. **dishwasher** *n* lavapiatti *m*.

dishearten [dis'haɪtn] *v* scoraggiare.

dishevelled [di'ʃevəld] *adj* scapigliato, arruffato.

dishonest [dis'onist] *adj* disonesto. **dishonesty** *n* disonestà *f*.

dishonour [dis'onə] *v* disonorare. *n* disonore *m*, infamia *f*. **dishonourable** *adj* disonorevole.

disillusion [disi'luːʒən] *v* disilludere, disingannare. *n* disillusione *f*, disinganno *m*.

disinfect [disin'fekt] *v* disinfettare. **disinfectant** *nm*, *adj* disinfettante.

disinherit [disin'herit] *v* diseredare.

disintegrate [dis'intiˌgreit] *v* disintegrare, disgregare, disfare, disfarsi. **disintegration** *n* disfacimento *m*, sfacelo *m*, disintegrazione *f*.

disinterested [dis'intristid] *adj* disinteressato.

disjointed [dis'dʒointid] *adj* sconnesso, incoerente.

dislike [dis'laik] *v* detestare, sentire antipatia per. *n* antipatia *f*, avversione *f*.

dislocate ['disləˌkeit] *v* dislocare; (*joint*) lussare. **dislocation** *n* dislocazione *f*; lussazione *f*.

dislodge [dis'lodʒ] *v* sloggiare, scacciare.

disloyal [dis'loiəl] *adj* sleale, infedele. **disloyalty** *n* slealtà *f*, infedeltà *f*.

dismal ['dizməl] *adj* triste, lugubre, malinconico.

dismantle [dis'mantl] *v* smantellare.

dismay [dis'mei] *v* costernare, sgomentare. *n* costernazione *f*, sgomento *m*.

dismiss [dis'mis] *v* (*send away*) respingere; (*discard*) scartare; (*discharge*) licenziare. **dismissal** *n* licenziamento *m*.

dismount [dis'maunt] *v* smontare.

disobey [disə'bei] *v* disubbidire, disobbedire. **disobedience** *n* disubbidienza *f*. **disobedient** *adj* disubbidiente.

disorder [dis'oɪdə] *n* disordine *m*, confusione *f*; (*med*) disturbo *m*. **disorderly** *adj* disordinato.

disorganized [dis'oɪgənaizd] *adj* disorganizzato. **disorganization** *n* disorganizzazione *f*.

disown [dis'oun] *v* ripudiare, rinnegare.

disparage [di'sparidʒ] *v* denigrare, screditare.

disparity [dis'pariti] *n* disparità *f*.

dispassionate [dis'paʃənit] *adj* spassionato, obiettivo.

dispatch [di'spatʃ] *v* spedire, inviare; (*settle*) sbrigare; (*kill*) spacciare. *n* spedizione *f*; (*mil*) dispaccio *m*; (*speed*) prontezza *f*, sollecitudine *f*.

dispel [di'spel] *v* dissipare, scacciare.

dispense [di'spens] *v* dispensare, distribuire; (*justice*) amministrare. **dispense with** fare a meno di. **dispensary** *n* dispensario *m*, farmacia *f*.

disperse [di'spəɪs] *v* disperdere, sparpagliare, dileguarsi. **dispersion** *n* dispersione *f*, diffusione *f*.

displace [dis'pleis] *v* spostare; (*take place of*) soppiantare. **displaced person** profugo (*pl* -ghi) *m*, -a *f*. **displacement** *n* spostamento *m*.

display [di'splei] *v* mostrare, esibire, ostentare, manifestare. *n* mostra *f*, manifestazione *f*, esposizione *f*.

displease [dis'pliɪz] *v* spiacere, dispiacere, scontentare. **displeasure** *n* dispiacere *m*, ira *f*.

dispose [di'spouz] *v* disporre, sistemare. **dispose of** sbarazzarsi di, eliminare. **disposal** *n* (*control*) disposizione *f*; (*act of disposing*) sistemazione *f*. **disposed** *adj* disposto, intenzionato. **disposition** *n* disposizione *f*, tendenza *f*; (*character*) indole *f*.

disprove [dis'pruɪv] *v* confutare.

dispute [di'spjuɪt] *n* disputa *f*, vertenza *f*; (*quarrel*) lite *f*. *v* contestare.

disqualify [dis'kwoliˌfai] *v* (*sport*) squalificare; (*render unfit*) incapacitare; (*law*) interdire. **disqualification** *n* squalifica *f*, incapacità *f*, interdizione *f*.

disregard [disrə'gaɪd] *v* non far caso a, ignorare. *n* noncuranza *f*, inosservanza *f*.

disreputable [dis'repjutəbl] *adj* malfamato, vergognoso.

disrespect [disrə'spekt] *n* mancanza di rispetto *f*, irreverenza *f*. **disrespectful** *adj* poco rispettoso, che non mostra rispetto.

disrupt [dis'rʌpt] *v* scompigliare, mettere in confusione. **disruption** *n* scompiglio *m*.

dissatisfy [di'satisfai] *v* scontentare. **dissatisfaction** *n* insoddisfazione *f*.

dissect [di'sekt] *v* sezionare; (*corpse*) dissecare; (*analyse*) analizzare. **dissection** *n* sezionamento *m*; dissezione *f*; analisi *f*.

dissent [di'sent] *n* dissenso *m*. *v* dissentire.

dissident ['disidənt] *n(m+f)*, *adj* dissidente.

dissimilar [di'similǝ] *adj* dissimile.
dissipated ['disipeitid] *adj* dissoluto.
dissociate [di'sousieit] *v* dissociare, sdoppiare. **dissociation** *n* dissociazione *f*, sdoppiamento *m*.
dissolve [di'zolv] *v* sciogliere, sciogliersi, dissolvere. **dissolute** *adj* dissoluto, licenzioso.
dissuade [di'sweid] *v* dissuadere, distogliere. **dissuasion** *n* dissuasione *f*, distoglimento *m*.
distance ['distǝns] *n* distanza *f*, lontananza *f*; (*reserve*) riserbo *m*. **distant** *adj* distante, lontano, remoto; riservato.
distaste [dis'teist] *n* avversione *f*. **distasteful** *adj* sgradevole.
distemper [di'stempǝ] *n* (*paint*) intonaco *m*; (*canine*) cimurro *m*. *v* intonacare.
distended [di'stendid] *adj* dilatato.
distil [di'stil] *v* distillare. **distillation** *n* distillazione *f*. **distillery** *n* distilleria *f*.
distinct [di'stiŋkt] *adj* differente, diverso; distinto; (*clear*) chiaro. **distinction** *n* distinzione *f*; differenza *f*. **distinctive** *adj* caratteristico, distintivo.
distinguish [di'stiŋgwiʃ] *v* distinguere, differenziare, individuare. **distinguish oneself** farsi notare. **distinguishable** *adj* distinguibile. **distinguished** *adj* distinto, insigne.
distort [di'stoːt] *v* deformare, alterare. **distortion** *n* deformazione *f*, alterazione *f*.
distract [di'strakt] *v* distrarre; (*disturb*) turbare. **distraction** *n* distrazione *f*.
distraught [di'stroːt] *adj* turbato.
distress [di'stres] *n* (*anxiety*) angoscia *f*; (*poverty*) miseria *f*; (*ship*) pericolo *m*; (*worry*) preoccupazione *f*. *v* angosciare, affliggere, preoccupare. **distressed** *adj* dolente, angosciato. **distressing** *adj* penoso, doloroso.
distribute [di'stribjut] *v* distribuire. **distribution** *n* distribuzione *f*. **distributor** *n* distributore *m*.
district ['distrikt] *n* distretto *m*, quartiere *m*, zona *f*.
distrust [dis'trʌst] *v* diffidare di, sospettare, non aver fiducia in. *n* sospetto *m*, sfiducia *f*, diffidenza *f*.
disturb [di'stɔːb] *v* disturbare, incomodare. **disturbance** *n* disturbo *m*; (*breach of peace*) sommossa *f*.
ditch [ditʃ] *n* fossa *f*, fossato *m*. *v* (*abandon*) piantare.
ditto ['ditou] *adv* idem.

divan [di'van] *n* divano *m*.
dive [daiv] *v* tuffarsi, fare un tuffo, sommergersi. *n* (*plunge*) tuffo *m*; (*coll*) taverna *f*, bettola *f*. **diver** *n* palombaro *m*. **diving board** trampolino *m*. **diving suit** scafandro *m*.
diverge [dai'vǝːdʒ] *v* divergere.
diversify [dai'vǝːsifai] *v* diversificare, differenziare.
divert [dai'vǝːt] *v* deviare; distrarre; (*amuse*) divertire. **diversion** *n* (*distraction*) diversivo *m*, distrazione *f*; (*mil*) diversione *f*; deviazione *f*.
divide [di'vaid] *v* dividere, separare. **divided** *adj* diviso. **dividers** *pl n* compasso *m sing*. **division** *n* divisione *f*.
dividend ['dividend] *n* dividendo *m*.
divine [di'vain] *adj* divino, sacro. *n* teologo *m*, sacerdote *m*. *v* scoprire, indovinare; (*prophesy*) pronosticare. **diviner** *n* (*soothsayer*) indovino, -a *m*, *f*; (*user of divining rod*) rabdomante *m*. **divinity** *n* divinità *f*.
divorce [di'vois] *n* divorzio *m*. *v* divorziare, divorziarsi.
divulge [dai'vʌldʒ] *v* divulgare, diffondere.
dizzy ['dizi] *adj* vertiginoso. **feel dizzy** avere il capogiro; sentirsi girare la testa. **dizziness** *n* capogiro *m*, vertigine *f*.
*do [duː] *v* fare; (*suffice*) bastare; (*achieve*) compiere; (*carry out*) eseguire. **do away with** abolire; (*kill*) uccidere. **do-it-yourself** *adj* da fare da soli. **do out of** deprivare di. **do up** (*clothes, etc.*) abbottonare. **do without** fare a meno di. **how do you do?** come sta? (*polite*) come stai? **make do** arrangiarsi.
docile ['dousail] *adj* docile, mansueto.
dock[1] [dok] *n* (*wharf*) banchina *f*; (*waterway*) bacino *m*; (*port area*) zona portuale *f*. *v* attraccare. **docker** *n* portuale *m*. **dockyard** *n* cantiere navale *m*.
dock[2] [dok] *v* mozzare, troncare.
dock[3] [dok] *n* (*law*) banco degli imputati *m*.
docket ['dokit] *n* bolletta *f*.
doctor ['doktǝ] *n* dottore, -essa *m*, *f*; (*med*) medico, -chessa *m*, *f*. **doctorate** *n* dottorato *m*.
doctrine ['doktrin] *n* dottrina *f*. **doctrinal** *adj* dottrinale.
document ['dokjumǝnt] *n* documento *m*. *v* documentare. **documentary** *n* documentario *m*. **documentation** *n* documentazione *f*.

dodge [dodʒ] *v* schivare, scansare. *n* sotterfugio *m*, stratagemma *f*.

doe [dou] *n* selvaggina femmina *f*; (*deer*) daina *f*; (*rabbit*) femmina del coniglio *f*; (*hare*) lepre femmina *f*.

dog [dog] *n* cane *m*. **dog-eared** *adj* (*page*) accartocciato, con le orecchie. **dogrose** *n* rosa canina *f*. **dog-tired** *adj* stanco morto. **dogtooth** *n* dente canino *m*. *v* pedinare. **be dogged by** essere perseguitato da. **dogged** *adj* ostinato, accanito.

doge [doudʒ] *n* doge *m*.

dogma ['dogmə] *n* dogma *m*. **dogmatic** *adj* dogmatico.

dole [doul] *n* sussidio di disoccupazione *m*. *v* **dole out** distribuire.

doll [dol] *n* bambola *f*, pupa *f*. *v* **doll up** agghindarsi, abbellirsi.

dollar ['dolə] *n* dollaro *m*.

dolphin ['dolfin] *n* delfino *m*.

domain [də'mein] *n* (*land*) proprietà *f*; (*law*) demanio *m*; (*control, sphere of activity*) dominio *m*.

dome [doum] *n* cupola *f*.

domestic [də'mestik] *adj* domestico; (*not foreign*) nazionale. *n* domestico, -a *m*, *f*. **domesticate** *v* addomesticare. **domesticity** *n* domesticità *f*.

domicile ['domisail] *n* domicilio *m*.

dominate ['domi,neit] *v* dominare. **dominant** *adj* dominante.

domineer [domi'niə] *v* signoreggiare. **domineering** *adj* imperioso; (*overbearing*) prepotente.

dominion [də'minjən] *n* dominio *m*; autorità *f*.

domino ['dominou] *n* domino *m*.

don¹ [don] *v* vestire, indossare.

don² [don] *n* (*Spanish title*) don *m invar*; (*scholar*) docente universitario, -a *m*, *f*.

donate [də'neit] *v* donare. **donation** *n* dono *m*, donazione *f*. **donor** *n* donatore, -trice *m*, *f*.

done [dʌn] *V* **do**.

donkey ['doŋki] *n* asino, -a *m*, *f*; somaro, -a *m*, *f*.

doom [duːm] *n* destino *m*, sorte *f*; (*ruin*) rovina *f*. *v* destinare, condannare. **doomed** *adj* condannato. **doomsday** *n* giorno del giudizio *m*.

door [doː] *n* porta *f*, uscio *m*. **doorbell** *n* campanello *m*. **door-handle** *n* maniglia *f*. **door-keeper** *n* portiere, -a *m*, *f*, portinaio, -a *m*, *f*. **door-knocker** *n* battiporta *m*,

batacchio *m*. **doormat** *n* zerbino *m*, stoino *m*. **doorstep** *n* soglia *f*. **doorway** *n* entrata *f*, portone *m*.

dope [doup] *n* (*slang: drug*) stupefacente *m*, droga *f*; (*slang: information*) notizie *f pl*. *v* drogare. **dopey** *adj* inebetito.

dormant ['doːmənt] *adj* addormentato, latente.

dormitory ['doːmitəri] *n* dormitorio *m*.

dormouse ['doː,maus] *n* ghiro *m*.

dose [dous] *n* dose *f*. *v* dosare.

dot [dot] *n* punto *m*. *v* punteggiare. **on the dot** in orario. **dotty** *adj* (*coll*) picchiatello.

dote [dout] *v* **dote on** essere infatuato di.

double ['dʌbl] *v* raddoppiare. **double up** piegare *or* piegarsi in due; contorcersi. *adj* doppio. *n* doppio *m*; (*person*) sosia *m invar*. **at the double** a passo di corsa. **double-barrelled** *adj* a doppia canna. **double bass** contrabbasso *m*. **double bed** letto matrimoniale *m*. **double-breasted** *adj* a doppio petto. **double-cross** *v* fare il doppio gioco, tradire.

doubt [daut] *n* dubbio *m*, incertezza *f*. *v* dubitare, mettere in dubbio. **doubtful** *adj* dubbio, incerto, problematico. **doubtless** *adv* senza dubbio.

dough [dou] *n* pasta *f*; (*slang*) quattrini *m pl*. **doughnut** *n* ciambella *f*, krapfen *m invar*.

dove [dʌv] *n* colomba *f*. **dovecot** *n* colombaia *f*. **dovetail** *v* (*carpentry*) incastrare a coda di rondine; (*fit exactly*) combaciare, far combaciare.

dowdy ['daudi] *adj* sciatto, trasandato.

down¹ [daun] *adv* giù, di sotto, per terra. *adj* depresso, abbattuto. **down and out** ridotto in miseria. *v* **down tools** abbandonare il lavoro.

down² [daun] *n* (*plumage*) piumino *m*, lanugine *f*; (*soft hair*) peluria *f*.

downcast ['daun,kaɪst] *adj* abbattuto, depresso.

downfall ['daun,foɪl] *n* rovina *f*, caduta *f*.

downhearted [,daun'haɪtid] *adj* depresso, scoraggiato.

downhill [,daun'hil] *adv* in discesa.

downpour ['daun,poɪ] *n* acquazzone *m*.

downright ['daun,rait] *adv* categoricamente, nettamente.

downstairs [,daun'steəz] *adv* da basso, al piano inferiore. **go downstairs** scendere le scale.

downstream [‚daun'striːm] *adv* a valle, seguendo la corrente.

downtrodden ['daun‚trodn] *adj* oppresso.

downward ['daunwəd] *adj* discendente.

downwards ['daunwədz] *adv* in giù, verso il basso.

dowry ['dauəri] *n* dote *f.*

doze [douz] *v* sonnecchiare, fare un pisolino. **doze off** assopirsi. **dozy** *adj* sonnolento.

dozen ['dʌzn] *n* dozzina *f.*

drab [drab] *adj* squallido, scialbo.

draft [draːft] *n* (*sketch*) abbozzo *m*; (*preliminary copy*) brutta copia *f*; (*conscription*) leva *f*; (*written order*) tratta *f*, cambiale *f*; (*bank*) assegno circolare *m. v* abbozzare, delineare; (*conscript*) chiamare sotto le armi, arruolare.

drag [drag] *v* trascinare; (*search*) dragare; (*extract*) strappare. *n* trazione *f.* **in drag** vestito da donna.

dragon ['dragən] *n* drago *m*; (*woman*) megera *f.* **dragon-fly** *n* libellula *f.*

drain [drein] *n* fogna *f*, tubo di scarico *m. v* (*draw off*) scolare, prosciugare; (*med*) drenare; (*exhaust*) esaurire; (*drink up*) bere fino all'ultimo. **drainage** *n* scarico *m*, fognatura *f*, drenaggio *m.* **draining board** scolatoio *m.* **drainpipe** *n* grondaia *f.*

drama ['draːmə] *n* dramma *m.* **dramatic** *adj* drammatico, impressionante. **dramatist** *n* drammaturgo, -a *m, f.* **dramatize** *v* drammatizzare.

drank [draŋk] *V* **drink**.

drape [dreip] *v* drappeggiare.

draper ['dreipə] *n* negoziante di tessuti *m, f.* **drapery** *n* tessuti *m pl*; tendaggio *m.*

drastic ['drastik] *adj* drastico.

draught or *US* **draft** [draːft] *n* (*air current*) corrente d'aria *f*; (*drink*) sorso *m*; (*pull*) tiro *m*; (*fishing*) retata *f.* **draughts** *n* gioco della dama *m.* **draughtsman** *n* disegnatore, -trice *m, f*, progettista *m, f*; (*of documents*) compilatore, -trice *m, f.* **it's draughty** c'è una corrente d'aria.

***draw** [droː] *v* (*pull*) tirare; (*attract*) attirare, attrarre; (*picture*) disegnare; (*sport*) pareggiare; (*extract*) estrarre. **draw back** ritirarsi. **drawback** *n* inconveniente *m.* **drawbridge** *n* ponte levatoio *m.* **draw near** avvicinarsi. **draw on** (*funds*) attingere (a). *n* (*sport*) pareggio *m.* **drawing** *n* disegno *m.* **drawing-board** *n* tavola

da disegno *f.* **drawing-pin** *n* puntina da disegno *f.* **drawing-room** *n* salotto *m.*

drawer ['droːə] *n* cassetto *m.* **chest of drawers** cassettone *m.* **drawers** *pl n* (*underclothes*) mutandine *f pl.*

drawl [droːl] *v* strascicare le parole.

drawn [droːn] *V* **draw**.

dread [dred] *v* aver paura di. *n* timore *m*, paura *f*, fobia *f.* **dreadful** *adj* spaventoso.

***dream** [driːm] *n* sogno *m*; visione *f. v* sognare; immaginare. **dreamer** *n* sognatore, -trice *m, f*; visionario, -a *m, f.* **dreamy** *adj* (*vague*) vago.

dreamt [dremt] *V* **dream**.

dreary ['driəri] *adj* triste; (*boring*) noioso. **dreariness** *n* tristezza *f.*

dredge [dredʒ] *v* dragare.

dregs [dregz] *pl n* feccia *f sing*; (*coffee*) fondo *m sing.*

drench [drentʃ] *v* inzuppare, bagnare.

dress [dres] *v* (*clothe*) vestire; (*salad, etc.*) condire; (*wounds*) bendare. *n* abito *m*, vestito *m.* **dress circle** prima galleria *f.* **dressmaker** *n* sarta *f.* **dressmaking** *n* confezione di abiti da donna *f.* **dress rehearsal** prova generale *f.* **dressing** *n* condimento *m*; benda *f.* **dressing down** rimprovero *m.* **dressing-gown** *n* vestaglia *f.* **dressing-room** *n* camerino *m.* **dressing-table** *n* toilette (*pl* -s) *f.*

dresser[1] ['dresə] *n* (*furniture*) credenza *f.*

dresser[2] ['dresə] *n* (*theatre*) vestiarista *m, f*; (*med*) assistente medico, -a *m, f.*

drew [druː] *V* **draw**.

dribble ['dribl] *v* sbavare; (*trickle*) gocciolare; (*ball*) palleggiare. *n* bava *f*; gocciolamento *m*; palleggio *m.*

drier ['draiə] *n* (*clothes*) asciugatrice *f*; (*hair*) asciugacapelli *m.*

drift [drift] *v* andare alla deriva; (*wander aimlessly*) lasciarsi andare. **drift apart** perdersi di vista. *n* tendenza *f*, direzione *f*; (*movement*) deriva *f*; (*current*) corrente *f.*

drill[1] [dril] *n* trivella *f*, sonda *f*, trapano *m. v* trapanare, sondare.

drill[2] [dril] *n* esercitazioni *f pl*, addestramento *m. v* esercitare, fare esercitazioni, addestrare.

***drink** [driŋk] *v* bere. *n* bibita *f*, bevanda *f.* **drinkable** *adj* bevibile, potabile. **drinking fountain** fontanella *f.* **drinking water** acqua potabile *f.*

drip [drip] *v* gocciolare. *n* gocciolio *m*, gocciolatura *f*; (*slang*) persona insulsa *f.*

dripping n stillicidio m; (fat) grasso colato m.
***drive** [draiv] v condurre; (car) guidare; (push) spingere. **drive away** scacciare. n (road) viale m; (trip) corsa f, giro m; energia f, iniziativa f; (golf) colpo forte m. **driver** n guidatore, -trice m, f. **driving-licence** n patente di guida f. **driving-test** n esame di guida m.
drivel ['drivl] n (nonsense) sciocchezze f pl. v dir sciocchezze.
driven ['drivn] V **drive**.
drizzle ['drizl] v piovigginare. n pioggerella f.
drone [droun] n (bee) fuco m, pecchione m; (idler) fannullone m; (hum) ronzio m. v (hum) ronzare. **droning** adj ronzante, monotono.
droop [druːp] v afflosciarsi, accasciarsi. n accasciamento m. **drooping** adj piegato in giù, floscio.
drop [drop] n goccia f; (fall) caduta f. v (fall) cadere; (let fall) far cadere; (lower) calare; diminuire, abbassarsi. **dropper** n contagocce m. **droppings** pl n sterco m sing.
dropout ['dropaut] n emarginato, -a m, f. v **drop out** ritirarsi, rinunciare.
drought [draut] n siccità f.
drove [drouv] V **drive**.
drown [draun] v annegare, affogare.
drowsy ['drauzi] adj sonnolento, assopito.
drudge [drʌdʒ] v sfacchinare, sgobbare. n sgobbone, -a m, f. **drudgery** n sfacchinata f.
drug [drʌg] n medicinale m, droga f, stupefacente m. **drug-addict** n drogato, -a m, f, tossicomane m, f. v narcotizzare, drogare.
drum [drʌm] n tamburo m, timpano m; (cylinder) cilindro m, rullo m. **drumstick** n bacchetta da tamburo f; (chicken) coscia di pollo f. v suonare il tamburo; (beat) tamburellare. **drummer** n tamburo m.
drunk [drʌŋk] V **drink**. adj ubriaco (m pl -chi), sbronzo. **get drunk** ubriacarsi. **drunkard** n ubriacone, -a m, f; sbronzo, -a m, f. **drunkenness** n ubriachezza f.
dry [drai] adj asciutto, secco; (uninteresting) monotono; (caustic) mordace. v asciugare, seccare. **dry-clean** v lavare a secco. **dry-cleaning** n lavaggio a secco m. **dry rot** carie del legno f.

dual ['djuəl] adj doppio, duplice.
dubbed ['dʌbd] adj (film) doppiato; (name) qualificato.
dubious ['djuːbiəs] adj dubbio, equivoco, incerto. **dubiousness** n incertezza f.
duchess ['dʌtʃis] n duchessa f.
duck¹ [dʌk] n (zool) anitra f. **duckling** n anatroccolo m.
duck² [dʌk] v (plunge) tuffare, immergere; (dodge) schivare; (lower the head) chinarsi di colpo.
dud [dʌd] adj inutile. n (explosive) proiettile che non esplode m.
due [djuː] adj (owing) da pagarsi; (rightful, proper) debito; (attributable) dovuto; (expected) atteso, in arrivo. adv direttamente. **due to** a causa di. **dues** pl n dazio m sing, diritti m pl.
duel ['djuəl] n duello m, lotta f.
duet [dju'et] n duetto m.
duffel bag ['dʌfəl] n sacca da viaggio f.
duffel coat ['dʌfəl] n montgomery m invar.
dug [dʌg] V **dig**.
duke [djuːk] n duca m.
dull [dʌl] adj (unintelligent) ottuso; (boring) noioso; (slow) lento; monotono; (not sharp) non tagliente; (weather) grigio. v attutire, attenuare, intorpidire. **dullness** n lentezza f; noia f.
duly ['djuːli] adv debitamente.
dumb [dʌm] adj muto, reticente; (slang: foolish) scemo. **dumbfound** v sbalordire, stupire.
dummy ['dʌmi] adj falso, finto. n (man of straw) uomo di paglia m; (cards) morto m; (baby's) biberon m invar, poppatoio m; (model) manichino m.
dump [dʌmp] n (tip) luogo di scarico m; (coll) posto triste m. v (get rid of) scartare, disfarsi di; (unload) scaricare.
dunce [dʌns] n ignorante m, f.
dune [djuːn] n duna f.
dung [dʌŋ] n letame m, sterco m.
dungarees [ˌdʌŋgə'riːz] pl n (overalls) tuta f sing.
dungeon ['dʌndʒən] n segreta f, cella sotterranea f.
duplicate ['djuːplikət; v 'djuːplikeit] adj duplice, doppio. n duplicato m, duplice copia f, doppione m. v duplicare.
durable ['djuərəbl] adj durevole, duraturo.
duration [dju'reiʃən] n durata f.

during ['djuriŋ] *prep* durante, nel corso di.

dusk [dʌsk] *n* crepuscolo *m*.

dust [dʌst] *n* polvere *f*. *v* (*clean*) spolverare; (*sprinkle*) cospargere. **dustbin** *n* pattumiera *f*. **dustman** *n* spazzino *m*. **dustpan** *n* paletta per la spazzatura *f*. **duster** *n* spolverino *m*, strofinaccio *m*. **dusty** *adj* polveroso.

Dutch [dʌtʃ] *adj* olandese. **Dutch person** olandese *m*, *f*. **go Dutch** fare *or* pagare alla romana.

duty ['djuɪti] *n* dovere *m*; (*customs*) dogana *f*.

duvet ['durvei] *n* piumino *m*.

dwarf [dwoɪf] *n* nano *m*. *v* (*make appear small*) far sembrar piccolo; (*render insignificant*) sminuire.

*dwell [dwel] *v* (*reside*) dimorare. **dwell on** soffermarsi su. **dwelling** *n* dimora *f*, abitazione *f*.

dwelt [dwelt] *V* **dwell**.

dwindle ['dwindl] *v* diminuire; (*decline*) deperire.

dye [dai] *n* colorante *m*, tintura *f*. *v* colorare, tingere. **dyed in the wool** inveterato, radicato. **dyer** *n* tintore *m*.

dyke [daik] *n* diga *f*, argine *m*.

dynamic [dai'namik] *adj* dinamico. **dynamics** *n* dinamica *f*.

dynamite ['dainǝˌmait] *n* dinamite *f*.

dynamo ['dainǝˌmou] *n* dinamo *f invar*.

dynasty ['dinǝsti] *n* dinastia *f*.

dysentery ['disǝntri] *n* dissenteria *f*.

dyslexia [dis'leksiǝ] *n* dislessia *f*.

dyspepsia [dis'pepsiǝ] *n* dispepsia *f*.

E

each [iɪtʃ] *adj* ogni, ciascuno. *pron* ognuno. *adv* (*apiece*) l'uno, l'una. **each other** l'un l'altro.

eager ['iɪgǝ] *adj* avido, premuroso; impaziente. **eagerness** *n* impazienza *f*; zelo *m*; brama *f*.

eagle ['iɪgl] *n* aquila *f*.

ear[1] [iǝ] *n* orecchio *m*. **be up to one's ears in ...** aver ... fin sopra i capelli. **earache** *n* mal d'orecchi *m*. **eardrum** *n* timpano *m*. **earmark** *v* contrassegnare; (*set aside*) mettere da parte; (*money*) stanziare. **ear-plug** *n* tappo per orecchi *m*. **ear-ring** *n* orecchino *m*. **ear-splitting**

adj assordante. **within earshot** a portata d'orecchio.

ear[2] [iǝ] *n* spiga *f*.

earl [ǝil] *n* conte *m*.

early ['ǝili] *adv* presto, di buon'ora. *adj* primo; (*morning*) mattiniero, mattutino; (*before time*) prematuro; (*ancient*) antico (*m pl* -chi).

earn [ǝin] *v* guadagnare, meritare. **earnings** *pl n* guadagni *m pl*, stipendio *m*.

earnest ['ǝinist] *adj* serio, coscienzioso. **be in earnest** fare sul serio. **earnestness** *n* serietà *f*.

earth [ǝiθ] *n* terra *f*; (*world*) mondo *m*; (*soil*) terreno *m*. **earthquake** *n* terremoto *m*. *v* (*elec*) mettere a terra. **earthenware** *n* terraglia *f*. **earthly** *adj* terrestre. **earthy** *adj* (*coarse*) grossolano; robusto.

earwig ['iǝwig] *n* forbicina *f*.

ease [iɪz] *n* agio *m*, comodo *m*. **at ease** tranquillo. **ill at ease** a disagio. *v* agevolare, alleggerire.

easel ['iɪzl] *n* cavalletto ·*m*.

east [iɪst] *adj* orientale, dell'est. *n* oriente *m*, est *m*. **Middle/Near/Far East** medio/prossimo/estremo oriente *m*. **eastward** *adv*, *adj* verso est, ad est, verso oriente.

Easter ['iɪstǝ] *n* Pasqua *f*.

easy ['iɪzi] *adj* facile, semplice; (*informal*) disinvolto; (*compliant*) accomodante. **easy chair** poltrona *f*. **easy-going** *adj* (*placid*) bonaccione, pacione; indolente; tollerante.

*eat [iɪt] *v* mangiare. **eatable** *adj* mangiabile, mangereccio.

eaten ['iɪtn] *V* **eat**.

eavesdrop ['iɪvzdrop] *v* origliare.

ebb [eb] *n* riflusso *m*; declino *m*. *v* rifluire; declinare.

eccentric [ik'sentrik] *nm*, *adj* eccentrico. **eccentricity** *n* eccentricità *f*.

ecclesiastical [iklizii'astikl] *adj* ecclesiastico.

echo ['ekou] *v* echeggiare, far eco a. *n* eco *f*, *m* (*pl* -i *m*).

eclair [ei'kleǝ] *n* bignè *m invar*.

eclipse [i'klips] *n* eclissi *f*. *v* eclissare.

ecology [i'kolǝdʒi] *n* ecologia *f*.

economy [i'konǝmi] *n* economia *f*. **economical** *or* **economic** *adj* economico, a buon prezzo; (*thrifty*) frugale. **economics** *n* economia *f*, scienze economiche *f pl*. **economist** *n* economista *m*, *f*. **economize** *v* economizzare, fare economia.

ecstasy ['ekstəsi] *n* estasi *f*. **ecstatic** *adj* estatico.

eczema ['eksimə] *n* eczema *m*.

edge [edʒ] *n* orlo *m*, margine *m*; (*blade*) filo *m*; (*road*) ciglio *m*; (*river*) sponda *f*. **be on edge** avere i nervi. *v* orlare.

edible ['edəbl] *adj* mangereccio, mangiabile.

Edinburgh ['edinbərə] *n* Edimburgo *f*.

edit ['edit] *v* curare, redigere, dirigere. **editor** *n* redattore, -trice *m*, *f*; (*newspaper*) direttore, -trice *m*, *f*. **editorial** *n* articolo di fondo *m*. **edition** *n* edizione *f*.

educate ['edju‚keit] *v* educare, istruire. **educated** *adj* colto, istruito. **education** *n* educazione *f*, istruzione *f*; (*teaching*) insegnamento *m*, pedagogia *f*.

eel [iɪl] *n* anguilla *f*.

eerie ['iəri] *adj* (*strange*) misterioso; (*causing fear*) pauroso.

effect [i'fekt] *n* effetto *m*; conseguenza *f*, risultato *m*; impressione *f*. **take effect** entrare in vigore. **with effect from** a partire da. *v* effettuare, realizzare. **effective** *adj* efficace, efficiente.

effeminate [i'feminət] *adj* effeminato.

effervescent [‚efə'vesənt] *adj* effervescente.

efficient [i'fiʃənt] *adj* efficiente, capace. **efficiency** *n* efficienza *f*, capacità *f*; (*machine*) rendimento *m*.

effigy ['efidʒi] *n* effigie *f*.

effort ['efət] *n* sforzo *m*, fatica *f*. **make an effort** sforzarsi, fare di tutto. **effortless** *adj* senza sforzo.

egg [eg] *n* uovo *m* (*pl* -a *f*). **egg-cup** *n* portauovo *m*. **egg-shaped** *adj* ovale. **egg-shell** *n* guscio d'uovo *m*. **egg-whisk** *n* frullino *m*. *v* **egg on** aizzare.

ego ['iɪgou] *n* ego *m*. **egocentric** *adj* egocentrico. **egoism** *n* egoismo *m*. **egoist** *n* egoista *m*, *f*. **egoistic(al)** *adj* egoista, egoistico. **egotism** *n* egotismo *m*. **egotist** *n* egotista *m*, *f*. **egotistic(al)** *adj* egotista.

Egypt ['iɪdʒipt] *n* Egitto *m*. **Egyptian** *n*, *adj* egiziano, -a; (*ancient*) egizio, -a.

eiderdown ['aidədaun] *n* piumino *m*.

eight [eit] *nm*, *adj* otto. **eighth** *nm*, *adj* ottavo.

eighteen [ei'tiɪn] *nm*, *adj* diciotto. **eighteenth** *nm*, *adj* diciottesimo.

eighty ['eiti] *nm*, *adj* ottanta. **eightieth** *nm*, *adj* ottantesimo.

either ['aiðə] *pron*, *adj* l'uno o l'altro; (*each*) ciascuno dei due, tutti e due. *adv*

nemmeno, neppure, neanche. *conj* **either ... or ...** o ... o ..., sia ... che ..., sia ... sia ....

ejaculate [i'dʒakjuleit] *v* eiaculare; esclamare. **ejaculation** *n* eiaculazione *f*, esclamazione *f*.

eject [i'dʒekt] *v* espellere, gettar fuori. **ejector seat** sedile eiettabile *m*.

eke [iɪk] *v* **eke out** supplire. **eke out a living** sbarcare il lunario.

elaborate [i'labəreit; *adj* i'labərət] *v* elaborare, sviluppare. *adj* elaborato, minuzioso.

elapse [i'laps] *v* passare, decorrere.

elastic [i'lastik] *nm*, *adj* elastico.

elated [i'leitid] *adj* giubilante, euforico.

elbow ['elbou] *n* gomito *m*. **elbow-room** *n* libertà di movimento *f*. *v* (*jostle*) dar gomitate.

elder[1] ['eldə] *adj* più vecchio, maggiore. *n* anziano, -a *m*, *f*. **elderly** *adj* di una certa età, anziano.

elder[2] ['eldə] *n* sambuco (*pl* -chi) *m*. **elderberry** *n* bacca di sambuco *f*.

eldest ['eldist] *adj* più vecchio, maggiore, primogenito.

elect [i'lekt] *v* eleggere, scegliere. *adj* eletto, scelto. **election** *n* elezione *f*. **electioneering** *n* campagna elettorale *f*. **electorate** *n* elettorato *m*. **elector** *n* elettore, -trice *m*, *f*.

electricity [elek'trisəti] *n* elettricità *f*. **electric** *adj* elettrico. **electric appliances** elettrodomestici *m pl*. **electrician** *n* elettricista *m*. **electrify** *v* elettrificare. **electrocution** *n* elettroesecuzione *f*. **electrode** *n* elettrodo *m*. **electrolysis** *n* elettrolisi *f*. **electron** *n* elettrone *m*. **electronic** *adj* elettronico. **electronics** *n* elettronica *f*.

elegant ['eligənt] *adj* elegante, fine. **elegance** *n* eleganza *f*, finezza *f*.

elegy ['elidʒi] *n* elegia *f*. **elegiac** *adj* elegiaco.

element ['eləmənt] *n* elemento *m*, fattore *m*. **elemental** *adj* fondamentale. **elementary** *adj* elementare.

elephant ['elifənt] *n* elefante *m*. **elephantine** *adj* elefantesco.

elevate ['eliveit] *v* elevare, innalzare; (*exalt*) esaltare. **elevated** *adj* elevato, eminente. **elevation** *n* (*altitude*) altezza *f*; (*drawing*) proiezione ortogonale *f*; (*grandeur*) elevatezza *f*. **elevator** *n* (*lift*) ascensore *m*.

eleven [i'levn] *nm, adj* undici. **eleventh** *nm, adj* undicesimo.

elf [elf] *n* elfo *m*, folletto *m*.

eligible ['elidʒəbl] *adj* eleggibile; desiderabile.

eliminate [i'limineit] *v* eliminare, scartare. **elimination** *n* eliminazione *f*.

elite [ei'liːt] *n* élite (*pl* -s) *f*, fior fiore *m invar*.

ellipse [i'lips] *n* ellisse *f*.

elm [elm] *n* olmo *m*.

elocution [elə'kjuːʃən] *n* elocuzione *f*.

elope [i'loup] *v* fuggire. **elopement** *n* fuga *f*.

eloquent ['eləkwənt] *adj* eloquente, rettorico. **eloquence** *n* eloquenza *f*, rettorica *f*.

else [els] *adv, pron* altro, altrimenti. **elsewhere** *adv* altrove.

elucidate [i'luːsideit] *v* chiarire, spiegare.

elude [i'luːd] *v* eludere, evitare. **elusive** *adj* evasivo, elusivo.

emaciated [i'meisieitid] *adj* scarno, emaciato.

emanate ['eməneit] *v* emanare, emettere, scaturire. **emanation** *n* emanazione *f*, emissione *f*.

emancipate [i'mansipeit] *v* emancipare. **emancipation** *n* emancipazione *f*.

embalm [im'baːm] *v* imbalsamare.

embankment [im'baŋkmənt] *n* argine *m*, lungofiume *m*.

embargo [im'baːgou] *n* embargo *m*, sanzioni *f pl*, proibizione *f*.

embark [im'baːk] *v* imbarcare. **embark on** intraprendere.

embarrass [im'barəs] *v* mettere in imbarazzo. **embarrassment** *n* imbarazzo *m*.

embassy ['embəsi] *n* ambasciata *f*.

embellish [im'beliʃ] *v* abbellire, ornare. **embellishment** *n* abbellimento *m*.

ember ['embə] *n* tizzone *m*. **embers** *pl n* brace *f pl*.

embezzle [im'bezl] *v* appropriarsi indebitamente. **embezzlement** *n* appropriazione indebita *f*, malversazione *f*. **embezzler** *n* malversatore, -trice *m, f*.

embitter [im'bitə] *v* rendere amaro, amareggiare.

emblem ['embləm] *n* emblema *m*, simbolo *m*.

embody [im'bodi] *v* incorporare; (*comprise*) comprendere; incarnare; concretare.

emboss [im'bos] *v* sbalzare, fare in rilievo, scolpire in rilievo.

embrace [im'breis] *v* abbracciare. *n* abbraccio *m*.

embroider [im'broidə] *v* ricamare; (*embellish*) abbellire. **embroidery** *n* ricamo *m*.

embryo ['embriou] *n* embrione *m*. **embryonic** *adj* embrionale.

emerald ['emərəld] *n* smeraldo *m*.

emerge [i'məːdʒ] *v* emergere.

emergency [i'məːdʒənsi] *n* emergenza *f*, caso imprevisto *m*. **emergency exit** uscita di sicurezza *f*. **in case of emergency** in caso di urgenza.

emigrate ['emigreit] *v* emigrare. **emigration** *n* emigrazione *f*.

eminent ['eminənt] *adj* eminente, distinto.

emit [i'mit] *v* emettere, emanare. **emission** *n* emissione *f*.

emotion [i'mouʃən] *n* emozione *f*, sentimento *m*, commozione *f*. **emotional** emotivo; impressionabile.

empathy ['empəθi] *n* empatia *f*, immedesimazione *f*.

emphasis ['emfəsis] *n*, *pl* -ses enfasi *f*, veemenza *f*, rilievo *m*. **emphasize** *v* dare rilievo a, mettere in evidenza. **emphatic** *adj* enfatico, risoluto, intenso.

empire ['empaiə] *n* impero *m*. **emperor** *n* imperatore *m*. **empress** *n* imperatrice *f*.

empirical [im'pirikəl] *adj* empirico.

employ [im'ploi] *v* impiegare; (*use*) adoperare, usare. **employee** *n* impiegato, -a *m, f*. **employer** *n* padrone, -a *m, f*; datore, -trice di lavoro *m, f*. **employment** *n* impiego (*pl* -ghi) *m*, lavoro *m*. **employment agency** ufficio di collocamento *m*.

empower [im'pauə] *v* autorizzare.

empty ['empti] *adj* vuoto. *v* vuotare, scaricare. **empty-handed** *adj* a mani vuote.

emulate ['emjuleit] *v* emulare. **emulation** *n* emulazione *f*.

emulsion [i'mʌlʃən] *n* emulsione *f*.

enable [i'neibl] *v* mettere in grado di, permettere; (*law*) abilitare.

enact [i'nakt] *v* (*ordain*) ordinare; (*decree*) decretare; (*put into operation*) promulgare; (*theatre*) recitare.

enamel [i'naməl] *n* smalto *m*. *v* smaltare.

enamoured [i'naməd] *adj* innamorato.

enchant [in'tʃaint] *v* incantare, affascinare, ammaliare. **enchanting** *adj* incantevole. **enchantment** *n* incanto *m*, incantesimo *m*, fascino *m*.

encircle [in'səikl] *v* cingere, accerchiare. **encirclement** *n* accerchiamento *m*.
enclose [in'klouz] *v* rinchiudere; (*letter*) allegare. **enclosure** *n* recinto *m*; (*letter*) allegato *m*; (*rel*) clausura *f*.
encore ['oŋkoɪ] *nm, interj* bis.
encounter [in'kauntə] *v* incontrare, affrontare. *n* incontro *m*; (*battle*) lotta *f*.
encourage [in'kʌridʒ] *v* incoraggiare, favorire, stimolare. **encouragement** *n* incitamento *m*, stimolo *m*.
encroach [in'kroutʃ] *v* **encroach on** abusare di; (*intrude on*) invadere.
encumber [in'kʌmbə] *v* ingombrare, impacciare; (*burden*) sopraffare. **encumbrance** *n* (*hindrance*) impaccio *m*; (*burden*) carico (*pl* -chi) *m*.
encyclopedia [insaiklə'piːdiə] *n* enciclopedia *f*.
end [end] *n* fine *f*, termine *m*; (*purpose*) scopo *m*; (*result*) conclusione *f*. **in the end** infine. **make ends meet** sbarcare il lunario. *v* finire, concludere, terminare. **endless** *adj* interminabile, senza fine.
endanger [in'deindʒə] *v* mettere in pericolo, compromettere.
endear [in'diə] *v* rendere caro. **endearing** *adj* simpatico, amabile.
endeavour [in'devə] *v* cercare, tentare. *n* sforzo *m*, tentativo *m*.
endemic [en'demik] *n* endemico.
endive ['endiv] *n* indivia *f*, cicoria *f*.
endorse [in'doɪs] *v* approvare; (*sign*) vistare; (*cheque*) girare; (*record infringement*) annotare le infrazioni commesse. **endorsement** *n* visto *m*, girata *f*, annotazione delle infrazioni commesse *f*.
endow [in'dau] *v* dotare, fornire. **endowment** *n* dotazione *f*, donazione *f*.
endure [in'djuə] *v* tollerare, sopportare; (*last*) durare; resistere. **endurance** *n* resistenza *f*.
enema ['enəmə] *n* clistere *m*, enteroclisma *m*.
enemy ['enəmi] *n* nemico, -a *m, f*; avversario, -a *m, f*.
energy ['enədʒi] *n* energia *f*. **energetic** *adj* energico.
enfold [in'fould] *v* avvolgere.
enforce [in'foɪs] *v* imporre, far valere, far rispettare. **enforced** *adj* obbligatorio, imposto. **enforcement** *n* imposizione *f*, applicazione *f*.
engage [in'geidʒ] *v* (*employ*) assumere, impiegare; (*occupy*) impegnare,

occupare; (*mil*) attaccare; (*interlock*) ingranare, innestare; (*reserve*) prenotare. **engaged** *adj* (*busy*) occupato; (*betrothed*) fidanzato. **get engaged** fidanzarsi. **engagement** *n* fidanzamento *m*; (*employment*) impiego (*pl* -ghi) *m*; (*obligation*) impegno *m*; (*appointment*) appuntamento *m*.
engine ['endʒin] *n* motore *m*, macchina *f*; (*rail*) locomotiva *f*.
engineer [endʒi'niə] *n* ingegnere, -a *m, f*; meccanico, -a *m, f*; tecnico, -a *m, f*; (*mil*) geniere *m*. *v* (*construct*) costruire; (*contrive*) macchinare, tramare. **engineering** *n* costruzione *f*; (*study, science*) ingegneria *f*.
England ['iŋglənd] *n* Inghilterra *f*. **English** *n*(*m* + *f*), *adj* inglese.
engrave [in'greiv] *v* incidere, intagliare; (*printing*) imprimere. **engraver** *n* incisore *m*. **engraving** *n* incisione *f*.
engrossed [in'groust] *adj* preso (da), immerso.
engulf [in'gʌlf] *v* ingolfare.
enhance [in'hains] *v* intensificare, aumentare, migliorare.
enigma [i'nigmə] *n* enigma *m*. **enigmatic** *adj* enigmatico, misterioso.
enjoy [in'dʒoi] *v* godere, apprezzare. **enjoy oneself** divertirsi. **enjoyable** *adj* divertente, piacevole. **enjoyment** *n* piacere *m*, godimento *m*, gioia *f*, divertimento *m*.
enlarge [in'laidʒ] *v* ingrandire. **enlarge on** dilungarsi su. **enlargement** *n* ingrandimento *m*; (*med*) ipertrofia *f*.
enlighten [in'laitn] *v* illuminare, chiarire. **enlightenment** *n* schiarimento *m*, delucidazione *f*; (*history*) illuminismo *m*.
enlist [in'list] *v* arruolare; (*obtain*) ottenere. **enlistment** *n* arruolamento *m*.
enliven [in'laivn] *v* animare, ravvivare.
enmity ['enməti] *n* ostilità *f*.
enormous [i'noɪməs] *adj* enorme, immenso.
enough [i'nʌf] *adv* abbastanza, sufficientemente. *adj* sufficiente, abbastanza, bastante. **be enough** bastare. *interj* basta!
enquire [in'kwaiə] *V* **inquire**.
enrage [in'reidʒ] *v* far arrabbiare. **enraged** *adj* arrabbiato, furioso.
enrich [in'ritʃ] *v* arricchire, abbellire.
enrol [in'roul] *v* (*mil*) arruolare; (*college, etc.*) iscrivere. **enrolment** *n* arruolamento *m*; iscrizione *f*.

enslave [in'sleiv] *v* far schiavo, assoggettare. **enslavement** *n* schiavitù *f*.
ensue [in'sjuɪ] *v* seguire, risultare.
ensure [in'ʃuə] *v* assicurare, garantire.
entail [in'teil] *v* comportare, implicare.
entangle [in'taŋgl] *v* impigliare, aggrovigliare; (*involve*) coinvolgere. **entanglement** *n* impiccio *m*, imbroglio *m*.
enter ['entə] *v* entrare (in); penetrare; (*join*) iscriversi a; (*record*) notare.
enterprise ['entə,praiz] *n* impresa *f*, iniziativa *f*. **enterprising** *adj* intraprendente, pieno d'iniziativa.
entertain [,entə'tein] *v* (*amuse*) divertire; (*receive guests*) ricevere ospitare; (*consider*) concepire, prendere in considerazione. **entertainer** *n* (*actor*) attore, -trice *m*, *f*; (*singer*) cantante *m*, *f*. **entertaining** *adj* divertente, piacevole. **entertainment** *n* divertimento *m*, spettacolo *m*.
enthral [in'θrɔil] *v* affascinare.
enthusiasm [in'θuɪzi,azəm] *n* entusiasmo *m*. **enthusiast** *n* entusiasta *m*, *f*; (*fam*) tifoso, -a *m*, *f*. **enthusiastic** *adj* entusiastico, appassionato.
entice [in'tais] *v* sedurre, allettare. **enticement** *n* seduzione *f*, allettamento *m*.
entire [in'taiə] *adj* intero, completo, assoluto. **in its entirety** nel suo insieme.
entitle [in'taitl] *v* dar diritto a, qualificare; (*name*) intitolare. **entitlement** *n* diritto *m*, titolo *m*.
entity ['entəti] *n* entità *f*.
entrails ['entreilz] *pl n* viscere *f pl*.
entrance¹ ['entrəns] *n* entrata *f*, ingresso *m*, ammissione *f*.
entrance² [in'traɪns] *v* incantare, estasiare.
entrant ['entrənt] *n* candidato, -a *m*, *f*; concorrente *m*, *f*.
entreat [in'triɪt] *v* supplicare, implorare. **entreaty** *n* supplica *f*, preghiera *f*.
entrée ['ontrei] *n* (*main course*) piatto principale *m*, secondo piatto *m*; (*first course*) primo piatto *m*.
entrench [in'trentʃ] *v* trincerare, rafforzare. **entrenched** *adj* (*set*) radicato.
entrepreneur [,ontrəprə'nəɪ] *n* imprenditore, -trice *m*, *f*.
entrust [in'trʌst] *v* affidare.
entry ['entri] *n* entrata *f*; (*book-keeping*) partita *f*; annotazione *f*.
entwine [in'twain] *v* intrecciare.
enumerate [i'njuɪməreit] *v* annoverare, elencare.

enunciate [i'nʌnsi,eit] *v* enunciare; articolare.
envelop [in'veləp] *v* avvolgere.
envelope ['envə,loup] *n* busta *f*.
environment [in'vaiərənmənt] *n* ambiente *m*.
envisage [in'vizidʒ] *v* contemplare, immaginare.
envoy ['envoi] *n* inviato, -a *m*, *f*.
envy ['envi] *n* invidia *f*. *v* invidiare. **envious** *adj* invidioso.
enzyme ['enzaim] *n* enzima *m*.
ephemeral [i'femərəl] *adj* effimero, passeggero.
epic ['epik] *adj* epico. *n* epopea *f*.
epicure ['epikjuə] *n* epicureo *m*; (*gourmet*) buongustaio, -a *m*, *f*.
epidemic [epi'demik] *n* epidemia *f*. *adj* epidemico.
epilepsy ['epilepsi] *n* epilessi *f*. **epileptic** *nm*, *adj* epilettico.
epilogue ['epilog] *n* epilogo (*pl* -ghi) *m*.
Epiphany [i'pifəni] *n* Epifania *f*.
episcopal [i'piskəpəl] *adj* vescovile.
episode ['episoud] *n* episodio *m*, incidente *m*.
epitaph ['epi,taɪf] *n* epitaffio *m*.
epitome [i'pitəmi] *n* epitome *f*, compendio *m*.
epoch ['iɪpok] *n* epoca *f*.
equable ['ekwəbl] *adj* equanime, sereno, uniforme.
equal ['iɪkwəl] *adj* eguale, uguale, pari. *v* uguagliare; (*in calculations*) fare. **equality** *n* uguaglianza *f*, parità *f*. **equalize** *v* ragguagliare; (*sport*) pareggiare.
equanimity [ekwə'niməti] *n* equanimità *f*, serenità *f*.
equate [i'kweit] *v* uguagliare, paragonare. **equation** *n* equazione *f*.
equator [i'kweitə] *n* equatore *m*.
equestrian [i'kwestriən] *adj* equestre.
equilateral [,iɪkwi'latərəl] *adj* equilatero.
equilibrium [,iɪkwi'libriəm] *n* equilibrio *m*. **equilibrate** *v* equilibrare, bilanciare.
equinox ['ekwinoks] *n* equinozio *m*.
equip [i'kwip] *v* (*array*) allestire; (*furnish*) attrezzare, fornire (di), dotare (di). **equipment** *n* equipaggiamento *m*, attrezzatura *f*.
equity ['ekwəti] *n* giustizia *f*; imparzialità *f*; (*property*) valore netto *m*; (*securities*) azioni ordinarie *f pl*.
equivalent [i'kwivələnt] *nm*, *adj* equivalente.

era ['ɪərə] *n* era *f*, epoca *f*.
eradicate [i'radiˌkeit] *v* sradicare, estirpare.
erase [i'reiz] *v* cancellare.
erect [i'rekt] *v* erigere, costruire. *adj* eretto, dritto. **erection** *n* erezione *f*.
ermine ['əːmin] *n* ermellino *m*.
erode [i'roud] *v* erodere. **erosion** *n* erosione *f*.
erotic [i'rotik] *adj* erotico.
err [əː] *v* errare; (*make mistakes*) sbagliare; (*sin*) peccare.
errand ['erənd] *n* commissione *f*. **errandboy** *n* fattorino *m*.
erratic [i'ratik] *adj* erratico.
error ['erə] *n* errore *m*, sbaglio *m*, torto *m*. **erroneous** *adj* erroneo.
erudite ['erudait] *adj* erudito, dotto. **erudition** *n* erudizione *f*.
erupt [i'rʌpt] *v* (*volcano*) eruttare; (*burst out*) erompere. **eruption** *n* eruzione *f*.
escalate ['eskəˌleit] *v* intensificare. **escalation** *n* intensificazione *f*. **escalator** *n* scala mobile *f*.
escalope ['eskəˌlop] *n* scaloppina *f*.
escape [is'keip] *v* fuggire, sfuggire; (*avoid*) evitare. *n* fuga *f*, evasione *f*. **escapism** *n* evasione dalla realtà *f*.
escort ['eskɔːt; *v* i'skɔːt] *n* scorta *f*. *v* scortare.
esoteric [esə'terik] *adj* esoterico.
especial [i'speʃəl] *adj* notevole, particolare. **especially** *adv* specie, specialmente.
espionage ['espiəˌnaːʒ] *n* spionaggio *m*.
esplanade [ˌesplə'neid] *n* spianata *f*; lungomare *m*.
essay ['esei] *n* saggio *m*, tema *m*.
essence ['esns] *n* essenza *f*; (*gist*) nocciolo *m*.
essential [i'senʃəl] *adj* essenziale, indispensabile.
establish [i'stabliʃ] *v* stabilire, fondare; (*ascertain*) constatare; (*set up*) istituire, instaurare; (*fix*) determinare. **established** *adj* (*set*) radicato; (*beyond question*) indubbio. **establishment** *n* costituzione *f*, fondazione *f*; (*house*) casa *f*; (*organization*) personale effettivo *m*.
estate [i'steit] *n* (*property*) tenuta *f*; (*possessions*) beni *m pl*, patrimonio *m*. **estate agent** agente immobiliare *m*. **estate car** giardinietta *f*. **housing estate** quartiere residenziale *m*.
esteem [i'stiːm] *n* stima *f*, considerazione *f*. *v* stimare, apprezzare.

estimate ['estiˌmeit; *n* 'estimət] *v* (*value*) valutare; (*judge*) stimare; (*assess cost*) preventivare. *n* preventivo *m*; valutazione *f*. **estimation** *n* valutazione *f*; considerazione *f*.
estrange [i'streindʒ] *v* alienare. **estrangement** *n* alienazione *f*; allontanamento *m*.
estuary ['estjuəri] *n* estuario *m*.
eternal [i'təːnl] *adj* eterno. **eternity** *n* eternità *f*.
ether ['iːθə] *n* etere *m*.
ethereal [i'θiəriəl] *adj* etereo, evanescente.
ethical ['eθikl] *adj* etico, morale. **ethics** *pl n* etica *f sing*, morale *f sing*.
ethnic ['eθnik] *adj* etnico. **ethnology** *n* etnologia *f*.
etiquette ['etiˌket] *n* etichetta *f*, comportamento *m*, cerimoniale *m*.
etymology [ˌeti'molədʒi] *n* etimologia *f*. **etymological** *adj* etimologico.
Eucharist ['juːkərist] *n* eucaristia *f*.
eunuch ['juːnək] *n* eunuco (*pl* -chi) *m*.
euphemism ['juːfəˌmizəm] *n* eufemismo *m*. **euphemistic** *adj* eufemistico.
euphoria [juː'fɔːriə] *n* euforia *f*. **euphoric** *adj* euforico.
Europe ['juərəp] *n* Europa *f*. **European** *n*, *adj* europeo, -a. **European Economic Community** Comunità Economica Europea *f*.
euthanasia [ˌjuːθə'neiziə] *n* eutanasia *f*.
evacuate [i'vakjuˌeit] *v* evacuare, sfollare. **evacuation** *n* evacuazione *f*, sfollamento *m*.
evade [i'veid] *v* evadere, evitare, eludere. **evasion** *n* evasione *f*. **evasive** *adj* evasivo, elusivo.
evaluate [i'valjuˌeit] *v* valutare. **evaluation** *n* valutazione *f*.
evangelical [ˌiːvan'dʒelikəl] *adj* evangelico. **evangelist** *n* evangelista *m*.
evaporate [i'vapəˌreit] *v* evaporare, far evaporare. **evaporation** *n* evaporazione *f*.
eve [iːv] *n* vigilia *f*.
even ['iːvən] *adj* (*flat*) piano, piatto; (*regular*) uniforme, regolare; (*not odd*) pari. *adv* (*still*) ancora; (*indeed*) perfino. **even if** benchè, sebbene, quantunque. *v* livellare, uguagliare.
evening ['iːvniŋ] *n* sera *f*, serata *f*. **evening class** classe *or* scuola serale *f*. **evening dress** abito da sera *m*.
evensong ['iːvənˌsoŋ] *n* vespro *m*.

event [i'vent] *n* avvenimento *m*, evento *m*; (*outcome*) eventualità *f*; (*sport*) gara *f*.
eventful *adj* ricco di vicende, memorabile. **eventual** *adj* finale, contingente. **eventually** *adv* alla fine, ultimamente.
ever ['evə] *adv* sempre, mai. **ever since** da quando, da allora. **evergreen** *nm, adj* sempreverde. **everlasting** *adj* eterno, perpetuo, perenne. **hardly ever** quasi mai.
every ['evri] *adj* ogni, ognuno, ciascuno. **everybody** *or* **everyone** *pron* ognuno, tutti *pl*. **everyday** *adj* quotidiano, normale. **every now and then** di tanto in tanto. **every other day** un giorno si un giorno no. **everything** *pron* tutto, ogni cosa. **everywhere** *adv* dovunque, dappertutto.
evict [i'vikt] *v* sfrattare. **eviction** *n* sfratto *m*.
evidence ['evidəns] *n* prova *f*, evidenza *f*; (*law*) testimonianza *f*, deposizione *f*. **give evidence** (*law*) deporre, testimoniare. **evident** *adj* evidente, manifesto, ovvio.
evil ['iːvl] *adj* cattivo, malvagio. *n* male *m*, peccato *m*. **evil-doer** malfattore, -trice *m*, *f*. **evil eye** malocchio *m*. **evil-looking** *adj* losco. **evil-minded** *adj* malintenzionato.
evoke [i'vouk] *v* evocare.
evolve [i'volv] *v* evolvere, sviluppare. **evolution** *n* evoluzione *f*.
ewe [juː] *n* pecora (femmina) *f*.
exacerbate [ig'zasə,beit] *v* esacerbare, inasprire, irritare.
exact [ig'zakt] *adj* esatto, preciso. *v* esigere, richiedere. **exacting** *adj* esigente, impegnativo. **exactitude** *n* esattezza *f*, precisione *f*.
exaggerate [ig'zadʒə,reit] *v* esagerare. **exaggeration** *n* esagerazione *f*.
exalt [ig'zolt] *v* esaltare; (*praise*) vantare, lodare. **exaltation** *n* esaltazione *f*.
examine [ig'zamin] *v* esaminare; verificare; (*med*) visitare; (*law*) interrogare. **examination** *n* esame *m*; verifica *f*; visita medica *f*; (*law*) interrogatorio *m*. **examiner** *n* ispettore, -trice *m*, *f*.
example [ig'zaːmpl] *n* esempio *m*; (*specimen*) esemplare *m*. **for example** per esempio.
exasperate [ig'zaːspə,reit] *v* esasperare; esacerbare; irritare. **exasperating** *adj* esasperante. **exasperation** *n* esasperazione *f*.

excavate ['ekskə,veit] *v* scavare. **excavation** *n* scavo *m*.
exceed [ik'siːd] *v* eccedere, superare. **exceedingly** *adv* estremamente.
excel [ik'sel] *v* eccellere.
excellent ['eksələnt] *adj* eccellente, ottimo. **excellence** *n* eccellenza *f*, superiorità *f*. **Excellency** *n* Eccellenza *f*.
except [ik'sept] *prep* eccetto, salvo, tranne, all'infuori di. *v* escludere, eccettuare.
excerpt ['eksəːpt] *n* estratto *m*, brano *m*.
excess [ik'ses] *n* eccesso *m*, sovrabbondanza *f*. **excess baggage** eccedenza di bagaglio *f*. **excess weight** soprappeso *m*. **excessive** *adj* eccessivo, smoderato.
exchange [iks'tʃeindʒ] *n* cambio *m*, scambio *m*; (*phone*) centralino *m*. **rate of exchange** cambio *m*. *v* cambiare, scambiare.
exchequer [iks'tʃekə] *n* tesoro *m*, erario *m*.
excise ['eksaiz] *n* imposta di consumo *f*. *v* recidere, tagliar via.
excite [ik'sait] *v* eccitare, stimolare, provocare. **excitable** *adj* eccitabile, impressionabile. **excitement** *n* eccitamento *m*, agitazione *f*, emozione *f*.
exclaim [ik'skleim] *v* esclamare. **exclamation** *n* esclamazione *f*. **exclamation mark** punto esclamativo *m*.
exclude [ik'skluːd] *v* escludere. **excluding** *prep* escluso, eccetto. **exclusion** *n* esclusione *f*. **exclusive** *adj* esclusivo. **exclusivity** *n* esclusiva *f*.
excommunicate [ekskə'mjuːni,keit] *v* scomunicare. **excommunication** *n* scomunica *f*.
excrement ['ekskrəmənt] *n* sterco *m*, feci *f pl*. **excrete** *v* defecare. **excretion** *n* escrezione *f*.
excruciating [ik'skruːʃieitiŋ] *adj* atroce.
excursion [ik'skəːʃən] *n* escursione *f*, gita *f*.
excuse [ik'skjuːz] *n* scusa *f*, pretesto *m*. **make excuses** scusarsi. *v* scusare, perdonare; giustificare. **excuse from** esentare da. **excuse me!** scusi!
execute ['eksi,kjuːt] *v* eseguire, mettere in esecuzione, effettuare; (*kill*) giustiziare. **execution** *n* esecuzione *f*; (*death*) esecuzione capitale *f*. **executioner** *n* boia *m invar*.
executive [ig'zekjutiv] *adj* esecutivo. *n* (*body*) esecutivo *m*; (*person*) funzionario,

-a *m, f.* **executor** *n* esecutore, -trice *m, f.* testamentario, -a *m, f.*

exemplify [ig'zempli,fai] *v* esemplificare, illustrare.

exempt [ig'zempt] *v* esentare, esonerare. *adj* esente. **exemption** *n* esenzione *f*, dispensa *f.*

exercise ['eksə,saiz] *n* esercizio *m*, uso *m*; (*task*) compito *m*; (*mil*) manovra *f. v* esercitare, usare. **exercise-book** *n* quaderno *m.*

exert [ig'zəɪt] *v* esercitare. **exert oneself** sforzarsi. **exertion** *n* sforzo *m.*

exhale [eks'heil] *v* emanare; (*breathe out*) esalare.

exhaust [ig'zoɪst] *v* stancare, esaurire, estenuare. *n* scarico (*pl* -chi) *m*, scappamento *m.* **exhausted** *adj* sfinito, esausto. **exhausting** *adj* faticoso, estenuante. **exhaustion** *n* esaurimento *m.*

exhibit [ig'zibit] *v* esibire, esporre. *n* oggetto per mostra *m*; (*law*) oggetto di appoggio *m.* **exhibition** *n* mostra *f*, esposizione *f.* **exhibitionism** *n* esibizionismo *m.* **exhibitionist** *n* esibizionista *m, f.* **exhibitor** *n* esibitore, -trice *m, f.*

exhilarating [ig'zilareitiŋ] *adj* esilarante, rallegrante.

exigency [ig'zidʒənsi] *n* esigenza *f*, necessità *f.*

exile ['eksail] *n* (*expulsion*) esilio *m*; (*person*) esule *m, f*, esiliato, -a *m, f. v* esiliare, mettere al bando.

exist [ig'zist] *v* esistere, vivere. **existence** *n* esistenza *f*, vita *f.* **existentialism** *n* esistenzialismo *m.* **existing** *adj* esistente, attuale.

exit ['egzit] *n* uscita *f. v* uscire.

exodus ['eksədəs] *n* esodo *m.*

exonerate [ig'zonə,reit] *v* esonerare, assolvere.

exorbitant [ig'zoɪbitənt] *adj* esorbitante, esagerato.

exorcize ['eksoɪsaiz] *v* esorcizzare. **exorcism** *n* esorcismo *m.* **exorcist** *n* esorcista *m, f.*

exotic [ig'zotik] *adj* esotico; (*strange*) strano.

expand [ik'spand] *v* espandere, estendere. **expansion** *n* espansione *f.*

expanse [ik'spans] *n* spazio *m*, distesa *f.*

expatriate [eks'peitrieit; *n, adj* eks'peitriət] *v* espatriare, emigrare. *n, adj* espatriato, -a.

expect [ik'spekt] *v* (*await*) aspettare;

anticipare; (*believe*) credere. **expectant** *adj* in attesa. **expectation** *n* aspettativa *f*, attesa *f*, prospettiva *f.*

expedient [ik'spiɪdiənt] *n* espediente *m*, accorgimento *m.* *adj* opportuno, conveniente.

expedition [,ekspi'diʃən] *n* spedizione *f.* **expeditious** *adj* sbrigativo.

expel [ik'spel] *v* espellere, scacciare.

expenditure [ik'spenditʃə] *n* spesa *f*, consumo *m.*

expense [ik'spens] *n* spesa *f.* **expense account** conto spese *m.* **expensive** *adj* caro, costoso.

experience [ik'spiəriəns] *v* provare, subire. *n* esperienza *f*; incidente *m*, avventura *f.*

experiment [ik'sperimənt] *n* esperimento *m*, prova *f. v* sperimentare, provare, fare esperimenti. **experimental** *adj* sperimentale.

expert ['ekspəɪt] *adj* esperto, perito, competente. *n* esperto, -a *m, f*, perito, -a *m, f*; conoscitore, -trice *m, f.*

expertise [,ekspəɪ'tiɪz] *n* perizia *f*, maestria *f.*

expire [ik'spaiə] *v* scadere, terminare; (*die*) morire. **expiry** *n* termine *m*, scadenza *f.*

explain [ik'splein] *v* spiegare, chiarire. **explanation** *n* spiegazione *f*, chiarimento *m.* **explanatory** *adj* esplicativo.

expletive [ek'spliɪtiv] *n* (*profanity*) bestemmia *f.*

explicit [ik'splisit] *adj* esplicito, chiaro.

explode [ik'sploud] *v* esplodere, far saltare, scoppiare; (*discredit*) screditare. **explosion** *n* esplosione *f.*

exploit[1] ['eksploit] *n* impresa *f.* **exploits** *pl* *n* gesta *f pl.*

exploit[2] [ik'sploit] *v* sfruttare, valorizzare. **exploitation** *n* sfruttamento *m*, valorizzazione *f.*

explore [ik'sploɪ] *v* esplorare; studiare. **exploration** *n* esplorazione *f*; studio *m.* **exploratory** *adj* esploratorio.

exponent [ik'spounənt] *n* esponente *m, f*; (*representative*) interprete *m, f*, rappresentante *m, f.* **exponential** *adj* esponenziale.

export ['ekspoɪt; *v* ik'spoɪt] *n* esportazione *f. v* esportare.

expose [ik'spouz] *v* esporre, mostrare; (*reveal*) svelare; (*unmask*) smascherare. **exposition** *n* spiegazione *f*; mostra *f.*

exposure *n* esposizione *f*; smascheramento *m*; rivelazione *f*; (*phot*) posa *f*.
express [ik'spres] *adj* espresso, esplicito. **express train** direttissimo *m*, rapido *m*. *v* esprimere. **expression** *n* espressione *f*; manifestazione *f*; (*phrase*) modo di dire *m*. **expressionless** *adj* impassibile.
expressway (*mot*) *n* autostrada
expulsion [ik'spʌlʃən] *n* espulsione *f*.
expurgate ['ekspəgeit] *v* espurgare.
exquisite ['ekswizit] *adj* squisito; (*intense*) vivo, acuto.
extend [ik'stend] *v* estendere, prolungare. **extension** *n* estensione *f*; (*time*) proroga *f*; (*phone*) telefono interno *m*. **extensive** *adj* esteso, vasto.
extent [ik'stent] *n* estensione *f*; limite *m*.
extenuating [ik'stenjueitiŋ] *adj* attenuante.
exterior [ik'stiəriə] *nm, adj* esterno.
exterminate [ik'stəːmiˌneit] *v* sterminare, annientare. **extermination** *n* sterminio *m*, annientamento *m*.
external [ik'stəːnl] *adj* esterno.
extinct [ik'stiŋkt] *adj* estinto.
extinguish [ik'stiŋgwiʃ] *v* estinguere, spegnere. **fire extinguisher** estintore *m*.
extol [ik'stoul] *v* esaltare, lodare.
extort [ik'stoːt] *v* estorcere, strappare. **extortion** *n* estorsione *f*. **extortionate** *adj* esorbitante, esagerato.
extra ['ekstrə] *adj* extra *invar*, straordinario, supplementare, in più. *n* (*theatre*) comparsa *f*; (*additional charge*) spesa extra *f*. *adv* in più.
extract [ik'strakt] *v* estrarre; (*tooth*) cavare. **extraction** *n* estrazione *f*; origine *f*.
extradite ['ekstrəˌdait] *v* estradare. **extraditable** *adj* passibile di estradizione. **extradition** *n* estradizione *f*.
extramural [ˌekstrə'mjuərəl] *adj* fuori le mura; (*university*) al di fuori dell'università. **extramural course** corso libero *m*.
extraneous [ik'streiniəs] *adj* estraneo.
extraordinary [ik'stroːdənəri] *adj* straordinario, eccezionale, fenomenale.
extravagant [ik'stravəgənt] *adj* stravagante; (*wasteful*) prodigo, spendereccio; (*exaggerated*) esagerato. **extravagance** *n* stravaganza *f*, prodigalità *f*.
extreme [ik'striːm] *adj* estremo, ultimo. *n* estremo *m*. **extremist** *n* estremista *m, f*.
extremity *n* estremità *f*.

extricate ['ekstriˌkeit] *v* **extricate oneself** districarsi, tirarsi d'impaccio, liberarsi.
extrovert ['ekstrəvəːt] *nm, adj* estroverso.
exuberant [ig'zjuːbərənt] *adj* esuberante. **exuberance** *n* esuberanza *f*.
exude [ig'zjuːd] *v* emanare.
exult [ig'zʌlt] *v* esultare. **exultant** *adj* esultante, trionfante. **exultation** *n* esultazione *f*, trionfo *m*.
eye [ai] *n* occhio *m*; (*needle*) cruna *f*. **see eye to eye (with)** vederla allo stesso modo (di). *v* adocchiare, osservare.
eyeball ['aibɔːl] *n* bulbo oculare *m*.
eyebrow ['aibrau] *n* sopracciglio *m*.
eyelash ['ailaʃ] *n* ciglio *m* (*pl* -a *f*).
eyelet ['ailit] *n* occhiello *m*.
eyelid ['ailid] *n* palpebra *f*.
eye-opener *n* fatto rivelatore *m*.
eye shadow *n* bistro *m*, ombretto *m*.
eyesight ['aisait] *n* vista *f*, visione *f*.
eyesore ['aisɔː] *n* pugno in un occhio *m*.
eyewitness ['aiˌwitnis] *n* testimonio oculare *m*.

F

fable ['feibl] *n* favola *f*.
fabric ['fabrik] *n* (*cloth*) tessuto m, stoffa *f*; (*structure*) struttura *f*.
fabricate ['fabrikeit] *v* (*make up*) inventare; (*fake*) falsificare; (*construct*) fabbricare. **fabrication** *n* costruzione *f*, invenzione *f*.
fabulous ['fabjuləs] *adj* favoloso.
façade [fə'saːd] *n* facciata *f*.
face [feis] *n* faccia *f*, volto *m*, viso *m*; (*clock*) quadrante *m*; (*type*) carattere *m*. *v* (*look towards*) fronteggiare; (*confront*) affrontare; (*cover*) rivestire. **face-cloth** *n* pezzuola per lavarsi *f*. **face-lift** *n* plastica facciale *f*; (*restyling*) restauro *m*. **face-pack** *n* maschera di bellezza *f*. **face value** valore nominale *m*. **lose face** perdere prestigio.
facet ['fasit] *n* (*small plane*) faccetta *f*; (*aspect*) aspetto *m*.
facetious [fə'siːʃəs] *adj* arguto, spiritoso.
facial ['feiʃəl] *adj* facciale.
facile ['fasail] *adj* (*glib*) superficiale, pronto; (*easy*) facile.
facilitate [fə'siliˌteit] *v* facilitare, agevolare.

facility [fə'silәti] *n* facilità *f*; (*help*) facilitazione *f*, agevolazione *f*; opportunità *f*. **facilities** *pl n* servizi *m pl*.

facing ['feisiŋ] *n* (*covering*) rivestimento *m*; (*dress*) risvolto *m*.

facsimile [fak'simәli] *n* facsimile *m invar*.

fact [fakt] *n* fatto *m*, verità *f*. **as a matter of fact** in effetti. **fact-finding** *adj* di inchiesta. **in fact** infatti. **factual** *adj* effettivo.

faction ['fakʃәn] *n* fazione *f*, dissenso *m*. **factious** *adj* fazioso, partigiano.

factor ['faktә] *n* fattore *m*; agente *m*, *f*.

factory ['faktәri] *n* fabbrica *f*, stabilimento *m*.

faculty ['fakәlti] *n* facoltà *f*.

fad [fad] *n* capriccio *m*; (*fashion*) moda *f*.

fade [feid] *v* (*colour*) sbiadire; (*lose freshness*) appassire; (*disappear*) svanire. **fade away** affievolirsi.

fag [fag] *v* sfacchinare. *n* (*hard work*) sgobbata *f*; (*slang*) sigaretta *f*. **fag-end** *n* cicca *f*. **fagged out** stanco morto.

fail [feil] *v* fallire; (*fall short*) mancare; (*not pass*) bocciare, essere respinto. **without fail** senza fallo. **failure** *n* insuccesso *m*, mancanza *f*.

failing ['feiliŋ] *n* debole *m*, difetto *m*. *adj* debile. *prep* salvo.

faint [feint] *v* svenire. *adj* fiacco, tenue, appena percettibile. **feel faint** sentirsi venir meno. **not have the faintest idea** non avere la più pallida idea.

fair¹ [feә] *adj* (*colouring*) biondo, chiaro; (*unbiased*) giusto, imparziale; (*moderately good*) discreto. **fair copy** bella copia *f*. **fair play** comportamento leale *m*. *adv* secondo le regole. **fairly** *adv* (*moderately*) abbastanza; (*properly*) giustamente. **in all fairness** in tutta franchezza.

fair² [feә] *n* fiera *f*, mercato *m*.

fairy ['feәri] *n* fata *f*. **fairy-tale** *n* fiaba *f*.

faith [feiθ] *n* (*belief*) fede *f*; (*confidence*) fiducia *f*. **faith-healer** *n* guaritore, -trice per suggestione *m*, *f*. **faithful** *adj* fedele. **faithless** *adj* che non ha fede, sleale.

fake [feik] *v* contraffare, fingere. *n* (*object*) contraffazione; (*person*) impostore, -a *m*, *f*.

falcon ['fɔːlkәn] *n* falco *m*, falcone *m*.

***fall** [fɔːl] *v* cadere, cascare; (*collapse*) crollare; (*lower*) abbassarsi. **fall asleep** addormentarsi. **fall back on** riccorrere a. **fall behind** rimanere indietro; (*fig*) essere in arretrato. **fall ill** ammalarsi. **fall-out** *n* pioggia radioattiva *f*. **fall through** fallire.

n caduta *f*; crollo *m*, rovina *f*; abbassamento *m*; (*autumn*) autunno *m*.

fallacy ['falәsi] *n* falsità *f*. **fallacious** *adj* fallace, falso.

fallen ['fɔːlәn] *V* **fall**.

fallible ['falәbl] *adj* fallibile. **fallibility** *n* fallibilità *f*.

fallow ['falou] *adj* a maggese.

false [fɔːls] *adj* falso, artificiale, finto. **false alarm** falso allarme *m*. **false pretences** (*law*) millantato credito *m*. **false teeth** denti artificiali *m pl*. **falsehood** *n* menzogna *f*. **falseness** *n* perfidia *f*. **falsify** *v* falsificare.

falsetto [fɔːl'setou] *n* falsetto *m*.

falter ['fɔːltә] *v* (*waver*) vacillare, titubare; (*speak hesitatingly*) balbettare. **faltering** *adj* titubante.

fame [feim] *n* fama *f*, rinomanza *f*. **famed** *adj* rinomato.

familiar [fә'miljә] *adj* familiare; intimo; (*impudent*) sfacciato; (*well-known*) noto. **be on familiar terms with** aver dimestichezza con. **familiarity** *n* familiarità *f*; intimità *f*; (*impertinence*) sfacciataggine *f*.

family ['famәli] *n* famiglia *f*. **family allowance** assegni familiari *m pl*. **family tree** albero genealogico *m*.

famine ['famin] *n* carestia *f*.

famished ['famiʃt] *adj* affamato.

famous ['feimәs] *adj* famoso, celebre.

fan¹ [fan] *n* ventaglio *m*; (*mechanical*) ventilatore *m*. **fan-belt** *n* cinghia per ventilatore *f*. *v* (*flames*) soffiare su; (*excite*) aizzare. **fan oneself** farsi vento.

fan² [fan] *n* (*admirer*) tifoso, -a *m*, *f*.

fanatic [fә'natik] *n*, *adj* fanatico, -a; (*sport*) tifoso, -a. **fanaticism** *n* fanatismo *m*; tifo *m*.

fancy ['fansi] *adj* elaborato, raffinato, di fantasia. **fancy-dress** *n* costume *m*. **fancy-dress ball** ballo in maschera *m*. *n* immaginazione *f*, fantasia *f*, capriccio *m*. *v* desiderare, immaginare. **fanciful** *adj* fantasioso, capriccioso.

fanfare ['fanfeә] *n* fanfara *f*.

fang [faŋ] *n* zanna *f*.

fantastic [fan'tastik] *adj* fantastico, strano.

fantasy ['fantәsi] *n* fantasia *f*, capriccio *m*.

far [faː] *adv*, *adj* lontano, distante; (*much*) molto. **as far as** (*place*) fino a. **as far as I know** a quanto sappia. **far-fetched** *adj* improbabile, forzato. **far-reaching** *adj* di gran portata. **far-sighted** adj (*prudent*) previdente. **so far** (*up to this point*) fin qui.

farce [faɪs] n farsa f.

fare [feə] n tariffa f, prezzo del biglietto m; (*person*) viaggiatore, -trice m, f; (*food*) vitto m. v vivere, trovarsi.

farewell [feə'wel] n addio m, congedo m. *interj* addio!

farm [faɪm] n fattoria f, podere m. **farmhouse** n casa colonica f. v coltivare, fare l'agricoltore. **farm out** dare in appalto. **farmer** n agricoltore m, contadino, -a m, f. **farming** n agricoltura f, coltivazione f.

fart [faɪt] (*vulgar*) n scoreggia f. v fare scoregge.

farther ['faɪðə] adj, adv più lontano; ulteriore. **farthest** adj il più lontano.

fascinate ['fasiˌneit] v affascinare, incantare. **fascinating** adj affascinante, avvincente. **fascination** n fascino m, attrattiva f.

fascism ['faʃizəm] n fascismo m. **fascist** n(m+f), adj fascista.

fashion ['faʃən] n (*manner*) modo m, maniera f; (*dress*) moda f; (*style*) stile m; (*vogue*) voga f. **after a fashion** in un certo modo. **in fashion** alla moda. **out of fashion** fuori moda. v foggiare, modellare. **fashionable** adj elegante, di moda.

fast¹ [faɪst] adj rapido, veloce; (*firmly held*) fisso, saldo; (*colour*) solido. adv presto, rapidamente. **the clock is . . . fast** l'orologio va avanti di . . . .

fast² [faɪst] n digiuno m. v digiunare.

fasten ['faɪsn] v legare, fissare, agganciare, attaccare. **fastener** or **fastening** n chiusura f, fermaglio m.

fastidious [fa'stidiəs] adj meticoloso, schifiltoso.

fat [fat] adj, nm grasso. **fatten** v ingrassare. **fatty** adj grasso, untuoso.

fatal ['feitl] adj fatale, ineluttabile. **fatalism** n fatalismo m. **fatalist** n fatalista m, f. **fatality** n fatalità f.

fate [feit] n fato m, destino m. **fated** adj destinato. **fateful** adj decisivo.

father ['faɪðə] n padre m; (*coll*) babbo m. v procreare, originare. **fatherhood** n paternità f. **father-in-law** n suocero m. **fatherland** n patria f. **fatherly** adj paterno.

fathom ['faðəm] v (*understand*) indovinare, penetrare; (*depth*) sondare. n braccio m.

fatigue [fə'tiːg] n stanchezza f, esaurimento m. v stancare.

fatuous ['fatjuəs] adj fatuo, frivolo, vuoto.

fault [foɪlt] n (*flaw*) difetto m, imperfezione f; errore m; (*cause for blame*) colpa f; (*geol*) faglia f; (*tennis*) fallo m. **be at fault** essere colpevole. **find fault with** criticare, biasimare. **faultless** adj senza colpa. **faulty** adj difettoso.

favour ['feivə] n favore m, piacere m. v favorire, favoreggiare, preferire. **favourable** adj favorevole, vantaggioso.

favourite ['feivrit] adj preferito. n favorito, -a m, f.

fawn¹ [foɪn] n (*zool*) daino m, cerbiatto m. adj (*colour*) fulvo.

fawn² [foɪn] v **fawn on** adulare.

fear [fiə] v temere, aver paura di. n timore m, paura f. **fearful** adj terribile, spaventoso. **fearless** adj intrepido.

feasible ['fiːzəbl] adj fattibile, realizzabile. **feasibility** n praticabilità f.

feast [fiɪst] n festa f, banchetto m.

feat [fiɪt] n impresa f, azione f.

feather ['feðə] n penna f, piuma f. **feather-bed** n letto di piume m. **feathered** adj pennuto.

feature ['fiɪtʃə] n caratteristica f, tratto distintivo m; (*newspaper*) elzeviro m; (*geog*) configurazione f. **features** pl n (*anat*) lineamenti m pl. v dar rilievo a; (*theatre*) presentare. **featureless** adj scialbo.

February ['februəri] n febbraio m.

fed [fed] V **feed**.

federal ['fedərəl] adj federale. **federation** n federazione f.

fee [fiɪ] n onorario m, parcella f; (*school*) retta f; (*entrance fee*) tassa d'iscrizione f.

feeble ['fiːbl] adj debole, fiacco. **feeble-minded** adj cretino, debole di mente. **feebleness** n debolezza f.

*****feed** [fiɪd] v nutrire; (*supply*) alimentare; (*eat*) mangiare, nutrirsi. n mangime m, nutrimento m; (*baby*) poppata f. **feedback** n retroreazione f, feedback m invar; (*response*) reazione f. **fed up** (*coll*) stufo.

*****feel** [fiɪl] v (*touch*) tastare, toccare; (*emotion*) sentire. **feel like** sentirsi disposto a. **feeler** n tentacolo m; (*proposal*) sondaggio m. **feeling** n (*physical*) senso m, sensazione f; (*emotion*) sensibilità f, suscettibilità f; (*affection*) affetto m.

feet [fiːt] *V* **foot.**

feign [fein] *v* fingere, simulare, far finta.

feline ['fiːlain] *adj* felino.

fell¹ [fel] *V* **fall.**

fell² [fel] *v* (*cut down*) abbattere; (*strike down*) atterrare.

fellow ['felou] *n* individuo *m*, tipo *m*; (*companion*) compagno *m*, collega *m, f*; (*member*) membro *m*, socio *m*. **fellowcountryman** *n* compatriota *m, f*. **fellowship** *n* (*companionship*) cameratismo *m*; (*rel*) comunità *f*; (*allowance*) borsa di studio *f*.

felony ['felɔni] *n* crimine *m*. **felon** *n* delinquente *m, f*.

felt¹ [felt] *V* **feel.**

felt² [felt] *n* feltro *m*.

female ['fiːmeil] *n* femmina *f*. *adj also* **feminine** femminile.

feminism ['feminizɔm] *n* femminismo *m*. **feminist** *n* femminista *m, f*.

fence [fens] *n* (*barrier*) steccato *m*, palizzata *f*; (*receiver of stolen goods*) riçettatore, -trice *m, f*. *v* (*sport*) tirar di scherma. **fence in** recintare. **fencing** *n* recinto *m*; (*sport*) scherma *f*.

fend [fend] *v* **fend for oneself** provvedere a sè stesso, arrangiarsi. **fend off** parare, schivare.

fender ['fendɔ] *n* paracenere *m invar*; (*US*) paraurti *m*.

fennel ['fenl] *n* finocchio *m*.

ferment ['fɔːment; *v* fɔ'ment] *n* fermento *m*. *v* fermentare. **fermentation** *n* fermentazione *f*.

fern [fɔːn] *n* felce *f*.

ferocious [fɔ'rouʃɔs] *adj* feroce. **ferocity** *n* ferocia *f*.

ferret ['ferit] *n* furetto *m*. *v* **ferret out** scovare.

ferry ['feri] *n* traghetto *m*. *v* traghettare.

fertile ['fɔːtail] *adj* fertile, fecondo. **fertility** *n* fertilità *f*, fecondità *f*. **fertilize** *v* (*enrich*) fertilizzare; fecondare. **fertilizer** *n* fertilizzante *m*, concime *m*.

fervent ['fɔːvɔnt] *adj* fervente, fervido. **fervour** *n* fervore *m*, ardore *m*.

fester ['festɔ] *v* suppurare; (*rankle*) bruciare.

festival ['festɔvɔl] *n* festival *m invar*, festa *f*.

festoon [fɔ'stuːn] *v* decorare con festoni. *n* festone *m*.

fetch [fetʃ] *v* andare a prendere; (*call*) chiamare; (*a price*) realizzare. **fetching** *adj* attraente.

fête [feit] *n* festa *f*. *v* festeggiare.

fetid ['fiːtid] *adj* fetido, puzzolente.

fetish ['fetiʃ] *n* feticcio *m*, idolo *m*.

fetter ['fetɔ] *n* catena *f*. *v* incatenare.

feud [fjuːd] *n* lite *f*. *v* essere in lotta.

feudal ['fjuːdl] *adj* feudale. **feudalism** *n* feudalesimo *m*.

fever ['fiːvɔ] *n* febbre *f*. **feverish** *adj* febbricitante; (*restless*) febbrile.

few [fjuː] *pron, adj* pochi, -e. **a few** alcuni, -e. **quite a few** parecchi, parecchie. **fewer** *adj* meno *invar*. **fewest** *adj* meno *invar*.

fiancé [fi'onsei] *n* fidanzato *m*. **fiancée** *n* fidanzata *f*.

fiasco [fi'askou] *n* fiasco *m*.

fib [fib] (*coll*) *n* frottola *f*. *v* raccontar frottole.

fibre ['faibɔ] *n* fibra *f*. **fibreglass** *n* fibra di vetro *f*. **fibrous** *adj* fibroso.

fickle ['fikl] *adj* volubile. **fickleness** *n* volubilità *f*.

fiction ['fikʃɔn] *n* (*invention*) finzione *f*; (*novels, etc.*) novellistica *f*, narrativa *f*. **fictional** *or* **fictitious** *adj* fittizio, immaginario.

fiddle ['fidl] *n* violino *m*; (*coll: fraud*) imbroglio *m*, truffa *f*. *v* suonare il violino; (*coll: cheat*) truffare, imbrogliare. **fit as a fiddle** sano come un pesce.

fidelity [fi'delɔti] *n* fedeltà *f*.

fidget ['fidʒit] *v* muoversi irrequietamente, dimenarsi. **fidgety** *adj* irrequieto, nervoso.

field [fiːld] *n* campo *m*; (*of knowledge, etc.*) settore *m*. **field glasses** binoccolo *m sing*. **field marshal** maresciallo *m*.

fiend [fiːnd] *n* demonio *m*. **fiendish** *adj* infernale, diabolico.

fierce [fiɔs] *adj* feroce, intenso.

fiery ['faiɔri] *adj* focoso, ardente.

fifteen [fif'tiːn] *nm, adj* quindici. **fifteenth** *nm, adj* quindicesimo.

fifth [fifθ] *nm, adj* quinto.

fifty ['fifti] *nm, adj* cinquanta. **fiftieth** *nm, adj* cinquantesimo.

fig [fig] *n* fico *m*.

***fight** [fait] *v* lottare, combattere. *n* lotta *f*, combattimento *m*; (*scuffle*) zuffa *f*.

figment ['figmɔnt] *n* **figment of the imagination** finzione *f*.

figure ['figɔ] *n* (*numeral*) cifra *f*; (*shape*) forma *f*; (*pictorial*) figura *f*; (*character*) personaggio *m*; (*bodily form*) linea *f*.

figurehead n (naut) polena f; (derog) uomo di paglia m. **figure of speech** modo di dire m. v (appear) apparire. **figure out** calcolare.

filament ['filəmənt] n filamento m.

file[1] [fail] n (dossier) pratica f; archivio m; (for papers) cartella f; (card with details) scheda f; (row) fila f. v archiviare, mettere in ordine, registrare. **filing** n schedare m. **filing cabinet** schedario m. **single file** fila indiana f.

file[2] [fail] n (tool) lima f. v limare, levigare.

filial ['filiəl] adj filiale.

fill [fil] v riempire; (tooth) otturare. **fill in** completare, inserire. **fill up** (mot) fare il pieno. **filling** n (cookery) ripieno m; (tooth) otturazione f. **filling station** stazione di rifornimento f.

fillet ['filit] n (meat) filetto m. v disossare.

film [film] n pellicola f; (phot, cinema) film m invar. **film star** divo, -a del cinema m, f. v girare un film.

filter ['filtə] n filtro m. **filter-tip** n filtro m. v filtrare.

filth [filθ] n sudiciume m, sporcizia f; oscenità f. **filthy** adj sudicio, sporco; lurido, osceno.

fin [fin] n pinna f.

final ['fainl] adj finale, ultimo. n finale f. **finalist** n finalista m, f. **finally** adv infine.

finance [fai'nans] n finanza f. v finanziare. **financial** adj finanziario. **financier** n finanziere m, finanziatore m.

finch [fintʃ] n fringuello m.

***find** [faind] v scoprire, trovare. **find out** scoprire.

fine[1] [fain] adj (high quality) pregiato, raffinato; (minute) fine; (accomplished) bravo; (beautiful) bello. adv bene.

fine[2] [fain] n (penalty) multa f. v multare.

finesse [fi'nes] n finezza f.

finger ['fingə] n dito m (pl dita f). **cross one's fingers** toccar ferro. **finger bowl** lavadita m invar. **finger-mark** n ditata f. **fingernail** n unghia f. **fingerprint** n impronta digitale f. **fingertip** n punta delle dita f. v (touch) palpare.

finish ['finiʃ] v finire, concludere. n fine f, conclusione f; (surface) finitura f; (textile) appretto m.

finite ['fainait] adj limitato, circoscritto; (math) finito.

Finland ['finlənd] n Finlandia f. **Finn** n

finlandese m, f. **Finnish** nm, adj finlandese.

fir [fəː] n abete m.

fire ['faiə] n fuoco m; (conflagration) incendio m; (heater) stufa f. **catch fire** prender fuoco. **hang fire** indugiare. **set fire to** appiccare il fuoco a, incendiare. v (shoot) sparare; (dismiss) licenziare, silurare; (inflame) eccitare, infiammare; (inspire) ispirare.

fire alarm n allarme d'incendio m.

firearm ['faiəˌaːm] n arma da fuoco f.

fire brigade n corpo dei vigili del fuoco m.

fire door n esercitazione antincendio f.

fire drill n pompa antincendio f.

fire engine n uscita di sicurezza f.

fire escape n uscita di sicurezza f.

fire extinguisher n estintore m.

firefly ['faiəflai] n lucciola f.

fire-guard n parafuoco m, paracenere m invar.

fireman ['faiəmən] n pompiere m, vigile del fuoco m.

fireplace ['faiəˌpleis] n focolare m, camino m, caminetto m.

fireproof ['faiəˌpruːf] adj incombustibile, resistente al fuoco.

fireside ['faiəˌsaid] n focolare m.

fire station n caserma dei pompieri f.

firewood ['faiəˌwud] n legna da ardere f.

fireworks ['faiəˌwəːks] pl n fuochi d'artifizio m pl.

firing squad n plotone d'esecuzione m.

firm[1] [fəːm] adj fermo; (steady) saldo; (steadfast) risoluto; solido; stabile. **stand firm** tener duro. **firmness** n fermezza f; saldezza f; risolutezza f.

firm[2] [fəːm] n (comm) ditta f, azienda f.

first [fəːst] adj primo. adv prima; in primo luogo; anzitutto. **first aid** pronto soccorso m. **first-class** adj ottimo, di prima qualità, eccellente; (rail, etc.) di prima classe. **first floor** primo piano m. **first-hand** adj, adv di prima mano. **first name** nome di battesimo m.

fiscal ['fiskəl] adj fiscale.

fish [fiʃ] n pesce m. v pescare. **fishy** adj (coll) losco.

fishbone ['fiʃboun] n lisca f.

fisherman ['fiʃəmən] n pescatore m.

fish fingers pl n bastoncini di pesce m pl.

fishing ['fiʃiŋ] n pesca f. **fishing boat** peschereccio m. **fishing rod** canna da pesca f.

fishmonger ['fiʃˌmʌŋgə] n pescivendolo, -a m, f.
fishpond ['fiʃˌpond] n vivaio m.
fission ['fiʃən] n fissione f.
fissure ['fiʃə] n fessura f.
fist [fist] n pugno m.
fit[1] [fit] adj (suitable) adatto; competente; (healthy) sano. **keep fit** mantenersi sano, mantenersi in forma. n misura f. v (clothes, etc.) star bene; (suit) adeguare, convenire. **fit in** incastrare. **fitting** adj conveniente, adatto. **fittings** pl n suppellettili m pl, arredi m pl.
fit[2] [fit] n accesso m, attacco m. **fitful** adj intermittente.
five [faiv] nm, adj cinque.
fix [fiks] v fissare, stabilire. **fix up** sistemare, mettere a posto. n (coll) difficoltà f, guaio m. **fixation** n fissazione f. **fixed** adj fisso, stabile. **fixture** n (accessory) attrezzatura f; (sport) avvenimento sportivo m.
fizz [fiz] v frizzare. n spumante m. **fizzy** adj effervescente, frizzante.
fizzle ['fizl] v **fizzle out** far cilecca.
flabbergast ['flabəgɑist] v sbalordire.
flabby ['flabi] adj floscio, flaccido.
flag[1] [flag] n (banner) bandiera f. **flag-pole** n asta di bandiera f. **flagship** n nave ammiraglia f. v **flag down** intimare di fermarsi.
flag[2] [flag] v (tire) indebolirsi, accasciarsi.
flag[3] [flag] n (stone) lastra (di pietra) f.
flagon ['flagən] n bottiglione m.
flagrant ['fleigrənt] adj flagrante.
flair [fleə] n intuito m, inclinazione f.
flake [fleik] v sfaldare, sfaldarsi. n falda f, scaglia f. **flaky** adj a scaglie. **flaky pastry** sfoglia f.
flamboyant [flam'boiənt] adj sgargiante.
flame [fleim] n fiamma f. v fiammeggiare, risplendere. **burst into flames** divampare. **flaming** adj fiammeggiante, violento.
flamingo [flə'miŋgou] n fiammingo m.
flan [flan] n sformato m, torta f.
flank [flaŋk] v fiancheggiare. n fianco m, lato m.
flannel ['flanl] n (fabric) flanella f; (facecloth) pezzuola per lavarsi f. v (slang) abbindolare con le chiacchiere.
flap [flap] v agitare; (wings) battere; (coll) agitarsi. n lembo m; (wings) colpo m; panico m.
flare [fleə] n fiammata f, bagliore m; (rocket) razzo m. v brillare; (clothes)

svasare. **flare up** divampare; (anger, etc.) arrabbiarsi.
flash [flaʃ] n baleno m, lampo m. v balenare. **flashback** n scena retrospettiva f, flashback m invar. **flash bulb** lampadina flash f. **flashlight** n fotolampo m, flash m invar.
flask [flɑisk] n flacone m, borraccia f.
flat[1] [flat] adj piatto, piano; (tyre) a terra; (net) netto; (stale) svanito, insipido. n (music) bemolle m. **flat-footed** adj con i piedi piatti. **flat out** a briglia sciolta. n (music) bemolle m. **flatten** v appiattire, livellare.
flat[2] [flat] n appartamento m.
flatter ['flatə] v adulare, lusingare. **flatterer** n adulatore, -trice m, f. **flattering** adj lusinghiero. **flattery** n lusinghe f pl, adulazione f.
flatulence ['flatjuləns] n flatulenza f. **flatulent** adj flatulento.
flaunt [floint] v ostentare, pavoneggiarsi.
flautist ['floitist] n flautista m, f.
flavour ['fleivə] n sapore m, gusto m. v condire. **flavouring** n condimento m.
flaw [floi] n tacca f, difetto m. **flawed** adj difettoso. **flawless** adj perfetto.
flax [flaks] n lino m. **flaxen** adj di lino; (colour) biondissimo.
flea [flii] n pulce f.
fleck [flek] n chiazza f, macchia f. v chiazzare, macchiare.
fled [fled] V flee.
***flee** [flii] v fuggire, scappare.
fleece [fliis] n vello m. v (coll) pelare, derubare.
fleet [fliit] n flotta f; (of cars) parco m.
fleeting ['fliitiŋ] adj fugace, transitorio.
Flemish ['flemiʃ] nm, adj fiammingo.
flesh [fleʃ] n carne f; (fruit) polpa f.
flew [flui] V fly[1].
flex [fleks] v flettere. n filo or cavo elettrico m. **flexible** adj flessibile. **flexibility** n flessibilità f.
flick [flik] n colpetto m. v dare un colpetto a.
flicker ['flikə] v tremolare. n tremolio m.
flight[1] [flait] n (flying) volo m; (steps) rampa f. **flighty** adj frivolo.
flight[2] [flait] n (fleeing) fuga f.
flimsy ['flimzi] adj tenue, fragile; (inadequate) insufficiente.
flinch [flintʃ] v (wince) sussultare; (shrink from) sottrarsi a. **without flinching** senza batter ciglio.

*fling [fliŋ] v lanciare, scagliare, buttare. **n have one's fling** godersela.
flint [flint] n selce f; (*lighter*) pietrina f.
flip [flip] n colpetto m. v dare un colpetto a. **flip a coin** fare testa e croce. **flip through** sfogliare, dare una scorsa a.
flippant ['flipənt] adj poco serio, frivolo.
flippancy n mancanza di serietà f.
flirt [flɜɪt] v flirtare. n dongiovanni m; civetta f.
flit [flit] v svolazzare; (*disappear*) squaliarsela.
float [flout] v galleggiare, stare a galla. n galleggiante m; (*angling*) sughero m; (*procession*) carro m.
flock¹ [flok] n (*animals*) branco m; (*birds*) stormo m; (*sheep*) gregge m; (*crowd*) folla f. v accorrere in massa, affluire. **flock together** radunarsi.
flock² [flok] n fiocco m; (*mattress filling*) borra f.
flog [flog] v bastonare, frustare; (*sell*) spacciare.
flood [flʌd] v inondare, allagare. n inondazione f, alluvione f, diluvio m; (*outpouring*) torrente m, ondata f. **floodlight** n riflettore m. **floodlit** adj illuminato a giorno.
floor [flɔɪ] n pavimento m; (*storey*) piano m. **floorboard** n tavola di pavimento f. **take the floor** (*speak*) prendere la parola; (*dance*) ballare. v pavimentare; (*knock down*) atterrare.
flop [flop] n tonfo m; (*coll*) fiasco m. v cader di schianto; (*coll*) fallire.
Florence ['florəns] n Firenze f. **Florentine** n, adj fiorentino, -a.
florist ['florist] n fioraio, -a m, f; fiorista m, f.
flotsam ['flotsəm] n relitti m pl. **flotsam and jetsam** (*people*) relitti umani m pl.
flounce¹ [flauns] v dimenare.
flounce² [flauns] n balza f.
flounder ['flaundə] v dibattersi, dimenarsi; (*speech*) impappinarsi. n passera di mare f.
flour ['flauə] n farina f. **floury** adj farinoso.
flourish ['flʌriʃ] v (*prosper*) fiorire; (*brandish*) brandire. n (*fanfare*) squillo di tromba m; (*writing*) ghirigoro m; (*speech*) fiorettatura f; (*gesture*) largo gesto m.
flout [flaut] v sprezzare, schernire.

flow [flou] n corrente f, flusso m. v scorrere, circolare.
flower ['flauə] n fiore m. **flower-bed** n aiuola f. **flower-pot** n vaso da fiori m. v fiorire, essere in fiore. **flowering** adj in fiore. **flowery** adj fiorito.
flown [floun] V **fly¹**.
flu [fluɪ] n influenza f.
fluctuate ['flʌktjuˌeit] v fluttuare. **fluctuation** n fluttuazione f.
flue [fluɪ] n gola del camino f.
fluent ['fluənt] adj corrente, scorrevole. **speak fluently** parlare correntemente.
fluff [flʌf] n lanugine f, peluria f.
fluid ['fluid] nm, adj fluido, liquido.
fluke [fluɪk] n (*lucky chance*) colpo fortunato m.
flung [flʌŋ] V **fling**.
fluorescent [fluə'resnt] adj fluorescente.
fluoride ['fluəraid] n fluoruro m. **fluoridation** n fluorizzazione f.
flush¹ [flʌʃ] n (*colouring*) rossore m; (*rush of liquid*) flusso m; (*blushing*) vampa f; (*poker*) flush m invar. v (*wash out*) pulire con un getto d'acqua; (*lavatory*) vuotare; (*redden*) arrossire, avvampare.
flush² [flʌʃ] adj (*level*) a livello, rasente; (*slang: rich*) ben fornito.
fluster ['flʌstə] v turbare, confondere.
flute [fluɪt] n flauto m.
flutter ['flʌtə] v battere; agitare, confondere; (*fly*) svolazzare. n battito m, agitazione f; (*bet*) scommessa f.
flux [flʌks] n flusso m.
*fly¹ [flai] v volare; (*flutter*) svolazzare; (*flag*) sventolare; (*flee*) fuggire, scappare. **fly away** or **off** volar via. **flyleaf** n risguardo m. **flyover** n cavalcavia m invar. **flysheet** n volantino m. **flywheel** n volano m. **flying squad** squadra mobile f.
fly² [flai] n (*insect*) mosca f.
foal [foul] n puledro m.
foam [foum] n schiuma f. **foam rubber** gomma piuma f. v spumeggiare.
focus ['foukəs] n fuoco m, centro m. v concentrare; (*bring into focus*) mettere a fuoco. **focal** adj focale.
fodder ['fodə] n mangime m, foraggio m.
foe [fou] n nemico, -a m, f; avversario, -a m, f.
foetus ['fiɪtəs] n feto m.
fog [fog] n nebbia f. **fog-bound** adj fermo per la nebbia. **fog-horn** n sirena da nebbia f. **foggy** adj nebbioso.

foible ['foibl] *n* debole *m*.
foil¹ [foil] *v* frustrare, sventare.
foil² [foil] *n* lamina (di metallo) *f*; (*tinfoil*) stagnolo *m*; (*contrast*) contrappeso *m*.
foist [foist] *v* rifilare, affibbiare.
fold¹ [fould] *v* piegare; (*envelop*) avvolgere. **fold one's arms** incrociare le braccia. **fold (up)** (*collapse*) chiudere, cessare l'esercizio. *n* piega *f*, ripiegatura *f*. **folder** *n* cartella *f*. **folding** *adj* pieghevole.
fold² [fould] *n* (*enclosure*) ovile *m*.
foliage ['fouliidʒ] *n* fogliame *m*.
folk [fouk] *n* gente *f*, popolo *m*. **folk dance** danza rustica *f*. **folklore** *n* folclore *m*. **folk song** canto popolare *m*.
follicle ['folikl] *n* follicolo *m*.
follow ['folou] *v* seguire, succedere; (*understand*) capire; (*result*) risultare, conseguire. **follower** *n* seguace *m*, *f*. **following** *adj* seguente, successivo.
folly ['foli] *n* follia *f*.
fond [fond] *adj* affettuoso, affezionato. **become fond of** affezionarsi a. **be fond of** voler bene a; (*person*) amare.
fondle ['fondl] *v* accarezzare, coccolare.
font [font] *n* fonte battesimale *f*.
food [fuid] *n* cibo *m*, vitto *m*; (*foodstuffs*) generi alimentari *m pl*.
fool [fuil] *n* sciocco, -a *m*, *f*; cretino, -a *m*, *f*; (*jester*) buffone, -a *m*, *f*, pagliaccio *m*. **foolhardy** *adj* temerario. **foolproof** *adj* sicurissimo. *v* (*deceive*) ingannare. **foolish** *adj* sciocco, insensato. **foolishness** *n* sciocchezza *f*.
foolscap ['fuilskap] *n* carta protocollo *f*.
foot [fut] *n, pl* **feet** piede *m*; (*birds, animals*) zampa *f*. *v* **foot the bill** saldare il conto. **on foot** a piedi. **put one's foot down** farsi valere. **put one's foot in it** fare una gaffe.
football ['fut,boil] *n* football *m invar*, pallone *m*. **footballer** *n* calciatore *m*.
foot-bridge ['fut,bridʒ] *n* passerella *f*.
foothold ['fut,hould] *n* punto d'appoggio *m*.
footing ['futiŋ] *n* (*foundation*) base *f*; (*mutual standing*) relazioni *f pl*.
footlights ['fut,laits] *pl n* luci della ribalta *f pl*.
footnote ['fut,nout] *n* postilla *f*, nota in calce *f*.
footpath ['fut,paiθ] *n* sentiero *m*.
footprint ['fut,print] *n* orma *f*.
footstep ['fut,step] *n* passo *m*.

footwear ['fut,weə] *n* calzatura *f*.
for [foi] *prep* per, a favore di, a, di, da. *conj* poiché.
forage ['foridʒ] *v* foraggiare. *n* foraggio *m*.
forbade [foi'bad] *V* **forbid**.
*forbear [foi'beə] *v* astenersi da, pazientare.
*forbid [foi'bid] *v* proibire, vietare. **forbidding** *adj* austero, formidabile.
forbidden [foi'bidn] *V* **forbid**.
force [fois] *n* forza *f*. **in force** in vigore. *v* forzare; (*compel*) costringere. **forceful** *adj* energico.
forceps ['foiseps] *pl n* forcipe *m sing*.
ford [foid] *n* guado *m*. *v* guadare.
fore [foi] *adj* anteriore. **come to the fore** venire alla ribalta.
forearm ['foiraim] *n* avambraccio *m*.
forebear ['foibeə] *n* antenato, -a *m*, *f*.
foreboding [foi'boudiŋ] *n* presagio *m*.
*forecast ['foikaist] *n* previsione *f*, pronostico *m*. *v* prevedere.
forecourt ['foikoit] *n* cortile *m*.
forefather ['foifaiðə] *n* antenato *m*, avo *m*.
forefinger ['foifiŋgə] *n* indice *m*.
forefront ['foifrʌnt] *n* prima linea *f*.
foreground ['foigraund] *n* primo piano *m*.
forehand ['foihand] *nm, adj* (*tennis*) diritto.
forehead ['forid] *n* fronte *f*.
foreign ['forən] *adj* straniero, forestiero; (*trade, etc.*) estero; (*not belonging*) estraneo. **foreigner** *n* straniero, -a *m*, *f*; forestiero, -a *m*, *f*.
foreleg ['foileg] *n* zampa anteriore *f*.
foreman ['foimən] *n* caposquadra (*pl* capisquadra) *m*, capo operaio *m*; (*jury*) presidente *m*.
foremost ['foimoust] *adj* principale, primo. *adv* in primo luogo. **first and foremost** anzitutto.
forename ['foineim] *n* nome di battesimo *m*.
forensic [fə'rensik] *adj* forense. **forensic medicine** medicina legale *f*.
forerunner ['foirʌnə] *n* precursore *m*.
*foresee [foi'sii] *v* prevedere. **foreseeable** *adj* prevedibile.
foreshadow [foi'ʃadou] *v* adombrare.
foreshorten [foi'ʃoitn] *v* scorciare. **foreshortened** *adj* di scorcio.
foresight ['foisait] *n* (*prevision*) preveggenza *f*; (*care for future*) previdenza *f*.

foreskin ['fɔːskin] *n* prepuzio,*m*.
forest ['fɔrist] *n* foresta *f*. **forester** *n* guardia forestale *f*. **forestry** *n* selvicoltura *f*.
forestall [fɔːˈstɔːl] *v* anticipare, prevenire.
foretaste ['fɔːteist] *n* pregustazione *f*.
*foretell [fɔːˈtel] *v* predire, pronosticare.
forethought ['fɔːθɔːt] *n* premeditazione *f*, previdenza *f*.
forever [fɔrˈevə] *adv* per sempre.
foreword ['fɔːwɔːd] *n* prefazione *f*.
forfeit ['fɔːfit] *n* (*pawn*) pegno *m*; (*fine*) multa *f*. *v* (*give up*) dover abbandonare; pagare il fio.
forgave [fəˈgeiv] *V* **forgive**.
forge[1] [fɔːdʒ] *v* (*counterfeit*) falsificare, contraffare; (*metal*) forgiare. *n* fucina *f*. **forger** *n* falsario, -a *m, f*. **forgery** *n* contraffazione *f*, falso *m*.
forge[2] [fɔːdʒ] *v* avanzare. **forge ahead** farsi strada; (*take lead*) distanziarsi, staccarsi.
*forget [fəˈget] *v* dimenticare, scordare, non ricordarsi di. **forget-me-not** *n* nontiscordardimè *m*. **forget oneself** lasciarsi andare. **forgetful** *adj* smemorato.
*forgive [fəˈgiv] *v* perdonare, rimettere. **forgiveness** *n* perdono *m*, indulgenza *f*. **forgiving** *adj* clemente, indulgente.
forgiven [fəˈgivn] *V* **forgive**.
*forgo [fɔːˈgou] *v* rinunciare a.
forgot [fəˈgot] *V* **forget**.
forgotten [fəˈgotn] *V* **forget**.
fork [fɔːk] *n* (*cutlery*) forchetta *f*; (*agriculture*) forca *f*, forcone *m*; (*road*) bivio *m*; (*branching*) biforcazione *f*. *v* forcare; biforcarsi. **fork out** (*slang: pay*) metter mano alla borsa.
forlorn [fəˈlɔːn] *adj* disperato, desolato.
form [fɔːm] *n* forma *f*; (*document*) modulo *m*; (*bench*) banco *m*; (*school*) classe *f*. *v* formare. **formation** *n* formazione *f*. **formative** *adj* formativo.
formal ['fɔːməl] *adj* formale, esplicito. **formality** *n* formalità *f*, cerimonia *f*.
format ['fɔːmat] *n* formato *m*.
former ['fɔːmə] *adj* precedente, anteriore. **the former** il primo. **formerly** *adv* in passato, già, in altri tempi.
formidable ['fɔːmidəbl] *adj* formidabile, spaventoso, terribile.
formula ['fɔːmjulə] *n, pl* -ae formula *f*.
formulate ['fɔːmjuˌleit] *v* formulare. **formulation** *n* formulazione *f*.

*forsake [fəˈseik] *v* abbandonare.
forsaken [fəˈseikn] *V* **forsake**.
forsook [fəˈsuk] *V* **forsake**.
fort [fɔːt] *n* fortezza *f*, forte *m*.
forth [fɔːθ] *adv* avanti; (*out of concealment*) fuori. **and so forth** e così via. **forthcoming** *adj* imminente, prossimo. **forthright** *adj* franco, schietto. **forthwith** *adv* immediatamente.
fortify ['fɔːtiˌfai] *v* fortificare, rafforzare, dar forza a; (*wine*) alcolizzare. **fortification** *n* fortificazione *f*.
fortitude ['fɔːtiˌtjuːd] *n* forza d'animo *f*; (*virtue*) fortezza *f*.
fortnight ['fɔːtnait] *n* quindicina *f*, due settimane *f pl*. **fortnightly** *nm, adj* quindicinale, bimensile.
fortress ['fɔːtris] *n* fortezza *f*.
fortuitous [fɔːˈtjuːitəs] *adj* fortuito.
fortune ['fɔːtʃən] *n* fortuna *f*; (*riches*) ricchezza *f*; futuro *m*. **fortune-teller** *n* chiromante *m, f*. **fortune-telling** *n* chiromanzia *f*. **fortunate** *adj* fortunato.
forty ['fɔːti] *nm, adj* quaranta. **fortieth** *nm, adj* quarantesimo.
forum ['fɔːrəm] *n* foro *m*; (*court*) tribuna *f*.
forward ['fɔːwəd] *adj* avanzato; presuntuoso. *adv* also **forwards** avanti, in avanti. **look forward to** anticipare con piacere. **put forward** proporre. *v* spedire, inoltrare; (*mail*) rispedire.
fossil ['fɔsl] *n* fossile *m*. **fossilized** *adj* fossilizzato.
foster ['fɔstə] *v* (*child*) allevare; incoraggiare; nutrire, alimentare. **foster-child** *n* figlio adottivo *m*. **foster-parents** *pl n* genitori adottivi *m pl*.
fought [fɔːt] *V* **fight**.
foul [faul] *adj* lurido, schifoso; (*weather*) pessimo. **foul play** (*crime*) delitto *m*; (*sport*) gioco falloso *m*.
found[1] [faund] *V* **find**.
found[2] [faund] *v* fondare, istituire, basare. **foundation** *n* fondazione *f*; istituto *m*; (*base*) fondamento *m*, base *f*. **founder** *n* fondatore, -trice *m, f*.
founder ['faundə] *v* (*sink*) colare a picco.
foundry ['faundri] *n* fonderia *f*.
fountain ['fauntin] *n* fontana *f*. **fountain pen** penna stilografica *f*.
four [fɔː] *nm, adj* quattro. **foursome** *n* quattro *m*. **on all fours** (a) carponi.
fourth *nm, adj* quarto.

fourteen [fo'tiːn] *nm, adj* quattordici. **fourteenth** *nm, adj* quattordicesimo.

fowl [faul] *n* pollame *m*; (*chicken*) pollo *m*.

fox [foks] *n* volpe *f*; (*sly person*) furbacchione *m*, furbo, -a *m, f*. **foxglove** *n* digitale *f*. **fox-hound** *n* bracco *m*. *v* (*coll*) ingannare. **foxed** *adj* perplesso.

foyer ['foiei] *n* ridotto *m*.

fraction ['frakʃən] *n* frazione *f*.

fracture ['fraktʃə] *n* frattura *f*, rottura *f*. *v* rompere, fratturare.

fragile ['fradʒail] *adj* fragile; (*delicate*) gracile.

fragment ['fragmənt] *n* frammento *m*.

fragrant ['freigrənt] *adj* fragrante, profumato. **fragrance** *n* profumo *m*.

frail [freil] *adj* fragile, gracile.

frame [freim] *n* struttura *f*; (*skeleton*) ossatura *f*; (*picture*) cornice *f*; (*machine*) telaio *m*. **frame of mind** disposizione d'animo *f*, umore *m*. **framework** *n* (*mech*) intelaiatura *f*; (*outline*) abbozzo *m*. *v* incorniciare, costruire; (*compose*) redigere; (*fabricate evidence*) calunniare.

France [frɑːns] *n* Francia *f*.

franchise ['frantʃaiz] *n* (*privilege*) franchigia *f*; (*comm*) concessione *f*.

frank [fraŋk] *adj* sincero, schietto. **frankness** *n* sincerità *f*, schiettezza *f*.

frantic ['frantik] *adj* frenetico.

fraternal [frə'təːnl] *adj* fraterno. **fraternity** *n* fratellanza *f*; (*friendship*) fraternità *f*. **fraternize** *v* fraternizzare.

fraud [froːd] *n* (*deceit*) frode *f*, inganno *m*; (*deceiver*) impostore, -a *m, f*, truffatore, -trice *m, f*. **fraudulent** *adj* fraudolento, doloso.

fraught [froːt] *adj* (*tense*) nervoso. **fraught with** pieno *or* denso di.

fray[1] [frei] *v* (*unravel*) logorare, consumare. **frayed** *adj* (*clothes, etc*.) logoro dall'uso, liso. **frayed nerves** nervi scoperti *m pl*.

fray[2] [frei] *n* (*brawl*) mischia *f*.

freak [friːk] *n* fenomeno *m*; figura grottesca *f*, mostro *m*.

freckle ['frekl] *n* lentiggine *f*. **freckled** *adj* lentigginoso.

free [friː] *adj* libero; (*without payment*) gratis, gratuito; (*unconstrained*) disinvolto, sciolto; (*lavish*) generoso. **free from** esente da. **freehold** *n* proprietà fondiaria assoluta *f*. **freelance** *adj* indipendente. **Freemason** *n* massone *m*.

free speech libertà di parola *f*. **free trade** libero scambio *m*. **free will** libero arbitrio *m*. *v* liberare. **freedom** *n* libertà *f*.

freesia ['friːziə] *n* fresia *f*.

***freeze** [friːz] *v* gelare, congelare; (*block*) bloccare. *n* gelo *m*. **freezer** *n* congelatore *m*, freezer *m invar*. **freezing** *adj* gelido. **below freezing** sotto zero. **freezing point** punto di congelamento *m*.

freight [freit] *n* (*cargo*) carico *m*; (*charge*) nolo *m*; (*conveyance*) trasporto *m*. **freight train** treno merci *m*. *v* trasportare. **freighter** *n* nave da carico *f*.

French [frentʃ] *nm, adj* francese. **French bean** *n* fagiolino verde *m*, cornetto *m*. **French horn** corno (a pistoni) *m*. **Frenchman/woman** *n* francese *m, f*. **french fries** *pl n* patatine fritte *f pl*

frenzy ['frenzi] *n* frenesia *f*. **frenzied** *adj* frenetico.

frequent ['friːkwənt; *v* fri'kwent] *adj* frequente. *v* frequentare. **frequency** *n* frequenza *f*.

fresco ['freskou] *n* affresco *f*.

fresh [freʃ] *adj* fresco; (*water*) dolce; (*brisk*) vigoroso; (*cheeky*) insolente. **fresh from** appena venuto da. **freshman** *n* matricola *f*. **freshen** *v* rinfrescare, rinnovare. **freshness** *n* freschezza *f*, vigore *m*.

fret[1] [fret] *v* inquietarsi. **fretful** *adj* irritabile.

fret[2] [fret] *n* (*pattern*) fregio *m*. *v* ornare con fregi, traforare. **fretwork** *n* lavoro di traforo *m*.

friar ['fraiə] *n* frate *m*. **friary** *n* convento di frati *m*.

friction ['frikʃən] *n* attrito *m*; (*conflict*) dissenso *m*.

Friday ['fraidei] *n* venerdì *m*.

fridge [fridʒ] *n* (*coll*) frigorifero *m*.

fried [fraid] *adj* fritto.

friend [frend] *n* amico, -a *m, f*. **make friends** fare amicizia. **friendless** *adj* senza amici. **friendliness** *n* amichevolezza *f*, cordialità *f*. **friendly** *adj* amichevole, cordiale, gentile. **be friendly with** essere amico di. **friendship** *n* amicizia *f*.

frieze [friːz] *n* fregio *m*.

frigate ['frigit] *n* fregata *f*.

fright [frait] *n* spavento *m*. **frighten** *v* spaventare, allarmare. **be frightened** aver paura. **frightening** *adj* spaventevole, terribile. **frightful** *adj* terribile.

73 furniture

frigid ['fridʒid] *adj* freddo; *(woman)* frigido. **frigidity** *n* freddezza *f*; frigidità *f*.
frill [fril] *n* fronzolo *m*. **frilly** *adj* carico di fronzoli.
fringe [frindʒ] *n* (*border*) orlo *m*; limite *m*; (*ornamental border, hair*) frangia *f*; periferia *f*. *v* ornare di frange.
frisk [frisk] *v* saltellare; (*search*) perquisire. **frisky** *adj* vivace.
fritter¹ ['fritə] *v* **fritter away** sprecare.
fritter² ['fritə] *n* (*cookery*) frittella *f*.
frivolity [fri'voliti] *n* frivolezza *f*. **frivolous** *adj* superficiale, frivolo.
frizz [friz] *v* arricciare. *n* ricciolo *m*. **frizzy** *adj* ricciuto.
fro [frou] *adv* **to and fro** avanti e indietro.
frock [frok] *n* vestito *m*.
frog [frog] *n* rana *f*. **frogman** *n* uomo rana *m*.
frolic ['frolik] *v* trastullarsi, scherzare. *n* scherzo *m*.
from [from] *prep* da, per, da parte di.
front [frʌnt] *n* parte anteriore *f*; (*mil, pol*) fronte *m*; (*arch*) facciata *f*; (*seaside*) lungomare *m*. *adj* primo, anteriore. **front door** portone *m*. **in front of** davanti a.
frontier ['frʌntiə] *n* frontiera *f*, confine *m*.
frost [frost] *n* gelo *m*. **frost-bite** *n* gelone *m*. *v* brinare; (*cookery*) glassare. **frosted glass** vetro smerigliato *m*. **frosty** *adj* (*weather*) gelido; (*manner*) freddo.
froth [froθ] *n* schiuma *f*. *v* spumare, schiumare.
frown [fraun] *v* aggrottare le ciglia, corrugare la fronte. **frown at** guardare in cagnesco. *n* cipiglio *m*, viso arcigno *m*.
froze [frouz] *V* **freeze**.
frozen ['frouzn] *V* **freeze**. *adj* gelato, congelato; bloccato.
frugal ['fruːgəl] *adj* frugale, sobrio.
fruit [fruːt] *n* frutto *m*; (*collectively*) frutta *f*; (*result*) risultato *m*. **fruit salad** macedonia di frutta *f*. *v* (*bear fruit*) fruttare. **fruiterer** *n* fruttivendolo, -a *m, f*. **fruitful** *adj* fecondo; (*profitable*) redditizio. **fruition** *n* realizzazione *f*. **fruitless** *adj* infruttuoso; inutile. **fruity** *adj* saporito; di frutta; (*wine*) dal gusto d'uva.
frustrate [frʌ'streit] *v* frustrare. **frustration** *n* frustrazione *f*.
fry [frai] *v* friggere. **frying pan** padella *f*.
fuchsia ['fjuːʃə] *n* fucsia *f*.
fuck [fʌk] *v* (*vulgar*) fottere, chiavare.
fuel ['fjuəl] *n* combustibile *m*; (*mot*) carburante *m*. **fuel oil** gasolio *m*, nafta *f*. *v* alimentare.
fugitive ['fjuːdʒitiv] *adj* (*runaway*) fuggitivo, fuggiasco; (*fleeting*) effimero, fugace. *n* fuggiasco, -a *m, f*; profugo, -a *m, f*.
fugue [fjuːg] *n* fuga *f*.
fulcrum ['fulkrəm] *n* fulcro *m*.
fulfil [ful'fil] *v* adempiere, compiere, soddisfare. **fulfilment** *n* adempimento *m*, realizzazione *f*.
full [ful] *adj* pieno; completo; intero. **full-length** *adj* di lunghezza normale; (*portrait*) in piedi. **full moon** luna piena *f*. **full-sized** *adj* di grandezza naturale. **full stop** punto *m*. **full-time** *adj, adv* a tempo intero, a orario completo. **fully** *adv* completamente.
fumble ['fʌmbl] *v* brancolare.
fume [fjuːm] *v* emettere fumo; (*coll: rage*) arrabbiarsi, imperversare. *n* fumo *m*, esalazione *f*.
fumigate ['fjuːmigeit] *v* suffumicare.
fun [fʌn] *n* spasso *m*, divertimento *m*, scherzo *m*. **funfair** *n* luna park *m invar*. **in fun** per ridere. **make fun of** prendere in giro.
function ['fʌŋkʃən] *n* funzione *f*; (*purpose*) scopo *m*; (*duty*) mansione *f*; (*ceremony*) cerimonia *f*. *v* funzionare. **functional** *adj* funzionale.
fund [fʌnd] *n* fondo *m*, riserva *f*, capitale *m*. **funds** *pl n* soldi *m pl*.
fundamental [fʌndə'mentl] *adj* fondamentale, basilare.
funeral ['fjuːnərəl] *n* funerale *m*. *adj* funebre. **funereal** *adj* funereo.
fungus ['fʌŋgəs] *n, pl* -gi fungo *m*. **fungicide** *n* anticrittogamico *m*.
funnel ['fʌnl] *n* imbuto *m*; (*ship*) ciminiera *f*.
funny ['fʌni] *adj* divertente, comico; (*odd*) strano. **funny story** barzelletta *f*. **the funny thing is** il bello è.
fur [fəː] *n* (*skin*) pelo *m*; pelliccia *f*. *v* incrostarsi. **furrier** *n* pellicciaio *m*. **furry** *adj* peloso.
furious ['fjuəriəs] *adj* furibondo, arrabbiatissimo.
furnace ['fəːnis] *n* fornace *f*.
furnish ['fəːniʃ] *v* (*supply*) fornire, dotare; (*house, etc.*) arredare, ammobiliare.
furniture ['fəːnitʃə] *n* mobilio *m*, mobili *m pl*; (*fittings*) attrezzatura *f*.

furrow ['fʌrou] *n* solco *m*; (*brow*) ruga *f*, grinza *f*.

further ['fəɪðə] *adj* ulteriore, più lontano. *adv* più lontano, oltre. **furthermore** *adv* inoltre. **further on** più avanti. **further up** più in su. *v* favorire, promuovere.

furthest ['fəɪðist] *adj* in più lontano, estremo.

furtive ['fəɪtiv] *adj* furtivo, di soppiatto.

fury ['fjuəri] *n* furia *f*.

fuse[1] [fjuɪz] *n* (*elec*) valvola *f*, fusibile *m*. **blow a fuse** saltare la corrente. *v* (*melt*) fondere; (*blend*) amalgamare, unire. **fusion** *n* fusione *f*.

fuse[2] [fjuɪz] *n* (*bomb*) detonatore *m*.

fuselage ['fjuɪzə,laɪʒ] *n* fusoliera *f*.

fuss [fʌs] *v* lamentarsi, agitarsi. **fuss over** affaccendarsi attorno a. *n* scalpore *m*, trambusto *m*. **make a fuss** fare un gran chiasso. **fussy** *adj* pignolo, meticoloso.

futile ['fjuɪtail] *adj* vano, inutile. **futility** *n* inutilità *f*.

future ['fjuɪtʃə] *n* futuro *m*, avvenire *m*. *adj* futuro.

fuzz [fʌz] *n* lanugine *f*, peluria *f*. **fuzzy** *adj* peloso; (*unclear*) sfocato.

G

gabble ['gabl] *v* borbottare. *n* borbottio *m*.

gaberdine [gabə'diɪn] *n* gabardina *f*.

gable ['geibl] *n* pigna *f*, frontone *m*.

gadget ['gadʒit] *n* congegno *m*, dispositivo *m*.

gag[1] [gag] *n* bavaglio *m*. *v* imbavagliare.

gag[2] [gag] *n* (*joke*) battuta *f*.

gaiety ['geiəti] *n* allegria *f*.

gaily ['geili] *adv* allegramente.

gain [gein] *n* guadagno *m*, profitto *m*. *v* guadagnare; (*obtain*) ottenere.

gait [geit] *n* andatura *f*, passo *m*.

gala ['gaɪlə] *n* festa *f*.

galaxy ['galəksi] *n* galassia *f*.

gale [geil] *n* bufera *f*, burrasca *f*.

gallant ['galənt] *adj* (*courageous*) prode; (*courtly*) galante. *n* cavaliere *m*. **gallantry** *n* valore *m*, coraggio *m*; galanteria *f*.

gall-bladder ['goɪl,bladə] *n* cistifellea *f*, vescica biliare *f*.

galleon ['galiən] *n* galeone *m*.

gallery ['galəri] *n* galleria *f*; (*theatre*) loggione *m*.

galley ['gali] *n* (*naut*) galea *f*; (*kitchen*) cambusa *f*.

gallop ['galəp] *n* galoppo *m*; galoppata *f*. *v* galoppare, andare al galoppo.

gallows ['galouz] *n* patibolo *m*.

gallstone ['goɪlstoun] *n* calcolo biliare *m*.

galore [gə'loɪ] *adv* in quantità.

galvanize ['galvənaiz] *v* galvanizzare. **galvanometer** *n* galvanometro *m*.

gambit ['gambit] *n* gambetto *m*.

gamble ['gambl] *v* (*risk*) rischiare, arrischiare; (*game*) giocare. *n* impresa rischiosa *f*, speculazione *f*. **gambler** *n* giocatore, -trice *m*, *f*. **gambling** *n* gioco d'azzardo *m*.

game [geim] *n* gioco *m*; (*match*) partita *f*; (*hunting*) selvaggina *f*. **gamekeeper** *n* guardacaccia *m*. *adj* (*plucky*) che ha del fegato.

gammon ['gamən] *n* prosciutto *m*.

gander ['gandə] *n* papero *m*.

gang [gan] *n* squadra *f*, gruppo *m*; (*youths, thieves, etc.*) banda *f*. *v* **gang up** allearsi. **gangster** *n* gangster *m invar*, bandito *m*.

gangling ['ganglin] *adj* allampanato.

gangrene ['gangriɪn] *n* cancrena *f*.

gangway ['ganwei] *n* passaggio *m*, corsia *f*; (*naut*) barcarizzo *m*.

gaol *V* **jail**.

gap [gap] *n* (*breach*) breccia *f*; (*opening*) apertura *f*; (*hole*) buco *m*; (*vacant space*) vuoto *m*; intervallo *m*; (*divergence*) distacco *m*.

gape [geip] *v* stare a bocca aperta; (*open wide*) spalancare.

garage ['garaɪʒ] *n* garage *m invar*; (*repairs*) autorimessa *f*.

garbage ['gaɪbidʒ] (*US*) *n* rifiuti *m pl*. **garbage can** bidone della spazzatura *m*.

garble ['gaɪbl] *v* mutilare.

garden ['gaɪdn] *n* giardino *m*. *v* fare del giardinaggio. **gardener** *n* giardiniere, -a *m*, *f*. **gardening** *n* giardinaggio *m*.

gargle ['gaɪgl] *v* gargarizzare. *n* gargarismo *m*.

garish ['geəriʃ] *adj* vistoso.

garland ['gaɪlənd] *n* ghirlanda *f*. *v* inghirlandare.

garlic ['gaɪlik] *n* aglio *m*.

garment ['ga:mənt] *n* indumento *m*, capo di vestiario *m*.

garnish ['gaɪniʃ] *v* guarnire, adornare. *n* ornamento *m*, guarnizione *f*.

garret ['garət] *n* soffitta *f*.
garrison ['garisn] *n* guarnigione *f*, presidio *m*. *v* presidiare.
garrulous ['garələs] *adj* loquace.
garter ['gaitə] *n* giarrettiera *f*.
gas [gas] *n* gas *m invar*; (*US: petrol*) benzina *f*. **gas cooker** fornello a gas *m*. **gas fire** stufa a gas *f*. **gas mask** maschera antigas *f*. *v* asfissiare.
gash [gaʃ] *n* sfregio *m*, squarcio *m*. *v* sfregiare, squarciare.
gasket ['gaskit] *n* guarnizione *f*.
gasoline ['gasə,liin] *n* (*US*) benzina *f*.
gasp [gaisp] *v* boccheggiare, ansimare. *n* rantolo *m*.
gastric ['gastrik] *adj* gastrico.
gastronomy [ga'stronəmi] *n* gastronomia *f*. **gastronomic** *adj* gastronomico.
gate [geit] *n* cancello *m*, porta *f*. **gatecrash** *v* fare il portoghese, entrare senza invito *or* pagare. **gatepost** *n* montante del cancello *m*. **gateway** *n* entrata *f*, portone *m*.
gateau ['gatou] *n* pasticcino *m*, gateau *m*.
gather ['gaðə] *v* cogliere; (*bring together*) raccogliere; (*infer*) dedurre; (*assemble*) radunarsi. **gathering** *n* riunione *f*, adunata *f*.
gaudy ['goidi] *adj* vistoso.
gauge [geidʒ] *n* (*measure*) misura *f*; (*instrument*) calibro *m*; (*rail*) scartamento *m*. *v* misurare, calibrare.
gaunt [goint] *adj* emaciato, desolato.
gauze [goiz] *n* garza *f*.
gave [geiv] *V* give.
gay [gei] *adj* vivace, allegro; (*slang*) omosessuale.
gaze [geiz] *v* mirare, guardare fissamente. **gaze at** fissare. *n* sguardo fisso *m*.
gazelle [gə'zel] *n* gazzella *f*.
gazette [gə'zet] *n* gazzetta ufficiale *f*.
gazetteer [gazə'tiə] *n* dizionario geografico *m*.
gear [giə] *n* (*mot*) marcia *f*, velocità *f*; (*equipment, tools*) arnesi *m pl*, attrezzatura *f*; (*belongings*) roba *f*. **change gear** cambiare velocità. **gearbox** *n* scatola del cambio *f*. **gear lever** leva del cambio *f*. *v* preparare, adattare.
gelatine ['dʒelə,tiin] *n* gelatina *f*.
gelignite ['dʒelig,nait] *n* gelatina esplosiva *f*.
gem [dʒem] *n* gemma *f*.
Gemini ['dʒemini] *n* Gemelli *m pl*.

gender ['dʒendə] *n* genere *m*, sesso *m*.
gene [dʒiin] *n* gene *m*.
genealogy [dʒiini,alədʒi] *n* genealogia *f*. **genealogical** *adj* genealogico.
general ['dʒenərəl] *nm, adj* generale. **general practitioner** medico generico *m*. **generalization** *n* generalizzazione *f*. **generalize** *v* generalizzare.
generate ['dʒenəreit] *v* generare, produrre. **generation** *n* generazione *f*. **generator** *n* generatore *m*.
generic [dʒi'nerik] *adj* generico.
generous ['dʒenərəs] *adj* generoso. **generosity** *n* generosità *f*.
genetic [dʒi'netik] *adj* genetico. **geneticist** *n* genetista *m, f*. **genetics** *n* genetica *f*.
Geneva [dʒi'niivə] *n* Ginevra *f*.
genial ['dʒiiniəl] *adj* gioviale, simpatico.
genital ['dʒenitl] *adj* genitale. **genitals** *pl n* organi genitali *m pl*.
genius ['dʒiinjəs] *n* genio *m*.
Genoa ['dʒenouə] *n* Genova *f*. **Genoese** *n(m+f), adj* genovese.
genteel [dʒen'tiil] *adj* signorile. **gentility** *n* signorilità *f*.
gentle ['dʒentl] *adj* tenero; (*mild*) mite; (*not steep*) dolce. **gentleman** *n* signore *m*; (*of good breeding, etc.*) gentiluomo *m*. **gentlemanly** *adj* signorile. **gentleness** *n* dolcezza *f*. **gently** *adv* dolcemente; adagio, piano.
gentry ['dʒentri] *n* piccola nobiltà *f*.
gents [dʒents] *n* (*sign*) uomini, signori.
genuine ['dʒenjuin] *adj* genuino, autentico; sincero. **genuinely** *adv* (*really*) veramente.
genus ['dʒiinəs] *n* genere *m*.
geography [dʒi'ogrəfi] *n* geografia *f*. **geographer** *n* geografo, -a *m, f*. **geographical** *adj* geografico.
geology [dʒi'olədʒi] *n* geologia *f*. **geological** *adj* geologico. **geologist** *n* geologo, -a *m, f*.
geometry [dʒi'omətri] *n* geometria *f*. **geometric** *adj* geometrico.
geranium [dʒə'reiniəm] *n* geranio *m*.
geriatric [dʒeri'atrik] *adj* geriatrico. **geriatrics** *n* geriatria *f*.
germ [dʒəim] *n* germe *m*.
Germany ['dʒəiməni] *n* Germania *f*. **German** *n, adj* tedesco, -a. **German measles** rosolia *f*, rubeola *f*.
germinate ['dʒəimineit] *v* germinare. **germination** *n* germinazione *f*.

gerund ['dʒerənd] *n* gerundio *m*.
gesticulate [dʒe'stikjuˌleit] *v* gesticolare.
gesticulation *n* gesticolazione *f*.
gesture ['dʒestʃə] *n* gesto *m*. *v* gesticolare, fare gesti.
***get** [get] *v* (*obtain*) ottenere, procurare; (*fetch*) andare a prendere; (*receive*) ricevere; (*understand*) capire; (*become*) diventare; (*reach*) arrivare. **get across** attraversare; (*make understand*) far capire. **get along with** andare d'accordo con. **get at** (*reach*) raggiungere; (*hint*) alludere. **getaway** *n* fuga *f*. **get off** scendere. **get out** uscire. **get up** alzarsi.
geyser ['giːzə] *n* (*geog*) geyser *m*; (*water-heater*) scaldabagno *m*.
ghastly ['gaːstli] *adj* orrendo; (*pale*) spettrale.
gherkin ['gəːkin] *n* cetriolino *m*.
ghetto ['getou] *n* ghetto *m*.
ghost [goust] *n* fantasma *m*, spettro *m*. **ghostly** *adj* spettrale.
giant ['dʒaiənt] *n* gigante, -essa *m*, *f*. *adj* gigantesco, gigante.
gibberish ['dʒibəriʃ] *n* discorso incomprensibile *m*.
gibe [dʒaib] *n* beffa *f*; scherno *m*. *v* **gibe at** beffarsi di, beffare.
giblets ['dʒiblits] *pl n* rigaglie *f pl*, frattaglie *f pl*.
giddy ['gidi] *adj* (*flighty*) incostante, volubile; (*dizzy*) preso da vertigini; (*height*) vertiginoso. **feel giddy** avere il capogiro. **giddiness** *n* capogiro *m*, vertigini *f pl*.
gift [gift] *n* dono *m*, regalo *m*. **gifted** *adj* dotato.
gigantic [dʒai'gantik] *adj* gigantesco.
giggle ['gigl] *v* ridere scioccamente. *n* risatina sciocca *f*. **have the giggles** avere la ridarella.
gill [gil] *n* (*fish*) branchia *f*; (*mushroom*) lamella *f*.
gilt [gilt] *n* doratura *f*. *adj* dorato.
gimmick ['gimik] *n* (*coll: device*) congegno *m*; stratagemma *m*.
gin [dʒin] *n* gin *m invar*.
ginger ['dʒindʒə] *n* zenzero *m*. *adj* fulvo.
gingerly ['dʒindʒəli] *adj* cauto.
gipsy ['dʒipsi] *n* zingaro, -a *m*, *f*.
giraffe [dʒi'raːf] *n* giraffa *f*.
girder ['gəːdə] *n* trave maestra *f*, putrella *f*.
girdle ['gəːdl] *n* busto *m*, cintura *f*. *v* cingere.

girl [gəːl] *n* ragazza *f*. **girlfriend** *n* amica *f*. **girlish** *adj* da ragazza.
giro ['dʒairou] *n* giroconto *m*, postagiro *m*.
girth [gəːθ] *n* circonferenza *f*.
gist [dʒist] *n* nocciolo *m*.
***give** [giv] *v* dare; (*present*) regalare; (*relinquish*) cedere. **give away** regalare; (*betray*) tradire; (*secret*) rivelare. **give back** restituire. **give in** cedere. **give oneself up** costituirsi. **give out** distribuire. **give rise to** risultare in. **give up** abbandonare; (*cease*) smettere. *n* elasticità *f*.
given ['givn] *V* give.
glacier ['glasiə] *n* ghiacciaio *m*.
glad [glad] *adj* lieto, contento. **gladden** *v* rallegrare. **gladly** *adv* con piacere.
glamour [glamə] *n* fascino *m*. **glamorous** *adj* affascinante.
glance [glaɪns] *n* sguardo *m*. **at a glance** a prima vista. *v* dare un'occhiata.
gland [gland] *n* ghiandola *f*. **glandular** *adj* ghiandolare.
glare [gleə] *n* (*light*) bagliore *m*; (*fierce look*) sguardo torvo *m*. *v* **glare at** guardare con cipiglio, guardare con occhio torvo.
glass [glaɪs] *n* vetro *m*; (*container*) bicchiere *m*. **glasses** *pl n* occhiali *m pl*. **glassy** *adj* vitreo.
glaze [gleiz] *n* smalto *m*, patina *f*. *v* smaltare, verniciare; (*fit with glass*) fornire di vetri.
gleam [gliːm] *v* luccicare. *n* barlume *m*, luccichio *m*.
glean [gliːn] *v* racimolare.
glee [gliː] *n* gioia *f*. **gleeful** *adj* pieno di gioia.
glib [glib] *adj* facondo.
glide [glaid] *v* scivolare, scorrere; (*aero*) planare. **glider** *n* aliante *m*. **gliding** *n* volo a vela *m*.
glimmer ['glimə] *v* luccicare; (*of dawn*) albeggiare. *n* barlume *m*, luccichio *m*.
glimpse [glimps] *n* occhiata *f*, visione *f*. *v* intravedere.
glint [glint] *n* luccichio *m*. *v* luccicare, scintillare.
glisten ['glisn] *v* luccicare, brillare.
glitter ['glitə] *v* brillare, scintillare. *n* lucentezza *f*.
gloat [glout] *v* gongolare (malignamente).

globe [gloub] *n* globo *m*. **global** *adj* globale.

gloom [gluːm] *n* (*darkness*) oscurità *f*; (*depression*) malinconia *f*, tristezza *f*. **gloomy** *adj* malinconico, triste.

glory ['gloːri] *n* gloria *f*, splendore *m*. **glorify** *v* glorificare. **glorious** *adj* illustre, splendido.

gloss[1] [glos] *n* (*lustre*) lucentezza *f*; (*appearance*) apparenza *f*. **glossy** *adj* lucido.

gloss[2] [glos] *n* (*explanation*) chiosa *f*. *v* chiosare, commentare.

glossary ['glosəri] *n* lessico *m*.

glove [glʌv] *n* guanto *m*.

glow [glou] *v* risplendere; ardere. *n* rossore *m*; (*colour*) luminosità *f*. **glowing** *adj* acceso, ardente; fervente.

glucose ['gluːkous] *n* glucosio *m*.

glue [gluː] *n* colla *f*. *v* incollare.

glum [glʌm] *adj* tetro, cupo.

glut [glʌt] *n* sovrabbondanza *f*. *v* saturare.

glutton ['glʌtən] *n* ghiottone, -a *m*, *f*; goloso, -a *m*, *f*. **gluttonous** *adj* ghiotto, goloso. **gluttony** *n* golosità *f*.

gnarled [naːld] *adj* nodoso.

gnash [naʃ] *v* **gnash one's teeth** digrignare i denti.

gnat [nat] *n* zanzara *f*.

gnaw [noː] *v* rodere, rosicchiare. **gnawing** *adj* rosicante.

gnome [noum] *n* gnomo *m*.

***go** [gou] *v* andare; (*become*) diventare. **go away** andarsene. **go back** ritornare. **go-between** *n* intermediario *m*. **go by** passare; (*be guided by*) regolarsi su. **go down** scendere; (*sink*) affondare. **go in** entrare. **go off** esplodere; (*spoil*) guastarsi; (*leave*) andarsene. **go on** continuare. **go out** uscire. **go up** salire. **go without** fare a meno di. *n* energia *f*; (*try*) colpo *m*. **on the go** molto attivo.

goad [goud] *n* pungolo *m*. *v* incitare.

goal [goul] *n* (*aim*) meta *f*; (*sport*) porta *f*, rete *f*. **goalkeeper** *n* portiere *m*. **goal-post** *n* palo della porta *m*.

goat [gout] *n* capra *f*.

gobble ['gobl] *v* inghiottire.

goblin ['goblin] *n* folletto *m*.

god [god] *n* dio (*pl* dei) *m*. **goddaughter** *n* figlioccia *f*. **godfather** *n* padrino *m*. **godmother** *n* madrina *f*. **godson** *n* figlioccio *m*. **goddess** *n* dea *f*.

goggles ['goglz] *pl n* occhiali di protezione *m pl*.

gold [gould] *n* oro *m*. **goldfinch** *n* cardellino *m*. **goldfish** *n* pesce dorato *or* rosso *m*. **gold mine** miniera d'oro *f*. **goldsmith** *n* orefice *m*. **golden** *adj* d'oro; (*colour*) aureo. **golden rule** regola d'oro *f*.

golf [golf] *n* golf *m*. **golf course** campo di golf *m*. **golfer** *n* giocatore, -trice di golf *m*, *f*.

gondola ['gondələ] *n* gondola *f*.

gone [gon] *V* **go**.

gong [goŋ] *n* gong *m invar*.

gonorrhoea [ˌgonə'riə] *n* gonorrea *f*.

good [gud] *adj* buono; valido; (*well-behaved, clever*) bravo. **good afternoon** buon giorno; (*later*) buona sera. **goodbye** *interj* addio; arrivederci; (*coll*) ciao. **good-for-nothing** *n* buono a nulla *m*. **good-looking** *adj* bello. **good morning** buon giorno. **goodnight** *interj* buona notte. **goodwill** *n* benevolenza *f*; (*comm*) avviamento *m*. *n* bene *m*, vantaggio *m*. **be no good** non servire. **for good** per sempre. **goodness** *n* bontà *f*, gentilezza *f*, virtù *f*.

Good Friday *n* Venerdì Santo *m*.

goods [gudz] *pl n* merce *f pl*, beni *m pl*. **goods train** treno merci *m*.

goose [guːs] *n*, *pl* **geese** oca *f*.

gooseberry ['guzbəri] *n* uva spina *f*.

gore [goː] *v* trafiggere.

gorge [goːdʒ] *n* (*geol*) gola *f*. *v* rimpinzarsi (di).

gorgeous ['goːdʒəs] *adj* splendido.

gorilla [gə'rilə] *n* gorilla *m invar*.

gorse [goːs] *n* ginestrone *m*.

gory [goːri] *adj* cruento.

gosling ['gozliŋ] *n* papero, -a *m*, *f*.

gospel ['gospəl] *n* vangelo *m*; (*coll: truth*) verità implicita *f*.

gossip ['gosip] *n* ciarla *f*, pettegolezzo *m*; (*person*) ciarlone, -a *m*, *f*, chiacchierone, -a *m*, *f*. *v* ciarlare, chiacchierare.

got [got] *V* **get**.

Gothic ['goθik] *adj* gotico.

gourd [guəd] *n* zucca *f*.

gourmet ['guəmei] *n* buongustaio, -a *m*, *f*.

gout [gaut] *n* gotta *f*.

govern ['gʌvən] *v* governare *f*; (*gramm*) reggere. **governess** *n* governante *f*. **government** *n* governo *m*. **governor** *n* governatore *m*; (*coll: boss*) capo *m*.

gown [gaun] *n* (*dress*) veste *f*; (*robe*) toga *f*.

grab [grab] v arraffare. n strappo m.
grace [greis] n grazia f, eleganza f. v adornare. **graceful** adj grazioso. **gracious** adj benigno.
grade [greid] n grado m; (level) livello m; classe f. v classificare.
gradient ['greidiənt] n gradiente m; (slope) pendio m.
gradual ['gradjuəl] adj graduale. **gradually** adv poco a poco.
graduate ['gradjuət; v 'gradjueit] n laureato, -a m, f. v laurearsi.
graft¹ [graift] n (bot) innesto m; (med) trapianto m; (hard work) sgobbata f. v innestare; trapiantare; sgobbare.
graft² [graift] n (bribery) corruzione f. v corrompere.
grain [grein] n (seed) chicco m, granello m; (wheat) grano m; (wood) venatura f; (leather) grana f. **against the grain** contro pelo.
gram [gram] n grammo m.
grammar ['gramə] n grammatica f. **grammatical** adj grammaticale.
gramophone ['graməfoun] n grammofono m.
granary ['granəri] n granaio m.
grand [grand] adj (imposing) grandioso; (first rate) splendido. **grandchild** n nipote m, f; nipotino, -a m, f. **grandfather** n nonno m. **grandmother** n nonna f. **grand piano** pianoforte a coda m. **grandstand** n tribuna coperta f. **grand total** somma f.
grandeur n grandiosità f.
granite ['granit] n granito m.
grant [graint] v (confer) concedere, accordare; (give) dare; (admit) ammettere. **take for granted** ritenere per certo. n (student) borsa di studio f; concessione f.
granule ['granjuil] n granello m.
grape [greip] n acino m, chicco d'uva m. **grapes** pl n uva f sing. **grapevine** n vite f; (coll) canali confidenziali m pl.
grapefruit ['greipfruit] n pompelmo m.
graph [graf] n (math) grafico m; diagramma m. **graphic** adj grafico. **graph paper** carta millimetrata f.
grapple ['grapl] v **grapple with** venire alle prese con.
grasp [graisp] v afferrare; (understand) capire. n stretta f. **grasping** adj avaro.
grass [grais] n erba f; (lawn) prato m. **grasshopper** n cavalletta f. **grassy** adj erboso.

grate¹ [greit] n graticola f. **grating** n inferriata f.
grate² [greit] v grattugiare; (sound harshly) stridere; (irritate) dare sui nervi.
grateful ['greitful] adj riconoscente, grato.
gratify ['grati,fai] v appagare.
gratitude ['gratitjuid] n gratitudine f.
gratuitous [grə'tjuitəs] adj (free) gratuito; (without cause) ingiustificato.
gratuity [grə'tjuəti] n (tip) mancia f; (unsolicited gift) gratifica f.
grave¹ [greiv] n tomba f, sepolcro m. **gravedigger** n becchino m. **gravestone** n lapide funeraria f. **graveyard** n cimitero m.
grave² [greiv] adj grave.
gravel ['gravəl] n ghiaia f.
gravity ['gravəti] n gravità f. **gravitate** v gravitare.
gravy ['greivi] n sugo di carne m; salsa f.
graze¹ [greiz] v (touch) sfiorare; (scrape) scalfire. n scalfitura f, lesione superficiale f.
graze² [greiz] v (animal) pascolare.
grease [griis] n grasso m, unto m. **greaseproof paper** carta oleata f. v ungere, ingrassare. **greasy** adj grasso, unto; (slippery) scivoloso.
great [greit] adj grande; (very good) magnifico; (very large) grandissimo. **Great Britain** Gran Bretagna f. **greatly** adv molto. **greatness** n grandezza f.
Greece [griis] n Grecia f. **Greek** n, adj greco (pl -ci), -a.
greed [griid] n ingordigia f. **greedy** adj ingordo.
green [griin] adj verde. n verde m; (land) prato m; (golf) green m. **greenfly** n afide m. **greengage** n prugna verde f. **greengrocer** n erbivendolo, -a m, f, fruttivendolo, -a m, f. **greenhouse** n serra f. **green light** luce verde f. **greens** pl n verdura f sing.
Greenland ['griinlənd] n Groenlandia f. **Greenlander** n groenlandese m, f.
greet [griit] v salutare. **greeting** n saluto m.
gregarious [gri'geə,riəs] adj gregario, socievole.
grenade [grə'neid] n granata f.
grew [gruu] V grow.
grey [grei] adj grigio.
grid [grid] n (network) rete f; (map) reticolo m; (grating) grata f.

grief [griːf] *n* dolore *m*, afflizione *f*. **come to grief** far fiasco *or* cilecca.

grieve [griːv] *v* (*upset*) affliggere, addolorare; (*sorrow*) affliggersi. **grievance** *n* (*injustice*) ingiustizia *f*; (*complaint*) lamentela *f*. **grievous** *adj* doloroso, atroce.

grill [gril] *n* (*cookery*) graticola *f*, gratella *f*; (*grilled meat*) carne ai ferri *f*. *v* (*cookery*) cucinare ai ferri; (*question severely*) sottoporre a un interrogatorio severo.

grille [gril] *n* inferriata *f*, grata *f*.

grim [grim] *adj* (*unrelenting*) inesorabile; (*fierce*) feroce; (*forbidding*) arcigno. **grimly** *adv* con severità.

grimace [gri'meis] *n* smorfia *f*. *v* fare smorfie.

grime [graim] *n* sudiciume *m*. **grimy** *adj* sudicio.

grin [grin] *v* fare un largo sorriso. *n* largo sorriso *m*.

*****grind** [graind] *v* (*pulverize*) macinare; (*sharpen*) affilare; (*teeth*) digrignare. *n* (*coll: hard work*) sgobbata *f*.

grip [grip] *v* stringere; (*hold interest*) avvincere; (*take firm hold*) far presa. *n* presa *f*, stretta *f*; (*control*) padronanza *f*. **come to grips with** venire alle prese con.

gripe [graip] *n* colica *f*. *v* (*coll*) lagnarsi.

grisly ['grizli] *adj* orribile, macabro.

gristle ['grisl] *n* cartilagine *f*. **gristly** *adj* cartilaginoso.

grit [grit] *n* (*sand*) sabbia *f*; (*mech*) graniglia *f*; (*coll: courage*) fegato *m*. *v* (*teeth*) digrignare. **gritty** *adj* sabbioso.

groan [groun] *n* gemito *m*, lamento *m*. *v* gemere, lamentarsi.

grocer ['grousə] *n* droghiere, -a *m, f*. **grocer's** *n* (*shop*) drogheria *f*. **groceries** *pl n* generi coloniali *m pl*.

groin [groin] *n* inguine *m*.

groom [gruːm] *n* stalliere *m*; (*bridegroom*) sposo *m*. *v* preparare; (*horse*) strigliare.

groove [gruːv] *n* solco *m*. *v* scanalare.

grope [group] *v* brancolare. **grope for** cercare a tentoni, brancolare in cerca di.

gross [grous] *adj* grossolano, volgare; (*not net*) lordo. *v* (*income*) avere un introito lordo di. *n* grossa *f*.

grotesque [grə'tesk] *adj* fantastico; (*incongruous*) grottesco.

grotto ['grotou] *n* grotta *f*.

ground¹ [graund] *V* **grind**.

ground² [graund] *n* (*soil*) terreno *m*;

(*earth*, *floor*) terra *f*; (*sport*) campo *m*; (*reason*) motivo *m*; (*bottom*) fondo *m*. **ground floor** pianterreno *m*. **grounds** *pl n* (*sediment*) deposito *m sing*; (*dregs*) fondi *m pl*. *v* (*base*) fondare; (*teach*) insegnare i primi elementi; (*aircraft*) impedire di volare. **grounding** *n* base *f*. **groundless** *adj* infondato.

group [gruːp] *n* gruppo *m*. *v* raggruppare, disporre.

grouse¹ [graus] *n* (*bird*) urogallo *m*.

grouse² [graus] (*coll*) *v* brontolare, lamentarsi. *n* lagnanza *f*.

grove [grouv] *n* boschetto *m*.

grovel ['grovl] *v* umiliarsi; (*cringe*) striciare.

*****grow** [grou] *v* crescere; (*thrive*) prosperare; (*become*) diventare. **grown-up** *n, adj* adulto, -a. **grow on** piacere sempre più. **grow up** crescere, sorgere. **grower** *n* coltivatore, -trice *m, f*. **growth** *n* crescita *f*, progresso *m*; (*med*) escrescenza *f*, tumore *m*.

growl [graul] *v* ringhiare; (*rumble*) brontolare. *n* ringhio *m*; brontolio *m*.

grown [groun] *V* **grow**.

grub [grʌb] *n* (*insect*) larva *f*, bruco *m*; (*coll*) roba da mangiare *f*. *v* ripulire; (*uproot*) sradicare.

grubby ['grʌbi] *adj* (*dirty*) sudicio; (*contemptible*) abietto.

grudge [grʌdʒ] *n* rancore *m*. **bear a grudge against** nutrire rancore verso. *v* (*give reluctantly*) dare malvolentieri; (*resent*) invidiare. **grudgingly** *adv* malvolentieri.

gruelling ['gruəliŋ] *adj* faticoso.

gruesome ['gruːsəm] *adj* raccapricciante.

gruff [grʌf] *adj* (*surly*) burbero; (*hoarse*) rauco; (*harsh*) aspro.

grumble ['grʌmbl] *v* (*complain*) lagnarsi; (*growl*) brontolare. *n* lagnanza *f*, brontolio *m*.

grumpy ['grʌmpi] *adj* scontroso.

grunt [grʌnt] *v* grugnire. *n* grugnito *m*.

guarantee [garən'tiː] *v* garantire, rispondere di. *n* garanzia *f*.

guard [gaɪd] *v* (*keep safe*) custodire; (*watch over*) sorvegliare; (*keep watch*) stare in guardia. **guard against** badare a. *n* guardia *m, f*; (*appliance*) protezione *f*; (*railway*) capotreno *m*. **guarded** *adj* cauto. **guardian** *n* custode *m*; (*legal*) tutore *m*.

guerrilla [gə'rilə] *n* guerrigliero *m*. **guerrilla warfare** guerriglia *f*.
guess [ges] *n* congettura *f*, supposizione *f*. **at a rough guess** a occhio e croce. *v* indovinare.
guest [gest] *n* ospite *m*, *f*; (*of hotel*) cliente *m*, *f*. **guest-house** *n* pensione *f*.
guide [gaid] *n* guida *f*; (*of tourists*) cicerone *m*. **guidebook** *n* guida *f*. *v* guidare; (*advise*) consigliare; (*direct*) dirigere. **be guided by** seguire il consiglio di. **guidance** *n* (*leadership*) guida *f*; (*instruction*) norma *f*.
guild [gild] *n* corporazione *f*.
guile [gail] *n* astuzia *f*. **guileless** *adj* ingenuo.
guillotine ['gilətiːn] *n* ghigliottina *f*.
guilt [gilt] *n* colpa *f*. **guiltless** *adj* innocente. **guilty** *adj* colpevole. **have a guilty conscience** avere la coscienza sporca *or* cattiva.
guinea-pig ['ginipig] *n* cavia *f*.
guitar [gi'taɪ] *n* chitarra *f*. **guitarist** *n* chitarrista *m*, *f*.
gulf [gʌlf] *n* (*geog*) golfo *m*; (*wide separation*) abisso *m*.
gull [gʌl] *n* gabbiano *m*.
gullet ['gʌlit] *n* (*throat*) gola *f*; (*oesophagus*) esofago *m*.
gullible ['gʌləbl] *adj* credulo. **gullibility** *n* credulità *f*.
gully ['gʌli] *n* (*canyon*) burrone *m*; (*ditch*) cunetta *f*.
gulp [gʌlp] *n* (*food*) boccone *m*; (*drink*) sorso *m*. *v* (*food*) ingoiare; (*drink*) tracannare; (*choke*) soffocare.
gum[1] [gʌm] *n* (*secretion*) gomma *f*; (*glue*) colla *f*. *v* ingommare; incollare.
gum[2] [gʌm] *n* (*mouth*) gengiva *f*.
gun [gʌn] *n* fucile *m*; cannone *m*. **gunfire** *n* sparatoria *f*. **gunman** *n* bandito armato *m*. **gunner** *n* artigliere *m*. **gunpowder** *n* polvere da sparo *f*. **gunshot** *n* colpo di fucile *m*.
gurgle ['gəːgl] *v* gorgogliare. *n* gorgoglio *m*.
gush [gʌʃ] *n* sgorgo *m*; (*language*) torrente *m*. *v* (*liquid*) scaturire; (*speech*) parlare con effusione.
gust [gʌst] *n* raffica *f*.
gusto ['gʌstou] *n* fervore *m*.
gut [gʌt] *n* budello *m* (*pl* -a *f*). **guts** *pl n* (*coll*) fegato *m sing*. *v* sbudellare.
gutter ['gʌtə] *n* (*house*) grondaia *f*; (*street*) cunetta *f*; (*conduit*) condotto *m*. **guttersnipe** *n* scugnizzo *m*.
guy[1] [gai] *n* tipo *m*, individuo *m*.
guy[2] [gai] *n* (*rope*) tirante *m*.
gymnasium [dʒim'neiziəm] *n* palestra *f*. **gymnast** *n* ginnasta *m*, *f*. **gymnastics** *n* ginnastica *f*.
gynaecology [gainə'kolədʒi] *n* ginecologia *f*. **gynaecological** *adj* ginecologico. **gynaecologist** *n* ginecologo, -a *m*, *f*.
gypsum ['dʒipsəm] *n* gesso *m*.
gyrate [ˌdʒai'reit] *v* girare, roteare.
gyroscope ['dʒairəˌskoup] *n* giroscopio *m*.

H

haberdasher ['habədaʃə] *n* merciaio, -a *m*, *f*. **haberdashery** *n* merceria *f*.
habit ['habit] *n* abitudine *f*; (*dress*) tonaca *f*. **habitual** *adj* abituale. **habitually** *adv* di solito.
habitable ['habitəbl] *adj* abitabile.
habitat ['habitat] *n* ambiente *m*.
hack[1] [hak] *v* tagliare, troncare. **hacksaw** *n* seghetto *m*.
hack[2] [hak] *n* (*horse*) ronzino *m*; (*writer*) scribacchino *m*.
hackneyed ['haknid] *adj* trito, comune.
had [had] *V* **have**.
haddock ['hadək] *n* eglefino *m*.
haemorrhage ['heməridʒ] *n* emorragia *f*.
haemorrhoids ['heməroidz] *pl n* emorroidi *f pl*.
hag [hag] *n* vecchiaccia *f*, strega *f*.
haggard ['hagəd] *adj* smunto, scarno.
haggle ['hagl] *v* mercanteggiare.
Hague [heig] *n* l'Aia *f*.
hail[1] [heil] *n* grandine *f*. **hailstone** *n* chicco di grandine *m*. *v* grandinare.
hail[2] [heil] *v* salutare; (*call*) chiamare. **hail from** essere oriundo di. *interj* salve! *n* saluto *m*.
hair [heə] *n* capelli *m pl*; (*single strand*) capello *m*; (*of animals*) pelo *m*. **split hairs** cercare il pelo nell'uovo. **hairy** *adj* capelluto; peloso.
hairbrush ['heəbrʌʃ] *n* spazzola per capelli *f*.
haircut ['heəkʌt] *n* taglio dei capelli *m*. **have a haircut** farsi tagliare i capelli.
hairdresser ['heəˌdresə] *n* parrucchiere, -a *m*, *f*.

hair-dryer ['heə,draiə] *n* asciugacapelli *m invar*.

hairpin ['heəpin] *n* forcina *f*.

hair-raising ['heə,reizin] *adj* raccapricciante.

hake [heik] *n* nasello *m*.

half [haɪf] *adj* mezzo. *n* mezzo *m*, metà *f*; (*sport: period*) tempo *m*. **in half** in due.

half-and-half *adj*, *adv* metà e metà.

half-back ['haɪfbak] *n* mediano *m*.

half-baked [,haɪf'beikt] *adj* (*coll*) inesperto, immaturo.

half-breed ['haɪfbriɪd] *nm*, *adj* ibrido.

half-brother ['haɪfbrʌðə] *n* fratellastro *m*.

half-hearted [,haɪf'haɪtid] *adj* esitante, poco entusiasta.

half-hour [,haɪf'auə] *n* mezz'ora *f*.

half-mast [,haɪf'maɪst] *n* **at half-mast** a mezz'asta.

half-moon [,haɪf'muɪn] *n* mezzaluna *f*.

half-sister ['haɪfsistə] *n* sorellastra *f*.

half-time [,haɪf'taim] *n* intervallo *m*.

half-tone ['haɪftoun] *n* mezzatinta *f*, fotoriproduzione *f*.

halfway [,haɪf'wei] *adj*, *adv* a metà strada. **meet halfway** giungere a un compromesso.

half-witted [,haɪf'witid] *adj* scemo, deficiente.

halibut ['halibət] *n* halibut *m invar*, ippoglosso *m*.

hall [hoɪl] *n* (*entrance*) entrata *f*; (*room*) sala *f*, salone *m*; (*building*) villa *f*, casa signorile *f*.

hallmark ['hoɪlmaɪk] *n* marchio d'autenticità *m*; elemento caratteristico *m*. *v* marcare.

hallowed ['haloud] *adj* venerato.

hallucination [hə,luɪsi'neiʃən] *n* allucinazione *f*.

halo ['heilou] *n* aureola *f*; (*astron*) alone *m*.

halt [hoɪlt] *n* fermata *f*; (*temporary*) sosta *f*. *v* sostare, fermare, fermarsi. *interj* alt!

halter ['hoɪltə] *n* capestro *m*; cavezza *f*.

halve [haɪv] *v* dimezzare, ridurre della *or* alla metà.

ham [ham] *n* prosciutto *m*.

hamburger ['hambəɪgə] *n* hamburger *m invar*.

hammer ['hamə] *n* martello *m*. *v* martellare.

hammock ['hamək] *n* amaca *f*.

hamper¹ ['hampə] *v* intralciare, ostacolare.

hamper² ['hampə] *n* paniere *m*.

hamster ['hamstə] *n* criceto *m*.

hand [hand] *n* mano (*pl* -i) *f*; (*clock*) lancetta *f*; (*worker*) operaio, -a *m*, *f*. **at hand** a portata di mano. **by hand** a mano. **hands down** completamente, con facilità. **hands off!** via le mani! **hands up!** alto le mani! **in hand** (*under control*) sotto controllo; (*available*) a disposizione; (*being dealt with*) in corso. **on hand** presente; (*available*) disponibile. **on the other hand** d'altra parte. *v* (*give*) dare, porgere. **hand down** trasmettere, tramandare. **hand in** *or* **over** consegnare. **hand out** distribuire. **handful** *n* manata *f*; piccolo gruppo *m*.

handbag ['handbag] *n* borsetta *f*.

handbill ['handbil] *n* volantino *m*.

handbook ['handbuk] *n* manuale *m*.

handbrake ['handbreik] *n* freno a mano *m*.

handcuff ['handkʌf] *n* manetta *f*. *v* ammanettare.

handicap ['handikap] *n* svantaggio *m*, impedimento *m*; (*sport*) handicap *m invar*. *v* impedire.

handicraft ['handikraɪft] *n* artigianato *m*; (*trade*) mestiere *m*.

handiwork ['handiwəɪk] *n* (*personal work*) opera *f*.

handkerchief ['hankətʃif] *n* fazzoletto *m*.

handle ['handl] *n* manico *m*; (*door*) maniglia *f*; (*crank*) manovella *f*. *v* (*manipulate*) maneggiare; (*deal with*) trattare. **handlebar** *n* manubrio *m*.

handmade [,hand'meid] *adj* fatto a mano.

hand-out ['handaut] *n* comunicato *m*, campione pubblicitario *m*.

hand-pick [hand'pik] *v* scegliere a mano.

handrail ['handreil] *n* ringhiera *f*.

handshake ['handʃeik] *n* stretta di mano *f*.

handsome ['hansəm] *adj* bello; generoso, considerevole.

handstand ['hand,stand] *n* posata verticale sulle mani *f*.

hand-towel ['hand,tauəl] *n* asciugamano *m*.

handwriting ['hand,raitin] *n* calligrafia *f*.

handy ['handi] *adj* (*accessible*) a portata di mano; (*deft*) destro, abile; (*convenient*) comodo.

*hang [han] *v* pendere, appendere, sospendere; (*execute*) impiccare. **hang around** bazzicare. **hanger** *n* (*clothes*) attaccapanni *m invar*. **hanger-on** *n* scroccone *m*. **hangman** *n* boia *m invar*. **hang on** persistere, indugiare; (*phone*) restare in linea. **hangover** *n* postumi di una sbornia *m pl*.

hangar ['haŋə] *n* hangar *m invar*; aviorimessa *f*.

hanker ['haŋkə] *v* **hanker after** bramare. **hankering** *n* forte desiderio *m*, brama *f*.

haphazard [ˌhap'hazəd] *adj* casuale.

happen ['hapən] *v* (*take place*) accadere, succedere. **as it happens** per caso. **happening** *n* avvenimento *m*.

happy ['hapi:] *adj* felice, contento, lieto; (*in greetings*) buono. **happy-go-lucky** *adj* spensierato. **happiness** *n* felicità *f*, contentezza *f*.

harass ['harəs] *v* molestare, tormentare, irritare. **harassment** *n* tormento *m*, molestia *f*.

harbour ['haɪbə] *n* porto *m*. *v* (*shelter*) dare asilo a.

hard [haɪd] *adj* duro; difficile; severo. *adv* molto; (*solidly*) sodo. **hard and fast** immutabile. **hard-boiled** *adj* (*egg*) sodo; (*person*) duro. **hard core** nucleo *m*. **hard-headed** *adj* accorto, pratico. **hard-hearted** *adj* insensibile. **hard up** al corto di quattrini. **hardware** *n* ferramenta *f pl*; (*computer*) meccanismo *m*. **hard-wearing** *adj* duraturo, durevole. **hard work** lavoro faticoso *m*. **try hard** provare assiduamente. **work hard** lavorar sodo. **hardness** *n* durezza *f*. **hardship** *n* privazione *f*.

hardly ['haɪdli] *adv* (*not quite*) non esattamente; (*barely, almost not*) quasi, appena; (*with difficulty*) a stento.

hardy ['haɪdi] *adj* robusto, resistente; (*courageous*) coraggioso.

hare [heə] lepre *f*. **hare-brained** *adj* scervellato.

harm [haɪm] *n* male *m*, danno *m*. *v* nuocere a, far male a. **harmful** *adj* nocivo, dannoso. **harmless** *adj* innocuo, inoffensivo.

harmony ['haɪməni] *n* armonia *f*, accordo *m*. **harmonic** *adj* armonico, armonioso. **harmonize** *v* armonizzare.

harness ['haɪnis] *n* briglia *f*. *v* imbrigliare.

harp [haɪp] *n* arpa *f*. **harpist** *n* arpista *m*, *f*.

harpoon [haɪ'puɪn] *n* rampone *m*. *v* ramponare.

harpsichord [ˌhaɪpsiˌkɔɪd] *n* clavicembalo *m*.

harrowing ['harouiŋ] *adj* straziante.

harsh [haɪʃ] *adj* aspro, duro. **harshness** *n* asprezza *f*, durezza *f*.

harvest ['haɪvist] *n* raccolto *m*. *v* raccogliere, mietere.

has [haz] *V* **have**.

hash [haʃ] *n* carne tritata *f*; (*coll: mess*) confusione *f*, pasticcio *m*. **make a hash of** sciupare, mandare a rotoli.

hashish ['haʃiːʃ] *n* (h)ascisc *m invar*.

haste [heist] *n* fretta *f*. **hasten** *v* precipitare, affrettarsi. **hasty** *adj* frettoloso.

hat [hat] *n* cappello *m*.

hatch[1] [hatʃ] *v* (*bring forth*) covare; (*contrive*) tramare.

hatch[2] [hatʃ] *n* (*naut*) boccaporto *m*; (*opening*) portello *m*, sportello *m*.

hatchet ['hatʃit] *n* accetta *f*.

hate [heit] *v* odiare. *n also* **hatred** odio *m*. **hateful** *adj* odioso.

haughty ['hɔɪti] *adj* altezzoso, arrogante.

haul [hɔɪl] *n* tiro *m*; (*fish*) retata *f*; (*coll: booty*) bottino *m*. *v* tirare.

haunch [hɔɪntʃ] *n* anca *f*.

haunt [hɔɪnt] *v* perseguitare, ossessionare. *n* ritrovo *m*. **haunting** *adj* ossessionante.

*have [hav] *v* avere. **have to** avere da, dovere. **have it in for** avercela con. **have on** (*wear*) portare; (*have planned*) aver intenzione di fare, aver da fare; (*coll: tease*) prendere in giro.

haven ['heivn] *n* (*harbour*) porto *m*; (*shelter*) rifugio *m*.

haversack ['havəsak] *n* bisaccia *f*.

havoc ['havək] *n* **play havoc with** rovinare, far strage di.

hawk[1] [hɔɪk] *n* falco *m*, falcone *m*.

hawk[2] [hɔɪk] *v* spacciare; fare il venditore ambulante.

hawthorn ['hɔɪθɔɪn] *n* biancospino *m*.

hay [hei] *n* fieno *m*. **go haywire** perdere le staffe. **hay fever** raffreddore del fieno *m*. **haystack** *n* fienile *m*.

hazard ['hazəd] *n* (*danger*) pericolo *m*; (*risk*) rischio *m*. *v* azzardare. **hazardous** *adj* pericoloso, rischioso.

haze [heiz] *n* foschia *f*. **hazy** *adj* nebuloso, indistinto.

hazel ['heizl] *n* (*tree*) nocciolo *m*. **hazelnut** *n* nocciola *f*. *adj* color nocciola *invar*.

he [hiɪ] *pron* egli, lui. **he who** colui che.

head [hed] *n* testa *f*; (*leader*) capo *m*. *v* (*lead*) essere a capo di; (*direct*) dirigere.

headache ['hedeik] *n* mal di testa *m*; (*coll*) preoccupazione *f*.

headdress ['heddres] *n* copricapo *m*.

heading *n* (*title*) intestazione *f*; (*topic*) voce *f*.

headlamp ['hedlamp] *n also* **headlight** (*mot*) faro *m*, fanale *m*.

headland ['hedlənd] *n* promontorio *m*.

headline ['hedlain] *n* titolo *m*. **headlines** *pl n* (*news*) sommario *m sing*.

headlong ['hedloŋ] *adv* a capofitto.

headmaster [‚hed'maistə] *n* preside *m*.

headphones ['hedfounz] *pl n* cuffia *f sing*.

headquarters [‚hed'kwoitəz] *n* (*mil*) quartiere generale *m*; (*office*) sede *f*, direzione *f*.

headrest ['hedrest] *n* appoggiatesta *m invar*.

headscarf ['hedskaif] *n* foulard *m invar*.

headstrong ['hedstroŋ] *adj* testardo, cocciuto.

headway ['hedwei] *n* progresso *m*. **make headway** fare strada.

heady ['hedi] *adj* impetuoso; (*intoxicating*) che dà alla testa.

heal [hiil] *v* guarire, sanare.

health [helθ] *n* salute *f*. **healthy** *adj* (*person*) sano; (*climate, etc.*) salubre.

heap [hiip] *n* mucchio *m*. *v* ammucchiare.

***hear** [hiə] *v* udire, sentire; (*be informed of*) venire a sapere. **hear about** aver notizie di. **hear from** aver notizie da. **hearing** *n* udito *m*; (*audience*) udienza *f*. **hearsay** *n* voce *f*.

heard [həid] *V* **hear**.

hearse [həis] *n* carro funebre *m*.

heart [hait] *n* cuore *m*; (*feeling*) animo *m*; (*essential part*) parte centrale *f*, centro *m*. **by heart** a memoria. **hearts** *pl n* (*cards*) cuori *m pl*. **take to heart** prendersi a cuore.

heart attack *n* attacco cardiaco *m*.

heartbeat ['haitbiit] *n* battito del cuore *m*.

heart-breaking ['haitbreikiŋ] *adj* straziante. **heart-broken** *adj* accorato, affranto.

heartburn ['haitbəin] *n* bruciore di stomaco *m*.

heartening ['haitniŋ] *adj* incoraggiante.

heartfelt ['haitfelt] *adj* sincero.

hearth [haiθ] *n* focolare *m*.

heartless ['haitləs] *adj* spietato, insensibile.

hearty ['haiti] *adj* (*warm-hearted*) caloroso; sincero; vigoroso.

heat [hiit] *n* calore *m*, caldo *m*; (*sport*) batteria *f*; (*oestrum*) estro *m*. **heat wave** calura *f*. *v* scaldare, riscaldare. **heated** *adj* animato. **heater** *n* riscaldatore *m*; stufa elettrica *f*. **heating** *n* riscaldamento *m*.

heath [hiiθ] *n* brughiera *f*.

heathen ['hiiðn] *n, adj* pagano, -a.

heather ['heðə] *n* erica *f*.

heave [hiiv] *v* sollevare; (*retch*) avere i conati di vomito. **heave a sigh** tirare un sospiro. *n* sollevamento *m*.

heaven ['hevn] *n* cielo *m*, paradiso *m*. **for heaven's sake!** per l'amor del cielo! **good heavens!** santo cielo! **heavenly** *adj* divino, delizioso.

heavy ['hevi] *adj* pesante, forte. **heavyweight** *n* peso massimo *m*.

Hebrew ['hiibrui] *n* (*language*) ebraico *m*; (*person*) ebreo, -a *m, f*. *adj* ebraico; ebreo.

heckle ['hekl] *v* interrompere con domande imbarazzanti.

hectare ['hektai] *n* ettaro *m*.

hectic ['hektik] *adj* febbrile.

hedge [hedʒ] *n* siepe *f*; (*bet*) copertura *f*. *v* (*bet*) coprire dai rischi. **as a hedge against** per mettersi al riparo contro.

hedgehog ['hedʒhog] *n* riccio *m*.

heed [hiid] *v* badare a, dar retta a. **heedless** *adj* noncurante.

heel [hiil] *n* (*anat*) calcagno *m*; (*shoe*) tacco *m*. **Achilles' heel** tallone d'Achille *m*.

hefty ['hefti] *adj* robusto.

heifer ['hefə] *n* giovenca *f*.

height [hait] *n* altezza *f*; (*hill*) collina *f*; (*highest degree*) colmo *m*; (*highest point*) culmine *m*. **heighten** *v* intensificare.

heir [eə] *n* erede *m, f*.

held [held] *V* **hold**[1].

helicopter ['helikoptə] *n* elicottero *m*.

hell [hel] *n* inferno *m*. **hellish** *adj* infernale.

hello [hə'lou] *interj* (*on meeting*) ciao! (*phone*) pronto!

helm [helm] *n* timone *m*.

helmet ['helmit] *n* elmo *m*, elmetto *m*; (*motorcyclist, airman*) casco *m*.

help [help] *n* aiuto *m*, assistenza *f*; (*remedy*) rimedio *m*. *v* aiutare, assistere. **helpful** *adj* utile, vantaggioso. **helping** *n* porzione *f*. **helpless** *adj* impotente, indifeso.

hem [hem] *n* orlo *m*. *v* orlare. **hem in** rinchiudere, accerchiare.

hemisphere ['hemi‚sfiə] *n* emisfera *f*.

hemp [hemp] *n* canapa *f*.

hen [hen] *n* gallina *f*.

hence [hens] *adv* quindi.

henna ['henə] *n* tintura di henna *f*.

her [hɜɪ] *pron* (*direct object*) la; (*indirect object*) le; (*after prep*) lei. *adj* (il) suo, (la) sua; (*pl*) (i) suoi, (le) sue.

herald ['herəld] *n* araldo *m*, messaggero *m*.

heraldry ['herəldri] *n* araldica *f*.

herbs [hɜɪbz] *pl n* erbe aromatiche *f pl*.

herd [hɜɪd] *n* gregge *m*, mandria *f*; (*people*) massa *f*. **herd together** raggruppare, radunare.

here [hiə] *adv* qui, qua; (*emphasizing*) ecco. **here I am!** eccomi qua!

hereabouts ['hiərəˌbauts] *adv* qui vicino.

hereafter [ˌhiərˈaɪftə] *adv* d'ora innanzi, in futuro. *n* **the hereafter** l'al di là *m*.

hereby [ˌhiəˈbai] *adv* così, con questo.

hereditary [hiˈreditri] *adj* ereditario.

heredity [hiˈredəti] *n* eredità *f*.

heresy ['herəsi] *n* eresia *f*. **heretic** *n* eretico, -a *m*, *f*. **heretical** *adj* eretico.

herewith [ˌhiəˈwið] *adv* con questo; (*correspondence*) con la presente.

heritage ['heritidʒ] *n* patrimonio *m*.

hermit ['hɜɪmit] *n* eremita *m*.

hernia ['hɜɪniə] *n* ernia *f*.

hero ['hiərou] *n* eroe *m*; (*principal character*) protagonista *m*. **heroic** *adj* eroico. **heroine** *n* eroina *f*; protagonista *f*.

heroin ['herouin] *n* eroina *f*.

heron ['herən] *n* airone *m*.

herring ['heriŋ] *n* aringa *f*. **herring-bone** *adj* a lisca di pesce.

hers [hɜɪz] *pron* il suo, la sua; (*pl*) i suoi, le sue.

herself [hɜɪˈself] *pron* lei stessa; (*after prep*) sè (stessa); (*reflexive*) si; (*emphatic*) proprio lei.

hesitate ['heziteit] *v* esitare. **hesitant** *adj* esitante. **hesitation** *n* esitazione *f*. **without hesitation** decisamente.

heterogeneous [hetərəˈdʒiːniəs] *adj* eterogeneo.

heterosexual [hetərəˈsekʃuəl] *adj* eterosessuale.

hexagon ['heksəgən] *n* esagono *m*. **hexagonal** *adj* esagonale.

heyday ['heidei] *n* (*prime*) fiore *m*; più bel periodo *m*; (*splendour*) fulgore *m*.

hiatus [haiˈeitəs] *n* interruzione *f*; (*med*) iato *m*.

hibernate ['haibəneit] *v* svernare; (*of animals*) ibernare.

hiccup ['hikʌp] *n* singhiozzo *m*. *v* singhiozzare. **have hiccups** avere il singhiozzo.

hid [hid] *V* **hide**[1].

hidden ['hidn] *V* **hide**[1].

***hide**[1] [haid] *v* nascondere, nascondersi. **hide-out** *n* nascondiglio *m*.

hide[2] [haid] *n* (*raw*) pelle *f*; (*dressed*) cuoio *m*. **hidebound** *adj* gretto, di mentalità ristretta.

hideous ['hidiəs] *adj* orrendo, ripugnante.

hiding[1] ['haidiŋ] *n* **be in hiding** essere *or* tenersi nascosto. **go into hiding** nascondersi, darsi alla macchia.

hiding[2] ['haidiŋ] *n* (*beating*) batosta *f*.

hierarchy ['haiəraɪki] *n* gerarchia *f*.

high [hai] *adj* alto, elevato; (*of meat*) andato a male. **it's high time** è ora. **leave high and dry** piantare in asso. *adv* in alto. *n* culmine *f*; (*weather*) anticiclone *m*. **highness** *n* altezza *f*.

highbrow ['haibrau] *n*(*m+f*), *adj* intellettuale.

high chair *n* seggiolina *f*.

high-fidelity *adj* ad alta fedeltà.

high frequency *adj* ad alta frequenza.

high jump *n* salto in alto *m*.

highlight ['hailait] *v* mettere in rilievo. *n* clou *m invar*, culmine *m*.

high-pitched [ˌhaiˈpitʃd] *adj* acuto.

high point *n* culmine *m*.

high-powered *adj* potente, dinamico.

high pressure *n* alta pressione *f*. **high-pressure** *adj* ad alta pressione; (*coll*) aggressivo.

high-rise block *adj* a molti piani.

high-spirited [ˌhaiˈspiritid] *adj* vivace. **high spirits** *pl n* buonumore *m sing*.

high street *n* corso *m*.

highway ['haiwei] *n* strada maestra *f*. **highway code** codice della strada *m*.

hijack ['haidʒak] *v* (*goods*) rubare in transito; (*aero*) dirottare. **hijacker** *n* dirottatore *m*, pirata dell'aria *m*. **hijacking** *n* dirottamento *m*.

hike [haik] *n* gita a piedi *f*. *v* fare una gita *or* escursione a piedi.

hilarious [hiˈleəriəs] *adj* divertente, allegro.

hill [hil] *n* colle *m*, collina *f*; (*slope*) salita *f*.

him [him] *pron* (*direct object*) lo; (*indirect object*) gli; (*after prep*) lui.

himself [him'self] *pron* lui stesso; *(after prep)* sè (stesso); *(reflexive)* si; *(emphatic)* proprio lui.

hinder ['hində] *v* *(make difficult)* intralciare; *(make impossible)* impedire.

Hindu [hin'duɪ] *n(m+f)*, *adj* indù *invar*. **Hinduism** *n* induismo *m*.

hinge [hindʒ] *n* cardine *m*, perno *m*. *v* *(depend)* dipendere (da).

hint [hint] *n* cenno *m*, allusione *f*; *(clue)* suggerimento *m*; *(slight amount)* traccia *f*. *v* far capire, accennare, alludere.

hip [hip] *n* fianco *m*, anca *f*.

hippopotamus [hipə'potəməs] *n* ippopotamo *m*.

hire [haiə] *v* prendere a nolo, noleggiare. **hire out** dare a nolo, noleggiare. *n* nolo *m*, noleggio *m*. **hire purchase** vendita a rate *f*.

his [hiz] *adj* (il) suo, (la) sua; *(pl)* (i) suoi, (le) sue. *pron* il suo, la sua; *(pl)* i suoi, le sue.

hiss [his] *v* sibilare. *n* sibilo *m*. **hissing** *adj* sibilante.

history ['histəri] *n* storia *f*; *(past)* passato *m*. **historian** *n* storico *m*. **historic** *adj* storico; memorabile.

*****hit** [hit] *n* colpo *m*, botta *f*; successo *m*. *v* colpire, battere. **hit on** scoprire. **hit-or-miss** *adv* alla buona.

hitch [hitʃ] *v* attaccare. **hitch-hike** *v* fare l'autostop. **hitch up** tirar su. *n* *(obstacle)* intoppo *m*; *(knot)* nodo *m*.

hitherto [ˌhiðə'tuɪ] *adv* finora.

hive [haiv] *n* alveare *m*.

hoard [hoɪd] *n* scorta *f*, mucchio *m*. *v* ammucchiare.

hoarding ['hoɪdiŋ] *n* *(billboard)* tabellone *m*.

hoarse [hoɪs] *adj* rauco. **hoarseness** *n* raucedine *f*.

hoax [houks] *n* beffa *f*.

hobble ['hobl] *v* zoppicare.

hobby ['hobi] *n* passatempo *m*, hobby *m* *invar*.

hock¹ [hok] *n* *(joint)* garretto *m*.

hock² [hok] *n* *(wine)* vino bianco del Reno *m*.

hockey ['hoki] *n* hockey *m* *invar*.

hoe [hou] *n* zappa *f*. *v* zappare.

hog [hog] *n* maiale *m*, porco *m*. *v* *(coll)* monopolizzare.

hoist [hoist] *n* montacarichi *m* *invar*. *v* sollevare.

*****hold¹** [hould] *n* presa *f*, stretta *f*; *(dominating influence)* ascendente *m*. **get hold of** *(grasp)* afferrare; *(obtain)* ottenere. *v* tenere; contenere; esser valido. **hold back** trattenere. **hold out** resistere. **hold up** *(delay)* ostacolare; *(stop by force)* fermare per derubare; *(exhibit)* esibire. **hold-up** *n* intoppo *m*; *(robbery)* rapina a mano armata *f*. **holder** *n* supporto *m*; detentore *m*. **holding** *n* *(land)* tenuta *f*; *(shares)* pacchetto (di azioni) *m*.

hold² [hould] *n* *(naut)* stiva *f*.

hole [houl] *n* buco *m*; *(in the ground)* buca *f*; *(burrow)* tana *f*; *(predicament)* guaio *m*.

holiday ['holədi] *n* *(day)* giorno festivo *m*, festa *f*; *(period)* vacanza *f*. **go on holiday** andare in vacanza *or* villeggiatura. **holiday-maker** *n* villeggiante *m*, *f*.

Holland ['holənd] *n* Olanda *f*.

hollow ['holou] *adj* cavo; concavo; *(not solid)* vuoto; *(of sound)* cupo; falso. *n* buca *f*, cavità *f*; *(anat)* cavo *m*.

holly ['holi] *n* agrifoglio *m*.

holster ['houlstə] *n* fondina *f*.

holy ['houli] *adj* santo, sacro.

homage ['homidʒ] *n* omaggio *m*. **pay homage to** rendere omaggio a.

home [houm] *n* *(house)* casa *f*, domicilio *m*; *(land)* patria *f*; *(institution)* ricovero *m*, rifugio *m*; *(habitat)* ambiente naturale *m*. **at home** a casa. **feel at home** sentirsi a proprio agio. **leave home** lasciare la casa paterna. *adj* domestico, casalingo. *adv* a casa; in patria; *(all the way)* a fondo. **strike home** colpire nel vivo.

homecoming ['houmˌkʌmiŋ] *n* ritorno in casa *or* patria *m*.

home-grown [houm'groun] *adj* nostrano.

homeless ['houmləs] *adj* senza tetto.

homely ['houmli] *adj* semplice, senza pretese; *(unattractive)* brutto.

home-made [ˌhoum'meid] *adj* fatto in casa.

homesick ['houmsik] *adj* nostalgico.

homework ['houmwɜɪk] *n* compiti di casa *m pl*.

homicide ['homisaid] *n* *(crime)* omicidio *m*; *(murderer)* omicida *m*, *f*. **homicidal** *adj* micidiale.

homogeneous [homə'dʒiɪniəs] *adj* omogeneo.

homosexual [homə'sekʃuəl] *n(m+f)*, *adj* omosessuale.

honest ['onist] *adj* onesto. **honestly!** *interj* davvero! **honesty** *n* onestà *f*.
honey ['hʌni] *n* miele *m*. **honeycomb** *n* favo *m*. **honeymoon** *n* luna di miele *f*.
honeysuckle ['hʌnisʌkl] *n* caprifoglio *m*.
honour ['onə] *n* onore *m*; (*respect*) stima *f*. *v* onorare; (*comm*) far onore a. **honours** *pl n* (*titles*) onorificenza *f sing*. **honorary** *adj* onorario. **honourable** *adj* onorevole, stimato, probo.
hood [hud] *n* cappuccio *m*; (*mot*) cappotta *f*.
hoof [huːf] *n* zoccolo *m*.
hook [huk] *n* gancio *m*; (*fishing*) amo *m*. *v* agganciare.
hooligan ['huːligən] *n* teppista *m*.
hoop [huːp] *n* cerchio *m*.
hoot [huːt] *v* (*car*) suonare il clacson; (*shriek*) stridere; (*hiss*) fischiare. **hooter** *n* sirena *f*; (*car*) clacson *m invar*.
hop¹ [hop] *v* salterellare. *n* salterello *m*.
hop² [hop] *n* (*bot*) luppolo *m*.
hope [houp] *n* speranza *f*. *v* sperare. **hopeful** *adj* pieno di speranza, fiducioso; (*promising*) promettente. **hopeless** *adj* senza speranza, disperato; (*not resolvable*) irrimediabile.
horde [hoːd] *n* banda *f*.
horizon [hə'raizn] *n* orizzonte *m*. **horizontal** *adj* orizzontale.
hormone ['hoːmoun] *n* ormone *m*.
horn [hoːn] *n* corno (*pl* -a) *m*; (*mot*) clacson *m invar*.
hornet ['hoːnit] *n* calabrone *m*.
horoscope ['horəskoup] *n* oroscopo *m*.
horrible ['horibl] *adj also* **horrid** orribile, orrendo.
horrify ['horifai] *v* inorridire, raccapricciare. **horrifying** *adj* raccapricciante.
horror ['horə] *n* orrore *m*, spavento *m*.
hors d'oeuvre [oː'dəːvr] *n* antipasto *m*.
horse [hoːs] *n* cavallo *m*.
horseback ['hoːsbak] *n* **on horseback** a cavallo.
horse-chestnut *n* ippocastano *m*.
horse-fly *n* tafano *m*.
horseman ['hoːsmən] *n* cavaliere *m*.
horsepower ['hoːs,pauə] *n* cavallo vapore *m*.
horse-race *n* corsa ippica *f*.
horseradish ['hoːs,radiʃ] *n* cren *m invar*; (*plant*) barbaforte *m*.
horseshoe ['hoːʃʃuː] *n* ferro di cavallo *m*.
horsewoman ['hoːs,wumən] *n* cavallerizza *f*.

horticulture ['hoːtikʌltʃə] *n* orticultura *f*.
hose [houz] *n* (*stocking*) calza *f*, calzino *m*; (*pipe*) tubo flessibile *m*, manichetta *f*. *v* **hose (down)** dare una lavata a, annaffiare.
hosiery ['houziəri] *n* calzetteria *f*.
hospitable [ho'spitəbl] *adj* ospitale.
hospital ['hospitl] *n* ospedale *m*. **hospitalize** far ricoverare in ospedale.
hospitality [,hospi'taliti] *n* ospitalità *f*.
host¹ [houst] *n* oste *m*, ospite *m*. **hostess** *n* ospite *f*, ostessa *f*.
host² [houst] *n* moltitudine *f*, gran numero *m*.
host³ [houst] *n* (*rel*) ostia *f*.
hostage ['hostidʒ] *n* ostaggio *m*.
hostel ['hostəl] *n* ostello *m*, alloggio *m*.
hostile ['hostail] *adj* ostile. **hostility** *n* antagonismo *m*. **hostilities** *pl n* ostilità *f pl*.
hot [hot] *adj* caldo; ardente, impetuoso; (*pungent, peppery*) forte, piccante. **be hot** aver caldo. **hot-blooded** *adj* dal sangue caldo. **hot-headed** *adj* impetuoso. **hothouse** *n* serra *f*. **hotplate** *n* scaldavivande *m invar*; (*hob*) fornello *m*. **hot-tempered** *adj* irascibile.
hotel [hou'tel] *n* albergo *m*. **hotel-keeper** *n* albergatore, -trice *m*, *f*.
hound [haund] *n* bracco *m*.
hour ['auə] *n* ora *f*. **hours** *pl n* (*time spent*) orario *m sing*. **kilometres/miles per hour** chilometri/miglia all'ora.
hourly ['auəli] *adj* orario. *adv* (*every hour*) ogni ora; (*hour by hour*) d'ora in ora, continuamente.
house [haus; *v* hauz] *n* casa *f*; (*theatre attendance*) sala *f*; (*audience*) pubblico *m*; (*dynasty*) dinastia *f*, famiglia *f*; (*comm*) ditta *f*. *v* (*shelter*) alloggiare; (*put in safe place*) mettere al sicuro.
houseboat ['hausbout] *n* casa galleggiante *f*, houseboat *f invar*.
housebound ['hausbaund] *adj* costretto a stare a casa.
housebreaking ['haus,breikiŋ] *n* scasso *m*.
household ['haushould] *n* famiglia *f*, casa *f*. *adj* casalingo, domestico.
housekeeper ['haus,kiːpə] *n* massaia *f*, governante *f*. **housekeeping** *n* economia domestica *f*.
housemaid ['hausmeid] *n* domestica *f*, cameriera *f*.

house-to-house *adj* di porta in porta.
housewife ['hauswaif] *n* massaia *f*, casalinga *f*.
housework ['hauswɔɪk] *n* lavori di casa *m pl*.
housing ['hauziŋ] *n* alloggio *m*. **housing estate** quartiere residenziale *m*.
hovel ['hovəl] *n* tugurio *m*.
hover ['hovə] *v* librarsi. **hovercraft** *n* hovercraft *m invar*.
how [hau] *adv* come, in che modo; *(to what extent)* quanto. **how are you?** come sta? **how do you do** *(after introduction)* piacere; buon giorno. **how much** quanto. **how many** quanti. **how often** quante volte. *conj* che.
however [hau'evə] *adv* comunque, tuttavia. *conj* nonostante, tuttavia.
howl [haul] *v* ululare, lamentarsi. *n* ululato *m*, lamento *m*.
hub [hʌb] *n* parte centrale *f*; *(of wheel)* mozzo *m*. **hub cap** coppa *f*.
hubbub ['hʌbʌb] *n* baccano *m*.
huddle ['hʌdl] *v* **huddle together** affollarsi, accalcarsi.
hue [hjuɪ] *n* colore *m*, tinta *f*.
huff [hʌf] *n* stizza *f*, risentimento *m*. **in a huff** offeso.
hug [hʌg] *v* abbracciare. *n* abbraccio *m*.
huge [hjuɪdʒ] *adj* enorme, immenso.
hulk [hʌlk] *n* carcassa *f*. **hulking** *adj* goffo.
hull [hʌl] *n* *(shell)* guscio *m*; *(husk)* buccia *f*; *(of nuts)* mallo *m*; *(pod)* baccello *m*; *(naut)* scafo *m*.
hum [hʌm] *v* ronzare; cantare a bocca chiusa, canterellare. *n* ronzio *m*.
human ['hjuɪmən] *adj* umano. **human being** essere umano *m*.
humane [hjuɪ'mein] *adj* umanitario, umano, compassionevole.
humanism ['hjuɪmənizəm] *n* umanesimo *m*. **humanist** *n* umanista *m*, *f*.
humanitarian [hjuɪˌmani'teəriən] *adj* filantropico. *n* filantropo, -a *m*, *f*.
humanity [hjuɪ'manəti] *n* umanità *f*; compassione *f*.
humble ['hʌmbl] *adj* umile, modesto. *v* umiliare.
humdrum ['hʌmdrʌm] *adj* monotono, noioso.
humid ['hjuɪmid] *adj* umido. **humidity** *n* umidità *f*.
humiliate [hjuɪ'milieit] *v* umiliare.
humility [hjuɪ'miləti] *n* umiltà *f*.

humour ['hjuɪmə] *n* *(mood)* umore *m*; stato d'animo *m*, disposizione *f*; *(comic quality)* comicità *f*. *v* compiacere, accontentare. **humorist** *n* umorista *m*, *f*. **humorous** *adj* divertente, spiritoso.
hump [hʌmp] *n* gobba *f*; *(hill)* cresta *f*.
hunch [hʌntʃ] *n* gobba *f*. **have a hunch** *(coll)* avere un sospetto. **hunchback** *n* gobbo *m*. **hunchbacked** *adj* gobbo.
hundred ['hʌndrəd] *nm, adj* cento. **hundredth** *nm, adj* centesimo.
hung [hʌŋ] *V* **hang**.
Hungary ['hʌŋgəri] *n* Ungheria *f*. **Hungarian** *n*(*m*+*f*), *adj* ungherese.
hunger ['hʌŋgə] *n* fame *f*, appetito *m*. **hungry** *adj* affamato. **be hungry** aver fame.
hunt [hʌnt] *n* caccia *f*; *(pursuit)* inseguimento *m*; *(search)* ricerca affannosa *f*. *v* andare a caccia di; inseguire; cercare affannosamente. **hunter** *n* cacciatore *m*.
hurdle ['hɔɪdl] *n* ostacolo *m*. *v* fare la corsa a ostacoli.
hurl [hɔɪl] *v* scagliare, scaraventare.
hurrah [hu'raɪ] *interj* evviva!
hurricane ['hʌrikən] *n* uragano *m*. **hurricane lamp** lanterna controvento *f*.
hurry ['hʌri] *n* fretta *f*. **be in a hurry** aver fretta. *v* affrettare. **hurry up** sbrigarsi.
***hurt** [hɔɪt] *v* far male a, nuocere a; *(wound)* ferire; *(feel painful)* dolere. *n* dolore *m*, male *m*; ferita *f*; offesa *f*. **feel hurt** rimanere offeso.
husband ['hʌzbənd] *n* marito *m*.
hush [hʌʃ] *n* silenzio *m*. *interj* zitto! *v* far tacere. **hush-hush** *adj* *(coll)* segretissimo. **hush up** nascondere, dissimulare; *(suppress)* soffocare.
husk [hʌsk] *n* guscio *m*, baccello *m*.
husky ['hʌski] *adj* *(of voice)* rauco, fioco; *(burly)* grande e grosso.
hustle ['hʌsl] *n* spintone *m*. *v* spingere, sbrigarsi.
hut [hʌt] *n* capanna *f*, baracca *f*.
hutch [hʌtʃ] *n* conigliera *f*.
hyacinth ['haiəsinθ] *n* giacinto *m*.
hybrid ['haibrid] *nm, adj* ibrido.
hydrant ['haidrənt] *n* idrante *m*.
hydraulic [hai'drɔɪlik] *adj* idraulico.
hydrocarbon [ˌhaidrou'kaɪbən] *n* idrocarburo *m*.
hydro-electric [ˌhaidroui'lektrik] *adj* idroelettrico.
hydrofoil ['haidroufoil] *n* aliscafo *m*.

hydrogen ['haidrədʒən] *n* idrogeno *m*.
hyena [hai'iːnə] *n* iena *f*.
hygiene ['haidʒiːn] *n* igiene *f*. hygienic *adj* igienico.
hymn [him] *n* inno *m*, canto sacro *m*.
hyphen ['haifən] *n* lineetta *f*.
hypnosis [hip'nousis] *n* ipnosi *f*. hypnotic *adj* ipnotico. hypnotism *n* ipnotismo *m*, ipnosi *f*. hypnotist *n* ipnotizzatore, -trice *m*, *f*.
hypochondria [haipə'kondriə] *n* ipocondria *f*. hypochondriac *n*, *adj* ipocondriaco, -a.
hypocrisy [hi'pokrəsi] *n* ipocrisia *f*. hypocrite *n* ipocrita *m*, *f*. hypocritical *adj* ipocrita.
hypodermic [haipə'dəːmik] *adj* ipodermico.
hypotenuse [hai'potənjuːz] *n* ipotenusa *f*.
hypothesis [hai'poθəsis] *n*, *pl* -ses ipotesi *f*. hypothetical *adj* ipotetico.
hysterectomy [histə'rektəmi] *n* isterectomia *f*.
hysteria [his'tiəriə] *n* isterismo *m*. hysterical *adj* isterico. hysterics *pl n* crisi isterica *f* *sing*.

I

I [ai] *pron* io.
ice [ais] *n* ghiaccio *m*. iceberg *n* iceberg *m* *invar*. ice-cold *adj* freddo come il ghiaccio, glaciale, gelido. ice cream gelato *m*. ice lolly ghiacciolo *m*. ice rink pista di pattinaggio *f*. *v* (*cookery*) glassare; (*cover with ice*) ghiacciare. icing *n* glassa *f*. icy *adj* glaciale, gelido.
Iceland ['aislənd] *n* Islanda *f*. Icelander *n* islandese *m*, *f*. Icelandic *adj* islandese.
icicle ['aisikl] *n* ghiacciolo *m*.
icon ['aikon] *n* icona *f*. iconoclast *n* iconoclasta *m*, *f*.
idea [ai'diə] *n* idea *f*, concetto *m*, impressione *f*.
ideal [ai'diəl] *nm*, *adj* ideale. idealist *n* idealista *m*, *f*. idealistic *adj* idealistico. idealize *v* idealizzare.
identical [ai'dentikəl] *adj* identico.
identify [ai'dentifai] *n* identificare. identification *n* identificazione *f*.
identity [ai'dentiti] *n* identità *f*. identity card carta d'identità *f*. identity parade

confronto all'americana *m*. mistaken identity errore di persona *m*.
ideology [aidi'olədʒi] *n* ideologia *f*. ideological *adj* ideologico.
idiom ['idiəm] *n* (*expression*) frase idiomatica *f*; (*language*) idioma *m*.
idiosyncrasy [ˌidiə'siŋkrəsi] *n* idiosincrasia *f*.
idiot ['idiət] *n* idiota *m*, *f*; cretino, -a *m*, *f*. idiotic *adj* idiota, cretino, imbecille.
idle ['aidl] *adj* (*lazy*) pigro; (*doing nothing*) disoccupato; (*machine*) fermo; (*worthless*) vano. *v* stare senza far nulla; (*machine*) girare a folle. idler *n* fannullone, -a *m*, *f*.
idol ['aidl] *n* idolo *m*. idolatry *n* idolatria *f*. idolize *v* idoleggiare.
idyllic [i'dilik] *adj* idillico.
if [if] *conj* se. as if come se. if not se no. if you please per piacere.
ignite [ig'nait] *v* accendere, dar fuoco a; (*catch fire*) prender fuoco.
ignition [ig'niʃən] *n* accensione *f*. ignition key interruttore dell'accensione *m*.
ignorant ['ignərənt] *adj* ignorante. be ignorant of ignorare. ignorance *n* ignoranza *f*.
ignore [ig'noː] *v* (*disregard*) non badare a, trascurare; (*refrain from seeing/recognizing/hearing*) fingere di non vedere/riconoscere/sentire.
ill [il] *adj* (*sick*) malato; (*bad*) cattivo. *nm*, *adv* male. ill-advised *adj* malavveduto. ill-bred *or* ill-mannered *adj* maleducato. ill-treat *v* maltrattare. illness *n* malattia *f*.
illegal [i'liːgəl] *adj* illegale.
illegible [i'ledʒəbl] *adj* illeggibile.
illegitimate [ˌili'dʒitimit] *adj* illegittimo.
illicit [i'lisit] *adj* illecito.
illiterate [i'litərit] *n*(*m*+*f*), *adj* analfabeta.
illogical [i'lodʒikəl] *adj* illogico.
illuminate [i'luːmiˌneit] *v* illuminare, rischiarare. illuminating *adj* illuminante. illumination *n* illuminazione *f*.
illusion [i'luːʒən] *n* illusione *f*.
illustrate ['iləˌstreit] *v* illustrare. illustration *n* illustrazione *f*.
illustrious [i'lʌstriəs] *adj* illustre, celebre.
image ['imidʒ] *n* immagine *f*, ritratto *m*. imagery *n* immagini *f* *pl*.
imagine [i'madʒin] *v* farsi un'idea di, immaginarsi; (*suppose*) supporre; (*believe*) credere. imaginary *adj* immaginario. imagination *n* immaginazione *f*, fantasia *f*.

imbalance [im'balans] *n* squilibrio *m*.
imbecile ['imbə‚siːl] *n*(*m*+*f*), *adj* imbecille.
imitate ['imi‚teit] *v* imitare, contraffare. **imitation** *n* imitazione *f*, copia *f*, contraffattura *f*.
immaculate [i'makjulit] *adj* immacolato.
immaterial [‚imə'tiəriəl] *adj* (*unimportant*) di nessuna importanza.
immature [‚imə'tjuə] *adj* immaturo. **immaturity** *n* immaturità *f*.
immediate [i'miːdiət] *adj* immediato. **immediately** *adv* immediatamente, subito.
immense [i'mens] *adj* immenso.
immerse [i'məis] *v* immergere. **immersion** *n* immersione *f*. **immersion heater** riscaldatore a immersione *m*.
immigrate ['imi‚greit] *v* immigrare. **immigrant** *n*(*m*+*f*), *adj* immigrante. **immigration** *n* immigrazione *f*.
imminent ['iminənt] *adj* imminente.
immobile [i'moubail] *adj* immobile, fermo. **immobilize** *v* immobilizzare.
immoral [i'morəl] *adj* immorale. **immorality** *n* immoralità *f*.
immortal [i'moitl] *adj* immortale. **immortality** *n* immortalità *f*. **immortalize** *v* immortalare.
immovable [i'muːvəbl] *adj* inamovibile, fisso.
immune [i'mjuin] *adj* immune. **immunity** *n* immunità *f*. **immunization** *n* immunizzazione *f*. **immunize** *v* immunizzare.
imp [imp] *n* folletto *m*.
impact ['impakt] *n* urto *m*, scontro *m*; (*effect*) impressione *f*.
impair [im'peə] *v* danneggiare, menomare.
impale [im'peil] *v* impalare.
impart [im'paɪt] *v* impartire.
impartial [im'paɪʃəl] *adj* imparziale. **impartiality** *n* imparzialità *f*.
impasse [am'pais] *n* impasse *m*, intoppo *m*.
impatient [im'peiʃənt] *adj* impaziente. **get impatient** impazientirsi. **impatience** *n* impazienza *f*.
impeach [im'piɪtʃ] *v* accusare; (*call in question*) mettere in dubbio, imputare.
impeccable [im'pekəbl] *adj* impeccabile.
impede [im'piɪd] *v* ostacolare, impedire.
impediment [im'pedimənt] *n* impedimento *m*, ostacolo *m*. **speech impediment** difetto *or* impedimento di lingua *m*.
impel [im'pel] *v* spingere, impellere.

impending [im'pendiŋ] *adj* imminente.
imperative [im'perətiv] *nm*, *adj* imperativo.
imperfect [im'pəɪfikt] *nm*, *adj* imperfetto.
imperial [im'piəriəl] *adj* imperiale. **imperialism** *n* imperialismo *m*.
imperil [im'perəl] *v* mettere in pericolo, compromettere.
impersonal [im'pəɪsənl] *adj* impersonale, comune.
impersonate [im'pəɪsə‚neit] *v* impersonare; (*theatre*) interpretare.
impertinent [im'pəɪtinənt] *adj* impertinente. **impertinence** *n* impertinenza *f*.
impervious [im'pəɪviəs] *adj* impervio; impermeabile; (*fig*) sordo.
impetuous [im'petjuəs] *adj* impetuoso.
impetus ['impətəs] *n* impeto *m*, slancio *m*.
impinge [im'pindʒ] *v* **impinge on** colpire.
implement ['implimənt; *v* 'impliment] *n* attrezzo *m*, utensile *m*. *v* adempire. **implementation** *n* adempimento *m*.
implicate ['implikeit] *v* implicare, coinvolgere. **implication** *n* implicazione *f*.
implicit [im'plisit] *adj* implicito.
implore [im'ploɪ] *v* supplicare.
imply [im'plai] *v* (*mean*) significare; (*suggest*) far pensare a.
impolite [impə'lait] *adj* scortese, sgarbato.
import [im'poɪt] *v* importare. *n* (*comm*) importazione *f*; importanza *f*. **importer** *n* importatore *m*.
importance [im'poɪtəns] *n* importanza *f*. **important** *adj* importante.
impose [im'pouz] *v* imporre. **impose on** abusare di. **imposing** *adj* imponente. **imposition** *n* imposizione *f*.
impossible [im'posəbl] *adj* impossibile. **impossibility** *n* impossibilità *f*.
impostor [im'postə] *n* impostore *m*.
impotent ['impətənt] *adj* impotente. **impotence** *n* impotenza *f*.
impound [im'paund] *v* confiscare.
impoverish [im'povəriʃ] *v* impoverire.
impractical [im'praktikəl] *adj* (*person*) privo di senso pratico; (*thing*) inservibile, non pratico.
impregnate ['impreg‚neit] *v* impregnare. **impregnation** *n* impregnazione *f*.
impress [im'pres] *v* colpire, fare impressione su; (*urge*) raccomandare; (*print*) imprimere, stampare. **impression** *n* impressione *f*; (*print*) stampa *f*, ristampa *f*. **impressive** *adj* impressionante.

imprint ['imprint] *n* impronta *f*.
imprison [im'prizn] *v* carcerare. **imprisonment** *n* carcerazione *f*.
improbable [im'probəbl] *adj* improbabile. **improbability** *n* improbabilità *f*.
impromptu [im'promptjuɪ] *adj* improvvisato. *adv* all'improvviso.
improper [im'propə] *adj* (*inappropriate*) improprio; (*unseemly*) indecente, indecoroso.
improve [im'pruɪv] *v* migliorare; (*increase value*) valorizzare; (*get better*) star meglio. **improve on** perfezionare. **improvement** *n* miglioramento *m*; (*making more valuable*) miglioria *f*.
improvise ['imprəˌvaiz] *v* improvvisare. **improvisation** *n* improvvisazione *f*.
impudent ['impjudənt] *adj* sfacciato. **impudence** *n* sfacciataggine *f*.
impulse ['impʌls] *n* impulso *m*, stimolo *m*. **impulsive** *adj* impulsivo.
impure [im'pjuə] *adj* impuro. **impurity** *n* impurità *f*.
in [in] *prep* in; (*within*) tra, entro. *adv* dentro, a casa, in sede.
inability [ˌinə'biləti] *n* incapacità *f*.
inaccessible [ˌinak'sesəbl] *adj* inaccessibile.
inaccurate [in'akjurit] *adj* inesatto. **inaccuracy** *n* inesattezza *f*.
inactive [in'aktiv] *adj* inattivo, passivo.
inadequate [in'adikwit] *adj* inadeguato, insufficiente, inetto. **inadequacy** *n* inadeguatezza *f*.
inadmissible [inəd'misəbl] *adj* inammissibile.
inadvertent [ˌinəd'vəɪtənt] *adj* involontario.
inane [in'ein] *adj* insensato, futile.
inanimate [in'animit] *adj* (*not animate*) inanimato; (*lifeless*) esanime.
inarticulate [ˌinɑɪ'tikjulit] *adj* (*person*) che non sa esprimersi; inarticolato.
inasmuch [ˌinəz'mʌtʃ] *conj* dacchè, poichè.
inaudible [in'ɔɪdəbl] *adj* inaudibile.
inaugurate [i'nɔɪgjuˌreit] *v* inaugurare. **inaugural** *adj* inaugurale. **inauguration** *n* inaugurazione *f*.
inauspicious [inɔɪ'spiʃəs] *adj* infausto.
inbred [ˌin'bred] *adj* (*inborn*) innato; (*resulting from. inbreeding*) endogamo. **inbreeding** *n* endogamia *f*.
incalculable [in'kalkjuləbl] *adj* incalcolabile, imprevedibile.

incapable [in'keipəbl] *adj* incapace, inetto.
incendiary [in'sendiəri] *adj* incendiario.
incense¹ ['insens] *n* incenso *m*.
incense² [in'sens] *v* irritare, provocare.
incentive [in'sentiv] *n* incentivo *m*.
incessant [in'sesənt] *adj* continuo.
incest ['insest] *n* incesto *m*. **incestuous** *adj* incestuoso.
inch [intʃ] *n* pollice *m*. **inch by inch** gradatamente. *v* **inch forward** avanzare poco alla volta.
incident ['insidənt] *n* caso *m*, episodio *m*; (*event with serious consequences*) incidente *f*. **incidental** *adj* incidentale. **incidentally** *adv* tra parentesi, a proposito.
incinerator [in'sinəˌreitə] *n* inceneritore *m*. **incinerate** *v* incenerire.
incisive [in'saisiv] *adj* acuto.
incite [in'sait] *v* incitare, spronare. **incitement** *n* incitamento *m*.
incline [in'klain] *v* inclinare, chinare. **be inclined to** essere propenso *or* disposto a. *n* piano inclinato *m*, pendio *m*. **inclination** *n* inclinazione *f*; propensione *f*.
include [in'kluɪd] *v* includere. **inclusion** *n* inclusione *f*. **inclusive** *adj* compreso.
incoherent [ˌinkə'hiərənt] *adj* incoerente.
income ['inkʌm] *n* entrata *f*, reddito *m*. **income tax** imposta sull'entrata *f*. **incoming** *adj* in arrivo.
incompatible [inkəm'patəbl] *adj* incompatibile. **incompatibility** *n* incompatibilità *f*.
incompetent [in'kompitənt] *adj* incompetente. **incompetence** *n* incompetenza *f*.
incomplete [ˌinkəm'pliɪt] *adj* incompleto.
incomprehensible [inˌkompri'hensəbl] *adj* incomprensibile.
inconceivable [inkən'siɪvəbl] *adj* inconcepibile.
inconclusive [inkən'kluɪsiv] *adj* inconcludente.
incongruous [in'kongruəs] *adj* incongruo.
inconsiderate [ˌinkən'sidərit] *adj* sconsiderato; (*person*) che manca di riguardo.
inconsistent [ˌinkən'sistənt] *adj* inconsistente. **inconsistency** *n* inconsistenza *f*.
incontinence [in'kontinəns] *n* incontinenza *f*. **incontinent** *adj* incontinente.
inconvenience [inkən'viɪnjəns] *n* sconvenienza *f*. *v* sconvenire, disturbare. **inconvenient** *adj* sconveniente, scomodo.

incorporate [in'kɔɪpə‚reit] *v* incorporare.
incorrect [inkə'rekt] *adj* scorretto.
increase [in'kriɪs] *v* aumentare, ingrandirsi, crescere. *n* aumento *m*. increasingly *adv* sempre più.
incredible [in'kredəbl] *adj* incredibile.
incredulous [in'kredjuləs] *adj* incredulo.
increment ['iŋkrəmənt] *n* incremento *m*, aumento *m*.
incriminate [in'krimineit] *v* incolpare.
incubate ['iŋkju‚beit] *v* incubare. incubation *n* incubazione *f*. incubator *n* incubatrice *f*.
incumbent [in'kʌmbənt] *adj* be incumbent on spettare a.
incur [in'kəi] *v* incorrere in.
incurable [in'kjuərəbl] *adj* incurabile.
indebted [in'detid] *adj* (*owing money*) indebitato; (*under obligation*) riconoscente.
indecent [in'diɪsnt] *adj* indecente. indecency *n* indecenza *f*; (*law*) oltraggio al pudore *m*.
indeed [in'diɪd] *adv* infatti, effettivamente, proprio. *interj* davvero!
indefatigable [indi'fatigəbl] *adj* indefesso.
indefinite [in'definit] *adj* indefinito, vago, illimitato.
indelible [in'deləbl] *adj* indelebile; (*memory*) indimenticabile.
indemnity [in'demnəti] *n* indennità *f*; (*sum paid*) indennizzo *m*. indemnify *v* indennizzare.
indent [in'dent] *v* (*notch*) dentellare; (*make recess*) incavare. indentation *n* incavo *m*, dentellatura *f*, rientranza *f*; (*printing*) capoverso *m*.
independent [‚indi'pendənt] *adj* indipendente. independence *n* indipendenza *f*.
index ['indeks] *n* indice *m*. index card scheda *f*. index finger indice *m*.
India ['indjə] *n* India *f*. India rubber gomma *f*. Indian *n*, *adj* indiano, -a. Indian ink inchiostro di china *m*.
indicate ['indikeit] *v* indicare.
indict [in'dait] *v* accusare. indictment *n* accusa *f*; (*law*) atto d'accusa *m*.
indifferent [in'difrənt] *adj* indifferente. indifference *n* indifferenza *f*.
indigenous [in'didʒinəs] *adj* indigeno.
indigestion [‚indi'dʒestʃən] *n* indigestione *f*.
indignant [in'dignənt] *adj* sdegnato. feel indignant indignarsi, sdegnarsi (contro).

indignity [in'dignəti] *n* indegnità *f*.
indirect [‚indi'rekt] *adj* indiretto.
indiscreet [‚indi'skriɪt] *adj* indiscreto. indiscretion *n* indiscrezione *f*.
indiscriminate [‚indi'skriminit] *adj* indiscriminato.
indispensable [‚indi'spensəbl] *adj* indispensabile.
indisposed [‚indi'spouzd] *adj* indisposto.
individual [‚indi'vidjuəl] *n* individuo *m*. *adj* individuale, particolare.
indoctrinate [in'doktri‚neit] *v* indottrinare. indoctrination *n* indottrinamento *m*.
indolent ['indələnt] *adj* indolente. indolence *n* indolenza *f*.
indoor ['indoɪ] *adj* di *or* da casa. indoors *adv* in casa, all'interno, dentro.
induce [in'djuɪs] *v* indurre.
indulge [in'dʌldʒ] *v* (*gratify*) appagare, soddisfare; essere indulgente verso. indulge in abbandonarsi a, dedicarsi a. indulgence *n* indulgenza *f*. indulgent *adj* indulgente.
industry ['indəstri] *n* industria *f*; diligenza *f*, zelo *m*. industrial *adj* industriale. industrialize *v* industrializzare. industrious *adj* diligente, operoso.
inebriated [i'niɪbrieitid] *adj* ubriaco.
inedible [in'edibl] *adj* immangiabile.
inefficient [‚ini'fiʃnt] *adj* inefficiente. inefficiency *n* inefficienza *f*.
inept [i'nept] *adj* inetto, incapace.
inequality [‚ini'kwoləti] *n* ineguaglianza *f*.
inert [i'nəit] *adj* inerte. inertia *n* inerzia *f*.
inevitable [in'evitəbl] *adj* inevitabile.
inexcusable [inik'skjuɪzəbl] *adj* imperdonabile, ingiustificabile.
inexhaustible [inig'zoɪstəbl] *adj* inesauribile.
inexpensive [‚inik'spensiv] *adj* a buon mercato, poco caro.
inexperienced [‚inik'spiəriənst] *adj* inesperto.
inexplicable [inik'splikəbl] *adj* inspiegabile.
infallible [in'faləbl] *adj* infallibile. infallibility *n* infallibilità *f*.
infamous ['infəməs] *adj* infame. infamy *n* infamia *f*.
infancy ['infənsi] *n* infanzia *f*.
infant ['infənt] *n* infante *m*, bambino, -a *m*, *f*. infantile *adj* infantile, puerile. infant prodigy bambino prodigio *m*.

infantry ['infəntri] *n* fanteria *f.*
infatuated [in'fatjueitid] *adj* infatuato. **be infatuated** prendere una cotta.
infect [in'fekt] *v* infettare. **infection** *n* infezione *f.* **infectious** *adj* infettivo.
infer [in'fəɪ] *v* dedurre, desumere. **inferable** *adj* deducibile. **inference** *n* inferenza *f,* deduzione *f.*
inferior [in'fiəriə] *n(m+f),* *adj* inferiore. **inferiority** *n* inferiorità *f.*
infernal [in'fəɪnl] *adj* infernale.
infest [in'fest] *v* infestare.
infidelity [,infi'deliti] *n* infedeltà *f.*
infiltrate [in'fil,treit] *v* infiltrare. **infiltration** *n* infiltrazione *f.*
infinite ['infinit] *nm, adj* infinito. **infinity** *n* infinità *f,* infinito *m.*
infinitive [in'finitiv] *nm, adj* infinito.
infirm [in'fəɪm] *adj* infermo. **infirmity** *n* infermità *f.*
inflame [in'fleim] *v* infiammare. **inflammable** *adj* infiammabile. **inflammation** *n* infiammazione *f.*
inflate [in'fleit] *v* gonfiare. **inflation** *n* inflazione *f.*
inflection [in'flekʃən] *n* inflessione *f.*
inflexible [in'fleksəbl] *adj* inflessibile.
inflict [in'flikt] *v* infliggere.
influence ['influəns] *n* influenza *f,* ascendente *m. v* influire su, influenzare. **influential** *adj* autorevole, importante.
influenza [,influ'enzə] *n* influenza *f.*
influx ['inflʌks] *n* afflusso *m,* affluenza *f.*
inform [in'fɔɪm] *v* informare, far sapere a. **inform against** *or* **on** *(denounce)* denunziare. **informant** *n* informatore, -trice *m, f.* **informer** *n* spia *f,* delatore, -trice *m, f.*
informal [in'fɔɪml] *adj* alla buona, senza cerimonia, non ufficiale. **informality** *n* mancanza di formalità *f.*
information [,infə'meiʃən] *n* informazioni *f pl,* notizie *f pl.* **for your information** a titolo d'informazione.
infra-red [,infrə'red] *adj* infrarosso.
infrequent [in'friːkwənt] *adj* raro.
infringe [in'frindʒ] *v* violare, trasgredire. **infringement** *n* violazione *f.*
infuriate [in'fjuəri,eit] *v* fare arrabbiare. **be infuriated** essere furibondo *or* arrabbiatissimo.
ingenious [in'dʒiɪnjəs] *adj* ingegnoso. **ingenuity** *n* ingegnosità *f.*
ingot ['iŋgət] *n* lingotto *m.*
ingredient [in'griːdjənt] *n* ingrediente *m.*

inhabit [in'habit] *v* abitare, vivere, dimorare. **inhabitant** *n* abitante *m, f.*
inhale [in'heil] *v* inalare.
inherent [in'hiərənt] *adj* inerente.
inherit [in'herit] *v* ereditare. **inheritance** *n* eredità *f.*
inhibit [in'hibit] *v* inibire. **inhibition** *n* inibizione *f.*
inhuman [in'hjuɪmən] *adj* inumano. **inhumanity** *n* inumanità *f.*
iniquity [i'nikwəti] *n* iniquità *f.* **iniquitous** *adj* iniquo.
initial [i'niʃl] *nf, adj* iniziale. *v* siglare.
initiate [i'niʃi,eit] *v* iniziare, istituire. **initiation** *n* iniziazione *f,* inizio *m.*
initiative [i'niʃiətiv] *n* iniziativa *f.*
inject [in'dʒekt] *v* iniettare; *(introduce)* immettere. **injection** *n* iniezione *f.*
injure ['indʒə] *v (damage)* danneggiare; *(hurt)* far male a; *(wound)* ferire; *(law)* ledere. **injurious** *adj* dannoso, nocivo. **injury** *n* male *m;* danno *m;* torto *m;* ferita *f.*
injustice [in'dʒʌstis] *n* ingiustizia *f.*
ink [iŋk] *n* inchiostro *m.* **ink-well** *n* calamaio *m.*
inkling ['iŋkliŋ] *n* sospetto *m,* sentore *m.*
inland ['inlənd; *adv* in'land] *adj* interno. *adv* all' *or* nell'interno.
in-laws ['in,lɔɪs] *pl n (coll)* parenti acquisiti *m pl.*
*inlay ['inlei] *v* intarsiare. *n* intarsio *m.*
inlet ['inlet] *n (geog)* insenatura *f.*
inmate ['inmeit] *n (of hospital, etc.)* ricoverato, -a *m, f; (of prison)* carcerato, -a *m, f.*
inn [in] *n* locanda *f,* osteria *f,* albergo *m.* **innkeeper** *n* locandiere, -a *m, f;* oste, -essa *m, f;* albergatore, -trice *m, f.*
innate [i'neit] *adj* innato.
inner ['inə] *adj* interno, interiore; *(thoughts, etc.)* intimo. **inner tube** camera d'aria *f.*
innocent ['inəsnt] *n(m+f), adj* innocente. **innocence** *n* innocenza *f.*
innocuous [i'nokjuəs] *adj* innocuo.
innovation [inə'veiʃən] *n* innovazione *f,* novità *f.* **innovate** *v* innovare. **innovator** *n* innovatore, -trice *m, f.*
innuendo [,inju'endou] *n* insinuazione *f.*
innumerable [i'njuɪmərəbl] *adj* innumerevole.
inoculate [i'nokju,leit] *v* inoculare. **inoculation** *n* inoculazione *f.*

inorganic [ˌinɔːˈganik] *adj* inorganico.
input [ˈinput] *n* (*elec*) alimentazione *f*; (*computer*) input *m* invar.
inquest [ˈinkwest] *n* inchiesta *f*, istruttoria *f*.
inquire [inˈkwaiə] *v* chiedere, domandare.
inquiry *n* domanda *f*, informazione *f*, inchiesta *f*.
inquisition [ˌinkwiˈziʃən] *n* inquisizione *f*, inchiesta *f*.
inquisitive [inˈkwizətiv] *adj* curioso.
insane [inˈsein] *adj* pazzo, matto. insanity *n* pazzia *f*, follia *f*.
insatiable [inˈseiʃəbl] *adj* insaziabile.
inscribe [inˈskraib] *v* (*enrol*) inscrivere; (*engrave*) incidere. inscription *n* iscrizione *f*, dedica *f*.
insect [ˈinsekt] *n* insetto *m*. insecticide *n* insetticida *m*.
insecure [ˌinsiˈkjuə] *adj* malsicuro, instabile. insecurity *n* incertezza *f*, instabilità *f*.
inseminate [inˈsemineit] *v* inseminare. insemination *n* inseminazione *f*.
insensible [inˈsensəbl] *adj* insensibile; (*unconscious*) privo di sensi.
insensitive [inˈsensətiv] *adj* insensibile, indifferente.
inseparable [inˈsepərəbl] *adj* inseparabile.
insert [inˈsəɪt; *n* ˈinsəɪt] *v* inserire. *n also* insertion inserzione *f*.
inshore [ˌinˈʃɔɪ] *adj* costiero. *adv* verso la riva.
inside [ˌinˈsaid] *adv* dentro, internamente. *prep* dentro, all'interno. *adj* interno, interiore; (*confidential*) riservato. *n* interno *m*; (*soccer*) mezzala *f*. inside out a rovescio.
insidious [inˈsidiəs] *adj* insidioso, perfido.
insight [ˈinsait] *n* discernimento *m*, intuito *m*.
insignificant [ˌinsigˈnifikənt] *adj* insignificante.
insincere [ˌinsinˈsiə] *adj* insincero.
insinuate [inˈsinjueit] *v* insinuare, dare ad intendere. insinuation *n* insinuazione *f*.
insipid [inˈsipid] *adj* insipido.
insist [inˈsist] *v* insistere. insistence *n* insistenza *f*. insistent *adj* insistente.
insolent [ˈinsələnt] *adj* impertinente. insolence *n* impertinenza *f*.
insoluble [inˈsoljubl] *adj* insolubile; (*not solvable*) insolvibile.
insomnia [inˈsomniə] *n* insonnia *f*. insomniac *n* insonne *m*, *f*.

inspect [inˈspekt] *v* ispezionare, verificare; (*troops*) passare in rivista. inspection *n* ispezione *f*, verifica *f*; rivista *f*. inspector *n* ispettore, -trice *m*, *f*; (*bus*, *train*) controllore, -a *m*, *f*; (*police*) commissario *m*.
inspire [inˈspaiə] *v* ispirare, infondere. inspiration *n* ispirazione *f*.
instability [ˌinstəˈbiləti] *n* instabilità *f*.
install [inˈstoil] *v* installare. installation *n* installazione *f*.
instalment [inˈstoilmənt] *n* (*comm*) rata *f*; (*serial*) puntata *f*.
instance [ˈinstəns] *n* esempio *m*. for instance per esempio.
instant [ˈinstənt] *adj* immediato; urgente; (*comm*) corrente; (*of food*) istantaneo. *n* istante *m*, momento *m*. instantaneous *adj* istantaneo.
instead [inˈsted] *adv* invece.
instep [ˈinstep] *n* (*anat*) collo del piede *m*; (*shoe*) collo della scarpa *m*.
instigate [ˈinstigeit] *v* istigare. instigation *n* istigazione *f*.
instil [inˈstil] *v* instillare, infondere.
instinct [ˈinstiŋkt] *n* istinto *m*. instinctive *adj* istintivo.
institute [ˈinstitjuɪt] *n* istituto *m*. *v* istituire, iniziare. institution *n* istituzione *f*.
instruct [inˈstrʌkt] *v* (*teach*) istruire; (*direct*) dare istruzioni *or* disposizioni a. instruction *n* istruzione *f*, disposizioni *f* pl. instructive *adj* istruttivo. instructor *n* istruttore, -trice *m*, *f*, insegnante *m*, *f*.
instrument [ˈinstrəmənt] *n* strumento *m*; (*tool*) arnese *m*; (*law*) titolo *m*, atto *m*. instrumental *adj* strumentale. be instrumental in essere utile a.
insubordinate [ˌinsəˈbɔidənət] *adj* insubordinato. insubordination *n* insubordinazione *f*.
insufficient [ˌinsəˈfiʃənt] *adj* insufficiente.
insular [ˈinsjulə] *adj* insulare; (*outlook*) gretto.
insulate [ˈinsjuleit] *v* isolare. insulating tape nastro isolante *m*. insulation *n* isolamento *m*.
insulin [ˈinsjulin] *n* insulina *f*.
insult [inˈsʌlt; *n* ˈinsʌlt] *v* insultare, offendere. *n* insulto *m*, offesa *f*.
insure [inˈʃuə] *v* assicurare. insurance *n* assicurazione *f*.
intact [inˈtakt] *adj* intatto.

intake ['inteik] *n* (*consumption*) consumo *m*; (*employment*) assunzione *f*; (*people newly taken on*) reclute *f pl*.

intangible [in'tandʒəbl] *adj* intangibile.

integral ['intigrəl] *adj* integrale.

integrate ['intigreit] *v* integrare. **integration** *n* integrazione *f*.

integrity [in'tegrəti] *n* integrità *f*.

intellect ['intilekt] *n* intelletto *m*. **intellectual** *n*(*m*+*f*), *adj* intellettuale.

intelligent [in'telidʒənt] *adj* intelligente. **intelligence** *n* intelligenza *f*; informazioni *f pl*. **intelligentsia** *n* intellighenzia *f*.

intelligible [in'telidʒəbl] *adj* intelligibile.

intend [in'tend] *v* intendere, aver l'intenzione di. **intended** *adj* premeditato, voluto.

intense [in'tens] *adj* intenso, profondo.

intent[1] [in'tent] *n* intento *m*, proposito *m*, intenzione *f*. **to all intents and purposes** a tutti gli effetti.

intent[2] [in'tent] *adj* intento, assorto. **intent on** deciso a.

intention [in'tenʃən] *n* intenzione *f*, proposito *m*. **intentional** *adj* intenzionale.

inter [in'tɜɪ] *v* seppellire. **interment** *n* sepoltura *f*.

interact [ˌintər'akt] *v* esercitare un'azione reciproca, interagire. **interaction** *n* azione reciproca *f*.

intercede [ˌintə'siɪd] *v* intercedere.

intercept [ˌintə'sept] *v* intercettare. **interception** *n* intercettazione *f*.

interchange [ˌintə'tʃəindʒ] *v* scambiare. **interchangeable** *adj* intercambiabile, scambievole.

intercom ['intəˌkom] *n* citofono *m*.

intercourse ['intəkɔɪs] *n* rapporti *m pl*.

interest ['intrist] *v* interessare. **be interested in** interessarsi di. *n* interesse *m*. **interesting** *adj* interessante.

interfere [ˌintə'fiə] *v* interferire, immischiarsi. **interference** *n* interferenza *f*.

interim ['intərim] *n* interim *m*. *adj* provvisorio, temporaneo.

interior [in'tiəriə] *nm*, *adj* interno. **interior decorator** arredatore, -trice *m*, *f*.

interjection [ˌintə'dʒekʃən] *n* interiezione *f*.

interlude ['intəluɪd] *n* interludio *m*.

intermediary [intə'miɪdiəri] *n* intermediario *m*.

intermediate [ˌintə'miɪdiət] *adj* intermedio.

interminable [in'tɜɪminəbl] *adj* senza fine.

intermission [ˌintə'miʃən] *n* interruzione *f*.

intermittent [ˌintə'mitənt] *adj* intermittente.

intern [in'tɜɪn] *v* internare. **internment** *n* internamento *m*.

internal [in'tɜɪnl] *adj* interno, interiore.

international [ˌintə'naʃənl] *adj* internazionale.

interpose [ˌintə'pouz] *v* frapporre.

interpret [in'tɜɪprit] *v* interpretare. **interpretation** *n* interpretazione *f*. **interpreter** *n* interprete *m*, *f*.

interrogate [in'terəgeit] *v* interrogare. **interrogation** *n* interrogazione *f*. **interrogative** *adj*, *nm* interrogativo.

interrupt [ˌintə'rʌpt] *v* interrompere. **interruption** *n* interruzione *f*.

intersect [ˌintə'sekt] *v* intersecare. **intersection** *n* intersezione *f*.

intersperse [ˌintə'spəɪs] *v* cospargere.

interval ['intəvəl] *n* intervallo *m*.

intervene [ˌintə'viɪn] *v* intervenire. **intervention** *n* intervento *m*.

interview ['intəvjuɪ] *n* intervista *f*, colloquio *m*. *v* intervistare.

intestine [in'testin] *n* intestino *m*. **intestinal** *adj* intestinale.

intimate[1] ['intimət] *adj* intimo, familiare. **intimacy** *n* intimità *f*.

intimate[2] ['intimeit] *v* intimare, suggerire. **intimation** *n* intimazione *f*.

intimidate [in'timideit] *v* intimidire, intimorire. **intimidation** *n* intimidazione *f*.

into ['intu] *prep* in, dentro.

intolerable [in'tolərəbl] *adj* insopportabile, intollerabile.

intolerant [in'tolərənt] *adj* intollerante. **intolerance** *n* intolleranza *f*.

intonation [ˌintə'neiʃən] *n* intonazione *f*.

intoxicate [in'toksikeit] *v* intossicare; (*with drink*) ubriacare; (*excite*) esaltare. **intoxicated** *adj* ubriaco, eccitato.

intransigent [in'transidʒənt] *adj* intransigente.

intransitive [in'transitiv] *adj* intransitivo.

intravenous [ˌintrə'viɪnəs] *adj* endovenoso.

intrepid [in'trepid] *adj* intrepido.

intricate ['intriket] *adj* complicato, complesso. **intricacy** *n* complicazione *f*.

intrigue ['intriɪg; *v* in'triɪg] *n* intrigo (*pl*

-ghi) *m. v (plot)* intrigare; *(excite curiosity)* incuriosire. **intriguing** *adj* interessante, affascinante.

intrinsic [in'trinsik] *adj* intrinseco.

introduce [ˌintrə'djuɪs] *v* introdurre; *(people)* presentare. **introduction** *n* introduzione *f*, presentazione *f*. **introductory** *adj* introduttorio, introduttivo.

introspective [ˌintrə'spektiv] *adj* introspettivo. **introspection** *n* introspezione *f*.

introvert ['intrəˌvəɪt] *adj, n* introverso, -a.

intrude [in'truɪd] *v* intrudere. **intrusion** *n* intrusione *f*.

intuition [ˌintjuɪ'iʃən] *n* intuito *m*; *(psychol, etc.)* intuizione *f*. **intuitive** *adj* intuitivo.

inundate ['inʌndeit] *v* inondare, allagare. **inundation** *n* allagamento *m*.

invade [in'veid] *v* invadere. **invader** *n* invasore *m*. **invasion** *n* invasione *f*.

invalid¹ ['invəlid] *n, adj* invalido, -a; malato, -a.

invalid² [in'valid] *adj (not valid)* invalido, senza validità, nullo. **invalidate** *v* invalidare, annullare.

invaluable [in'valjuəbl] *adj* inestimabile, incalcolabile.

invariable [in'veəriəbl] *adj* invariabile, costante.

invective [in'vektiv] *n* invettiva *f*.

invent [in'vent] *v* inventare. **invention** *n* invenzione *f*.

inventory ['invəntri] *n* inventario *m*.

invert [in'vəɪt] *v* invertire; *(inside out)* rovesciare; *(upside down)* capovolgere. **inverted commas** virgolette *f pl*. **inversion** *n* inversione *f*, rovesciamento *m*.

invertebrate [in'vəɪtibrət] *nm, adj* invertebrato.

invest [in'vest] *v* investire. **investment** *n* investimento *m*.

investigate [in'vestigeit] *v* investigare, svolgere indagini. **investigation** *n* indagine *f*.

invigorating [in'vigəreitiŋ] *adj* che invigorisce, fortificante.

invincible [in'vinsəbl] *adj* invincibile.

invisible [in'vizəbl] *adj* invisibile. **invisibility** *n* invisibilità *f*.

invite [in'vait] *v* invitare; provocare; *(lay oneself open to)* esporsi a. **invitation** *n* invito *m*. **inviting** *adj* attraente, seducente.

invoice ['invois] *n* fattura *f. v* fatturare.

invoke [in'vouk] *v* invocare. **invocation** *n* invocazione *f*.

involuntary [in'voləntəri] *adj* involontario.

involve [in'volv] *v (imply)* implicare; *(implicate)* coinvolgere; *(entail)* comportare. **involvement** *n* implicazione *f*.

inward ['inwəd] *adj* interno, intimo. **inwardly** *adv* interiormente. **inwards** *adv* verso il centro.

iodine ['aiədiɪn] *n* iodio *m*.

ion ['aiən] *n* ione *m*.

irate [ai'reit] *adj* arrabbiato.

Ireland ['aiələnd] *n* Irlanda *f*. **Irish** *n(m+f), adj* irlandese.

iris ['aiəris] *n (anat)* iride *f*; *(bot)* giaggiolo *m*.

irk [əɪk] *v* infastidire, dar noia a. **irksome** *adj* seccante, noioso.

iron ['aiən] *n* ferro *m*; *(for pressing)* ferro da stiro *m*. **iron curtain** cortina di ferro *f*. **ironmonger's** *n* ferramenta *f. v* stirare. **ironing board** tavola da stiro *f*.

irony ['aiərəni] *n* ironia *f*. **ironic** *adj* ironico.

irrational [i'raʃənl] *adj* irrazionale.

irregular [i'regjulə] *adj* irregolare. **irregularity** *n* irregolarità *f*.

irrelevant [i'reləvənt] *adj* non pertinente.

irreparable [i'repərəbl] *adj* irreparabile.

irresistible [ˌiri'zistəbl] *adj* irresistibile.

irrespective [ˌiri'spektiv] *adj* **irrespective of** senza riguardo a, senza tener conto di.

irresponsible [ˌiri'sponsəbl] *adj* irresponsabile. **irresponsibility** *n* irresponsabilità *f*.

irrevocable [i'revəkəbl] *adj* irrevocabile.

irrigate ['irigeit] *v* irrigare. **irrigation** *n* irrigazione *f*.

irritate ['iriteit] *v* irritare. **irritating** *adj* irritante. **irritation** *n* irritazione *f*.

Islam ['izlaɪm] *n* Islam *m*. **Islamic** *adj* islamico.

island ['ailənd] *n* isola *f*.

isolate ['aisəleit] *v* isolare. **isolation** *n* isolamento *m*.

issue ['iʃuɪ] *n* questione *f*, problema *m*; *(outcome)* conclusione *f*; edizione *f*; *(shares, etc.)* emissione *f. v* pubblicare; emettere; uscire.

isthmus ['isməs] *n* istmo *m*.

it [it] *pron (subject)* esso, -a; *(direct object)* lo, la; *(indirect object)* gli, le.

italic [i'talik] *adj (handwriting)* italico;

(*printing*) corsivo. **in italics** in (carattere) corsivo.

Italy ['itəli] *n* Italia *f*. **Italian** *n*, *adj* italiano, -a; (*language*) italiano *m*.

itch [itʃ] *n* (*sensation*) prurito *m*; (*desire*) gran voglia *f*. *v* sentire prurito.

item ['aitəm] *n* voce *f*, capo *m*, pezzo *m*.

itinerary [ai'tinərəri] *n* itinerario *m*.

its [its] *adj* (il) suo, (la) sua; (*pl*) (i) suoi, (le) sue.

itself [it'self] *pron* (*reflexive*) si; (*after prep*) sè; (*emphatic*) se esso, -a, se stesso, -a.

ivory ['aivəri] *n* avorio *m*.

ivy ['aivi] *n* edera *f*.

J

jab [dʒab] *n* puntura *f*. *v* pungere, punzecchiare.

jack [dʒak] *n* (*car*) cricco *m*; (*cards*) fante *m*; (*bowls*) boccino *m*. *v* **jack up** alzare.

jackdaw ['dʒakdɔi] *n* taccola *f*.

jacket ['dʒakit] *n* giacca *f*; (*of book*) copertina *f*; (*boiler, etc.*) rivestimento *m*. **jacket potato** patata in camicia *f*.

jack-knife ['dʒaknaif] *n* coltello a serramanico *m*.

jackpot ['dʒakpot] *n* posta intera *f*, monte premi *m*. **hit the jackpot** avere un colpo di fortuna.

jade [dʒeid] *n* giada *f*.

jaded ['dʒeidid] *adj* stracco, spossato.

jagged ['dʒagid] *adj* scabro, intaccato, dentellato.

jaguar ['dʒagjuə] *n* giaguaro *m*.

jail *or* **gaol** [dʒeil] *n* prigione *f*, carcere *m*. *v* incarcerare, mettere in prigione.

jam¹ [dʒam] *v* (*block*) bloccare; (*cause to stop functioning*) intralciare; (*squeeze*) pigiare; (*radio*) disturbare; (*traffic*) intasare. **jam on the brakes** bloccare i freni. *n* (*traffic*) intasamento *m*. **get into a jam** mettersi nei pasticci.

jam² [dʒam] *n* marmellata *f*, conserva di frutta *f*.

janitor ['dʒanitə] *n* portinaio, -a *m, f*.

January ['dʒanjuəri] *n* gennaio *m*.

Japan [dʒə'pan] *n* Giappone *m*. **Japanese** *n*(*m+f*), *adj* giapponese.

jar¹ [dʒai] *n* (*vessel*) brocca *f*; (*usually with lid*) barattolo *m*.

jar² [dʒai] *v* vibrare; produrre un suono aspro. **jarring** *adj* discorde.

jargon ['dʒaigən] *n* gergo *m*.

jasmine ['dʒazmin] *n* gelsomino *m*.

jaundice ['dʒɔindis] *n* itterizia *f*. **jaundiced** *adj* distorto, invelenito.

jaunt [dʒɔint] *n* gita *f*.

jaunty ['dʒɔinti] *adj* vivace, disinvolto.

javelin ['dʒavəlin] *n* giavellotto *m*.

jaw [dʒɔi] *n* (*upper*) mascella *f*; (*lower*) mandibola *f*.

jay [dʒei] *n* ghiandaia *f*.

jazz [dʒaz] *n* jazz *m invar*.

jealous ['dʒeləs] *adj* geloso. **become jealous** ingelosirsi. **make jealous** ingelosire. **jealousy** *n* gelosia *f*.

jeans [dʒiins] *pl n* jeans *m pl*.

jeep [dʒiip] *n* jeep *f invar*.

jeer [dʒiə] *v* schernire, canzonare. *n* derisione *f*, scherno *m*.

jelly ['dʒeli] *n* gelatină *f*, budino di gelatina *m*.

jeopardize ['dʒepədaiz] *v* mettere a repentaglio, arrischiare. **jeopardy** *n* repentaglio *m*.

jerk [dʒəik] *n* (*shock*) scossa *f*; (*pull*) strappo *m*; (*sudden start*) scatto *m*. *v* scuotere; dare uno strappoa; scattare.

jersey ['dʒəizi] *n* (*fabric*) jersey *m invar*; (*garment*) maglione *m*.

jest [dʒest] *n* scherzo *m*, burla *f*. *v* scherzare. **jester** *n* buffone *m*.

Jesuit ['dʒezjuit] *adj, nm* gesuita. **Jesuitical** *adj* gesuitico.

Jesus ['dʒiizəs] *n* Gesù *m*. **Jesus Christ** Gesù Cristo.

jet [dʒet] *n* getto *m*, zampillo *m*; (*spout*) becco *m*; (*aero*) aviogetto *m*, aeroplano a reazione *m*. **jet-black** *adj* (nero) ebano *invar*. **jet engine** motore a reazione *m*.

jettison ['dʒetisn] *v* buttar via, disfarsi di.

jetty ['dʒeti] *n* molo *m*, banchina *f*.

Jew [dʒui] *n* ebreo, -a *m, f*. **Jewish** *adj* (*person*) ebreo; (*thing*) ebraico.

jewel ['dʒuiəl] *n* gioiello *m*; (*watch*) rubino *m*; (*treasure*) tesoro *m*. **jeweller** *n* gioielliere *m*. **jewellery** *n* gioielleria *f*.

jib¹ [dʒib] *n* (*sail*) fiocco *m*; (*crane*) braccio *m*.

jib² [dʒib] *v* **jib at** essere restio *or* ritroso a.

jig¹ [dʒig] *n* (*machine tool*) maschera di montaggio *f*. *v* lavorare con maschere.

jig² *n* (*dance*) giga *f*. *v* ballare la giga. **jig up and down** salterellare su e giù.

jiggle ['dʒigl] *v* dondolare, muoversi in qua e in là.

jigsaw ['dʒigsɔɪ] *n* sega da traforo *f*. **jigsaw puzzle** puzzle *m*.

jilt [dʒilt] *v* piantare in asso.

jingle ['dʒiŋgl] *n* (*sound*) tintinnio *m*; (*song*) ritornello *m*, cantilena *f*. *v* tintinnare.

jinx [dʒiŋks] *n* malocchio *m*.

job [dʒob] *n* impiego (*pl* -ghi) *m*, lavoro *m*; (*coll*) affare *m*, mestiere *m*.

jockey ['dʒoki] *n* fantino *m*. *v* maneggiare.

jocular ['dʒokjulə] *adj* faceto.

jodhpurs ['dʒodpəz] *pl n* calzoni da equitazione *m pl*.

jog [dʒog] *v* (*sport*) fare il footing; (*horse*) andare al piccolo trotto. **jog the memory** richiamare alla memoria. *n* (*push*) spinta *f*; (*nudge*) colpetto *m*; (*elbowing*) gomitata *f*; (*trot*) piccolo trotto *m*.

join [dʒoin] *n* giuntura *f*. *v* unire, congiungere, unirsi a; (*become member*) iscriversi a, entrare. **join in** entrare a far parte di.

joiner ['dʒoinə] *n* falegname *m*.

joint [dʒoint] *n* (*join*) giuntura *f*; articolazione *f*; (*plant*) nodo *m*; (*meat*) taglio (di carne) *m*; (*coll: bar, etc.*) bettola *f*. *adj* comune, collettivo.

joist [dʒoist] *n* trave *f*, travicello *m*.

joke [dʒouk] *n* scherzo *m*, barzelletta *f*. **no joke** un affare serio *m*. *v* scherzare. **joker** *n* burlone *m*; (*cards*) jolly *m invar*, matta *f*.

jolly ['dʒoli] *adj* divertente, ameno, gaio. *adv* molto.

jolt [dʒoult] *v* scuotere, far sobbalzare. *n* scossa *f*, sobbalzo *m*.

jostle ['dʒosl] *n* (*push*) spinta *f*; (*elbowing*) gomitata *f*. *v* fare a gomitate, spingersi avanti.

journal ['dʒəɪnl] *n* periodico *m*; (*daily record*) diario *m*, giornale *m*; (*day-book*) brogliaccio *m*. **journalism** *n* giornalismo *m*. **journalist** *n* giornalista *m, f*.

journey ['dʒəɪni] *n* viaggio *m*. *v* viaggiare. **go on a journey** andare *or* mettersi in viaggio.

jovial ['dʒouviəl] *adj* gioviale, lieto.

jowl [dʒaul] *n* (*jaw*) mascella *f*; (*flesh*) gota *f*.

joy [dʒoi] *n* gioia *f*, allegrezza *f*, allegria *f*. **joyful** *or* **joyous** *adj* gioioso.

jubilant ['dʒuɪbilənt] *adj* giubilante.

jubilee ['dʒuɪbiliɪ] *n* giubileo *m*.

Judaism ['dʒuɪdeiˌizəm] *n* giudaismo *m*.

judge [dʒʌdʒ] *n* giudice *m*; (*of competition*) arbitro *m*; (*expert*) intenditore, -trice *m, f*. *v* giudicare, considerare. **judgment** *n* giudizio *m*; (*law*) sentenza *f*; (*opinion*) parere *m*. **Last Judgment** giudizio universale *m*.

judicial [dʒuɪ'diʃəl] *adj* giudiziario; legale.

judiciary [dʒuˈdiʃiəri] *n* magistratura *f*.

judicious [dʒuɪˈdiʃəs] *adj* giudizioso, prudente.

judo ['dʒuɪdou] *n* judo *m invar*, giudò *m*.

jug [dʒʌg] *n* brocca *f*, caraffa *f*.

juggernaut ['dʒʌgənoit] *n* (*lorry*) grosso autotreno *m*.

juggle ['dʒʌgl] *v* giocolare, prestigiare; (*trick*) truffare. **juggle with** svisare, travisare. **juggler** *n* giocoliere, -a *m, f*; prestigiatore, -trice *m, f*.

jugular ['dʒʌgjulə] *adj* giugulare.

juice [dʒuɪs] *n* succo *m*, sugo *m*. **juicy** *adj* sugoso, succolento.

jukebox ['dʒuɪkboks] *n* jukebox *m invar*.

July [dʒu'lai] *n* luglio *m*.

jumble ['dʒʌmbl] *n* miscuglio *m*, confusione *f*. **jumble sale** bazar di beneficenza *m invar*.

jump [dʒʌmp] *n* salto *m*; (*sudden rise*) balzo *m*; (*nervous*) sussulto *m*. **long/high jump** salto in lungo/alto *m*. *v* saltare, fare un salto; sussultare; (*of prices*) rincarare. **jump at** accettare con entusiasmo. **jump off** lanciarsi da. **jump over** scavalcare.

jumper ['dʒʌmpə] *n* (*pullover*) maglione *m*, pullover *m invar*; (*jacket*) casacca *f*; (*person*) saltatore, -trice *m, f*.

junction ['dʒʌŋktʃən] *n* congiunzione *f*; (*rail*) nodo ferroviario *m*.

juncture ['dʒʌŋkʃə] *n* frangente *m*, momento (critico) *m*.

June [dʒuɪn] *n* giugno *m*.

jungle ['dʒʌŋgl] *n* giungla *f*.

junior ['dʒuɪnjə] *adj* minore, più giovane.

juniper ['dʒuɪnipə] *n* ginepro *m*.

junk[1] [dʒʌŋk] *n* (*rubbish*) roba vecchia *f*, robaccia *f*, rifiuti *m pl*.

junk[2] [dʒʌŋk] *n* (*boat*) giunca *f*.

junta ['dʒʌntə] *n* giunta *f*.

jurisdiction [dʒuəris'dikʃən] *n* giurisdizione *f*.

jury ['dʒuəri] *n* giuria *f*. **juror** *n* giurato, -a *m, f*.

just [dʒʌst] *adj* giusto, preciso. *adv* giusto, per l'appunto, proprio; (*barely*) appena; (*not more than*) soltanto.
justice ['dʒʌstis] *n* giustizia *f*; (*judge*) giudice *m*, magistrato *m*. **do justice to** (*show appreciation*) far onore a; (*concede what is due*) apprezzare, stimare.
justify ['dʒʌstifai] *v* giustificare, scusare. **justifiable** *adj* giustificabile, scusabile, legittimo. **justification** *n* giustificazione *f*, scusa *f*.
jut [dʒʌt] *v* sporgere, protendere (in fuori).
jute [dʒuːt] *n* giuta *f*.
juvenile ['dʒuːvənail] *adj* giovanile, per ragazzi, minorenne.
juxtapose [,dʒʌkstə'pouz] *v* giustapporre. **juxtaposition** *n* giustapposizione *f*.

K

kaleidoscope [kə'laidəskoup] *n* caleidoscopio *m*.
kangaroo [kaŋgə'ruː] *n* canguro *m*.
karate [kə'raiti] *n* karatè *m invar*.
keel [kiːl] *n* chiglia *f*. *v* **keel over** capovolgersi.
keen [kiːn] *adj* (*cutting*) tagliente; (*sharp*) aguzzo; (*perceptive*) vivo, perspicace; (*biting*) mordace; (*eager*) appassionato, entusiasta. **keenness** *n* passione *f*, entusiasmo *m*, intensità *f*; (*eagerness*) ardore *m*.
*****keep** [kiːp] *v* tenere; mantenere; conservare; (*hold in custody*) custodire; (*manage*) gestire; (*observe*) osservare, rispettare. **keep at** persistere, continuare a fare. **keep back** (*stay behind*) stare indietro; (*withhold*) trattenere. **keep down** reprimere. **keep good time** (*watch*) funzionare bene. **keep in with** mantenersi in buoni rapporti con. **keep on** continuare. **keep out** non lasciar entrare; restar fuori. **keep to** aderire a. *n* **earn one's keep** mantenersi. **for keeps** per sempre.
keeper ['kiːpə] *n* guardiano, -a *m*, *f*; custode *m*, *f*.
keeping ['kiːpiŋ] *n* custodia *f*. **in keeping with** conforme *or* consono a.
keepsake ['kiːpseik] *n* ricordo *m*.
keg [keg] *n* barilotto *m*.
kennel ['kenl] *n* canile *m*.
kept [kept] *V* **keep**.

kerb [kəːb] *n* banchina *f*.
kernel ['kəːnl] *n* nocciolo *m*, nucleo *m*.
kerosene ['kerəsiːn] *n* cherosene *m*.
kettle ['ketl] *n* bollitore *m*, pentola *f*.
kettledrum ['ketldrʌm] *n* timpano *m*.
key [kiː] *n* chiave *f*; (*part of keyboard*) tasto *m*. **keyboard** *n* tastiera *f*. **keyhole** *n* buco della chiave *m*. **keynote** *n* nota determinante *f*.
khaki ['kaiki] *adj* cachi.
kick [kik] *v* dare un calcio a, dare una pedata a; protestare. **kick off** iniziare. **kick out** buttar fuori. **kick up** scatenare, provocare. *n* calcio *m*, pedata *f*; (*force*) forza *f*.
kid[1] [kid] *n* (*child*) bimbo, -a *m*, *f*; (*goat*) capretto *m*. **handle with kid gloves** trattare coi guanti.
kid[2] [kid] *v* (*coll*) prendere in giro.
kidnap ['kidnap] *v* rapire. **kidnapper** *n* rapitore, -trice *m*, *f*.
kidney ['kidni] *n* (*organ*) rene *m*; (*food*) rognone *f*. **kidney bean** fagiolo *m*.
kill [kil] *v* uccidere, ammazzare. **killer** *n* assassino, -a *m*, *f*.
kiln [kiln] *n* forno *m*.
kilo ['kiːlou] *n* chilo *m*. **kilogram** *n* chilogrammo *m*.
kilometre ['kiləmiːtə] *n* chilometro *m*.
kilt [kilt] *n* gonnellino scozzese *m*.
kin [kin] *n* parenti *m pl*; (*kinship*) parentela *f*. **kinsman** *n* parente *m*. **next of kin** parente prossimo *m*.
kind[1] [kaind] *adj* gentile, cortese, buono; (*well-meant*) cordiale. **kind-hearted** *adj* benevolo. **kindly** *adv* gentilmente; (*please*) per cortesia, per favore. **kindness** *n* gentilezza *f*, cortesia *f*.
kind[2] [kaind] *n* genere *m*, specie *f*, razza *f*.
kindergarten ['kindəgaitn] *n* giardino d'infanzia *m*, asilo (infantile) *m*.
kindle ['kindl] *v* accendere; (*excite*) eccitare.
kindred ['kindrid] *n* parentela *f*. *adj* affine, simile. **kindred spirit** anima gemella *f*.
kinetic [kin'etik] *adj* chinetico.
king [kiŋ] *n* re *m invar*. **kingdom** *n* regno *m*.
kingfisher ['kiŋ,fiʃə] *n* martin pescatore *m*.
kink [kiŋk] *n* attorcigliamento *m*, piega *f*; (*whim*) ghiribizzo *m*. **kinky** *adj* (*odd*) strambo; (*coll*) pervertito.

kiosk ['kiɪosk] n chiosco m; (newsagent) edicola f.
kipper ['kipə] n aringa affumicata f.
kiss [kis] n bacio m. v baciare.
kit [kit] n (tools) attrezzi m pl, utensili m pl; (outfit) corredo m. v attrezzare. **kit out** equipaggiare.
kitchen ['kitʃin] n cucina f.
kite [kait] n aquilone m; (bird) nibbio m.
kitten ['kitn] n micio m, gattino m.
kitty ['kiti] n (joint pool) fondo comune m; (cards) posta f.
kleptomania [kleptə'meiniə] n cleptomania f. **kleptomaniac** n cleptomane m, f.
knack [nak] n destrità f, bernoccolo m.
knapsack ['napsak] n zaino m.
knave [neiv] n furfante m; (cards) fante m.
knead [niɪd] v impastare.
knee [niɪ] n ginocchio m (pl -a f). **kneecap** n rotula f, patella f. **knee-deep** adj che arriva fino al ginocchio; (submerged) sommerso.
***kneel** [niɪl] v inginocchiarsi, mettersi in ginocchio.
knelt [nelt] V **kneel**.
knew [njuɪ] V **know**.
knickers ['nikəz] pl n mutandine f pl.
knife [naif] n coltello m. v accoltellare.
knight [nait] n cavaliere m.
***knit** [nit] v lavorare a maglia, fare la calza; (join together) unire. **knit one's brows** aggrottare le ciglia. **knitting needle** ferro da calza m. **knitwear** n maglieria f.
knob [nob] n pomo m, manopola f; (protuberance) bitorzolo m. **knobbly** adj bitorzoluto, nodoso.
knock [nok] v (at door) bussare; (hit) colpire, battere; (of motor engine) battere in testa. **knock about** (mistreat) malmenare; (wander aimlessly) fare vita randagia. **knock down** (strike) abbattere; demolire; (lower) abbassare. **knock-kneed** adj dalle gambe a X. **knock off** (stop work) tralasciare, smettere; (deduct) dedurre; (coll: steal) far man bassa, portar via; (complete hurriedly) buttar giù. **knock out** (stun) far perdere i sensi a; (put out of action) mettere fuori combattimento. **knock together** (make hurriedly) acciabattare. **knock up** (wake) svegliare; (tennis) fare del palleggio. n colpo m; bussata f; (blow) batosta f.
knocker n battiporta m invar, picchiotto m.

knot [not] n nodo m. v annodare. **knotted** adj nodoso, annodato, pieno di nodi.
knotty adj pieno di nodi; difficile, complesso.
***know** [nou] v (facts) sapere; (be acquainted with) conoscere; (understand) capire; (recognize) riconoscere. **as far as is known** per quanto si sappia. **know about** essere informato su, essere al corrente di. **know how to** sapere. n **in the know** (coll) al corrente. **knowing** adj accorto, intelligente. **known** adj noto, conosciuto. **make known** far sapere or conoscere, divulgare, render noto.
knowledge ['nolidʒ] n cognizione f, conoscenze f pl.
known [noun] V **know**.
knuckle ['nʌkl] n nocca f. **knuckle down** applicarsi. **knuckle under** sottomettersi, piegarsi.
kosher ['kouʃə] adj kasher, cascer.

L

label ['leibl] n etichetta f; (strip of paper) cartellino m; definizione f. v etichettare, qualificare.
laboratory [lə'borətəri] n laboratorio m.
labour ['leibə] n (toil) lavoro m; (hard work, task) fatica f; (effort) sforzo m; (workforce) manodopera f; (childbirth) doglie del parto f pl, travaglio del parto m. **Labour Party** partito laburista m. **labour-saving** adj che risparmia fatica. v faticare, lavorare. **labour under** essere vittima di. **laborious** adj laborioso, faticoso.
laburnum [lə'bəɪnəm] n laburno m.
labyrinth ['labərinθ] n labirinto m.
lace [leis] n pizzo m, merletto m, brina f; (string, cord) laccio m; (braid) gallone m. v (fasten) allacciare; (trim with lace) ornare di pizzi; (add to drink) correggere.
lacemaker n trinaia f.
lacerate ['lasəreit] v lacerare.
lack [lak] n mancanza f, insufficienza f. v mancare (di).
lackadaisical [ˌlakə'deizikəl] adj svogliato, infingardo.
lacquer ['lakə] n lacca f. v laccare.
lad [lad] n ragazzo m, giovanotto m.

ladder ['ladə] n scala f; (stocking) smagliatura f. v smagliarsi. **ladder-proof** adj indemagliabile.

laden ['leidn] adj carico (m pl -chi).

ladle ['leidl] n (dish-shaped) mestolo m; (cup-shaped) ramaiuolo m, cucchiaione m. v scodellare.

lady ['leidi] n signora f. **lady of the house** padrona di casa f.

ladybird ['leidibəɪd] n coccinella f.

lag[1] [lag] v avanzare lentamente. **lag behind** rimanere indietro. n ritardo m, intervallo m.

lag[2] [lag] v (cover) rivestire di materiale isolante, isolare. **lagging** n rivestimento isolante m.

lager ['laɪgə] n birra (chiara) f.

lagoon [lə'guɪn] n laguna f.

laid [leid] V lay[1].

lain [lein] V lie[1].

lair [leə] n tana f.

laity ['leiəti] n the laity i laici m pl.

lake [leik] n lago m.

lamb [lam] n agnello m.

lame [leim] adj zoppo, storpio; (poor) debole, insufficiente. **lame duck** fallito m.

lament [lə'ment] n lamento m. v lamentare, compiangere. **lamented** adj compianto.

laminate ['lamineit] v laminare.

lamp [lamp] n lampada f, lume m; (of car, ship) fanale m. **lamp-holder** n portalampada m. **lamp-post** n lampione m. **lampshade** n paralume m.

lance [laɪns] n lancia f. v incidere col bisturi. **lancet** n bisturi m invar.

land [land] n terra f; (country) paese m; (agricultural area) campagna f; (site, soil) terreno m. v (put on shore) sbarcare, approdare; (from the air) atterrare; (obtain) ottenere. **landing** n sbarco m; atterraggio m; (of stairs) pianerottolo m.

landlady ['landleidi] n padrona di casa f, proprietaria f.

landlord ['landloɪd] n padrone di casa m, proprietario m; (of inn) oste m.

landmark ['landmaɪk] n punto di riferimento m.

landscape ['landskeip] n paesaggio m.

landslide ['landslaid] n frana f.

lane [lein] n (between houses) vicolo m; (track) sentiero m; (part of road, sports track) corsia f.

language ['laŋgwidʒ] n (of a nation) lingua f; (means of expression) linguaggio m.

languish ['laŋgwiʃ] v languire.

lanky ['laŋki] adj alto e magro.

lantern ['lantən] n lanterna f.

lap[1] [lap] n (anat) grembo m; (loose fold) falda f, piega f; (circuit) giro m; (part of journey) tappa f.

lap[2] [lap] v lambire. **lap up** lappare; (coll) ascoltare or accettare con avidità.

lapel [lə'pel] n risvolto m.

Lapland ['lapland] n Lapponia f. **Lapp** n(m+f), adj lappone.

lapse [laps] n svista f, errore m; (time) corso m, periodo m; (law) scadenza f; decadenza f. v (become void) scadere; (decline) decadere; (time) trascorrere. **lapsed** adj (law) decaduto; (rel) apostata.

larceny ['laɪsəni] n furto m.

larch [laɪtʃ] n larice m.

lard [laɪd] n strutto m.

larder ['laɪdə] n dispensa f.

large [laɪdʒ] adj grande, ampio. **at large** in libertà; (in general) in complesso.

lark[1] [laɪk] n (bird) allodola f.

lark[2] [laɪk] (coll) n burla f. v **lark about** divertirsi.

larva ['laɪvə] n, pl **larvae** larva f.

larynx ['lariŋks] n laringe f. **laryngitis** n laringite f.

laser ['leizə] n laser m invar.

lash [laʃ] n sferzata f; (eye) ciglio m (pl -a f). v (whip) sferzare; (tie) legare. **lash out** menar colpi; (coll: money) non badare a spese. **lash out at** inveire contro.

lass [las] n fanciulla f, giovane f.

lassitude ['lasitjuɪd] n stanchezza f.

lasso [la'suɪ] n lasso m, laccio m. v catturare al lasso or laccio.

last[1] [laɪst] adj finale, ultimo; (past) scorso, passato. **last but one** penultimo. **last night** ieri sera. adv (after all others) per ultimo; (most recently) l'ultima volta; finalmente. **at last** alla fine, finalmente.

last[2] [laɪst] v durare. **lasting** adj durevole.

latch [latʃ] n saliscendi m invar, chiavistello m. v chiudere con saliscendi. **latch on to** afferrare.

late [leit] adj tardo; recente; (former) precedente; (dead) defunto, fu. adv (not on time) in ritardo; (not early) tardi. **lately** adv recentemente. **lateness** n ritardo

m. **later** *adv* più tardi, dopo. **see you later!** a più tardi! **latest** *adj* ultimo; recentissimo. **at the latest** al più tardi.
latent ['leitənt] *adj* latente.
lateral ['latərəl] *adj* laterale.
lathe [leið] *n* tornio *m.*
lather ['laɪðə] *n* schiuma *f.* *v* (*of soap*) far schiuma.
Latin ['latin] *nm, adj* latino.
latitude ['latitjuɪd] *n* latitudine *f.*
latrine [lə'triɪn] *n* latrina *f.*
latter ['latə] *adj* secondo, ultimo. **the latter** il secondo, questo.
lattice ['latis] *n* traliccio *m,* grata *f.*
laugh [laɪf] *v* ridere. **laugh at** ridere per *or* di. *n* risata *f;* (*coll*) spasso *m.* **have a laugh** fare una risata. **laughable** *adj* ridicolo, risibile. **laughing stock** zimbello *m.* **laughter** *n* riso *m* (*pl* -a *f*), risata *f.*
launch¹ [loɪntʃ] *v* varare; (*give a start*) lanciare; (*attack*) sferrare.
launch² [loɪntʃ] *n* (*naut*) lancia *f.*
launder ['loɪndə] *v* fare il bucato, lavare e stirare. **launderette** *n* lavanderia automatica *f,* lavanderia a gettoni *f.* **laundry** *n* (*place*) lavanderia *f;* (*clothes, etc.*) bucato *m.*
laurel ['lorəl] *n* alloro *m,* lauro *m.*
lava ['laɪvə] *n* lava *f.*
lavatory ['lavətəri] *n* gabinetto *m,* ritirata *f.*
lavender ['lavində] *n* lavanda *f.*
lavish ['laviʃ] *adj* prodigo, generoso. *v* dispensare *or* spendere largamente.
law [loɪ] *n* legge *f;* (*profession*) diritto *m;* (*rule*) norma *f,* regola *f.* **law-abiding** *adj* ligio alla legge. **lawsuit** *n* causa *f,* processo *m.* **lawful** *adj* legittimo, lecito. **lawyer** *n* avvocato, -essa *m, f.*
lawn [loɪn] *n* prato rasato *m.* **lawn-mower** *n* falciatrice *or* tosatrice per prati *f.*
lax [laks] *adj* rilassato; negligente.
laxative ['laksətiv] *nm, adj* lassativo.
***lay¹** [lei] *v* posare, mettere; (*eggs*) deporre; (*table*) apparecchiare. **lay-by** *n* area *or* piazzola di sosta *or* parcheggio *f.* **lay down** posare per terra; stabilire. **lay off** (*workers*) sospendere. **lay on** disporre, installare. **layout** *n* disposizione *f;* (*sketch*) tracciato *m,* pianta *f.* **lay out** (*spread*) stendere; (*coll: spend*) sborsare. **be laid up** essere costretto di rimanere a letto.
lay² [lei] *adj* laico; non professionale. **layman** *n* laico, -a *m, f;* profano, -a *m, f.*

lay³ [lei] *V* **lie¹**.
layer ['leiə] *n* strato *m.*
lazy ['leizi] *adj* pigro, indolente. **laziness** *n* pigrizia *f.*
***lead¹** [liɪd] *v* condurre; influenzare; (*bring*) portare; (*be at head of*) essere in testa di, essere al comando di; (*act as guide*) guidare; (*make go*) indurre. *n* direzione *f,* comando *m;* (*for dog*) guinzaglio *m;* (*theatre*) primo attore, prima attrice *m, f.* **be in the lead** (*sport*) essere in testa. **take the lead** (*sport*) passare in testa. **leader** *n* capo *m,* dirigente *m, f;* (*newspaper*) articolo di fondo *m.* **leadership** *n* direzione *f,* comando *m.* **leading** *adj* principale, primo.
lead² [led] *n* piombo *m.* **leaden** *adj* di piombo.
leaf [liɪf] *n* (*plant*) foglia *f;* (*paper*) foglio *m;* (*table*) asse *f.* *v* **leaf through** sfogliare. **leaflet** *n* volantino *m,* manifestino *m.*
league [liɪg] *n* lega *f;* classe *f.*
leak [liɪk] *n* (*escape*) fuga *f;* (*crack*) fessura *f;* (*boat*) falla *f;* (*news*) trapelamento *m.* *v* perdere; (*boat*) far acqua; trapelare.
***lean¹** [liɪn] *v* appoggiare, inclinare, pendere. **lean against** appoggiarsi a. **lean out** sporgersi. **lean towards** tendere verso. **leaning** *n* inclinazione *f,* propensione *f.*
lean² [liɪn] *adj* magro, scarno; (*poor*) povero.
leant [lent] *V* **lean¹**.
***leap** [liɪp] *n* salto *m,* balzo *m.* **by leaps and bounds** a passi da gigante. *v* saltare, balzare. **leap-frog** *n* cavallina *f.* **leap year** anno bisestile *m.*
leapt [lept] *V* **leap**.
***learn** [ləɪn] *v* imparare, studiare; (*become informed*) sentire, apprendere. **learned** *adj* dotto, erudito, colto. **learner** *n* (*beginner*) principiante *m, f;* allievo, -a *m, f;* apprendista *m, f.* **learning** *n* cultura *f,* erudizione *f.*
learnt [ləɪnt] *V* **learn**.
lease [liɪs] *n* affitto *m,* contratto d'affitto *m.* *v* affittare.
leash [liɪʃ] *n* guinzaglio *m.*
least [liɪst] *adj* minimo. *pron, adv* (il) meno. **at least** almeno. **not in the least** per nulla, affatto.
leather ['leðə] *n* cuoio *m,* pelle *f.* **leather goods** pelletteria *f sing.*
***leave¹** [liɪv] *v* lasciare; abbandonare; (*go out from*) uscire da; (*depart*) partire. **leave alone** lasciar stare, lasciare in pace.

leave home andar via. **leave out** omettere. **be left** rimanere. **be left over** avanzare.
leave² [liːv] *n* permesso *m*; (*holiday*) licenza *f*, congedo *m*.
lecherous ['letʃərəs] *adj* lussurioso, lascivo. **lecher** *n* libertino *m*. **lechery** *n* lascivia *f*.
lectern ['lektən] *n* leggio *m*.
lecture ['lektʃə] *n* lezione *f*, conferenza *f*; (*reprimand*) ramanzina *f*, sgridata *f*. *v* tenere una conferenza; dare un corso di lezioni; (*rebuke*) predicare, fare una paternale a. **lecturer** *n* conferenziere, -a *m, f*; (*university*) docente *m, f*.
led [led] *V* **lead¹**.
ledge [ledʒ] *n* (*window*) davanzale *m*; (*projecting part*) sporgenza *f*.
ledger ['ledʒə] *n* (libro) mastro *m*.
lee [liː] *n* (*shelter*) riparo *m*; (*naut*) sottovento *m*. **leeward** *adj, adv* sottovento.
leech [liːtʃ] *n* sanguisuga *f*.
leek [liːk] *n* porro *m*.
leer [liə] *v* guardare di sbieco. *n* sguardo sbieco *m*.
leeway ['liːwei] *n* (*naut*) deriva *f*. **make up leeway** recuperare lo svantaggio.
left¹ [left] *V* **leave¹**.
left² [left] *adj* sinistro. *n* sinistra *f*. **the Left** (*pol*) la Sinistra. *adv* a sinistra, verso sinistra, sulla sinistra. **left-hand** *adj* sinistro. **left-handed** *adj* mancino.
leg [leg] *n* gamba *f*; (*furniture*) piede *m*; (*lap*) tappa *f*; (*poultry*) coscia *f*; (*meat*) cosciotto *m*.
legacy ['legəsi] *n* lascito *m*, eredità *f*.
legal ['liːgəl] *adj* lecito, legittimo, legale. **legality** *n* legalità *f*. **legalize** *v* legalizzare, legittimare.
legend ['ledʒənd] *n* leggenda *f*. **legendary** *adj* leggendario.
Leghorn [ˌleg'hoːn] *n* Livorno *m*.
legible ['ledʒəbl] *adj* leggibile. **legibility** *n* leggibilità *f*.
legion ['liːdʒən] *n* legione *f*.
legislate ['ledʒisleit] *v* promulgare leggi. **legislation** *n* legislazione *f*.
legitimate [lə'dʒitimət] *adj* legittimo, lecito. *v* legittimare. **legitimacy** *n* legittimità *f*.
leisure ['leʒə] *n* agio *m*, tempo libero *m*. **leisurely** *adj* fatto con comodo.
lemon ['lemən] *n* limone *m*. *adj* color limone *invar*. **lemonade** *n* limonata *f*. **lemon juice** succo di limone *m*.

*lend [lend] *v* prestare, dare in prestito.
length [leŋθ] *n* lunghezza *f*; (*time*) durata *f*; (*cloth*) taglio *m*. **at length** per disteso.
lengthen *v* allungare. **lengthy** *adj* lungo.
lenient ['liːniənt] *adj* benigno, indulgente. **leniency** *n* indulgenza *f*.
lens [lenz] *n* lente *f*; (*camera*) obiettivo *m*.
lent [lent] *V* **lend**.
Lent [lent] *n* quaresima *f*.
lentil ['lentil] *n* lenticchia *f*.
Leo ['liːou] *n* Leone *m*.
leopard ['lepəd] *n* leopardo *m*.
leotard ['liːətaːd] *n* calzamaglia (*pl* calzemaglie) *f*.
leper ['lepə] *n* lebbroso, -a *m, f*. **leprosy** *n* lebbra *f*.
lesbian ['lezbiən] *n* lesbica *f*.
less [les] *adj* minore, meno. *nm, adv, prep* meno. **lessen** *v* diminuire. **lesser** *adj* minore, inferiore.
lesson ['lesn] *n* lezione *f*.
lest [lest] *conj* per paura che.
*let [let] *v* lasciare, permettere; (*rent*) affittare. **let down** (*lower*) calare; (*hair*) sciogliere; (*disappoint*) deludere; (*dress*) allungare. **let in** fare entrare. **let know** far sapere. **let out** far uscire, liberare; (*dress*) allargare; (*secret*) lasciar sfuggire; (*emit*) fare.
lethal ['liːθəl] *adj* letale.
lethargy ['leθədʒi] *n* letargia *f*. **lethargic** *adj* letargico.
letter ['letə] *n* lettera *f*; (*character*) carattere *m*. **letter-box** *n* buca delle lettere *f*. **lettering** *n* iscrizione *f*.
lettuce ['letis] *n* lattuga *f*.
leukaemia [luː'kiːmiə] *n* leucemia *f*.
level ['levl] *n* livello *m*, piano *m*; (*height, position*) altezza *f*. *v* livellare, spianare. *adj* piano, uniforme; (*equal*) pari. **be level with** essere a livello di. **level crossing** passaggio a livello *m*. **level-headed** *adj* equilibrato.
lever ['liːvə] *n* leva *f*. **leverage** *n* leva *f*, stimolo *m*.
levy ['levi] *n* imposta *f*, contributo *m*. *v* imporre, esigere.
lewd [luːd] *adj* lascivo, osceno.
liable ['laiəbl] *adj* responsabile. **liable to** soggetto a, passibile di. **liability** *n* obbligo *m*, responsabilità *f*; (*comm*) passività *f*, deficit *m invar*.

liaison [li:'eizon] *n* legame *m*; (*sexual*) relazione amorosa *f*.

liar ['laiə] *n* bugiardo, -a *m*, *f*.

libel ['laibəl] *n* diffamazione *f*, calunnia *f*. *v* diffamare, calunniare. **libellous** *adj* diffamatorio, calunnioso.

liberal ['libərəl] *adj* liberale, generoso. *n* liberale *m*, *f*. **liberalism** *n* liberalismo *m*.

liberate ['libəreit] *v* liberare, mettere in libertà. **liberation** *n* liberazione *f*.

liberty ['libəti] *n* libertà *f*.

Libra ['li:brə] *n* Libra *f*.

library ['laibrəri] *n* biblioteca *f*. **librarian** *n* bibliotecario, -a *m*, *f*.

libretto [li'bretou] *n* libretto *m*.

lice [lais] *V* **louse**.

licence ['laisəns] *n* licenza *f*, permesso *m*; (*driving*) patente (di guida) *f*; (*arms*) porto d'armi *m*. **license** *v* autorizzare. **licensee** *n* gestore autorizzato *m*, concessionario *m*.

lichen ['laikən] *n* lichene *m*.

lick [lik] *v* leccare. *n* leccata *f*.

lid [lid] *n* coperchio *m*.

***lie¹** [lai] *v* giacere, stare sdraiato. **lie down** coricarsi, sdraiarsi. **lie in** (*stay in bed*) restare a letto; (*consist of*) consistere di. **lie with** spettare a.

lie² [lai] *n* (*untruth*) bugia *f*, menzogna *f*. *v* mentire, dire una bugia.

lieu [lu:] *n* **in lieu of** invece di.

lieutenant [ləf'tenənt] *n* tenente *m*.

life [laif] *n* vita *f*. **lifeless** *adj* esanime.

lifebelt ['laifbelt] *n* salvagente *m*.

lifeboat ['laifbout] *n* scialuppa di salvataggio *f*.

life insurance *n* assicurazione sulla vita *f*.

life-jacket *n* cintura di salvataggio *f*.

lifeline ['laiflain] *n* linea di communicazione vitale *f*.

lifelong ['laiflɔŋ] *adj* di tutta la vita.

lifetime ['laiftaim] *n* vita *f*, durata della vita *f*.

lift [lift] *n* ascensore *m*; (*coll: ride*) autostop *m*. *v* sollevare, alzare.

***light¹** [lait] *n* luce *f*, lume *m*; illuminazione *f*. **switch on/off the light** accendere/spegnere la luce. *adj* chiaro. **light bulb** ampolla *f*. **lighthouse** *n* faro *m*. **light-year** *n* anno luce *m*. *v* accendere. **lighten** *v* rischiarare, illuminare. **lighter** *n* (*for cigarette*) accendino *m*. **lighting** *n* illuminazione *f*.

light² [lait] *adj* leggero. **light-headed** *adj*

frivolo; (*giddy*) preso da vertigini. **light-hearted** *adj* gaio. **lighten** *v* alleggerire, alleviare. **lightness** *n* leggerezza *f*.

***light³** [lait] *v* **light upon** imbattersi in.

lightning ['laitniŋ] *n* fulmine *m*, lampo *m*. **lightning conductor** *n* parafulmine *m*.

like¹ [laik] *adj* simile, uguale. *prep* come. **be** *or* **look like** rassomigliare a. **liken** *v* paragonare. **likeness** *n* somiglianza *f*; (*portrait*) ritratto *m*. **likewise** *adv* parimenti, altrettanto.

like² [laik] *v* gradire; (*want*) volere. **I like ...** mi piace .... **likeable** *adj* simpatico. **liking** *n* simpatia *f*, gusto *m*. **have a liking for** trovar simpatico *or* gradevole.

likely ['laikli] *adj* probabile, verosimile. *adv* probabilmente. **likelihood** *n* probabilità *f*.

lilac ['lailək] *nm*, *adj* lilla *invar*.

lily ['lili] *n* giglio *m*. **lily-of-the-valley** *n* mughetto *m*.

limb [lim] *n* arto *m*, membro *m* (*pl* -a *f*).

limbo ['limbou] *n* limbo *m*.

lime¹ [laim] *n* calce *f*. **limestone** *n* calcare *m*.

lime² [laim] *n* (*fruit*) limetta *f*; (*linden*) tiglio *m*.

limelight ['laim,lait] *n* luci della ribalta *f pl*. **be in the limelight** essere alla ribalta.

limit ['limit] *n* limite *m*, ambito *m*. *v* limitare. **limitation** *n* limitazione *f*. **limitless** *adj* illimitato.

limousine ['limə,zi:n] *n* berlina *f*, limousine *f invar*.

limp¹ [limp] *v* zoppicare. *n* zoppicamento *m*.

limp² [limp] *adj* floscio; (*weak*) debole.

limpet ['limpit] *n* patella *f*.

line [lain] *n* linea *f*; (*row*) fila *f*; (*string*) corda *f*; (*wrinkle*) ruga *f*; (*of letters*) riga *f*. *v* rigare; (*clothes*) foderare; (*border*) fiancheggiare. **line up** allineare. **linear** *adj* lineare.

linen ['linin] *n* lino *m*; (*sheets, etc.*) biancheria *f*. *adj* di lino.

liner ['lainə] *n* (*naut*) transatlantico *m*; (*aero*) aereo di linea *m*.

linger ['liŋgə] *v* indugiare, soffermarsi. **lingering** *adj* protratto.

lingerie ['lãʒəri:] *n* biancheria per signora *f*.

linguist ['liŋgwist] *n* linguista *m*, *f*; poliglotta *m*, *f*. **linguistic** *adj* linguistico. **linguistics** *n* linguistica *f*.

lining ['lainiŋ] n (clothes) fodera f; rivestimento interno m.

link [liŋk] n (of chain) anello m; (bond) legame m; (mech) collegamento m. v collegare, congiungere.

linoleum [li'nouliəm] n linoleum m invar.

linseed ['lin,siːd] n semi di lino m pl. **linseed oil** olio di semi di lino m.

lint [lint] n filaccia (di lino) f.

lion ['laiən] n leone m. **lioness** n leonessa f.

lip [lip] n labbro m (pl -a f). **lip-read** v capire dal movimento delle labbra. **lipstick** n rossetto m.

liqueur [li'kjuə] n liquore m.

liquid ['likwid] nm, adj liquido. **liquidate** v liquidare; eliminare. **liquidation** n liquidazione f.

liquor ['likə] n bevanda alcoolica f.

liquorice ['likəris] n liquirizia f.

lisp [lisp] v essere or parlar bleso. n blesità f.

list¹ [list] n lista f, elenco m. v elencare, registrare.

list² [list] v (naut) sbandare. n sbandamento m.

listen ['lisn] v ascoltare; (heed) badare. **listener** n ascoltatore, -trice m, f.

listless ['listlis] adj languido, svogliato.

lit [lit] V **light**.

litany ['litəni] n litania f.

literal ['litərəl] adj letterale. **literally** adv alla lettera, letteralmente.

literary ['litərəri] adj (writing) letterario; (people) letterato.

literate ['litərət] adj che sa leggere e scrivere. **literacy** n il saper leggere e scrivere m.

literature ['litrətʃə] n letteratura f.

litigation [liti'geiʃən] n lite f, causa f. **litigate** v essere in causa.

litre ['liːtə] n litro m.

litter ['litə] n rifiuti m pl, immondizia f; (zool) figliata f; (bed, etc.) lettiga f. v sparpagliare, lasciare in disordine.

little ['litl] adj piccolo, piccino; (not much) un po' di, poco; (short) breve. nm, adv poco. **little by little** a poco a poco.

liturgy ['litədʒi] n liturgia f.

live¹ [liv] v vivere; (reside) abitare, stare. **live by** or **on** vivere di. **live down** far dimenticare. **live up to** mettere in pratica, giustificare.

live² [laiv] adj vivo; (broadcast) dal vivo, in ripresa diretta; (coal, etc.) ardente; (wire) sotto tensione.

livelihood ['laivlihud] n vita f.

lively ['laivli] adj vivace, animato. **liveliness** n vivacità f.

liven ['laivn] v **liven up** animare.

liver ['livə] n fegato m.

livestock ['laivstok] n bestiame m.

livid ['livid] adj livido.

living ['liviŋ] adj vivente, vivo. n vita f. **living room** stanza di soggiorno f.

lizard ['lizəd] n lucertola f.

load [loud] n carico (pl -chi) m; (weight) peso m; (quantity carried) portata f; (elec) carica f. v caricare. **loaded** adj caricato, carico; (question) insidioso; (slang) ricco.

loaf¹ [louf] n pane m.

loaf² [louf] v oziare, girellare, stare con le mani in mano. **loafer** n bighellone, -a m, f; fannullone, -a m, f.

loan [loun] n prestito m. v prestare, dare in prestito.

loathe [louð] v aborrire, detestare. **loathing** n disgusto m. **loathsome** adj disgustoso.

lob [lob] (sport) n pallonetto m. v fare un pallonetto.

lobby ['lobi] n atrio m, anticamera f; (theatre) ridotto m. v influenzare con manovre di anticamera.

lobe [loub] n (anat) lobo m.

lobster ['lobstə] n aragosta f.

local ['loukəl] adj locale, del luogo. **locality** n località f. **localize** v circoscrivere, delimitare.

locate [lə'keit] v individuare; determinare la posizione di; situare. **location** n posizione f, sito m; (cinema) set m invar.

lock¹ [lok] n serratura f; (canal) conca f. **locksmith** n magnano m. **lock, stock, and barrel** barca e barattini. **under lock and key** sotto chiave. v serrare, chiudere a chiave; (mech) bloccare. **lock away** mettere al sicuro. **lock in** rinchiudere. **lock out** chiudere fuori; (workers) fare una serrata. **lock up** chiudere a chiave, mettere sotto chiave.

lock² [lok] n (of hair) ciocca f, ricciolo m.

locker ['lokə] n armadietto m.

locket ['lokit] n medaglione m.

locomotive [,loukə'moutiv] n locomotiva f.

locust ['loukəst] n cavalletta f.

lodge [lodʒ] n capanna f; (porter's) portineria f. v alloggiare; (put in place, deposit) deporre, collocare; (report) presentare. **lodge a complaint** sporgere querela. **lodger** n pensionante m, f. **lodging** n alloggio m.

loft [loft] n solaio m, soffitta f. **lofty** adj alto; (style) nobile.

log [log] n ceppo m, tronco m. **logbook** n registro m; (naut) giornale di bordo m; (mot) libretto di circolazione m. v registrare.

logarithm ['logəriðəm] n logaritmo m.

loggerheads ['logəhedz] n **be at loggerheads** prendersi i capelli, essere ai ferri corti.

logic ['lodʒik] n logica f. **logical** adj logico.

loin [loin] n (cookery) lombata f. **gird up one's loins** apprestarsi.

loiter ['loitə] v bighellonare, passare oziando.

lollipop ['loli,pop] n lecca lecca m invar.

London ['lʌndən] n Londra f.

lonely ['lounli] adj solitario, solo. **loneliness** n solitudine f.

long[1] [loŋ] adj lungo. adv a lungo. **as long as** finquanto. **long-distance** adj a lunga distanza; (phone) interurbano. **long-playing record** disco microsolco m. **long-range** adj (distance) a lunga portata; (time) a lunga scadenza. **long-sighted** adj presbite; (having foresight) previdente. **long-standing** adj di vecchia data. **long-wave** adj (radio) a onde lunghe. **long-winded** adj prolisso.

long[2] [loŋ] v bramare, aver gran desiderio (di). **longing** n brama f, desiderio ardente m.

longevity [lon'dʒevəti] n longevità f.

longitude ['londʒitjuɪd] n longitudine f.

loo [luɪ] n (coll) gabinetto m.

look [luk] n sguardo m, occhiata f; (appearance) aspetto m; espressione f. v guardare; (appear, seem) sembrare, parere. **look after** (care for) occuparsi di, badare a. **look at** guardare, considerare. **look down on** guardare con disprezzo. **look for** cercare. **look forward to** aspettare con impazienza. **look out** guardar fuori, affacciarsi; (be on guard) stare attento. **look over** ripassare, riesaminare.

loom[1] [luɪm] v apparire (indistintamente), intravedere; (be imminent) incombere.

loom[2] [luɪm] n telaio m.

loop [luɪp] n cappio m, laccio m, anello m. v fare un cappio or laccio, allacciare.

loophole ['luɪphoul] n scappatoia f.

loose [luɪs] adj sciolto, libero; (tooth) caduco. **come** or **get loose** allentarsi. **let loose** liberare. **loose-fitting** adj ampio. **loose-leaf** adj a fogli staccati. **loosely** adv scioltamente; in senso lato. **loosen** v sciogliere, allentare.

loot [luɪt] n bottino m. v far man bassa, saccheggiare. **looting** n saccheggio m.

lop [lop] v potare. **lop off** mozzare.

lopsided [,lop'saidid] adj sbilenco, asimmetrico.

lord [loɪd] n signore m; (English title) lord m invar. **lordship** n signoria f.

lorry ['lori] n autocarro m, camion m invar. **lorry-driver** n camionista m.

***lose** [luɪz] v perdere, smarrire; (clock) ritardare. **lose interest** non interessarsi più. **lose one's temper** arrabbiarsi.

loss [los] n perdita f, danno m. **be at a loss** non sapere cosa fare, essere disorientato.

lost [lost] V lose. adj perso, smarrito. **lost cause** causa persa f. **lost property** oggetti smarriti m pl.

lot [lot] n (destiny) sorte f; (of land) lotto m; (method of decision) sorteggio m; (comm) partita f; (coll: large amount) grande quantità f. **a lot of** molto. **lots of** tanti. **the whole lot** tutto quanto. **what a lot of** quanto.

lotion ['louʃən] n lozione f.

lottery ['lotəri] n lotteria f.

lotus ['loutəs] n loto m.

loud [laud] adj forte, alto; (gaudy) vistoso. adv forte. **loud-mouthed** adj sguaiato. **loudspeaker** n altoparlante m. **loudness** n forza f, altezza di voce f.

lounge [laundʒ] n salotto m; sala di ritrovo f. v oziare, dondolarsi.

louse [laus] n, pl **lice** pidocchio m. **lousy** adj pidocchioso; (slang: bad) schifoso.

love [lʌv] n amore m; (tennis) zero m. **fall in love (with)** innamorarsi (di). **love affair** relazione amorosa f. **make love (to)** fare all'amore (con). **with love** (in letter) affettuosamente. v amare, voler bene a. **lovable** adj amabile, simpatico. **lovely** adj bello, grazioso, incantevole. **lover** n amante m, f; (enthusiast) appassionato, -a m, f. **loving** adj affettuoso.

low [lou] adj basso; (coll) depresso; volgare. adv basso, in basso. **lowbrow** adj incolto, popolare. **low-lying** adj situato in pianura. **low-necked** adj scollato. **lowly** adj umile, dimesso.

lower ['louə] *adj* più basso, inferiore. *v* abbassare, ridurre; (*flag*) ammainare; degradare.

loyal ['loiəl] *adj* fedele, devoto, leale. **loyalty** *n* fedeltà *f*, devozione *f*, lealtà *f*.

lozenge ['lozindʒ] *n* pastiglia *f*, pasticca *f*.

lubricate ['luːbrikeit] *v* lubrificare. **lubricant** *nm, adj* lubrificante. **lubrication** *n* lubrificazione *f*.

lucid ['luːsid] *adj* (*easily understood*) chiaro; (*clear*) limpido; (*bright*) lucido.

luck [lʌk] *n* fortuna *f*; (*chance*) sorte *f*. **bad luck** sfortuna *f*. **be in/out of luck** essere fortunato/sfortunato. **good luck** buona fortuna *f*. **lucky** *adj* fortunato.

lucrative ['luːkrətiv] *adj* lucroso, redditizio.

ludicrous ['luːdikrəs] *adj* ridicolo, irrisorio.

lug [lʌg] *v* tirare, trascinare.

luggage ['lʌgidʒ] *n* bagaglio *m*. **hand luggage** bagaglio a mano *m*. **left luggage** deposito bagagli *m*. **luggage rack** *n* (*rail*) rete portabagagli *f*.

lukewarm ['luːkwoːm] *adj* tiepido.

lull [lʌl] *n* momento di calma *m*; (*truce*) tregua *f*. *v* (*put to sleep*) far addormentare; calmare.

lumbago [lʌm'beigou] *n* lombaggine *f*.

lumber¹ ['lʌmbə] *n* legname *m*; (*useless articles*) cianfrusaglie *f pl*. *v* (*encumber*) ingombrare, accatastare. **lumberjack** *n* boscaiolo *m*.

lumber² ['lʌmbə] *v* (*move clumsily*) muoversi pesantemente *or* goffamente.

luminous ['luːminəs] *adj* luminoso.

lump [lʌmp] *n* massa *f*; (*swelling*) gonfiore *m*. **lump sum** somma globale *f*. **lump together** mettere insieme. **lumpy** *adj* grumoso.

lunacy ['luːnəsi] *n* pazzia *f*.

lunar ['luːnə] *adj* lunare.

lunatic ['luːnətik] *n, adj* pazzo, -a, matto, -a. **lunatic asylum** manicomio *m*.

lunch [lʌntʃ] *n* colazione *f*, pranzo *m*. *v* far colazione, pranzare.

lung [lʌŋ] *n* polmone *m*.

lunge [lʌndʒ] *v* scagliarsi. *n* rapido movimento in avanti *m*.

lurch¹ [ləːtʃ] *v* barcollare, sbandare. *n* barcollamento *m*, sbandamento *m*.

lurch² [ləːtʃ] *n* **leave in the lurch** piantare in asso.

lure [luə] *n* (*bait*) esca *f*; (*fascination*) fascino *m*. *v* adescare, attirare, affascinare.

lurid ['luərid] *adj* raccapricciante.

lurk [ləːk] *v* (*be in hiding*) nascondersi; (*lie in wait*) stare in agguato.

luscious ['lʌʃəs] *adj* succulento.

lush [lʌʃ] *adj* lussureggiante.

lust [lʌst] *n* brama *f*; (*sexual*) libidine *f*; concupiscenza *f*. *v* **lust after** aver brama *or* sete di.

lustre ['lʌstə] *n* splendore *m*.

lute [luːt] *n* liuto *m*.

Luxembourg ['lʌksəmˌbəːg] *n* Lussemburgo *m*.

luxury ['lʌkʃəri] *n* lusso *m*. **luxuriant** *adj* lussureggiante, rigoglioso. **luxurious** *adj* lussuoso, di lusso.

lynch [lintʃ] *v* linciare.

lynx [links] *n* lince *f*.

lyre [laiə] *n* lira *f*.

lyrical ['lirikəl] *adj* lirico.

lyrics ['liriks] *pl n* parole (di una canzone) *f pl*.

M

mac [mak] *n* (*coll*) impermeabile *m*.

macabre [mə'kaːbr] *adj* macabro.

macaroni [makə'rouni] *n* maccheroni *m pl*.

mace¹ [meis] *n* (*club*) mazza *f*.

mace² [meis] *n* (*spice*) macis *f invar*.

machine [mə'ʃiːn] *n* macchina *f*. **machine-gun** *n* mitragliatrice *f*. **machine tool** macchina utensile *f*. *v* lavorare a macchina. **machinery** *n* macchinario *m*; meccanismo *m*; (*system*) organizzazione *f*. **machinist** *n* macchinista *m, f*.

mackerel ['makrəl] *n* sgombro *m*.

mackintosh ['makinˌtoʃ] *n* impermeabile *m*.

mad [mad] *adj* matto, pazzo; furioso. **drive mad** far impazzire. **go mad** impazzire. **madden** *v* far impazzire. **madness** *n* pazzia *f*.

madam ['madəm] *n* signora *f*.

made [meid] *V* **make**.

magazine [ˌmagə'ziːn] *n* (*publication*) rivista *f*, periodico *m*; (*phot*) magazzino *m*; (*rifle*) caricatore *m*.

maggot ['magət] *n* larva *f*.

magic ['madʒik] *adj* magico. *n* magia *f*, incanto *m*. **magician** *n* mago *m*, stregone *m*; (*conjurer*) illusionista *m*.

magistrate ['madʒistreit] n magistrato m, pretore m. magistrature n magistratura f, pretura f.

magnanimous [mag'naniməs] adj magnanimo. magnanimity n magnanimità f.

magnate ['magneit] n magnate m.

magnet ['magnət] n magnete m, calamita f. magnetic adj magnetico. magnetism n magnetismo m. magnetize v magnetizzare.

magnificent [mag'nifisnt] adj magnifico, splendido. magnificence n magnificenza f.

magnify ['magnifai] v magnificare, ingrandire. magnifying glass lente d'ingrandimento f. magnification n ingrandimento m.

magnitude ['magnitjuid] n grandezza f.

magnolia [mag'nouliə] n magnolia f.

magpie ['magpai] n gazza f.

mahogany [mə'hogəni] n mogano m.

maid [meid] n domestica f, donna di servizio f. old maid vecchia zitella f.

maiden ['meidən] n fanciulla f. adj primo; (journey) inaugurale. maiden lady signorina f. maiden name nome da ragazza m.

mail¹ [meil] n posta f. mail order vendita per catalogo f. v imbucare, mandare per posta.

mail² [meil] n (armour) maglia di ferro f. mailed fist pugno di ferro m.

maim [meim] v mutilare, storpiare.

main [mein] adj principale, essenziale. mainland n terra ferma f. mainspring n (of watch) molla principale f; (impelling cause) movente principale f. mainstay n (chief support) sostegno m, braccio destro m. mainstream n tendenza dominante f. n (gas, water, etc.) conduttura principale f. in the main nel complesso, in genere. mainly adv sopratutto; in genere.

maintain [mein'tein] v mantenere; (support) sostenere; (assert) affermare. maintenance n mantenimento m; (machinery, etc.) manutenzione f; (alimony) alimenti m pl.

maisonette [meizə'net] n casetta f.

maize [meiz] n mais m invar, granturco m invar.

majesty ['madʒəsti] n maestà f. majestic adj maestoso.

major ['meidʒə] nm, adj maggiore. majority n maggioranza f; (age) maggiore età f.

*make [meik] v fare; produrre. make

believe dare da intendere, far finta di. make-believe n finzione f, illusione f. make do arrangiarsi. make out preparare; decifrare; (understand) capire. make up costituire, costruire; inventare; compensare; (cosmetics) truccare. make-up n trucco m, truccatura f; composizione f; costituzione f. maker n creatore, -trice m, f; fabbricante m, f.

makeshift ['meikʃift] adj di fortuna, improvvisato. n espediente m.

maladjusted [malə'dʒʌstid] adj disadattato.

malaise [ma'leiz] n malessere m.

malaria [mə'leəriə] n malaria f.

male [meil] n maschio m. adj maschio, maschile.

malevolent [mə'levələnt] adj malevolo. malevolence n malevolenza f.

malfunction [mal'fʌŋkʃən] n funzionamento difettoso m.

malice ['malis] n malizia f, malignità f. with malice aforethought con premeditazione maliziosa. malicious adj malizioso, maligno.

malignant [mə'lignənt] adj maligno. malignancy n malignità f.

malinger [mə'liŋgə] v darsi malato, scansar fatiche. malingerer n scansafatiche m, f invar.

mallet ['malit] n maglio m, martello (di legno) m. malleable adj malleabile.

malnutrition [malnju'triʃən] n malnutrizione f.

malt [moilt] n malto m.

Malta ['moiltə] n Malta f. Maltese n(m+f), adj maltese.

maltreat [mal'triit] v maltrattare. maltreatment n maltrattamento m.

mammal ['maməl] n mammifero m.

mammoth ['maməθ] n mammut m. adj enorme, mastodontico.

man [man] n, pl men uomo (pl uomini) m. v equipaggiare, presidiare. manly adj virile.

manage ['manidʒ] v dirigere, amministrare; (cope) farcela. manage to riuscire a, fare in modo da. manage without fare a meno di. manageable adj (people) trattabile, docile; (things) maneggevole. management n amministrazione f, direzione f. manager n direttore m. manageress n direttrice f. managing director consigliere delegato m.

mandarin ['mandərin] *n* mandarino *m*.
mandate ['mandeit] *n* mandato *m*.
mandatory *adj* mandatario.
mandolin ['mandəlin] *n* mandolino *m*.
mane [mein] *n* criniera *f*.
mange [meindʒ] *n* rogna *f*. **mangy** *adj* rognoso.
mangle¹ ['maŋgl] *v* (*disfigure*) deformare, mutilare.
mangle² ['maŋgl] *n* (*wringer*) mangano *m*. *v* manganare.
manhandle [man'handl] *v* manovrare a mano; (*treat harshly*) malmenare.
manhole ['manhoul] *n* botola *f*. **manhole cover** tombino *m*.
mania ['meiniə] *n* mania *f*. **maniac** *n* maniaco, -a *m*, *f*. **maniacal** *adj* maniaco.
manicure ['manikjuə] *n* manicure *f invar*.
manifest ['manifest] *adj* evidente, palese. *v* manifestare, dimostrare. *n* (*comm*) manifesto (di bordo) *m*, nota di carico *f*.
manifesto [mani'festou] *n* manifesto *m*, proclama *m*.
manifold ['manifould] *adj* molteplice, vario. *n* (*tech*) collettore *m*.
manipulate [mə'nipjuleit] *v* maneggiare. **manipulation** *n* maneggio *m*. **manipulative** *adj* manipolatore.
mankind [man'kaind] *n* umanità *f*, genere umano *m*.
man-made [man'meid] *adj* artificiale, sintetico.
manner ['manə] *n* modo *m*, maniera *f*; stile *m*; sorta *f*, specie *f*. **manners** *pl n* maniere *f pl*, educazione *f sing*. **mannerism** *n* affettazione *f*, manierismo *m*.
manoeuvre [mə'nuːvə] *n* manovra *f*. *v* manovrare, maneggiare.
manor ['manə] *n* castello *m*, maniero *m*.
manpower ['man,pauə] *n* manodopera *f*; forze di lavoro *f pl*; capacità lavorativa *f*.
mansion ['manʃən] *n* palazzo *m*, casa signorile *f*.
mantelpiece ['mantlpiːs] *n* mensola (del caminetto) *f*.
manual ['manjuəl] *nm, adj* manuale. **manually** *adv* a mano.
manufacture [manju'faktʃə] *n* manifattura *f*, fabbricazione *f*, confezione *f*. *v* fabbricare. **manufacturer** *n* fabbricante *m*.
manure [mə'njuə] *n* concime *f*, fertilizzante *m*.
manuscript ['manjuskript] *nm, adj* manoscritto.

many ['meni] *adj, pron* molti, -e. **as many** altrettanti, -e. **how many** quanti, -e. **so many** tanti, -e. **too many** troppi, -e.
map [map] *n* mappa *f*, carta geografica *f*; (*of town*) pianta *f*. **off the map** remoto. *v* **map out** tracciare.
maple ['meipl] *n* acero *m*.
mar [maː] *v* guastare, rovinare.
marathon ['marəθən] *n* maratona *f*.
marble ['maːbl] *n* marmo *m*; (*glass ball*) bilia *f*. *adj* di marmo, marmoreo.
march [maːtʃ] *n* marcia *f*. *v* marciare. **march-past** *n* sfilata *f*.
March [maːtʃ] *n* marzo *m*.
marchioness [maːʃə'nes] *n* marchesa *f*.
mare [meə] *n* cavalla *f*.
margarine [maːdʒə'riːn] *n* margarina *f*.
margin ['maːdʒin] *n* margine *m*. **marginal** *adj* marginale.
marguerite [maːgə'riːt] *n* margherita *f*.
marigold ['marigould] *n* calendola *f*.
marijuana [mari'waːnə] *n* marijuana *f invar*, canapa indiana *f*.
marina [mə'riːnə] *n* porticciuolo *m*.
marinade [mari'neid] *n* marinata *f*. *v* marinare.
marine [mə'riːn] *adj* marino, marittimo. *n* (*fleet*) marina *f*; (*soldier*) soldato di marina *m*.
marital ['maritl] *adj* coniugale.
maritime ['maritaim] *adj* marittimo.
marjoram ['maːdʒərəm] *n* maggiorana *f*.
mark¹ [maːk] *n* segno *m*; (*brand*) marchio *m*; (*rating*) voto *m*; (*trace*) traccia *f*. **marksman** *n* tiratore scelto *m*. *v* segnare; notare; osservare; (*correct, grade*) dare i voti a. **mark off** delimitare. **mark out** tracciare. **marking** *n* marchio *m*. **markings** *pl n* segni caratteristici *m pl*.
mark² [maːk] *n* (*money*) marco *m*.
market ['maːkit] *n* mercato *m*. **market garden** orto *m*. **market research** ricerca di mercato *f*. *v* mettere in vendita. **marketing** *n* marketing *m invar*.
marmalade ['maːməleid] *n* marmellata *f*.
maroon¹ [mə'ruːn] *nm, adj* (*colour*) marrone rossastro.
maroon² [mə'ruːn] *v* abbandonare.
marquee [maː'kiː] *n* grande tenda *f*; padiglione *m*.
marquess ['maːkwis] *n* marchese *m*.
marriage ['maridʒ] *n* matrimonio *m*. **marriage licence** dispensa di matrimonio *f*.

marrow ['marou] *n* zucca *f.*
marry ['mari] *v* sposare. **married** *adj* sposato. **get married** sposarsi.
Mars [maɪz] *n* Marte *m.* **Martian** *n, adj* marziano, -a.
marsh [maɪʃ] *n* palude *f.* **marshy** *adj* paludoso.
marshal ['maɪʃəl] *v* disporre; (*mil*) schierare. *n* maresciallo *m.*
martial ['maɪʃəl] *adj* marziale.
martin ['maɪtin] *n* balestruccio *m.*
martyr ['maɪtə] *n* martire *m, f. v* martirizzare. **martyrdom** *n* martirio *m.*
marvel ['maɪvəl] *n* meraviglia *f. v* meravigliarsi. **marvel at** stupirsi di, ammirare.
marvellous ['maɪvələs] *adj* meraviglioso.
marzipan [maɪzi'pan] *n* marzapane *m.*
mascara [ma'skaɪrə] *n* mascara *m invar.*
mascot ['maskət] *n* portafortuna *m invar,* mascotte *f.*
masculine ['maskjulin] *adj* maschile, virile. **masculinity** *n* mascolinità *f,* virilità *f.*
mash [maʃ] *v* ridurre in polpa, schiacciare; (*cookery*) fare un purè di. *n* (*cookery*) passata *f,* purè *m.*
mask [maɪsk] *n* maschera *f. v* mascherare; (*hide*) nascondere.
masochist ['masəkist] *n* masochista *m, f. adj* masochistico. **masochism** *n* masochismo *m.*
mason ['meisn] *n* muratore *m;* (*freemason*) massone *m.* **masonic** *adj* massonico. **masonry** *n* muratura *f.*
masquerade [maskə'reid] *n* mascherata *f. v* **masquerade as** mascherarsi da, farsi passare per.
mass¹ [mas] *n* massa *f,* (*bulk*) mole *f;* (*great number*) gran numero *m;* (*large amount*) grande quantità *f.* **masses** *pl n* (*coll*) mucchio *m sing.* **mass meeting** adunata popolare *f.* **mass-produced** *adj* prodotto in serie. **mass-production** *n* produzione in serie *or* massa *f.*
mass² [mas] *n* (*rel*) messa *f.*
massacre ['masəkə] *n* massacro *m,* strage *f. v* massacrare, far strage di.
massage ['masaɪʒ] *n* massaggio *m. v* massaggiare. **masseur** *n* massaggiatore *m.* **masseuse** *n* massaggiatrice *f.*
massive ['masiv] *adj* massiccio, solido.
mast [maɪst] *n* albero *m.*
mastectomy [ma'stektəmi] *n* mastectomia *f.*

master ['maɪstə] *n* padrone *m,* signore *m;* (*of ship*) capitano *m;* (*school*) professore *m.* **masterpiece** *n* capolavoro *m. v* dominare, impadronirsi di; (*learn*) conoscere a perfezione. **masterly** *adj* magistrale.
masturbate ['mastəbeit] *v* masturbarsi. **masturbation** *n* masturbazione *f.*
mat [mat] *n* (*covering*) tappeto *m;* (*for floor*) stuoia *f;* (*at door*) zerbino *m;* (*on table*) sottopiatto *m.*
match¹ [matʃ] *n* (*light*) fiammifero *m.* **matchbox** *n* scatola da fiammiferi *f.*
match² [matʃ] *v* (*clothes, colours, etc.*) andare bene insieme; corrispondere; (*oppose*) opporre; (*equal*) uguagliare. *n* (*equal*) uguale *m, f,* pari *m, f;* (*contest, partner*) partita *f.* **matchmaker** *n* sensale di matrimoni. **meet one's match** trovare un degno avversario.
mate [meit] *n* compagno, -a *m, f;* (*help*) aiuto *m,* assistente *m, f;* (*naut*) secondo *m.*
material [mə'tiəriəl] *n* (*substance*) sostanza *f,* materia *f;* materiale *m;* (*fabric*) stoffa *f. adj* materiale, essenziale. **materialize** *v* realizzarsi, prender corpo.
maternal [mə'təɪnl] *adj* materno. **maternity** *n* maternità *f.*
mathematics [maθə'matiks] *n* matematica *f.* **mathematical** *adj* matematico. **mathematician** *n* matematico, -a *m, f.*
matinee ['matinei] *n* rappresentazione diurna *f.*
matins ['matinz] *n* mattutino *m.*
matriarch ['meitriaɪk] *n* matrona *f.* **matriarchal** *adj* matriarcale.
matrimony ['matriməni] *n* matrimonio *m.* **matrimonial** *adj* matrimoniale.
matrix ['meitriks] *n* matrice *f.*
matron ['meitrən] *n* (*hospital*) capoinfermiera *f;* (*institution*) direttrice *f.*
matt [mat] *adj* matto, opaco.
matter ['matə] *v* importare. *n* materia *f;* (*thing, affair*) cosa *f,* affare *m;* (*of book, etc.*) argomento *m,* questione *f.* **as a matter of fact** in realtà, fatto sta che. **matter-of-fact** *adj* pratico. **what's the matter?** cosa c'è?
mattress ['matris] *n* materasso *m.*
mature [mə'tjuə] *v* maturare; (*become due*) scadere. **maturity** *n* maturità *f.*
maudlin ['moɪdlin] *adj* lamentevole, querulo.

maul [mɔɪl] *v* dilaniare.
mausoleum [mɔɪsə'lɪəm] *n* mausoleo *m*.
mauve [mouv] *adj* (color) malva *invar*.
maxim ['maksim] *n* massima *f*.
maximum ['maksiməm] *nm, adj* massimo.
***may** [mei] *v* potere. **maybe** può darsi, forse.
May [mei] *n* maggio *m*.
mayonnaise [ˌmeɪə'neiz] *n* maionese *f*.
mayor [meə] *n* sindaco *m*.
maze [meiz] *n* labirinto *m*.
me [mɪɪ] *pron* mi; (*after prep*) me. **it's me** sono io.
meadow ['medou] *n* prato *m*.
meagre ['mɪɪgə] *adj* scarso.
meal¹ [mɪɪl] *n* (*food*) pasto *m*.
meal² [mɪɪl] *n* (*grain*) farina *f*.
***mean¹** [mɪɪn] *v* significare, voler dire; intendere; destinare.
mean² [mɪɪn] *adj* gretto; (*miserly*) avaro; (*shabby*) meschino; (*low*) basso. **meanness** *n* grettezza *f*; avarizia *f*.
mean³ [mɪɪn] *n* (*average*) media *f*. *adj* medio.
meander [mi'andə] *v* divagare.
meaning ['mɪɪnɪŋ] *n* significato *m*, senso *m*. *adj* significativo.
means [mɪɪnz] *n* mezzi *m pl*. **by means of** per mezzo di. **by no means** niente affatto. **by some means or other** in qualche modo.
meant [ment] *V* **mean¹**.
meanwhile ['mɪɪnwail] *adv also* **in the meantime** nel frattempo, intanto.
measles ['mɪɪzlz] *n* morbillo *m*. **German measles** *n* rosolio *f*, rubeola *f*. **measly** *adj* (*wretched*) miserabile.
measure ['meʒə] *n* misura *f*; (*action*) provvedimento *m*. **made to measure** fatto su misura. *v* misurare; (*estimate*) valutare. **measurement** *n* misura *f*. **measurements** *pl n* dimensioni *f pl*.
meat [mɪɪt] *n* carne *f*. **meaty** *adj* sostanzioso.
mechanic [mi'kanik] *n* meccanico *m*. **mechanical** *adj* meccanico. **mechanism** *n* meccanismo *m*. **mechanized** *adj* meccanizzato.
medal ['medl] *n* medaglia *f*.
meddle ['medl] *v* immischiarsi, intromettersi. **meddler** *n* ficcanaso *m invar*.
media ['mɪɪdɪə] *pl n* mezzi di comunicazione *m pl*.
median ['mɪɪdɪən] *adj* mediano. *n* mediana *f*.

mediate ['mɪɪdieit] *v* fare da mediatore *or* intermediario. **mediation** *n* mediazione *f*.
mediator *n* mediatore, -trice *m, f*.
medical ['medikəl] *adj* medico. *n* (*examination*) esame medico *m*. **medication** *n* medicazione *f*. **medicinal** *adj* medicinale.
medicine *n* (*science*) medicina *f*; (*substance*) medicinale *m*, farmaco *m*.
medieval [medi'ɪɪvəl] *adj* medievale.
mediocre [mɪɪdi'oukə] *adj* mediocre. **mediocrity** *n* mediocrità *f*.
meditate ['mediteit] *v* meditare. **meditation** *n* meditazione *f*.
Mediterranean [ˌmeditə'reiniən] *n* Mediterraneo *m*. *adj* mediterraneo.
medium ['mɪɪdiəm] *n* (*spiritualist*) medium *m, f invar*; (*biology*) brodo (di coltura) *m*; (*agency*) mezzo *m*. **happy medium** giusto mezzo *m*. *adj* medio.
medley ['medli] *n* miscuglio *m*, pasticcio *m*.
meek [mɪɪk] *adj* mansueto, mite. **meekness** *n* mansuetudine *f*.
***meet** [mɪɪt] *v* incontrare; (*by arrangement*) trovare; (*gather*) riunirsi. **meeting** *n* incontro *m*; riunione *f*.
megaphone ['megəfoun] *n* megafono *m*.
melancholy ['melənkəli] *n* malinconia *f*. *adj also* **melancholic** malinconico.
mellow ['melou] *adj* maturo; (*wine*) amabile; (*soft*) morbido. *v* maturare; (*person*) intenerirsi.
melodrama ['melədraɪmə] *n* melodramma *m*. **melodramatic** *adj* melodrammatico.
melody ['melədi] *n* melodia *f*. **melodious** *adj* melodioso.
melon ['melən] *n* melone *m*.
melt [melt] *v* fondere, sciogliere; (*feeling*) intenerire. **melt down** fondere. **melting point** punto di fusione *m*. **melting pot** crogiuolo *m*.
member ['membə] *n* membro *m*; (*of society, club, etc.*) socio, -a *m, f*; (*of parliament*) deputato, -a *m, f*. **membership** *n* (*number*) numero dei soci *m*; (*condition*) l'essere socio *m*.
membrane ['membrein] *n* membrana *f*.
memento [mə'mentou] *n* ricordo *m*.
memo ['memou] *n* appunto *m*.
memoirs ['memwaɪz] *pl n* memorie *f pl*.
memorandum [memə'randəm] *n* appunto *m*, promemoria *m invar*; (*document*) memorandum *m invar*.

memorial [mi'moɪrɪəl] *n* monumento *m*. *adj* commemorativo.
memory ['meməri] *n* (*faculty*) memoria *f*; (*recollection*) ricordo *m*. **memorable** *adj* memorabile. **memorize** *v* imparare a memoria.
men [men] *V* **man**.
menace ['menis] *n* minaccia *f*. *v* minacciare. **menacing** *adj* minaccioso.
menagerie [mi'nadʒəri] *n* serraglio *m*.
mend [mend] *v* riparare, aggiustare; (*get better*) migliorare. **mend one's ways** ravvedersi. *n* **be on the mend** stare rimettendosi. **mending** *n* rammendo *m*.
menial ['miːnɪəl] *adj* servile, umile.
meningitis [ˌmenin'dʒaitis] *n* meningite *f*.
menopause ['menəpoɪz] *n* menopausa *f*.
menstrual ['menstruəl] *adj* mestruale. **menstruate** *v* mestruare. **menstruation** *n* mestruazione *f*.
mental ['mentl] *adj* mentale; (*home, hospital*) psichiatrico. **mentality** *n* mentalità *f*.
menthol ['menθəl] *n* mentolo *m*.
mention ['menʃən] *v* accennare a, parlare di, citare. **don't mention it!** prego! *n* menzione *f*, cenno *m*; citazione *f*.
menu ['menjuɪ] *n* menu *m invar*, lista dei cibi *f*.
mercantile ['məɪkənˌtail] *adj* mercantile.
mercenary ['məɪsinəri] *nm*, *adj* mercenario.
merchandise ['məɪtʃəndaiz] *n* merce *f*.
merchant ['məɪtʃənt] *n* commerciante *m*, *f*. **merchant navy** marina mercantile *f*.
mercury ['məɪkjuri] *n* mercurio *m*.
mercy ['məɪsi] *n* pietà *f*, carità *f*. **at the mercy of** alla mercè di. **merciful** *adj* pietoso, caritatevole.
mere [miə] *adj* puro, mero.
merge [məɪdʒ] *v* fondere, amalgamare. **merger** *n* fusione *f*.
meridian [mə'ridiən] *n* meridiano *m*.
meringue [mə'raŋ] *n* meringa *f*.
merit ['merit] *n* merito *m*, valore *m*. *v* meritare.
mermaid ['məɪmeid] *n* sirena *f*.
merry ['meri] *adj* allegro; (*coll*) brillo. **merry-go-round** *n* carosello *m*. **merry-making** *n* festa *f*.
mesh [meʃ] *n* maglia *f*; (*net*) rete *f*. **in mesh** ingranato.
mesmerize ['mezməraiz] *v* ipnotizzare; affascinare.

mess [mes] *n* confusione *f*, pasticcio *m*; (*eating place*) mensa *f*. **be in a mess** (*of things*) essere in disordine; (*of people*) trovarsi nei guai. **make a mess of** rovinare. *v* **mess about** perdersi in cose inutili; (*inconvenience*) disturbare. **mess up** rovinare. **messy** *adj* confuso, disordinato; (*dirty*) sporco.
message ['mesidʒ] *n* messaggio *m*. **messenger** *n* messaggero *m*; (*errand boy*) fattorino *m*.
met [met] *V* **meet**.
metabolism [mi'tabəlizm] *n* metabolismo *m*. **metabolic** *adj* metabolico.
metal ['metl] *n* metallo *m*. **metallic** *adj* metallico. **metallurgy** *n* metallurgia *f*.
metamorphosis [metə'moɪfəsis] *n* metamorfosi *f invar*.
metaphor ['metəfə] *n* metafora *f*. **metaphoric(al)** *adj* metaforico.
metaphysics [ˌmetə'fiziks] *n* metafisica *f*. **metaphysical** *adj* metafisico.
meteor ['miɪtiə] *n* meteora *f*. **meteoric** *adj* meteorico; rapidissimo.
meteorology [ˌmiɪtiə'rolədʒi] *n* meteorologia *f*. **meteorological** *adj* meteorologico. **meteorologist** *n* meteorologo, -a *m*, *f*.
meter ['miɪtə] *n* contatore *m*; (*parking*) parchimetro *m*. *v* misurare.
methane ['miɪθein] *n* metano *m*.
method ['meθəd] *n* metodo *m*, modo *m*. **methodical** *adj* metodico, sistematico.
methylated spirits ['meθileitid] *n* alcool denaturato *m*.
meticulous [mi'tikjuləs] *adj* meticoloso.
metre ['miɪtə] *n* metro *m*. **metric** *adj* metrico.
metronome ['metrənoum] *n* metronomo *m*.
metropolis [mə'tropəlis] *n* metropoli *f*. **metropolitan** *adj* metropolitano.
mettle ['metl] *n* **put someone on his mettle** mettere qualcuno alla prova.
mews [mjuɪz] *n* vicolo *m*.
miaow [mi'au] *v* miagolare.
mice [mais] *V* **mouse**.
microbe ['maikroub] *n* microbo *m*.
microfilm ['maikrəˌfilm] *n* microfilm *m invar*.
microphone ['maikrəfoun] *n* microfono *m*.
microscope ['maikrəskoup] *n* microscopio *m*. **microscopic** *adj* microscopico. **microscopy** *n* microscopia *f*.

mid [mid] *adj* **in mid** ... **a metà** ..., **in mezzo a** ..., **in pieno** .... **midday** *n* mezzogiorno *m*. **midnight** *n* mezzanotte *f*. **mid-ocean** *n* alto mare *m*. **midsummer** *n* mezza estate *f*. **midway** *adv* a metà strada.

middle ['midl] *n* mezzo *m*, centro *m*. *adj* medio. **middle-aged** *adj* di mezza età. **Middle Ages** Medio Evo *m sing*. **middleclass** *adj* borghese. **middle man** *n* intermediario *m*.

midge [midʒ] *n* zanzara *f*.

midget ['midʒit] *n* nano *m*.

midst [midst] *n* mezzo *m*, centro *m*. **in the midst of** nel mezzo di, in mezzo a, fra.

midwife ['midwaif] *n* levatrice *f*. **midwifery** *n* ostetricia *f*.

might¹ [mait] *V* **may**.

might² [mait] *n* (*power*) forza *f*, potenza *f*.

mighty ['maiti] *adj* forte, potente. *adv* (*coll*) estremamente.

migraine ['miːgrein] *n* emicrania *f*.

migrate [mai'greit] *v* migrare. **migrant** *n, adj* migratore, -trice. **migration** *n* migrazione *f*. **migratory** *adj* migratorio.

Milan [mi'lan] *n* Milano *f*. **Milanese** *n(m+f), adj* milanese.

mild [maild] *adj* mite. **mildness** *n* mitezza *f*.

mildew ['mildjuː] *n* muffa *f*. **mildewy** *adj* ammuffito.

mile [mail] *n* miglio *m* (*pl* -a *f*). **mileage** *n* distanza percorsa in miglia *f*, chilometraggio *m*. **mileometer** *n* contachilometri *m invar*.

militant ['militənt] *n(m+f), adj* militante, attivista.

military ['militəri] *adj* militare. **militarism** *n* militarismo *m*. **militate** *v* militare. **militia** *n* milizia *f*.

milk [milk] *n* latte *m*. **milkman** *n* lattaio *m*. *v* mungere; (*exploit*) sfruttare.

mill [mil] *n* (*flour*) mulino *m*; (*textiles*) stabilimento *m*; (*tech*) fresa *f*; (*coffee*) macinino *m*. **millstone** *n* macina *f*; (*burden*) macigno *m*. *v* macinare; (*metal*) laminare; (*crowd*) circolare. **milling** *n* (*corn*) macinatura *f*; (*metal*) laminatura *f*; (*tech*) fresatura *f*; (*coins*) zigrinatura *f*.

millennium [mi'leniəm] *n* millennio *m*.

millet ['milit] *n* miglio *m*.

milligram ['miliˌgram] *n* milligrammo *m*.

millilitre ['miliˌliːtə] *n* millilitro *m*.

millimetre ['miliˌmiːtə] *n* millimetro *m*.

milliner ['milinə] *n* modista *f*.

million ['miljən] *n* milione *m*. **millionaire** *n* milionario, -a *m, f*. **millionth** *nm, adj* milionesimo.

mime [maim] *n* (*art*) mimica *f*; (*artist*) mimo, -a *m, f*. *v* mimare.

mimic ['mimik] *v* contraffare; (*ape*) scimmiottare. *n* imitatore, -trice *m, f*; contraffattore, -trice *m, f*. **mimicry** *n* mimica *f*; (*zool*) mimetismo *m*.

mimosa [mi'mouzə] *n* mimosa *f*.

minaret [minə'ret] *n* minareto *m*.

mince [mins] *v* tritare, tagliuzzare. **not mince one's words** parlare apertamente. *n* (*meat*) carne tritata *f*. **make mincemeat of** (*coll*) demolire. **mincer** *n* tritatutto *m invar*.

mind [maind] *n* mente *f*, intelletto *m*, spirito *m*; (*reason*) ragione *f*; (*opinion*) parere *m*. **bear in mind** tenere a mente. **make up one's mind** decidersi. **peace of mind** serenità *f*. **piece of one's mind** (*reprimand*) rimprovero *m*. **speak one's mind** parlar chiaro. **state of mind** stato d'animo *m*. *v* badare a, occuparsi di; (*watch out*) far attenzione. **do you mind if** ...? ti dispiace se ...? **never mind!** non importa! **mindful** *adj* attento. **mindless** *adj* (*heedless*) sbadato; (*senseless*) insensato.

mine¹ [main] *pron* il mio, la mia; (*pl*) i miei, le mie.

mine² [main] *n* miniera *f*; (*explosive*) mina *f*. *v* (*dig*) scavare; (*extract*) estrarre; (*mil*) minare. **mine-detector** *n* rilevatore di mine *m*. **minefield** *n* campo minato *m*. **minesweeper** *n* dragamine *m invar*. **miner** *n* minatore *m*.

mineral ['minərəl] *nm, adj* minerale.

mingle ['miŋgl] *v* mescolare, mischiarsi.

miniature ['minitʃə] *n* miniatura *f*. *adj* in miniatura.

minim ['minim] *n* (*music*) minima *f*.

minimum ['miniməm] *n* minimo *m*. **minimal** *adj* minimo. **minimize** *v* minimizzare.

mining ['mainiŋ] *n* estrazione *f*, scavo *m*; (*mil*) posa di mine *f*. *adj* minerario.

minister ['ministə] *n* (*pol*) ministro, -a *m, f*; (*rel*) sacerdote *m*; (*diplomat*) incaricato, -a *m, f*. *v* **minister to** soccorrere. **minister to the needs of** provvedere ai bisogni di. **ministerial** *adj* ministeriale. **ministry** *n* ministero *m*; (*clergy*) clero *m*.

mink [miŋk] *n* visone *m*.

minor ['mainə] *adj* minore, più piccolo, meno importante. *n* minorenne *m, f.*

minority *n* minoranza *f*; (*age*) minorità *f*, età minore *f.*

minstrel ['minstrəl] *n* menestrello *m,* cantante *m.*

mint[1] [mint] *n* (*bot*) menta *f.*

mint[2] [mint] *n* zecca *f.* **be in mint condition** essere nuovo di zecca. **have a mint of money** avere un mucchio di soldi. *v* coniare.

minuet [minju'et] *n* minuetto *m.*

minus ['mainəs] *prep* meno.

minute[1] ['minit] *n* minuto *m*; momento *m.* **minutes** *pl n* (*of meeting*) verbale *m sing. v* (*record*) prendere nota; (*enter in minutes*) mettere agli atti.

minute[2] [mai'njuit] *adj* minuto; (*detailed*) minuzioso.

minx [miŋks] *n* (*coll*) civetta *f.*

miracle ['mirəkl] *n* miracolo *m.* **miraculous** *adj* miracoloso.

mirage ['mira:ʒ] *n* miraggio *m.*

mirror ['mirə] *n* specchio *m. v* riflettere, rispecchiare.

mirth [mə:θ] *n* ilarità *f*, allegria *f.*

misadventure [misəd'ventʃə] *n* infortunio *m*, disavventura *f.*

misanthropist [miz'anθrəpist] *n* misantropo, -a *m, f.* **misanthropic** *adj* misantropico. **misanthropy** *n* misantropia *f.*

misapprehension [misapri'henʃən] *n* equivoco *m*, malinteso *m.* **misapprehend** *v* fraintendere.

misbehave [misbi'heiv] *v* comportarsi male. **misbehaviour** *n* cattiva condotta *f.*

miscalculate [mis'kalkjuleit] *v* calcolar male. **miscalculation** *n* calcolo errato *m.*

miscarriage [mis'karidʒ] *n* (*med*) aborto *m.* **miscarry** *v* abortire.

miscellaneous [misə'leiniəs] *adj* miscellaneo.

mischance [mis'tʃa:ns] *n* sventura *f.*

mischief ['mistʃif] *n* (*harm*) danno *m*; (*of child, etc.*) fastidi *m pl*; (*teasing*) malizia *f.* **be up to mischief** combinare un brutto tiro. **make mischief** creare discordia. **mischief-maker** *n* attaccabrighe *m invar.* **mischievous** *adj* malizioso; (*of child*) birichino.

misconception [miskən'sepʃən] *n* malinteso *m.*

misconduct [mis'kondʌkt] *n* cattiva condotta *f.*

misdeed [mis'di:d] *n* misfatto *m*, delitto *m.*

misdemeanour [misdi'mi:nə] *n* (*misbehaviour*) cattiva condotta *f*; (*crime*) delitto *m.*

miser ['maizə] *n* avaro, -a *m, f.* **miserly** *adj* avaro.

miserable ['mizərəbl] *adj* (*unhappy*) infelice, triste; (*pitiful*) pietoso; (*painful*) penoso; depresso.

misery ['mizəri] *n* miseria *f*; sofferenze *f pl.*

misfire [mis'faiə] *v* fare cilecca *or* fiasco.

misfit ['misfit] *n* (*person*) spostato, -a *m, f.*

misfortune [mis'fɔ:tʃən] *n* sfortuna *f*, disgrazia *f.*

misgiving [mis'giviŋ] *n* dubbio *m.*

misguided [mis'gaidid] *adj* fuori posto, sviato.

mishap ['mishap] *n* disgrazia *f*, contrattempo *m.*

misjudge [mis'dʒʌdʒ] *v* farsi un'idea sbagliata di, giudicare male.

***mislay** [mis'lei] *v* smarrire.

***mislead** [mis'li:d] *v* ingannare. **misleading** *adj* ingannevole.

misnomer [mis'noumə] *n* termine improprio *m.*

misplace [mis'pleis] *v* mettere fuori posto.

misprint ['misprint] *n* errore tipografico *m.*

miss[1] [mis] *n* colpo mancato *m. v* mancare (a); (*not catch*) perdere; (*skip*) saltare; (*not find*) non trovare; (*regret absence of*) sentire la mancanza di. **miss out** omettere. **be missing** mancare.

miss[2] [mis] *n* signorina *f.*

missile ['misail] *n* missile *m.*

mission ['miʃən] *n* missione *f.* **missionary** *n, adj* missionario, -a.

mist [mist] *n* caligine *f*, foschia *f. v* offuscare. **misty** *adj* caliginoso, fosco.

***mistake** [mi'steik] *n* errore *m*, sbaglio *m.* **by mistake** per errore. **make a mistake** sbagliare, fare un errore. *v* (*confuse*) confondere, scambiare. **mistaken** *adj* sbagliato, falso.

mistletoe ['misltou] *n* vischio *m.*

mistress ['mistris] *n* padrona *f*; (*school*) insegnante *f*; (*lover*) amante *f.*

mistrust [mis'trʌst] *v* diffidare di, non aver fiducia in. *n* diffidenza *f*, sfiducia *f.* **mistrustful** *adj* diffidente.

***misunderstand** [misʌndə'stand] *v*

fraintendere, capir male. **misunderstanding** n malinteso m, equivoco m. **misunderstood** adj incompreso.
misuse [mis'juɪs; v mis'juɪz] n abuso m; uso incorretto m. v abusare; (ill-treat) maltrattare; (use badly) adoperare male.
mitigate ['mitigeit] v mitigaɾe; (law) attenuare. **mitigation** n (law) attenuante f.
mitre ['maitə] n (rel) mitra f; (carpentry) ugnatura f. v ugnare.
mitten ['mitn] n mezzo quanto m, muffola f.
mix [miks] v mescolare, mischiare; combinare. **mix up** v confondere. **mix-up** n confusione f. **mixed** adj misto. **mixer** n (tech) agitatore m. **be a good mixer** essere socievole. **mixture** n miscela f; miscuglio m.
moan [moun] n (complaint) lamento m; (groan) gemito m. v lamentarsi; gemere.
moat [mout] n fosso m, fossato m.
mob [mob] n folla f, marmaglia f, plebaglia f. v molestare, assalire.
mobile ['moubail] adj mobile. **mobility** n mobilità f. **mobilization** n mobilitazione f. **mobilize** v mobilitare.
moccasin ['mokəsin] n mocassino m.
mock [mok] v deridere, canzonare. adj finto, falso. **mockery** n presa in giro f, derisione f. **mocking** adj beffardo. **mocking-bird** n mimo m.
mode [moud] n modo m, maniera f.
model ['modl] n modello m; (art) modello, -a m, f; (fashion) indossatore, -trice m, f. adj modello, esemplare. v modellare, fare l'indossatore.
moderate ['modərət; v 'modəreit] adj misurato, moderato; (price) modico. v moderare. **moderation** n misura f, moderazione f. **in moderation** moderatamente.
modern ['modən] adj moderno. **modernization** n rimodernamento m. **modernize** v rimodernare.
modest ['modist] adj modesto. **modesty** n modestia f.
modify ['modifai] v modificare. **modification** n modifica f.
modulate ['modjuleit] v modulare. **modulation** n modulazione f.
module ['modjuɪl] n modulo m.
mohair ['mouheə] n mohair m invar.
moist [moist] adj umido. **moisten** v inumidire; (surface) umettare. **moisture** n umidità f. **moisturize** v umidificare.

molar ['moulə] nm, adj molare.
molasses [mə'lasiz] n melassa f.
mold (US) V **mould**.
mole[1] [moul] n (on skin) neo m.
mole[2] [moul] n (zool) talpa f.
molecule ['molikjuɪl] n molecola f. **molecular** adj molecolare.
molest [mə'lest] v molestare.
mollify ['molifai] v placare.
mollusc ['moləsk] n mollusco m.
mollycoddle ['molikodl] v coccolare.
molt (US) V **moult**.
molten ['moultən] adj fuso.
moment ['moumənt] n momento m, istante m. **at the moment** attualmente. **momentary** adj momentaneo. **momentous** adj grave, importante. **momentum** n impeto m, slancio m.
Monaco ['monəkou] n Monaco f.
monarch ['monək] n monarca m, f. **monarchist** n, adj monarchico, -a. **monarchy** n monarchia f.
monastery ['monəstəri] n monastero m. **monastic** adj monastico.
Monday ['mʌndi] n lunedì m.
money ['mʌni] n denaro m, soldi m pl. **money-box** n salvadanaio m. **money-lender** n usuraio m. **money order** vaglia m invar. **monetary** adj monetario.
mongol ['mongəl] adj mongolo; (med) mongoloide. **Mongolia** n Mongolia f.
mongrel ['mʌngrəl] nm, adj bastardo.
monitor ['monitə] n (radio) ascoltatore m; (tech) monitor m invar. v (radio) ascoltare; controllare. **monitoring service** servizio d'ascolto m.
monk [mʌnk] n monaco m, frate m.
monkey ['mʌnki] n scimmia f.
monogamy [mə'nogəmi] n monogamia f. **monogamous** adj monogamo.
monogram ['monəgram] n monogramma m.
monograph ['monəgraɪf] n monografia f.
monolithic [,monə'liθik] adj monolitico.
monologue ['monəlog] n monologo (pl -ghi) m.
monopolize [mə'nopəlaiz] v monopolizzare. **monopoly** n monopolio m.
monosyllable ['monəsiləbl] n monosillabo m. **monosyllabic** adj monosillabico, monosillabo.
monotony [mə'notəni] n monotonia f. **monotone** n tono uniforme m. **monotonous** adj monotono.

monsoon [mon'suːn] *n* monsone *m*.
monster ['monstə] *n* moṣtro *m*. **monstrosity** *n* mostruosità *f*. **monstrous** *adj* mostruoso.
month [mʌnθ] *n* mese *m*.
monthly ['mʌnθli] *n* (*periodical*) rivista mensile *f*. *adj* mensile. *adv* al mese, mensilmente.
monument ['monjument] *n* monumento *m*. **monumental** *adj* monumentale.
mood[1] [muːd] *n* umore *m*, stato d'animo *m*. **feel in the mood to** sentirsi disposto a, aver voglia di. **moodiness** *n* malumore *m*; volubilità *f*. **moody** *adj* capriccioso; (*sulky*) di malumore.
mood[2] [muːd] *n* (*gramm*) modo *m*.
moon [muːn] *n* luna *f*. **moonlight** *n* chiaro di luna *m*.
moor[1] [muə] *n* brughiera *f*. **moorhen** *n* gallinella d'acqua *f*.
moor[2] [muə] *v* ormeggiare, ancorare. **mooring** *n* ormeggio *m*, ancoraggio *m*.
moose [muːs] *n* alce *m*.
moot [muːt] *adj* discutibile.
mop [mop] *n* scopa di cotone per lavaggio *f*; (*of hair*) zazzera *f*. *v* **mop one's brow** asciugarsi la fronte. **mop up** asciugare; rastrellare.
mope [moup] *v* fare il broncio, immusonirsi.
moped ['mouped] *n* ciclomotore *m*.
moral ['morəl] *nf, adj* morale. **morals** *pl n* morale *f sing*. **morale** *n* morale *m*. **moralist** *n* moralista *m, f*. **morality** *n* moralità *f*, buon costume *m*.
morbid ['moːbid] *adj* morboso, patologico.
more [moː] *adv* più, di più; (*again*) ancora. *nm, adj* più. **more and more** sempre più. **more than** più di *or* che.
moreover [moː'rouvə] *adv* inoltre, per di più.
morgue [moːg] *n* obitorio *m*.
morning ['moːniŋ] *n* mattina *m*, mattinata *f*. **this morning** stamane. **tomorrow morning** domattina. *adj* del mattino, mattutino.
moron ['moːron] *n* deficiente *m, f*. **moronic** *adj* deficiente, scemo.
morose [mə'rous] *adj* scontroso.
morphine ['moːfiːn] *n* morfina *f*.
Morse code [moːs] *n* alfabeto Morse *m*.
morsel ['moːsəl] *n* boccone *m*.
mortal ['moːtl] *n(m+f), adj* mortale. **mortality** *n* mortalità *f*.

mortar ['moːtə] *n* (*vessel, arms*) mortaio *m*; (*building*) malta *f*.
mortgage ['moːgidʒ] *n* ipoteca *f*. *v* ipotecare, impegnare.
mortify ['moːtifai] *v* mortificare. **mortification** *n* mortificazione *f*.
mortuary ['moːtʃuəri] *n* camera ardente *or* mortuaria *f*.
mosaic [mə'zeiik] *n* mosaico *m*.
Moscow ['moskou] *n* Mosca *f*.
mosque [mosk] *n* moschea *f*.
mosquito [mə'skiːtou] *n* zanzara *f*.
moss [mos] *n* muschio *m*, musco *m*. **mossy** *adj* muscoso.
most [moust] *adj* (*majority*) la maggior parte di, il più di; (*greatest*) il più grande, il maggiore. *n* il più *m*; (*greatest part*) la maggior parte *f*; (*majority*) la maggioranza *f*, i più *m pl*. *adv* il più; (*very*) molto, assai.
motel [mou'tel] *n* motel *m invar*, autostello *m*.
moth [moθ] *n* lepidottero *m*. **clothes moth** tarma *f*. **mothball** *n* pallina antitarmica *f*.
mother ['mʌðə] *n* madre *f*; (*coll*) mamma *f*. *v* aver cura di come una madre. **mother-in-law** *n* suocera *f*. **mother-of-pearl** *n* madreperla *f*. **mother tongue** madrelingua *f*. **motherly** *adj* materno.
motion ['mouʃən] *n* moto *m*, movimento *m*; (*proposal*) mozione *f*; (*law*) istanza *f*. **go through the motions** far finta. **set in motion** avviare, mettere in moto. *v* accennare a, far cenno a. **motionless** *adj* immobile.
motivate ['moutiveit] *v* motivare, spingere. **motivation** *n* spinta *f*, stimolo *m*.
motive ['moutiv] *n* motivo *m*, ragione *f*.
motor ['moutə] *nm, adj* motore. **motorboat** *n* motoscafo *m*. **motor car** automobile *f*, macchina *f*. **motorcycle** *n* motocicletta *f*. **motorcyclist** *n* motociclista *m, f*. **motorway** *n* autostrada *f*. *v* andare in macchina. **motoring** *n* automobilismo *m*. **motorist** *n* automobilista *m, f*. **motorize** *v* motorizzare.
mottled ['motld] *adj* chiazzato.
motto ['motou] *n* motto *m*, massima *f*.
mould[1] *or US* **mold** [mould] *n* stampo *m*, forma *f*. *v* formare, foggiare, modellare.
mould[2] *or US* **mold** [mould] *n* muffa *f*. **mouldy** *adj* ammuffito. **go mouldy** ammuffire.

moult *or US* **molt** [moult] *v* mutare, fare la muta.

mound [maund] *n* tumulo *m*; (*heap*) mucchio *m*.

mount[1] [maunt] *v* montare. *n* (*setting*) montatura *f*.

mount[2] [maunt] *n* monte *m*.

mountain ['mauntən] *n* montagna *f*. **mountaineer** *n* alpinista *m*, *f*. **mountaineering** *n* alpinismo *m*. **mountainous** *adj* montuoso, alpestre.

mourn [moɪn] *v* rimpiangere, essere in lutto per. **mourning** *n* lutto *m*, cordoglio *m*. **mournful** *adj* triste; lugubre.

mouse [maus] *n*, *pl* **mice** topo *m*. **mousetrap** *n* trappola (per topi) *f*. **mousy** *adj* (*colour*) grigio topo; timido.

mousse [muɪs] *n* mousse *f*, spuma *f*.

moustache [mə'staɪʃ] *n* baffi *m pl*.

mouth [mauθ] *n* bocca *f*; (*of river*) foce *f*. **mouth organ** armonica *f*. **mouthpiece** *n* (*spokesman*) portavoce *m invar*; (*of pipe*) bocchino *m*. *v* declamare. **mouthful** *n* boccone *m*.

move [muɪv] *v* muovere, spostare; (*house*) traslocare; (*arouse feelings*) commuovere; (*propose*) proporre. **move away** *or* **off** allontanare; (*depart*) partire. **move back** indietreggiare; (*return*) tornare. **move forward** avanzare. **move in** occupare. **move out** uscire, sgombrare. **move up** (*raise*) salire; (*get closer*) avvicinarsi. *n* mossa *f*, passo *m*; (*house*) trasloco *m*. **movable** *adj* movibile. **movement** *n* movimento *m*; (*sign*) cenno *m*; (*tech*) meccanismo *m*. **moving** *adj* commovente; (*in motion*) in moto.

movie ['muɪvi] *n* (*US*) film *m invar*.

*****mow** [mou] *v* falciare.

mown [moun] *V* **mow**.

Mr ['mistə] *n* signor *m*.

Mrs ['misiz] *n* signora *f*.

much [mʌtʃ] *pron*, *adj* molto. *adv* molto, assai. **as much as** (tanto) quanto. **how much** quanto. **so much** tanto. **too much** troppo.

muck [mʌk] *n* letame *m*; (*coll: filth*) porcheria *f*. *v* **muck about** (*coll*) bighellonare. **muck up** (*coll*) rovinare.

mucus ['mjuɪkəs] *n* muco *m*. **mucous membrane** mucosa *f*.

mud [mʌd] *n* fango *m*. **mudguard** *n* parafango *m*. **mudslinger** *n* maldicente *m*, *f*. **muddy** *adj* fangoso, inzaccherato.

muddle ['mʌdl] *n* confusione *f*, pasticcio *m*. *v* **muddle through** arrabattarsi. **muddle up** confondere. **muddler** *n* confusionario, -a *m*, *f*.

muff [mʌf] *n* manicotto *m*. *v* mancare, sbagliare.

muffle ['mʌfl] *v* smorzare, attutire.

mug [mʌg] *n* (*cup*) tazza *f*; (*coll: face*) muso *m*, ceffo *m*; (*slang: fool*) gonzo *m*. *v* assalire.

mulberry ['mʌlbəri] *n* (*fruit*) mora di gelso *f*; (*tree*) gelso *m*.

mule[1] [mjuɪl] *n* (*zool*) mulo *m*. **mulish** *adj* (*stubborn*) duro.

mule[2] [mjuɪl] *n* (*slipper*) ciabatta *f*, pianella *f*.

mullet ['mʌlit] *n* (*grey*) muggine *m*; (*red*) triglia *f*.

multicoloured [ˌmʌlti'kʌləd] *adj* multicolore.

multimillionaire [ˌmʌltimiljə'neə] *n* multimilionario, -a *m*, *f*.

multiple ['mʌltipl] *adj* multiplo, molteplice. *n* multiplo *m*.

multiply ['mʌltiplai] *v* moltiplicare. **multiplication** *n* moltiplicazione *f*. **multiplicity** *n* varietà *f*.

multiracial [ˌmʌlti'reiʃəl] *adj* multirazziale.

multitude ['mʌltitjuɪd] *n* moltitudine *f*, massa *f*.

mum [mʌm] *adj* **keep mum** star zitto.

mumble ['mʌmbl] *v* borbottare.

mummy[1] ['mʌmi] *n* (*corpse*) mummia *f*. **mummify** *v* mummificare.

mummy[2] ['mʌmi] *n* (*coll: mother*) mamma *f*, mammina *f*.

mumps [mʌmps] *n* orecchioni *m pl*.

munch [mʌntʃ] *v* sgranocchiare.

mundane [mʌn'dein] *adj* mondano.

municipal [mju'nisipəl] *adj* municipale. **municipality** *n* comune *m*.

mural ['mjuərəl] *n* pittura murale *f*.

murder ['məɪdə] *n* assassinio *m*. *v* assassinare, ammazzare; (*coll*) massacrare. **murderer** *n* assassino *m*. **murderess** *n* assassina *f*. **murderous** *adj* micidiale.

murmur ['məɪmə] *n* mormorio *m*. *v* mormorare.

muscle ['mʌsl] *n* muscolo *m*.

muse[1] [mjuɪz] *n* musa *f*.

muse[2] [mjuɪz] *v* meditare, riflettere.

museum [mju'ziəm] *n* museo *m*.

mushroom ['mʌʃrum] *n* fungo *m*. *v* (*gather*) raccogliere funghi; (*spread*) dilagare, svilupparsi rapidamente.

music ['mjuːzik] *n* musica *f.* **musician** *n* musicista *m*, *f.*

musical ['mjuːzikl] *adj* musicale; (*gifted*) dotato per la musica. *n* musical *m invar.*

musk [mʌsk] *n* (*zool*) muschio *m.*

musket ['mʌskit] *n* moschetto *m.*

Muslim ['mʌzlim] *n*, *adj* musulmano, -a.

muslin ['mʌzlin] *n* mussola *f.*

mussel ['mʌsl] *n* mitilo *m*, cozza *f.*

*must¹ [mʌst] *v* dovere. *n* (*coll*) cosa essenziale *f.*

must² [mʌst] *n* (*wine*) mosto *m.*

mustard ['mʌstəd] *n* senape *f*, mostarda *f.*

muster ['mʌstə] *v* radunare. **muster up courage** farsi coraggio. *n* **pass muster** essere accettabile.

mute [mjuːt] *adj* muto, taciturno. *n* muto, -a *m*, *f*; (*music*) sordina *f.*

mutilate ['mjuːtileit] *n* mutilare, mozzare. **mutilation** *n* mutilazione *f.*

mutiny ['mjuːtini] *n* ammutinamento *m*, ribellione *f.* *v* ammutinarsi, ribellarsi. **mutinous** *adj* ammutinato, ribelle.

mutter ['mʌtə] *v* brontolare, borbottare.

mutton ['mʌtn] *n* carne ovina *f*, castrato *m.* **dead as mutton** morto stecchito.

mutual ['mjuːtʃuəl] *adj* mutuo, reciproco; comune.

muzzle ['mʌzl] *n* (*gun*) imboccatura *f*; (*animal*) muso *m*; (*device*) museruola *f.* *v* mettere la museruola a; (*silence*) far tacere.

my [mai] *adj* (il) mio, (la) mia; (*pl*) (i) miei, (le) mie.

myself [mai'self] *pron* io stesso; (*after prep*) me stesso; (*reflexive*) mi.

myopia [mai'oupiə] *n* miopia *f.* **myopic** *adj* miope.

mystery ['mistəri] *n* mistero *m*, segretò *m.* **mysterious** *adj* misterioso, strano.

mystic ['mistik] *n* mistico, -a *m*, *f.* **mystical** *adj* mistico, misterioso. **mysticism** *n* misticismo *m*, mistica *f.*

mystify ['mistifai] *v* mistificare, disorientare.

mystique [mi'stiːk] *n* mistica *f.*

myth [miθ] *n* mito *m.* **mythical** *adj* mitico. **mythological** *adj* mitologico. **mythology** *n* mitologia *f.*

N

nag¹ [nag] *v* rimbrottare, brontolare. **nagging** *adj* bisbetico.

nag² [nag] *n* ronzino *m.*

nail [neil] *n* (*anat*) unghia *f*; (*metal*) chiodo *m.* **nail-brush** *n* spazzolino per le unghie *m.* **nail-file** *n* lima per le unghie *f.* **nail polish** smalto per le unghie *m.* **nail-scissors** *pl n* forbici per le unghie *f pl.*

naive [nai'iːv] *adj* ingenuo. **naivety** *n* ingenuità *f.*

naked ['neikid] *adj* nudo, scoperto. **strip naked** spogliare. **nakedness** *n* nudità *f.*

name [neim] *v* chiamare. *n* nome *m.* **go by the name of** chiamarsi. **my name is . . .** mi chiamo . . . . **namesake** *n* omonimo *m.* **nameless** *adj* anonimo. **namely** *adv* cioè.

nanny ['nani] *n* bambinaia *f.*

nap¹ [nap] *n* (*doze*) pisolino *m.* *v* fare *or* schiacciare un pisolino.

nap² [nap] *n* (*cloth*) pelo *m.*

nape [neip] *n* nuca *f.*

napkin ['napkin] *n* tovagliolo *m.*

nappy ['napi] *n* pannolino *m.*

narcotic [naːˈkotic] *nm*, *adj* narcotico.

narrate [nəˈreit] *v* narrare, raccontare. **narration** *n* racconto *m.* **narrative** *n* narrativa *f.* **narrator** *n* narratore, -trice *m*, *f.*

narrow ['narou] *adj* stretto; limitato; (*person, mind, etc.*) ristretto. **narrow-gauge** *adj* (*railway*) a scartamento ridotto. **narrow-minded** *adj* gretto, di mente ristretta. *v* restringere, limitare. **narrowly** *adv* per un pelo, a stento.

nasal ['neizəl] *adj* nasale.

nasturtium [nəˈstəːʃəm] *n* nasturzio *m.*

nasty ['naːsti] *adj* (*filthy*) disgustoso; (*offensive*) ripugnante; (*unpleasant*) cattivo, sgradevole. **nastiness** *n* cattiveria *f.*

nation ['neiʃən] *n* nazione *f.* **national** *adj* nazionale. **national insurance** assicurazione sociale *f.* **nationalism** *n* nazionalismo *m.* **nationalist** *n(m+f)*, *adj* nazionalista. **nationality** *n* nazionalità *f.* **nationalization** *n* nazionalizzazione *f.* **nationalize** *v* nazionalizzare.

native ['neitiv] *n*, *adj* (*original inhabitant*) indigeno, -a; (*of town, etc.*) nativo, -a, oriundo, -a.

nativity [nəˈtivəti] *n* natività *f.*

natural ['natʃərəl] *adj* naturale; normale;

istintivo. **naturalization** *n* naturalizzazione *f*. **naturalize** *v* naturalizzare.

nature ['neitʃə] *n* natura *f*; (*condition*) indole *f*; disposizione *f*.

naught [nɔɪt] *n* nulla *m*. **come to naught** ridurre a zero.

naughty ['nɔɪti] *adj* cattivo; (*mischievous*) birichino; indecente, spinto.

nausea ['nɔɪziə] *n* nausea *f*; fastidio *m*. **nauseous** *adj* nauseabondo, disgustoso.

nautical ['nɔɪtikəl] *adj* nautico.

naval ['neivəl] *adj* navale, marittimo.

nave¹ [neiv] *n* (*of church*) navata *f*.

nave² [neiv] *n* (*hub*) mozzo *m*.

navel ['neivəl] *n* ombelico *m*.

navigate ['navigeit] *v* navigare, pilotare. **navigable** *adj* navigabile. **navigation** *n* navigazione *f*. **navigator** *n* navigatore *m*; (*officer*) ufficiale di rotta *m*.

navy ['neivi] *n* marina militare *f*. **navy blue** *adj* blu marino.

near [niə] *adj* vicino. *prep* vicino a, accanto a. *adv* vicino. *v* avvicinare. **near at hand** a portata di mano. **near-sighted** *adj* miope. **nearby** *adj, adv, prep* vicino (a). **nearly** *adv* quasi.

neat [niɪt] *adj* (*orderly*) ordinato, accurato; elegante; (*undiluted*) liscio. **neatness** *n* ordine *m*; eleganza *f*.

nebulous ['nebjuləs] *adj* vago, nebuloso.

necessary ['nesisəri] *adj* necessario, indispensabile. **necessity** *n* necessità *f*, bisogno *m*.

neck [nek] *n* (*anat*) collo *m*; (*of dress*) scollatura *f*. **have a stiff neck** avere il torcicollo. **neck and neck** testa a testa. **necklace** *n* collana *f*. **necktie** *n* cravatta *f*.

nectar ['nektə] *n* nettare *m*. **nectarine** *n* pesca noce *f*.

née [nei] *adj* nata.

need [niɪd] *n* bisogno *m*, necessità *f*; (*poverty*) miseria *f*. **if need be** caso mai, se c'è bisogno. *v* aver bisogno di; (*require*) richiedere. **needed** *adj* necessario. **needless** *adj* inutile, superfluo. **needy** *adj* indigente, bisognoso.

needle ['niɪdl] *n* ago *m*; (*knitting*) ferro *m*; (*gramophone*) puntina *f*. **needlework** *n* (*sewing*) cucitura *f*; (*embroidery*) ricamo *m*. *v* (*coll*) punzecchiare.

negative ['negətiv] *adj* negativo. *n* negativa *f*. **answer in the negative** rispondere di no.

neglect [ni'glekt] *n* negligenza *f*, trascuratezza *f*. *v* trascurare. **neglect to** mancare di. **negligent** *adj* negligente. **negligible** *adj* trascurabile.

negligée ['negliʒei] *n* negligé *m invar*, vestaglia *f*.

negotiate [ni'gouʃieit] *v* trattare, negoziare; (*obstacle, etc.*) superare. **negotiable** *adj* negoziabile. **negotiation** *n* trattativa *f*, negoziato *m*.

Negro ['niɪgrou] *nm, adj* negro. **Negress** *n* negra *f*.

neigh [nei] *v* nitrire. *n* nitrito *m*.

neighbour ['neibə] *n* vicino, -a *m, f*. **next-door neighbour** vicino di casa *m*. **neighbourhood** *n* vicinanza *f*, paraggi *m pl*. **neighbouring** *adj* adiacente, vicino. **neighbourly** *adj* socievole, da buon vicino.

neither ['naiðə] *adj* nè l'uno nè l'altro. *adv* **neither ... nor ...** nè ... nè .... *pron* nessuno, nè l'uno nè l'altro.

neon ['niɪon] *n* neon *m*.

nephew ['nefjuɪ] *n* nipote *m*.

nepotism ['nepətizəm] *n* nepotismo *m*.

nerve [nəɪv] *n* nervo *m*; coraggio *m*; (*coll: cheek*) sfacciataggine *f*, faccia tosta *f*. **get on the nerves of** dare sui nervi a. **nerve-racking** *adj* snervante. **nervous** *adj* nervoso; apprensivo. **get nervous** inquietarsi. **nervous breakdown** esaurimento nervoso *m*.

nest [nest] *n* nido *m*. **nest egg** gruzzolo *m*. *v* annidarsi.

nestle ['nesl] *v* annidarsi, accoccolarsi.

net¹ [net] *n* rete *f*. **network** *n* rete *f*. *v* (*enclose*) cintare con reti; (*catch*) prendere con reti; (*ball*) mandare in rete. **netting** *n* reticolato *m*.

net² [net] *adj* netto.

Netherlands ['neðələndz] *pl n* Paesi Bassi *m pl*.

nettle ['netl] *n* ortica *f*. **nettle-rash** *n* orticaria *f*. *v* irritare.

neurosis [nju'rousis] *n* nevrosi *f*. **neurotic** *n, adj* nevrotico, -a.

neuter ['njuɪtə] *adj* neutro. *v* castrare.

neutral ['njuɪtrəl] *adj* neutrale; (*tech*) neutro. *n* neutrale *m, f*. **neutrality** *n* neutralità *f*. **neutralize** *v* neutralizzare. **neutron** *n* neutrone *m*.

never ['nevə] *adv* (non ...) mai. **never-ending** *adj* interminabile.

nevertheless [nevəðə'les] *adv, conj* ciononostante, tuttavia.

new [njuɪ] *adj* nuovo. **new-born** *adj* neonato. **newcomer** *n* nuovo venuto, nuova venuta *m, f.*

news [njuɪz] *n* novità *f pl,* notizie *f pl,* informazioni *f pl.* **news agency** agenzia d'informazioni *f.* **newsagent** *n* giornalaio *m.* **news bulletin** notiziario *m;* (*radio*) giornale radio *m.* **news item** notizia *f.* **newspaper** *n* giornale *m.* **newsprint** *n* carta da giornale *f.* **newsreel** *n* cinegiornale *m.*

newt [njuɪt] *n* tritone *m.*

New Year *n* Anno nuovo *m.* **Happy New Year!** Buon Anno! **New Year's Day** il Capodanno *m.* **New Zealand** *n* Nuova Zelanda *f.* **New Zealander** neozelandese *m, f.*

next [nekst] *adj* prossimo; (*nearest*) più vicino; (*following*) successivo, seguente. *adv* (*after*) dopo, poi; (*later*) in seguito. **next-of-kin** *n* parente prossimo *m, f.*

nib [nib] *n* pennino *m.*

nibble ['nibl] *n* (*morsel*) bocconcino *m. v* rosicchiare.

nice [nais] *adj* bello; piacevole, simpatico; (*subtle*) sottile; delicato; (*refined*) elegante, fine. **nicely** *adv* proprio bene. **nicety** *n* esattezza *f.* **niceties** *pl n* finezze *f pl,* sfumature *f pl.*

niche [nitʃ] *n* nicchia *f.*

nick [nik] *v* intaccare; (*slang: steal*) arraffare; (*slang: catch*) acchiappare. *n* tacca *f.* **in the nick of time** all'ultimo momento.

nickel ['nikl] *n* nichel *m;* (*US: coin*) nichelino *m.*

nickname ['nikneim] *n* nomignolo *m,* soprannome *m. v* soprannominare.

nicotine ['nikətim] *n* nicotina *f.*

niece [niːs] *n* nipote *f.*

niggling ['niglin] *adj* insignificante.

night [nait] *n* notte *f;* (*evening*) sera *f.* **have a good/bad night** dormir bene/male. **night-club** *n* night *m invar.* **nightdress** *n* camicia da notte *f.* **nightfall** *n* tramonto *m.* **nightmare** *n* incubo *m.* **nightmarish** *adj* opprimente, spaventoso. **stay the night** pernottare.

nightingale ['naitiŋˌgeil] *n* usignolo *m.*

nightly ['naitli] *adj* notturno; (*every night*) di tutte le sere. *adv* ogni notte *or* sera.

nil [nil] *n* nulla *m,* niente *m,* zero *m.*

nimble ['nimbl] *adj* agile, svelto. **nimbleness** *n* agilità *f.*

nine [nain] *nm, adj* nove. **ninepins** *n* birilli *m pl.* **ninth** *nm, adj* nono.

nineteen [nain'tiɪn] *nm, adj* diciannove. **nineteenth** *nm, adj* diciannovesimo.

ninety ['nainti] *nm, adj* novanta. **ninetieth** *nm, adj* novantesimo.

nip¹ [nip] *v* pizzicare; (*bite*) morsicare. **nip in** intromettersi, entrare lestamente. **nip in the bud** stroncare sul nascere. **nip out** fare un salto. *n* (*frost*) gelo *m;* (*bite*) morso *m.* **nippy** *adj* (*speedy*) svelto; (*cold*) frizzante.

nip² [nip] *n* (*drop*) bicchierino *m,* sorso *m.*

nipple ['nipl] *n* capezzolo *m;* (*tech*) rubinetto *m.*

nit [nit] *n* lendine *m;* (*coll*) stupido, -a *m, f.*

nitrogen ['naitrədʒən] *n* azoto *m.*

no [nou] *adj* nessuno, neppure uno; (*forbidden*) vietato. *adv* no; (*with comparative*) non. *n* no *m invar.*

noble ['noubl] *n(m+f), adj* nobile. **nobility** *n* nobiltà *f.*

nobody ['noubodi] *pron* nessuno. *n* zero *m,* sconosciuto, -a *m, f.*

nocturnal [nok'təɪnəl] *adj* notturno.

nod [nod] *n* cenno col capo *m. v* fare un cenno col capo; (*doze*) sonnecchiare; (*assent*) annuire; (*greet*) salutare. **nodding acquaintance** conoscenza superficiale *f.*

noise [noiz] *n* rumore *m;* (*loud*) baccano *m.* **background noise** rumori di fondo *m pl.* **big noise** (*coll*) pezzo grosso *m.* **noiseless** *adj* silenzioso. **noisy** *adj* rumoroso, chiassoso.

nomad ['noumad] *n(m+f), adj* nomade.

nominal ['nominl] *adj* nominale; simbolico.

nominate ['nomineit] *v* nominare; (*propose*) proporre. **nomination** *n* nomina *f.*

nominative ['nominətiv] *nm, adj* nominativo.

nonchalant ['nonʃələnt] *adj* indifferente, noncurante. **nonchalance** *n* indifferenza *f,* noncuranza *f.*

nonconformist [nonkən'foːmist] *n(m+f), adj* dissidente, anti-conformista.

nondescript ['nondiskript] *adj* inclassificabile, qualunque.

none [nʌn] *pron* nessuno, nulla, niente. *adv* affatto, punto. **none other than** nientedimeno che.

nonentity [non'entəti] *n* nullità *f,* zero *m.*
nonetheless [ˌnʌnðə'les] *adv* ciononostante, tuttavia.
nonsense ['nonsəns] *n* nonsenso *m,* assurdo *m;* (*coll*) sciocchezze *f pl.* **nonsensical** *adj* assurdo, sciocco. **talk nonsense** dire sciocchezze.
non-stop [non'stop] *adj* continuo, ininterrotto.
noodles ['nuːdlz] *pl n* tagliatelle *f pl,* taglierini *m pl.*
nook [nuk] *n* cantuccio *m,* angolo *m.*
noon [nuːn] *n* mezzogiorno *m.*
no-one ['nouwʌn] *pron* nessuno.
noose [nuːs] *n* nodo scorsoio *m,* laccio *m.*
nor [noɪ] *conj* nè, neppure, nemmeno.
norm [noːm] *n* norma *f,* modello *m.* **normal** *adj* normale, regolare. **normally** *adv* di solito.
north [noːθ] *n* nord *m,* settentrione *m. adj also* **northern** del nord, settentrionale. **northerly** *adj* di nordo; da nordo; a nordo. **north-east** *n* nordest *m.* **north-eastern** del nordest. **north-west** *n* nordovest *m.* **north-western** del nordovest.
Norway ['noːwei] *n* Norvegia *f.* **Norwegian** *n*(*m*+*f*), *adj* norvegese.
nose [nouz] *n* naso *m;* (*of animal, aeroplane, etc.*) muso *m. v* fiutare. **nose around** esplorare. **nosy** *adj* (*coll*) curioso.
nostalgia [no'staldʒə] *n* nostalgia *f,* rimpianto *m.* **nostalgic** *adj* nostalgico.
nostril ['nostrəl] *n* narice *f.*
not [not] *adv* non. **not at all** niente affatto. **not even** neppure, neanche.
notable ['noutəbl] *adj* notevole, degno di nota.
notary ['noutəri] *n* notaio *m.*
notch [notʃ] *n* tacca *f,* intaglio *m. v* intaccare.
note [nout] *n* nota *f,* appunto *m,* commento *m;* (*money*) biglietto *m.* **note-book** *n* taccuino *m.* **notepaper** *n* carta da lettere *or* scrivere. **noteworthy** *adj* degno di nota, notevole. **take note of** prendere atto di. **take notes** prendere appunti.
notation *n* notazione *f. v* notare; osservare. **noted** *adj* noto, rinomato.
nothing ['nʌθiŋ] *n* niente *m,* zero *m. adv* per nulla, niente (affatto). **next to nothing** quasi nulla. **nothing but** null'altro che. **nothing less than** semplicemente.
notice ['noutis] *n* avviso *m,* annuncio *m;*

(*advance warning*) preavviso *m;* (*criticism*) recensione *f.* **give notice** (*dismiss*) licenziare. **notice-board** *n* tabellone *m.* **take notice of** fare attenzione a. *v* notare, rilevare. **noticeable** *adj* apparente, percettibile.
notify ['noutifai] *v* notificare, avvertire. **notification** *n* notifica *f.*
notion ['noufən] *n* nozione *f,* idea *f.*
notorious [nou'toːriəs] *adj* notorio, famigerato. **notoriety** *n* notorietà *f.*
notwithstanding [notwið'standiŋ] *prep* nonostante, malgrado. *adv* ciononostante, con tutto ciò.
nougat ['nuːgat] *n* torrone *m.*
nought [noːt] *n* zero *m.*
noun [naun] *n* nome *m,* sostantivo *m.*
nourish ['nʌriʃ] *v* nutrire, alimentare. **nourishing** *adj* nutriente. **nourishment** *n* cibo *m,* alimento *m.*
novel[1] ['novəl] *n* romanzo *m.* **novelist** *n* romanziere, -a *m, f.*
novel[2] ['novəl] *adj* nuovo, originale; (*unusual*) insolito. **novelty** *n* novità *f.*
November [nə'vembə] *n* novembre *m.*
novice ['novis] *n* novizio, -a *m, f.*
now [nau] *adv* ora, adesso. **from now on** d'ora in poi. **just now** or ora. **nowadays** *adv* oggigiorno, al giorno d'oggi. **now and again** ogni tanto, di quando in quando. **until now** finora.
nowhere ['nouweə] *adv* in nessun luogo.
noxious ['nokʃəs] *adj* nocivo, malefico.
nozzle ['nozl] *n* (*spout*) becco *m;* (*tech*) ugello *m.*
nuance ['njuːãs] *n* sfumatura *f.*
nuclear ['njuːkliə] *adj* nucleare.
nucleus ['njuːkliəs] *n* nucleo *m.*
nude ['njuːd] *n, adj* nudo, -a. **nudism** *n* nudismo *m.* **nudist** *n* nudista *m, f.* **nudity** *n* nudità *f.*
nudge [nʌdʒ] *n* colpetto *m. v* dare un colpetto a.
nugget ['nʌgit] *n* pepita *f.*
nuisance ['njuːsns] *n* fastidio *m,* seccatura *f;* (*law*) infrazione *f.* **make a nuisance of oneself** seccare tutti.
null [nʌl] *adj* nullo. **null and void** senza validità legale.
numb [nʌm] *adj* intorpidito; (*stunned*) intontito. *v* intorpidire, paralizzare. **numbness** *n* torpore *m.*
number ['nʌmbə] *n* numero *m;* (*numeral*) cifra *f;* quantità *f.* **number plate** targa *f. v*

numerare, contare. **numberless** *adj* innumerevole.
numeral ['njuːmərəl] *n* cifra *f.*
numerical [njuːˈmerikl] *adj* numerico.
numerous ['njuːmərəs] *adj* numeroso.
nun [nʌn] *n* monaca *f,* suora *f.* **become a nun** prendere il velo. **nunnery** *n* convento *m.*
nurse [nəːs] *v* curare, fare l'infermiere; (*suckle*) allattare; (*hope, grievance, etc.*) nutrire, covare. *n* infermiere, -a *m, f;* (*children's*) balia *f,* bambinaia *f.* **nursing** *n* professione d'infermiere *f.* **nursing home** casa di cura *f,* clinica *f.*
nursery ['nəːsəri] *n* (*children's*) camera dei bambini *f;* (*plants, etc.*) vivaio *m,* serra *f.* **day nursery** asilo infantile *m.* **nursery rhyme** filastrocca *f.* **nursery school** giardino d'infanzia *m.*
nurture ['nəːtʃə] *v* (*feed*) nutrire; (*rear*) allevare. *n* nutrimento *m;* allevamento *m.*
nut [nʌt] *n* noce *f;* (*tech*) dado *m;* (*coll: head*) zucca *f.* **be nuts** (*coll*) essere matto. **in a nutshell** in poche parole. **nutcrackers** *pl n* schiaccianoci *m invar.* **nutmeg** *n* noce moscata *f.* **nut-tree** *n* noce *m.*
nutrient ['njuːtriənt] *adj* nutriente. *n* nutrimento *m.*
nutrition [njuˈtriʃən] *n* alimentazione *f.* **nutritious** *adj* nutriente.
nuzzle ['nʌzl] *v* accucciolarsi, rannicchiarsi.
nylon ['nailon] *n* nailon *m.*
nymph [nimf] *n* ninfa *f.* **nymphomaniac** *n* ninfomane *f.*

O

oak [ouk] *n* quercia *f.*
oar [oɪ] *n* remo *m.*
oasis [ouˈeisis] *n, pl* -ses oasi *f invar.*
oath [ouθ] *n* (*promise*) giuramento *m;* (*profanity*) bestemmia *f.*
oats [outs] *pl n* avena *f sing.* **oatmeal** *n* farina d'avena *f.*
obedient [əˈbiːdiənt] *adj* ubbidiente, obbediente. **obedience** *n* ubbidienza *f,* obbedienza *f.*
obese [əˈbiːs] *adj* obeso. **obesity** *n* obesità *f.*
obey [əˈbei] *v* ubbidire, obbedire.
obituary [əˈbitjuəri] *n* necrologia *f.*

object ['obʒikt; *v* əbˈʒekt] *n* oggetto *m;* (*aim*) scopo *m. v* obiettare, protestare. **objection** *n* obiezione *f,* protesta *f.* **have no objection to** aver nulla in contrario a. **objectionable** *adj* offensivo, sgradevole, riprensibile. **objective** *nm, adj* obiettivo.
oblige [əˈblaidʒ] *v* costringere, obbligare; fare un favore a. **be obliged to** (*have to*) dovere; (*be grateful to*) essere riconoscente a. **obligation** *n* (*law*) obbligazione *f;* (*binding promise*) obbligo (*pl* -ghi) *m;* (*duty*) dovere *m.* **obligatory** *adj* obbligatorio. **obliging** *adj* cortese, accomodante.
oblique [əˈbliːk] *adj* obliquo; indiretto.
obliterate [əˈblitəreit] *v* obliterare, cancellare; (*destroy*) distruggere. **obliteration** *n* distruzione *f.*
oblivion [əˈbliviən] *n* oblio *m.* **oblivious** *adj* dimentico (*m pl* -chi).
oblong ['oblon] *adj* bislungo.
obnoxious [əbˈnokʃəs] *adj* odioso, offensivo.
oboe ['oubou] *n* oboe *m.* **oboist** *n* oboista *m, f.*
obscene [əbˈsiːn] *adj* osceno. **obscenity** *n* oscenità *f.*
obscure [əbˈskjuə] *adj* (*not clear*) ambiguo, oscuro; (*inconspicuous*) vago. *v* offuscare, velare. **obscurity** *n* oscurità *f.*
observe [əbˈzəːv] *v* (*see*) osservare; notare, rilevare; (*rel*) praticare. **observance** *n* osservanza *f.* **observant** *adj* osservante. **observation** *n* osservazione *f,* attenzione *f.* **keep under observation** tenere in osservazione. **observatory** *n* osservatorio *m.* **observer** *n* osservatore, -trice *m, f.*
obsess [əbˈses] *v* ossessionare. **obsession** *n* ossessione *f.*
obsolescent [obsəˈlesnt] *adj* che sta cadendo in disuso.
obsolete ['obsəliːt] *adj* caduto in disuso; antiquato.
obstacle ['obstəkl] *n* ostacolo *m.*
obstetrics [obˈstetriks] *n* ostetricia *f.* **obstetrician** *n* ostetrico, -a *m, f.*
obstinate ['obstinət] *adj* ostinato. **obstinacy** *n* ostinatezza *f.*
obstreperous [əbˈstrepərəs] *adj* ribelle.
obstruct [əbˈstrʌkt] *v* impacciare, ostacolare. **obstruction** *n* impaccio *m,* ostacolo *m.*
obtain [əbˈtein] *v* ottenere, procurare. **obtainable** *adj* ottenibile, raggiungibile.

obtrusive [əb'truːsiv] *adj* importuno; invadente. **obtrusion** *n* invadenza *f*.

obtuse [əb'tjuːs] *adj* ottuso.

obverse ['obvəːs] *n* faccia *f*, diritto *m*; (*counterpart*) inverso *m*.

obvious ['obviəs] *adj* ovvio, evidente.

occasion [ə'keiʒən] *v* causare. *n* (*time*) occasione *f*, volta *f*; (*cause*) motivo *m*, ragione *f*. **rise to the occasion** mostrarsi all'altezza. **occasional** *adj* saltuario, sporadico. **occasionally** *adv* ogni tanto.

occult ['okʌlt] *adj* occulto. *n* forze occulte *f pl*.

occupy ['okjupai] *v* occupare. **occupant** *or* **occupier** *n* occupante *m*, *f*. **occupation** *n* occupazione *f*; (*trade*) mestiere *m*, professione *f*. **occupational** *adj* del lavoro, professionale.

occur [ə'kəː] *v* succedere, capitare; (*come to mind*) venire in mente. **occurrence** *n* avvenimento *m*, caso *m*.

ocean ['ouʃən] *n* oceano *m*.

ochre ['oukə] *n* ocra *f*. *adj* (*color*) ocra.

o'clock [ə'klok] *adv* **one o'clock** l'una. **two/three/etc. o'clock** le due/tre/etc.

octagon ['oktəgən] *n* ottagono *m*. **octagonal** *adj* ottagonale.

octane ['oktein] *n* ottano *m*.

octave ['oktiv] *n* ottava *f*.

October [ok'toubə] *n* ottobre *m*.

octopus ['oktəpəs] *n* polpo *m*.

oculist ['okjulist] *n* oculista *m*, *f*.

odd [od] *adj* (*not even*) dispari; (*not paired*) scompagnato; (*strange*) strano, bizzarro; casuale; (*approximately*) circa. **oddity** *n* stranezza *f*; (*person*) eccentrico, -a *m*, *f*. **oddments** *pl n* rimasugli *m pl*, scampoli *m pl*.

odds [odz] *pl n* probabilità *f pl*, differenza *f sing*; (*betting*) posta *f sing*. **be at odds with** essere in disaccordo con. **lay odds** scommettere. **odds and ends** cosette varie *f pl*, rimasugli *m pl*.

ode [oud] *n* ode *f*.

odious ['oudiəs] *adj* odioso.

odour ['oudə] *n* odore *m*. **odourless** *adj* inodoro.

oesophagus [iː'sofəgəs] *n* esofago *m*.

of [ov] *prep* di.

off [of] *adv* via, distante. *prep* lontano da, fuori (di). *adj* (*holiday*) libero; (*food*) marcio, non buono. **be off** (*cancelled*) non aver luogo.

offal ['ofəl] *n* frattaglie *f pl*.

offend [ə'fend] *v* offendere. **offence** *n* offesa *f*; (*law*) infrazione alla legge *f*. **take offence** offendersi. **offender** *n* colpevole *m*, *f*; trasgreditore, -trice *m*, *f*.

offensive [ə'fensiv] *adj* offensivo; (*disagreeable*) sgradevole; insolente. *n* offensiva *f*.

offer ['ofə] *v* offrire, presentare, dare. *n* offerta *f*, proposta *f*.

offhand [of'hand] *adj* noncurante. *adv* all'improvviso.

office ['ofis] *n* (*place*) ufficio *m*; (*post, function*) carica *f*. **head office** *n* sede (centrale) *f*. **officer** *n* funzionario, -a *m*, *f*; (*mil, etc.*) ufficiale *m*.

official [ə'fiʃəl] *adj* ufficiale. *n* funzionario, -a *m*, *f*.

officious [ə'fiʃəs] *adj* inframmettente, invadente.

offing ['ofiŋ] *n* **in the offing** in vista.

off-load [of'loud] *v* scaricare.

off-peak [of'piːk] *adj* non di punta.

off-putting ['of,putiŋ] *adj* sconcertante, che lascia perplesso.

off-season [of'siːzn] *adj* fuori stagione.

offset [of'set; *n* 'ofset] *v* compensare, controbilanciare. *n* (*print*) offset *m invar*.

offshoot ['ofʃuːt] *n* ramo *m*.

offshore ['ofʃoː] *adv* al largo. *adj* di terra.

offside [of'said] *adv*, *adj* fuori gioco.

offspring ['ofspriŋ] *n* prole *f*; frutto *m*.

offstage ['ofsteidʒ] *adv*, *adj* fuori scena.

often ['ofn] *adv* spesso, sovente, molte volte. **how often** quante volte. **too often** troppe volte.

ogre ['ougə] *n* orco *m*.

oil [oil] *n* olio *m*; petrolio *m*; gasolio *m*. **oilfield** *n* giacimento petrolifero *m*. **oil-fired** *adj* a gasolio *or* nafta. **oil-painting** *n* pittura a olio *f*. **oilskin** *n* tela impermeabile *f*. **oil-well** *n* pozzo petrolifero *m*. *v* ungere, lubrificare. **oily** *adj* oleoso, untuoso.

ointment ['ointmənt] *n* unguento *m*.

old [ould] *adj* vecchio, antico (*m pl* -chi); (*not new*) usato. **old age** vecchiaia *f*. **old-fashioned** *adj* fuori moda. **old man** vecchio *m*. **old people** vecchi *m pl*. **old woman** vecchia *f*. **oldish** *adj* vecchiotto.

olive ['oliv] *n* oliva *f*. **olive green** *adj* verde oliva. **olive grove** oliveto *m*. **olive oil** olio d'oliva *m*. **olive-tree** *n* olivo *m*.

Olympic [ə'limpik] *adj* olimpico. **Olympic Games** olimpiadi *f pl*.

omelette ['omlɪt] *n* frittata *f.*
omen ['oumən] *n* presagio *m*, segno *m.*
ominous ['ominəs] *adj* sinistro, minaccioso.
omit [ou'mit] *v* omettere, tralasciare. **omission** *n* omissione *f.*
omnipotent [om'nipətənt] *adj* onnipotente. **omnipotence** *n* onnipotenza *f.*
on [on] *prep* su, sopra; a. *adv* su. *adj (gas, elec, etc.)* acceso; *(tap)* aperto.
once [wʌns] *adv* una volta. **all at once** ad un tratto. **at once** subito.
one [wʌn] *n, adj* uno, -a. *pron* uno; *(impersonal)* si. **oneself** *pron* sè (stesso); *(reflexive)* si. **one by one** a uno a uno. **one-sided** *adj* unilaterale; parziale; ineguale. **one-way street** senso unico *m.* **the one** quello, -a. **which one?** quale?
onion ['ʌnjən] *n* cipolla *f.*
onlooker ['onlukə] *n* spettatore, -trice *m, f.*
only ['ounli] *adj* solo, unico. *conj* ma. *adv* solo, soltanto. **only just** appena.
onset ['onset] *n* inizio *m.*
onshore ['onʃoɪ] *adv* a terra.
onslaught ['onsloɪt] *n* attacco *m*, assalto *m.*
onus ['ounəs] *n* onere *m*, obbligo *(pl* -ghi) *m.*
onward ['onwəd] *adj* che progredisce *or* avanza. **onwards** *adv* (in) avanti.
onyx ['oniks] *n* onice *m.*
ooze [uɪz] *v* colare, trasudare.
opal ['oupəl] *n* opale *m.*
opaque [ə'paik] *adj* opaco *(m pl* -chi). **opacity** *n* opacità *f.*
open ['oupən] *v* aprire; iniziare; inaugurare. **open wide** spalancare. *nm, adj* aperto. **lay oneself open to** esporsi a. **open-handed** *adj* generoso. **open-hearted** *adj* sincero. **open-minded** *adj* spregiudicato, libero da preconcetti. **open-mouthed** *adj, adv* a bocca aperta.
opening ['oupəniŋ] *adj* introduttivo, inaugurale. *n* apertura *f*; inaugurazione *f.*
opera ['opərə] *n* opera *f.* **opera glasses** binocoli da teatro *m pl.* **opera house** teatro dell'opera *m.* **opera singer** cantante lirico, -a *m, f.* **operetta** *n* operetta *f.*
operate ['opəreit] *v* operare. **operation** *n* operazione *f*; *(activity)* attività *f*; *(surgical)* intervento (chirurgico) *m.* **come into operation** entrare in vigore. **operative** *adj*

operativo; attivo; *(surgical)* operatorio.
operator *n* operatore, -trice *m, f*; *(phone)* telefonista *m, f.*
ophthalmic [of'θalmik] *adj* oftalmico.
opinion [ə'pinjən] *n* opinione *f*, parere *m*, giudizio *m.* **in the opinion of** secondo. **opinionated** *adj* dogmatico, intransigente.
opium ['oupiəm] *n* oppio *m.*
opponent [ə'pounənt] *n* avversario, -a *m, f.*
opportune [opə'tjuɪn] *adj* opportuno, giusto.
opportunity [opə'tjuɪnəti] *n* occasione *f.*
oppose [ə'pouz] *v* opporre, combattere; contrastare. **opposed** *adj* opposto, contrario. **opposition** *n* opposizione *f.*
opposite ['opəzit] *nm, adj* opposto, contrario. *prep* di fronte a, dirimpetto a.
oppress [ə'pres] *v* opprimere. **oppression** *n* oppressione *f.* **oppressive** *adj* oppressivo, opprimente. **oppressor** *n* oppressore *m.*
opt [opt] *v* optare. **opt out** decidere di non partecipare.
optical ['optikl] *adj* ottico. **optician** *n* ottico *m.* **optics** *n* ottica *f.*
optimism ['optimizəm] *n* ottimismo *m.* **optimist** *n* ottimista *m, f.* **optimistic** *adj* ottimistico.
optimum ['optiməm] *n* optimum *m*, meglio *m. adj* migliore.
option ['opʃən] *n* opzione *f*, scelta *f.* **optional** *adj* facoltativo.
opulent ['opjulənt] *adj* opulento. **opulence** *n* opulenza *f.*
or [oɪ] *conj* o, oppure. **either ... or ...** o ... o .... **or else** altrimenti.
oracle ['orəkl] *n* oracolo *m.*
oral ['oɪrəl] *adj* orale.
orange ['orindʒ] *n (fruit)* arancia *f*; *(tree, colour)* arancio *m. adj (colour)* arancio, arancione. **orange juice** succo d'arancio *m*; *(drink)* spremuta d'arancio *f.* **orange squash** aranciata *f.*
orator ['orətə] *n* oratore, -trice *m, f.* **oration** *n* orazione *f.*
orbit ['oɪbit] *n* orbita *f.*
orchard ['oɪtʃəd] *n* frutteto *m.*
orchestra ['oɪkəstrə] *n* orchestra *f.* **orchestral** *adj* orchestrale. **orchestrate** *v* orchestrare. **orchestration** *n* orchestrazione *f.*
orchid ['oɪkid] *n* orchidea *f.*
ordain [oɪ'dein] *v* ordinare.
ordeal [oɪ'diɪl] *n* dura prova *f*, travaglio *m.*

order ['ɔɪdə] *n* ordine *m*; comando *m*; classe *f*, grado *m*; (*commission*) ordinazione *f*. **in order that** affinché, perché. **in order to** per, allo scopo di. **out of order** guasto. *v* ordinare. **order about** mandar qua e là.

orderly ['ɔɪdəli] *adj* ordinato, regolare. *n* attendente *m*, inserviente *m*.

ordinal ['ɔɪdinl] *adj* ordinale.

ordinary ['ɔɪdənəri] *nm*, *adj* ordinario, solito, comune.

ore [ɔɪ] *n* minerale *m*.

oregano [ori'gainou] *n* origano *m*.

organ ['ɔɪgən] *n* organo *m*. **organ-pipe** *n* canna d'organo *f*. **organic** *adj* organico.

organist *n* organista *m*, *f*.

organism ['ɔɪgənizəm] *n* organismo *m*.

organize ['ɔɪgənaiz] *v* organizzare. **organization** *n* organizzazione *f*. **organizer** *n* organizzatore, -trice *m*, *f*.

orgasm ['ɔɪgazəm] *n* orgasmo *m*.

orgy ['ɔɪdʒi] *n* orgia *f*.

orient ['ɔɪriənt] *n* oriente *m*. *v* orientare. **oriental** *adj* orientale.

orientate ['ɔɪriənteit] *v* orientare. **orientation** *n* orientamento *m*.

origin ['ɔridʒin] *n* origine *f*. **originate** *v* originare. **originate from** derivare *or* provenire da. **originator** *n* creatore, -trice *m*, *f*; originatore, -trice *m*, *f*.

original [ə'ridʒinl] *adj* originale; (*authentic, primitive*) originario. *n* originale *m*. **originality** *n* originalità *f*. **originally** *adv* in origine.

ornament ['ɔɪnəmənt] *n* ornamento *m*; (*music*) abbellimento *m*; (*object, fitting*) suppellittile *f*. *v* abbellire. **ornamentation** *n* abbellimento *m*.

ornate [ɔɪ'neit] *adj* ornato.

ornithology [ɔɪni'θolədʒi] *n* ornitologia *f*. **ornithologist** *n* ornitologo, -a *m*, *f*.

orphan ['ɔɪfən] *n* orfano, -a *m*, *f*. *v* rendere orfano. **be orphaned** rimanere orfano. **orphanage** *n* orfanotrofio *m*.

orthodox ['ɔɪθədoks] *adj* ortodosso. **orthodoxy** *n* ortodossia *f*.

orthopaedic [ɔɪθə'piːdik] *adj* ortopedico. **orthopaedics** *n* ortopedia *f*. **orthopaedist** *n* ortopedico, -a *m*, *f*.

oscillate ['osileit] *v* (far) oscillare; (*fluctuate*) vacillare. **oscillation** *n* oscillazione *f*.

ostensible [o'stensəbl] *adj* ostensibile.

ostentatious [osten'teiʃəs] *adj* ostentato, ostentoso.

osteopath ['ostiəpaθ] *n* osteologo, -a *m*, *f*.

ostracize ['ostrəsaiz] *v* osteggiare, mettere al bando.

ostrich ['ostritʃ] *n* struzzo *m*.

other ['ʌðə] *adj* altro, diverso. **on the other hand** d'altra parte. **other people** gli altri. *pron* altro. **each other** l'un l'altro. **otherwise** ['ʌðəwaiz] *adv* altrimenti.

otter ['otə] *n* lontra *f*.

***ought** [ɔɪt] *v* dovere.

our [auə] *adj* (il) nostro, (la) nostra; (*pl*) (i) nostri, (le) nostre.

ours [auəz] *pron* il nostro, la nostra; (*pl*) i nostri, le nostre.

ourselves [auə'selvz] *pron* noi (stessi); (*reflexive*) ci.

oust [aust] *v* espellere, soppiantare.

out [aut] *adj* (*not alight*) spetto. *adv* via, fuori; (*to the end*) alla fine. **feel out of it** sentirsi a disagio. **out of** (*without*) senza. **out of action** fuori servizio, guasto. **out of date** antiquato; (*ticket, etc.*) scaduto. **out of doors** all'aperto. **out of place** inopportuno. **out of pocket** in perdita. **out of print** esaurito, fuori stampa. **out of tune** stonato. **out of work** disoccupato.

outboard ['autbɔɪd] *adj* fuoribordo.

outbreak ['autbreik] *n* scoppio *m*; (*riot*) sommossa; eruzione *f*; epidemia *f*.

outbuilding ['autbiːdiŋ] *n* edificio annesso *m*, dipendenza *f*.

outburst ['autbəɪst] *n* scoppio *m*; (*invective*) tirata *f*.

outcast ['autkaɪst] *n*, *adj* proscritto, -a, reietto, -a.

outcome ['autkʌm] *n* esito *m*, risultato *m*.

outcry ['autkrai] *n* grido *m*, scalpore *m*.

***outdo** [aut'duɪ] *v* sorpassare.

outdoor ['autdɔɪ] *adj* all'aperto.

outer ['autə] *adj* esterno, esteriore.

outfit ['autfit] *n* corredo *m*, equipaggiamento *m*; (*coll*) compagnia *f*.

outgoing ['autgouiŋ] *adj* uscente, in partenza; (*person*) estroverso, espansivo. **outgoings** *pl n* spese *f pl*.

***outgrow** [aut'grou] *v* (*grow taller than*) sorpassare in altezza; (*clothes*) diventare troppo grande per.

outhouse ['authaus] *n* fabbricato annesso *m*.

outing ['autiŋ] *n* gita *f*, scampagnata *f*.

outlandish [aut'landiʃ] *adj* esotico.

outlast [aut'laɪst] *v* durare più a lungo di, sopravvivere a.

outlaw ['autlɔɪ] *n* fuorilegge *m*, *f invar*. *v* mettere al bando, proscrivere.

outlay ['autlei] *n* spesa *f*, dispendio *m*.

outlet ['autlit] *n* sfogo *m*, sbocco *m*.

outline ['autlain] *v* delineare; (*draft*) abbozzare. *n* contorno *m*; (*general sketch*) abbozzo *m*. **outlines** *pl n* elementi *m pl*.

outlive [aut'liv] *v* sopravvivere a.

outlook ['autluk] *n* (*view*) veduta *f*; (*future prospect*) prospettiva *f*; (*mental view*) modo di vedere *m*, vedute *f pl*.

outlying ['autlaiiŋ] *adj* periferico, lontano.

outnumber [aut'nʌmbə] *v* superare in numero.

outpatient ['autpeiʃənt] *n* paziente esterno *or* ambulatoriale *m*, *f*.

outpost ['autpoust] *n* avamposto *m*.

output ['autput] *n* produzione *f*; (*yield*) rendimento *m*.

outrage ['autreidʒ] *n* oltraggio *m*. *v* oltraggiare.

outrageous [aut'reidʒəs] *adj* (*disgraceful*) vergognoso; offensivo; (*excessive*) esagerato.

outright ['autrait; *adv* aut'rait] *adj* completo, categorico. *adv* (*at once*) subito; (*entirely*) completamente; (*openly*) apertamente.

outset ['autset] *n* **at the outset** al principio.

outside [aut'said; *adj* 'autsaid] *adj* esterno, esteriore; (*extraneous*) estraneo. *adv* fuori, all'aperto. *prep* fuori di; (*except*) all'infuori di. *n* esterno *m*. **at the outside** (*coll*) tutt'al più. **outsider** *n* estraneo *m*; (*sport*) outsider *m invar*.

outsize ['autsaiz] *adj* di taglia forte, fuori misura.

outskirts ['autskəɪtz] *pl n* dintorni *m pl*, periferia *f sing*.

outspoken [aut'spoukən] *adj* franco, esplicito, schietto.

outstanding [aut'standiŋ] *adj* (*striking*) eminente, notevole; (*unpaid*) in sospeso, arretrato.

outstrip [aut'strip] *v* distanziare.

outward ['autwəd] *adj* esterno, esteriore, superficiale; (*journey*) d'andata. **outwardly** *adv* in apparenza.

outweigh [aut'wei] *v* superare in importanza.

outwit [aut'wit] *v* superare in astuzia.

oval ['ouvəl] *nm*, *adj* ovale.

ovary ['ouvəri] *n* ovaia *f*.

ovation [ou'veiʃən] *n* ovazione *f*.

oven ['ʌvn] *n* forno *m*.

over ['ouvə] *adv* oltre, al di sopra; (*in excess*) in più; (*finished*) finito. *prep* su, sopra; (*across*) al di là di; (*more than*) più di. **over here** qui, da questa parte. **over there** là, laggiù.

overall ['ouvərɔɪl] *adj* globale, completo. *n* (*workman's*) tuta *f*; (*scientist's*) camice *m*; (*woman's*) grembiulone *m*. *adv* in complesso.

overbalance [ouvə'baləns] *v* sbilanciare, perdere l'equilibrio.

overbearing [ouvə'beəriŋ] *adj* prepotente, altezzoso.

overboard ['ouvəbɔɪd] *adv* in mare *or* acqua.

overcast [ouvə'kaɪst] *adj* coperto, nuvoloso.

overcharge [ouvə'tʃaidʒ] *v* far pagare troppo.

overcoat ['ouvəkout] *n* cappotto *m*, soprabito *m*.

*overcome [ouvə'kʌm] *v* superare. *adj* sopraffatto, commosso.

overcrowded [ouvə'kraudid] *adj* sovraffollato. **overcrowding** *n* sovraffollamento *m*.

*overdo [ouvə'duɪ] *v* esagerare; (*overcook*) stracuocere.

overdose ['ouvədous] *n* dose eccessiva *f*.

overdraft ['ouvədraɪft] *n* scoperto (di conto) *m*.

*overdraw [ouvə'drɔɪ] *v* andare allo scoperto.

overdrive ['ouvədraiv] *n* marcia sovramoltiplicata *f*.

overdue [ouvə'djuɪ] *adj* in ritardo, tardivo; (*bill*) scaduto.

overestimate [ouvə'estimeit] *v* sopravvalutare.

overexpose [ouvəik'spouz] *v* sovraesporre. **overexposure** *n* sovraesposizione *f*.

overflow [ouvə'flou; *n* 'ouvəflou] *v* (*flood*) inondare; (*river*) straripare; (*vessel*) traboccare. *n* (*outlet*) troppopieno *m*. **overflow pipe** scarico del troppopieno *m*.

overgrown [ouvə'groun] *adj* ricoperto di vegetazione.

*overhang [ouvə'haŋ; *n* 'ouvəhaŋ] *v* sporgere sopra; (*impend*) incombere su, minacciare. *n* aggetto *m*; (*mountaineering*) strapiombo *m*.

overhaul [ouvə'hɔil] *v* (*investigate*) esaminare; (*repair*) ripassare, riparare. *n* esame minuzioso *m*.

overhead [ouvə'hed] *adv* in alto, di sopra. *adj* di sopra, aereo. **overheads** *pl n* spese generali *f pl*.

*overhear [ouvə'hiə] *v* udire per caso; (*eavesdrop*) origliare.

overheat [ouvə'hiit] *v* surriscaldare.

overjoyed [ouvə'dʒoid] *adj* felicissimo, colmo di gioia.

overland [ouvə'land] *adj, adv* per terra.

overlap [ouvə'lap] *v* sovrapporre, accavallare; coincidere *or* corrispondere in parte con.

*overlay ['ouvəlei; *v* ouvə'lei] *n* copertura *f*. *v* ricoprire; incrostare.

overleaf [ouvə'liif] *adv* **see overleaf** vedi retro.

overload [ouvə'loud; *n* 'ouvəloud] *v* sovraccaricare. *n* sovraccarico *m*.

overlook [ouvə'luk] *v* (*miss*) lasciarsi sfuggire, non rilevare; condonare; (*ignore*) non tener conto di, trascurare; (*house, etc.*) dare su.

overnight [ouvə'nait] *adv* di notte; (*suddenly*) d'un tratto. **stay overnight** pernottare.

overpower [ouvə'pauə] *v* sopraffare, dominare. **overpowering** *adj* irresistibile.

overrate [ouvə'reit] *v* sopravvalutare.

overreach [ouvə'riitʃ] *v* **overreach oneself** sopravvalutare le proprie forze.

overriding [ouvə'raidiŋ] *adj* di primaria importanza.

overrule [ouvə'ruil] *v* (*decision*) annullare; (*plea*) respingere.

*overrun [ouvə'rʌn] *v* invadere, infestare.

overseas [ouvə'siiz] *adv* oltremare. *adj* d'oltremare, straniero.

overseer [ouvə'siə] *n* ispettore, -trice *m, f*, sorvegliante *m, f*.

overshadow [ouvə'ʃadou] *v* oscurare; (*render insignificant*) eclissare.

*overshoot [ouvə'ʃuit] *v* (*miss*) fallire; (*go beyond*) oltrepassare. **overshoot the mark** passare il segno. **overshoot the runway** atterrare lungo.

oversight ['ouvəsait] *n* svista *f*, inavvertenza *f*.

*oversleep [ouvə'sliip] *v* dormire troppo a lungo, dormire oltre all'ora stabilita.

overspill ['ouvəspil] *n* sovrappiù *m*.

overt [ou'vəit] *adj* manifesto, palese.

*overtake [ouvə'teik] *v* sorpassare.

*overthrow [ouvə'θrou; *n* 'ouvəθrou] *v* rovesciare, sconfiggere. *n* rovesciamento *m*.

overtime ['ouvətaim] *n* ore straordinarie *f pl*.

overtone ['ouvətoun] *n* (*implication*) sfumatura *f*.

overture ['ouvətjuə] *n* (*music*) ouverture *f*, preludio *m*; (*proposal*) proposta *f*; (*political*) apertura *f*.

overturn [ouvə'təin] *v* rovesciare, capovolgere.

overweight [ouvə'weit] *adj* **be overweight** pesare troppo.

overwhelm [ouvə'welm] *v* (*defeat*) sopraffare; (*crush*) schiacciare; (*with kindness, etc.*) colmare. **overwhelmingly** *adv* in modo schiacciante.

overwork [ouvə'wəik] *v* (far) lavorar troppo. *n* eccesso di lavoro *m*.

overwrought [ouvə'roit] *adj* teso, turbato, agitato.

ovulate ['ovjuleit] *v* ovulare. **ovulation** *n* ovulazione *f*.

owe [ou] *v* dovere. **owing** *adj* dovuto. **owing to** dovuto a, grazie a.

owl [aul] *n* gufo *m*, civetta *f*.

own [oun] *adj* proprio. **get one's own back** rendere pan per focaccia. **on one's own** da solo. *v* possedere; (*recognize*) riconoscere; confessare. **owner** *n* proprietario, -a *m, f*. **ownership** *n* proprietà *f*, possesso *m*.

ox [oks] *n, pl* **oxen** bue (*pl* buoi) *m*. **oxtail** *n* coda di bue *f*.

oxygen ['oksidʒən] *n* ossigeno *m*.

oyster ['oistə] *n* ostrica *f*.

ozone ['ouzoun] *n* ozono *m*.

P

pace [peis] *n* passo *m*; (*speed*) velocità *f*. **keep pace with** (*walking*) camminare di pari passo con; (*keep up to date*) tenersi al corrente di. *v* **pace off** misurare a passi. **pace up and down** andare su e giù.

Pacific [pə'sifik] *nm, adj* pacifico.

pacifism ['pasifizəm] *n* pacifismo *m*. **pacifist** *n* pacifista *m, f*.

pacify ['pasifai] *v* pacificare.

pack [pak] *n* (*parcel, package*) pacco *m*; (*of goods*) imballo *m*; (*rucksack*) zaino *m*; (*cards*) mazzo *m*; (*thieves*) banda *f*;

(*hounds*) muta *f.* **pack of lies** tessuto di bugie *m.* *v* imballare; (*suitcases*) fare (le valige); (*cram*) pigiare. **packed** *adj* (*full*) pieno zeppo. **packing** *n* confezione *f,* imballaggio *m;* (*tech*) guarnizione *f.* **do one's packing** fare le valige, fare i bagagli.

package ['pakidʒ] *n* pacco *m. adj* (*deal, etc.*) comprensivo.

packet ['pakit] *n* pacchetto *m.*

pact [pakt] *n* patto *m.*

pad¹ [pad] *n* (*cushion*) cuscinetto *m,* tampone *m;* (*notepaper*) taccuino *m;* (*paw*) zampa *f. v* imbottire. **pad out** (*speech, essay, etc.*) infarcire. **padding** *n* imbottitura *f;* infarcimento *m.*

pad² [pad] *v* camminare a passo felpato.

paddle¹ ['padl] *n* (*of boat*) pagaia *f;* (*tech*) spatola *f;* (*zool*) pinna *f.* **paddle-boat** *n* piroscafo a ruote *m. v* remare piano.

paddle² ['padl] *v* sguazzare (nell'acqua). **paddling pool** piscina per bambini *f.*

paddock ['padək] *n* recinto *m;* (*racing*) paddock *m invar.*

paddy-field ['padifiːld] *n* risaia *f.*

padlock ['padlok] *n* lucchetto *m. v* chiudere col lucchetto.

paediatric [piːdi'atrik] *adj* pediatrico. **paediatrician** *n* pediatra *m, f.* **paediatrics** *n* pediatria *f.*

pagan ['peigən] *n, adj* pagano, -a.

page¹ [peidʒ] *n* (*book*) pagina *f.*

page² [peidʒ] *n also* **page-boy** paggio *m;* (*hotel*) piccolo *m. v* (*coll*) chiamare.

pageant ['padʒənt] *n* corteo storico *m.* **pageantry** *n* fasto *m.*

paid [peid] *V* **pay.**

pain [pein] *n* dolore *m,* sofferenza *f.* **be at pains to** sforzarsi di. **on pain of** sotto pena di. **painkiller** *n* analgesico *m.* **painstaking** *adj* laborioso. *v* addolorare, far male a. **painful** *adj* dóloroso. **painless** *adj* indolore.

paint [peint] *v* dipingere, pitturare; (*decorate*) verniciare. *n* colore *m,* vernice *f.* **paint-box** *n* scatola di colori *f.* **paintbrush** *n* pennello *m.* **painter** *n* pittore, -trice *m, f;* decoratore *m.* **painting** *n* guadro *m,* pittura *f.*

pair [peə] *n* paio *m* (*pl* -a *f*), coppia *f. v* accoppiare.

pal [pal] *n* (*coll*) compagno, -a *m, f.*

palace ['paləs] *n* palazzo *m.* **palatial** *adj* sontuoso.

palate ['palit] *n* palato *m.* **palatable** *adj* saporito.

pale¹ [peil] *adj* pallido. *v* impallidire. **paleness** *n* pallore *m.*

pale² [peil] *n* (*stake*) palo *m.* **beyond the pale** *adj* (*coll*) impossibile.

palette ['palit] *n* tavolozza *f.* **palette knife** spatola *f.*

pall¹ [poil] *v* smettere *or* cessare di interessare; (*weary*) stancare.

pall² [poil] *n* drappo funebre *m.*

palm¹ [paim] *n* (*of hand*) palmo *m. v* **palm off** affibbiare. **palmist** *n* chiromante *m, f.* **palmistry** *n* chiromanzia *f.*

palm² [paim] *n* (*tree*) palma *f.* **Palm Sunday** Domenica delle Palme *f.*

palpitation [ˌpalpi'teiʃən] *n* palpitazione *f.*

pamper ['pampə] *v* viziare.

pamphlet ['pamflit] *n* opuscolo *m;* (*polemical*) libello *m.*

pan [pan] *n* pentola *f,* casseruola *f,* padella *f.* **pancake** *n* fritella *f.* **Pancake Tuesday** martedì grasso *m.*

pancreas ['paŋkriəs] *n* pancreas *m invar.* **pancreatic** *adj* pancreatico.

panda ['pandə] *n* panda *m invar.*

pander ['pandə] *v* **pander to** favorire, andare incontro a.

pane [pein] *n* vetro *m.*

panel ['panl] *n* pannello *m;* (*jury*) lista *f;* (*instruments*) cruscotto *m.* **panelling** *n* rivestimento a pannelli *m.*

pang [paŋ] *n* dolore acuto *m,* spasimo *m.*

panic ['panik] *n* panico *m,* allarme *m.* **panic-stricken** *adj* colto dal panico. *v* essere in preda al panico. **panicky** *adj* apprensivo.

panorama [ˌpanə'raimə] *n* panorama *m.*

pansy ['panzi] *n* (*flower*) viola del pensiero *f;* (*coll: homosexual*) finocchio *m.*

pant [pant] *v* anelare, sbuffare.

panther ['panθə] *n* pantera *f.*

pantomime ['pantəmaim] *n* pantomina *f;* (*Christmas*) spettacolo di Natale *m.*

pantry ['pantri] *n* dispensa *f.*

pants [pants] *pl n* mutande *f pl.*

papal ['peipl] *adj* papale. **papacy** *n* papato *m.*

paper ['peipə] *n* carta *f;* documento *m;* (*treatise*) discorso *m;* (*news*) giornale *m.* **paperback** *n* edizione economica *f.* **paper-clip** *n* fermaglio *m,* agrafe *f.* **paper-mill** *n* cartiera *f.* **paperweight** *n* fermacarte *m invar.* **paperwork** *n* lavoro d'ufficio *m*; documenti *m pl. v* tappezzare.

paprika ['paprikə] *n* paprica *f*.

par [paɪ] *n* **above/below par** sopra/sotto la pari. **feel below par** sentirsi (un po') giù. **on a par with** alla pari con.

parable ['parəbl] *n* parabola *f*.

parabola [pə'rabələ] *n* parabola *f*.

parachute ['parəʃuɪt] *n* paracadute *m invar. v* scendere col paracadute. **parachutist** *n* paracadutista *m, f*.

parade [pə'reid] *n* (*display*) sfoggio *m*; (*mil*) sfilata *f*; (*sea-front*) lungomare *m. v* ostentare, sfoggiare; sfilare.

paradise ['parədais] *n* paradiso *m*.

paradox ['parədoks] *n* paradosso *m*. **paradoxical** *adj* paradossale.

paraffin ['parəfin] *n* paraffina liquida *f*; (*oil*) cherosene *m*, petrolio da illuminazione *m*.

paragraph ['parəgraɪf] *n* paragrafo *m*; (*news item*) trafiletto *m*.

parallel ['parəlel] *adj* parallelo. **parallel line** parallela *f*. *n* parallelo *m*; (*comparison*) paragone *m*.

paralyse ['parəlaiz] *v* paralizzare. **paralysis** *n*, *pl* -ses paralisi *f*. **paralytic** *n, adj* paralitico, -a.

parameter [pə'ramitə] *n* parametro *m*.

paramilitary [ˌparə'militəri] *adj* paramilitare.

paramount ['parəmaunt] *adj* sommo, supremo.

paranoia [ˌparə'noiə] *n* paranoia *f*. **paranoiac** *or* **paranoid** *n, adj* paranoico, -a.

parapet ['parəpit] *n* parapetto *m*.

paraphernalia [ˌparəfə'neiliə] *n* oggetti vari *m pl*, cianfrusaglie *f pl*.

paraphrase ['parəfreiz] *n* parafrasi *f. v* parafrasare.

paraplegic [ˌparə'pliːdʒik] *n, adj* paraplegico, -a. **paraplegia** *n* paraplegia *f*.

parasite ['parəsait] *n* parassita *m, f*. **parasitic** *adj* parassita, parassitico.

parasol ['parəsol] *n* parasole *m*.

paratrooper ['parəˌtruɪpə] *n* (soldato) paracadutista *m*.

parcel ['paɪsəl] *n* pacco *m*, pacchetto *m*. **by parcel post** a mezzo pacco postale. **part and parcel of** parte integrale di. *v* **parcel up** impacchettare.

parched [paɪtʃt] *adj* riarso. **be parched with thirst** morire dalla sete.

parchment ['paɪtʃmənt] *n* pergamena *f*,

cartapecora *f*. **parchment paper** carta pergamenata *f*.

pardon ['paɪdn] *n* perdono *m*; (*law*) grazia *f*; (*for minor fault*) scusa *f*. **I beg your pardon** mi scusi. *v* scusare; perdonare; graziare. *interj* prego? **pardonable** *adj* perdonabile.

pare [peə] *v* sbucciare, pelare. **pare down** ridurre.

parent ['peərənt] *n* padre, madre *m, f*. **parents** *pl n* genitori *m pl*. **parental** *adj* dei genitori. **parenthood** *n* l'essere genitori *m*.

parenthesis [pə'renθəsis] *n, pl* -ses parentesi *f*.

pariah [pə'raiə] *n* paria *m invar*.

Paris ['paris] *n* Parigi *f*. **Parisian** *n, adj* parigino, -a.

parish ['pariʃ] *n* parrocchia *f*; (*civil*) comune *m*. **parish priest** parroco (*pl* -chi) *m*. **parishioner** *n* parrocchiano, -a *m, f*.

parity ['pariti] *n* parità *f*.

park [paɪk] *n* parco *m. v* parcheggiare, posteggiare. **parking** *n* posteggio *m*, parcheggio *m*. **parking meter** parchimetro *m*.

parliament ['paɪləmənt] *n* parlamento *m*. **member of parliament** deputato *m*. **parliamentary** *adj* parlamentare.

parlour ['paɪlə] *n* salotto *m*. **parlour game** gioco di società *m*.

Parmesan [ˌpaɪmi'zan] *n* (*cheese*) (formaggio) parmigiano *m*, grana *m invar*.

parochial [pə'roukiəl] *adj* provinciale.

parody ['parədi] *n* parodia *f. v* parodiare.

parole [pə'roul] *v* rilasciare sulla parola. *n* rilascio sulla parola *m*.

paroxysm ['parəksizəm] *n* parossismo *m*, accesso *m*.

parrot ['parət] *n* pappagallo *m*.

parsley ['paɪsli] *n* prezzemolo *m*.

parsnip ['paɪsnip] *n* pastinaca *f*.

parson ['paɪsn] *n* prete *m*, parroco *m*. **parsonage** *n* casa parrocchiale *f*, presbiterio *m*.

part [paɪt] *n* parte *f*; (*theatre*) ruolo *m*; (*district*) quartiere *f*. **part-time** *adv, adj* a mezzo tempo. **spare part** pezzo di ricambio *m*. **take part** prender parte. *v* separare, spartire; (*hair*) dividere. **part with** rinunciare a. **parting** *n* separazione *f*, addio *m*; (*hair*) divisa dei capelli *f*, riga *f*.

*partake [paɪteik] *v* **partake of** consumare.

partial ['paɪʃəl] *adj* parziale. **be partial to** avere un debole per. **partiality** *n* preferenza *f*. **partially** *adv* in parte.
participate [paɪ'tisipeit] *v* partecipare. **participant** *n* partecipante *m, f*. **participation** *n* partecipazione *f*.
participle ['paɪtisipl] *n* participio *m*.
particle ['paɪtikl] *n* particella *f*.
particular [pə'tikjulə] *adj* particolare, speciale; (*exacting*) esigente. *n* particolare *m*, dettaglio *m*. **particularly** *adv* in particolare, specie.
partisan [paɪti'zan] *n, adj* partigiano, -a.
partition [paɪ'tiʃən] *n* spartizione *f*; (*of room*) tramezzo *m*. *v* spartire; tramezzare.
partly ['paɪtli] *adv* in parte.
partner ['paɪtnə] *n* (*comm*) socio *m*; compagno, -a *m, f*, partner (*pl* -s) *m, f*. *v* far da compagno a, associarsi a. **partnership** *n* società *f*, associazione *f*.
partridge ['paɪtridʒ] *n* pernice *f*.
party ['paɪti] *n* (*group*) compagnia *f*, gruppo *m*; (*entertainment*) festa *f*, trattenimento *m*; (*pol*) partito *m*; (*law*) parte *f*. **third party** terzi *m pl*.
pass [pais] *n* (*mountain*) passo *m*, valico (*pl* -chi) *m*; (*permit*) permesso *m*; (*mil*) libera uscita *f*; (*school*) promozione *f*; (*sport*) allungo *m*. *v* passare, superare; promuovere; allungare. **pass by** (*disregard*) non curarsi di; (*in front of*) passare davanti a. **pass off** far passare (per). **pass on** trasmettere; (*die*) morire. **pass out** (*faint*) svenire.
passage ['pasidʒ] *n* passaggio *m*; (*in book*) brano *m*.
passenger ['pasindʒə] *n* viaggiatore, -trice *m, f*. **passenger train** treno viaggiatori *m*.
passer-by [,paɪsə'bai] *n* passante *m, f*.
passing ['paɪsiŋ] *adj* passeggero, transitorio; casuale. **in passing** di passaggio *or* sfuggita; (*by the way*) tra parentesi.
passion ['paʃən] *n* passione *f*, entusiasmo *m*. **passionate** *adj* appassionato, ardente.
passive ['pasiv] *nm, adj* passivo. **passivity** *n* passività *f*.
Passover ['paɪsouvə] *n* Pasqua degli ebrei *f*.
passport ['paɪspoɪt] *n* passaporto *m*.
password ['paɪswɔɪd] *n* parola d'ordine *f*.
past [paist] *prep* al di là di, oltre; (*after*) dopo. **five past six** le sei e cinque. *adj* passato, scorso; (*former*) ex. *adv* davanti, oltre. *n* passato *m*.

pasta ['pastə] *n* pasta *f*, pastasciutta *f*.
paste [peist] *n* pasta *f*; (*adhesive*) colla *f*. *v* incollare.
pastel ['pastəl] *n* pastello *m*.
pasteurize ['pastʃəraiz] *v* pastorizzare. **pasteurization** *n* pastorizzazione *f*.
pastime ['paɪstaim] *n* passatempo *m*.
pastoral ['paɪstərəl] *adj* pastorale.
pastry ['peistri] *n* pasta *f*. **pastry-cook** *n* pasticciere, -a *m, f*.
pasture ['paɪstʃə] *n* pascolo *m*, pastura *f*. *v* pascolare.
pasty[1] ['peisti] *adj* pallido; (*consistency*) pastoso.
pasty[2] ['pasti] *n* (*pie*) pasticcio *m*.
pat[1] [pat] *adj* pronto, apposito. *adv* (*aptly*) a proposito; (*exactly*) precisamente.
pat[2] [pat] *n* (*light blow*) colpetto *m*; (*of butter*) pezzetto *m*. *v* dare un colpetto a.
patch [patʃ] *n* (*material*) pezza *f*, toppa *f*; (*land*) pezzo *m*. **go through a bad patch** attraversare un momento brutto. *v* rattoppare. **patch up** rattoppare, accomodare; (*quarrel*) comporre. **patchy** *adj* rattoppato; (*not uniform*) irregolare.
pâté ['patei] *n* pasticcio *m*, pâté *m invar*.
patent ['peitənt] *adj* manifesto, ovvio. **patent leather** pelle verniciata *f*. **patent medicine** specialità medicinale *f*. *n* brevetto *m*. *v* brevettare.
paternal [pə'təɪnl] *adj* paterno. **paternity** *n* paternità *f*.
path [paɪθ] *n* sentiero *m*; (*course, way*) via *f*, strada *f*.
pathetic [pə'θetik] *adj* patetico, commovente.
pathology [pə'θolədʒi] *n* anatomia patologica *f*. **pathological** *adj* patologico. **pathologist** *n* anatomo patologo, anatoma patologa *m, f*.
patient ['peiʃənt] *adj* paziente. *n* paziente *m, f*, malato, -a *m, f*. **be patient** pazientare, aver pazienza. **patience** *n* pazienza *f*.
patio ['patiou] *n* patio *m invar*.
patriarchal ['peitriaɪkəl] *adj* patriarcale. **patriarch** *n* patriarca *m*.
patriot ['patriət] *n* patriota *m, f*. **patriotic** *adj* patriottico. **patriotism** *n* patriottismo *m*.
patrol [pə'troul] *n* pattuglia *f*. *v* andare in pattuglia, ispezionare.
patron ['peitrən] *n* patrono *m*, protettore *m*; (*customer*) cliente abituale *m, f*,

avventore, -a *m, f.* **patronage** *n* protezione *f*, auspici *m pl.* **patronize** *v* favorire, proteggere; frequentare. **patronizing** *adj* condiscendente.

patter[1] ['patə] *v* (*sound*) picchiettare. *n* picchiettio *m.*

patter[2] ['patə] *n* (*speech*) cicalata *f*, ciancia *f. v* cicalare, cianciare.

pattern ['patən] *n* modello *m*, tipo *m*; disegno *m. v* modellare.

paunch [pɔintʃ] *n* pancia *f.* **paunchy** *adj* panciuto.

pauper ['pɔipə] *n* povero, -a *m, f*; mendicante *m, f.* **pauperize** *v* impoverire.

pause [pɔiz] *n* pausa *f*; esitazione *f. v* fare una pausa; esitare.

pave [peiv] *v* pavimentare. **pave the way** preparare il terreno. **pavement** *n* marciapiede *m.* **paving stone** lastra da selciato *f.*

pavilion [pə'viljən] *n* padiglione *m.*

paw [pɔi] *n* zampa *f. v* (*ground*) scalpitare; (*handle*) palpeggiare.

pawn[1] [pɔin] *n* (*deposit*) pegno *m.* **pawnbroker** *n* prestatore su pegno *m.* **pawnshop** *n* monte di pietà *m. v* pignorare, dare in pegno.

pawn[2] [pɔin] *n* (*chess*) pedina *f.*

*****pay** [pei] *n* paga *f*, stipendio *m.* **in the pay of** al servizio di. **pay-roll** *n* organico *m. v* pagare; (*settle*) saldare; (*profit*) rendere; (*attention, etc.*) fare. **pay back** rimborsare, restituire. **pay in** versare. **pay off** liquidare. **payable** *adj* pagabile. **payee** *n* beneficiario, -a *m, f.* **payment** *n* pagamento *m*, versamento *m.*

pea [pii] *n* pisello *m.*

peace [piis] *n* pace *f*; tranquillità *f.* **breach of the peace** violazione dell'ordine pubblico *f.* **peace-loving** *adj* pacifico. **peace offering** dono propiziatorio *m.* **peace-time** *n* tempo di pace *m.* **peaceful** *adj* pacifico.

peach [piitʃ] *n* (*fruit*) pesca *f*; (*tree*) pesco *m.*

peacock ['piikok] *n* pavone *m.* **peacock blue** *nm, adj.* blu pavone. **peahen** *n* pavona *f.*

peak [piik] *n* cima *f*, vetta *f*; (*highest point*) massimo *m*; (*on cap*) visiera *f.* **peak hours** ore di punta *f pl.* **peak load** carico massimo *m. v* raggiungere il massimo.

peal [piil] *n* (*bells*) scampanio *m*; (*thunder, laughter*) scoppio *m*, scroscio *m. v* scampanare; (*thunder*) rimbombare.

peanut ['piinʌt] *n* arachide *f.*

pear [peə] *n* (*fruit*) pera *f*; (*tree*) pero *m.*

pearl [pəil] *n* perla *f.* **pearly** *adj* (*like pearl*) perlaceo; (*adorned with pearls*) perlato.

peasant ['peznt] *n* contadino, -a *m, f.*

peat [piit] *n* torba *f.*

pebble ['pebl] *n* ciottolo *m.* **pebbly** *adj* ciottoloso.

peck [pek] *v* beccare; (*food*) mangiucchiare; (*kiss*) dare un bacetto a, baciucchiare. *n* beccata *f*; baciucchio *m.*

peckish ['pekiʃ] *adj* **feel peckish** sentirsi vuoto *or* affamato.

peculiar [pi'kjuiljə] *adj* strano, particolare. **peculiarity** *n* particolarità *f*, stranezza *f.*

pedal ['pedl] *n* pedale *m. v* pedalare.

pedantic [pi'dantik] *adj* pedante. **pedant** *n* pedante *m, f.* **pedantry** *n* pedanteria *f.*

peddle ['pedl] *v* spacciare.

pedestal ['pedistl] *n* piedistallo *m.*

pedestrian [pi'destriən] *adj* pedonale; (*commonplace*) pedestre. *n* pedone *m.* **pedestrian precinct** zona pedonale *f.*

pedigree ['pedigrii] *n* genealogia *f*; (*of animals*) pedigree *m invar. adj* di razza.

pedlar ['pedlə] *n* (*salesman*) venditore ambulante *m.*

peel [piil] *n* buccia *f. v* sbucciare; (*paint, skin*) staccarsi. **peeler** *n* sbucciatore *m.* **peelings** *pl n* bucce *f pl.*

peep [piip] *n* occhiata (furtiva) *f*, sguardo furtivo *m. v* dare un'occhiatina, spiare. **peep-hole** *n* spiraglio *m.* **peep out** mostrarsi appena.

peer[1] [piə] *v* **peer at** scrutare, guardare da presso.

peer[2] [piə] *n* pari *m.* **peerage** *n* nobiltà *f.*

peevish ['piiviʃ] *adj* permaloso, scontroso.

peg [peg] *n* piolo *m*; (*violin, etc.*) bischero *m*; (*washing*) molletta *f.* **off the peg** *adj* pronto. *v* (*prices*) stabilire. **peg out** (*coll: die*) crepare.

pejorative [pə'dʒorətiv] *adj* peggiorativo.

Peking [pii'kiŋ] *n* Pechino *f.* **Pekingese** *n* (*dog*) (cane) pechinese *m.*

pelican ['pelikən] *n* pellicano *m.*

pellet ['pelit] *n* pallottola *f*, pallina *f*; (*pill*) pillola *f.*

pelmet ['pelmit] *n* mantovana *f.*

pelt[1] [pelt] *v* scagliare; (*rain*) piovere

dirottamente, diluviare. *n* **at full pelt** a piena velocità.

pelt² [pelt] *n* pelliccia *f*.

pelvis ['pelvis] *n* pelvi *f*, bacino *m*. **pelvic** *adj* pelvico.

pen¹ [pen] *n* (*for writing*) penna *f*. *v* scrivere.

pen² [pen] *n* recinto *m*; (*for sheep*) ovile *m*; (*for pigs*) porcile *m*. *v* **pen in** rinchiudere.

penal ['piːnl] *adj* penale. **penalize** *v* punire. **penalty** *n* pena *f*; (*fine*) multa *f*. **penalty kick** (*sport*) calcio di rigore *m*.

penance ['penəns] *n* penitenza *f*.

pencil ['pensl] *n* matita *f*. **pencil-sharpener** *n* temperamatite *m invar*.

pendant ['pendənt] *n* ciondolo *m*.

pending ['pendiŋ] *adj* in sospeso. *prep* in attesa di.

pendulum ['pendjuləm] *n* pendolo *m*. **pendulum clock** orologio a pendolo *m*.

penetrate ['penitreit] *v* penetrare. **penetration** *n* penetrazione *f*.

pen-friend *n* amico, -a per corrispondenza *m, f*.

penguin ['peŋgwin] *n* pinguino *m*.

penicillin [peni'silin] *n* penicillina *f*.

peninsula [pə'ninsjulə] *n* penisola *f*. **peninsular** *adj* peninsulare.

penis ['piːnis] *n* pene *m*.

penitent ['penitənt] *n*(*m*+*f*), *adj* penitente. **penitence** *n* penitenza *f*, pentimento *m*. **penitentiary** *n* (*prison*) penitenziario *m*; (*church dignitary*) penitenziere *m*.

penknife ['pennaif] *n* temperino *m*.

pen-name *n* pseudonimo *m*.

pennant ['penənt] *n* pennello *m*.

penniless ['peniləs] *adj* al verde, senza un soldo.

pension ['penʃən] *n* pensione *f*. *v* **pension off** mettere a riposo, mettere in pensione. **pensioner** *n* pensionato, -a *m, f*.

pensive ['pensiv] *adj* pensoso, pensieroso, preoccupato.

pentagon ['pentəgən] *n* pentagono *m*. **pentagonal** *adj* pentagonale.

penthouse ['penthaus] *n* attico *m*.

pent-up [ˌpent'ʌp] *adj* represso.

penultimate [pi'nʌltimit] *adj* penultimo.

people ['piːpl] *n* popolo *m*, nazione *f*. *pl n* gente *f sing*; (*coll: family*) i suoi *m pl*. *v* popolare.

pepper ['pepə] *n* pepe *m*. **peppercorn** *n* grano di pepe *m*. **pepper-mill** *n*

macinapepe *m invar*. **peppermint** *n* (*herb*) menta piperita *f*; (*sweet*) mentina *f*. **pepper-pot** *n* pepaiola *f*. *v* (*season*) pepare; (*dot*) cospargere; (*hit*) tempestare.

per [pəː] *prep* a. **as per** secondo. **per cent** percento. **percentage** *n* percentuale *f*.

perceive [pə'siːv] *v* rilevare, scorgere, accorgersi di.

perceptible [pə'septibl] *adj* percettibile; visibile. **perceptibility** *n* percettibilità *f*; visibilità *f*.

perception [pə'sepʃən] *n* percezione *f*. **perceptive** *adj* percettivo, sensibile.

perch¹ [pəːtʃ] *n* posatoio *m*. *v* posarsi.

perch² [pəːtʃ] *n* (*fish*) pesce persico *m*.

percolate ['pəːkəleit] *v* filtrare. **percolator** *n* percolatore *m*.

percussion [pə'kʌʃən] *n* percussione *f*.

perennial [pə'reniəl] *adj* perenne; perpetuo. *v* pianta perenne *f*.

perfect ['pəːfikt; *v* pə'fekt] *adj* perfetto, ideale; (*real*) vero. *v* perfezionare. **perfection** *n* perfezione *f*.

perforate ['pəːfəreit] *v* perforare. **perforation** *n* perforazione *f*.

perform [pə'fɔːm] *v* eseguire, compire; (*music, theatre*) recitare. **performance** *n* esecuzione *f*; recita *f*; (*show*) spettacolo *m*. **performer** *n* artista *m, f*.

perfume ['pəːfjuːm] *n* profumo *m*. *v* profumare. **perfumery** *n* profumeria *f*.

perfunctory [pə'fʌŋktəri] *adj* fatto alla buona, meccanico, indifferente.

perhaps [pə'haps] *adv* forse, magari.

peril ['peril] *n* rischio *m*. **perilous** *adj* rischioso, pericoloso.

perimeter [pə'rimitə] *n* perimetro *m*.

period ['piəriəd] *n* periodo *m*; (*full stop*) punto fermo *m*; (*med*) mestruazione *f*. *adj* antico (*m pl* -chi), storico. **periodic** *adj* periodico. **periodical** *nm, adj* periodico.

peripheral [pə'rifərəl] *adj* periferico. **periphery** *n* periferia *f*.

periscope ['periskoup] *n* periscopio *m*.

perish ['periʃ] *v* perire; (*food, etc.*) guastarsi, deperire. **perishable** *adj* deperibile.

perjure ['pəːdʒə] *v* spergiurare. **perjurer** *n* spergiuro, -a *m, f*. **perjury** *n* spergiuro *m*, giuramento falso *m*.

perk [pəːk] *v* **perk up** rianimarsi, ravvivarsi. **perky** *adj* vispo.

perm [pəːm] *n* permanente *f*. **have a perm** farsi fare la permanente.

permanent ['pɜːmənənt] *adj* permanente.
permeate ['pɜːmieit] *v* permeare.
permit ['pɜːmit; *v* pə'mit] *n* permesso *m*, licenza *f*. *v* permettere. permissible *adj* permissibile. permission *n* permesso *m*. permissive *adj* permissivo.
permutation [pɜːmju'teiʃən] *n* permutazione *f*.
pernicious [pə'niʃəs] *adj* pernicioso.
pernickety [pə'nikəti] *adj* pignolo.
perpendicular [ˌpɜːpen'dikjulə] *nf, adj* perpendicolare.
perpetrate ['pɜːpitreit] *v* commettere. perpetration *n* perpetrazione *f*. perpetrator *n* perpetratore, -trice *m, f*.
perpetual [pə'petʃuəl] *adj* perpetuo.
perpetuate [pə'petʃueit] *v* perpetuare. perpetuation *n* perpetuazione *f*. in perpetuity in perpetuo.
perplex [pə'pleks] *v* confondere, rendere perplesso. perplexed *adj* perplesso, confuso. perplexing *adj* imbarazzante. perplexity *n* perplessità *f*, imbarazzo *m*.
persecute ['pɜːsikjuːt] *v* perseguitare. persecution *n* persecuzione *f*.
persevere [ˌpɜːsi'viə] *v* perseverare. perseverance *n* perseveranza *f*, assiduità *f*. persevering *adj* perseverante, assiduo.
persist [pə'sist] *v* persistere, ostinarsi, perseverare. persistence *n* perseveranza *f*, persistenza *f*, ostinazione *f*. persistent *adj* ostinato, persistente.
person ['pɜːsn] *n* persona *f*, individuo *m*. personage *n* personaggio *m*. personal *adj* personale; (*disparaging*) offensivo, di carattere personale. personality *n* personalità *f*; carattere *m*; celebrità *f*.
personify [pə'sonifai] *v* personificare. personification *n* personificazione *f*.
personnel [ˌpɜːsə'nel] *n* personale *m*, impiegati *m pl*.
perspective [pə'spektiv] *n* prospettiva *f*.
perspire [pə'spaiə] *v* sudare. perspiration *n* sudore *m*.
persuade [pə'sweid] *v* persuadere. persuasion *n* persuasione *f*. persuasive *adj* persuasivo.
pert [pɜːt] *adj* (*lively*) vispo; impudente, insolente.
pertain [pə'tein] *v* pertain to riguardare, appartenere a. pertinent *adj* pertinente, a proposito. pertinence *n* pertinenza *f*.
perturb [pə'tɜːb] *v* turbare, sconcertare.
peruse [pə'ruːz] *v* leggere attentamente.

pervade [pə'veid] *v* pervadere. pervasive *adj* penetrante.
perverse [pə'vɜːs] *adj* perverso. perversity *n* perversità *f*.
pervert ['pɜːvɜːt; *v* pə'vɜːt] *n* pervertito, -a *m, f*. *v* pervertire. perversion *n* perversione *f*, pervertimento *m*.
pessimism ['pesimizəm] *n* pessimismo *m*. pessimist *n* pessimista *m, f*. pessimistic *adj* pessimista, pessimistico.
pest [pest] *n* animale *or* parassita nocivo *m*; (*coll: nuisance*) seccatore *m*. pest control disinfestazione *f*. pesticide *n* pesticida *m*.
pester ['pestə] *v* seccare.
pet [pet] *n* animale favorito *m*; (*favourite*) cocco, -a *m, f*. *adj* prediletto. pet aversion avversione spiccata *f*. pet name nomignolo *m*. *v* coccolare. petting *n* (*slang*) carezze amorose *f pl*.
petal ['petl] *n* petalo *m*.
petition [pə'tiʃən] *n* petizione *f*, supplica *f*. *v* presentare una petizione *or* supplica.
petrify ['petrifai] *v* pietrificare, paralizzare. petrified *adj* allibito, pietrificato.
petrol ['petrəl] *n* benzina *f*. petrol-tank *n* serbatoio *m*.
petroleum [pə'trouliəm] *n* petrolio *m*.
petticoat ['petikout] *n* sottana *f*.
petty ['peti] *adj* insignificante; (*mean*) meschino. petty cash piccola cassa *f*, fondo per le piccole spese *m*. petty officer capo *m*. pettiness *n* piccolezza *f*, meschinità *f*.
petulant ['petjulənt] *adj* scontroso, irritabile. petulance *n* scontrosità *f*, irritabilità *f*.
pew [pjuː] *n* banco (di chiesa) *m*.
pewter ['pjuːtə] *n* peltro *m*.
phantom ['fantəm] *n* fantasma *m*.
pharmacy ['faːməsi] *n* farmacia *f*. pharmaceutical *adj* farmaceutico. pharmacist *n* farmacista *m, f*.
pharynx ['fariŋks] *n* faringe *f*.
phase [feiz] *n* fase *f*.
pheasant ['feznt] *n* fagiano *m*.
phenomenon [fə'nomənən] *n, pl* -ena fenomeno *m*. phenomenal *adj* fenomenale.
phial ['faiəl] *n* fiala *f*.
philanthropy [fi'lanθrəpi] *n* filantropia *f*. philanthropic *adj* filantropico. philanthropist *n* filantropo, -a *m, f*.
philately [fi'latəli] *n* filatelia *f*. philatelist *n* filatelico, -a *m, f*.

philosophy [fi'losəfi] *n* filosofia *f.* **philosopher** *n* filosofo, -a *m, f.* **philosophical** *adj* filosofico.

phlegm [flem] *n* (*mucus*) muco *m*; (*sluggishness*) flemma *f.*

phlegmatic [fleg'matik] *adj* flemmatico.

phobia ['foubiə] *n* fobia *f.*

phone [foun] *n* (*coll*) telefono *m.* *v* telefonare (a).

phonetic [fə'netik] *adj* fonetico. **phonetics** *n* fonetica *f.*

phoney ['founi] (*coll*) *adj* falso, fasullo. *n* ipocrita *m, f*; impostore *m.*

phosphate ['fosfeit] *n* fosfato *m.*

phosphorescence [fosfə'resəns] *n* fosforescenza *f.* **phosphorescent** *adj* fosforescente.

phosphorus ['fosfərəs] *n* fosforo *m.*

photo ['foutou] *n* (*coll*) foto *f.*

photocopy ['foutou,kopi] *n* fotocopia *f.* *v* fotocopiare.

photogenic [,foutou'dʒenik] *adj* fotogenico.

photograph ['foutəgraɪf] *n* fotografia *f.* *v* fotografare. **photographer** *n* fotografo *m.* **photographic** *adj* fotografico. **photography** *n* fotografia *f.*

phrase [freiz] *n* frase *f*, modo di dire *m.* *v* esprimere, formulare.

physical ['fizikəl] *adj* fisico.

physician [fi'ziʃən] *n* medico *m.*

physics ['fiziks] *n* fisica *f.* **physicist** *n* fisico, -a *m, f.*

physiology [,fizi'olədʒi] *n* fisiologia *f.* **physiological** *adj* fisiologico. **physiologist** *n* fisiologo, -a *m, f.*

physiotherapy [,fiziou'θerəpi] *n* fisioterapia *f.* **physiotherapist** *n* fisioterapista *m, f.*

physique [fi'ziɪk] *n* fisico *m.*

piano [pi'anou] *n* pianoforte *m.* **pianist** *n* pianista *m, f.*

pick¹ [pik] *v* (*choose*) scegliere; (*pluck*) cogliere. **pick out** scegliere. **pickpocket** *n* borsaiolo *m.* **pick up** raccogliere; (*recover*) star meglio; (*passenger*) far salire; (*learn*) imparare. **pick-up** *n* pick-up *m.* *n* (*choice*) scelta *f*; (*best*) fior fiore *m.*

pick² [pik] *n* piccone *m.*

picket ['pikit] *n* picchetto *m.* *v* picchettare.

pickle ['pikl] *v* marinare; (*in vinegar*) mettere sott'aceto. *n* (*coll: predicament*) pasticcio *m.* **pickles** *pl n* sottaceti *m pl.* **pickled** *adj* sottaceto.

picnic ['piknik] *n* picnic *m invar*, colazione all'aperto *f.*

pictorial [pik'toɪriəl] *adj* illustrato.

picture ['piktʃə] *v* immaginare, figurare. *n* (*painting*) quadro *m*; foto *f*; (*image*) immagine *f*; film *m.* **be in the picture** essere informato. **pictures** *n* (*coll*) cinema *m.* **put in the picture** mettere al corrente.

picturesque [piktʃə'resk] *adj* pittoresco.

pidgin ['pidʒən] *n* linguaggio bastardo *or* maccheronico *m.*

pie [pai] *n* pasticcio *m*; (*sweet*) crostata *f.*

piece [piɪs] *n* pezzo *m.* **piecemeal** *adv* gradualmente, un po' alla volta. **piecework** *n* lavoro a cottimo *m.* *v* rappezzare. **piece together** aggiustare, mettere assieme.

Piedmont ['piɪdmənt] *n* Piemonte *m.*

pier [piə] *n* molo *m*, banchina *f.*

pierce [piəs] *v* forare, penetrare. **piercing** *adj* acuto, penetrante; (*wind*) pungente.

piety ['paiəti] *n* devozione religiosa *f.*

pig [pig] *n* maiale *m*, porco (*pl* -ci) *m.* **pigheaded** *adj* ostinato, testardo. **pigheadedness** *n* testardaggine *f.* **pig-iron** *n* ghisa *f.* **piglet** *n* porcellino *m.* **pigskin** *adj* cinghiale. **pigsty** *n* porcile *m.* **pigtail** *n* codino *m.*

pigeon ['pidʒən] *n* piccione *m.* **carrier pigeon** piccione viaggiatore *m.* **clay pigeon** piattello *m.*

pigeon-hole *n* casella *f.* *v* incasellare.

pigment ['pigmənt] *n* pigmento *m.*

pike [paik] *n* (*fish*) luccio *m.*

pilchard ['piltʃəd] *n* sardina *f*, sarda *f.*

pile¹ [pail] *n* (*heap*) mucchio *m*; (*building*) fabbricato *m.* *v* accumulare. **pile on** (*coll*) esagerare. **pile up** accatastare.

pile² [pail] *n* (*post*) palo *m.* **pile-driver** *n* battipalo *m.*

pile³ [pail] *n* (*of carpet, etc.*) pelo *m.*

piles [pailz] *pl n* (*med*) emorroidi *f pl.*

pilfer ['pilfə] *v* rubacchiare. **pilferer** *n* ladruncolo *m.*

pilgrim ['pilgrim] *n* pellegrino *m.* **pilgrimage** *n* pellegrinaggio *m.*

pill [pil] *n* pillola *f.* **pillbox** *n* scatoletta per pillole *f*; (*mil*) casamatta *f.*

pillage ['pilidʒ] *n* saccheggio *m.* *v* saccheggiare.

pillar ['pilə] *n* pilastro *m*, colonna *f.* **pillar-box** *n* buca delle lettere *f.*

pillion ['piljən] *n* sella posteriore *f*, sedile posteriore *m.* **ride pillion** viaggiare sul sedile posteriore.

pillow ['pilou] *n* guanciale *m.* **pillowslip** *n* federa *f.*

pilot ['pailət] *n* pilota *m, f. v* pilotare.

pimento [pi'mentou] *n* (*allspice*) pimento *m*; (*capsicum*) peperone *m.*

pimp [pimp] *n* ruffiano *m.*

pimple ['pimpl] *n* pustoletta *f*, foruncolo *m.*

pin [pin] *n* spillo *m*; (*brooch*) spilla *f.* **pincushion** *n* portaspilli *m invar.* **pinpoint** *v* determinare con precisione. **pinprick** *n* (*annoyance*) seccatura *f. v* puntare. **pin down** inchiodare. **pin-up** *n* (*girl*) ragazza da copertina *f*, pin-up *f invar.*

pinafore ['pinəfoɪ] *n* grembiulino *m.*

pincers ['pinsəz] *pl n* pinza *f sing*, tenaglia *f sing.*

pinch [pintʃ] *v* pizzicare; (*hurt*) far male a; (*coll: steal*) rubare; (*coll: catch*) acchiappare. *n* (*nip*) pizzicotto *m*; (*small quantity*) pizzico (*pl* -chi) *m.* **at a pinch** caso mai.

pine¹ [pain] *n* (*tree*) pino *m.* **pine-cone** *n* pigna *f.*

pine² [pain] *v* languire. **pine for** desiderare ardentemente.

pineapple ['painapl] *n* ananas *m.*

pinion¹ ['pinjən] *n* (*tech*) pignone *m.*

pinion² ['pinjən] *v* (*shackle*) legare.

pink [piŋk] *adj* rosa *invar. n* (*colour*) rosa *m invar*; (*flower*) garofano *m.* **in the pink of condition** in ottima forma.

pinnacle ['pinəkl] *n* cima *f*, colmo *m*; (*arch*) pinnacolo *m.*

pioneer [,paiə'niə] *n* pioniere, -a *m, f. v* aprire la strada a.

pious ['paiəs] *adj* pio, devoto.

pip¹ [pip] *n* (*seed*) seme *m*, granello *m.*

pip² [pip] *n* (*phone*) segnale acustico *m.*

pipe [paip] *n* tubo *m*, condotto *m*; (*for smoking*) pipa *f.* **pipe-cleaner** *n* nettapipe *m invar.* **pipedream** *n* illusione *f.* **pipeline** *n* oleodotto *m*; linea di comunicazione *f. v* **pipe down!** sta zitto! **pipe up** farsi sentire. **piping** *n* (*sewing*) cordonetto *m.* **piping hot** caldo bollente.

piquant ['piːkənt] *adj* piccante, mordace.

pique [piːk] *n* dispetto *m. v* **feel piqued** risentirsi.

pirate ['paiərət] *n* pirata *m.* **pirate radio** radiopirata *m. v* (*radio*) servirsi abusivamente di; (*book*) plagiare. **piracy** *n* pirateria *f.*

pirouette [piru'et] *n* piroetta *f. v* piroettare.

Pisces ['paisiɪz] *n* Pesci *m pl.*

piss [pis] (*vulgar*) *n* piscia *f. v* pisciare. **pissed** *adj* sbronzo.

pistachio [pi'staɪʃiou] *n* pistacchio *m.*

pistol ['pistl] *n* pistola *f.*

piston ['pistən] *n* pistone *m.*

pit [pit] *n* fossa *f*; (*theatre*) platea *f*; (*scar*) buttero *m. v* **pit against** opporre.

pitch¹ [pitʃ] *n* lancio *m*; (*degree*) grado *m*; (*music*) tono *m*, registro *m*; (*sport*) campo *m*, terreno *m. v* lanciare; (*tent*) piantare; (*fix*) fissare; (*ship*) beccheggiare. **pitchfork** *n* forcone *m.*

pitch² [pitʃ] *n* pece *f.* **pitch-dark** *adj* buio pesto.

pitfall ['pitfoɪl] *n* trappola *f*, tranello *m.*

pith [piθ] *n* midollo *m.* **pithy** *adj* succinto.

pittance ['pitəns] *n* somma irrisoria *f.*

pituitary [pi'tjuɪitəri] *n* ipofisi *f*, glandola pituitaria *f.*

pity ['piti] *n* pietà *f*, compassione *f*; (*shame*) peccato *m.* **what a pity!** che peccato! *v* avere pietà di, compatire. **pitiful** *adj* (*wretched*) pietoso; (*contemptible*) miserabile. **pitiless** *adj* spietato.

pivot ['pivət] *n* perno *m*, fulcro *m. v* imperniare.

placard ['plakaɪd] *n* cartellone *m.*

placate [plə'keit] *v* placare, conciliare.

place [pleis] *n* luogo *m*, posto *m.* **out of place** inopportuno. **put in one's place** umiliare. **take place** aver luogo, accadere. *v* mettere, posare, porre; (*order*) piazzare.

placenta [plə'sentə] *n* placenta *f.*

placid ['plasid] *adj* placido.

plagiarize ['pleidʒəraiz] *v* plagiare. **plagiarism** *n* plagio *m.* **plagiarist** *n* plagiario, -a *m, f.*

plague [pleig] *n* (*disease*) peste *f*; (*calamity*) piaga *f. v* tormentare, affliggere.

plaice [pleis] *n* passera di mare *f.*

plaid [plad] *n* plaid *m invar.*

plain [plein] *adj* chiaro; (*simple*) semplice; (*frank*) schietto; (*not patterned*) a tinta unita; (*unattractive*) brutto. **in plain clothes** in borghese. **plain cooking** cucina semplice *or* casalinga *f. n* pianura *f.*

plaintiff ['pleintif] *n* querelante *m*, *f*; attore, -trice *m*, *f*.

plaintive ['pleintiv] *adj* querulo, lamentoso.

plait [plat] *n* (*braid*) treccia *f*; (*pleat*) piega *f*. *v* intrecciare; piegare.

plan [plan] *n* piano *m*, progetto *m*; intenzione *f*; (*drawing*) disegno *m*; (*map*) pianta *f*. *v* progettare; intendere; (*econ*) pianificare.

plane[1] [plein] *n* (*flat surface*) piano *m*, livello *m*; (*coll*) aereo *m*. *adj* piano.

plane[2] [plein] *n* (*tool*) pialla *f*. *v* piallare.

plane[3] [plein] *n* (*tree*) platano *m*.

planet ['planit] *n* pianeta *m*. **planetarium** *n* planetario *m*. **planetary** *adj* planetario.

plank [plaŋk] *n* asse *f*, tavola *f*.

plankton ['plaŋktən] *n* plancton *m invar*.

plant [plaint] *n* (*bot*) pianta *f*; (*manufacturing*) impianto *m*, stabilimento *m*. *v* piantare. **plantation** *n* piantagione *f*.

plaque [plaik] *n* placca *f*.

plasma ['plazmə] *n* plasma *m*.

plaster ['plaistə] *n* intonaco *m*; (*med*) impiastro *m*; (*for wound*) cerotto *m*. **plaster of Paris** gesso *m*. *v* intonacare; impiastrare; ingessare.

plastic ['plastik] *adj* plastico. *n* plastica *f*.

plate [pleit] *n* (*dish*) piatto *m*; (*of metal*) lamiera *f*, lastra *f*; (*denture*) dentiera *f*; (*metallic ware*) argenteria *f*; (*in book*) tavola *f*, illustrazione *f*. **plate-glass** *n* cristallo *m*. *v* galvanizzare; (*silver*) argentare.

plateau ['platou] *n* altipiano *m*.

platform ['platfoim] *n* piattaforma *f*; (*rail*) binario *m*.

platinum ['platinəm] *n* platino *m*.

platonic [plə'tonik] *adj* platonico.

platoon [plə'tuin] *n* plotone *m*.

plausible ['ploizəbl] *adj* ammissibile, credibile.

play [plei] *v* giocare; (*musical instrument*) suonare; (*act*) recitare. **play down** minimizzare. **play fair** comportarsi lealmente. **play truant** marinare la scuola. *n* gioco *m*, divertimento *m*; (*theatre*) spettacolo *m*. **playboy** *n* playboy *m*, buontempone *m*. **playground** *n* cortile di scuola *m*. **playmate** *n* compagno, -a di gioco *m*, *f*. **play-pen** *n* recinto per bambini *m*, box *m invar*. **play-school** *n* asilo *m*. **playwright** *n* commediografo, -a *m*, *f*; drammaturgo, -a *m*, *f*. **player** *n* giocatore, -trice *m*, *f*; (*music*) suonatore, -trice *m*, *f*; (*theatre*) attore, -trice *m*, *f*. **playful** *adj*

scherzoso, giocoso. playing card carta da gioco *f*. **playing field** campo sportivo *m*.

plea [plii] *n* difesa *f*, supplica *f*; (*excuse*) scusa *f*.

plead [pliid] *v* implorare; perorare. **plead guilty/innocent** dichiararsi colpevole/innocente. **plead with** intercedere presso. **pleading** *n* perorazione *f*.

please [pliiz] *v* piacere (a), contentare, soddisfare. **please oneself** fare il proprio comodo. *adv* per favore, per cortesia. **pleased** *adj* contento, lieto, soddisfatto. **pleasing** *adj* piacevole, gradevole. **pleasure** *n* piacere *m*, favore *m*.

pleat [pliit] *n* piega *f*. *v* pieghettare.

pledge [pledʒ] *n* promessa solenne *f*; (*undertaking*) impegno *m*. *v* impegnare, garantire; promettere solennemente.

plenty ['plenti] *n* abbondanza *f*. **in plenty** in abbondanza. **plenty of** abbastanza. **plentiful** *adj* abbondante.

pleurisy ['pluərisi] *n* pleurite *f*.

pliable ['plaiəbl] *adj* flessibile. **pliability** *n* flessibilità *f*.

pliers ['plaiəz] *pl n* pinza *f sing*, tenaglia *f sing*.

plight [plait] *n* stato *m*.

plimsoll ['plimsəl] *n* scarpa da tennis *f*.

plod [plod] *v* **plod along** tirare avanti. **plodder** *n* sgobbone, -a *m*, *f*.

plonk [ploŋk] *n* (*coll*) vino comune *m*.

plot[1] [plot] *n* (*story*) trama *f*, intreccio *m*; (*secret plan*) congiura *f*, complotto *m*. *v* tramare, complottare; (*trace*) tracciare. **plotter** *n* cospiratore, -trice *m*, *f*.

plot[2] [plot] *n* (*land*) lotto *or* pezzo di terreno *m*.

plough [plau] *n* aratro *m*. *v* arare; (*coll: fail exam*) trombare. **plough back** riinvestire. **plough through** (*book, etc.*) leggere con fatica.

pluck [plʌk] *v* cogliere; (*feathers*) spennare; (*tug at*) strappare. **pluck up courage** farsi coraggio. *n* (*courage*) fegato *m*. **be plucky** aver fegato.

plug [plʌg] *n* tappo *m*; (*elec*) spina *f*; (*mot*) candela *f*. *v* tappare.

plum [plʌm] *n* (*fruit*) prugna *f*, susina *f*; (*tree*) prugno *m*, susino *m*. *adj* (*colour*) prugna.

plumage ['pluimidʒ] *n* piumaggio *m*.

plumb [plʌm] *adj* verticale. *adv* a piombo; (*absolutely*) proprio. *n* piombo

m, scandaglio *m.* *v* sondare; *(naut)* scandagliare. **plumber** *n* idraulico *m.*
plume [pluɪm] *n* penna *f,* piuma *f;* *(on helmet)* pennacchio *m.*
plummet ['plʌmit] *v* piombare.
plump¹ [plʌmp] *adj (fat)* grassoccio, paffuto.
plump² [plʌmp] *v* **plump for** scegliere.
plunder ['plʌndə] *n* bottino *m.* *v* spogliare, depredare.
plunge [plʌndʒ] *n* tuffo *m.* *v* tuffare; immergere; *(rush)* lanciarsi. **plunger** *n* *(tech)* stantuffo *m.*
pluperfect [pluɪ'pəfikt] *n* trapassato remoto *m.*
plural ['pluərəl] *nm, adj* plurale. **in the plural** al plurale.
plus [plʌs] *adj* addizionale. *prep* più.
plush [plʌʃ] *n* felpa *f. adj* lussuoso.
plutocrat ['pluɪtəkrat] *n* plutocrate *m, f.*
ply¹ [plai] *v (travel)* viaggiare regolarmente; *(trade)* esercitare.
ply² [plai] *n (layer)* strato *m;* *(wool)* filo *m.* **plywood** *n* legno compensato *m.*
pneumatic [njuˈmatik] *adj* pneumatico.
pneumonia [njuˈmouniə] *n* polmonite *f.*
poach¹ [poutʃ] *v (game)* cacciare di frodo; *(fish)* pescare di frodo; *(encroach on)* usurpare. **poacher** *n* bracconiere *m.*
poach² [poutʃ] *v (cookery)* lessare. **poached egg** uovo affogato *m,* uovo in camicia *m.*
pocket ['pokit] *n* tasca *f,* taschino *m;* *(billiards)* buca *f.* **be out of pocket** rimetterci. *v* intascare. *adj* tascabile. **pocketbook** *n* taccuino *m.* **pocket-knife** *n* temperino *m.* **pocket-money** *n* soldi per le piccole spese *m pl.*
pod [pod] *n* baccello *m.*
podgy ['podʒi] *adj* grassotto, paffuto.
poem ['pouim] *n* poesia *f.*
poet ['pouit] *n* poeta *m.* **poetess** *n* poetessa *f.* **poetic** *adj* poetico. **poetry** *n* poesia *f.*
poignant ['poinjənt] *adj* intenso, vivo, commovente.
point [point] *n* punto *m;* *(sharp end)* punta *f;* *(elec)* presa *f.* **be on the point of** stare per. **make a point of** insistere su.
point-blank *adv* a bruciapelo; *(coll)* di punto in bianco. *v* indicare, additare; *(aim)* puntare; *(brickwork)* affilettare.
pointed *adj* acuto. **pointer** *n (hint)* indicazione *f;* *(dog)* pointer *m.* **pointing** *n* affilettatura *f.* **pointless** *adj* inutile.

poise [poiz] *n* equilibrio *m,* compostezza *f,* portamento *m.* *v* equilibrare, essere in equilibrio.
poison ['poizən] *n* veleno *m.* *v* avvelenare. **poisonous** *adj* velenoso.
poke [pouk] *n* spinta *f,* gomitata *f.* *v (stick into)* ficcare; *(thrust)* cacciare; *(fire)* attizzare. **poke about** frugare. **poke fun at** beffarsi di. **poker** *n* attizzatoio *m.* **poky** *adj* meschino, piccolo.
poker ['poukə] *n (cards)* poker *m.* **poker-faced** *adj* impassibile.
Poland ['poulənd] *n* Polonia *f.* **Pole** *n* polacco, -a *m, f.* **Polish** *nm, adj* polacco.
polar ['poulə] *adj* polare. **polar bear** orso bianco *m.* **polarize** *v* polarizzare. **polarity** *n* polarità *f.*
pole¹ [poul] *n (post)* palo *m,* asta *f.* **pole-vault** *n* salto all'asta *m.*
pole² [poul] *n (geog)* polo *m.*
police [pə'liːs] *n* polizia *f.* **policeman** *n* carabiniere *m,* poliziotto *m,* vigile *m.* **police station** questura *f.* *v* mantenere l'ordine, sorvegliare, vigilare.
policy¹ ['poləsi] *n* politica *f,* linea di condotta *f.*
policy² ['poləsi] *n (insurance)* polizza *f.*
polio ['pouliou] *n* poliomielite *f.*
polish ['poliʃ] *n (for shoes, etc.)* lucido *m;* *(for nails)* smalto *m;* raffinatezza *f.* *v* lucidare, lustrare. **polish off** *(dispose of quickly)* sbrigare; liquidare. **polish up** ripassare.
polite [pə'lait] *adj* cortese, garbato. **politeness** *n* cortesia *f,* garbo *m.*
politics ['politiks] *n* politica *f.* **politic** *adj* espediente. **political** *adj* politico. **politician** *n* uomo politico *m.*
polka ['polkə] *n* polca *f.*
poll [poul] *n* elezione *f;* *(casting of votes)* votazione *f;* *(votes cast)* voti *m pl.* **opinion poll** sondaggio d'opinioni *m.* *v* ottenere voti. **polling booth** cabina elettorale *f.*
pollen ['polən] *n* polline *m.* **pollinate** *v* impollinare. **pollination** *n* impollinazione *f.*
pollute [pə'luːt] *v* inquinare. **pollution** *n* inquinamento *m.*
polo ['poulou] *n* polo *m.* **polo-neck** *n* collo ciclista *m.* **polo-neck sweater** ciclista *f.*
polygamy [pə'ligəmi] *n* poligamia *f.* **polygamist** *n* poligamo *m.* **polygamous** *adj* poligamo.

polygon ['poligən] *n* poligono *m*. **polygonal** *adj* poligonale.
polytechnic [,poli'teknik] *n* politecnico *m*.
polythene ['poliθiin] *n* politene *m*.
pomegranate ['pomigranit] *n* melagrana *f*.
pomp [pomp] *n* pompa *f*, sfarzo *m*. **pompous** *adj* pomposo, ampolloso.
pond [pond] *n* stagno *m*.
ponder ['pondə] *v* ponderare; valutare. **ponderous** *adj* ponderoso, pesante.
pontiff ['pontif] *n* pontefice *m*, papa *m*. **pontifical** *adj* pontificio. **pontificate** *v* pontificare.
pontoon [pon'tuin] *n* pontone *m*; (*cards*) ventuno *m*.
pony ['pouni] *n* pony *m*.
poodle ['puidl] *n* cane barbone *m*.
poof [puif] *n* (*derog*) finocchio *m*.
pool[1] [puil] *n* (*pond*) stagno *m*; (*puddle*) pozzanghera *f*; (*swimming*) piscina *f*.
pool[2] [puil] *v* mettere in comune. *n* fondo comune *m*; (*football*) totocalcio *m*.
poor [puə] *adj* povero; mediocre; (*meagre*) magro; (*not good*) cattivo.
poorly ['puəli] *adj* malaticcio. *adv* male. **feel poorly** non sentirsi troppo bene.
pop[1] [pop] *v* schioccare, saltare. **pop in** fare una breve visita. **pop out** saltar fuori. **pop up** apparire. *n* schiocco *m*; (*drink*) bibita gassata *f*.
pop[2] [pop] *adj* popolare. **pop-art** *n* pop-art *f*. **pop music** musica pop *f*.
pope [poup] *n* papa *m*.
poplar ['poplə] *n* pioppo *m*.
poppy ['popi] *n* papavero *m*.
popular ['popjulə] *adj* popolare; (*favourite*) ben visto. **popularity** *n* popolarità *f*. **popularize** *v* divulgare.
population [,popju'leifən] *n* popolazione *f*. **populate** *v* popolare.
porcelain ['poislin] *n* porcellana *f*.
porch [poitf] *n* portico *m*.
porcupine ['poikjupain] *n* porcospino *m*.
pore[1] [poi] *n* (*opening*) poro *m*.
pore[2] [poi] *v* **pore over** meditare su, essere assorto in.
pork [poik] *n* carne suina *f*, carne di maiale *f*.
pornography [poi'nogrəfi] *n* pornografia *f*. **pornographic** *adj* pornografico.
porous ['poirəs] *adj* poroso.
porpoise ['poipəs] *n* focena *f*.
porridge ['poridʒ] *n* pappa di fiocchi d'avena *f*.

port[1] [poit] *n* (*harbour*) porto *m*.
port[2] [poit] *n* (*naut: left*) sinistra *f*, babordo *m*.
port[3] [poit] *n* (*wine*) porto *m invar*.
portable ['poitəbl] *adj* portatile.
portent ['poitent] *n* (*omen*) presagio *m*; (*marvel*) portento *m*. **portentous** *adj* prodigioso, portentoso; grave.
porter ['poitə] *n* (*janitor*) portinaio, -a *m*, *f*; (*carrier*) facchino *m*.
portfolio [poit'fouliou] *n* (*pol*) portafoglio *m*; (*case*) cartella *f*.
porthole ['poithoul] *n* oblò *m*.
portion ['poifən] *n* porzione *f*. *v* ripartire.
portrait ['poitrət] *n* ritratto *m*. **portrait-painter** *n* ritrattista *m*, *f*.
portray [poi'trei] *v* rappresentare.
Portugal ['poitjugl] *n* Portogallo *m*. **Portuguese** *n*(*m* + *f*), *adj* portoghese.
pose [pouz] *n* posa *f*; (*posture*) atteggiamento *m*. *v* posare, atteggiarsi (a); (*propound*) porre.
posh [pof] *adj* elegante.
position [pə'zifən] *n* posizione *f*, situazione *f*; (*employment*) posto *m*. *v* collocare, piazzare.
positive ['pozətiv] *adj* positivo; (*certain*) sicuro. *n* (*phot*) positiva *f*; (*gramm*) positivo *m*.
possess [pə'zes] *v* possedere, avere. **possessed** *adj* ossesso, frenetico. **possession** *n* possesso *m*. **possessions** *pl n* (*goods*) beni personali *m pl*. **possessive** *nm*, *adj* possessivo. **possessor** *n* possessore *m*, posseditrice *f*.
possible ['posəbl] *adj* possibile. **possibility** *n* possibilità *f*. **possibly** *adv* (*perhaps*) forse, può darsi; (*if possible*) possibilmente.
post[1] [poust] *n* (*pole*) palo *m*. *v* affiggere.
post[2] [poust] *n* (*job*) posto *m*. *v* collocare.
post[3] [poust] *n* (*mail*) posta *f*. **post-box** *n* buca da lettere *f*. **postcard** *n* cartolina *f*. **postman** *n* postino *m*. **postmark** *n* timbro postale *m*. **postmarked** *adj* timbrato. **post office** posta *f*, ufficio postale *m*. **post office box** casella postale *f*. *v* imbucare; (*book-keeping*) registrare. **keep posted** tenere al corrente. **postage** *n* tariffa postale *f*. **postage stamp** francobollo *m*. **postal** *adj* postale. **postal order** vaglia postale *m invar*.
poste restante [poust'restät] *adv* fermo posta.

poster ['poustə] *n* cartellone *m*, manifesto *m*, avviso pubblicitario *m*.

posterior [po'stiəriə] *adj* posteriore.

posterity [po'sterəti] *n* posterità *f*.

postgraduate [poust'gradjuit] *adj* di perfezionamento *or* specializzazione. *n* laureato, -a che continua gli studi universitari *m*, *f*.

posthumous ['postjuməs] *adj* postumo.

post-mortem [poust'mɔɪtəm] *n* autopsia *f*.

postpone [pous'poun] *v* posporre, rinviare. **postponement** *n* rinvio *m*.

postscript ['pousskript] *n* poscritto *m*.

postulate ['postjuleit; *n* 'postjulət] *v* postulare. *n* postulato *m*.

posture ['postʃə] *n* posizione *f*; (*attitude*) atteggiamento *m*. *v* assumere una posa.

pot [pot] *n* vaso *m*; (*pan*) pentola *f*; (*container*) recipiente *m*. *v* (*plant*) piantare in vaso; (*billiards*) mandare in buca. **pot-belly** *n* pancione *m*. **pot-bellied** *adj* panciuto. **take pot luck** mangiare alla buona.

potassium [pə'tasjəm] *n* potassio *m*. **potash** *n* potassa *f*.

potato [pə'teitou] *n* patata *f*.

potent ['poutənt] *adj* potente, forte. **potency** *n* potenza *f*.

potential [pə'tenʃəl] *adj*, *nm* potenziale.

pot-hole ['pothoul] *n* (*cave*) spelonca *f*; (*in road*) buca *f*. **pot-holer** *n* speleologo, -a *m*, *f*. **pot-holing** *n* speleologia *f*.

potion ['pouʃən] *n* pozione *f*.

potter[1] ['potə] *v* **potter about** lavoricchiare.

potter[2] ['potə] *n* ceramista *m*, *f*, vasaio, -a *m*, *f*.

pottery ['potəri] *n* (*ware*) ceramica *f*; (*workshop*) laboratorio di ceramiche *m*.

potty[1] ['poti] *adj* (*coll*) matto.

potty[2] ['poti] *n* (*coll*) vaso da notte *m*, pitale *m*.

pouch [pautʃ] *n* borsa *f*, tasca *f*, sacchetto *m*.

poultice ['poultis] *n* cataplasma *m*.

poultry ['poultri] *n* pollame *m*. **poulterer** *n* pollivendolo, -a *m*, *f*.

pounce [pauns] *n* sbalzo *m*. *v* balzare. **pounce on** piombare su, saltare addosso a.

pound[1] [paund] *v* (*hit*) pestare, battere. *n* colpo *m*.

pound[2] [paund] *n* (*weight*) libbra *f*; (*sterling*) lira sterlina *f*.

pound[3] [paund] *n* (*enclosure*) recinto *m*.

pour [pɔɪ] *v* versare, riversarsi; (*rain*) scrosciare.

pout [paut] *v* fare il broncio. *n* broncio *m*.

poverty ['povəti] *n* povertà *f*, miseria *f*. **poverty-stricken** *adj* bisognoso, indigente.

powder ['paudə] *n* polvere *f*; (*cosmetic*) cipria *f*. **powder compact** portacipria *m invar*. **powder puff** piumino per la cipria *m*. *v* polverizzare, incipriare. **powdery** *adj* polveroso.

power ['pauə] *n* potere *m*; (*pol*, *phys*, *etc*.) potenza *f*; (*tech*) energia *f*, forza *f*. **powers** *pl n* facoltà *f pl*. **power station** centrale elettrica *f*. **powerful** *adj* potente. **powerless** *adj* impotente, incapace.

practicable ['praktikəbl] *adj* fattibile.

practical ['praktikəl] *adj* pratico. **for practical purposes** in pratica. **practical joke** beffa *f*. **practically** *adv* in effetto, quasi.

practice ['praktis] *n* pratica *f*; esercizio *m*; clientela *f*; (*sport*) allenamento *m*. **normal practice** regola *f*. **out of practice** fuori esercizio.

practise ['praktis] *v* praticare, esercitare; (*music*) esercitarsi; (*sport*) allenarsi. **practised** *adj* esperto, pratico. **practising** *adj* (*rel*) praticante.

practitioner [prak'tiʃənə] *n* **general practitioner** medico generico *m*.

pragmatic [prag'matik] *adj* prammatico; (*officious*) inframmettente; dogmatico. **pragmatism** *n* pragmatismo *m*; dogmatismo *m*.

Prague [praɪg] *n* Praga *f*.

prairie ['preəri] *n* prateria *f*.

praise [preiz] *n* lode *f*, elogio *m*. *v* lodare, elogiare. **praiseworthy** *adj* lodevole.

pram [pram] *n* carrozzella *f*.

prance [prains] *v* pavoneggiarsi; (*child*) saltellare; (*horse*) impennarsi.

prank [praŋk] *n* burla *f*, tiro *m*. **play a prank on** fare un tiro a.

prattle ['pratl] *v* cianciare, ciarlare.

prawn [prɔin] *n* gambero *m*, palemone *m*.

pray [prei] *v* pregare. **prayer** *n* preghiera *f*. **prayer-book** *n* libro di preghiere *m*; (*missal*) messale *m*.

preach [priitʃ] *v* predicare. **preach a sermon** fare una predica. **preacher** *n* predicatore *m*.

preamble [prii'ambl] *n* preambolo *m*.

prearrange [priiə'reindʒ] *v* predisporre.

precarious [pri'keəriəs] *adj* precario, incerto.
precaution [pri'kɔɪʃən] *n* precauzione *f*.
precede [pri'siːd] *v* precedere. **precedence** *n* precedenza *f*. **precedent** *n* precedente *m*.
precinct ['priːsiŋkt] *n* (*area*) zona *f*; ambito *m*.
precious ['preʃəs] *adj* prezioso.
precipice ['presipis] *n* precipizio *m*.
precipitate [pri'sipiteit; *adj* pri'sipitət] *v* precipitare; (*hurry up*) affrettare. *n* precipitato *m*. *adj* precipitoso.
précis ['preisi] *n* sunto *m*.
precise [pri'sais] *adj* preciso, esatto; (*strict*) puntiglioso. **precision** *n* precisione *f*, esattezza *f*.
preclude [pri'kluːd] *v* precludere.
precocious [pri'kouʃəs] *adj* precoce. **precociousness** *n* precocità *f*.
preconceive [ˌpriːkən'siːv] *v* avere preconcetti su. **preconception** *n* preconcetto *m*.
precursor [ˌpriː'kɔːsə] *n* precursore *m*.
predatory ['predətəri] *adj* predatore, rapace.
predecessor ['priːdisesə] *n* predecessore *m*.
predestine [pri'destin] *v* predestinare. **predestination** *n* predestinazione *f*.
predicament [pri'dikəmənt] *n* situazione imbarazzante *f*, pasticcio *m*.
predicate ['predikət] *n* predicato *m*.
predict [pri'dikt] *v* predire, pronosticare. **predictable** *adj* prevedibile. **prediction** *n* predizione *f*.
predispose [ˌpriːdi'spouz] *v* predisporre. **predisposition** *n* predisposizione *f*.
predominate [pri'domineit] *v* predominare, prevalere. **predominance** *n* predominio *m*, ascendente *m*.
pre-eminent [priː'eminənt] *adj* preminente, per eccellenza. **pre-eminence** *n* preminenza *f*.
preen [priːn] *v* **preen oneself** (*bird*) lisciarsi le penne; (*person*) agghindarsi.
prefabricate [priː'fabrikeit] *v* prefabbricare. **prefab** *n* (*coll*) casa prefabbricata *f*.
preface ['prefis] *n* prefazione *f*. *v* premettere.
prefect ['priːfekt] *n* prefetto *m*; (*school*) capoclasse *m*.
prefer [pri'fəː] *v* preferire. **preferable** *adj* preferibile. **preference** *n* preferenza *f*. **preference shares** azioni privilegiate *f pl*. **preferential** *adj* preferenziale, di favore.

prefix ['priːfiks] *n* prefisso *m*. *v* prefiggere.
pregnant ['pregnənt] *adj* incinta; (*animal*) gravida. **pregnancy** *n* gravidanza *f*.
prehistoric [ˌpriːhi'storik] *adj* preistorico. **prehistory** *n* preistoria *f*.
prejudice ['predʒədis] *n* pregiudizio *m*, prevenzione *f*. **have a prejudice against** esser prevenuto contro. *v* pregiudicare, compromettere. **prejudiced** *adj* prevenuto.
preliminary [pri'liminəri] *nm*, *adj* preliminare.
prelude ['preljuːd] *n* preludio *m*.
premarital [priː'maritl] *adj* prematrimoniale.
premature [premə'tʃuə] *adj* prematuro.
premeditate [priː'mediteit] *v* premeditare. **premeditation** *n* premeditazione *f*.
premier ['premiə] *adj* primo, primario. *n* primo ministro *m*.
premiere ['premieə] *n* prima (rappresentazione) *f*.
premise ['premis] *n* premessa *f*. **premises** *n* locali *m pl*. **off the premises** fuori. **on the premises** sul posto.
premium ['priːmiəm] *n* premio *m*; (*finance*) aggio *m*. **at a premium** (*econ*) sopra la pari.
premonition [ˌpremə'niʃən] *n* premonizione *f*.
preoccupied [priː'okjupaid] *adj* preoccupato. **preoccupation** *n* preoccupazione *f*.
prepare [pri'peə] *v* preparare. **preparation** *n* preparazione *f*. **preparatory** *adj* preparatorio.
preposition [ˌprepə'ziʃən] *n* preposizione *f*.
preposterous [pri'postərəs] *adj* assurdo.
prerequisite [priː'rekwizit] *n* requisito (principale) *m*.
prerogative [pri'rogətiv] *n* prerogativa *f*.
prescribe [pri'skraib] *v* prescrivere. **prescription** *n* prescrizione *f*; (*med*) ricetta medica *f*.
presence ['prezns] *n* presenza *f*; (*appearance*) aspetto *m*.
present[1] ['preznt] *adj* presente, attuale. *n* (*time*) presente *m*. **at present** attualmente. **for the present** per ora. **presently** *adv* quanto prima.
present[2] [pri'zent; *n* 'preznt] *v* presentare, offrire. *n* (*gift*) regalo *m*. **presentable** *adj* presentabile. **presentation** *n* presentazione *f*.

preserve [pri'zəɪv] v conservare, preservare; (*appearances*) salvare. n (*food*) conserva f; (*reserve*) riserva f. **preservation** n preservazione f. **preservative** nm, adj preservativo.

preside [pri'zaid] v **preside over** presiedere a.

president ['prezidənt] n presidente m. **presidency** n presidenza f. **presidential** adj presidenziale.

press [pres] v premere; (*squeeze*) comprimere, schiacciare; far pressione su; insistere su; (*iron*) stirare. **press-button** n pulsante m. **press-stud** n bottone automatico m. n (*newspapers*) stampa f; (*printing*) macchina da stampa f; (*publishing house*) casa editrice f; (*tech*) torchio m. **press cutting** ritaglio (di giornale) m. **pressing** adj urgente.

pressure ['preʃə] n pressione m. **pressure-cooker** n pentola a pressione f. **pressurize** v pressurizzare; (*force*) far pressione su.

prestige [pre'stiːʒ] n prestigio m.

presume [pri'zjuːm] v presumere, supporre. **presumption** n presunzione f, supposizione f; arroganza f. **presumptuous** adj presuntuoso. **presumptive** adj presunto.

pretend [pri'tend] v pretendere; (*feign*) fingere, far finta. **pretence** n pretesa f; (*pretext*) pretesto m. **pretension** n pretensione f. **pretentious** adj pretenzioso, pieno di pretese.

pretext ['priːtekst] n pretesto m.

pretty ['priti] adj carino, simpatico. adv (*quite*) piuttosto, abbastanza; (*moderately*) quasi.

prevail [pri'veil] v prevalere. **prevail upon** persuadere, indurre. **prevalent** adj prevalente.

prevent [pri'vent] v impedire. **prevention** n prevenzione f; (*med*) profilassi f.

preview ['priːvjuː] n anteprima f.

previous ['priːviəs] adj precedente, anteriore. **previously** adv prima.

prey [prei] n preda f. **be/fall a prey to** essere/cadere in preda a. v **prey on** predare; (*fear, etc.*) rodere.

price [prais] n prezzo m. **price-list** n listino dei prezzi m. v valutare, fare il prezzo di. **priceless** adj impagabile; (*very amusing*) divertentissimo.

prick [prik] v pungere, punzecchiare.

prick up one's ears drizzare le orecchie. n puntura f.

prickle ['prikl] n spina f. **prickly** adj spinoso; (*sensitive*) difficile. **prickly pear** fico d'India m.

pride [praid] n orgoglio m, amor proprio m; (*best part*) fiore m. v **pride oneself on** essere orgoglioso di.

priest [priːst] n prete m, sacerdote m. **priesthood** n sacerdozio m.

prig [prig] n borioso, -a m, f. **priggish** adj borioso.

prim [prim] adj affettato, compassato; (*formal*) cerimonioso.

primary ['praiməri] adj primario, fondamentale, primo. **primary school** scuola elementare f.

primate ['praimət] n primate m. **primacy** n primato m.

prime [praim] adj primo; di prima qualità. n fiore m, primavera f. v (*arms*) innescare; (*paint*) mesticare; (*information*) mettere al corrente; (*pump*) adescare. **primer** n (*book*) testo elementare m; (*paint*) mestica f.

primitive ['primitiv] adj primitivo.

primrose ['primrouz] n primula f.

primus stove ['praiməs] n fornello a petrolio m.

prince [prins] n principe m. **princess** n principessa f.

principal ['prinsəpəl] adj principale, primo. n (*of business*) principale m, f; (*of school*) direttore, -trice m, f; (*comm*) capitale m.

principle ['prinsəpəl] n principio m.

print [print] v stampare, imprimere; (*handwriting*) scrivere a stampatello. n stampa f; impressione f; (*phot*) copia f. **out of print** esaurito. **printer** n tipografo m. **printing** n tipografia f; (*edition*) tiratura f.

prior[1] ['praiə] adj precedente, anteriore. **prior to** prima di. **priority** n precedenza f.

prior[2] ['praiə] n priore m. **prioress** n priora f. **priory** n convento m, monastero m.

prise [praiz] v far leva su. **prise open** forzare.

prism ['prizm] n prismo m.

prison ['prizn] n prigione f. **prisoner** n prigioniero, -a m, f. **take prisoner** far prigioniero.

private ['praivət] adj privato, personale. n soldato semplice m. **privacy** n intimità f.

privet ['privət] *n* ligustro *m*.

privilege ['privəlidʒ] *n* privilegio *m*.

privy ['privi] *adj* privato. **be privy to** essere a conoscenza di.

prize [praiz] *n* (*reward*) premio *m*. **prizefighter** *n* pugile *m*. **prize-giving** *n* distribuzione dei premi *f*. **prizewinner** *n* vincitore, -trice *m, f*. *v* apprezzare, valutare.

probable ['probəbl] *adj* probabile. **probability** *n* probabilità *f*.

probation [prə'beiʃən] *n* (*law*) libertà condizionata *f*; (*for job*, *etc*.) periodo di prova *m*. **probationary** *adj* di prova.

probe [proub] *v* esplorare, sondare. *n* (*investigation*) sondaggio *m*, inchiesta *f*; (*instrument*) sonda *f*.

problem ['probləm] *n* problema *m*. **problematic** *adj* problematico.

proceed [prə'siːd] *v* procedere, proseguire. **proceeds** *pl n* ricavo *m sing*, incasso *m sing*. **procedure** *n* procedura *f*; (*proceeding*) procedimento *m*.

process ['prouses] *n* processo *m*, andamento *m*; (*procedure*) procedimento *m*. *v* trattare, trasformare. **processed cheese** formaggio fuso *m*.

procession [prə'seʃən] *n* processione *f*, sfilata *f*.

proclaim [prə'kleim] *v* proclamare. **proclamation** *n* proclama *m*.

procrastinate [prə'krastineit] *v* procrastinare.

procreate ['proukrieit] *v* procreare. **procreation** *n* procreazione *f*.

procure [prə'kjuə] *v* procurare. **procurement** *n* approvvigionamento *m*.

prod [prod] *v* (*incite*) sollecitare; (*push*) spingere.

prodigy ['prodidʒi] *n* prodigio *m*.

produce [prə'djuːs; *n* 'prodjuːs] *v* produrre; (*pull out*) tirar fuori; (*theatre*) mettere in scena. *n* prodotti *or* generi agricoli *m pl*. **producer** *n* produttore, -trice *m, f*; (*theatre, etc*.) regista *m, f*. **product** *n* prodotto *m*, frutto *m*. **production** *n* produzione *f*; messa in scena *f*. **productive** *adj* produttivo; fertile. **productivity** *n* produttività *f*.

profane [prə'fein] *adj* profano. **profanity** *n* profanità *f*; (*language*) bestemmia *f*.

profess [prə'fes] *v* professare, manifestare; (*practise*) esercitare; (*imply*) pretendere di. **professed** *adj* (*avowed*)

dichiarato. **profession** *n* professione *f*; dichiarazione *f*.

professional [prə'feʃənl] *n* professionista *m, f*. *adj* professionale. **professionalism** *n* professionismo *m*.

professor [prə'fesə] *n* professore, -essa *m, f*.

proficient [prə'fiʃənt] *adj* competente, provetto. **proficiency** *n* perizia *f*, competenza *f*.

profile ['proufail] *n* profilo *m*.

profit ['profit] *n* profitto *m*, guadagno *m*. *v* (*be of benefit to*) giovare a, essere utile a. **profit from** approfittare di, trarre profitto da. **profitable** *adj* vantaggioso; lucroso.

profound [prə'faund] *adj* profondo.

profuse [prə'fjuːs] *adj* abbondante, prodigo. **apologize profusely** profondersi in scuse. **profusion** *n* abbondanza *f*.

prognosis [prog'nousis] *n* prognosi *f*.

programme ['prougram] *n* programma *m*. *v* programmare.

progress ['prougres] *v* progredire, avanzare. *n* progresso *m*, andamento *m*. **progression** *n* progressione *f*. **progressive** *adj* progressivo.

prohibit [prə'hibit] *v* proibire, vietare. **prohibition** *n* proibizione *f*, divieto *m*; (*of alcohol*) proibizionismo *m*.

project ['prodʒekt; *v* prə'dʒekt] *n* progetto *m*, disegno *m*. *v* (*plan*) progettare; (*math, screen*) proiettare; (*protrude*) sporgere. **projectile** *n* proiettile *m*. **projection** *n* proiezione *f*; sporgenza *f*. **projector** *n* proiettore *m*.

proletariat [proulə'teəriət] *n* proletariato *m*. **proletarian** *n, adj* proletario, -a.

proliferate [prə'lifəreit] *v* proliferare.

prolific [prə'lifik] *adj* prolifico.

prologue ['proulog] *n* prologo (*pl* -ghi) *m*.

prolong [prə'loŋ] *v* prolungare.

promenade [promə'naid] *v* fare una passeggiata. *n* passeggiata *f*; (*sea-front*) lungomare *m*.

prominent ['prominənt] *adj* prominente; eminente, importante. **prominence** *n* prominenza; eminenza *f*. **give prominence to** dar risalto a.

promiscuous [prə'miskjuəs] *adj* indiscriminato. **promiscuity** *n* promiscuità *f*.

promise ['promis] *v* promettere, assicurare. *n* promessa *f*, assicurazione *f*. **promising** *adj* che promette bene.

promontory ['promantari] *n* promontorio *m*.

promote [pra'mout] *v* promuovere; (*comm*) lanciare. **promotion** *n* promozione *f*; lancio *m*.

prompt [prompt] *adj* pronto, sollecito. *v* ispirare, suggerire.

prone [proun] *adv* bocconi. **be prone to** essere disposto *or* propenso a.

prong [proŋ] *n* rebbio *m*. *v* infilzare.

pronoun ['prounaun] *n* pronome *m*.

pronounce [pra'nauns] *v* pronunciare; dichiarare. **pronounced** *adj* pronunciato, spiccato. **pronouncement** *n* dichiarazione *f*. **pronunciation** *n* pronuncia *f*.

proof [pruːf] *n* prova *f*; (*printing*) bozza *f*. *adj* impenetrabile, resistente (a). *v* impermeabilizzare.

prop[1] [prop] *n* appoggio *m*, sostegno *m*; (*building*) puntello *m*. *v* **prop up** sorreggere, appoggiare; puntellare.

prop[2] [prop] *n* (*coll*) oggetto teatrale *m*.

propaganda [propa'ganda] *n* propaganda *f*.

propagate ['propageit] *v* propagare. **propagation** *n* propagazione *f*.

propel [pra'pel] *v* spingere avanti, azionare. **propellant** *n* propellente *m*. **propeller** *n* elica *f*.

proper ['propa] *adj* proprio; (*right*) particolare; (*good*) buono. **properly** *adv* come si deve; correttamente; (*well*) bene.

property ['propati] *n* proprietà *f*; possesso *m*, beni *m pl*.

prophecy ['profasi] *n* profezia *f*. **prophesy** *v* fare il profeta, predire.

prophet ['profit] *n* profeta *m*. **prophetess** *n* profetessa *f*. **prophetic** *adj* profetico.

propitious [pra'piʃas] *adj* propizio, favorevole.

proportion [pra'pɔːʃan] *n* proporzione *f*. **out of proportion** sproporzionato, smisurato. **proportional** *adj* proporzionale.

propose [pra'pouz] *v* proporre, intendere; fare una proposta di matrimonio. **proposal** *n* proposta *f*; offerta di matrimonio *f*.

proposition *n* proposta *f*; (*gramm*) proposizione *f*.

proprietor [pra'praiata] *n* proprietario *m*, padrone *m*. **proprietress** *n* proprietaria *f*, padrona *f*.

propriety [pra'praiati] *n* decoro *m*, decenza *f*.

propulsion [pra'pʌlʃan] *n* propulsione *f*.

prose [prouz] *n* prosa *f*. **prosaic** *adj* prosaico, banale.

prosecute ['prosikjuːt] *v* citare in giudizio, processare. **prosecution** *n* processo *m*. **prosecutor** *n* procuratore *m*, pubblico ministero *m*.

prospect ['prospekt; *v* pra'spekt] *n* prospettiva *f*, aspettativa *f*; (*view*) prospetto *m*. *v* esplorare. **prospective** *adj* futuro.

prospectus [pra'spektas] *n* prospetto *m*.

prosper ['prospa] *v* prosperare. **prosperity** *n* prosperità *f*. **prosperous** *adj* prospero, benestante.

prostitute ['prostitjuːt] *v* prostituire. *n* prostituta *f*, puttana *f*. **prostitution** *n* prostituzione *f*.

prostrate [pro'streit; *adj* 'prostreit] *v* prostrare, prosternare. *adj* abbattuto.

protagonist [prou'taganist] *n* protagonista *m, f*.

protect [pra'tekt] *v* proteggere. **protection** *n* protezione *f*. **protective** *adj* protettivo. **protector** *n* protettore, -trice *m, f*. **protectorate** *n* protettorato *m*.

protégé ['protaʒei] *n* protetto, -a *m, f*.

protein ['proutiːn] *n* proteina *f*.

protest [pra'test; *n* 'proutest] *v* protestare. *n* protesta *f*; (*comm*) protesto *m*; (*pol*) contestazione *f*. **under protest** protestando.

Protestant ['protistant] *n(m+f)*, *adj* protestante. **Protestantism** *n* protestantesimo *m*.

protocol ['proutakol] *n* protocollo *m*.

proton ['prouton] *n* protone *m*.

protoplasm ['proutaplazam] *n* protoplasma *m*.

prototype ['proutataip] *n* prototipo *m*.

protract [pra'trakt] *v* protrarre, prolungare.

protractor [pra'trakta] *n* goniometro *m*.

protrude [pra'truːd] *v* sporgere.

proud [praud] *adj* orgoglioso, fiero.

prove [pruːv] *v* dimostrare, confermare.

proverb ['provaːb] *n* proverbio *m*.

provide [pra'vaid] *v* provvedere, fornire. **provide against** premunirsi contro. **provided that** purchè. **providence** *n* provvidenza *f*.

province ['provins] *n* provincia *f*. **provincial** *adj* provinciale.

provision [pra'viʒan] *n* provvedimento *m*. **provisions** *pl n* viveri *m pl*, provviste *f pl*. **provisional** *adj* provvisorio.

proviso [pra'vaizou] *n* stipulazione *f*, condizione *f*.

provoke [prə'vouk] *v* provocare, irritare.
provocation *n* provocazione *f*. **provocative** *adj* provocativo.
prow [prau] *n* prua *f*, prora *f*.
prowess ['prauis] *n* (*ability*) bravura *f*;. (*bravery*) prodezza *f*, valore *m*.
prowl [praul] *v* girare furtivamente, vagare.
proximity [prok'siməti] *n* prossimità *f*.
proxy ['proksi] *n* (*agency, authorization*) procura *f*; (*person*) procuratore, -trice *m*, *f*.
prude [pruːd] *n* persona che affetta pudore, puritano, -a *m, f*. **prudish** *adj* che affetta pudore, puritano.
prudent ['pruːdənt] *adj* prudente, cauto. **prudence** *n* prudenza *f*, avvedutezza *f*.
prune[1] [pruːn] *v* sfrondare; (*tree*) potare.
prune[2] [pruːn] *n* prugna secca *f*.
pry [prai] *v* curiosare, ficcare il naso (in).
psalm [saːm] *n* salmo *m*.
pseudonym ['sjuːdənim] *n* pseudonimo *m*.
psychedelic [,saikə'delik] *adj* psichedelico.
psychiatry [sai'kaiətri] *n* psichiatria *f*. **psychiatric** *adj* psichiatrico. **psychiatrist** *n* psichiatra *m, f*.
psychic ['saikik] *adj* psichico.
psychoanalysis [,saikouə'naləsis] *n* psicanalisi *f*. **psychoanalyse** *v* psicanalizzare. **psychoanalyst** *n* psicanalista *m, f*. **psychoanalytic** *adj* psicanalitico.
psychology [sai'kolədʒi] *n* psicologia *f*. **psychological** *adj* psicologico. **psychologist** *n* psicologo, -a *m, f*.
psychopath ['saikəpaθ] *n* psicopatico, -a *m, f*.
psychosis [sai'kousis] *n* psicosi *f*. **psychotic** *n, adj* psicotico, -a.
psychosomatic [,saikəsə'matik] *adj* psicosomatico.
psychotherapy [,saikə'θerəpi] *n* psicoterapia *f*. **psychotherapist** *n* psicoterapista *m, f*.
pub [pʌb] *n* bar *m* invar.
puberty ['pjuːbəti] *n* pubertà *f*.
pubic ['pjuːbik] *adj* pubico.
public ['pʌblik] *nm, adj* pubblico. **public holiday** festa civile *f*. **public library** biblioteca comunale *f*. **public school** collegio privato *m*. **public-spirited** *adj* dotato di senso civico. **publican** proprietario del bar *m*, oste *m*.
publication [,pʌbli'keiʃən] *n* pubblicazione *f*.

publicity [pʌb'lisəti] *n* pubblicità *f*. **publicist** *n* pubblicista *m, f*.
publicize ['pʌblisaiz] *v* divulgare; (*advertise*) fare la pubblicità a.
publish ['pʌbliʃ] *v* pubblicare. **publisher** *n* (*person*) editore *m*; (*firm*) casa editrice *f*.
pucker ['pʌkə] *v* corrugare, raggrinzare.
pudding ['pudiŋ] *n* budino *m*, dolce *m*.
puddle ['pʌdl] *n* pozzanghera *f*.
puerile ['pjuərail] *adj* puerile.
puff [pʌf] *n* (*of wind*) soffio *m*; (*of smoke*) buffata *f*; (*of breath*) alito *m*; (*powder*) piumino *m*; (*pipe, cigarette*) boccata *f*. **puff pastry** pasta sfoglia *f*. *v* sbuffare.
pull [pul] *n* tirata *f*, strappo *m*; (*influence*) ascendente *m*. *v* tirare; (*haul*) trascinare. **pull back** tirare indietro, trattenere. **pull down** tirar giù; demolire. **pull in** (*train*) entrare in stazione. **pull oneself together** riprendere animo. **pull up** tirar su; (*plant, etc.*) strappare; (*stop*) fermarsi.
pulley ['puli] *n* puleggia *f*.
pullover ['pul,ouvə] *n* pullover *m* invar.
pulp [pʌlp] *n* polpa *f*. *v* ridurre in polpa.
pulpit ['pulpit] *n* pulpito *m*.
pulsate [pʌl'seit] *v* palpitare, pulsare. **pulsation** *n* pulsazione *f*.
pulse[1] [pʌls] *n* (*beat*) polso *m*; (*elec*) impulso *m*; vitalità *f*. *v* pulsare.
pulse[2] [pʌls] *n* (*vegetables*) legumi *m pl*.
pulverize ['pʌlvəraiz] *v* polverizzare.
pump [pʌmp] *n* pompa *f*. **petrol pump** distributore di benzina *m*. *v* pompare; (*bullets*) scaricare.
pumpkin ['pʌmpkin] *n* zucca *f*.
pun [pʌn] *n* gioco di parole *m*. *v* fare giochi di parole.
punch[1] [pʌntʃ] *v* (*hit*) picchiare, dare un pugno *or* cazzotto a. *n* pugno *m*; (*coll*) cazzotto *m*; (*energy*) forza *f*. **punch-drunk** *adj* stordito.
punch[2] [pʌntʃ] *n* (*drink*) ponce *m*.
punch[3] [pʌntʃ] *n* (*tool*) punzone *m*. *v* (*tickets*) forare; (*tech*) punzonare; (*stamp*) timbrare.
punctual ['pʌŋktʃuəl] *adj* puntuale. **punctuality** *n* puntualità *f*.
punctuate ['pʌŋktʃueit] *v* interrompere ripetutamente; (*sentence*) mettere la punteggiatura. **punctuation** *n* punteggiatura *f*.
puncture ['pʌŋktʃə] *n* puntura *f*; (*tyre*) foratura *f*. **have a puncture** avere una gomma a terra. *v* forare, bucare.

pungent ['pʌndʒənt] *adj* pungente, aspro; caustico.

punish ['pʌnɪʃ] *v* punire, castigare. **punishment** *n* punizione *f*, castigo (*pl* -ghi) *m*. **punitive** *adj* punitivo.

punt¹ [pʌnt] *n* (*boat*) barchino *m*.

punt² [pʌnt] *v* (*bet*) puntare. **punter** *n* giocatore d'azzardo *m*, scommettitore *m*.

puny ['pjuːnɪ] *adj* sparuto, debole.

pupil¹ ['pjuːpl] *n* (*school*) allievo, -a *m, f*, alunno, -a *m, f*.

pupil² ['pjuːpl] *n* (*anat*) pupilla *f*.

puppet ['pʌpɪt] *n* burattino *m*.

puppy ['pʌpɪ] *n* cagnolino *m*.

purchase ['pəːtʃəs] *v* acquistare, comprare. *n* acquisto *m*; (*tech*) presa *f*. **purchaser** *n* compratore, -trice *m, f*.

pure ['pjuə] *adj* puro. **purify** *v* purificare, depurare. **purity** *n* purezza *f*.

purée ['pjuərei] *n* puré *m*.

purgatory ['pəːgətəri] *n* purgatorio *m*.

purge [pəːdʒ] *v* (*purify*) purgare; (*pol*) epurare. *n* purga *f*, epurazione *f*.

puritan ['pjuərɪtən] *n, adj* puritano, -a. **puritanism** *n* puritanesimo *m*.

purl [pəːl] *v* (*knitting*) lavorare a punto rovescio; (*edge*) smerlare. *n* punto rovescio *m*; punto smerlo *m*.

purple ['pəːpl] *n* porpora *f*. *adj* purpureo; (*of face*) paonazzo.

purpose ['pəːpəs] *n* scopo *m*, proposito *m*. **on purpose** apposta.

purr [pəː] *n* fusa *f pl*. *v* far le fusa.

purse [pəːs] *n* borsa *f*; (*for money*) borsellino *m*. *v* contrarre.

purser ['pəːsə] *n* commissario di bordo *m*.

pursue [pə'sjuː] *v* (*seek to attain*) perseguire; (*follow closely*) perseguitare; (*continue*) seguire, proseguire. **pursuit** *n* (*quest*) ricerca *f*; (*chase*) inseguimento *m*; (*activity*) impiego (*pl* -ghi) *m*.

pus [pʌs] *n* pus *m*, materia *f*.

push [puʃ] *n* spinta *f*; (*effort*) sforzo *m*, energia *f*; iniziativa *f*. **push-chair** *n* carozzina *f*. *v* spingere; (*urge*) spronare; (*product*) lanciare. **push away** allontanare. **push back** respingere. **push-over** *n* vittima facile *f*. **pushing** *adj* energico, aggressivo.

*****put** [put] *v* mettere, porre; (*question*) rivolgere; (*idea*) esprimere. **put about** (*rumour*) diffondere. **put across** (*explain*) spiegare. **put aside** *or* **by** mettere da parte, risparmiare. **put down** (*suppress*) sopprimere; (*land*) atterrare; (*ascribe*)

attribuire. **put forward** proporre, nominare. **put off** rinviare; (*get rid of*) sbarazzarsi di; (*cause to dislike*) ripugnare. **put out** (*extinguish*) spegnere; (*inconvenience*) disturbare. **put up** (*lodge*) offrire alloggio a; (*stay*) prendere alloggio; (*raise*) alzare; (*notice, etc.*) affiggere. **put up with** sopportare.

putrid ['pjuːtrɪd] *adj* putrido.

putt [pʌt] *v* colpire leggermente, fare il putting. *n* colpo leggero *m*, putting *m invar*.

putty ['pʌtɪ] *n* stucco *m*. *v* stuccare.

puzzle ['pʌzl] *n* indovinello *m*; enigma *m*. *v* confondere, rendere perplesso. **puzzled** *adj* perplesso.

pygmy ['pigmi] *n, adj* pigmeo, -a.

pyjamas [pə'dʒɑːməz] *pl n* pigiama *m sing*.

pylon ['pailən] *n* pilone *m*.

pyramid ['pirəmid] *n* piramide *f*.

python ['paiθən] *n* pitone *m*.

Q

quack¹ [kwak] *v* (*duck*) schiamazzare.

quack² [kwak] *n* (*med*) ciarlatano *m*, medicastro *m*.

quadrangle ['kwodraŋgl] *n* (*math*) quadrangolo *m*; (*arch*) corte quadrangolare *f*.

quadrant ['kwodrənt] *n* quadrante *m*.

quadrilateral [kwodrə'latərəl] *nm, adj* quadrilatero.

quadruped ['kwodruped] *n* quadrupede *m*.

quadruple [kwod'ruːpl] *adj* quadruplo.

quagmire ['kwagmaiə] *n* pantano *m*.

quail¹ [kweil] *n* (*bird*) quaglia *f*.

quail² [kweil] *v* aver paura, sgomentarsi.

quaint [kweint] *adj* interessante *or* pittoresco in un modo insolito.

quake [kweik] *v* tremare; (*person*) fremere. *n* (*coll: earthquake*) terremoto *m*.

Quaker ['kweikə] *n* quacchero, -a *m, f*.

qualify ['kwolifai] *v* qualificare; (*define*) precisare. **qualification** *n* qualifica *f*; (*limitation*) riserva *f*. **qualified** *adj* qualificato, idoneo; (*limited*) condizionato.

quality ['kwoləti] *n* qualità *f*.

qualm [kwaɪm] *n* scrupolo *m*, apprensione *f*.

quandary ['kwondəri] *n* situazione difficile *f*, imbarazzo *m*.

quantify ['kwontifai] *v* quantificare.

quantity ['kwontəti] *n* quantità *f*.

quantum ['kwontəm] *n* quanto *m*.

quarantine ['kworəntiɪn] *n* quarantena *f*. *v* mettere in quarantena.

quarrel ['kworəl] *n* lite *f*, bisticcio *m*. **pick a quarrel** attaccar briga. *v* litigare, bisticciare. **quarrelsome** *adj* litigioso.

quarry[1] ['kwori] *n* (*prey*) preda *f*.

quarry[2] ['kwori] *n* (*mining*) cava *f*. *v* scavare.

quarter ['kwoɪtə] *n* quarto *m*; (*three months*) trimestre *m*; (*district, mercy*) quartiere *m*. **at close quarters** da vicino. **quarters** *pl n* (*mil*) accantonamento *m sing*. *v* dividere in quattro; (*mil*) acquartierare. **quarterly** *nm, adj* trimestrale.

quartet [kwoɪ'tet] *n* quartetto *m*.

quartz [kwoɪts] *n* quarzo *m*.

quash [kwoʃ] *v* sopprimere; (*law*) annullare, cassare.

quaver ['kweivə] *n* (*music*) croma *f*; (*shaky voice*) tremolio *m*. *v* tremolare.

quay [kiɪ] *n* banchina *f*.

queasy ['kwiɪzi] *adj* che sente nausea.

queen [kwiɪn] *n* regina *f*.

queer [kwiə] *adj* strambo, bizzarro. **feel queer** sentirsi male. *n* (*coll: homosexual*) finocchio *m*.

quell [kwel] *v* reprimere, sopprimere.

quench [kwentʃ] *v* spegnere. **quench one's· thirst** dissetarsi.

query ['kwiəri] *n* domanda *f*, quesito *m*. *v* chiedersi; (*raise doubt*) mettere in dubbio.

quest [kwest] *n* ricerca *f*.

question ['kwestʃən] *n* questione *f*, domanda *f*; (*gramm*) interrogazione *f*; problema *m*. **question mark** punto interrogativo *m*. *v* interrogare; (*query*) mettere in dubbio.

queue [kjuɪ] *n* coda *f*. *v* fare la coda, mettersi in coda.

quibble ['kwibl] *n* cavillo *m*. *v* cavillare.

quick [kwik] *adj* rapido, veloce; (*lively*) vivace. **quicksand** *n* sabbia mobile *f*. **quicksilver** *n* argento vivo *m*. **quick-tempered** *adj* impulsivo. **quick-witted** *adj* sveglio. *adv* presto. *n* **cut to the quick**

toccare sul vivo. **quicken** *v* affrettare, accelerare.

quid [kwid] *n* (*coll*) sterlina *f*.

quiet ['kwaiət] *adj* tranquillo, quieto. **keep quiet** tacere, star zitto. *n* quiete *f*, tranquillità *f*, silenzio *m*. **on the quiet** di nascosto. **quieten** *v* calmare, acquietare.

quill [kwil] *n* penna *f*.

quilt [kwilt] *v* trapuntare. *n* trapunta *f*; (*duvet*) piumino *m*.

quince [kwins] *n* cotogna *f*.

quinine [kwi'niɪn] *n* chinino *m*.

quinsy ['kwinzi] *n* angina *f*.

quintet [kwin'tet] *n* quintetto *m*.

quirk [kwəɪk] *n* ticchio *m*, vezzo *m*.

*quit [kwit] *v* lasciare, abbandonare; (*depart*) partire.

quite [kwait] *adv* perfettamente, bene, affatto, proprio; (*somewhat*) abbastanza.

quits [kwits] *adj* pari. **call it quits** far pari e patta. **double or quits** lascia o raddoppia.

quiver[1] ['kwivə] *v* fremere; (*voice*) tremolare. *n* fremito *m*; tremolio *m*.

quiver[2] ['kwivə] *n* (*arrows*) faretra *f*.

quiz [kwiz] *n* quiz *m invar*. *v* interrogare. **quizzical** *adj* (*odd*) curioso; (*ridiculing*) beffardo.

quota ['kwoutə] *n* quota *f*, rata *f*; (*trade*) contingente *m*.

quote [kwout] *v* citare; (*price*) quotare. **quotation** *n* citazione *f*. **quotation marks** virgolette *f pl*.

quotient ['kwouʃnt] *n* quoziente *m*.

R

rabbi ['rabai] *n* rabbino *m*.

rabbit ['rabit] *m* coniglio *m*.

rabble ['rabl] *n* plebaglia *f*.

rabies ['reibiɪz] *n* rabbia *f*. **rabid** *adj* (*med*) idrofobo; furioso; fanatico.

race[1] [reis] *n* (*sport*) corsa *f*, gara *f*. **racecourse** *n* ippodromo *m*. **racehorse** *n* cavallo da corsa *m*. **race-track** *n* pista *f*. *v* correre; (*compete*) gareggiare con. **racing** *adj* da corsa. **racy** *adj* vivace, piccante.

race[2] [reis] *n* razza *f*. **racial** *adj* razziale. **racialism** *or* **racism** *n* razzismo *m*. **racialist** *or* **racist** *n*(*m+f*), *adj* razzista.

rack[1] [rak] *n* rastrelliera *f*; (*for plates*) scolapiatti *m invar*; (*tech*) cremagliera *f*;

(*for luggage*) rete *f*. *v* **rack one's brains** scervellarsi, lambiccarsi il cervello.

rack² [rak] *n* **go to rack and ruin** andare in malora.

racket¹ ['rakit] *n* (*bat*) racchetta *f*.

racket² ['rakit] *n* (*noise*) baccano *m*, chiasso *m*; (*dishonest scheme*) truffa *f*.

radar ['reidaɪ] *n* radar *m*.

radial ['reidiəl] *adj* radiale.

radiant ['reidiənt] *adj* raggiante; splendido; (*joyful*) esultante; (*phys*, *tech*) radiante. **radiance** *n* splendore *m*.

radiate ['reidieit] *v* irradiare, raggiare. **radiation** *n* irradiazione *f*; (*phys*) radiazione *f*. **radiator** *n* (*car*) radiatore *m*; (*central heating*) termosifone *m*.

radical ['radikəl] *n*(*m*+*f*), *adj* radicale.

radio ['reidiou] *nf invar*, *adj* radio.

radioactive [reidiou'aktiv] *adj* radioattivo. **radioactivity** *n* radioattività *f*.

radiography [reidi'ogrəfi] *n* radiografia *f*.

radiology [reidi'olədʒi] *n* radiologia *f*. **radiologist** *n* radiologo, -a *m*, *f*.

radish ['radiʃ] *n* ravanello *m*.

radium ['reidiəm] *n* radio *m*.

radius ['reidiəs] *n* raggio *m*.

raffia ['rafiə] *n* rafia *f*.

raffle ['rafl] *n* riffa *f*.

raft [raɪft] *n* zattera *f*.

rafter ['raɪftə] *n* trave *f*.

rag¹ [rag] *n* (*cloth*) straccio *m*, cencio *m*; (*derog: newspaper*) giornalaccio *m*. **ragged** *adj* lacero, cencioso.

rag² [rag] (*coll*) *v* prendere in giro. *n* baldoria *f*.

rage [reidʒ] *n* rabbia *f*, collera *f*; (*enthusiasm*) passione *f*, moda *f*. **be in a rage** essere furioso *or* arrabbiato. **fly into a rage** infuriarsi. *v* montare su tutte le furie, infuriarsi; (*storm*, *etc.*) imperversare. **rage against** inveire contro. **raging** *adj* furioso, violento.

raid [reid] *n* incursione *f*, razzia *f*. *v* fare un'incursione in, razziare, invadere. **raider** *n* razziatore *m*.

rail [reil] *n* (*bar*) sbarra *f*; (*barrier*) ringhiera *f*; (*handrail*) corrimano *m invar*; (*for train*) rotaia *f*, binario *m*. **by rail** col treno. **go off the rails** perdere le staffe. **railway** *n* ferrovia *f*.

railings ['reiliŋz] *pl n* cancellata *f sing*, inferriata *f sing*.

rain [rein] *n* pioggia *f*. **rainbow** *n* arcobaleno *m*. **raincoat** *n* impermeabile *m*. **raindrop** *n* goccia di pioggia *f*. *v*

piovere. **rain cats and dogs** piovere a catinelle. **rainy** *adj* piovoso.

raise [reiz] *v* (*lift up*) alzare; (*rear*) allevare; (*bring up*) sollevare; (*increase*) aumentare; (*cause*) suscitare.

raisin ['reizən] *n* uva secca *f*.

rake [reik] *n* (*tool*) rastrello *m*. *v* rastrellare. **rake up the past** rivangare il passato.

rally ['rali] *n* (*meeting*) raduno *m*; (*mot*) rally *m invar*; (*recovery*) ricupero di forze *m*, ripresa *f*; (*tennis*, *etc.*) scambio di colpi *m*. *v* radunare; riprendersi.

ram [ram] *n* montone *m*. *v* ficcare; (*ships*) speronare.

ramble ['rambl] *n* gita *f*, giro *m*. *v* vagare, girovagare; (*speech*) divagare; (*mind*) delirare. **rambling** *adj* (*unconnected*) sconnesso, sconclusionato. **rambling rose** rosa rampicante *f*.

ramp [ramp] *n* rampa *f*.

rampage [ram'peidʒ] *n* **go on the rampage** andare su tutte le furie.

rampant ['rampənt] *adj* (*unchecked*) sfrenato; (*heraldry*) rampante.

rampart ['rampaɪt] *n* bastione *m*.

ramshackle ['ramʃakl] *adj* cadente.

ran [ran] *V* **run**.

ranch [raɪntʃ] *n* fattoria (per l'allevamento di bestiame) *f*, ranch *m invar*.

rancid ['ransid] *adj* rancido.

rancour ['raŋkə] *n* amarezza *f*, rancore *m*.

random ['randəm] *adj* casuale, fortuito. *n* **at random** a casaccio.

randy ['randi] *adj* lascivo.

rang [raŋ] *V* **ring²**.

range [reindʒ] *n* (*assortment*) gamma *f*; (*mountains*) catena *f*; (*scope*) portata *f*; (*for shooting*) campo di tiro *m*; (*of voice*) estensione *f*; (*stove*) fornello *m*. **out of range** fuori tiro. **range-finder** *n* telemetro *m*. **within range** a portata; (*of gun*) a tiro. *v* (*arrange*) disporre; (*set in order*) schierare; (*between limits*) estendersi, variare.

rank¹ [raŋk] *n* (*class*) grado *m*; (*row*) fila *f*. **ranks** *pl n* truppe *f pl*. *v* (*arrange*) schierare; classificare; considerare.

rank² [raŋk] *adj* (*excessive*) rigoglioso; (*utter*) assoluto; (*smell*) puzzolente.

rankle ['raŋkl] *v* bruciare; (*cause bitterness*) amareggiare.

ransack ['ransak] *v* mettere sossopra, rovistare.

ransom ['ransəm] *n* riscatto *m*. *v* riscattare.

rap [rap] *v* picchiare, colpire. **rap over the knuckles** rimproverare. *n* colpetto *m*. **take the rap** accollarsi il biasimo.

rape [reip] *n* stupro *m*, violenza carnale *f*; (*abduction*) rapimento *m*. *v* violentare, stuprare; rapire.

rapid ['rapid] *adj* rapido, veloce. **rapidity** *n* rapidità *f*.

rapier ['reipiə] *n* spada *f*, stocco *m*.

rapture ['raptʃə] *n* estasi *f*. **rapturous** *adj* estatico.

rare[1] ['reə] *adj* (*scarce*) raro. **rarity** *n* rarità *f*.

rare[2] ['reə] *adj* (*meat*) al sangue.

rascal ['raiskəl] *n* briccone *m*, mascalzone *m*.

rash[1] [raʃ] *adj* avventato, sconsiderato. **rashness** *n* avventatezza *f*, imprudenza *f*.

rash[2] [raʃ] *n* (*med*) eruzione *f*.

rasher ['raʃə] *n* fetta (di prosciutto) *f*.

raspberry ['raizbəri] *n* lampone *m*. **blow a raspberry** (*coll*) fare una pernacchia.

rat [rat] *n* ratto *m*; (*coll: traitor*) traditore *m*. **smell a rat** (*coll*) avere dei sospetti.

rate [reit] *n* (*charge*) tasso *m*; (*speed*) velocità *f*, passo *m*; (*degree*) grado *m*. **at any rate** comunque. **at this rate** così, a questo passo. **ratepayer** *n* contribuente *m*, *f*. **rates** *pl n* imposta *f sing*. *v* stimare, valutare, considerare.

rather ['raiðə] *adv* piuttosto, anzi. *interj* certo! altro che! **I would rather ...** preferirei ....

ratify ['ratifai] *v* ratificare. **ratification** *n* ratifica *f*.

ratio ['reiʃiou] *n* rapporto *m*, proporzione *f*.

ration ['raʃən] *n* razione *f*. **rations** *pl n* viveri *m pl*. *v* razionare.

rational ['raʃənl] *adj* razionale.

rattle ['ratl] *v* sbatacchiare; (*disconcert*) sconcertare. *n* sbatacchio *m*; (*toy, instrument*) raganella *f*; (*in throat*) rantolo *m*.

raucous ['roikəs] *adj* rauco.

ravage ['ravidʒ] *v* devastare. *n* devastazione *f*.

rave [reiv] *v* delirare. **rave about** andar pazzo di.

raven ['reivən] *n* corvo *m*.

ravenous ['ravənəs] *adj* vorace. **be ravenous** avere una fame da lupo.

ravine [rə'viin] *n* burrone *m*.

ravish ['raviʃ] *v* (*delight*) incantare; (*rape*) violentare. **ravishing** *adj* incantevole.

raw [roi] *adj* (*not cooked*) crudo; (*not refined*) greggio; (*untrained*) inesperto. **raw material** materia prima *f*. **touch on the raw** toccare sul vivo.

ray[1] [rei] *n* raggio *m*.

ray[2] [rei] *n* (*fish*) razza *f*.

rayon ['reion] *n* raion *m*.

razor ['reizə] *n* rasoio *m*. **razor blade** lametta *f*.

reach [riitʃ] *n* portata *f*; (*continuous stretch*) tratto *m*. **out of reach** fuori mano. **within reach** a portata di mano. *v* (*get to*) raggiungere; (*hand*) porgere.

react [ri'akt] *v* reagire. **reaction** *n* reazione *f*. **reactionary** *n*, *adj* reazionario, -a. **reactor** *n* reattore *m*.

*****read** [riid] *v* leggere; studiare. **well-read** *adj* istruito. **readable** *adj* leggibile. **reader** *n* lettore, -trice *m*, *f*. **readership** *n* lettori *m pl*. **reading** *n* lettura *f*; interpretazione *f*.

readjust [riiə'dʒʌst] *v* raggiustare.

ready ['redi] *adj* pronto, preparato; (*willing*) disposto. **get ready** preparare, prepararsi. **ready-made** *adj* confezionato. **ready money** contanti *m pl*.

real [riəl] *adj* reale, effettivo, genuino. **real estate** beni immobili *m pl*. **realism** *n* realismo *m*. **realist** *n* realista *m*, *f*. **realistic** *adj* realistico. **reality** *n* realtà *f*.

realize ['riəlaiz] *v* realizzare. **realization** *n* realizzazione *f*.

really ['riəli] *adv* effettivamente; (*before adj*) proprio. *interj* davvero.

realm [relm] *n* dominio *m*; (*special field*) campo *m*.

reap [riip] *v* mietere; (*profit*, *etc*.) raccogliere.

reappear [riiə'piə] *v* riapparire. **reappearance** *n* ricomparsa *f*.

rear[1] [riə] *n* (*back*) dietro *m*, parte posteriore *f*; (*mil*) retroguardia *f*. **at the rear of** dietro a. **rear-view mirror** retrovisore *m*. **stay in the rear** restare per ultimo. *adj* posteriore.

rear[2] [riə] *v* (*raise*) allevare; (*horse*, *etc*.) impennarsi; (*elevate*) innalzare.

rearm [ri'aim] *v* riarmare. **rearmament** *n* riarmo *m*.

rearrange [riiə'reindʒ] *v* riordinare. **rearrangement** *n* riordinamento *m*.

reason ['riːzn] *n* ragione *f*, causa *f*; *(judgment)* ragionevolezza *f*. **it stands to reason** è evidente. *v* ragionare. **reasonable** *adj* ragionevole, giusto. **reasoning** *n* modo di ragionare *m*.

reassure [riə'ʃuə] *v* rassicurare. **reassurance** *n* rassicurazione *f*.

rebate ['riːbeit] *n* sconto *m*.

rebel ['rebl] *v* ribellarsi. *n* ribelle *m, f*. **rebellion** *n* ribellione *f*. **rebellious** *adj* ribelle.

rebound [ri'baund; *n* 'riːbaund] *v* rimbalzare. *n* rimbalzo *m*.

rebuff [ri'bʌf] *v* respingere, rifiutare. *n* scacco *m*, rifiuto *m*.

*rebuild [riː'bild] *v* ricostruire. **rebuilding** *n* ricostruzione *f*.

rebuke [ri'bjuːk] *n* rimprovero *m*. *v* rimproverare.

recall [ri'koːl] *v* richiamare; *(remember)* rievocare, ricordare. *n* richiamo *m*, memoria *f*. **past recall** irrevocabile.

recap ['riːkap] *(coll)* *v* ricapitolare. *n* ricapitolazione *f*.

recede [ri'siːd] *v* recedere, inclinarsi all'indietro.

receipt [rə'siːt] *v* quietanzare. *n* ricevuta *f*. **receipts** *pl n* incasso *m sing*, entrate *f pl*.

receive [rə'siːv] *v* ricevere; *(sustain)* sostenere, riportare; *(stolen goods)* ricettare. **receiver** *n* ricettatore, -trice *m, f*; *(bankruptcy)* curatore fallimentare *m*; *(phone)* ricevitore *m*.

recent ['riːsnt] *adv* recente. **recently** *adv* di recente, poco fa.

receptacle [rə'septəkl] *n* recipiente *m*; *(bot)* ricettacolo *m*.

reception [rə'sepʃən] *n* ricevimento *m*; *(radio)* ricezione *f*. **receptionist** *n* segretaria *f*, receptionist *f invar*. **receptive** *adj* ricettivo.

recess [ri'ses] *n* nicchia *f*; pausa *f*; *(holiday)* vacanza *f*. **recesses** *pl n* *(of mind, etc.)* recessi *m pl*.

recession [rə'seʃən] *n* recessione *f*.

recharge [riː'tʃɑɪdʒ] *v* ricaricare.

recipe ['resəpi] *n* ricetta *f*.

recipient [rə'sipiənt] *n* destinatario, -a *m, f*. *adj* ricevente.

reciprocate [rə'siprəkeit] *v* contraccambiare, reciprocare; *(tech)* alternarsi. **reciprocal** *adj* reciproco. **reciprocity** *n* reciprocità *f*.

recite [rə'sait] *v* recitare. **recital** *n* *(narrative)* racconto *m*; *(entertainment)* recital *m invar*. **recitation** *n* recitazione *f*.

reckless ['rekləs] *adj* imprudente, avventato. **recklessness** *n* avventatezza *f*.

reckon ['rekən] *v* contare; *(consider)* giudicare. **reckon on** contare su. **reckon with** prendere in considerazione. **reckoning** *n* *(bill)* resa dei conti *f*.

reclaim [ri'kleim] *v* redimere; *(land)* bonificare; *(material)* ricuperare. **reclamation** *n* bonifica *f*.

recline [rə'klain] *v* appoggiarsi.

recluse [rə'kluːs] *n* eremita *m*.

recognize ['rekəgnaiz] *v* riconoscere. **recognition** *n* riconoscimento *m*. **recognizable** *adj* riconoscibile.

recoil [rə'koil] *v* rinculare. **recoil from** rifuggire da. *n* rinculo *m*.

recollect [rekə'lekt] *v* rammentarsi di. **recollection** *n* memoria *f*, ricordo *m*.

recommence [riːkə'mens] *v* ricominciare.

recommend [rekə'mend] *v* raccomandare, consigliare. **recommendation** *n* raccomandazione *f*.

recompense ['rekəmpens] *v* compensare, risarcire. *n* indennizzo *m*, risarcimento *m*.

reconcile ['rekənsail] *v* mettere d'accordo, riconciliare. **reconcile oneself to** rassegnarsi a. **reconciliation** *n* rappacificazione *f*.

reconnoitre [rekə'noitə] *v* fare un sopralluogo; *(mil)* fare una ricognizione. **reconnaissance** *n* esplorazione *f*, sopralluogo *(pl -ghi)* *m*; *(mil)* ricognizione *f*.

reconstruct [riːkən'strʌkt] *v* ricostruire. **reconstruction** *n* ricostruzione *f*.

record [rə'koːd; *n* 'rekoːd] *v* registrare; notare; *(as document)* mettere a verbale. *n* nota *f*. registro *m*; *(court report)* verbale *m*; *(sport)* record *m invar*; disco *m*; *(dossier)* stato di servizio *m*. **keep a record of** prendere nota di. **off the record** ufficiosamente. **record-player** *n* giradischi *m invar*. **recorder** *n* *(music)* flautino *m*. **recording** *n* registrazione *f*.

recount [ri'kaunt] *v* riferire, raccontare.

recoup [ri'kuːp] *v* rifarsi di, compensare.

recourse [rə'koːs] *n* **have recourse to** ricorrere a. **without recourse** senza rivalsa.

recover [rə'kʌvə] *v* *(get back)* riprendere, ricuperare; *(regain health)* rimettersi.

recovery *n* ricupero *m*; (*health*) guarigione *f*.

recreation [rekri'eiʃən] *n* ricreazione *f*, passatempo *m*, svago *m*.

recrimination [rəkrimi'neiʃən] *n* recriminazione *f*.

recruit [rə'kruit] *n* recluta *f*. *v* arruolare. **recruitment** *n* reclutamento *m*.

rectangle ['rektaŋgl] *n* rettangolo *m*. **rectangular** *adj* rettangolare.

rectify ['rektifai] *v* rettificare; (*elec*) raddrizzare.

rectum ['rektəm] *n* retto *m*.

recuperate [rə'kjuipəreit] *v* ricuperare; (*get well again*) rimettersi. **recuperation** *n* ricupero *m*.

recur [ri'kəi] *v* ricorrere, ritornare. **recurrence** *n* ricorrenza *f*; (*of illness*) ricaduta *f*. **recurrent** *adj* ricorrente.

red [red] *adj* rosso. **go red** (*person*) arrossire; (*thing*) diventar rosso. **redcurrant** *n* ribes *m invar*. **red-handed** *adj* in flagrante. **red herring** diversivo *m*. **redhot** *adj* rovente. **Red Indian** *n* pellerossa (*pl* pellirosse) *m*, *f*. *n* **in the red** scoperto. **reddish** *adj* rossastro.

redeem [rə'diːm] *v* redimere, estinguere, svincolare. **redeeming feature** particolare che salva *m*. **redeemable** *adj* redimibile. **redemption** *n* redenzione *f*; salvezza *f*; liberazione *f*.

redress [rə'dres] *n* riparazione *f*, soddisfazione *f*. *v* soddisfare, correggere.

reduce [rə'djuis] *v* ridurre. **reduced** *adj* ridotto. **reduction** *n* riduzione *f*.

redundant [rə'dʌndənt] *adj* superfluo. **make redundant** (*employee*) mettere in cassa d'integrazione.

reed [riːd] *n* canna *f*; (*of musical instrument*) linguetta *f*.

reef [riːf] *n* scogliera *f*.

reek [riːk] *v* puzzare. *n* puzzo *m*.

reel[1] [riːl] *n* rocchetto *m*; (*fishing*) mulinello *m*; (*film*) rotolo *m*. *v* arrotolare. **reel off** rifilare.

reel[2] [riːl] *v* (*sway*) barcollare; (*of head*) girare.

refectory [rə'fektəri] *n* refettorio *m*.

refer [rə'fəi] *v* (*report, ascribe*) riferire; (*consult*) ricorrere, rivolgersi; (*send back*) rimandare. **referring to** con riferimento a. **reference** *n* riferimento *m*; (*testimonial*) referenza *f*, attestato *m*.

referee [refə'riː] *n* arbitro *m*. *v* arbitrare.

referendum [refə'rendəm] *n* referendum *m*.

refill ['riːfil] *n* refill *m invar*, pezzo di ricambio *m*.

refine [rə'fain] *v* raffinare. **refined** *adj* raffinato, squisito. **refinement** *n* (*tech*) raffinazione *f*; (*manners*) raffinatezza *f*. **refinery** *n* raffineria *f*.

reflation [rə'fleiʃn] *n* reflazione *f*.

reflect [rə'flekt] *v* riflettere; (*manifest*) rispecchiare. **reflection** *n* riflessione *f*. **on reflection** a pensarci su. **reflector** *n* riflettore *m*; (*of vehicle*) catarifrangente *m*.

reflex ['riːfleks] *nm*, *adj* riflesso. **reflexive** *adj* riflessivo.

reform [rə'foim] *n* riforma *f*. *v* riformare, correggere. **reformation** *n* riforma *f*. **reformatory** *n* riformatorio *m*. **reformer** *n* riformatore, -trice *m*, *f*.

refract [rə'frakt] *v* rifrangere. **refraction** *n* rifrazione *f*.

refractory [rə'fraktəri] *adj* refrattario; (*stubborn*) ostinato.

refrain[1] [rə'frein] *v* astenersi, trattenersi.

refrain[2] [rə'frein] *n* ritornello *m*, ripresa *f*.

refresh [rə'freʃ] *v* rinfrescare, ristorare. **refresher course** corso di aggiornamento *m*. **refreshments** *pl n* rinfreschi *m pl*.

refrigerator [rə'fridʒəreitə] *n* frigorifero *m*.

refuel [riː'fjuiəl] *v* rifornirsi di carburante.

refuge ['refjuidʒ] *n* rifugio *m*. **take refuge** rifugiarsi. **refugee** *n* profugo, -a *m*, *f*.

refund [ri'fʌnd; *n* 'riːfʌnd] *v* rimborsare. *n* rimborso *m*.

refuse[1] [rə'fjuiz] *v* rifiutare, dire di no; (*deny*) negare, respingere; (*prohibit*) vietare. **refusal** *n* rifiuto *m*; (*option*) diritto di opzione *m*.

refuse[2] ['refjuis] *n* rifiuti *m pl*, immondizia *f*.

refute [ri'fjuit] *v* confutare.

regain [ri'gein] *v* riacquistare, riprendere. **regain consciousness** riprendere i sensi, rianimarsi.

regal ['riːgəl] *adj* regale.

regard [rə'gaid] *v* (*consider*) stimare; (*concern*) riguardare. *n* riguardo *m*; rispetto *m*; considerazione *f*; deferenza *f*. **with regard to** riguardo a, per quanto riguarda. **regardless of** senza badare *or* riguardo a.

regatta [rə'gatə] *n* regata *f*.

regent ['riːdʒənt] *n* reggente *m*. **regency** *n* reggenza *f*.

regime [rei'ʒıım] *n* regime *m*.
regiment ['redʒımənt] *n* reggimento *m*. *v* irreggimentare. **regimental** *adj* reggimentale. **regimentation** *n* irreggimentazione *f*.
region ['rıidʒən] *n* regione *f*, zona *f*. **regional** *adj* regionale.
register ['redʒıstə] *n* registro *m*; (*voting*) lista elettorale *f*; (*professional*) albo *m*. *v* registrare; (*show*) indicare; (*enter formally*) iscriversi. **registered letter** (lettera) raccomandata *f*. **registered office** sede legale *f*. **registrar** *n* segretario *m*; ufficiale di stato civile *m*. **registration** *n* registrazione *f*; iscrizione *f*. **registry office** ufficio di stato civile *m*.
regress [ri'gres] *v* regredire. **regression** *n* regressione *f*. **regressive** *adj* regressivo.
regret [rə'gret] *n* dispiacere *m*, rammarico *m*. **regrets** *pl n* (*sorrow*) rimorsi *m pl*; (*excuses*) scuse *f pl*. *v* rimpiangere, rammicarsi di. **regretful** *adj* spiacente. **regrettable** *adj* spiacevole.
regular ['regjulə] *adj* regolare. **regularity** *n* regolarità *f*.
regulate ['regjuleit] *v* regolare. **regulation** *n* regolamento *m*; (*rule*) regola *f*.
rehabilitate [rıihə'biliteit] *v* riabilitare. **rehabilitation** *n* riabilitazione *f*.
rehearse [rə'həıs] *v* (*theatre*) provare; (*enumerate*) ripetere, recitare. **rehearsal** *n* prova *f*. **dress rehearsal** prova generale *f*.
reign [rein] *n* regno *m*. *v* regnare; prevalere.
reimburse [rıiim'bəıs] *v* rimborsare. **reimbursement** *n* rimborso *m*.
rein [rein] *n* redine *f*, briglia *f*. **give free rein to** dare libero sfogo a. *v* **rein in** frenare.
reincarnation [rıiinkaı'neiʃən] *n* reincarnazione *f*.
reindeer ['reindiə] *n* renna *f*.
reinforce [rıiin'fɔis] *v* rinforzare. **reinforced concrete** cemento armato *m*. **reinforcement** *n* rinforzo *m*.
reinstate [ˌrıiin'steit] *v* reintegrare. **reinstatement** *n* reintegrazione *f*.
reinvest [rıiin'vest] *v* rinvestire.
reissue [rıi'iʃuı] *n* nuova emissione *f*, ristampa *f*. *v* emettere di nuovo, ristampare.
reject [rə'dʒekt; *n* 'rıidʒekt] *v* rifiutare, respingere; (*discard*) scartare. *n* scarto *m*. **rejection** *n* rifiuto *m*.

rejoice [rə'dʒois] *v* rallegrarsi, gioire. **rejoicing** *n* allegrezza *f*, allegria *f*.
rejoin [rə'dʃoin] *v* (*join again*) ricongiungere; (*come back to*) tornare a; (*answer*) rispondere; (*law*) replicare. **rejoinder** *n* risposta *f*, replica *f*.
rejuvenate [rə'dʒuivəneit] *v* ringiovanire. **rejuvenation** *n* ringiovanimento *m*.
relapse [rə'laps] *v* ricadere; (*med*) riammalarsi. *n* ricaduta *f*.
relate [rə'leit] *v* (*tell*) narrare; (*refer*) riferire, riguardare; (*be connected*) aver rapporto. **related** *adj* associato, congiunto; (*family*) parente.
relation [rə'leiʃn] *n* (*family*) parente *m*, *f*; (*connection*) rapporto *m*; (*narration*) racconto *m*. **relationship** *n* parentela *f*, rapporto *m*.
relative ['relətiv] *adj* relativo. **relative to** (*concerning*) riguardante. *n* parente *m*, *f*. **relativity** *n* relatività *f*.
relax [rə'laks] *v* rilassare, allentare; (*rest*) riposarsi. **relaxation** *n* distensione *f*, riposo *m*; (*entertainment*) svago *m*.
relay ['rıilei; *v* ri'lei] *n* (*shift*) turno *m*; (*elec*) relè *m invar*, soccorritore *m*; (*radio*) trasmissione *f*. **relay race** (corsa a) staffetta *f*. *v* trasmettere.
release [rə'liis] *v* liberare, rimettere in libertà; (*launch*) lanciare, (*let go*) mollare; (*publication*) mettere in circolazione. *n* liberazione *f*; lancio *m*; (*press*) comunicato stampa *m*.
relent [rə'lent] *v* placarsi, cedere. **relentless** *adj* inesorabile, spietato.
relevant ['reləvənt] *adj* pertinente, a proposito. **relevance** *n* pertinenza *f*.
reliable [ri'laiəbl] *adj* fidato; sicuro; (*information*) attendibile. **reliability** *n* sicurezza *f*; (*person*) fidatezza *f*; attendibilità *f*.
relic ['relik] *n* reliquia *f*.
relief [rə'liif] *n* (*alleviation*) sollievo *m*; (*help*) soccorso *m*; (*prominence*) rilievo *m*. **relief map** *n* plastico *m*, levata topografica *f*.
relieve [rə'liiv] *v* alleviare; (*help*) soccorrere. **feel relieved** sentirsi sollevato.
religion [rə'lidʒən] *n* religione *f*. **religious** *adj* religioso, devoto.
relinquish [rə'linkwiʃ] *v* abbandonare, rinunziare a.
relish ['reliʃ] *v* apprezzare, godere. *n* piacere *m*, godimento *m*.

reluctant [rə'lʌktənt] *adj* restio, riluttante. **reluctance** *n* riluttanza *f*. **reluctantly** *adv* di malavoglia, a malincuore.

rely [rə'lai] *v* contare, fare assegnamento, fidarsi (di).

remain [rə'mein] *v* rimanere, restare. **remainder** *n* resto *m*, avanzo *m*. **remains** *pl n* resti *m pl*; (*mortal*) spoglie *f pl*.

remand [rə'maind] *v* rinviare. *n* rinvio *m*.

remark [rə'maik] *n* nota *f*, osservazione *f*, commento *m*. *v* notare, osservare. **remarkable** *adj* notevole.

remarry [rii'mari] *v* risposarsi.

remedy ['remədi] *n* rimedio *m*. *v* rimediare, correggere; (*heal*) curare. **remedial** *adj* (*school*) correttivo; (*law*) riparatore.

remember [ri'membə] *v* ricordare, ricordarsi (di), rammentare. **remembrance** *n* memoria *f*, ricordo *m*.

remind [rə'maind] *v* ricordare, rammentare, richiamare alla mente. **reminder** *n* promemoria *m invar*, ricordo *m*.

reminiscence [remə'nisens] *n* reminiscenza *f*. **reminiscent of** che rammenta.

remiss [rə'mis] *adj* negligente, disattento.

remit [rə'mit] *v* (*transmit*) rimettere; (*abate*) mitigare; (*send back*) rinviare; perdonare. **remittance** *n* rimessa *f*.

remnant ['remnənt] *n* scampolo *m*, resto *m*.

remorse [rə'mois] *n* rimorso *m*. **remorseful** *adj* preso *or* tormentato dal rimorso. **remorseless** *adj* spietato.

remote [rə'mout] *adj* remoto, lontano; (*faint*) pallido. **remote control** telecomando *m*.

remove [rə'muiv] *v* (*take off*) togliere; (*do away with*) eliminare; (*withdraw*) ritirare; (*move house*) traslocare. **removal** *n* (*house*) trasloco *m*; (*med*) ablazione *f*; (*act of removing*) rimozione *f*.

remunerate [rə'mjuinəreit] *v* ricompensare. **remuneration** *n* ricompensa *f*, rimunerazione *f*. **remunerative** *adj* rimunerativo.

renaissance [rə'neisəns] *n* rinascimento *m*.

rename [rii'ņeim] *v* rinominare.

render ['rendə] *v* rendere; rappresentare; (*give back*) restituire; (*cookery*) struggere, (*building*) incalcinare.

rendezvous ['rondivui] *n* appuntamento *m*, convegno *m*.

renegade ['renigeid] *n, adj* rinnegato, -a.

renew [rə'njui] *v* rinnovare. **renewal** *n* rinnovamento *m*.

renounce [ri'nauns] *v* rinunciare a, ripudiare. **renouncement** *or* **renunciation** *n* rinunzia *f*.

renovate ['renəveit] *v* rinnovare, ripristinare; (*buildings*) restaurare. **renovation** *n* ripristinamento *m*; restauro *m*.

renown [rə'naun] *n* fama *f*. **renowned** *adj* rinomato, famoso, celebre.

rent[1] [rent] *v* affittare; (*take, occupy*) prendere in affitto; (*let out*) dare in affitto. *n* affitto *m*.

rent[2] [rent] *n* (*tear*) strappo *m*, rottura *f*.

reopen [rii'oupən] *v* riaprire. **reopening** *n* riapertura *f*.

reorganize [rii'oigənaiz] *v* riorganizzare. **reorganization** *n* riorganizzazione *f*.

rep[1] [rep] *n* (*coll*) teatro stabile, compagnia stabile *f*.

rep[2] [rep] *n* (*coll*) rappresentante *m, f*.

repair [ri'peə] *v* riparare, aggiustare. *n* riparazione *f*. **beyond repair** irreparabile. **in good/bad repair** in buono/cattivo stato. **repairer** *n* riparatore, -trice *m, f*.

repartee [repa'tii] *n* battuta di spirito *f*.

repatriate [rii'patrieit] *v* rimpatriare. **repatriation** *n* rimpatrio *m*.

***repay** [ri'pei] *v* ripagare; (*refund*) rimborsare. **repayment** *n* rimborso *m*; ricompensa *f*.

repeal [rə'piil] *v* revocare, annullare. *n* revoca *f*, annullamento *m*.

repeat [rə'piit] *v* ripetere; (*food*) tornare a gola. *n* ripetizione *f*; (*music*) ripresa *f*.

repel [rə'pel] *v* respingere. **repellent** *adj* repellente.

repent [rə'pent] *v* pentirsi. **repentance** *n* penitenza *f*; (*regret*) pentimento *m*.

repercussion [riipə'kʌʃən] *n* ripercussione *f*.

repertoire ['repətwai] *n* repertorio *m*.

repertory ['repətəri] *n* teatro stabile *m*. **repertory company** compagnia stabile *f*.

repetition [repə'tiʃn] *n* ripetizione *f*. **repetitive** *adj* che si ripete.

replace [rə'pleis] *v* rimpiazzare; (*put back*) rimettere a posto; sostituire. **replaceable** *adj* sostituibile. **replacement** *n* sostituzione *f*.

replay ['riiplei; *v* rii'plei] *n* rivincita *f*. *v* fare la rivincita.

replenish [rə'pleniʃ] *v* rifornire. **replenishment** *n* rifornimento *m*.

replica ['replikə] *n* facsimile *m invar*, copia *f.*
reply [rə'plai] *n* risposta *f. v* rispondere.
report [rə'poɪt] *n* rapporto *m*, relazione *f*; (*school*) pagella *f*; (*rumour*) voce *f*; (*noise*) scoppio *m. v* (*relate*) riferire, fare un rapporto; denunciare; presentarsi.
reporter *n* cronista *m*, *f*; reporter *m invar.*
repose [rə'pouz] *n* riposo *m. v* riposarsi.
reprehensible [repri'hensəbl] *adj* biasimevole, riprensibile.
represent [reprə'zent] *v* rappresentare; (*depict*) raffigurare. **representation** *n* rappresentazione *f.*
representative [reprə'zentətiv] *adj* rappresentativo, caratteristico. *m* rappresentante *m*, *f*; (*pol*) deputato, -a *m*, *f.*
repress [rə'pres] *v* reprimere. **repressed** *adj* represso. **repression** *n* repressione *f.* **repressive** *adj* repressivo.
reprieve [rə'priɪv] *v* graziare. *n* grazia *f.*
reprimand ['reprimaɪnd] *v* rimproverare, sgridare. *n* rimprovero *m*, predica *f.*
reprint [riɪ'print; *n* 'riɪprint] *v* ristampare. *n* ristampa *f.*
reprisal [rə'praizəl] *n* rappresaglia *f.*
reproach [rə'proutʃ] *v* rimproverare, biasimare. *n* rimprovero *m*, biasimo *m.*
reproduce [riɪprə'djuɪs] *v* riprodurre. **reproduction** *n* riproduzione *f.* **reproductive** *adj* riproduttivo.
reprove [rə'pruɪv] *v* rimproverare, sgridare. **reproof** *n* rimprovero *m.*
reptile ['reptail] *n* rettile *m.*
republic [rə'pʌblik] *n* repubblica *f.* **republican** *n*, *adj* repubblicano, -a.
repudiate [rə'pjuɪdieit] *v* ripudiare; (*disown*) disconoscere; (*reject*) respingere. **repudiation** *n* ripudio *m.*
repugnant [rə'pʌgnənt] *adj* ripugnante. **repugnance** *n* ripugnanza *f.*
repulsion [rə'pʌlʃn] *n* ripulsione *f*, ripugnanza *f.* **repulsive** *adj* ributtante, schifoso.
repute [rə'pjuɪt] *v* reputare, stimare. *n also* **reputation** reputazione *f*, fama *f.* **reputable** *adj* rispettabile, stimabile, onorevole. **reputedly** *adv* presumibilmente.
request [ri'kwest] *n* richiesta *f*, domanda *f. v* richiedere, domandare, sollecitare.
requiem ['rekwiəm] *n* requiem *m invar.*
require [rə'kwaiə] *v* richiedere; (*demand*)

esigere, pretendere; rendere necessario.
requirement *n* esigenza *f*, bisogno *m.*
requisite ['rekwizit] *adj* necessario, indispensabile. *n* requisito *m.*
requisition [rekwi'ziʃən] *v* requisire. *n* (*mil*) requisizione *f*, ordine *m.*
re-route [riɪ'ruɪt] *v* deviare.
resale [riɪ'seil] *n* rivendita *f.*
rescue ['reskjuɪ] *n* salvataggio *m*, soccorso *m. v* liberare; soccorrere. **rescuer** *n* liberatore, -trice *m*, *f*; soccorritore, -trice *m*, *f.*
research [ri'səɪtʃ] *n* ricerca *f*, indagine *f. v* fare *or* compiere ricerche, indagare. **researcher** *n* ricercatore, -trice *m*, *f.*
resemble [rə'zembl] *v* somigliare, rassomigliare. **resemblance** *n* somiglianza *f*, rassomiglianza *f.*
resent [ri'zent] *v* risentirsi di, offendersi *or* sdegnarsi per. **resentful** *adj* offeso, sdegnoso. **resentment** *n* risentimento *m*, sdegno *m*, rancore *m.*
reserve [rə'zəɪv] *v* riservare. *n* riserva *f*; (*manner*) riserbo *m*; (*circumspection*) riservatezza *f.* **reservation** *n* riserva *f*; (*booking*) prenotazione *f.*
reservoir ['rezəvwaɪ] *n* cisterna *f*, serbatoio *m*; (*artificial lake*) lago artificiale *m*, bacino di riserva *m.*
reside [rə'zaid] *v* dimorare, risiedere. **residence** *n* residenza *f*, dimora *f.* **residence permit** permesso di soggiorno *m.* **resident** *n*(*m*+*f*), *adj* residente. **residential** *adj* residenziale.
residue ['rezidjuɪ] *n* residuo *m.* **residual** *adj* residuo, rimanente.
resign [rə'zain] *v* dimettersi, rassegnare le dimissioni; (*surrender*) rinunciare a. **resign oneself to** rassegnarsi a. **resignation** *n* dimissioni *f pl*, rassegnazione *f.* **resigned** *adj* rassegnato.
resilient [rə'ziliənt] *adj* flessibile. **be resilient** (*person*) aver capacità di ricupero. **resilience** *n* flessibilità *f*, resilienza *f*; capacità di ricupero *f.*
resin ['rezin] *n* resina *f.* **resinous** *adj* resinoso.
resist [rə'zist] *v* resistere (a). **resistance** *n* resistenza *f.* **resistant** *adj* resistente.
*resit [riɪ'sit] *v* ripetere.
resolute ['rezəluɪt] *adj* deciso, risoluto. **resolution** *n* risoluzione *f*; (*determination*) risolutezza *f*; decisione *f.*
resolve [rə'zolv] *v* risolvere; decidere; (*clear up*) chiarire. *n* decisione *f.*

resonant ['rezənənt] *adj* risonante.
resonance *n* risonanza *f*.
resort [rə'zɔit] *v* resort to ricorrere a. *n*
(*recourse*) ricorso *m*; (*expedient*) risorsa
f; (*holiday*, etc.) luogo di soggiorno *m*,
stazione di villeggiatura *f*.
resound [rə'zaund] *v* risonare, echeggiare.
resource [rə'zɔis] *n* risorsa *f*. **resourceful**
adj pieno di risorse, ingegnoso.
respect [rə'spekt] *v* rispettare, aver
riguardo per. *n* rispetto *m*; (*esteem*)
stima *f*, riguardo *m*; (*detail*) aspetto *m*.
pay one's respects to rendere omaggio a.
with due respect coi debiti riguardi. **with
respect to** riguardo a, quanto a. **respectable** *adj* rispettabile; onesto; consider-
avole. **respectful** *adj* rispettoso. **respec-
tively** *adv* rispettivamente.
respiration [respə'reiʃn] *n* respirazione *f*.
respirator *n* (*med*) respiratore *m*; (*gas
mask*) maschera antigas *f*. **respiratory** *adj*
respiratorio.
respite ['respait] *n* tregua *f*, proroga *f*.
respond [rə'spond] *v* rispondere; reagire.
respondent *n* (*law*) imputato, -a *m*, *f*.
response *n* risposta *f*; reazione *f*;
(*church*) responsorio *m*. **responsive** *adj*
sensibile.
responsible [rə'sponsəbl] *adj* responsabile. **responsibility** *n* responsabilità *f*.
rest[1] [rest] *v* riposarsi; (*place*) posare;
(*stay*) stare, fermarsi. *n* riposo; (*support*)
appoggio *m*. **restful** *adj* riposante,
tranquillo. **restive** *adj* restio. **restless** *adj*
inquieto, irrequieto.
rest[2] [rest] *n* resto *m*.
restaurant ['restront] *n* ristorante *m*, trattoria *f*. **restaurant car** vagone ristorante
m.
restore [rə'stɔi] *v* ristabilire; (*building*,
etc.) restaurare. **restoration** *n* ristabili-
mento *m*; restauro *m*; (*history*) restaura-
zione *f*.
restrain [rə'strein] *v* trattenere, reprimere,
frenare. **restraint** *n* freno *m*, ritegno *m*;
limitazione *f*.
restrict [rə'strikt] *v* restringere, limitare.
restriction *n* restrizione *f*, limitazione *f*.
restrictive *adj* restrittivo.
result [rə'zʌlt] *n* risultato *m*, esito *m*. *v*
risultare, derivare. **resultant** *adj*
risultante.
resume [rə'zjuim] *v* riprendere; riassumere. **resumption** *n* ripresa *f*.
résumé ['reizumei] *n* riassunto *m*.

resurgence [ri'sɔidʒəns] *n* risurrezione *f*,
rinascita *f*.
resurrect [rezə'rekt] *v* risuscitare. **resurrection** *n* risurrezione *f*.
resuscitate [rə'sʌsəteit] *v* risuscitare.
retail ['riiteil] *n* vendita al dettaglio *or*
minuto *f*. *v* (*sell*) vendere al dettaglio *or*
minuto; (*tell*) raccontare, dettagliare.
adv, *adj* al dettaglio *or* minuto. **retailer** *n*
dettagliante *m*.
retain [rə'tein] *v* ritenere, mantenere.
retainer (*law*) caparra *f*.
retaliate [rə'talieit] *v* contraccambiare,
rendere la pariglia. **retaliation** *n* contraccambio *m*, rappresaglia *f*.
retard [rə'taid] *v* ritardare, ostacolare.
retarded *adj* tardivo.
retch [retʃ] *v* aver conati di vomito.
reticent ['retisənt] *adj* reticente, riservato,
taciturno. **reticence** *n* reticenza *f*,
riservatezza *f*, taciturnità *f*.
retina ['retinə] *n* retina *f*.
retinue ['retinjui] *n* seguito *m*.
retire [rə'taiə] *v* ritirarsi; (*go to bed*)
andare a letto; (*give up work*) andare in
pensione. **retired** *adj* in pensione, a
riposo; (*withdrawn*) ritirato, appartato.
retirement *n* ritirata *f*; riposo *m*.
retort[1] [rə'tɔit] *v* ribattere, rimbeccare. *n*
(*reply*) ritorsione *f*, rimbecco *m*.
retort[2] [rə'tɔit] *n* (*chem*) storta *f*.
retrace [ri'treis] *v* (*follow up*) rintracciare;
(*go back over*) ripercorrere; risalire alle
origini di.
retract [rə'trakt] *v* (*withdraw*) ritirare, far
rientrare; (*disown*) disdire.
retreat [rə'trit] *n* ritiro *m*; rifugio *m*,
asilo *m*; (*mil*) ritirata *f*. *v* ritirarsi, indietreggiare.
retrieve [rə'triv] *v* ricuperare; riparare;
rimediare. **retrieval** *n* ricupero *m*. **retriever** *n* (*dog*) cane da riporto *m*.
retrograde ['retrəgreid] *adj* retrogrado.
retrospect ['retrəspekt] *n* in retrospect
guardando indietro. **retrospective** *adj*
retrospettivo.
return [rə'tɜin] *v* tornare, ritornare; (*put
back*) rimettere; (*reciprocate*) contraccambiare; (*give back*) restituire; (*send
back*) rinviare. *n* ritorno *m*; restituzione
f; rinvio *m*; (*profit*) utile *m*; (*report*) relazione *f*, rapporto *m*; (*statement*)
rendiconto *m*. **by return of post** a giro di
posta. **in return for** in cambio di. **return**

match rivincita *f.* **return ticket** biglietto di andata e ritorno *m.*

reunite [riːjuˈnait] *v* riunire. **reunion** *n* riunione *f.*

rev [rev] *v (mot)* imballare. *n* giro *m.* **rev counter** contagiri *m invar.*

reveal [rəˈviːl] *v* rivelare, manifestare. **revelation** *n* rivelazione *f.*

revel [ˈrevl] *v (take pleasure)* trovar diletto; *(make merry)* far baldoria. *n also* **revelry** baldoria *f.*

revenge [rəˈvendʒ] *n* vendetta *f.* *v* vendicare.

revenue [ˈrevinjuː] *n (income)* rendita *f;* *(yield)* reddito *m;* *(of state)* erario *m;* *(department)* fisco *m.*

reverberate [rəˈvɜːbəreit] *v (sound)* risonare, riecheggiare; *(heat, light)* riverberare. **reverberation** *n* riverberazione *f.*

reverence [ˈrevərəns] *n* riverenza *f,* venerazione *f.* **reverend** *nm, adj* reverendo. **reverent** *adj* riverente. **reverential** *adj* reverenziale.

reverse [rəˈvɜːs] *v* rovesciare; *(inside out)* rivoltare; *(mot)* far marcia indietro. **reverse the charges** addebitare al destinatario. *adj* contrario, rovescio, inverso. *n* contrario *m,* rovescio *m,* inverso *m;* *(mot)* retromarcia *f.* **reversal** *n* rovesciamento *m;* *(law)* revoca *f.* **reversible** *adj* reversibile; *(law)* revocabile; *(fabric)* a due diritti.

revert [rəˈvɜːt] *v* ritornare.

review [rəˈvjuː] *n (survey)* rassegna *f,* esame *m;* critica *f,* recensione *f;* *(mil, periodical)* rivista *f.* *v* riesaminare; fare la critica di; passare in rivista. **reviewer** *n* critico *m.*

revise [rəˈvaiz] *v* rivedere, correggere. **revision** *n* revisione *f.*

revive [rəˈvaiv] *v* rianimare, risvegliare; *(restore to use)* ripristinare. **revival** *n* risveglio *m;* ripristino *m;* *(theatre)* ripresa *f.*

revoke [rəˈvouk] *v* revocare.

revolt [rəˈvoult] *v* ribellarsi; *(feel disgust)* provare orrore; *(cause disgust)* disgustare. **revolting** *adj* rivoltante, disgustoso; *(rebellious)* ribelle.

revolution [revəˈluːʃən] *n* rivoluzione *f;* *(turn)* giro *m.* **revolutionary** *n, adj* revoluzionario, -a.

revolve [rəˈvolv] *v (turn)* girare; *(depend)* basarsi (su), dipendere (da). **revolver** *n*

rivoltella *f.* **revolving** *adj (door)* girevole; *(credit)* rotativo.

revue [rəˈvjuː] *n* rivista *f.*

revulsion [rəˈvʌlʃən] *n* ripugnanza *f,* disgusto *m;* *(med)* revulsione *f.*

reward [rəˈwoːd] *n* ricompensa *f,* compenso *m.* *v* ricompensare, rimunerare. **rewarding** *adj* rimunerativo.

rhetoric [ˈretərik] *n* retorica *f.* **rhetorical** *adj* retorico.

rheumatism [ˈruːmətizəm] *n* reumatismo *m.* **rheumatic** *adj* reumatico.

Rhine [rain] *n* Reno *m.*

rhinoceros [raiˈnosərəs] *n* rinoceronte *m.*

rhododendron [roudəˈdendrən] *n* rododendro *m.*

rhombus [ˈrombəs] *n* rombo *m.*

rhubarb [ˈruːbaːb] *n* rabarbaro *m.*

rhyme [raim] *n* rima *f.* *v* rimare, far rima.

rhythm [ˈriðəm] *n* ritmo *m.* **rhythmic** *adj* ritmico.

rib [rib] *n* costola *f.* **ribbed** *adj* a coste, scanalato.

ribbon [ˈribən] *n* nastro *m.* **torn to ribbons** ridotto a brandelli.

rice [rais] *n* riso *m.*

rich [ritʃ] *adj* ricco; *(full)* pieno, abbondante; *(food)* pesante; *(colour)* intenso. **riches** *pl n* ricchezza *f sing.* **richness** *n* ricchezza *f.*

rickety [ˈrikəti] *adj* traballante, instabile; *(med)* rachitico.

***rid** [rid] *v* liberare, sbarazzare. **get rid of** sbarazzarsi di. **good riddance!** che liberazione!

ridden [ˈridn] *V* ride.

riddle¹ [ˈridl] *n* indovinello *m,* enigma *m.* **speak in riddles** parlare per enigmi.

riddle² [ˈridl] *v* crivellare.

***ride** [raid] *n (on horseback)* passeggiata a cavallo *f;* *(on bicycle)* passeggiata in bicicletta *f;* *(in vehicle)* corsa *f,* giro *m.* **take for a ride** *(make fun of)* prendere in giro; *(deceive)* imbrogliare. *v* cavalcare, andare a cavallo. **rider** *n (horse)* cavallerizzo, -a *m, f;* ciclista *m, f;* motociclista *m, f;* *(additional clause)* clausola aggiunta *f,* codicillo *m.* **riding school** maneggio *m.*

ridge [ridʒ] *n (geog)* cresta *f;* *(raised strip)* costa *f;* *(roof)* colmo *m;* *(meteorology)* espansione di alta pressione *f.* *v* corrugare, incresparsi.

ridicule [ˈridikjuːl] *v* mettere in ridicolo, canzonare. *n* ridicolo *m.* **be an object of**

ridicule esser posto in ridicolo. **ridiculous** *adj* ridicolo, assurdo.

rife [raif] *adj* diffuso, corrente.

rifle¹ ['raifl] *n* fucile *m*. **rifle-range** *n* poligono di tiro *m*.

rifle² ['raifl] *v* svaligiare. **rifle through** rovistare *or* frugare in.

rift [rift] *n* crepa *f*, spacco *m*; (*in relations*) disaccordo *m*, screzio *m*; (*geol*) falda *f*.

rig [rig] *n* (*naut*) attrezzatura *f*; (*industry*) impianto *m*; (*fraudulent dealing*) broglio *m*, manipolazione *f*. *v* attrezzare; (*equip*) montare; manipolare, manovrare.

right [rait] *adj* corretto, giusto; (*geom*) retto; (*not left*) destro. **be right** aver ragione. **right-angled** *adj* ad angolo retto. **right-hand man** braccio destro *m*. **right wing** (*pol*) destra *f*. **right-winger** *n* persona di destra *f*. *n* bene *m*, giusto *m*; (*law*) diritto *m*; (*not left*) destra *f*. **right of way** (*vehicles*) precedenza *f*; (*law*) servitù di passaggio *f*; (*path*) passaggio pubblico *m*. *adv* bene; (*exactly*) proprio; direttamente; completamente; (*direction*) a destra. **right away** subito. *v* (*restore to position*) raddrizzare; (*correct*) aggiustare, accomodare, metere a posto; (*redress*) riparare. **rightful** *adj* legittimo. **rightly** *adv* giustamente.

righteous ['raitʃəs] *adj* retto, giusto. **righteousness** *n* rettitudine *f*.

rigid ['ridʒid] *adj* rigido, inflessibile, rigoroso. **rigidity** *n* rigidezza *f*; (*stiffness*) rigidità *f*.

rigmarole ['rigməroul] *n* (*long procedure*) trafila *f*; (*nonsense*) filastrocca *f*.

rigour ['rigə] *n* rigore *m*. **rigorous** *adj* rigoroso, rigido.

rim [rim] *n* orlo *m*, bordo *m*; (*of wheel*) cerchio *m*; (*of spectacles*) montatura *f*.

rind [raind] *n* (*fruit*) buccia *f*, scorza *f*; (*cheese*) crosta *f*.

ring¹ [riŋ] *n* anello *m*; (*enclosure*) recinto *m*, pista *f*; (*boxing*) quadrato *m*, ring *m* *invar*. *v* cingere, circondare. **ringlet** *n* (*curl*) ricciolo *m*.

*ring² [riŋ] *n* (*sound*) suono *m*, squillo *m*; (*inherent quality*) tono *m*; (*coll*) telefonata *f*, colpo di telefono *m*. *v* suonare; (*echo*) risonare, echeggiare; telefonare (a).

rink [riŋk] *n* pista di pattinaggio *f*.

rinse [rins] *v* sciacquare, risciacquare. *n* risciacquatura *f*; (*hair*) cachet *m*.

riot ['raiət] *n* rivolta *f*, sommossa *f*; (*uproar*) baccano *m*, fracasso *m*; (*profusion*) orgia *f*. **riot squad** squadra mobile *or* volante *f*. *v* insorgere, far baccano.

riotous *adj* tumultuoso; (*noisy*) chiassoso, clamoroso; dissoluto.

rip [rip] *n* strappo *m*, squarcio *m*. *v* strappare, squarciare. **let rip** (*give vent to*) dare libero sfogo a.

ripe [raip] *adj* maturo. **ripen** *v* (far) maturare. **ripeness** *n* maturità *f*. **ripening** *n* maturazione *f*.

ripple ['ripl] *n* increspamento *m*, crespa *f*; (*sound*) mormorio *m*. *v* increspare, mormorare.

*rise [raiz] *v* sorgere; (*get up*) alzarsi, levarsi; (*increase*) aumentare, salire; (*swell*) gonfiarsi; (*rebel*) insorgere. *n* salita *f*; aumento *m*. **give rise to** causare.

risen ['rizn] *V* rise.

risk [risk] *v* rischiare, arrischiare, correre il rischio di. *n* rischio *m*. **at the risk of a** rischio di. **risky** *adj* rischioso.

rissole ['risoul] *n* polpetta *f*, crocchetta *f*.

rite [rait] *n* rito *m*.

ritual ['ritʃuəl] *nm*, *adj* rituale.

rival ['raivəl] *n*(*m+f*), *adj* rivale. *v* rivaleggiare, competere. **rivalry** *n* rivalità *f*.

river ['rivə] *n* fiume *m*.

rivet ['rivit] *n* rivetto *m*. *v* rivettare. **riveting** *adj* affascinante.

road [roud] *n* strada *f*, via *f*. **road-block** *n* posto di blocco *m*. **road sign** cartello stradale *m*. **road-works** *pl n* lavori stradali *m pl*. **roadworthy** *adj* atto a prendere la strada.

roam [roum] *v* vagare, errare.

roar [rɔi] *v* (*wild beast*) ruggire, urlare; (*sea*) muggire. **roar with laughter** scoppiare dalle risa. *n* ruggito *m*, urlo *m*; muggito *m*; (*thunder*) rombo *m*; (*laughter*) scroscio *m*.

roast [roust] *v* arrostire; (*coffee*) tostare. *n* arrosto *m*.

rob [rob] *v* derubare, rapinare; (*plunder*) svaligiare. **robber** *n* ladro *m*, rapinatore *m*. **robbery** *n* rapina *f*. **armed robbery** rapina a mano armata *f*.

robe [roub] *n* abito lungo *m*, toga *f*.

robin ['robin] *n* pettirosso *m*.

robot ['roubot] *n* automa *m*.

robust [rə'bʌst] *adj* robusto.

rock¹ [rok] *n* (*stone*) roccia *f*, scoglio *m*; (*support*) rocca *f*. **on the rocks** (*coll: without money*) al verde; (*coll: with ice*) con

ghiaccio. **rock-bottom** *adj* bassissimo.
rock-crystal *n* cristallo di rocca *m*. **rock-salt** *n* salgemma *m*. **rocky** *adj* roccioso.
rock² [rok] *v* dondolare, oscillare; *(baby)* cullare. **off one's rocker** *(coll)* matto.
rocking-chair *n* sedia a dondolo *f*. **rocking-horse** *n* cavallo a dondolo *m*.
rocket ['rokit] *n* razzo *m*; *(reprimand)* cicchetto *m*. *v (increase sharply)* andare alle stelle.
rod [rod] *n* bastone *m*, stecca *f*; *(fishing)* canna (da pesca) *f*; *(piston)* biella *f*.
rode [roud] *V* ride.
rodent ['roudənt] *nm, adj* roditore.
roe¹ [rou] *n (deer)* capriolo *m*.
roe² [rou] *n (hard)* uova di pesce *f pl*; *(soft)* latte di pesce *m*.
rogue [roug] *n (dishonest person)* mariolo *m*; *(rascal)* briccone *m*, furfante *m*. **roguery** *n* bricconeria *f*. **roguish** *adj* bricconesco; *(mischievous)* furbo.
role [roul] *n* ruolo *m*, funzione *f*.
roll [roul] *v* rullare; *(wave)* ondeggiare; *(rotate)* roteare; *(ship)* rollare. **be rolling in money** guazzare nel denaro. **roll out** *(pastry)* spianare. **roll up** arrotolare. *n* rotolo *m*; *(bread)* panino *m*. **roll-call** *n* appello *m*. **roller** *n* cilindro *m*, rullo *m*. **roller-skate** *n* schettino *m*, pattino a rotelle *m*. **rolling-pin** *n* matterello *m*.
romance [rou'mans] *n* romanzo (cavalleresco) *m*; *(medieval tale)* romanza *f*; *(love affair)* idillio *m*, avventura amorosa *f*. **romantic** *adj* romantico; *(fanciful)* romanzesco.
Romania [ruː'meinjə] *n* Romania *f*. **Romanian** *n, adj* romeno, -a.
Rome [roum] *n* Roma *f*. **Roman** *n, adj* romano, -a. **Roman Catholic** *adj* cattolico (romano).
romp [romp] *v* giocare rumorosamente, ruzzare. **romp home** *(win easily)* vincere facilmente. **romp through** *(exam)* superare con facilità. *n* trambusto *m*; *(coll)* cagnara *f*.
roof [ruːf] *n, pl* **-s** tetto *m*. **hit the roof** *(coll)* andare su tutte le furie. **roof of the mouth** palato *m*.
rook [ruk] *n (bird)* corvo *m*; *(chess)* torre *f*; *(swindler)* truffatore, -trice *m, f*. *v* barare, truffare.
room [ruːm] *n* stanza *f*, sala *f*, camera *f*; *(space)* posto *m*, spazio *m*; opportunità *f*. **room temperature** temperatura ambiente *f*. *v* alloggiare. **roomy** *adj* spazioso, vasto.

roost [ruːst] *n (building)* pollaio *m*; *(pole)* posatoio *m*. **rule the roost** fare il gallo del pollaio. *v* appollaiarsi.
root¹ [ruːt] *n* radice *f*; *(cause)* fondo *m*. **root and branch** radicalmente. **root cause** causa prima *f*. **take root** mettere radice. *v* piantare, abbarbicare; *(become fixed)* mettere radici, radicare.
root² [ruːt] *v* grufolare; *(search)* frugacchiare. **root for** *(slang)* sostenere. **root out** scovare.
rope [roup] *n* corda *f*, fune *f*. **know the ropes** esser pratico, saperla lunga. **learn the ropes** familiarizzarsi.
rosary ['rouzəri] *n* rosario *m*.
rose¹ [rouz] *V* rise.
rose² [rouz] *n* rosa *f*. **rose-bush** *n* rosa *f*, rosaio *m*. **rosy** *adj* roseo.
rosé ['rouzei] *n* rosato *m*.
rosemary ['rouzməri] *n* rosmarino *m*.
rosette [rou'zet] *n* coccarda *f*, rosetta *f*.
roster ['rostə] *n* turno di servizio *m*; *(mil)* ruolino *m*.
rostrum ['rostrəm] *n* tribuna *f*, piattaforma *f*.
rot [rot] *v* putrefare, marcire; *(teeth, wood)* cariare. *n* putrefazione *f*; *(rotten matter)* marciume *m*; *(coll: nonsense)* sciocchezze *f pl*; declino *m*. **rotten** *adj* marcio; *(coll: annoying)* seccante.
rota ['routə] *n* turno (di servizio) *m*, lista *f*.
rotate [rou'teit] *v* rotare; *(crops)* avvicendare. **rotary** *adj (motion)* rotatorio; *(tech)* rotativo. **rotation** *n* rotazione *f*; avvicendamento *m*.
rouge [ruːʒ] *n* belletto *m*, rossetto *m*.
rough [rʌf] *adj (coarse)* ruvido; *(person)* rozzo; *(ground)* malagevole, irregolare; *(sea, weather)* agitato, tempestoso; approssimativo; *(unrefined)* greggio. **rough-and-ready** *adj* improvvisato. **rough-and-tumble** *n* zuffa *f*, mischia *f*. *v* **rough it** vivere primitivamente. **rough out** abbozzare. **roughen** *v* irruvidire. **roughness** *n* ruvidezza *f*.
roulette [ruː'let] *n* roulette *f*.
round [raund] *adj* tondo, rotondo; circolare; sferico. *prep* tutto intorno a. *n* tondo *m*, cerchio *m*; *(tour)* giro *m*; *(game)* partita *f*; *(boxing)* ripresa *f*; *(ammunition)* scarica *f*; *(applause)* salva *f*. *adv* in giro. **all year round** tutto l'anno. **show round** fare da guida a. *v* **round off**

completare. **round up** (*number*) arrotondare.

roundabout ['raundəbaut] *n* anello stradale *m*. *adj* indiretto, obliquo.

rouse [rauz] *v* destare. **rousing** *adj* stimolante.

route [ruːt] *n* strada *f*, rotta *f*. **en route** per strada.

routine [ruːˈtiːn] *n* uso *m*, abitudine *f*.

rove [rouv] *v* errare, vagabondare.

row¹ [rou] *n* fila *f*.

row² [rou] *v* remare. *n* remata *f*. **rowing boat** barca a remi *f*.

row³ [rau] *n* (*quarrel*) rissa *f*, lite *f*; (*noise*) chiasso *m*, baccano *m*. *v* litigarsi.

rowdy ['raudi] *adj* chiassoso, turbolento. *n* attaccabrighe *m*, *f invar*.

royal ['roiəl] *adj* reale, regio, regale. **royalist** *n*(*m*+*f*), *adj* realista. **royalties** *pl n* diritti d'autore *m pl*. **royalty** *n* (*people*) reali *m pl*; (*status*) regalità *f*, dignità di re *f*.

rub [rʌb] *v* fregare, strofinare. **rub down** (*clean*) pulire fregando; (*dry*) asciugare fregando. **rub out** cancellare. **rub shoulders** venire in contatto.

rubber ['rʌbə] *n* gomma *f*, caucciù *m*.

rubbish ['rʌbiʃ] *n* (*waste*) immondizia *f*; (*derog*) robaccia *f*; (*nonsense*) sciocchezze *f pl*. **rubbish bin** pattumiera *f*.

rubble ['rʌbl] *n* frantumi *m pl*, macerie *f pl*.

ruby ['ruːbi] *n* rubino *m*. *adj* (color) rubino *or* vermiglio.

rucksack ['rʌksak] *n* sacco da montagna *m*, zaino *m*.

rudder ['rʌdə] *n* timone *m*.

rude [ruːd] *adj* (*discourteous*) scortese; (*unmannerly*) rozzo, grossolano; (*sturdy*) robusto. **rudeness** *n* scortesia *f*; grossolanità *f*; robustezza *f*.

rudiment ['ruːdimənt] *n* rudimento *m*.

rueful ['ruːfəl] *adj* triste, lamentevole.

ruff [rʌf] *n* gorgiera *f*.

ruffian ['rʌfiən] *n* ruffiano *m*, farabutto *m*.

ruffle ['rʌfl] *v* arruffare, increspare.

rug [rʌg] *n* tappeto *m*; (*travelling*) coperta da viaggio *f*; (*bedside*) scendiletto *m*.

rugby ['rʌgbi] *n* rugby *m invar*, palla ovale *f*.

rugged ['rʌgid] *adj* irregolare; rude.

ruin ['ruːin] *n* rovina *f*. *v* rovinare. **ruinous** *adj* rovinoso.

rule [ruːl] *n* regola *f*, norma *f*; (*ruler*) regolo *m*. **as a rule** di regola *or* solito. *v* regolare, dirigere; decidere, (*mark with lines*) rigare. **rule out** escludere. **ruler** *n* sovrano *m*, governatore *m*; (*school*) regolo *m*. **ruling** *n* direttiva *f*, decisione *f*.

rum [rʌm] *n* rum *m*.

rumble ['rʌmbl] *v* rimbombare, brontolare; (*stomach*) gorgogliare; (*coll: detect*) scoprire. *n* brontolio *m*, gorgoglio *m*.

rummage ['rʌmidʒ] *v* frugare, rovistare.

rummy ['rʌmi] *n* ramino *m*.

rumour ['ruːmə] *n* diceria *f*, voce *f*. *v* far correre voce.

rump [rʌmp] *n* groppa *f*, culatta *f*. **rump steak** bistecca *f*.

*run [rʌn] *n* corsa *f*; (*outing*) gita *f*; serie *f invar*; durata *f*. **in the long run** a lungo andare. **on the run** in fuga. *v* correre; (*flow*) scorrere; funzionare; (*colour*) spandere; (*stockings*) smagliare; (*manage*) dirigere. **run away** *or* **off** fuggire. **runaway** *n*, *adj* fuggiasco, -a. **run down** (*slow*) rallentarsi; (*car, etc.*) investire; (*disparage*) parlar male di; (*find*) trovare. **run in** rodare. **run into** (*encounter*) incontrare per caso, imbattersi; (*collide with*) urtare; (*amount to*) raggiungere. **run out** (*supplies, etc.*) esaurirsi. **run over** (*car, etc.*) investire; (*overflow*) traboccare; (*rehearse*) ripassare. **runway** *n* pista di decollo *or* atterraggio *f*. **runner** *n* corridore *m*; (*messenger*) fattorino *m*; (*carpet*) passatoia *f*; (*plant*) pollone *m*. **runner bean** fagiolo (rampicante) *m*. **runner-up** *n* secondo arrivato, seconda arrivata *m*, *f*.

rung¹ [rʌŋ] *n* piolo *m*.

rung² [rʌŋ] *V* **ring²**.

running ['rʌniŋ] *n* corsa *f*; funzionamento *m*; (*competition*) gara *f*. **be in the running** aver possibilità di vincere. **make the running** fare l'andatura. *adj* funzionante; regolare; consecutivo.

rupture ['rʌptʃə] *n* rottura *f*; (*med*) ernia *f*. *v* rompere.

rural ['ruərəl] *adj* campestre, rurale.

rush¹ [rʌʃ] *v* precipitarsi, avventarsi; (*convey with haste*) precipitare, spostare in fretta. *n* corsa precipitosa *f*; (*intense activity*) trambusto *m*; (*haste*) fretta e furia *f*; (*sudden coming*) accesso *m*. **rush hour** ora di punta *f*.

rush² [rʌʃ] *n* (*plant*) giunco *m*.

rusk [rʌsk] *n* biscotto (non dolce) *m*.

Russia ['rʌʃə] *n* Russia *f.* **Russian** *n, adj*
russo, -a.
rust [rʌst] *n* ruggine *f.* **rustproof** *adj* inossidabile. *v* arrugginirsi. **rusty** *adj* arrugginito, rugginoso; (*out of practice*) fuori
d'esercizio.
rustic ['rʌstik] *adj* rustico.
rustle ['rʌsl] *n* fruscio *m.* *v* frusciare,
stormire.
rut [rʌt] *n* solco *m,* carreggiata *f;* (*fixed
habit*) abitudine fissa *f.*
ruthless ['ruːθlis] *adj* spietato, implacabile.
rye [rai] *n* segala *f.*

S

sabbatical [sə'batikəl] *adj* sabbatico.
sable ['seibl] *n* zibellino *m. adj* di zibellino.
sabotage ['sabətaɪʒ] *n* sabotaggio *m. v*
sabotare. **saboteur** *n* sabotatore, -trice *m,
f.*
sabre ['seibə] *n* sciabola *f.* **sabre-rattling** *n*
minaccia di guerra *f,* bravata *f.*
saccharin ['sakərin] *n* saccarina *f.*
sachet ['saʃei] *n* sacchetto profumato *m.*
sack [sak] *n* sacco *m;* (*coll; dismissal*)
licenziamento *m.* **get the sack** (*coll*)
essere mandato a spasso. *v* (*coll*)
mandare a spasso.
sacrament ['sakrəmənt] *n* sacramento *m.*
sacramental *adj* sacramentale.
sacred ['seikrid] *adj* sacro, sacrosanto.
sacrifice ['sakrifais] *n* sacrificio *m;*
(*comm*) perdita *f. v* sacrificare; (*comm*)
vendere sottocosto.
sacrilege ['sakrəlidʒ] *n* sacrilegio *m.* **sacrilegious** *adj* sacrilego (*m pl* -ghi).
sad [sad] *adj* triste. **sadden** *v* rattristare.
sadness *n* tristezza *f.*
saddle ['sadl] *n* sella *f. v* sellare.
sadism ['seidizəm] *n* sadismo *m.* **sadist** *n*
sadico, -a *m, f.* **sadistic** *adj* sadico.
safe [seif] *adj* sicuro; (*unharmed*) salvo;
innocuo. **safe and sound** sano e salvo.
safe-conduct *n* salvacondotto *m.* **safeguard** *v* salvaguardare; proteggere. **safe
keeping** custodia *f. n* cassaforte *f.* **safety**
n sicurezza *f,* salvezza *f.* **safety-belt** *n* cintura di sicurezza *f.* **safety-catch** *n* sicura
f. **safety-pin** *n* spillo di sicurezza *m.*
saffron ['safrən] *n* zafferano *m.*

sag [sag] *v* incurvarsi, piegarsi.
saga ['saɪgə] *n* saga *f.*
sage[1] [seidʒ] *n, adj* saggio, -a. **sagacious**
adj sagace, avveduto.
sage[2] [seidʒ] *n* (*herb*) salvia *f.*
Sagittarius [sadʒi'teəriəs] *n* Sagittario *m.*
sago ['seigou] *n* sagù *m.*
said [sed] *V* say.
sail [seil] *v* navigare; (*leave*) salpare. *n*
vela *f.* **sailcloth** *n* tela olona *f.* **sailing** *n*
vela *f,* sport della vela *m.* **sailing boat**
barca a vela *f.* **sailor** *n* marinaio *m.*
saint [seint] *n* santo, -a *m, f. adj* santo.
saintly *adj* santo, pio.
sake [seik] *n* beneficio *m,* interesse *m,*
bene *m.* **for God's sake** per l'amor di
Dio. **for the sake of** (*in order to*) tanto
per. **for your own sake** per il tuo bene.
salad ['saləd] *n* insalata *f.*
salami [sə'laɪmi] *n* salame *m.*
salary ['saləri] *n* stipendio *m.*
sale [seil] *n* vendita *f;* (*clearance*) liquidazione *f,* saldo *m.* **for** *or* **on sale** in
vendita. **salesgirl** *n* commessa *f.* **salesman**
n commesso *m.* **travelling salesman** commesso viaggiatore *m.*
saline ['seilain] *adj* salino. **salinity** *n* salin-
ità *f.*
saliva [sə'laivə] *n* saliva *f.* **salivary** *adj*
salivare. **salivate** *v* salivare.
sallow ['salou] *adj* giallastro, olivastro.
salmon ['samən] *n* salmone *m.*
salon ['salon] *n* salone *m.*
saloon [sə'luːn] *n* salone *m;* (*ship*) ritrovo
per passeggeri *m.* **saloon car** berlina *f.*
salt [soːlt] *n* sale *m.* **salt-cellar** *n* saliera *f.*
adj also **salty** salato, piccante. *v* salare.
salubrious [sə'luːbriəs] *adj* salubre.
salute [sə'luːt] *n* saluto *m. v* salutare.
salvage ['salvidʒ] *n* salvataggio *m,*
ricupero *m. v* salvare, ricuperare.
salvation [sal'veiʃən] *n* salvezza *f;* (*theology*) salvazione *f.*
same [seim] *adj* stesso, medesimo;
(*unchanged*) immutato. *pron* lo stesso, il
medesimo. **all the same** (*nevertheless*)
malgrado tutto. **at the same time** nello
stesso tempo; (*notwithstanding*) con tutto
ciò. ciononostante. **the same to you!**
altrettanto! **sameness** *n* somiglianza *f,*
uniformità *f,* monotonia *f.*
sample ['saːmpl] *n* campione *m;* (*specimen*) saggio *m. v* campionare; (*test*)
assaggiare. **sampling** *n* campionatura *f.*

sanatorium [sanə'tɔːrɪəm] n sanatorio m.
sanctify ['saŋktifai] v santificare, consacrare.
sanctimonious [saŋkti'mounɪəs] adj santocchio, santerello.
sanction ['saŋkʃən] n sanzione f. v sanzionare, sancire.
sanctity ['saŋktəti] n santità f.
sanctuary ['saŋktʃuəri] n santuario m; (refuge) asilo m, rifugio m.
sand [sand] n sabbia f. v (sprinkle) insabbiare; (smooth) smerigliare. sand-blast v pulire con un getto di sabbia. sandpaper n carta vetrata f. sandy adj (consistency) sabbioso; (colour) biondo rossiccio.
sandal ['sandl] n sandalo m.
sandwich ['sanwidʒ] n sandwich m invar, panino imbottito m. v inserire.
sane [sein] adj equilibrato, sano di mente. sanity n sanità di mente f, equilibrio m.
sang [saŋ] V sing.
sanitary ['sanitəri] adj igienico, sanitario. sanitary towel n pannolino igienico m.
sank [saŋk] V sink.
sap¹ [sap] n (plant) linfa f.
sap² [sap] v (undermine) minare, indebolire.
sapphire ['safaiə] n zaffiro m. adj zaffirino.
sarcasm ['saɪkazəm] n sarcasmo m. sarcastic adj sarcastico.
sardine [saɪ'diːn] n sardina f.
Sardinia [saɪ'dinjə] n Sardegna f. Sardinian n, adj sardo, -a.
sardonic [saɪ'donik] adj sardonico.
sash¹ [saʃ] n (scarf) sciarpa f.
sash² [saʃ] n (frame) telaio m. sash-cord n corda del contrappeso f. sash-window n finestra alla ghigliottina f.
sat [sat] V sit.
satchel ['satʃəl] n cartella f.
satellite ['satəlait] nm, adj satellite. satellite town città satellite f.
satin ['satin] nm, adj raso.
satire ['sataiə] n satira f. satirical adj satirico. satirist n satirista m, f.
satisfy ['satisfai] v soddisfare. satisfaction n soddisfazione f. satisfactory adj soddisfacente.
saturate ['satʃəreit] v saturare. saturated adj saturo. saturation n saturazione f.
Saturday ['satədi] n sabato m.
sauce [sɔːs] n salsa f; (coll) impertinenza f. saucy adj impertinente, sfacciato. sauciness n impertinenza f, sfacciataggine f.

saucepan ['sɔːspən] n casseruola f, pentola f.
saucer ['sɔːsə] n piattino m, sottocoppa f.
sauerkraut ['sauəkraut] n sarcrauti m pl.
sauna [soːnə] n sauna f.
saunter [sɔːntə] v girovagare, andare a passeggio, girare. n giro m.
sausage ['sosidʒ] n salsiccia f, salame m.
savage ['savidʒ] adj selvaggio; feroce, crudele. v assalire, ferire. savagery n selvatichezza f; ferocia f, crudeltà f.
save¹ [seiv] v salvare; (keep) conservare; (put aside) risparmiare. saver n risparmiatore, -trice m, f. saving n economia f. savings pl n risparmi m pl.
save² [seiv] prep (except) salvo, eccetto.
saviour ['seivjə] n liberatore, -trice m, f; (rel) redentore m.
savoury. ['seivəri] adj (appetizing) saporito, gustoso; (piquant) piccante. n piatto appetitoso m.
*saw¹ [sɔː] n sega f. sawdust n segatura f. sawmill n segheria f. v segare.
saw² [sɔː] V see¹.
sawn [sɔːn] V saw¹.
saxophone ['saksəfoun] n sassofono m.
*say [sei] v dire; (declare) dichiarare, affermare. I say! senti! guarda un po'! (let's) say (as an estimate) mettiamo, facciamo. n have no say non aver voce. have one's say dire la sua. saying n massima f, motto m, proverbio m.
scab [skab] n crosta f; (biol) scabbia f, rogna f; (derog: non-striker) crumiro, -a m, f. scabby adj rognoso, scabbioso.
scaffold ['skafəld] n (execution) patibolo m. scaffolding n impalcatura f, ponteggio m; (theatre) palco m.
scald [skɔːld] n scottatura f. v scottare.
scale¹ [skeil] n (thin plate) lamina f; (of fish, etc.) scaglia f, squama f; tartaro m; incrostazione f. v squamare; incrostare. scaly adj squamoso.
scale² [skeil] n (music, math, etc.) scala f. to scale in proporzione. v (climb) scalare; (climb over) scavalcare. scale down ridurre proporzionalmente.
scales [skeilz] pl n bilancia f sing. tip the scales dare il crollo alla bilancia.
scallop ['skaləp] n (zool) pettine m; (shell) conchiglia f; (edging) dentellatura f.
scalp [skalp] n scalpo m. v scalpare.
scalpel ['skalpəl] n scalpello m.

scampi ['skampi] *pl n* scampi *m pl.*

scan [skan] *v* scrutare; (*radar, etc.*) analizzare, sondare; (*poetry*) scandire; (*glance at*) dare una scorsa a. **scanner** *n* analizzatore *m*, dispositivo di esplorazione *m.*

scandal ['skandl] *n* scandalo *m*; (*gossip*) maldicenza *f*, diceria *f*. **scandalmonger** *n* maldicente *m, f*. **scandalize** *v* scandalizzare. **scandalous** *adj* scandaloso.

scanty ['skanti] *adj also* **scant** scarso, insufficiente. **scantily dressed** vestito succintamente.

scapegoat ['skeipgout] *n* capro espiatorio *m.*

scar [skaɪ] *n* cicatrice *f*, sfregio *m*. *v* (*mark*) sfregiare; (*heal*) cicatrizzare. **scarred** *adj* sfregiato.

scarce [skeəs] *adj* scarso, raro. **scarcely** *adv* appena. **scarcity** *n* scarsezza *f.*

scare [skeə] *n* paura *f*, panico *m*. *v* impaurire, spaventare. **be scared** avere paura. **be scared stiff** avere una paura matta. **scarecrow** *n* spauracchio *m*. **scaremonger** *n* allarmista *m, f.*

scarf [skaɪf] *n* sciarpa *f*; (*square*) foulard *m invar.*

scarlet ['skaɪlit] *adj* scarlatto. **scarlet fever** scarlattina *f*. **scarlet runner** fagiolo di Spagna *m.*

scathing ['skeiðiŋ] *adj* sprezzante, sdegnoso.

scatter ['skatə] *v* spargere, disperdere, diffondere. **scatterbrained** *adj* scervellato, distratto.

scavenge ['skavindʒ] *v* (*streets*) spazzare; (*zool*) nutrirsi di cadaveri. **scavenger** *n* (*street cleaner*) spazzino *m*; (*zool*) animale necrofago *m.*

scene [siɪn] *n* scena *f*, spettacolo *m*. **scenario** *n* scenario *m.*

scenery ['siɪnəri] *n* (*landscape*) paesaggio *m*, veduta *f*; (*theatre*) scenario *m.*

scent [sent] *n* profumo *m*, odore *m*; (*track*) pista *f*. **throw off the scent** far perdere la traccia. *v* (*detect*) fiutare; (*perfume*) profumare.

sceptic ['skeptik] *n* scettico, -a *m, f*. **sceptical** *adj* scettico. **scepticism** *n* scetticismo *m.*

sceptre ['septə] *n* scettro *m.*

schedule ['ʃedjuɪl] *n* programma *m*; (*timetable*) orario *m*; lista *f*, specchietto *m*. **according to schedule** secondo il previsto

or programma. *v* programmare; (*list*) elencare.

scheme [skiɪm] *n* schema *m*, progetto *m*, piano *m*; intrigo (*pl* -ghi) *m*, trama *f*. *v* progettare; tramare. **schematic** *adj* schematico.

schizophrenia [ˌskitsə'friɪniə] *n* schizofrenia *f*. **schizophrenic** *n, adj* schizofrenico, -a.

scholar ['skolə] *n* persona erudita *f*, studioso, -a *m, f*; studente, -essa *m, f*. **scholarly** *adj* erudito, dotto. **scholarship** *n* erudizione *f*; studio *m*; (*award*) borsa di studio *f.*

scholastic [skə'lastik] *adj* scolastico.

school[1] [skuɪl] *n* scuola *f*. **schoolboy** *n* scolaro *m*. **schoolfellow** *n* compagno, -a di scuola *m, f*. **schoolgirl** *n* scolara *f*. **schoolmaster** *n* maestro *m*; insegnante *m*. **schoolmistress** *n* maestra *f*, insegnante *f*. *v* istruire, ammaestrare.

school[2] [skuɪl] *n* (*of fish*) banco *m*, frotta *f.*

schooner ['skuɪnə] *n* goletta *f.*

sciatica [sai'atikə] *n* sciatica *f*. **sciatic** *adj* sciatico.

science ['saiəns] *n* scienza *f*. **science fiction** fantascienza *f*. **scientific** *adj* scientifico. **scientist** *n* scienziato, -a *m, f.*

scissors ['sizəz] *pl n* forbici *f pl.*

scoff[1] [skof] *v* (*mock*) beffare, schernire. *n* beffa *f.*

scoff[2] [skof] *v* (*coll: eat*) pappare.

scold [skould] *v* sgridare, rimproverare. **scolding** *n* sgridata *f*, lavata di capo *f.*

scone [skon] *n* focaccia *f.*

scoop [skuɪp] *n* (*kitchen*) mestolo *m*; (*dredge*) benna *f*; (*coll*) colpo *m*. *v* scavare. **scoop out** scodellare. **scoop up** raccogliere, tirar su.

scooter ['skuɪtə] *n* motoretta *f*, scooter *m invar*; (*child's*) monopattino *m.*

scope [skoup] *n* (*extent*) portata *f*; opportunità *f*; possibilità *f*; (*space for activity*) campo libero *m.*

scorch [skoɪtʃ] *n* scottatura *f*. *v* abbruciacchiare. **scorcher** *n* (*coll*) giornata caldissima *f.*

score [skoɪ] *n* (*sport*) punteggio *m*; (*account*) conto *m*; (*debt*) debito *m*; (*ground*) causa *f*; (*music*) partitura *f*. **scoreboard** *n* tabellone *m*. *v* (*sport*) segnare; (*points*) notare; marcare; (*notches*) intaccare; orchestrare. **score off** aver la meglio su.

scorn [skoɪn] *n* disprezzo *m*, sdegno *m*. *v* sdegnare, sprezzare. **scornful** *adj* sdegnoso, sprezzante.

Scorpio ['skoɪpiou] *n* Scorpione *m*.

scorpion ['skoɪpiən] *n* scorpione *m*.

scotch [skotʃ] *v* sopprimere.

Scotland ['skotlənd] *n* Scozia *f*. **Scot** *n* scozzese *m*, *f*. **Scotch** *n* (*whisky*) scotch *m* *invar*, whisky scozzese *m*. **Scottish** *or* **Scots** *adj* scozzese.

scoundrel ['skaundrəl] *n* furfante *m*, mascalzone *m*.

scour[1] [skauə] *v* (*clean*) pulire sfregando; (*rub*) fregare, forbire.

scour[2] [skauə] *v* (*search*) perlustrare.

scout [skaut] *v* esplorare, perlustrare. *n* (*mil*) vedetta *f*; (*boy*) giovane esploratore *m*; osservatore *m*.

scowl [skaul] *n* cipiglio *m*, guardataccia *f*. *v* accigliarsi.

scramble ['skrambl] *v* (*move hastily*) sgambettare; (*climb*) arrampicarsi; (*struggle*) azzuffarsi, battagliare; (*radio, etc.*) disturbare. **scrambled eggs** uova strapazzate *f pl*. *n* confusione *f*, parapiglia *f*; (*struggle*) lotta *f*.

scrap [skrap] *n* (*small piece*) pezzetto *m*, frammento *m*; (*metal*) rottame *m*. **scrapbook** *n* album *m invar*. **scraps** *pl n* rifiuti *m pl*; (*leftovers*) avanzi *m pl*, rimasugli *m pl*. *v* scartare, mettere fuori servizio. **scrappy** *adj* frammentario.

scrape [skreip] *v* raschiare, grattare. **scrape through** cavarsela; (*exam*) passare per il buco della serratura. **scrape together** racimolare, raccogliere. *n* (*embarrassing situation*) impaccio *m*.

scratch [skratʃ] *v* graffiare, grattare; cancellare; (*withdraw*) ritirarsi. *n* graffiatura *f*. **from scratch** da zero. **up to scratch** all'altezza della situazione.

scrawl [skroɪl] *n* scarabocchio *m*. *v* scarabocchiare.

scream [skriɪm] *v* strillare. *n* strillo *m*; (*coll: funny person*) spasso *m*.

screech [skriɪtʃ] *v* stridere, cigolare. *n* strido *m* (*pl* -a *f*).

screen [skriɪn] *n* paravento *m*; (*shelter*) riparo *m*; (*film, etc.*) schermo *m*. *v* (*hide*) nascondere; (*protect*) proteggere; (*check*) vagliare; (*cinema*) proiettare.

screw [skruɪ] *n* vite *f*. **screwdriver** *n* cacciavite *m invar*. *v* avvitare. **screw up one's courage** farsi coraggio.

scribble ['skribl] *n* sgorbio *m*. *v*

scribacchiare. **scribbler** *n* scribacchino, -a *m*, *f*.

script [skript] *n* (*handwriting*) scrittura *f*; manuscritto *m*; (*theatre*) copione *m*.

Scripture ['skriptʃə] *n* Sacra Scrittura *f*, Bibbia *f*.

scroll [skroul] *n* (*roll*) rotolo *m*; (*ornament*) voluta *f*.

scrounge [skraundʒ] (*coll*) *v* scroccare. **scrounger** *n* scroccone, -a *m*, *f*.

scrub[1] [skrʌb] *v* lavare *or* pulire fregando forte. **scrubbing brush** spazzola dura *f*, spazzolone per lavare *m*.

scrub[2] [skrʌb] *n* (*bush*) macchia *f*.

scruffy ['skrʌfi] *adj* trasandato.

scruple ['skruɪpl] *n* scrupolo *m*. **scrupulous** *adj* scrupoloso.

scrutiny ['skruɪtəni] *n* esame accurato *m*. **scrutinize** *v* esaminare accuratamente.

scuffle ['skʌfl] *n* tafferuglio *m*. *v* azzuffarsi.

scullery ['skʌləri] *n* retrocucina *f*.

sculpt [skʌlpt] *v* scolpire. **sculptor** *n* scultore *m*. **sculptress** *n* scultrice *f*. **sculptural** *adj* scultorio. **sculpture** *n* scultura *f*.

scum [skʌm] *n* (*on liquids*) schiuma *f*; (*on metals*) scoria *f*; (*worthless people*) feccia *f*.

scurf [skəɪf] *n* forfora *f*. **scurfy** *adj* forforoso.

scurrilous ['skʌriləs] *adj* scurrile.

scurvy ['skəɪvi] *n* scorbuto *m*.

scuttle[1] ['skʌtl] *n* (*for coal*) secchio da carbone *m*.

scuttle[2] ['skʌtl] *v* (*run*) scorrazzare.

scuttle[3] ['skʌtl] *v* (*sink*) affondare.

scythe [saið] *n* falce *f*. *v* falciare.

sea [siɪ] *n* mare *m*. **at sea** in mare; perplesso. **by sea** per mare. **put out to sea** prendere il largo.

sea bed *n* fondo del mare *m*.

seafaring ['siɪˌfeəriŋ] *adj* navigatore, -trice; marinaro. **seafarer** *n* navigatore *m*.

seafood ['siɪfuɪd] *n* frutti di mare *m pl*.

sea front *n* marina *f*.

seagoing ['siɪgouiŋ] *adj* d'alto mare.

sea-gull *n* gabbiano *m*.

sea-horse *n* cavalluccio marino *m*.

seal[1] [siɪl] *n* (*stamp*) sigillo *m*; chiusura *f*. *v* sigillare; (*close*) chiudere. **sealing wax** ceralacca *f*.

seal[2] [siɪl] *n* (*animal*) foca *f*. **sealskin** *n* pelle di foca *f*.

sea-level *n* livello del mare *m*.
sea-lion *n* leone marino *m*.
seam [siːm] *n* cucitura *f*, giuntura *f*; (*geol*) vena *f*. *v* cucire.
seaman ['siːmən] *n* marinaio *m*.
search [səːtʃ] *v* frugare, rovistare. *n* (*act*) ricerca *f*; esame minuto *m*; (*for something hidden*) perquisizione *f*. **searchlight** *n* proiettore *m*. **search-party** *n* squadra di ricerca *f*. **search-warrant** *n* mandato di perquisizione *m*. **searching** *adj* (*careful*) minuzioso; (*observing*) indagatore, -trice *m, f*.
seashore ['siːʃoɪ] *n* spiaggia *f*, costa *f*.
seasick ['siːsik] *adj* **be seasick** avere il mal di mare. **seasickness** *n* mal di mare *m*.
seaside ['siːsaid] *n* **at** *or* **to the seaside** al mare.
season ['siːzn] *n* stagione *f*. **season ticket** abbonamento *m*. *v* (*wood*) stagionare; (*spice*) condire. **seasonable** *adj* (*timely*) opportuno. **seasoning** *n* condimento *m*.
seat [siːt] *n* sedile *m*; (*chair*) sedia *f*; (*place*) posto *m*; (*coll: behind*) sedere *m*; (*location*) sede *f*. **take a seat** accomodarsi. *v* (*cause to sit*) far sedere; (*provide with seat*) provvedere di posti (a sedere).
seaweed ['siːwiːd] *n* alga *f*.
seaworthy ['siːwəɪði] *adj* atto a tenere il mare.
secluded [si'kluːdid] *adj* isolato, appartato. **seclusion** *n* isolamento *m*.
second ['sekənd] *n* secondo *m*; (*day*) due *m*; (*gear*) seconda *f*. *adj* secondo. **on second thoughts** ripensandoci bene. **second-hand** *adj* di seconda mano. **second-rate** *adj* mediocre. **second sight** chiaroveggenza *f*.
secondary ['sekəndəri] *adj* secondario.
secret ['siːkrit] *nm, adj* segreto. **top secret** *adj* riservatissimo. **secrecy** *n* segretezza *f*. **secretive** *adj* riservato, reticente.
secretary ['sekrətəri] *n* segretario, -a *m, f*. **secretarial** *adj* segretariale. **secretariat** *n* segreteria *f*, segretariato *m*.
secrete [si'kriːt] *v* (*biol*) secernere; (*conceal*) celare. **secretion** *n* secrezione *f*.
sect [sekt] *n* setta *f*. **sectarian** *adj* settario.
section ['sekʃən] *n* sezione *f*, parte *f*.
sector ['sektə] *n* settore *m*.
secular ['sekjulə] *adj* secolare; profano; laico.
secure [si'kjuə] *adj* sicuro; solido. *v* mettere al sicuro, assicurare; garantire;

procurarsi. **security** *n* sicurezza *f*, garanzia *f*. **securities** *pl n* titoli *m pl*, obbligazioni *f pl*.
sedate [si'deit] *adj* pacato, posato. . *v* calmare, tranquillizzare. **sedative** *n* sedativo *m*; calmante *m*.
sediment ['sedimənt] *n* sedimento *m*. **sedimentation** *n* sedimentazione *f*.
seduce [si'djuːs] *v* sedurre. **seducer** *n* seduttore, -trice *m, f*. **seduction** *n* seduzione *f*. **seductive** *adj* seducente.
see[1] [siː] *v* vedere. **see about** *or* **to** occuparsi di. **see home** accompagnare a casa. **see through** penetrare.
see[2] [siː] *n* (*bishop's*) diocesi *f*. **Holy See** Santa Sede *f*.
seed [siːd] *n* seme *m*; (*collective*) semenza *f*. **go to seed** (*bot*) sementire; (*decay*) scadere, declinare. *v* seminare. **seedling** *n* germoglio *m*, semenzale *m*. **seedy** *adj* (*shabby*) malconcio; indisposto.
seek [siːk] *v* cercare.
seem [siːm] *v* sembrare, parere. **seeming** *adj* apparente.
seen [siːn] *V* **see**[1].
seep [siːp] *v* infiltrare.
seesaw ['siːsoɪ] *n* altalena (a bilico) *f*. *adj* oscillante. *v* altalenare.
seethe [siːð] *v* bollire; (*be agitated*) fremere. **seethe with rage** fremere di rabbia.
segment ['segmənt] *n* segmento *m*, sezione *f*.
segregate ['segrigeit] *v* segregare. **segregation** *n* segregazione *f*.
seize [siːz] *v* (*grasp*) afferrare; (*by force*) impadronirsi di; confiscare. **seize up** grippare, ingranarsi. **seizure** *n* confisca *f*; conquista *f*; (*med*) attacco *m*.
seldom ['seldəm] *adv* raramente, di rado.
select [sə'lekt] *adj* scelto, distinto. *v* scegliere. **selection** *n* selezione *f*, scelta *f*. **selective** *adj* selettivo. **selectivity** *n* selettività *f*.
self [self] *n* io *m*, persona *f*.
self-assured *adj* sicuro di sè. **self-assurance** sicurezza di sè *f*.
self-centred *adj* egocentrico, egoista.
self-confident *adj* sicuro di sè. **self-confidence** *n* fiducia in sè.
self-conscious *adj* impacciato. **self-consciousness** *n* impaccio *m*.
self-contained *adj* (*not shared*) indipendente; (*uncommunicative*) riservato; (*self-sufficient*) autosufficiente.

self-critical *adj* autocritico. **self-criticism** *n* autocritica *f.*
self-defence *n* autodifesa *f*; (*law*) legittima difesa *f.*
self-discipline *n* autodisciplina *f.*
self-employed *adj* be self-employed lavorare in proprio.
self-evident *adj* manifesto, palese.
self-explanatory *adj* ovvio.
self-expression *n* espressione della propria personalità *f.*
self-government *n* autonomia *f.*
self-interest *n* interesse personale *m.*
selfish ['selfiʃ] *adj* egoista, egoistico. **selfishness** *n* egoismo *m.*
selfless ['selflis] *adj* altruista, altruistico. **selflessness** *n* altruismo *m.*
self-pity *n* autocommiserazione *f.*
self-portrait *n* autoritratto *m.*
self-possessed *adj* composto, padrone di sè.
self-preservation *n* conservazione *f.*
self-propelled *adj* che si muove per forza propria.
self-respect *n* amor proprio *m.* **self-respecting** *adj* dignitoso.
self-restraint *n* autocontrollo *m.*
self-righteous *adj* compiaciuto di sè stesso. **self-righteousness** *n* autocompiacimento *m.*
self-sacrifice *n* abnegazione *f.*
selfsame ['selfseim] *adj* identico, proprio lo stesso.
self-satisfied *adj* contento di sè. **self-satisfaction** *n* autocompiacimento *m.*
self-service *n* self-service *m invar.*
self-styled *adj* sedicente.
self-sufficient *adj* autosufficiente. **self-sufficiency** *n* autosufficienza *f.*
self-willed *adj* ostinato; (*wilful*) caparbio.
***sell** [sel] *v* vendere. **seller** *n* venditore, -trice *m, f.*
sellotape ® ['seləteip] *n* scotch ® *m invar*, nastro autoadesivo *m.*
semantic [sə'mantik] *adj* semantico. **semantics** *n* semantica *f.*
semaphore ['seməfoɪ] *n* semaforo *m.*
semen ['siːmən] *n* sperma *m.*
semibreve ['semibriːv] *n* semibreve *f.*
semicircle ['semisəɪkl] *n* semicerchio *m.* **semicircular** *adj* semicircolare.
semicolon [ˌsemi'koulən] *n* punto e virgola *m.*
semifinal [semi'fainl] *n* semifinale *f.* **semifinalist** *n* semifinalista *m, f.*

seminar ['seminaɪ] *n* seminario *m.*
seminary ['seminəri] *n* seminario *m.*
semi-precious *adj* semiprezioso.
semiquaver ['semikweivə] *n* semicroma *f.*
semitone ['semitoun] *n* semitono *m.*
semolina [ˌsemə'liːnə] *n* semolino *m.*
senate ['senit] *n* senato *m.* **senator** *n* senatore *m.*
***send** [send] *v* mandare; (*dispatch*) spedire; trasmettere. **send for** (*person*) mandare a chiamare; (*thing*) mandare a prendere. **send in** sottoporre. **send on** (*readdress*) inoltrare. **sender** *n* mittente *m, f.*
senile ['siːmail] *adj* senile. **senility** *n* (*old age*) senilità *f*; (*mental infirmity*) senilismo *m.*
senior ['siːnjə] *adj* più anziano, maggiore. *n* anziano, -a *m, f*; superiore, -a *m, f.* **seniority** *n* anzianità *f.*
sensation [sen'seiʃən] *n* sensazione *f.* **cause a sensation** far sensazione *or* colpo. **sensational** *adj* sensazionale, che fa colpo.
sense [sens] *n* senso *m.* **take leave of one's senses** perder la ragione. **talk sense** parlare sensatamente. *v* intuire, capire.
sensible ['sensəbl] *adj* sensato, ragionevole; (*appreciable*) sensibile. **sensibility** *n* sensibilità *f.*
sensitive ['sensitiv] *adj* sensibile; delicato; (*physiology*) sensitivo. **sensitivity** *n* sensibilità *f*; suscettibilità *f*; delicatezza *f.*
sensual ['sensjuəl] *adj* sensuale. **sensuality** *n* sensualità *f.*
sensuous ['sensjuəs] *adj* gradevole ai sensi, voluttuoso.
sent [sent] *V* **send.**
sentence ['sentəns] *n* (*gramm*) frase *f*; (*law*) condanna *f*, pena *f.* **pass sentence** pronunciare (una) sentenza. *v* condannare.
sentiment ['sentimənt] *n* sentimento *m.* **sentimental** *adj* sentimentale. **sentimentality** *n* sentimentalità *f.*
sentry ['sentri] *n* sentinella *f.* **stand sentry** fare la guardia.
separate ['sepərət; *v* 'sepəreit] *adj* separato; distinto; indipendente. *v* separare. **separation** *n* separazione *f.*
September [sep'tembə] *n* settembre *m.*
septic ['septik] *adj* settico. **septicaemia** *n* setticemia *f.*

sequel ['siːkwəl] *n* seguito *m*; conseguenza *f*.

sequence ['siːkwəns] *n* successione *f*; (*math*, *cards*) sequenza *f*. **in sequence** in ordine successivo.

sequin ['siːkwin] *n* lustrino *m*.

serenade [serə'neid] *n* serenata *f*. *v* fare una serenata a.

serene [sə'riːn] *adj* sereno. **serenity** *n* serenità *f*.

sergeant ['saɪdʒənt] *n* (*mil*) sergente *m*; (*police*) brigadiere *m*.

serial ['siəriəl] *n* (*novel*) romanzo a puntate *m*; (*play*) commedia a puntate *f*. *adj* (*in instalments*) a puntate; (*tech*) di *or* in serie. **serialize** *v* pubblicare *or* trasmettere a puntate.

series ['siəriːz] *n* serie *f*.

serious ['siəriəs] *adj* serio, grave. **are you serious?** dice sul serio? **seriousness** *n* serietà *f*.

sermon ['səːmən] *n* predica *f*.

serpent ['səːpənt] *n* serpente *m*. **serpentine** *adj* serpentino; (*winding*) serpeggiante.

serum ['siərəm] *n* siero *m*.

servant ['səːvənt] *n* domestico, -a *m*, *f*; servo, -a *m*, *f*.

serve [səːv] *v* servire. **it serves you right!** ti sta bene! te lo sei meritato!

service ['səːvis] *n* servizio *m*; (*disposal*) disposizione *f*; (*rel*) ufficio divino *m*. **of service** d'aiuto, utile. **service area/station** area/stazione di servizio *f*. *v* provvedere alla manutenzione di, controllare. **serviceable** *adj* pratico, funzionale.

serviette [ˌsəːvi'et] *n* tovagliolo *m*.

servile ['səːvail] *adj* servile. **servility** *n* servilità *f*.

session ['seʃən] *n* seduta *f*, sessione *f*.

***set** [set] *adj* fisso; (*ready*) pronto; prescritto; deciso; preparato; (*prearranged*) stabilito. *n* serie *f*, assortimento *m*; (*theatre*, *etc.*) set *m invar*, scenario *m*; (*tennis*) set *m invar*, partita *f*. *v* (*place*) mettere, posare; (*fix*) fissare; (*solidify*) indurirsi, rapprendersi; (*sun*) tramontare; (*jewel*) incastonare; (*hair*) mettere in piega; (*bones*) mettere a posto. **set about** (*begin to*) accingersi a; (*attempt*) cercare di; (*coll*) attaccare. **set aside** *or* **by** mettere da parte. **set back** (*hinder*) impedire; (*delay*) ritardare. **setback** *n* regresso *m*, contrattempo *m*. **set free** liberare. **set off** far esplodere; (*depart*) mettersi in viaggio; (*intensify*) mettere in risalto; compensare. **set out** partire. **set up** (*erect*) erigere; (*establish*) stabilire, metter su; (*prepare*) allestire.

setting *n* (*environment*) ambiente *m*; (*jewel*) montatura *f*; (*theatre*) scenario *m*, messa in scena *f*; (*music*) messa in musica *f*; (*sun*) tramonto *m*.

settee [se'tiː] *n* canapè *m*, sofà *m*.

settle ['setl] *v* fissare, determinare; (*pay*) regolare, saldare; (*compose*) sistemare; decidere. **settle down** stabilizzarsi; (*live*) stabilirsi. **settlement** *n* decisione *f*; saldo *m*; colonia *f*. **settler** *n* colonizzatore, -trice *m*, *f*.

seven ['sevn] *nm*, *adj* sette. **seventh** *nm*, *adj* settimo.

seventeen [sevn'tiːn] *nm*, *adj* diciassette. **seventeenth** *adj* diciassettesimo.

seventy ['sevnti] *nm*, *adj* settanta. **seventieth** *adj* settantesimo.

sever ['sevə] *v* staccare.

several ['sevrəl] *pron* parecchi, diversi. *adj* parecchi, diversi; separato; (*own*) proprio.

severe [sə'viə] *adj* severo; grave; (*weather*) rigido; (*pain*, *etc.*) violento, vivo. **severity** *n* severità *f*, rigore *m*; violenza *f*.

***sew** [sou] *v* cucire. **sewing** *n* cucito *m*. **sewing machine** macchina da cucire *f*.

sewage ['sjuidʒ] *n* acque di scolo *or* scarico *f pl*.

sewer ['sjuə] *n* fogna *f*. **sewerage** *n* fognatura *f*.

sewn [soun] *V* **sew.**

sex [seks] *n* sesso *m*. **sexual** *adj* sessuale. **sexuality** *n* sessualità *f*.

sextet [seks'tet] *n* sestetto *m*.

shabby ['ʃabi] *adj* (*of poor appearance*) malconcio, trasandato; (*badly worn*) logoro, frusto; (*contemptible*) meschino.

shack [ʃak] *n* baracca *f*.

shade [ʃeid] *n* ombra *f*; (*colour*) tinta *f*; (*lamp*) paralume *m*. *v* ombreggiare; (*protect*) proteggere (dalla luce); (*drawing*) sfumare. **shading** *n* sfumatura *f*.

shadow ['ʃadou] *n* ombra *f*. *v* ombreggiare; (*follow*) pedinare. **shady** *adj* ombreggiato; (*dubious*) disonesto, losco.

shaft [ʃaːft] *n* (*pole*) asta *f*; (*passageway*) condotto *m*; (*handle*) manico *m*; (*light*) fascio *m*; (*sarcasm*) frecciata *f*.

shaggy ['ʃagi] *adj* peloso, irsuto.

*shake [ʃeik] n scossa f. **no great shakes**
di poco conto. v scuotere; agitare; (tremble) tremare; (disturb) fremere. **shake
hands** stringere la mano. **shake off** liberarsi da. **shake-up** n riorganizzazione f.
shaky adj tremolante; (insecure) malsicuro; precario.
shaken ['ʃeikn] V shake.
shall [ʃal] aux translated by future tense.
shallot [ʃə'lot] n scalogno m.
shallow ['ʃalou] adj poco profondo, basso,
superficiale. **shallows** pl n bassofondo (pl
bassifondi) m sing.
sham [ʃam] adj finto, falso. n finzione f,
inganno m. v fingere, simulare.
shambles ['ʃamblz] n macello m.
shame [ʃeim] v svergognare. n vergogna f.
bring shame on recar onta a, disonorare.
shamefaced adj timido, vergognoso. **what
a shame!** che peccato! **shameful** adj
vergognoso. **shameless** adj svergognato,
spudorato; (brazen) sfacciato. **shamelessness** n spudoratezza f, sfacciataggine f.
shampoo [ʃam'puɪ] n shampoo m invar. v
shampoo one's hair lavarsi i capelli.
shamrock ['ʃamrok] n trifoglio d'Irlanda
m.
shanty[1] ['ʃanti] n (hut) capanna f. **shanty
town** baraccopoli f, bidonville (pl -s) f.
shanty[2] ['ʃanti] n (song) canzone
marinaresca f.
shape [ʃeip] n forma f; condizione f. **take
shape** concretizzarsi, prender forma. v
formare, dar forma a; modellare; adattare. **shapeless** adj informe, confuso.
shapely adj ben fatto, bello.
share [ʃeə] n porzione f, parte f; (comm)
azione f. **shareholder** n azionista m, f. v
dividere; (jointly) condividere. **share in**
prender parte a. **share out** distribuire.
shark [ʃaɪk] n pescecane (pl pescicani) m.
sharp [ʃaɪp] adj (cutting) tagliente; (not
blunt) aguzzo; brusco; (distinct) netto;
(flavour) aspro, piccante; acuto; (alert)
sveglio; (biting) mordace; (shrewd) scaltro. adv bruscamente; (punctually) in
punto. n (music) diesis m. **sharpen** v affilare; (pencil) far la punta a; rendere più
acuto.
shatter ['ʃatə] v (break into fragments)
frantumare; (destroy) rovinare. **shattering**
adj (coll) schiacciante.
shave [ʃeiv] n rasatura f. **have a close
shave** cavarsela per un pelo. v farsi la

barba; (cut closely) radere, rasare. **shaving brush/soap** pennello/sapone da
barba m. **shaving cream** crema da barba
f.
shawl [ʃoɪl] n scialle m.
she [ʃiɪ] pron ella, lei. **she who** colei che.
sheaf [ʃiɪf] n fascio m; (cereals) covone m.
*shear [ʃiə] v tosare; (tech) spezzarsi;
(deprive) privare. **shears** pl n cesoie f pl.
sheath [ʃiɪθ] n guaina f. **sheathe** v rivestire; (sword) ringuainare.
*shed[1] [ʃed] v (let fall) versare; (lose)
perdere. **shed light on** far luce su.
shed[2] [ʃed] n capannone m; (outhouse)
capanna f, rimessa f.
sheen [ʃiɪn] n lucentezza f.
sheep [ʃiɪp] n pecora f. **sheep-dog** n (cane
da) pastore m. **sheepish** adj timido.
sheer[1] [ʃiə] adj (mere) mero; assoluto;
(steep) a piombo; trasparente.
sheer[2] [ʃiə] v cambiar rotta.
sheet [ʃiɪt] n (bedding) lenzuolo m (pl -a
f); (paper) foglio m; (iron, etc.) lamiera f;
(glass) lastra f. **sheet lightning** lampeggio
m.
shelf [ʃelf] n (support) mensola f, ripiano
m; (ledge) sporgenza f; (rock) scogliera f.
set of shelves scaffale m.
shell [ʃel] n (of egg, etc.) guscio m; (of
fish) conchiglia f; (mil) proiettile m;
(hollow casing) involucro m. **shellfish** n
crostaceo m, mollusco m; (pl: as food)
frutti di mare m pl. **shell-shock** n psicosi
traumatica da guerra f. v (mil)
bombardare; (eggs, etc.) sgusciare; (peas)
sgranare.
shelter ['ʃeltə] n riparo m, rifugio m;
protezione f. **take shelter** ripararsi,
rifugiarsi. v proteggere, dare asilo a.
shelve [ʃelv] v (put aside) mettere da parte; (postpone) rimandare, archiviare.
shepherd ['ʃepəd] n pastore m. **shepherdess** n pastora f.
sheriff ['ʃerif] n sceriffo m.
sherry ['ʃeri] n sherry m invar.
shield [ʃiɪld] n schermo m; (armour) scudo m. v proteggere.
shift [ʃift] v spostare, trasferire; (free oneself from) liberarsi da. **shift for oneself**
fare da sè. n turno m; (change) cambiamento m; (artifice) espediente m. **shifting**
adj instabile, mutevole; (sands) mobile.
shifty adj malizioso.
shimmer ['ʃimə] v luccicare. n luccichio
m.

shin [ʃin] *n* stinco *m*.

*shine [ʃain] *n* splendore *m*. *v* brillare, risplendere; (*polish*) lustrare.

shingle ['ʃiŋgl] *n* (*roof*) lastra di copertura *f*; (*stone*) ciottolo *m*; (*extent of pebbles*) ghiaia *f*.

shingles ['ʃiŋglz] *n* erpete *m*; (*coll*) fuoco di Sant'Antonio *m*.

ship [ʃip] *n* nave *f*. **shipowner** *n* armatore *m*. **shipshape** *adv* in ordine perfetto. **shipwreck** *n* naufragio *m*. **be shipwrecked** naufragare. **shipyard** *n* cantiere navale *m*. *v* spedire. **shipper** *n* spedizioniere *m*.

shirk [ʃəik] *v* evitare, scansare. **shirker** *n* scansafatiche *m*, *f* invar.

shirt [ʃəit] *n* camicia *f*.

shit [ʃit] *n* (*vulgar*) *n* merda *f*. *v* cacare.

shiver ['ʃivə] *v* tremare, rabbrividire. *n* brivido *m*, tremito *m*. **have the shivers** (*cold*) avere i brividi; (*fear*) avere la tremarella.

shoal [ʃoul] *n* frotta *f*; (*fish*) banco *m*.

shock[1] [ʃok] *n* colpo *m*; (*encounter*) scontro *m*; (*elec*) scossa *f*; (*med*) shock *m* invar; impressione *f*. **shock absorber** ammortizzatore *m*. *v* colpire; disgustare; impressionare; dare una scossa a. **shocking** *adj* terribile; ripugnante, disgustoso.

shock[2] [ʃok] *n* (*hair*) chioma *f*.

shod [ʃod] *V* **shoe**.

shoddy ['ʃodi] *adj* scadente.

*shoe [ʃuː] *n* scarpa *f*. **shoe-lace** *n* laccio delle scarpe *m*. **shoemaker** *n* calzolaio *m*. *v* (*horse*) ferrare.

shone [ʃon] *V* **shine**.

shook [ʃuk] *V* **shake**.

*shoot [ʃuːt] *v* tirare, sparare; (*hit*) ferire; (*kill*) uccidere; (*film*) girare; (*bot*) germogliare. *n* (*plant*) rampollo *m*, germoglio *m*; (spedizione di) caccia *f*. **shooting** *n* tiro *m*, caccia *f*; (*firing*) sparatoria *f*. **shooting pain** dolore lancinante *m*. **shooting star** stella filante *f*.

shop [ʃop] *n* negozio *m*, bottega *f*; (*in factory*, *etc.*) officina *f*. **shopkeeper** *n* negoziante *m*, *f*. **shoplifter** *n* taccheggiatore, -trice *m*, *f*. **shoplifting** *n* taccheggio *m*. **shop-soiled** *adj* sciupato. **shop-window** *n* vetrina *f*. **shut up shop** chiudere bottega. **talk shop** parlare d'affari. *v* fare gli acquisti, fare la spesa. **shopper** *n* acquirente *m*, *f*. **shopping** *n* acquisti *m pl*. **go shopping** fare la spesa. **shopping bag** borsa per la spesa *f*.

shore[1] [ʃoi] *n* sponda *f*, riva *f*. **on shore** a terra.

shore[2] [ʃoi] *v* **shore up** puntellare.

shorn [ʃoin] *V* **shear**.

short [ʃoit] *adj* (*not long*) corto; breve; (*not tall*) basso; brusco. *adv* bruscamente; (*suddenly*) di botto. **in short** in breve. **nothing short of** addirittura. **run short** scarseggiare. **to cut a long story short** a farla breve. *n* (*film*) short *m* invar, cortometraggio *m*. **shortage** *n* mancanza *f*, carenza *f*. **shorten** *v* accorciare, abbreviare. **shortly** *adv* presto.

shortbread ['ʃoitbred] *n* biscotto di pasta frolla *m*.

short-circuit *n* corto circuito *m*. *v* mettere in corto circuito.

shortcoming ['ʃoitkʌmiŋ] *n* difetto *m*.

short cut *n* scorciatoia *f*.

shorthand ['ʃoithand] *n* stenografia *f*. **shorthand typist** *n* stenodattilografo, -a *m*, *f*.

short list *n* rosa dei candidati *f*. *v* mettere nella rosa dei candidati.

short-lived *adj* di poca durata.

shorts [ʃoits] *pl n* shorts *m pl*; calzoncini corti *m pl*.

short-sighted *adj* miope; (*lacking foresight*) imprevidente. **short-sightedness** *n* miopia *f*; imprevidenza *f*.

short story *n* novella *f*.

short-tempered *adj* irascibile.

short-term *adj* a breve scadenza.

short-wave *adj* a onde corte.

shot[1] [ʃot] *V* **shoot**.

shot[2] [ʃot] *n* sparo *m*, colpo *m*; (*pellet*) pallottola *f*; (*pellets*) pallini di piombo *m pl*; (*person*) tiratore *m*; (*phot*) istantanea *f*; (*film*) ripresa *f*. **off like a shot** via come un bolide. **shotgun** *n* fucile da caccia *m*.

should[1] [ʃud] *aux translated by conditional tense*.

should[2] [ʃud] *aux translated by conditional tense of* dovere.

shoulder ['ʃouldə] *n* spalla *f*; (*road*) banchina *f*. **give the cold shoulder** trattare con freddezza. **shoulder-blade** *n* scapola *f*. **shoulder-strap** *n* spallina *f*. *v* caricarsi sulle spalle; (*assume as burden*) addossarsi.

shout [ʃaut] *v* gridare, urlare. *n* grido *m* (*pl* -a *f*), urlo *m* (*pl* -a *f*). **shout at** sgridare, alzar la voce con. **shout down** far tacere a forza di grida.

shove [ʃʌv] *n* spinta *f*. *v* spingere.
shovel ['ʃʌvl] *v* spalare. *n* pala *f*. **shovelful** *n* palata *f*.
*****show** [ʃou] *n* (*display*) mostra *f*, esposizione *f*; (*theatre*) spettacolo *m*; apparenza *f*; ostentazione *f*. **give the show away** rivelare tutto. **run the show** essere in controllo. **show business** mondo dello spettacolo *m*. **show-case** *n* vetrina *f*. **show-down** *n* (*final reckoning*) resa dei conti *f*. **showman** *n* (*theatre*) impresario *m*; showman *m invar*. **show-room** *n* sala d'esposizione *f*. *v* mostrare, manifestare, indicare, dimostrare. **show off** ostentare, darsi delle arie. **show up** (*reveal*) svelare; (*display*) far risaltare; (*appear*) presentarsi.
shower ['ʃauə] *n* (*bath*) doccia *f*; (*rain*) acquazzone *m*; (*blows*) grandine *f*. **have a shower** fare la doccia. *v* **shower with** tempestare di, inondare di.
shown [ʃoun] *V* **show**.
shrank [ʃraŋk] *V* **shrink**.
shred [ʃred] *n* (*piece torn off*) brandello *m*; (*bit, scrap*) briciolo *m*. *v* fare a brandelli *or* pezzetti.
shrew [ʃruː] *n* (*woman*) bisbetica *f*; (*zool*) toporagno *m*.
shrewd [ʃruːd] *adj* accorto, scaltro. **shrewdness** *n* accortezza *f*, scaltrezza *f*.
shriek [ʃriːk] *v* strillare. *n* strillo *m*.
shrill [ʃril] *adj* stridulo, acuto.
shrimp [ʃrimp] *n* gamberetto *m*.
shrine [ʃrain] *n* santuario *m*, reliquario *m*, tempio *m*.
*****shrink** [ʃriŋk] *v* (*become tight*) restringersi; (*withdraw*) ritirarsi; (*become less*) ridursi. **shrink from** rifuggire da. **shrinkage** *n* restringimento *m*.
shrivel ['ʃrivl] *v* raggrinzirsi.
shroud [ʃraud] *n* lenzuolo funebre *m*; (*mist*) velo *m*. *v* avvolgere.
Shrove Tuesday [ʃrouv] *n* martedì grasso *m*.
shrub [ʃrʌb] *n* arbusto *m*.
shrug [ʃrʌg] *v* scrollare (le spalle). **shrug off** (*minimize*) prendere alla leggera; (*shake off*) scrollarsi di dosso. *n* scrollata (di spalle) *f*.
shrunk [ʃrʌŋk] *V*. **shrink**.
shudder ['ʃʌdə] *n* brivido *m*, tremito *m*. *v* rabbrividire.
shuffle ['ʃʌfl] *v* mettere in disordine; rimaneggiare; (*cards*) mescolare; (*feet*) strascicare.

shun [ʃʌn] *v* scansare, sfuggire (a).
shunt [ʃʌnt] *v* (*rail*) smistare; (*get rid of*) mettere da parte; (*elec*) shuntare. *n* (*rail*) scambio *m*; (*elec*) shunt *m invar*.
*****shut** [ʃʌt] *adj* chiuso. *v* chiudere. **shut down** (*work*) sospendere l'attività. **shut off** bloccare, sottrarsi a. **shut out** non lasciar entrare. **shut up** star zitto.
shutter ['ʃʌtə] *n* (*window*) persiana *f*; (*phot*) otturatore *m*.
shuttle ['ʃʌtl] *n* spola *f*, navetta *f*. **shuttlecock** *n* volano *m*. **shuttle service** servizio di spola *m*, servizio pendolare *m*.
shy [ʃai] *adj* timido, schivo. *v* (*horse*) scartare. **shy from** rifuggire da; (*shun*) schivare. **shyness** *n* timidezza *f*, diffidenza *f*.
sick [sik] *adj* malato; (*fed up*) stanco, stufo. **be sick** essere malato, star male; vomitare. **feel sick** sentirsi male, avere la nausea. **make sick** (*infuriate*) mandare in bestia; disgustare; far vomitare. **sick-bay** *n* infermeria *f*. *n* vomito *m*. **sicken** *v* ammalarsi. **sickening** *adj* nauseabondo, disgustante. **sickness** *n* malattia *f*.
sickle ['sikl] *n* falce *f*.
side [said] *n* lato *m*, fianco *m*; (*lake, etc.*) riva *f*; (*in battle, quarrel, etc.*) partito *m*, parte *f*. **on the other side** d'altra parte. **sideboard** *n* credenza *f*. **side-issue** *n* questione secondaria *f*. **sidelight** *n* (*mot*) luce di posizione *f*. **sidelong** *adj* di traverso, furtivo. **sidestep** *v* schivare. **side-street** *n* via laterale *f*. **sidetrack** *v* distrarre. **sideways** *adv* lateralmente; obliquamente. *v* **side with** essere dalla parte di. **siding** *n* binario di raccordo *m*.
sidle ['saidl] *v* andare a sghembo. **sidle up to** accostarsi furtivamente a.
siege [siːdʒ] *n* assedio *m*. **lay siege** assediare. **raise the siege** togliere l'assedio.
sieve [siv] *n* setaccio *m*. *v* setacciare.
sift [sift] *v* setacciare; (*examine*) vagliare.
sigh [sai] *v* sospirare. *n* sospiro *m*.
sight [sait] *n* vista *f*; (*coll*) spettacolo *m*; (*tech*) mirino *m*. **catch sight of** intravedere. **know by sight** conoscere di vista. **lose sight of** perdere di vista. **sights** *pl n* luoghi d'interesse *m pl*. **sightseeing** *n* turismo *m*.
sign [sain] *n* segno *m*, cenno *m*; (*inscription*) insegna *f*, segnale *m*; (*trace*) traccia *f*. **signpost** *n* indicatore *m*. *v* firmare,

ratificare. **sign off** ritirarsi. **sign on** (*employ*) assumere; (*commit oneself*) impegnarsi.
signal ['signəl] *n* segnale *m*. *v* segnalare.
signature ['signətʃə] *n* firma *f*. **signatory** *n* firmatario, -a *m, f*.
signify ['signifai] *v* significare; (*mean*) voler dire; (*be of consequence*) importare.
significance *n* importanza *f*; (*meaning*) significato *m*. **significant** *adj* significativo, espressivo.
silence ['sailəns] *n* silenzio *m*. *v* ridurre al silenzio, far tacere; (*put to rest*) porre fine a. **silencer** *n* silenziatore *m*.
silent ['sailənt] *adj* silenzioso; tacito; muto. **keep silent** tacere, rimaner zitto.
silhouette [silu'et] *n* silhouette (*pl* -s) *f*.
silk [silk] *n* seta *f*. **silkworm** *n* baco da seta *m*. **silken** *adj* di seta. **silky** *adj* di seta; (*lustrous*) lucido; (*smooth*) morbido.
sill [sil] *n* (*window*) davanzale *m*.
silly ['sili] *adj* sciocco. **silliness** *n* sciocchezza *f*.
silt [silt] *n* limo *m*. *v* **silt up** insabbiarsi.
silver ['silvə] *n* argento *m*; (*cutlery, etc.*) argenteria *f*. *adj* d'argento, argenteo. *v* argentare.
similar ['similə] *adj* simile. **similarity** *n* somiglianza *f*.
simile ['siməli] *n* (*figure of speech*) similitudine *f*; (*example*) paragone *m*.
simmer ['simə] *v* sobbollire.
simple ['simpl] *adj* semplice. **simpleton** *n* sempliciotto, -a *m, f*. **simplicity** *n* semplicità *f*. **simplification** *n* semplificazione *f*. **simplify** *v* semplificare.
simulate ['simjuleit] *v* simulare, fingere. **simulation** *n* simulazione *f*, finzione *f*.
simultaneous [siməl'teinjəs] *adj* simultaneo.
sin [sin] *n* peccato *m*. *v* peccare. **sinful** *adj* peccaminoso. **sinner** *n* peccatore, -trice *m, f*.
since [sins] *adv* (*from then*) da allora; (*subsequently*) poi; (*ago*) fa. *prep* da. *conj* (*period*) da quando; dacchè; (*because*) poichè.
sincere [sin'siə] *adj* sincero. **sincerity** *n* sincerità *f*.
sinew ['sinjuː] *n* tendine *m*; (*force*) nerbo *m*.
***sing** [siŋ] *v* cantare. **singer** *n* cantante *m, f*. **singing** *n* canto *m*.
singe [sindʒ] *v* strinare; (*scorch*) bruciacchiare.

single ['siŋgl] *adj* (*one only*) singolo, solo; (*unmarried*) celibe. **single-breasted** *adj* a un petto. **single file** fila indiana *f*. **single-handed** *adj* (*unaided*) solo, senza aiuto. **single-minded** *adj* deciso, fermo, tenace. **single mindedness** *n* fermezza *f*, tenacia *f*. **single ticket** biglietto di andata solo *m. n* singolo *m. v* **single out** scegliere.
singular ['siŋgjulə] *nm, adj* singolare.
sinister ['sinistə] *adj* (*ominous*) di cattivo augurio.
***sink** [siŋk] *n* lavandino *m. v* (*submerge, go under*) affondare; (*go down*) calare, abbassarsi.
sinuous ['sinjuəs] *adj* tortuoso.
sinus ['sainəs] *n* seno *m*; (*nasal*) seno paranasale *m*. **sinusitis** *n* sinusite *f*.
sip [sip] *n* sorso *m. v* sorseggiare, bere a piccoli sorsi.
siphon ['saifən] *n* sifone *m. v* travasare con un sifone.
sir [səː] *n* signore *m*.
siren ['saiərən] *n* sirena *f*.
sirloin ['səːloin] *n* lombata *f*.
sister ['sistə] *n* sorella *f*; (*nursing*) infermiera capo sala *f*; (*rel*) suora *f*. **sister-in-law** *n* cognata *f*.
***sit** [sit] *v* sedere; posare; (*garment*) cadere; (*exam*) dare; (*be convened*) essere in seduta. **sit down** sedersi, mettersi a sedere. **sit on the fence** non prendere partito. **sit tight** non lasciarsi smuovere. **sitting** *n* seduta *f*. **sitting room** salotto *m*.
site [sait] *n* posizione *f*; (*building*) cantiere edile *m. v* situare.
situation [sitju'eiʃən] *n* situazione *f*; (*post*) posizione *f*. **situated** *adj* situato.
six [siks] *nm, adj* sei. **sixth** *nm, adj* sesto.
sixteen [siks'tiːn] *nm, adj* sedici. **sixteenth** *nm, adj* sedicesimo.
sixty ['siksti] *nm, adj* sessanta. **sixtieth** *nm, adj* sessantesimo.
size¹ [saiz] *n* dimensione *f*, grandezza *f*; (*garments*) misura *f*, taglia *f. v* **size up** valutare. **sizeable** *adj* notevole.
size² [saiz] *n* (*glue*) bozzima *f. v* imbozzimare.
sizzle ['sizl] *v* sfriggere. *n* sfrigolio *m*.
skate¹ [skeit] *v* pattinare. *n* pattino. **skater** *n* pattinatore, -trice *m, f*. **skating** *m* pattinaggio *m*.
skate² [skeit] *n* (*fish*) razza *f*.
skeleton ['skelitn] *n* scheletro *m*.

sketch [sketʃ] *n* abbozzo *m*; (*theatre*) bozzetto *m*. *v* abbozzare; delineare. **sketchbook** *n* albo di *or* per schizzi *m*. **sketchy** *adj* impreciso, superficiale.

skewer ['skjuə] *n* spiedo *m*.

ski [skiː] *n* sci *m*. **ski-lift** *n* sciovia *f*. *v* sciare. **skier** *n* sciatore, -trice *m*, *f*. **skiing** *n* sci *m*.

skid [skid] *v* slittare; (*car*) sbandare; (*plane*) derapare. *n* slittamento *m*; sbandamento *m*.

skill [skil] *n* abilità *f*, destrezza *f*. **skilful** *adj* abile, esperto. **skilled** *adj* abile, esperto; (*worker*) specializzato.

skim [skim] *v* (*milk*) scremare; (*glide over*) rasentare. **skim over** sfiorare; (*reading*) sfogliare.

skimp [skimp] *v* (*food, expense, etc.*) lesinare, risparmiare; (*person*) tenere a stecchetto; (*scrimp*) fare economia. **skimpy** *adj* (*scanty*) scarso; (*mean*) tirchio.

skin [skin] *n* pelle *f*; (*fruit*) buccia *f*, scorza *f*; (*film*) pellicola *f*; (*colouring*) carnagione *f*. **by the skin of one's teeth** per il rotto della cuffia. **skin-deep** *adj* superficiale. **skin-diving** *n* pesca subacquea *f*. **skinflint** *n* spilorcio *m*. **skin-graft** *n* innesto epidermico *m*. *v* sbucciare; (*animals*) scorticare. **skinny** *adj* magro, ossuto.

skip [skip] *v* saltare; (*leap*) balzellare. *n* balzo *m*.

skipper ['skipə] *n* capitano *m*.

skirmish ['skəːmiʃ] *n* scaramuccia *f*. *v* scontrarsi.

skirt [skəːt] *n* gonna *f*, sottana *f*. *v* costeggiare; (*edge*) orlare. **skirting board** zoccolo *m*.

skittle ['skitl] *n* birillo *m*.

skull [skʌl] *n* cranio *m*, teschio *m*. **skullcap** *n* calotta *f*, papalina *f*.

skunk [skʌŋk] *n* moffetta *f*; (*coll*) farabutto *m*.

sky [skai] *n* cielo *m*. **blow sky-high** far saltare per aria. **sky-blue** *adj* celeste. **skylark** *n* allodola *f*. **skylight** *n* lucernario *m*. **skyline** *n* profilo *m*, orizzonte *m*. **skyscraper** *n* grattacielo *m*.

slab [slab] *n* piastra *f*; (*thick piece*) fetta *f*.

slack [slak] *adj* (*loose*) lento; (*inactive*) fiacco; (*negligent*) indolente. *n* (*rope*) imbando *m*; (*comm*) attività ridotta *f*. *v* (*neglect duty*) trascurare. **slacken** *v* rallentare.

slacks [slaks] *pl n* calzoni sportivi *m pl*.

slag [slag] *n* scoria *f*.

slalom ['slailəm] *n* slalom *m*.

slam [slam] *v* sbattere. *n* (*bridge*) slam *m* invar.

slander ['slaində] *n* diffamazione *f*. *v* diffamare. **slanderer** *n* diffamatore, -trice *m*, *f*. **slanderous** *adj* diffamatorio.

slang [slaŋ] *n* gergo *m*. *v* vituperare. **slanging match** battibecco *m*.

slant [slaint] *v* inclinare, inclinarsi; (*news*) presentare in modo tendenzioso. *n* (*slope*) inclinazione *f*; (*point of view*) punto di vista *m*; (*bias*) tendenza *f*.

slap [slap] *n* schiaffo *m*; (*rebuke*) rabbuffo *m*. **slap in the face** insulto *m*, umiliazione *f*. **slap on the back** felicitazione *f*. *v* schiaffeggiare. **slap-bang** *adv* (*right*) in pieno; (*suddenly*) di colpo. **slapdash** *adj* fatto a casaccio, abborracciato. **slap-happy** *adj* incosciente.

slash [slaʃ] *v* tagliare, squarciare. *n* taglio *m*.

slat [slat] *n* stecca *f*, assicella *f*.

slate [sleit] *n* lavagna *f*; (*geol*) ardesia *f*. **have a clean slate** aver la fedina pulita. **wipe the slate clean** ricominciare dimenticando il passato.

slaughter ['sloitə] *n* macello *m*; (*massacre*) strage *f*. *v* macellare, far strage di. **slaughterhouse** *n* macello *m*.

slave [sleiv] *n* schiavo, -a *m*, *f*. **slave-driver** *n* negriero, -a *m*, *f*. **slave labour** lavori forzati *m pl*. *v* sgobbare.

sledge [sledʒ] *n* slitta *f*.

sledgehammer ['sledʒhamə] *n* mazza *f*. **sledgehammer blow** mazzata *f*.

sleek [sliːk] *adj* (*glossy*) lucido; (*smooth*) liscio; (*soft*) morbido; (*unctuous*) mellifluo.

*****sleep** [sliːp] *n* sonno *m*. **go to sleep** addormentarsi, prendere sonno. **have a good sleep** fare una bella dormita. *v* dormire; (*accommodate*) alloggiare. **sleep on** dormirci su. **sleeper** *n* dormiente *m*, *f*; (*timber beam*) traversina *f*; (*on train*) vagone letto *m*. **be a heavy/light sleeper** avere il sonno pesante/leggero. **sleeping bag** sacco a pelo *m*. **sleeping partner** (*econ*) socio accomandante *m*. **sleeping pill** sonnifero *m*. **sleepless** *adj* insonne. **sleepy** *adj* sonnolento.

sleet [sliːt] *n* nevischio *m*.

sleeve [sliːv] *n* manica *f*; (*tech*) manicotto *m*; (*record*) copertina *f*. **up one's sleeve** di riserva.

sleigh [slei] *n* slitta *f*. *v* andare in slitta.

slender ['slendə] *adj* snello; (*small*) esiguo, scarso.

slept [slept] *V* **sleep**.

slice [slais] *n* fetta *f*; parte *f*, porzione , (*spatula*) paletta *f*. *v* affettare, tagliare a fette; (*sport*) tagliare.

slick [slik] *adj* (*sleek*) lucido; (*coll: smooth*) untuoso; (*coll: shrewd*) spigliato, scaltro.

slid [slid] *V* **slide**.

***slide** [slaid] *n* (*inclined plane*) scivolo *m*; (*microscope*) vetrino *m*; (*phot*) diapositiva *f*; (*hair*) fibbia *f*; (*act of sliding*) scivolata *f*. **slide-rule** *n* regolo calcolatore *m*. *v* scivolare. **let slide** lasciar correre. **sliding scale** scala mobile *f*.

slight [slait] *adj* leggero; (*frail*) esile. *n* affronto *m*, dispetto *m*, mancanza di rispetto *f*. *v* mancare di rispetto, ignorare.

slim [slim] *adj* magro, snello; (*poor*) povero; (*scant*) minimo. *v* dimagrare. **slimming** *adj* dimagrante.

slime [slaim] *n* melma *f*; (*secretion*) bava *f*. **slimy** *adj* melmoso; bavoso; (*servile*) untuoso.

***sling** [sliŋ] *n* (*weapon*) fionda *f*; (*bandage*) benda *f*, fascia *f*; (*rifle*) cinghia *f*; (*hoist*) braca *f*. **have one's arm in a sling** portare un braccio al collo. *v* (*throw*) lanciare, gettare; (*suspend*) sospendere.

***slink** [sliŋk] *v* sgattaiolare.

slip [slip] *n* errore *m*, svista *f*; (*garment*) sottana *f*; (*skid*) scivolata *f*; (*plant*) rampollo *m*; (*of paper*) pezzetto *m*. **slip of the tongue** lapsus linguae *m invar*. *v* scivolare. **let slip** lasciar scappare. **slip away** andarsene. **slip-knot** *n* nodo scorsoio *m*. **slip-road** *n* raccordo *m*. **slip up** fare uno sbaglio, prendere una papera.

slipper ['slipə] *n* pantofola *f*, ciabatta *f*.

slippery ['slipəri] *adj* scivoloso.

***slit** [slit] *n* taglio *m*, fessura *f*. *v* tagliare, squarciare.

slither ['sliðə] *v* scivolare.

slobber ['slobə] *v* sbavare.

sloe [slou] *n* (*fruit*) prugnola *f*; (*tree*) prugnolo *m*.

slog [slog] *v* (*walk*) avanzare a fatica; (*toil*) faticare. *n* camminata dura *f*; faticata *f*.

slogan ['slougən] *n* motto *m*, slogan *m invar*.

slop [slop] *v* versare; (*spill over*) traboccare. **slops** *pl n* (*food*) pappa *f sing*; (*dirty water*) lavatura *f sing*.

slope [sloup] *n* pendio *m*. *v* inclinarsi, pendere. **sloping** *adj* inclinato, obliquo.

sloppy ['slopi] *adj* (*wet*) bagnato; (*careless*) abborracciato; (*untidy*) scatto; sentimentale.

slot [slot] *n* fessura *f*, apertura *f*. **slot-machine** *n* (*vending*) apparecchio a gettoni *m*; (*gambling*) slot-machine *m invar*. *v* **slot into** incanalare.

slouch [slautʃ] *v* (*walk*) camminare dinoccolato; (*droop*) languire. *n* andatura dinoccolata *f*.

slovenly ['slʌvnli] *adj* sciatto, trascurato.

slow [slou] *adj* lento; (*late*) tardo; (*clock*) indietro *invar*. *adv* piano, adagio. *v* **slow down** rallentare.

slug [slʌg] *n* lumaca *f*.

sluggish ['slʌgiʃ] *adj* lento, inerte.

sluice [sluːs] *n* chiusa *f*. *v* (*flush*) lavare abbondantemente.

slum [slʌm] *n* quartiere povero *or* basso *m*; (*tumbledown house*) tugurio *m*, catapecchia *f*.

slumber ['slʌmbə] *v* sonnecchiare. *n* (*heavy*) dormita *f*; (*light*) dormiveglia *m invar*.

slump [slʌmp] *n* crollo *m*, caduta *f*. *v* cadere, crollare.

slung [slʌŋ] *V* **sling**.

slunk [slʌŋk] *V* **slink**.

slur [sləː] *v* (*speech*) biascicare; (*disparage*) denigrare; (*music*) legare. **slur over** passar sopra a. *n* affronto *m*; (*blot*) macchia *f*.

slush [slʌʃ] *n* melma *f*. **slushy** *adj* melmoso.

slut [slʌt] *n* (*immoral*) sgualdrina *f*; (*slovenly*) sciattona *f*.

sly [slai] *adj* astuto, scaltro. **on the sly** in sordina.

smack[1] [smak] *n* (*hit*) schiaffo *m*; (*sound*) schiocco *m*; (*kiss*) bacione *m*. **smack in the eye** (*snub*) rabbuffo *m*; (*disappointment*) delusione *f*. *v* schiaffeggiare, schioccare. **smack one's lips** leccarsi i baffi.

smack[2] [smak] *n* sapore *m*. *v* **smack of** (*taste*) sapere di; (*suggest*) ricordare.

small [smɔːl] *adj* piccolo; (*low*) basso; (*humble*) umile; insignificante. **small change** spiccioli *m pl*. **small fry** persone

di poco conto *f pl.* **small-minded** *adj* gretto. **smallpox** *n* vaiolo *m.* **small talk** chiacchera *f,* cicaleccio *m.*
smart [smɑɪt] *adj* (*sharp*) acuto; intelligente; (*shrewd*) sveglio; elegante; brillante. *v* bruciare, sentire un vivo dolore.
smarten *v* abbellire, ravvivarsi.
smash [smaʃ] *n* (*collision*) scontro *m;* (*ruin*) rovina *f,* disastro *m;* (*tennis*) smash *m invar.* **smash-and-grab raid** (*coll*) spaccata *f. v* (*shatter*) fracassare; (*destroy*) annientare. **smashing** *adj* (*coll*) magnifico.
smear [smiə] *v* (*grease*) ungere; (*daub*) spalmare; (*soil*) macchiare; (*defame*) calunniare. *n* macchia *f;* (*slur*) calunnia *f.*
*smell [smel] *n* odore *m,* profumo *m;* (*faculty*) odorato *m. v* sentire l'odore di; (*perceive*) fiutare; (*stink*) puzzare. **smell a rat** fiutare un imbroglio. **smell of** aver odore di.
smelt [smelt] *V* **smell.**
smile [smail] *n* sorriso *m. v* sorridere.
smirk [smɔɪk] *n* sorriso compiaciuto *m. v* sorridere con aria compiaciuta.
smock [smok] *n* camiciotto *m;* (*artists'*) blusa *f.* **smocking** *n* nido d'ape *m,* punto smock *m.*
smog [smog] *n* smog *m invar.*
smoke [smouk] *n* fumo *m.* **smoke-screen** *n* cortina di fumo *f.* **smoke-stack** *n* fumaiolo *m. v* fumare; (*cure*) affumicare. **smokeless** *adj* senza fumo. **smoker** *n* (*person*) fumatore, -trice *m, f;* (*compartment*) scompartimento per fumatori *m.* **smoky** *adj* fumoso, che sa di fumo.
smooth [smuːð] *adj* (*not rough*) liscio; (*unruffled*) calmo; (*not harsh*) gradevole. *v* lisciare, spianare, facilitare.
smother ['smʌðə] *v* soffocare, sopprimere.
smoulder ['smouldə] *v* covare (sotto la cenere).
smudge [smʌdʒ] *n* sgorbio *m. v* sgorbiare.
smug [smʌg] *adj* soddisfatto di sè.
smuggle ['smʌgl] *v* **smuggle in/out** far entrare/uscire di contrabbando. **smuggler** *n* contrabbandiere, -a *m, f.* **smuggling** *n* contrabbando *m.*
snack [snak] *n* (*light meal*) spuntino *m.*
snag [snag] *n* (*impediment*) intoppo *m. v* (*stocking*) smagliare.
snail [sneil] *n* chiocciola *f,* lumaca *f.*
snake [sneik] *n* serpente *m.*
snap [snap] *v* (*noise*) schioccare; (*break suddenly*) spezzarsi; (*phot*) scattare. **snap**

out of it riprenderci. **snap up** non lasciarsi sfuggire. *n* schiocco *m;* rottura improvvisa *f;* (*sudden bite*) morsicata *f;* (*phot*) istantanea *f;* (*short spell*) ondata *f.*
snapdragon *n* bocca di leone *f. adj* istantaneo. **snappy** *adj* irritabile; (*lively*) vivace.
snare [sneə] *n* laccio *m,* lacciolo *m. v* prendere al laccio; accalappiare.
snarl[1] [snɑːl] *v* (*growl*) ringhiare. *n* ringhio *m.*
snarl[2] [snɑːl] *n* (*tangle*) groviglio *m. v* aggrovigliare.
snatch [snatʃ] *v* ghermire, agguantare. *n* strappo *m;* (*scrap*) frammento *m.*
sneak [sniːk] *v* muoversi furtivamente; (*coll: steal*) squagliarsela; (*slang: tell tales*) spifferare. *n* (*coll*) spifferone, -a *m, f;* (*despicable person*) vigliacco, -a *m, f.*
sneakers *pl n* scarpe da tennis *or* ginnastica *f pl.*
sneer [sniə] *n* (*derisory*) ghigno *m;* (*contemptuous*) sogghigno *m. v* ghignare; sogghignare. **sneer at** canzonare, burlarsi di.
sneeze [sniːz] *n* starnuto *m. v* starnutire. **sneeze at** (*coll*) sprezzare.
sniff [snif] *n* annusare, fiutare; aspirare col naso. *n* annusata *f,* fiuto *m.*
snigger ['snigə] *v* ridere sotto i baffi, ridacchiare. *n* ghigno *m.*
snip [snip] *v* tagliuzzare; (*cut off*) spuntare. *n* (*piece*) ritaglio *m;* (*bargain*) occasione *f.*
snipe [snaip] *n* (*bird*) beccaccino *m. v* sparare di sorpresa. **sniper** *n* tiratore scelto che spara di soppiatto *m.*
snivel ['snivl] *v* moccicare; (*whine*) frignare. **sniveller** *n* moccioso, -a *m, f;* frignone, -a *m, f.*
snob [snob] *n* snob *m, f invar.*
snoop [snuːp] *v* curiosare.
snooty ['snuːti] *adj* (*coll*) sdegnoso, altezzoso.
snooze [snuːz] *v* sonnecchiare. *n* pisolino *m.*
snore [snɔɪ] *v* russare, ronfare.
snorkel ['snɔːkəl] *n* respiratore a tubo *m.*
snort [snɔɪt] *n* sbuffata *f. v* sbuffare.
snout [snaut] *n* muso *m;* (*pig*) grugno *m;* (*nozzle*) becco *m.*
snow [snou] *n* neve *f.* **snowball** *n* palla di neve *f.* **snowbound** *adj* bloccato dalla neve. **snow-drift** *n* cumulo *or* banco di neve *m.* **snowdrop** *n* bucaneve *m invar.*

snowfall *n* nevicata *f*. **snowflake** *n* fiocco di neve *m*. **snowman** *n* pupazzo di neve *m*. **snow-plough** *n* spazzaneve *m invar*. **snowstorm** *n* tormenta *f*. *v* nevicare. **snowy** *adj* nevoso; (*colour*) niveo, candido.

snub [snʌb] *n* rabbuffo *m*, affronto *m*. *v* trattare con disprezzo. **snub-nosed** *adj* camuso.

snuff¹ [snʌf] *v* fiutare, aspirare. *n* tabacco da fiuto *m*. **snuffbox** *n* tabacchiera *f*.

snuff² [snʌf] *v* **snuff it** (*coll: die*) crepare. **snuff out** spegnere.

snug [snʌg] *adj* (*comfortable*) comodo; (*cosy*) intimo; (*close-fitting*) aderente.

snuggle ['snʌgl] *v* rannicchiarsi; (*cuddle*) coccolare.

so [sou] *adv* così, tanto; (*to that extent*) talmente. *conj* perciò, quindi. **and so on** eccetera. **if so** in tal caso. **in so far as** per quanto. **so-called** *adj* cosiddetto. **so far** finora. **so long as** finché. **so much** tanto. **so-so** *adv* discretamente, così così. **so to speak** per così dire.

soak [souk] *v* inzuppare, imbevere. **be soaked through** essere bagnato fradicio. **soak in** penetrare. **soak up** assorbire.

soap [soup] *n* sapone *m*. **soap-dish** *n* portasapone *m invar*. **soap flakes/powder** sapone in scaglie/polvere *m*. **soap-suds** *n* saponata *f sing*. *v* insaponare. **soapy** *adj* (*covered with soap*) insaponato; (*like soap*) saponoso.

soar [soɪ] *v* librarsi; (*rise*) salire.

sob [sob] *n* singhiozzo *m*. *v* singhiozzare.

sober ['soubə] *adj* sobrio, calmo. *v* **sober down** calmarsi. **sober up** smaltire una sbornia. **sobriety** *n* moderatezza *f*, serietà *f*.

soccer ['sokə] *n* calcio *m*, football *m invar*.

sociable ['souʃəbl] *adj* socievole. **sociability** *n* socievolezza *f*.

social ['souʃəl] *adj* (*of a community*) sociale; (*disposition*) socievole; (*of polite society*) mondano. **social security** previdenza sociale *f*. **social worker** assistente sociale *m*. **socialism** *n* socialismo *m*. **socialist** *n*(*m*+*f*), *adj* socialista.

society [sə'saiəti] *n* società *f*, compagnia *f*.

sociology [sousi'olədʒi] *n* sociologia *f*. **sociological** *adj* sociologico. **sociologist** *n* sociologo, -a.

sock¹ [sok] *n* (*short*) calzino *m*; (*long*) calza *f*.

sock² [sok] (*slang*) *n* colpo *m*. *v* picchiare; (*punch*) prendere a pugni.

socket ['sokit] *n* cavità *f*; (*eye*) orbita *f*, occhiaia *f*; (*elec*) presa *f*.

soda ['soudə] *n* (*water*) seltz *m invar*; (*sodium carbonate*) soda *f*; soda caustica *f*.

sodden ['sodn] *adj* fradicio.

sofa ['soufə] *n* sofà *m invar*.

soft [soft] *adj* (*not hard*) molle; (*not rough*) morbido, soffice; (*pleasant*) mite, dolce; (*soothing*) tenero; (*water*) dolce. *adv* piano. **soften** *v* ammorbidire, intenerirsi. **softly** *adv* pian piano, adagio, dolcemente.

soggy ['sogi] *adj* fradicio, inzuppato.

soil¹ [soil] *n* suolo *m*, terra *f*.

soil² [soil] *v* sporcare, insudiciare.

solar ['soulə] *adj* solare.

sold [sould] *V* **sell**.

solder ['soldə] *n* saldatura *f*. *v* saldare. **soldering iron** saldatore *m*.

soldier ['souldʒə] *n* soldato *m*. *v* **soldier on** tirare avanti.

sole¹ [soul] *adj* solo, unico.

sole² [soul] *n* (*foot*) pianta *f*; (*shoe, tech*) suola *f*.

sole³ [soul] *n* (*fish*) sogliola *f*.

solemn ['soləm] *adj* solenne, serio.

solicitor [sə'lisitə] *n* avvocato, -essa *m*, *f*.

solicitous [sə'lisitəs] *adj* premuroso.

solid ['solid] *adj* solido, sodo, compatto; (*sound*) serio. *n* (corpo) solido *m*. **solidarity** *n* solidarietà *f*. **solidity** *n* solidità *f*; serietà *f*.

solitary ['solitəri] *adj* solitario, solo, isolato. **solitary confinement** *n* reclusione *or* segregazione cellulare *f*.

solitude ['solitjuɪd] *n* solitudine *f*, isolamento *m*.

solo ['soulou] *n* assolo *m*. *adj* solo, solitario. **soloist** *n* solista *m*, *f*.

solstice ['solstis] *n* solstizio *m*.

soluble ['soljubl] *adj* solubile.

solution [sə'luɪʃən] *n* soluzione *f*.

solve [solv] *v* risolvere. **solvent** *nm*, *adj* solvente. **solvency** *n* solvenza *f*.

sombre ['sombə] *adj* tetro, fosco.

some [sʌm] *adj* del, della; (*pl*) dei, delle; qualche; (*certain*) alcuni. *pron* alcuni, -e; (*before verb*) ne. **somebody** *or* **someone** *pron* qualcuno. **somebody else** qualcun altro. **some day** un bel giorno. **somehow**

adv in qualche modo, in un modo o in un altro. **some ... some ...** gli uni ... gli altri .... **something** *pron* qualcosa. **something else** qualcos'altro. **sometime** *adv* un giorno o l'altro, presto o tardi. **sometimes** *adv* qualche volta; (*now and then*) di tanto in tanto. **somewhat** *adv* piuttosto. **somewhere** *adv* in qualche parte. **somewhere else** altrove.

somersault ['sʌməsɔɪlt] *n* capriola *f*, salto mortale *m*. *v* fare una capriola, fare un salto mortale.

son [sʌn] *n* figlio *m*. **son-in-law** *n* genero *m*.

sonata [sə'naɪtə] *n* sonata *f*.

song [sɒŋ] *n* canzone *f*; (*act of singing*) canto *m*. **for a song** per una sciocchezza.

sonic ['sɒnik] *adj* sonico. **sonic bang** *or* **boom** boato sonico *m*.

sonnet ['sɒnit] *n* sonetto *m*.

soon [suːn] *adv* presto, tra poco. **as soon as** appena. **how soon?** fra quanto tempo? **soon after** subito dopo. **too soon** in anticipo. **very soon** tra breve, quanto prima. **no sooner said than done** detto fatto. **sooner or later** presto o tardi, prima o poi.

soot [sut] *n* fuliggine *f*. **sooty** *adj* fuligginoso.

soothe [suːð] *v* calmare, mitigare.

sophisticated [sə'fistikeitid] *adj* raffinato, sofisticato.

sopping ['sɒpiŋ] *adj* fradicio.

soprano [sə'prɑːnou] *n* soprano *m*, *f*.

sordid ['sɔɪdid] *adj* sordido.

sore [sɔɪ] *adj* doloroso. **sore throat** mal di gola *m*. *n* piaga *f*, ulcera *f*.

sorrow ['sɒrou] *n* dolore *m*, dispiacere *m*; (*cause of regret*) rincrescimento *m*. **sorrowful** *adj* triste, addolorato; (*distressing*) penoso.

sorry ['sɒri] *adj* dolente, spiacente, triste; (*wretched*) meschino, miserabile. **feel sorry for** compatire. **I'm sorry** mi dispiace *or* rincresce. *interj* pardon! scusi! scusate!

sort [sɔɪt] *n* sorta *f*, specie *f invar*. **a good sort** una brava persona *f*. **out of sorts** giù di giri. *v* classificare, raggruppare. **sort out** smistare; (*choose*) scegliere.

soufflé ['suːflei] *n* soufflé *m invar*.

sought [sɔɪt] *V* **seek**.

soul [soul] *n* anima *f*, spirito *m*.

sound[1] [saund] *n* suono *m*; (*noise*) rumore

m. **sound effect** effetto sonoro *m*. **soundproof** *adj* fonoassorbente, impenetrabile al suono. **sound-track** *n* colonna sonora *f*. *v* suonare; (*seem*) sembrare.

sound[2] [saund] *adj* (*not damaged*) sano; valido, legittimo; (*sleep, etc.*) profondo.

sound[3] [saund] *n* (*med*) sonda *f*. *v* sondare; (*naut*) scandagliare.

soup [suːp] *n* minestra *f*; (*broth*) brodo *m*; (*with bread*) zuppa *f*. **be in the soup** trovarsi nei pasticci. **soup-ladle** *n* cucchiaione *m*. **soup-plate** *n* fondina *f*.

sour [sauə] *adj* acido; (*tart, harsh*) acerbo, agro.

source [sɔɪs] *n* sorgente *f*, origine *f*.

south [sauθ] *n* sud *m*; (*of country*) meridione *m*. *adj also* **southern, southerly** del sud; meridionale. *adv* (*direction*) verso sud; (*location*) al sud; (*origin*) dal sud. **south-east** *n* sudest *m*. **South Pole** polo sud *m*. **south-west** *n* sudovest *m*. **southernmost** *adj* il più a sud.

souvenir [suːvə'niə] *n* ricordo *m*.

sovereign ['sɒvrin] *n*, *adj* sovrano, -a. **sovereignty** *n* sovranità *f*.

***sow**[1] [sou] *v* seminare; disseminare.

sow[2] [sau] *n* scrofa *f*.

sown [soun] *V* **sow**[1].

soya ['sɔiə] *n* soia *f*.

spa [spɑː] *n* terme *f pl*, stazione termale *f*.

space [speis] *n* spazio *m*. *v* scaglionare; (*printing*) spaziare. **spaceman** *n* astronauta *m*. **spaceship** *n* astronave *f*. **spacious** *adj* ampio, spazioso.

spade [speid] *n* badile *m*, vanga *f*. **call a spade a spade** dire pane al pane.

spades [speidz] *pl n* (*cards*) picche *f pl*.

Spain [spein] *n* Spagna *f*. **Spaniard** *n* spagnolo, -a *m*, *f*. **Spanish** *nm*, *adj* spagnolo.

span [span] *n* (*hand*) spanna *f*; (*bridge*) arco *m*; (*extent*) portata *f*; (*time*) durata *f*. *v* stendersi attraverso.

spaniel ['spanjəl] *n* spaniel *m invar*.

spank [spaŋk] *v* sculacciare.

spanner ['spanə] *n* chiave *f*; (*adjustable*) chiave inglese *f*.

spare [speə] *adj* di riserva *or* scorta; (*surplus*) in più, disponibile; frugale; (*lean*) magro. **spare part** pezzo di ricambio *m*. **spare room** camera in più *f*. **spare time** tempo disponibile *m*. **spare wheel** ruota di scorta *f*. *v* (*not harm*) risparmiare; (*do without*) fare a meno di. **spare no**

expense non badare a spese. **sparing** *adj* parco, sobrio, limitato.

spark [spɑːk] *n* scintilla *f*; (*gleam*) barlume *m*. *v* emettere scintille, scintillare; (*elec*) accendere. **sparking-plug** *n* candela (d'accensione) *f*.

sparkle ['spɑːkl] *n* scintilla *f*, splendore *m*. *v* scintillare, brillare, risplendere. **sparkling** *adj* brillante; (*wine*) spumante.

sparrow ['sparou] *n* passero *m*.

sparse [spɑːs] *adj* rado, scarso. **sparsely** *adv* poco.

spasm ['spazəm] *n* accesso *m*; (*muscular*) spasmo *m*. **spasmodic** *adj* spasmodico.

spastic ['spastik] *n*, *adj* spastico, -a.

spat [spat] *V* **spit**[1].

spate [speit] *n* piena *f*.

spatial ['speiʃl] *adj* spaziale.

spatula ['spatjulə] *n* spatola *f*.

spawn [spɔːn] *n* (*zool*) uova *f pl*; (*brood*) progenie *f*. *v* deporre uova; (*give rise to*) generare, produrre (in abbondanza); (*derog*) figliare.

*****speak** [spiːk] *v* parlare. **so to speak** per così dire. **speaking of** a proposito di. **speak out** parlare apertamente. **speak up** (*loudly*) parlare ad alta voce, parlare più forte. **speak up for** parlare a favore di. **strictly speaking** per essere precisi. **speaker** *n* oratore *m*; (*pol*) presidente *m*; (*hi-fi*) cassa acustica.

spear [spiə] *n* lancia *f*. *v* trafiggere.

special ['speʃəl] *adj* speciale, particolare; straordinario. **specialist** *n* specialista *m*, *f*. **speciality** *n* specialità *f*. **specialization** *n* specializzazione *f*. **specialize** *v* specializzare.

species ['spiːʃiːz] *n* specie *f invar*, genere *m*.

specify ['spesifai] *v* specificare, precisare. **specific** *adj* specifico, preciso. **specification** *n* specificazione *f*; (*detailed description*) specifica *f*.

specimen ['spesimin] *n* esemplare *m*, modello *m*; (*for test*) campione *m*.

speck [spek] *n* (*spot*) macchia *f*; (*particle*) granello *m*. **speckle** *n* macchia *f*, chiazza *f*. **speckled** *adj* chiazzato.

spectacle ['spektəkl] *n* spettacolo *m*. **spectacles** *pl n* occhiali *m pl*. **spectacled** *adj* occhialuto.

spectator [spek'teitə] *n* spettatore, -trice *m*, *f*.

spectrum ['spektrəm] *n* spettro *m*.

speculate ['spekjuleit] *v* speculare,

meditare. **speculation** *n* speculazione *f*. **speculative** *adj* speculativo. **speculator** *n* speculatore, -trice *m*, *f*.

sped [sped] *V* **speed**.

speech [spiːtʃ] *n* (*faculty*) parola *f*; discorso *m*. **speechless** *adj* muto, senza parole.

*****speed** [spiːd] *n* velocità *f*. **at full speed** a tutta corsa, a velocità massima. **speed-boat** *n* fuoribordo *m*. **speed limit** limite di velocità *m*. **speedometer** *n* tachimetro *m*. *v* andare in fretta. **speed up** accelerare. **speedy** *adj* veloce; (*ready*) pronto.

*****spell**[1] [spel] *v* (*read*) compitare, sillabare; (*write*) scrivere; significare. **spelling** *n* ortografia *f*.

spell[2] [spel] *n* (*magic*) incanto *m*, incantesimo *m*; fascino *m*. **cast a spell** incantare. **spellbind** *v* affascinare.

spell[3] [spel] *n* periodo *m*; (*work*) turno *m*; (*bout*) attacco *m*.

spelt [spelt] *V* **spell**[1].

*****spend** [spend] *v* spendere; (*employ*) impiegare, dedicare; (*time*) trascorrere, passare; (*consume*) esaurire. **spendthrift** *n*, *adj* prodigo, -a.

spent [spent] *V* **spend**.

sperm [spəːm] *n* sperma *m*.

spew [spjuː] *n* vomito *m*. *v* vomitare.

sphere [sfiə] *n* sfera *f*. **spherical** *adj* sferico.

spice [spais] *n* (*cookery*) spezie *f invar*; (*flavour*) gusto *m*, sapore *m*. *v* condire (con spezie); dar gusto *or* interesse a. **spicy** *adj* piccante, aromatico; salace.

spider ['spaidə] *n* ragno *m*. **spider's web** ragnatela *f*.

spike [spaik] *n* punta *f*, chiodo *m*. *v* inchiodare; (*frustrate*) rendere inservibile.

*****spill** [spil] *v* spandere, versare. **spill over** traboccare.

spilt [spilt] *V* **spill**.

*****spin** [spin] *v* (*thread*) filare; (*rotate*) (far) girare. **spin-drier** *n* centrifuga *f*, idroestrattore *m*. **spin-dry** *v* asciugare con la centrifuga. **spin out** prolungare. **spin a yarn** raccontare una frottola. *n* rotazione *f*; (*phys*) spin *m invar*; (*short trip*) giro *m*.

spinach ['spinidʒ] *n* spinaci *m pl*.

spindle ['spindl] *n* fuso *m*. **spindly** *adj* esile, affusolato.

spine [spain] *n* (*anat*) spina dorsale *f*; (*book*) dorso *m*. **spinal** *adj* spinale,

vertebrale. **spine-chilling** *adj* agghiacciante. **spineless** *adj* smidollato, debole.
spinster ['spinstə] *n* nubile *f*; (*coll*) zitella *f*.
spiral ['spaiərəl] *n* spirale *f*. *adj* a spirale. **spiral staircase** scala a chiocciola *f*.
spire ['spaiə] *n* guglia *f*.
spirit ['spirit] *n* spirito *m*; (*drink*) superalcolico *m*. **be in high spirits** avere il morale alto; essere allegro. **spirit-level** *n* livella a bolla d'aria *f*. **that's the spirit!** così va bene! **spirited** *adj* vivace, vigoroso. **spiritless** *adj* (*without vigour*) fiacco; (*not lively*) abbattuto. **spiritual** *adj* spirituale. **spiritualism** *n* spiritismo *m*; (*philos*) spiritualismo *m*. **spiritualist** *n* spiritista *m*, *f*.
*spit[1] [spit] *v* sputare; (*rain*) piovigginare; (*cat*) soffiare. **the spitting image of** ... ... nato e sputato. *n also* **spittle** sputo *m*, saliva *f*.
spit[2] [spit] *n* (*skewer*) spiedo *m*; (*land*) lingua di terra *f*. *v* (*skewer*) infilzare.
spite [spait] *n* dispetto *m*. **in spite of** nonostante, malgrado. *v* far dispetto a; (*annoy*) indispettire. **spiteful** *adj* dispettoso, maligno.
splash [splaʃ] *v* (*spatter*) spruzzare; (*mark with colour*) macchiare, chiazzare. *n* spruzzata *f*; (*sound*) tonfo *m*; (*liquid splashed*) spruzzo *m*; (*patch*) macchia *f*; (*showy display*) sfoggio *m*.
spleen [spliːn] *n* (*med*) milza *f*; (*peevishness*) malumore *m*. **vent one's spleen on** sfogarsi su.
splendid ['splendid] *adj* splendido, stupendo. **splendour** *n* splendore *m*.
splice [splais] *v* (*rope*) impiombare; (*tape*) giuntare. *n* impiombatura *f*; giuntura *f*.
splint [splint] *n* stecca *f*.
splinter ['splintə] *n* scheggia *f*. *v* frantumarsi.
*split [split] *v* (*cleave*) spaccare; dividere, separare. **split hairs** cavillare. **split on** (*coll*) denunciare. **split up** dividersi, suddividere. *n* fenditura *f*; (*into fractions*) scissione *f*; separazione *f*. *adj* spaccato.
splutter ['splʌtə] *v* (*spit*) sputacchiare; (*talk confusedly*) farfugliare; (*splash*) spruzzare; (*engine*) scoppiettare.
*spoil [spoil] *v* rovinare, sciupare; (*indulge*) viziare. **be spoiling for** aver una gran voglia di. **spoil-sport** *n* guastafeste *m*, *f invar*. **spoils** *pl n* spoglie *f pl*.
spoilt [spoilt] *V* **spoil**.

spoke[1] [spouk] *V* **speak**.
spoke[2] [spouk] *n* raggio *m*; (*rung*) piolo *m*. **put a spoke in someone's wheel** mettere un bastone fra le ruote a qualcuno.
spoken ['spoukn] *V* **speak**.
spokesman ['spouksmən] *n* portavoce *m*, *f invar*.
sponge [spʌndʒ] *n* spugna *f*. **sponge-cake** *n* pan di Spagna *m*. **throw in the sponge** gettare la spugna. *v* lavare con la spugna; (*coll: cadge*) scroccare. **sponger** *n* scroccone, -a *m*, *f*. **spongy** *adj* spugnoso.
sponsor ['sponsə] *n* garante *m*, *f*; (*TV, etc.*) finanziatore, -trice *m*, *f*. *v* essere garante di; rendersi responsabile di; finanziare; (*lend support*) patrocinare. **sponsorship** *n* garanzia *f*; finanziamento *m*.
spontaneous [spon'teinjəs] *adj* spontaneo. **spontaneity** *n* spontaneità *f*.
spool [spuːl] *n* rocchetto *m*.
spoon [spuːn] *n* cucchiaio *m*. **spoonfeed** *v* scodellare la pappa a. **spoonful** *n* cucchiaiata *f*.
sporadic [spə'radik] *adj* isolato.
sport [spoːt] *n* sport *m invar*; (*jesting*) scherzo *m*. **be a sport!** sii bravo! **sportsman** *n* sportivo *m*. **sportsmanship** *n* abilità sportiva *f*; spirito sportivo *m*. **sportswoman** *n* sportiva *f*. *v* (*display*) sfoggiare. **sporting** *adj* sportivo. **sporting chance** possibilità di successo *f*.
spot [spot] *n* (*mark*) macchia *f*, puntino *m*; (*pimple*) piccolo foruncolo *m*; (*place*) posto *m*, località *f*. **on the spot** sul posto. **spot check** controllo saltuario *m*. **spotlight** *n* riflettore *m*. *v* macchiare, punteggiare; (*see*) riconoscere, scoprire, osservare. **spotless** *adj* immacolato. **spotter** *n* osservatore, -trice *m*, *f*.
spouse [spaus] *n* sposo, -a *m*, *f*, coniuge *m*, *f*.
spout [spaut] *n* becco *m*, beccuccio *m*; (*chute*) scivolo *m*; (*jet*) getto *m*. **up the spout** (*lost*) perduto; (*in a bad way*) ridotto male. *v* (*discharge*) scaricare, gettare; (*gush out*) scaturire; (*coll; talk*) declamare.
sprain [sprein] *v* (*strain*) storcere; (*wrench*) slogare. *n* storta *f*; slogatura *f*.
sprang [spraŋ] *V* **spring**.
sprawl [sprɔːl] *v* stendersi lungo disteso; (*spread out*) estendersi. **send sprawling** mandare a gambe all'aria.

spray¹ [sprei] *n* (*jet*) spruzzo *m*; (*appliance*) spray *m invar*, atomizzatore *m*; (*hail*) raffica *f*. *v* spruzzare, atomizzare; (*scatter*) spargere.

spray² [sprei] *n* (*branch*) frasca *f*.

*spread [spred] *v* (*lay out*) stendere; (*distribute*) spargere; (*disseminate*) diffondere; (*apply layer*) spalmare. *n* estensione *f*, diffusione *f*; (*cover*) coperta *f*; (*coll: feast*) banchetto *m*.

spree [sprii] *n* baldoria *f*.

sprig [sprig] *n* ramoscello *m*.

sprightly ['spraitli] *adj* vivace.

*spring [sprin] *v* (*rise suddenly*) saltare, balzare; (*move rapidly*) scattare. **spring a leak** aprire una falla. **spring from** derivare *or* provenire da. **spring up** (*arise*) nascere; (*originate*) sorgere; (*jump up*) balzare; (*come forth*) spuntare. *n* (*beginning*) origine *f*; (*source of water*) sorgente *f*; (*season*) primavera *f*; (*coil*) molla *f*. *adj* primaverile, giovane. **spring-board** *n* trampolino *m*. **spring onion** cipollina *f*.

sprinkle ['sprinkl] *v* spargere, cospargere; (*liquid*) spruzzare. **sprinkler** *n* (*watering can*) annaffiatoio *m*; (*fire*) nebulizzatore (antincendio) *m*. **sprinkling** *n* (*of knowledge*) infarinatura *f*.

sprint [sprint] *n* (*sport*) sprint *m invar*; volata *f*. *v* correre di volata, scattare. **sprinter** *n* sprinter *m, f invar*, velocista *m, f*.

sprout [spraut] *v* germogliare. *n* germoglio *m*. **Brussels sprouts** cavolini di Bruxelles *m pl*.

spruce [spruis] *n* abete *m*.

sprung [sprʌn] *V* spring.

spun [spʌn] *V* spin.

spur [spəi] *n* sprone *m*. **on the spur of the moment** lì per lì. *v* **spur on** incitare.

spurious ['spjuəriəs] *adj* falso, spurio.

spurn [spəin] *v* sdegnare; rifiutare.

spurt [spəit] *n* (*gush*) getto improvviso *m*, zampillo *m*; (*burst*) scatto *m*; (*effort*) sforzo *m*. *v* zampillare.

spy [spai] *n* spia *f*. *v* spiare, fare la spia. **spying** *n* spionaggio *m*.

squabble ['skwobl] *v* litigare, bisticciarsi. *n* alterco *m*, bisticcio *m*, lite *f*.

squad [skwod] *n* squadra *f*.

squadron ['skwodrən] *n* squadriglia *f*.

squalid ['skwolid] *adj* squallido.

squall [skwoil] *n* raffica *f*.

squander ['skwondə] *v* sprecare, sperperare. **squanderer** *n* sprecone, -a *m, f*.

square [skweə] *n* quadrato *m*; (*street*) piazza *f*; (*instrument*) squadra *f*. *adj* quadro; (*math*) quadrato; (*corner*) ad angolo retto; perpendicolare; (*settled*) saldato; (*straightforward*) diretto, netto. **square meal** pasto sostanzioso *m*. *v* (*math*) quadrare; (*accounts*) saldare; (*regulate*) mettere a punto; (*coll: bribe*) corrompere. **square up to** affrontare.

squash [skwoʃ] *v* schiacciare, spremere; (*suppress*) sopprimere; ridurre al silenzio, umiliare. *n* (*drink*) spremuta *f*; (*sport*) squash *m invar*; (*crowd*) ressa *f*.

squat [skwot] *v* rannicchiarsi, accovacciarsi; (*occupy illegally*) occupare abusivamente. *adj* tarchiato, tozzo.

squawk [skwoik] *v* schiamazzare. *n* schiamazzo *m*.

squeak [skwiik] *v* stridere, cigolare. *n* strido *m*, cigolio *m*. **have a narrow squeak** scamparla bella.

squeal [skwiil] *v* strillare; (*coll: complain*) protestare. *n* strillo *m*.

squeamish ['skwiimiʃ] *adj* schizzinoso, schifiltoso.

squeeze [skwiiz] *v* (*press*) spremere; (*force*) pigiare; (*embrace*) stringere; (*press together*) comprimere. *n* stretta *f*; (*crowd*) calca *f*; (*comm*) restrizioni *f pl*.

squid [skwid] *n* calamaro *m*, seppia *f*.

squiggle ['skwigl] *n* sgorbio *m*. *v* sgorbiare.

squint [skwint] *v* (*be cross-eyed*) essere guercio *or* strabico; (*glance sideways*) guardare di traverso. *n* sguardo torto *m*, strabismo *m*. **squint-eyed** *adj* guercio, strabico.

squire ['skwaiə] *n* gentiluomo *m*, proprietario di terre *m*.

squirm [skwəim] *v* (*wriggle*) dimenarsi, contorcersi; (*feel embarrassed*) essere sulle spine.

squirrel ['skwirəl] *n* scoiattolo *m*.

squirt [skwəit] *v* schizzare. *n* (*jet*) schizzo *m*; (*syringe*) schizzetto *m*; (*derog*) ometto *m*, tizio *m*.

stab [stab] *v* pugnalare, accoltellare. **stab in the back** pugnalare alle spalle. *n* pugnalata *f*, coltellata *f*; (*try*) tentativo *m*. **have a stab at** tentare di.

stabilize ['steibilaiz] *v* stabilizzare. **stabilization** *n* stabilizzazione *f*. **stabilizer** *n* stabilizzatore *m*.

stable¹ ['steibl] *n* stalla *f*; (*racing*) scuderia *f*.

stable² ['steibl] *adj* stabile; (*firm*) saldo; permanente. **stability** *n* stabilità *f*, fermezza *f*.

staccato [stə'kaɪtou] *adj* staccato.

stack [stak] *n* (*heap*) catasta *f*, mucchio *m*; (*chimney*) fumaiolo *m*. *v* accatastare, ammucchiare.

stadium ['steidiəm] *n* stadio *m*.

staff [staɪf] *n* (*stick*) bastone *m*; (*flag-pole*) asta *f*; (*personnel*) personale *m*; (*mil*) stato maggiore *m*. *v* fornire di personale, impiegare.

stag [stag] *n* cervo *m*. **stag-beetle** *n* cervo volante *m*.

stage [steidʒ] *n* (*phase*) fase *f*; (*lap*) tappa *f*; periodo *m*, momento *m*; teatro *m*; (*platform*) palcoscenico *m*. **at this stage** a questo punto. **go on the stage** fare l'attore. **stage-coach** *n* diligenza *f*. **stage-craft** *n* scenotecnica *f*. **stage fright** timor panico *m*. **stage-manager** *n* direttore di scena *m*. *v* rappresentare, mettere in scena. **staging** *n* messa in scena *f*.

stagger ['stagə] *v* barcollare; (*shock*) colpire, impressionare; (*arrange*) scaglionare. **staggering** *adj* sconcertante.

stagnant ['stagnənt] *adj* stagnante, inattivo. **stagnate** *v* ristagnare. **stagnation** *n* ristagno *m*.

staid [steid] *adj* posato, serio.

stain [stein] *n* macchia *f*; tinta *f*, colore *m*. **stain remover** smacchiatore *m*. *v* macchiare; colorire. **stainless steel** acciaio inossidabile *m*.

stair [steə] *n* (*step*) scalino *m*, gradino *m*. **staircase** *n* scala *f*. **stairs** *pl n* scale *f pl*.

stake¹ [steik] *n* (*post*) palo *m*; (*execution*) rogo *m*. *v* (*support*) palare. **stake out** cintare. **stake out a claim** reclamare.

stake² [steik] *n* (*bet*) posta *f*, scommessa *f*. **at stake** in gioco. *v* mettere in gioco, scommettere. **stake one's life** scommettere l'osso del collo.

stale [steil] *adj* vecchio, stantio; (*bread*) raffermo.

stalemate ['steilmeit] *n* stallo *m*; (*deadlock*) punto morto *m*. **reach stalemate** giungere a una posizione di stallo.

stalk¹ [stoɪk] *n* stelo *m*, gambo *m*.

stalk² [stoɪk] *v* (*follow*) inseguire furtivamente; (*stride haughtily*) camminare impettito.

stall¹ [stoɪl] *n* banco *m*, chiosco *m*; (*newspapers*) edicola *f*; (*theatre*) poltrona di platea *f*. **stalls** *pl n* (*theatre*) platea *f sing*. *v* (*engine*) imballare; (*aeroplane*) picchiare; (*stop*) fermarsi.

stall² [stoɪl] *v* (*delay*) tirar per le lunghe; (*act evasively*) cercar pretesti.

stallion ['staljən] *n* stallone *m*.

stamina ['staminə] *n* vigore *m*, capacità di resistenza *f*.

stammer ['stamə] *v* balbettare. *n* balbuzie *f*. **stammerer** *n* balbuziente *m*, *f*.

stamp [stamp] *v* marcare, imprimere; (*envelope*) affrancare; (*print on*) timbrare; (*documents*) bollare; (*with foot*) pestare. **stamp out** domare, annientare. *n* (*impression*) impronta *f*; marchio *m*; (*document*) bollo *m*; (*postage*) francobollo *m*; (*implement*) stampiglia *f*; (*rubber*) timbro *m*. **stamp-collector** *n* filatelico, -a *m*, *f*.

stampede [stam'piːd] *n* fuga precipitosa *f*. *v* fuggire in disordine.

***stand** [stand] *n* posizione *f*; (*platform*) tribuna *f*; (*exhibition*) stand *m invar*; (*music, etc.*) leggio *m*. *v* stare, essere; (*be upright*) stare in piedi; (*remain*) restare; (*tolerate*) sopportare, tollerare. **stand by** (*wait*) rimanere in attesa; (*help*) aiutare; (*remain faithful*) restar fedele a. **stand-by** *n* riserva *f*, scorta *f*. **stand for** significare; (*support*) sostenere. **stand-in** *n* controfigura *f*. **stand-offish** *adj* riservato. **stand out** (*project*) spiccare; (*be conspicuous*) risaltare. **standstill** *n* arresto *m*, fermata *f*. **come to a standstill** fermarsi. **stand up** alzarsi. **stand up for** prender la parte di. **stand up to** resistere a.

standard ['standəd] *n* standard *m invar*, modello *m*, campione *m*; (*level*) livello *m*; (*flag*) stendardo *m*, bandiera *f*. *adj* standard *invar*, normale. **standard lamp** torciera *f*, piantana *f*.

standing ['standiŋ] *n* posizione *f*, reputazione *f*; (*period*) durata *f*. *adj* fermo, fisso; permanente; abituale; (*upright*) in piedi. **leave standing** abbandonare sul posto.

stank [staŋk] *V* **stink**.

stanza ['stanzə] *n* strofa *f*.

staple¹ [steipl] *n* graffa *f*; (*stationery*) punto metallico *m*. *v* graffare; cucire (con punti metallici). **stapler** *n* cucitrice *f*.

staple² [steipl] *n* prodotto principale *m*; (*textile*) fiocco *m*. *adj* principale, base *invar*.

star [staɪ] *n* stella *f*; (*actor*) divo, -a *m, f*. **starfish** *n* stella di mare *f. adj* principale. *v* (*cinema, etc.*) primeggiare. **starry** *adj* stellato. **starry-eyed** *adj* (*coll*) ingenuo.

starboard ['staɪbəd] *n* dritta *f*.

starch [staɪtʃ] *n* amido *m*, fecola *f. v* inamidare. **starchy** *adj* (*food*) ricco d'amido; (*manner*) rigido.

stare [steə] *v* fissare; (*gaze fixedly*) sgranare gli occhi. **stare in the face** (*be obvious*) saltare agli occhi, essere ovvio. *n* sguardo fisso *m*.

stark [staɪk] *adj* rigido; (*bleak*) brullo. **stark mad** matto da legare. **stark naked** completamente nudo, nudo nato.

starling ['staɪlɪŋ] *n* storno *m*, stornello *m*.

start [staɪt] *n* (*beginning*) inizio *m*; (*point of departure*) partenza *f*; (*sudden movement*) soprassalto *m*; (*lead*) vantaggio *m*. **by fits and starts** a sbalzi. *v* iniziare, cominciare; partire; (*jump*) sussultare; (*set in motion*) mettere in moto. **to start with** per cominciare. **starter** *n* starter *m invar*, motorino d'avviamento *m*.

startle ['staɪtl] *v* (*far*) trasalire, sbigottire. **startling** *adj* sorprendente.

starve [staɪv] *v* affamare; (*to death*) (*far*) morire di fame; (*be very hungry*) soffrire la fame. **starve of** (*far*) soffrire per mancanza di. **starvation** *n* fame *f*.

state [steit] *n* stato *m*; pompa *f*; (*coll*) ansietà *f*. **statesman** *n* uomo di stato *m*. *adj* statale; solenne. *v* dichiarare, affermare; specificare; indicare. **stateless** *adj* apolide. **stately** *adj* solenne, maestoso. **statement** *n* affermazione *f*, dichiarazione *f*; (*bank, etc.*) estratto conto *m*.

static ['statik] *adj* fisso, statico. **statics** *n* statica *f*.

station ['steiʃən] *n* stazione *f*; (*headquarters*) sede *f*; (*rank*) condizione sociale *f*. **station-master** *n* capostazione (*pl* capistazione) *m*. **station-wagon** *n* (*US*) giardinetta *f*. *v* appostare, collocare.

stationary ['steiʃənəri] *adj* fermo; costante, fisso.

stationer ['steiʃənə] *n* cartolaio, -a *m, f*. **stationer's** *n* cartoleria *f*. **stationery** *n* oggetti di cancelleria *m pl*.

statistics [stə'tistiks] *n* statistica *f*. **statistical** *adj* statistico. **statistician** *n* statistico, -a *m, f*.

statue ['statjuɪ] *n* statua *f*.

stature ['statʃə] *n* statura *f*.

status ['steitəs] *n* posizione sociale *f*, rango *m*, prestigio *m*.

statute ['statjuɪt] *n* decreto *m*, legge *f*.

staunch [stɔɪntʃ] *adj* fedele, leale. *v* stagnare.

stay [stei] *n* soggiorno *m*; arresto *m*; (*law*) sospensione *f*. *v* (*remain*) restare, rimanere; (*on holiday, etc.*) soggiornare; (*at hotel*) alloggiare (in); (*stop*) sostare; sospendere. **stay in** non uscire, restare a casa. **stay on** trattenersi. **stay out** rimaner fuori, non rientrare.

steadfast ['stedfaɪst] *adj* risoluto, saldo.

steady ['stedi] *adj* fermo, stabile; (*responsible*) serio; regolare; costante. *v* reggersi, tener fermo; calmare.

steak [steik] *n* (*meat*) bistecca *f*; (*fish*) trancia *f*.

***steal** [stiɪl] *v* rubare. **steal away** andarsene di nascosto. **steal a march on** prevenire.

stealthy ['stelθi] *adj* clandestino. **stealthily** *adv* di nascosto *or* soppiatto.

steam [stiɪm] *n* vapore *m*; (*coll: energy*) carica *f*. **let off steam** (*coll*) sfogarsi. *v* emettere vapore; (*cook*) cucinare a vapore. **steam up** appannarsi. **steamer** *n* (*boat*) piroscafo *m*; (*cookery*) pentola a vapore *f*. **steamy** *adj* pieno di vapore.

steam-roller *n* rullo compressore *m*; (*coll*) forza irresistibile *f*. *v* sopraffare.

steel [stiɪl] *n* acciaio *m*. *v* indurire. **steely** *adj* d'acciaio, inflessibile.

steep¹ [stiɪp] *adj* (*sheer*) ripido; (*coll: unreasonable*) eccessivo.

steep² [stiɪp] *v* (*soak*) inzuppare; (*tech*) macerare.

steeple ['stiɪpl] *n* (*spire*) guglia *f*; (*tower*) campanile *m*.

steer¹ [stiə] *n* (*ox*) manzo *m*.

steer² [stiə] *v* guidare, dirigere. **steer clear of** evitare. **steering-wheel** *n* volante *m*.

stem¹ [stem] *n* (*stalk*) gambo *m*; (*of pipe*) cannello; (*branch*) ramo *m*; (*of word*) radice *f*. *v* **stem from** derivare da.

stem² [stem] *v* contenere, arginare.

stench [stentʃ] *n* puzzo *m*.

stencil ['stensl] *n* (*device*) stampino *m*; (*duplicating machine*) ciclostile *m*. *v* stampinare; ciclostilare.

step [step] *n* passo *m*; (*stair*) gradino *m*; (*measure*) provvedimento *m*. **out of step** non conforme. **step by step** un poco alla volta, per gradi. **step-ladder** *n* scala a libretto *f*, scaleo *m*. **watch one's step**

stare attenti. *v* fare un passo; (*walk*) camminare. **step down** scendere; (*retire*) ritirarsi. **step in** entrare; intervenire. **step up** salire; aumentare; accelerare.
stepbrother ['stepbrʌðə] *n* fratellastro *m*.
stepdaughter ['stepdɔɪtə] *n* figliastra *f*.
stepfather ['stepfaɪðə] *n* patrigno *m*.
stepmother ['stepmʌðə] *n* matrigna *f*.
stepsister ['stepsistə] *n* sorellastra *f*.
stepson ['stepsʌn] *n* figliastro *m*.
stereo ['steriou] *adj* stereo. **stereophonic** *adj* stereofonico.
stereotype ['steriətaip] *n* cliché *m*; (*tech*) stereotipia *f*. **stereotyped** *adj* (*trite*) stereotipato; (*tech*) stereotipo.
sterile ['sterail] *adj* sterile. **sterility** *n* sterilità *f*. **sterilization** *n* sterilizzazione *f*. **sterilize** *v* sterilizzare.
sterling ['stəːliŋ] *n* sterlina *f*. *adj* genuino.
stern[1] [stəːn] *adj* (*harsh*) severo; (*strict*) rigoroso.
stern[2] [stəːn] *n* (*ship*) poppa *f*.
stethoscope ['steθəskoup] *n* stetoscopio *m*.
stew [stjuː] *n* spezzatino *m*, stufato *m*. **be in a stew** essere preoccupato *or* turbato. *v* cuocere (a fuoco lento).
steward ['stjuəd] *n* amministratore, -trice *m*, *f*; (*ship*) cameriere di bordo *m*, steward *m invar*. **stewardess** *n* stewardess *f invar*, assistente di volo *f*. **stewardship** *n* gestione *f*; (*office*) carica di amministratore *f*.
stick[1] [stik] *n* (*wood*) bastone *m*; (*celery*, *etc*.) gambo *m*; (*small rod*) bastoncino *m*. **be in a cleft stick** non sapere che pesci pigliare.
*stick[2] [stik] *v* attaccare, appiccicare; (*stab*) ficcare; (*remain*) rimanere. **stick it out** tener duro. **stick out** (*be conspicuous*) saltare agli occhi; (*put out*) tirar fuori. **stick to** (*not digress*) attenersi a, non divagare da; (*remain loyal*) restar fedele a. **stick up for** difendere, battersi per. **sticky** *adj* attaccaticcio; adesivo; (*weather*) pesante; (*coll*; *difficult*) complesso.
stickler ['stiklə] *n* pignolo, -a *m*, *f*. **stickler for ...** persona ligia a ....
stiff [stif] *adj* rigido; (*hard to move, difficult*) duro; (*formal*) freddo. *adv* (*coll*) a morte. **stiffen** *v* irrigidire. **stiffness** *n* rigidezza *f*; durezza *f*.
stifle ['staifl] *v* soffocare.
stigma ['stigmə] *n* segno *m*, marchio *m*; (*disgrace*) stigma *m*.

stile [stail] *n* scaletta *f*.
still[1] [stil] *adj* (*quiet*) tranquillo; (*motionless*) immobile. *adv* ancora, tuttora. **stillborn** *adj* nato morto. *n* silenzio *m*; (*phot*) posa *f*. *v* calmare. **stillness** *n* silenzio *m*, tranquillità *f*.
still[2] [stil] *n* distilleria *f*; (*retort*) storta *f*.
stilt [stilt] *n* trampolo *m*; (*building*) palafitta *f*. **stilted** *adj* artificiale; (*pompous*) ampolloso.
stimulus ['stimjuləs] *n pl* -**li** stimolo *m*. **stimulant** *nm*, *adj* stimolante. **stimulate** *v* stimolare. **stimulation** *n* stimolo *m*.
*sting [stiŋ] *v* (*wound*) pungere; (*incite*) spronare; (*coll*: *cheat*) truffare. *n* puntura *f*; (*pang*) morso *m*; (*incitement*) sprone *m*.
stingy ['stindʒi] *adj* tirchio, spilorcio. **stinginess** *n* tirchieria *f*, spilorceria *f*.
*stink [stiŋk] *n* puzzo *m*. *v* puzzare. **stinking** *adj* puzzolente, fetente.
stint [stint] *n* dovere *m*, periodo di lavoro *m*. *v* risparmiare, fare economia.
stipulate ['stipjuleit] *v* pattuire, convenire. **stipulation** *n* patto *m*, condizione *f*, convenzione *f*.
stir [stəː] *v* mescolare, agitare; (*budge*) muoversi. **stir up** eccitare, incitare. *n* (*excitement*) scalpore *m*; confusione *f*. **stirring** *adj* (*touching*) commovente; eccitante.
stirrup ['stirəp] *n* staffa *f*.
stitch [stitʃ] *n* (*sewing*) punto *m*; (*knitting*) maglia *f*. *v* cucire; (*sew on*) attaccare; (*med*) suturare.
stoat [stout] *n* ermellino *m*.
stock [stok] *n* (*goods*) provvista *f*, stock *m invar*, riserva *f*; (*standing*) credito *m*; famiglia *f*; (*cookery*) brodo *m*. **stockbroker** *n* agente di cambio *m*. **stock exchange** borsa valori *f*. **stockholder** *n* azionista *m*, *f*. **stockpile** *v* far scorta di. **stocks and shares** titoli *m pl*. **stocktaking** *n* inventario *m*. *v* (*supply*) fornire, rifornire; tenere in magazzino.
stocking ['stokiŋ] *n* calza *f*.
stocky ['stoki] *adj* tarchiato, tozzo.
stodge [stodʒ] (*coll*) *n* (*food*) cibo pesante *m*; (*dull matter*) mattone *m*. **stodgy** *adj* pesante; (*tedious*) noioso.
stoical ['stouikl] *adj* stoico. **stoic** *n* stoico, -a *m*, *f*.
stoke [stouk] *v* alimentare. **stoke up** rimpinzarsi. **stoker** *n* fuochista *m*.

stole 180

stole¹ [stoul] *V* steal.
stole² [stoul] *n* stola *f.*
stolen ['stoulǝn] *V* steal.
stomach ['stʌmǝk] *n* stomaco *m.* stomach-
ache *n* mal di stomaco *m. v* (*tolerate*)
sopportare.
stone [stoun] *n* pietra *f;* (*pebble*) sasso *m;*
(*fruit*) nocciolo *m;* (*med*) calcolo *m.* a
stone's throw from a due passi da. stone-
deaf *adj* sordo come una campana.
stonemason *n* muratore *m.* stoneware *n*
gres *m invar. v* prendere a sassate; (*fruit*)
snocciolare.
stood [stud] *V* stand.
stool [stuːl] *n* sgabello *m.* stool-pigeon *n*
spia *f.*
stoop [stuːp] *v* curvare, chinarsi; (*condescend*) abbassarsi. *n* walk with a stoop
camminar curvo.
stop [stop] *n* (*halt*) sosta *f,* fermata *f;*
(*punctuation*) punto *m;* (*organ*) registro
m. v finire, smettere; (*halt*) fermare; (*prevent*) impedire; (*withhold*) trattenere;
(*block*) turare. stop-press *n* ultimissime *f*
pl. stop-watch *n* cronometro a scatto *m.*
stoppage *n* fermata *f,* arresto *m;* sospensione *f;* (*med*) blocco *m.* stopper *n* (*bung*)
tappo *m.*
store [stoɪ] *n* (*supply*) provvista *f,* riserva
f; (*shop*) bottega *f;* (*warehouse*) magazzino *m.* storekeeper *n* magazziniere *m. v*
fare provviste di; conservare; accumulare; mettere in magazzino. storage *n*
immagazzinamento *m;* (*comm*) magazzinaggio *m.*
storey ['stoɪri] *n* piano *m.*
stork [stoɪk] *n* cicogna *f.*
storm [stoɪm] *n* tempesta *f;* (*thunder*)
temporale *m. v* (*rage*) infuriarsi; (*rush*)
precipitarsi; (*mil*) prendere d'assalto.
stormy *adj* burrascoso.
story ['stoɪri] *n* storia *f,* racconto *m;*
(*news*) fatto di cronaca *m.*
stout [staut] *adj* (*fat*) grasso; intrepido;
robusto.
stove [stouv] *n* stufa *f;* (*cooker*) cucina *f.*
stow [stou] *v* stivare; (*fill*) riempire (di).
stow away mettere da parte; (*on boat,
etc.*) imbarcarsi clandestinamente.
stowaway *n* passeggero clandestino *m.*
stowage *n* stivaggio *m.*
straddle ['stradl] *v* stare a cavalcioni,
cavalcare.
straggle ['stragl] *v* disperdersi; (*lag

behind) rimanere indietro. straggler *n*
ritardatario, -a *m, f.*
straight [streit] *adj* diritto; (*open*) franco,
aperto. *adv* diritto, in linea retta; (*directly*) direttamente. straight away subito.
straightforward *adj* franco, aperto; onesto; semplice. straighten *v* raddrizzare;
(*order*) assettare.
strain¹ [strein] *v* filtrare, passare; (*force*)
sforzare; (*sprain*) storcere. *n* sforzo *m,*
tensione *f;* (*med*) storta *f;* (*tune*) melodia
f. strained *adj* forzato; filtrato. strainer *n*
filtro *m,* colino *m.*
strain² [strein] *n* (*race*) stirpe *f,* famiglia *f.*
strait [streit] *n* (*geog*) stretto *m.* straits *pl*
n difficoltà *f pl. adj* strait-laced *adj*
rigoroso, puritano.
strand¹ [strand] *n* (*hair*) ciocca *f;* (*rope*)
fune *f.*
strand² [strand] *n* (*shore*) spiaggia *f,*
sponda *f. v* arenare, incagliarsi.
strange [streindʒ] *adj* strano, misterioso;
(*unaccountable*) inspiegabile. stranger *n*
sconosciuto, -a *m, f;* estraneo, -a *m, f;*
(*foreigner*) straniero, -a *m, f.*
strangle ['strangl] *v* strangolare. strangulation *n* strangolamento *m.*
strap [strap] *n* cinghia *f;* (*on garment*)
spallina *f;* (*watch*) cinturino *m. v* strap up
assicurare con cinghia; (*med*) fissare con
cerotto. strapping *adj* robusto.
strategy ['stratǝdʒi] *n* strategia *f.* strategic
adj strategico.
stratum ['straɪtǝm] *n, pl* -ta strato *m.*
straw [stroɪ] *n* paglia *f;* (*drinking*) cannuccia *f.*
strawberry ['stroɪbǝri] *n* fragola *f.*
stray [strei] *v* (*lose one's way*) smarrirsi;
(*roam*) vagare. stray from deviare *or*
allontanarsi da. *adj* (*animal*) randagio;
(*lost*) smarrito; (*occasional*) isolato.
streak [striːk] *n* (*mark*) riga *f,* striscia *f;*
(*vein*) vena *f;* (*lightning*) lampo *m. v*
striare; venare; (*rush*) filare.
stream [striːm] *n* corso d'acqua *m;*
(*brook*) ruscello *m;* corrente *f.* streamline
v sveltire. streamlined *adj* aerodinamico,
sveltito. *v* grondare, riversarsi. streaming
cold forte raffreddore *m.*
street [striːt] *n* strada *f,* via *f.* street-
cleaner *n* spazzino *m.* street-light *n* lampione *m.* the man in the street l'uomo
qualunque *m.*
strength [strenθ] *n* forza *f;* intensità *f;*

validità f; (mil) effettivo m. **strengthen** v rinforzare; (give weight to) convalidare.

strenuous ['strenjuəs] adj energico, fervente; (activity) arduo, duro.

stress [stres] n tensione f; pressione f, spinta f; (emphasis) rilievo m; accento m; (med) stress m invar. v mettere in rilievo, sottolineare; accentare; sottoporre a tensione.

stretch [stretʃ] v (pull) tirare; (extend) stendere; (reach) estendersi. **stretch one's legs** sgranchirsi le gambe. **stretch out** allungare, sdraiarsi. n (expanse) tratto m; (time) periodo m. **stretcher** n barella f, lettiga f.

stricken ['strikən] adj colpito.

strict [strikt] adj severo, rigoroso; esatto, (absolute) stretto.

*__stride__ [straid] v camminare a grandi passi. n passo m. **take in one's stride** (do easily) superare con facilità; (adjust to) prendersela con calma.

strife [straif] n lotta f, conflitto m.

*__strike__ [straik] v colpire; (deal a blow) battere; (match) accendere; (oil) scoprire; (not work) scioperare. **strike home** colpire nel segno. **strike off** radiare. **strike up** (enter upon) stringere. n sciopero m; (discovery) scoperta f. **striking** adj sorprendente, impressionante.

*__string__ [striŋ] n spago m, corda f; (series) fila f. **pull strings** manovrare, raccomandare. **strings** pl n (music) strumenti a corda m pl. v (music) incordare; (racket) mettere le corde a; (beads) infilare.

stringent ['strindʒənt] adj rigoroso, severo.

strip[1] [strip] v spogliare, denudare; (car, etc.) smontare; (paint) togliere. **strip of** privare di. **strip-tease** n spogliarello m.

strip[2] [strip] n striscia f, nastro m; (comic) fumetto m.

stripe [straip] n riga f, striscia f; (mil) gallone m. **striped** adj a righe or strisce.

*__strive__ [straiv] v (try hard) sforzarsi, adoperarsi; (struggle) lottare.

striven ['strivn] V strive.

strode [stroud] V stride.

stroke[1] [strouk] n colpo m; (mark) sbarra f; (swimming) bracciata f; (med) colpo apoplettico m; (clock) tocco m; (tech) corsa f. **stroke of genius** lampo di genio m. **stroke of lightning** fulmine m.

stroke[2] [strouk] v accarezzare, lisciare.

stroll [stroul] n passeggiatina f. **go for a stroll** andare a far quattro passi. v girovagare.

strong [stroŋ] adj forte, robusto, resistente. **stronghold** n roccaforte f. **strong language** parole grosse f pl. **strong-minded** adj risoluto. **strong point** forte m.

strove [strouv] V strive.

struck [strʌk] V strike.

structure ['strʌktʃə] n struttura f. **structural** adj strutturale.

struggle ['strʌgl] n (fight) lotta f; (effort) sforzo m. v lottare; sforzarsi.

strum [strʌm] v strimpellare.

strung [strʌŋ] V string.

strut[1] [strʌt] v (prance) camminare impettito.

strut[2] [strʌt] n (support) puntone m.

stub [stʌb] n (cigarette, pencil, etc.) mozzicone m; (cheque) matrice f; (tree) ceppo m. v urtare. **stub out** spegnere.

stubble ['stʌbl] n stoppia f; (beard) barba ispida f. **stubbly** adj pieno di stoppie; ispido.

stubborn ['stʌbən] adj ostinato, testardo. **stubbornness** n ostinatezza f, testardaggine f.

stuck [stʌk] V stick[2].

stud[1] [stʌd] n (ornament) borchia f; (nail) ribattino m; (button) bottoncino m. v guarnire di borchie; (jewel) tempestare.

stud[2] [stʌd] n scuderia f. **stud-horse** n stallone m.

student ['stjuːdənt] n (pupil) studente, -essa m, f; (scholar) studioso, -a m, f.

studio ['stjuːdiou] n studio m.

study ['stʌdi] n studio m. v studiare; esaminare attentamente. **studied** adj studiato, premeditato. **studious** adj studioso, attento, premuroso.

stuff [stʌf] n roba f; (substance) sostanza f; (fabric) tessuto m. **know one's stuff** sapere il fatto proprio. v (cookery) farcire; (animal) imbalsamare; (fill) imbottire. **stuffing** n imbottitura f; (cookery) ripieno m. **stuffy** adj soffocante; (tedious) noioso; (blocked up) intasato; (prim) rigido, conservatore.

stumble ['stʌmbl] v inciampare, fare un passo falso; (speech) impaperarsi. **stumbling block** ostacolo m.

stump [stʌmp] n (tree) ceppo m; (limb) moncone m.

stun [stʌn] v stordire; (astound) sbalordire. **stunning** adj sbalorditivo, stupefacente.

stung [stʌŋ] V sting.

stunk [stʌŋk] V stink.

stunt[1] [stʌnt] v arrestare la crescita di.

stunt[2] [stʌnt] n bravata f; acrobazia f; trovata pubblicitaria f.

stupid ['stjuːpid] adj stupido, sciocco. **stupidity** n stupidità f.

stupor ['stjuːpə] n stupore m, torpore m.

sturdy ['stəːdi] adj vigoroso, robusto. **sturdiness** n vigoria f.

sturgeon ['stəːdʒən] n storione m.

stutter ['stʌtə] n balbuzie f. v balbettare. **stutterer** n balbuziente m, f.

sty [stai] n porcile m.

stye [stai] n orzaiolo m.

style [stail] n stile m. **stylish** adj elegante. **stylist** n stilista m, f.

stylus ['stailəs] n puntina f.

suave [swaɪv] adj cortese, affabile.

subconscious [sʌb'kɒnʃəs] nm, adj subcosciente.

subcontract [sʌbkən'trakt] n subappalto m. v dare in subappalto.

subdivision [ˌsʌbdi'viʒən] n suddivisione f. **subdivide** v suddividere.

subdue [səb'djuː] v (conquer) soggiogare; (repress) reprimere; (reduce intensity) attenuare. **subdued** adj inibito; intimidito; attenuato.

subject ['sʌbdʒikt; v səb'dʒekt] n soggetto m, argomento m; (study) materia f; (pol) suddito, -a m, f. adj **subject to** soggetto a. v (bring under control) sottomettere; (expose) esporre, sottoporre. **subjective** adj soggettivo. **subjectivity** n soggettività f.

subjunctive [səb'dʒʌŋktiv] nm, adj congiuntivo.

***sublet** [ˌsʌb'let] v subaffittare.

sublimate ['sʌblimeit] v sublimare. n sublimato m. **sublimation** n sublimazione f.

sublime [sə'blaim] adj sublime.

submarine ['sʌbməriːn] n sottomarino m.

submerge [səb'məːdʒ] v sommergere. **submersion** n sommersione f.

submit [səb'mit] v (yield) sottomettersi, rassegnarsi; deferire; (present) sottoporre. **submission** n sottomissione f, rassegnazione f; (theory) tesi f.

subnormal [sʌb'nɔːməl] adj subnormale.

subordinate [sə'bɔːdinət] adj subordinato, inferiore. n subalterno m. v subordinare. **subordination** n subordinazione f.

subscribe [səb'skraib] v sottoscrivere, aderire; (newspapers, etc.) abbonarsi. **subscriber** n abbonato, -a m, f. **subscription** n abbonamento m; (dues) quota f; (fund raised) sottoscrizione f.

subsequent ['sʌbsikwənt] adj successivo, susseguente.

subservient [səb'səːviənt] adj subordinato; (servile) umile.

subside [səb'said] v decrescere, diminuire; (give way) cedere, avvallare; (abate) quietarsi. **subsidence** n avvallamento m.

subsidiary [səb'sidiəri] adj sussidiario; (comm) consociato.

subsidize ['sʌbsidaiz] v sovvenzionare. **subsidy** n sovvenzione f.

subsist [səb'sist] v sostentarsi. **subsistence** n sostentamento m. **subsistence money** acconto paga m, trasferta f.

substance ['sʌbstəns] n sostanza f, materia f; realtà f; (wealth) beni m pl. **substantial** adj sostanziale; (meal) sostanzioso; (considerable) notevole.

substitute ['sʌbstitjuːt] n (person) sostituto, -a m, f; (thing) surrogato m. v sostituire, rimpiazzare. **substitution** n sostituzione f.

subterfuge ['sʌbtəfjuːdʒ] n sotterfugio m.

subterranean [sʌbtə'reiniən] adj sotterraneo.

subtitle ['sʌbtaitl] n sottotitolo m.

subtle ['sʌtl] adj sottile, delicato; astuto, ingegnoso. **subtlety** n sottigliezza f, finezza f; astuzia f.

subtract [səb'trakt] v dedurre, sottrarre. **subtraction** n sottrazione f.

suburb ['sʌbəːb] n sobborgo m. **suburban** adj suburbano.

subvert [səb'vəːt] v sovvertire. **subversion** n sovversione f. **subversive** n, adj sovversivo, -a.

subway ['sʌbwei] n sottopassaggio m; (US) metropolitana f.

succeed [sək'siːd] v riuscire; (be successful) aver successo; (follow) succedere. **success** n successo m, buona riuscita f. **successful** adj (person) che ha successo; vittorioso; prospero, arrivato; (thing) riuscito. **succession** n successione f. **successive** adj successivo. **successor** n successore m.

succinct [sək'siŋkt] adj succinto.

succulent ['sʌkjulənt] *adj* succulento.
succumb [sə'kʌm] *v* soccombere.
such [sʌtʃ] *adj* tale; *(like)* del genere, simile. *adv* così. **such and such** tale dei tali. **such as** come. **such as it is** così com'è.
suck [sʌk] *v* succhiare; *(breast)* poppare. **suck up** assorbire; *(slang)* fare il leccapiedi.
sucker ['sʌkə] *n* *(plant)* pollone *m*; *(device)* ventosa *f*; *(slang: fool)* gonzo *m*.
suckle ['sʌkl] *v* allattare.
suction ['sʌkʃən] *n* aspirazione *f*. **suction pump** pompa aspirante *f*.
sudden ['sʌdən] *adj* improvviso, subitaneo. **all of a sudden** ad un tratto, all'improvviso.
suds [sʌdz] *pl n* saponata *f sing*.
sue [suɪ] *v* *(law)* citare, chiamare in giudizio, querelare. **sue for peace** chiedere *or* sollecitare la pace.
suede [sweid] *nm, adj* scamosciato.
suet ['suit] *n* grasso di rognone *m*.
suffer ['sʌfə] *v* soffrire, patire; tollerare; *(undergo)* subire. **on sufferance** per tacita tolleranza. **suffering** *n* sofferenza *f*, dolore *m*.
sufficient [sə'fiʃənt] *adj* sufficiente. **sufficiency** *n* sufficienza *f*.
suffix ['sʌfiks] *n* suffisso *m*.
suffocate ['sʌfəkeit] *v* soffocare. **suffocation** *n* soffocazione *f*.
sugar ['ʃugə] *n* zucchero *m*. **sugar-beet** *n* barbabietola (da zucchero) *f*. **sugar-cane** *n* canna da zucchero *f*. **sugary** *adj* zuccherino, melliffuo.
suggest [sə'dʒest] *v* suggerire; proporre. **suggestible** *adj* suggestionabile. **suggestion** *n* suggerimento *m*; proposta *f*; *(psych)* suggestione *f*.
suicide ['suisaid] *n* *(deed)* suicidio *m*; *(person)* suicida *m, f*. **commit suicide** suicidarsi. **suicidal** *adj* suicida.
suit [suit] *n* *(garment)* abito *m*; *(law)* causa *f*; *(cards)* seme *m*, colore *m*; *(request)* preghiera *f*. **follow suit** seguire l'esempio; *(cards)* rispondere a colore. **suitcase** *n* valigia *f*. *v* accontentare, convenire a, soddisfare. **suit yourself!** fa come ti pare! **suitable** *adj* adatto; conveniente, opportuno. **suitability** *n* convenienza *f*.
suite [swiit] *n* *(music)* suite *f invar*; *(retinue)* seguito *m*; *(furniture)* mobilia *f invar*; *(rooms)* fuga di stanze *f*.

sulk [sʌlk] *v* tenere il broncio. **sulky** *adj* imbronciato.
sullen ['sʌlən] *adj* accigliato, imbronciato.
sulphur ['sʌlfə] *n* zolfo *m*.
sultan ['sʌltən] *n* sultano *m*.
sultana [sʌl'tɑːnə] *n* uva sultanina *f*.
sultry ['sʌltri] *adj* afoso; *(person)* eccitante.
sum [sʌm] *n* somma *f*, addizione *f*; *(amount)* importo *m*, totale *m*. **do sums** far calcoli. *v* **sum up** riassumere. **summing-up** *n* riassunto *m*, riepilogo (*pl* -ghi) *m*.
summarize ['sʌməraiz] *v* riassumere. **summary** *nm, adj* sommario.
summer ['sʌmə] *n* estate *f*. *adj* d'estate, estivo.
summit ['sʌmit] *n* cima *f*, vertice *m*.
summon ['sʌmən] *v* convocare; *(law)* citare, chiamare in giudizio. **summon up courage** farsi coraggio.
summons ['sʌmənz] *v* citare in giudizio. *n* citazione *f*. **answer a summons** presentarsi in giudizio.
sumptuous ['sʌmptʃuəs] *adj* sontuoso.
sun [sʌn] *n* sole *m*. *v* **sun oneself** prendere il sole. **sunny** *adj* soleggiato; *(cheerful)* allegro.
sunbathe ['sʌnbeið] *v* fare i bagni di sole. **sunbathing** *n* bagni di sole *m pl*.
sunburn ['sʌnbəːn] *n* *(pain)* scottatura solare *f*, eritema solare *m*; *(tan)* abbronzatura *f*. **sunburnt** *adj* scottato dal sole; abbronzato.
Sunday ['sʌndi] *n* domenica *f*.
sundial ['sʌndaiəl] *n* meridiana *f*.
sundry ['sʌndri] *adj* diversi, parecchi. **all and sundry** tutti quanti.
sunflower ['sʌnˌflauə] *n* girasole *m*.
sung [sʌŋ] *V* sing.
sun-glasses ['sʌnglɑːsiz] *pl n* occhiali da sole *m pl*.
sunk [sʌŋk] *V* sink.
sunlight ['sʌnlait] *n* luce del sole *f*.
sunrise ['sʌnraiz] *n* alba *f*.
sunset ['sʌnset] *n* tramonto *m*.
sunshine ['sʌnʃain] *n* sole *m*; *(good weather)* bel tempo *m*. **sunshine roof** tetto scorrevole *m*.
sunstroke ['sʌnstrouk] *n* colpo di sole *m*, insolazione *f*.
sun-tan ['sʌntan] *n* abbronzatura *f*.
super ['suipə] *adj* *(coll)* magnifico.
superannuation [ˌsuipəranju'eiʃən] *n*

(*retirement*) collocamento a riposo *m*; (*pension*) vitalizio *m*.

superb [suɪ'pɔɪb] *adj* superbo, magnifico.

supercilious [ˌsuɪpə'siliəs] *adj* altero, borioso.

superficial [ˌsuɪpə'fiʃəl] *adj* superficiale.

superfluous [su'pəɪfluəs] *adj* superfluo.

superhuman [suɪpə'hjuɪmən] *adj* sovrumano.

superimpose [ˌsuɪpərim'pouz] *v* sovraporre.

superintendent [ˌsuɪpərin'tendənt] *n* soprintendente *m*; (*police*) commissario *m*.

superior [suɪpiəriə] *adj* superiore. *n* superiore, -a *m*, *f*. **superiority** *n* superiorità *f*.

superlative [suɪ'pəɪlətiv] *nm*, *adj* superlativo.

supermarket ['suɪpəˌmaɪkit] *n* supermercato *m*.

supernatural [ˌsuɪpə'natʃərəl] *nm*, *adj* soprannaturale.

supersede [ˌsuɪpə'siɪd] *v* rimpiazzare, sostituire.

supersonic [ˌsuɪpə'sonik] *adj* supersonico.

superstition [suɪpə'stiʃən] *n* superstizione *f*. **superstitious** *adj* superstizioso.

supervise ['suɪpəvaiz] *v* sorvegliare, soprintendere. **supervision** *n* sorveglianza *f*, soprintendenza *f*. **supervisor** *n* soprintendente *m*, *f*, sorvegliante *m*, *f*, ispettore, -trice *m*, *f*.

supper ['sʌpə] *n* cena *f*. **have supper** cenare.

supple ['sʌpl] *adj* flessibile; agile. **suppleness** *n* flessibilità *f*; agilità *f*.

supplement ['sʌpləmənt] *n* supplemento *m*, aggiunta *f*. *v* completare, integrare. **supplementary** *adj* supplementare.

supply [sə'plai] *n* provvista *f*, rifornimento *m*; (*econ*) offerta *f*. *v* provvedere, fornire. **supplier** *n* fornitore *m*.

support [sə'pɔɪt] *n* appoggio *m*, sostegno *m*. **means of support** mezzi di sostentamento *m pl*. *v* reggere, sostenere; (*keep*) mantenere; (*tolerate*) sopportare.

suppose [sə'pouz] *v* supporre; (*think*) ritenere, pensare. **supposed** *adj* presunto. **be supposed to** dovere. **supposedly** *adv* per supposizione. **supposing** *conj* supponiamo che. **supposition** *n* supposizione *f*.

suppository [sə'pozitri] *n* supposta *f*.

suppress [sə'pres] *v* sopprimere; (*check*) soffocare; (*hide*) nascondere.

supreme [su'priɪm] *adj* supremo, massimo. **supremacy** *n* supremazia *f*.

surcharge ['sɔɪtʃaɪdʒ] *n* soprattassa *f*.

sure [ʃuə] *adj* certo, sicuro. **make sure** assicurarsi.

surety ['ʃuərəti] *n* certezza *f*; garanzia *f*. **stand surety for** farsi garante per.

surf [sɔɪf] *n* frangente *m*, risacca *f*. **surfing** *n* surfing *m invar*, sport dell'acquaplano *m*.

surface ['sɔɪfis] *n* superficie *f*, faccia *f*. *adj* superficiale, esterno. *v* venire a galla, affiorare.

surfeit ['sɔɪfit] *n* eccesso *m*.

surge [sɔɪdʒ] *n* ondata *f*, riflusso *m*. *v* fluttuare, rifluire.

surgeon ['sɔɪdʒən] *n* chirurgo *m*. **surgery** *n* (*subject*) chirurgia *f*; (*consulting room*) gabinetto medico *m*, infermeria *f*. **surgical** *adj* chirurgico.

surly ['sɔɪli] *adj* scontroso.

surmount [sə'maunt] *v* superare.

surname ['sɔɪneim] *n* cognome *m*.

surpass [sə'paɪs] *v* sorpassare, superare.

surplus ['sɔɪpləs] *n* eccesso *m*, avanzo *m*, residuato *m*.

surprise [sə'praiz] *n* sorpresa *f*; (*astonishment*) stupore *m*, meraviglia *f*. **take by surprise** (*amaze*) stupire; (*come upon unawares*) cogliere all'improvviso. *adj* (*unexpected*) inaspettato. *v* sorprendere; cogliere all'improvviso; stupire.

surrealism [sə'riəlizəm] *n* surrealismo *m*. **surrealist** *n*(*m*+*f*), *adj* surrealista.

surrender [sə'rendə] *v* cedere; (*mil*) arrendersi. *n* resa *f*.

surreptitious [ˌsʌrəp'tiʃəs] *adj* furtivo, clandestino. ·

surround [sə'raund] *v* circondare; (*encircle*) accerchiare. *n* bordura *f*. **surrounding** *adj* circostante. **surroundings** *pl n* dintorni *m pl*; (*environment*) ambiente *m sing*.

survey ['sɔɪvei; *v* sə'vei] *n* quadro generale *m*; (*official examination*) perizia *f*; rapporto *m*; valutazione *f*; (*of land*) agrimensura *f*; (*geog*) rilievo topografico *m*; (*poll*) sondaggio *m*. *v* contemplare; esaminare, fare una perizia di; prendere i rilievi di. **surveyor** *n* ispettore, -trice *m*, *f*; (*land*) agrimensore *m*; (*house*) geometra *m*, *f*; (*geog*) topografo, -a *m*, *f*.

survive [sə'vaiv] *v* sopravvivere. **survival** *n* sopravvivenza *f*. **survivor** *n* superstite *m*, *f*.

susceptible [sə'septəbl] *adj* suscettibile; predisposto. **susceptibility** *n* suscettibilità *f*; predisposizione *f*.

suspect [sə'spekt; *n, adj* 'sʌspekt] *v* sospettare; (*surmise*) dubitare. *n* persona sospetta *f*. *adj* sospetto.

suspend [sə'spend] *v* sospendere. **suspense** *n* incertezza *f*, apprensione *f*. **in suspense** in sospeso. **suspension** *n* sospensione *f*. **suspension bridge** ponte sospeso *m*.

suspicion [sə'spiʃən] *n* sospetto *m*, dubbio *m*. **suspicious** *adj* (*distrustful*) sospettoso, diffidente; (*questionable*) sospetto.

sustain [sə'stein] *v* sostenere; (*injury, etc.*) subire.

swab [swob] *n* tampone *m*; (*sample*) prelievo *m*.

swagger ['swagə] *v* (*strut*) pavoneggiarsi; (*boast*) boriarsi, grandeggiare. *n* boria *f*, andatura spavalda *f*.

swallow¹ ['swolou] *v* inghiottire, ingoiare; (*coll: believe*) bere; (*suppress*) reprimere. *n* gorgata *f*.

swallow² ['swolou] *n* (*bird*) rondine *f*.

swam [swam] *V* swim.

swamp [swomp] *n* palude *f*. *v* (*flood*) inondare, allagare; (*overwhelm*) travolgere.

swan [swon] *n* cigno *m*.

swank [swaŋk] (*coll*) *v* darsi delle arie. *n* boria *f*.

swap *or* **swop** [swop] *n* scambio *m*. *v* scambiare.

swarm [swoːm] *n* (*bees*) sciame *m*; (*crowd*) folla *f*. *v* sciamare; (*throng*) accalcarsi; (*teem*) brulicare.

swarthy ['swoːði] *adj* di carnagione scura.

swat [swot] *v* schiacciare.

sway [swei] *v* oscillare, vacillare; inclinare; influenzare. *n* oscillazione *f*. **hold sway over** esercitare potere su.

*swear [sweə] *v* (*declare solemnly*) giurare; (*curse*) bestemmiare. **swear by** giurare su. **swear in** far prestare giuramento, insediare. **swear-word** *n* bestemmia *f*.

sweat [swet] *v* sudare. *n* sudore *m*. **sweat-shirt** *n* argentina *f*. **sweater** *n* maglione *m*.

swede [swiːd] *n* ravizzone *m*.

Sweden ['swiːdn] *n* Svezia *f*. **Swede** *n* svedese *m*, *f*. **Swedish** *nm, adj* svedese.

*sweep [swiːp] *v* spazzare; (*view*) percorrere. **sweep aside** scartare. **sweep the board** far piazza pulita. **sweep** *n* spazzata *f*; curva *f*; (*chimney*) spazzacamino *m*. **sweeping** *adj* radicale, di lunga portata. **sweeping statement** asserzione gratuita *f*.

sweet [swiːt] *adj* dolce; fresco; (*smell*) profumato; (*sound*) armonioso; (*temper*) amabile, carino. *n* caramella *f*; (*dessert*) dolce *m*. **sweet-and-sour** *adj* agrodolce. **sweetbread** *n* animella *f*. **sweetheart** *n* amoroso, -a *m*, *f*. **sweet pea** pisello odoroso *m*. **sweeten** *v* addolcire; alleviare. **sweetener** *n* dolcificante *m*; (*bribe*) bustarella *f*. **sweetness** *n* dolcezza *f*; (*taste*) sapore dolce *m*.

*swell [swel] *v* aumentare, gonfiarsi. *n* (*sea*) ondata *f*. **swelling** *n* gonfiore *m*, tumore *m*, tumefazione *f*.

swelter ['sweltə] *v* soffocare *or* morire dal caldo. **sweltering** *adj* soffocante.

swept [swept] *V* sweep.

swerve [swəːv] *v* (*change direction abruptly*) scartare; deviare, scostarsi. *n* scarto *m*; deviazione *f*.

swift [swift] *adj* lesto; (*prompt*) pronto. *n* rondone *m*.

swig [swig] *v* tracannare. *n* sorso *m*.

swill [swil] *v* (*swig*) tracannare; (*rinse*) risciacquare. *n* (*rubbish*) rifiuti *m pl*; (*slops*) intruglio *m*; (*for pigs*) broda (per maiali) *f*.

*swim [swim] *v* nuotare. *n* nuotata *f*. **go for a swim** andare a nuotare. **in the swim** attivo. **swimmer** *n* nuotatore, -trice *m*, *f*. **swimming** *n* nuoto *m*. **swimming costume** costume da bagno *m*. **swimming pool** *or* **baths** piscina *f*. **swimming trunks** calzoncini da bagno *m pl*.

swindle ['swindl] *v* truffare, imbrogliare. *n* truffa *f*. **swindler** *n* truffatore, -trice *m*, *f*, imbroglione, -a *m*, *f*.

swine [swain] *n* maiale *m*, porco (*pl* -ci) *m*.

*swing [swiŋ] *v* dondolare, oscillare; (*club, etc.*) vibrare; influenzare. **swing open** spalancarsi. **swing round** voltarsi di scatto. *n* oscillazione *f*, ritmo *m*; (*in playground*) altalena *f*. **in full swing** in piena attività. **swing-door** *n* porta a due battenti *f*.

swipe [swaip] (*coll*) *n* botta *f*. *v* dare una botta (a); (*steal*) fregare.

swirl [swɜːl] v turbinare. n turbine m.
swish [swiʃ] v (sound) sibilare; (move) brandire; (rustle) frusciare. n (whip) sferza f; (sound) sibilo m.
Swiss [swis] n, adj svizzero, -a.
switch [switʃ] n (elec) interruttore m; (whip) sferza f; (change) svolta f, cambiamento m. **switchback** n montagne russe f pl. **switchboard** n tavolo di controllo m; (phone) centralino m. v spostare, scambiare. **switch off** spegnere. **switch on** accendere. **switch over** commutare.
Switzerland ['switsələnd] n Svizzera f.
swivel ['swivl] n perno m. **swivel chair** sedia girevole f. v girare, rotare.
swollen ['swoulən] V **swell**. adj gonfio.
swoop [swuːp] v piombare, avventarsi. n calata improvvisa f. **at one fell swoop** d'un sol colpo.
swop V **swap**.
sword [sɔːd] n spada f. **cross swords** (fight) battersi; (argue) venire alle mani. **swordfish** n pesce spada m.
swore [swɔː] V **swear**.
sworn [swɔːn] V **swear**.
swot [swot] (coll) v sgobbare. n secchione, -a m, f.
swum [swʌm] V **swim**.
swung [swʌŋ] V **swing**.
sycamore ['sikəmɔː] n sicomoro m.
syllable ['siləbl] n sillaba f.
syllabus ['siləbəs] n programma m, prospetto m.
symbol ['simbl] n simbolo m. **symbolic** adj simbolico. **symbolism** n simbolismo m. **symbolize** v simboleggiare.
symmetry ['simitri] n simmetria f. **symmetrical** adj simmetrico.
sympathy ['simpəθi] n simpatia f, comprensione f; compassione f. **sympathetic** adj simpatico, simpatizzante; compassionevole. **sympathetic to** favorevole a, ben disposto verso. **sympathize** v simpatizzare; essere d'accordo; compatire. **sympathizer** n simpatizzante m, f.
symphony ['simfəni] n sinfonia f. **symphony orchestra** orchestra sinfonica f. **symphonic** adj sinfonico.
symposium [sim'pouziəm] n simposio m.
symptom ['simptəm] n sintomo m. **symptomatic** adj sintomatico.
synagogue ['sinəgog] n sinagoga f.
synchromesh ['siŋkroumeʃ] n sincronizzatore m.
synchronize ['siŋkrənaiz] v sincronizzare.

syndicate ['sindikit] n sindacato m.
syndrome ['sindroum] n sindrome f.
synod ['sinəd] n sinodo m.
synonym ['sinənim] n sinonimo m. **synonymous** adj sinonimo.
synopsis [si'nopsis] n, pl -ses sinossi f; (film, etc.) sinopsi f. **synoptic** adj sinottico.
syntax ['sintaks] n sintassi f. **syntactic** adj sintattico.
synthesis ['sinθisis] n, pl -ses sintesi f. **synthesize** v sintetizzare. **synthetic** adj sintetico.
syphilis ['sifilis] n sifilide f.
syringe [si'rindʒ] n siringa f. v siringare; (inject) iniettare.
syrup ['sirəp] n sciroppo m; (golden) melassa f. **syrupy** adj sciropposo.
system ['sistəm] n sistema m. **systematic** adj sistematico.

T

tab [tab] n cartellino m, etichetta f. **keep tabs on** tener d'occhio.
tabby ['tabi] n (gatto) soriano or tigrato m.
table ['teibl] n tavola f; (with modifier) tavolo m; (multiplication) tavola pitagorica f; (synopsis) tabella f. **lay/clear the table** apparecchiare/sparecchiare la tavola. **table-cloth** n tovaglia f. **table-mat** n sottopiatto m. **table-napkin** n tovagliolo m. **tablespoon** n cucchiaio da tavola m; (spoonful) cucchiaiata f. **table tennis** tennis da tavolo m. **turn the tables** rovesciare le posizioni. v intavolare.
table d'hôte [taːblə'dout] adj a prezzo fisso.
tablet ['tablit] n tavoletta f; (med) pastiglia f.
taboo [tə'buː] nm, adj tabù.
tabulate ['tabjuleit] v presentare in forma sinottica.
tacit ['tasit] adj tacito.
tack [tak] n (pin) puntina f; (naut) bordata f; (stitch) punto lungo m. **get down to brass tacks** venire ai fatti. v (sewing) imbastire; (sailing) bordeggiare. **tack on** aggiungere. **tacking** n imbastitura f. **tacky** adj appiccicaticcio, appiccicoso.

tackle ['takl] *n* attrezzatura *f*; (*fishing*) arnesi da pesca *m pl*; (*hoisting*) paranco *m*; (*football*) carica *f*; (*rugby*) placcaggio *m*. *v* venire alle prese con, affrontare; caricare; placcare.

tact [takt] *n* tatto *m*, riguardo *m*. **tactful** *adj* riguardoso, diplomatico. **tactless** *adj* mancante di riguardo, senza tatto.

tactics ['taktiks] *pl n* tattica *f sing*. **tactical** *adj* tattico. **tactician** *n* tattico, -a *m*, *f*.

tadpole ['tadpoul] *n* girino *m*.

taffeta ['tafitə] *n* taffettà *m*.

tag [tag] *n* (*stub*) talloncino *m*; (*label*) etichetta *f*, cartellino *m*; (*refrain*) ritornello *m*; (*saying*) locuzione *f*. *v* **tag along** seguire. **tag on** aggiungere.

tail [teil] *n* coda *f*. **tail-board** *n* ribalta *f*. **tail-end** *n* finalino *m*. **tail-light** *n* fanalino *m*. **tails** *pl n* (*dress*) frac *m invar*; (*coin*) croce *f sing*.

tailor ['teilə] *n* sarto, -a *m*, *f*. **tailoring** *n* mestiere del sarto *m*.

taint [teint] *n* tara *f*, traccia di marcio *f*. *v* (*spoil*) guastare, contaminare. **tainted** *adj* tarato.

***take** [teik] *v* prendere; (*carry*, *convey*) portare; (*require*) volerci; (*bath*, *walk*, *etc.*) fare. **take after** assomigliare a. **take back** riportare. **take care** badare, far attenzione. **take care of** curarsi di. **take down** tirar giù; (*dictation*) prender nota di. **take in** (*visitors*) dare alloggio a; (*reduce*) stringere; (*understand*) comprendere; (*deceive*) ingannare. **take off** (*remove*) togliere; (*aero*) decollare; (*mimic*) parodiare. **take-off** *n* decollo *m*; caricatura *f*. **take on** assumere; (*fight*) affrontare. **take out** tirar fuori; accompagnare. **take over** (*assume control*) rilevare. **take-over** *n* rilievo *m*. **take place** accadere, aver luogo. **take to** affezionarsi a; (*addict*) darsi a.

taken ['teikn] *V* take.

talcum powder ['talkəm] *n* talco in polvere *m*; borotalco *m*.

tale [teil] *n* storia *f*, racconto *m*; (*gossip*) diceria *f*.

talent ['talənt] *n* talento *m*; (*gift*) dote *f*; (*aptitude*) attitudine *f*. **talented** *adj* dotato.

talk [toık] *n* discorso *m*, conversazione *f*; (*lecture*) conferenza *f*; (*chat*) chiacchierata *f*. *v* parlare; conversare; chiacchierare. **talk about** parlare di. **talk nonsense** dire sciocchezze. **talk over** discutere. **talk**

round persuadere. **talk sense** dire cose sensate. **talkative** *adj* loquace.

tall [toıl] *adj* alto. **tallboy** *n* canterano *m*. **tall order** impresa difficile *f*. **tall story** storia inverosimile *f*, frottola *f*.

tally ['tali] *n* (*score*) punteggio *m*; (*account*) conto *m*; (*label*) etichetta *f*, scontrino *m*. *v* corrispondere; coincidere (con).

talon ['talən] *n* artiglio *m*.

tambourine [tambə'riın] *n* tamburello *m*.

tame [teim] *adj* docile, domestico. *v* addomesticare, domare.

tamper ['tampə] *v* **tamper with** alterare, falsificare; (*meddle*) ingerirsi in; (*bribe*) subornare.

tampon ['tampon] *n* tampone *m*.

tan [tan] *v* (*leather*) conciare; (*sun*) abbronzare. *n* (*colour*) castano *m*; abbronzatura *f*. *adj* castano.

tandem ['tandəm] *n* tandem *m invar*. **in tandem** in tandem.

tangent ['tandʒənt] *n* tangente *f*. **fly off at a tangent** pigliare un dirizzone.

tangerine [tandʒə'riın] *n* mandarino *m*.

tangible ['tandʒəbl] *adj* tangibile.

tangle ['tangl] *n* groviglio *m*, confusione *f*. *v* ingarbugliare, imbrogliare. **tangle with** (*fight*) lottare con *or* contro.

tank [taŋk] *n* serbatoio *m*; (*pool*) vasca *f*; (*mil*) carro armato *m*. **tanker** *n* (*ship*) nave cisterna *f*; (*lorry*) autocisterna *f*.

tankard ['taŋkəd] *n* boccale *m*.

tantalize ['tantəlaiz] *v* tormentare.

tantamount ['tantəmaunt] *adj* **be tantamount to** equivalere a, essere come.

tantrum ['tantrəm] *n* accesso d'ira *m*, bizza *f*. **have tantrums** fare le bizze.

tap¹ [tap] *v* (*strike*) picchiare, dare un colpetto a; (*knock*) bussare. *n* colpetto *m*.

tap² [tap] *n* rubinetto *m*; (*on cask*) spina *f*, cannella *f*. **on tap** (*beer*) alla spina; (*ready*) a disposizione, pronto. *v* (*draw off*) spillare; (*phone*) intercettare; utilizzare.

tape [teip] *n* nastro *m*. **red tape** burocrazia *f*. **tape-measure** *n* metro *m*. **tape-recorder** *n* registratore a nastro *m*. *v* (*tie*) allacciare; (*record*) registrare.

taper ['teipə] *v* affusolare, assottigliarsı. **taper off** finire a punta. *n* cerino *m*, candela sottile *f*. **tapering** *adj* affusolato, a punta.

tapestry ['tapəstri] *n* arazzo *m*, tappezzeria *f*.

tapioca [tapi'oukə] *n* tapioca *f*.

tar [taɪ] *n* catrame *m*. *v* incatramare.

tarantula [tə'rantjulə] *n* tarantola *f*.

target ['taɪgit] *n* bersaglio *m*, obiettivo *m*.

tariff ['tarif] *n* tariffa *f*.

tarmac ['taɪmak] *n* macadam al catrame; (*runway*) pista *f*.

tarnish ['taɪniʃ] *v* annerire, offuscare; (*stain*) macchiare. *n* annerimento *m*; macchia *f*.

tarpaulin [taɪ'pɔːlin] *n* copertone *m*.

tarragon ['tarəgən] *n* dragoncello *m*.

tart¹ [taɪt] *adj* aspro, agro. **tartness** *n* asprezza *f*.

tart² [taɪt] *n* torta *f*, crostata *f*; (*slang*) puttana *f*.

tartan ['taɪtən] *n* tartan *m invar*, tessuto scozzese *m*.

tartar ['taɪtə] *n* tartaro *m*. **cream of tartar** cremor di tartaro *m*.

task [taɪsk] *n* compito *m*, dovere *m*. **take to task** rimproverare.

tassel ['tasəl] *n* nappa *f*, nappina *f*.

taste [teist] *n* gusto *m*, sapore *m*; (*liking*) amore *m*, apprezzamento *m*; (*small sample*) assaggio *m*. *v* assaggiare, gustare. **taste of** sapere di. **tasteful** *adj* squisito, di buon gusto. **tasteless** *adj* insipido; di cattivo gusto. **tasty** *adj* saporito, appetitoso.

tattered ['tatəd] *adj* stracciato, a brandelli.

tattoo¹ [tə'tuɪ] *n* tatuaggio *m*. *v* tatuare.

tattoo² [tə'tuɪ] *n* (*mil*) ritirata *f*.

taught [tɔɪt] *V* teach.

taunt [tɔɪnt] *v* rinfacciare, schernire. *n* derisione *f*, scherno *m*.

Taurus ['tɔɪrəs] *n* Toro *m*.

taut [tɔɪt] *adj* teso.

tavern ['tavən] *n* osteria *f*, trattoria *f*, taverna *f*.

tawdry ['tɔɪdri] *adj* vistoso, volgare.

tax [taks] *n* tassa *f*, imposta *f*. **tax-collector** *n* esattore fiscale *m*. **tax evasion** evasione fiscale *f*. **taxpayer** *n* contribuente *m*, *f*. *v* tassare, imporre una tassa su; (*make demands*) mettere alla prova. **taxation** *n* tassazione *f*, tasse *f pl*.

taxi ['taksi] *n* tassì *m*. **taxi-driver** *n* tassista *m*, *f*. **taxi rank** posteggio (per tassì) *m*. *v* (*aero*) rullare.

tea [tiɪ] *n* tè *m*. **teacup** *n* tazza da tè *f*. **teapot** *n* teiera *f*. **teaspoon** *n* cucchiaino *m*. **tea-towel** *n* canovaccio *m*.

*teach [tiɪtʃ] *v* insegnare. **teacher** *n* insegnante *m*, *f*; (*primary school*) maestro, -a *m*, *f*; (*secondary school, university*) professore, -essa *m*, *f*. **teaching** *n* insegnamento *m*. **teachings** *pl n* dottrina *f sing*, precetti *m pl*.

teak [tiɪk] *n* tek *m*.

team [tiɪm] *n* squadra *f*; (*animals*) tiro *m*. **teamwork** *n* affiatamento *m*. *v* **team up with** mettersi insieme a, collaborare con.

*tear¹ [teə] *n* strappo *m*. *v* strappare. **be torn between** dibattersi tra. **tear off** strappar via; (*run*) scappar via. **tear up** stracciare. **tearing** *adj* impetuoso, terribile.

tear² [tiə] *n* lacrima *f*. **burst into tears** scoppiare in lacrime. **in tears** sciolto in lacrime. **tear-gas** *n* gas lacrimogeno *m*. **tearful** *adj* lacrimoso.

tease [tiɪz] *v* stuzzicare, canzonare; irritare.

teat [tiɪt] *n* (*nipple*) capezzolo *m*; (*rubber*) tettarella *f*.

technical ['teknikəl] *adj* tecnico. **technicality** *n* tecnicismo *m*. **technician** *n* tecnico, -a *m*, *f*. **technique** *n* tecnica *f*. **technological** *adj* tecnologico. **technologist** *n* tecnologo, -a *m*, *f*. **technology** *n* tecnologia *f*.

teddy bear ['tediˌbeə] *n* orsacchiotto *m*.

tedious ['tiɪdiəs] *adj* noioso. **tedium** *n* noia *f*.

tee [tiɪ] *n* tee *m invar*. *v* **tee off** cominciare (dal tee). **tee up** preparare, collocare sul tee.

teem [tiɪm] *v* (*rain*) grondare. **teem with** formicolare *or* brulicare di.

teenage ['tiɪneidʒ] *adj* adolescente. **teenager** *n* adolescente *m*, *f*.

teeth [tiɪθ] *V* tooth.

teethe [tiɪð] *v* mettere i denti. **teething** *n* dentizione *f*. **teething-ring** *n* dentaruolo *m*. **teething troubles** difficoltà iniziali *f pl*.

teetotal [tiɪ'toutl] *adj* astemio. **teetotaller** *n* astemio, -a *m*, *f*.

telecommunications [ˌtelikəmjuɪni'keiʃənz] *pl n* telecomunicazioni *f pl*.

telegram ['teligram] *n* telegramma *m*.

telegraph ['teligraɪf] *n* telegrafo *m*. *v* telegrafare. **telegraphic** *adj* telegrafico.

telepathy [tə'lepəθi] *n* telepatia *f*. **telepathic** *adj* telepatico.

telephone ['telifoun] *n* telefono *m*. *v* telefonare. **telephone box** cabina telefonica *f*. **telephone call** telefonata *f*, colpo di telefono *m*. **telephone exchange** centralino *m*. **telephone operator** telefonista *m*, *f*.
teleprinter ['teliprintə] *n* telescrivente *m*.
telescope ['teliskoup] *n* telescopio *m*. *v* incastrare, far scorrere l'uno nell'altro; (*shorten*) condensare. **telescopic** *adj* telescopico.
television ['teliviʒən] *n* televisione *f*. **television screen** video *m*. **television set** televisore *m*. **televise** *v* teletrasmettere, trasmettere per televisione.
telex ['teleks] *n* telex *m*. *v* trasmettere per telex.
*tell [tel] *v* dire, raccontare; distinguere. **tell off** (*scold*) sgridare. **telling-off** *n* ramanzina *f*, sgridata *f*. **telling** *adj* efficace, indicativo.
temper ['tempə] *n* (*mood*) umore *m*, disposizione *f*; (*metal*) tempra *f*. **keep one's temper** contenersi, rimaner calmo. **lose one's temper** arrabbiarsi, andare in collera. *v* moderare, temperare; (*metal*) temprare.
temperament ['tempərəmənt] *n* temperamento *m*, indole *f*. **temperamental** *adj* capriccioso.
temperate ['tempərət] *adj* temperato.
temperature ['temprətʃə] *n* temperatura *f*. **have a temperature** (*med*) avere la febbre.
tempestuous [tem'pestjuəs] *adj* tempestoso, burrascoso.
temple¹ ['templ] *n* (*rel*) tempio *m*.
temple² ['templ] *n* (*anat*) tempia *f*.
tempo ['tempou] *n* tempo *m*; ritmo *m*, andamento *m*.
temporary ['tempərəri] *adj* temporaneo.
tempt [tempt] *v* tentare. **temptation** *n* tentazione *f*. **tempter** *n* tentatore *m*. **tempting** *adj* allettante, seducente; (*food*) appetitoso. **temptress** *n* tentatrice *f*.
ten [ten] *nm*, *adj* dieci. **tenth** *nm*, *adj* decimo.
tenable [tenəbl] *adj* sostenibile, tenibile.
tenacious [tə'neiʃəs] *adj* tenace, ostinato; (*persistent*) accanito. **tenacity** *n* tenacia *f*, ostinazione *f*; accanimento *m*.
tenant ['tenənt] *n* inquilino, -a *m*, *f*. **tenancy** *n* affitto *m*.
tend¹ [tend] *v* (*be inclined*) tendere. **tendency** *n* tendenza *f*, inclinazione *f*. **tendentious** *adj* tendenzioso.

tend² [tend] *v* (*care for*) curare, assistere, soccorrere.
tender¹ ['tendə] *adj* tenero, delicato; (*affectionate*) affettuoso; (*sensitive*) sensibile. **tenderness** *n* tenerezza *f*; affettuosità *f*.
tender² ['tendə] *n* offerta *f*; (*comm*) preventivo *m*, appalto *m*. *v* offrire; appaltare, preventivare. **tender one's resignation** dare *or* rassegnare le dimissioni.
tendon ['tendən] *n* tendine *m*.
tendril ['tendril] *n* viticcio *m*.
tenement ['tenəmənt] *n* casamento *m*, casa popolare *f*.
tennis ['tenis] *n* tennis *m*. **tennis-ball/racket** *n* palla/racchetta da tennis *f*. **tennis-court** *n* campo da tennis *m*. **tennis player** giocatore, -trice di tennis *m*, *f*.
tenor ['tenə] *n* tenore *m*.
tense¹ [tens] *adj* teso, rigido. **tension** *n* tensione *f*; (*mech*) trazione *f*.
tense² [tens] *n* tempo *m*.
tent [tent] *n* tenda *f*.
tentacle ['tentəkl] *n* tentacolo *m*.
tentative ['tentətiv] *adj* di prova, sperimentale; (*hesitant*) titubante.
tenterhooks ['tentəhuks] *pl n* **on tenterhooks** sulle spine.
tenuous ['tenjuəs] *adj* tenue.
tenure ['tenjə] *n* tenuta *f*, possesso *m*, esercizio *m*.
tepid ['tepid] *adj* tiepido.
term [təːm] *n* termine *m*; durata *f*; (*school*) trimestre *m*. **come to terms with** venire a patti con. **terms** *pl n* tariffa *f* *sing*; condizioni *f pl*; (*footing*) relazioni *f pl*.
terminal ['təːminəl] *n* (*elec*) terminale *m*; (*aero*) terminal *m invar*. *adj* finale, estremo.
terminate ['təːmineit] *v* terminare, porre termine a. **termination** *n* (*act*) terminazione *f*; (*end*) termine *m*, conclusione *f*.
terminology [təːmi'nolədʒi] *n* terminologia *f*.
terminus ['təːminəs] *n* stazione di testa *f*, capolinea (*pl* capilinea) *m*.
terrace ['terəs] *n* terrazzo *m*; (*row of houses*) fila di case *f*.
terrain [tə'rein] *n* terreno *m*.
terrestrial [tə'restriəl] *adj* terrestre.
terrible ['terəbl] *adj* terribile, spaventoso.
terrier ['teriə] *n* terrier *m invar*.

terrific [tə'rifik] *adj* (*coll*) tremendo, fantastico.

terrify ['terifai] *v* atterrire. **be terrified** avere una paura matta. **terrifying** *adj* spaventoso.

territory ['teritəri] *n* territorio *m*. **territorial** *adj* territoriale.

terror ['terə] *n* terrore *m*. **terror-stricken** *adj* terrorizzato, atterrito. **terrorism** *n* terrorismo *m*. **terrorist** *n* terrorista *m*, *f*. **terrorize** *v* terrorizzare.

test [test] *n* prova *f*; esame *m*; analisi *f*; (*psych*) test *m invar*; (*industry*) collaudo *m*. **test-tube** *n* provetta *f*. *v* provare; esaminare; analizzare; collaudare.

testament ['testəmənt] *n* testamento *m*.

testicle ['testikl] *n* testicolo *m*.

testify ['testifai] *v* testimoniare, attestare.

testimonial [testi'mouniəl] *n* benservito *m*, attestato di buona condotta *m*.

testimony ['testiməni] *n* testimonianza *f*, deposizione *f*; (*proof*) prova *f*.

tetanus ['tetənəs] *n* tetano *m*.

tether ['teðə] *v* impastoiare. *n* pastoia *f*. **be at the end of one's tether** non poterne più, essere agli sgoccioli.

text [tekst] *n* testo *m*. **textbook** *n* libro di testo *m*. **textual** *adj* testuale.

textile ['tekstail] *nm*, *adj* tessile.

texture ['tekstjuə] *n* struttura *f*; (*surface*) grana *f*.

Thames [temz] *n* Tamigi *m*.

than [ðən] *conj* di, che.

thank [θaŋk] *v* ringraziare. **thank you** grazie. **thanks** *pl n* grazie *f pl*. **thanks to** grazie a. **thankful** *adj* riconoscente, grato.

that [ðat] *adj*, *pron* quel(lo), quella. **that is** cioè. **that's all!** ecco tutto! *adv* talmente. *conj* che.

thatch [θatʃ] *n* (copertura di) paglia *f*. *v* coprire di paglia.

thaw [θɔɪ] *n* disgelo *m*. *v* disgelare.

the [ðə] *art* il *or* lo, la; (*pl*) i *or* gli, le.

theatre ['θiətə] *n* teatro *m*; (*hospital*) sala operatoria *f*. **theatrical** *adj* teatrale.

theft [θeft] *n* furto *m*.

their [ðeə] *adj* (il) loro, (la) loro; (*pl*) (i) loro, (le) loro.

theirs [ðeəz] *pron* il loro, la loro; (*pl*) i loro, le loro.

them [ðem] *pron* (*before verb*) li, le; (*after verb or prep*) loro. **both of them** tutti e due. **none of them** nessuno di loro.

theme [θiːm] *n* tema *m*. **theme song** sigla (musicale) *f*. **thematic** *adj* tematico.

themselves [ðəm'selvz] *pron* loro stessi, -e; (*reflexive*) si; (*after prep*) sè stessi, -e.

then [ðen] *adv* (*at that time*) allora; (*next in time*) poi, dopo. **by then** a quel punto. **now and then** di tanto in tanto. *conj* dunque, allora. *adj* di allora.

theology [θi'olədʒi] *n* teologia *f*. **theologian** *n* teologo *m*. **theological** *adj* teologico.

theorem ['θiərəm] *n* teorema *m*.

theory ['θiəri] *n* teoria *f*. **theoretical** *adj* teorico.

therapy ['θerəpi] *n* terapia *f*. **therapeutic** *adj* terapeutico. **therapist** *n* terapista *m*, *f*.

there [ðeə] *adv* lì, là; (*to that place*) ci, vi. **thereabouts** *adv* da quelle parti, all'incirca. **thereafter** *adv* quindi, in seguito. **there are** ci sono. **thereby** *adv* così, in tal modo. **therefore** *adv* dunque, perciò, quindi. **there is** c'è; (*calling attention*) ecco. **there it is!** eccolo! **thereupon** *adv* quindi, subito dopo.

thermal ['θəɪməl] *adj* termico; (*waters*) termale.

thermodynamics [θəɪmoudai'namiks] *n* termodinamica *f*.

thermometer [θə'momitə] *n* termometro *m*.

thermonuclear [θəɪmou'njukliə] *adj* termonucleare.

thermos ® ['θəɪməs] *n* thermos ® *m invar*.

thermostat ['θəɪməstat] *n* termostato *m*.

these [ðiɪz] *pron*, *adj* questi, -e.

thesis ['θiɪsis] *n*, *pl* -ses tesi *f*.

they [ðei] *pron* essi, -e, loro.

thick [θik] *adj* spesso; (*hair*) folto; (*fog*) fitto; stupido. **thick as thieves** amici per la pelle. **thickset** *adj* (*heavily built*) tarchiato; (*dense*) folto, fitto. **thick-skinned** *adj* insensibile. **through thick and thin** nella buona e nella cattiva sorte. **thicken** *v* addensare, ispessire, infittire. **thickness** *n* spessore *m*; (*layer*) strato *m*.

thief [θiɪf] *n* ladro, -a *m*, *f*. **thieve** *v* rubare. **thieving** *n* ruberia *f*, il rubare *m*.

thigh [θai] *n* coscia *f*.

thimble ['θimbl] *n* ditale *m*.

thin [θin] *adj* sottile, fine; (*lean*) magro; (*not dense*) rado, sparso; (*weak*) debole. *v* diradare; (*lose weight*) dimagrare; (*dilute*) allungare. **thinner** *n* diluente *m*.

thing [θiŋ] *n* cosa *f*, oggetto *m*. **for one thing ... for another ...** anzitutto ... e poi .... **things** *pl n* (*implements, possessions etc.*) roba *f sing*, cose *f pl*.

*think [θiŋk] v pensare; (believe) credere, ritenere; (imagine) figurarsi. **thinker** n pensatore, -trice m, f.

thinking ['θiŋkiŋ] adj pensante, ragionevole. n pensiero m, il ragionare m. **to my way of thinking** a mio avviso.

third [θɜid] nm, adj terzo. **third party** terzi m pl.

thirst [θɜist] n sete f. v aver sete. **thirst for** or **after** bramare. **thirsty** adj assetato. **be thirsty** aver sete.

thirteen [θɜ'tiin] nm, adj tredici. **thirteenth** nm, adj tredicesimo.

thirty ['θɜiti] nm, adj trenta. **thirtieth** nm, adj trentesimo.

this [ðis] pron, adj questo, -a.

thistle ['θisl] n cardo m.

thorn [θoin] n spina f; (shrub) spino m. **thorny** adj spinoso.

thorough ['θʌrə] adj accurato; profondo; radicale; diligente. **thoroughly** adv a fondo.

thoroughbred ['θʌrəbred] n purosangue m. adj di razzo, di puro sangue.

thoroughfare ['θʌrəfeə] n via f, passaggio m.

those [ðouz] pron, adj quei or quegli, quelle.

though [ðou] conj (in spite of) sebbene, benchè; (yet, still) tuttavia, pure. **as though** come se. **even though** anche se. **it looks as though** sembra che.

thought [θoit] V think. n pensiero m; idea f. **on second thoughts** ripensandoci (su). **thoughtful** adj (reflective) pensoso; (thought out) profondo; (considerate) premuroso, sollecito; (careful) attento, prudente. **thoughtless** adj (careless) imprudente; (heedless) sbadato; (unthinking) avventato; (inconsiderate) irrispettoso.

thousand ['θauzənd] adj mille. n mille m invar, migliaio (pl -a) m. **thousandth** nm, adj millesimo.

thrash [θraʃ] v battere, bastonare. **thrash out** discutere a fondo. **thrashing** n (defeat) batosta f; (beating) botte f pl.

thread [θred] n filo m; (screw) filetto m, passo m. v infilare; filettare. **threadbare** adj logoro.

threat [θret] n minaccia f. **threaten** v minacciare. **threatening** adj minaccioso; (letter) minatorio.

three [θrii] nm, adj tre. **three-cornered** adj triangolare, a tre punte. **three-dimensional** adj tridimensionale. **three-ply** adj (wood) a tre strati; (wool) a tre capi. **three-quarter** adj a tre quarti. **three-speed** adj a tre marce.

thresh [θreʃ] v (corn, etc.) trebbiare; battere. **threshing** n trebbiatura f.

threshold ['θreʃould] n soglia f.

threw [θrui] V throw.

thrift [θrift] n frugalità f, economia f. **thrifty** adj frugale, parsimonioso. **be thrifty** fare economia.

thrill [θril] n brivido m, fremito m; (excitement) emozione f. v far rabbrividire; emozionare; entusiasmare. **be thrilled with** essere entusiasta di. **thriller** n (book, film) giallo m. **thrilling** adj emozionante, eccitante.

thrive [θraiv] v fiorire, riuscire. **thrive on** approfittare di. **thriving** adj prospero, fiorente.

throat [θrout] n gola f. **have a sore throat** aver mal di gola. **throaty** adj gutturale.

throb [θrob] v battere, palpitare. n battito m, palpito m. **throbbing** adj palpitante, pulsante.

throes [θrouz] pl n **in the throes of** alle prese con.

thrombosis [θrom'bousis] n trombosi f.

throne [θroun] n trono m.

throng [θroŋ] n folla f, calca f. v affollarsi, stiparsi.

throttle ['θrotl] v strozzare; (suppress) soffocare; (mot) regolare. n (valve) valvola a farfalla f.

through [θrui] adj diretto, di transito; finito. adv da una parte all'altra; (to the end) fino alla fine. prep da, per; (place) attraverso; (time) durante; (by means of) tramite, per mezzo di; (past) al di là di. **get through** (phone) ottenere la comunicazione; (finish) sbrigare. **throughout** adv completamente; (time) durante; (always) sempre.

*throw [θrou] n lancio m, tiro m. v lanciare, gettare; (coll: confuse) lasciare perplesso, sconcertare. **throw away** buttar via. **throwaway** adj (casual) spigliato; (remark) lasciato cadere; (to be discarded) da buttar via. **throw in** buttar dentro; (sport) rimettere in gioco; (include) comprendere. **throw out** buttar fuori, mettere alla porta; (put forward) dare. **throw up** lanciare in aria; (be sick) rigettare.

thrown [θroun] *V* **throw**.
thrush¹ [θrʌʃ] *n* (*bird*) tordo *m*.
thrush² [θrʌʃ] *n* (*med*) mughetto *m*.
*thrust [θrʌst] *n* spinta *f*, botta *f*; (*mil*) attacco *m*. *v* spingere, ficcare, lanciarsi. **thrust oneself on** imporsi a.
thud [θʌd] *n* tonfo *m*.
thug [θʌg] *n* delinquente *m*.
thumb [θʌm] *n* pollice *m*. **thumbmark** *n* impronta digitale *f*. *v* **thumb a lift** fare l'autostop.
thump [θʌmp] *n* tonfo *m*. *v* picchiare, battere.
thunder ['θʌndə] *n* tuono *m*. **thunderbolt** *n* fulmine *m*. **thunderstorm** *n* temporale *m*. **thunderstruck** *adj* sbalordito. *v* tuonare. **thundering** *adj* (*coll*) enorme. **thundery** *adj* temporalesco; (*menacing*) minaccioso.
Thursday ['θəɪzdi] *n* giovedì *m*.
thus [ðʌs] *adv* così.
thwart [θwoɪt] *v* frustrare.
thyme [taim] *n* timo *m*.
thyroid ['θairoid] *n* tiroide *f*.
tiara [ti'aɪrə] *n* diadema *m*.
tick¹ [tik] *n* (*sound*) tictac *m invar*, ticchettio *m*; (*mark*) contrassegno *m*, visto *m*; (*moment*) attimo *m*. *v* ticchettare, fare tictac; contrassegnare, vistare. **tick off** (*coll: scold*) sgridare. **ticking-off** *n* (*coll*) lavata di capo *f*. **tick over** (*engine*) girare in folle.
tick² [tik] *n* (*insect*) zecca *f*, acaro *m*.
ticket ['tikit] *n* biglietto *m*; (*label, counterfoil*) scontrino *m*. **ticket collector** bigliettario, -a *m, f*. **ticket office** biglietteria *f*.
tickle ['tikl] *v* solleticare; (*make itch*) fare il solletico; (*gratify*) lusingare; (*amuse*) divertire. *n* irritazione *f*; (*itch*) prurito *m*.
ticklish *adj* (*person*) che sente il solletico; (*tricky*) delicato, scabroso.
tide [taid] *n* marea *f*; corrente *f*. **tidemark** *n* battigia *f*. *v* **tide over** superare.
tidy ['taidi] *adj* ordinato; (*neat*) ben curato *or* tenuto; (*coll: considerable*) bello. *v* mettere in ordine. **tidy up** far pulizia. **tidiness** *n* ordine *m*.
tie [tai] *v* legare; (*join*) attaccare; (*lace up*) allacciare; (*sport*) pareggiare. **tie down** limitare, obbligare. **tie up** (*property, capital etc.*) vincolare. *n* legame *m*; (*neck*) cravatta *f*; (*bond*) vincolo *m*; pareggio *m*; (*music*) legatura *f*.
tier [tiə] *n* (*row*) fila *f*; (*rank*) gradino *m*; (*layer*) strato *m*.

tiger ['taigə] *n* tigre *f*.
tight [tait] *adj* stretto; (*fitting closely*) aderente; (*taut*) teso; (*coll: drunk*) brillo; (*coll: mean*) tirchio. **in a tight corner** con le spalle al muro. *adv* **hold tight** stringere, tenersi fermo. **sit tight** non muoversi. **tighten** *v* stringere, serrare. **tights** *pl n* collant *m invar*.
tile [tail] *n* (*roof*) tegola *f*; (*floor, wall*) piastrella *f*, mattonella *f*. *v* coprire con tegole *or* piastrelle.
till¹ [til] *V* **until**.
till² [til] *n* cassa *f*.
till³ [til] *v* coltivare; (*plough*) arare.
tiller ['tilə] *n* (*rudder*) barra del timone *f*.
tilt [tilt] *v* inclinare. *n* inclinazione *f*. **at full tilt** di gran carriera, a tutta velocità.
timber ['timbə] *n* legname *m*; (*beam*) trave *f*. **timbered** *adj* costruito in legno, coperto di legno; (*wooded*) alberato.
time [taim] *n* tempo *m*, periodo *m*; (*occasion*) volta *f*; (*clock*) ora *f*; epoca *f*. **for a long time** (*past*) da molto tempo; (*future*) per molto tempo. **for the time being** per ora. **from time to time** ogni tanto, di quando in quando. **have a good time** divertirsi. **in time** a tempo; (*eventually*) alla fine. **one at a time** uno alla volta. **on time** in orario. **take one's time** fare con comodo. **time bomb** bomba a orologeria *f*. **timekeeper** *n* (*sport*) cronometrista *m*; (*overseer*) controllore *m*. **time-signal** *n* segnale orario *m*. **timetable** *n* orario *m*. *v* misurare il tempo; (*sport*) cronometrare; (*choose moment*) scegliere il momento. **timeless** *adj* eterno, permanente. **timely** *adj* opportuno, tempestivo.
timid ['timid] *adj* timido. **timidity** *n* timidezza *f*.
tin [tin] *n* (*metal*) stagno *m*; (*can*) latta *f*, scatola *f*. **tin-opener** *n* apriscatole *m invar*. *v* inscatolare; stagnare. **tinny** *adj* (*sound*) metallico.
tinge [tindʒ] *n* sfumatura *f*, tocco *m*. *v* **tinged with** misto a.
tingle ['tiŋgl] *v* formicolare. *n* formicolio *m*, prurito *m*.
tinker ['tiŋkə] *v* (*repair*) rabberciare, rattoppare; (*busy oneself*) affaccendarsi.
tinkle ['tiŋkl] *v* (far) tintinnare, squillare. *n* tintinnio *m*, squillo *m*.
tinsel ['tinsəl] *n* orpello *m*.
tint [tint] *n* tono *m*, tinta *f*. *v* colorire.

tiny ['taini] *adj* piccino, minuto.
tip¹ [tip] *n* (*end*) punta *f*, estremità *f*; (*summit*) cima *f*. **tiptoe** *v* camminare in punta di piedi. **on tiptoe** in punta di piedi.
tip² [tip] *v* (*topple*) rovesciare; (*dump*) scaricare. *n* luogo di scarico *m*.
tip³ [tip] *n* (*money*) mancia *f*; (*hint*) consiglio *m*; informazione riservata *f*. *v* dare la mancia. **tip off** avvertire, prevenire.
tipsy ['tipsi] *adj* (*coll*) brillo. **get tipsy** ubriacarsi leggermente.
tire¹ ['taiə] *v* stancarsi, stancare; (*get fed up*) stufarsi. **tired** *adj* stanco; (*fed up*) stufo. **tireless** *adj* infaticabile; (*unceasing*) indefesso. **tiresome** *adj* noioso, seccante. **tiring** *adj* faticoso.
tire² (*US*) *V* **tyre**.
tissue ['tiʃuɪ] *n* tessut ɔ *m*; (*handkerchief*) fazzoletto di carta *m*. **tissue paper** carta velina *f*.
tit [tit] *n* (*bird*) cincia *f*.
title ['taitl] *n* titolo *m*; (*law*) diritto *m*. **title-page** *n* frontespizio *m*. **title-role** *n* parte principale *f*. *v* intitolare.
to [tu] *prep* a, in; (*in order to*) per; (*towards*) verso; da. *adv* **to and fro** avanti e indietro. **to-do** *n* (*coll*) trambusto *m*.
toad [toud] *n* rospo *m*. **toadstool** *n* fungo *m*.
toast [toust] *n* (*bread*) toast *m invar*; (*speech*, *drink*) brindisi *m*. **drink a toast to** bere alla salute di. *v* tostare. **toaster** *n* tostapane *m invar*.
tobacco [tə'bakou] *n* tabacco *m*. **tobacconist** *n* tabaccaio, -a *m*, *f*.
toboggan [tə'bogən] *n* toboga *m invar*. *v* andare in toboga.
today [tə'dei] *adv* oggi; (*nowadays*) oggigiorno. **a week/fortnight today** oggi a otto/quindici. *n* oggi *m*.
toddler ['todlə] *n* bambino, -a *m*, *f*, piccino, -a *m*, *f*. **toddle** *v* sgambettare.
toe [tou] *n* dito del piede *m*; (*shoe*) punta *f*. **tread on someone's toes** pestare i piedi a qualcuno.
toffee ['tofi] *n* caramella mou *f*.
together [tə'geðə] *adv* insieme, assieme. **together with** insieme con, assieme a.
toil [toil] *n* fatica *f*. *v* faticare.
toilet ['toilit] *n* (*lavatory*) gabinetto *m*; (*dressing*, *etc.*) toilette (*pl* -s) *f*, toletta *f*. **toilet-paper** *n* carta igienica *f*. **toilet water** acqua da toletta *f*.

token ['toukən] *n* segno *m*, simbolo *m*; (*gift*) omaggio *m*; (*coin*) gettone *m*.
Tokyo ['toukiou] *n* Tokio *f*.
told [tould] *V* **tell**.
tolerate ['toləreit] *v* tollerare, sopportare. **tolerable** *adj* tollerabile. **tolerance** *n* tolleranza *f*. **tolerant** *adj* tollerante.
toll¹ [toul] *n* pedaggio *m*; (*duty*) dazio *m*.
toll² [toul] *n* (*bell*) rintocco *m*. *v* rintoccare.
tomato [tə'maɪtou] *n* pomodoro *m*. **tomato juice/paste** succo/estratto di pomodoro *m*. **tomato sauce** salsa di pomodoro *f*.
tomb [tuɪm] *n* tomba *f*. **tombstone** *n* pietra tombale *f*.
tomorrow [tə'morou] *nm*, *adv* domani. **the day after tomorrow** dopodomani. **tomorrow morning** domattina. **tomorrow week** domani a otto.
ton [tʌn] *n* tonnellata *f*. **tonnage** *n* tonnellaggio *m*.
tone [toun] *n* tono *m*. *v* armonizzare. **tone down** attenuare, smorzare. **tonality** *n* tonalità *f*.
tongs [toŋz] *pl n* pinza *f sing*; (*fire*) molle *f pl*.
tongue [tʌŋ] *n* lingua *f*. **hold one's tongue** star zitto, tacere. **tongue-tied** *adj* ammutolito; (*speech defect*) scilinguato.
tonic ['tonik] *n* ricostituente *m*; (*water*) acqua brillante *f*; (*music*) tonica *f*. *adj* tonico.
tonight [tə'nait] *adj* (*evening*) stasera; (*night*) stanotte.
tonsil ['tonsil] *n* tonsilla *f*. **tonsillitis** *n* tonsillite *f*.
too [tuɪ] *adv* (*also*) anche, pure; (*moreover*) inoltre; (*more than enough*) troppo. **too many** troppi. **too much** troppo.
took [tuk] *V* **take**.
tool [tuɪl] *n* attrezzo *m*, arnese *m*; strumento *m*. **tool-shed** *n* ripostiglio per attrezzi *m*. **tools of the trade** ferri del mestiere *m pl*. *v* lavorare.
tooth [tuɪθ] *n*, *pl* **teeth** dente *m*. **have a sweet tooth** essere ghiotto di dolci. **have a tooth out** farsi cavare un dente. **in the teeth of** (*in defiance of*) a dispetto di; (*in the presence of*) in cospetto di. **toothache** *n* mal di denti *m*. **tooth-brush** *n* spazzolino da denti *m*. **toothpaste** *n* dentifricio *m*. **toothpick** *n* stuzzicadenti *m*. **toothless** *adj* sdentato.

top¹ [top] *n* (*highest point*) cima *f*, vertice *m*; (*leading position*) testa *f*, capo *m*; (*lid*) coperchio *m*. **at the top of one's voice** a voce altissima; (*shouting*) a squarciagola. **from top to toe** da capo a piedi. **on top of** (*upon*) sopra, su; (*at the head of*) in testa a; (*following*) dopo, in seguito a. *adj* (*uppermost*) superiore, ultimo; (*greatest*) più alto; (*foremost*) principale. **at top speed** a velocità massima. **top-heavy** *adj* sovraccarico (*m pl* -chi); (*unbalanced*) sbilanciato. **topsoil** *n* terriccio *m*. *v* sorpassare, superare; (*be above*) sovrastare a; (*prune*) scapezzare. **top up** *v* riempire. **topless** *adj* (*dress*) a petto scoperto. **topmost** *adj* il più alto.

top² [top] *n* (*toy*) trottola *f*.

topaz ['toupaz] *n* topazio *m*.

topic ['topik] *n* argomento *m*. **topical** *adj* di attualità.

topography [tə'pogrəfi] *n* topografia *f*.

topple ['topl] *v* (far) cadere *or* crollare.

topsy-turvy [topsi'tɜɪvi] *adv* sottosopra.

torch [tɔɪtʃ] *n* fiaccola *f*; (*electric*) lampadina tascabile *f*, torcia elettrica *f*.

tore [tɔɪ] *V* tear¹.

torment ['tɔɪment; *v* tɔɪ'ment] *n* supplizio *m*, tortura *f*. *v* tormentare, angosciare.

torn [tɔɪn] *V* tear¹.

tornado [tɔɪ'neidou] *n* tornado *m*, turbine *m*.

torpedo [tɔɪ'piɪdou] *n* siluro *m*, torpedine *f*. *v* silurare. **torpedo-boat** *n* torpediniera *f*.

torrent ['tɔrənt] *n* torrente *m*. **torrential** *adj* torrenziale.

torso ['tɔɪsou] *n* torso *m*.

tortoise ['tɔɪtəs] *n* tartaruga *f*. **tortoise-shell** *nf, adj* tartaruga.

tortuous ['tɔɪtʃuəs] *adj* tortuoso.

torture ['tɔɪtʃə] *n* tortura *f*. *v* torturare.

Tory ['tɔɪri] *n, adj* (*coll*) conservatore, -trice.

toss [tos] *v* (*throw*) lanciare; (*pitch*) sballottare; (*move restlessly*) agitarsi. **toss aside** buttar via. **toss back** rilanciare. **toss up** (*coin*) far testa o croce; tirare a sorte. **toss-up** *n* questione di fortuna *f*. *n* **toss of the head** scrollata del capo *f*.

tot¹ [tot] *n* (*child*) bimbo, -a *m, f*, piccino, -a *m, f*; (*drink*) bicchierino *m*.

tot² [tot] *v* **tot up** sommare, fare la somma di.

total ['toutəl] *n* totale *m*, ammontare *m*.

adj totale, globale. *v* (*add up*) fare la somma di; (*add up to*) ammontare a.

totter ['totə] *v* barcollare, vacillare. **tottering** *adj* barcollante; (*shaky*) malsicuro.

touch [tʌtʃ] *n* (*sense*) tatto *m*; contatto *m*; (*music, painting*) tocco *m*; (*hint*) accenno *m*; (*med*) attacco leggero *m*. **touchstone** *n* pietra di paragone *f*, criterio *m*. *v* toccare; (*lightly*) sfiorare; (*handle*) maneggiare, tastare; (*move*) commuovere. **touch-and-go** *adj* rischioso. **touch down** (*plane*) atterrare. **touch up** ritoccare, ripassare. **touch wood!** tocca ferro! **touched** *adj* commosso. **touching** *adj* commovente; adiacente. **touchy** *adj* permaloso.

tough [tʌf] *adj* (*hard*) duro; (*hardy*) tenace; robusto; resistente; difficile. *n* teppista *m*. **toughen** *v* indurire, rinforzare. **toughness** *n* robustezza *f*; durezza *f*; resistenza *f*.

toupee ['tuɪpei] *n* toupet *m invar*, parrucca *f*.

tour [tuə] *n* giro *m*, viaggio *m*; (*theatre, sport*) tournée (*pl* -s) *f*. *v* viaggiare, fare un giro; fare una tournée. **tourism** *n* turismo *m*. **tourist** *n* turista *m, f*.

tournament ['tuənəmənt] *n* torneo *m*.

tow¹ [tou] *n* (*hemp*) stoppa *f*.

tow² [tou] *v* rimorchiare. *n* **in tow** rimorchio. **tow-rope** *n* rimorchio *m*. **tow-path** *n* alzaia *f*.

towards [tə'wɔɪdz] *prep* verso, incontro a.

towel ['tauəl] *n* asciugamano *m*. *v* asciugarsi. **towelling** *n* spugna *f*.

tower ['tauə] *n* torre *f*. *v* elevarsi. **tower above** dominare. **towering** *adj* dominante; (*very great*) smisurato; violento.

town [taun] *n* città *f*; (*smaller*) cittadina *f*. **go to town** andare in città; (*do thoroughly*) mettercela tutta. **town clerk** segretario comunale *m*. **town hall** municipio *m*. **town planner** urbanista *m, f*. **town planning** urbanistica *f*.

toxic ['toksik] *adj* tossico. **toxicity** *n* tossicità *f*.

toy [toi] *n* giocattolo *m*. *v* (*play*) giocherellare; (*trifle*) dilettarsi.

trace [treis] *n* traccia *f*. *v* (*indicate, sketch*) tracciare; (*follow, discover*) rintracciare. **traceable** *adj* rintracciabile.

track [trak] *n* (*footpath*) sentiero *m*; (*mark, trace*) traccia *f*, orma *f*; (*sport*) pista *f*; (*set course*) percorso *m*; (*record*) banda *f*. **keep track of** seguire. **off the**

beaten **track** fuori mano. **on the right
track** sulla strada buona. *v* inseguire.
track down scovare.

tract¹ [trakt] *n* (*region*) zona *f*; (*anat*)
apparato *m*.

tract² [trakt] *n* (*treatise*) trattato *m*; (*pamphlet*) manifesto *m*.

tractor ['traktə] *n* trattore *m*.

trade [treid] *n* (*work*) mestiere *m*; commercio *m*, traffico *m*; (*business*) affari *m pl*. **trademark** *n* marchio depositato *m*. **tradesman** *n* fornitore *m*, esercente *m*, negoziante *m*. **trade union** sindacato *m*. **trade unionist** sindacalista *m*, *f*. *v* fare affari, commerciare. **trade on** approfittare di. **trader** *n* commerciante *m*, *f*.

trading ['treidiŋ] *n* commercio *m*. *adj* commerciale.

tradition [trə'diʃən] *n* tradizione *f*. **traditional** *adj* tradizionale.

traffic ['trafik] *n* traffico *m*. **traffic jam** intasamento or ingorgo (del traffico) *m*. **traffic-light** *n* semaforo *m*. *v* trafficare.

tragedy ['tradʒədi] *n* tragedia *f*. **tragic** *adj* tragico.

trail [treil] *n* traccia *f*, pista *f*. *v* (*follow*) inseguire; (*drag*) trascinare. **trailer** *n* rimorchio *m*.

train [trein] *n* (*rail*) treno *m*; (*dress*) strascico *m*; (*following*) seguito *m*; serie *f*. **train of events** svolgimento *m*. *v* (*teach*) istruire; (*impart skill*) addestrare, ammaestrare; (*sport*) allenare. **trainee** *n* allievo, -a *m*, *f*; (*apprentice*) apprendista *m*, *f*. **trainer** *n* allenatore, -trice *m*, *f*. **training** *n* addestramento *m*; allenamento *m*.

trait [treit] *n* caratteristica *f*.

traitor ['treitə] *n* traditore *m*. **traitress** *n* traditrice *f*. **turn traitor** passare al nemico.

tram [tram] *n* tram *m invar*.

tramp [tramp] *n* (*person*) vagabondo *m*; (*walk*) passeggiata *f*; (*sound*) calpestio *m*. *v* vagabondare, percorrere a piedi.

trample ['trampl] *v* calpestare. **trample on** pestare.

trampoline ['trampəliin] *n* trampolino *m*.

trance [trains] *n* trance *f invar*; (*daze*) stupore *m*.

tranquil ['traŋkwil] *adj* sereno, calmo. **tranquillity** *n* serenità *f*, calma *f*. **tranquillizer** *n* tranquillante *m*, sedativo *m*.

transact [tran'zakt] *v* **transact business**

trattare, entrare in trattative. **transaction** *n* affare *m*, trattativa *f*.

transcend [tran'send] *v* trascendere, superare. **transcendental** *adj* trascendentale.

transcribe [tran'skraib] *v* trascrivere. **transcript** or **transcription** *n* trascrizione *f*.

transept ['transept] *n* transetto *m*.

transfer ['transfəɪ; *v* trans'fəɪ] *n* trasferimento *m*; (*design*) decalcomania *f*. *v* trasferire; (*drawing*) riportare. **transferable** *adj* trasferibile.

transform [trans'foɪm] *v* trasformare. **transformation** *n* trasformazione *f*, mutamento *m*; (*phys*) conversione *f*. **transformer** *n* trasformatore *m*.

transfuse [trans'fjuɪz] *v* trasfondere. **transfusion** *n* trasfusione *f*.

transgress [trans'gres] *v* trasgredire. **transgression** *n* trasgressione *f*, infrazione *f*.

transient ['tranziənt] *adj* transitorio, passeggero; (*phys*) transiente.

transistor [tran'zistə] *n* transistor *m invar*, transistore *m*. **transistorize** *v* transistorizzare.

transit ['transit] *n* passaggio *m*, transito *m*. **in transit** durante il trasporto, in transito. *adj* di passaggio or transito.

transition [tran'ziʃən] *n* transizione *f*; (*music*) modulazione *f*.

transitive ['transitiv] *adj* transitivo.

translate [trans'leit] *v* tradurre. **translation** *n* traduzione *f*. **translator** *n* traduttore, -trice *m*, *f*.

translucent [trans'luɪsnt] *adj* semitrasparente, traslucido.

transmit [tranz'mit] *v* trasmettere. **transmission** *n* trasmissione *f*. **transmitter** *n* (*radio set*) trasmettitore *m*; (*station*) trasmittente *f*.

transparent [trans'peərənt] *adj* trasparente. **transparency** *n* trasparenza *f*; (*phot*) diapositiva *f*.

transplant [trans'plaɪnt; *n* 'transplaɪnt] *v* trapiantare. *n* trapianto *m*.

transport ['transpoɪt; *v* trans'poɪt] *n* trasporto *m*. *v* trasportare. **transportation** *n* trasporto *m*.

transpose [trans'pouz] *v* trasporre. **transposition** *n* trasposizione *f*.

transverse ['tranzvəɪs] *adj* traverso, trasversale.

trap [trap] *n* trappola *f*; (*trick*) tranello

m; (*vehicle*) carrozzetta *f*. **trapdoor** *n* trabocchetto *m*. *v* prendere in trappola.
trapeze [trə'piːz] *n* trapezio *m*.
trash [traʃ] *n* (*rubbish*) robaccia *f*; rifiuti *m pl*; (*nonsense*) sciocchezze *f pl*. **trashy** *adj* di nessun valore.
trauma ['troɪmə] *n* trauma *m*. **traumatic** *adj* traumatico.
travel ['travl] *n* viaggiare *m*, viaggi *m pl*. **travel agency** agenzia di viaggi *f*. *v* viaggiare. **traveller** *n* viaggiatore, -trice *m*, *f*. **traveller's cheque** assegno turistico *m*.
travesty ['travəsti] *n* travestimento *m*, parodia *f*.
trawl [trɔːl] *n* strascico (*pl* -chi) *m*. *v* pescare con strascico. **trawler** *n* peschereccio *m*.
tray [trei] *n* vassoio *m*.
treachery ['tretʃəri] *n* tradimento *m*, perfidia *f*. **treacherous** *adj* traditore, -trice, perfido; (*unreliable*) falso; (*dangerous*) pericoloso.
treacle ['triːkl] *n* melassa *f*.
*tread [tred] *v* (*trample*) calcare, calpestare; (*walk*) camminare. *n* passo *m*; (*stair*) gradino *m*; (*tyre*) battistrada *m invar*.
treason ['triːzn] *n* tradimento *m*.
treasure ['treʒə] *n* tesoro *m*. *v* (*cherish*) aver caro; (*prize*) apprezzare; (*retain carefully*) tener caro. **treasurer** *n* tesoriere, -a *m*, *f*. **treasury** *n* tesoreria *f*. **Treasury** *n* Ministero del Tesoro *m*.
treat [triːt] *v* trattare; (*med*) curare. *n* piacere *m*. **treatment** *n* trattamento *m*.
treatise ['triːtiz] *n* trattato *m*, dissertazione *f*.
treaty ['triːti] *n* trattato *m*.
treble ['trebl] *adj* triplo, triplice; di soprano. *n* soprano. *v* triplicare. *adv* tre volte tanto.
tree [triː] *n* albero *m*.
trek [trek] *v* viaggiare (scomodamente). *n* viaggio (scomodo) *m*, migrazione *f*.
trellis ['trelis] *n* pergolato *m*, graticcio *m*.
tremble ['trembl] *v* tremare; (*be agitated*) fremere. *n* tremito *m*; fremito *m*.
tremendous [trə'mendəs] *adj* enorme; (*coll*) straordinario.
tremor ['tremə] *n* tremore *m*.
trench [trentʃ] *n* (*ditch*) fosso *m*; (*mil*) trincea *f*. **trenchant** *adj* tagliente, caustico.
trend [trend] *n* tendenza *f*; direzione *f*; (*fashion*) moda *f*. **trendy** *adj* di moda.

trespass ['trespəs] *v* trasgredire; (*rel*) peccare. *n* trasgressione *f*; peccato *m*.
trestle ['tresl] *n* trespolo *m*.
trial ['traiəl] *n* (*law*) processo *m*; (*test*) esame *m*, prova *f*; esperimento *m*; (*trouble*) disperazione *f*, dolore *m*. **by trial and error** (a) tentoni.
triangle ['traiaŋgl] *n* triangolo *m*. **triangular** *adj* triangolare.
tribe [traib] *n* tribù *f*. **tribal** *adj* tribale. **tribesman** *n* membro di tribù *m*.
tribunal [trai'bjuːnl] *n* tribunale *m*.
tributary ['tribjutəri] *nm*, *adj* tributario.
tribute ['tribjuːt] *n* tributo *m*, omaggio *m*. **pay tribute to** rendere omaggio a.
trick [trik] *n* espediente *m*; (*prank*) tiro *m*; (*artifice*) trucco *m*; (*cards*) bazza *f*. **confidence trick** truffa all'americana *f*. **do the trick** ottenere l'effetto voluto. *v* ingannare, abbindolare. **trickery** *n* inganno *m*. **tricky** *adj* (*crafty*) furbo; complicato, delicato.
trickle ['trikl] *v* gocciolare. *n* gocciolio *m*; flusso irregolare *m*. **trickle of water** filo d'acqua *m*.
tricycle ['traisikl] *n* triciclo *m*.
trifle ['traifl] *n* sciocchezza *f*, inezia *f*; (*food*) zuppa inglese *f*. **a trifle** (*a little*) un po', alquanto. *v* scherzare. **trifling** *adj* insignificante.
trigger ['trigə] *n* grilletto *m*. *v* **trigger off** far scattare.
trigonometry [trigə'nomətri] *n* trigonometria *f*.
trill [tril] *n* trillo *m*. *v* trillare; (*continuous*) trilleggiare.
trilogy ['trilədʒi] *n* trilogia *f*.
trim [trim] *adj* ordinato, ben messo *or* tenuto, assettato. *n* assetto *m*; (*ornament*) guarnizione *f*. *v* (*neaten*) assettare; guarnire; (*hair*) spuntare. **trimmings** *pl n* guarnizioni *f pl*.
trinket ['triŋkit] *n* gingillo *m*.
trio ['triːou] *n* trio *m*.
trip [trip] *n* (*excursion*) gita *f*; (*journey*) viaggio *m*; (*stumble*) passo falso *m*. *v* (*step lightly*) saltellare; (*stumble*) inciampare. **trip up** far cadere, fare lo sgambetto, inciampare. **tripper** *n* escursionista *m*, *f*.
tripe [traip] *n* trippa *f*.
triple ['tripl] *adj* triplo, triplice. *v* triplicare. **triplet** *n* trigemino, -a *m*, *f*.

tripod ['traipod] *n* cavalletto *m*, treppiede *m*.

trite [trait] *adj* banale, comune.

triumph ['traiʌmf] *n* trionfo *m*. *v* trionfare, esultare. **triumphant** *adj* trionfante.

trivial ['triviəl] *adj* insignificante, banale. **triviality** *n* affare di nessuna importanza *m*.

trod [trod] *V* **tread**.

trodden ['trodn] *V* **tread**.

trolley ['troli] *n* carrello *m*.

trombone [trom'boun] *n* trombone *m*.

troop [truːp] *n* banda *f*, gruppo *m*; (*mil*) truppa *f*. *v* **troop along** sfilare. **troop in/out** entrare/uscire in gruppo.

trophy ['troufi] *n* trofeo *m*.

tropic ['tropik] *n* tropico *m*. **tropical** *adj* tropicale.

trot [trot] *v* trottare. *n* trotto *m*, trottata *f*. **on the trot** (*coll*) di seguito. **trotter** *n* (*horse*) trottatore *m*; (*pig's foot*) zampa *f*.

trouble ['trʌbl] *n* disturbo *m*; difficoltà *f*; (*unpleasantness*) dispiacere *m*; preoccupazione *f*; (*annoyance*) fastidio *m*. **make trouble** creare guai. **the trouble is** il guaio è. **troublemaker** *n* sobillatore, -trice *m*, *f*. *v* disturbare, dare fastidio. **troubled** *adj* turbato, preoccupato, agitato. **troublesome** *adj* noioso, fastidioso.

trough [trof] *n* trogolo *m*; (*drinking*) abbeveratoio *m*.

trousers ['trauzəz] *pl n* calzoni *m pl*, pantaloni *m pl*.

trout [traut] *n* trota *f*.

trowel ['trauəl] *n* (*plastering*) cazzuola *f*; (*gardening*) vanghetto *m*.

truant ['truːənt] *n* **play truant** marinare la scuola; (*shirk duty*) batter la fiacca.

truce [truːs] *n* tregua *f*.

truck [trʌk] *n* autocarro *m*, camion *m*.

trudge [trʌdʒ] *v* trascinarsi, camminare a stento.

true [truː] *adj* vero; corretto; genuino; (*mech*) centrato. **come true** avverarsi. **hold true for** valere per.

truffle ['trʌfl] *n* tartufo *m*.

trump [trʌmp] *n* briscola *f*; (*bridge*) atout *m invar*. **trump card** (*coll*) forte *m*. *v* (*cards*) tagliare; (*beat*) battere. **trump up** fabbricare.

trumpet ['trʌmpit] *n* tromba *f*. **blow one's own trumpet** vantare i propri meriti. *v* (*proclaim loudly*) strombazzare; (*elephant*) barrire.

truncheon ['trʌntʃən] *n* manganello *m*, bastone *m*.

trunk' [trʌŋk] *n* tronco *m*; (*chest*) baule *m*; torso *m*; (*elephant*) proboscide *f*. (*car*)|portabagagli *m* **trunk call** telefonata interurbana *f*. **trunk road** strada maestra *or* statale *f*. **trunks** *pl n* calzoncini *m pl*.

truss [trʌs] *v* legare. *n* (*framework*) travatura *f*; (*bundle*) fastello; (*med*) cinto erniario *m*.

trust [trʌst] *n* fiducia *f*; (*hope*) fede *f*; (*law*) fedecommesso *m*; (*comm*) trust *m invar*. **trustworthy** *adj* degno di fiducia, fidato. *v* fidarsi di, aver fiducia in; (*hope*) augurarsi. **trustee** *n* fidecommissario *m*; curatore, -trice *m*, *f*. **trusty** *adj* fedele, leale.

truth [truːθ] *n* verità *f*, vero *m*. **truthful** *adj* veritiero, sincero.

try [trai] *v* tentare; (*test*) provare; (*law*) giudicare, processare; (*taste*) assaggiare. **try on** provare. *n* tentativo *m*; (*rugby*) meta *f*. **trying** *adj* difficile; (*distressing*) penoso; (*irritating*) seccante.

tsar [zɑː] *n* zar *m invar*.

T-shirt ['tiːʃəːt] *n* maglietta *f*.

tub [tʌb] *n* tino *m*; (*bath*) vasca *f*. **tubby** *adj* grassoccio.

tuba ['tjuːbə] *n* tuba *f*.

tube [tjuːb] *n* tubo *m*; (*for toothpaste, etc.*) tubetto *m*; (*rail*) metropolitana *f*. **inner tube** *n* camera d'aria *f*. **tubing** *n* tubo *m*. **tubular** *adj* tubolare.

tuber ['tjuːbə] *n* tubero *m*.

tuberculosis [tjubəːkjuˈlousis] *n* tubercolosi *f*.

tuck [tʌk] *n* piega *f*, rimbocco *m*. **tuckshop** *n* spaccio di dolciumi *m*. *v* (*thrust into*) stipare; (*needlework*) rimboccare. **tuck in** ripiegare; (*coll: eat*) pappare, farsi una mangiata. **tuck up in bed** mettere a letto, coricare.

Tuesday ['tjuːzdi] *n* martedì *m*.

tuft [tʌft] *n* ciuffo *m*, fiocco *m*.

tug [tʌg] *v* (*pull*) tirare, dare uno strappo a; (*drag*) trascinare. *n* strappo *m*; (*boat*) rimorchiatore *m*.

tuition [tjuˈiʃən] *n* insegnamento *m*, istruzione *f*.

tulip ['tjuːlip] *n* tulipano *m*.

tumble ['tʌmbl] *v* cascare, ruzzolare; (*somersault*) fare un capitombolo. **tumble down** crollare. *n* caduta *f*, capitombolo *m*. **tumbler** *n* (*glass*) bicchiere *m*.

tummy ['tʌmi] (*coll*) *n* pancia *f*. **tummy-ache** *n* mal di pancia *m*.
tumour ['tjuːmə] *n* tumore *m*.
tumult ['tjuːmʌlt] *n* tumulto *m*. **tumultuous** *adj* tumultuoso.
tuna ['tjuːnə] *n also* **tunny** tonno *m*.
tune [tjuːn] *n* motivo *m*; melodia *f*, aria *f*. **call the tune** essere in comando. **in tune** in tono, intonato. **out of tune** fuori tono, stonato. **sing out of tune** stonare. **to the tune of** alla bellezza di. *v* accordare; (*radio*) sintonizzare. **tuner** *n* sintonizzatore *m*.
tunic ['tjuːnik] *n* tunica *f*.
tunnel ['tʌnl] *n* tunnel *m invar*, traforo *m*. *v* traforare.
tunny ['tʌni] *V* **tuna**.
turban ['təːbən] *n* turbante *m*.
turbid ['təːbid] *adj* torbido.
turbine ['təːbain] *n* turbina *f*.
turbot ['təːbət] *n* rombo *m*.
turbulent ['təːbjulənt] *adj* turbolento. **turbulence** *n* turbolenza *f*.
tureen [tə'riːn] *n* zuppiera *f*.
turf [təːf] *n* zolla erbosa *f*; (*sod*) piota *f*; (*peat*) torba *f*; (*horse-racing*) ippica *f*. *v* piotare. **turf out** (*coll*) buttar fuori.
turkey ['təːki] *n* tacchino *m*.
Turkey ['təːki] *n* Turchia *f*. **Turk** *n* turco, -a *m, f*. **Turkish** *nm, adj* turco.
turmeric ['təːmərik] *n* curcuma *f*.
turmoil ['təːmoil] *n* scompiglio *m*, confusione *f*.
turn [təːn] *v* girare, voltare; (*change*) cambiare; (*change direction*) svoltare. **turn against** alienare, ribellarsi a. **turn away** voltarsi da parte, guardar via; (*refuse admission*) mandar via. **turncoat** *n* rinnegato, -a *m, f*. **turn down** (*fold*) risvoltare; (*lower*) abbassare; (*reject*) rifiutare. **turn into** far diventare, convertire in. **turn off** (*stop flow*) chiudere; (*switch off*) spegnere; (*change direction*) voltare. **turn on** (*start flow*) aprire; (*switch on*) accendere; (*coll*) eccitare; (*attack*) aggredire. **turn out** (*switch off*) spegnere; produrre; (*send away*) cacciar via; (*empty*) vuotare; risultare; (*clothe*) vestire. **turn over** rovesciare. **turnover** *n* (*comm*) giro d'affari *m*; (*cookery*) pasticcio *m*. **turnstile** *n* tornello *m*. **turntable** *n* (*records*) giradischi *m invar*; (*rail*) piattaforma girevole *f*. **turn up** (*arrive*) capitare; (*come to light*) ricomparire;

(*increase intensity*) alzare; (*occur*) succedere. *n* giro *m*, rivoluzione *f*; (*change of direction*) svolta *f*; (*in rota, game, etc.*) turno *m*. **turning** *n* curva *f*, svolta *f*. **turning point** momento critico *or* decisivo *m*.
turnip ['təːnip] *n* rapa *f*.
turpentine ['təːpəntain] *n* trementina *f*; (*oil*) essenza di trementina *f*.
turquoise ['təːkwoiz] *n* (*stone*) turchese *f*; (*colour*) turchese *m*. *adj* turchese.
turret ['tʌrit] *n* torretta *f*.
turtle ['təːtl] *n* testuggine *f*, tartaruga *f*. **turn turtle** cappottare, capovolgersi. **turtle-dove** *n* tortora *f*.
Tuscany ['tʌskəni] *n* Toscana *f*. **Tuscan** *n, adj* toscano, -a.
tusk [tʌsk] *n* zanna *f*.
tussle ['tʌsl] *n* zuffa *f*. *v* venire alle mani, azzuffarsi.
tutor ['tjuːtə] *n* insegnante (privato) *m*; (*coach*) ripetitore, -trice *m, f*. **tutorial** *n* periodo di istruzione (privata) *m*.
tuxedo [tʌk'siːdou] *n* smoking *m invar*.
tweed [twiːd] *n* tweed *m invar*, tessuto di lana scozzese *m*.
tweezers ['twiːzəz] *pl n* pinzette *f pl*.
twelve [twelv] *nm, adj* dodici. **twelfth** *nm, adj* dodicesimo.
twenty ['twenti] *nm, adj* venti. **twentieth** *nm, adj* ventesimo.
twice [twais] *adv* due volte; (*doubly*) il doppio.
twiddle ['twidl] *v* (far) girare. **twiddle one's thumbs** tener le mani in mano.
twig [twig] *n* ramoscello *m*.
twilight ['twailait] *n* crepuscolo *m*, penombra *f*.
twin [twin] *n, adj* gemello, -a. **twin beds** letti gemelli *m pl*.
twine [twain] *n* spago *m*, corda *f*. *v* attorcigliare.
twinge [twindʒ] *n* spasimo *m*.
twinkle ['twiŋkl] *v* scintillare, luccicare; (*wink*) ammiccare, strizzare l'occhio. *n* luccichio *m*; strizzata d'occhio *f*.
twirl [twəːl] *v* girare rapidamente, piroettare.
twist [twist] *v* torcere, intrecciare; (*sprain*) slogarsi; alterare. *n* movimento rotatorio *m*; (*curve*) svolta *f*; (*thread*) filo ritorto *m*. **twister** *n* (*cheat*) imbroglione, -a *m, f*.
twit [twit] *n* (*coll*) scemo, -a *m, f*.
twitch [twitʃ] *v* (*jerk*) strappare, dare uno strattone; (*body*) storcere. *n* contorsione *f*, spasimo *m*. **twitching** *adj* convulsivo.

twitter ['twitə] *v* cinguettare. *n* cinguettio *m*.

two [tuɪ] *nm, adj* due. **in twos** due a due.

two-faced *adj* falso. **two-piece** *n* (*garment*) duepezzi *m invar*. **two-seater** *adj* a due posti. **two-way** *adj* a doppio senso; (*elec*) bipolare.

tycoon [tai'kuɪn] *n* magnate *m*.

type [taip] *n* tipo *m*, genere *m*; (*print*) carattere *m*. **typescript** *n* dattiloscritto *m*. **typesetter** *n* compositore *m*. **typewriter** *n* macchina da scrivere *f*. **typewritten** *adj* scritto a macchina, dattiloscritto. *v* dattilografare. **typical** *adj* tipico, caratteristico. **typify** *v* servire da esempio, simbolizzare. **typist** *n* dattilografo, -a *m, f*.

typhoid ['taifoid] *n* tifo *m*.

typhoon [tai'fuɪn] *n* tifone *m*.

typographical [ˌtaipə'grafikl] *adj* tipografico.

tyrant ['tairənt] *n* tiranno *m*. **tyrannical** *adj* tirannico. **tyranny** *n* tirannia *f*.

tyre *or US* **tire** ['taiə] *n* gomma *f*, copertone *m*.

U

ubiquitous [ju'bikwitəs] *adj* onnipresente.

udder ['ʌdə] *n* mammella *f*.

ugly ['ʌgli] *adj* (*not pretty*) brutto; (*not agreeable*) antipatico, sgradevole; (*vicious*) vile. **ugliness** *n* bruttezza *f*.

ulcer ['ʌlsə] *n* ulcera *f*.

ulterior [ʌl'tiəriə] *adj* ulteriore. **ulterior motive** secondo fine *m*.

ultimate ['ʌltimət] *adj* finale, definitivo, assoluto. **ultimately** *adv* alla fine. **ultimatum** *n* ultimatum *m invar*.

ultraviolet [ʌltrə'vaiələt] *adj* ultravioletto.

umbilical [ʌm'bilikəl] *adj* ombilicale.

umbrella [ʌm'brelə] *n* ombrello *m*.

umpire ['ʌmpaiə] *n* arbitro *m*. *v* arbitrare.

umpteen [ʌmp'tiːn] (*coll*) *adj* innumerevole. **umpteenth** *adj* ennesimo.

unable [ʌn'eibl] *adj* incapace. **be unable to** non potere.

unacceptable [ʌnək'septəbl] *adj* inaccettabile.

unaccompanied [ʌnə'kumpənid] *adj* solo, non accompagnato.

unaccountable [ʌnə'kauntəbl] *adj* inspiegabile.

unaccustomed [ʌnə'kʌstəmd] *adj* (*not used to*) poco abituato; (*unusual*) insolito.

unadulterated [ʌnə'dʌltəreitid) *adj* sincero.

unanimous [ju'nanimmʌs] *adj* unanime.

unapproachable [ʌnə'proutʃəbl] *adj* inaccessibile.

unarmed [ʌn'aɪmd] *adj* disarmato.

unashamed [ʌnə'ʃeimd] *adj* svergognato, senza vergogna.

unattainable [ʌnə'teinəbl] *adj* irraggiungibile.

unattractive [ʌnə'traktiv] *adj* poco attraente, antipatico.

unauthorized [ʌn'ɔiθəraizd] *adj* non autorizzato, illecito.

unavoidable [ʌnə'voidəbl] *adj* inevitabile.

unaware [ʌnə'weə] *adj* ignaro. **be unaware of** ignorare. **unawares** *adv* di sorpresa.

unbalanced [ʌn'balənst] *adj* squilibrato.

unbearable [ʌn'beərəbl] *adj* insopportabile.

unbelievable [ʌnbi'liɪvəbl] *adj* incredibile.

***unbend** [ʌn'bend] *v* raddrizzare. **unbending** *adj* rigido, inflessibile.

unbiased [ʌn'baiəst] *adj* imparziale.

unbreakable [ʌn'breikəbl] *adj* infrangibile.

unbridled [ʌn'braidld] *adj* sfrenato.

unbroken [ʌn'broukn] *adj* intatto; ininterrotto; (*not beaten*) imbattuto.

unbutton [ʌn'butn] *v* sbottonare.

uncalled-for [ʌn'kɔɪldfoɪ] *adj* immeritato, gratuito.

uncanny [ʌn'kani] *adj* strano, misterioso.

uncertain [ʌn'sɔitn] *adj* incerto, dubbio. **uncertainty** *n* incertezza *f*.

unchanged [ʌn'tʃeindʒd] *adj* immutato, invariato.

uncharitable [ʌn'tʃaritəbl] *adj* aspro, crudele.

uncivilized [ʌn'sivilaizd] *adj* barbaro.

uncle ['ʌŋkl] *n* zio *m*.

uncomfortable [ʌn'kʌmfətəbl] *adj* scomodo. **feel uncomfortable** sentirsi a disagio.

uncommon [ʌn'komən] *adj* poco comune, insolito.

uncompromising [ʌn'komprəmaiziŋ] *adj* intrattabile, intransigente.

unconditional [ʌnkən'diʃənl] *adj* incondizionale, senza riserve, categorico.

unconscious [ʌn'konʃəs] *adj* (*unaware*) inconscio, inconsapevole; (*med*) privo di coscienza. *n* inconscio *m*. **become unconscious** svenire, perdere conoscenza. **be unconscious of** essere ignaro di, non accorgersi di. **unconsciously** *adv* senza rendersene conto.

uncontrollable [ʌnkən'troʊləbl] *adj* incontrollabile, irreprimibile.

unconventional [ʌnkən'venʃənl] *adj* anticonformista; non convenzionale.

unconvincing [ʌnkən'vinsiŋ] *adj* poco convincente. **unconvinced** *adj* non convinto, poco persuaso.

uncooked [ʌn'kukt] *adj* crudo, non cotto.

uncouth [ʌn'kuːθ] *adj* rozzo, grossolano.

uncover [ʌn'kʌvə] *v* scoprire, rivelare, esporre.

uncut [ʌn'kʌt] *adj* non tagliato, integro.

undecided [ʌndi'saidid] *adj* indeciso, irresoluto.

undeniable [ʌndi'naiəbl] *adj* innegabile, incontestabile.

under ['ʌndə] *adv*, *prep* sotto, al di sotto (di). **be under the weather** sentirsi poco bene. **under age** minorenne. **under lock and key** sottochiave. **under one's breath** sottovoce. **under the circumstances** in queste circostanze.

undercharge [ʌndə'tʃaːdʒ] *v* far pagare meno del dovuto, non far pagare abbastanza.

underclothes ['ʌndəkloʊðz] *pl n* biancheria intima *f sing.*

undercoat ['ʌndəkout] *n* (*paint*) prima mano *f.*

undercover [ʌndə'kʌvə] *adj* segreto.

***undercut** [ʌndə'kʌt] *v* (*comm*) offrire a un prezzo inferiore a.

underdeveloped [ʌndədi'veləpt] *adj* sottosviluppato.

underdog ['ʌndədog] *n* vittima *f*, persona che ha la peggio *f.*

underdone [ʌndə'dʌn] *adj* (*meat*) al sangue.

underestimate [ʌndə'estimeit] *v* sottovalutare.

underexpose [ʌndərik'spouz] *v* sottoesporre.

underfoot [ʌndə'fut] *adv* sotto i piedi.

***undergo** [ʌndə'gou] *v* subire, supportare.

undergraduate [ʌndə'gradjuət] *n* studente universitario, studentessa universitaria *m, f.*

underground ['ʌndəgraund; *adv*

ʌndə'graund] *adj* sotterraneo; (*secret*) segreto; clandestino. **underground passage** sottopassaggio *m. adv* sottoterra. *n* resistenza *f*; (*railway*) metropolitana *f.*

undergrowth ['ʌndəgrouθ] *n* boscaglia *f*, macchia *f.*

underhand [ʌndə'hand] *adj* clandestino; (*dubious*) losco.

***underlie** [ʌndə'lai] *v* sottostare a; essere alla base di.

underline [ʌndə'lain] *v* sottolineare.

undermine [ʌndə'main] *v* minare, insidiare.

underneath [ʌndə'niːθ] *adv*, *prep* sotto, al di sotto (di).

undernourished [ʌndə'nʌriʃt] *adj* malnutrito.

underpants ['ʌndəpants] *pl n* mutande *f pl.*

underpass ['ʌndəpaːs] *n* sottopassaggio *m.*

underprivileged [ʌndə'privilidʒd] *adj* non privilegiato, derelitto.

underrate [ʌndə'reit] *v* sottovalutare.

understaffed [ʌndə'staːft] *adj* a corto di personale *or* manodopera.

***understand** [ʌndə'stand] *v* capire, comprendere; (*realize*) rendersi conto; (*believe*) credere. **understandable** *adj* comprensibile.

understanding [ʌndə'standiŋ] *n* comprensione *f*; (*knowledge*) conoscenza *f*; (*agreement*) accordo *m*. **on the understanding that** a condizione *or* premesso che. *adj* comprensivo, indulgente.

understate [ʌndə'steit] *v* minimizzare, attenuare. **understatement** *n* atto del minimizzare *m.*

understudy ['ʌndəstʌdi] *v* sostituire. *n* sostituto, -a *m, f*, attore, -trice supplente *m, f.*

***undertake** [ʌndə'teik] *v* intraprendere; (*accept obligation*) impegnarsi; (*warrant*) garantire. **undertaker** *n* imprenditore di pompe funebri *m*, becchino *m*. **undertaking** *n* impresa *f*; (*pledge*) impegno *m*, promessa *f.*

undertone ['ʌndətoun] *n* fondo *m*, senso occulto *m*. **in an undertone** a basso voce.

underwear ['ʌndəweə] *n* biancheria *or* maglieria intima *f.*

underwater ['ʌndəwɔːtə; *adv* ʌndə'wɔːtə] *adj* subacqueo. *adv* sott'acqua.

underweight [ʌndə'weit] *adj* di peso insufficiente.

underworld ['ʌndəwəːld] *n* (*myth*) inferno *m*; (*crime*) malavita *f*.

*****underwrite** [ʌndə'rait] *v* sottoscrivere; (*support*) sostenere; (*finance*) garantire; (*insurance*) riassicurare. **underwriter** *n* riassicuratore *m*, garante di una emissione *m*.

undesirable [ʌndi'zaiərəbl] *adj* indesiderabile, sgradito.

undignified [ʌn'dignifaid] *adj* poco dignitoso.

*****undo** [ʌn'duː] *v* disfare, sciogliere, annullare; rovinare. **leave undone** tralasciare di fare. **undoing** *n* rovina *f*.

undoubted [ʌn'dautid] *adj* indubbio, incontestato, certo.

undress [ʌn'dres] *v* svestire, spogliarsi.

undue [ʌn'djuː] *adj* indebito, eccessivo.

undulate ['ʌndjuleit] *v* ondeggiare.

unearth [ʌn'əːθ] *v* scoprire, dissotterrare.

unearthly *adj* (*ghostly*) spettrale; (*coll*) assurdo.

uneasy [ʌn'iːzi] *adj* turbato, imbarazzato, a disagio.

uneducated [ʌn'edjukeitid] *adj* ignorante, senza coltura.

unemployed [ʌnem'ploid] *adj* disoccupato. **the unemployed** i disoccupati *m pl*. **unemployment** *n* disoccupazione *f*.

unending [ʌn'endiŋ] *adj* interminabile, che non finisce più.

unequal [ʌn'iːkwəl] *dj* disuguale; (*unevenly matched*) impari. **unequal to** non all'altezza di. **unequalled** *adj* senza pari.

uneven [ʌn'iːvn] *adj* (*not level*) irregolare; ineguale; (*odd*) dispari.

unexpected [ʌneks'pektid] *adj* inatteso.

unfailing [ʌn'feiliŋ] *adj* infallibile, immancabile.

unfair [ʌn'feə] *adj* ingiusto; (*dishonest*) sleale; (*sport*) non sportivo. **unfairness** *n* ingiustizia *f*; slealtà *f*.

unfaithful [ʌn'feiθfəl] *adj* infedele, disonesto; inesatto. **unfaithfulness** *n* infedeltà *f*.

unfamiliar [ʌnfə'miljə] *adj* (*not conversant*) poco familiare *or* pratico; (*not well-known*) poco conosciuto *or* noto.

unfasten [ʌn'faːsn] *v* slegare, sciogliere, disfare.

unfavourable [ʌn'feivərəbl] *adj* sfavorevole.

unfit [ʌn'fit] *adj* (*unsuitable*) inadatto, non idoneo; (*unable*) inabile; (*unwell*) indisposto.

unfold [ʌn'fould] *v* (*open out*) schiudere; (*develop*) sviluppare; (*reveal*) rivelare.

unforeseen [ʌnfoː'siːn] *adj* imprevisto. **unforeseeable** *adj* imprevedibile.

unfortunate [ʌn'foːtʃənət] *adj* sfortunato, disgraziato; (*unsuitable, unhappy*) infelice. **unfortunately** *adv* purtroppo.

unfriendly [ʌn'frendli] *adj* freddo; ostile.

unfurnished [ʌn'fəːniʃd] *adj* non ammobiliato.

ungrateful [ʌn'greitfəl] *adj* ingrato.

unguarded [ʌn'gaːdid] *adj* incustodito, indifeso; imprudente, indiscreto.

unhappy [ʌn'hapi] *adj* infelice, triste; inopportuno; (*infelicitous*) poco felice. **unhappily** *adv* sfortunatamente. **unhappiness** *n* infelicità *f*, tristezza *f*.

unhealthy [ʌn'helθi] *adj* malsano; (*morbid*) morboso.

unhurried [ʌn'hʌrid] *adj* calmo, senza fretta.

unhurt [ʌn'həːt] *adj* incolume.

unicorn ['juːnikoːn] *n* unicorno *m*.

uniform ['juːnifoːm] *adj* uniforme, costante. *n* uniforme *f*, divisa *f*. **uniformity** *n* uniformità *f*.

unify ['juːnifai] *v* unificare. **unification** *n* unificazione *f*.

unilateral [juːni'latərəl] *adj* unilaterale.

unimaginable [ʌni'madʒinəbl] *adj* inconcepibile. **unimaginative** *adj* poco immaginativo.

unimpaired [ʌnim'peəd] *adj* intatto, in pieno vigore.

uninhabited [ʌnin'habitid] *adj* disabitato, deserto. **uninhabitable** *adj* inabitabile.

unintentional [ʌnin'tenʃənl] *adj* involontario.

uninterested [ʌn'intristid] *adj* disinteressato. **uninteresting** *adj* poco interessante, noioso.

union ['juːnjən] *n* unione *f*, unificazione *f*; associazione *f*; (*trade*) sindacato *f*; (*tech*) collegamento *m*.

unique [juː'niːk] *adj* unico, solo.

unison ['juːnisn] *n* unisono *m*. **in unison** all'unisono.

unit ['juːnit] *n* unità *f*; (*whole*) insieme *m*.

unite [juː'nait] *v* unire, combinare, congiungere. **united** *adj* unito. **United Kingdom** Regno Unito *m*. **United Nations** Nazioni Unite *f pl*. **United States of America** Stati Uniti d'America *m pl*.

unity ['juːniti] *n* unità *f*.
universe ('juːnivəːs] *n* universo *m*. **universal** *adj* universale.
university [juːni'vəːsəti] *n* università *f*. *adj* universitario.
unjust [ʌn'dʒʌst] *adj* ingiusto.
unkempt [ʌn'kempt] *adj* spettinato; (*untidy*) sciatto.
unkind [ʌn'kaind] *adj* poco gentile; crudele.
unknown [ʌn'noun] *adj* sconosciuto, ignoto. *n* ignoto *m*; (*math*) incognita *f*. **unknown to** all'insaputa di.
unlawful [ʌn'lɔːfəl] *adj* illegale; illecito.
unless [ʌn'les] *conj* a meno che non, se non.
unlike [ʌn'laik] *adj* dissimile *or* diverso (da). **be unlike** non rassomigliarsi. **not unlike** assai simile a. *prep* a differenza di, all'inverso di.
unlikely [ʌn'laikli] *adj* improbabile, inverosimile.
unload [ʌn'loud] *v* scaricare, liberarsi di.
unlock [ʌn'lok] *v* aprire.
unlucky [ʌn'lʌki] *adj* sfortunato, disgraziato.
unmarried [ʌn'marid] *adj* non sposato; (*bachelor*) celibe; (*spinster*) nubile. **unmarried mother** ragazza madre *f*.
unmistakable [ʌnmi'steikəbl] *adj* inequivocabile, manifesto.
unnatural [ʌn'natʃərəl] *adj* contro natura; (*lacking natural feelings*) snaturato, disumano; anormale; forzato.
unnecessary [ʌn'nesəsəri] *adj* inutile, non necessario.
unnoticed [ʌn'noutist] *adj* inavvertito.
unobtainable [ʌnəb'teinəbl] *adj* irreperibile.
unoccupied [ʌn'okjupaid] *adj* libero, vacante, vuoto.
unofficial [ʌnə'fiʃəl] *adj* ufficioso.
unopposed [ʌnə'pouzd] *adj* incontrastato.
unpack [ʌn'pak] *v* (*case*) disfare (le valige); (*contents*) disimballare.
unpaid [ʌn'peid] *adj* non retribuito *or* rimunerato; (*debt, etc.*) non saldato *or* pagato.
unpardonable [ʌn'paːdnəbl] *adj* imperdonabile.
unpleasant [ʌn'pleznt] *adj* spiacevole, sgradevole, antipatico. **unpleasantness** *n* spiacevolezza *f*; (*disagreement*) dissenso *m*.

unpopular [ʌn'popjulə] *adj* impopolare. **be unpopular with** esser malvisto da.
unprecedented [ʌn'presidentid] *adj* inaudito, senza precedenti.
unpredictable [ʌnprə'diktəbl] *adj* imprevedibile.
unqualified [ʌn'kwolifaid] *adj* non qualificato; senza diploma; categorico, assoluto.
unquestionable [ʌn'kwestʃənəbl] *adj* indiscutibile, fuori questione. **unquestioned** *adj* indiscusso, incontestato.
unravel [ʌn'ravəl] *v* sciogliere, sbrogliare; (*clear*) chiarire.
unreadable [ʌn'riːdəbl] *adj* illeggibile; (*tedious*) noioso.
unreal [ʌn'riəl] *adj* irreale.
unreasonable [ʌn'riːzənəbl] *adj* irragionevole.
unrecognizable [ʌn,rekəg'naizəbl] *adj* irriconoscibile.
unrelenting [ʌnri'lentiŋ] *adj* inesorabile; (*dogged*) accanito.
unreliable [ʌnri'laiəbl] *adj* da non fidarsene; (*news*) inattendibile.
unrepetant [ʌnri'pentənt] *adj* impenitente.
unrest [ʌn'rest] *n* agitazione *f*, fermento *m*.
unripe [ʌn'raip] *adj* immaturo, acerbo.
unruly [ʌn'ruːli] *adj* indisciplinato, turbolento.
unsafe [ʌn'seif] *adj* malsicuro, pericoloso.
unsatisfactory [ʌnsatis'faktəri] *adj* poco soddisfacente, che lascia desiderare.
unsavoury [ʌn'seivəri] *adj* sgradevole; (*coll*) disgustoso, poco pulito.
unscrew [ʌn'skruː] *v* svitare.
unscrupulous [ʌn'skruːpjuləs] *adj* senza scrupoli.
unselfish [ʌn'selfiʃ] *adj* altruistico.
unsettle [ʌn'setl] *v* turbare; disturbare; sconcertare. **unsettled** *adj* (*weather*) variabile; (*account*) non saldato; (*not fixed*) non sistemato; (*uncertain*) incerto.
unsightly [ʌn'saitli] *adj* brutto, spiacevole a vedersi.
unskilled [ʌn'skild] *adj* inesperto, non qualificato. **unskilled worker** *n* manovale *m*.
unsociable [ʌn'souʃəbl] *adj* poco socievole, scontroso.
unsound [ʌn'saund] *adj* imperfetto, difettoso; erroneo; (*ill-founded*) poco profondo.

unspeakable [ʌn'spiːkəbl] *adj* indicibile, inesprimibile; (*very bad*) inqualificabile.
unstable [ʌn'steibl] *adj* instabile.
unsteady [ʌn'stedi] *adj* malfermo, instabile; incostante; (*wavering*) traballante, barcollante.
unsuccessful [ʌnsək'sesfəl] *adj* non *or* mal riuscito, sfortunato, fallito.
unsuitable [ʌn'suːtəbl] *adj* inadatto; inopportuno; sconveniente. **unsuited** *adj* non idoneo, disadatto, sconvenevole.
unsure [ʌn'ʃuə] *adj* malsicuro, incerto.
untangle [ʌn'taŋgl] *v* districare.
unthinkable [ʌn'θiŋkəbl] *adj* inconcepibile, assurdo.
untidy [ʌn'taidi] *adj* disordinato, trascurato. **untidiness** *n* disordine *m*. trascuratezza *f*.
untie [ʌn'tai] *v* sciogliere, slegare.
until [ən'til] *prep* fino a; (*before*) prima di. *conj* finchè, fino a quando; fino al momento in cui.
untimely [ʌn'taimli] *adj* inopportuno, intempestivo, prematuro.
untoward [ʌntə'woːd] *adj* disgraziato.
untrue [ʌn'truː] *adj* non vero, falso, erroneo; infedele; inesatto.
unusual [ʌn'juːʒuəl] *adj* insolito, straordinario, eccezionale.
unwanted [ʌn'wontid] *adj* indesiderato, superfluo.
unwelcome [ʌn'welkəm] *adj* (*person*) malaccolto; (*news, etc.*) sgradito, spiacevole.
unwell [ʌn'wel] *adj* indisposto, ammalato.
unwieldy [ʌn'wiːldi] *adj* ingombrante.
unwilling [ʌn'wiliŋ] *adj* restio, riluttante; (*given reluctantly*) dato controvoglia.
***unwind** [ʌn'waind] *v* dipanare; (*relax*) rilassarsi.
unwise [ʌn'waiz] *adj* imprudente, insensato.
unwittingly [ʌn'witiŋli] *adv* senza saperlo, per inavvertenza.
unworthy [ʌn'wəːði] *adj* indegno. **unworthy of** che non merita.
unwrap [ʌn'rap] *v* disfare.
up [ʌp] *adv* su; (*erect*) in piedi; (*out of bed*) alzato. **be up against** essere alle prese con. **be up to** (*capable of*) essere all'altezza di; (*mischief*) tramare. **up here** quassù. **up there** lassù. **up to** fino a. **what's up?** cosa succede? *prep* su, su per. *n* **ups and downs** alti e bassi *m pl*.

upbringing ['ʌpbriŋiŋ] *n* educazione *f*.
update [ʌp'deit] *v* aggiornare.
upheaval [ʌp'hiːvl] *n* commozione *f*, sconvolgimento *m*.
uphill [ʌp'hil] *adv* in salita, in su. *adj* in salita, ascendente; difficile.
***uphold** [ʌp'hould] *v* sostenere, appoggiare.
upholster [ʌp'houlstə] *v* tappezzare. **upholsterer** *n* tappezziere *m*. **upholstery** *n* tappezzeria *f*.
upkeep ['ʌpkiːp] *n* mantenimento *m*. manutenzione *f*.
uplift [ʌp'lift] *v* edificare, incoraggiare. *n* edificazione *f*, incoraggiamento *m*.
upon [ə'pon] *prep* su, sopra.
upper ['ʌpə] *adj* superiore, più alto. **get the upper hand** prevalere. *n* tomaia *f*. **be on one's uppers** essere alle strette. **uppermost** *adj* il più alto.
upright ['ʌprait] *adj* verticale, in piedi; (*righteous*) retto, onesto.
uprising ['ʌpraiziŋ] *n* insurrezione *f*.
uproar ['ʌproː] *n* tumulto, fracasso. **uproarious** *adj* tumultuoso, chiassoso. **uproariously funny** da crepar dal ridere.
uproot [ʌp'ruːt] *v* sradicare.
***upset** [ʌp'set; *n* 'ʌpset] *v* sconvolgere, disturbare; (*knock over*) rovesciare. *adj* sconvolto, turbato; rovesciato. *n* disturbo *m*, contrattempo *m*. **upsetting** *adj* turbante, preoccupante.
upshot ['ʌpʃot] *n* conclusione *f*, effetto *m*.
upside down [ʌpsai'daun] *adv, adj* sottosopra, in disordine.
upstairs [ʌp'steəz] *adv* di sopra, al piano superiore.
upstream [ʌp'striːm] *adv* a monte, controcorrente.
uptight ['ʌptait] *adj* (*coll*) nervoso.
up-to-date [ʌptə'deit] *adj* aggiornato, di moda.
upward ['ʌpwəd] *adj* in salita, rivolto in alto. **upwards** *adv* in su, in alto; (*more*) più.
uranium [ju'reiniəm] *n* uranio *m*.
urban ['əːbən] *adj* urbano.
urchin ['əːtʃin] *n* monello, -a *m, f*.
urge [əːdʒ] *n* sprone *m*, impulso *m*. *v* esortare, spingere; insistere.
urgent ['əːdʒənt] *adj* urgente. **urgency** *n* urgenza *f*.
urine ['juːrin] *n* orina *f*. **urinal** *n* orinatoio *m*. **urinary** *adj* urinario. **urinate** *v* orinare.

urn [ɜːn] *n* urna *f.*
us [ʌs] *pron* ci, ce; *(after prep)* noi.
usage ['juːzidʒ] *n* uso *m,* usanza *f.*
use [juːs; *v* juːz] *n* uso *m,* impiego *(pl
-ghi) m;* utilità *f.* **it's no use!** è inutile!
what's the use? a cosa serve? *v* usare,
impiegare, adoperare. **use up** consumare.
used *adj (car)* d'occasione. **be used to**
essere abituato a. **useful** *adj* utile. **useless**
adj inutile.
usher ['ʌʃə] *n* usciere *m. v* **usher in** far
entrare, introdurre. **usherette** *n* maschera
f.
usual ['juːzuəl] *adj* solito, usuale. **as usual**
come di solito. **usually** *adv* di solito,
generalmente.
usurp [ju'zɜːp] *v* usurpare.
utensil [ju'tensl] *n* utensile *m,* arnese *m.*
uterus ['juːtərəs] *n* utero *m.*
utility [ju'tiləti] *n* utilità *f,* vantaggio *m;*
servizio pubblico *m.* **utilize** *v* utilizzare.
utmost ['ʌtmoust] *adj* massimo, supremo.
n massimo *m,* possibile *m.* **do one's
utmost** fare del proprio meglio.
utter[1] ['ʌtə] *v (say)* pronunciare, emettere.
utter[2] ['ʌtə] *adj (absolute)* completo,
assoluto.
U-turn ['juːtɜːn] *n* cambio di direzione *m.*

V

vacant ['veikənt] *adj* libero, vuoto; vacuo.
vacancy *n (job)* posto libero *m; (room)*
camera libera *f.* **vacate** *v* lasciar libero,
sgomberare.
vaccine ['vaksiːn] *n* vaccino *m.* **vaccinate** *v*
vaccinare. **vaccination** *n* vaccinazione *f.*
vacillate ['vasileit] *v* vacillare.
vacuum ['vakjum] *n* vuoto *m.* **vacuum
cleaner** *n* aspirapolvere *m invar.* **vacuum
flask** *n* thermos   *m invar.*
vagina [və'dʒainə] *n* vagina *f.* **vaginal** *adj*
vaginale.
vagrant ['veigrənt] *n, adj* vagabondo, -a.
vagrancy *n* vagabondaggio *m.*
vague [veig] *adj* vago.
vain [vein] *adj (worthless)* vano, inutile;
(conceited) vanitoso. **in vain** invano.
valiant ['valiənt] *adj* valoroso.
valid ['valid] *adj (ticket, etc.)* valevole;
(sound) valido. **validity** *n* validità *f.*
valley ['vali] *n* valle *f.*

value ['valjuː] *n* valore *m. v* valutare,
stimare; dare importanza a. **valuable** *adj*
prezioso, di valore. **valuables** *pl n* valori
m pl, oggetti di valore *m pl.*
valve [valv] *n* valvola *f.*
vampire ['vampaiə] *n* vampiro *m.*
van[1] [van] *n (vehicle)* furgone *m,* camion
f.
van[2] [van] *n (forefront)* avanguardia *f.*
vandal ['vandl] *n* vandalo *m.* **vandalism** *n*
vandalismo *m.*
vanilla [və'nilə] *n* vaniglia *f.*
vanish ['vaniʃ] *v* sparire.
vanity ['vanəti] *n* vanità *f.*
vapour ['veipə] *n* vapore *m.* **vaporize** *v*
vaporizzare.
variance ['veəriəns] *n* variazione *f.* **at variance** in disaccordo.
varicose veins ['varikous] *pl n* vene varicose *f pl.*
variety [və'raiəti] *n* varietà *f,* diversità *f.*
various ['veəriəs] *adj* vario, diverso.
varnish ['vaːniʃ] *n* vernice *f,* lacca *f. v*
verniciare, laccare.
vary ['veəri] *v* variare; modificare; differire. **variant** *n* variante *f.* **variation** *n* variazione *f.* **varied** *adj* vario, svariato.
vase [vaːz] *n* vaso *m.*
vasectomy [və'sektəmi] *n* vasectomia *f.*
vast [vaːst] *adj* vasto, immenso.
vat [vat] *n* tino *m.*
Vatican ['vatikən] *n* Vaticano *m.* **Vatican
City** la Città del Vaticano *f.*
vault[1] [vɔːlt] *n* volta *f; (cellar)* cantina *f;
(safe)* camera di sicurezza *f.*
vault[2] [vɔːlt] *v* saltare, volteggiare. *n* salto
m.
veal [viːl] *n* vitello *m.*
veer [viə] *v* virare, cambiar direzione.
vegetable ['vedʒtəbl] *n* ortaggio *m,*
verdura *f. adj* vegetale; *(food)* di verdura.
vegetarian *n, adj* vegetariano, -a. **vegetate**
v vegetare. **vegetation** *n* vegetazione *f.*
vehement ['viːəmənt] *adj* violento,
impetuoso.
vehicle ['viːəkl] *n* veicolo *m; (means)* mezzo *m.*
veil [veil] *n* velo *m. v* velare; *(hide)* nascondere.
vein [vein] *n* vena *f; (leaf, marking)*
venatura *f.*
velocity [və'losəti] *n* velocità *f.*
velvet ['velvit] *n* velluto *m.* **velvety** *adj*
vellutato.

vending machine ['vendiŋ] *n* distributore automatico *m*.

veneer [və'niə] *n* piallaccio *m*; (*superficial layer*) vernice *f*.

venerate ['venəreit] *v* venerare. **venerable** *adj* venerabile.

venereal disease [və'niəriəl] *n* malattia venerea *f*.

Venetian blind [və'niːʃən] *n* veneziana *f*.

vengeance ['vendʒəns] *n* vendetta *f*. **with a vengeance** (*unexpectedly*) in modo insospettato; (*with violence*) violentemente.

Venice ['venis] *n* Venezia *f*.

venison ['venisn] *n* cacciagione *f*.

venom ['venəm] *n* veleno *m*; (*spite*) malignità *f*, cattiveria *f*. **venomous** *adj* velenoso; maligno, cattivo.

vent [vent] *n* (*outlet*) apertura *f*, sbocco *m*. **give vent to** sfogare. *v* esprimere, sfogare.

ventilate ['ventileit] *v* ventilare. **ventilation** *n* ventilazione *f*.

venture ['ventʃə] *n* impresa (rischiosa) *f*, avventura *f*. *v* azzardare, arrischiare.

venue ['venjuː] *n* sede *f*; (*place*) posto *m*.

verb [vəːb] *n* verbo *m*. **verbal** *adj* verbale. **verbatim** *adj* parola per parola.

verdict ['vəːdikt] *n* verdetto *m*, giudizio *m*.

verge [vəːdʒ] *n* orlo *m*, limite *m*. **on the verge of** sul punto di. *v* **verge on** tendere a, avvicinarsi a.

verify ['verifai] *v* verificare, confermare. **verification** *n* verifica *f*.

vermin ['vəːmin] *pl n* animali nocivi *m pl*, parassiti *m pl*; (*scum*) feccia *f sing*.

vermouth ['vəːməθ] *n* vermut *m invar*.

vernacular [və'nakjulə] *adj* indigeno, dialettale; volgare. *n* **in the vernacular** in volgare.

versatile ['vəːsətail] *adj* versatile, eclettico.

verse [vəːs] *n* verso *m*; (*poem*) poesia *f*. **in verse** in versi.

version ['vəːʃən] *n* versione *f*.

versus ['vəːsəs] *prep* contro.

vertebra ['vəːtibrə] *n, pl* **-brae** vertebra *f*. **vertebral** *adj* vertebrale. **vertebrate** *nm, adj* vertebrato.

vertical ['vəːtikl] *nf, adj* verticale.

vertigo ['vəːtigou] *n* vertigini *f pl*.

very ['veri] *adv* molto, assai. **the very next day** proprio il giorno dopo. *adj* proprio; esatto; (*same*) stesso; (*mere*) solo.

vessel ['vesl] *n* (*container*) recipiente *m*, vaso *m*; (*ship*) nave *f*, bastimento *m*.

vest [vest] *n* maglia *f*, maglietta *f*. *v* conferire, assegnare.

vestige ['vestidʒ] *n* vestigio *m*, traccia *f*.

vestry ['vestri] *n* sagrestia *f*.

vet [vet] (*coll*) *v* controllare, esaminare. *n* veterinario, -a *m, f*.

veteran ['vetərən] *n* veterano *m*; (*mil*) reduce *m*.

veterinary ['vetərinəri] *adj* veterinario. **veterinary surgeon** *n* veterinario, -a *m, f*.

veto ['viːtou] *n* veto *m*.

vex [veks] *v* vessare, irritare. **vexed question** argomento dibattuto *m*.

via [vaiə] *prep* per, attraverso, tramite.

viable ['vaiəbl] *adj* vitale, capace a vivere; (*workable*) praticabile, possibile; (*road*) transitabile. **viability** *n* praticabilità *f*; (*biol*) vitalità *f*.

viaduct ['vaiədʌkt] *n* viadotto *m*.

vibrate [vai'breit] *v* (far) vibrare. **vibration** *n* vibrazione *f*.

vicar ['vikə] *n* parroco *m*, vicario *m*. **vicarage** *n* parrocchia *f*.

vicarious [vi'keəriəs] *adj* vicario.

vice¹ [vais] *n* (*evil*) vizio *m*; (*fault*) difetto *m*.

vice² [vais] *n* (*tool*) morsa *f*.

vice-chancellor [vais'tʃaːnsələ] *n* (*university*) rettore *m*.

vice-president [vais'prezidənt] *n* vice-presidente *m*.

vice versa [vaisi'vəːsə] *adv* viceversa.

vicinity [vi'sinəti] *n* vicinanza *f*, prossimità *f*; (*neighbourhood*) vicinanze *f pl*, dintorni *m pl*.

vicious ['viʃəs] *adj* (*bad*) cattivo; (*crude*) crudele, maligno. **vicious circle** circolo vizioso *m*.

victim ['viktim] *n* vittima *f*. **fall victim to** essere preda a. **victimize** *v* perseguitare *or* punire ingiustamente; sacrificare.

victory ['viktəri] *n* vittoria *f*. **victorious** *adj* vittorioso.

video-tape ['vidiouteip] *n* video-cassetta *f*.

vie [vai] *v* gareggiare.

Vienna [vi'enə] *n* Vienna *f*.

view [vjuː] *n* vista *f*; (*scene, opinion*) veduta *f*. **in view of** in vista di; (*considering*) dato; (*on account of*) grazie a, a causa di. **on view** esposto. **viewfinder** *n* mirino *m*. **viewpoint** *n* punto di vista *m*. **with a view to** allo scopo di. *v* vedere;

osservare; ispezionare. **viewer** *n* spettatore, -trice *m*, *f*; telespettatore, -trice *m*, *f*.

vigil ['vidʒil] *n* veglia *f*; vigilia *f*. **vigilant** *adj* vigile.

vigour ['vigə] *n* vigore *m*. **vigorous** *adj* vigoroso; robusto.

vile [vail] *adj* vile, spregevole.

villa ['vilə] *n* villa *f*.

village ['vilidʒ] *n* villaggio *m*, paese *m*.

villain ['vilən] *n* farabutto *m*, villano *m*.

vindicate ['vindikeit] *v* rivendicare, giustificare; (*exonerate*) discolpare. **vindication** *n* rivendicazione *f*, giustificazione *f*; discolpa *f*.

vindictive [vin'diktiv] *adj* vendicativo, malevolo.

vine [vain] *n* vite *f*. **vineyard** *n* vigna *f*.

vinegar ['vinigə] *n* aceto *m*.

vintage ['vintidʒ] *n* vendemmia *f*; (*year*) annata *f*. *adj* (*wine*) pregiato; (*car*) d'epoca.

vinyl ['vainil] *adj* vinilico.

viola [vi'oulə] *n* viola *f*.

violate ['vaiəleit] *v* violare, trasgredire. **violation** *n* violazione *f*, trasgressione *f*.

violence ['vaiələns] *n* violenza *f*. **violent** *adj* violento.

violet ['vaiəlit] *n* (*colour*) (color) viola *m*, violetto *m*; (*flower*) viola *f*, violetta *f*. *adj* viola *invar*, violetto.

violin [vaiə'lin] *n* violino *m*. **violinist** *n* violinista *m*, *f*.

viper ['vaipə] *n* vipera *f*.

virgin ['vəidʒin] *nf*, *adj* vergine. **virginity** *n* verginità *f*.

Virgo ['vəigou] *n* Vergine *f*.

virile ['virail] *adj* virile. **virility** *n* virilità *f*.

virtual ['vəitʃuəl] *adj* effettivo, in pratica.

virtue ['vəitʃui] *n* virtù *f*; (*admirable quality*) pregio *m*. **by virtue of** in virtù di, grazie a. **virtuoso** *n* virtuoso, -a *m*, *f*. **virtuous** *adj* virtuoso.

virulent ['virələnt] *adj* virulento. **virulence** *n* virulenza *f*.

virus ['vaiərəs] *n* virus *m invar*. **viral** *adj* virale.

visa ['viizə] *n* visto *m*.

viscount ['vaikaunt] *n* visconte *m*. **viscountess** *n* viscontessa *f*.

viscous ['viskəs] *adj* viscoso. **viscosity** *n* viscosità *f*.

visible ['vizəbl] *adj* visibile; (*obvious*) evidente. **visibility** *n* visibilità *f*.

vision ['viʒən] *n* visione *f*; (*wisdom*) sagacia *f*. **visionary** *n*, *adj* visionario, -a.

visit ['vizit] *n* visita *f*. *v* visitare; (*person*) fare una visita a, andare a trovare; (*place*) andare a vedere; (*doctor*) consultare. **visitor** *n* visitatore, -trice *m*, *f*; (*guest*) ospite *m*, *f*.

visor ['vaizə] *n* visiera *f*.

visual ['viʒuəl] *adj* visivo, visuale. **visualize** *v* immaginare, concepire.

vital ['vaitl] *adj* vitale, essenziale; capitale. **vitality** *n* vitalità *f*.

vitamin ['vitəmin] *n* vitamina *f*.

vivacious [vi'veiʃəs] *adj* vivace, animato. **vivacity** *n* vivacità *f*.

vivid ['vivid] *adj* vivido, vivace.

vixen ['viksn] *n* volpe femmina *f*.

vocabulary [və'kabjuləri] *n* vocabolario *m*.

vocal ['voukəl] *adj* vocale; orale.

vocation [vou'keiʃən] *n* vocazione *f*; professione *f*; (*role*) funzione *f*. **vocational** *adj* vocazionale, professionale.

vociferous [və'sifərəs] *adj* rumoroso, chiassoso.

vodka ['vodkə] *n* vodka *f*.

voice [vois] *n* voce *f*. *v* esprimere, formulare, manifestare.

void [void] *nm*, *adj* vuoto. *v* vuotare; (*law*) annullare.

volatile ['volətail] *adj* (*chem*) volatile; capriccioso; (*unpredictable*) imprevedibile; esplosivo.

volcano [vol'keinou] *n* vulcano *m*. **volcanic** *adj* vulcanico.

volley ['voli] *n* raffica *f*, scarica *f*; (*tennis*) volata *f*. **volleyball** *n* pallavolo *f*.

volt [voult] *n* volt *m invar*. **voltage** *n* tensione *f*, voltaggio *m*.

volume ['voljum] *n* volume *m*. **voluminous** *adj* voluminoso.

volunteer [volən'tiə] *n* volontario, -a *m*, *f*. *v* offrirsi volontariamente; (*mil*) arruolarsi volontario; (*offer*) dare *or* offrire spontaneamente. **voluntary** *adj* volontario.

voluptuous [və'lʌptʃuəs] *adj* voluttuoso, sensuale.

vomit ['vomit] *v* vomitare. *n* vomito *m*.

voodoo ['vuidui] *n* vodù *m*.

voracious [və'reiʃəs] *adj* vorace, insaziabile. **voracity** *n* voracità *f*.

vote [vout] *n* voto *m*, diritto di voto *m*, suffragio *m*. *v* votare, dare il proprio voto; (*agree generally*) convenire. **voter** *n* elettore, -trice *m, f*.

vouch [vautʃ] *v* **vouch for** garantire, attestare. **vouchsafe** *v* degnarsi di dare, concedere.

voucher ['vautʃə] *n* buono *m*, tagliando *m*.

vow [vau] *n* voto *m*, giuramento *m*. *v* giurare; fare voto di.

vowel ['vauəl] *n* vocale *f*.

voyage ['vɔiidʒ] *n* viaggio *m*, escursione *f*; (*crossing*) traversata *f*. *v* viaggiare; attraversare.

vulgar ['vʌlgə] *adj* volgare. **vulgarity** *n* volgarità *f*. **vulgarize** *v* divulgare, volgarizzare; (*debase*) degradare.

vulnerable ['vʌlnərəbl] *adj* vulnerabile.

vulture ['vʌltʃə] *n* avvoltoio *m*.

W

wad [wod] *n* tampone *m*; pacchetto *m*; (*roll*) rotolo *m*. **wadding** *n* (*padding*) imbottitura *f*.

waddle ['wodl] *v* camminare dondolandosi. *n* andatura dondolante *f*.

wade [weid] *v* guadare, avanzare con fatica. **wader** *n* (*bird*) trampoliere *m*.

wafer ['weifə] *n* cialda *f*, wafer *m invar*; (*church*) ostia *f*.

waft [woft] *v* diffondere. *n* zaffata *f*.

wag [wag] *v* agitare, scuotere; (*tail*) dimenare. **set tongues wagging** suscitare pettegolezzi.

wage [weidʒ] *n* salario *m*, paga *f*. *v* **wage war** muover guerra.

wager ['weidʒə] *n* scommessa *f*. *v* scommettere.

wagon ['wagən] *n* vagone *m*, carrozza *f*. **be on the wagon** (*coll*) essere astemio.

waif [weif] *n* senzatetto *m invar*; (*foundling*) trovatello, -a *m, f*.

wail [weil] *n* gemito *m*, lamento *m*. *v* gemere, emettere un lamento.

waist [weist] *n* vita *f*. **waistcoat** *n* gilè *m*. **waistline** *n* misura *or* circonferenza della vita *f*.

wait [weit] *v* aspettare, attendere; servire, sostare. *n* attesa *f*; sosta *f*. **lie in wait** stare in agguato. **waiter** *n* cameriere *m*. **waiting-room** *n* sala d'aspetto *f*. **waitress** *n* cameriera *f*.

waive [weiv] *v* rinunciare. **waiver** *n* rinuncia *f*; (*document*) atto di rinuncia *m*.

*****wake**[1] [weik] *v also* **wake up** svegliare, svegliarsi. *n* veglia *f*.

wake[2] [weik] *n* scia *f*. **in the wake of** subito dopo, nella scia di.

Wales [weilz] *n* Galles *m*.

walk [wɔk] *v* camminare; (*go on foot*) andare a piedi. **walk in** entrare. **walk out on** piantare. **walkover** *n* vittoria incontestata *or* facile *f*. *n* cammino *m*, passeggiata *f*; (*gait*) passo *m*. **walker** *n* camminatore, -trice *m, f*; (*sport*) podista *m, f*.

wall [wɔl] *n* muro *m*; (*internal*) parete *f*. **wallpaper** *n* carta da parati *f*.

wallet ['wolit] *n* portafoglio *m*.

wallop ['woləp] (*coll*) *v* (*thrash*) battere, picchiare. *n* (*blow*) colpo violento *m*.

wallow ['wolou] *v* sguazzare.

walnut ['wɔlnʌt] *n* (*tree*) noce *m*; (*fruit*) noce *f*.

walrus ['wɔlrəs] *n* tricheco *m*. **walrus moustache** baffi spioventi *m pl*.

waltz [wɔlts] *n* valzer *m invar*. *v* ballare il valzer. **waltz through** (*coll*) superare facilmente.

wand [wond] *n* bacchetta *f*.

wander ['wondə] *v* vagare, girare; (*stray*) allontanarsi, delirare.

wane [wein] *v* calare, declinare. *n* declino *m*; (*moon*) calare *m*.

wangle ['waŋgl] (*coll*) *n* trucco *m*, intrigo (*pl* -ghi) *m*. *v* procurare con astuzia.

want [wont] *v* volere, desiderare, aver voglia di; (*lack*) mancare di; (*ought*) dovere. *n* (*need*) bisogno *m*, esigenza *f*; (*deficiency*) mancanza *f*. **wanted** *adj* (*asked for*) richiesto; (*police*) ricercato; (*advertisement*) cercasi.

wanton ['wontən] *adj* deliberato, gratuito, sfrenato. *n* libertino *m*, sgualdrina *f*.

war [wɔ] *n* guerra *f*. **warfare** *n* guerra *f*. **warmonger** *n* guerrafondaio *m*. **wartime** *n* tempo di guerra *m*. *v* far guerra, combattere.

warble ['wɔbl] *n* trillo *m*. *v* trillare. **warbler** *n* uccello canoro *m*.

ward [wɔd] *n* (*district*) distretto *m*; (*hospital*) corsia *f*, padiglione *m*; (*law*) pupillo, -a *m, f*. *v* **ward off** parare, scansare.

warden ['wɔdn] *n* guardiano, -a *m, f*, custode *m, f*.

warder ['wɔdə] *n* carceriere, -a *m, f*.

wardrobe ['wɔɪdroub] *n* guardaroba *m invar*; (*cupboard*) armadio *m*.

warehouse ['weəhaus] *n* magazzino *m*.

warm [wɔɪm] *adj* caldo; cordiale, caloroso; (*lively*) animato; (*enthusiastic*) ardente. **be warm** aver caldo. **get warm** scaldarsi. *v* riscaldare. **warmth** *n* caldo *m*; calore *m*; animazione *f*; ardore *m*.

warn [wɔɪn] *v* mettere in guardia, ammonire; (*notify*) avvertire, preavvisare. **warning** *n* ammonimento *m*; preavviso *m*; allarme *m*.

warp [wɔɪp] *v* deformare. *n* ordito *m*.

warrant ['wɔrənt] *n* autorizzazione *f*, diritto *m*; (*law*) mandato *m*. *v* autorizzare; giustificare; garantire. **warranty** *n* (*comm*) garanzia *f*.

warren ['wɔrən] *n* (*rabbit*) garenna *f*.

warrior ['wɔriə] *n* guerriero *m*. **unknown warrior** *n* milite ignoto *m*.

Warsaw ['wɔɪsɔɪ] *n* Varsavia *f*.

wart [wɔɪt] *n* verruca *f*.

wary ['weəri] *adj* diffidente, cauto. **be wary of** diffidare di; guardarsi dal.

was [wɔz] *V* **be**.

wash [wɔʃ] *v* lavare. **wash away** portare via; (*obliterate*) cancellare. **wash-basin** *n* lavandino *m*. **wash-out** *n* (*slang*) fiasco *m*. **wash up** lavare i piatti. *n* lavata *f*; (*clothes, etc.*) bucato *m*; (*painting*) acquerello *m*, guazzo *m*. **have a wash** lavarsi. **washable** *adj* lavabile. **washing** *n* bucato *m*. **washing-machine** *n* lavatrice automatica *f*.

washer ['wɔʃə] *n* rondella *f*.

wasp [wɔsp] *n* vespa *f*.

waste [weist] *v* sprecare, sciupare. **waste away** deperire. *n* spreco *m*; (*rubbish*) immondizia *f*; (*scrap*) scarti *m pl*, cascami *m pl*; (*geog*) deserto *m*. **waste-paper basket** cestino da rifiuti *m*. **waste-pipe** *n* tubo di scarico *m*. **wasteful** *adj* dispendioso, sprecone.

watch [wɔtʃ] *v* guardare, osservare; (*as spectator*) assistere a; (*keep an eye on*) tener d'occhio. **watch out** stare attento. **watch over** sorvegliare. *n* (*time*) orologio *m*; osservazione *f*; guardia *f*, sorveglianza *f*. **keep watch** fare la guardia. **watch-dog** *n* cane da guardia *m*. **watchful** *adj* vigile.

water ['wɔɪtə] *n* acqua *f*. *v* annaffiare, irrigare. **water down** diluire; moderare, attenuare. **watery** *adj* acquoso; (*colour*) scialbo.

water-closet *n* gabinetto *m*.

water-colour *n* acquerello *m*.

watercress ['wɔɪtəkres] *n* crescione *m*.

waterfall ['wɔɪtəfɔɪl] *n* cascata *f*.

waterfront ['wɔɪtəfrʌnt] *n* lungomare *m*; (*wharf*) zona portuale *f*.

watering-can *n* annaffiatoio *m*.

water-lily *n* ninfea *f*.

waterlogged ['wɔɪtəlogd] *adj* saturo d'acqua; (*ground*) acquitrinoso.

water-melon *n* cocomero *m*.

water-mill *n* mulino ad acqua *m*.

water polo *n* pallanuoto *f*.

waterproof ['wɔɪtəpruf] *nm*, *adj* impermeabile. *v* impermeabilizzare.

watershed ['wɔɪtəʃed] *n* spartiacque *m invar*.

water-ski *n* sci nautico *m*. *v* fare dello sci nautico. **water-skiing** *n* sci nautico *m*.

watertight ['wɔɪtətait] *adj* stagno; (*irrefutable*) inconfutabile.

water-way *n* corso navigabile *m*.

waterworks ['wɔɪtəwɜɪks] *n* impianto idrico *m*. **turn on the waterworks** (*coll*) mettersi a piangere.

watt [wɔt] *n* watt *m invar*. **wattage** *n* wattaggio *m*.

wave [weiv] *n* onda *f*; (*surge*) ondata *f*; (*sign*) cenno *m*. **waveband** *n* gamma di lunghezze d'onda *f*. *v* sventolare, far segno con; (*hair*) ondulare. **wave aside** scartare. **wavy** *adj* (*hair*) ondulato; (*line*) ondeggiante.

waver ['weivə] *v* (*vacillate*) titubare, esitare.

wax[1] [waks] *n* cera *f*. *v* dar la cera a, lucidare.

wax[2] [waks] *v* (*increase*) crescere; (*become*) diventare.

way [wei] *n* (*manner*) modo *m*; (*respect*) rispetto *m*, particolare *m*; (*street*) strada *f*; passaggio *m*. **by the way** a proposito. **give way** cedere; (*traffic*) dare la precedenza. **in a way** in un certo modo. **make way for** fare largo a. **out of the way** (*place*) fuori strada; (*unusual*) fuori del comune. **way in** entrata *f*. **way out** uscita *f*.

*****waylay** [wei'lei] *v* abbordare; (*ambush*) tendere un agguato a.

wayward ['weiwəd] *adj* capriccioso, ribelle.

we [wiɪ] *pron* noi.

weak [wiːk] *adj* debole. **weaken** *v* indebolire. **weakling** *n* persona debole *f*. **weakness** *n* debolezza *f*; (*inclination*) debole *m*.
wealth [welθ] *n* ricchezza *f*; abbondanza *f*. **wealthy** *adj* ricco.
wean [wiːn] *v* svezzare.
weapon ['wepən] *n* arma *f*.
*****wear** [weə] *v* portare, indossare; (*deteriorate*) consumare; (*last*) durare. **wear off** passare, dissiparsi. **wear out** consumare, indebolire; (*tire*) stancare. *n* (*use*) uso *m*; (*clothing*) abiti *m pl*, abbigliamento *m*; (*deterioration*) usura *f*.
weary ['wiəri] *adj* stanco, stufo. *v* stancare, stufare.
weasel ['wiːzl] *n* donnola *f*.
weather ['weðə] *n* tempo *m*. **weather-beaten** *adj* segnato dalle intemperie. **weather forecast** bollettino meteorologico *m*. *v* (*expose*) esporre all'aria, stagionare; (*overcome*) superare.
*****weave** [wiːv] *v* tessere; (*devise*) ordire. *n* armatura *f*. **weaver** *n* tessitore *m*. **weaving** *n* tessitura *f*.
web [web] *n* tessuto *m*; (*spider*) ragnatela *f*. **webbed foot** piede palmato *m*.
wedding ['wediŋ] *n* matrimonio *m*; (*ceremony*) nozze *f pl*. **wedding-dress** *n* abito nuziale *m*. **wedding-ring** *n* fede *f*.
wedge [wedʒ] *n* cuneo *m*. *v* incuneare, incastrare.
Wednesday ['wenzdi] *n* mercoledì *m*.
weed [wiːd] *n* erbaccia *f*, malerba *f*. **weedkiller** *n* erbicida *m*. *v* diserbare, sarchiare. **weedy** *adj* coperto di erbacce; (*person*) sparuto.
week [wiːk] *n* settimana *f*. **weekday** *n* giorno feriale *or* lavorativo *m*. **weekend** *n* fine settimana *f*, week-end *m invar*.
weekly ['wiːkli] *nm, adj* settimanale. *adv* ogni settimana.
*****weep** [wiːp] *v* piangere. **weeping** *n* pianto *m*. **weeping willow** salice piangente *m*.
weepy *adj* (*coll*) lacrimoso, sentimentale.
weigh [wei] *v* pesare; (*have importance*) valere. **weigh anchor** salpare. **weighbridge** *n* pesa a ponte *f*, pesa pubblica *f*. **weigh up** soppesare, valutare. **weight** *n* peso *m*. **carry weight** aver peso. **lose weight** dimagrire. **put on weight** ingrassare. **weighty** *adj* pesante; importante.
weird [wiəd] *adj* strano, misterioso.
welcome ['welkəm] *interj* benvenuto! **welcome home!** ben tornato! *n* benvenuto

m, buona *or* cordiale accoglienza *f*. *adj* benvenuto, gradito. *v* accogliere; (*greet*) dare il benvenuto a; (*accept gladly*) gradire.
weld [weld] *v* saldare. *n* saldatura *f*.
welfare ['welfeə] *n* benessere *m*; assistenza sociale *f*. **welfare worker** *n* assistente sociale *m, f*.
well[1] [wel] *n* pozzo *m*; (*stairs*) tromba *f*.
well[2] [wel] *adv* bene. *interj* beh! allora! **as well** (*also*) anche.
well-behaved *adj* educato, beneducato.
well-being *n* benessere *m*, bene *m*.
well-bred *adj* educato, beneducato.
well-built *adj* ben costruito.
wellingtons ['weliŋtənz] *pl n* stivali impermeabili *m pl*, stivali di gomma *m pl*.
well-known *adj* ben noto.
well-meaning *adj* ben intenzionato. **well-meant** *adj* fatto a fin di bene.
well-off *adj* benestante, agiato.
well-paid *adj* ben pagato *or* retribuito.
well-read *adj* colto.
well-spoken *adj* che parla bene.
well-to-do *adj* benestante, abbiente.
well-worn *adj* logoro; (*hackneyed*) trito.
Welsh [welʃ] *n*(*m*+*f*), *adj* gallese.
went [went] *V* go.
wept [wept] *V* weep.
were [wəː] *V* be.
west [west] *n* ovest *m*, occidente *m*. *adv* *also* **westward(s)** verso ovest, in direzione ovest.
western ['westən] *adj* occidentale, dell'ovest. *n* (*film*) western *m*.
wet [wet] *adj* bagnato, umido; (*rainy*) piovoso; (*paint, ink, etc.*) fresco. **wet blanket** guastafeste *m, f invar*. **wet through** bagnato fradicio; (*person*) bagnato fino alle ossa. *v* bagnare.
whack [wak] (*coll*) *n* colpo *m*; (*part*) fetta *f*. *v* colpire. **be whacked** essere sfinito.
whale [weil] *n* balena *f*. **have a whale of a time** (*coll*) divertirsi un mondo. **whaling** *n* caccia alla balena *f*.
wharf [woːf] *n* banchina *f*, scalo *m*.
what [wot] *pron* (che) cosa; (*relative*) quello che. *adj* che, quale. **what a ... !** che ... ! **what for?** perché? **what is the matter?** cosa c'è? cosa succede?
whatever [wot'evə] *pron* qualsiasi *or* qualunque cosa. *adj* qualsiasi, qualunque. **none whatever** nessuno. **nothing whatever** assolutamente nulla.

wheat [wiːt] *n* grano *m*, frumento *m*.
wheel [wiːl] *n* ruota *f*; (*pottery*) tornio *m*; (*steering*) volante *m*. **wheelbarrow** *n* carretta *f*, carriola *f*. **wheelchair** *n* sedia a rotelle *f*. *v* (*make turn*) far rotare; (*push*) spingere.
wheeze [wiːz] *v* ansimare. *n* respiro affannoso *m*.
whelk [welk] *n* buccino *m*.
when [wen] *adv* quando. *conj* quando; (*after which*) appena; (*whereas*) mentre. **whenever** *adv* qualora, ogni volta che.
where [weə] *conj*, *adv* dove. **whereabouts** *adv* dove, da che parte. **whereas** *conj* mentre. **whereby** *conj*, *adv* onde, per cui. **whereupon** *conj* dopoché, dal momento che. **wherever** *conj* dovunque. **wherewithal** *n* necessario *m*.
whether ['weðə] *conj* se.
which [witʃ] *pron* quale; (*relative*) il quale, la quale; che. *adj* quale. **which way?** da che parte?
whichever [witʃevə] *adj* qualunque, qualsiasi. *pron* quello che; (*person*) chiunque.
whiff [wif] *n* buffata *f*, zaffata *f*.
while [wail] *conj* mentre. *n* momento *m*. **a long while ago** molto tempo fa.
whim [wim] *n* capriccio *m*.
whimper ['wimpə] *v* piagnucolare. *n* piagnucolio *m*.
whimsical ['wimzikl] *adj* bizzarro, eccentrico.
whine [wain] *v* gemere; (*complain*) uggiolare. *n* uggiolio *m*, gemito *m*.
whip [wip] *n* frusta *f*. **whip-round** (*coll*) colletta *f*. *v* frustare; (*cookery*) frullare. **whipped cream** panna montata *f*.
whippet ['wipit] *n* levriere inglese *m*.
whirl [wəːl] *n* turbine *m*, giro vertiginoso *m*. **whirlpool** *n* vortice *m*. **whirlwind** *n* turbine *m*, tromba d'aria *f*. *v* girare (rapidamente).
whisk [wisk] *v* (*dust*) spolverare; (*cookery*) frullare. *n* piumino *m*; frullino *m*.
whisker ['wiskə] *n* pelo *m*. **whiskers** *pl n* basette *f pl*; (*moustache, cat*) baffi *m pl*.
whisky ['wiski] *n* whisky *m invar*.
whisper ['wispə] *v* bisbigliare, mormorare. *n* bisbiglio *m*, mormorio *m*.
whist [wist] *n* whist *m invar*.
whistle ['wisl] *v* fischiare; (*tune*) fischiettare. *n* (*sound*) fischio *m*; (*instrument*) fischietto *m*.
white [wait] *n* bianco *m*. *adj* bianco.

whitebait *pl n* bianchetti *m pl*. **whiten** *v* imbiancare.
whitewash ['waitwoʃ] *n* intonaco *m*; (*cover-up*) riabilitazione *f*. *v* imbiancare, intonacare; (*cover up*) scolpare.
whiting ['waitiŋ] *n* (*fish*) merlango *m*.
Whitsun ['witsn] *n* Pentecoste *f*.
whizz [wiz] *v* (*hum*) sibilare; (*move*) guizzare.
who [huː] *pron* chi; (*relative*) che, il quale, la quale. **whoever** *pron* chiunque.
whole [houl] *n* totale *m*, insieme *m*. **as a whole** nell'insieme. **on the whole** tutto considerato, in fin dei conti. *adj* intero, tutto; intatto. **wholehearted** *adj* generoso. **wholemeal** *adj* integrale. **wholesale** *adv* all'ingrosso. **wholesaler** *n* grossista *m, f*. **wholesome** *adj* sano.
whom [huːm] *pron* che; (*relative*) il quale, la quale; (*after prep*) cui.
whooping cough ['huːpiŋ] *n* pertosse *f*.
whore [hoː] *n* (*derog*) puttana *f*.
whose [huːz] *pron* di chi. *adj* di cui; (*relative*) il cui, la cui.
why [wai] *adv*, *conj* perché, per cui.
wick [wik] *n* stoppino *m*.
wicked ['wikid] *adj* cattivo, malvagio. **wickedness** *n* cattiveria *f*, malvagità *f*.
wicker ['wikə] *n* vimini *m pl*.
wicket ['wikit] *n* porta *f*, sportello *m*. **a sticky wicket** una situazione scabrosa.
wide [waid] *adj* largo; (*spacious*) ampio. *adv* lontano. **open wide** *v* spalancare. **wide apart** spaziati. **wide awake** completamente sveglio; (*alert*) vigilante. **wide open** spalancato. **widespread** *adj* esteso, diffuso. **widen** *v* estendere, allargare.
widow ['widou] *n* vedova *f*. **widower** *n* vedovo *m*.
width [widθ] *n* larghezza *f*; (*cloth*) altezza *f*.
wield [wiːld] *v* (*weapon*) brandire; (*power*) esercitare.
wife [waif] *n* moglie *f*.
wig [wig] *n* parrucca *f*.
wiggle ['wigl] *v* dimenare.
wild [waild] *adj* selvatico; (*animal, place*) selvaggio; (*unrestrained*) feroce. **spread like wildfire** divampare. **wild with anger** fuori di sè dalla rabbia. **wild with joy** folle di gioia.
wilderness ['wildənəs] *n* deserto *m*, solitudine *f*.
wilful ['wilfəl] *adj* intenzionale; premeditato; ostinato.

will[1] [wil] *aux translated by future tense.*
will[2] [wil] *n* volontà *f*; (*law*) testamento *m*. **against one's will** malvolentieri, controvoglia. **at will** a piacere.
willing ['wiliŋ] *adj* (*disposed*) disposto; (*ready*) pronto, volonteroso. **willingness** *n* prontezza *f*; buona volontà *f*.
willow ['wilou] *n* salice *m*.
wilt [wilt] *v* appassire.
***win** [win] *v* vincere. **win back** riguadagnare. *n* vittoria *f*; (*games*) vincita *f*. **winner** *n* vincitore *m*.
wince [wins] *v* trasalire. *n* sussulto *m*, trasalimento *m*.
winch [wintʃ] *n* argano *m*. *v* **winch up** sollevare con l'argano.
wind[1] [wind] *n* vento *m*; (*breath*) fiato *m*. **get wind of** aver sentore di, fiutare. *v* sfiatare. **windy** *adj* esposto al vento.
***wind**[2] [waind] *v* (*twist*) serpeggiare. **wind up** (*roll up*) avvolgere; concludere; (*end up*) andare a finire; (*clock*) caricare; (*business*) liquidare.
wind-cheater *n* giacca a vento *f*.
windfall ['windfoil] *n* frutto fatto cadere dal vento *m*; fortuna inaspettata *f*.
windlass ['windləs] *n* verricello *m*.
windmill ['wind,mil] *n* mulino a vento *m*.
window ['windou] *n* finestra *f*; (*train*) finestrino *m*; (*car*) cristallo *m*; (*cashier's*) sportello *m*. **French window** *n* portafinestra *f*. **window-dressing** *n* mostra *f*; (*show*) bella mostra *f*, inganno *m*. **window-sill** *n* davanzale *m*.
windpipe ['windpaip] *n* trachea *f*.
windshield ['windʃiild] *n* parabrezza *m invar*. **windshield wiper** tergicristallo *m*.
windswept ['windswept] *adj* battuto dai venti.
wine [wain] *n* vino *m*. **wineglass** *n* bicchiere da vino *m*. **wine list** carta dei vini *f*.
wing [wiŋ] *n* ala *f*. **in the wings** (*theatre*) tra le quinte. **wingspan** *n* apertura alare *f*.
wink [wiŋk] *v* strizzare l'occhio, ammiccare. *n* (*signal*) cenno *m*; (*instant*) attimo *m*. **have forty winks** schiacciare un pisolino.
winkle ['wiŋkl] *n* chiocciola di mare *f*.
winter ['wintə] *n* inverno *m*. **wintry** *adj* invernale.
wipe [waip] *v* strofinare; (*dry*) asciugare. **wipe away** *or* **off** cancellare, allontanare. **wipe out** eliminare; (*debts, etc.*)

liquidare; (*annihilate*) annientare. **wiper** *n* strofinaccio *m*; (*windscreen*) tergicristallo *m*.
wire [waiə] *n* filo *m*; telegramma *m*. **wireless** *n* radio *f invar*. *v* (*elec*) montare; (*fasten*) legare con filo metallico; telegrafare. **wiry** *adj* secco, nerboruto.
wisdom ['wizdəm] *n* saggezza *f*. **wisdom tooth** *n* dente del giudizio *m*.
wise [waiz] *adj* saggio. **wisecrack** *n* battuta *f*.
wish [wiʃ] *n* desiderio *m*, voglia *f*. **wishes** *pl n* auguri *m pl*. *v* desiderare, volere; (*greeting*) augurare. **wishful thinking** pio desiderio *m*.
wisp [wisp] *n* (*hair*) ciocca *f*; (*smoke*) filo *m*.
wistful ['wistfəl] *adj* pensoso, malinconico.
wit [wit] *n* spirito *m*; arguzia *f*, intelligenza *f*; (*person*) uomo di spirito *m*. **be at one's wits' end** non saper più cosa fare. **live by one's wits** vivere di espedienti.
witch [witʃ] *n* strega *f*. **witchcraft** *n* stregoneria *f*. **witch-doctor** *n* stregone *m*.
with [wið] *prep* con; (*together with*) insieme a; (*because of*) per, a causa di.
***withdraw** [wið'droi] *v* ritirare; (*cash*) prelevare. **withdrawal** *n* ritiro *m*; (*mil*) ritirata *f*; prelevamento *m*.
wither ['wiðə] *v* (*lose freshness*) appassire; atrofizzare; (*decay*) avvizzire.
***withhold** [wið'hould] *v* trattenere; (*hide*) nascondere.
within [wi'ðin] *adv* dentro. *prep* entro, in. **within reach** a portata.
without [wi'ðaut] *prep* senza. *adv* fuori. **do without** fare a meno (di).
***withstand** [wið'stand] *v* resistere a.
witness ['witnis] *n* (*evidence*) testimonianza *f*; (*person*) testimone *m*, *f*. *v* testimoniare, attestare.
witty ['witi] *adj* spiritoso, arguto.
wizard ['wizəd] *n* mago *m*.
wobble ['wobl] *v* vacillare, traballare.
woke [wouk] *V* **wake**[1].
woken ['woukn] *V* **wake**[1].
wolf [wulf] *n* lupo *m*. **cry wolf** gridare al lupo. *v* divorare.
woman ['wumən] *n, pl* **women** donna *f*. **old woman** *n* vecchia *f*. **young woman** giovane *f*. **womanly** *adj* femminile.
womb [wuim] *n* utero *m*.

won [wʌn] *V* **win.**

wonder ['wʌndə] *n* meraviglia *f*; miracolo *m*. *v* meravigliarsi; (*ask oneself*) domandarsi. **wonderful** *adj* meraviglioso.

wood [wud] *n* (*material*) legno *m*; (*as fuel*) legna *f*; (*forest*) bosco *m*. **wooden** *adj* di legno; rigido. **woody** *adj* (*wooded*) boscoso; (*tough*) legnoso.

woodcock ['wudkok] *n* beccaccia *f*.

woodcut ['wudkʌt] *n* silografia *f*, incisione su legno *f*.

woodland ['wudlənd] *n* boscaglia *f*.

woodpecker ['wudpekə] *n* picchio *m*.

wood-pigeon *n* colombaccio *m*.

wood-wind *n* strumenti a fiato *m pl*.

woodwork ['wudwəːk] *n* (*carpentry*) lavoro in legno *m*, falegnameria *f*; (*wooden parts*) parti in legno *f pl*.

woodworm ['wudwəːm] *n* tarlo *m*.

wool [wul] *n* lana *f*. **dyed in the wool** *adj* radicato, convinto. **woollen** *adj* di lana; (*industry*) laniero. **woolly** *adj* di lana, lanoso; confuso.

word [wəːd] *n* parola *f*. **in other words** altrimenti detto. **word for word** alla lettera. *v* esprimere, redigere. **wording** *n* espressione *f*, formulazione *f*.

wore [woɪ] *V* **wear.**

work [wəːk] *n* lavoro *m*; (*toil*) fatica *f*; (*product*) opera *f*. **workman** *n* operaio *m*. **works** *n* (*factory*) fabbrica *f*, stabilimento *m*. **workshop** *n* officina *f*. *v* lavorare; (*machine, etc.*) (far) funzionare. **work out** risolvere; risultare. **worker** *n* lavoratore, -trice *m*, *f*, operaio, -a *m*, *f*. **working** *n* operazione *f*, funzionamento *m*. **working class** classe operaia *f*. **working order** buon ordine *m*.

world [wəːld] *n* mondo *m*. **world war** guerra mondiale *f*. **world-wide** *adj* mondiale, universale. **worldly** *adj* temporale; mondano.

worm [wəːm] *n* verme *m*. *v* insinuarsi.

worn [woɪn] *V* **wear.**

worry ['wʌri] *n* preoccupazione *f*, ansia *f*. *v* preoccupare; molestare. **worrying** *adj* preoccupante.

worse [wəːs] *adj* peggio, peggiore. *nm*, *adv* peggio. **from bad to worse** di male in peggio. **get worse** peggiorare. **worsen** *v* peggiorare.

worship ['wəːʃip] *n* adorazione *f*, omaggio *m*; (*rel*) culto *m*, servizio religioso *m*. *v* adorare; andare a messa, andare in chiesa.

worst [wəːst] *adj* peggiore, il più brutto. *nm*, *adv* peggio.

worsted ['wustid] *nm*, *adj* pettinato.

worth [wəːθ] *adj* **be worth** valere. **be worthless** non valere nulla. **be worthwhile** valere la pena. *n* merito *m*, valore *m*. **worthy** *adj* degno.

would [wud] *aux translated by conditional or imperfect tense.*

wound[1] [wuɪnd] *n* ferita *f*. *v* ferire; offendere. **wounded** *adj* ferito.

wound[2] [waund] *V* **wind**[2].

wove [wouv] *V* **weave.**

woven ['wouvn] *V* **weave.**

wrangle ['raŋgl] *v* litigare, disputare. *n* lite *f*, disputa *f*.

wrap [rap] *v* (*envelop*) avvolgere; (*cover*) coprire; (*parcel*) incartare. *n* (*shawl*) scialle *m*; (*dressing-gown*) vestaglia *f*. **wrapper** *n* involucro *m*; (*book*) copertina *f*.

wreath [riːθ] *n* ghirlanda *f*, corona *f*. **wreathe** *v* incoronare. **wreathed in smiles** raggiante.

wreck [rek] *n* (*ship*) naufragio *m*; (*ruin*) relitto *m*, rovina *f*. *v* rovinare; demolire; naufragare. **wreckage** *n* rottami *m pl*.

wren [ren] *n* scricciolo *m*.

wrench [rentʃ] *v* storcere. **wrench open** forzare. *n* (*movement*) strappo *m*; (*injury*) storta *f*; (*spanner*) chiave *f*.

wrestle ['resl] *v* lottare. **wrestling** *n* lotta *f*.

wretch [retʃ] *n* (*unfortunate*) disgraziato, -a *m*, *f*; (*despicable*) incosciente *m*, *f*. **wretched** *adj* disgraziato, miserabile; (*pitiful*) pietoso.

wriggle ['rigl] *v* dimenarsi.

***wring** [riŋ] *v* torcere. **wring out** strizzare. **wringer** *n* strizzatoio *m*. **wringing wet** fradicio.

wrinkle ['riŋkl] *n* crespa *f*; (*face*) ruga *f*. *v* increspare; corrugare.

wrist [rist] *n* polso *m*.

writ [rit] *n* mandato *m*.

***write** [rait] *v* scrivere. **write down** trascrivere, registrare. **write off** (*comm*) cancellare. **writer** *n* scrittore, -trice *m*, *f*. **writing** *n* calligrafia *f*. **writings** *pl n* scritti *m pl*.

writhe [raið] *v* contorcersi.

written ['ritn] *V* **write.**

wrong [roŋ] *adv* male. *adj* (*not moral*) peccato; (*incorrect*) sbagliato. **be wrong** (*person*) aver torto, sbagliarsi. *n* torto *m*; ingiustizia *f*; (*law*) violazione *f*. *v* **far**

torto a, maltrattare. **wrongful** *adj* ingiustificato.

wrote [rout] *V* **write.**

wrought iron [ˌrɔɪt'aɪən] *n* ferro battuto *m*.

wrung [rʌŋ] *V* **wring.**

wry [rai] *adj* ironico, perverso; (*askance*) di sbieco.

X

xenophobia [ˌzenə'foubiə] *n* xenofobia *f*. **xenophobic** *adj* xenofobo.

Xmas ['krisməs] *V* **Christmas.**

X-ray ['eksrei] *n* raggio X *m*; (*photo*) radiografia *f*. *v* radiografare.

xylophone ['zailəfoun] *n* xilofono *m*.

Y

yacht [jot] *n* panfilo *m*. **yachting** *n* velismo *m*.

yank [jaŋk] *v* (*coll*) dare uno strattone a, tirare con violenza.

yap [jap] *v* guaire. *n* guaito *m*.

yard [jaɪd] *n* cortile *m*; (*site*) cantiere *m*; (*railway*) scalo merci *m*. **yardstick** *n* (*measure*) metro *m*; (*standard*) pietra di paragone *f*.

yarn [jaɪn] *n* (*thread*) filo *m*, filato *m*; storia *f*.

yawn [jɔɪn] *v* sbadigliare. *n* sbadiglio *m*.

year [jiə] *n* anno *m*, annata *f*. **year-book** *n* annuario *m*. **yearly** *adj* annuo, annuale.

yearn [jəɪn] *v* languire. **yearn for** bramare, desiderare vivamente. **yearning** *n* vivo desiderio *m*, brama *f*.

yeast [jiɪst] *n* lievito *m*.

yell [jel] *v* gridare, urlare. *n* grido *m*, urlo *m*.

yellow ['jelou] *adj* giallo; (*coll: cowardly*) vigliacco. *n* giallo *m*. *v* ingiallire. **yellowy** *adj* giallastro.

yelp [jelp] *v* (*dog*) uggiolare. **yelp with pain** gridare per il dolore. *n* uggiolio *m*; grido di dolore *m*.

yes [jes] *nm, adv* sì.

yesterday ['jestədi] *nm, adv* ieri.

yet [jət] *adv* ancora; (*already*) già. *conj* ma, tuttavia. **as yet** finora.

yew [juɪ] *n* tasso *m*.

yield [jiɪld] *v* produrre; (*surrender*) cedere; (*profit, interest, etc.*) rendere, fruttare. *n* frutto *m*, prodotto *m*; (*tech*) resa *f*; (*finance*) reddito *m*; (*harvest*) raccolto *m*.

yoga ['jougə] *n* yoga *m*.

yoghurt ['yogət] *m* iogurt *m*.

yoke [jouk] *n* giogo *m*; (*dress*) carrè *m*.

yolk [jouk] *n* tuorlo *m*.

you [juɪ] *pron* (*subject: fam*) tu; (*subject: pl*) voi; (*subject: fml*) Lei; (*direct object*) ti, vi, la; (*indirect object*) ti *or* te, vi *or* ve, le; (*after prep*) te, voi, Lei. **if I were you** se fossi (in) te.

young [jʌŋ] *adj* giovane. **youngster** *n* (*child*) bambino, -a *m, f*; (*youth*) ragazzo, -a *m, f*.

your [jɔɪ] *adj* (*fam*) (il) tuo, (la) tua, (i) tuoi, (le) tue; (*pl*) (il) vostro, (la) vostra, (i) vostri, (le) vostre; (*fml*) (il) suo, (la) sua, (i) suoi, (le) sue.

yours [jɔɪz] *pron* (*fam*) il tuo, la tua, i tuoi, le tue; (*pl*) il vostro, la vostra, i vostri, le vostre; (*fml*) il suo, la sua, i suoi, le sue.

yourself [jə'self] *pron* (*fam*) tu stesso; (*fml*) Lei stesso; (*reflexive*) ti, si; (*after prep*) te stesso, Lei stesso.

yourselves [jə'selvz] *pron* voi stessi; (*reflexive*) vi.

youth [juɪθ] *n* gioventù *f*; (*boy*) giovane *m*.

Yugoslavia [juɪgou'slaɪvjə] *n* Iugoslavia *f*. **Yugoslav** *n, adj* iugoslavo, -a.

Z

zeal [ziɪl] *n* zelo *m*. **zealous** *adj* zelante.

zebra ['zebrə] *n* zebra *f*. **zebra crossing** passaggio zebrato *m*.

zero ['ziərou] *n* zero *m*. *v* mettere a zero, azzerare.

zest [zest] *n* (*enjoyment*) gusto *m*, entusiasmo *m*; (*piquancy*) nota piccante *f*.

zigzag ['zigzag] *nm, adj* zigzag. *v* andare a zigzag, serpeggiare.

zinc [ziŋk] *n* zinco *m*.

zip [zip] *n* chiusura *or* cerniera lampo *f*. *v* **zip up** chiudere la (cerniera) lampo.

zodiac ['zoudiak] *n* zodiaco *m*.

zone [zoun] *n* zona *f*.

zoo [zuː] *n* giardino zoologico *m*, zoo *m* invar. **zoologist** *n* zoologo, -a *m, f.* **zoology** *n* zoologia *f.*
zoom [zuːm] *v* (*noise*) ronzare; (*aircraft*) salire in candela; (*film*) zumare. *n* ronzio *m.* **zoom lens** zoom *m* invar, obiettivo zoom *m.*

Italian—Inglese

A

a, ad [a, ad] *prep* to; (*stato in luogo*) at, in; (*prezzo, ora, età*) at. **a 10 metri da** 10 metres away from. **a due a due** two by two. **alle dozzina** by the dozen. **andare a casa** go home. **100 km all'ora** 100 km an hour.

abate [a'bate] *sm* abbot.

abbagliare [abba'ʎare] *v* dazzle.

abbaiare [abba'jare] *v* bark. **abbaiata** *sf* bark.

abbaino [abba'ino] *sm* attic, garret.

abbandonare [abbando'nare] *v* abandon, leave. **abbandonarsi a** (*darsi senza ritegno*) indulge in; give in to. **abbandono** *sm* neglect; desertion.

abbassare [abbas'sare] *v* lower, reduce. **abbasso** *avv* down. **abbasso ...** ! *inter* down with ... !

abbastanza [abbas'tantsa] *avv* enough.

abbattere [ab'battere] *v* knock down, fell; (*uccidere*) kill; (*deprimere*) depress. **abbattersi** *v* become disheartened.

abbazia [abba'tsia] *sf* abbey.

abbellire [abbel'lire] *v* embellish, adorn.

abbiente [ab'bjɛnte] *agg* prosperous, well-to-do.

abbigliare [abbi'ʎare] *v* dress. **abbigliamento** *sm* clothes *pl*; (*modo*) dress.

abboccare [abbok'kare] *v* bite. **abboccato** *agg* (*vino*) medium sweet.

abbonarsi [abbo'narsi] *v* subscribe; take out a season ticket (for). **abbonamento** *sm* subscription; season ticket. **abbonato, -a** *sm, sf* subscriber; ticket-holder.

abbondare [abbon'dare] *v* be plentiful, abound. **abbondante** *agg* plentiful, abundant. **abbondanza** *sf* abundance, plenty.

abbordare [abbor'dare] *v* approach; (*introdurre*) broach.

abborracciare [abborrat'tʃare] *v* botch.

abbottonare [abbotto'nare] *v* button up.

abbozzare [abbot'tsare] *v* sketch, outline. **abbozzare un sorriso** give a faint smile. **abbozzo** *sm* sketch.

abbracciare [abbrat'tʃare] *v* embrace. **abbraccio** *sm* embrace, hug.

abbreviare [abbre'vjare] *v* abbreviate, shorten. **abbreviazione** *sf* abbreviation.

abbronzare [abbron'dzare] *v* tan. **abbronzatura** *sf* (sun-)tan.

abbrustolire [abbrusto'lire] *v* toast.

abbuono [ab'bwɔno] *sm* allowance; (*sport*) handicap.

abdicare [abdi'kare] *v* abdicate. **abdicazione** *sf* abdication.

aberrazione [aberra'tsjone] *sf* aberration.

abete [a'bete] *sm* fir(-tree). **abete rosso** spruce.

abietto [a'bjɛtto] *agg* abject. **abiezione** *sf* low spirits *pl*.

abile ['abile] *agg* clever, good (at); (*adatto*) suitable. **abilità** *sf* cleverness, skill; (*destrezza*) dexterity.

abilitare [abili'tare] *v* train; (*a una professione*) qualify. **abilitazione** *sf* qualification, diploma.

abisso [a'bisso] *sm* abyss.

abitare [abi'tare] *v* live. **abitante** *s(m+f)* inhabitant. **abitazione** *sf* home, dwelling.

abitato [abi'tato] *agg* inhabited. *sm* built-up area; (*villaggio*) hamlet.

abito ['abito] *sm* suit; dress; (*rel, abitudine*) habit. **abituale** *agg* customary, usual; habitual.

abituarsi [abitu'arsi] *v* **abituarsi a** get used to, become accustomed to.

abitudine [abi'tudine] *sf* habit, custom. **avere l'abitudine di** be in the habit of. **d'abitudine** as a rule.

abolire [abo'lire] *v* abolish. **abolizione** *sf* abolition.

abominevole [abomi'nevole] *agg* abominable.
aborigeno [abo'ridʒeno] *sm* aborigine. *agg* aboriginal.
aborrire [abor'rire] *v* abhor, loathe.
abortire [abor'tire] *v* miscarry; fail. **aborto** *sm* miscarriage. **aborto procurato** abortion.
abrasivo [abra'zivo] *sm, agg* abrasive.
abrasione *sf* abrasion.
abside ['abside] *sf* apse.
abusare [abu'zare] *v* abuse. **abusivo** *agg* unauthorized, improper. **abuso** *sm* abuse.
accademia [akka'dɛmja] *sf* academy. **accademico** *sm, agg* academic.
*accadere [akka'dere] *v* happen. **accaduto** *sm* occurrence.
accampare [akkam'pare] *v* camp; (*avanzare*) put forward. **accampamento** *sm* camp. *r:*
accanirsi [akka'nirsi] *v* rage; persist.
accanito *agg* (*ostinato*) dogged, stubborn; (*spietato*) merciless; (*violento*) fierce.
accanto [ak'kanto] *avv* nearby; (*casa*) next door. **accanto a** next to, near to, beside.
accantonare [akkanto'nare] *v* set aside.
accaparrare [akkapar'rare] *v* corner.
accappatoio [akkappa'tojo] *sm* bathrobe.
accarezzare [akkaret'tsare] *v* caress, stroke.
accasciare [akka'ʃare] *v* crush. **accasciarsi** *v* collapse.
accattone [akkat'tone], **-a** *sm, sf* scrounger.
accavallare [akkaval'lare] *v* (*sovrapporre*) overlap; (*accumulare*) pile up; (*incrociare*) cross.
accecare [attʃe'kare] *v* blind; block up. **accecante** *agg* blinding.
*accedere [at'tʃedere] *v* accede.
accelerare [attʃele'rare] *v* accelerate, speed up. **accelerato** *sm* local train. **acceleratore** *sm* accelerator. **accelerazione** *sf* acceleration.
*accendere [at'tʃendere] *v* light; (*luce, radio*) switch on, turn on. **accendino** *sm* (*fam*) lighter.
accennare [attʃen'nare] *v* make a sign, nod; refer to, hint at, touch on. **accenno** *sm* indication, mention.
accensione [attʃen'sjone] *sf* ignition.
accento [at'tʃento] *sm* accent, stress; tone. **accentare** *v* accent.

accentrare [attʃen'trare] *v* centralize, concentrate.
accentuare [attʃentu'are] *v* stress; (*aumentare*) heighten.
accerchiare [attʃer'kjare] *v* encircle. **accerchiamento** *sm* encirclement.
accertare [attʃer'tare] *v* verify, ascertain; (*dir*) establish. **accertamento** *sm* verification; establishment.
acceso [at'tʃezo] *agg* alight, switched on; (*colore*) vivid; (*eccitato*) burning.
accessibile [attʃes'sibile] *agg* (*luogo*) accessible; (*persona*) approachable.
accesso [at'tʃesso] *sm* access; (*med*) attack, fit.
accessorio [attʃes'sɔrjo] *agg* complementary, secondary. *sm* accessory, fitting.
accetta [at'tʃetta] *sf* hatchet.
accettare [attʃet'tare] *v* accept; admit. **accettabile** *agg* acceptable. **accettazione** *sf* acceptance; (*sala*) reception. **bene accetto** welcome. **male accetto** unwelcome.
acchiappare [akkjap'pare] *v* catch, grab (hold of), seize.
acciaio [at'tʃajo] *sm* steel. **acciaieria** *sf* steelworks.
accidente [attʃi'dɛnte] *sm* accident, mishap. **mandare un accidente a** (*fam*) curse. **non capire un accidente** not understand a thing. **accidenti!** *inter* my goodness! (*ira*) damn it! **accidenti a lui!** blast him! **accidentale** *agg* accidental.
accigliarsi [attʃiʎ'ʎarsi] *v* frown. **accigliato** *agg* frowning.
*accingersi [at'tʃindʒersi] *v* **accingersi a** set about; be on the point of.
acciuffare [attʃuf'fare] *v* seize.
acciuga [at'tʃuga] *sf* anchovy.
acclamare [akkla'mare] *v* acclaim. **acclamazione** *sf* acclamation.
acclimatare [akklima'tare] *v* acclimatize.
*accludere [ak'kludere] *v* enclose.
accoccolarsi [akkokko'larsi] *v* squat.
*accogliere [ak'kɔʎʎere] *v* receive, accept, welcome; contain. **accoglienza** *sf* welcome, reception.
accomodare [akkomo'dare] *v* (*riparare*) mend, fix; (*mettere in ordine*) arrange, tidy; (*sistemare*) settle. **accomodarsi** *v* make oneself comfortable; take a seat; (*mettersi d'accordo*) agree. **accomodamento** *sm* agreement; compromise. **accomodante** *agg* accommodating.

accompagnare [akkompa'ɲare] *v* accompany. **accompagnatore, -trice** *sm, sf* escort; (*musica*) accompanist.

acconciare [akkon'tʃare] *v* prepare; arrange. **acconciarsi i capelli** do one's hair. **acconciatura** *sf* hair-style.

***accondiscendere** [akkondi'ʃɛndere] *v* comply (with); condescend.

acconsentire [akkonsen'tire] *v* consent; acquiesce.

accoppare [akkop'pare] *v* (*fam*) kill, slaughter.

accorciare [akkor'tʃare] *v* shorten.

accordare [akkor'dare] *v* (*uniformare*) match; harmonize; (*concedere*) grant; (*musica*) tune. **accordarsi** *v* agree.

accordo [ak'kɔrdo] *sm* agreement. **essere** or **andare d'accordo** agree. **d'accordo!** agreed!

***accorgersi** [ak'kɔrdʒersi] *v* notice. **accorgimento** *sm* expedient, stratagem.

***accorrere** [ak'korrere] *v* come running, rush.

accorto [ak'kɔrto] *agg* shrewd. **fare accorto** warn, caution. **stare accorto** be wary. **accortezza** *sf* shrewdness.

accostare [akkos'tare] *v* approach. **accosto** *avv* near.

accovacciarsi [akkovat'tʃarsi] *v* crouch, huddle.

accreditare [akkredi'tare] *v* accredit.

***accrescere** [ak'kreʃere] *v* increase.

accumulare [akkumu'lare] *v* accumulate, heap. **accumulatore** *sm* accumulator.

accurato [akku'rato] *agg* accurate, thorough. **accuratezza** *sf* thoroughness, care.

accusare [akku'zare] *v* accuse; (*notificare*) acknowledge. **accusa** *sf* accusation, charge.

acerbo [a'tʃɛrbo] *agg* (*immaturo*) unripe; (*aspro*) sour.

acero ['atʃero] *sm* maple.

aceto [a'tʃeto] *sm* vinegar.

acido ['atʃido] *sm* acid. *agg* acid, sour. **acidità** *sf* acidity.

acne ['akne] *sf* acne.

acqua ['akkwa] *sf* water. **acqua ossigenata** hydrogen peroxide. **acqua in bocca!** keep mum!

acquaforte [akkwa'fɔrte] *sf, pl* **acqueforti** etching.

acquaio [ak'kwajo] *sm* kitchen sink.

acquaragia [akkwa'radʒa] *sf* turpentine, turps.

acquario [ak'kwarjo] *sm* aquarium.

acquatico [ak'kwatiko] *agg* aquatic, water.

acquavite [akkwa'vite] *sf* rough brandy.

acquazzone [akkwat'tsone] *sm* shower.

acquedotto [akkwe'dotto] *sm* aqueduct.

acquerello [akkwe'rɛllo] *sm* water-colour.

acquistare [akkwis'tare] *v* buy; (*ottenere*) acquire; (*guadagnare*) gain. **acquistarsi fama di** gain the reputation of. **acquisto** *sm* purchase. **buon acquisto** bargain.

acquoso [ak'kwozo] *agg* watery; (*terreno*) marshy.

acre ['akre] *agg* acrid, sharp.

acrilico [a'kriliko] *agg* acrylic.

acrobata [a'krɔbata] *s(m+f)* acrobat. **acrobatico** *agg* acrobatic. **acrobazia** *sf* acrobatics *pl*.

aculeo [a'kuleo] *sm* sting.

acustica [a'kustika] *sf* acoustics *pl*. **acustico** *agg* acoustic. **apparecchio acustico** *sm* hearing-aid.

acuto [a'kuto] *agg* acute, intense; (*aguzzo*) pointed; (*perspicace*) shrewd. *sm* (*musica*) top note.

ad *V* a.

adagiarsi [ada'dʒarsi] *v* lie down.

adagio [a'dadʒo] *avv* slowly; gently. *sm* (*musica*) slow movement, adagio.

adattabile [adat'tabile] *agg* adaptable. **adattabilità** *sf* adaptability.

adattare [adat'tare] *v* adapt. **adattarsi** *v* adapt oneself, resign oneself. **adatto** *agg* suitable (for); (*qualificato*) suited (to).

addebitare [addebi'tare] *v* charge.

addensare [adden'sare] *v* thicken; (*raccogliere*) gather.

addestrare [addes'trare] *v* train. **addestramento** *sm* training.

addetto [ad'detto] *agg* employed (in); destined (for), intended (for); assigned. *sm* (*pol*) attaché.

addietro [ad'djɛtro] *avv* (*fa*) ago; (*prima*) before.

addio [ad'dio] *inter* goodbye, farewell. *sm* parting, farewell.

addirittura [addirit'tura] *avv* (*persino*) even; (*direttamente*) straight away; absolutely.

additare [addi'tare] *v* point at; (*mostrare*) point out, show.

additivo [addi'tivo] *sm* additive.

addizionare [additsjo'nare] *v* add up. **addizionale** *agg* additional. **addizione** *sf* addition.

addolcire [addol'tʃire] *v* sweeten; *(miti-gare)* soften.

addolorare [addolo'rare] *v* distress.

addome [ad'dɔme] *sm* abdomen. **addominale** *agg* abdominal.

addomesticare [addomesti'kare] *v* tame.

addormentare [addormen'tare] *v* put to sleep. **addormentarsi** *v* fall asleep, go to sleep. **addormentato** *agg* sleeping; *(di mente)* dull; *(intorpidito)* numb.

addossare [addos'sare] *v* lean; *(mettere a carico)* saddle with. **addossarsi** *v* shoulder.

addosso [ad'dɔsso] *avv, prep* on. **d'addosso** off. **essere uno addosso all'altro** be crowded together.

***addurre** [ad'durre] *v* advance, put forward; produce.

adeguare [ade'gware] *v* adjust.

adempiere [a'dempjere] *v also* **adempire** carry out.

adenoidi [ade'nɔidi] *sf pl* adenoids *pl*.

aderire [ade'rire] *v* adhere, stick. **aderire a** comply with; accept; *(associarsi)* join. **aderente** *agg* close; *(abito)* close-fitting. **aderenza** *sf* adhesion. **aderenze** *sf pl* *(fam)* contacts *pl*.

adescare [ades'kare] *v* lure.

adesione [ade'zjone] *sf* adhesion; *(consenso)* assent; support. **adesivo** *sm, agg* adhesive.

adesso [a'dɛsso] *avv* now; nowadays; *(poco fa)* just (now); *(fra poco)* any minute (now). **per adesso** for the time being.

adiacente [adja'tʃɛnte] *agg* adjacent. **adiacente a** next to.

adibire [adi'bire] *v* turn (into).

adirarsi [adi'rarsi] *v* get angry.

adito ['adito] *sm* entry. **dare adito a** give rise to.

adocchiare [adok'kjare] *v* spot.

adolescente [adole'ʃɛnte] *agg* adolescent. *s(m+f)* adolescent, teenager. **adolescenza** *sf* adolescence.

adombrare [adom'brare] *v* shade; *(celare)* hide. **adombrarsi** *v* take umbrage; *(cavalli)* shy.

adoperare [adope'rare] *v* use. **adoperarsi** *v* do one's best.

adorare [ado'rare] *v* adore, worship. **adorabile** *agg* adorable. **adoratore, -trice** *sm, sf* admirer. **adorazione** *sf* worship.

adornare [ador'nare] *v* adorn, decorate. **adorno** *agg* adorned, decked out.

adottare [adot'tare] *v* adopt, foster. **adottivo** *agg* adoptive. **adozione** *sf* adoption.

adrenalina [adrena'lina] *sf* adrenaline.

adulazione [adula'tsjone] *sf* flattery. **adulare** *v* flatter. **adulatore, -trice** *sm, sf* flatterer.

adulterare [adulte'rare] *v* adulterate; *(corrompere)* debase.

adultero [a'dultero], **-a** *sm, sf* adulterer, -ess. *agg* adulterous. **adulterio** *sm* adultery.

adulto [a'dulto], **-a** *s, agg* adult, grown-up.

adunare [adu'nare] *v* assemble. **adunanza** *sf* assembly. **adunata** *sf* meeting, gathering; *(mil)* parade.

aerare [ae'rare] *v* air, ventilate. **aeratore** *sm* ventilator.

aereo [a'ɛreo] *agg* aerial, air. *sm* aeroplane.

aerodinamica [aerodi'namika] *sf* aerodynamics. **aerodinamico** *agg* streamlined.

aerodromo [ae'rɔdromo] *sm* aerodrome.

aerolinea [aero'linea] *sf* airline.

aeronautica [aero'nautika] *sf* aeronautics; aviation; *(mil)* air-force. **aeronautico** *agg* aeronautical.

aeroplano [aero'plano] *sm* aeroplane, aircraft. **aeroplano a reazione** jet. **aeroplano di bombardamento** bomber. **aeroplano di combattimento** fighter.

aeroporto [aero'pɔrto] *sm* airport.

aerosol [aero'sɔl] *sm invar* aerosol.

afa ['afa] *sf* oppressive heat.

affabile [af'fabile] *agg* affable. **affabilità** *sf* affability.

affaccendarsi [affattʃen'darsi] *v* busy oneself. **affaccendato** *agg* busy.

affacciarsi [affat'tʃarsi] *v* show oneself, appear.

affamato [affa'mato] *agg* starving; *(bramoso)* eager (for). **affamare** *v* reduce to starvation.

affannare [affan'nare] *v* worry. **affannarsi** *v* do one's utmost. **affanno** *sm* *(difficoltà di respiro)* breathlessness; anxiety, worry. **affannoso** *agg* difficult.

affare [af'fare] *sm* affair, business; *(questione)* matter; *(fam)* thing; *(acquisto vantaggioso)* bargain. **affari** *sm pl* *(comm)* business *sing*. **affarista** *s(m+f)* speculator.

affascinare [affaʃi'nare] *v* fascinate, charm.

affastellare [affastel'lare] *v* tie in bundles; (*ammucchiare*) pile up; (*frasi, ecc.*) string together.

affaticare [affati'kare] *v* tire, strain.

affatto [af'fatto] *avv* quite; (*con negazione*) at all.

affermare [affer'mare] *v* affirm; assert. **affermarsi** *v* be successful.

afferrare [affer'rare] *v* seize, grab, clutch at.

affettare[1] [affet'tare] *v* affect, pretend. **affettato** *agg* affected; mannered.

affettare[2] [affet'tare] *v* slice. **affettato** *sm* sliced salami *or* ham.

affetto[1] [af'fetto] *sm* affection, feeling. **affettuoso** *agg* affectionate, loving.

affetto[2] [af'fetto] *agg* affected (by); (*med*) suffering (from).

affezionarsi [affetsjo'narsi] *v* become fond (of). **affezionato** *agg* fond, devoted. **affezione** *sf* fondness, affection; (*med*) disorder.

affibbiare [affib'bjare] *v* saddle with.

affidare [affi'dare] *v* entrust. **affidare alla memoria** commit to memory. **affidamento** *sm* trust. **dare affidamento** inspire confidence. **fare affidamento su** rely on.

*affiggere [af'fiddʒere] *v* affix; (*manifesto*) put up.

affilare [affi'lare] *v* sharpen.

affiliare [affi'ljare] *v* (*dir*) foster; (*iscrivere*) enrol.

affinché [affin'ke] *cong* so that, in order that.

affinità [affini'ta] *sf* affinity. **affine** *agg* related. **affini** *sm pl* in-laws *pl*.

affissione [affis'sjone] *sf* bill-posting.

affisso [af'fisso] *agg* exhibited. *sm* poster, bill.

affittare [affit'tare] *v* rent, lease; (*dare in affitto*) let. **affitto** *sm* (*prezzo*) rent; (*locazione*) lease.

*affliggere [af'fliddʒere] *v* afflict. **affliggersi** *v* grieve, worry. **afflizione** *sf* affliction.

*affluire [afflu'ire] *v* flow; (*gente*) flock. **affluente** *sm* (*geog*) tributary. **affluenza** *sf* flow; (*di gente*) influx. **afflusso** *sm* flow.

affogare [affo'gare] *v* drown. **uovo affogato** *sm* poached egg.

affollare [affol'lare] *v* crowd. **affollamento** *sm* (*atto*) crowding; (*folla*) crowd.

affondare [affon'dare] *v* sink.

affrancare [affran'kare] *v* stamp. **affrancatura** *sf* postage.

affranto [af'franto] *agg* distraught.

affresco [af'fresko] *sm* fresco.

affrettare [affret'tare] *v* hurry, speed up.

affrontare [affron'tare] *v* face. **affronto** *sm* affront.

affumicare [affumi'kare] *v* (*annerire*) blacken (with smoke); (*gastr*) smoke; (*snidare*) smoke out. **affumicato** *agg* smoked.

afoso [a'fozo] *agg* sultry.

Africa ['afrika] *sf* Africa. **africano, -a** *s*, *agg* African.

agenda [a'dʒɛnda] *sf* diary.

agente [a'dʒɛnte] *sm* agent. **agente delle tasse** tax inspector. **agente di polizia** police officer.

agenzia [adʒen'tsia] *sf* agency.

agevole [a'dʒevole] *agg* easy. **agevolare** *v* facilitate. **agevolazione** *sf* concession.

agganciare [aggan'tʃare] *v* fasten, hook up.

aggettivo [addʒet'tivo] *sm* adjective.

agghiacciare [aggjat'tʃare] *v* freeze. **far agghiacciare il sangue** make one's blood run cold.

aggiornare [addʒor'nare] *v* bring up to date; (*rinviare*) postpone. **aggiornato** *agg* up-to-date.

aggirarsi [addʒi'rarsi] *v* **aggirarsi su** (*approssimarsi*) be about *or* around.

aggiudicare [addʒudi'kare] *v* award.

*aggiungere [ad'dʒundʒere] *v* add. **aggiungersi** *v* join. **aggiunta** *sf* addition. **aggiuntivo** *agg* additional. **aggiunto** *sm* assistant.

aggiustare [addʒus'tare] *v* repair, adjust; (*ordinare*) tidy, arrange.

aggrappare [aggrap'pare] *v* clutch. **aggrapparsi a** cling to.

aggravare [aggra'vare] *v* make worse. **aggravarsi** *v* deteriorate.

aggredire [aggre'dire] *v* attack.

aggregare [aggre'gare] *v* aggregate. **aggregato** *sm*, *agg* aggregate.

aggressione [aggres'sjone] *sf* aggression, attack. **aggressivo** *agg* aggressive. **aggressore** *sm* aggressor, assailant.

aggrottare [aggrot'tare] *v* **aggrottare le ciglia** frown, knit one's brows.

aggruppare [aggrup'pare] *v* group.

agguato [ag'gwato] *sm* ambush, trap. **stare in agguato** lie in wait.

agiato [a'dʒato] *agg* well-off. **agiatezza** *sf* prosperity.

agile ['adʒile] *agg* agile, nimble. **agilità** *sf* agility.

agio ['adʒo] *sm* comfort, ease; (*di tempo*) leisure; (*mec*) play. **sentire a proprio agio** feel at ease.

agire [a'dʒire] *v* act; (*comportarsi*) behave; (*dir*) take legal action.

agitare [adʒi'tare] *v* wave, shake; (*incitare*) stir. **agitato** *agg* agitated, disturbed. **agitatore, -trice** *sm, sf* agitator.

agli ['aʎi] *prep + art* a gli.

aglio ['aʎo] *sm* garlic.

agnello [a'ɲello] *sm* lamb.

agnostico [a'ɲostiko], **-a** *s, agg* agnostic.

ago ['ago] *sm* needle. **ago da calza** knitting-needle. **lavoro ad ago** *sm* needlework.

agonia [ago'nia] *sf* agony. **agonizzare** *v* agonize, suffer anguish.

agonismo [ago'nizmo] *sm* fighting spirit.

agopuntura [agopun'tura] *sf* acupuncture.

agosto [a'gosto] *sm* August.

agrario [a'grarjo] *sm* land-owner. *agg* agrarian, agricultural. **riforma agraria** *sf* land reform. **agraria** *sf* agricultural science.

agricoltore [agrikol'tore] *sm* farmer.

agrifoglio [agri'foʎʎo] *sm* holly.

agro ['agro] *agg* sour, sharp, tart.

agrumi [a'grumi] *sm pl* citrus fruit *pl*.

aguzzare [agut'tsare] *v* sharpen.

ahimé [ai'mɛ] *inter* alas!

ai ['ai] *prep + art* a i.

Aia ['aja] *sf* **L'Aia** The Hague.

airone [ai'rone] *sm* heron.

aiuola [a'jwɔla] *sf* flower-bed.

aiutare [aju'tare] *v* help. **aiuto** *sm* help, aid; assistant.

aizzare [ait'tsare] *v* incite, provoke.

al [al] *prep + art* a il.

ala ['ala] *sf* wing; (*di cappello*) brim. **apertura alare** *sf* wing-span.

alabastro [ala'bastro] *sm* alabaster.

alano [a'lano] *sm* Great Dane.

alba ['alba] *sf* dawn. **albeggiare** *v* dawn.

albatro ['albatro] *sm* albatross.

albergare [alber'gare] *v* give hospitality to; shelter, harbour.

albergo [al'bergo] *sm* hotel. **albergatore** *sm* innkeeper. **alberghiero** *agg* hotel.

albero ['albero] *sm* tree; (*mar*) mast. **albero a camme** camshaft.

albicocca [albi'kɔkka] *sf* apricot. **albicocco** *sm* apricot tree.

albo ['albo] *sm* roll, register; (*tavola*) notice-board. .

album ['album] *sm* album.

alcali ['alkali] *sm* alkali. **alcalino** *agg* alkaline.

alchimia [alki'mia] *sf* alchemy. **alchimista** *sm* alchemist.

alcool ['alkool] *sm* alcohol.

alco(o)lismo [alko(o)'lizmo] *sm* alcoholism. **alco(o)lici** *sm pl* alcoholic drinks *pl*, spirits *pl*. **alco(o)lico** *agg* alcoholic. **alco(o)lizzato, -a** *sm, sf* alcoholic.

alcunché [alkun'ke] *pron* something, anything.

alcuno [al'kuno] *agg* some, any, a few. *pron* anyone, anybody. **alcuni** *pron* some, a few.

alfabeto [alfa'bɛto] *sm* alphabet.

alfiere[1] [al'fjɛre] *sm* (*portabandiera*) standard-bearer; (*fig*) forerunner.

alfiere[2] [al'fjɛre] *sm* (*scacchi*) bishop.

alfine [al'fine] *avv* in the long run.

alga ['alga] *sf* alga.

algebra ['aldʒebra] *sf* algebra.

aliante [ali'ante] *sm* glider. **aliantista** *s(m + f)* glider-pilot.

alibi ['alibi] *sm* alibi.

alice [a'litʃe] *sf* anchovy.

alienare [alje'nare] *v* alienate. **alienato** *agg* alienated; (*pazzo*) insane. **alienazione** *sf* alienation; (*pazzia*) madness.

alieno [a'ljɛno] *agg* alien, foreign.

alimentare [alimen'tare] *agg* alimentary. *v* feed. **alimentari** *sm pl* foodstuffs *pl*. **alimentazione** *sf* feeding; (*tec*) feed. **alimenti** *sm pl* alimony *sing*. **alimento** *sm* food.

aliquota [a'likwota] *sf* quota, share.

aliscafo [alis'kafo] *sm* hydrofoil.

alito ['alito] *sm* breath.

all' [all] *prep + art* a l'.

alla ['alla] *prep + art* a la.

allacciare [allat'tʃare] *v* tie up, fasten; (*amicizia, relazioni*) establish; (*tec*) connect.

allagare [alla'gare] *v* flood. **allagamento** *sm* flooding.

allargare [allar'gare] *v* broaden; (*sport*) open up.

allarmare [allar'mare] *v* alarm. **allarme** *sm* alarm. **allarmista** *s(m + f)* scaremonger, alarmist. **allarmistico** *agg* alarmist.

alle ['alle] *prep + art* a le.

alleanza [alle'antsa] *sf* alliance. **alleare** *v* ally.

alleato [alle'ato], **-a** *agg* allied. *sm, sf* ally.

allegare¹ [alle'gare] *v* enclose.

allegare² [alle'gare] *v* advance, put forward.

alleggerire [alleddʒe'rire] *v* lighten; (*sofferenza*) ease.

allegoria [allego'ria] *sf* allegory. **allegorico** *agg* allegorical.

allegro [al'legro] *agg* cheerful, merry. *sm* (*musica*) fast movement, allegro. **allegria** *sf* gaiety, fun, cheerfulness.

allenare [alle'nare] *v* train, coach. **allenatore, -trice** *sm, sf* trainer, coach.

allentare [allen'tare] *v* loosen. **allentare il passo** slow down.

allergia [aller'dʒia] *sf* allergy. **allergico** *agg* allergic.

allestire [alles'tire] *v* prepare, get ready; (*teatro*) stage; (*arredare*) fit out, equip. **allestimento** *sm* preparation; staging; fitting out.

allettare [allet'tare] *v* entice, tempt. **alettante** *agg* enticing, tempting.

allevare [alle'vare] *v* (*bambini*) bring up; (*animali*) breed, keep; (*piante*) grow. **allevamento** *sm* bringing up; (*educazione*) upbringing; (*cavalli*) stud farm; (*cani*) kennels *pl*. **allevatore, -trice** *sm, sf* breeder.

alleviare [alle'vjare] *v* relieve, alleviate.

allibratore [allibra'tore] *sm* bookmaker.

allievo [al'ljɛvo], **-a** *sm, sf* pupil, student; (*apprendista*) trainee. **allievo ufficiale** (*mil*) cadet.

alligatore [alliga'tore] *sm* alligator.

allineare [alline'are] *v* line up; (*adeguare*) adjust. **allineamento** *sm* alignment, coming into line.

allo ['allo] *prep* + *art* **a lo.**

allocco [al'lɔkko] *sm* tawny owl.

allodola [al'lɔdola] *sf* lark.

alloggiare [allod'dʒare] *v* house, put up; (*mil*) billet; (*prendere alloggio*) stay, lodge. **alloggio** *sm* accommodation; lodgings *pl*.

allontanare [allonta'nare] *v* move away; (*tener lontano*) keep away; (*pericolo, ecc.*) avert; (*licenziare*) dismiss. **allontanarsi** *v* go away, leave. **allontanamento** *sm* removal.

allora [al'lora] *avv* then; in that case. **da allora** since then, from that time on. **fino allora** until then.

alloro [al'lɔro] *sm* laurel; (*gastr*) bay leaf.

alluce ['allutʃe] *sm* big toe.

allucinazione [alluʃina'tsjone] *sf* hallucination. **allucinare** *v* hallucinate; (*abbagliare*) dazzle.

***alludere** [al'ludere] *v* allude, hint (at).

alluminio [allu'minjo] *sm* aluminium.

allungare [allun'gare] *v* lengthen, stretch; (*diluire*) water down; pass. **allungare gli orecchi** strain one's ears. **allungare il muso** (*fam*) make a long face. **allungare la strada** go the long way round. **allungamento** *sm* extension, lengthening.

allusione [allu'zjone] *sf* allusion.

almeno [al'meno] *avv* at least; if only.

Alpi ['alpi] *sf pl* **le Alpi** the Alps *pl*. **alpino** *agg* alpine.

alpinismo [alpi'nizmo] *sm* mountaineering.

alquanto [al'kwanto] *pron, agg* some; a fair amount of. **alquanti** *pron, agg* several; a number of. *avv* somewhat, rather.

alt [alt] *sm, inter* stop.

altalena [alta'lena] *sf* (*sospesa*) swing; (*a bilico*) see-saw; (*fig*) ups and downs *pl*.

altare [al'tare] *sm* altar.

alterare [alte'rare] *v* alter, change; (*falsificare*) forge; (*svisare*) distort; (*turbare*) upset, make angry; (*andare a male*) go off, spoil. **alterazione** *sf* alteration; forgery; deterioration.

alternare [alter'nare] *v* alternate; (*agric*) rotate. **alternarsi** *v* take turns. **alternativa** *sf* alternative. **alternato** *agg* alternating. **alterno** *agg* alternating, alternate.

altero [al'tɛro] *agg* haughty.

altezza [al'tettsa] *sf* height; (*profondità*) depth; (*di tessuto*) width; (*quota*) altitude; nobility; (*titolo*) Highness. **essere all'altezza di** be equal to, be up to.

altitudine [alti'tudine] *sf* height, altitude.

alto ['alto] *agg* high; (*statura*) tall; (*tessuto*) wide; (*suono forte*) loud; (*suono acuto*) shrill; (*profondo*) deep; (*geog*) northern; (*nobile*) lofty; (*di grado elevato*) high-ranking. *avv* high. *sm* top, upper part. **alti e bassi** ups and downs *pl*.

altoforno [alto'forno] *sm, pl* **altiforni** blast furnace.

altoparlante [altopar'lante] *sm* loudspeaker.

altopiano [alto'pjano] *sm, pl* **altipiani** plateau.

altrettanto [altret'tanto] *pron, agg* as much *or* many (again); (*medesimo*) the same. **altrettanto ... quanto ...** as ... as .... *avv* as, as much.

altri ['altri] *pron* others *pl*, another (person), someone else.

altro ['altro] *agg* other; another; (*in più*) more; (*ulteriore*) further; (*prossimo*) next. *pron* other (one), another (one); (*persona*) somebody else. **cos'altro?** what else? **l'un l'altro** one another, each other. **l'uno e l'altro** both. **nè l'uno nè l'altro** neither. **nessun'altro** nobody else. **nient'altro** nothing else. **non altro che** nothing but. **più che altro** more than anything. **qualcos'altro** something else. **se non altro** at least. **senz'altro** certainly. **tra l'altro** among other things. **tutt'altro!** far from it!

altronde [al'tronde] *avv* **d'altronde** on the other hand, however.

altrove [al'trove] *avv* elsewhere.

altrui [al'trui] *agg invar* other people's, someone else's.

altruista [altru'ista] *s(m+f)* altruist, unselfish person. **altruismo** *sm* altruism, unselfishness. **altruistico** *agg* unselfish, altruistic.

alunno [a'lunno], **-a** *sm*, *sf* pupil.

alveare [alve'are] *sm* beehive.

alzaia [al'tsaja] *sf* tow-line; (*strada*) towpath.

alzare [al'tsare] *v* raise, lift; (*raccogliere*) pick up; (*carte da gioco*) cut. **alzarsi** *v* get up, rise. **alzare le spalle** shrug one's shoulders.

amaca [a'maka] *sf* hammock.

almalgamare [amalga'mare] *v* amalgamate, combine. **amalgama** *sm* amalgam.

amante [a'mante] *s(m+f)* lover. *agg* fond (of), keen (on).

amare [a'mare] *v* love, like. **amato** *agg* beloved. **amatore** *sm* lover; (*conoscitore*) connoisseur.

amarena [ama'rena] *sf* sour cherry, black cherry.

amaro [a'maro] *agg* bitter; (*doloroso*) painful. *sm* bitterness; (*bibita*) bitters *pl*. **amarezza** *sf* bitterness.

ambasciata [amba'ʃata] *sf* embassy; message. **ambasciatore, -trice** *sm*, *sf* ambassador, ambassadress.

ambedue [ambe'due] *pron*, *agg* both.

ambidestro [ambi'dɛstro] *agg* ambidextrous.

ambientarsi [ambjen'tarsi] *v* accustom oneself, settle down. **ambiente** *sm* environment, milieu; atmosphere. **temperatura ambiente** *sf* room temperature.

ambiguo [am'biguo] *agg* ambiguous; (*equivoco*) dubious; (*fam*) shady. **ambiguità** *sf* ambiguity; duplicity.

ambito¹ ['ambito] *sm* limits *pl*; sphere.

ambito² [am'bito] *agg* longed-for, coveted. **ambire** *v* covet.

ambivalente [ambiva'lɛnte] *agg* ambivalent.

ambizione [ambi'tsjone] *sf* ambition. **ambizioso** *agg* ambitious.

ambo ['ambo] *agg* both.

ambra ['ambra] *sf*, *agg* amber. **ambra grigia** ambergris.

ambulante [ambu'lante] *agg* wandering. **biblioteca ambulante** *sf* mobile library. **venditore ambulante** *sm* pedlar.

ambulanza [ambu'lantsa] *sf* ambulance; (*infermeria mobile*) field hospital.

ambulatorio [ambula'tɔrjo] *sm* outpatients' department, clinic.

ameba [a'mɛba] *sf* amoeba.

ameno [a'mɛno] *agg* agreeable; (*divertente*) entertaining.

America [a'mɛrika] *sf* America. **americano, -a** *s*, *agg* American.

ametista [ame'tista] *sf* amethyst.

amianto [a'mjanto] *sm* asbestos.

amichevole [ami'kevole] *agg* friendly.

amico [a'miko], **-a** *sm*, *sf* friend. *agg* friendly. **amicizia** *sf* friendship.

amido ['amido] *sm* starch.

ammaccare [ammak'kare] *v* dent. **ammaccatura** *sf* dent.

ammaestrare [ammaes'trare] *v* teach, train. **ammaestramento** *sm* teaching, training.

ammalarsi [amma'larsi] *v* fall ill.

ammansire [amman'sire] *v* tame, subdue.

ammassare [ammas'sare] *v* amass.

ammazzare [ammat'tsare] *v* kill, murder.

ammenda [am'mɛnda] *sf* (*dir*) fine. **fare ammenda di** make amends for.

*****ammettere** [am'mettere] *v* admit; permit; suppose; take for granted. **ammesso che** given that.

ammezzato [ammed'dzato] *agg* mezzanine. *sm* mezzanine floor.

ammiccare [ammik'kare] *v* wink (at).

amministrare [amminis'trare] *v* administer, manage, run. **amministrativo** *agg* administrative. **amministratore, -trice** *sf* director. **amministratore delegato** managing director. **amministrazione** *sf* administration, management. **consiglio d'amministrazione** *sm* board of directors.

223   **anestetico**

ammiraglio [ammi'raʎo] *sm* admiral.
ammiragliato *sm* admiralty.
ammirare [ammi'rare] *v* admire.
ammiratore, -trice *sm*, *sf* admirer, fan.
ammirazione *sf* admiration. ammirevole
agg admirable.
ammissibile [ammis'sibile] *agg* admissible, acceptable.
ammissione [ammis'sjone] *sf* admission,
admittance. esame d'ammissione *sm*
entrance examination. tassa
d'ammissione *sf* entrance fee.
ammobiliare [ammobi'ljare] *v* furnish.
ammollare¹ [ammol'lare] *v* soften;
(*nell'acqua*) soak.
ammollare² [ammol'lare] *v* let go, slacken.
ammoniaca [ammo'niaka] *sf* ammonia.
ammonire [ammo'nire] *v* warn; reprimand. ammonimento *sm* warning;
reproof.
ammontare [ammon'tare] *sm*, *v* amount.
ammorbidire [ammorbi'dire] *v* soften.
ammortire [ammor'tire] *v* deaden.
ammucchiare [ammuk'kjare] *v* pile up.
ammuffire [ammuf'fire] *v* go mouldy.
ammuffito *agg* mouldy.
ammutinamento [ammutina'mento] *sm*
mutiny.
amnistia [amnis'tia] *sf* amnesty.
amo ['amo] *sm* hook. abboccare all'amo
swallow the bait.
amorale [amo'rale] *agg* amoral.
amore [a'more] *sm* love; (*persona grazi-
osa*) darling. amor proprio self-respect.
per amore di for the sake of. amoroso
agg loving.
ampère [ã'pɛr] *sm invar* ampere, amp.
ampio ['ampjo] *agg* wide, spacious;
(*abbondante*) full.
amplificare [amplifi'kare] *v* amplify,
enlarge. amplificatore *sm* amplifier.
ampolloso [ampol'loso] *agg* pompous.
amputare [ampu'tare] *v* amputate.
amputazione *sf* amputation.
anacronismo [anakro'nizmo] *sm* anachronism.
anagrafe [a'nagrafe] *sf* register office.
anagramma [ana'gramma] *sm* anagram.
analcolico [anal'kɔliko] *agg* non-alcoholic.
sm soft drink.
anale [a'nale] *agg* anal.
analfabeta [analfa'bɛta] *agg*, *s(m+f)* illiterate. analfabetismo *sm* illiteracy.
analgesico [anal'dʒeziko] *agg*, *sm* analge-
sic.

analizzare [analid'dzare] *v* analyse. analisi
sf analysis (*pl* -ses). in ultima analisi
when all is said and done. analista
s(m+f) analyst. analitico *agg* analytic.
analogo [a'nalogo] *agg*, *m pl* -ghi analogous. analogia *sf* analogy.
ananas ['ananas] *sm* pineapple.
anarchico [a'narkiko], -a *agg* anarchic(al).
sm, *sf* anarchist. anarchia *sf* anarchy.
anatema [ana'tɛma] *sm* anathema.
anatomia [anato'mia] *sf* anatomy.
anatomia patologica pathology.
anatomico *agg* anatomical. anatomista
s(m+f) anatomist.
anatra ['anatra] *sf* duck. anatroccolo *sm*
duckling.
anca ['anka] *sf* hip.
anche ['anke] *cong* too, as well, also;
(*inoltre*) besides; (*perfino*) even.
ancora¹ ['ankora] *sm* anchor. ancoraggio
sm moorings *pl*. ancorare *v* anchor.
ancora² [an'kora] *avv* still; (*in frasi negative*) yet; (*di nuovo*) again; (*un altro*)
another; (*persino*) even. ancora un po'
little more; (*tempo*) a little longer.
*andare [an'dare] *v* go; (*funzionare*) work,
run; (*calzare*) fit; (*essere adatto*) suit;
(*dovere*) must be, have to be. a lungo
andare in the long run. andare a genio be
to one's liking. andare a piedi walk.
andare a spasso go for a walk. andare
avanti proceed, progress, go on. andar
bene go well; fit; (*salute*) be well. andare
in bicicletta cycle. andare incontro a go
towards, go and meet. andarsene go
away, leave.
andata [an'data] *sf* biglietto d'andata *sm*
single ticket.
andirivieni [andiri'vjeni] *sm* coming and
going; (*risposta evasiva*) prevarication.
andito ['andito] *sm* passage.
aneddoto [a'nɛddoto] *sm* anecdote.
anelare [ane'lare] *v* pant; (*aspirare*) yearn
(for). anelante *agg* panting, out of
breath.
anello [a'nɛllo] *sm* ring. anello matrimoni-
ale/di fidanzamento wedding/
engagement ring.
anemia [ane'mia] *sf* anaemia. anemico
agg anaemic.
anemone [a'nɛmone] *sm* anemone.
anestetico [anes'tɛtiko] *agg*, *sm* anaesthetic. anestesia *sf* anaesthesia. anesteti-
sta *s(m+f)* anaesthetist.

anfetamina [anfeta'mina] *sf* amphetamine.

anfibio [an'fibjo] *sm, agg* amphibian.

angariare [anga'rjare] *v* harass.

angelica [an'dʒɛlika] *sf* angelica.

angelo ['andʒelo] *sm* angel; (*pesce*) angelfish. **angelo custode** guardian angel.

angelico *agg* angelic.

anglicano [angli'kano], **-a** *s, agg* Anglican. **anglicanesimo** *sm* Anglicanism.

angolo ['angolo] *sm* corner; (*geom, ecc.*) angle. **angolare** *agg* angular. **pietra angolare** *sf* cornerstone.

angoscia [an'gɔʃa] *sf* anxiety, anguish. **angosciare** *v* distress. **angoscioso** *agg* distressed; distressing.

anguilla [an'gwilla] *sf* eel.

anguria [an'gurja] *sf* water-melon.

anice ['anitʃe] *sm* aniseed.

anima ['anima] *sf* soul; (*parte centrale*) core; (*fervore*) heart; (*di arma da fuoco*) bore. **rodersi l'anima** torment oneself.

animale [ani'male] *sm* animal; (*persona*) brute. *agg* animal.

animare [ani'mare] *v* animate; stimulate. **animato** *agg* animate; (*vivace*) spirited. **disegno** *or* **cartone animato** *sm* cartoon. **essere animato da** be inspired by.

animo ['animo] *sm* mind; (*cuore, coraggio*) heart; (*carattere*) nature. **farsi animo** pluck up courage. **in fondo all'animo** at the back of one's mind. **mettersi l'animo in pace** resign oneself. **stato d'animo** *sm* mood.

animosità [animozi'ta] *sf* animosity, spite.

annacquare [annak'kware] *v* water down.

annaffiare [annaf'fjare] *v* water.

annali [an'nali] *sm pl* annals *pl*.

annata [an'nata] *sf* year; (*raccolto*) crop; (*di vino*) vintage; (*importo*) income.

annebbiare [anneb'bjare] *v* become foggy; (*fig*) dim, cloud.

annegare [anne'gare] *v* drown. **annegamento** *sm* drowning.

***annettere** [an'nɛttere] *v* (*pol*) annex; attach. **annesso** *sm* annexe, appendage.

annichilare [anniki'lare] *v* annihilate, destroy.

annientare [annjen'tare] *v* annihilate, destroy. **annientamento** *sm* (total) destruction.

anniversario [anniver'sarjo] *sm, agg* anniversary.

anno ['anno] *sm* year. **anno bisestile** leap-year. **anno luce** light-year.

annodare [anno'dare] *v* knot *or* tie (together).

annoiare [anno'jare] *v* bore.

annotare [anno'tare] *v* note, jot down; (*postillare*) annotate.

annoverare [annove'rare] *v* number; enumerate.

annuale [annu'ale] *agg* annual, yearly.

annuario [annu'arjo] *sm* yearbook.

annuire [annu'ire] *v* nod in agreement; (*acconsentire*) agree.

annullare [annul'lare] *v* cancel; (*matrimonio*) annul; (*legge*) repeal. **annullamento** *sm* cancellation; annulment; repeal.

annunciare [annun'tʃare] *v* announce; (*precorrere*) herald. **annunciatore, -trice** *sm, sf* announcer. **annuncio** *sm* announcement, notice; (*pubblicità*) advertisement.

Annunciazione [annuntʃa'tsjone] *sf* Annunciation.

annuo ['annuo] *agg* yearly, annual.

annusare [annu'zare] *v* sniff; (*intuire*) smell.

annuvolare [annuvo'lare] *v* cloud (over).

ano ['ano] *sm* anus.

anodo ['anodo] *sm* anode.

anomalia [anoma'lia] *sf* anomaly. **anomalo** *agg* anomalous.

anonimo [a'nɔnimo] *agg* anonymous. **società anonima** *sf* limited company.

anormale [anor'male] *agg* abnormal. **anormalità** *sf* abnormality.

ansare [an'sare] *v* puff, pant.

ansia ['ansja] *sf* anxiety; (*angoscia*) dread; (*desiderio*) longing. **ansioso** *agg* anxious; longing; (*impaziente*) restless.

antagonismo [antago'nizmo] *sm* antagonism. **antagonista** *s(m+f)* adversary.

antartico [an'tartiko] *agg* antarctic.

antenato [ante'nato] *sm* forefather, ancestor.

antenna [an'tenna] *sf* (*zool*) antenna; (*radio, TV*) aerial.

anteprima [ante'prima] *sf* preview.

anteriore [ante'rjore] *agg* (*nel tempo*) preceding, previous; (*nello spazio*) front, fore.

antiabbagliante [antiabba'ʎante] *agg* anti-dazzle. **fari antiabbaglianti** *sm pl* dipped headlights *pl*.

antiaereo [antia'ɛreo] *agg* anti-aircraft.

antibiotico [antibi'ɔtiko] *agg, sm* antibiotic.

anticamera [anti'kamera] *sf* lobby, waiting-room. **fare anticamera** be kept waiting. **far fare anticamera** keep waiting.

antichità [antiki'ta] *sf* antiquity; (*oggetto*) antique.

anticiclone [antitʃi'klone] *sm* anticyclone.

anticipare [antitʃi'pare] *v* anticipate; advance; pay in advance. **anticipato** *agg* advanced; (*prima del tempo*) in advance. **anticipazione** *sf* anticipation; (*soldi*) advance.

anticipo [an'titʃipo] *sm* advance, deposit. **in anticipo** early; (*orologio*) fast.

antico [an'tiko] *agg, m pl* **-chi** old; ancient; antique. **all'antica** *agg* old-fashioned.

anticoncezionale [antikontʃetsjo'nale] *agg, sm* contraceptive.

anticonformista [antikonfor'mista] *agg, s(m + f)* non-conformist.

anticongelante [antikondʒe'lante] *sm* anti-freeze.

anticorpo [anti'kɔrpo] *sm* antibody.

antidoto [an'tidoto] *sm* antidote.

antifecondativo [antifekonda'tivo] *sm, agg* contraceptive.

antifurto [anti'furto] *sm* burglar alarm.

antilope [an'tilope] *sf* antelope.

antincendio [antin'tʃendjo] *agg* **equipaggiamento antincendio** fire-fighting equipment.

antiorario [antio'rarjo] *agg* anti-clockwise.

antipasto [anti'pasto] *sm* hors d'oeuvre, starter.

antipatia [antipa'tia] *sf* dislike, antipathy. **prendere in antipatia** take a dislike to. **antipatico** *agg* disagreeable, unpleasant.

antiquario [anti'kwarjo] *sm* antique dealer. **antiquariato** *sm* antique trade; (*negozio*) antique shop.

antiquato [anti'kwato] *agg* (*fuori moda*) old-fashioned; (*disusato*) obsolete.

antisemita [antise'mita] *s(m + f)* anti-Semite. *agg* anti-Semitic. **antisemitismo** *sm* anti-Semitism.

antisettico [anti'sɛttiko] *sm, agg* antiseptic.

antisociale [antiso'tʃale] *agg* antisocial.

antistaminico [antista'miniko] *sm* antihistamine.

antitesi [an'titezi] *sf* antithesis (*pl* -ses).

antologia [antolo'dʒia] *sf* anthology.

antro ['antro] *sm* cave.

antropologia [antropolo'dʒia] *sf* anthropology. **antropologico** *agg* anthropological. **antropologo, -a** *sm, sf* anthropologist.

anulare [anu'lare] *agg* annular, ring-shaped. *sm* ring-finger.

anzi ['antsi] *cong* on the contrary; (*invece*) as a matter of fact; (*o meglio*) or better, better still; (*di più*) indeed.

anziano [an'tsjano], **-a** *agg* elderly; aged; senior. *sm, sf* elderly person.

anziché [antsi'ke] *cong* (*piuttosto*) rather than; (*invece*) instead of.

anzitutto [antsi'tutto] *avv* above all, first of all.

apatia [apa'tia] *sf* apathy.

ape ['ape] *sf* bee.

aperitivo [aperi'tivo] *sm* aperitif.

aperto [a'pɛrto] *agg* open; (*pronto*) quick. **all'aperto** in the open, outdoors.

apice ['apitʃe] *sm* apex, top.

apocrifo [a'pɔkrifo] *agg* apocryphal.

apolide [a'pɔlide] *agg* stateless.

apostolo [a'pɔstolo] *sm* apostle. **apostolico** *agg* apostolic.

apostrofo [a'pɔstrofo] *sm* apostrophe.

appagare [appa'gare] *v* satisfy.

appalto [ap'palto] *sm* contract.

appannare [appan'nare] *v* (*vista*) dim, blur; (*vetri*) mist up.

apparato [appa'rato] *sm* show, display; (*tec*) machinery; (*biol*) system, apparatus. **apparato scenico** set.

apparecchiare [apparek'kjare] *v* prepare. **apparecchiare la tavola** lay the table. **apparecchio** *sm* set; device, instrument, appliance; (*fam*) (aero)plane; (*fam*) (tele)phone.

apparenza [appa'rɛntsa] *sf* appearance. **apparente** *agg* apparent. **apparentemente** *avv* apparently; (*a prima vista*) to all appearances.

***apparire** [appa'rire] *v* appear; (*sembrare*) look, seem. **appariscente** *agg* striking.

appartamento [apparta'mento] *sm* flat, apartment.

appartare [appar'tare] *v* put aside. **appartarsi** *v* withdraw. **appartato** *agg* secluded.

***appartenere** [apparte'nere] *v* belong.

appassionare [appassjo'nare] *v* move, arouse passion; arouse interest. **appassionarsi per** be very fond of.

appena [ap'pena] *avv* barely, hardly; (*soltanto*) only; (*solo un po'*) only just; (*da poco*) just (recently). *cong* **appena** ... **che** ... no sooner ... than ....

*****appendere** [ap'pɛndere] *v* hang.

appendice [appen'ditʃe] *sm* appendix.

appendicite *sf* appendicitis.

appetito [appe'tito] *sm* appetite. **aver appetito** have an appetite, be hungry.

appetitoso *agg* appetizing; tempting.

appianare [appja'nare] *v* level; (*dissidio, ecc.*) smooth (over), settle.

appiccare [appik'kare] *v* (*appendere*) hang; (*cominciare*) set off. **appiccar fuoco a** set fire to.

appiccicare [appittʃi'kare] *v* stick. **appiccicaticcio** *agg* sticky.

appigionare [appidʒo'nare] *v* let.

appioppare [appjop'pare] *v* give; (*affibbiare*) saddle with.

appisolarsi [appizo'larsi] *v* doze.

applaudire [applau'dire] *v* applaud.

applauso *sm* applause.

applicare [appli'kare] *v* apply. **applicazione** *sf* application; concentration; (*dir*) enforcement. **applique** *sf, pl* -s wall-bracket.

appoggiare [appod'dʒare] *v* lean; (*posare*) lay; (*fondare*) base; (*favorire*) support. **appoggio** *sm* support.

*****apporre** [ap'porre] *v* affix, append.

apportare [appor'tare] *v* bring about, produce. **apporto** *sm* contribution.

apposito [ap'pɔzito] *agg* special; (*adatto*) suitable. **appositamente** *avv* suitably; (*apposta*) deliberately; (*espressamente*) specially.

apposta [ap'pɔsta] *avv* deliberately, on purpose, specially. *agg invar* special.

*****apprendere** [ap'prɛndere] *v* learn. **apprendista** *s*(*m*+*f*) apprentice, learner. **apprendistato** *sm* apprenticeship.

apprensione [appren'sjone] *sm* apprehension, concern. **apprensivo** *agg* apprehensive, uneasy.

appresso [ap'prɛsso] *avv* close by, at hand; (*con sè*) with one; (*in sequito*) later. *prep* close to; (*dietro*) close behind. *agg invar* following.

apprestare [appres'tare] *v* prepare; (*porgere*) bring.

apprezzare [appret'tsare] *v* appreciate. **apprezzamento** *sm* appreciation; (*giudizio*) opinion; (*osservazione*) remark.

approfittare [approfit'tare] *v* profit (by), take advantage (of).

approfondire [approfon'dire] *v* deepen; (*studiare*) probe, go into.

approntare [appron'tare] *v* get ready.

approssimativo [approssima'tivo] *agg* approximate, rough. **approssimare** *v* approximate. **approssimarsi (a)** approach. **approssimazione** *sf* approximation.

approvare [appro'vare] *v* approve (of). **approvazione** *sf* approval.

appuntamento [appunta'mento] *sm* appointment; (*fam*) date.

appunto¹ [ap'punto] *sm* note; (*osservazione*) remark. **muovere** *or* **fare un appunto a** blame, find fault with.

appunto² [ap'punto] *avv* precisely, just.

appurare [appu'rare] *v* verify.

aprile [a'prile] *sm* April.

*****aprire** [a'prire] *v* open; (*luce, radio, ecc.*) switch on. **apribottiglie** *sm invar* bottle-opener. **apriscatole** *sm invar* tin-opener.

aquila ['akwila] *sf* eagle. **aquilone** *sm* kite.

Arabia [a'rabja] *sf* Aràbia. **arabo, -a** *s, agg* Arab; *sm* (*lingua*) Arabic.

arachide [a'rakide] *sf* ground-nut, peanut.

aragosta [ara'gosta] *sf* lobster.

araldo [a'raldo] *sm* herald. **araldica** *sf* heraldry. **araldico** *agg* heraldic.

arancio [a'rantʃo] *sm* orange tree. *agg invar* (*colore*) orange. **arancia** *sf* orange. **arancione** *sm, agg invar* orange.

arare [a'rare] *v* plough. **aratro** *sm* plough.

arazzo [a'rattso] *sm* tapestry.

arbitrare [arbi'trare] *v* arbitrate; (*sport*) referee. **arbitro** *sm* referee, umpire.

arbitrio [ar'bitrjo] *sm* will. **arbitrario** *agg* arbitrary.

arbusto [ar'busto] *sm* bush.

arca ['arka] *sf* ark.

arcaico [ar'kaiko] *agg* archaic.

arcata [ar'kata] *sf* arcade; (*di ponte*) span; (*anat*) arch.

archeologia [arkeolo'dʒia] *sf* archaeology. **archeologico** *agg* archaeological. **archeologo, -a** *sm, sf* archaeologist.

archetipo [ar'kɛtipo] *sm* archetype. *agg* archetypal.

archetto [ar'ketto] *sm* bow.

architetto [arki'tetto] *sm* architect. **architettonico** *agg* architectural. **architettura** *sf* architecture.

archivio [ar'kivjo] *sm* archives *pl*; (*comm*) file. **archiviare** *v* (place on) file;

(*questione*, *ecc.*) pigeon-hole. **archivista** *s*(*m*+*f*) archivist; (*comm*) filing clerk.

arciduca [artʃi'duka] *sm* archduke.

arciere [ar'tʃɛre] *sm* archer.

arcigno [ar'tʃiɲo] *agg* sullen.

arcipelago [artʃi'pɛlago] *sm*, *pl* -**ghi** archipelago.

arcivescovo [artʃi'veskovo] *sm* archbishop. **arcivescovado** *sm* archbishop's palace; (*dignità*) archbishopric.

arco ['arko] *sm* bow; (*anat*, *arch*) arch; (*geom*) arc. **quartetto d'archi** *sm* string quartet. **strumenti ad arco** *sm pl* strings *pl*. **tiro all'arco** *sm* archery.

arcobaleno [arkoba'leno] *sm* rainbow.

arcuato [arku'ato] *agg* arched. **dalle gambe arcuate** bow-legged.

*****ardere** ['ardere] *v* burn. **ardente** *agg* burning; (*colore*) fiery; (*appassionato*) ardent.

ardesia [ar'dɛzja] *sf* slate.

ardire [ar'dire] *v* dare. **ardito** *agg* bold, daring; risky. **ardore** *sm* (*calore*) heat; passion.

arduo ['arduo] *agg* arduous, laborious; (*ripido*) steep.

area ['area] *sf* area; (*terreno*) land, ground.

arena[1] [a'rɛna] *sf* arena.

arena[2] [a'rena] *sf* (*sabbia*) sand.

arenaria [are'narja] *sf* sandstone.

arenarsi [are'narsi] *v* run aground; (*fermarsi*) come to a standstill.

argano ['argano] *sm* winch; (*mar*) capstan.

argentina [ardʒen'tina] *sf* polo-neck sweater.

argento [ar'dʒɛnto] *sm* silver. **argento vivo** quicksilver. **argentare** *v* silver(-plate). **argentato** *agg* silver-plated; (*colore*) silver. **argenteria** *sf* silver, silverware.

argilla [ar'dʒilla] *sf* clay.

argine ['ardʒine] *sm* embankment; barrier. **arginare** *v* stem, check.

argomento [argo'mento] *sm* argument, reason; (*materia*) subject, topic. **argomentare** *v* discuss, argue.

arguto [ar'guto] *agg* (*spiritoso*) witty; shrewd. **arguzia** *sf* wit, humour; shrewdness.

aria ['arja] *sf* air; (*aspetto*) look; (*musica*) tune; (*opera*) aria. **all'aria aperta** in the open, out-of-doors. **corrente d'aria** *sf* draught. **darsi delle arie** put on airs.

arido ['arido] *agg* dry, arid.

arieggiare [arjed'dʒare] *v* air.

ariete [a'rjɛte] *sm* ram. **Ariete** *sm* Aries.

aringa [a'ringa] *sf* herring.

arioso [a'rjozo] *agg* airy.

aristocratico [aristo'kratiko], -**a** *sm*, *sf* aristocrat. *agg* aristocratic. **aristocrazia** *sf* aristocracy.

aritmetica [arit'mɛtika] *sf* arithmetic. **aritmetico** *agg* arithmetic(al).

armadio [ar'madjo] *sm* cupboard; (*per abiti*) wardrobe.

armare [ar'mare] *v* arm; (*mar*) rig up; reinforce. **armarsi** *v* take up arms; (*provvedersi*) arm oneself. **arma** *sf*, *pl* -**i** weapon, arms *pl*; (*mil*) force. **armamento** *sm* armament; (*tec*) equipment.

armata [ar'mata] *sf* army; (*flotta*) fleet.

armato [ar'mato] *agg* armed; equipped.

armatura [arma'tura] *sf* scaffolding; (*elett*) armature.

armonia [armo'nia] *sf* harmony. **in armonia con** in keeping with. **armonica** *sf* harmonics. **armonica a bocca** mouth-organ. **armonico** *agg* harmonic. **armonioso** *agg* melodious. **armonizzare** *v* harmonize; (*colori*, *ecc.*) match.

arnese [ar'neze] *sm* tool; gadget. **arnese da cucina** kitchen utensil. **bene/male in arnese** in good/poor shape.

arnia ['arnja] *sf* beehive.

aroma [a'rɔma] *sm* aroma; aromatic herb, spice. **aromatico** *agg* aromatic.

arpa ['arpa] *sf* harp. **arpeggio** *sm* arpeggio. **arpista** *s*(*m*+*f*) harpist.

arpione [ar'pjone] *sm* hook; (*arma*) harpoon; (*cardine*) hinge.

arrabbiarsi [arrab'bjarsi] *v* become angry or annoyed. **far arrabbiare** annoy, anger. **arrabbiato** *agg* angry; (*cane*) rabid; (*furioso*) enraged.

arraffare [arraf'fare] *v* snatch.

arrampicarsi [arrampi'karsi] *v* climb (up). **arrampicata** *sf* climbing, climb.

arrangiare [arran'dʒare] *v* (*aggiustare*) mend; improvise; (*fam*) fix; (*musica*) arrange. **arrangiarsi** *v* manage; come to an agreement.

arrecare [arre'kare] *v* cause, bring about.

arredare [arre'dare] *v* furnish. **arredamento** *sm* furnishing; (*mobilio*) furniture. **arredatore, -trice** *sm*, *sf* interior decorator; (*cinema*) set decorator.

*****arrendersi** [ar'rɛndersi] *v* surrender, give oneself up. **arrendevole** *agg* yielding.

arrestare [arres'tare] *v* stop; (*dir*) arrest. **arresto** *sm* stop, stoppage; arrest. **arresto cardiaco** heart failure.

arretrato [arre'trato] *agg* behind; (*non fatto*) outstanding, overdue; (*non sviluppato*) backward; (*numero di rivista, ecc.*) back. **arretrati** *sm pl* arrears *pl*; (*di paga*) back-pay *sing*.

arricchire [arrik'kire] *v* enrich. **arricchirsi** become rich.

arricciare [arrit'tʃare] *v* curl. **arricciare il naso** pull a face. **arricciare il pelo** bristle.

arringa [ar'ringa] *sf* address.

arrischiare [arris'kjare] *v* risk, venture. **arrischiato** *agg* risky; (*imprudente*) rash.

arrivare [arri'vare] *v* arrive; succeed; (*capitare*) happen. **arrivare a** (*riuscire*) manage to; (*giungere*) reach, get to; (*essere ridotto a*) be reduced to. **arrivare fino a** reach, get as far as. **ben arrivato!** welcome! **arrivo** *sm* arrival.

arrivederci [arrive'dertʃi] *inter* goodbye! (*fam*) see you!

arrogante [arro'gante] *agg* arrogant. **arroganza** *sf* arrogance.

arrossire [arros'sire] *v* blush.

arrostire [arros'tire] *v* roast. **arrosto** *sm*, *agg invar* roast.

arrotare [arro'tare] *v* sharpen. **arrotino** *sm* knife-grinder.

arrotolare [arroto'lare] *v* roll up.

arrotondare [arroton'dare] *v* round off.

arroventato [arroven'tato] *agg* red-hot.

arruffare [arruf'fare] *v* ruffle; (*confondere*) muddle.

arrugginirsi [arruddʒi'nirsi] *v* rust. **arrugginito** *agg* rusty.

arruolare [arrwo'lare] *v* enlist.

arsenale [arse'nale] *sm* arsenal; (*mar*) (naval) dockyard.

arsenico [ar'sɛniko] *sm* arsenic.

arso ['arso] *agg* burnt, parched.

arte ['arte] *sf* art; (*attività*) craft; (*abilità*) skill; (*astuzia*) cunning. **ad arte** on purpose; (*con artifizio*) cunningly. **artefice** *sm* craftsman.

arteria [ar'tɛria] *sf* artery. **arteria di traffico** main road, thoroughfare.

artico ['artiko] *agg* arctic.

articolare [artiko'lare] *v* articulate; (*suddividere*) split up.

articolo [ar'tikolo] *sm* article. **articoli** *sm pl* goods *pl*. **articolo di cronaca** news item. **articolo di fondo** leading article, leader.

artificiale [artifi'tʃale] *agg* artificial.

artificio [arti'fitʃo] *sm* stratagem, device. **fuochi d'artificio** *sm pl* fireworks *pl*.

artigiano [arti'dʒano] *sm* craftsman. **artigianato** *sm* craftsmanship; (*prodotti*) handicraft; (*classe*) craftsmen *pl*.

artiglieria [artiʎe'ria] *sf* artillery.

artiglio [ar'tiʎo] *sm* claw, talon. **cadere negli artigli di** fall into the clutches of.

artista [ar'tista] *s(m+f)* artist. **artistico** artistic.

arto ['arto] *sm* limb.

artrite [ar'trite] *sf* arthritis.

asbesto [az'bɛsto] *sm* asbestos.

ascella [a'ʃɛlla] *sf* armpit.

***ascendere** [a'ʃendere] *v* rise.

ascensore [aʃer'sore] *sm* elevator.

ascesa [a'ʃeza] *sf* also **ascensione** ascent, climb.

ascesso [a'ʃɛsso] *sm* abscess.

asceta [a'ʃɛta] *s(m+f)* ascetic. **ascetico** *agg* ascetic. **ascetismo** *sm* asceticism.

ascia ['aʃa] *sf* axe.

asciugare [aʃu'gare] *v* dry. **asciugamano** *sm* towel. **asciugatoio** *sm* bath towel. **carta asciugante** *sf* blotting-paper.

asciutto [a'ʃutto] *agg* dry. **essere all'asciutto** (*salvo*) be safe; (*al verde*) be broke. **pasta asciutta** *sf* pasta.

ascoltare [askol'tare] *v* listen (to); heed, pay attention (to); (*lezioni, messa, ecc.*) attend. **ascoltatore, -trice** *sm*, *sf* listener. **dare ascolto a** pay attention to.

asfalto [as'falto] *sm* asphalt. **asfaltare** *v* asphalt.

Asia ['azja] *sf* Asia. **asiatico** *sm*, *agg* Asian, Asiatic.

asilo [a'zilo] *sm* refuge, shelter; (*pol*) asylum. **asilo infantile** kindergarten, nursery school. **dare asilo a** shelter.

asino ['azino] *sm* ass, donkey. **asineria** *sf* stupidity. **asinino** *agg* asinine. **tosse asinina** *sf* whooping cough.

asma ['azma] *sm* asthma. **asmatico** *agg* asthmatic.

asola ['azola] *sf* buttonhole.

asparago [as'parago] *sm* asparagus.

aspettare [aspet'tare] *v* await, wait (for). **aspettare con desiderio** look forward to. **aspettare un bambino** be expecting a baby. **aspettativa** *sf* expectation; (*licenza*) leave of absence.

aspetto¹ [as'pɛtto] *sm* appearance, look. **sotto questo aspetto** from this point of view.

aspetto² [as'pɛtto] *sm* waiting. **sala d'aspetto** *sf* waiting-room.
aspirare [aspi'rare] *v* inhale, breathe in; (*desiderare*) aspire. **aspirapolvere** *sm invar* vacuum cleaner.
aspirina [aspi'rina] *sf* aspirin.
asportare [aspor'tare] *v* remove, take away.
aspro ['aspro] *agg* sour, tart; (*vino*) rough; (*suono*) harsh; (*clima*) raw; (*fig*) hard. **asprezza** *sf* sourness; harshness.
assaggiare [assad'dʒare] *v* taste, try. **assaggio** *sm* taste; (*campione*) sample.
assai [as'sai] *avv* very; (very) much; (*abbastanza*) enough.
assalire [assa'lire] *v* assail, attack.
assalto [as'salto] *sm* attack.
assassinare [assassi'nare] *v* murder. **assassinio** *sm* murder. **assassino, -a** *sm*, *sf* murderer, murderess.
asse¹ ['asse] *sm* axis; (*mec*) axle.
asse² ['asse] *sf* (*tavola*) board, plank. **asse da stiro** ironing-board.
assediare [asse'djare] *v* besiege. **assedio** *sm* siege. **stato d'assedio** *sm* state of emergency.
assegnare [asse'ɲare] *v* assign, allot. **assegnazione** *sf* allocation.
assegno [as'seɲno] *sm* check. **assegno circolare** banker's draft. **assegno in bianco** blank check. **assegno sbarrato** crossed check. **assegno turistico** traveller's check.
assemblea [assem'blɛa] *sf* assembly, meeting.
assenso [as'sɛnso] *sm* assent, agreement.
assente [as'sɛnte] *agg* absent. **assentarsi** *v* absent oneself, stay away. **assenteismo** *sm* absenteeism. **assenza** *sf* absence; (*mancanza*) lack.
assentire [assen'tire] *v* assent, approve.
asserire [asse'rire] *v* assert, affirm. **asserzione** *sf* assertion, statement.
assessore [asses'sore] *sm* (*dir*) assessor; (*comunale*) councillor.
assestare [asses'tare] *v* arrange, settle.
assetato [asse'tato] *agg* thirsty.
assettare [asset'tare] *v* tidy, put in order.
assicurare [assiku'rare] *v* assure; (*dir*) insure; (*rendere certo*) ensure; (*procurare*) secure; (*lettera*) register. **assicurarsi** *v* take out insurance. **assicuratore** *sm* underwriter. **assicurazione** *sf* insurance.
assiduo [as'siduo] *agg* assiduous.

assieme [as'sjɛme] *avv* together.
assieparsi [assje'parsi] *v* crowd (round).
assillare [assil'lare] *v* pester.
assimilare [assimi'lare] *v* assimilate. **assimilazione** *sf* assimilation.
Assise [as'size] *sf* **corte d'Assise** *sf* Assizes *pl*.
assistente [assis'tɛnte] *s(m+f)* assistant; (*universitario*) lecturer; (*di volo*) steward, stewardess. **assistente sociale** social worker. **assistenza** *sf* assistance; (*sociale*) welfare.
***assistere** [as'sistere] *v* (*aiutare*) assist, help; be present at; (*sport*) watch; (*lezione*) attend.
asso ['asso] *sm* ace; champion. **piantare in asso** leave in the lurch.
associare [asso'tʃare] *v* associate, join. **associarsi** *v* join; become a partner *or* member. **associazione** *sf* association, society; (*comm*) partnership.
assoggettare [assoddʒet'tare] *v* subject.
assoluto [asso'luto] *agg* absolute, complete.
***assolvere** [as'sɔlvere] *v* (*rel*) absolve; (*dir*) discharge, acquit. **assoluzione** *sf* absolution; discharge, acquittal. **assolvimento** *sm* fulfilment.
assomigliare [assomi'ʎare] *v* resemble.
assonnato [asson'nato] *agg* sleepy; (*torpido*) sluggish.
assopirsi [asso'pirsi] *v* nod off; calm *or* cool down.
assorbire [assor'bire] *v* absorb. **assorbente** *agg* absorbent. **assorbente (igienico)** *sm* sanitary towel. **carta assorbente** *sf* blotting-paper.
assordare [assor'dare] *v* deafen; (*attutire un suono*) deaden.
assortire [assor'tire] *v* sort out. **assortimento** *sm* assortment.
***assuefare** [assue'fare] *v* accustom.
***assumere** [as'sumere] *v* assume; (*personale*) take on, engage; (*procurarsi*) obtain.
assunzione [assun'tsjone] *sf* engagement; (*di un obbligo*) undertaking; (*elevazione*) ascent; (*filos*) assumption. **Assunzione** *sf* (*rel*) Assumption.
assurdo [as'surdo] *agg* absurd, preposterous. *sm* absurdity.
asta ['asta] *sf* pole; (*mec*) rod; (*scrittura*) stroke. **a mezz'asta** at half-mast. **vendita all'asta** *sf* auction.

astante [as'tante] *s(m+f)* bystander.
astemio [as'tɛmjo], **-a** *sm*, *sf* teetotaller. *agg* teetotal.
*****astenersi** [aste'nersi] *v* abstain, refrain.
asterisco [aste'risko] *sm* asterisk.
astinenza [asti'nɛntsa] *sf* abstinence.
astio ['astjo] *sm* rancour, resentment. **portar astio** bear a grudge.
*****astrarre** [as'trarre] *v* abstract. **astratto** *sm*, *agg* abstract. **astrazione** *sf* abstraction.
astro ['astro] *sm* star.
astrologia [astrolo'dʒia] *sf* astrology. **astrologico** *agg* astrological. **astrologo, -a** *sm*, *sf* astrologer.
astronauta [astro'nauta] *s(m+f)* astronaut.
astronomia [astrono'mia] *sf* astronomy. **astronomico** *agg* astronomic(al). **astronomo, -a** *sm*, *sf* astronomer.
astuccio [as'tuttʃo] *sm* case.
astuto [as'tuto] *agg* astute, shrewd. **astuzia** *sf* shrewdness, cunning; (*azione*) trick.
Atene [a'tɛne] *sf* Athens. **ateniese** *s(m+f)*, *agg* Athenian.
ateo ['ateo], **-a** *sm*, *sf* atheist. *agg* atheistic.
atlante [at'lante] *sm* atlas.
atlantico [at'lantiko] *agg* Atlantic.
atleta [at'lɛta] *s(m+f)* athlete. **atletica** *sf* athletics. **atletico** *agg* athletic.
atmosfera [atmos'fɛra] *sf* atmosphere. **atmosferico** *agg* atmospheric.
atomo ['atomo] *sm* atom. **atomico** *agg* atomic.
atrio ['atrjo] *sm* (*entrance*) hall, lobby.
atroce [a'trɔtʃe] *agg* dreadful, terrible; (*feroce*) cruel. **atrocità** *sf* atrocity.
attaccare [attak'kare] *v* attach, fasten; (*appendere*) hang (up); (*incollare*) stick (on); apply; pass on; (*assalire, corrodere*) attack; (*iniziare*) begin. **attaccabottoni** *s(m+f)* *invar* (*fam*) bore. **attaccabrighe** *s(m+f)* *invar* (*fam*) troublemaker. **attaccapanni** *sm* (*gruccia*) coat-hanger; (*mobilia*) coat-rack. **attaccar briga** *or* **lite** pick a quarrel. **attaccaticcio** *agg* sticky. **attacco** *sm* attack; (*inizio*) opening; (*giuntura*) joint, fastening; (*elett*) plug.
attecchire [attek'kire] *v* (*radicarsi*) take root; (*diffondersi*) catch on.
atteggiare [atted'dʒare] *v* assume. **atteggiarsi** *v* pose. **atteggiamento** *sm* attitude, expression.

*****attendere** [at'tɛndere] *v* await, wait (for); (*dedicarsi*) devote oneself to, look after. **attendibile** *agg* reliable, trustworthy.
*****attenersi** [atte'nersi] *v* **attenersi a** keep to.
attentato [atten'tato] *sm* attack; attempted murder *or* assassination.
attento [at'tɛnto] *agg* attentive, alert; careful. **stare attento** pay attention, mind. *inter* careful! mind! look out!
attenzione [atten'tsjone] *sf* attention, care. **fare attenzione a** pay attention to.
atterrare [atter'rare] *v* (*di aereo*) land; (*gettare a terra*) knock down. **atterraggio** *sm* landing.
attesa [at'teza] *sf* wait; (*aspettativa*) expectation.
attestare [attes'tare] *v* certify, attest. **attestato** *sm* certificate, testimonial.
attiguo [at'tiguo] *agg* adjoining.
attimo ['attimo] *sm* instant, moment.
attirare [atti'rare] *v* attract, draw.
attitudine¹ [atti'tudine] *sf* (*disposizione*) aptitude, bent.
attitudine² [atti'tudine] *sf* attitude.
attivare [atti'vare] *v* activate, bring into action.
attivo [at'tivo] *agg* active; (*diligente*) busy. **bilancio attivo** *sm* credit balance. *sm* asset.
attizzare [attit'tsare] *v* poke; (*fig*) stir up.
atto¹ ['atto] *agg* suitable, fit.
atto² ['atto] *sm* action, act; gesture; (*dir*) deed. **atto di accusa** indictment. **atto di citazione** summons. **atto di nascita/morte** birth/death certificate. **atto matrimoniale** marriage certificate. **dare atto** give notice. **in atto** in progress.
attonito [at'tɔnito] *agg* astonished.
attorcigliare [attortʃi'ʎare] *v* twist.
attore [at'tore] *sm* actor; (*dir*) plaintiff.
attorniare [attor'njare] *v* surround.
attorno [at'torno] *avv* round, around, about. **guardarsi attorno** look round; (*fig*) be wary. **qui attorno** hereabouts.
*****attrarre** [at'trarre] *v* attract. **attrattiva** *sf* attraction, fascination. **attrazione** *sf* attraction.
attraversare [attraver'sare] *v* cross; go through. **attraversamento** *sm* crossing.
attrezzo [at'trettso] *sm* tool, appliance. **attrezzi** *sm pl* equipment *sing*; kitchen utensils *pl*; (*teatro*) props *pl*. **attrezzare** *v*

equip; furnish. **attrezzatura** *sf* equipment.

attribuire [attribu'ire] *v* ascribe, attribute; *(assegnare)* award. **attributo** *sm* attribute.

attrice [at'tritʃe] *sf* actress.

attrito [at'trito] *sm* friction.

attuale [attu'ale] *agg* present, current; *(valido)* topical; *(filos)* actual. **attualmente** *avv* at present.

attualità [attuali'ta] *sf* topicality. *sf pl* news *sing*, current events *pl*. **di attualità** topical; *(di moda)* fashionable. **tornare di attualità** come back into fashion.

attuare [attu'are] *v* carry out, put into effect. **attuarsi** *v* come true, be fulfilled.

attutire [attu'tire] *v* mitigate; *(suono)* muffle.

audace [au'datʃe] *agg* daring, bold; risky, rash. **audacia** *sf* boldness, daring.

audiovisivo [audjovi'zivo] *agg* audio-visual.

auditorio [audi'tɔrjo] *sm* auditorium, studio.

audizione [audi'tsjone] *sf* audition; *(dir)* hearing.

augurare [augu'rare] *v* wish. **augurarsi** *v* hope. **augurio** *sm* wish; *(presagio)* omen.

aula ['aula] *sf* classroom; *(università)* lecture theatre; courtroom.

aumentare [aumen'tare] *v* increase. **aumentare di peso** put on weight. **aumento** *sm* increase.

aureo ['aureo] *agg* golden.

aureola [au'rɛola] *sf* halo.

aurora [au'rora] *sf* dawn.

ausiliare [auzi'ljare] *sm*, *agg* *also* **ausiliario** auxiliary.

austero [aus'tɛro] *agg* austere.

Australia [aus'tralja] *sf* Australia. **australiano, -a** *s*, *agg* Australian.

Austria ['austrja] *sf* Austria. **austriaco, -a** *s*, *agg* Austrian.

autarchia [autar'kia] *sf* self-sufficiency. **autarchico** *agg* self-sufficient.

autentico [au'tɛntiko] *agg* authentic, genuine. **autenticare** *v* authenticate.

autista[1] [au'tista] *s(m+f)* driver. **autista di piazza** taxi-driver.

autista[2] [au'tista] *agg* autistic.

auto ['auto] *sf* *(fam)* car.

autobiografia [autobiogra'fia] *sf* autobiography. **autobiografico** *agg* autobiographical.

autoblinda [auto'blinda] *sf* armoured car.

autobus ['autobus] *sm* bus.

autocarro [auto'karro] *sm* truck.

autocolonna [autoko'lonna] *sf* convoy.

autocontrollo [autokon'trɔllo] *sm* self-control.

autocratico [auto'kratiko] *agg* autocratic.

autodidatta [autodi'datta] *s(m+f)* self-taught person.

autofurgone [autofur'gone] *sm* van.

autolettiga [autolet'tiga] *sf* ambulance.

autolinea [auto'linea] *sf* bus route.

automa [au'tɔma] *sm* automaton, robot.

automatico [auto'matiko] *agg* automatic. **distributore automatico** slot-machine. **automatizzare** *v* automate.

automezzo [auto'mɛddzo] *sm* motor vehicle.

automobile [auto'mobile] *sf* car. **automobilismo** *sm* motoring. **automobilista** *s(m+f)* motorist. **automobilistico** *agg* motor.

autonomo [au'tɔnomo] *agg* autonomous. **autonomia** *sf* autonomy.

autopsia [autop'sia] *sf* post-mortem, autopsy.

autore [au'tore], **-trice** *sm*, *sf* author; artist.

autorevole [auto'revole] *agg* authoritative.

autorimessa [autori'messa] *sf* garage.

autorità [autori'ta] *sf* authority. **autoritario** *agg* authoritarian.

autoritratto [autori'tratto] *sm* self-portrait.

autorizzare [autorid'dzare] *v* authorize. **autorizzazione** *sf* authorization; permit.

autostop [autos'tɔp] *sm invar* hitch-hiking. **fare l'autostop** hitch-hike.

autostrada [autos'trada] *sf* expressway.

autosufficiente [autosuffi'tʃɛnte] *agg* self-sufficient.

autotreno [auto'trɛno] *sm* articulated lorry.

autoveicolo [autove'ikolo] *sm* motor vehicle.

autunno [au'tunno] *sm* autumn. **autunnale** *agg* autumnal.

avambraccio [avam'brattʃo] *sm* forearm.

avanguardia [avan'gwardja] *sf* forefront; *(mil)* vanguard; *(arte)* avant-garde.

avanti [a'vanti] *avv* forward, ahead; *(prima)* before. **andare avanti** go forward, proceed. **avanti a** before, in front of. **avanti e indietro** backwards and forwards, to and fro. **d'ora in avanti** from now on. **tirare avanti** *(fam)* scrape along, get by. *inter* come in! (*andiamo*) come now!

avantieri [avan'tjɛri] *avv* the day before yesterday.

avanzare[1] [avan'tsare] *v* advance; (*presentare*) put forward. **avanzata** *sf* advance.

avanzare[2] [avan'tsare] *v* be owed; remain, be left over. **avanzo** *sm* remainder; (*cibo*) left-overs *pl*.

avaro [a'varo], **-a** *agg* mean. *sm, sf* miser. **avarizia** *sf* meanness, stinginess.

avena [a'vena] *sf* oats *pl*. **farina d'avena** *sf* oatmeal.

***avere** [a'vere] *v* have; get. **aver caldo/freddo** be hot/cold. **aver fame/sete** be hungry/thirsty. **aver fretta** be in a hurry. **aver paura/sonno** be afraid/sleepy. *sm* (*comm*) credit; belongings *pl*; property.

aviazione [avja'tsjone] *sf* aviation, flying; (*arma*) air-force. **aviatore, -trice** *sm, sf* aviator, pilot.

avido ['avido] *agg* avid, eager.

aviolinea [avjo'linea] *sf* airline.

avo ['avo] *sm* (*nonno*) grandfather; (*antenato*) forefather, ancestor. **avito** *agg* ancestral.

avocado [avo'kado] *sm* avocado.

avorio [a'vɔrjo] *sm* ivory.

avvampare [avvam'pare] *v* blaze, flare up.

avvantaggiare [avvantad'dʒare] *v* profit, benefit.

***avvedersi** [avve'dersi] *v* become aware.

avvelenare [avvele'nare] *v* poison. **avvelenamento** *sm* poisoning. **avvelenatore, -trice** *sm, sf* poisoner.

***avvenire** [avve'nire] *v* happen. *sm* future. **avvenimento** *sm* event, occurrence.

avventato [avven'tato] *agg* rash, reckless.

avventare *v* hurl; (*azzardare*) venture.

avventore [avven'tore], **-a** *sm, sf* patron, regular customer.

avventurare [avventu'rare] *v* venture, risk. **avventura** *sf* adventure; (*amorosa*) love affair. **avventuriere** *sm* adventurer.

avverbio [av'verbio] *sm* adverb.

avversario [avver'sario], **-a** *sm, sf* adversary, opponent. *agg* opposing.

avversione [avver'sjone] *sf* dislike, aversion.

avversità [avversi'ta] *sf* adversity.

avverso [av'vɛrso] *agg* adverse; opposing.

avvertire [avver'tire] *v* (*osservare*) notice; (*percepire*) feel; (*ammonire*) warn; (*avvisare*) inform. **avvertenza** *sf* warning, notice; (*attenzione*) care; (*istruzioni*) directions *pl*.

avvezzare [avvet'tsare] *v* (*educare*) train; (*abituare*) accustom.

avviare [avvi'are] *v* start (up), set going; (*comm*) set up; direct. **scuola d'avviamento** *sf* training college, technical college. **avviato** *agg* under way; (*prospero*) thriving.

avvicinare [avvitʃi'nare] *v* approach; (*portar vicino*) bring near.

avvilire [avvi'lire] *v* disgrace; (*scoraggiare*) dishearten; humiliate. **avvilito** *agg* down-hearted; demoralized.

avviluppare [avvilup'pare] *v* entangle; (*avvolgere*) wrap up.

avvincente [avvin'tʃɛnte] *agg* fascinating.

avvisare [avvi'zare] *v* let know, advise; (*ammonire*) warn. **avviso** *sm* notice, note; announcement; (*pubblicità*) advertisement; opinion. **avviso circolare** circular. **come d'avviso** as advised.

avvizzire [avvit'tsire] *v* wither.

avvocato [avvo'kato] *sm* lawyer, barrister, solicitor; advocate, champion. **avvocatura** *sf* legal profession.

***avvolgere** [av'vɔldʒere] *v* envelop, wrap up; (*arrotolare*) roll up, wind.

avvoltoio [avvol'tojo] *sm* vulture.

azalea [adza'lɛa] *sf* azalea.

azienda [a'dzjɛnda] *sf* firm, business, company; (*impresa*) undertaking. **azienda agricola** farm. **aziendale** *agg* business.

azione [a'tsjone] *sf* action; (*atto*) deed; (*mec*) movement, motion; (*dir*) lawsuit; (*comm*) share. **azionista** *s(m+f)* shareholder.

azoto [a'dzɔto] *sm* nitrogen.

azzardare [addzar'dare] *v* risk, venture. **azzardarsi** *v* dare. **azzardato** *agg* risky, rash. **azzardo** *sm* risk.

azzuffarsi [addzuf'farsi] *v* brawl, come to blows.

azzurro [ad'dzurro] *agg, sm* (sky) blue.

B

babbo ['babbo] *sm* (*fam*) dad, daddy.
babbuino [babbu'ino] *sm* baboon.
babordo [ba'bordo] *sm* port.
bacca ['bakka] *sf* berry.
baccalà [bakka'la] *sm* dried salt cod.
baccano [bak'kano] *sm* row, din, uproar.
baccello [bat'tʃɛllo] *sm* pod.
bacchetta [bak'kɛtta] *sf* rod, stick; (*musica*) baton.
baciare [ba'tʃare] *v* kiss. **bacio** *sm* kiss.
bacino [ba'tʃino] *sm* basin; (*anat*) pelvis.
baco ['bako] *sm* larva; (*da seta*) silkworm.
bada ['bada] *sf* **tenere a bada** hold at bay.
badare [ba'dare] *v* **badare a** pay attention to, take care to. **badare di** be careful to. **senza badare a** regardless of.
badessa [ba'dessa] *sf* abbess.
badia [ba'dia] *sf* abbey.
badile [ba'dile] *sm* spade.
baffo ['baffo] *sm* **farsene un baffo** (*fam*) not care a damn. **baffi** *sm pl* moustache *sing*. **leccarsi i baffi** lick one's lips. **ridere sotto i baffi** laugh up one's sleeve.
bagaglio [ba'gaʎo] *sm* baggage. **bagagliaio** *sm* (*ferr*) luggage van; (*auto*) boot. **deposito bagagli** *sm* left luggage.
bagattella [bagat'tɛlla] *sf* (*gioco*) bagatelle; (*inezia*) trifle.
bagliore [ba'ʎore] *sm* flash.
bagnare [ba'ɲare] *v* wet. **bagnato** *agg* wet.
bagnino [ba'ɲino] *sm* beach attendant, lifeguard.
bagno ['baɲo] *sm* bath; (*locale*) bathroom. **fare il bagno** take a bath. **bagnante** *s(m+f)* bather. **bagnomaria** *sm* bain-marie.
baia ['baja] *sf* (*geog*) bay.
baionetta [bajo'netta] *sf* bayonet.
balbettare [balbet'tare] *v* stammer.
balbuziente [balbut'tsjɛnte] *s(m+f)* stammerer.
balcone [bal'kone] *sm* balcony. **balconata** *sf* (*teatro, ecc.*) gallery.
baldacchino [baldak'kino] *sm* canopy; (*rel*) baldachin.
baldanza [bal'dantsa] *sf* self-confidence; audacity. **baldanzoso** *agg* self-confident; audacious.
baldoria [bal'dɔrja] *sf* merrymaking. **far baldoria** make merry.
balena [ba'lena] *sf* whale.
balenare [bale'nare] *v* flash (with lightning); (*apparire subitamente*) come in a flash. **baleno** *sm* flash.

balia¹ ['balja] *sf* nurse.
balia² [ba'lia] *sf* **in balia di** in the power of, at the mercy of.
balistica [ba'listika] *sf* ballistics. **balistico** *agg* ballistic.
balla ['balla] *sf* (*involto*) bale; (*frottola*) fib, lie.
ballare [bal'lare] *v* dance.
ballata [bal'lata] *sf* ballad.
ballerino [balle'rino], **-a** *sm, sf* ballet-dancer.
balletto [bal'letto] *sm* ballet.
ballo ['ballo] *sm* ball; dance. **essere in ballo** be at stake.
ballottaggio [ballottad'dʒo] *sm* ballot. **ballottare** *v* ballot.
balneare [balne'are] *agg* bathing.
balocco [ba'lɔkko] *sm* toy, plaything.
balordo [ba'lordo] *agg* senseless, absurd; (*tonto*) dull.
balsamo ['balsamo] *sm* balsam; (*lenimento*) balm.
balza ['baltsa] *sf* (*rupe*) cliff; (*frangia*) fringe.
balzare [bal'tsare] *v* bounce, leap.
bambagia [bam'badʒa] *sf* cotton wool. **tenere nella bambagia** pamper, spoil.
bambinaia [bambi'naja] *sf* (children's) nurse, nanny.
bambino [bam'bino], **-a** *sm, sf* child (*pl* -ren). **bambinata** *sf* childishness. **bambinesco** *adj* puerile.
bamboccio [bam'bɔttʃo] *sm* (*scioccone*) simpleton; (*fantoccio*) rag-doll; (*bambino*) bonny child.
bambola ['bambola] *sf* doll.
bambù [bam'bu] *sm* bamboo.
banale [ba'nale] *adj* banal.
banana [ba'nana] *sf* banana. **banano** *sm* banana tree.
banca ['banka] *sf* bank. **bancario** *agg* bank, banking. **banchiere** *sm* banker.
bancarella [banka'rɛlla] *sf* barrow, stall.
bancarotta [banka'rotta] *sf* bankruptcy.
banchetto [ban'ketto] *sm* banquet. **banchettare** *v* banquet, feast.
banchina [ban'kina] *sf* (*porto*) wharf, quay; (*stazione*) platform.
banco ['banko] *sm* bench; (*di vendita*) counter; (*banca*) bank. **bancogiro** *sm* giro. **banconota** *sf* banknote.
banda¹ ['banda] *sf* (*lato*) side.
banda² ['banda] *sf* (*striscia*) stripe; (*radio*) band. **banda sonora** sound-track.

banda³ ['banda] *sf* group, band; *(delinquenti)* gang.

bandiera [ban'djɛra] *sf* flag, banner. **bandiera di comodo** flag of convenience.

banderuola *sf* pennant; *(ventaruola)* weather-vane; *(girella)* fickle person.

bandire [ban'dire] *v* proclaim; *(esiliare)* banish. **bandito** *sm* bandit. **banditore** *sm* town-crier. **bando** *sm* proclamation; banishment.

bangio ['bandʒo] *sm invar* banjo.

bar [bar] *sm invar* bar, café.

bara ['bara] *sf* bier, coffin. **aver un piede nella bara** have one foot in the grave.

baracca [ba'rakka] *sf* hut. **mandare avanti la baracca** carry on. **piantare baracca e burattini** abandon everything. **baraccone** *sm* stall, stand.

baraonda [bara'onda] *sf* hubbub, confusion.

barare [ba'rare] *v* cheat. **baro** *sm* cheat.

barattare [barat'tare] *v* barter. **baratto** *sm* barter, exchange.

barattolo [ba'rattolo] *sm* jar, tin.

barba ['barba] *sf* beard. **che barba!** what a bore! **barbuto** *adj* bearded.

barbabietola [barba'bjɛtola] *sf* beetroot.

barbaro ['barbaro] *sm* barbarian. *adj* barbarous.

barbiere [bar'bjɛre] *sm* barber.

barbiturato [barbitu'rato] *sm* barbiturate.

barca ['barka] *sf* boat. **barca a remi** rowing-boat. **barca a vela** sailing-boat. **barca a motore** motor boat. **barcamenarsi** *v* manage.

barcollare [barkol'lare] *v* totter, stagger.

bardare [bar'dare] *v* harness.

barella [ba'rella] *sf* stretcher. **barelliere** *sm* stretcher-bearer.

barile [ba'rile] *sm* barrel, cask.

barista [ba'rista] *sm* barman. *sf* barmaid.

baritono [ba'ritono] *sm* baritone.

barlume [bar'lume] *sm* glimmer.

barocco [ba'rokko] *sm, agg* baroque.

barometro [ba'rɔmetro] *sm* barometer.

barone [ba'rone] *sm* baron; *(dell'industria)* tycoon. **baronessa** *sf* baroness.

barra ['barra] *sf* bar, rod.

barricare [barri'kare] *v* barricade. **barricata** *sf* barricade.

barriera [bar'rjɛra] *sf* barrier.

baruffa [ba'ruffa] *sf* brawl.

barzelletta [bardzel'letta] *sf* joke, funny story.

bascula ['baskula] *sf* weighing machine.

base ['baze] *sf* basis *(pl* -ses); *(tec)* base. **a base di** made up of. **in base a** on the basis of. **basamento** *sm* pedestal; foundation. **basare** *v* base, found.

basetta [ba'zetta] *sf* sideburn.

basilica [ba'zilika] *sf* basilica.

basilico [ba'ziliko] *sm* basil.

basso ['basso] *agg* low, low-lying; *(poco profondo)* shallow. *avv* low, low down. *sm (musica)* bass. **a basso ... !** down with ... !

bassofondo [basso'fondo] *sm* shallows *pl.* **bassifondi** *sm pl (quartieri)* slums *pl; (strati sociali)* underworld *sing.*

bassotto [bas'sɔtto] *sm* dachshund.

bastardo [bas'tardo], **-a** *s, agg* bastard; *(non di razza)* mongrel.

bastare [bas'tare] *v* suffice, be enough. **basta!** *inter* enough! *(silenzio)* quiet! **basta che** provided that.

bastimento [basti'mento] *sm* ship.

bastonare [basto'nare] *v* beat, cane. **bastonata** *sf* caning, beating.

bastone [bas'tone] *sm* stick, cane; golf-club. **bastone da passeggio** walking stick.

battaglia [bat'taʎa] *sf* battle; campaign. **cavallo di battaglia** hobby-horse.

battaglio [bat'taʎʎo] *sm (campana)* clapper; *(porta)* door-knocker.

battaglione [batta'ʎone] *sm* battalion.

battello [bat'tɛllo] *sm* boat.

battere ['battere] *v* beat. **battere a macchina** type. **battere le mani** clap (one's hands). **in un batter d'occhio** in a flash. **senza batter ciglio** without batting an eyelid.

batteria [batte'ria] *sf* battery; *(sport)* heat; *(insieme)* set.

batterio [bat'tɛrjo] *sm* bacterium *(pl* -a). **batteriologia** *sf* bacteriology. **batteriologo, -a** *sm, sf* bacteriologist.

battesimo [bat'tezimo] *sm* baptism, christening. **battesimale** *adj* baptismal. **battezzare** *v* baptize, christen.

battibecco [batti'bekko] *sm* quarrel.

batticuore [batti'kwɔre] *sm* avere il batticuore have palpitations. **far venire il batticuore** make anxious.

battimani [batti'mani] *sm* applause.

battistero [battis'tɛro] *sm* baptistry.

battito ['battito] *sm* beat, pulsation.

battitore [batti'tore] *sm (sport)* server, striker; *(caccia)* beater.

battuta [bat'tuta] *sf* (*colpo*) blow; (*spiritosaggine*) witty remark; (*musica*) beat; (*sport*) service.

batuffolo [ba'tuffolo] *sm* wad.

baule [ba'ule] *sm* trunk. **fare i bauli** (*fam*) go away.

bava ['bava] *sf* dribble.

bavaglino [bava'ʎino] *sm* bib.

bavaglio [ba'vaʎo] *sm* gag. **mettere il bavaglio a** gag.

bavero ['bavero] *sm* collar.

bazzicare [battsi'kare] *v* associate with; frequent.

beatitudine [beati'tudine] *sf* beatitude.

beato [be'ato] *agg* blessed. **beato te!** lucky you!

bebè [be'bɛ] *sm* baby.

beccaccia [bek'kattʃa] *sf* woodcock. **beccaccino** *sm* snipe.

beccare [bek'kare] *v* peck; (*fam*) catch, collar.

becchino [bek'kino] *sm* undertaker; gravedigger.

becco¹ ['bekko] *sm* beak; (*bruciatore*) burner.

becco² ['bekko] *sm* (*caprone*) goat; (*cornuto*) cuckold.

Befana [be'fana] *sf* Epiphany.

beffare [bef'fare] *v* mock. **beffarsi di** make fun of. **beffa** *sf* jest, practical joke.

begli ['beʎi] *V* **bello.**

bei ['bɛi] *V* **bello.**

bel ['bel] *V* **bello.**

belare [be'lare] *v* bleat.

Belgio ['bɛldʒo] *sm* Belgium. **belga** *s*(*m*+*f*), *agg*, *m pl* -**gi** Belgian.

belletto [bel'letto] *sm* make-up, rouge.

bellezza [bel'lettsa] *sf* beauty. **che bellezza!** how lovely!

bello ['bɛllo] *agg* beautiful; fine; fair. **il bello è che** the odd thing is (that). **nel bel mezzo** right in the middle. **oh bella!** you don't say! **questa à bella!** (*ironico*) that's a good one! **sul più bello** at the crucial moment.

belva ['belva] *sf* wild animal.

bemolle [be'mɔlle] *sm* (*musica*) flat.

benché [ben'ke] *cong* although.

bendare [ben'dare] *v* (*fasciare*) bandage; (*coprire gli occhi*) blindfold. **benda** *sf* bandage; blindfold.

bene ['bɛne] *avv* well. **star bene** feel well; (*abito*) suit. **va bene** all right. *sm* good; (*amore*) love; wealth, property. **beni di consumo** consumer goods *pl*. **voler bene**

a be fond of. **benino** *avv* fairly well, reasonably.

*****benedire** [bene'dire] *v* bless, consecrate. **benedetto** *agg* blessed. **benedetti voi!** lucky you!

beneducato [benedu'kato] *agg* well-mannered.

beneficenza [benefi'tʃɛntsa] *sf* charity.

beneficio [bene'fitʃo] *sm* profit; advantage. **benefico** *agg* beneficial.

benessere [be'nɛssere] *sm* well-being, welfare.

benestante [benes'tante] *agg* comfortably off, well-to-do. **benestare** *sm* well-being; (*autorizzazione*) consent.

benevolo [be'nɛvolo] *agg* kindly, well-disposed.

beninteso [benin'tezo] *avv* naturally, of course.

benvenuto [benve'nuto] *sm*, *agg* welcome. **dare il benvenuto a** welcome.

benzina [ben'dzina] *sf* gasoline. **far benzina** fill up. **distributore di benzina** *sm* gasoline station or pump.

*****bere** ['bere] *v* drink.

bernoccolo [ber'nokkolo] *sm* bump; (*disposizione*) flair.

berretto [ber'retto] *sm* cap, hat.

bersaglio [ber'saʎo] *sm* target.

bestemmia [bes'temmja] *sf* swear-word, curse. **bestemmiare** *v* swear, curse.

bestia ['bestja] *sf* animal, beast; ignoramus. **bestiale** *agg* bestial, brutal; (*fam: intenso*) beastly.

bestiame [bes'tjame] *sm* livestock.

betoniera [beto'njɛra] *sf* cement-mixer.

bettola ['bettola] *sf* low dive.

betulla [be'tulla] *sf* birch.

bevanda [be'vanda] *sf* drink, beverage. **bevibile** *agg* drinkable.

biada ['bjada] *sf* fodder, forage.

biancheria [bjanke'ria] *sf* (*indumenti intimi*) underwear; (*da casa*) linen.

bianchetti [bjan'ketti] *sm pl* whitebait *pl*.

bianchetto [bjan'ketto] *sm* whitewash.

bianco ['bjanko] *agg* white; (*non scritto*) blank. **sm** white.

biancospino [bjanko'spino] *sm* hawthorn.

biascicare [bjaʃi'kare] *v* (*cibo*) munch; (*parole*) mumble.

biasimare [bjazi'mare] *v* blame. **biasimo** *sm* blame.

Bibbia ['bibbja] *sf* Bible. **biblico** *agg* biblical.

bibita ['bibita] *sf* (soft) drink, beverage.
bibliografia [bibljogra'fia] *sf* bibliography.
bibliografico *agg* bibliographical. **bibliografo, -a** *sm, sf* bibliographer.
biblioteca [bibljo'tɛka] *sf* library. **bibliotecario, -a** *sm, sf* librarian.
bicchiere [bik'kjɛre] *sm* glass, tumbler.
bicicletta [bitʃi'kletta] *sf* bicycle. **andare in bicicletta** cycle.
bicipite [bi'tʃipite] *sm* biceps.
bidè [bi'dɛ] *sm* bidet.
bidone [bi'done] *sm* drum, can.
bieco ['bjɛko] *agg* **guardare con occhio bieco** look askance at.
biennale [bien'nale] *agg* biennial. *sf* biennial event.
bietta ['bjetta] *sf* wedge.
biforcarsi [bifor'karsi] *v* branch off, fork. **biforcazione** *sf* fork, junction.
bigamia [biga'mia] *sf* bigamy. **bigamo** *sm* bigamist.
bighellonare [bigello'nare] *v* idle; (*girellare*) saunter.
bigio ['bidʒo] *agg* grey; (*tempo*) dull.
bigliardo [bi'ʎardo] *sm* billiards.
biglietto [bi'ʎetto] *sm* ticket; note; card. **bigliettaio, -a** *sm, sf* conductor. **biglietteria** *sf* booking-office.
bigodino [bigo'dino] *sm* curler, roller.
bigotto [bi'gɔtto], **-a** *sm, sf* bigot. *agg* bigoted.
bilancia [bi'lantʃa] *sf* scales *pl*; (*comm*) balance. **Bilancia** *sf* Libra. **bilanciare** *v* balance; (*pesare*) weigh.
bilancio [bi'lantʃo] *sm* balance sheet; budget.
bile ['bile] *sf* bile.
bilico ['biliko] *sm* **in bilico** in the balance.
bilingue [bi'lingwe] *agg* bilingual.
bilione [bi'ljone] *sm* a thousand millions.
bimbo ['bimbo], **-a** *sm, sf* child (*pl* -ren).
bimensile [bimen'sile] *agg* fortnightly.
binario [bi'narjo] *agg* binary. *sm* rails *pl*, railway line.
binocolo [bi'nɔkolo] *sm* binoculars *pl*.
biochimico [bio'kimiko], **-a** *agg* biochemical. *sm, sf* biochemist. *sf* (*scienza*) biochemistry.
biografia [biogra'fia] *sf* biography. **biografico** *agg* biographical. **biografo, -a** *sm, sf* biographer.
biologia [biolo'dʒia] *sf* biology. **biologico** *agg* biological. **biologo, -a** *sm, sf* biologist.

biondo ['bjondo] *agg* blond, fair-haired.
birbante [bir'bante] *sm* rascal, knave.
birbone [bir'bone] *sm* rogue, scamp.
birichino [biri'kino], **-a** *sm, sf* imp, mischievous child. *agg* impish, cheeky. **birichinata** *sf* childish prank.
birillo [bi'rillo] *sm* skittle.
birra ['birra] *sf* beer. **birreria** *sf* public house.
bis [bis] *inter* encore! **dare il bis** give an encore.
bisaccia [bi'zattʃa] *sf* knapsack, saddlebag.
bisbetico [biz'bɛtiko] *agg* cantankerous, peevish.
bisbigliare [bizbi'ʎare] *v* whisper. **bisbiglio** *sm* whisper.
biscia ['biʃa] *sf* snake.
biscotto [bis'kɔtto] *sm* biscuit.
bisestile [bizes'tile] *agg* **anno bisestile** leap-year.
bisognare [bizo'ɲare] *v* be necessary. **bisogno** *sm* need, requirement. **aver bisogno di** need. **non c'è bisogno** there is no need. **bisognoso** *agg* needy.
bistecca [bis'tekka] *sf* steak.
bisticciare [bistit'tʃare] *v* quarrel. **bisticcio** *sm* quarrel.
bistrattare [bistrat'tare] *v* ill-treat.
bitorzolo [bi'tortsolo] *sf* pimple.
bivio ['bivjo] *sm* junction, fork.
bizzarro [bid'dzarro] *agg* strange, odd.
bizzeffe [bid'dzɛffe] *avv* **a bizzeffe** galore.
blandire [blan'dire] *v* caress, entice. **blandizie** *sf pl* flattery *sing*.
blando ['blando] *agg* bland, mellow.
blasfemo [blas'fɛmo] *agg* blasphemous.
blatta ['blatta] *sf* cockroach.
blesità [blezi'ta] *sf* lisp. **parlar bleso** lisp.
bloccare [blok'kare] *v* block, blockade. **blocco** *sm* block; (*massa*) lump; blockade; (*ostruzione*) blockage. **in blocco** in bulk.
blu [blu] *agg* blue. **bluastro** *agg* bluish.
blusa ['bluza] *sf* blouse.
boa¹ ['bɔa] *sm invar* (*zool*) boa.
boa² *sf* (*mar*) buoy.
boato [bo'ato] *sm* roar, rumble. **boato sonico** sonic bang.
bobina [bo'bina] *sf* bobbin, reel.
bocca ['bokka] *sf* mouth; (*apertura*) opening. **in bocca al lupo!** good luck!
boccale [bok'kale] *sm* tankard.
boccata [bok'kata] *sf* mouthful.

bocchino [bok'kino] *sm* mouthpiece; cigarette-holder.

boccia ['bɔttʃa] *sf* (*sport*) bowl; (*vaso*) decanter; (*bot*) bud.

bocciare [bot'tʃare] *v* (*dir*) repeal; (*esami*) fail.

boccio ['bɔttʃo] *sm also* **bocciolo** bud.

boccone [bok'kone] *sm* mouthful.

bocconi [bok'koni] *avv* prone, flat on one's face.

bofonchiare [bofon'kjare] *v* snort.

boia ['bɔja] *sm invar* executioner. **boiata** *sf* (*fam*) rubbish.

boicottare [boikot'tare] *v* boycott. **boicottaggio** *sm* boycott.

bolide ['bɔlide] *sm* fire-ball. **andare come un bolide** go like a bomb. **passare come un bolide** flash past.

bolla[1] ['bolla] *sf* bubble; (*med*) blister.

bolla[2] ['bolla] *sf* (*sigillo*) seal; (*papale*) bull; (*comm*) bill.

bollare [bol'lare] *v* seal, stamp.

bolletta [bol'letta] *sf* (*comm*) bill, receipt. **essere in bolletta** (*fam*) be broke. **bollettino** *sm* bulletin, list.

bollire [bol'lire] *v* boil. **bollente** *agg* boiling. **bollito** *sm* boiled meat. **bollitore** *sm* kettle.

bollo ['bollo] *sm* stamp, seal. **bollo di circolazione** tax disc.

bomba ['bomba] *sf* bomb.

bombardare [bombar'dare] *v* bomb, shell. **bombardamento** *sm* bombardment, shelling.

bombetta [bom'betta] *sf* bowler hat.

bombola ['bombola] *sf* gas cylinder.

bonario [bo'narjo] *agg* good-natured.

bontà [bon'ta] *sf* goodness.

borbottare [borbot'tare] *v* mutter; rumble.

bordello [bor'dɛllo] *sm* brothel; (*confusione*) uproar.

bordo ['bordo] *sm* (*mar*) side; (*orlo*) border, edge. **a bordo** on board. **giornale di bordo** *sm* (ship's) log. **virare di bordo** (*mar*) tack.

borghese [bor'geze] *agg* bourgeois, middle-class; civilian. *s(m+f)* middle-class person; civilian. **in borghese** in civilian *or* plain clothes. **borghesia** *sf* middle class, bourgeoisie.

borgo ['borgo] *sm* (*paesello*) hamlet; (*sobborgo*) suburb.

boria ['bɔrja] *sf* conceit, arrogance. **metter**

su boria put on airs. **borioso** arrogant, conceited.

borotalco [boro'talko] *sm invar* talcum powder.

borsa[1] ['borsa] *sf* bag; (*della spesa*) shopping bag; (*per documenti*) brief-case; (*diplomatica*) attaché case; (*dell'acqua*) hot-water bottle. **borsa di studio** scholarship, grant. **borsaiolo** *sm* pickpocket. **borsetta** *sf* handbag. **borsista** *s(m+f)* scholarship-holder.

borsa[2] ['borsa] *sf* (*comm*) stock exchange. **borsa nera** black market. **borsista** *sm* stockbroker.

bosco ['bɔsko] *sm* wood, forest. **boscaglia** *sf* thicket. **boschereccio** *agg* woody. **boschetto** *sm* grove. **boscoso** *agg* wooded.

botanico [bo'taniko], **-a** *agg* botanical. *sm, sf* botanist. *sf* botany.

botta ['bɔtta] *sf* blow. **fare a botte** come to blows. **dare le botte a** spank, slap.

botte ['botte] *sf* cask, barrel.

bottega [bot'tega] *sf* shop; (*laboratorio*) workshop. **bottegaio**, **-a** *sm, sf* shopkeeper. **botteghino** *sm* small shop; (*teatro*) box-office.

bottiglia [bot'tiʎa] *sf* bottle.

bottone [bot'tone] *sm* button. **attaccare un bottone a** (*fam*) buttonhole. **bottoni gemelli** cuff-links *pl*.

bozza ['bɔttsa] *sf* draft, sketch; (*stampa*) galley proof. **bozzetto** *sm* sketch.

bozzolo ['bɔttsolo] *sm* cocoon.

braccetto [brat'tʃetto] *sm* **a braccetto** arm in arm.

braccialetto [brattʃa'letto] *sm* bracelet.

bracciante [brat'tʃante] *sm* labourer.

bracciata [brat'tʃata] *sf* armful.

braccio ['brattʃo] *sm, pl* **-a** *f in anat sense* arm. **prendere in braccio** take into one's arms. **bracciolo** *sm* (*sedia*) arm.

braciola [bra'tʃɔla] *sf* chop.

bramare [bra'mare] *v* yearn *or* long for. **brama** *sf* longing, strong desire.

branchia ['brankja] *sf* gill.

branco ['branko] *sm* flock, drove, herd.

brancolare [branko'lare] *v* grope.

branda ['branda] *sf* camp-bed.

brandello [bran'dello] *sm* shred, tatter.

brandire [bran'dire] *v* brandish.

brano ['brano] *sm* (*pezzo*) shred, piece; (*frammento di opera*) passage, extract.

branzino [bran'dzino] *sm* sea bass.

brasare [bra'zare] *v* braise. **brasato** *sm* braised beef.

bravo ['bravo] *agg* good; capable; (*dabbene*) decent. *inter* well done! **bravura** *sf* skill.

breccia ['brettʃa] *sf* breach.

bretelle [bre'tɛlle] *sf pl* braces *pl*.

breve ['brɛve] *agg* brief, short. *sf* breve. **per farla breve** to cut a long story short. **tra breve** shortly. **brevità** *sf* brevity.

brevetto [bre'vetto] *sm* patent. **brevettare** *v* patent.

brezza ['brettsa] *sf* breeze.

bricco ['brikko] *sm* jug, pot.

briccone [brik'kone] *sm* knave, rascal. *agg* knavish, mischievous.

briciola ['britʃola] *sf* crumb. **briciolo** *sm* tiny piece, morsel.

bridge ['bridʒ] *sm invar* (*carte*) bridge.

briga ['briga] *sf* trouble. **attaccar briga** pick a quarrel. **darsi** *or* **prendersi la briga di** go to the trouble of.

brigadiere [briga'djɛre] *sm* sergeant-major; (*generale*) brigadier.

brigante [bri'gante] *sm* brigand, bandit.

brigata [bri'gata] *sf* company, group; (*mil*) brigade; (*uccelli*) flock.

briglia ['briʎa] *sf* bridle. **tenere in briglia** rein in, restrain.

brillare [bril'lare] *v* shine, sparkle, glitter. **brillante** *agg* sparkling, brilliant. **brillo** *agg* tipsy.

brina ['brina] *sf* rime, hoar-frost.

brindare [brin'dare] *v* **brindare a** drink to, toast.

brindello [brin'dɛllo] *sm* shred, tatter.

brindisi ['brindizi] *sm* toast. **fare un brindisi a** drink to, toast.

brio ['brio] *sm* liveliness, vivacity.

britannico [bri'tanniko], **-a** *agg* British. *sm, sf* Briton, British person.

brivido ['brivido] *sm* shudder, shiver. **aver dei brividi** shudder, shiver.

brocca ['brɔkka] *sf* jug, pitcher.

broccolo ['brɔkkolo] *sm* broccoli.

brodo ['brɔdo] *sm* broth, soup. **tutto fa brodo** it is all grist to the mill.

broglio ['brɔʎo] *sm* malpractice, racket.

bronchite [bron'kite] *sf* bronchitis.

broncio ['brontʃo] *sm* **tenere** *or* **portare il broncio** sulk.

brontolare [bronto'lare] *v* mutter, grumble. **brontolone**, **-a** *sm, sf* grumbler.

bronzo ['brondzo] *sm* bronze.

bruciapelo [brutʃa'pelo] *sm* **a bruciapelo** point-blank.

bruciare [bru'tʃare] *v* burn, scorch. **bruciare le tappe** hurry. **bruciatura** *sf* burn, scald. **bruciore** *sm* burning sensation, intense desire.

bruco ['bruko] *sm* larva, caterpillar.

brufolo ['brufolo] *sm* pimple.

brughiera [bru'gjɛra] *sf* heath, moor.

brulicare [bruli'kare] *v* swarm, crawl, teem. **brulichio** *sm* swarming, teeming.

brullo ['brullo] *agg* bleak; barren.

bruno ['bruno] *agg* brown; dark.

brusco ['brusko] *agg* sharp; brusque, harsh; (*improvviso*) sudden.

brusio [bru'zio] *sm* bustle, hum.

bruto ['bruto] *sm, agg* brute. **brutale** *agg* brutal.

brutto ['brutto] *agg* ugly, plain; (*non buono*) bad. **avere brutta cera** look poorly. **far brutta figura** cut a sorry figure, disgrace oneself. **il brutto è che** the worst is (that), the difficulty is (that).

buca ['buka] *sf* hole, pit. **buca delle lettere** *sf* letter-box. **bucare** *v* make a hole in; (*biglietto*) punch; (*gomma*) puncture. **bucatura** *sf* puncture.

bucaneve [buka'neve] *sm invar* snowdrop.

bucato [bu'kato] *sm* washing. **fare il bucato** do the washing.

buccia ['buttʃa] *sf* peel, skin, rind.

buco ['buko] *sm* hole. **buco nell'acqua** failure.

buddismo [bud'dizmo] *sm* Buddhism. **buddista** *s(m+f)*, *agg* Buddhist.

budello [bu'dɛllo] *sm* gut.

budino [bu'dino] *sm* pudding.

bue ['bue] *sm, pl* **buoi** ox (*pl* -en); (*carne*) beef.

bufalo ['bufalo], **-a** *sm, sf* buffalo.

bufera [bu'fɛra] *sf* gale, blizzard.

buffè [buf'fɛ] *sm invar* (*credenza*) sideboard; (*gastr*) buffet.

buffo ['buffo] *agg* comic(al), amusing. *sm* (*teatro*) comic. **il buffo è che** the odd thing is (that).

bugia[1] [bu'dʒia] *sf* lie. **dire bugie** tell lies. **bugiardo**, **-a** *sm, sf* liar.

bugia[2] [bu'dʒia] *sf* candlestick.

buio ['bujo] *sm, agg* dark. **al buio** in the dark. **buio pesto** pitch-dark.

bulbo ['bulbo] *sm* bulb. **bulbo oculare** eyeball.

Bulgaria [bulga'ria] *sf* Bulgaria. **bulgaro**, **-a** *s*, *agg* Bulgarian.

bullone [bul'lone] *sm* bolt.

buono¹ ['bwɔno], **-a** *agg* good; kind; (*giusto*) right. **a buon conto** apropos. **a buon mercato** cheap(ly). **alla buona** simply. **buoncostume** *sm* good conduct. **buongustaio, -a** *sm, sf* gourmet. **buongusto** *sm* good taste. **buono a nulla** *sm, agg* good-for-nothing. **buonsenso** *sm* good sense. **con le buone o con le cattive** by hook or by crook. *sm, sf* good person.
buono² ['bwɔno] *sm* (*documento*) bond, coupon, voucher.
buonora [bwo'nora] *sf* **alla buonora!** at last! **di buonora** early.
burattino [burat'tino] *sm* puppet.
burbero ['burbero], **-a** *agg* grumpy, gruff. *sm, sf* grumpy person.
burlare [bur'lare] *v* make a fool of; (*scherzare*) joke. **burlarsi di** make fun of. **burla** *sf* joke, jest.
burocrate [bu'rɔkrate] *sm* bureaucrat. **burocratico** *agg* bureaucratic. **burocrazia** *sf* bureaucracy; (*fam*) red tape.
burrasca [bur'raska] *sf* blizzard, storm. **burrascoso** *agg* stormy.
burro ['burro] *sm* butter.
burrone [bur'rone] *sm* ravine.
bussare [bus'sare] *v* knock.
bussola ['bussola] *sf* compass.
busta ['busta] *sf* envelope.
bustarella [busta'rella] *sf* bribe.
busto ['busto] *sm* bust; (*indumento*) corset.
buttare [but'tare] throw. **buttar giù** (*cibo*) gulp down; (*scritto*) jot down; (*gastr*) put in boiling water.

C

cabina [ka'bina] *sf* (*aero, mar*) cabin; (*telefono, ecc.*) booth; (*ascensore*) cage.
cablogramma [kablo'gramma] *sm* cable.
cacao [ka'kao] *sm* cocoa.
cacare [ka'kare] *v* (*volg*) shit.
caccia¹ ['kattʃa] *sf* hunt, chase; (*ricerca*) pursuit, search. **a caccia di** in search of. **caccia grossa** big game. **dar la caccia** pursue.
caccia² ['kattʃa] *sm invar* (*aero*) fighter; (*mar*) destroyer.
cacciagione [kattʃa'dʒone] *sf* game.
cacciare [kat'tʃare] *v* hunt; (*espellere*) throw *or* drive out; (*introdurre*) thrust; (*mettere*) stick, put.

cacciavite [kattʃa'vite] *sm* screwdriver.
cachi ['kaki] *agg, sm* khaki.
cacio ['katʃo] *sm* cheese.
cactus ['kaktus] *sm* cactus.
cadauno [kada'uno] *agg, pron* each.
cadavere [ka'davere] *sm* corpse.
***cadere** [ka'dere] *v* fall; (*aero*) crash. **cader dalle nuvole** be dumbfounded. **lasciar cadere** drop. **caduta** *sf* fall; (*aero*) crash.
cadetto [ka'detto] *sm* younger son; (*mil*) cadet.
caffè [kaf'fɛ] *sm* coffee; (*locale*) café. **caffettiera** *sf* coffee-pot; (*macchina*) coffee-maker.
caffeina [kaffe'ina] *sf* caffeine.
cafone [ka'fone] *sm* (*fam*) lout.
cagionare [kadʒo'nare] *v* cause. **cagione** *sf* cause, reason. **a cagion di** on account of, owing to.
cagna ['kaɲa] *sf* bitch.
cagnara [ka'ɲara] *sf* (*fam*) row, uproar.
calabrone [kala'brone] *sm* hornet.
calamaio [kala'majo] *sm* inkstand, inkwell.
calamaro [kala'maro] *sm* squid.
calamita [kala'mita] *sf* magnet.
calamità [kalami'ta] *sf* calamity.
calare [ka'lare] *v* lower, let down; (*maglia*) decrease, cast off; (*scendere*) go down; (*abbassarsi*) drop. **calata** *sf* descent; (*banchina*) quay.
calcagno [kal'kaɲo] *sm* heel. **stare alle calcagna di** follow closely.
calcare¹ [kal'kare] *v* press (hard); (*disegno*) trace. **calco** *sm* (*impronta di rilievo*) cast; (*disegno*) tracing.
calcare² [kal'kare] *sm* limestone.
calce ['kaltʃe] *sf* lime.
calcestruzzo [kaltʃes'truttso] *sm* concrete.
calcio¹ ['kaltʃo] *sm* (*chim*) calcium.
calcio² ['kaltʃo] *sm* (*fucile*) (rifle) butt.
calcio³ ['kaltʃo] *sm* kick; (*sport*) football. **calcio di rigore** penalty (kick). **dare un calcio** kick.
calcolare [kalko'lare] *v* calculate; consider. **calcolatore, -trice** *sm, sf* calculator, computer.
calcolo¹ ['kalkolo] *sm* calculation; (*congettura*) reckoning; (*mat*) calculus. **a calcoli fatti** all things considered.
calcolo² ['kalkolo] *sm* (*med*) calculus, stone.

caldaia [kal'daja] *sf* boiler.

caldo ['kaldo] *agg* warm; (*molto*) hot. *sm* warmth; heat. **aver** *or* **far caldo** be hot.

caleidoscopio [kaleido'skɔpjo] *sm* kaleidoscope.

calendario [kalen'darjo] *sm* calendar.

calibro ['kalibro] *sm* calibre; (*mec*) gauge; (*strumento*) callipers *pl*.

calice ['kalitʃe] *sm* goblet; (*rel*) chalice; (*bot*) calyx.

caligine [ka'lidʒine] *sf* fog.

calligrafia [kalligra'fia] *sf* handwriting.

callo ['kallo] *sm* corn. **callifugo** *sm, pl* -**ghi** corn-plaster.

calmare [kal'mare] *v* calm; ease. **calmarsi** *v* calm down. **calma** *sf* calm, tranquillity. **perdere la calma** lose one's temper. **prendersela con calma** take it easy. **calmante** *sm* sedative. **calmo** *agg* calm.

calore [ka'lore] *sm* heat; (*cordialità*) warmth.

caloria [kalo'ria] *sf* calorie.

calorifero [kalo'rifero] *sm* radiator.

caloroso [kalo'rozo] *agg* warm.

calpestare [kalpes'tare] *v* trample on.

calunnia [ka'lunnja] *sf* calumny; (*diffamazione orale*) slander; (*scritta*) libel. **calunniare** *v* slander; libel.

calvo ['kalvo] *agg* bald. **calvizie** *sf* baldness.

calza ['kaltsa] *sf* (*corta*) sock; (*lunga*) stocking. **fare la calza** knit. **ferro da calza** *sm* knitting-needle.

calzare [kal'tsare] *v* put on; (*portare*) wear; (*convenire*) fit. **calzatura** *sf* footwear.

calzolaio [kaltso'lajo] *sm* shoemaker. **calzoleria** *sf* shoe shop.

calzoni [kal'tsoni] *sm pl* trousers *pl*.

camaleonte [kamale'onte] *sm* chameleon.

cambiale [kam'bjale] *sf* bill of exchange.

cambiare [kam'bjare] *v* change. **cambiar casa** move. **tanto per cambiare** just for a change. **cambiamento** *sm* change.

cambio ['kambjo] *sm* change; (*econ*) exchange; (*auto*) transmission, gearbox.

camera ['kamera] *sf* room; (*da letto*) bedroom; (*assemblea, tec*) chamber. **camera d'aria** (*pneumatico*) inner tube. **musica da camera** *sf* chamber music.

camerata¹ [kame'rata] *sf* dormitory.

camerata² [kame'rata] *s(m + f)* comrade; (*fam*) mate.

cameriera [kame'rjɛra] *sf* (*albergo*) chamber-maid; (*ristorante*) waitress; (*domestica*) maid.

cameriere [kame'rjɛre] *sm* (*ristorante*) waiter; servant.

camicia [ka'mitʃa] *sf* shirt; (*da donna*) blouse; (*tec*) jacket. **camicia da notte** night-gown. **camicia di forza** strait-jacket. **camiciola** *sf* (*maglia*) vest; T-shirt.

camino [ka'mino] *sm* fireplace; chimney.

camion [ka'mjon] *sm invar* truck. **camioncino** *sm* van.

cammello [kam'mɛllo] *sm* camel.

camminare [kammi'nare] *v* walk; (*procedere*) go. **camminata** *sf* walk.

cammino [kam'mino] *sm* way; (*percorso*) journey; (*sentiero*) path. **mettersi in cammino** set out.

camorra [ka'mɔrra] *sf* racket. **camorrista** *s(m + f)* racketeer.

camoscio [ka'mɔʃo] *sm* chamois; (*pelle*) chamois leather.

campagna [kam'paɲa] *sf* country; (*paesaggio*) countryside; (*terreno*) land; (*villeggiatura*) holidays *pl*; (*mil, propaganda, ecc.*) campaign. **campagnolo** *agg* rural, country.

campana [kam'pana] *sf* bell; (*di lampada*) lampshade. **campanello** *sm* bell. **campanile** *sm* bell tower.

campare [kam'pare] *v* live.

campeggiare [kamped'dʒare] *v* camp. **campeggio** *sm* camping; (*terreno*) campsite.

campestre [kam'pɛstre] *agg* rural, country.

campione [kam'pjone] *sm* (*sport, difensore*) champion; (*piccola quantità*) sample; (*di tessuto*) pattern. **campionario** *sm* sample collection; pattern book. **campionessa** *sf* champion.

campo ['kampo] *sm* field. **campo di golf** golf-course. **campo di tennis** tennis court.

camposanto [kampo'santo] *sm* cemetery.

camuffamento [kamuffa'mento] *sm* disguise; (*mil*) camouflage. **camuffare** *v* disguise; camouflage.

camuso [ka'muzo] *agg* snub-nosed.

Canada ['kanada] *sm* Canada. **Canadese** *s(m + f), agg* Canadian.

canaglia [ka'naʎa] *sf* scoundrel; (*marmaglia*) rabble.

canale [ka'nale] *sm* canal; (*radio, TV*) channel. **Canale della Manica** (English)

Channel. **canale di scarico** drain. **canale di scolo** gutter.

canapa ['kanapa] *sf* hemp.

canapè [kana'pɛ] *sm* (*mobile*) settee; (*tartina*) canapé.

canarino [kana'rino] *sm* canary. *agg* canary yellow.

cancellare [kantʃel'lare] *v* cancel, wipe out; (*con gomma*) rub out; (*con penna*) cross out.

cancelliere [kantʃel'ljɛre] *sm* chancellor.

cancelleria *sf* chancellery, chancery; (*cartoleria*) stationery.

cancello [kan'tʃello] *sm* gate. **cancellata** *sf* railings *pl*.

cancro [kan'kro] *sm* cancer. **Cancro** *sm* Cancer.

cancrena [kan'krena] *sf* gangrene.

candeggiare [kanded'dʒare] *v* bleach. **candeggina** *sf* bleach.

candela [kan'dela] *sf* candle; (*auto*) sparking-plug. **precipitare in candela** do a nose-dive. **candelabro** *sm* candlestick; (*a bracci*) candelabra.

candidato [kandi'dato], **-a** *sm, sf* candidate. **candidatura** *sf* candidature.

candido ['kandido] *agg* spotless, snow-white; (*sincero*) candid.

candito [kan'dito] *agg* candied, crystallized.

cane ['kane] *sm* dog. **cane bastardo** mongrel. **cane da guardia** watch-dog. **cane da salotto** lap-dog.

canestro [ka'nɛstro] *sm* basket.

canguro [kan'guro] *sm* kangaroo.

canicola [ka'nikola] *sm* heat-wave.

canile [ka'nile] *sm* kennel.

canino [ka'nino] *agg* canine.

canna ['kanna] *sf* cane; (*pianta*) reed; (*fucile*) barrel; (*bicicletta*) cross-bar; (*pesca*) rod; (*tubo, organo*) pipe. **cannello** *sm* tube; (*per saldare*) blowpipe.

cannella [kan'nɛlla] *sf* cinnamon.

cannibale [kan'nibale] *sm* cannibal.

cannocchiale [kannok'kjale] *sm* telescope.

cannone [kan'none] *sm* cannon. **cannonata** *sf* cannon shot. **è una cannonata!** (*fam*) it's terrific!

cannuccia [kan'nuttʃa] .*sf* (*per bibite*) (drinking) straw; (*di pipa*) stem.

canoa [ka'nɔa] *sf* canoe.

canone ['kanone] *sm* canon; (*soldi dovuti*) fee; (*per affitto*) rent.

canonico [ka'nɔniko] *agg* canonical. **diritto canonico** *sm* canon law. **canonica** *sf* rectory.

canonizzare [kanonid'dzare] *v* canonize.

canottaggio [kanot'taddʒo] *sm* rowing. **canottiere** *sm* oarsman.

canottiera [kanot'tjera] *sf* T-shirt.

canotto [ka'nɔtto] *sm* rowing-boat; (*di salvataggio*) lifeboat.

canovaccio [kano'vattʃo] *sm* (*per stoviglie*) dishcloth; (*teatro*) plot.

cantare [kan'tare] *v* sing; (*del gallo*) crow; (*cinguettare*) chirp; (*fam*: *fare la spia*) squeal. **cantata** *sf* singsong; (*musica*) cantata. **canterellare** *or* **canticchiare** *v* hum.

cantiere [kan'tjere] *sm* yard; (*mar*) shipyard, dockyard.

cantilena [kanti'lena] *sf* singsong.

cantina [kan'tina] *sf* cellar.

canto¹ ['kanto] *sm* song; (*poesia*) lyric; (*liturgia*) chant. **canto popolare** folksong.

canto² ['kanto] *sm* (*angolo*) corner; (*parte*) side. **da canto** aside. **d'altro canto** on the other hand. **da un canto** in a way.

cantone¹ [kan'tone] *sm* corner. **cantonata** *sf* (street-)corner; (*errore*) blunder. **prendere una cantonata** blunder.

cantone² [kan'tone] *sm* (*geog*) canton.

cantoniere [kanto'njere] *sm* (*ferr*) signalman.

canuto [ka'nuto] *agg* white-haired.

canzonare [kantso'nare] *v* make fun of, tease, mock. **canzonatore, -trice** *sm, sf* mocker. **canzonatura** *sf* mockery.

canzone [kan'tsone] *sf* song; (*discorso noioso*) old story. **canzonetta** *sf* pop song.

caos ['kaos] *sm* chaos. **caotico** *agg* chaotic.

capace [ka'patʃe] *agg* (*abile*) capable; (*in grado di*) able. **capacità** *sf* capacity; ability.

capanna [ka'panna] *sf* hut. **capannone** *sm* shed; (*aero*) hangar.

caparbio [ka'parbjo] *agg* stubborn.

caparra [ka'parra] *sf* deposit.

capello [ka'pello] *sm* hair. **capelli** *sm pl* hair *sing*. **averne fin sopra i capelli** (**di**) be heartily sick (of). **capelluto** *agg* hairy. **cuoio capelluto** *sm* scalp.

capezzale [kapet'tsale] *sm* **al capezzale** at the bedside.

capezzolo [ka'pettsolo] *sm* nipple.

capire [ka'pire] *v* understand; (*rendersi*

conto) realize. **farsi capire** make oneself understood. **si capisce** naturally.

capitale [kapi'tale] *sm* (*econ*) capital. *sf* capital (city). *agg* capital. fundamental; (*principale*) main. **capitalismo** *sm* capitalism. **capitalista** *s(m+f)*, *agg* capitalist.

capitano [kapi'tano] *sm* captain.

capitare [kapi'tare] *v* (*giungere*) turn up; (*presentarsi*) arise, come up; (*accadere*) happen. **capitar bene** strike lucky. **dove capita** anywhere.

capitello [kapi'tɛllo] *sm* capital.

capitolo [ka'pitolo] *sm* chapter. **aver voce in capitolo** have a say in the matter.

capo ['kapo] *sm* head; (*pezzo*) item; (*geog*) cape. **da capo** again, from the beginning. **da capo a fondo** from top to bottom. **da un capo all'altro** from one end to the other. **in capo a** within. **per sommi capi** briefly, in short. **venire a capo di** get to the bottom of.

capobanda [kapo'banda] *sm invar* ringleader; (*musica*) bandmaster.

capodanno [kapo'danno] *sm* New Year's Day.

capofitto [kapo'fitto] *agg* **a capofitto** headlong; (*con massimo impegno*) wholeheartedly.

capogiro [kapo'dʒiro] *sm* giddiness, dizzy spell. **fare venire il capogiro a** make dizzy.

capolavoro [kapola'voro] *sm* masterpiece.

capolinea [kapo'linea] *sm*, *pl* **capilinea** terminus.

capoluogo [kapo'lwɔgo] *sm*, *pl* **-ghi** main town, capital.

capomastro [kapo'mastro] *sm* foreman.

capoofficina [kapoofi'tʃina] *sm*, *pl* **capiofficina** foreman.

caporale [kapo'rale] *sm* corporal.

caposala [kapo'sala] *s(m+f)*, *pl* **capisala**, **caposala** (*fabbrica*) foreman; (*albergo*) head-waiter; (*ospedale*) ward sister.

capostazione [kaposta'tsjone] *sm*, *pl* **capistazione** station-master.

capotare [kapo'tare] *v* (*auto*) overturn; (*mar*) capsize.

capote [ka'pɔt] *sf*, *pl* **-s** (*auto*) hood.

capotreno [kapo'treno] *sm* guard.

*capovolgere [kapo'vɔldʒere] *v* overturn; (*fig*) turn upside down, reverse; (*mar*) capsize. **capovolgimento** *sm* reversal.

cappa ['kappa] *sf* cloak; (*di camino*) hood.

cappella¹ [kap'pɛlla] *sf* chapel. **cappellano** *sm* chaplain.

cappella² [kap'pɛlla] *sf* (*di fungo*) cap.

cappello [kap'pɛllo] *sm* hat. **cappellaio** *sm* hatter.

cappero ['kappero] *sm* caper. **capperi!** *inter* gosh! good heavens!

cappotta [kap'pɔtta] *sf* (*auto*) hood.

cappotto [kap'pɔtto] *sm* coat; (*bridge*) slam.

cappuccino [kapput'tʃino] *sm* coffee with milk, cappuccino; (*rel*) Capuchin friar.

cappuccio [kap'puttʃo] *sm* hood; (*tec*) cap; (*rel*) cowl.

capra ['kapra] *sf* goat. **capretto** *sm* kid. **capro** *sm* he-goat. **capro espiatorio** scapegoat.

capriccio [ka'prittʃo] *sm* whim, fancy. **fare i capricci** have tantrums.

Capricorno [kapri'kɔrno] *sm* Capricorn.

caprifoglio [kapri'fɔʎʎo] *sm* honeysuckle.

capriola¹ [kapri'ɔla] *sf* somersault, jump.

capriola² [kapri'ɔla] *sf* (*zool*) roe deer. **capriolo** *sm* roebuck.

capsico [kap'siko] *sm* capsicum.

capsula ['kapsula] *sf* capsule; (*di dente*) crown.

carabiniere [karabi'njɛre] *sm* policeman, soldier in police corps.

caraffa [ka'raffa] *sf* carafe, jug.

caramella [kara'mɛlla] *sf* sweet. **caramellato** *agg* candied; (*zucchero*) caramelized.

carato [ka'rato] *sm* carat.

carattere [ka'rattere] *sm* (*indole*) nature; (*forza, lettera*) character; characteristic; (*teatro*) role; type. **caratteristica** *sf* characteristic, (*distinctive*) feature; (*tec*) specification. **caratteristico** *agg* typical, distinctive.

carboidrato [karboi'drato] *sm* carbohydrate.

carbonchio [kar'bonkjo] *sm* carbuncle; (*vet*) anthrax; (*agric*) blight.

carbone [kar'bone] *sm* coal. **carbone coke** coke. **carbone di legna** charcoal. **carboncino** *sm* (*disegno*) charcoal.

carbonio [kar'bɔnjo] *sm* carbon.

carburante [karbu'rante] *sm* fuel.

carburatore [karbura'tore] *sm* carburettor.

carcassa [kar'kassa] *sf* carcass; (*fam*) wreck.

carcere ['kartʃere] *sm* prison, jail. **carcerato, -a** *sm*, *sf* prisoner. **carceriere, -a** *sm*, *sf* jailer.

carciofo [kar'tʃɔfo] *sm* artichoke.
cardiaco [kar'diako] *agg* cardiac. **attacco cardiaco** *sm* heart attack. **cardiologo, -a** *sm, sf* heart specialist, cardiologist.
cardinale [kardi'nale] *sm, agg* cardinal.
cardine ['kardine] *sm* hinge; (*fig*) cornerstone.
cardo ['kardo] *sm* (*bot*) thistle.
carena [ka'rɛna] *sf* hull. (**bacino di**) **carenaggio** *sm* dry dock.
carestia [kares'tia] *sf* famine.
carezzare [karet'tsare] *v* stroke, caress. **carezza** *sf* caress. **fare le carezze a** pat, stroke.
cariarsi [ka'rjarsi] *v* decay.
carica ['karika] *sf* (*impiego*) position; (*ufficio pubblico*) office; (*mil, elett*) charge; (*sport*) tackle.
caricare [kari'kare] *v* load; (*riempire*) fill; (*mil, elett*) charge; (*sport*) tackle; (*orologio, molla*) wind up.
caricatura [karika'tura] *sf* caricature.
carico ['kariko] *sm, pl* **-chi** (*di nave*) cargo; (*peso*) burden; (*tec*) load. **a carico di** (*contro*) against; (*a spese di*) at the expense of, chargeable to. **testimone a carico** witness for the prosecution. *agg* loaded, filled (with), full (of).
carie ['karje] *sf* (*dentaria*) tooth decay; (*di legno, cereali, ecc.*) rot.
carino [ka'rino] *agg* lovely, charming.
carità [kari'ta] *sf* charity; (*misericordia*) compassion. **aver carità di** take pity on. **fare la carità** give alms. **per carita!** God forbid!
carlinga [kar'linga] *sf* fuselage.
carnagione [karna'dʒone] *sf* complexion, skin.
carne ['karne] *sf* flesh; (*alimento*) meat. **carne di manzo/maiale/vitello** beef/pork/veal. **carnale** *agg* carnal. **carnoso** *agg* fleshy.
carneficina [karnefi'tʃina] *sf* slaughter. **carnefice** *sm* executioner.
carnevale [karne'vale] *sm* carnival.
carnivoro [kar'nivoro], **-a** *sm, sf* carnivore. *agg* carnivorous.
caro ['karo] *agg* dear. **aver caro** hold dear. **pagar caro** pay a lot for; (*fig*) pay dearly for. **cari** *sm pl* loved ones *pl*.
carogna [ka'roɲa] *sf* carrion; (*fam*) bastard, sod.
carosello [karo'zɛllo] *sm* merry-go-round.
carota [ka'rɔta] *sf* carrot.

carovana [karo'vana] *sf* caravan; procession.
carpione [kar'pjone] *sm* **in carpione** soused.
carponi [kar'poni] *avv* on all fours.
carrabile [kar'rabile] *agg* **passo carrabile** *sm* passageway.
carreggiata [karred'dʒata] *sf* carriageway, track. **rimettersi in carreggiata** catch up. **uscire di carreggiata** go off the road; (*fig*) go astray.
carrello [kar'rɛllo] *sm* (*vagoncino*) trolley; (*mec*) (under-)carriage.
carretta [kar'retta] *sf* cart.
carriera [kar'rjɛra] *sf* career; (*velocità*) full speed. **fare carriera** get on, make good.
carriola [karri'ɔla] *sf* wheelbarrow.
carro ['karro] *sm* (*a quattro ruote*) wagon; (*a due ruote*) cart. **carro armato** armoured vehicle, tank. **carro attrezzi** breakdown van. **carro funebre** hearse. **carro merci** goods wagon.
carrozza [kar'rottsa] *sf* coach. **carrozza letto** sleeping-car, sleeper. **in carrozza!** all aboard!
carrucola [kar'rukola] *sf* pulley.
carta ['karta] *sf* paper; (*geog*) map; (*da gioco, documento*) card; (*statuto*) charter. **carta asciugante** *or* **assorbente** blotting paper. **carta carbone** carbon paper. **carta da parati** wallpaper. **cartapecora** *sf* parchment. **cartapesta** *sf* papier mâché. **cartastraccia** *sf* waste paper.
cartella [kar'tɛlla] *sf* (*custodia per fogli*) folder; (*busta di pelle*) brief-case; (*per scolari*) satchel; (*scheda*) card, file.
cartellino [kartel'lino] *sm* tag.
cartello [kar'tɛllo] *sm* (*insegna*) sign; (*indicatore*) signpost, road sign; (*avviso*) notice, poster. **cartellone** *sm* poster.
cartilagine [karti'ladʒine] *sf* cartilage.
cartolaio [karto'lajo], **-a** *sm, sf* stationer. **cartoleria** *sf* stationer's (shop).
cartolina [karto'lina] *sf* postcard.
cartone [kar'tone] *sm* cardboard; (*disegno*) cartoon. **cartoni animati** (*cinema*) cartoons *pl*. **cartoncino** *sm* card.
cartuccia [kar'tuffʃa] *sf* cartridge.
casa ['kaza] *sf* home; (*edificio, dinastia*) house; (*comm*) firm. **a casa** (*stato in luogo*) at home; (*moto a luogo*) home. **a casa del diavolo** off the beaten track. **cambiar casa** move house. **casa di cura** nursing home. **casa popolare** council house.

casalinga [kaza'linga] *sf* housewife.
casalinghi *sm pl* household goods *pl.*
casalingo *agg* domestic; (*semplice*) homely, plain.
cascame [kas'kame] *sm* waste.
cascare [kas'kare] *v* fall; (*capelli, denti*) fall out; (*muri, ecc.*) fall down. cascata *sf* fall; (*d'acqua*) waterfall; (*perle, ecc.*) cascade.
cascina [ka'ʃina] *sf* dairy farm; (*casa colonica*) farmhouse.
casco ['kasko] *sm* helmet; (*parrucchieri*) hair-drier.
caseggiato [kazed'dʒato] *sm* block of buildings.
casella [ka'zɛlla] *sf* (*riquadro*) square; (*scompartimento*) compartment. casella postale post-office box. casellario *sm* (*mobile*) filing cabinet; (*ufficio*) registry.
casello [ka'zɛllo] *sm* (*ferr*) signal-box; (*autostrada*) toll-booth.
caserma [ka'zɛrma] *sm* barracks *pl.*
casino [ka'zino] *sm* (*fam: confusione*) row, racket; (*postribolo*) brothel; (*casa signorile*) lodge.
casinò [kazi'nɔ] *sm* casino.
caso ['kazo] *sm* case; (*affare*) matter; (*combinazione, destino*) chance; possibility. a caso at random. fare caso a heed, attach importance to. in caso in case. in caso diverso *or* contrario otherwise. in ogni caso in any case, at any rate. per caso by chance. poniamo il caso let us suppose.
cassa ['kassa] *sf* case, box; (*istituzione*) fund; (*dove si paga*) cash desk. cassa da morto coffin. cassa pronta ready cash. libro di cassa cash-book.
casseruola [kasse'rwɔla] *sf* casserole, saucepan.
cassetta [kas'setta] *sf* box; (*teatro*) takings *pl.* cassetto *sm* drawer. cassettone *sm* chest of drawers.
cassiere [kas'sjɛre], -a *sm, sf* cashier.
casta ['kasta] *sf* caste.
castagno [kas'taɲo] *sm* chestnut tree; (*colore*) chestnut. *agg* chestnut. castagna *sf* chestnut. castagnola *sf* (*petardo*) cracker.
castello [kas'tɛllo] *sm* castle; (*impalcatura*) scaffolding. castello di poppa quarterdeck. castello di prua forecastle.
castigare [kasti'gare] *v* punish. castigo *sm*, *pl* -ghi punishment.

casto ['kasto] *agg* chaste. castità *sf* chastity.
castoro [kas'tɔro] *sm* beaver.
castrare [kas'trare] *v* castrate, geld. castrato *sm* (*carne*) lamb.
casuale [kazu'ale] *agg* fortuitous, accidental; (*dir*) contingent. casualmente *avv* by chance.
catacomba [kata'komba] *sf* catacomb.
catafascio [kata'faʃo] *sm* andare a catafascio go to rack and ruin.
catalizzatore [kataliddza'tore] *sm* catalyst. *agg* catalytic.
catalogo [ka'talogo] *sm, pl* -ghi catalogue, list. catalogare *v* catalogue, list.
catapulta [kata'pulta] *sf* catapult; (*missili*) launcher. catapultare *v* launch.
catarifrangente [katarifran'dʒɛnte] *sm* reflector.
catarro [ka'tarro] *sm* catarrh.
catasta [ka'tasta] *sf* pile.
catastrofe [ka'tastrofe] *sf* catastrophe. catastrofico *agg* catastrophic.
catechismo [kate'kizmo] *sm* catechism.
categoria [katego'ria] *sf* category, class. categorico *agg* categorical, absolute, explicit.
catena [ka'tena] *sf* chain. catena di montaggio assembly line. catenaccio *sm* bolt; (*fam: macchina vecchia*) old crock; (*sport*) defensive tactics *pl.*
cateratta [kate'ratta] *sf* cataract; (*chiusa*) floodgate.
catetere [kate'tɛre] *sm* catheter.
catino [ka'tino] *sm* basin. piovere a catinelle rain cats and dogs.
catodo ['katodo] *sm* cathode.
catrame [ka'trame] *sm* tar.
cattedra ['kattedra] *sf* (*tavola*) desk; (*ufficio di insegnante*) teaching post; (*carica universitaria*) chair.
cattedrale [katte'drale] *sf* cathedral.
cattivarsi [katti'varsi] *v* win, gain.
cattivo [kat'tivo] *agg* bad; (*in senso morale*) wicked; (*scortese*) nasty; (*capriccioso*) naughty. cattiveria *sf* wickedness, naughtiness; (*parole cattive*) spiteful remark.
cattolico [kat'tɔliko], -a *s, agg* Catholic. Cattolicesimo *sm* Catholicism.
catturare [kattu'rare] *v* capture, arrest. cattura *sf* capture, arrest.
caucciù [kaut'tʃu] *sm* rubber.
causa ['kauza] *sf* cause; (*dir*) lawsuit,

245 **centrale**

action. **a causa di** because of, on account of. **fare causa a** sue. **causale** *agg* causal.

causare [kau'zare] *v* cause, give rise to, bring about.

caustico ['kaustiko] *agg* caustic.

cauto ['kauto] *agg* cautious, careful. **cautela** *sf* caution; (*precauzione*) care.

cauzione [kau'tsjone] *sf* (*caparra*) security, bail. **rilasciare su cauzione** release on bail. **cauzionare** *v* pay a deposit.

cava ['kava] *sf* quarry.

cavalcare [kaval'kare] *v* ride; (*ponte*) span. **cavalcata** *sf* ride. **cavalcavia** *sm invar* flyover. **a cavalcioni** astride.

cavaliere [kava'ljɛre] *sm* knight; (*chi cavalca*) rider.

cavalleria [kavalle'ria] *sf* (*mil*) cavalry; (*medievale, cortesia*) chivalry. **cavalleresco** *agg* chivalrous. **cavallerizza** *sf* horsewoman; (*maneggio*) riding school. **cavallerizzo** *sm* horseman; (*chi insegna*) riding master.

cavalletta [kaval'letta] *sf* grasshopper.

cavalletto [kaval'letto] *sm* (*sostegno*) trestle, stand; (*da pittore*) easel.

cavallo [ka'vallo] *sm* horse; (*scacchi*) knight. **a cavallo** on horseback. **a cavallo di** astride, straddling. **andare a cavallo** ride. **cavallo dei pantaloni** crotch. **cavalla** *sf* mare. **cavallina** *sf* filly. **correre la cavallina** sow one's wild oats.

cavare [ka'vare] *v* draw *or* pull out. **cavarsela** *v* get by, manage. **cavarsi** *v* (*togliersi*) take off. **cavatappi** *sm invar* corkscrew.

caverna [ka'vɛrna] *sf* cave. **cavernoso** *agg* cavernous, hollow.

cavia ['kavia] *sf* guinea pig.

caviale [ka'vjale] *sm* caviar.

caviglia [ka'viʎa] *sf* ankle.

cavillare [kavil'lare] *v* quibble.

cavo[1] ['kavo] *sm*, *agg* (*vuoto*) hollow.

cavo[2] ['kavo] *sm* cable.

cavolo ['kavolo] *sm* cabbage. **cavoli di Bruxelles** Brussels sprouts *pl*. **cavolfiore** *sm* cauliflower. **testa di cavolo** (*fam*) clot.

cazzo ['kattso] *sm* (*volg*) prick.

cazzotto [kat'tsɔtto] *sm* (*fam*) punch. **fare a cazzotti** fight.

ce [tʃe] *V* **ci**.

cece ['tʃetʃe] *sm* chick-pea.

cecità [tʃetʃi'ta] *sf* blindness.

Cecoslovacchia [tʃekozlo'vakkja] *sf* Czechoslovakia. **ceco(slovacco)**, **-a** *s*, *agg* Czech(oslovak).

cedere ['tʃɛdere] *v* yield; (*trasferire*) hand over; (*piegarsi*) give way. **cedere il passo** make way. **cedere il posto** give up one's seat.

cedola ['tʃɛdola] *sf* (*scontrino*) coupon; (*di titolo*) dividend voucher.

cedro[1] ['tʃedro] *sm* (*agrume*) citron.

cedro[2] ['tʃedro] *sm* (*conifera*) cedar.

ceffone [tʃef'fone] *sm* slap (in the face).

celare [tʃe'lare] *v* conceal, hide.

celebrare [tʃele'brare] *v* celebrate.

celebre ['tʃɛlebre] *agg* famous. **celebrità** *sf* fame; (*persona*) celebrity.

celere ['tʃelere] *agg* rapid. *sf* flying squad.

celeste [tʃe'lɛste] *agg*, *sm* sky-blue.

celibe ['tʃɛlibe] *agg* single. *sm* bachelor.

cella ['tʃɛlla] *sf* cell. **cella frigorifera** cold storage.

cellula ['tʃɛllula] *sf* cell.

cellulosa [tʃellu'loza] *sf* cellulose.

cemento [tʃe'mento] *sm* cement. **cemento armato** reinforced concrete. **cementare** *v* cement.

cena ['tʃena] *sf* supper, dinner. **cenare** *v* have supper *or* dinner.

cencio ['tʃentʃo] *sm* rag; (*per stoviglie*) dishcloth; (*per spolverare*) duster. **cencioso** *agg* ragged, tattered.

cenere ['tʃenere] *sf* ash. **Ceneri** *sf pl* Ash Wednesday *sing*.

cenno ['tʃenno] *sm* sign, gesture; (*col capo*) nod; (*con gli occhi*) wink; (*con la mano*) wave; (*allusione*) mention.

censimento [tʃensi'mento] *sm* census.

censurare [tʃensu'rare] *v* (*biasimare*) censure; (*sottoporre a censura*) censor. **censura** *sf* censorship; (*riprovazione*) censure.

centenario [tʃente'narjo], **-a** *sm*, *sf* centenarian. *sm* (*ricorrenza*) centenary. *agg* hundred-year-old.

centesimo [tʃen'tɛzimo] *sm* hundredth; (*soldo*) cent. *agg* hundredth.

centigrado [tʃen'tigrado] *agg* centigrade.

centimetro [tʃen'timetro] *sm* centimetre; (*nastro per misurare*) tape-measure.

cento ['tʃɛnto] *agg*, *sm* hundred. **per cento** per cent. **centinaio** *sm*, *pl* **-a** *f* hundred; (*circa cento*) about a hundred. **a centinaia** by the hundred, in hundreds.

centrale [tʃen'trale] *agg* central, principal. *sf* (*deposito*) main depot; (*del telefono*) exchange; (*di energia*) power station; (*di amministrazione*) head office. **centralino** *sm* switchboard. **centralista** *s(m+f)* switchboard operator.

centro ['tʃɛntro] *sm* centre; *(mezzo)* middle; *(luogo di soggiorno)* resort; *(fam: colpo centrato)* bull's-eye.

ceppo ['tʃeppo] *sm (razza)* stock; *(base di albero)* stump; *(pezzo di legno)* block; *(auto)* brake-block. **ceppi** *sm pl* fetters *pl*.

cera¹ ['tʃera] *sf* wax; *(per lucidare)* polish. **dare la cera** wax. **ceralacca** *sf* sealing-wax.

cera² ['tʃera] *sf (aspetto)* air, expression. **aver buona/brutta cera** look well/ill. **far buona cera a** welcome heartily.

ceramica [tʃe'ramika] *sf (oggetto)* piece of pottery; *(materiale)* earthenware; *(arte)* pottery. **ceramiche** *sf pl* pottery *sing*. **ceramista** *s(m+f)* potter.

cercare [tʃer'kare] *v* look for, search for; *(nei libri)* look up; *(tentare)* try; *(volere)* want. **cerca** *sf* search; *(questua)* begging.

cerchia ['tʃerkja] *sf* circle.

cerchio ['tʃerkjo] *sm* circle; *(giocattolo, di botte)* hoop. **fare cerchio intorno a** circle round.

cereale [tʃere'ale] *sm, agg* cereal.

cerebrale [tʃere'brale] *agg* cerebral.

cerimonia [tʃeri'mɔnja] *sf* ceremony. **far cerimonie** stand on ceremony. **senza cerimonie** without fuss. **cerimoniale** *sm, agg* ceremonial.

cerino [tʃe'rino] *sm (candela)* taper; *(fiammifero)* wax match.

cerniera [tʃer'njɛra] *sf* hinge; *(di borsetta)* clasp. **cerniera lampo** zip fastener.

cernita ['tʃernita] *sf* choice.

cero ['tʃero] *sm* (church) candle.

cerotto [tʃe'rɔtto] *sm* plaster.

certezza [tʃer'tettsa] *sf* certainty.

certificare [tʃertifi'kare] *v* certify. **certificato** *sm* certificate.

certo ['tʃɛrto] *agg* certain. *avv* certainly. **dare** *or* **sapere per certo** know for a fact. **tenere per certo** have no doubts about.

certuni [tʃer'tuni] *pron* some (people).

cervello [tʃer'vɛllo] *sm* brain; *(intelligenza, cibo)* brains *pl*. **dare al cervello** go to one's head.

cervo ['tʃervo] *sm* deer, stag. **cervo volante** *(insetto)* stag beetle; *(aquilone)* kite. **cerva** *sf* deer, doe, hind.

cesello [tʃe'zɛllo] *sm (strumento)* engraving tool, small chisel. **cesellare** *v* engrave, chisel; *(fare con cura)* polish.

cesoie [tʃe'zɔje] *sf pl* shears *pl*.

cespo ['tʃespo] *sm (di erbe)* tuft; *(di fiori)* cluster. **cespo di lattuga** head of lettuce.

cespuglio [tʃes'puʎo] *sm* shrub, bush.

cessare [tʃes'sare] *v* cease, stop. **cessate il fuoco** *sm* cease-fire. **cessazione** *sf* cessation; *(comm)* termination, stoppage.

cessione [tʃes'sjone] *sf* relinquishment; *(dir)* transfer, assignment.

cesso ['tʃesso] *sm (fam)* loo, lavatory.

cesta ['tʃesta] *sf* basket.

cestino [tʃes'tino] *sm* waste-paper basket; *(da lavoro)* work-basket. **cestino da viaggio** packed lunch. **cestinare** *v* throw away; *(scritti)* reject.

cesto ['tʃesto] *sm* basket.

ceto ['tʃɛto] *sm* class.

cetriolo [tʃetri'ɔlo] *sm* cucumber. **cetriolino** *sm* gherkin.

che¹ [ke] *pron (persone: soggetto)* who; *(persone: oggetto)* whom, that; *(cose)* which, that; *(quando)* when; *(dove)* where; *(interrogativo)* what; *(indefinito)* something. *inter* what! *(come)* how! *agg (quale)* what; *(numero limitato)* which. **non è un gran che** it's nothing much.

che² [ke] *cong* that; *(comparativa)* than; *(quando)* when; *(dopo)* after; *(eccettuativa)* but.

checché [ke'ke] *pron* whatever.

chi [ki] *pron (soggetto)* who; *(oggetto)* whom; *(colui che)* he who; *(colei che)* she who; *(coloro che)* those who; *(chiunque)* whoever. **chi ... chi ...** some ... others .... **di chi** whose.

chiacchierare [kjakkje'rare] *v* chat. **chiacchiera** *sf* chat; *(discorso inutile)* idle talk. **far due** *or* **quattro chiacchiere** chat. **chiacchierata** *sf* chat.

chiacchierone [kjakkje'rone], **-a** *agg* talkative; *(pettegolo)* gossipy. *sm, sf* chatterbox, gossip.

chiamare [kja'mare] *v* call; *(far venire)* send for; *(al telefono)* ring (up). **chiamare in giudizio** sue. **chiamare sotto le armi** call up. **chiamata** *sf* call. **chiamata in giudizio** summons. **chiamata urbana/interurbana** local/trunk call.

chiarire [kja'rire] *v* clarify; *(spiegare)* explain.

chiaro ['kjaro] *agg* clear; *(luminoso)* bright; *(non scuro)* light. *sm* light. *avv* clearly, distinctly. **chiaro e tondo** blunt. **mettere in chiaro** clear up.

chiasso ['kjasso] *sm* noise, racket, row. **far chiasso** kick up a row. **chiassoso** *agg* rowdy, noisy; *(colore)* loud.

chiavare [kja'vare] *v* (*volg*) screw, fuck.
chiave ['kjave] *sf* key; (*tec*) spanner; (*segno musicale*) clef. **chiave apritutto** master key. **chiave inglese** adjustable spanner.
chiavistello [kjavis'tɛllo] *sm* bolt, latch.
chiazzare [kjat'tsare] *v* spot; (*con colori diversi*) mottle. **chiazza** *sf* spot; (*sulla pelle*) patch, blotch. **chiazzato** *agg* spotty; blotchy; mottled.
chicco ['kikko] *sm* grain; (*di caffè*) bean; (*d'uva*) grape; (*di grandine*) hailstone; (*del rosario*) bead.
*chiedere ['kjɛdere] *v* ask; (*per avere*) ask for; (*di diritto*) demand; (*vivamente*) beg; (*richiedere*) require; (*prezzo*) charge. **chiedersi** *v* wonder.
chiesa ['kjɛza] *sf* church.
chiglia ['kiʎa] *sf* keel.
chilo ['kilo] *sm* kilo.
chilometro [ki'lɔmetro] *sm* kilometre.
chimera [ki'mɛra] *sf* chimera.
chimico ['kimiko] *agg* chemical. *sm* chemist. **chimica** *sf* (*scienza*) chemistry; (*persona*) chemist.
china[1] ['kina] *sf* slope; decline.
china[2] ['kina] *sf* **inchiostro di china** *sm* Indian ink.
chinare [ki'nare] *v* bend; (*occhi*) lower. **chinarsi** *v* stoop.
chincaglieria [kinkaʎe'ria] *sf* fancy goods *pl*.
chiocciare [kjot'tʃare] *v* cluck; (*covare*) brood. **chioccia** *sf* broody hen.
chiocciola ['kjɔttʃola] *sf* snail; (*anat*) cochlea. **scala a chiocciola** *sf* spiral staircase.
chiodo ['kjɔdo] *sm* nail; fixed idea; (*fam*) debt. **chiodato** *agg* nailed; (*scarpe*) hobnailed.
chioma ['kjɔma] *sf* hair.
chiosco ['kjɔsko] *sm* kiosk, stall.
chiostro ['kjɔstro] *sm* cloister.
chiromante [kiro'mante] *s(m+f)* fortune-teller. **chiromanzia** *sf* fortune-telling.
chirurgia [kirur'dʒia] *sf* surgery. **chirurgico** *agg* surgical. **chirurgo** *sm* surgeon.
chissà [kis'sa] *avv* who knows, goodness knows; (*forse*) perhaps.
chitarra [ki'tarra] *sf* guitar.
*chiudere ['kjudere] *v* close, shut; (*a chiave*) lock (up); (*sbattendo*) slam; (*spegnere*) turn *or* switch off; (*tappare*)

stop up; (*recingere*) enclose. **chiudere bottega** shut up shop. **chiuder dentro** shut in. **chiudere in attivo/perdita** show a profit/loss.
chiunque [ki'unkwe] *pron* whoever; (*qualunque persona*) anyone.
chiusa ['kjuza] *sf* (*parte finale*) close; (*recinto*) enclosure; (*sbarramento artificiale*) lock; (*diga*) dam.
chiuso ['kjuzo] *agg* closed, shut.
chiusura [kju'zura] *sf* (*termine*) end; (*serratura*) fastener; (*il chiudere*) closing, shut-down.
ci [tʃi], **ce** *pron* (to) us; (*riflessivo*) ourselves; (*reciproco*) each other; (*impersonale*) one; (*di ciò*) about it *or* that. **ci conto su** I'm counting on it. **ci penso io** I'll think about it. *avv* (*lì*) there; (*qui*) here.
ciabatta [tʃa'batta] *sf* slipper.
cialda ['tʃalda] *sf* waffle; (*cialdino*) wafer.
ciambella [tʃam'bɛlla] *sf* (*pasta*) doughnut; (*cuscino*) rubber ring; (*di salvataggio*) lifebuoy.
ciambellano [tʃambel'lano] *sm* chamberlain.
cianciare [tʃan'tʃare] *v* prattle away, talk idly.
cianfrusaglia [tʃanfru'zaʎa] *sf* knick-knack, junk.
cianuro [tʃa'nuro] *sm* cyanide.
ciao ['tʃao] *inter* (*incontrandosi*) hello! (*congedandosi*) cheerio! goodbye!
ciarlare [tʃar'lare] *v* chatter, chat. **ciarla** *sf* (*chiacchiera*) chat; (*pettegolezzo*) gossip.
ciarlatano [tʃarla'tano] *sm* charlatan.
ciascuno [tʃas'kuno] *agg* each; (*ogni*) every. *pron* each one; (*ognuno*) everyone.
cibare [tʃi'bare] *v* feed. **cibo** *sm* food.
cicala [tʃi'kala] *sf* cicada.
cicalino [tʃika'lino] *sm* buzzer.
cicatrice [tʃika'tritʃe] *sf* scar.
cicca ['tʃikka] *sf* (*mozzicone*) fag end. **non valere una cicca** be not worth a thing.
cicchetto [tʃik'ketto] *sm* (*bicchierino*) nip; (*rimprovero*) dressing-down.
cicerone [tʃitʃe'rone] *sm* (tourist) guide.
ciclamino [tʃikla'mino] *sm* cyclamen.
ciclismo [tʃi'klizmo] *sm* cycling. **ciclista** *s(m+f)* cyclist.
ciclo ['tʃiklo] *sm* cycle. **ciclico** *agg* cyclical.
ciclomotore [tʃiklomo'tore] *sm* moped.
ciclone [tʃi'klone] *sm* cyclone.

cicogna [tʃi'koɲa] *sf* stork.
cicoria [tʃi'korja] *sf* chicory. **cicoria belga** endive.
cicuta [tʃi'kuta] *sf* hemlock.
cieco ['tʃɛko], **-a** *agg* blind. *sm, sf* blind person.
cielo ['tʃɛlo] *sm* sky; (*sede divina*) heaven. **a cielo aperto** in the open. **per amor del cielo!** for heaven's sake!
cifra ['tʃifra] *sf* figure, number; (*somma*) amount; (*codice segreto*) cipher.
ciglio ['tʃiʎo] *sm, pl* **-a** *f in anat sense* eyelash; (*bordo*) edge. **non batter ciglio** not bat an eyelid.
cigno ['tʃiɲo] *sm* swan.
cigolare [tʃigo'lare] *v* creak, squeak. **cigolio** *sm* creaking, squeaking.
cilecca [tʃi'lekka] *sf* **far cilecca** misfire.
ciliegia [tʃi'ljɛdʒa] *sf* cherry. **ciliegio** *sm* cherry tree.
cilindro [tʃi'lindro] *sm* cylinder; (*rullo*) roller; (*cappello*) top hat.
cima ['tʃima] *sf* top, summit. **da cima a fondo** from top to bottom. **cimare** *v* (*piante*) trim, clip; (*tessuti*) shear.
cimelio [tʃi'mɛljo] *sm* (*oggetto prezioso*) treasure; (*ricordo*) relic, memento.
cimice ['tʃimitʃe] *sf* bedbug.
ciminiera [tʃimi'njɛra] *sf* chimney.
cimitero [tʃimi'tɛro] *sm* cemetery.
cimurro [tʃi'murro] *sm* distemper.
Cina ['tʃina] *sf* China. **cinese** *agg, s(m+f)* Chinese.
cincia ['tʃintʃa] *sf* tit(mouse). **cinciallegra** *sf* (great) tit.
cincin [tʃin'tʃin] *inter* cheers!
cinema ['tʃinema] *sm invar* cinema. **cinematografico** *agg* film. **cinematografo** *sm* cinema.
cinetico [tʃi'nɛtiko] *agg* kinetic. **cinetica** *sf* kinetics.
***cingere** ['tʃindʒere] *v* surround, encircle. **cingere d'assedio** besiege.
cinghia ['tʃingja] *sf* belt.
cinghiale [tʃin'gjale] *sm* (wild) boar; (*pelle*) pigskin.
cinguettare [tʃingwet'tare] *v* twitter. **cinguettio** *sm* twittering.
cinico ['tʃiniko], **-a** *agg* cynical. *sm, sf* cynic. **cinismo** *sm* cynicism.
cinquanta [tʃin'kwanta] *sm, agg* fifty. **cinquantesimo** *sm, agg* fiftieth.
cinque ['tʃinkwe] *sm, agg* five.
cintura [tʃin'tura] *sf* belt; (*giro della vita*)

waist. **cintura di sicurezza** safety-belt.
cinturino *sm* strap.
ciò [tʃɔ] *pron* this, that. **ciò che** what. **ciò detto** having said this. **ciònondimeno** *or* **ciònonostante** nevertheless, just the same. **con ciò** therefore. **e con ciò?** so what?
cioccolata [tʃokko'lata] *sf* chocolate; (*bevanda*) (drinking) chocolate. **cioccolatino** *sm* (piece of) chocolate. **cioccolato** *sm* chocolate.
cioè [tʃo'ɛ] *avv* that is; (*o piuttosto*) or better.
ciondolo ['tʃondolo] *sm* pendant. **ciondolare** *v* dangle; (*bighellonare*) hang about.
ciotola ['tʃotola] *sf* bowl.
ciottolo ['tʃottolo] *sm* pebble.
cipiglio [tʃi'piʎo] *sm* frown.
cipolla [tʃi'polla] *sf* onion.
cipresso [tʃi'presso] *sm* cypress.
cipria ['tʃiprja] *sf* powder.
Cipro ['tʃipro] *sm* Cyprus. **cipriota** *agg, s(m+f)* Cypriot.
circa ['tʃirka] *prep* (*riguardo a*) about, concerning. *avv* (*pressappoco*) about, approximately.
circo ['tʃirko] *sm* circus.
circolare[1] [tʃirko'lare] *sf, agg* circular. **assegno circolare** *sm* banker's draft.
circolare[2] [tʃirko'lare] *v* circulate. **circolatorio** *agg* circulatory. **circolazione** *sf* circulation.
circolo ['tʃirkolo] *sm* circle.
***circoncidere** [tʃirkon'tʃidere] *v* circumcise. **circoncisione** *sf* circumcision.
circondare [tʃirkon'dare] *v* surround.
circonferenza [tʃirkonfe'rentsa] *sf* circumference.
circonvallazione [tʃirkonvalla'tsjone] *sf* ring-road.
***circoscrivere** [tʃirkos'krivere] *v* circumscribe.
circostante [tʃirkos'tante] *agg* surrounding.
circostanza [tʃirkos'tantsa] *sf* circumstances *pl*; (*condizione particolare*) occurrence. **di circostanza** fitting.
circuito [tʃir'kuito] *sm* circuit; (*sport*) (race-)track.
cisterna [tʃis'tɛrna] *sf* cistern; (*serbatoio*) tank. **nave cisterna** tanker.
citare [tʃi'tare] *v* (*riportare parole*) quote; (*nominare*) cite; (*dir: convocare*) summon(s). **citazione** *sf* quotation; summons.

citofono [tʃi'tɔfono] *sm* (*fam*) intercom.
città [tʃit'ta] *sf* town, city. **cittadina** *sf* small town; (*persona*) citizen. **cittadinanza** *sf* citizenship, nationality; (*popolazione*) people. **cittadino** *sm* citizen.
ciuco ['tʃuko] *sm* donkey.
ciuffo ['tʃuffo] *sm* tuft.
ciurma ['tʃurma] *sf* crew; (*ciurmaglia*) riff-raff.
civetta [tʃi'vetta] *sf* (*uccello*) owl; (*donna*) flirt. **civettare** *v* flirt.
civico ['tʃiviko] *agg* civic.
civile [tʃi'vile] *agg* civil; (*non militare*) civilian; (*incivilito*) civilized. **civilizzare** *v* civilize. **civismo** *sm* public spirit.
civiltà [tʃivil'ta] *sf* civilization; (*cortesia*) good breeding.
clacson ['klakson] *sm invar* horn, hooter.
clamore [kla'more] *sm* clamour; (*fig*) outcry, sensation. **clamoroso** *agg* noisy, sensational.
clandestino [klandes'tino] *agg* clandestine.
clarinetto [klari'netto] *sm* clarinet.
classe ['klasse] *sf* class; (*scuola*) form.
classico ['klassiko] *agg* classic, classical; typical. *sm* classic.
classificare [klassifi'kare] *v* classify. **classificatore** *sm* file. **classificazione** *sf* classification.
classismo [klas'sizmo] *sm* class-consciousness. **classista** *agg* class-conscious.
clausola ['klauzola] *sf* clause.
claustrofobia [klaustrofo'bia] *sf* claustrophobia.
clavicembalo [klavi'tʃembalo] *sm* harpsichord.
clavicola [kla'vikola] *sf* collar-bone.
clemenza [kle'mentsa] *sf* clemency; (*tempo*) mildness. **clemente** *agg* mild, clement.
cleptomane [klep'tɔmane] *s(m+f)*, *agg* kleptomaniac. **cleptomania** *sf* kleptomania.
clero ['klɛro] *sm* clergy. **clericale** *agg* clerical.
cliché [kli'ʃe] *sm* (*stampa*) block; (*luogo comune*) cliché.
cliente [kli'ente] *s(m+f)* (*di negozio*) customer; (*di professionista*) client; (*di albergo*) guest. **cliente abituale** patron. **clientela** *sf* customers *pl*, clientele; (*di professionista*) practice.
clima ['klima] *sm* climate. **climatico** *agg* climatic.

clinica ['klinika] *sf* clinic. **clinico** *agg* clinical.
cloro ['klɔro] *sm* chlorine.
clorofilla [kloro'filla] *sf* chlorophyll.
cloroformio [kloro'fɔrmjo] *sm* chloroform.
cloruro [klo'ruro] *sm* chloride.
coabitare [koabi'tare] *v* cohabit.
coagulare [koagu'lare] *v* coagulate; (*latte*) curdle; (*sangue*) clot. **coagulazione** *sf* coagulation; curdling; clotting.
coalizione [koali'tsjone] *sf* coalition. **coalizzarsi** *v* unite.
coatto [ko'atto] *agg* compulsory.
cobalto [ko'balto] *sm* cobalt.
cobra ['kɔbra] *sm invar* cobra.
cocaina [koka'ina] *sf* cocaine. **cocainomane** *s(m+f)* cocaine addict.
coccarda [kok'karda] *sf* rosette.
cocchio ['kɔkkjo] *sm* carriage, coach. **cocchiere** *sm* coachman.
coccinella [kottʃi'nɛlla] *sf* ladybird.
coccio ['kɔttʃo] *sm* (*terracotta*) earthenware; (*rottame*) piece, crock.
cocciuto [kot'tʃuto] *agg* stubborn, pig-headed. **cocciutaggine** *sf* stubbornness, pig-headedness.
cocco¹ ['kɔkko], **-a** *sm, sf* (*fam: amore*) pet, darling.
cocco² ['kɔkko] *sm* coconut tree *or* palm. **noce di cocco** *sf* coconut.
coccodrillo [kokko'drillo] *sm* crocodile.
cocente [ko'tʃɛnte] *agg* burning, scorching.
cocomero [ko'kɔmero] *sm* water-melon.
cocuzzolo [ko'kuttsolo] *sm* tip.
coda ['koda] *sf* tail; (*fila*) queue; (*musica*) coda. **con la coda dell'occhio** out of the corner of one's eye. **fare la coda** queue (up).
codardo [ko'dardo] *agg* cowardly.
codeina [kode'ina] *sf* codeine.
codesto [ko'desto] *agg* that. *pron* that (one).
codice ['kɔditʃe] *sm* code. **codice della strada** highway code.
coefficiente [koeffi'tʃɛnte] *sm* coefficient; (*causa*) contributory factor.
coerente [koe'rɛnte] *agg* coherent; (*fig*) consistent.
coesistere [koe'zistere] *v* coexist. **coesistenza** *sf* coexistence.
coetaneo [koe'taneo], **-a** *s, agg* contemporary.

cofano ['kɔfano] *sm* (*auto*) bonnet; (*forziere*) chest.

*cogliere ['kɔʎere] *v* (*staccare*) pick; (*sorprendere, capire*) catch; (*colpire*) hit. **cogliere la palla al balzo** seize the opportunity.

coglione [koˈʎone] (*volg*) *sm* testicle; (*sciocco*) fool. **coglioneria** *sf* foolishness.

cognato [koˈɲato] *sm* brother-in-law. **cognata** *sf* sister-in-law.

cognizione [koɲiˈtsjone] *sf* knowledge; (*dir*) cognizance.

cognome [koˈɲome] *sm* surname.

coi ['koi] *prep + art* **con i.**

*coincidere [koinˈtʃidere] *v* coincide. **coincidenza** *sf* coincidence; (*treno, ecc.*) connection.

*coinvolgere [koinˈvɔldʒere] *v* involve.

coito ['kɔito] *sm* coitus, sexual intercourse.

col [kol] *prep + art* **con il.**

colare [koˈlare] *v* (*filtrare*) sieve, strain; (*gocciolare*) drip, trickle; (*fondere*) melt, cast; (*a picco*) sink. **colabrodo** *or* **colapasta** *sm invar* strainer, colander. **colatoio** *sm* strainer. **colino** *sm* sieve.

colazione [kolaˈtsjone] *sf* (*del mattino*) breakfast; (*di mezzogiorno*) lunch. **far colazione** (have) breakfast; (have) lunch.

colei [koˈlɛi] *pron* (*soggetto*) she; (*oggetto*) her. **colei che** (she) who.

colera [koˈlɛra] *sm invar* cholera.

colesterolo [kolesteˈrɔlo] *sm* cholesterol.

coll' [koll] *prep + art* **con l'.**

colla ['kɔlla] *sf* glue, paste.

collaborare [kollaboˈrare] *v* collaborate; (*giornale*) contribute. **collaboratore, -trice** *sm, sf* collaborator; contributor. **collaborazione** *sf* collaboration; contribution.

collana [kolˈlana] *sf* necklace; (*raccolta*) collection.

collants [kɔlˈlã] *sm pl* tights *pl*.

collare [kolˈlare] *sm* collar.

collasso [kolˈlasso] *sm* collapse. **collasso cardiaco** heart failure.

collaterale [kollateˈrale] *agg* collateral.

collaudare [kollauˈdare] *v* test. **collaudo** *sm* test.

colle¹ ['kɔlle] *sm* (*altura*) hill.

colle² ['kɔlle] *sm* (*valico*) pass.

collega [kolˈlɛga] *s(m + f)*, *m pl* **-ghi** colleague.

collegare [kolleˈgare] *v* connect, link (up).

collegarsi *v* (*telefono*) get through. **collegamento** *sm* connection, link; (*mil*) liaison.

collegio [kolˈlɛdʒo] *sm* college; (*convitto*) boarding school; (*consiglio*) board. **collegio di difesa** counsel for the defence. **collegio elettorale** constituency.

collegiale [kolleˈdʒale] *s(m + f)* boarder. *agg* (*collettivo*) corporate, collective; (*di collegio*) college, boarding-school.

collera ['kɔllera] *sf* anger, rage.

colletta [kolˈlɛtta] *sf* collection.

collettivo [kolletˈtivo] *agg* collective.

colletto [kolˈlɛtto] *sm* collar.

collettore [kolletˈtore] *sm* collector; (*tec*) manifold.

collezionare [kolletsjoˈnare] *v* collect. **collezione** *sf* collection.

collina [kolˈlina] *sf* hill.

collisione [kolliˈzjone] *sf* collision.

collo¹ ['kɔllo] *sm* neck. **collo del piede** instep.

collo² ['kɔllo] *sm* (*pacco*) parcel, package; (*bagaglio*) item of luggage.

collocare [kolloˈkare] *v* place. **collocare a riposo** retire, pension off. **collocamento** *sm* (*occupazione*) employment, job; (*il collocare*) placing, setting; (*vendita*) sale. **collocamento a riposo** retirement. **ufficio di collocamento** *sm* employment exchange.

colloide [kolˈlɔide] *sm* colloid. *agg* colloidal.

colloquio [kolˈlɔkwjo] *sm* conversation, talk; (*intervista*) interview; (*esame*) oral (examination).

colmare [kolˈmare] *v* fill; (*fino all'orlo*) fill to the brim; (*coprire di*) shower. **colmo** *sm* top, summit; (*culmine*) height; (*situazione paradossale*) last straw, limit.

colombo [koˈlombo], **-a** *sm, sf* dove, pigeon. **colombaia** *sf* dovecote.

colonia [koˈlɔnja] *sf* colony; (*per bambini*) holiday camp; (*per lavoro*) settlement. **coloniale** *agg* colonial.

colonna [koˈlonna] *sf* column; (*sostegno*) pillar; (*fila*) line, queue. **colonna vertebrale** spinal column, backbone.

colonnello [kolonˈnɛllo] *sm* colonel.

colore [koˈlore] *sm* colour; (*sostanza colorante*) paint, dye, tint; (*carte da gioco*) suit. **farne di tutti i colori** get up to all sorts of mischief. **colorante** *sm* dye. **colorare** *v* colour.

colorire [kolo'rire] *v* colour; *(arrossire)* blush.

colorito [kolo'rito] *sm (carnagione)* complexion; *(tinta)* colour(ing). *agg* colourful.

coloro [ko'loro] *pron (soggetto)* they; *(oggetto)* them. **coloro che** (those) who.

colossale [kolos'sale] *agg* colossal, tremendous. **colosso** *sm (statua)* colossus; *(uomo)* giant.

colpa ['kolpa] *sf* fault; *(colpevolezza)* guilt; *(peccato)* sin. **dare la colpa a** blame. **per colpa di** through, because of. **prendersi la colpa** take the blame.

colpevole [kol'pevole] *agg (persona)* guilty; *(azione)* culpable. *s(m+f)* culprit. **dichiararsi colpevole** plead guilty.

colpire [kol'pire] *v* hit, strike.

colpo ['kolpo] *sm* stroke, blow; *(arma da fuoco)* shot; *(impresa)* move, raid. **colpo d'aria** draught. **far colpo** impress, cause a stir, make a hit.

coltello [kol'tɛllo] *sm* knife. **coltellata** *sf* stab.

coltivare [kolti'vare] *v* cultivate; *(far crescere)* grow. **coltivatore** *sm* grower. **coltivazione** *sf* cultivation; growing.

colto[1] ['kolto] *agg* cultivated, cultured.

coltura [kol'tura] *sf* cultivation; *(allevamento)* breeding; *(med)* culture.

colui [ko'lui] *pron (soggetto)* he; *(oggetto)* him. **colui che** (he) who.

coma ['kɔma] *sm invar* coma. **comatoso** *agg* comatose.

comandare [koman'dare] *v (reggere comando)* be in command, command; *(chiedere)* order; *(mec)* control. **comandamento** *sm* commandment. **comandante** *sm* commander. **comando** *sm* command; *(sede)* headquarters; *(mec)* control, drive. **comando a distanza** remote control.

combaciare [komba'tʃare] *v* coincide.

combattere [kom'battere] *v* fight. **combattente** *sm* serviceman. **combattimento** *sm* fight. **combattivo** *agg* pugnacious. **combattuto** *agg* undecided, torn.

combinare [kombi'nare] *v* combine; *(mettere d'accordo)* agree; *(concludere)* arrange, bring off, achieve. **combinazione** *sf* combination; *(caso)* chance.

combustibile [kombus'tibile] *sm* fuel. *agg* combustible.

combustione [kombus'tjone] *sf* combustion.

come ['kome] *avv* as; *(somiglianza)* like; *(in qual modo)* how.

comedone [kome'done] *sm* blackhead.

cometa [ko'meta] *sf* comet.

comico ['kɔmiko], **-a** *sm, sf* comic, comedian. *agg* comic(al), funny; *(commedia)* dramatic.

comignolo [ko'miɲolo] *sm* chimney-pot.

cominciare [komin'tʃare] *v* begin, start. **a cominciare da** from.

comitato [komi'tato] *sm* committee.

comitiva [komi'tiva] *sf* party.

comizio [ko'mitsjo] *sm* meeting.

commedia [kom'mɛdja] *sf* play, comedy; *(finzione)* play-acting, sham; *(scena comica)* farce. **commediante** *s(m+f) (fam)* ham; *(ipocrita)* humbug. **commediografo** *sm* playwright.

commemorare [kommemo'rare] *v* commemorate. **commemorativo** *agg* memorial.

commentare [kommen'tare] *v* comment (on). **commentario** *sm* commentary. **commentatore, -trice** *sm, sf* commentator. **commento** *sm* comment; *(radio)* commentary.

commercio [kom'mɛrtʃo] *sm* trade, commerce. **commercio all'ingrosso/al minuto** wholesale/retail trade. **mettere in commercio** put on sale.

commesso [kom'messo], **-a** *sm, sf (di negozio)* (shop) assistant; *(d'ufficio)* clerk. **commesso viaggiatore** travelling salesman.

commestibile [kommes'tibile] *agg* edible. **commestibili** *sm pl* foodstuffs *pl*, provisions *pl*.

*****commettere** [kom'mettere] *v (fare)* commit; *(mettere insieme)* fit together, join; *(ordinare)* commission.

commissariato [kommissa'rjato] *sm (polizia)* police station. **commissario** *sm (polizia)* police inspector; *(sovietico)* commissar; *(amministratore)* commissioner.

commissione [kommis'sjone] *sf* commission; *(incombenza)* errand; *(ordinazione)* order; *(comitato)* board. **fare delle commissioni** go shopping.

commosso [kom'mɔsso] *agg* moved, touched.

commozione [kommo'tsjone] *sf* deep feelings *pl*; *(med)* concussion.

*****commuovere** [kom'mwɔvere] *v* move,

touch. **commovente** *agg* moving, touching.

commutare [kommu'tare] *v* commute.

comò [ko'mɔ] *sm* chest of drawers.

comodino [komo'dino] *sm* bedside table.

comodo ['kɔmodo] *sm* convenience. *agg* comfortable; (*opportuno*) convenient; (*utile*) useful, handy. **far comodo** be useful *or* handy; (*garbare*) please, suit. **fare con comodo** take one's time. **comodare** *v* suit. **comodità** *sf* comfort.

compagnia [kompa'ɲia] *sf* company.

compagno [kom'paɲo], **-a** *sm*, *sf* companion, mate, friend. **compagno d'armi** fellow-soldier. **compagno di prigionia/viaggio** fellow-prisoner/traveller. **compagno di scuola** classmate.

*comparire [kompa'rire] *v* appear. **comparsa** *sf* appearance; (*film*) extra.

compartimento [komparti'mento] *sm* compartment.

compassione [kompas'sjone] *sf* pity. **far compassione** arouse pity. **per compassione** out of pity. **compassionevole** *agg* (*che fa compassione*) pitiful; (*che ha compassione*) compassionate.

compasso [kom'passo] *sm* compasses *pl*.

compatire [kompa'tire] *v* be sorry for. **compatibile** *agg* compatible; (*perdonabile*) excusable.

compatriota [kompatri'ɔta] *s(m+f)* compatriot.

compatto [kom'patto] *agg* compact, dense; (*fig*) united. **compattezza** *sf* compactness; unity.

compendio [kom'pɛndjo] *sm* (*riassunto*) summary; (*trattato*) outline. **compendioso** *agg* brief.

compensare [kompen'sare] *v* compensate; (*ricompensare*) reward. (**legno**) **compensato** *sm* plywood. **compensazione** *sf* compensation; (*econ*) clearing. **compenso** *sm* compensation; reward. **in compenso** in return, in exchange.

competente [kompe'tɛnte] *agg* competent, qualified; (*adeguato*) fair. **competenza** *sf* experience, authority; (*dir*) competence.

competere [kom'pɛtere] *v* (*spettare*) be due; (*gareggiare*) compete, rival. **competitivo** *agg* competitive.

*compiacere [kompja'tʃere] *v* please. **compiacersi** *v* be pleased, rejoice; congratulate; (*degnarsi*) be good enough. **compiaciuto** *agg* pleased, satisfied.

*compiangere [kom'pjandʒere] *v* pity; (*rimpiangere*) mourn. **compianto** *sm* grief.

compiere ['kompjere] *v* (*finire*) complete; (*adempiere*) carry out, fulfil. **compiere ... anni** be ... years old. **compimento** *sm* fulfilment.

compilare [kompi'lare] *v* compile, draw up.

compito ['kompito] *sm* task; (*dovere*) duty; (*scuola*) homework.

compleanno [komple'anno] *sm* birthday.

complementare [komplemen'tare] *agg* complementary; (*secondario*) subsidiary. **complemento** *sm* complement; (*gramm*) object.

complesso [kom'plɛsso] *agg* complex; complicated. *sm* (*insieme*) whole; (*industria*) combine, group; (*psic*) complex; (*musica*) ensemble, band. **in complesso** (*tutto sommato*) on the whole; (*in tutto*) in all, altogether. **nel complesso** as a whole.

completo [kom'plɛto] *agg* complete; (*pieno*) full (up); (*assoluto*) total. *sm* (*abito*) suit; (*di maglia*) twin set; (*in generale*) outfit. **al completo** (*pieno*) full up; (*esaurito*) sold out; (*tutti presenti*) in full force. **completare** *v* complete, finish.

complicare [kompli'kare] *v* complicate; (*aggravare*) worsen. **complicato** *agg* complicated, complex; (*intricato*) involved. **complicazione** *sf* complication.

complice ['komplitʃe] *s(m+f)* accomplice; (*dir*) accessory. **essere complice in** be a party to. **complicità** *sf* complicity.

complimento [kompli'mento] *sm* compliment. **complimenti** *sm pl* (*cerimonie*) ceremony *sing*; (*ossequi*) regards *pl*; (*auguri*) congratulations *pl*. **far complimenti** stand on ceremony. **complimentare** *v* compliment.

complotto [kom'plɔtto] *sm* plot. **complottare** *v* plot.

componente [kompo'nɛnte] *agg* component. *s(m+f)* component, member.

*comporre [kom'porre] *v* (*costituire*) make up; (*assestare*) tidy; (*mettere assieme*) assemble, put together; (*musica*) compose; (*atteggiare*) put on. **comporre una lite** settle a quarrel.

comportare [kompor'tare] *v* (*richiedere*) involve; (*portare con sè*) imply; (*consentire*) permit. **comportarsi** *v* behave. **comportamento** *sm* behaviour.

compositore [kompozi'tore], **-trice** *sm, sf*
(*musica*) composer; type-setter.
composizione [kompozi'tsjone] *sf* composition.
composto [kom'posto] *sm* compound,
mixture. *agg* (*decoroso*) dignified; (*assestato*) neat; (*costituito*) made up (of), consisting (of); (*mat*) compound. **compostezza** *sf* self-possession; decorum; neatness.
comprare [komp'rare] *v* buy; (*corrompere*)
bribe. **comprare all'ingrosso** buy wholesale. **compratore, -trice** *sm, sf* buyer.
***comprendere** [kom'prendere] *v* include;
(*capire*) understand. **comprensibile** *agg*
understandable, intelligible. **comprensione** *sf* understanding. **comprensivo** *agg*
(*che include*) inclusive, comprehensive;
(*tollerante*) understanding. **compreso** *agg*
inclusive; (*capito*) understood.
compressa [kom'pressa] *sf* tablet, pill;
(*garza*) compress.
compressore [kompres'sore] *sm* compressor.
***comprimere** [kom'primere] *v* compress;
(*reprimere*) suppress.
***compromettere** [kompro'mettere] *v*
compromise. **compromesso** *sm* compromise. **compromettente** *agg* compromising.
comprovare [kompro'vare] *v* confirm.
compunto [kom'punto] *agg* contrite.
comune [ko'mune] *agg* common. *sm* commune, municipality; (*autorità*) town
council. **avere in comune** share. **fuori del
comune** uncommon, unusual.
comunicare [komuni'kare] *v* communicate, announce; (*malattia*) pass on; (*rel*)
administer Communion. **comunicarsi** *v*
spread; receive Communion. **comunicato**
sm communiqué, bulletin. **comunicato
stampa** press release.
comunione [komu'njone] *sf* community;
(*rel*) (Holy) Communion.
comunismo [komu'nizmo] *sm* communism. **comunista** *s(m+f)*, *agg* communist.
comunità [komuni'ta] *sf* community.
comunque [ko'munkwe] *avv* (*in ogni
modo*) anyhow, at any rate. *cong* however, no matter how.
con [kon] *prep* with; (*mezzo*) with, by.
conca ['konka] *sf* basin; (*valle*) depression.
concavo [kon'kavo] *agg* concave.

***concedere** [kon'tʃedere] *v* grant, award;
(*permettere*) allow.
concentrare [kontʃen'trare] *v* concentrate.
concentramento *sm* concentration. **concentrato** *sm* concentrate.
concentrico [kon'tʃentriko] *agg* concentric.
concepire [kontʃe'pire] *v* conceive;
(*capire*) understand; (*nutrire*) entertain,
cherish. **concepibile** *agg* conceivable.
conceria [kontʃe'ria] *sf* tannery.
concernere [kon'tʃernere] *v* concern,
regard. **per quanto mi concerne** as far as
I am concerned.
concerto [kon'tʃerto] *sm* concert.
concessione [kontʃes'sjone] *sf* concession.
concetto [kon'tʃetto] *sm* concept, notion,
idea.
concezione [kontʃe'tsjone] *sf* conception;
(*pensiero*) concept.
conchiglia [kon'kiʎa] *sf* shell.
conciare [kon'tʃare] *v* (*pelli*) tan; (*tabacco*) cure; (*ridurre male*) get into a mess;
spoil. **conciare per le feste** (*fam*) give a
thrashing.
conciliare [kontʃi'ljare] *v* reconcile.
concilio [kon'tʃiljo] *sm* council.
concime [kon'tʃime] *sm* manure;
(*artificiale*) fertilizer.
conciso [kon'tʃizo] *agg* concise, to the
point.
concittadino [kontʃitta'dino], **-a** *sm, sf*
fellow-citizen.
conclave [kon'klave] *sm* conclave.
***concludere** [kon'kludere] *v* conclude;
(*operare con profitto*) achieve. **conclusione** *sf* conclusion, result. **in conclusione**
to sum up, in short. **conclusivo** *agg* final,
conclusive; (*determinante*) decisive.
concordare [konkor'dare] *v* agree, fix.
concordato *sm* agreement.
concorrente [konkor'rente] *agg* concurrent; (*rivale*) competing. *s(m+f)* competitor; (*a un concorso*) candidate, applicant. **concorrenza** *sf* competition. **far
concorrenza** compete (with).
***concorrere** [kon'korrere] *v* contribute;
(*gareggiare*) compete (for); (*convergere*)
come together.
concorso [kon'korso] *sm* (*affluire*) concourse, gathering; contribution; contest,
competition; (*esame*) competitive examination.
concreto [kon'krɛto] *sm, agg* concrete.
concretare *v* get done.

condannare [kondan'nare] *v* condemn; (*dichiarare colpevole*) sentence. **condanna** *sf* conviction, sentence. **condannato, -a** *sm, sf* condemned person.

condensazione [kondensa'tsjone] *sf* condensation. **condensare** *v* condense.

condire [kon'dire] *v* season; (*insalata*) dress. **condimento** *sm* seasoning, dressing.

***condividere** [kondi'videre] *v* share.

condizione [kondi'tsjone] *sf* condition. **condizioni** *sf pl* state *sing*; (*comm*) terms *pl*. **condizioni di vita** standard of living *sing*. **essere in condizione di** be able to. **mettere in condizione di** enable to. **condizionale** *sm, agg* conditional.

condoglianza [kondo'ʎantsa] *sf* condolence. **fare le condoglianze** express one's sympathy.

condonare [kondo'nare] *v* remit, condone. **condono** *sm* remission.

condotta [kon'dotta] *sm* (*comportamento*) conduct, behaviour; (*di un'azione, ecc.*) handling; (*tubazione*) piping.

***condurre** [kon'durre] *v* (*portare*) lead; (*accompagnare*) take; (*auto*) drive; (*dirigere*) manage, run; (*eseguire, fis*) conduct; (*ridurre*) reduce. **condursi** *v* behave.

conduttore [kondut'tore] *agg* conducting. *sm* (*fis*) conductor; (*conducente*) driver. **conduttura** *sf* (*tubazione*) piping; (*condotto*) pipe.

confederazione [konfedera'tsjone] *sf* federation.

conferenza [konfe'rentsa] *sf* (*congresso*) conference; (*discorso*) lecture. **conferenza stampa** press conference. **conferenziere, -a** *sm, sf* lecturer, speaker.

conferire [konfe'rire] *v* award, confer; (*dare*) give.

confermare [konfer'mare] *v* confirm, **conferma** *sf* confirmation.

confessare [konfes'sare] *v* confess. **confessione** *sf* confession. **confessore** *sm* confessor.

confetto [kon'fetto] *sm* sugared almond.

confettura [konfet'tura] *sf* preserve.

confezionare [konfetsjo'nare] *v* make up. **confezione** *sf* (*involucro*) wrapping; (*lavorazione*) manufacture. **confezioni** *sf pl* (*abiti pronti*) ready-made clothes *pl*.

confidare [konfi'dare] *v* trust, confide. **confidenza** *sf* confidence. **dar confidenza**

a be familiar with. **prendersi la confidenza** take the liberty. **confidenziale** *agg* confidential.

confinare [konfi'nare] *v* border (on); (*relegare*) confine; (*pol*) intern, banish. **confine** *sm* border.

confiscare [konfis'kare] *v* seize, confiscate. **confisca** *sf* seizure, confiscation.

conflitto [kon'flitto] *sm* conflict.

***confondere** [kon'fondere] *v* confuse; (*scambiare*) mistake for; (*mettere in imbarrazzo*) embarrass. **confondersi** *v* become mixed up.

conformare [konfor'mare] *v* conform, adapt. **conforme a** *agg* in conformity with, true to. **conformista** *s(m+f)* conformist.

confortare [konfor'tare] *v* comfort, console. **confortevole** *agg* comforting; (*comodo*) comfortable. **conforto** *sm* comfort.

confrontare [konfron'tare] *v* compare; (*dir*) confront. **confronto** *sm* comparison; (*dir*) confrontation. **a confronto di** compared with. **senza confronto** far away.

confusione [konfu'zjone] *sf* confusion; (*ressa*) bustle; (*chiasso*) din, turmoil. **confusione mentale** mental aberration. **confuso** *agg* confused, muddled; vague; (*turbato*) bewildered.

congedare [kondʒe'dare] *v* dismiss; (*mil*) discharge. **congedarsi** *v* say goodbye (to); take leave (of). **congedo** *sm* (*commiato*) leave; discharge.

congegno [kon'dʒeɲo] *sm* device, gadget. **congegnare** *v* plan, devise.

congelare [kondʒe'lare] *v* freeze. **congelatore** *sm* freezer.

congenito [kon'dʒenito] *agg* congenital.

congestionato [kondʒestjo'nato] *agg* congested; (*traffico*) blocked; (*viso*) flushed. **congestione** *sf* congestion; (*traffico*) jam.

***congiungere** [kon'dʒundʒere] *v* (*unire*) join; (*collegare*) connect, link (up). **congiuntivite** *sf* conjunctivitis. **congiuntivo** *sm* subjunctive. **congiuntura** *sf* (*punto di unione*) joint; (*circostanza*) juncture; economic situation. **congiunzione** *sf* conjunction.

congiura [kon'dʒura] *sf* plot, conspiracy. **congiurato, -a** *sm, sf* plotter, conspirator.

congratularsi [kongratu'larsi] *v* congratulate.

congregare [kongre'gare] v congregate, gather. congrega sf band. congregazione sf congregation.

congresso [kon'grɛsso] sm congress.

congruo ['kongruo] agg adequate, fair.

coniare [ko'njare] v coin. conio sm coining; (impronta, qualità) stamp; (matrice) minting die.

conico ['kɔniko] agg conical.

conifero [ko'nifero] agg coniferous. conifera sf conifer.

coniglio [ko'niʎo] sm rabbit.

coniugare [konju'gare] v conjugate.

coniuge ['kɔnjudʒe] s(m+f) spouse. coniugale agg conjugal.

*connettere [kon'nɛttere] v connect, link; associate; (ragionare) think straight. connessione sf connection.

connotati [konno'tati] sm pl description sing, distinguishing features pl.

cono ['kɔno] sm cone.

*conoscere [ko'nɔʃere] v know; (fare la conoscenza) meet. conoscere di fama/vista know by reputation/sight. conoscente s(m+f) acquaintance. conoscenza sf knowledge; (conoscente) acquaintance; (coscienza) consciousness, senses pl. conoscitore, -trice sm, sf expert, connoisseur. conosciuto agg (well-)known, renowned.

conquistare [konkwis'tare] v conquer; (fig) gain. conquista sf conquest. conquistatore, -trice sm, sf conqueror.

consacrare [konsa'krare] v consecrate, dedicate.

consanguineo [konsan'gwineo], -a agg related (by blood). sm, sf blood relation.

consapevole [konsa'pevole] agg aware, conscious. consapevolezza sf awareness, consciousness.

consecutivo [konseku'tivo] agg consecutive; (seguente) following.

consegnare [konse'ɲare] v deliver, hand over; (mil) confine to barracks. consegna sf delivery; (merce ordinata) consignment; (custodia) care; (deposito) (safe) custody; (mil: ordine) order; (mil: punizione) confinement.

conseguire [konse'gwire] v • (ottenere) obtain, get; (raggiungere) achieve; (risultare) follow, ensue. conseguenza sf consequence, result; (malattia) aftereffect. di conseguenza consequently, as a result.

consenso [kon'sɛnso] sm approval; (accordo) agreement; (permesso) consent.

consentire [konsen'tire] v (essere d'accordo) agree; (accondiscendere) consent; (permettere) allow. consenziente agg consenting.

conservare [konser'vare] v keep, preserve. conserva sf preserve. mettere in conserva preserve; (in scatola) tin; (in bottiglia) bottle. conservatore, -trice s, agg conservative. conservazione sf preservation.

considerare [konside'rare] v consider; (guardare) examine; (stimare) esteem, think highly of; (tener conto) bear in mind. consideratezza sf caution. considerato agg careful, wary. considerazione sf (prudenza) caution; (risguardo) consideration; (stima) esteem, regard. considerevole agg considerable.

consigliare [konsi'ʎare] v advise, recommend. consigliere sm counsellor. consigliere comunale town councillor. consigliere delegato managing director. consiglio sm advice; (organo amministrativo) board; (ente pubblico) council; (colloquio) meeting. consiglio d'amministrazione board of directors.

*consistere [kon'sistere] v consist. consistente agg substantial; (convincente) sound. consistenza sf consistency; (fondamento) basis. consistenza di cassa/magazzino cash/stock in hand.

consolare [konso'lare] v console, comfort; (rallegrare) cheer (up). consolazione sf consolation, comfort; (piacere) delight.

console ['kɔnsole] sm consul. consolare agg consular. consolato sm consulate.

consolidare [konsoli'dare] v consolidate; (rinforzare) reinforce.

consonante [konso'nante] sf consonant.

consono ['kɔnsono] agg consono a in keeping with; in accordance with.

consorte [kon'sɔrte] s(m+f), agg consort.

consorzio [kon'sɔrtsjo] sm partnership; (impresa commerciale, banca) consortium, trust; (imprese riunite) syndicate, cooperative.

constare [kon'stare] v consist. a quanto mi consta to my knowledge, as far as I know.

constatare [konsta'tare] v (notare) see; (accertare) ascertain, verify; (riconoscere) recognize. constatazione sf verification; recognition.

consueto [konsu'ɛto] *agg* (*solito*) usual; (*abituato*) used. **come di consueto** as usual. **di consueto** usually. **consuetudine** *sf* habit, custom.

consulente [konsu'lɛnte] *s(m+f)*, *agg* consultant. **consulenza** *sf* advice. **consultare** *v* consult. **consultazione** *sf* consultation; (*biblioteca*) reference. **consultivo** *agg* consultative, advisory.

consumare¹ [konsu'mare] *v* consume, use up; (*logorare*) wear out; (*dissipare*) squander; (*mangiare*) eat. **consumazione** *sf* (*bibita*) drink; (*spuntino*) snack. **consumismo** *sm* consumer society. **consumo** *sm* consumption; (*spreco*) waste. **articoli di consumo** *sm pl* consumer goods *pl*.

consumare² [konsu'mare] *v* (*portare a compimento*) consummate. **consumazione** *sf* consummation.

consuntivo [konsun'tivo] *sm* balance sheet.

contabile [kon'tabile] *s(m+f)* bookkeeper; (*ragioniere*) accountant. **valore contabile** *sm* book value. **contabilità** *sf* bookkeeping; accountancy. **tenere la contabilità** keep the books.

contachilometri [kontaki'lɔmetri] *sm invar* mileometer; (*tachimetro*) speedometer.

contadino [konta'dino], **-a** *agg* (*della campagna*) rustic; (*dei contadini*) peasant. *sm*, *sf* peasant; (*agricoltore*) farmer.

contagioso [konta'dʒozo] *agg* contagious, catching. **contagiare** *v* infect, contaminate.

contagiri [konta'dʒiri] *sm invar* rev(olution) counter.

contaminare [kontami'nare] *v* contaminate.

contanti [kon'tanti] *sm pl* cash *sing*, ready money *sing*.

contare [kon'tare] *v* count; (*proporsi*) think. **contato** *agg* limited. **ho i giorni contati** my days are numbered. **ho i minuti contati** I have no time to waste. **contatore** *sm* meter.

contatto [kon'tatto] *sm* contact. **essere/mantenersi/mettersi in contatto** be/keep/get in touch.

conte ['konte] *sm* count. **contea** *sf* (*suddivisione amministrativa*) county; (*titolo, dominio di conti*) earldom. **contessa** *sf* countess.

conteggio [kon'tɛddʒo] *sm* count, counting. **conteggiare** *v* (*calcolare*) count; (*far pagare*) charge.

contegno [kon'teɲo] *sm* bearing, behaviour. **darsi** *or* **assumere un contegno** strike an attitude. **contegnoso** *agg* dignified, reserved.

contemplare [kontem'plare] *v* contemplate; consider, provide for. **contemplazione** *sf* contemplation.

contempo [kon'tɛmpo] *sm* **nel contempo** in the meantime, meanwhile.

contemporaneo [kontempo'raneo], **-a** *sm*, *sf* contemporary. *agg* contemporary; simultaneous.

*****contendere** [kon'tɛndere] *v* dispute; (*litigarsi*) quarrel (over); oppose. **contendente** *s(m+f)* competitor.

*****contenere** [konte'nere] *v* contain, hold; (*trattenere*) hold back. **contenersi** *v* (*dominarsi*) restrain oneself; (*comportarsi*) act. **contenitore** *sm* container.

contentare [konten'tare] *v* (*appagare*) satisfy; (*far contento*) please. **contentarsi** *v* be satisfied. **contentezza** *sf* satisfaction, contentment; (*gioia*) joy. **contento** *agg* (*soddisfatto*) pleased, satisfied; (*felice*) happy; (*allegro*) cheerful.

contenuto [konte'nuto] *sm* (*recipiente*) contents *pl*; (*argomento*) content. *agg* reserved, restrained.

contestare [kontes'tare] *v* contest; (*dir*) charge (with); (*impugnare*) challenge. **contestazione** *sf* dispute; notification.

contiguo [kon'tiguo] *agg* neighbouring, adjoining.

continente [konti'nɛnte] *sm*, *agg* continent. **continentale** *agg* continental. **continenza** *sf* continence.

contingente [kontin'dʒɛnte] *sm* quota; (*mil*) contingent. **contingenza** *sf* circumstance; contingency. **indennità di contingenza** *sf* cost of living allowance.

continuare [kontinu'are] *v* continue, carry on; (*riprendere*) resume; (*insistere*) keep on. **continuazione** *sf* continuation. **continuità** *sf* continuity. **continuo** *agg* endless; (*costante*) continual; (*ininterrotto*) continuous.

conto ['kɔnto] *sm* account; (*somma da pagare*) bill; calculation. **a conti fatti** all things considered. **a (ogni) buon conto** in any case. **far conto che** *or* **di** suppose, imagine; (*proporsi*) intend. **fare conto su** rely on. **per conto di** on behalf of. **per**

conto mio as far as I'm concerned; (*da solo*) on my own. **tener conto di** make a note of; consider, take into account.

*__contorcere__ [kon'tɔrtʃere] *v* twist. **contorcersi** *v* writhe. **contorsione** *sf* contortion. **contorsionista** *s(m+f)* contortionist.

contorno [kon'torno] *sm* (*linea*) outline; (*gastr*) vegetables *pl*, side-dish; (*ornamento*) surround, border.

contrabbandare [kontrabban'dare] *v* smuggle. **contrabbando** *sm* contraband, smuggling. **merce di contrabbando** *sf* smuggled goods *pl*.

contrabbasso [kontrab'basso] *sm* double-bass.

contraccambiare [kontrakkam'bjare] *v* reciprocate. **in contraccambio di** in return for.

contraccolpo [kontrak'kolpo] *sm* counter-blow; (*fig*) repercussion.

*__contraddire__ [kontrad'dire] *v* contradict. **contraddizione** *sf* contradiction. **spirito di contraddizione** *sm* contrariness.

contraddittorio [kontraddit'tɔrjo] *agg* contradictory. *sm* (*dir*) cross-examination.

contraente [kontra'ɛnte] *agg* contracting.

contraereo [kontra'ɛreo] *agg* anti-aircraft.

*__contraffare__ [kontraf'fare] *v* imitate; (*falsificare*) forge, counterfeit. **contraffattore, -trice** *sm, sf* counterfeiter, forger; imitator. **contraffazione** *sf* forgery.

contralto [kon'tralto] *sm* contralto. *agg* alto.

*__contrapporre__ [kontrap'porre] *v* oppose, contrast. **contrapposizione** *sf* opposition, contrast.

contrariare [kontra'rjare] *v* irritate, oppose.

contrario [kon'trarjo] *agg* opposite, contrary; (*avverso*) unfavourable. *sm* contrary, opposite. **al contrario** on the contrary. **al contrario di** unlike. **essere contrario a** be opposed to.

*__contrarre__ [kon'trarre] *v* contract.

contrassegnare [kontrasse'ɲare] *v* mark. **contrassegno** *sm* mark.

contrastare [kontras'tare] *v* (*ostacolare*) bar, oppose; (*essere in conflitto*) clash; dispute. **contrasto** *sm* contrast; conflict.

contrattaccare [kontrattak'kare] *v* counter-attack. **contrattacco** *sm* counter-attack.

contrattempo [kontrat'tɛmpo] *sm* hitch.

contratto [kon'tratto] *sm* contract. **contrattare** *v* negotiate; (*mercanteggiare*) haggle.

contravvenzione [kontravven'tsjone] *sf* (*violazione*) infringement; (*multa*) fine. **contravventore, -trice** *sm, sf* offender.

contrazione [kontra'tsjone] *sf* contraction.

contribuire [kontribu'ire] *v* contribute. **contribuente** *sm, sf* taxpayer. **contributo** *sm* contribution; (*dir*) tax.

contristare [kontris'tare] *v* sadden.

contrito [kon'trito] *agg* contrite.

contro ['kontro] *prep, avv* against.

controbattere [kontro'battere] *v* rebut.

controbilanciare [kontrobilan'tʃare] *v* counterbalance.

controfirmare [kontrofir'mare] *v* counter-sign. **controfirma** *sf* countersignature.

controllare [kontrol'lare] *v* control; (*esaminare*) check. **controllo** *sm* control; (*verifica*) check; inspection. **controllo delle nascite** birth-control. **controllore** *sm* inspector.

contromano [kontro'mano] *avv* in the opposite direction.

contromarcia [kontro'martʃa] *sf* reverse (gear).

contropelo [kontro'pelo] *avv* against the grain.

controproducente [kontroprodu'tʃɛnte] *agg* self-defeating, counter-productive.

contrordine [kon'trordine] *sm* counter-mand. **dare un contrordine** countermand.

controsenso [kontro'sɛnso] *sm* nonsense, contradiction in terms.

controversia [kontro'vɛrsja] *sf* controversy. **controverso** *agg* controversial.

controvoglia [kontro'vɔʎa] *avv* unwillingly.

conturbare [kontur'bare] *v* perturb.

contusione [kontu'zjone] *sf* bruise. **contuso** *agg* bruised.

convalescenza [konvale'ʃɛntsa] *sf* convalescence. **convalescente** *s(m+f), agg* convalescent. **convalescenziario** *sm* convalescent home.

convalidare [konvali'dare] *v* confirm. **convalida** or **convalidazione** *sf* confirmation.

convegno [kon'veɲo] *sm* meeting, rendez-vous. **darsi convegno** make a date; meet.

*__convenire__ [konve'nire] *v* (*venire insieme*) come together, meet; (*essere d'accordo*) agree; (*ammettere*) admit; (*essere vantaggioso*) suit, pay, be worth it. **conveniente** *agg* (*vantaggioso*) favourable, reasonable; (*adatto, adeguato*) suitable. **convenienza** *sf* (*utilità*) convenience; (*decoro*) propriety; (*l'essere adatto*) suitability.

convento [kon'vɛnto] *sm* convent.

convenzione [konven'tsjone] *sf* (*patto*) agreement; (*uso*) custom, convention.

***convergere** [kon'verdʒere] *v* converge. **convergente** *agg* converging.

conversare [konver'sare] *v* converse. **conversazione** *sf* conversation, talk.

conversione [konver'sjone] *sf* conversion; (*trasformazione*) change, turn(ing).

convertire [konver'tire] *v* convert, turn. **convertibile** *agg* convertible. **convertito, -a** *sm, sf* convert.

convesso [kon'vɛsso] *agg* convex.

***convincere** [kon'vintʃere] *v* convince. **convincente** *agg* convincing. **convinto** *agg* (*persuaso*) convinced; (*dimostrato colpevole*) convicted; (*fedele*) staunch. **convinzione** *sf* conviction.

convitato [konvi'tato] *sm* guest.

convito [kon'vito] *sm* banquet.

convitto [kon'vitto] *sm* boarding-school.

convocare [konvo'kare] *v* convoke, convene; (*radunare*) call together, rally.

convoglio [kon'vɔʎo] *sm* convoy. **convoglio funebre** funeral procession. **convogliare** *v* (*scortare*) convoy; (*condurre, trasportare*) convey.

convulsione [konvul'sjone] *sf* convulsion. **convulsivo** *agg* convulsive. **convulso** *agg* convulsed.

cooperare [koope'rare] *v* cooperate, collaborate; contribute. **cooperativa** *sf* cooperative. **cooperazione** *sf* cooperation, collaboration.

coordinare [koordi'nare] *v* coordinate. **coordinata** *sf* coordinate.

coperchio [ko'pɛrkjo] *sm* lid, cover.

coperta [ko'pɛrta] *sf* (*drappo*) blanket; (*riparo*) cover. **copertina** *sf* (*quaderno*) cover; (*libro*) dust-jacket.

coperto¹ [ko'pɛrto] *agg* covered; (*riparato*) sheltered; (*chiuso*) closed; (*nuvoloso*) overcast; (*nascosto*) concealed. *sm* **al coperto** under cover. **mettersi al coperto** shelter.

coperto² [ko'pɛrto] *sm* (*a tavola*) place (-setting); (*prezzo*) cover charge.

copertone [koper'tone] *sm* (*pneumatico*) tyre; (*telone*) tarpaulin.

copia ['kɔpja] *sf* copy; (*fig*) image. **bella/brutta copia** fair/rough copy. **copiare**

v copy. **carta copiativa** *sf* carbon paper. **matita copiativa** *sf* indelible pencil. **copiatura** *sf* copy; (*trascrizione*) copying.

copioso [ko'pjozo] *agg* copious.

coppa ['kɔppa] *sf* cup; (*auto*) sump.

coppia ['kɔppja] *sf* couple. **a coppie** in pairs, in twos.

***coprire** [ko'prire] *v* cover; (*nascondere*) hide. **coprire un rumore** drown a noise.

coraggio [ko'raddʒo] *sm* courage, bravery; (*sfacciataggine*) nerve; (*cuore*) heart. **farsi coraggio** pluck up courage. **perdere coraggio** lose heart. **coraggioso** *agg* courageous, brave; (*ardito*) bold.

corallo [ko'rallo] *sm* coral.

corazzare [korat'tsare] *v* armour. **corazza** *sf* armour. **corazzata** *sf* battleship.

corbelleria [korbelle'ria] *sf* (*detto*) nonsense; (*atto*) foolery.

corda ['kɔrda] *sf* cord; (*cordicella, musica*) string; (*fune*) rope; (*geom*) chord. **avere la corda al collo** have one's back to the wall. **essere giù di corda** feel low. **tagliar la corda** (*andarsene di soppiatto*) sneak off; (*fuggire*) cut and run.

cordiale [kor'djale] *agg* cordial, warm. **cordiali saluti** kind regards *pl*. **cordialità** *sf* friendliness.

cordoglio [kor'dɔʎo] *sm* grief. **esprimere il proprio cordoglio** offer one's condolences.

cordone [kor'done] *sm* cord; (*schieramento*) cordon.

coreografo [kore'ɔgrafo] *sm* choreographer. **coreografia** *sf* choreography.

coriandoli [ko'rjandoli] *sm pl* confetti *sing*.

coricare [kori'kare] *v* lay down; (*mettere a letto*) put to bed. **coricarsi** *v* lie down; go to bed.

cornacchia [kor'nakkja] *sf* crow.

cornamusa [korna'muza] *sf* bagpipes *pl*.

cornetto [kor'netto] *sm* (*musica*) cornet; (*telefono*) receiver.

cornice [kor'nitʃe] *sf* frame; (*ambiente*) setting; (*arch*) cornice.

corno ['kɔrno] *sm, pl* **-a** *f* in zool sense horn; (*ramificato*) antler; (*musica*) French horn. **corno da caccia** bugle. **corno inglese** cor anglais. **dire corna di** run down. **fare le corna** (*non essere fedele*) be unfaithful; (*gesto*) make a V-sign. **non capire un corno** not understand a thing. **non valere un corno** not be worth a brass farthing. **cornuto** *agg* horned.

coro ['kɔro] *sm* choir; (*canto*) chorus. **in coro** in chorus, all together.

corpo ['kɔrpo] *sm* body; (*mil, ecc.*) corps. **a corpo morto** headlong, whole-heartedly. **corpo a corpo** hand to hand. **corporatura** *sf* build. **corporeo** *agg* bodily.

corporazione [korpora'tsjone] *sf* guild, association.

corpulento [korpu'lɛnto] *agg* stout.

corpuscolo [kor'puskolo] *sm* corpuscle.

corredo [kor'rɛdo] *sm* outfit; (*mil*) equipment. **corredare** *v* fit out, equip; (*fig*) furnish (with).

***correggere** [kor'reddʒere] *v* correct; (*bevanda*) lace.

corrente [kor'rɛnte] *agg* current; (*che scorre*) running; (*andante*) common or garden. **essere/tenere al corrente** be/keep informed *or* up-to-date. **mettere al corrente** acquaint, inform. *sf* current, stream; (*tendenza, moda*) trend. **corrente d'aria** draught.

***correre** ['korrere] *v* run; (*veicoli*) go; (*circolare*) circulate. **correre dietro a** run after.

corretto [kor'rɛtto] *agg* correct, right, exact. **correttezza** *sf* fairness; (*educazione*) propriety.

correzione [korre'tsjone] *sf* correction. **correzione di bozze** proof-reading.

corridoio [korri'dojo] *sm* passage, corridor.

corridore [korri'dore] *sm* runner; (*automobilista*) racing-driver; (*ciclista*) racing-cyclist. **cavallo corridore** *sm* racehorse.

corriera [kor'rjɛra] *sf* coach.

corriere [kor'rjɛre] *sm* messenger, courier; (*merci*) carrier; (*posta*) mail.

corrimano [korri'mano] *sm* handrail.

***corrispondere** [korris'pondere] *v* correspond; (*accordarsi*) agree; (*pagare*) pay; (*ricambiare*) reciprocate. **corrispondente** *s(m + f)* correspondent. **corrispondenza** *sf* correspondence; (*posta*) mail; (*conformità*) relation; (*somiglianza*) likeness.

corroborare [korrobo'rare] *v* corroborate; (*rinforzare*) strengthen.

***corrodere** [kor'rodere] *v* corrode. **corrosione** *sf* corrosion.

***corrompere** [kor'rompere] *v* corrupt;

(*con denaro*) bribe; (*guastare*) spoil. **corrotto** *agg* corrupt.

corrucciarsi [korrut'tʃarsi] *v* be angered and upset (by).

corrugare [korru'gare] *v* crease, wrinkle. **corrugare la fronte** knit one's brow.

corruzione [korru'tsjone] *sf* corruption; (*con denaro*) bribery.

corsa ['korsa] *sf* (*gara*) race; (*azione*) racing; (*atletica*) running; (*percorso*) run. **andare di corsa** (be in a) hurry. **di gran corsa** in a great hurry, in great haste. **fare una corsa (da)** (*fam*) pop over *or* round (to).

corsia [kor'sia] *sf* (*teatro, ecc.*) gangway; (*ospedale*) ward; (*autostrada*) lane; (*tappeto*) runner.

corsivo [kor'sivo] *agg* italic. *sm* italics *pl*.

corso[1] ['korso] *sm* course; (*econ*) circulation; (*quotazione*) rate; (*strada principale*) high street. **in corso** in progress; (*in sospeso*) pending; (*corrente*) present.

corso[2] ['kɔrso], **-a** *s, agg* Corsican.

corte ['korte] *sf* court; (*cortile*) courtyard. **corte marziale** court-martial. **fare la corte (a)** (*ragazza*) court; (*lusingare*) play up (to). **corteggiare** *v* court. **corteggio** *sm* retinue.

corteccia [kor'tettʃa] *sf* (*albero*) bark; (*frutto*) rind; (*anat*) cortex.

corteo [kor'tɛo] *sm* procession.

cortese [kor'teze] *agg* polite, courteous; (*gentile*) kind. **cortesia** *sf* politeness, courtesy; kindness. **avere la cortesia di** be so kind as to. **per cortesia** (*per favore*) please, kindly; (*per ragioni di cortesia*) out of politeness.

cortile [kor'tile] *sm* courtyard; (*casa colonica*) farmyard. **animali da cortile** *sm pl* farmyard animals *pl*.

cortina [kor'tina] *sf* curtain. **cortina di ferro** iron curtain. **cortina di fumo** smoke-screen.

corto ['kɔrto] *agg* short. **a farla corta** to come to the point. **essere a corto di** be short of.

corvo ['kɔrvo] *sm* (*imperiale*) raven; (*comune*) rook.

cosa ['kɔza] *pron* what. **a cosa serve?** what is it for? *sf* thing; (*qualcosa*) something; (*faccenda*) matter. **a cose fatte** after the event. **cosa da nulla** nothing. **cosa da poco** trifle. **gran cosa** much. **qualsiasi** *or* **qualunque cosa** anything. **tante cose** (*augurio*) best wishes *pl*.

coscia ['kɔʃa] *sf* thigh; (*gastr*) leg.

cosciente [koʃɛnte] *agg* aware. **coscienza** *sf* conscience; (*conoscenza*) consciousness; (*impegno*) conscientiousness. **avere la coscienza pulita/sporca** have a clear/guilty conscience. **in coscienza** morally, honestly. **coscienzioso** *agg* conscientious.

coscrizione [koskri'tsjone] *sf* draft, conscription. **coscritto** *sm* conscript, recruit.

così [ko'zi] *avv* (*in questo modo*) like this or that; (*tanto*) so; (*con agg qualificante un sostantivo*) such. *cong* so. **così ... come ...** as ... as .... **così così** so-so. **cosiddetto** *agg* so-called.

cosmetico [koz'metiko] *sm*, *agg* cosmetic. **cosmesi** or **cosmetica** *sf* beauty culture.

cosmo ['kɔzmo] *sm* cosmos. **cosmonauta** *s(m + f)* astronaut. **cosmonautica** *sf* astronautics.

cosmopolita [kozmo'pɔlita] *s(m + f)*, *agg* cosmopolitan.

coso ['kozo] *sm* (*fam*) thingummy.

***cospargere** [kos'pardʒere] *v* strew.

cospicuo [kos'pikuo] *agg* conspicuous; (*grande*) considerable.

cospirare [kospi'rare] *v* plot.

costa ['kɔsta] *sf* coast, coastline; (*litorale*) shore; (*coltello, libro*) back; (*costola*) rib.

costà [kos'ta] *avv* (over) there.

costante [kos'tante] *agg* constant, firm; (*saldo*) steady. *sf* constant. **costanza** *sf* steadfastness, firmness.

costare [kos'tare] *v* cost. **costar caro** be expensive. **mi è costato caro** I have paid dearly for it.

costeggiare [kosted'dʒare] *v* skirt; (*costa*) follow the coast.

costei [kos'tɛi] *pron* this woman.

costellare [kostel'lare] *v* stud.

costellazione [kostella'tsjone] *sf* constellation.

costernare [koster'nare] *v* dismay.

costiero [kos'tjɛra] *agg* coastal.

costipato [kosti'pato] *agg* (*stitico*) constipated; (*fam: raffreddato*) having a bad cold.

costituire [kostitu'ire] *v* (*formare*) set up, form; (*dar luogo*) constitute; (*dichiarare*) appoint. **costituirsi** *v* (*presentarsi spontaneamente*) give oneself up. **costituirsi parte civile** take legal proceedings. **costituzione** *sf* constitution.

costo ['kɔsto] *sm* cost, price. **costoso** *agg* costly, dear.

costola ['kɔstola] *sf* rib.

costoro [kos'toro] *pron* these people.

***costringere** [kos'trindʒere] *v* force, compel.

***costruire** [kostru'ire] *v* build, construct. **costruzione** *sf* construction; (*edificio*) building.

costui [kos'tui] *pron* this man.

costume [kos'tume] *sm* (*usanza*) custom, use; (*condotta*) behaviour; (*indumento*) costume; (*abitudine personale*) habit. **il buon costume** morality.

costura [kos'tura] *sf* seam.

cotogna [ko'toɲa] *sf* quince.

cotoletta [koto'letta] *sf* cutlet.

cotone [ko'tone] *sm* cotton. **cotone idrofilo** cotton-wool. **cotoniero** *agg* cotton. **cotonificio** *sm* cotton mill.

cotta ['kɔtta] *sf* **prendere una cotta** (*fam*) fall in love.

cottimo ['kɔttimo] *sm* piece-work.

cotto ['kɔtto] *agg* cooked; (*carne*) done; (*in forno*) baked. **farne di cotte e di crude** be up to all sorts of tricks. **nè cotto nè crudo** neither one thing nor the other.

cottura [kot'tura] *sf* cooking; (*in forno*) baking.

covare [ko'vare] *v* hatch; (*fig*) brood over; (*sotto la cenere*) smoulder. **covata** *sf* brood.

covo ['kovo] *sm* lair, den.

cozza ['kɔttsa] *sf* mussel.

cozzare [kot'tsare] *v* collide or clash (with); (*con le corna*) butt. **cozzo** *sm* collision, clash; butt.

crampo ['krampo] *sm* cramp.

cranio ['kranjo] *sm* skull.

cratere [kra'tɛre] *sm* crater.

cravatta [kra'vatta] *sf* tie.

creanza [kre'antsa] *sf* (good) manners *pl*, breeding.

creare [kre'are] *v* create, give rise to; (*eleggere*) appoint. **creatore** *sm* maker, creator. **creatura** *sf* creature. **creazione** *sf* creation.

credenza[1] [kre'dɛntsa] *sf* belief (*pl* -s), opinion; (*fede*) faith; (*comm*) credit.

credenza[2] [kre'dɛntsa] *sf* (*mobile*) sideboard.

credere ['krɛdere] *v* believe; (*pensare*) think; (*aver fiducia*) trust. **credibile** *agg* credible, believable. **credibilità** *sf* credibility.

credito ['kredito] *sm* credit; (*stima*) esteem. **creditore** *sm* creditor.

credulo ['krɛdulo] *agg* credulous. **credulone, -a** *sm, sf* gullible person.

crema ['krɛma] *sf* cream. **cremoso** *agg* creamy.

cremare [kre'mare] *v* cremate. **crematorio** *sm* crematorium. **cremazione** *sf* cremation.

cremisi ['krɛmizi] *agg, sm* crimson.

cren ['krɛn] *sm* horse-radish.

crepare [kre'pare] *v* burst, crack; (*fam: morire*) die, kick the bucket. **crepacuore** *sm* heartbreak.

crepitare [krepi'tare] *v* crackle. **crepitio** *sm* crackle, crackling.

crepuscolo [kre'puskolo] *sm* twilight, dusk; decline.

***crescere** ['kreʃere] *v* grow; (*maturarsi*) grow up; (*aumentare*) rise; (*sovrabbondare*) be left over. **crescita** *sf* growth.

crescione [kre'ʃone] *sm* (*d'acqua*) watercress; (*inglese*) mustard and cress.

cresima ['krɛzima] *sf* confirmation. **cresimare** *v* confirm.

crespa ['krespa] *sf* (*ruga*) wrinkle; (*stoffa*) crease; (*piccola ondulazione*) ripple.

crespo ['krespo] *agg* frizzy. *sm* crepe.

cresta ['kresta] *sf* crest.

creta ['krɛta] *sf* clay.

cretino [kre'tino], **-a** *sm, sf* idiot, fool. *agg* idiotic, foolish. **cretineria** *sf* stupidity; (*discorso, azione*) foolish thing.

cricca ['krikka] *sf* clique, gang.

cricco ['krikko] *sm* jack.

criceto [kri'tʃɛto] *sm* hamster.

criminale [krimi'nale] *agg, s(m + f)* criminal. **crimine** *sm* crime. **criminoso** *agg* criminal.

criniera [kri'njɛra] *sf* mane.

cripta ['kripta] *sf* crypt.

crisalide [kri'zalide] *sf* chrysalis.

crisantemo [krizan'tɛmo] *sm* chrysanthemum.

crisi ['krizi] *sf* crisis (*pl* -ses); (*med*) fit, attack.

cristallizzare [kristallid'dzare] *v* crystallize.

cristallo [kris'tallo] *sm* crystal; (*vetro*) plate-glass; (window) pane. **cristallino** *agg* crystalline; pure, limpid.

cristiano [kris'tjano], **-a** *agg* Christian. *sm, sf* Christian; (*essere umano*) soul.

Cristo ['kristo] *sm* Christ. **non c'è cristo** (*possibilità*) there isn't a chance. **povero cristo** poor devil.

criterio [kri'tɛrjo] *sm* criterion (*pl* -a), norm; sense.

critico ['kritiko] *agg* critical. *sm* critic. **critica** *sf* criticism; (*scritto*) review; (*persona*) critic. **criticare** *v* criticize; review; (*biasimare*) blame.

crivellare [krivel'lare] *v* riddle. **crivello** *sm* sieve.

croccante [krok'kante] *agg* crisp. *sm* (*dolce*) praline.

crocchia ['krɔkkja] *sf* bun, chignon.

crocchio ['krɔkkjo] *sm* cluster.

croce ['krotʃe] *sf* cross. **a occhio e croce** roughly. **croce uncinata** swastika. **crocevia** *sm invar* crossroads. **fare a testa e croce** toss a coin. **punto a croce** *sm* cross-stitch.

crociare [kro'tʃare] *v* cross. **crociata** [kro'tʃata] *sf* crusade. **crociato** *sm* crusader.

crocicchio [kro'tʃikkjo] *sm* crossroads. **crociera** [kro'tʃɛra] *sf* cruise.

***crocifiggere** [krotʃifid'dʒere] *v* crucify. **crocifisso** [krotʃi'fisso] *sm* crucifix. *agg* crucified.

croco ['krɔko] *sm* crocus.

crogiolarsi [krodʒo'larsi] *v* bask. **crogiolo** *sm* crucible; (*fig*) melting-pot.

crollare [krol'lare] *v* (*cadere*) collapse, slump; (*spalle*) shrug. **crollo** *sm* collapse, slump.

croma ['krɔma] *sf* quaver.

cromo ['krɔmo] *sm* (*metallo*) chromium. **giallo cromo** chrome yellow. **cromatura** *sf* chromium-plating.

cromosoma [kromo'sɔma] *sm* chromosome.

cronaca ['krɔnaka] *sf* (*narrazione*) chronicle; (*radio, TV, stampa*) news, review.

cronico ['krɔniko] *agg* chronic. *sm* chronic invalid.

cronista [kro'nista] *s(m + f)* reporter.

cronologico [krono'lɔdʒiko] *agg* chronological.

cronometro [kro'nɔmetro] *sm* chronometer, stop-watch. **cronometrare** *v* time.

crosta ['krɔsta] *sf* crust; (*ferita*) scab. **crostata** *sf* tart.

crostacei [kros'tatʃei] *sm pl* crustaceans *pl*, shellfish *pl*.

crucciare [krut'tʃare] *v* distress, worry.

cruciale [kru'tʃale] *agg* crucial.

cruciverba [krutʃi'vɛrba] *sm invar* cross-word.

crudele [kru'dɛle] *agg* cruel; (*duro, aspro*) harsh; (*doloroso*) bitter. **crudeltà** *sf* cruelty; (*asprezza*) harshness.

crudo ['krudo] *agg* raw; (*rigido*) harsh; (*brusco*) crude; (*volgare*) coarse.

crumiro [kru'miro], **-a** *sm, sf* blackleg.

cruna ['kruna] *sf* eye (of a needle).

crusca ['kruska] *sf* bran.

cruscotto [krus'kɔtto] *sm* instrument panel; (*auto*) dashboard.

cubo ['kubo] *sm* cube. **cubico** *agg* cubic. **cubismo** *sm* cubism.

cuccagna [kuk'kaɲa] *sf* (*abbondanza*) plenty; (*allegria*) fun.

cuccetta [kut'tʃetta] *sf* couchette.

cucchiaio [kuk'kjajo] *sm* spoon; (*contenuto*) spoonful; (*da tavola*) tablespoon. **cucchiaino** *sm* teaspoon.

cucciolo ['kuttʃolo] *sm* puppy.

cucina [ku'tʃina] *sf* (*luogo*) kitchen; (*atto del cucinare*) cooking; (*cibo*) food; (*apparecchio*) cooker. **cucina casalinga** home cooking. **cucinare** *v* cook.

cucire [ku'tʃire] *v* sew, stitch; (*con cucitrice*) staple. **cucirino** *sm* sewing thread. **cucito** *sm* sewing, needlework. **cucitrice** *sf* (*persona*) seamstress; (*apparecchio*) stapler. **cucitura** *sf* seam.

cuculo ['kukulo] *sm* cuckoo.

cuffia ['kuffja] *sf* cap; bonnet; (*telefono, radio*) earphones *pl*, headphones *pl*.

cugino [ku'dʒino], **-a** *sm, sf* cousin.

cui ['kui] *pron* (*persone*) whom; (*cose*) which. **il cui, la cui, ecc.** whose. **in cui** (*quando*) when; (*dove*) where.

culla ['kulla] *sf* cradle. **cullare** *v* rock, lull. **cullarsi** *v* (*illudersi*) delude oneself.

culmine ['kulmine] *sm* summit, height. **culminare** *v* culminate.

culo ['kulo] *sm* (*fam*) bottom; (*volg*) arse.

culto ['kulto] *sm* worship; (*religione*) cult.

cultura [kul'tura] *sf* culture, learning; cultivation. **culturale** *agg* cultural.

cumulo ['kumulo] *sm* pile, heap.

cuneo ['kuneo] *sm* wedge.

cunetta [ku'netta] *sf* gutter.

*****cuocere** ['kwɔtʃere] *v* (*cucinare*) cook; (*al forno*) bake; (*a lesso*) boil; (*alla griglia*) grill; (*arrosto*) roast; (*in umido*) stew; (*ceramica, ecc.*) fire. **cuocere a fuoco lento** simmer. **cuoco, -a** *sm, sf* cook.

cuoio ['kwɔjo] *sm* leather; (*pelle*) hide.

cuoio capelluto scalp. **cuoio scamosciato** chamois leather, suede.

cuore ['kwɔre] *sm* heart. **di cuore** heartily. **di tutto cuore** with all one's heart. **mettersi il cuore in pace** set one's mind at rest. **nel cuore di** at the height of; (*notte*) at dead of. **senza cuore** heartless.

cupido ['kupido] *agg* greedy. **cupidigia** *sf* greed.

cupo ['kupo] *agg* (*profondo, suono*) deep; (*privo di luce, colore*) dark.

cupola ['kupola] *sf* dome.

cura ['kura] *sf* care; (*med*) cure, treatment. **curare** *v* look after, take care of; cure, treat. **curarsi** *v* mind *or* care about. **curativo** *agg* curative.

curatore [kura'tore], **-trice** *sm, sf* guardian. **curatela** *sf* guardianship.

curioso [ku'rjozo] *agg* curious; (*strano*) odd. **curiosità** *sf* curiosity. **curiosare** *v* pry.

curvare [kur'vare] *v* bend. **curvare il capo** bow one's head. **curva** *sf* bend, curve. **curvatura** *sf* curvature, sweep. **curvo** *agg* curved, bent.

cuscino [ku'ʃino] *sm* cushion; (*guanciale*) pillow. **cuscinetto** *sm* (*a sfere*) ball-bearing; (*a rulli*) roller-bearing. **stato cuscinetto** *sm* buffer state.

custode [kus'tɔde] *s(m+f)* keeper, caretaker. **custodia** *sf* custody, care, safe keeping; (*astuccio*) case. **custodire** *v* keep; look after; (*sorvegliare*) guard.

cutaneo [ku'taneo] *agg* cutaneous, skin.

D

da [da] *prep* from; (*moto a luogo*) to; (*stato in luogo*) at; (*durata*) for; (*fin da*) since; (*causa*) of, from; (*segno distintivo*) with; (*come*) as, like. **da allora** since then. **da allora in poi** ever since. **da lontano** from afar. **da molto** for a long time. **da noi** at home; (*al mio paese*) in my country.

dabbasso [dab'basso] *avv* downstairs.

dabbene [dab'bene] *agg* decent, honest.

daccapo [dak'kapo] *avv* (*di nuovo*) again, once more; (*da principio*) from the beginning, all over again.

dacché [dak'ke] *cong* since.

dado ['dado] *sm* die (*pl* dice); (*gastr*) cube; (*mec*) nut.

daffare [daf'fare] *sm invar* work, business.

dagli[1] ['daʎi] *prep+art* da gli.

dagli[2] ['daʎi] *inter (forza)* go on! come on! *(noioso)* not again! pack it in!

dai ['dai] *prep+art* da i.

daino ['daino] *sm* (fallow) deer. **daina** *sf* doe. **pelle di daino** *sf* buckskin.

dal [dal] *prep+art* da il.

dalia ['dalja] *sf* dahlia.

dall' [dall] *prep+art* da l'.

dalla ['dalla] *prep+art* da la.

dalle ['dalle] *prep+art* da le.

dallo ['dallo] *prep+art* da lo.

daltonismo [dalto'nizmo] *sm* colour-blindness. **daltonico** *agg* colour-blind.

dama ['dama] *sf* lady, noblewoman; *(gioco)* draughts; *(carta)* queen.

damasco [da'masko] *sm* damask.

dancing ['daɪnsiŋ] *sm invar* dance-hall.

Danimarca [dani'marka] *sf* Denmark. **danese** *sm, agg* Danish; *s(m+f)* Dane.

dannare [dan'nare] *v* damn. **dannato, -a** *s, agg* damned. **dannazione** *sf* damnation; *(tormento)* trial.

danneggiare [danned'dʒare] *v (guastare)* damage; *(nuocere)* injure, harm. **danno** *sm* damage; injury, harm; *(pregiudizio)* detriment. **danno doloso** wilful damage. **dannoso** *agg* harmful.

danzare [dan'tsare] *v* dance. **danza** *sf* dancing; *(ballo)* dance. **danzatore, -trice** *sm, sf* dancer.

dappertutto [dapper'tutto] *avv* everywhere, all over the place.

dappoco [dap'pɔko] *agg invar* worthless; *(inetto)* good-for-nothing.

dappresso [dap'presso] *avv* close to, close up.

dapprima [dap'prima] *avv* at first.

dardeggiare [darded'dʒare] *v* dart. **dardo** *sm* dart.

*dare ['dare] *v* give; *(avere come risultato)* make, come to; *(esame)* take; apply; *(colpire)* hit; *(fruttare)* yield. **dare ai** *or* **sui nervi a qualcuno** get on someone's nerves. **dare alla luce** give birth to. **dar da fare a** keep busy. **dar fine a** put an end to. **dare nell'occhio** catch the eye. **dare per scontato** take for granted. **dar retta a** listen to. **dare su** look out on to; *(affacciare)* face. **darsi a** *(dedicarsi)* devote oneself to; *(applicarsi)* go in for.

darsena ['darsena] *sf* dock.

data ['data] *sf* date. **di fresca data** recent. **di vecchia data** of long standing. **in che**

data? when? **datare** *v* date; *(risalire)* go back (to).

dato ['dato] *agg* given; *(in vista)* considering, in view of. **dato che** supposing that, as, since. *sm* data. **dato di fatto** fact. **datore di lavoro** *sm* employer.

dattero ['dattero] *sm (frutto)* date; *(albero)* date-palm.

dattilografo [datti'lɔgrafo], **-a** *sm, sf* typist. **dattilografare** *v* type.

davanti [da'vanti] *avv* in front. *sm, agg* front. **davanti a** in front of; *(dirimpetto)* facing; *(in presenza di)* before.

davanzale [davan'tsale] *sm* window-sill.

davvero [dav'vero] *avv* really. **dici davvero?** do you (really) mean it?

dazio ['datsjo] *sm (imposta)* duty; *(ufficio)* customs (office).

dea ['dɛa] *sf* goddess.

debito[1] ['debito] *agg* due.

debito[2] ['debito] *sm* debt; *(comm)* debit; *(dovere)* duty. **estinguere/fare un debito** settle/incur a debt. **sentirsi in debito** be indebted. **debitore** *sm* debtor.

debole ['debole] *agg* weak, feeble; *(luce, suono, speranza)* faint. *sm (persona)* weakling; *(punto)* weak point; *(inclinazione)* weakness, foible. **debolezza** *sf* weakness; *(difetto)* failing.

debuttare [debut'tare] *v* make one's debut. **debutto** *sm* debut.

decade ['dɛkade] *sf* ten days *pl*.

*decadere [deka'dere] *v* decline. **decadere da** *(dir)* forfeit. **decadente** *agg* decadent. **decadenza** *sf* decline; *(dir)* forfeiture, lapse. **decaduto** *agg* impoverished; *(scaduto)* fallen into disuse.

decalcomania [dekalkoma'nia] *sf* transfer.

decano [de'kano] *sm* dean; *(diplomatico)* doyen.

decantare[1] [dekan'tare] *v (lodare)* sing the praises of.

decantare[2] [dekan'tare] *v (liquido)* decant.

decapitare [dekapi'tare] *v* behead.

deceduto [detʃe'duto] *agg* deceased.

decennio [de'tʃɛnnjo] *sm* decade.

decente [de'tʃɛnte] *agg* decent. **decenza** *sf* decency, propriety.

decentrare [detʃen'trare] *v* decentralize. **decentramento** *sm* decentralization.

decesso [de'tʃesso] *sm* death.

decibel [detʃi'bɛl] *sm invar* decibel.

*decidere [de'tʃidere] *v* decide (on); *(risolvere, determinare)* settle. **decidersi**

make up one's mind; (*indursi*) bring oneself to.

deciduo [de'tʃiduo] *agg* deciduous.

decifrare [detʃi'frare] *v* decipher; (*fam*) make out.

decimale [detʃi'male] *agg, sm* decimal.

decimo ['dɛtʃimo] *sm, agg* tenth.

decina [de'tʃina] *sf* ten; (*circa dieci*) ten or so. **a decine** (*fig*) by the dozen.

decisione [detʃi'zjone] *sf* decision, resolution; (*dir*) ruling. **decisivo** *agg* decisive; (*prova*) conclusive; (*voto*) casting.

deciso [de'tʃizo] *agg* (*fermo*) decided, firm, resolute; (*definito, risolto*) settled, resolved; (*spiccato*) decided, marked. **decisamente** *avv* decidedly; definitely.

declamare [dekla'mare] *v* declaim; (*protestare*) rail.

declinare [dekli'nare] *v* decline. **declinazione** *sf* (*fis*) declination; (*gramm*) declension. **declino** *sm* decline.

declivio [de'klivjo] *sm* slope.

decollare [dekol'lare] *v* take off. **decollo** *sm* take-off.

*decomporsi [dekom'porsi] *v* disintegrate, decompose. **decomposizione** *sf* disintegration, decomposition.

decorare [deko'rare] *v* decorate. **decorazione** *sf* decoration.

decoro [de'kɔro] *sm* dignity; (*orgoglio*) pride. **decoroso** *agg* proper.

decorrere [de'korrere] *v* elapse. **con decorrenza da ...** with effect from. **decorso** *sm* (*svolgimento*) course; (*periodo*) lapse.

decrepito [de'krɛpito] *agg* decrepit.

decrescente [dekre'ʃɛnte] *agg* decreasing, diminishing; (*luna*) on the wane.

decreto [de'kreto] *sm* decree, order. **decreto di citazione** writ; (*testimone*) subpoena. **decretare** *v* decree, order; (*concedere*) award.

dedalo ['dɛdalo] *sm* maze.

dedicare [dedi'kare] *v* dedicate, devote; consecrate; (*intitolare*) name after. **dedicarsi a** (*occuparsi di*) take up, go in for. **dedica** *sf* dedication.

dedito ['dɛdito] *agg* devoted; (*assorbito*) engrossed (in); (*vizio*) addicted.

*dedurre [de'durre] *v* deduce; (*desumere*) infer; (*prendere, derivare*) take, draw; (*sottrarre*) deduct. **deduzione** *sf* deduction.

defalcare [defal'kare] *v* deduct.

deferire [defe'rire] *v* defer, refer. **deferire al tribunale** sue. **deferente** *agg* deferential.

deficiente [defi'tʃɛnte] *agg* deficient; insufficient; (*inferiore alla media*) backward; (*fam*) moronic. *s(m+f)* moron, half-wit. **deficienza** *sf* deficiency, lack; (*scarsità*) shortage; (*idiozia*) mental deficiency.

deficit ['dɛfitʃit] *sm invar* deficit. **bilancio deficitario** *sm* debit balance.

definire [defi'nire] *v* define; (*risolvere*) settle. **definitivo** *agg* definitive. **in definitiva** (*dopo tutto*) after all; to sum up; (*in fin dei conti*) all things considered. **definizione** *sf* definition; settlement.

deflazione [defla'tsjone] *sf* deflation. **deflazionare** *v* deflate. **deflazionistico** *agg* deflationary.

*deflettere [de'flettere] *v* deviate. **deflessione** *sf* deflection; deviation.

deformare [defor'mare] *v* deform, distort; (*mec*) warp; (*senso*) twist. **deformazione** *sf* deformation, distortion; warping. **deforme** *agg* deformed, misshapen; (*viso*) disfigured.

defunto [de'funto], **-a** *s, agg* deceased.

degenerare [dedʒene'rare] *v* degenerate. **degenerato, -a** *s, agg* degenerate.

degente [de'dʒɛnte] *agg* bedridden. **degenza** *sf* (*a letto*) stay in bed; (*in ospedale*) stay in hospital.

degli ['deʎi] *prep + art* di gli.

degnare [de'ɲare] *v* deign; deem *or* consider worthy. **degnarsi di** condescend to. **degno** *agg* worthy, deserving. **degno di fiducia** trustworthy. **degno di lode** praiseworthy. **degno di nota** noteworthy.

degradare [degra'dare] *v* degrade. **degradazione** *sf* degradation.

degustare [degus'tare] *v* taste, sample.

dei[1] ['dei] *prep + art* di i.

dei[2] ['dei] *V* dio.

deificare [deifi'kare] *v* deify.

del [del] *prep + art* di il.

delatore [dela'tore], **-trice** *sm, sf* informer. **delazione** *sf* denouncement; (*fam*) tip-off.

delegare [dele'gare] *v* delegate. **delega** *sf* (*procura*) proxy; (*dir*) power of attorney. **delegato, -a** *sm, sf* delegate. **delegazione** *sf* delegation.

deleterio [dele'tɛrjo] *agg* harmful.

delfino [del'fino] *sm* dolphin.

deliberare [delibe'rare] *v* deliberate;

(*decidere*) resolve. **deliberato** *agg* determined, resolved. **deliberazione** *sf* deliberation, decision.

delicato [deli'kato] *agg* delicate; (*gusto*) refined. **delicatezza** *sf* delicacy; (*tatto*) tact; refinement.

delimitare [delimi'tare] *v* define, circumscribe. **delimitazione** *sf* demarcation.

delineare [deline'are] *v* sketch, outline. **delinearsi** *v* (*presentarsi*) appear, emerge; (*apparire*) loom up, take shape.

delinquente [delin'kwɛnte] *s(m+f)* delinquent, criminal; (*mascalzone*) rascal. **delinquenza** *sf* criminality.

deliquio [de'likwio] *sm* **cadere in deliquio** faint. **essere in deliquio** be in a faint.

delirare [deli'rare] *v* be delirious; (*farneticare*) rave. **delirio** *sm* delirium; (*follia*) frenzy.

delitto [de'litto] *sm* crime; (*reato*) offence; (*grave*) felony; (*lieve*) misdemeanour. **delittuoso** *agg* criminal.

delizia [de'litsja] *sf* delight. **delizioso** *agg* delightful; (*sapore*) delicious.

dell' [dell] *prep + art* **di l'**.

della ['della] *prep + art* **di la**.

delle ['delle] *prep + art* **di le**.

dello ['dello] *prep + art* **di lo**.

delta ['delta] *sm invar* delta.

*deludere [de'ludere] *v* disappoint; (*render vano*) frustrate.

delusione [delu'zjone] *sf* disappointment. **deluso** *agg* disappointed.

demente [de'mente] *agg* insane. *s(m+f)* lunatic. **demenza** *sf* madness, insanity; (*med*) dementia.

democratico [demo'kratiko], **-a** *sm*, *sf* democrat. *agg* democratic. **democrazia** *sf* democracy.

democristiano [demokris'tjano], **-a** *sm*, *sf* Christian Democrat. *agg* Christian Democratic.

demografia [demogra'fia] *sf* demography. **demografico** *agg* demographic.

demolire [demo'lire] *v* demolish. **demolizione** *sf* demolition.

demone ['dɛmone] *sm* demon; (*potenza ispiratrice*) genius; passion. **demonico** *agg* demonic.

demonio [de'mɔnjo] *sm* devil. **brutto come il demonio** as ugly as sin. **demoniaco** *agg* demoniacal, devilish.

demoralizzare [demoralid'dzare] *v* demoralize. **demoralizzarsi** *v* lose heart.

denaro [de'naro] *sm* money; (*grossezza di filo*) denier. **denaro spicciolo** small change.

denigrare [deni'grare] *v* denigrate; (*fam*) run down. **denigratorio** *agg* disparaging. **denigrazione** *sf* denigration, disparagement.

denominatore [denomina'tore] *sm* denominator. **denominare** *v* name. **denominazione** *sf* naming; (*nome*) name.

denotare [deno'tare] *v* denote, show.

denso ['dɛnso] *agg* dense, thick. **densità** *sf* density; (*spessore*) thickness.

dente ['dɛnte] *sm* tooth (*pl* teeth); (*ruota*) cog; (*forchetta*) prong. **a denti stretti** tight-lipped. **avere il dente avvelenato contro** have it in for. **dente del giudizio** wisdom tooth. **dente di latte** milk-tooth. **dente finto** false tooth. **dente sporgente** buck-tooth. **mettere i denti** teethe, cut one's teeth. **restare a denti asciutti** go hungry; (*fig*) go away empty-handed. **dentario** *agg* dental. **dentato** *agg* toothed.

dentellare [dentel'lare] *v* indent, notch. **dentellatura** *sf* indentation.

dentice ['dɛntitʃe] *sm* sea bream.

dentiera [den'tjɛra] *sf* denture.

dentifricio [denti'fritʃo] *sm* toothpaste.

dentista [den'tista] *s(m+f)* dentist.

dentro ['dentro] *avv* in; (*all'interno*) inside. *prep* in, inside; (*in casa*) indoors. **andar dentro** (*fam*) go to jail.

denunziare [denun'tsjare] *v* **also denunciare** denounce; (*riferire*) report; (*dichiarare*) declare; (*disdire*) terminate; (*rendere palese*) show. **denunzia** *or* **denuncia** *sf* report; (*accusa*) charge; declaration; notice of termination.

deodorante [deodo'rante] *agg, sm* deodorant.

deperire [depe'rire] *v* (*piante*) wither; (*animali*) waste away; (*persone*) get run down; (*cibi*) perish. **deperibile** *agg* perishable.

depilatorio [depila'torjo] *agg* depilatory. *sm* hair-remover.

depliant [depli'ã] *sm*, *pl* **-s** leaflet.

deplorare [deplo'rare] *v* (*compiangere*) lament, regret; (*biasimare*) deplore, regret. **deplorevole** *agg* deplorable.

*deporre [de'porre] *v* put *or* set down, deposit, lay; (*testimoniare*) (bear) witness. **deporre in giudizio** give evidence. **deposizione** *sf* deposition, testimony.

deportare [depor'tare] *v* deport. **deportato, -a** *sm, sf* deportee. **deportazione** *sf* deportation.
deposito [de'pɔzito] *sm* deposit; (*magazzino*) warehouse, store. **deposito bagagli** left-luggage office. **depositare** *v* deposit. **depositario** *sm* trustee.
depravare [depra'vare] *v* deprave.
depredare [depre'dare] *v* plunder.
depresso [de'prɛsso] *agg* depressed. **depressione** *sf* depression. **depressivo** *agg* depressive, depressant.
***deprimere** [de'primere] *v* depress. **deprimente** *agg* depressing.
depurare [depu'rare] *v* purify. **depuratore** *sm* purifier. **depurazione** *sf* purification.
deputare [depu'tare] *v* delegate. **deputato, -a** *sm, sf* deputy; delegate; Member of Parliament.
deragliare [dera'ʎare] *v* be derailed, go off the rails. **deragliamento** *sm* derailment.
derapare [dera'pare] *v* skid.
derelitto [dere'litto], **-a** *agg* forsaken. *sm, sf* down-and-out; (*trovatello*) foundling.
deretano [dere'tano] *sm* behind.
***deridere** [de'ridere] *v* laugh at, mock, deride. **derisione** *sf* derision, ridicule. **derisorio** *agg* derisory, laughable.
deriva [de'riva] *sf* **alla deriva** adrift. **andare alla deriva** drift.
derivare [deri'vare] *v* derive; (*conseguire*) follow, result; (*sviare*) divert. **derivata** *sf* (*mat*) derivative. **derivato** *sm* (*chim*) derivative; (*sottoprodotto*) by-product. **derivazione** *sf* derivation, origin. **collegare in derivazione** (*elett, radio*) shunt.
dermatite [derma'tite] *sf* dermatitis. **dermatologo, -a** *sm, sf* dermatologist.
derogare [dero'gare] *v* deviate (from), depart (from); (*non osservare*) not comply (with); (*dir*) waive. **deroga** *sf* departure. **in deroga a** notwithstanding; (*dir*) waiving. **derogabile** *agg* not binding.
derrate [der'rate] *sf pl* provisions *pl*; (*alimentari*) foodstuffs *pl*.
derubare [deru'bare] *v* rob.
***descrivere** [des'krivere] *v* describe. **descrittivo** *agg* descriptive. **non descrivibile** indescribable. **descrizione** *sf* description, account.
deserto [de'zɛrto] *sm* desert, wilderness.

agg (*vuoto*) deserted; (*disabitato*) uninhabited.
desiderare [dezide'rare] *v* wish; (*volere*) want; (*bramare*) long for, desire. **lasciare a desiderare** leave to be desired. **desiderabile** *agg* desirable.
desiderio [dezi'dɛrjo] *sm* wish; (*brama, rimpianto*) longing, desire. **aver desiderio di** wish *or* want to. **pio desiderio** wishful thinking.
designare [dezi'ɲare] *v* designate; (*denominare*) call; (*nominare, stabilire*) appoint.
desinare [dezi'nare] *sm* lunch, dinner. *v* lunch, dine.
desinenza [dezi'nɛntsa] *sf* ending.
***desistere** [de'zistere] *v* desist. **desistere da** give up.
desolato [dezo'lato] *agg* (*afflitto*) distressed; (*deserto*) desolate; (*devastato*) desolated. **desolante** *agg* distressing. **desolazione** *sf* desolation; distress.
despota ['dɛspota] *sm* despot.
destare [des'tare] *v* awake, rouse; (*suscitare*) arouse, awaken. **destar meraviglia** cause wonder.
destinare [desti'nare] *v* destine; (*assegnare*) intend, assign; (*dedicare*) devote; (*riservare*) set aside; (*indirizzare*) address; decide. **destinatario, -a** *sm, sf* (*lettera*) addressee; (*merci*) consignee. **esser destinato a** (*decretato dalla sorte*) be bound *or* destined to; (*condannato*) be doomed to. **destinazione** *sf* destination. **destino** *sm* destiny, fate.
destituire [destitu'ire] *v* dismiss. **destituito** *agg* dismissed; (*privo*) devoid. **destituzione** *sf* dismissal.
desto ['desto] *agg* (*sveglio*) (wide-)awake; (*vivace*) lively.
destra ['dɛstra] *sf* (*lato*) right, right-hand side; (*mano*) right hand; (*pol*) right (wing). **a destra** on *or* to the right. **tenere la destra** keep (to the) right.
destro ['dɛstro] *agg* (*lato*) right(-hand); (*abile*) skilful, dextrous; (*accorto*) clever. **destrezza** *sf* ability, skill, dexterity. **destrorso** *agg* from left to right; (*in senso orario*) clockwise.
detenere [dete'nere] *v* hold; (*trattenere in prigione*) detain. **detenuto, -a** *sm, sf* detainee. **detenzione** *sf* detention. **detenzione abusiva** unlawful possession.
detergente [deter'dʒɛnte] *sm, agg* detergent.

deteriorare [deterjo'rare] *v* deteriorate.
deterioramento *sm* deterioration.
determinare [determi'nare] *v* determine; (*causare*) bring about. **determinante** *agg* determining, decisive. **determinato** *agg* (*preciso*) definite, distinct; (*stabilito*) appointed; (*noto*) given; (*particolare*) special; (*deciso*) determined. **determinazione** *sf* determination.
deterrente [deter'rɛnte] *sm, agg* deterrent.
detersivo [deter'sivo] *sm, agg* detergent.
detestare [detes'tare] *v* detest, loathe. **detestabile** *agg* hateful, odious.
detonatore [detona'tore] *sm* detonator. **detonante** *sm, agg* explosive. **capsula detonante** *sf* percussion cap.
***detrarre** [det'rarre] *v* deduct, take away; (*nuocere a*) detract (from).
detrimento [detri'mento] *sm* detriment, prejudice.
detrito [de'trito] *sm* debris; (*geol*) detritus.
dettagliare [detta'ʎare] *v* (*particolareggiare*) detail; (*vendere al minuto*) retail. **dettagliante** *s(m+f)* retailer. **dettaglio** *sm* detail; retail.
dettare [det'tare] *v* dictate. **dettar legge** lay down the law. **dettato** *sm* dictation.
detto ['detto] *agg* (*già citato*) above-mentioned, aforesaid; (*chiamato*) known as, alias. **detto fatto** no sooner said than done. **detto fra noi** between you and me. *sm* saying.
deturpare [detur'pare] *v* disfigure, deface. **devastare** [devas'tare] *v* ravage, devastate. **devastazione** *sf* devastation, destruction. **devastatore** [devasta'tore] *agg* devastating, destructive. *sm* devastator, destroyer.
deviare [devi'are] *v* deviate; (*spostare in altra direzione*) divert. **deviazione** *sf* deviation; (*fis*) deflection; (*traffico*) diversion, detour.
devolvere [de'vɔlvere] *v* devolve, assign.
devoto [de'vɔto] *agg* (*rel*) devout; (*dedicato, affezionato*) devoted. **devozione** *sf* devotion; devoutness.
di [di] *prep* of; (*partitivo*) some, any; (*moto da luogo*) from; (*paragone*) than.
diabete [dia'bɛte] *sm* diabetes. **diabetico, -a** *s, agg* diabetic.
diacono [di'akono] *sm* deacon.
diadema [dia'dɛma] *sm* diadem, tiara.
diaframma [dia'framma] *sm* diaphragm; (*divisione*) partition.

diagnosi ['djaɲozi] *sf* diagnosis (*pl* -ses). **fare la diagnosi di** diagnose.
diagonale [djago'nale] *sf, agg* diagonal.
diagramma [dia'gramma] *sm* diagram; (*grafico*) chart, curve.
dialetto [dia'lɛtto] *sm* dialect. **dialettale** *agg* dialect.
dialogo ['djalogo] *sm, pl* -ghi dialogue; (*trattative*) negotiations *pl*; (*colloquio*) conversation, talk.
diamante [dia'mante] *sm* diamond.
diametro ['djametro] *sm* diameter. **diametrale** *agg* diametrical.
diamine ['djamine] *inter* heavens! **che diamine ... !** what on earth ... !
diapason [di'apazon] *sm* tuning fork; (*tono*) pitch; (*estensione di voce*) range.
diapositiva [diapozi'tiva] *sf* transparency, slide.
diario [di'arjo] *sm* diary, journal. **diario di bordo** log-book.
diarrea [diar'rɛa] *sf* diarrhoea.
diavolo ['djavolo] *sm* devil. **che diavolo ... !** what the devil ... ! **un buon diavolo** a good chap. **diavoleria** *sf* mischief. **diavoletto** *sm* imp; (*bigodino*) roller, curler.
dibattere [di'battere] *v* debate. **dibattersi** *v* struggle. **dibattimento** *sm* hearing. **dibattito** *sm* debate. **dibattuto** *agg* (*discusso*) controversial, vexed; (*tormentato*) troubled.
dicastero [dikas'tɛro] *sm* ministry.
dicembre [di'tʃɛmbre] *sm* December.
diceria [ditʃe'ria] *sf* rumour, gossip.
dichiarare [dikja'rare] *v* declare; (*gioco di carte*) bid. **dichiarazione** *sf* declaration; bid; (*attestazione*) statement; (*amore*) proposal. **dichiarazione dei redditi** tax return.
diciannove [ditʃan'nɔve] *agg, sm* nineteen. **diciannovesimo** *sm, agg* nineteenth.
diciassette [ditʃas'sɛtte] *agg, sm* seventeen. **diciassettesimo** *sm, agg* seventeenth.
diciotto [di'tʃɔtto] *agg, sm* eighteen. **diciottesimo** *sm, agg* eighteenth.
dicitura [ditʃi'tura] *sf* caption.
didascalia [didaska'lia] *sf* caption; (*cinema*) subtitle; (*teatro*) stage directions *pl*.
didattico [di'dattiko] *agg* didactic.
didentro [di'dɛntro] **al/dal didentro** on/from the inside.

didietro [di'djɛtro] *sm* behind.
dieci ['djɛtʃi] *sm, agg* ten.
diesis [di'ɛzis] *sm* (*musica*) sharp.
dieta ['djɛta] *sf* diet. **essere a dieta** be on a diet.
dietro ['djɛtro] *avv* behind. *prep* (*luogo*) behind; (*tempo*) after; (*su, in seguito a*) on. **dietro front** about turn.
difatti [di'fatti] *cong* in fact.
***difendere** [di'fɛndere] *v* defend.
difensiva [difen'siva] *sf* defensive. **difensivo** *agg* defensive.
difensore [difen'sore] *sm* defender. **avvocato difensore** *sm* counsel for the defence.
difesa [di'feza] *sf* defence. **difesa legittima** self-defence. **senza difesa** defenceless. **stare sulla difesa** be on the defensive.
difeso [di'fezo] *agg* (*riparato*) sheltered; (*fortificato*) defended, protected.
difetto [di'fɛtto] *sm* (*mancanza*) lack; (*imperfezione*) defect, fault. **difettare** *v* also **far difetto** lack; (*venir meno*) fail; (*essere difettoso*) be defective *or* faulty. **difettoso** *agg* defective, faulty.
diffamare [diffa'mare] *v* denigrate; (*a voce*) slander; (*per iscritto*) libel. **diffamatorio** *agg* defamatory; slanderous; libellous. **diffamatore, -trice** *sm, sf* libeller; slanderer.
differente [diffe'rente] *agg* different, unlike.
differenza [diffe'rentsa] *sf* difference. **a differenza di** unlike. **differenziale** *sm, agg* differential. **differenziare** *v* differentiate.
differire [diffe'rire] *v* (*rimandare*) defer; (*esser diverso*) differ, be different.
difficile [dif'fitʃile] *agg* difficult; (*improbabile*) unlikely; (*duro*) hard. *sm* difficulty. *s*(*m+f*) difficult person.
difficoltà [diffikol'ta] *sf* difficulty; (*ostacolo*) trouble. **difficoltoso** *agg* difficult.
diffidare [diffi'dare] *v* (*non fidarsi*) mistrust, be suspicious of; (*avvisare*) warn, caution. **diffida** *sf* warning, notice. **diffidente** *agg* suspicious. **diffidenza** *sf* suspicion.
***diffondere** [dif'fondere] *v* spread; (*luce, calore, ecc.*) diffuse; (*dilungarsi*) dwell; (*comm*) promote.
diffusione [diffu'zjone] *sf* spreading, diffusion; (*giornali*) circulation. **diffuso** *agg* widespread; diffused; widely circulated; (*prolisso*) long-winded.

diga ['diga] *sf* dam, barrier.
digerire [didʒe'rire] *v* digest; (*assimilare*) take in; (*tollerare*) stand, bear; (*credere*) swallow. **digeribile** *agg* digestible. **digestione** *sf* digestion. **digestivo** *sm, agg* digestive.
digitale [didʒi'tale] *agg* **impronta digitale** *sf* finger-print.
digiunare [didʒu'nare] *v* also **stare a digiuno** fast. **digiuno** *sm* fast. **a digiuno** on an empty stomach. **essere a digiuno di** (*fig*) be without.
dignità [diɲi'ta] *sf* dignity; (*ufficio*) (high) rank. *sf pl* dignitaries *pl*. **dignitoso** *agg* dignified.
digredire [digre'dire] *v* digress.
digressione [digres'sjone] *sf* digression.
digrignare [digri'ɲare] *v* **digrignare i denti** gnash one's teeth; (*animali*) bare the teeth.
dilagare [dila'gare] *v* flood, spread. **dilagamento** *sm* flooding.
dilaniare [dila'njare] *v* rend.
dilapidare [dilapi'dare] *v* squander.
dilatare [dila'tare] *v* dilate, open (wide). **dilatazione** *sf* dilation.
dilatorio [dila'tɔrjo] *agg* dilatory. **dilazione** *sf* delay, deferment.
dileguare [dile'gware] *v* dispel. **dileguarsi** *v* disappear, fade.
dilemma [di'lemma] *sm* dilemma.
dilettante [dilet'tante] *agg, s*(*m+f*) amateur. **dilettantesco** *agg* amateurish.
dilettare [dilet'tare] *v* delight; (*far divertire*) amuse. **dilettarsi** *v* delight in, enjoy.
diletto¹ [di'letto] *sm* (*piacere*) delight, pleasure; (*godimento*) enjoyment.
diletto² [di'letto] *agg* beloved; (*preferito*) favourite.
diligente [dili'dʒente] *agg* (*che lavora*) industrious; (*accurato*) conscientious; painstaking.
diligenza¹ [dili'dʒentsa] *sf* industry, conscientiousness. **con diligenza** conscientiously.
diligenza² [dili'dʒentsa] *sf* (*carrozza*) stage-coach.
diluire [dilu'ire] *v* dilute; (*allungare con acqua*) water down; (*vernice, ecc.*) thin (down).
dilungarsi [dilun'garsi] *v* (*andar per le lunghe*) talk at length, dwell.
diluvio [di'luvjo] *sm* flood, deluge.

dimagrire [dima'grire] *v also* **dimagrare** lose weight; (*di proposito*) slim; (*far sembrare snello*) make look slimmer.

dimenare [dime'nare] *v* wave (about); (*coda*) wag. **dimenarsi** *v* fidget, toss about.

dimensione [dimen'sjone] *sf* dimension. **a due/tre dimensioni** two-/three-dimensional.

dimenticare [dimenti'kare] *v* forget; (*perdonare*) forget about; (*trascurare*) neglect. **dimenticarsi (di)** forget (about). **dimentico** *agg, m pl* **-chi** forgetful; (*noncurante*) oblivious.

dimestichezza [dimesti'kettsa] *sf* familiarity. **aver dimestichezza con** be familiar with.

dimettere [di'mettere] *v* discharge; (*licenziare*) dismiss. **dimettersi** *v* resign.

dimezzare [dimed'dzare] *v* halve.

diminuire [diminu'ire] *v* diminish, reduce; (*calare*) drop; (*lavoro a maglia*) cast off, decrease. **diminuire di peso** lose weight. **diminuire di prezzo** cost less. **diminuire di valore** fall in value, be worth less. **diminutivo** *agg* diminutive. **diminuzione** *sf* decrease; drop, cut, fall.

dimissione [dimis'sjone] *sf* resignation. **dare** *or* **rassegnare le dimissioni** resign. **dimissionario** *agg* outgoing.

dimorare [dimo'rare] *v* stay, live. **dimora** *sf* (*abitazione*) home, abode; (*soggiorno*) stay, residence.

dimostrare [dimos'trare] *v* demonstrate; (*manifestare*) show, display; prove. **dimostrabile** *agg* demonstrable. **dimostrante** *s(m+f)* demonstrator. **dimostrativo** *agg* demonstrative. **dimostratore, -trice** *sm, sf* demonstrator. **dimostrazione** *sf* demonstration; (*prova*) proof.

dinamica [di'namika] *sf* dynamics. **dinamico** *agg* dynamic, forceful.

dinamite [dina'mite] *sf* dynamite.

dinamo ['dinamo] *sf invar* dynamo.

dinanzi [di'nantsi] *avv* ahead, forward. *agg invar* (*dirimpetto*) facing; (*precedente*) previous. *prep* **dinanzi a** (*davanti a*) in front of; (*dirimpetto*) opposite; in the presence of, before.

dinastia [dinas'tia] *sf* dynasty. **dinastico** *agg* dynastic.

dinoccolato [dinokko'lato] *agg* shambling. **camminare dinoccolato** *v* slouch.

dinosauro [dino'sauro] *sm* dinosaur.

dintorno [din'torno] *avv* around, about.

dintorni *sm pl* outskirts *pl*, surroundings *pl*.

dio ['dio] *sm, pl* **dei** god. **come un dio** wonderfully, beautifully.

diocesi ['diɔtʃezi] *sf* diocese.

diodo ['diodo] *sm* diode.

dipanare [dipa'nare] *v* unravel.

dipartimento [diparti'mento] *sm* department, district.

dipendente [dipen'dɛnte] *s(m+f)* (*impiegato*) employee. *agg* dependent, subordinate. **dipendenza** *sf* dependence; (*edificio*) annexe; (*filiale*) branch. **essere alle dipendenze di** be in the employ of.

*dipendere [di'pɛndere] *v* depend (on); (*derivare*) be due (to), be caused (by). **dipende!** that depends! **dipende da te!** it is up to you!

*dipingere [di'pindʒere] *v* paint; (*rappresentare*) depict. **dipingersi** *v* (*truccarsi*) make up. **dipinto** *sm* painting.

diploma [di'plɔma] *sm* diploma, certificate, qualification. **diplomarsi** *v* obtain a certificate, qualify.

diplomatico [diplo'matiko], **-a** *agg* diplomatic. *sm, sf* diplomat. **diplomazia** *sf* diplomacy.

diporto [di'pɔrto] *sm* pleasure, pastime.

diradare [dira'dare] *v* thin; (*nebbia*) clear.

diramare [dira'mare] *v* issue, broadcast. **diramarsi** *v* branch out *or* off. **diramazione** *sf* branch; (*comunicato, ecc.*) broadcasting, circulation.

*dire ['dire] *v* say; (*raccontare, ordinare*) tell; (*significare*) mean. **a chi lo dici!** don't I know! **aver da dire su** find fault with. **è tutto dire** which is saying a lot. **inutile dire** it goes without saying. *sm* speech, words *pl*. **a dire di tutti** by all accounts. **oltre ogni dire** beyond all description.

diretto [di'rɛtto] *agg* direct; (*inteso*) meant, destined; (*guidato*) conducted. *sm* (*ferr*) through train. **direttissimo** *sm* (*ferr*) express train. **direttiva** *sf* directive; (*condotta*) policy. **direttivo** *agg* (*che dirige*) guiding; (*proprio alla direzione*) managerial. **direttore** *sm* manager; (*scuola*) headmaster; (*giornale*) editor; (*orchestra*) conductor. **direttrice** *sf* manageress; headmistress.

direzione [dire'tsjone] *sf* direction; (*il dirigere*) management, administration; (*sede*) head office. **assumere la direzione**

take charge. **in che direzione?** which way?

*dirigere [di'ridʒere] *v* direct; (*rivolgere*) address; (*guidare*) lead; (*amministrare*) manage; (*giornale*) edit; (*orchestra*) conduct. **dirigersi verso** go towards, head for. **dirigibile** *sm* airship.

dirimpetto [dirim'petto] *agg invar, avv* opposite.

diritto¹ [di'ritto] *agg* (*non curvo*) straight; (*eretto, onesto*) upright; (*fam: astuto*) crafty; (*fam: accorto*) shrewd; (*destro*) right(-hand). *avv* straight. **andar diritto** go straight ahead *or* on. *sm* (*moneta*) obverse; (*lato buono*) good side; (*tennis*) forehand.

diritto² [di'ritto] *sm* (*legge*) law; (*pretesa*) right; (*tassa*) due, duty. **a buon diritto** with good cause. **diritti d'autore** copyright *sing*; (*compenso*) royalties *pl*. **diritto acquisito** vested interest.

diroccato [dirok'kato] *agg* dilapidated.

dirottare [dirot'tare] *v* divert; change course.

dirotto [di'rotto] *agg* (*pianto*) copious; (*pioggia*) pouring.

disabitato [dizabi'tato] *agg* uninhabited.

disabituare [dizabitu'are] *v* wean.

disaccordo [dizak'kordo] *sm* disagreement; variance. **essere** *or* **trovarsi in disaccordo su** disagree on, be at variance over.

disadatto [diza'datto] *agg* ill-suited.

disadorno [diza'dorno] *agg* bare.

disagevole [diza'dʒevole] *agg* uncomfortable.

disagio [di'zadʒo] *sm* (*imbarazzo*) uneasiness; (*mancanza di comodità*) discomfort. **essere a disagio** be ill at ease. **sentirsi a disagio** feel uneasy. **disagiato** *agg* uncomfortable; (*duro*) hard.

disamorarsi [dizamo'rarsi] *v* become estranged (from), cease to care (for).

disapprovare [dizappro'vare] *v* disapprove. **disapprovazione** *sf* disapproval.

disappunto [dizap'punto] *sm* disappointment.

disarmare [dizar'mare] *v* disarm; (*smantellare*) dismantle; (*edificio*) remove the scaffolding from. **disarmo** *sm* disarmament.

disarmonia [dizarmo'nia] *sf* discord.

disastro [di'zastro] *sm* disaster; (*incidente*) crash; (*fam: insuccesso*) utter failure.

combinare un disastro (*fam*) make a mess. **disastroso** *agg* disastrous.

disattento [dizat'tento] *agg* inattentive; (*sbadato*) careless. **disattenzione** *sf* carelessness; (*errore*) slip. **per disattenzione** through an oversight.

disavanzo [diza'vantso] *sm* deficit.

disavventura [dizavven'tura] *sf* misfortune.

disbrigo [diz'brigo] *sm, pl* **-ghi** settlement, dispatch.

discapito [dis'kapito] *sm* **a discapito di** at the cost of, to the prejudice of.

*discendere [di'ʃendere] *v* descend; (*andar giù*) go down; (*venir giù*) come down. **discendente** *s(m+f)* descendant. **discendenza** *sf* descent; (*collettivo*) offspring. **discensore** *sm* lift.

discepolo [di'ʃepolo] *sm* disciple.

discernere [di'ʃernere] *v* discern; distinguish.

discesa [di'ʃesa] *sf* descent; (*declivio*) slope. **discesa in picchiata** nose-dive. **in discesa** downhill.

*dischiudere [dis'kjudere] *v* open; (*svelare*) disclose.

*disciogliere [di'ʃɔʎere] *v* dissolve; (*liquefare*) melt.

disciplinare [diʃipli'nare] *v* discipline, control. *agg* disciplinary. **disciplina** *sf* discipline. **disciplinato** *agg* (well-)disciplined, orderly.

disco ['disko] *sm* disc; (*grammofono*) record; (*sport*) discus; (*hockey*) puck; (*telefono*) dial. **disco rosso/verde** red/green light.

discolo ['diskolo] *agg* mischievous.

discolpare [diskol'pare] *v* clear. **discolpa** *sf* justification, defence.

*disconoscere [disko'noʃere] *v* refuse to acknowledge.

discontinuo [diskon'tinuo] *agg* discontinuous; (*non regolare*) erratic.

discorde [dis'korde] *agg also* **discordante** discordant; (*contrastante*) conflicting; (*stonante*) clashing. **discordare** *v* disagree; conflict; clash. **discordia** *sf* disagreement.

*discorrere [dis'korrere] *v* talk. **discorrere del più e del meno** talk about this and that. **e via discorrendo** and so on.

discorso [dis'korso] *sm* conversation, talk; (*in pubblico, gramm*) speech. **cambiare discorso** change the subject. **senza tanti discorsi** quite frankly. **tenere**

un discorso make a speech, give an address.

discoteca [disko'tɛka] sf (locale) discotheque; record collection.

discreto [dis'kreto] agg fair, reasonable; (non importuno) tactful, discreet; (separato) discrete. discretamente avv moderately well. discrezionale agg discretionary. discrezione sf discretion, moderation, tact.

discriminazione [diskrimina'tsjone] sf discrimination. discriminare v discriminate; (dir) extenuate.

discussione [diskus'sjone] sf discussion, debate; (litigio) argument. mettere in discussione discuss, debate; (in dubbio) question.

discusso [dis'kusso] agg discussed, controversial.

*discutere [dis'kutere] v discuss, debate; (litigare) argue. discutibile agg debatable, questionable.

disdegnare [dizde'ɲare] v disdain, scorn. disdegno sm disdain, scorn.

*disdire [diz'dire] v (annullare) cancel; (negare) deny; (ritrattare) withdraw, take back; (mentire) refute. disdetta sf notice; (sfortuna) bad luck; cancellation.

disegnare [dize'ɲare] v draw; (progettare) design, sketch; (delineare) outline. disegnatore sm draughtsman. disegno sm drawing; (schizzo) sketch; (progetto) design, plan; (abbozzo) outline. a disegni patterned. disegno animato (cinema) cartoon. disegno di legge bill.

diseredare [dizere'dare] v disinherit. diseredato, -a s, agg destitute.

disertare [dizer'tare] v desert. disertore sm deserter. diserzione sf desertion.

*disfare [dis'fare] v undo; (smontare) take to pieces; (valigia) unpack; (sciogliere) melt. disfatta sf defeat. disfattismo sm defeatism. disfattista s(m+f), agg defeatist.

disgelare [dizdʒe'lare] v thaw (out); (frigorifero) defrost. disgelo sm thaw.

*disgiungere [diz'dʒundʒere] v detach, separate.

disgraziato [dizgra'tsjato], -a agg unfortunate, unlucky; (infelice) wretched. sm, sf (sventurato) wretch; (sciagurato) scoundrel. disgrazia sf misfortune; (incidente) accident, mishap; (sfavore) disgrace; (sfortuna) bad luck.

disgregare [dizgre'gare] v break up. disgregazione sf break-up.

disguido [diz'gwido] sm (equivoco) misunderstanding; (errore nel recapito) mistake in delivery.

disgustare [dizgus'tare] v disgust. disgusto sm disgust, revulsion, loathing. disgustoso agg disgusting, loathsome, revolting.

disidratare [dizidra'tare] v dehydrate.

*disilludere [dizil'ludere] v disillusion, disenchant. disillusione sf disenchantment, disillusion.

disimpegnare [dizimpe'ɲare] v free, release; (oggetto dato in pegno) redeem; (mil) relieve. disimpegnarsi v (cavarsela) acquit oneself, manage. disimpegno sm (adempimento) fulfilment; (politica) disengagement.

disinfettare [dizinfet'tare] v disinfect. disinfettante sm disinfectant. disinfezione sf disinfection.

disintegrare [dizinte'grare] v disintegrate; (fis) split, decay.

disinteressarsi [dizinteres'sarsi] v take no interest (in). disinteressato agg disinterested; (altruistico) unselfish.

disinvolto [dizin'vɔlto] agg unconstrained, self-possessed; (spigliato) free and easy, casual; (senza ritegno) uninhibited. disinvoltura sf ease, casualness; self-possession.

disistima [dizis'tima] sf lack of esteem; (disprezzo) contempt.

dislivello [dizli'vɛllo] sm difference (in level); (fig) inequality.

dislocare [dizlo'kare] v displace; (mil) detach.

dismisura [dizmi'zura] sf a dismisura excessively.

disoccupato [dizokku'pato], -a s, agg unemployed. disoccupazione sf unemployment. sussidio di disoccupazione sm unemployment benefit; (fam) dole.

disonesto [dizo'nɛsto] agg dishonest; (immorale) dishonourable; (impudico) shameless. disonestà sf dishonesty; dishonourable behaviour; shamelessness.

disonorare [dizono'rare] v dishonour, disgrace. disonore sm dishonour, disgrace. disonorevole agg dishonourable, disgraceful, shameful.

disopra [di'sopra] avv above; (al piano superiore) upstairs. agg invar (superiore) upper; (posto più in alto) higher up;

upstairs. *sm invar* top, upper part. **al disopra di** (*più di*) more than; (*superiore a*) above all; (*più alto di*) above. **dal disopra** from above.

disordinare [dizordi'nare] *v* upset, turn upside down. **disordinato** *agg* untidy; confuso; (*sregolato*) disorderly. **disordine** *sm* disorder; (*confusione*) muddle.

disorientare [dizorjen'tare] *v* (*confondere*) confuse, bewilder. **disorientarsi** *v* lose one's bearings, become confused.

disossare [dizos'sare] *v* bone.

disotto [di'sotto] *avv* below, underneath; (*al piano inferiore*) downstairs. *agg invar* below; (*tra due*) lower; (*in fondo*) bottom; downstairs.

dispaccio [dis'pattʃo] *sm* dispatch.

disparato [dispa'rato] *agg* dissimilar, different.

dispari ['dispari] *agg* odd.

disparte [dis'parte] *avv* **in disparte** aside, to one side. **tenersi in disparte** keep at a distance.

dispensa [dis'pɛnsa] *sf* distribution; (*mobile*) cupboard; (*locale*) pantry, larder; (*fascicolo*) number, issue; (*esonero*) exemption. **a dispense** in instalments. **dispensa ecclesiastica** dispensation. **dispensa universitaria** lecture notes *pl*. **dispensare** *v* dispense. **dispensario** *sm* clinic.

disperare [dispe'rare] *v* despair. **disperato** *agg* desperate. **disperazione** *sf* despair.

*****disperdere** [dis'pɛrdere] *v* disperse, scatter; dissipate; (*sprecare*) waste. **dispersione** *sf* dispersion; waste.

dispetto [dis'pɛtto] *sm* spite; (*irritazione*) annoyance. **a dispetto di** despite. **fare un dispetto** annoy. **per dispetto** out of spite. **dispettoso** *agg* spiteful, annoying.

*****dispiacere** [dispja'tʃere] *v* displease. **mi dispiace ...** (*non mi piace*) I don't like ... ; (*sono spiacente*) I'm sorry .... **ti dispiace ...?** do you mind ...? *sm* (*rammarico*) regret; (*noia*) displeasure; (*fastidio*) trouble, worry.

disponibile [dispo'nibile] *agg* available; (*libero*) vacant. **posto disponibile** *sm* vacancy.

disponibilità [disponibili'ta] *sf* availability. *sf pl* assets *pl*.

*****disporre** [dis'porre] *v* dispose; (*collocare in ordine, stabilire*) arrange; prepare; induce; order. **disporre di** have available,

have at one's disposal; (*avere*) have. **disporsi** *v* prepare, get ready; (*in fila*) line up.

dispositivo [dispozi'tivo] *sm* device.

disposizione [dispozi'tsjone] *sf* arrangement, layout; (*stato d'animo*) disposition; (*inclinazione*) bent; (*norma*) provision; (*comando*) order. **a disposizione** available.

disposto [dis'posto] *agg* arranged, laid out; (*pronto*) ready, willing; (*stabilito*) laid down.

disprezzare [dispret'tsare] *v* despise, scorn. **disprezzo** *sm* scorn, contempt.

disputare [dispu'tare] *v* dispute; (*litigare*) argue; (*contendere*) fight (over), strive (for); (*incontro*) play; (*corsa*) run. **disputa** *sf* dispute; (*lite*) argument.

dissanguare [dissan'gware] *v* bleed.

dissecare [disse'kare] *v* dissect.

disseccare [dissek'kare] *v* dry up.

disseminare [dissemi'nare] *v* scatter; (*diffondere*) spread.

dissenteria [dissente'ria] *sf* dysentery.

dissentire [dissen'tire] *v* dissent, disagree.

disseppellire [disseppel'lire] *v* unearth; (*esumare*) exhume.

dissertazione [disserta'tsjone] *sf* dissertation.

dissestare [disses'tare] *v* upset, unbalance. **dissestato** *agg* ruined; (*strada*) in poor condition; (*bilancio*) adverse.

dissetarsi [disse'tarsi] *v* quench one's thirst. **dissetante** *agg* thirst-quenching.

dissidente [dissi'dɛnte] *s(m+f)*, *agg* dissident; (*rel*) non-conformist.

dissidio [dis'sidjo] *sm* disagreement; (*lite*) quarrel.

dissimile [dis'simile] *agg* different, unlike.

dissimulare [dissimu'lare] *v* dissimulate; (*fingere*) pretend; (*nascondere*) hide.

dissipare [dissi'pare] *v* dissipate; (*sospetti, dubbi, ecc.*) dispel; (*sprecare*) squander.

dissociare [disso'tʃare] *v* dissociate. **dissociazione** *sf* dissociation.

dissoluto [disso'luto] *agg* dissolute.

dissoluzione [dissolu'tsjone] *sf* dissolution, break-up.

*****dissolvere** [dis'sɔlvere] *v* dispel; (*sciogliere*) dissolve.

dissotterrare [dissotter'rare] *v* unearth; (*esumare*) exhume.

*****dissuadere** [dissua'dere] *v* dissuade, deter.

distaccare [distak'kare] *v* detach; (*sport:*

lasciar dietro) leave behind. **distaccarsi** *v* (*spiccare*) stand out; (*allontanarsi*) withdraw. **distaccamento** *sm* (*mil*) detachment. **distacco** *sm* detachment; (*separazione*) parting, separation; (*sport: vantaggio*) lead.

distante [dis'tante] *agg* distant, remote, far. *avv* far, far off. **distanza** *sf* distance; (*tempo*) interval.

*****distare** [dis'tare] *v* be far (from).

*****distendere** [dis'tɛndere] *v* spread; (*allungare*) stretch; (*appendere*) hang (up); (*mettere giù*) lay; (*rilassare*) relax. **distendersi** *v* lie down, relax.

distensione [disten'sjone] *sf* stretching; relaxation; (*pol*) détente. **distensivo** *agg* relaxing.

distesa [dis'teza] *sf* expanse; (*fila*) row.

disteso [dis'tezo] *agg* (*teso*) stretched; (*coricato*) lying down; (*braccio*) outstretched; (*spiegato*) spread out; relaxed.

distillare [distil'lare] *v* distil. **distilleria** *sf* distillery.

*****distinguere** [dis'tingwere] *v* distinguish, tell; (*contrassegnare*) mark; draw a distinction; (*riconoscere*) recognize. **distinguibile** *agg* distinguishable; recognizable.

distinta [dis'tinta] *sf* list. **distinta delle spese** statement of expenses.

distintivo [distin'tivo] *agg* distinctive; (*atto a distinguere*) distinguishing. *sm* badge.

distinto [dis'tinto] *agg* distinct, different, separate; (*scelto, raffinato*) distinguished. **ben distinto** precise. **distinti saluti** yours faithfully.

distinzione [distin'tsjone] *sf* distinction. **fare una distinzione** make a distinction, discriminate. **senza distinzione** (*senza merito*) undistinguished; (*senza criterio*) indiscriminately; (*in modo equo*) impartially.

*****distogliere** [dis'tɔʎere] *v* divert, turn away.

distorsione [distor'sjone] *sf* distortion; (*med*) sprain.

*****distrarre** [dis'trarre] *v* distract; (*divertire*) amuse. **distrarsi** *v* amuse oneself; (*essere disattento*) be inattentive. **distratto** *agg* inattentive; (*assente*) absent-minded; (*sbadato*) careless. **distrazione** *sf* (*svago*) distraction, relaxation; (*sbadatezza*) carelessness; absent-mindedness; lack of attention.

distretto [dis'tretto] *sm* district.

distribuire [distribu'ire] *v* distribute; (*disporre*) arrange; (*assegnare*) hand out; (*le carte*) deal; (*posta*) deliver. **distributore** *sm* (*di accensione*) distributor; (*di benzina*) petrol pump, service station. **distribuzione** *sf* distribution; (*fornitura*) supply; arrangement; delivery. **distribuzione dei premi** prize-giving. **distribuzione dei ruoli** (*cinema*) casting.

districare [distri'kare] *v* disentangle; (*fig*) sort out. **districarsi** *v* extricate oneself.

*****distruggere** [dis'truddʒere] *v* destroy, ruin. **distruttivo** *agg* destructive. **distrutto** *agg* destroyed, ruined; (*fig*) broken. **distruzione** *sf* destruction, ruin.

disturbare [distur'bare] *v* disturb; (*molestare, seccare*) trouble, bother; (*recar fastidio*) inconvenience; (*radio*) jam. **disturbo** *sm* trouble; (*incomodo*) nuisance, inconvenience; (*indisposizione*) upset, disorder; (*radio*) jamming; atmospherics *pl*, interference. **recar disturbo** trouble, inconvenience.

disubbidire [dizubbi'dire] *v* disobey.

disuguale [dizu'gwale] *agg* unequal; (*non regolare*) irregular. **disuguaglianza** *sf* difference, disparity.

disunire [dizu'nire] *v* separate, divide.

disuso [di'zuzo] *sm* disuse. **andare** *or* **cadere in disuso** fall into disuse, become obsolete. **disusato** *agg* obsolete, out-of-date; (*fuori moda*) old-fashioned.

dito ['dito] *sm*, *pl* **-a** *f* finger. **dito anulare/indice/medio/mignolo** ring/index/middle/little finger. **dito del piede** toe. **ditale** *sm* (*cucire*) thimble; (*guanto*) finger-stall.

ditta ['ditta] *sf* firm, company.

dittatore [ditta'tore] *sm* dictator. **dittatorio** *agg* dictatorial. **dittatura** *sf* dictatorship.

dittico ['dittiko] *sm* diptych.

dittongo [dit'tɔngo] *sm* diphthong.

diurno [di'urno] *agg* day(-time). **spettacolo diurno** *sm* matinee.

diva ['diva] *sf* (film-)star.

divagare [diva'gare] *v* digress, wander; (*distrarre*) distract.

divampare [divam'pare] *v* flare up, blaze.

divano [di'vano] *sm* divan, settee, couch.

diventare [diven'tare] *v* *also* **divenire** become, turn *or* grow (into). **diventar matto** go mad. **diventar pallido/rosso** go *or* turn pale/red.

divergere [di'vɛrdʒere] *v* diverge; (*essere diverso*) differ. **divergenza** *sf* divergence; difference.
diversi [di'vɛrsi] *agg* several. *pron* (*parecchi*) several (people); (*alcuni*) some (people).
diversivo [diver'sivo] *agg* diverting; distracting. *sm* diversion; distraction.
diverso [di'vɛrso] *agg* different; distinct, separate; (*di genere diverso*) various; (*comm*) sundry. **in caso diverso** otherwise. **diversamente** *avv* differently; (*se no*) otherwise. **diversità** *sf* difference, diversity.
divertente [diver'tɛnte] *agg* amusing, enjoyable. **divertimento** *sm* entertainment, amusement. **buon divertimento!** enjoy yourself! have a good time!
divertire [diver'tire] *v* amuse; (*ricreare*) entertain. **divertirsi** *v* enjoy oneself.
dividendo [divi'dɛndo] *sm* dividend.
***dividere** [di'videre] *v* divide; (*condividere*) share. **dividersi** *v* separate, part, split (up).
divieto [di'vjɛto] *sm* prohibition. **divieto di sorpasso/sosta/transito** no overtaking/stopping/thoroughfare.
divinare [divi'nare] *v* divine; (*prevedere*) foretell.
divincolarsi [divinko'larsi] *v* wriggle.
divino [di'vino] *agg* sacred, holy; (*sublime*) divine, heavenly. **divinità** *sf* divinity.
divisa [di'viza] *sf* uniform; motto. **divisa estera** foreign currency.
divisibile [divi'zibile] *agg* divisible. **divisibilità** *sf* divisibility.
divisione [divi'zjone] *sf* division; (*reparto*) department.
diviso [di'vizo] *agg* divided, separated; (*condiviso*) shared. **divisore** *sm* divisor.
divisorio [divi'zɔrjo] *sm* partition. *agg* dividing.
divo ['divo] *sm* (film-)star.
divorare [divo'rare] *v* devour, eat up.
divorzio [di'vɔrtsjo] *sm* divorce. **divorziare** *v* divorce.
divulgare [divul'gare] *v* spread; (*rivelare*) divulge; (*rendere accessibile*) popularize. **divulgazione** *sf* spreading; (*notizie*) broadcasting; popularization.
dizionario [ditsjo'narjo] *sm* dictionary.
dizione [di'tsjone] *sf* diction.
doccia ['dottʃa] *sf* shower; (*grondaia*) gutter.

docente [do'tʃɛnte] *s(m+f)* lecturer, teacher.
docile ['dɔtʃile] *agg* docile, mild; (*materiale*) easily worked. **docilità** *sf* mildness, submissiveness; workability.
documento [doku'mento] *sm* document, paper. **documentare** *v* document. **documentario** *agg, sm* documentary. **documentazione** *sf* documentation; (*dir*) evidence.
dodici ['doditʃi] *agg, sm* twelve. **dodicesimo** *sm, agg* twelfth.
dogana [do'gana] *sf* customs. **doganale** *agg* customs. **doganiere** *sm* customs officer.
doge ['dɔdʒe] *sm* doge.
doglie ['dɔʎʎe] *sf pl* **doglie del parto** labour pains *pl*.
dogma ['dɔgma] *sm* dogma. **dogmatico** *agg* dogmatic.
dolce ['doltʃe] *agg* sweet; (*mite*) mild; (*morbido*) soft. *sm* sweet. **dolcezza** *sf* sweetness; mildness; softness.
***dolere** [do'lere] *v* (*far male*) ache, hurt. **mi duole di** *or* **che ...** I regret that ... , I'm sorry that ... .
dollaro ['dɔllaro] *sm* dollar.
dolo ['dɔlo] *sm* (*dir*) malice; (*inganno*) fraud.
dolore [do'lore] *sm* pain; (*male fisico*) ache; (*sofferenza morale*) sorrow; (*rincrescimento*) regret. **doloroso** *agg* painful; sorrowful.
domanda [do'manda] *sf* question; (*richiesta*) request; (*scritta*) application; (*econ*) demand; (*dir*) petition. **domandare** *v* (*per sapere*) ask; (*per avere*) ask for; (*esigere*) demand. **domandarsi** *v* wonder.
domani [do'mani] *avv* tomorrow. **a domani!** see you tomorrow! **domani a otto** tomorrow week. **domani l'altro** the day after tomorrow. *sm* tomorrow; future. **un domani** one day.
domare [do'mare] *v* tame; (*sedare*) put down; (*spegnere*) put out; (*frenare*) curb. **domatore** *sm* tamer.
domattina [domat'tina] *avv* tomorrow morning.
domenica [do'menika] *sf* Sunday.
domestico [do'mɛstiko] *agg* domestic; (*della casa*) household, home. **apparecchio domestico** household appliance. *sm* servant. **domestica** *sf* maid. **domestichezza** *sf* familiarity.

domiciliarsi [domitʃi'ljarsi] *v* settle.

domicilio [domi'tʃiljo] *sm* domicile, home.

dominare [domi'nare] *v* dominate; (*predominare*) prevail; (*frenare*) control; (*aver potestà*) rule. **dominio** *sm* domination; rule; (*territorio*) domain; (*proprietà*) possession. **pubblico dominio** (*proprietà*) common property; (*noto a tutti*) common knowledge.

domino ['dɔmino] *sm* (*gioco*) dominoes.

donare [do'nare] *v* give, present; (*star bene*) suit, become. **donatore, -trice** *sm, sf* donor. **donazione** *sf* donation, gift.

donde ['donde] *avv* (*da dove*) whence, from where; (*di che*) with which.

dondolare [dondo'lare] *v* swing, rock. **cavallo a dondolo** *sm* rocking-horse. **sedia a dondolo** *sf* rocking-chair.

donna ['dɔnna] *sf* woman (*pl* women); (*domestica*) maid, servant; (*giochi*) queen. **donnaiolo** *sm* philanderer. **donnesco** *agg* feminine.

donnola ['donnola] *sf* weasel.

dono ['dono] *sm* gift.

dopo ['dopo] *avv* after; (*poi*) then, afterwards; (*più tardi*) later (on); (*prossimo*) next. **a dopo!** see you later! **dopobarba** *agg, sm invar* after-shave. **dopo che** since. **dopo di che** whereupon. **dopodomani** *sm, avv* the day after tomorrow. **dopotutto** *avv* after all. **molto tempo dopo** long after.

dopopranzo [dopo'prantso] *avv* after lunch. *sm* afternoon.

doppiare¹ [dop'pjare] *v* (*cinema*) dub. **doppiaggio** *sm* dubbing.

doppiare² [dop'pjare] *v* double; (*sport*) lap.

doppio ['doppjo] *agg* double; (*insincero*) two-faced; (*duplice*) dual, twofold. **a doppio petto** double-breasted. **fare il doppio gioco** double-cross. *sm* double, twice as much *or* many. **doppione** *sm* duplicate.

dorare [do'rare] *v* gild; (*gastr*) coat with egg. **doratura** *sf* gilding, gold-plating.

dormicchiare [dormik'kjare] *v* doze, snooze.

dormire [dor'mire] *v* sleep; (*esser fermo*) lie dormant. **dormita** *sf* good sleep.

dormitorio [dormi'tɔrjo] *sm* dormitory.

dormiveglia [dormi'veʎa] *sm* **essere nel dormiveglia** be half-asleep.

dorso ['dorso] *sm* back; (*nuoto*) backstroke.

dose ['dɔze] *sf* dose; quantity. **dose eccessiva** overdose. **rincarare la dose** (*fam*) pile it on. **dosaggio** *sm* dosage.

dosso ['dɔsso] *sm* back. **togliersi un peso di dosso** take a weight off one's mind.

dotare [do'tare] *v* endow, provide. **dotato** *agg* gifted; endowed *or* provided (with); (*munito*) equipped (with). **dotazione** *sf* equipment; (*rendita*) endowment. **dote** *sf* (*matrimonio*) dowry; (*donazione*) endowment; (*qualità*) gift.

dotto¹ ['dɔtto] *agg* scholarly, learned. *sm* scholar.

dotto² ['dotto] *sm* (*condotto*) duct.

dottore [dot'tore] *-essa sm, sf* doctor.

dottrina [dot'trina] *sf* (*cultura*) learning; (*teoria, insieme di principi*) doctrine.

dove ['dove] *avv* where. *cong* (*se*) if; (*mentre*) whereas. **fin dove** as far as.

*****dovere** [do'vere] *v* must, have to; (*esser lecito*) may; (*essere inevitabile*) be bound to; (*esser causato da*) be due to; (*al condizionale*) should, ought to. **come si deve** properly; (*persona*) proper, decent. *sm* duty. **doveroso** *agg* right and proper; (*obbligato*) (duty-)bound. **dovuto** *agg, sm* due.

dovunque [do'vunkwe] *avv* (*dappertutto*) everywhere; (*in qualsiasi luogo*) anywhere. *cong* wherever.

dozzina [dod'dzina] *sf* dozen. **a dozzine** by the dozen. **da dozzina** cheap, poor.

dragare [dra'gare] *v* dredge; (*mine*) sweep. **draga** *sf* dredge, dredger. **dragamine** *sm invar* minesweeper.

drago ['drago] *sm* dragon; (*aquilone*) kite. **dragone** *sm* dragon; (*mil*) dragoon.

dramma ['dramma] *sm* play; tragedy. **drammatico** *agg* dramatic; (*esagerato*) theatrical. **drammatizzare** *v* dramatize. **drammaturgo** *sm* playwright, dramatist.

drappello [drap'pɛllo] *sm* squad, band.

drappo ['drappo] *sm* cloth; (*funebre*) pall. **drappeggiare** *v* drape.

drastico ['drastiko] *agg* drastic.

drenare [dre'nare] *v* drain. **drenaggio** *sm* drainage.

dritta ['dritta] *sf* (*mano*) right (hand); (*parte*) right(-hand side); (*mar*) starboard.

dritto ['dritto] *agg* (*fam*) astute. *sm* (*non rovescio*) right side; (*fam*) crafty person, fast worker.

drizzare [drit'tsare] *v* (*raddrizzare*)

straighten; (*erigere*) erect. **drizzare le orecchie** prick up one's ears.

droga ['drɔga] *sf* drug; (*sostanza aromatica*) spice. **drogare** *v* drug, dope; spice.

drogarsi *v* take drugs.

droghiere [dro'gjɛre], **-a** *sm, sf* grocer. **drogheria** *sf* grocer's shop. **articoli di drogheria** *sm pl* groceries *pl.*

dromedario [drome'darjo] *sm* dromedary.

dualismo [dua'lizmo] *sm* dualism.

dubbio ['dubbjo] *sm* doubt. **essere in dubbio** be in doubt, be uncertain. **mettere in dubbio** doubt, call in question. **senza dubbio** no doubt, doubtless. *agg also* **dubbioso** doubtful, uncertain; (*ambiguo*) dubious.

dubitare [dubi'tare] *v* doubt; (*essere in dubbio*) be in doubt; (*diffidare*) distrust. **non dubitare!** don't worry!

duca ['duka] *sm* duke.

duce ['dutʃe] *sm* leader.

duchessa [du'kessa] *sf* duchess.

due ['due] *sm, agg* two. **a due a due** two by two, in twos. **duepezzi** *sm invar* two-piece. **due punti** colon. **due volte** twice. **due volte tanto** twice as much *or* many. **nessuno dei due** neither of them. **tutti e due** both of them.

duello [du'ɛllo] *sm* duel. **duellare** *v* duel. **duellista** *or* **duellante** *sm* duellist.

duetto [du'etto] *sm* duet.

duna ['duna] *sf* dune.

dunque ['dunkwe] *cong* (*nel discorso*) well, now then; (*perciò*) so, therefore, hence; (*rafforzativo*) then. *sm* **trovarsi al dunque** come to the crunch. **venire al dunque** come to the point.

duo ['duo] *sm invar* duo.

duodeno [duo'dɛno] *sm* duodenum. **duodenale** *agg* duodenal.

duomo ['dwɔmo] *sm* cathedral.

duplex ['dupleks] *sm invar* (*telefono*) party-line.

duplicare [dupli'kare] *v* duplicate. **duplicato** *agg, sm* duplicate. **duplicatore** *sm* duplicator, copier. **duplice** *agg* double.

durare [du'rare] *v* last; (*cibo*) keep; (*abiti*) wear; (*sopportare*) endure.

durata [du'rata] *sf* length (of time), duration. **di breve durata** short(-lived), not lasting. **di lunga durata** lasting. **durata di una carica** term of office. **durevole** *agg* lasting.

duro ['duro] *agg* hard, tough. **aver la pelle dura** be thick-skinned. **aver la testa dura**

be stubborn. **tener duro** hold out. **durezza** *sf* hardness. **durone** *sm* callus.

duttile ['duttile] *agg* ductile.

E

e [e], **ed** *cong* and; (*invece*) and then. **e ... e ...** both ... and .... **tutti e due** both (of them). **tutti e tre** all three (of them).

ebano ['ebano] *sm* ebony. **d'ebano** (*colore*) jet-black. **ebanista** *sm* cabinet-maker.

ebbene [eb'bɛne] *cong* well (then).

ebbro ['ebbro] *agg* intoxicated, drunk. **ebbrezza** *sf* intoxication; (*fig*) rapture, elation.

ebdomadario [ebdoma'darjo] *agg, sm* weekly.

ebete ['ɛbete] *agg* dull-witted.

ebollizione [ebolli'tsjone] *sf* boiling. **punto di ebollizione** *sm* boiling point.

ebraico [e'braiko] *agg* Jewish, Hebrew. *sm* (*lingua*) Hebrew.

ebreo [e'brɛo], **-a** *sm, sf* Jew. *agg* Jewish.

eccedere [et'tʃedere] *v* exceed; surpass. **eccedere i limiti** go too far.

*eccellere [et'tʃellere] *v* excel, be outstanding. **eccellente** *agg* excellent. **eccellenza** *sf* excellence; (*titolo*) Excellency. **per eccellenza** par excellence.

eccentrico [et'tʃɛntriko] *agg, sm* eccentric. **eccentricità** *sf* eccentricity.

eccepibile [ettʃe'pibile] *agg* objectionable. **eccepire** *v* take exception (to), object (to).

eccesso [et'tʃesso] *sm* excess. **all'eccesso** excessively, to a fault. **eccesso di velocità** speeding. **eccessivo** *agg* excessive, exaggerated.

eccetera [et'tʃetera] etcetera, and so forth *or* on.

eccetto [et'tʃetto] *prep* except. **eccetto che** (*tranne che*) except for, but for; (*a meno che*) unless.

eccettuare [ettʃettu'are] *v* except, leave out.

eccezione [ettʃe'tsjone] *sf* exception. **ad eccezione di** except for. **eccezionale** *agg* exceptional.

eccidio [et'tʃidjo] *sm* slaughter.

eccitare [ettʃi'tare] *v* excite, stimulate; (*provocare*) stir up, rouse. **eccitamento** *sm* excitement; (*stimolo*) incitement. **eccitante** *sm* stimulant. **eccitazione** *sf* excitement.

ecclesiastico [ekkle'zjastiko] *agg* clerical, ecclesiastic(al). *sm* clergyman.

ecco ['ɛkko] *avv* this *or* that is; (*qui*) here is; (*li*) there is. **ecco fatto** that is that. **ecco tutto** that is all.

eccome [ek'kome] *avv*, *inter* and how, certainly.

echeggiare [eked'dʒare] *v* echo; (*risonare*) resound.

eclettico [e'klɛttiko] *agg* eclectic.

eclissare [eklis'sare] *v* eclipse. **eclisse** *or* **eclissi** *sf* eclipse.

eco ['ɛko] *s*(*m*+*f*), *pl* -**i** *m* echo. **echi di cronaca** gossip (column) *sing*. **far eco a** echo.

ecologia [ekolo'dʒia] *sf* ecology. **ecologico** *agg* ecological. **ecologo**, -**a** *sm*, *sf* ecologist.

economia [ekono'mia] *sf* economy; (*risparmio*) thrift, saving; (*scienza*) economics. **fare economie** economize, save. **economico** *agg* economic; (*a bassa spesa*) economical, cheap.

economizzare [ekonomid'dzare] *v* economize, save.

economo [e'kɔnomo] *sm* steward, supply officer.

ed [ed] *V* **e**.

edera ['edera] *sf* ivy.

edibile [e'dibile] *agg* edible.

edicola [e'dikola] *sf* bookstall.

edificare [edifi'kare] *v* (*erigere*) construct; (*stimolare al bene*) edify. **edificante** *agg* edifying. **edificio** *sm* building; (*fig*) structure.

edile [e'dile] *agg* building. *sm* builder. **edilizia** *sf* building trade. **edilizio** *agg* building.

Edimburgo [edim'burgo] *sf* Edinburgh.

editore [edi'tore], -**trice** *sm*, *sf* publisher. *agg* publishing. **edito** *agg* published.

editto [e'ditto] *sm* edict.

edizione [edi'tsjone] *sf* edition; (*tiratura*) issue.

educare [edu'kare] *v* educate; (*ammaestrare*) train. **educativo** *agg* educational. **educato** *agg* (*cortese*) polite. **bene/male educato** well-/ill-mannered. **educazione** *sf* education, upbringing; training; (*comportamento*) manners *pl*, breeding.

effeminato [effemi'nato] *agg* effeminate. **effeminatezza** *sf* effeminacy.

effervescente [efferve'ʃɛnte] *agg* effervescent, sparkling.

effetto [ef'fɛtto] *sm* effect; (*conseguenza*) result; impression; (*comm*) bill. **aver effetto** take effect. **dare effetto a** carry out. **fare effetto** work. **fare l'effetto di** give the impression of.

effettuare [effettu'are] *v* effect, bring about; (*realizzare*) carry out; (*fare*) make. **effettuabile** *agg* feasible. **effettuazione** *sf* execution.

efficace [effi'katʃe] *agg* effective, efficient. **efficacia** *sf* efficacy, effectiveness; force.

efficiente [effi'tʃɛnte] *agg* efficient. **efficienza** *sf* efficiency, effectiveness; (*mec*) working order.

effigie [ef'fidʒe] *sf* effigy; image.

effimero [ef'fimero] *agg* ephemeral.

effluente [efflu'ɛnte] *sm* effluent, sewage. **efflusso** *sm* outflow.

egida ['ɛdʒida] *sf* aegis.

Egitto [e'dʒitto] *sm* Egypt. **egiziano**, -**a** *s*, *agg* Egyptian. **egizio**, -**a** *s*, *agg* (ancient) Egyptian.

egli ['eʎi] *pron* he.

egocentrico [ego'tʃɛntriko] *agg* egocentric, self-centred.

egoista [ego'ista] *s*(*m*+*f*) egoist, selfish person. **egoistico** *agg* egoistic(al), selfish.

egotista [ego'tista] *s*(*m*+*f*) egotist, boaster. **egotistico** *agg* egotistic(al).

egregio [e'grɛdʒo] *agg* distinguished; (*in lettere*) dear.

eguale [e'gwale] *V* **uguale**.

egualitario [egwali'tarjo], -**a** *s*, *agg* egalitarian.

eiettore [ejet'tore] *sm* ejector. **sedile eiettore** *sm* ejector seat.

elaborare [elabo'rare] *v* elaborate, devise; (*dati*) process. **elaborato** *agg* elaborate. **elaboratore** *sm* (*elettronico*) computer; (*dati*) processor. **elaborazione** *sf* preparation, formulation; (*dati*) processing.

elargire [elar'dʒire] *v* lavish.

elastico [e'lastiko] *agg* elastic; (*molleggiante*) springy; (*fig*) flexible; (*agile*) nimble. *sm* elastic; (*anello*) elastic band; (*materasso*) spring.

elefante [ele'fante] *sm* elephant. **elefantesco** *agg* elephantine.

elegante [ele'gante] *agg* elegant; (*vestito*) smart; (*fine*) graceful; (*ingegnoso*) neat. **eleganza** *sf* elegance; smartness, stylishness.

*eleggere [e'leddʒere] *v* elect, nominate.
eleggibile *agg* eligible. **eleggibilità** *sf* eligibility.
elegia [ele'dʒia] *sf* elegy. **elegiaco** *agg* elegiac.
elemento [ele'mento] *sm* element; (*individuo*) fellow, individual. **elementare** *agg* elementary; (*naturale*) elemental.
elemosina [ele'mɔzina] *sf* alms, charity. **chiedere l'elemosina** beg. **fare l'elemosina** give alms.
elenco [e'lɛnko] *sm* list; (*telefonico*) directory; (*iscritti*) register. **elencare** *v* list; enumerate.
eletto [e'lɛtto] *agg* chosen; (*scelto*) select; (*nominato*) elected.
elettorale [eletto'rale] *agg* electoral, election. **collegio elettorale** *sm* constituency. **propaganda elettorale** *sf* electioneering. **scheda/urna elettorale** *sf* ballot-paper/box. **elettorato** *sm* electorate; (*diritto di eleggere*) franchise.
elettore [elet'tore], **-trice** *sm*, *sf* elector, voter; (*di collegio elettorale*) constituent.
elettrico [e'lɛttriko] *agg* electric(al). **elettricista** *sm* electrician. **elettricità** *sf* electricity.
elettrificare [elettrifi'kare] *v* electrify. **elettrificazione** *sf* electrification.
elettrizzare [elettrid'dzare] *v* electrify; (*fig*) thrill.
elettrodo [e'lɛttrodo] *sm* electrode.
elettrodomestico [elettrodo'mɛstiko] *sm* electric appliance.
elettrodotto [elettro'dotto] *sm* power line, mains.
elettrolisi [elet'trɔlizi] *sf* electrolysis. **elettrolitico** *agg* electrolytic.
elettrone [elet'trone] *sm* electron. **elettronica** *sf* electronics. **elettronico** *agg* electronic.
elettrotecnico [elettro'tɛkniko] *sm* electrical engineer.
elevare [ele'vare] *v* raise. **elevato** *agg* high; (*fig*) lofty. **elevazione** *sf* elevation; (*atto di alzare*) raising.
elezione [ele'tsjone] *sf* election. **elezioni politiche** general election *sing*.
elica ['ɛlika] *sf* propeller. **elicottero** *sm* helicopter.
eliminare [elimi'nare] *v* eliminate; (*escludere*) rule out. **eliminatoria** *sf* (*sport*) qualifying round. **eliminazione** *sf* elimination; exclusion.

elio ['ɛljo] *sm* helium.
ella ['ella] *pron* she; (*formula di cortesia*) you.
ellisse [el'lisse] *sf* ellipse. **ellittico** *agg* elliptical.
elmetto [el'metto] *sm also* **elmo** helmet.
elogio [e'lɔdʒo] *sm* praise. **elogiare** *v* praise.
eloquente [elo'kwɛnte] *agg* eloquent; (*significativo*) meaningful. **eloquenza** *sf* eloquence.
elsa ['elsa] *sf* hilt.
*eludere [e'ludere] *v* elude, dodge, evade.
emaciato [ema'tʃato] *agg* emaciated.
emanare [ema'nare] *v* emanate; (*diffondere*) give off, send out; (*promulgare*) issue. **emanazione** *sf* emanation; promulgation.
emancipare [emantʃi'pare] *v* emancipate. **emancipazione** *sf* emancipation.
embargo [em'bargo] *sm* embargo.
emblema [em'blɛma] *sm* emblem; symbol, model. **emblematico** *agg* emblematic, symbolic.
embolia [embo'lia] *sf* embolism. **embolo** *sm* embolus.
embrione [embri'one] *sm* embryo. **embrionale** *agg* embryonic.
emendare [emen'dare] *v* amend. **emendamento** *sm* amendment.
emergenza [emer'dʒɛntsa] *sf* emergency.
*emergere [e'mɛrdʒere] *v* emerge; (*distinguersi*) stand out; (*apparire*) appear.
*emettere [e'mettere] *v* emit, give out; (*ordine, azioni*) issue; (*giudizio*) deliver; (*grido*) utter.
emicrania [emi'krania] *sf* migraine.
emigrare [emi'grare] *v* emigrate; (*animali*) migrate. **emigrante** *s(m+f)* emigrant. **emigrato, -a** *sm*, *sf* emigrant; (*pol*) exile. **emigrazione** *sf* emigration, migration; (*econ*) flight.
eminente [emi'nɛnte] *agg* eminent, distinguished; (*elevato*) high. **eminenza** *sf* eminence.
emisfero [emis'fɛro] *sm* hemisphere. **emisferico** *agg* hemispheric(al).
emissario[1] [emis'sarjo] *sm* (*mandatario*) emissary.
emissario[2] [emis'sarjo] *sm* (*canale, ecc.*) outlet.
emissione [emis'sjone] *sf* emission; (*econ*) issue. **emittente** *agg* issuing; (*radio*) transmitting.

emolliente [emol'ljɛnte] *sm*, *agg* emollient.

emorragia [emorra'dʒia] *sf* haemorrhage, bleeding.

emorroidi [emor'rɔidi] *sf pl* piles *pl*.

emotivo [emo'tivo] *agg* emotional; (*impressionabile*) excitable; (*che provoca emozione*) emotive, thrilling.

emozione [emo'tsjone] *sf* emotion; excitement. **emozionante** *agg* exciting. **emozionare** *v* excite; (*commuovere*) move.

empio ['empjo] *agg* impious; (*crudele*) cruel.

empire [em'pire] *v* fill.

empirico [em'piriko] *agg* empirical.

emporio [em'pɔrjo] *sm* store.

emù [e'mu] *sm* emu.

emulare [emu'lare] *v* emulate. **emulazione** *sf* rivalry; (*dir*) nuisance.

emulsione [emul'sjone] *sf* emulsion.

enciclopedia [entʃiklope'dia] *sf* encyclopaedia. **enciclopedico** *agg* encyclopaedic.

encomio [en'kɔmjo] *sm* praise. **encomiabile** *agg* praiseworthy.

endemico [en'dɛmiko] *agg* endemic.

energia [ener'dʒia] *sf* energy. **energetico** *sm*, *agg* tonic. **energico** *agg* energetic; (*forte*) forceful, strong.

enfasi ['ɛnfazi] *sf* emphasis (*pl* -ses). **enfatico** *agg* emphatic.

enfiare [en'fjare] *v* swell, inflate.

enigma [e'nigma] *sm* puzzle, riddle; (*mistero, persona misteriosa*) enigma, mystery. **enigmatico** *agg* puzzling; mysterious.

ennesimo [en'nɛzimo] *agg* nth; (*fam*) umpteenth.

enorme [e'norme] *agg* enormous, huge. **enormità** *sf* (*causa di indignazione*) enormity; (*errore*) blunder.

ente ['ɛnte] *sm* (*filos*) being; (*azienda*) undertaking, concern; authority; (*istituzione*) body.

enteroclisi [entero'klizi] *sm* enema.

entità [enti'ta] *sf* entity; importance; (*consistenza*) extent.

entrambi [en'trambi] *agg*, *pron* both.

entrare [en'trare] *v* enter; (*andar dentro*) go in(to); (*con difficoltà*) get in(to); (*venir dentro*) come in(to); (*associarsi*) join. **entrare in ballo** come into play. **entrare in vigore** come into effect.

entrata [en'trata] *sf* entrance, entry; (*accesso*) admission. **entrate** *sf pl* (*redditi*) income *sing*, earnings *pl*; (*incassi*) receipts *pl*; (*di enti pubblici*) revenue *sing*.

entro ['entro] *prep* within; (*ora/data precisata*) by. **entro oggi** before the day is out.

entusiasmo [entu'zjazmo] *sm* enthusiasm. **entusiasmare** *v* thrill, excite. **entusiasta** *s*(*m + f*) enthusiast. **entusiastico** *agg* enthusiastic.

enumerare [enume'rare] *v* list. **enumerazione** *sf* listing; list.

enunciare [enun'tʃare] *v* enunciate; (*esprimere*) express; formulate.

enzima [en'dzima] *sm* enzyme.

epatite [epa'tite] *sf* hepatitis.

epico ['ɛpiko] *agg* epic, heroic. **epica** *sf* epic poetry.

epidemia [epide'mia] *sf* epidemic. **epidemico** *agg* epidemic.

Epifania [epifa'nia] *sf* Epiphany; (*festa*) Twelfth Night.

epigramma [epi'gramma] *sm* epigram. **epigrammatico** *agg* epigrammatic.

epilessia [epiles'sia] *sf* epilepsy. **epilettico, -a** *s*, *agg* epileptic.

epilogo [e'pilogo] *sm*, *pl* -ghi epilogue; (*fig*) end, conclusion.

episodio [epi'zɔdjo] *sm* episode. **episodico** *agg* episodic; (*frammentario*) bitty; (*accidentale*) incidental; isolated.

epistola [e'pistola] *sf* epistle. **epistolare** *agg* epistolary.

epitaffio [epi'taffjo] *sm* epitaph.

epiteto [e'piteto] *sm* epithet.

epoca ['ɛpoka] *sf* period; (*tempo*) time. **a quell'epoca** at that time. **che fa epoca** epoch-making. **da quell'epoca** from that time on, since then.

eppure [ep'pure] *cong* and yet.

epurare [epu'rare] *v* purge. **epurazione** *sf* purging; purge.

equanime [e'kwanime] *agg* (*imparziale*) fair; (*sereno*) even-tempered. **equanimità** *sf* fairness, equanimity.

equatore [ekwa'tore] *sm* equator. **equatoriale** *agg* equatorial.

equazione [ekwa'tsjone] *sf* equation.

equestre [e'kwɛstre] *agg* equestrian.

equilibrare [ekwili'brare] *v* balance. **equilibrio** *sm* balance, equilibrium; moderation, common sense; (*padronanza di sè*) poise. **perdere l'equilibrio** lose one's balance. **tenere in equilibrio** balance. **tenersi in equilibrio** keep one's balance. **equilibrista** *s*(*m + f*) acrobat.

equinozio [ekwi'nɔtsjo] *sm* equinox.
equipaggiare [ekwipad'dʒare] *v* (*fornire*) equip; (*nave*) man. **equipaggiamento** *sm* kit. **equipaggio** *sm* crew.
equiparare [ekwipa'rare] *v* level.
equitazione [ekwita'tsjone] *sf* (horse-)riding.
***equivalere** [ekwiva'lere] *v* be equivalent, correspond. **equivalente** *sm*, *agg* equivalent.
equivoco [e'kwivoko] *sm* (*errore*) mistake; (*malinteso*) misunderstanding. **a scanso di equivoci** to avoid misunderstandings. *agg* ambiguous; (*di dubbia moralità*) questionable, shady. **non equivoco** unambiguous, straightforward.
equo ['ɛkwo] *agg* fair.
era ['ɛra] *sf* era, age.
erario [e'rarjo] *sm* Treasury. **erariale** *agg* fiscal.
erba ['ɛrba] *sf* grass; (*gastr*) herb. **in erba** green; (*fig*) budding. **erbaceo** *agg* herbaceous.
erbaccia [er'battʃa] *sf* weed.
erbicida [erbi'tʃida] *sm* herbicide, weedkiller.
erbivendolo [erbi'vendolo], **-a** *sm*, *sf* greengrocer.
erbivoro [er'bivoro] *sm* herbivore. *agg* herbivorous.
erede [e'rɛde] *s*(*m*+*f*) heir, heiress. **erede apparente** heir presumptive. **erede universale** sole heir.
eredità [eredi'ta] *sf* inheritance, heritage. **ereditare** *v* inherit. **ereditario** *agg* inherited, hereditary. **principe ereditario** *sm* crown prince. **ereditiera** *sf* heiress.
eremita [ere'mita] *sm* hermit. **eremitaggio** *sm* hermitage.
eretico [e'rɛtiko], **-a** *sm*, *sf* heretic. *agg* heretical. **eresia** *sf* heresy; (*fam: sproposito*) rubbish.
eretto [e'rɛtto] *agg* erect, upright. **erettile** *agg* erectile.
erezione [ere'tsjone] *sf* erection.
ergastolo [er'gastolo] *sm* life imprisonment *or* sentence.
erica ['ɛrika] *sf* heather.
***erigere** [e'ridʒere] *v* raise, erect; (*fondare, considerare*) set up.
ermellino [ermel'lino] *sm* ermine; (*bruno*) stoat.
ermetico [er'mɛtiko] *agg* (*aria*) air-tight; (*acqua*) water-tight; obscure.

ernia ['ɛrnja] *sf* hernia, rupture.
***erodere** [e'rodere] *v* erode.
eroe [e'rɔe] *sm* hero. **eroico** *agg* heroic. **eroina** *sf* heroine. **eroismo** *sm* heroism; (*atto*) heroic deed.
erogare [ero'gare] *v* distribute, deliver; (*in donazione*) donate. **erogazione** *sf* distribution, delivery; donation.
eroina [ero'ina] *sf* (*stupefacente*) heroin.
erosione [ero'zjone] *sf* erosion.
erotico [e'rɔtiko] *agg* erotic. **erotismo** *sm* eroticism.
erpete ['ɛrpete] *sm* herpes.
erpice ['ɛrpitʃe] *sm* harrow.
errare [er'rare] *v* (*andare senza meta*) roam, wander; (*sbagliare*) err, be mistaken. **erratico** *agg* erratic. **errato** *agg* incorrect. **se non vado errato** if I am not mistaken.
erroneo [er'rɔneo] *agg* erroneous, wrong.
errore [er'rore] *sm* mistake, error. **errore giudiziario** miscarriage of justice. **per errore** by mistake, in error.
erudito [eru'dito] *agg* erudite, learned. **erudizione** *sf* learning.
eruttare [erut'tare] *v* (*ruttare*) belch; (*vulcano*) erupt; (*fig*) spew out. **eruzione** *sf* eruption.
esacerbare [ezatʃer'bare] *v* exacerbate.
esagerare [ezadʒe'rare] *v* exaggerate; (*caricare*) overdo. **esagerazione** *sf* exaggeration.
esagono [e'zagono] *sm* hexagon. **esagonale** *agg* hexagonal.
esalare [eza'lare] *v* exhale, give off. **esalazione** *sf* exhalation.
esaltare [ezal'tare] *v* exalt; (*lodare*) extol; (*entusiasmare*) thrill, stir. **esaltato, -a** *sm*, *sf* fanatic, hot-head.
esame [e'zame] *sm* examination, test; (*controllo*) inspection, check. **dare un esame** take an examination. **prendere in esame** consider, take into consideration.
esaminare [ezami'nare] *v* examine, test, check.
esanime [e'zanime] *agg* lifeless.
esasperare [ezaspe'rare] *v* (*irritare*) exasperate; (*inasprire*) sharpen, increase. **esasperazione** *sf* exasperation; sharpening, increase.
esatto [e'zatto] *agg* exact; correct; accurate; punctual. *avv* (*in punto*) exactly. **esattezza** *sf* exactness; accuracy, precision.

esattore [ezat'tore] *sm (tassa)* collector. **esattoria** *sf* tax office.

esaudire [ezau'dire] *v* grant.

esaurire [ezau'rire] *v* exhaust, use up; *(vendere completamente)* sell out; *(condurre a termine)* complete. **esaurirsi** *v* *(debilitarsi)* wear oneself out.

esca ['eska] *sf* bait; *(fig)* lure; *(per accendere)* tinder. **dar esca a** fan, stir up.

escandescenza [eskande'ʃɛntsa] *sf* **dare in escandescenze** flare up; *(fam)* fly off the handle.

eschimese [eski'meze] *s(m+f)*, *agg* Eskimo.

esclamare [eskla'mare] *v* exclaim, cry out. **punto esclamativo** *sm* exclamation mark. **esclamazione** *sf* exclamation.

*escludere [es'kludere] *v* exclude. **esclusione** *sf* exclusion. **ad esclusione di** except.

esclusivo [esklu'zivo] *agg* exclusive. **esclusiva** *sf (comm)* exclusive *or* sole right; *(rappresentanza)* sole agency. **escluso** *agg* excluded, impossible; *(eccettuato)* except; *(non compreso)* exclusive of, not including.

escogitare [eskodʒi'tare] *v* devise, think up.

escursione [eskur'sjone] *v* excursion, trip; *(a macchina)* drive; *(a piedi)* hike. **escursionista** *s(m+f)* tripper; hiker.

esecutivo [ezeku'tivo] *sm*, *agg* executive.

esecutore [ezeku'tore], **-trice** *sm*, *sf (dir)* executor; *(musica)* performer; *(carnefice)* executioner.

esecuzione [ezeku'tsjone] *sf* execution, performance.

eseguire [eze'gwire] *v* carry out; *(musica, teatro)* perform; *(dir)* execute.

esempio [e'zɛmpjo] *sm* example; model. **ad** *or* **per esempio** for instance. **dare l'esempio** set an example.

esemplare [ezem'plare] *agg* exemplary. *sm* example, model; *(tipico)* specimen. **esemplificare** *v* exemplify, illustrate.

esentare [ezen'tare] *v* exempt. **esentarsi da** get out of. **esente** *agg* exempt, free. **esenzione** *sf* exemption.

esequie [e'zɛkwje] *sf pl (cerimonie)* funeral rites *pl*; funeral *sing*.

esercente [ezer'tʃɛnte] *s(m+f)* retailer; *(negoziante)* shopkeeper. **esercire** *v* manage, run.

esercitare [ezertʃi'tare] *v* practise; *(usare)*

exercise. **esercitazione** *sf* practice; exercise; *(mil)* drill. **esercizio** *sm* exercise; *(attività)* practice; *(azienda)* concern.

esibire [ezi'bire] *v* exhibit. **esibirsi** *v (dar spettacolo)* perform; *(mettersi in mostra)* show off. **esibizione** *sf* exhibition, show, display. **esibizionismo** *sm* exhibitionism. **esibizionista** *s(m+f)* exhibitionist.

*esigere [e'zidʒere] *v* require, need, demand. **esigente** *agg* exacting. **esigenza** *sf* requirement; *(necessità)* need; *(pretesa)* demand. **esiguo** *agg* meagre.

esilarante [ezila'rante] *agg* exhilarating.

esile ['ezile] *agg* slender; *(debole)* feeble.

esiliare [ezi'ljare] *v* exile. **esiliarsi** *v* go into exile. **esiliato, -a** *sm*, *sf* exile. **esilio** *sm* exile.

*esimere [e'zimere] *v* exempt, free.

esimio [e'zimjo] *agg* distinguished, outstanding.

esistenzialismo [ezistentsja'lizmo] *sm* existentialism. **esistenzialista** *s(m+f)*, *agg* existentialist.

esistere [e'zistere] *v* exist, be. **esistente** *agg* existing. **esistenza** *sf* existence. **esistenza di cassa/magazzino** *(comm)* cash/stock in hand.

esitare [ezi'tare] *v* hesitate. **esitazione** *sf* hesitation.

esito ['ɛzito] *sm* outcome; *(dramma)* denouement. **buon esito** success.

esodo ['ɛzɔdo] *sm* exodus.

esofago [e'zɔfago] *sm* oesophagus; gullet.

esonerare [ezone'rare] *v* exempt. **esonero** *sm* exemption.

esorbitante [ezorbi'tante] *agg* exorbitant.

esorcizzare [ezortʃid'dzare] *v* exorcise. **esorcismo** *sm* exorcism.

esordire [ezor'dire] *v* start out; *(artista)* make one's debut. **esordio** *sm* start, debut.

esortare [ezor'tare] *v* urge. **esortazione** *sf* exhortation, encouragement.

esoso [e'zɔzo] *agg (avido)* greedy; exorbitant; odious.

esoterico [ezo'tɛriko] *agg* esoteric.

esotico [e'zɔtiko] *agg* exotic.

*espandere [es'pandere] *v* expand, extend. **espandersi** *v* spread. **espansione** *sf* expansion; *(effusione d'affetto)* effusiveness. **espansivo** *agg* effusive; *(forza)* expansive.

espatriare [espa'trjare] *v* emigrate. **espatrio** *sm* expatriation.

espediente [espe'djɛnte] *sm* expedient, device; (*soluzione*) way out. **vivere di espedienti** live on one's wits.

*espellere [es'pɛllere] *v* expel.

esperienza [espe'rjɛntsa] *sf* experience; experiment; (*conoscenza*) familiarity. **fare esperienza di** experience. **senza esperienza** inexperienced.

esperimento [esperi'mento] *sm* experiment; (*tentativo*) trial, test.

esperto [es'pɛrto], **-a** *sm, sf* expert, authority. *agg* expert (in); (*abile*) skilful (at); experienced (in).

espiare [espi'are] *v* expiate, atone. **capro espiatorio** *sm* scapegoat.

espletare [esple'tare] *v* accomplish.

esplicito [es'plitʃito] *agg* explicit. **esplicativo** *agg* explanatory.

*esplodere [es'plɔdere] *v* explode. **far esplodere** explode, blow up.

esplorare [esplo'rare] *v* explore; (*investigare*) probe. **esploratore, -trice** *sm, sf* explorer; (*mil*) scout. **giovani esploratori** Boy Scouts *pl.* **esplorazione** *sf* exploration; (*mil*) reconnaissance.

esplosione [esplo'zjone] *sf* explosion.

esplosivo [esplo'zivo] *sm, agg* explosive.

esponente [espo'nɛnte] *sm* exponent; representative. **esponenziale** *agg* exponential.

*esporre [es'porre] *v* expose; (*arrischiare*) risk; (*spiegare*) expound; (*mostrare*) exhibit, display.

esportare [espor'tare] *v* export. **esportatore, -trice** *sm, sf* exporter. **esportazione** *sf* export.

esposizione [espozi'tsjone] *sf* exhibition, show; (*spiegazione*) explanation; (*posizione, foto*) exposure.

esposto [es'posto] *agg* exhibited, displayed; exposed. *sm* statement.

espressione [espres'sjone] *sf* expression. **espressivo** *agg* expressive, eloquent.

espresso [es'prɛsso] *agg* express; (*manifestato*) expressed; (*dichiarato*) avowed, declared. **piatto espresso** *sm* specially prepared dish. *sm* (*lettera*) express letter; (*caffè*) espresso; (*ferr*) express train.

*esprimere [es'primere] *v* express.

espulsione [espul'sjone] *sf* expulsion.

essa ['essa] *pron* (*persona: soggetto*) she; (*persona: oggetto*) her; (*cosa, animale*) it.

esse ['esse] *pron* (*soggetto*) they; (*oggetto*) them.

essenza [es'sɛntsa] *sf* essence. **essenziale** *agg* essential.

*essere ['essere] *v* be; (*ausiliare con forma attiva*) have. *sm* being; (*fam*) person, creature; (*condizione*) existence.

essi ['essi] *pron* (*soggetto*) they; (*oggetto*) them.

essiccare [essik'kare] *v* dry. **essiccatoio** *sm* dryer.

esso ['esso] *pron* (*persona: soggetto*) he; (*persona: oggetto*) him; (*cosa, animale*) it.

est [est] *sm* east. **dell'est** east, eastern.

estasi ['ɛstazi] *sf* ecstasy. **estatico** *agg* ecstatic.

estate [es'tate] *sf* summer. **estate di San Martino** Indian summer.

*estendere [es'tɛndere] *v* extend, stretch; (*ampliare*) broaden. **estendersi** *v* (*stendersi*) stretch; (*diffondersi*) spread.

estensione [esten'sjone] *sf* extension; (*dimensione*) extent; (*distesa*) expanse; (*fig, musica*) range; (*significato*) wider sense.

estenuare [estenu'are] *v* exhaust. **estenuante** *agg* exhausting, wearing.

esteriore [este'rjore] *agg* outer, exterior, external. *sm* (*parte esterna*) outside; (*apparenze*) appearances *pl.*

esterno [es'tɛrno] *agg* external, outer, exterior. *sm* outside; (*scolaro*) day-boy; (*film*) exterior.

estero ['ɛstero] *agg* foreign. *sm* foreign countries *pl.* **all'estero** abroad.

esterrefatto [esterre'fatto] *agg* (*atterrito*) aghast, horrified; (*sbigottito*) amazed.

esteso [es'tezo] *agg* large, wide-ranging; (*fig*) thorough. **per esteso** in full.

estetica [es'tɛtika] *sf* aesthetics. **estetico** *agg* aesthetic.

estetista [este'tista] *s(m+f)* beauty specialist, beautician.

*estinguere [es'tingwere] *v* put out; (*far svanire*) extinguish; (*econ*) wipe out; (*debito*) pay off; (*sete*) quench. **estinguersi** *v* die out. **estinto** *agg* extinguished; (*scomparso*) extinct. **estinzione** *sf* extinction; (*sete*) quenching; (*econ*) discharge.

estirpare [estir'pare] *v* eradicate.

estivo [es'tivo] *agg* summer.

*estorcere [es'tɔrtʃere] *v* extort. **estorsione** *sf* extortion.

estradare [estra'dare] *v* extradite. **estradizione** *sf* extradition.

estraneo [es'traneo] *agg* extraneous, unrelated (to), unconnected (with); (*alieno*) foreign. **essere estraneo a** have no part in. **mantenersi estraneo a** have nothing to do with, keep clear of. *sm* stranger; unauthorized person. **estraniare** *v* estrange.

***estrarre** [es'trarre] *v* extract, draw (out); (*miniera*) mine; (*cava*) quarry. **estratto** *sm* extract; (*compendio*) abstract; (*stralcio*) excerpt. **estrazione** *sf* extraction.

estremo [es'trɛmo] *agg* extreme; (*ultimo*) final; (*grandissimo*) utmost. *sm* extreme; (*colmo*) height; (*estremità*) end, tip. **estremi** *sm pl* particulars *pl*; (*dir*) essential elements *pl*. **estremismo** *sm* extremism. **estremista** *s(m+f)* extremist.

estro ['ɛstro] *sm* (*ghiribizzo*) whim, fancy; (*impulso*) inspiration; (*venereo*) heat. **estroso** *agg* whimsical, capricious; inspired.

estrogeno [es'trɔdʒeno] *sm* oestrogen.

estroverso [estro'vɛrso], **-a** *sm, sf* extrovert. *agg* extroverted.

estuario [estu'arjo] *sm* estuary.

esuberante [ezube'rante] *agg* exuberant. **esuberanza** *sf* exuberance.

esule ['ɛzule] *s(m+f)* exile. **esulare** *v* lie outside, be beyond.

esultare [ezul'tare] *v* rejoice. **esultante** *agg* exultant.

esumare [ezu'mare] *v* exhume; (*fig*) unearth.

età [e'ta] *v* age. **all'età di dieci anni** at (the age of) ten. **età della ragione** age of discretion.

etere ['ɛtere] *sm* ether.

eterno [e'tɛrno] *agg* eternal, everlasting; (*lunghissimo*) interminable. **eternità** *sm* eternity; (*molto tempo*) ages *pl*.

eterodosso [etero'dɔsso] *agg* heterodox.

eterogeneo [etero'dʒɛneo] *agg* heterogeneous.

etica ['ɛtika] *sf* ethics. **etico** *agg* ethical.

etichetta¹ [eti'ketta] *sf* (*cartellino*) label.

etichetta² [eti'ketta] *sf* (*regole*) etiquette.

etimologia [etimolo'dʒia] *sf* etymology. **etimologico** *agg* etymological.

etnico ['ɛtniko] *agg* ethnic.

ettaro ['ɛttaro] *sm* hectare.

etto ['ɛtto] *sm* hundred grams.

eucalipto [euka'lipto] *sm* eucalyptus.

eufemismo [eufe'mizmo] *sm* euphemism.

eufemistico *agg* euphemistic.

eunuco [eu'nuko] *sm, pl* **-chi** eunuch.

Europa [eu'rɔpa] *sf* Europe. **europeo, -a** *s, agg* European.

eutanasia [eutana'zia] *sf* euthanasia.

evacuare [evaku'are] *v* evacuate.

***evadere** [e'vadere] *v* escape (from); (*sbrigare*) dispatch; (*fattura*) settle; (*ordini*) execute; (*fisco*) avoid.

evanescente [evane'ʃɛnte] *agg* (*suono*) fading; (*fugace*) fleeting; (*crema*) vanishing.

evangelista [evandʒe'lista] *sm* evangelist.

evangelico *agg* evangelical.

evaporare [evapo'rare] *v* evaporate. **evaporatore** *sm* humidifier. **evaporazione** *sf* evaporation.

evasione [eva'zjone] *sf* escape; (*fisco*) evasion; (*comm*) execution.

evasivo [eva'zivo] *agg* evasive.

evaso [e'vazo], **-a** *agg* escaped; (*comm*) dispatched, dealt with. *sm, sf* fugitive, escaped convict.

evento [e'vɛnto] *sm* event; (*eventualità*) eventuality. **in ogni evento** in any case, at all events.

eventuale [eventu'ale] *agg* possible, any. **eventualità** *sf* eventuality. **nell'eventualità di** *or* **che** in the event of. **eventualmente** *cong* if, in case.

evidente [evi'dente] *agg* obvious, manifest, clear; (*irrefutabile*) unmistakable. **evidenza** *sf* (*chiarezza*) clarity, obviousness. **mettere in evidenza** stress, emphasize. **mettersi in evidenza** make oneself conspicuous, draw attention to oneself. **tenere un'evidenza** (*comm*) keep pending.

evitare [evi'tare] *v* avoid; (*non arrecare*) spare, save.

evo ['ɛvo] *sm* **Medio Evo** Middle Ages *pl*.

evocare [evo'kare] *v* evoke.

evoluzione [evolu'tsjone] *sf* evolution. **evoluto** *agg* evolved, fully developed; advanced, progressive.

evviva [ev'viva] *inter* hurrah! **evviva ... !** long live ... !

extra ['ɛkstra] *agg invar* (*qualità*) first-rate; (*fuori del previsto*) additional. *sm invar* extra.

F

fa [fa] *avv* ago.

fabbisogno [fabbi'zoɲo] *sm* requirements *pl*.

fabbrica ['fabbrika] *sf* factory; (*officina*) works; (*edificio*) building. **fabbricante** *sm* manufacturer. **fabbricare** *v* manufacture, produce; (*costruire*) build; (*inventare*) make up. **fabbricato** *sm* building. **fabbricazione** *sf* manufacture, production.

fabbro ['fabbro] *sm* (*ferraio*) (black)smith.

faccenda [fat'tʃɛnda] *sf* matter; (*caso, circostanza*) business. **faccende domestiche** housework *sing*.

facchino [fak'kino] *sm* porter. **facchinaggio** *sm* porterage. **facchinata** *sf* (*lavoro*) drudgery.

faccia ['fattʃa] *sf* face; (*lato*) side. **avere una bella/brutta faccia** look well/unwell. **di faccia** opposite. **faccia tosta** (*fam*) cheek, nerve. **in faccia a** opposite. **facciata** *sf* front; (*pagina*) side.

facezia [fa'tʃɛtsja] *sf* pleasantry; (*detto spiritoso*) witticism. **faceto** *agg* facetious, witty.

facile ['fatʃile] *agg* easy; (*incline*) easily moved, prone. **facilità** *sf* ease, facility; (*l'esser facile*) easiness; (*capacità*) aptitude. **con facilità** with ease, readily; (*lingua*) fluently.

facilitare [fatʃili'tare] *v* facilitate; (*aiutare*) help. **facilitazione** *sf* facilitation, making easy. **facilitazioni di pagamento** easy terms *pl*.

facoltà [fakol'ta] *sf* faculty; (*potere*) power. **facoltativo** *agg* optional. **facoltoso** *agg* wealthy.

faggio ['faddʒo] *sm* beech.

fagiano [fa'dʒano] *sm* pheasant.

fagiolo [fa'dʒɔlo] *sm* bean. **andare a fagiolo** (*fam*) suit. **fagiolino** *sm* French bean.

fagotto [fa'gɔtto] *sm* bundle; (*musica*) bassoon. **far fagotto** pack up.

falcata [fal'kata] *sf* step.

falce ['faltʃe] *sf* sickle; (*manico lungo*) scythe.

falciare [fal'tʃare] *v* mow; (*fig*) mow down. **falciatrice** *sf* mower.

falco ['falko] *sm* hawk. **falcone** *sm* falcon; (*tec*) derrick.

falda ['falda] *sf* (*strato*) layer, sheet; (*di pendio*) foot; (*di cappello*) brim; (*di vestito*) skirt; (*di marsina*) tail.

falegname [fale'ɲame] *sm* joiner, carpenter. **falegnameria** *sf* (*arte*) joinery, carpentry; (*bottega*) joiner's shop.

falena [fa'lɛna] *sf* moth; (*cenere*) ash; (*persona fatua*) flighty person.

falla ['falla] *sf* leak. **aprire/chiudere una falla** spring/stop a leak.

fallace [fal'latʃe] *agg* fallacious.

fallire [fal'lire] *v* fail; (*non colpire*) miss; (*dir, comm*) go bankrupt. **fallimento** *sm* failure; bankruptcy.

fallito [fal'lito], -**a** *agg* unsuccessful. *sm, sf* bankrupt; (*fig*) failure.

fallo[1] ['fallo] *sm* (*errore*) fault; (*sport*) foul. **cogliere in fallo** find out. **essere in fallo** be at fault. **senza fallo** without fail, certainly.

fallo[2] ['fallo] *sm* (*membro virile*) phallus.

falò [fa'lo] *sm* bonfire.

falsare [fal'sare] *v* falsify; (*alterare*) distort. **falsario** *sm* (*documenti*) forger; (*monete*) counterfeiter.

falsariga [falsa'riga] *sf* (*modello*) pattern; (*norma*) lines *pl*.

falsificare [falsifi'kare] *v* falsify; (*arte*) fake. **falsificazione** *sf* falsification, faking; forgery, fake.

falso ['falso] *agg* false; (*falsificato*) counterfeit, faked, forged; (*fam*) bogus. *sm* (*non vero*) falsehood; (*reato*) forgery. **giurare il falso** commit perjury.

fama ['fama] *sf* fame, reputation.

fame ['fame] *sf* hunger; (*carestia*) famine. **aver fame** be hungry. **aver fame di** (*fig*) hunger for. **aver una fame da lupo** be ravenous. **fare la fame** go hungry. **morir di fame** starve to death; (*fig*) be starving.

famelico [fa'mɛliko] *agg* ravenous.

famigerato [famidʒe'rato] *agg* notorious.

famiglia [fa'miʎa] *sf* family. **in famiglia** at home.

familiare [fami'ljare] *agg* domestic; (*consueto, intimo*) familiar; (*semplice*) informal. *s(m+f)* (*parente*) relative. **familiarità** *sf* familiarity. **familiarizzarsi** *v* familiarize oneself.

famoso [fa'moso] *agg* famous, well-known; memorable.

fanale [fa'nale] *sm* lamp; (*auto*) light. **fanale anteriore** headlight. **fanale di coda** tail-light.

fanatico [fa'natiko], -**a** *agg* fanatical; (*fam: entusiasta*) wild (about). *sm, sf* fanatic; (*tifoso*) fan. **fanatismo** *sm* fanaticism.

fanciullo [fan'tʃullo], -**a** *sm, sf* child (*pl* -ren). **fanciullaggine** *sf* childish behaviour. **fanciullesco** *agg* childish, puerile;

(*innocente*) child-like. **fanciullezza** *sf* childhood.

fandonia [fan'dɔnja] *sf* nonsense.

fanfara [fan'fara] *sf* (brass-)band; (*composizione*) fanfare. **fanfaronata** *sf* boasting. **fanfarone, -a** *sm, sf* boaster.

fango ['fango] *sm* mud. **fare i fanghi** take mud-baths. **fangoso** *agg* muddy.

fannullone [fannul'lone], **-a** *sm, sf* idler, loafer.

fantascienza [fanta'ʃɛntsa] *sf* science fiction.

fantasia [fanta'zia] *sf* fantasy; (*capriccio*) fancy; imagination. *agg* (*moda*) fancy, patterned.

fantasma [fan'tazma] *sm* ghost, phantom.

fantasticare [fantasti'kare] *v* daydream, dream up. **fantastico** *agg* fantastic; (*non reale*) fanciful, strange.

fante ['fante] *sm* (*mil*) infantryman; (*carte*) knave, jack. **fanteria** *sf* infantry. **fantino** *sm* jockey.

fantoccio [fan'tɔttʃo] *sm* puppet.

farabutto [fara'butto] *sm* rascal, rogue.

faraona [fara'ona] *sf* guinea-fowl.

farcire [far'tʃire] *v* stuff.

fardello [far'dello] *sm* burden.

*fare ['fare] *v* (*agire*) do; (*produrre*) make; (*essere*) be; (*avere*) have; (*un mestiere, ecc.*) go in for, practise; (*comportarsi*) play; (*orologio*) say. **farcela** *v* (*riuscire*) manage; (*resistere*) be able to go on. **far attenzione** pay attention. **far bene** do good. **far bene a** be good for. **far chiamare** send for. **far entrare** let in. **fare il pieno** (*auto*) fill up. **far male** (*dolere*) hurt, ache; (*nuocere*) be bad for; (*agire male*) do the wrong thing. **far notare** point out. **fare per** be about to. **far vedere** show. **farsi** *v* (*diventare*) become, grow into; (*convertirsi*) turn into; (*tempo*) get.

farfalla [far'falla] *sf* butterfly; (*falena*) moth. **nuoto a farfalla** *sm* butterfly stroke.

farina [fa'rina] *sf* flour. **farina gialla** maize meal. **farina integrale** wholemeal. **farinaceo** *agg* floury, starchy. **farinoso** *agg* floury, mealy; (*neve*) powdery.

faringe [fa'rindʒe] *sf* pharynx. **faringite** *sf* pharyngitis.

farmacia [farma'tʃia] *sf* (*negozio*) chemist's (shop); (*scienza*) pharmacy. **farmacista** *s(m+f)* chemist. **farmaco** *sm* medicine.

farneticare [farneti'kare] *v* rave.

faro ['faro] *sm* lighthouse; (*lume, fig*) beacon; (*auto*) headlight.

farragine [far'radʒine] *sf* muddle, jumble.

farsa ['farsa] *sf* farce.

fascia ['faʃa] *sf* band; (*benda*) bandage; (*uniforme*) sash; (*postale*) wrapper; (*zona*) strip.

fasciare [fa'ʃare] *v* wrap; (*bambini*) swaddle; (*ferita*) dress, bandage.

fascicolo [fa'ʃikolo] *sm* (*opuscolo*) pamphlet, booklet; (*numero*) issue.

fascino ['faʃino] *sm* charm, fascination.

fascio ['faʃo] *sm* bundle, bunch.

fascismo [fa'ʃizmo] *sm* fascism. **fascista** *s(m+f)*, *agg* fascist.

fase ['faze] *sf* phase; (*auto*) stroke.

fastidio [fas'tidjo] *sm* trouble; (*avversione*) dislike; (*cosa fastidiosa*) bother, inconvenience. **dar fastidio** trouble; (*molestare*) annoy, bother. **darsi fastidio** put oneself out. **fastidioso** *agg* troublesome, annoying.

fasto ['fasto] *sm* pomp.

fasullo [fa'zullo] *agg* (*fam*) bogus, phoney.

fata ['fata] *sf* fairy.

fatale [fa'tale] *agg* inevitable; (*funesto*) fatal; (*decisivo*) fateful; irresistible.

fatica [fa'tika] *sf* (*sforzo*) effort, labour; (*stanchezza, tec*) fatigue. **a fatica** with difficulty. **costar fatica** require an effort. **durare fatica** find it difficult. **reggere alla fatica** stand the strain. **faticare** *v* labour; (*stentare*) have difficulty. **faticoso** *agg* tiring.

fatta ['fatta] *sf* kind.

fattezze [fat'tettse] *sf pl* features *pl*.

fattibile [fat'tibile] *agg* feasible.

fatto¹ ['fatto] *agg* made, done. **a conti fatti** all things considered. **detto fatto** no sooner said than done. **fatto a macchina/mano** machine-/hand-made. **fatto su misura** tailor-made.

fatto² ['fatto] *sm* fact; (*avvenimento*) event; (*azione*) deed; (*affare*) business. **cogliere sul fatto** catch in the act. **dire il fatto suo** have one's say. **fatto compiuto** fait accompli. **fatto sta** the fact remains. **in fatto di** regarding.

fattore [fat'tore] *sm* factor; (*capo di fattoria*) steward.

fattoria [fatto'ria] *sf* farm, estate.

fattorino [fatto'rino] *sm* messenger; (*di negozio*) errand-boy; (*di autobus*) conductor.

fattura [fat'tura] *sf* (*confezione*) making; (*lavorazione*) construction, workmanship; (*conto*) bill; (*comm*) invoice. **fatturare** *v* (*comm*) invoice; (*manipolare*) doctor. **fatturato** *sm* turnover.

fatuo ['fatuo] *agg* foolish, fatuous.

fauci ['fautʃi] *sf pl* jaws *pl*; (*fig*) clutches *pl*.

fauna ['fauna] *sf* fauna.

fausto ['fausto] *agg* propitious.

fautore [fau'tore], **-trice** *sm, sf* supporter.

fava ['fava] *sf* broad bean.

favilla [fa'villa] *sf* spark. **far faville** sparkle, shine.

favo ['favo] *sm* honeycomb.

favola ['favola] *sf* fable, story. **favoloso** *agg* fabulous.

favore [fa'vore] *sm* favour; (*appoggio*) support. **di favore** (*biglietto*) complimentary; (*prezzo*) special. **per favore** please.

favoreggiare [favored'dʒare] *v* favour; (*dir*) aid and abet.

favorevole [favo'revole] *agg* favourable, in favour.

favorire [favo'rire] *v* favour; (*sostenere*) support; (*promuovere*) promote, foster.

favorito, -a *s, agg* favourite. **favoritismo** *sm* favouritism.

fazione [fa'tsjone] *sf* faction, party. **fazioso** *agg* subversive.

fazzoletto [fattso'letto] *sm* handkerchief; (*da testa*) headsquare.

febbraio [feb'brajo] *sm* February.

febbre ['febbre] *sf* temperature, fever; (*fam: sulle labbra*) cold sore; (*brama*) lust, passion. **febbre da fieno** hay fever. **febbricitante** *agg* feverish.

feccia ['fettʃa] *sf* dregs *pl*.

feci ['fetʃi] *sf pl* faeces *pl*.

fecola ['fekola] *sf* starch.

fecondare [fekon'dare] *v* fertilize. **fecondazione** *sf* fertilization. **fecondazione artificiale** artificial insemination. **fecondità** *sf* fertility. **fecondo** *agg* fertile; prolific, fruitful.

fede ['fede] *sf* faith; (*fiducia*) confidence, trust; (*anello*) wedding ring; (*attestazione*) proof.

fedele [fe'dele] *agg* faithful, true. *s(m+f)* believer; (*seguace*) follower. **fedeltà** *sf* faithfulness, fidelity.

federa ['federa] *sf* pillow-case.

federale [fede'rale] *agg* federal.

federazione [federa'tsjone] *sf* federation, association.

fedina [fe'dina] *sf* police *or* criminal record.

fedine [fe'dine] *sf pl* side-whiskers *pl*.

fegato ['fegato] *sm* liver; (*coraggio*) guts *pl*. **mangiarsi il fegato** eat one's heart out.

felce ['feltʃe] *sf* fern; (*comune*) bracken.

felice [fe'litʃe] *agg* happy; (*fortunato*) lucky. **felicità** *sf* happiness, bliss. **felicitarsi con** congratulate. **felicitazioni** *sf pl* congratulations *pl*.

felino [fe'lino] *agg* feline.

felpa ['felpa] *sf* plush.

feltro ['feltro] *sm* felt.

femmina ['femmina] *sf* female; (*figlia*) daughter. *agg* female. **femminismo** *sm* feminism, women's movement. **femminista** *s(m+f)*, *agg* feminist.

femminile [femmi'nile] *agg* female; (*da donna*) feminine, womanly; (*gramm*) feminine. **scuola femminile** *sf* girls' school. *sm* feminine (gender). **femminilità** *sf* femininity.

femore ['femore] *sm* femur.

*****fendere** ['fendere] *v* split, pierce; (*solcare*) plough (through). **fenditura** *sf* cleft; (*fessura*) crack.

fenicottero [feni'kɔttero] *sm* flamingo.

fenomeno [fe'nɔmeno] *sm* phenomenon (*pl* -a); (*prodigio*) marvel. **fenomenale** *agg* phenomenal; (*eccezionale*) extraordinary, remarkable.

feretro ['feretro] *sm* coffin.

ferie ['fɛrje] *sf pl* holidays *pl*. **giorno feriale** *sm* weekday.

ferire [fe'rire] *v* wound, injure, hurt. **ferita** *sf* wound, injury; (*persona*) casualty. **ferito** *sm* casualty.

fermacarte [ferma'karte] *sm invar* (*a molla*) paper-clip; (*pesante*) paperweight.

fermaglio [fer'maʎo] *sm* clasp, clip.

fermare [fer'mare] *v* stop; (*arrestare*) check; (*fissare*) secure, fasten; (*prenotare*) book. **fermarsi** stop; (*rimanere*) stay. **fermata** *sf* stop; (*tappa*) stay; (*veicoli*) halt. **fermata facoltativa** request stop.

fermentare [fermen'tare] *v* ferment. **fermentazione** *sf* fermentation. **fermento** *sm* ferment; (*fig*) unrest.

fermo ['fermo] *agg* still; (*non in moto*) stationary; (*saldo*) firm, steady. **restar fermo** stand still; (*fig*) hold good. *sm* (*mec*) catch, fastener, lock; (*dir*) detention; (*sospensione*) stop.

feroce [fe'rotʃe] *agg* wild; (*crudele*) savage, ferocious; (*fig*) fierce. **ferocia** *sf* cruelty, ferocity.

ferragosto [ferra'gosto] *sm* mid-August holiday.

ferramenta [ferra'menta] *sf pl* ironmongery *sing*.

ferreo ['fɛrreo] *agg* iron.

ferro ['fɛrro] *sf* iron. **essere ai ferri corti** be at loggerheads. **ferro battuto** wrought iron. **ferro da calza** knitting needle. **ferro di cavallo** horseshoe. **tocca ferro!** touch wood!

ferrovia [ferro'via] *sf* railway. **ferroviario** *agg* rail(way), train. **ferroviere** *sm* railwayman.

fertile ['fɛrtile] *agg* fertile, fruitful. **fertilità** *sf* fertility, fruitfulness. **fertilizzante** *sm* fertilizer. **fertilizzare** *v* fertilize.

fervore [fer'vore] *sm* fervour. **fervente** *agg* fervent. **fervido** *agg* ardent; (*caloroso*) heartfelt; (*vivace*) lively.

fesso ['fesso] (*volg*) *agg*, *sm* idiot, fool. **fesseria** *sf* (*azione*) foolishness; (*parole*) nonsense; (*inezia*) trifle.

fessura [fes'sura] *sf* crack, slit; (*gettone, moneta*) slot.

festa ['festa] *sf* holiday; (*compleanno*) birthday; (*onomastico*) saint's day; (*festeggiamento*) celebration; (*ricevimento*) party. **far festa** (*non lavorare*) take a holiday, take time off; (*smettere il lavoro*) stop work; (*divertirsi*) make merry. **far festa a** give a warm welcome (to).

festeggiare [fested'dʒare] *v* celebrate; (*far festa*) give a hearty welcome (to). **festeggiamenti** *sm pl* festivities *pl*. **festeggiamento** *sm* celebration.

festività [festivi'ta] *sf* festivity, holiday. **festivo** *agg* (*della domenica*) Sunday; (*non-feriale*) holiday.

festone [fes'tone] *sm* festoon; (*ricamo*) scallop.

fetente [fe'tɛnte] *sm* (*volg*) stinker, scoundrel. *agg also* **fetido** stinking, foul. **fetore** *sm* stench.

feticcio [fe'tittʃo] *sm* fetish.

feto ['fɛto] *sm* foetus.

fetta ['fetta] *sf* slice. **tagliare a fette** slice, cut into slices. **fettuccia** *sf* (*nastro*) tape, ribbon. **fettuccine** *sf pl* noodles *pl*.

feudale [feu'dale] *agg* feudal. **feudalesimo** *sm* feudalism. **feudo** *sm* feud; (*proprietà terriera*) lands *pl*; (*fig*) domain.

fiaba ['fjaba] *sf* story, (fairy) tale.

fiacca ['fjakka] *sf* (*stanchezza*) weariness; (*pigrizia*) laziness; (*svogliatezza*) listlessness. **battere la fiacca** (*fam: stare in ozio*) kick one's heels; (*agire svogliatamente*) be sluggish. **fiaccare** *v* (*indebolire*) weaken; (*spossare*) wear out; (*spezzare*) break. **fiacco** *agg* (*debole*) weak; (*stanco*) exhausted, weary.

fiaccola ['fjakkola] *sf* torch. **alla luce di fiaccole** by torchlight.

fiala ['fjala] *sf* phial, medicine bottle.

fiamma ['fjamma] *sf* flame; (*improvvisa, irregolare*) flare; (*molto viva*) blaze. **in fiamme** on fire. **nuovo fiammante** brand-new. **fiammata** *sf* blaze, flare.

fiammeggiare [fjammed'dʒare] *v* blaze, flame.

fiammifero [fjam'mifero] *sm* match.

fiammingo [fjam'mingo] *agg* Flemish.

fiancheggiare [fjanked'dʒare] *v* flank; (*sostenere*) help.

fianco ['fjanko] *sm* side; (*mil*) flank. **di fianco a** (*vicino*) next to, by; (*lungo*) alongside.

fiasco ['fjasko] *sm* flask, (straw-covered) bottle; (*insuccesso*) flop. **far fiasco** flop.

fiatare [fja'tare] *v* breathe. **fiato** *sm* breath. **fiati** *sm pl* woodwind *pl*. **senza fiato** out of breath. **strumenti a fiato** *sm pl* wind instruments *pl*. **tutto d'un fiato** in one go.

fibbia ['fibbja] *sf* buckle.

fibra ['fibra] *sf* fibre; (*fig*) constitution.

ficcare [fik'kare] *v* poke, stick; (*fam: mettere*) put. **ficcanaso** *sm* busybody.

fico ['fiko] *sm* fig. **fico d'India** prickly pear. **non m'importa un fico (secco)** (*fam*) I couldn't care less. **non valere un fico** be worthless.

fidanzarsi [fidan'tsarsi] *v* get engaged. **fidanzamento** *sm* engagement. **fidanzato, -a** *sm*, *sf* fiancé, -e.

fidarsi [fi'darsi] *v* (*aver fiducia*) rely (on), trust; (*osare*) trust oneself, dare.

fido ['fido] *sm* (*econ*) credit.

fiducia [fi'dutʃa] *sf* trust, confidence. **aver fiducia in** trust. **di fiducia** (*fidato*) reliable, trustworthy; responsible. **fiduciario** *sm* (official) representative; (*dir*) trustee. **fiducioso** *agg* trusting.

fiele ['fjɛle] *sm* bile; (*fig*) ill-will.

fieno ['fjɛno] *sm* hay.

fiera ['fjɛra] *sf* fair; (*mostra*) exhibition; (*di beneficienza*) bazaar.

fiero ['fjɛro] *agg* (*orgoglioso*) proud; (*audace*) bold, spirited; (*feroce, violento*) fierce; (*austero*) severe. **fierezza** *sf* pride; boldness.

fifa ['fifa] (*fam*) *sf* fear. **aver fifa** be afraid. **fifone, -a** *sm, sf* coward.

figliastro [fi'ʎastro] *sm* stepson. **figliastra** *sf* stepdaughter.

figlio ['fiʎo] *sm* son; (*fig: frutto*) result, product. **figli** *sm pl* children *pl*. **figlia** *sf* daughter; (*comm*) counterfoil. **figliare** *v* give birth. **figliata** *sf* litter.

figlioccio [fi'ʎottʃo] *sm* godson. **figlioccia** *sf* goddaughter.

figliolo [fi'ʎolo] *sm* (*figlio*) son; (*ragazzo*) boy, young man; (*fam*) chap. **figliola** *sf* (*figlia*) daughter; (*ragazza*) girl. **figliolanza** *sf* offspring.

figura [fi'gura] *sf* figure; (*aspetto*) shape; (*illustrazione*) picture; (*tavola*) plate. **far bella figura** show up to advantage; make a good impression; (*riuscir bene*) do well. **far brutta figura** cut a sorry figure, disgrace oneself.

figurare [figu'rare] *v* represent, portray; (*simboleggiare*) stand for; (*mostrare*) pretend; (*risultare*) appear; (*far figura*) look smart. **figurarsi** *v* imagine. **figurati!** *inter* (*altro che*) of course! you bet! **figurina** *sf* figurine; (*cartoncino*) card. **figurino** *sm* fashion-plate; (*giornale*) fashion magazine. **figuro** *sm* shady character.

fila ['fila] *sf* row, line; (*coda*) queue; (*serie*) string. **di fila** (*di seguito*) in succession, in a row; (*senza interruzione*) on end, non-stop. **in fila indiana** in single file. **mettere in fila** line up. **mettersi in fila** queue up.

filantropo [fi'lantropo], **-a** *sm, sf* philanthropist. **filantropico** *agg* philanthropic.

filare [fi'lare] *v* spin; (*cavo, catena*) pay out; (*correre*) run, speed along.

filarmonico [filar'mɔniko] *agg* philharmonic.

filastrocca [filas'trɔkka] *sf* (*per bambini*) nursery rhyme; (*storia lunga*) tedious list, rigmarole.

filatelia [filate'lia] *sf* stamp-collecting, philately. **filatelico** *agg* stamp. **filatelista** *s(m+f)* stamp collector.

filatura [fila'tura] *sf* (*industria*) spinning; (*filanda*) spinning mill.

filetto [fi'letto] *sm* (*gastr*) fillet; border; (*filo sottile, mec*) thread; (*tipografia*) rule. **filettare** *v* (*ornare*) decorate; (*bordare*) edge; (*mec*) thread. **filettatura** *sf* edging, braid; threading.

filiale [fi'ljale] *sf* branch. *agg* filial.

filibustiere [filibus'tjɛre] *sm* pirate; (*imbroglione*) rogue.

filigrana [fili'grana] *sf* filigree; (*carta*) watermark.

film [film] *sm invar* film. **filmare** *v* film.

filo ['filo] *sm* thread; (*filato*) yarn; (*metallico*) wire; (*coltello*) edge; (*elettrico*) flex. **filo d'erba** blade of grass. **filo spinato** barbed wire. **lana a due/tre fili** *sf* two-/three-ply wool. **perdere il filo** (*discorso*) lose track; (*taglio*) become blunt. **per filo e per segno** in detail.

filodrammatico [filodram'matiko], **-a** *sm, sf* amateur actor, amateur actress. *agg* amateur theatrical.

filologo [fi'lologo], **-a** *sm, sf* philologist. **filologia** *sf* philology. **filologico** *agg* philological.

filone [fi'lone] *sm* seam, vein; (*pane*) French loaf; (*fig*) current, line.

filosofia [filozo'fia] *sf* philosophy. **filosofico** *agg* philosophical. **filosofo, -a** *sm, sf* philosopher.

filtrare [fil'trare] *v* filter. **filtro** *sm* filter; (*colino*) strainer.

filza ['filtsa] *sf* string.

finale [fi'nale] *agg* final; (*ultimo*) last. *sf* (*sport*) final; (*gramm*) ending. *sm* (*musica*) finale. **finalista** *s(m+f)* finalist. **finalità** *sf* (*scopo*) purpose, aim; (*filosofia*) finality.

finanza [fi'nantsa] *sf* finance; (*fam: risorse economiche*) finances *pl*. **finanze** *sf pl* (*entrate dello Stato*) public revenue *sing*. **guardia di finanza** *sf* customs officer.

finanziare [finan'tsjare] *v* finance. **finanziamento** *sm* financing; (*fondi*) funds *pl*. **finanziario** *agg* financial. **finanziatore, -trice** *sm, sf* backer. **finanziera** *sf* frock-coat.

finché [fin'ke] *cong* (*per tutto il tempo che*) as long as; (*fino a quando*) until, till.

fine[1] ['fine] *sf* end; (*libro, film, ecc.*) ending. *sm* (*scopo*) aim; (*esito*) conclusion. **alla fine** (*luogo*) at the end; (*tempo*) in the end; (*finalmente*) at last. **in fin dei conti** when all is said and done, in the end. **secondo fine** ulterior motive, hidden purpose. **senza fine** endless.

fine² ['fine] *agg* fine; (*signorile*) refined; (*acuto*) sharp; (*penetrante*) subtle. **finezza** *sf* fineness; (*raffinatezza*) finesse, polish; (*minuzie*) nicety.

fine-settimana [finesetti'mana] *s(m+f)* *invar* weekend.

finestra [fi'nɛstra] *sf* window.

*fingere ['findʒere] *v* pretend. **fingersi** *v* pretend to be.

finire [fi'nire] *v* finish; (*smettere*) stop; (*terminare, sboccare*) end; (*capitare*) end up. **andare a finire** (*capitare*) get to; (*concludersi*) turn out, end up. **finimondo** *sm* pandemonium. **finissaggio** *sm* finish. **finitura** *sf* finishing off; finishing touches *pl.*

Finlandia [fin'landja] *sf* Finland. **finlandese** *sm, agg* Finnish; *s(m+f)* (*abitante*) Finn.

fino¹ ['fino] *agg* fine, delicate; (*acuto*) subtle.

fino² ['fino] *avv* (*persino*) even. **fino a** (*tempo*) until, up to; (*luogo*) as far as. **fino a che punto?** how far? **fin da** (*passato*) since, as far back as; (*presente, futuro*) (as) from. **fin dove?** how far? **fino in fondo** right down, to the (very) end.

finocchio [fi'nɔkkjo] *sm* (*bot*) fennel; (*volg*) queer, gay.

finora [fi'nora] *avv* up to now, so far.

finta ['finta] *sf* pretence, sham; (*sport*) feint. **far finta di** pretend.

finto ['finto] *agg* false; (*simulato*) bogus; (*non reale*) mock; artificial. **fintapelle** *sf* imitation leather.

finzione [fin'tsjone] *sf* pretence; (*falsità*) falsehood; (*illusione*) fiction.

fio ['fio] *sm* **pagare il fio** pay the price.

fioccare [fjok'kare] *v* (*neve*) fall; (*fig*) come down thick and fast.

fiocco ['fjɔkko] *sm* flake; (*batuffolo*) flock; (*fibra tessile*) staple; (*nastro*) bow. **coi fiocchi** first-class, magnificent. **fiocchi d'avena** oatflakes *pl.* **fiocco di neve** snowflake.

fioco ['fjɔko] *agg* faint; (*luce*) dim.

fionda ['fjonda] *sf* catapult, sling.

fiordo ['fjɔrdo] *sm* fjord.

fiore ['fjore] *sm* flower; (*di albero*) blossom; (*meglio*) cream; (*carte da gioco*) club. **a fiori** floral. **fior di quattrini** pots of money *pl.* **in fiore** in bloom, in blossom. **fiorente** *agg* (*di fiore*) flowering; (*fig*) thriving, flourishing.

fiorentino [fjoren'tino], **-a** *s, agg* Florentine.

fioretto [fjo'retto] *sm* (*sport*) foil; (*musica, discorso*) embellishment.

fiorire [fjo'rire] *v* flower, bloom, blossom. **fioritura** *sf* flowering, blossoming; (*fiori*) bloom, blossom.

Firenze [fi'rɛntse] *sf* Florence.

firma ['firma] *sf* signature. **firmare** *v* sign. **firmatario** *sm* signatory.

fisarmonica [fizar'mɔnika] *sf* accordion.

fiscale [fis'kale] *agg* fiscal, tax. **fisco** *sm* treasury, tax authorities *pl.*

fischiare [fis'kjare] *v* whistle; (*disapprovare*) boo, hiss. **fischiata** *sf* booing, hissing. **fischiettare** *v* whistle (softly). **fischietto** *sm* whistle. **fischio** *sm* whistle, boo, hiss.

fisica ['fizika] *sf* physics; (*scienziata*) physicist.

fisico ['fiziko] *agg* physical. *sm* (*corpo*) body; (*costituzione*) make-up; (*scienziato*) physicist.

fisima ['fizima] *sf* whim, fancy.

fisiologia [fizjolo'dʒia] *sf* physiology. **fisiologico** *agg* physiological. **fisiologo, -a** *sm, sf* physiologist.

fisionomia [fizjono'mia] *sf* expression.

fisioterapia [fizjotera'pia] *sf* physiotherapy. **fisioterapista** *s(m+f)* physiotherapist.

fissare [fis'sare] *v* fix; (*attaccare*) fasten; (*guardare fissamente*) stare (at), gaze (at); (*prenotare*) book. **fissarsi di** be set on. **fissazione** *sf* fixation.

fissato [fis'sato] *agg* obsessed. *sm* (*fam*) fanatic, maniac. **essere fissato** have a bee in one's bonnet.

fissione [fis'sjone] *sf* fission.

fitta ['fitta] *sf* (*dolore*) twinge, sharp pain.

fittizio [fit'titsjo] *agg* fictitious.

fitto¹ ['fitto] *agg* thick, dense; (*conficcato*) stuck, driven in; (*tessuto, ecc.*) close. *sm* thick, middle. **a capo fitto** headlong. **buio fitto** pitch dark.

fitto² ['fitto] *sm* (*affitto*) rent.

fiume ['fjume] *sm* river; (*fig*) flood, stream. **fiumana** *sf* torrent.

fiutare [fju'tare] *v* smell; (*annusare rumorosamente*) sniff; (*intuire*) scent. **fiutare un inganno** (*fam*) smell a rat. **fiuto** *sm* scent, nose. **al fiuto** straight off, instinctively. **aver fiuto di** get wind of.

flaccido ['flattʃido] *agg* flabby, limp.

flacone [fla'kone] *sm* small bottle.

flagellare [fladʒel'lare] *v* flagellate, whip. **flagello** *sm* scourge, whip.

flagrante [fla'grante] *agg* flagrant. **cogliere in flagrante** catch in the act, catch red-handed.

flanella [fla'nɛlla] *sf* flannel.

flauto ['flauto] *sm* flute. **flauto dolce** recorder. **flautista** *s(m + f)* flautist.

flebile ['flɛbile] *agg* (*debole*) faint, feeble; (*lamentevole*) mournful, melancholy.

flemma ['flɛmma] *sf* coolness, imperturbability. **flemmatico** *agg* cool, self-possessed, phlegmatic.

flessibile [fles'sibile] *agg* flexible, pliable; versatile. **flessibilità** *sf* flexibility, pliability; versatility. **flessione** *sf* bending; (*diminuzione graduale*) drop, fall; (*ginnastica*) bend.

flessuoso [flessu'ozo] *agg* supple, lithe. **flessuosità** *sf* suppleness.

*__flettere__ ['flɛttere] *v* bend, bow; (*membra*) flex.

flipper ['flipper] *sm invar* pin-table.

flirt [flɔrt] *sm invar* (*amore superficiale*) flirtation; (*persona*) boy-friend, girl-friend. **flirtare** *v* flirt.

flora ['flɔra] *sf* flora.

florido ['flɔrido] *agg* (*prospero*) flourishing, thriving; (*colorito*) ruddy, glowing with health.

floscio ['flɔʃo] *agg* floppy, limp.

flotta ['flɔtta] *sf* fleet. **flottiglia** *sf* flotilla.

fluido ['fluido] *sm, agg* fluid. **fluidità** *sf* fluidity; (*scorrevolezza*) fluency; instability.

fluire [flu'ire] *v* flow.

fluorescente [fluore'ʃɛnte] *agg* fluorescent. **fluorescenza** *sf* fluorescence.

fluoro ['fluɔro] *sm* fluorine.

flusso ['flusso] *sm* flow, stream. **flusso e riflusso** ebb and flow. **flusso di sangue dal naso** nosebleed.

fluttuare [fluttu'are] *v* fluctuate.

fobia [fo'bia] *sf* phobia; (*fam*) (pet) aversion.

foca ['fɔka] *sf* seal.

focaccia [fo'kattʃa] *sf* bun. **rendere pan per focaccia** give as good as one gets.

focale [fo'kale] *agg* focal.

foce ['fotʃe] *sf* mouth, outlet.

focena [fo'tʃɛna] *sf* porpoise.

focolaio [foko'lajo] *sm* (*med*) focus; (*centro di diffusione*) hotbed, breeding ground.

focolare [foko'lare] *sm* hearth; (*fig*) fireside, home.

focoso [fo'kozo] *agg* fiery; (*ardente*) burning.

fodera ['fɔdera] *sf* lining; (*rivestimento*) cover. **foderare** *v* line; cover. **fodero** *sm* sheath.

foga ['foga] *sf* rush; (*ardore*) heat.

foggia ['fɔddʒa] *sf* fashion; (*forma*) shape. **foggiare** *v* shape, form, fashion.

foglia ['fɔʎʎa] *sf* leaf. **mettere le foglie** come into leaf. **fogliame** *sm* foliage.

foglio ['fɔʎʎo] *sm* sheet; (*giornale*) paper; (*banconota*) note. **foglio di via** travel-warrant. **foglio volante** leaflet.

fogna ['foɲa] *sf* sewer. **fognatura** *sf* sewerage.

foia ['fɔja] *sf* heat. **essere in foia** be on heat.

folata [fo'lata] *sf* gust.

folclore [fol'klɔre] *sm* folklore. **folcloristico** *agg* folk.

folgorare [folgo'rare] *v* flash; (*inveire*) rail; (*colpire con fulmine*) strike with lightning. **folgorare con lo sguardo** wither with a glance.

folla ['fɔlla] *sf* crowd; (*gran quantità*) host.

folle ['fɔlle] *agg* crazy; (*pazzo*) mad; (*sciocco*) foolish; (*auto*) neutral. **andare in folle** coast. **folletto** *sm* imp. **follia** *sf* madness, folly.

follicolo [fol'likolo] *sm* follicle.

folto ['folto] *sm, agg* thick.

fomentare [fomen'tare] *v* encourage; (*eccitare*) rouse. **fomento** *sm* (*impacco caldo*) poultice; (*sprone*) spur.

fonda ['fonda] *sf* anchorage.

fondamento [fonda'mento] *sm, pl* -a *f in literal sense* foundation. **fondamentale** *agg* fundamental, basic.

fondare [fon'dare] *v* found; (*istituire*) establish; base. **fondarsi su** be based on; (*fare assegnamento*) rely on. **fondatore, -trice** *sm, sf* founder. **fondazione** *sf* foundation, establishment.

*__fondere__ ['fondere] *v* melt, fuse; (*in una forma*) cast, mould; (*unire*) blend, merge.

fonderia [fonde'ria] *sf* foundry.

fondiario [fon'djarjo] *agg* land. **proprietà fondiaria** *sf* real estate.

fondina[1] [fon'dina] *sf* (*di pistola*) holster.

fondina[2] [fon'dina] *sf* (*piatto*) soup plate.

fondista [fon'dista] *s(m + f)* (*sport*) long

distance runner; (*giornalista*) leader writer.

fondo ['fondo] *agg* deep. *sm* bottom; (*feccia*) dregs *pl*; (*caffè*) grounds *pl*; (*estremità*) end; (*sfondo*) background; (*pittura*) primer; (*denaro*) fund; (*terreno*) estate. **a fondo** (*profondamente*) thoroughly; (*con tutte le forze*) wholeheartedly. **andare a fondo** sink. **andare a fondo di** get to the bottom of. **articolo di fondo** *sm* leading article. **dar fondo a** (*consumare*) use up. **fino in fondo** to the end. **fondo (di) cassa/magazzino** cash/stock in hand. **fondo stradale** road surface. **in fondo** (*sotto*) at *or* to the bottom; (*dietro*) at *or* to the back; (*in conclusione*) after all. **mandare a fondo** sink.

fonetica [fo'nɛtika] *sf* phonetics. **fonetico** *agg* phonetic.

fontana [fon'tana] *sf* fountain.

fonte ['fonte] *sf* spring; (*fig*) source. *sm* (*battesimale*) font.

foraggiare [forad'dʒare] *v* forage. **foraggio** *sm* forage.

forare [fo'rare] *v* perforate; (*gomma*) puncture; (*al trapano*) bore. **foratura** *sf* perforation; puncture.

forbici ['fɔrbitʃi] *sf pl* scissors *pl*; (*da siepe*, *cesoie*) shears *pl*; (*da potatura*) secateurs *pl*. **forbicina** *sf* earwig.

forbire [for'bire] *v* clean; (*fig*) polish.

forca ['forka] *sf* pitchfork; (*patibolo*) gallows. **va alla** *or* **sulla forca!** (*fam*) get stuffed! **forcella** *sf* fork; (*volatili*) wishbone.

forchetta [for'ketta] *sf* fork. **una buona forchetta** a hearty eater. **forchettata** *sf* forkful.

forcina [for'tʃina] *sf* hairpin.

forcipe ['fɔrtʃipe] *sm* forceps *pl*.

forense [fo'rɛnse] *agg* forensic.

foresta [fo'rɛsta] *sf* forest.

forestiero [fores'tjɛro], **-a** *agg* foreign. *sm*, *sf* foreigner.

forfait¹ [for'fɛ] *sm invar* (*contratto*) flat rate. **a forfait** all-in.

forfait² [for'fɛ] *sm invar* (*sport*) withdrawal. **dichiarare forfait** scratch.

forfora ['forfora] *sf* dandruff.

forma ['forma] *sf* form, shape; (*stampo*) mould; (*del calzolaio*) last. **a forma di X** X-shaped.

formaggio [for'maddʒo] *sm* cheese.

formale [for'male] *agg* formal. **formalità** *sf* formality.

formare [for'mare] *v* form; (*modellare*) shape; (*costituire*) make up; (*numero telefonico*) dial. **formarsi un'idea** get an idea. **formato** *sm* format, size. **formazione** *sf* formation; (*addestramento*) training.

formica [for'mika] *sf* ant. **formicaio** *sm* antheap; (*fig*) teeming crowd.

formicolare [formiko'lare] *v* swarm; (*provare sensazione*) tingle. **formicolio** *sm* swarming; (*sensazione*) pins and needles.

formidabile [formi'dabile] *agg* remarkable; (*molto forte*) powerful, formidable.

formula ['formula] *sf* formula (*pl* -ae).

formulare [formu'lare] *v* formulate; (*avanzare*) put forward; (*esprimere*) express. **formulario** *sm* (*modulo*) form.

fornace [for'natʃe] *sf* kiln, furnace.

fornaio [for'najo], **-a** *sm*, *sf* baker.

fornire [for'nire] *v* supply, furnish. **ben fornito** well-stocked. **fornitore** *sm* supplier. **fornitura** *sf* supply.

forno ['forno] *sm* oven. **fornello** *sm* cooker.

foro¹ ['foro] *sm* (*buco*) hole.

foro² ['fɔro] *sm* (*tribunale*) (law-)court; (*gli avvocati*) the bar; (*Roma*) forum.

forse ['forse] *avv* perhaps, maybe; (*circa*) about. **in forse** in doubt.

forsennato [forsen'nato] *agg* crazy, mad.

forte ['fɔrte] *agg* strong; (*grande*) large; (*bravo*) good; (*suono*) loud; (*intenso*) heavy. *avv* (*con forza*) hard; (*assai*) very much; (*velocemente*) fast; (*a voce alta*) loud. *sm* (*specialità*) strong point; (*persona*) powerful person; (*mil*) fort.

fortezza [for'tettsa] *sf* (*mil*) fortress; (*forza morale*) strength.

fortificare [fortifi'kare] *v* strengthen, fortify. **fortificazione** *sf* fortification.

fortuito [for'tuito] *agg* fortuitous, chance.

fortuna [for'tuna] *sf* fortune; (*buona sorte*) luck; success. **di fortuna** (*improvvisato*) makeshift; emergency. **fortuna che** fortunately. **fortunato** *agg* fortunate, lucky.

foruncolo [fo'runkolo] *sm* boil.

forza ['fɔrtsa] *sf* strength; (*potere, potenza*) power; (*fis, mil*) force. **a forza di** through, by dint of. **a tutta forza** with all one's strength. **bella forza!** there's nothing to it! **farsi forza** (*coraggio*) pluck up courage. **forza maggiore** force majeure, circumstances beyond one's control. **per forza** necessarily; (*controvoglia*) unwillingly. **per forza di cose** of necessity.

forzare [for'tsare] *v* force. **forzato** *sm* convict.

foschia [fos'kia] *sf* haze, mist.

fosco ['fosko] *agg* (*scuro*) dark; (*tetro*) gloomy.

fosfato [fos'fato] *sm* phosphate.

fosforescente [fosfore'ʃɛnte] *agg* phosphorescent. **fosforo** *sm* phosphorus.

fossa ['fossa] *sf* pit, hole; (*cimitero*) grave. **fossato** *sm* ditch; (*mil*) moat. **fossetta** *sf* dimple.

fossile ['fossile] *sm, agg* fossil.

fosso ['fosso] *sm* ditch. **saltare il fosso** (*fig*) take the plunge.

foto ['foto] *sf invar* (*fam*) snap, photo.

fotocopia [foto'kɔpja] *sf* photocopy.

fotogenico [foto'dʒɛniko] *agg* photogenic.

fotografare [fotogra'fare] *v* photograph. **fotografia** *sf* (*tecnica*) photography; (*copia*) photograph. **fotografico** *agg* photographic. **apparecchio fotografico** *sm* camera. **fotografo, -a** *sm, sf* photographer.

fottere ['fottere] (*volg*) *v* fuck. **fottuto** *agg* (*spacciato*) ruined, buggered.

fra [fra] *prep* (*fra due*) between; (*fra più di due*) among(st); (*entro*) in, within; (*partitivo*) of. **detto fra** (**di**) **noi** between ourselves. **fra l'altro** among other things; (*inoltre*) besides. **fra tutti** (*tutti insieme*) altogether, in all.

frac [frak] *sm invar* (*fam*) tails *pl*.

fracassare [frakas'sare] *v* smash. **fracassarsi** *v* break. **fracasso** *sm* (*chiasso*) racket, din, row; (*scalpore*) uproar.

fradicio ['fraditʃo] *agg* (*inzuppato*) sopping (wet), wet through; (*guasto*) rotten. **ubriaco fradicio** dead drunk.

fragile ['fradʒile] *agg* fragile; (*delicato*) frail.

fragola ['fragola] *sf* strawberry.

fragore [fra'gore] *sm* din. **fragoroso** *agg* roaring, resounding.

fragrante [fra'grante] *agg* fragrant.

***fraintendere** [frain'tɛndere] *v* misunderstand, misconstrue.

frammassone [frammas'sone] *sm* freemason. **frammassoneria** *sf* freemasonry.

frammento [fram'mento] *sm* fragment; (*scheggia*) splinter. **frammentario** *agg* fragmentary.

***frammettersi** [fram'mettersi] *v* (*interporsi*) come between; (*immischiarsi*) meddle.

frammezzo [fram'mɛddzo] *avv* **frammezzo a** in the midst of.

frana ['frana] *sf* landslide. **franare** *v* slide down; (*crollare*) cave in.

francamente [franka'mente] *avv* frankly.

franchezza [fran'kettsa] *sf* frankness.

franchigia [fran'kidʒa] *sf* exemption. **in franchigia** (*posta*) post-free; (*tassa*) tax-free.

Francia ['frantʃa] *sf* France. **francese** *sm, agg* French; *s*(*m + f*) French person.

franco¹ ['franko] *agg* (*schietto*) frank, open; (*disinvolto*) (self-)confident; (*libero*) free (of), exempt (from). **in porto franco** (*comm*) carriage paid.

franco² ['franko] *sm* (*moneta*) franc.

francobollo [franko'bollo] *sm* (postage) stamp.

***frangersi** ['frandʒersi] *v* break. **frangente** *sm* (*ondata*) breaker; (*crisi*) spot, predicament.

frangia ['frandʒa] *sf* fringe.

frantumare [frantu'mare] *v* crush. **in frantumi** in *or* to pieces.

***frapporre** [frap'porre] *v* interpose.

frase ['fraze] *sf* phrase; (*periodo*) sentence. **frase fatta** stock phrase.

frassino ['frassino] *sm* ash.

frastagliare [frasta'ʎare] *v* indent.

frastornato [frastor'nato] *agg* dizzy.

frastuono [fras'twono] *sm* din, uproar.

frate ['frate] *sm* friar.

fratello [fra'tɛllo] *sm* brother. **fratellanza** *sf* brotherhood. **fratellastro** *sm* stepbrother.

fraterno [fra'tɛrno] *agg* brotherly, fraternal. **fraternizzare** *v* fraternize.

frattaglie [frat'taʎe] *sf pl* offal *sing*; (*di pollame*) giblets *pl*.

frattanto [frat'tanto] *avv* also **nel frattempo** meanwhile, in the meantime.

frattura [frat'tura] *sf* fracture; (*fig*) break. **fratturare** *v* fracture, break.

frazione [fra'tsjone] *sf* fraction; (*borgata*) hamlet. **frazionare** *v* split up.

freccia ['frettʃa] *sf* arrow; (*auto*) indicator. **frecciata** *sf* shaft.

freddo ['freddo] *agg* cold; (*fig*) cool, chilly. *sm* cold. **aver freddo** be cold, feel cold. **fa freddo** it is cold. **fa un freddo cane** it is bitterly cold. **morir di freddo** be dying of cold. **soffrire il freddo** feel the cold.

freddura [fred'dura] *sf* pun.

fregare [fre'gare] *v* rub; (*per lucidare*) polish; (*per lavare*) scrub; (*fam*: *rubare*) pinch, swipe; (*volg*: *imbrogliare*) cheat. **fregata** *sf* rub(bing). **fregatura** *sf* (*volg*: *imbroglio*) swindle; (*fam*: *contrattempo*) wash-out, flop.

fregio ['fredʒo] *sm* ornament; (*arch*) frieze. **fregiare** *v* decorate.

fremere ['fremere] *v* quiver.

fremito ['fremito] *sm* quiver; (*di emozione*) thrill; (*brivido*) shudder.

frenare [fre'nare] *v* brake; (*fig*) restrain, control, check.

frenesia [frene'zia] *sf* frenzy. **frenetico** *agg* frenzied, raving.

freno ['freno] *sm* brake; (*fig*) check, restraint; (*cavallo*) bit. **allentare il freno** (*fig*) slacken the reins. **mordere il freno** champ at the bit. **stringere i freni** (*fig*) clamp down.

frequentare [frekwen'tare] *v* frequent, go to often; (*scuola, ecc.*) attend; (*persone*) mix with. **frequentatore, -trice** *sm, sf* regular. **frequente** *agg* frequent. **frequenza** *sf* frequency. **con frequenza** frequently.

fresa ['freza] *sf also* **fresatrice** cutter, milling machine.

fresco ['fresko] *agg* fresh; (*leggermente freddo*) cool. *sm* cool(ness); freshness; (*pittura*) fresco. **al fresco** in the cool; (*prigione*) in the cooler. **star fresco** (*nei guai*) be in a mess; (*sbagliarsi*) kid oneself.

fretta ['fretta] *sf* hurry. **aver fretta** be in a hurry. **far fretta a** hurry. **fatto in fretta** rushed, hurried. **frettoloso** *agg* rushed, hasty.

*****friggere** ['friddʒere] *v* fry; (*scoppiettare bollendo*) sizzle.

frigido ['fridʒido] *agg* cold, frigid. **frigidità** *sf* coldness, frigidity.

frigorifero [frigo'rifero] *sm* refrigerator. **frigo** *sm invar* (*fam*) fridge.

fringuello [frin'gwello] *sm* chaffinch.

frittata [frit'tata] *sf* omelette. **frittella** *sf* pancake.

fritto ['fritto] *agg* fried. *sm* fried food. **star fritto** (*fam*) be in trouble, be in for it. **frittura** *sf* (*vivanda*) fried food; (*atto del friggere*) frying.

frivolo ['frivolo] *agg* frivolous. **frivolezze** *sf* frivolity, trifle.

frizione [fri'tsjone] *sf* (*massaggio*) rub-down; (*auto*) clutch; (*attrito*) friction.

frizzare [frit'tsare] *v* tingle; (*bevande*) sparkle; (*metallo rovente*) hiss.

frodare [fro'dare] *v* defraud. **frode** *sf* fraud. **frodo** *sm* smuggling. **cacciare** *or* **pescare di frodo** poach. **cacciatore** *or* **pescatore di frodo** *sm* poacher.

frollare [frol'lare] *v* ripen. **frollo** *agg* ripe; (*carne*) tender; (*selvaggina*) high; (*pasta*) short.

fronda ['fronda] *sf* (leafy) branch; (*fig*) embellishment.

fronte ['fronte] *sf* (*testa*) forehead; (*faccia*) face; (*parte anteriore*) front; (*arch*) façade. *sm* (*mil*) front. **a fronte** (*in faccia*) facing. **di fronte** (*dirimpetto*) opposite; (*da davanti*) from the front. **far fronte a** face.

fronteggiare [fronted'dʒare] *v* face, stand up to.

frontespizio [frontes'pitsjo] *sm* title-page.

frontiera [fron'tjera] *sf* frontier, border.

fronzoli ['frondzoli] *sm pl* frills *pl*.

frotta ['frɔtta] *sf* flock, swarm.

frottola ['frɔttola] *sf* fib.

frugale [fru'gale] *agg* frugal.

frugare [fru'gare] *v* rummage, go through; (*perquisire*) search.

frullare [frul'lare] *v* whisk; (*fig*) whirl. **frullino** *sm* whisk.

frumento [fru'mento] *sm* wheat.

frusciare [fru'ʃare] *v* rustle.

frustare [frus'tare] *v* whip. **frusta** *sf* whip. **frustata** *sf* lash.

frustrazione [frustra'tsjone] *sf* frustration. **frustrare** *v* frustrate, thwart.

frutta ['frutta] *sf* fruit. **frutta cotta** stewed fruit. **fruttare** *v* bear fruit; yield; (*rendere*) bring in; (*procurare*) earn.

frutteto [frut'teto] *sm* orchard.

fruttifero [frut'tifero] *agg* fruitful; (*redditizio*) profitable.

fruttivendolo [frutti'vendolo], **-a** *sm, sf* fruiterer, greengrocer.

frutto ['frutto] *sm* fruit; (*interesse*) yield; (*rendita*) income; profit. **frutti di mare** seafood *sing*.

fu [fu] *agg invar* late, deceased.

fucilare [futʃi'lare] *v* shoot. **fucilata** *sf* shot. **fucilazione** *sf* execution. **fucile** *sm* rifle; (*da caccia*) shotgun.

fucina [fu'tʃina] *sf* forge.

fuco¹ ['fuko] *sm* (*ape*) drone.

fuco² ['fuko] *sm* (*alga*) fucus.

fucsia ['fuksja] *sf* fuchsia.

fuga ['fuga] *sf* escape; (*musica*) fugue; (*serie*) suite. **mettere in fuga** put to flight. **prendere la fuga** take flight, flee, escape. **fugace** *agg* transient.

fuggire [fud'dʒire] *v* flee, escape, run away. **fuggiasco** *sm*, *agg* fugitive; (*profugo*) refugee.

fulcro ['fulkro] *sm* fulcrum; (*fig*) heart.

fuliggine [fu'liddʒine] *sf* soot. **fuligginoso** *agg* sooty.

fulminare [fulmi'nare] *v* (*dal fulmine*) strike (by lightning); (*dalla corrente*) electrocute; (*con uno sguardo*) wither; (*allibire*) dumbfound. **fulmine** *sm* lightning, thunderbolt. **un fulmine a ciel sereno** a bolt from the blue.

fumaiolo [fuma'jɔlo] *sm* (*casa*) chimney-pot; (*nave*) funnel, smoke-stack.

fumare [fu'mare] *v* smoke; (*emettere vapore*) steam. **fumata** *sf* smoke. **fumatore, -trice** *sm*, *sf* smoker.

fumetto [fu'metto] *sm* comic-strip. **fumettista** *s(m+f)* comic-strip writer.

fumo ['fumo] *sm* smoke. **andare in fumo** go up in smoke.

funambolo [fu'nambolo], **-a** *sm*, *sf* tight-rope walker.

fune ['fune] *sf* rope, cable; (*per bucato*) washing line.

funebre ['funebre] *agg* funeral; (*lugubre*) funereal.

funerale [fune'rale] *sm* funeral. **funereo** *agg* funereal.

funesto [fu'nɛsto] *agg* fatal; (*doloroso*) distressing.

fungo ['fungo] *sm* mushroom; (*non mangereccio*) toadstool; (*bot*) fungus (*pl* -gi).

funicolare [funiko'lare] *sf* funicular railway.

funivia [funi'via] *sf* cable-car.

funzionare [funtsjo'nare] *v* function, work. **funzionale** *agg* functional, practical. **funzionamento** *sm* operation, working.

funzionario [funtsjo'narjo] *sm* official; (*impiegato statale*) civil servant.

funzione [fun'tsjone] *sf* function; (*carica*) office; (*compito*) duty. **entrare in funzione** come into operation. **essere in funzione di ...** act as ....

fuochista [fwo'kista] *sm* stoker.

fuoco ['fwɔko] *sm* fire; (*fis, mat, foto*) focus. **appiccare** *or* **dare fuoco a** set fire to. **a prova di fuoco** fireproof. **fuoco di Sant'Antonio** (*med*) shingles. **mettere a fuoco** (*foto*) focus. **prendere fuoco** catch fire.

fuorché [fwor'ke] *prep*, *cong* except.

fuori ['fwɔri] *avv* out; (*all'esterno*) outside. *prep also* **fuori di** *or* **da** out of. **esser fuori di sè** be beside oneself. **fuoribordo** *sm* (*motore*) outboard motor; (*barca*) motor boat. **fuori strada** (*veicoli*) off the road; (*fig*) on the wrong track. **mettere fuori combattimento** (*sport*) knock out; (*fig*) put out of the running.

furbo ['furbo] *agg* cunning, crafty. **furbacchione** *sm* cunning fellow. **furberia** *sf* cunning.

furetto [fu'retto] *sm* ferret.

furfante [fur'fante] *sm* rascal.

furgone [fur'gone] *sm* (delivery) van. **furgoncino** *sm* small (delivery) van.

furia ['furja] *sf* (*collera*) rage, fury; (*fretta*) rush, haste. **a furia di ...** by dint of ....

furibondo [furi'bondo] *agg* furious.

furioso [fu'rjozo] *agg* violent, furious.

furore [fu'rore] *sm* fury, rage.

furtivo [fur'tivo] *agg* furtive, stealthy.

furto ['furto] *sm* theft. **furto con scasso** burglary. **piccolo furto** petty theft, petty larceny.

fusa ['fuza] *sf pl* **fare le fusa** purr.

fuscello [fu'ʃɛllo] *sm* twig.

fusibile [fu'zibile] *agg* fusible. *sm* (*elett*) fuse.

fusione [fu'zjone] *sf* fusion; (*colata*) casting; (*scioglimento*) melting; (*fig*) merging; (*comm*) merger.

fuso¹ ['fuzo] *agg* (*liquefatto*) melted, molten; (*colato*) cast.

fuso² ['fuzo] *sm* spindle; (*ancora*) shank. **diritto come un fuso** (*eretto*) straight as a ramrod; (*difilato*) like a shot. **fuso orario** time zone.

fusoliera [fuzo'ljera] *sf* fuselage.

fustagno [fus'taɲo] *sm* fustian; (*a coste*) corduroy.

fustella [fus'tɛlla] *sf* (*tec*) die.

fustigare [fusti'gare] *v* flog; (*fig*) lash out at.

fusto ['fusto] *sm* trunk; (*ossatura*) frame; (*barile*) barrel, cask; (*recipiente di metallo*) drum.

futile ['futile] *agg* futile; (*meschino*) petty.

futuro [fu'turo] *agg*, *sm* future.

G

gabbare [gab'bare] *v* cheat.
gabbia ['gabbja] *sf* cage. **gabbia degli imputati** dock.
gabbiano [gab'bjano] *sm* seagull.
gabinetto [gabi'netto] *sm* study, office; (*di medico*) surgery; (*WC*) toilet, lavatory; (*pol*) cabinet; (*di scienze*) laboratory.
gaffe ['gaf] *sf, pl* -s blunder. **fare una gaffe** (*fam*) put one's foot in it.
gagà [ga'ga] *sm* (*fam*) dandy.
gagliardo [ga'ʎardo] *agg* vigorous; (*robusto*) strapping; (*coraggioso*) brave. **gagliardetto** *sm* pennant, flag.
gaio ['gajo] *agg* cheerful.
gala ['gala] *sf* (*ricevimento*) feast. *sm* (*mar*) flags *pl*. *sf* (*stoffa*) frill; (*cravatta*) bow-tie.
galantuomo [galan'twɔmo] *sm* (true) gentleman, man of honour. **galante** *agg* gallant, courteous.
galassia [ga'lassja] *sf* galaxy.
galateo [gala'tɛo] *sm* etiquette, good manners *pl*.
galea [ga'lɛa] *sf* galley.
galeotto [gale'ɔtto] *sm* (*carcerato*) convict; (*furfante*) scoundrel; (*vogatore forzato*) galley slave.
galera [ga'lɛra] *sf* prison.
galla ['galla] *sf* **stare** *or* **rimanere a galla** float, keep afloat. **tenersi a galla** keep afloat; (*fig*) keep one's head above water. **venire a galla** come to the surface; (*fig*) come to light, emerge.
galleggiare [galled'dʒare] *v* float. **galleggiante** *agg* floating. *sm* float; (*tec*) ballcock.
galleria [galle'ria] *sf* gallery; (*traforo*) tunnel; (*passaggio sotterraneo*) subway; (*cinema, ecc.*) circle, balcony.
Galles ['galles] *sm* Wales. **gallese** *sm, agg* Welsh; *s(m + f)* Welsh person.
gallo ['gallo] *sm* cock. **galletto** *sm* cockerel; (*tec*) wing-nut. **gallina** *sf* hen.
gallone¹ [gal'lone] *sm* (*misura*) gallon.
gallone² [gal'lone] *sm* braid; (*mil*) stripe.
galoppare [galop'pare] *v* gallop. **galoppata** *sf* gallop; (*lavora faticoso*) hard work. **galoppo** *sm* gallop.
galvanizzare [galvanid'dzare] *v* galvanize.
gamba ['gamba] *sf* leg. **andare a gambe all'aria** fall flat on one's back; (*fallire*) fail. **a tre gambe** three-legged. **darsela a gambe** take to one's heels. **gambe storte** bandy *or* bow legs *pl*. **in gamba** (*valente*) smart. *inter* take care!
gambero ['gambero] *sm* (*di acqua dolce*) crayfish; (*gamberetto*) shrimp; (*gamberone*) prawn. **rosso come un gambero** as red as a lobster.
gambo ['gambo] *sm* (*pianta*) stem, stalk; (*tec*) shank.
gamma ['gamma] *sf* range; (*lunghezza d'onda*) wave-band.
ganascia [ga'naʃa] *sf* jaw; (*freno*) brake-shoe.
gancio ['gantʃo] *sm* hook.
ganghero ['gangero] *sm* hinge. **essere fuori dai gangheri** be beside oneself. **uscire dai gangheri** lose one's head.
gara ['gara] *sf* competition; (*corsa*) race; (*comm*) tender.
garage [ga'raʒ] *sm, pl* -s garage.
garantire [garan'tire] *v* guarantee; (*rendersi garante*) vouch for; (*assicurare*) assure. **essere garante per** *or* **di** vouch for. **rendersi garante per** (*dir*) stand bail for.
garanzia [garan'tsia] *sf* guarantee.
garbare [gar'bare] *v* please, suit. **garbato** *agg* polite, well-mannered. **garbo** *sm* (*maniera*) good manners *pl*, politeness; (*gentilezza*) charm.
garbuglio [gar'buʎo] *sm* muddle.
gareggiare [gared'dʒare] *v* compete.
gargarismo [garga'rizmo] *sm* gargle. **fare i gargarismi** gargle.
garitta [ga'ritta] *sf* cabin; (*mil*) sentry-box.
garofano [ga'rɔfano] *sm* carnation. **chiodo di garofano** *sm* clove.
garrire [gar'rire] *v* twitter. **garrito** *sm* twitter.
garrulo ['garrulo] *agg* (*uccello*) twittering; (*persona loquace*) garrulous.
garza ['gardza] *sf* gauze.
garzone [gar'dzone] *sm* boy, mate.
gas ['gas] *sm* gas. **a gas** gas. **gas asfissiante/esilarante** poison/laughing gas. **gassoso** *agg* gaseous.
gasolio [ga'zɔljo] *sm* fuel oil, diesel fuel.
gassosa [gas'soza] *sf* fizzy drink, lemonade.
gastrico ['gastriko] *agg* gastric.

gastronomia [gastrono'mia] *sf* gastronomy, cooking. **gastronomico** *agg* gastronomic(al). **gastronomo** *sm* (*buongustaio*) gourmet.

gattabuia [gatta'buja] *sf* (*fam*) clink.

gatto ['gatto] *sm* cat. **gatta** *sf* she-cat. **comprare una gatta nel sacco** buy a pig in a poke. **gatta ci cova!** I smell a rat! **una gatta da pelare** a tricky job to do.

gattino *sm* kitten; (*bot*) catkin.

gazza ['gaddza] *sf* magpie.

gazzarra [gad'dzarra] *sf* uproar, row.

gazzella [gad'dzɛlla] *sf* gazelle.

gazzetta [gad'dzetta] *sf* gazette.

gelare [dʒe'lare] *v* freeze. **gelata** *sf* (hard) frost.

gelatina [dʒela'tina] *sf* gelatine.

gelato [dʒe'lato] *agg* frozen. *sm* ice-cream. **gelataio** *sm* ice-cream vendor. **gelateria** *sf* ice-cream shop *or* parlour.

gelido ['dʒɛlido] *agg* icy.

gelo ['dʒɛlo] *sm* frost; intense cold; (*sensazione*) chill.

gelone [dʒe'lone] *sm* chilblain.

gelosia[1] [dʒelo'zia] *sf* jealousy; (*cura attenta*) great care.

gelosia[2] [dʒelo'zia] *sf* (*finestra*) blind.

geloso [dʒe'lozo] *agg* jealous.

gelso ['dʒɛlso] *sm* (*mora*) mulberry; (*albero*) mulberry-tree.

gelsomino [dʒelso'mino] *sm* jasmine.

gemello [dʒe'mɛllo] *sm*, *agg* twin. **gemelli** *sm pl* (*di polsino*) cuff-links *pl*. **Gemelli** *sm pl* Gemini *sing*.

gemere ['dʒɛmere] *v* groan; (*colare*) drip, ooze; (*tubare*) coo. **gemito** *sm* groan.

gemma ['dʒɛmma] *sf* gem; (*bot*) bud.

gene ['dʒɛne] *sm* gene.

genealogia [dʒenealo'dʒia] *sf* (*scienza*) genealogy; (*stirpe*) pedigree. **albero genealogico** *sm* family tree.

generale [dʒene'rale] *sm*, *agg* general. **in generale** in general; (*di solito*) as a rule.

generalizzare [dʒeneralid'dzare] *v* generalize. **generalizzazione** *sf* generalization.

generare [dʒene'rare] *v* generate, produce. **generazione** *sf* generation.

genere ['dʒɛnere] *sm* kind, type; (*tipo di merce*) product, article; (*stile*) genre; (*gramm*) gender. **d'ogni genere** of all kinds. **il genere umano** mankind. **nel suo genere** in his way.

generico [dʒe'nɛriko] *agg* generic; general.

genero ['dʒɛnero] *sm* son-in-law.

generoso [dʒene'rozo] *agg* generous; (*vino*) full-bodied; (*cavallo*) thoroughbred.

genetica [dʒe'nɛtika] *sf* genetics. **genetico** *agg* genetic. **genetista** *s(m + f)* geneticist.

gengiva [dʒen'dʒiva] *sf* gum. **gengivite** *sf* gingivitis.

geniale [dʒe'njale] *agg* ingenious, clever. **genialità** *sf* brilliance.

genio[1] ['dʒɛnjo] *sm* genius; (*disposizione*) talent, gift; (*inclinazione*) taste. **andare a genio** be to one's liking, suit.

genio[2] ['dʒɛnjo] *sm* (*mil*) engineers *pl*.

genitali [dʒeni'tali] *sm pl* genitals *pl*.

genitore [dʒeni'tore] *sm* parent.

gennaio [dʒen'najo] *sm* January.

Genova ['dʒɛnova] *sf* Genoa. **genovese** *agg*, *s(m + f)* Genoese.

gente ['dʒɛnte] *sf* people *pl*.

gentile [dʒen'tile] *agg* kind; (*cortese*) polite; delicate. **gentilezza** *sf* kindness; politeness; (*atto gentile*) favour. **gentiluomo** *sm* (*nobile*) nobleman; (*persona retta*) gentleman.

genuino [dʒenu'ino] *agg* genuine, natural; authentic. **genuinità** *sf* authenticity, naturalness, spontaneity.

genziana [dʒen'tsjana] *sf* gentian.

geografia [dʒeogra'fia] *sf* geography. **geografico** *agg* geographical. **atlante geografico** *sm* atlas. **carta geografica** *sf* map. **geografo, -a** *sm*, *sf* geographer.

geologia [dʒeolo'dʒia] *sf* geology. **geologico** *agg* geological. **geologo, -a** *sm*, *sf* geologist.

geometra [dʒe'ɔmetra] *s(m + f)* surveyor.

geometria [dʒeome'tria] *sf* geometry. **geometrico** *agg* geometrical.

geranio [dʒe'ranjo] *sm* geranium.

gerarchia [dʒerar'kia] *sf* hierarchy. **gerarca** *sm* (*rel*) hierarch; (*capo*) leader. **gerarchico** *agg* hierarchical. **per via gerarchica** through official channels.

gerente [dʒe'rɛnte] *sm* manager.

gergo ['dʒɛrgo] *sm* slang, jargon.

geriatria [dʒerja'tria] *sf* geriatrics. **geriatrico** *agg* geriatric.

Germania [dʒer'manja] *sf* Germany. **germanico** *agg* German.

germe ['dʒɛrme] *sm* germ. **germinare** *v* germinate.

germogliare [dʒermoʎ'ʎare] *v* bud, sprout; (*fig*) germinate. **germoglio** *sm* shoot; (*origine*) germ.

gesso ['dʒɛsso] *sm* (*minerale*) gypsum; (*da disegno*) chalk; (*a pronta presa*) plaster (of Paris); (*opera*) plaster cast.

gesta ['dʒɛsta] *sf pl* (noble) deeds *pl*, feats *pl*.

gesticolare [dʒestiko'lare] *v* gesticulate.

gestire [dʒes'tire] *v* manage, run. **gestione** *sf* management.

gesto ['dʒɛsto] *sm* gesture; (*azione*) deed; (*del capo*) nod; (*della mano*) wave.

Gesù [dʒe'zu] *sm* Jesus.

gesuita [dʒezu'ita] *sm* Jesuit. **gesuitico** *agg* Jesuitical.

gettare [dʒet'tare] *v* throw; (*emettere*) let out; (*tec*) cast. **gettare i soldi dalla finestra** throw money down the drain. **gettare le fondamenta** lay the foundations. **gettar luce su ...** cast light on .... **gettata** *sf* cast; (*di reti*) casting.

getto ['dʒɛtto] *sm* (*lancio*) throw; (*di liquido o gas*) jet; (*metallo, ecc.*) casting.

gettone [dʒet'tone] *sm* counter, token.

ghermire [ger'mire] *v* clutch, grab.

ghetto ['getto] *sm* ghetto.

ghiacciaia [gjat'tʃaja] *sf* ice-box.

ghiacciaio [gjat'tʃajo] *sm* glacier.

ghiacciare [gjat'tʃare] *v* freeze. **ghiacciata** *sf* drink with crushed ice.

ghiaccio ['gjattʃo] *sm* ice. **di ghiaccio** (*freddissimo*) ice-cold, frozen; (*fig*) icy. **ghiacciolo** *sm* icicle; (*gelato*) ice lolly.

ghiaia ['gjaja] *sf* gravel.

ghianda ['gjanda] *sf* acorn.

ghiandaia [gjan'daja] *sf* jay.

ghiandola ['gjandola] *sf* gland. **ghiandolare** *agg* glandular.

ghigliottina [giʎot'tina] *sf* guillotine. **ghigliottinare** *v* guillotine.

ghignare [gi'ɲare] *v* sneer. **ghigno** *sm* sneer, smirk.

ghiotto ['gjotto] *agg* greedy; (*appetitoso*) inviting. **ghiottone, -a** *sm*, *sf* glutton, greedy person. **ghiottoneria** *sf* (*golosità*) gluttony; (*cibo ghiotto*) titbit.

ghiribizzo [giri'bittso] *sm* fancy, whim.

ghirigoro [giri'gɔro] *sm* flourish.

ghirlanda [gir'landa] *sf* garland, wreath.

ghiro ['giro] *sm* dormouse. **dormire come un ghiro** sleep like a log.

ghisa ['giza] *sf* cast iron.

già ['dʒa] *avv* already; (*un tempo*) once; (*ex*) formerly.

giacca ['dʒakka] *sf* coat; (*giacchetta*) jacket.

giacché [dʒak'ke] *cong* as, since.

giacchetta [dʒak'ketta] *sf* jacket.

*giacere [dʒa'tʃere] *v* lie; (*in sospeso*) be in abeyance. **mettersi a giacere** lie down.

giacenza *sf* abeyance; (*merce*) (unsold) stock; (*econ*) deposit. **giacimento** *sm* deposit.

giacinto [dʒa'tʃinto] *sm* hyacinth.

giada ['dʒada] *sf* jade.

giaggiolo [dʒad'dʒɔlo] *sm* iris.

giaguaro [dʒa'gwaro] *sm* jaguar.

giallo ['dʒallo] *agg* yellow. *sm* (*colore*) yellow; (*libro, film*) thriller. **giallo d'uovo** (egg) yolk. **giallastro** *agg* yellowish, sallow. **giallognolo** *agg* pale yellow, yellowish.

giammai [dʒam'mai] *avv* never. **se giammai** if ever.

Giappone [dʒap'pone] *sm* Japan. **giapponese** *s*(*m+f*), *agg* Japanese.

giardinetta [dʒardi'netta] *sf* estate car.

giardino [dʒar'dino] *sm* garden. **giardino d'infanzia** kindergarten, nursery school. **giardino zoologico** zoo. **giardinaggio** *sm* gardening. **giardiniere, -a** *sm*, *sf* gardener.

giarrettiera [dʒarret'tjɛra] *sf* suspender, garter.

giavellotto [dʒavel'lɔtto] *sm* javelin.

Gibilterra [dʒibil'terra] *sf* Gibraltar.

gigante [dʒi'gante] *sm*, *agg* giant. **gigantesco** *agg* gigantic, huge.

gigione [dʒi'dʒone] *sm* ham (actor). **fare il gigione** ham.

giglio ['dʒiʎo] *sm* lily.

gilè [dʒi'lɛ] *sm* waistcoat.

ginecologo [dʒine'kɔlogo], **-a** *sm*, *sf* gynaecologist. **ginecologia** *sm* gynaecology. **ginecologico** *agg* gynaecological.

ginepro [dʒi'nepro] *sm* juniper.

ginestra [dʒi'nɛstra] *sf* broom. **ginestrone** *sm* furze, gorse.

Ginevra [dʒi'nevra] *sf* Geneva.

gingillarsi [dʒindʒil'larsi] *v* (*divertirsi*) amuse oneself; (*perder tempo*) hang about.

ginnasio [dʒin'nazjo] *sm* secondary school.

ginnastica [dʒin'nastika] *sf* (*sport*) gymnastics; (*esercizi*) physical exercises *pl*.

ginocchio [dʒi'nokkjo] *sm pl* **-a** *f* knee. **ginocchioni** *avv* also **in ginocchio** on one's knees.

giocare [dʒo'kare] *v* play; (*in borsa*) gamble (on the Stock Exchange); (*scommettere*) bet. **giocata** *sf* (*partita*) game;

(*puntata*) stake, bet. **giocatore, -trice** *sm, sf* player; (*d'azzardo*) gambler.
giocattolo [dʒo'kattolo] *sm* toy.
giocherellare [dʒokerel'lare] *v* toy.
giochetto [dʒo'ketto] *sm* (*passatempo*) pastime; (*tranello*) trick; (*lavoro facile*) child's play.
gioco ['dʒɔko] *sm* (*divertimento, tec*) play; (*con regole, partita*) game; (*vizio*) gambling; (*combinazione di carte*) hand; (*posta*) stake; (*beffa*) trick. **entrare in gioco** come into play. **fare il doppio gioco** double-cross. **mettere in gioco** (*far agire*) bring into action; (*rischiare*) stake.
giocoliere [dʒoko'ljɛre] *sm* juggler.
giocondo [dʒo'kondo] *agg* cheerful, merry.
giogo ['dʒɔgo] *sm* yoke; (*valico*) pass; (*cima allungata*) ridge.
gioia¹ ['dʒɔja] *sf* joy, delight.
gioia² ['dʒɔja] *sf* (*gemma*) jewel.
gioire [dʒo'ire] *v* rejoice. **gioioso** *agg* joyful.
giornalaio [dʒorna'lajo], **-a** *sm, sf* newsagent.
giornale [dʒor'nale] *sm* (*quotidiano*) newspaper; (*registro*) journal; diary. **giornale di bordo** log(-book). **giornale radio** news (bulletin).
giornaliero [dʒorna'ljɛro] *agg* daily.
giornalismo [dʒorna'lizmo] *sm* journalism. **giornalista** *s(m+f)* journalist.
giornata [dʒor'nata] *sf* day. **a giornata** by the day. **di giornata** (*fresco*) fresh; (*di turno*) on duty. **donna a giornata** daily (woman). **vivere alla giornata** live from day to day.
giorno ['dʒorno] *sm* day. **a giorni** (*tra breve*) soon; (*a intervalli*) sometimes. **al giorno** a day. **al giorno d'oggi** nowadays. **che giorno è?** (*data*) what is the date? (*della settimana*) what day (of the week) is it? **da un giorno all'altro** (*improvvisamente*) suddenly; (*tra poco*) any day now. **di giorno** by day. **giorno festivo** holiday. **giorno libero** day off. **punto a giorno** *sm* hem-stitch. **un giorno o l'altro** one of these days.
giostra ['dʒɔstra] *sf* (*fiera*) merry-go-round; (*torneo*) tournament.
giovane ['dʒovane] *agg* young; (*giovanile*) youthful; (*non stagionato*) new. *sm* (*giovanotto*) young man, youth. *sf* young woman, girl. **giovanile** *agg* youthful, juvenile.

giovare [dʒo'vare] *v* help, do good.
giovedì [dʒove'di] *sm* Thursday.
giovenca [dʒo'vɛnka] *sf* heifer.
gioventù [dʒoven'tu] *sf* youth; (*i giovani*) young people *pl*.
giovevole [dʒo'vevole] *agg* useful.
gioviale [dʒo'vjale] *agg* genial, jolly.
giovinezza [dʒovi'nettsa] *sf* (*gioventù*) youth; (*qualità*) youthfulness. **seconda giovinezza** second childhood.
giradischi [dʒira'diski] *sm invar* record player.
giradito [dʒira'dito] *sm* whitlow.
giraffa [dʒi'raffa] *sf* giraffe.
giramento [dʒira'mento] *sm* **giramento di capo** dizzy spell; (*fit of*) dizziness.
girandola [dʒi'randola] *sf* (*fuochi d'artificio*) Catherine wheel; (*giocattolo*) toy windmill; (*fig*) fickle person.
girare [dʒi'rare] *v* turn; (*scansare*) get round, avoid; (*percorrere viaggiando*) travel, tour; (*andare da un posto all'altro*) go around; (*comm*) endorse; (*cinema*) shoot, take; (*camminare senza meta*) wander about; circulate. **girare a vuoto** (*mec*) idle. **mi gira la testa** I feel dizzy *or* giddy.
girarrosto [dʒirar'rɔsto] *sm* spit.
girasole [dʒira'sole] *sm* sunflower.
girino [dʒi'rino] *sm* tadpole.
giro ['dʒiro] *sm* turn; (*pista*) lap; (*percorso*) round; (*viaggio*) tour; (*passeggiata a piedi*) stroll, walk; (*in macchina*) drive; (*in bicicletta, a cavallo*) ride; (*periodo*) course, space; circulation; (*mec*) revolution. **andare in giro** go round. **essere in giro** (*fuori*) be out; (*in qualche posto*) be somewhere. **giro collo** neck. **giro d'affari** turnover. **giro d'orizzonte** survey. **giro manica** armhole. **guardarsi in giro** look around. **prendere in giro** make fun of.
gironzolare [dʒirondzo'lare] *v* stroll, wander (about).
girovago [dʒi'rovago] *sm, pl* **-ghi** vagabond, tramp. *agg* wandering. **girovagare** *v* stroll, wander (about).
gita ['dʒita] *sf* excursion, trip. **fare una gita** make an excursion, go on a trip.
giù [dʒu] *avv* down; (*dabbasso*) downstairs. **andare su e giù** (*salire e scendere*) go up and down; (*avanti e indietro*) go to and fro. **giù di lì** thereabouts. **in giù** (*moto*) down; (*stato*) low; (*in meno*) and under. **su per giù** thereabouts.

giubba ['dʒubba] *sf* jacket; (*mil*) tunic. **giubbotto di salvataggio** *sm* life-jacket.
giubilare [dʒubi'lare] *v* rejoice.
giubileo [dʒubi'lɛo] *sm* jubilee.
giudaismo [dʒuda'izmo] *sm* Judaism.
giudicare [dʒudi'kare] *v* judge; (*ritenere*) consider. **a giudicare da** judging by. **passare in giudicato** be beyond recall, be final.
giudice ['dʒuditʃe] *sm* judge. **giudice istruttore** examining magistrate.
giudiziario [dʒudi'tsjarjo] *agg* judicial.
giudizio [dʒu'ditsjo] *sm* judgment; (*parere*) opinion; (*dir*) sentence, verdict; (*buon senso*) common sense. **aver giudizio** be sensible. **citare in giudizio** summon. **comparire in giudizio** appear before a court. **dente del giudizio** *sm* wisdom tooth. **far giudizio** behave oneself. **rinviare a giudizio** commit for trial.
giudizioso *agg* sensible.
giugno ['dʒuɲo] *sm* June.
giulivo [dʒu'livo] *agg* merry.
giullare [dʒul'lare] *sm* (*cantastorie*) minstrel; (*buffone*) clown.
giunco ['dʒunko] *sm* rush.
***giungere** ['dʒundʒere] *v* arrive (at), reach; (*riuscire*) manage; (*arrivare al punto di*) go so far as. **mi è giunto** I have received. **mi giunge nuovo** it is news to me.
giungla ['dʒungla] *sf* jungle.
giunta¹ ['dʒunta] *sf* addition; (*peso*) makeweight; (*sartoria*) insert. **giuntare** *v* (*unire*) join; (*cucire*) sew together; (*cinema, nastro*) splice.
giunta² ['dʒunta] *sf* (*comitato*) council; (*mil*) junta.
giunto ['dʒunto] *sm* joint.
giuntura [dʒun'tura] *sf* joint; (*accoppiamento*) coupling.
giunzione [dʒun'tsjone] *sf* junction; (*giunto*) joint.
giurare [dʒu'rare] *v* swear. **giuramento** *sm* oath. **giuramento falso** (*spergiuro*) perjury. **mancare al giuramento** break an oath. **prestar giuramento** swear, take an oath.
giurato [dʒu'rato], **-a** *sm, sf* juror. *agg* sworn.
giuria [dʒu'ria] *sf* jury.
giuridico [dʒu'ridiko] *agg* legal.
giurisdizione [dʒurizdi'tsjone] *sf* jurisdiction.
***giustapporre** [dʒustap'porre] *v* juxtapose. **giustapposizione** *sf* juxtaposition.

giustezza [dʒus'tettsa] *sf* correctness; (*esattezza*) precision.
giustificare [dʒustifi'kare] *v* justify. **giustificazione** *sf* justification; (*scusa*) excuse.
giustizia [dʒus'titsja] *sf* justice; (*equità*) fairness. **assicurare alla giustizia** bring to justice. **fare** *or* **rendere giustizia** do justice.
giusto ['dʒusto] *agg* just; (*equo*) fair; (*legittimo*) rightful; (*corretto*) right. *avv* (*proprio, appena*) just; (*esattamente*) correctly. *sm* (*persona*) righteous man.
glaciale [gla'tʃale] *agg* glacial; (*fig*) icy.
gladiolo [gla'diolo] *sm* gladiolus.
glassa ['glassa] *sf* icing. **glassare** *v* ice.
gli¹ [ʎi] *art* the.
gli² [ʎi] *pron* (*persona*) (to) him; (*cosa, animale*) (to) it.
glicerina [glitʃe'rina] *sf* glycerine.
glicine ['glitʃine] *sm* wisteria.
globo ['globo] *sm* globe. **globo oculare** eyeball.
globulo ['globulo] *sm* globule; (*med*) corpuscle. **globulare** *agg* globular.
gloria ['glorja] *sf* glory; (*vanto*) pride. **gloriarsi** *v* glory (in); (*vantarsi*) boast (of).
glorificare [glorifi'kare] *v* glorify.
glucosio [glu'kɔzjo] *sm* glucose.
gnomo ['ɲomo] *sm* gnome.
gnomone [ɲo'mone] *sm* sundial.
gobba ['gobba] *sf* hump.
gobbo ['gobbo], **-a** *sm, sf* hunchback. *agg* hunchbacked.
goccia ['gottʃa] *sf* drop. **goccia a goccia** drop by drop; (*fig*) little by little. **una goccia nel mare** a drop in the ocean. **gocciolare** *v* drip.
***godere** [go'dere] *v* enjoy; (*rallegrarsi*) rejoice. **godimento** *sm* enjoyment; (*piacere*) pleasure.
goffo ['gɔffo] *agg* awkward, clumsy. **goffaggine** *sf* awkwardness, clumsiness; (*atto*) clumsy action; (*parola*) blunder.
gol [gɔl] *sm invar* goal.
gola ['gola] *sf* throat; (*golosità*) greed, gluttony. **aver l'acqua alla gola** be in deep water. **far gola** tempt.
golf¹ [gɔlf] *sm invar* (*sport*) golf.
golf² [gɔlf] *sm invar* (*maglione*) sweater, jumper; (*con bottoni*) cardigan.
golfo ['golfo] *sm* gulf.
goliardo [go'ljardo] *sm* (university) student. **goliardico** *agg* university.

goloso [go'lozo] *agg* greedy. **golosità** *sf* greediness, gluttony.

golpe¹ ['golpe] *sf* smut, blight.

golpe² ['golpe] *sm* coup (d'état).

gomito ['gomito] *sm* elbow. **gomitata** *sf* dig with the elbow. **farsi avanti a (forza di) gomitate** elbow one's way forward.

gomitolo [go'mitolo] *sm* ball.

gomma ['gomma] *sf* rubber; (*colla*) gum; (*pneumatico*) tyre. **gommapiuma** *sf* foam rubber. **gommato** *agg* rubberized; gummed. **gommoso** *agg* rubbery.

gondola ['gondola] *sf* gondola. **gondoliere** *sm* gondolier.

gonfalone [gonfa'lone] *sm* banner, standard.

gonfiare [gon'fjare] *v* swell (up); (*riempire di gas, ecc.*) inflate, blow up; (*montare*) puff up; exaggerate. **gonfiatura** *sf* blowing up, swelling up; (*gonfiore*) swelling; exaggeration. **gonfio** *agg* swollen, inflated. **gonfiore** *sm* swelling.

gong ['gɔng] *sm invar* gong.

gonna ['gonna] *sf also* **gonnella** skirt.

gonorrea [gonor'rɛa] *sf* gonorrhea.

gonzo ['gondzo] *sm* simpleton.

gorgheggiare [gorged'dʒare] *v* trill, warble. **gorgheggio** *sm* trill, warble; (*di uccello*) warbling.

gorgo ['gorgo] *sm* whirlpool.

gorgogliare [gorgo'ʎare] *v* gurgle; (*intestino*) rumble. **gorgoglio** *sm* rumble; gurgle.

gorilla [go'rilla] *sm invar* gorilla.

gotico ['gɔtiko] *agg* Gothic.

gotta ['gotta] *sf* gout.

governante [gover'nante] *sf* (*incaricata della casa*) housekeeper; (*istitutrice*) governess.

governare [gover'nare] *v* govern; (*dirigere*) run; (*dominare*) rule; (*pilotare*) steer. **governativo** *agg* government, governmental. **governatore** *sm* governor. **governo** *sm* government; (*dominio*) rule; (*amministrazione*) management. **governo della casa** housekeeping.

gozzo ['goddzo] *sm* crop; (*med*) goitre. **averla nel** *or* **sul gozzo** be unable to swallow.

gozzovigliare [goddzovi'ʎare] *v* revel, go on a spree.

gracchiare [grak'kjare] *v* croak.

gracidare [gratʃi'dare] *v* croak.

gracile ['gratʃile] *agg* frail. **gracilità** *sf* frailty.

gradasso [gra'dasso] *sm* boaster, braggart. **fare il gradasso** boast, brag.

gradazione [grada'tsjone] *sf* gradation; (*sfumatura*) shade. **gradazione alcolica** alcoholic strength.

gradevole [gra'devole] *agg* agreeable.

gradiente [gra'djɛnte] *sm* gradient.

gradimento [gradi'mento] *sm* (*approvazione*) liking; (*piacere*) pleasure.

gradino [gra'dino] *sm* step. **gradinata** *sf* flight of steps.

gradire [gra'dire] *v* (*trovar piacevole*) find agreeable; (*accogliere con gioia*) welcome; (*accettare*) accept; (*nelle richieste*) like.

grado¹ ['grado] *sm* degree; (*mil, rango*) rank. **a gradi** step by step. **avanzare di grado** be promoted. **essere in grado di** be able to.

grado² ['grado] *sm* **di buon grado** willingly.

graduale [gradu'ale] *agg* gradual.

graduare [gradu'are] *v* graduate. **graduatoria** *sf* (*elenco*) list; (*ordine*) classification.

graffa ['graffa] *sf* bracket; (*fermaglio*) (paper-)clip.

graffiare [graf'fjare] *v* scratch. **graffiatura** *sf* scratch. **graffio** *sm* scratch.

grafico [gra'fiko] *agg* graphic. *sm* (*diagramma*) chart, graph; (*persona*) graphic artist.

grafologo [gra'fɔlogo], **-a** *sm*, *sf* graphologist.

gramigna [gra'miɲa] *sf* couch-grass; (*malerba*) weed. **attaccarsi come la gramigna** cling like a leech.

grammatico [gram'matiko] *agg* grammatical. *sm* grammarian. **grammatica** *sm* grammar; (*persona*) grammarian.

grammo ['grammo] *sm* gram.

grammofono [gram'mɔfono] *sm* gramophone.

grana¹ ['grana] *sf* (*struttura*) grain. *sm* (*formaggio*) Parmesan (cheese).

grana² ['grana] *sf* (*seccatura*) nuisance. **piantare una grana** make trouble.

granaglie [gra'naʎe] *sf pl* cereals *pl*.

granaio [gra'najo] *sm* barn; (*zona produttrice di grano*) granary; (*locale sottotetto*) loft.

granata¹ [gra'nata] *sf* (*scopa*) broom.

granata² [gra'nata] *sf* (*mil*) grenade.

granata³ [gra'nata] *sf* (*frutto*) pomegranate; (*pietra*) garnet.

Gran Bretagna [gran bre'taɲa] *sf* Great Britain.

grancassa [gran'kassa] *sf* (*musica*) bass drum. **batter la grancassa** blow one's own trumpet.

granchio ['grankjo] *sm* crab. **prendere un granchio** make a blunder.

grande ['grande] *agg* big; (*ampio, numeroso*) large; (*largo*) wide; (*fig*) great; (*adulto*) grown-up. **in grande** on a large scale. **in gran parte** largely. **non ... un gran che** not ... much.

grandeggiare [granded'dʒare] *v* (*emergere*) tower, stand out; (*darsi arie*) show off.

grandezza [gran'dettsa] *sf* (*dimensione, taglia*) size; (*altezza*) height; (*larghezza*) width; (*ampiezza*) breadth; (*fig*) greatness; (*mat, fis*) magnitude.

grandinare [grandi'nare] *v* hail. **grandine** *sf* hail. **chicco di grandine** *sm* hailstone.

grandioso [gran'djozo] *agg* grand.

granduca [gran'duka] *sm, pl* -**chi** grand duke. **granducato** *sm* grand duchy. **granduchessa** *sf* grand duchess.

granello [gra'nɛllo] *sm* grain; (*di frutta*) pip. **granello di pepe** peppercorn.

granita [gra'nita] *sf* crushed-ice drink.

granito [gra'nito] *sm* granite.

grano ['grano] *sm* (*granello*) grain; (*frumento*) wheat; (*cereale in genere*) corn, cereal.

granturco [gran'turko] *sm* maize.

granulo ['granulo] *sm* granule. **granulare** *agg* granular.

grappolo ['grappolo] *sm* bunch.

grasso ['grasso] *agg* fat; (*unto*) greasy, oily; (*che contiene grasso*) fatty. *sm* fat; (*sostanza untuosa*) grease. **grassoccio** *agg* plump.

grata ['grata] *sf* grating, grille. **gratella** *sf* grill.

graticcio [gra'tittʃo] *sm* trellis.

graticola [gra'tikola] *sf* grill.

gratifica [gra'tifika] *sf* bonus.

gratis ['gratis] *agg* free. *avv* for nothing, for love.

gratitudine [grati'tudine] *sf* gratitude.

grato ['grato] *agg* grateful, obliged; (*gradevole*) pleasant; (*gradito*) welcome.

grattacapo [gratta'kapo] *sm* worry, headache.

grattacielo [gratta'tʃɛlo] *sm* skyscraper.

grattare [grat'tare] *v* scratch; (*grattugiare*) grate; (*raschiare*) scrape; (*fam: rubare*) pinch.

grattugiare [grattu'dʒare] *v* grate. **grattugia** *sf* grater.

gratuito [gra'tuito] *agg* free; (*non retribuito*) unpaid; (*ingiustificato*) gratuitous; (*infondato*) unfounded.

gravare [gra'vare] *v* burden.

grave ['grave] *agg* (*serio*) grave; (*pesante*) heavy; (*malattia*) serious; (*perdita*) grievous. **gravità** *sf* gravity. **gravoso** *agg* hard, onerous.

gravido ['gravido] *agg* pregnant. **gravidanza** *sf* pregnancy.

grazia ['gratsja] *sf* grace; (*fascino*) charm; (*clemenza*) pardon; favour. **grazie** *sm pl, inter* thanks. **grazie a** thanks to.

Grecia ['grɛtʃa] *sf* Greece. **greco, -a** *s, agg, m pl* -**ci** Greek. **naso greco** *sm* Grecian nose.

gregge ['greddʒe] *sm* flock, herd.

greggio ['greddʒo] *agg* raw, crude.

grembiule [grem'bjule] *sm* apron; (*con petto*) pinafore; (*con maniche*) overall.

grembo ['grembo] *sm* lap.

gremire [gre'mire] *v* fill (up). **gremirsi** *v* get crowded.

gres ['grɛs] *sm* stoneware.

gretto ['gretto] *agg* mean; (*idea, animo*) narrow-minded. **grettezza** *sf* meanness; narrow-mindedness.

gridare [gri'dare] *v* shout; (*strillare*) yell, scream. **gridare aiuto** call for help. **grido** *sm, pl* -**a** *f* shout; cry; scream, yell. **di grido** (*noto*) famous; (*di moda*) fashionable. **l'ultimo grido** the latest fashion, the last word.

griffa ['griffa] *sf* claw.

grigio ['gridʒo] *agg* grey; (*fig*) drab. *sm* grey. **grigiastro** *agg* greyish. **grigiore** *sm* greyness; (*fig*) drabness. **grigioverde** *sm, agg* grey-green, khaki.

griglia ['griʎa] *sf* grill; (*saracinesca*) shutter; (*schermo*) grille; (*radio*) grid; (*focolare*) grate.

grilletto [gril'letto] *sm* trigger.

grillo ['grillo] *sm* cricket; (*capriccio*) whim. **gli è saltato il grillo di** he got it into his head to.

grimaldello [grimal'dello] *sm* jemmy.

grinza ['grintsa] *sf* crease; (*ruga*) wrinkle. **non fare una grinza** (*calzare bene*) fit perfectly; (*filare bene*) be flawless.

gripparsi [grip'parsi] *v* (*auto*) seize up.

grondaia [gron'daja] *sf* gutter.

grondare [gron'dare] *v* drip; (*abbondantemente*) pour.

groppa ['grɔppa] *sf* back.

grossa ['grɔssa] *sf* (*comm*) gross. **dormire della grossa** sleep like a log.

grossezza [gros'settsa] *sf* (*volume*) bulk, size; (*spessore*) thickness.

grossista [gros'sista] *s(m+f)* wholesaler.

grosso ['grɔsso] *agg* large, big; (*spesso*) thick; (*non raffinato*) coarse; serious. **dirle grosse** tell fibs. **farne di grosse** cause all sorts of trouble. **grossolano** *agg* coarse, rough.

grotta ['grɔtta] *sf* cave; grotto.

grottesco [grot'tesko] *agg* grotesque.

groviera [gro'vjɛra] *s(m+f)* *also* **gruviera** (*formaggio*) gruyère.

groviglio [gro'viʎo] *sm* tangle; (*confusione*) mess.

gru [gru] *sf* crane.

gruccia ['gruttʃa] *sf* crutch; (*attaccapanni*) coat-hanger.

grugnire [gru'ɲire] *v* grunt. **grugnito** *sm* grunt.

grugno ['gruɲo] *sm* (*maiale*) snout; (*fam: muso*) mug.

grullo ['grullo] *agg* foolish.

grumo ['grumo] *sm* clot.

gruppo ['gruppo] *sm* group; (*mec*) unit.

gruviera [gru'vjɛra] *V* **groviera**.

gruzzolo ['gruttsolo] *sm* pile; (*risparmi*) nest-egg.

guadagnare [gwada'ɲare] *v* earn; (*ottenere*) gain; (*vincere*) win; (*raggiungere*) reach; (*risparmiare*) save.

guadagno [gwa'daɲo] *sm* (*retribuzione*) earnings *pl*; profit; advantage.

guado ['gwado] *sm* ford. **guadare** *v* wade.

guaina [gwa'ina] *sf* sheath.

guaio ['gwajo] *sm* trouble. **guai** *inter* woe betide you, us, etc.

guaire [gwa'ire] *v* whine, yelp. **guaito** *sm* whine, yelp.

guancia ['gwantʃa] *sf* cheek. **guanciale** *sm* pillow.

guanto ['gwanto] *sm* glove. **calzare come un guanto** fit like a glove. **gettare il guanto** throw down the gauntlet. **trattare coi guanti** treat with kid gloves.

guardaboschi [gwarda'bɔski] *sm* forester.

guardacaccia [gwarda'kattʃa] *sm invar* gamekeeper.

guardacoste [gwarda'kɔste] *sm invar* coastguard.

guardalinee [gwarda'linee] *sm invar* (*sport*) linesman.

guardamano [gwarda'mano] *sm invar* (*sciabola*) hilt; (*fucile*) guard; (*guanto*) protective glove.

guardare [gwar'dare] *v* look (at); (*affacciarsi*) look out; face; (*dare un'occhiata*) have a look; (*custodire*) look after, mind; (*stare a vedere*) watch; (*considerare*) view; (*cercare*) try to, be careful to. **andare a guardare** have a look. **Dio ne guardi!** God forbid! **guarda che roba!** just look at that! **guardar di sbieco** *or* **traverso** look askance (at). **guardare fisso** stare, gaze (at). **guarda un po'!** well, well!

guardaroba [gwarda'rɔba] *sm invar* (*luogo*) cloakroom; (*armadio*) wardrobe. **guardarobiera** *sf* cloakroom attendant.

guardarsi [gwar'darsi] *v* look at oneself. **guardarsi intorno** look around. **guardarsi da** (*fare attenzione a*) beware of; (*astenersi da*) refrain from. **me ne guardo bene!** heaven forbid!

guardata [gwar'data] *sf* look, glance.

guardavia [gwarda'via] *sm invar* guardrail.

guardia ['gwardja] *sf* (*custodia*) watch, guard; (*turno*) duty; (*custode*) keeper, watchman; (*sentinella*) sentry; (*sport*) guard. **essere di guardia** be on duty; (*mil*) be on guard duty. **fare la guardia** (*sorvegliare*) guard, watch; (*badare*) watch over. **guardia di finanza** (*corpo*) Customs *pl*; (*singolo*) Customs officer. **mettere in guardia** warn. **guardiano** *sm* keeper, guardian.

guardingo [gwar'dingo] *agg* cautious, wary.

guarire [gwa'rire] *v* cure; (*rimettersi in salute*) recover; (*ferita*) heal. **guarigione** *sf* recovery; healing.

guarnigione [gwarni'dʒone] *sf* garrison.

guarnire [gwar'nire] *v* decorate; (*vestiario*) trim; (*gastr*) garnish; (*corredare*) equip; (*mil*) garrison. **guarnizione** *sf* decoration, trimming, garnish; (*tec*) packing; (*auto*) gasket.

guastafeste [gwasta'feste] *s(m+f)* *invar* spoilsport.

guastamestieri [gwastames'tieri] *s(m+f) invar* bungler; (*fam*) menace.

guastare [gwas'tare] *v* spoil; (*rovinare*) ruin, damage. **guastarsi** *v* (*cibi*) go bad; (*mec*) break down; (*tempo*) change for the worse. **guasto** *agg* (*cibo*) bad, rotten; (*mec*) broken; (*salute, ecc.*) bad.

guazzabuglio [gwattsa'buʎo] *sm* hotchpotch, jumble.

guazzare [gwat'tsare] *v* splash about; (*fig*) wallow. **guazzo** *sm* pool; (*pittura*) gouache.

guercio ['gwertʃo] *agg* cross-eyed.

guerra ['gwɛrra] *sf* war; (*il guerreggiare*) warfare. **far guerra** wage war. **guerra mondiale** world war. **guerrafondaio** *sm, sf* warmonger.

guerreggiare [gwerred'dʒare] *v* fight.

guerresco [gwer'resko] *agg* (*bellicoso*) warlike; (*di guerra*) war.

guerriero [gwer'rjɛro] *agg* (*bellicoso*) warlike; (*combattivo*) aggressive. *sm* warrior.

guerriglia [gwer'riʎa] *sf* guerrilla warfare. **guerrigliero** *sm* guerrilla.

gufo ['gufo] *sm* owl.

guglia ['guʎa] *sf* (*arch*) spire; (*geog*) pinnacle.

guida ['gwida] *sf* guide; (*direzione, comando*) guidance, leadership; (*tappeto*) runner; (*elenco*) directory; (*auto*) drive, driving; (*comandi*) controls *pl*. **esame (di) guida** *sm* driving test. **guida a destra/sinistra** right-/left-hand drive. **scuola (di) guida** *sf* driving school.

guidare [gwi'dare] *v* guide; (*dirigere, comandare*) lead; (*auto*) drive; (*aero*) fly; (*nave*) steer; (*moto*) ride. **guidatore, -trice** *sm, sf* driver.

guinzaglio [gwin'tsaʎo] *sm* leash, lead. **mettere il guinzaglio** (*fig*) keep a tight rein (on). **tenere al guinzaglio** keep on a leash.

guisa ['gwiza] *sf* **a** *or* **in guisa di** in the manner of, like.

guizzare [gwit'tsare] *v* (*lampo*) flash; (*pesci*) dart; (*sfuggire*) wriggle; (*fiamma*) flicker. **guizzo** *sm* flash; dart; flicker.

guscio ['gufo] *sm* shell; (*legumi*) pod.

gustare [gus'tare] *v* taste; (*trovar buono*) enjoy. **gusto** *sm* taste; (*piacere*) enjoyment. **con gusto** tastefully. **di gusto** heartily. **non aver gusto** be tasteless. **prenderci gusto** take a liking (to). **senza gusto** tasteless.

gutturale [guttu'rale] *agg* guttural.

H

hascisc [a'ʃiʃ] *sm* hashish.
hockey ['hɔki] *sm* hockey.

I

i [i] *art* the.

iattanza [jat'tantsa] *sf* arrogance.

ibernazione [iberna'tsjone] *sf* hibernation. **ibernare** *v* hibernate.

ibrido ['ibrido] *sm, agg* hybrid.

Iddio [id'dio] *sm* God.

idea [i'dɛa] *sf* idea; opinion; (*proposito*) intention. **cambiare idea** change one's mind. **dare l'idea** give the impression.

ideale [ide'ale] *sm, agg* ideal. **idealismo** *sm* idealism. **idealista** *s*(*m*+*f*) idealist. **idealistico** *agg* idealistic.

identico [i'dɛntiko] *agg* identical.

identificare [identifi'kare] *v* identify. **identificazione** *sf* identification.

identità [identi'ta] *sf* identity.

ideologia [ideolo'dʒia] *sf* ideology. **ideologico** *agg* ideological.

idillio [i'dilljo] *sm* idyll. **idillico** *agg* idyllic.

idioma [i'djɔma] *sm* language. **frase idiomatica** *sf* idiom.

idiota [i'kjɔta] *s*(*m*+*f*) idiot, fool. *agg* idiotic, stupid.

idiotismo [idjo'tizmo] *sm* (*lingua*) idiom; (*med*) idiocy.

idiozia [idjo'tsia] *sf* idiocy; stupidity.

idolo ['idolo] *sm* idol. **idoleggiare** *v* idolize.

idoneo [i'dɔneo] *agg* fit, suitable; (*capace*) able. **non idoneo** unfit, unsuitable. **idoneità** *sf* ability, suitability.

idrante [i'drante] *sm* hydrant. **idratante** *agg* (*crema*) moisturizing.

idraulico [i'drauliko] *agg* hydraulic. *sm* plumber. **idraulica** *sf* hydraulics.

idroelettrico [idroe'lettriko] *agg* hydroelectric.

idroestrattore [idroestrat'tore] *sm* spindrier.

idrofilo [i'drɔfilo] *agg* **cotone idrofilo** *sm* cotton-wool.

idrofobia [i'drɔfobia] *sf* rabies, hydrophobia. **idrofobo** *agg* rabid, hydrophobic.
idrogeno [i'drɔdʒeno] *sm* hydrogen.
idrosci [idro'ʃi] *sm* water-skiing.
idrovolante [idrovo'lante] *sm* seaplane.
iena ['jɛna] *sf* hyena.
ieri ['jɛri] *avv, sm* yesterday. **ieri l'altro** the day before yesterday. **tutto ieri** all day yesterday.
iettatore [jetta'tore] *sm* jinx. **iettatura** *sf* bad luck; (*malocchio*) evil eye.
igiene [i'dʒɛne] *sf* hygiene. **igienico** *agg* hygienic; (*sano*) healthy. **assorbente igienico** *sm* sanitary towel. **carta igienica** *sf* toilet paper.
iglù [i'glu] *sm* igloo.
ignaro [i'ɲaro] *agg* unaware, ignorant.
ignobile [i'ɲɔbile] *agg* mean, base.
ignominia [iɲo'minja] *sf* disgrace.
ignorante [iɲo'rante] *agg* ignorant; (*non colto*) uneducated. *s(m+f)* ignoramus. **ignoranza** *sf* ignorance.
ignorare [iɲo'rare] *v* (*non sapere*) not know; (*trascurare, fingere di non conoscere*) ignore.
ignoto [i'ɲɔto] *agg* unknown. *sm* (*concetto*) unknown; (*persona*) unknown person.
ignudo [i'ɲudo] *agg* naked.
il [il] *art* the.
ilare ['ilare] *agg* cheerful. **ilarità** *sf* (*allegria*) cheerfulness; (*riso*) hilarity.
illecito [il'letʃito] *agg* illicit, unlawful.
illegale [ille'gale] *agg* illegal, unlawful. **illegalità** *sf* illegality.
illeggibile [illed'dʒibile] *agg* illegible; (*fig*) unreadable.
illegittimo [ille'dʒittimo] *agg* illegitimate. **illegittimità** *sf* illegitimacy.
illeso [il'lezo] *agg* unhurt.
illibato [illi'bato] *agg* pure, chaste.
illimitato [illimi'tato] *agg* unlimited, boundless.
illogico [il'lɔdʒiko] *agg* illogical, unsound. **illogicità** *sf* illogicality.
***illudere** [il'ludere] *v* deceive, fool. **illudersi** *v* delude oneself.
illuminare [illumi'nare] *v* light, illuminate; (*rischiarare*) light up; (*mostrare la verità*) enlighten; (*a giorno*) floodlight. **illuminazione** *sf* illumination, lighting. **illuminismo** *sm* Enlightenment.
illusione [illu'zjone] *sf* illusion; impression. **farsi (delle) illusioni** delude oneself;

(*fam*) kid oneself. **non farsi (delle) illusioni** have no illusions. **illusionista** *s(m+f)* conjurer.
illusorio [illu'zɔrjo] *agg* illusory, vain.
illustrare [illus'trare] *v* illustrate; (*spiegare*) explain. **illustrativo** *agg* explanatory. **illustrato** *agg* illustrated. **illustratore, -trice** *sm, sf* illustrator. **illustrazione** *sf* illustration, explanation.
illustre [il'lustre] *agg* famous, illustrious. **illustre ignoto** *sm* nobody.
imbacuccare [imbakuk'kare] *v* wrap up.
imballare¹ [imbal'lare] *v* pack; (*involucro*) wrap; (*in scatole*) box; (*in casse*) crate. **imballaggio** *sm* packing; wrapping; boxing; crating.
imballare² [imbal'lare] *v* (*auto*) race.
imbalsamare [imbalsa'mare] *v* embalm. **imbalsamatore, -trice** *sm, sf* embalmer; (*di animali*) taxidermist.
imbambolato [imbambo'lato] *agg* bewildered.
imbandierare [imbandje'rare] *v* deck with flags.
imbandire [imban'dire] *v* prepare.
imbarazzare [imbarat'tsare] *v* embarrass; (*impedire*) hamper; (*ostacolare*) block, hinder. **imbarazzo** *sm* embarrassment; (*impaccio*) hindrance, trouble. **essere in imbarazzo** be in a difficult situation, be in a fix; (*scelta difficile*) be in a quandary. **mettere in imbarazzo** (*in situazione difficile*) put in a spot; (*a disagio*) make ill at ease.
imbarcare [imbar'kare] *v* take aboard. **imbarcarsi** *v* embark. **imbarcazione** *sf* craft, boat. **imbarco** *sm* embarkation; (*merci*) shipment.
imbastire [imbas'tire] *v* (*cucire*) tack; (*tracciare sommariamente*) draw up, outline.
imbattersi [im'battersi] *v* come across; (*fam*) bump into.
imbattibile [imbat'tibile] *agg* invincible, unbeatable.
imbavagliare [imbava'ʎare] *v* gag.
imbecille [imbe'tʃille] *agg* stupid, idiotic. *s(m+f)* fool, idiot; (*med*) imbecile.
imbellettare [imbellet'tare] *v* make up; (*fig*) embellish.
imbellire [imbel'lire] *v* beautify.
imbevuto [imbe'vuto] *agg* steeped (in), imbued (with).
imbiancare [imbjan'kare] *v* whiten; (*muri*)

whitewash; (*candeggiare*) bleach. **imbianchino** *sm* house-painter.

imbizzarrirsi [imbiddzar'rirsi] *v* get excited.

imboccare [imbok'kare] *v* (*cibo*) feed; (*suggerire*) prompt; enter; (*portare alla bocca*) put to one's mouth. **imboccatura** *sf* mouth; entrance; (*bocchino*) mouthpiece.

imbonire [imbo'nire] *v* entice, talk into buying. **imbonimento** *sm* (*discorso*) salestalk; (*elogio immeritato*) build-up.

imboscata [imbos'kata] *sf* ambush. **imboscato** *sm* shirker, (draft-)dodger.

imbottigliare [imbotti'ʎare] *v* bottle; (*mil*) blockade; (*traffico*) jam.

imbottire [imbot'tire] *v* stuff; (*sarto*) pad, wad. **coperta imbottita** *sf* quilt. **panino imbottito** *sm* sandwich. **imbottitura** *sf* stuffing; padding; wadding.

imbrattare [imbrat'tare] *v* soil, dirty.

imbrigliare [imbri'ʎare] *v* bridle.

imbroccare [imbrok'kare] *v* (*azzeccare*) get right.

imbrogliare [imbro'ʎare] *v* (*gabbare*) cheat; (*mettere in disordine*) mix up, muddle up; (*ingarbugliare*) tangle (up). **imbroglio** *sm* (*faccenda confusa*) muddle, mess; (*groviglio*) tangle; (*raggiro*) trick, swindle. **imbroglione, -a** *sm, sf* cheat, trickster, swindler.

imbronciarsi [imbron'tʃarsi] *v* sulk; (*cielo*) cloud over.

imbrunire [imbru'nire] *v* darken, get dark. *sm* nightfall.

imbruttire [imbrut'tire] *v* spoil.

imbucare [imbu'kare] *v* post.

imburrare [imbur'rare] *v* butter.

imbuto [im'buto] *sm* funnel.

imitare [imi'tare] *v* imitate. **imitazione** *sf* imitation.

immagazzinare [immagaddzi'nare] *v* store.

immaginare [immadʒi'nare] *v* imagine. **s'immagini!** (*tutt'altro*) not in the least! (*certamente*) by all means! **immaginario** *agg* imaginary. **immaginazione** *sf* imagination.

immagine [im'madʒine] *sf* image; (*figura, ritratto*) picture. **immagine reflessa** reflection.

immancabile [imman'kabile] *agg* unfailing, certain.

immangiabile [imman'dʒabile] *agg* inedible, uneatable.

immatricolarsi [immatriko'larsi] *v* register, enrol.

immaturo [imma'turo] *agg* unripe; (*fig*) immature; (*prematuro*) untimely.

immedesimarsi [immedezi'marsi] *v* identify oneself (with).

immediato [imme'djato] *agg* immediate. **immediatamente** *avv* immediately; directly; (*subito*) at once.

immemorabile [immemo'rabile] *agg* immemorial.

immemore [im'mɛmore] *agg* heedless, forgetful.

immenso [im'menso] *agg* huge, vast; enormous. **immensità** *sf* hugeness, immensity; (*gran numero*) mass, enormous number.

***immergere** [im'mɛrdʒere] *v* immerse; (*intingere*) dip; (*con forza, tuffare*) plunge; (*sottomarino*) submerge. **immersione** *sf* immersion; (*tuffo*) dive.

immeritato [immeri'tato] *agg* undeserved. **immeritevole** *agg* undeserving.

***immettere** [im'mettere] *v* admit, introduce.

immigrare [immi'grare] *v* immigrate. **immigrante** *s(m + f)*, *agg* immigrant. **immigrato, -a** *s*, *agg* immigrant. **immigrazione** *sf* immigration.

imminente [immi'nɛnte] *agg* imminent. **imminenza** *sf* imminence.

immischiare [immis'kjare] *v* involve, mix up. **immischiarsi** *v* get involved, interfere.

immobile [im'mɔbile] *agg* (*che non si muove*) motionless, still; (*che non si può muovere*) immovable. **società immobiliare** *sf* building society. **immobilità** *sf* immobility, stillness. **beni immobili** *sm pl* real estate *sing*.

immobilizzare [immobilid'dzare] *v* immobilize; (*econ*) tie up.

immoderato [immode'rato] *agg* excessive. **immoderatezza** *sf* excessiveness; (*smoderatezza*) lack of moderation.

immodesto [immo'desto] *agg* conceited, immodest.

immolare [immo'lare] *v* sacrifice.

immondo [im'mondo] *agg* filthy. **immondezzaio** *sm* rubbish dump. **immondizia** *sf* (*sporcizia*) filth; (*spazzatura*) rubbish, garbage.

immorale [immo'rale] *agg* immoral.

immortale [immor'tale] *agg* immortal. **immortalare** *v* immortalize. **immortalità** *sf* immortality.

immune [im'mune] *agg* immune, free.
immunità *sf* immunity. **immunizzare** *v*
immunize.
immutabile [immu'tabile] *agg* immutable,
unchangeable; (*costante*) unswerving.
immutabilità *sf* immutability; firmness.
immutato *agg* unchanged, unfailing.
impacchettare [impakket'tare] *v* parcel
up, package.
impacciare [impat'tʃare] *v* hamper, hinder. **impaccio** *sm* obstacle, hindrance;
(*situazione imbarazzante*) fix, predicament. **impacciato** *agg* awkward;
(*imbarazzato*) ill at ease; (*goffo*) clumsy.
impadronirsi [impadro'nirsi] *v*
impadronirsi di seize, take possession of;
(*imparare a fondo*) master.
impagabile [impa'gabile] *agg* invaluable,
priceless.
impalcatura [impalka'tura] *sf* (*struttura
provvisoria*) scaffolding; (*struttura di sostegno*) framework; (*cervo*) antlers *pl*.
impallidire [impalli'dire] *v* turn pale; (*fig*)
fade; (*offuscarsi*) grow dim.
impanare[1] [impa'nare] *v* (*mec*) thread.
impanare[2] [impa'nare] *v* (*gastr*) dip in
breadcrumbs.
impannata [impan'nata] *sf* window-frame.
impantanarsi [impanta'narsi] *v* get
bogged down.
imparare [impa'rare] *v* learn. **imparare a
memoria** learn by heart.
impareggiabile [impared'dʒabile] *agg*
incomparable.
impari ['impari] *agg invar* unequal.
impartire [impar'tire] *v* give, impart.
imparziale [impar'tsjale] *agg* impartial,
unbiased; (*giusto*) fair.
impassibile [impas'sibile] *agg* impassive,
unmoved.
impastare [impas'tare] *v* (*pane*) knead;
(*lavorare*) mix; (*incollare*) paste. **impasta-
trice** *sf* mixer. **impasto** *sm* mixture.
impatto [im'patto] *sm* impact.
impaurire [impau'rire] *v* frighten.
impaziente [impa'tsjɛnte] *agg* impatient;
(*desideroso*) anxious. **impazientirsi** *v* lose
one's patience.
impazzare [impat'tsare] *v* be in full
swing; (*gastr*) curdle. **all'impazzata** wildly.
impazzire [impat'tsire] *v* go mad. **far
impazzire** drive mad.
impeccabile [impek'kabile] *agg* impeccable.

impedire [impe'dire] *v* prevent; (*sbarrare*)
block; (*impacciare*) hinder. **impedimento**
sm impediment; obstacle; (*l'impedire*)
prevention.
impegnare [impe'ɲare] *v* (*dare in pegno*)
pledge; (*tenere impegnato*) engage;
(*obbligare*) bind; (*tenere occupato*) take
up; (*prenotare*) book. **impegnarsi** *v*
undertake, strive. **impegnativo** *agg*
(*lavoro*) exacting, demanding; (*promessa*)
binding. **impegnato** *agg* engaged; (*vincolato*) pledged; (*pol*) committed. **impegno**
sm engagement; obligation; commitment; (*zelo*) eagerness, enthusiasm.
impenetrabile [impene'trabile] *agg*
impenetrable, impervious.
impenitente [impeni'tɛnte] *agg*
unrepentant. **scapolo impenitente** *sm*
confirmed bachelor.
impennarsi [impen'narsi] *v* flare up;
(*cavallo*) rear (up); (*aereo*) go into a
climb.
impensabile [impen'sabile] *agg* unthinkable.
impensato [impen'sato] *agg* unforeseen.
impensierirsi [impensje'rirsi] *v* worry.
imperativo [impera'tivo] *sm*, *agg* imperative. **imperare** *v* rule.
imperatore [impera'tore] *sm* emperor.
imperatrice *sf* empress.
impercettibile [impertʃet'tibile] *agg*
imperceptible.
imperdonabile [imperdo'nabile] *agg*
unforgivable.
imperfetto [imper'fetto] *agg* faulty, defective. *sm* imperfect (tense). **imperfezione**
sf defect.
imperioso [impe'rjozo] *agg* imperious;
(*ineluttabile*) pressing, impelling.
impermalirsi [imperma'lirsi] *v* take
umbrage, take offence.
impermeabile [imperme'abile] *sm* raincoat. *agg* impervious; (*all'acqua*) waterproof; (*all'aria*) airtight. **impermeabilizzare** *v* waterproof.
imperniare [imper'njare] *v* hinge;
(*fondare*) base.
impero [im'pero] *sm* (*territorio*) empire;
(*autorità*) rule.
imperscrutabile [imperskru'tabile] *agg*
inscrutable.
impersonale [imperso'nale] *agg* impersonal.

impersonare [imperso'nare] *v* (*simboleggiare*) personify; (*attore*) impersonate. **impersonarsi** *v* be the personification (of).

imperterrito [imper'tɛrrito] *agg* undaunted; unperturbed.

impertinente [imperti'nɛnte] *agg* impertinent, cheeky.

imperturbabile [impertur'babile] *agg* unruffled, imperturbable, calm. **imperturbato** *agg* unperturbed, unruffled.

impeto ['impeto] *sm* impetus, force; (*accesso*) outburst. **agire d'impeto** act on impulse.

impettito [impet'tito] *agg* stiff, erect. **camminare impettito** strut.

impetuoso [impe'twozo] *agg* impetuous.

impiallacciato [impjallat't∫ato] *agg* veneered. **impiallacciatura** *sf* veneer.

impiantare [impjan'tare] *v* set up; (*fondare*) establish; (*tec*) install. **impianto** *sm* plant, installation; (*fondazione*) establishment.

impiantito [impjan'tito] *sm* flooring.

impiastrare [impjas'trare] *v* smear. **impiastro** *sm* (*cataplasma*) poultice; (*persona uggiosa*) bore.

impiccare [impik'kare] *v* hang. **impiccato** *sm* hanged man.

impicciare [impit't∫are] *v* be in the way, hamper. **impicciarsi** *v* meddle, interfere.

impiccio [im'pitt∫o] *sm* (*ostacolo*) hindrance; (*guaio*) mess, trouble. **essere d'impiccio** *v* be in the way.

impiegare [impje'gare] *v* employ; spend. **impiegatizio** *agg* clerical. **impiegato, -a** *sm, sf* employee; (*funzionario*) official. **impiegati** *pl* (*collettivo*) staff *sing*, personnel *sing*.

impiego [im'pjɛgo] *sm*, *pl* -**ghi** use; (*denaro*) investment; (*posto, occupazione*) employment, job.

impietrito [impje'trito] *agg* petrified.

impigliarsi [impiʎ'ʎarsi] *v* get entangled, get mixed up.

impiparsi [impi'parsi] *v* (*fam*) not care a damn.

implacabile [impla'kabile] *agg* implacable.

implicare [impli'kare] *v* (*coinvolgere*) involve; (*comportare*) imply, entail.

implicito [im'plit∫ito] *agg* implicit.

implorare [implo'rare] *v* implore, entreat.

impolverare [impolve'rare] *v* cover with dust.

imponderabile [imponde'rabile] *agg* imponderable.

imponente [impo'nɛnte] *agg* imposing, impressive.

imponibile [impo'nibile] *agg* taxable. *sm* taxable income.

impopolare [impopo'lare] *agg* unpopular. **impopolarità** *sf* unpopularity.

*****imporre** [im'porre] *v* impose; (*costringere*) oblige; (*ordinare*) order; (*comportare*) involve. **imporsi** *v* (*farsi valere*) assert oneself; (*incontrar favore*) go down well; (*rendersi necessario*) become necessary.

importante [impor'tante] *agg* important. *sm* important thing, main point. **importanza** *sf* importance. **di nessuna importanza** unimportant.

importare [impor'tare] *v* (*aver peso*) matter; (*comportare*) involve; (*introdurre dall'estero*) import. **non importa!** it doesn't matter! never mind! **non me ne importa niente!** (*fam*) I couldn't care less!

importazione [importa'tsjone] *sf* import; (*atto*) importation.

importo [im'pɔrto] *sm* amount.

importunare [importu'nare] *v* trouble, bother. **importuno** *agg* troublesome, tiresome, boring.

imposizione [impozi'tsjone] *sf* imposition.

impossessarsi [imposses'sarsi] *v* get hold of, seize.

impossibile [impos'sibile] *agg* impossible. **fare l'impossibile** do all one can. **impossibilità** *sf* impossibility.

imposta¹ [im'pɔsta] *sf* (*finestra*) shutter.

imposta² [im'pɔsta] *sf* (*econ*) tax, duty.

impostare¹ [impos'tare] *v* (*spedire*) post.

impostare² [impos'tare] *v* (*avviare*) get under way; (*questione, ecc.*) set out, state; (*nave*) lay down; (*voce*) pitch. **impostazione** *sf* approach.

impostore [impos'tore] *sm* imposter.

impotente [impo'tɛnte] *agg* powerless; (*med*) impotent. **impotenza** *sf* powerlessness; impotence.

impoverire [impove'rire] *v* impoverish. **impoverimento** *sm* impoverishment.

impraticabile [imprati'kabile] *agg* (*strada*) impassable; (*campo sportivo*) unfit for play.

impratichirsi [imprati'kirsi] *v* practise.

imprecare [impre'kare] *v* curse. **imprecazione** *sf* curse.

impreciso [impre'tʃizo] *agg* (*inesatto*) inaccurate; (*indeterminato*) imprecise, vague. **imprecisabile** *agg* indefinable. **imprecisione** *sf* inaccuracy; vagueness.

impregnare [impre'ɲare] *v* impregnate; (*fig*) imbue; (*inzuppare*) soak.

imprenditore [imprendi'tore] *sm* contractor; entrepreneur. **imprenditore di pompe funebri** undertaker. **imprenditore edile** building contractor. **piccolo imprenditore** tradesman.

impreparato [imprepa'rato] *agg* unprepared; (*lavoro*) untrained. **impreparazione** *sf* unpreparedness; lack of training.

impresa [im'preza] *sf* undertaking, enterprise; (*azienda*) concern, firm; (*azione*) deed; (*azione pericolosa*) exploit. **impresario** *sm* entrepreneur; (theatre) manager, impresario.

imprescindibile [impreʃin'dibile] *agg* that cannot be disregarded.

impressionare [impressjo'nare] *v* make an impression; (*spaventare*) frighten; (*turbare*) shock, upset; (*foto*) expose. **impressionarsi** *v* be upset, be shocked; be affected. **impressionabile** *agg* impressionable, easily affected; easily frightened. **impressionante** *agg* striking, impressive; frightening; upsetting.

impressione [impres'sjone] *sf* impression; sensation.

imprestare [impres'tare] *v* lend.

imprevidenza [imprevi'dentsa] *sf* lack of foresight. **imprevedibile** *agg* unforeseeable. **imprevidente** *agg* heedless.

imprevisto [impre'visto] *agg* unforeseen. **salvo imprevisti** if all goes well.

imprigionare [impridʒo'nare] *v* imprison.

*imprimere [im'primere] *v* imprint, impress; (*dare*) impart; (*pittura*) prime.

improbabile [impro'babile] *agg* unlikely, improbable. **improbabilità** *sf* unlikelihood.

improduttivo [improdut'tivo] *agg* unproductive.

impronta [im'pronta] *sf* impression, mark, stamp. **impronta del piede** footprint. **impronta digitale** fingerprint. **improntare** *v* stamp. **all'impronto** at sight.

improprio [im'prɔprjo] *agg* (*inadatto*) inappropriate; (*inopportuno*) out of place; (*mat*) improper.

improrogabile [improro'gabile] *agg* **termine improrogabile** *sm* deadline.

improvvisare [improvvi'zare] *v* improvise. **improvvisamente** *avv* suddenly, all of a sudden. **improvvisata** *sf* surprise. **improvvisazione** *sf* improvisation.

imprudente [impru'dɛnte] *agg* rash, imprudent. **imprudenza** *sf* imprudence. **commettere un'imprudenza** do something rash.

impudente [impu'dɛnte] *agg* impudent.

impudico [impu'diko] *agg, m pl* -chi immodest.

impugnare[1] [impu'ɲare] *v* (*contestare*) challenge; (*dir*) contest.

impugnare[2] [impu'ɲare] *v* (*afferrare*) grasp. **impugnare le armi** take up arms. **impugnatura** *sf* handle; (*spada*) hilt; (*racchetta*) grip.

impulso [im'pulso] *sm* impulse. **dare impulso** boost. **impulsivo** *agg* impulsive.

impunemente [impune'mente] *avv* with impunity.

impunito [impu'nito] *agg* (*delitto*) unpunished.

impuntarsi [impun'tarsi] *v* refuse to budge, dig one's heels in.

impuro [im'puro] *agg* impure. **impurità** *sf* impurity.

imputare [impu'tare] *v* impute, attribute, ascribe; (*dir*) charge. **imputabile** *agg* attributable. **imputato, -a** *sm, sf* defendant, accused. **imputazione** *sf* charge.

imputridire [imputri'dire] *v* rot.

in [in] *prep* in; (*su, sopra*) on; (*moto a luogo*) to; (*dentro*) into; (*moto per luogo*) round, through; (*entro*) within; (*durante*) during.

inabile [in'abile] *agg* (*non capace*) unable, incapable; (*non idoneo*) unfit; (*per infortunio*) disabled; (*dir*) ineligible.

inabitabile [inabi'tabile] *agg* uninhabitable. **inabitato** *agg* uninhabited.

inaccessibile [inattʃes'sibile] *agg* inaccessible.

inaccettabile [inattʃet'tabile] *agg* unacceptable.

inadatto [ina'datto] *agg* unsuitable (for); (*incapace*) unfit (for).

inadeguato [inade'gwato] *agg* insufficient, inadequate.

inalare [ina'lare] *v* inhale.

inalienabile [ːnalje'nabile] *agg* inalienable.

inalterabile [inalte'rabile] *agg* unchangeable. **inalterato** *agg* unchanged.

inamidare [inami'dare] *v* starch.

inammissibile [innammis'sibile] *agg* inadmissible.

inanimato [inani'mato] *agg* inanimate, lifeless.

inappagabile [innappa'gabile] *agg* insatiable. **inappagato** *agg* unsatisfied.

inapplicabile [inappli'kabile] *agg* inapplicable.

inarcare [inar'kare] *v* arch, bend. **inarcare le sopracciglia** raise one's eyebrows.

inargentare [inardʒen'tare] *v* silver.

inaridire [inari'dire] *v* dry up.

inaspettato [inaspet'tato] *agg* unexpected.

inasprire [inas'prire] *v* exacerbate, make worse.

inattendibile [inatten'dibile] *agg* unreliable.

inatteso [inat'tezo] *agg* unexpected.

inattivo [inat'tivo] *agg* idle.

inattuabile [inat'twabile] *agg* impracticable.

inaudito [inau'dito] *agg* (*non udito prima*) unheard of; incredible, extraordinary.

inaugurare [inaugu'rare] *v* inaugurate, open. **inaugurazione** *sf* inauguration, opening.

inavveduto [inavve'duto] *agg* thoughtless, careless.

inavvertenza [inavver'tɛntsa] *sf* carelessness, oversight.

incagliarsi [inka'ʎarsi] *v* (*mar*) run aground; (*fig*) get stuck.

incalcolabile [inkalko'labile] *agg* incalculable.

incalzare [inkal'tsare] *v* follow closely; (*fig*) press.

incamminare [inkammi'nare] *v* start (off). **incamminarsi** *v* set off; (*avviarsi*) be on the way (to).

incanalare [inkana'lare] *v* channel.

incantare [inkan'tare] *v* enchant, charm. **incantarsi** *v* (*rimanere intontito*) be in a daze; (*mec*) jam, break down. **incantato** *agg* enchanted; (*intontito*) dazed, spellbound. **incantatore, -trice** *sm, sf* charmer. **incantesimo** *sm* charm, spell. **incantevole** *agg* charming, enchanting.

incanto[1] [in'kanto] *sm* spell, magic. **stare d'incanto** suit perfectly.

incanto[2] [in'kanto] *sm* (*vendita*) auction.

incapace [inka'patʃe] *agg* incapable.

incapacità *sf* inability; (*fisica*) disability; (*dir*) incapacity.

incappare [inkap'pare] *v* run into, come up against.

incarcerare [inkartʃe'rare] *v* imprison, jail.

incaricare [inkari'kare] *v* charge, entrust; order. **incaricarsi** *v* take charge. **incaricato, -a** *sm, sf* person in charge; (*università*) lecturer; (*funzionario*) official.

incarico [in'kariko] *sm, pl* -chi task, assignment, charge.

incarnare [inkar'nare] *v* embody; (*personaggio*) impersonate.

incartare [inkar'tare] *v* wrap (up).

incasellare [inkazel'lare] *v* pigeon-hole.

incassare [inkas'sare] *v* (*riscuotere*) collect, cash; (*sport*) take; (*inserire*) embed. **incasso** *sm* collection; (*entrata*) takings *pl.*

incastellatura [inkastella'tura] *sf* (*impalcatura*) scaffolding; (*mec*) casing.

incastonare [inkasto'nare] *v* set, mount. **incastonatura** *sf* setting, mounting.

incastrare [inkast'rare] *v* wedge, drive; (*imprigionare*) jam, sandwich; (*falegnameria*) mortise. **incastro** *sm* joint; (*cavità*) hollow, recess; mortise.

incatenare [inkate'nare] *v* chain; (*fig*) tie.

incatramare [inkatra'mare] *v* tar.

incauto [in'kauto] *agg* incautious.

incavare [inka'vare] *v* hollow out. **incavo** *sm* hollow; (*scanalatura*) groove.

incendiare [intʃen'djare] *v* set on fire; (*fig*) fire.

incendiario [intʃen'djarjo] *agg* incendiary. *sm* arsonist, fire-raiser.

incendio [in'tʃɛndjo] *sm* fire. **bocca d'incendio** *sf* (fire) hydrant. **incendio doloso** arson.

incenerire [intʃene'rire] *v* burn down; (*fig*) wither.

incenso [in'tʃɛnso] *sm* incense.

incensurabile [intʃensu'rabile] *agg* beyond reproach. **essere incensurato** have a clean record.

inceppare [intʃep'pare] *v* obstruct, hamper.

incertezza [intʃer'tettsa] *sf* uncertainty; (*dubbio*) doubt; (*indecisione*) hesitation.

incerto [in'tʃɛrto] *agg* uncertain; dubious; (*indeciso*) hesitant; (*malsicuro*) unsure. *sm* uncertainty.

incespicare [intʃespi'kare] *v* stumble, trip up.

incessante [intʃes'sante] *agg* ceaseless, constant.

incesto [in'tʃɛsto] *sm* incest. **incestuoso** *agg* incestuous.

incettare [intʃet'tare] *v also* **fare incetto di** corner, buy up. **incetta** *sf* cornering.

inchiesta [in'kjɛsta] *sf* inquiry, investigation; (*giornalismo*) report; (*scandalo*) probe.

inchinare [inki'nare] *v* bow, bend; (*abbassare*) lower. **inchinarsi** *v* bend down, bow; (*donna*) curtsey. **inchino** *sm* bow, curtsey.

inchiodare [inkjo'dare] *v* nail.

inchiostro [in'kjostro] *sm* ink. **inchiostro di china** Indian ink.

inciampare [intʃam'pare] *v* stumble (over), trip up. **inciampo** *sm* obstacle, stumbling block.

incidente [intʃi'dɛnte] *sm* (*episodio*) incident; (*infortunio*) accident; (*disputa*) argument.

incidenza [intʃi'dɛntsa] *sf* incidence.

***incidere*[1]** [in'tʃidere] *v* cut (into); carve; (*intagliare*) engrave; (*ad acquaforte*) etch; (*registrare*) record; (*med*) incise, lance. **incisione** *sf* incision; cut; engraving; etching; recording. **incisivo** *agg* incisive. **per inciso** by the way, incidentally. **incisore** *sm* engraver.

***incidere*[2]** [in'tʃidere] *v* **incidere su** affect.

incinta [in'tʃinta] *agg* pregnant.

incipriare [intʃi'prjare] *v* powder.

incitare [intʃi'tare] *v* incite. **incitamento** *sm* incitement, spur.

incivile [intʃi'vile] *agg* uncivilized; (*villano*) boorish, uncivil.

incivilire [intʃivi'lire] *v* civilize.

inclemente [inkle'mɛnte] *agg* harsh.

inclinare [inkli'nare] *v* incline; (*propendere*) tend, be inclined. **inclinazione** *sf* inclination; (*pendenza*) slope; (*disposizione d'animo*) leaning; (*simpatia*) liking; (*strada*) gradient. **incline** *agg* prone.

includere [in'kludere] *v* (*comprendere*) include; (*accludere*) enclose; (*implicare*) imply. **inclusione** *sf* inclusion. **incluso** *agg* included; (*comm*) inclusive.

incoerente [inkoe'rɛnte] *agg* incoherent; (*fig*) inconsistent.

incognita [in'kɔɲita] *sf* (*matematica*) unknown; (*fatto imprevedibile*) unknown factor, uncertainty; (*persona*) mystery, dark horse.

incognito [in'kɔɲito] *agg* unknown. *sm* incognito; (*ignoto*) unknown.

incollare [inkol'lare] *v* (*attaccare*) glue; (*spalmare*) paste.

incolore [inko'lore] *agg* colourless.

incolpare [inkol'pare] *v* blame.

incolto [in'kolto] *agg* (*non coltivato*) uncultivated; (*trascurato*) untidy; (*privo di coltura*) uncultured.

incolume [in'kɔlume] *agg* unharmed.

incombente [inkom'bɛnte] *agg* (*imminente*) impending; (*spettante*) incumbent.

incominciare [inkomin'tʃare] *v* begin, start. **(tanto) per cominciare** to begin with.

incomodo [in'kɔmodo] *agg* (*disagevole*) uncomfortable; (*inopportuno*) inconvenient. *sm* trouble, inconvenience. **il terzo incomodo** the odd man out. **incomodare** *v* inconvenience, trouble.

incomparabile [inkompa'rabile] *agg* incomparable.

incompatibile [inkompa'tibile] *agg* incompatible. **incompatibilità** *sf* incompatibility.

incompetente [inkompe'tɛnte] *agg* incompetent. *s(m+f)* incompetent person.

incompiuto [inkom'pjuto] *agg* unfinished.

incompleto [inkom'pleto] *agg* incomplete.

incomprensibile [inkompren'sibile] *agg* incomprehensible. **incomprensibilità** *sf* incomprehensibility.

incompreso [inkom'prezo] *agg* misunderstood.

inconcepibile [inkontʃe'pibile] *agg* inconceivable.

inconciliabile [inkontʃi'ljabile] *agg* irreconcilable.

inconcludente [inkonklu'dɛnte] *agg* inconclusive.

incondizionato [inkonditsjo'nato] *agg* unconditional; (*pieno*) complete.

inconsapevole [inkonsa'pevole] *agg* unaware, unconscious.

inconscio [in'kɔnʃo] *agg* unconscious; (*persona*) unaware. *sm invar* unconscious.

inconsiderabile [inkonside'rabile] *agg* negligible. **inconsiderato** *agg* thoughtless. **inconsideratezza** *sf* thoughtlessness.

inconsistente [inkonsis'tɛnte] *agg* flimsy; (*infondato*) groundless.

inconsolabile [inkonso'labile] *agg* inconsolable.

inconsueto [inkonsu'ɛto] *agg* unusual.

incontenibile [inkonte'nibile] *agg* uncontrollable.

incontentabile [inkonten'tabile] *agg* hard to please, exacting.

incontrare [inkon'trare] *v* meet; (*esser popolare*) be a success. **incontrar favore** find favour. **incontrarsi per caso** run into.

incontrario [inkon'trarjo] *sm* **all'incontrario** (*a rovescio*) the wrong way round.

incontrastato [inkontras'tato] *agg* unopposed.

incontro¹ [in'kontro] *sm* meeting; (*partita*) match; (*gioco*) game; (*favore*) reception, success. **incontro alla pari** (*sport*) tie, draw.

incontro² [in'kontro] *avv* towards. **all'incontro** on the contrary. **andare incontro a** go towards, approach; (*fig*) meet halfway.

incontrollabile [inkontrol'labile] *agg* uncontrollable.

inconveniente [inkonve'njɛnte] *sm* drawback, snag.

incoraggiare [inkorad'dʒare] *v* encourage.

incorniciare [inkorni'tʃare] *v* frame.

incoronare [inkoro'nare] *v* crown. **incoronazione** *sf* coronation.

incorporare [inkorpo'rare] *v* incorporate; annex.

incorreggibile [inkorred'dʒibile] *agg* incorrigible.

***incorrere** [in'korrere] *v* incur.

incorruttibile [inkorrut'tibile] *agg* incorruptible.

incosciente [inko'ʃɛnte] *agg* unconscious; (*sconsiderato*) irresponsible.

incredibile [inkre'dibile] *agg* incredible, unbelievable.

incredulo [in'krɛdulo] *agg* incredulous, disbelieving.

incremento [inkre'mento] *sm* (*aumento*) increase; (*sviluppo*) growth, expansion; (*mat*) increment. **incrementare** *v* increase; (*far prosperare*) promote.

increspare [inkres'pare] *v* (*acqua*) ripple; (*capelli*) curl. **increspare la fronte** frown.

incrinare [inkri'nare] *v* crack.

incrociare [inkro'tʃare] *v* cross. **incrociatore** *sm* cruiser. **incrocio** *sm* crossing; (*accoppiamento*) cross-breeding; (*frutto*) cross, hybrid.

incrostato [inkros'tato] *agg* encrusted.

incubatrice [inkuba'tritʃe] *sf* incubator. **incubazione** *sf* incubation.

incubo ['inkubo] *sm* nightmare.

incudine [in'kudine] *sf* anvil.

inculcare [inkul'kare] *v* inculcate.

incuneare [inkune'are] *v* wedge.

incurabile [inku'rabile] *agg* incurable.

incurante [inku'rante] *agg* heedless, unconcerned.

incuriosire [inkurjo'zire] *v* arouse curiosity.

incursione [inkur'sjone] *sf* incursion, raid. **incursione aerea** air-raid.

incustodito [inkusto'dito] *agg* unattended.

indagare [inda'gare] *v* investigate, inquire into. **indagine** *sf* inquiry, investigation; (*scientifica*) research; (*studio*) survey.

indebitamente [indebita'mɛnte] *avv* unduly; (*ingiustamente*) unlawfully.

indebitarsi [indebi'tarsi] *v* run into debt. **indebitato** *agg* indebted.

indebolire [indebo'lire] *v* weaken. **indebolimento** *sm* weakening; (*debolezza*) weakness.

indecente [inde'tʃɛnte] *agg* indecent. **indecenza** *sf* indecency; (*vergogna*) disgrace.

indecifrabile [indetʃi'frabile] *agg* illegible.

indecisione [indetʃi'zjone] *sf* indecision.

indeciso [inde'tʃizo] *agg* undecided; (*non risolto, instabile*) unsettled.

indefesso [inde'fɛsso] *agg* tireless.

indefinibile [indefi'nibile] *agg* indefinable.

indefinito [indefi'nito] *agg* indefinite; (*non risolto*) unsettled.

indegno [in'deɲo] *agg* unworthy. **indegnità** *sf* base action.

indelicato [indeli'kato] *agg* tactless; indiscreet.

indemagliabile [indema'ʎabile] *agg* non-run, ladder-proof.

indenne [in'dɛnne] *agg* unharmed, unscathed.

indennità [indenni'ta] *sf* (*risarcimento*) allowance; (*dir*) indemnity. **indennizzare** *v* compensate. **indennizzo** *sm* compensation.

inderogabile [indero'gabile] *agg* binding, irrevocable.

indescrivibile [indeskri'vibile] *agg* indescribable.

indesiderabile [indezide'rabile] *agg* undesirable.

indeterminabile [indetermi'nabile] *agg* indeterminate, imprecise.

indi ['indi] *avv* (*dopo*) then; (*da quel luogo*) from there. **indi a poco** soon after.

India ['indja] *sf* India. **indiano, -a** *s*, *agg* Indian.

indiavolato [indjavo'lato] *agg* (*molto agitato*) wild; (*eccessivo*) awful; (*indemoniato*) frenzied.

indicare [indi'kare] *v* indicate, show; (*significare*) mean. **indicativo** *agg* indicative. **indicato** *agg* indicated; (*adatto*) suitable.

indicatore [indika'tore] *sm* indicator; (*tec*) gauge; (*stradale*) signpost.

indicazione [indika'tsjone] *sf* indication; (*dato, notizia*) information; (*istruzione per l'uso*) direction.

indice ['inditfe] *sm* index; (*dito*) index finger; (*tec*) pointer.

indietreggiare [indjetred'dʒare] *v* draw back, withdraw.

indietro [in'djɛtro] *avv* (*in arretrato*) in arrears; (*debole*) weak; (*moto*) back(wards).

indifeso [indi'fezo] *agg* undefended; (*fig*) defenceless.

indifferente [indiffe'rɛnte] *agg* indifferent; (*lo stesso*) all the same; (*che non interessa*) unimportant. **indifferenza** *sf* indifference, lack of interest.

indigeno [in'didʒeno] *sm*, *agg* native.

indigesto [indi'dʒɛsto] *agg* indigestible; (*non digerito*) undigested.

indignare [indi'ɲare] *v* fill with indignation.

indimenticabile [indimenti'kabile] *agg* unforgettable.

indipendente [indipen'dɛnte] *agg* independent. **indipendenza** *sf* independence.

*indire [in'dire] *v* announce; (*radunare*) call.

indiretto [indi'rɛtto] *agg* indirect.

indirizzare [indirit'tsare] *v* address; (*rivolgere*) direct. **indirizzo** *sm* address; (*tendenza*) trend; direction.

indisciplinato [indiʃipli'nato] *agg* undisciplined.

indiscreto [indis'krɛto] *agg* indiscreet.

indiscusso [indis'kusso] *agg* beyond dispute, incontrovertible.

indispensabile [indispen'sabile] *agg* indispensable, essential.

indispettire [indispet'tire] *v* irritate.

indisposizione [indispozi'tsjone] *sf* indisposition, slight illness. **indisposto** *agg* indisposed, unwell.

indistinto [indis'tinto] *agg* indistinct. **indistinguibile** *agg* indistinguishable.

indivia [in'divja] *sf* endive.

individuale [individu'ale] *agg* individual.

individuare [individu'are] *v* (*determinare*) locate; (*riconoscere*) single out; (*scoprire*) discover, recognize.

individuo [indi'viduo] *sm* person; (*spreg*) fellow, character.

indivisibile [indivi'zibile] *agg* indivisible. **indiviso** *agg* undivided.

indizio [in'ditsjo] *sm* sign, indication; (*dir*) (circumstantial) evidence.

indole ['indole] *sf* nature, character.

indolenzire [indolen'tsire] *v* make sore, make ache. **indolenzito** *agg* sore, aching.

indomani [indo'mani] *sm* **l'indomani** the following day.

indossare [indos'sare] *v* (*mettersi indosso*) put on; (*portare*) wear. **indossatrice** *sf* model. **indosso** *avv* on.

indotto [in'dotto] *agg* induced.

indovinare [indovi'nare] *v* guess. **indovinato** *agg* (*riuscito*) successful; (*che sta bene*) becoming. **indovinello** *sm* puzzle, riddle. **indovino, -a** *sm*, *sf* fortune-teller.

indù [in'du] *s(m+f)*, *agg* Hindu.

indubbio [in'dubbjo] *agg* certain, unmistakable.

indubitabile [indubi'tabile] *agg* unquestionable. **indubitato** *agg* certain, unquestioned.

indugiare [indu'dʒare] *v* delay; (*soffermarsi*) linger (over). **indugio** *sm* delay.

indulgente [indul'dʒɛnte] *agg* lenient. **indulgenza** *sf* indulgence.

indumento [indu'mento] *sm* garment.

indurire [indu'rire] *v* harden. **indurimento** *sm* hardening.

*indurre [in'durre] *v* induce. **indurre in errore** mislead; (*fig*) lead astray. **indurre in tentazione** lead into temptation.

industria [in'dustrja] *sf* industry; (*attività industriale*) business.

industriale [indus'trjale] *agg* industrial. *sm* industrialist, manufacturer. **industrializzare** *v* industrialize. **industrializzazione** *sf* industrialization.

inebriare [inebri'are] *v* intoxicate.

inedito [in'ɛdito] *agg* unpublished.

ineducato [inedu'kato] *agg* ill-mannered.

ineguale [ine'gwale] *agg* unequal; (*non uniforme*) uneven.

ineluttabile [inelut'tabile] *agg* relentless; (*inevitabile*) unavoidable.

inerente [ine'rɛnte] *agg* (*riferentesi*) concerning; (*implicito*) inherent.

inerme [i'nɛrme] *agg* unarmed; (*senza difesa*) defenceless.

inerpicarsi [inerpi'karsi] *v* scramble up.

inerte [i'nɛrte] *agg* inert. **inerzia** *sf* sluggishness; (*fis*) inertia.

inesatto [ine'zatto] *agg* (*sbagliato*) wrong, incorrect; *imprecise*, inaccurate.

inesistente [inezis'tɛnte] *agg* non-existent.

inesorabile [inezo'rabile] *agg* inexorable.

inesperienza [inesper'jɛntsa] *sf* inexperience.

inesperto [ines'pɛrto] *agg* inexperienced.

inesplicabile [inespli'kabile] *agg* inexplicable.

inespressivo [inespres'sivo] *agg* expressionless.

inesprimibile [inespri'mibile] *agg* indescribable.

inetto [i'nɛtto] *agg* inept, inadequate; (*incapace*) unsuited (to), incapable (of).

inevaso [ine'vazo] *agg* outstanding.

inevitabile [inevi'tabile] *agg* unavoidable.

inezia [i'nɛtsja] *sf* trifle.

infagottare [infagot'tare] *v* bundle up, wrap up.

infallibile [infal'libile] *agg* infallible. **infallibilità** *sf* infallibility.

infame [in'fame] *agg* infamous, vile. **infamia** *sf* infamy, disgrace.

infangare [infan'gare] *v* muddy.

infante [in'fante] *s(m+f)* infant, newborn baby. **infantile** *agg* childlike; (*puerile*) childish, infantile. **asilo infantile** *sm* nursery school. **infanzia** *sf* infancy, childhood.

infarcire [infar'tʃire] *v* stuff.

infarinare [infari'nare] *v* (dip in) flour. **infarinatura** *sf* coating of flour; (*fig*) smattering.

infastidire [infasti'dire] *v* bother, trouble.

infaticabile [infati'kabile] *agg* tireless.

infatti [in'fatti] *cong* in fact, as a matter of fact, indeed.

infatuarsi [infatu'arsi] *v* become infatuated (with); fall (for).

infausto [in'fausto] *agg* inauspicious, unlucky.

infedele [infe'dele] *agg* unfaithful.

infelice [infe'litʃe] *agg* unhappy; (*inopportuno*) unfortunate; (*disgraziato*) wretched, unlucky; (*cattivo*) bad. *s(m+f)* unhappy person, wretch.

inferiore [infe'rjore] *agg* lower; (*di grado più basso*) inferior; (*numeri*) below, less than. **inferiorità** *sf* inferiority.

inferire [infe'rire] *v* (*arrecare*) inflict, cause; (*dedurre*) infer.

infermeria [inferme'ria] *sf* infirmary. **infermiere, -a** *sm, sf* nurse. **infermità** *sf* illness. **infermo** *sm, agg* invalid.

inferno [in'fɛrno] *sm* hell. **infernale** *agg* infernal, hellish.

inferriata [infer'rjata] *sf* grille.

infestare [infes'tare] *v* infest.

infettare [infet'tare] *v* infect; (*fig*) taint. **infettivo** *agg* infectious, catching. **infezione** *sf* infection.

infiacchire [infjak'kire] *v* weaken.

infiammare [am'mare] *v* set on fire; (*eccitare, med*) inflame. **infiammabile** *agg* inflammable. **infiammazione** *sf* inflammation.

infido [in'fido] *agg* untrustworthy.

infierire [infje'rire] *v* rage.

infilare [infi'lare] *v* thread, string; (*introdurre*) insert; (*imboccare*) turn into, take. **infilata** *sf* row, string.

infiltrarsi [infilt'rarsi] *v* infiltrate.

infimo ['infimo] *agg* (the) lowest.

infine [in'fine] *avv* in the end, finally.

infinito [infi'nito] *agg* infinite; (*interminabile*) endless; (*innumerevole*) countless. *sm* infinity; (*gramm*) infinitive. **infinità** *sf* infinity; (*gran numero*) large number, crowd.

infischiarsi [infis'kjarsi] *v* not give a damn.

infisso [in'fisso] *sm* frame.

inflazione [infla'tsjone] *sf* inflation.

inflessibile [infles'sibile] *agg* inflexible. **inflessione** *sf* inflection.

***infliggere** [in'fliddʒere] *v* inflict.

influenza [influ'ɛntsa] *sf* influence; (*med*) influenza, flu. **influenzare** *v* influence.

influire [influ'ire] *v* have an influence. **influire su** affect, influence. **influsso** *sm* influence.

infondato [infon'dato] *agg* groundless, unfounded.

*infondere [in'fondere] *v* instil, inspire.

informare [infor'mare] *v* inform, tell; (*plasmare*) form, shape. **informarsi** *v* inquire, find out. **informazione** *sf* information.

informe [in'forme] *agg* shapeless.

informicolirsi [informiko'lirsi] *v* have pins and needles.

infortunio [infor'tunjo] *sm* accident.

infossato [infos'sato] *agg* hollow.

*inframmettersi [infram'mettersi] *v* interfere.

*infrangere [in'frandʒere] *v* break. **infrangibile** *agg* unbreakable.

infrazione [infra'tsjone] *sf* infringement, breach.

infreddarsi [infred'darsi] *v* catch a cold. **infreddatura** *sf* cold.

infrequente [infre'qwente] *agg* infrequent.

infuori [in'fwori] *avv* **all'infuori di** apart from, except.

infuriare [infu'rjare] *v* rage. **infuriarsi** *v* fly into a temper.

ingannare [ingan'nare] *v* deceive; (*truffare*) cheat; (*essere infedele*) be unfaithful. **inganno** *sm* deceit, deception, trick.

ingarbugliarsi [ingarbu'ʎarsi] *v* get entangled.

ingegnarsi [indʒe'narsi] *v* get by, manage.

ingegnere [indʒe'nere] *sm* engineer. **ingegneria** *sf* engineering.

ingegno [in'dʒeno] *sm* genius, talent. **ingegnoso** *agg* ingenious, clever.

ingenuo [in'dʒenwo] *agg* ingenuous, naive. *sm* naive person. **fare l'ingenuo** feign innocence; pretend not to understand.

ingerirsi [indʒe'rirsi] *v* meddle, interfere.

ingessare [indʒes'sare] *v* put in plaster.

Inghilterra [ingil'terra] *sf* England.

inghiottire [ingjot'tire] *v* swallow.

inginocchiarsi [indʒinok'kjarsi] *v* kneel (down).

ingiuria [in'dʒurja] *sf* offence; insult; (*fig*) damage. **ingiuriare** *v* insult; (*oltraggiare*) offend. **ingiurioso** *agg* insulting, offensive.

ingiusto [in'dʒusto] *agg* unjust; unfair.

inglese [in'gleze] *sm* (*persona*) Englishman; (*lingua*) English. *sf* Englishwoman. *agg* English. **filare all'inglese** take French leave. **zuppa inglese** *sf* trifle.

ingoiare [ingo'jare] *v* gulp (down), swallow (down).

ingolfarsi [ingol'farsi] *v* (*auto*) flood; (*debiti*) be swamped.

ingombrare [ingomb'rare] *v* obstruct, get in the way.

ingombro [in'gombro] *agg* cluttered (with). *sm* obstruction; (*spazio*) space.

ingommare [ingom'mare] *v* stick.

ingordo [in'gordo] *agg* greedy. **ingordigia** *sf* greed.

ingorgarsi [ingor'garsi] *v* be blocked up. **ingorgo** *sm* obstruction; (traffic) jam.

ingranare [ingra'nare] *v* engage; (*fam*) get on. **ingranaggio** *sm* (*mec*) gear; (*fig*) works *pl*, mechanism.

ingrandire [ingran'dire] *v* enlarge, magnify. **ingrandimento** *sm* enlargement.

ingrassare [ingras'sare] *v* fatten, make fat; (*ungere*) grease. **ingrassarsi** *v* put on weight, get fat; (*arricchirsi*) profit.

ingrato [in'grato] *agg* ungrateful; (*sgradevole*) thankless. **ingratitudine** *sf* ingratitude.

ingrediente [ingre'djɛnte] *sm* ingredient.

ingresso [in'grɛsso] *sm* entrance; admission.

ingrossare [ingros'sare] *v* swell.

ingrosso [in'grɔsso] *avv* **all'ingrosso** wholesale.

inguacibile [ingwal'tʃibile] *agg* crease-resistant.

inguaribile [ingwa'ribile] *agg* incurable.

inguine ['ingwine] *sm* groin.

inibire [ini'bire] *v* inhibit, forbid. **inibizione** *sf* inhibition.

iniettare [injet'tare] *v* inject. **iniezione** *sf* injection.

inimicizia [inimi'tʃitsja] *sf* enmity, hostility.

inimitabile [inimi'tabile] *agg* inimitable.

inimmaginabile [inimmadʒi'nabile] *agg* unimaginable.

inintelligibile [ininntelli'dʒibile] *agg* unintelligible.

ininterrotto [ininter'rotto] *agg* uninterrupted, continuous.

iniziale [ini'tsjale] *agg* initial. *sf* initial (letter).

iniziare [ini'tsjare] *v* start, begin; (*avviare*) initiate. **iniziativa** *sf* initiative, enterprise. **inizio** *sm* beginning.

innaffiare [innaf'fjare] *v* water.

innalzare [innal'tsare] *v* raise.

innamorarsi [innamo'rarsi] *v* fall in love (with).

innanzi [in'nantsi] *prep* before. **innanzi tutto** first of all; (*sopratutto*) above all. *avv* (*prima*) before; (*avanti*) on, ahead. **d'ora innanzi** from now on, henceforth.

innato [in'nato] *agg* innate.

innegabile [inne'gabile] *agg* undeniable.

innestare [innes'tare] *v* (*piante*) graft; insert; (*med*) inoculate. **innestare una marcia** (*auto*) put into gear. **innesto** *sm* graft; (*auto*) clutch; (*med*) inoculation.

inno ['inno] *sm* hymn. **inno nazionale** national anthem.

innocente [inno'tʃɛnte] *agg* innocent. **dichiararsi innocente** (*dir*) plead not guilty. **innocenza** *sf* innocence.

innocuo [in'nɔkuo] *agg* innocuous, harmless.

innominabile [innomi'nabile] *agg* unmentionable.

innovare [inno'vare] *v* innovate. **innovatore, -trice** *sm*, *sf* innovator. **innovazione** *sf* innovation.

innumerevole [innume'revole] *agg* innumerable.

inoculare [inoku'lare] *v* inoculate.

inoffensivo [inoffen'sivo] *agg* inoffensive, harmless.

inoltrare [inol'trare] *v* send on, forward. **inoltrarsi** *v* advance.

inoltre [i'noltre] *avv* besides, furthermore.

inondare [inon'dare] *v* flood. **inondazione** *sf* flood.

inoperoso [inope'rozo] *agg* idle; (*econ*) unemployed.

inopportuno [inoppor'tuno] *agg* untimely; inopportune. **inopportunità** *sf* unsuitability; inappropriateness.

inorridire [inorri'dire] *v* horrify; be horrified.

inospitale [inospi'tale] *agg* inhospitable.

inosservato [inosser'vato] *agg* unobserved.

inossidabile [inossi'dabile] *agg* stainless.

inquadrare [inkwa'drare] *v* (*mettre in cornice*) frame; (*fig*) set; (*mil*) organize. **inquadratura** *sf* (*cine*, *TV*) shot.

inquietare [inkwje'tare] *v* worry. **inquietante** *agg* worrying. **inquieto** *agg* restless; (*preoccupato*) uneasy. **inquietudine** *sf* restlessness, worry.

inquilino [inkwi'lino], **-a** *sm*, *sf* tenant.

inquinare [inkwi'nare] *v* pollute. **inquinamento** *sm* pollution.

insabbiare [insab'biare] *v* (*pratica*) shelve.

insalata [insa'lata] *sf* salad; (*confusione*) muddle. **insalatiera** *sf* salad-bowl.

insalubre [insa'lubre] *agg* unhealthy.

insanabile [insa'nabile] *agg* incurable.

insanguinare [insangwi'nare] *v* stain with blood.

insaputa [insa'puta] *sf* **all'insaputa di** without the knowledge of.

insaziabile [insa'tsjabile] *agg* insatiable.

inscatolare [inskato'lare] *v* tin, can.

inscenare [inʃe'nare] *v* stage.

insegna [in'seɲa] *sf* (*emblema*) insignia *pl*; (*stemma*) coat of arms; motto; (*cartello*) sign.

insegnare [inse'ɲare] *v* teach. **insegnamento** *sm* teaching, education. **insegnante** *s(m+f)* teacher.

inseguire [inse'gwire] *v* pursue, chase. **inseguimento** *sm* pursuit, chase.

insensato [insen'sato] *agg* senseless, foolish.

insensibile [insen'sibile] *agg* (*leggerissimo*) imperceptible, very slight; (*indifferente*) insensitive, unfeeling.

inseparabile [insepa'rabile] *agg* inseparable.

inserire [inse'rire] *v* insert. **inserirsi** *v* introduce oneself, appear. **inserto** *sm* supplement. **inserzione** *sf* insertion; (*pubblicitaria*) advertisement.

inservibile [inser'vibile] *agg* useless.

inserviente [inser'vjɛnte] *s(m+f)* attendant.

insetto [in'sɛtto] *sm* insect. **insetticida** *sm* insecticide.

insicuro [insi'kuro] *agg* insecure.

insidia [in'sidja] *sf* snare, trap; (*pericolo*) danger. **insidioso** *agg* insidious.

insieme [in'sjeme] *avv* together; (*allo stesso tempo*) at the same time. *sm* whole; (*abbigliamento*) outfit.

insigne [in'siɲe] *agg* notable, illustrious.

insignificante [insiɲifi'kante] *agg* insignificant, trivial.

insignire [insi'ɲire] *v* decorate, honour.

insincero [insin'tʃero] *agg* insincere.

insinuare [insinu'are] *v* insinuate, creep. **insinuazione** *sf* insinuation.

insipido [in'sipido] *agg* insipid, tasteless.

*insistere [in'sistere] *v* insist (on). **insistente** *agg* insistent; (*incessante*) persistent, ceaseless. **insistenza** *sf* insistence.

insocievole [inso'tʃevole] *agg* unsociable.

insoddisfatto [insoddis'fatto] *agg* dissatisfied.

insofferente [insoffe'rɛnte] *agg* intolerant, impatient.

insoffribile [insof'fribile] *agg* unbearable.

insolazione [insola'tsjone] *sf* sunstroke.

insolente [inso'lɛnte] *agg* insolent. **insolenza** *sf* insolence.

insolito [in'sɔlito] *agg* unusual, strange.

insolubile [inso'lubile] *agg* insoluble. **insoluto** *agg* unsolved; (*non pagato*) outstanding.

insomma [in'somma] *inter* well! now then! *avv* (*in conclusione*) in short, in other words.

insonnia [in'sonnja] *sf* insomnia, sleeplessness. **insonne** *agg* sleepless; (*fig*) indefatigable.

insopportabile [insoppor'tabile] *agg* unbearable, intolerable.

*****insorgere** [in'sordʒere] *v* rebel, rise (up against); protest.

insormontabile [insormon'tabile] *agg* insurmountable.

insospettato [insospet'tato] *agg* unexpected, unsuspected.

insostenibile [insoste'nibile] *agg* (*non difensibile*) untenable; (*non sopportabile*) unbearable.

insostituibile [insostitu'ibile] *agg* irreplaceable.

insperato [inspe'rato] *agg* undreamt of, unexpected.

inspiegabile [inspje'gabile] *agg* inexplicable.

installare [instal'lare] *v* install, establish. **installarsi** *v* settle (down). **installazione** *sf* installation.

insù [in'su] *avv* up.

insubordinato [insubordi'nato] *agg* insubordinate.

insuccesso [insut'tʃesso] *sm* failure.

insudiciare [insudi'tʃare] *v* soil, dirty.

insufficiente [insuffi'tʃɛnte] *agg* insufficient, inadequate. **insufficienza** *sf* insufficiency; (*mancanza*) shortage.

insulina [insu'lina] *sf* insulin.

insultare [insul'tare] *v* insult. **insulto** *sm* insult, abuse; (*accesso*) fit.

insuperabile [insupe'rabile] *agg* insuperable, insurmountable; (*imbattibile*) unbeatable.

insurrezione [insurre'tsjone] *sf* insurrection.

insussistente [insussis'tɛnte] *agg* nonexistent, baseless.

intaccare [intak'kare] *v* attack; (*far tacche*) notch, nick; (*consumare*) eat into.

intagliare [inta'ʎare] *v* carve, cut.

intangibile [intan'dʒibile] *agg* intangible.

intanto [in'tanto] *avv* meanwhile, in the meantime; (*fam: invece*) but, whereas, while.

intasare [inta'zare] *v* clog, block. **intasamento** *sm* obstruction, blockage.

intascare [intas'kare] *v* pocket.

intatto [in'tatto] *agg* intact.

intavolare [intavo'lare] *v* (*iniziare*) begin.

integrale [integ'rale] *agg* complete, total. **calcolo integrale** *sm* integral calculus. **pane integrale** *sm* wholemeal bread.

integrare [integ'rare] *v* integrate.

integro ['integro] *agg* complete; (*onesto*) upright. **integrità** *sf* integrity.

intelletto [intel'letto] *sm* intellect. **intellettuale** $s(m+f)$, *agg* intellectual.

intelligente [intelli'dʒɛnte] *agg* intelligent. **intelligenza** *sf* intelligence. **intelligibile** *agg* intelligible.

intemperie [intem'pɛrje] *sf pl* bad weather *sing*.

intempestivo [intempes'tivo] *agg* untimely. **intempestività** *sf* untimeliness.

intendente [inten'dɛnte] *sm* superintendent, administrator. **intendenza** *sf* administration.

*****intendere** [in'tɛndere] *v* (*udire*) hear; (*comprendere*) understand; (*aver intenzione, volere*) intend; (*significare*) mean. **intendersi** *v* (*andar d'accordo*) agree, get on; (*essere competente*) be knowledgeable (about). **s'intende** of course, it goes without saying.

intenditore [intendi'tore], **-trice** *sm, sf* connoisseur, good judge.

intenso [in'tɛnso] *agg* intense. **intensificare** *v* intensify. **intensità** *sf* intensity.

intento [in'tɛnto] *agg* busy. *sm* object, end.

intenzione [inten'tsjone] *sf* intention. **aver l'intenzione di** intend to. **bene/male intenzionato** *agg* well-/ill-disposed.

intercettare [intertʃet'tare] *v* intercept.

*****interdire** [inter'dire] *v* (*proibire*) forbid; (*dir*) disqualify. **interdizione** *sf* ban, disqualification.

interessare [interes'sare] *v* interest; (*riguardare*) concern; (*stare a cuore*) matter. **interessarsi** *v* take an interest (in); (*prendersi cura*) look after, take care (of). **interessato** *agg* interested, concerned;

(*oppportunistico*) self-interested. **interesse** *sm* interest; (*tornaconto*) profit.

interferire [interfe'rire] *v* interfere. **interferenza** *sf* interference.

interiore [inte'rjore] *agg* inner, interior.

intermedio [inter'mɛdjo] *agg* intermediate. **intermediario, -a** *s, agg* intermediary.

interminabile [intermi'nabile] *agg* endless, never-ending.

internare [inter'nare] *v* intern; (*med*) commit. **internamento** *sm* internment; commitment. **internato** *sm* (*convitto*) boarding school; (*scolaro*) boarder.

internazionale [internatsjo'nale] *agg* international.

interno [in'tɛrno] *agg* inner, internal. *sm* inside, interior; (*telefono*) extension.

intero [in'tero] *sm, agg* whole. **per intero** in full.

interpellare [interpel'lare] *v* ask, consult.

interpretare [interpre'tare] *v* interpret, explain; (*teatro, ecc.*) play. **interpretazione** *sf* interpretation. **interprete** *s*(*m+f*) interpreter; (*teatro, ecc.*) actor, performer; (*cantante*) singer.

interrare [inter'rare] *v* inter, bury.

interrogare [interro'gare] *v* interrogate, question; examine, test; consult. **interrogatorio** *sm* examination; questioning. **interrogazione** *sf* interrogation; (*domanda*) question; (*dir*) questioning, examination.

*****interrompere** [inter'rompere] *v* interrupt, break (off).

interruttore [interrut'tore] *sm* switch.

interruzione [interru'tsjone] *sf* interruption, break.

interurbano [interur'bano] *agg* **chiamata** or **telefonata interurbana** *sf* trunk-call.

intervallo [inter'vallo] *sm* interval, break.

*****intervenire** [interve'nire] *v* intervene; (*assistere*) take part, attend; (*med*) operate. **intervento** *sm* intervention; operation.

intervista [inter'vista] *sf* interview. **intervistare** *v* interview. **intervistatore, -trice** *sm, sf* interviewer.

intesa [in'teza] *sf* agreement, understanding; (*pol*) entente. **inteso** *agg* (*volto a un fine*) intended, meant; (*compreso*) understood; (*convenuto*) agreed. **ben inteso** understood.

intestare [intes'tare] *v* head; (*mettere a nome di*) make out to. **intestatario, -a** *sm, sf* holder.

intestino [intes'tino] *sm* intestine.

intimare [inti'mare] *v* order; (*dichiarare*) declare.

intimidire [intimi'dire] *v* intimidate.

intimità [intimi'ta] *sf* intimacy; (*ambiente intimo, fig*) privacy.

intimo ['intimo] *agg* intimate; (*interno*) innermost. *sm* (*amico*) close friend; (*anima*) heart of hearts. **biancheria intima** *sf* underwear.

intimorire [intimo'rire] *v* intimidate, frighten.

*****intingere** [in'tindʒere] *v* dip.

intingolo [in'tingolo] *sm* (*piatto*) stew; (*salsa*) sauce, gravy.

intirizzire [intirit'tsire] *v* grow numb. **intirizzito** *agg* numb.

intitolare [intito'lare] *v* entitle; dedicate.

intollerabile [intolle'rabile] *agg* intolerable, unbearable.

intollerante [intolle'rante] *agg* intolerant.

intonaco [in'tɔnako] *sm* plaster. **intonacare** *v* plaster, whitewash.

intonare [into'nare] *v* (*accordare*) tune, (*cominciare a cantare*) intone, strike up; (*armonizzare*) match.

intontire [inton'tire] *v* daze.

intorno [in'torno] *avv* around; (*circa*) about; (*argomento*) on, about.

intorpidire [intorpi'dire] *v* grow numb.

intossicante [intossi'kante] *agg* poisoning. **intossicazione** *sf* poisoning.

intraducibile [intradu'tʃibile] *agg* untranslatable.

intralciare [intral'tʃare] *v* hold up, hinder. **intralcio** *sm* hindrance, obstacle.

intransigente [intransi'dʒɛnte] *agg* intransigent.

intransitivo [intransi'tivo] *agg* intransitive.

*****intraprendere** [intra'prɛndere] *v* undertake, take on, begin. **intraprendente** *agg* enterprising. **intraprendenza** *sf* enterprise, initiative.

intrattabile [intrat'tabile] *agg* intractable; (*fam*) impossible, difficult.

*****intrattenere** [intratte'nere] *v* entertain. **intrattenersi** *v* linger; (*indugiare su*) dwell (on).

*****intravedere** [intrave'dere] *v* catch a glimpse (of); (*intuire*) sense.

intreccio [in'trettʃo] *sm* plaiting; (*trama*) plot. **intrecciare** *v* intertwine; (*capelli*) braid.

intrepido [in'trepido] *agg* intrepid, brave.

intrigo [in'trigo] *sm, pl* **-ghi** plot, intrigue.

intrigare *v* plot, intrigue.

intrinseco [in'trinseko] *agg* intrinsic.

intriso [in'trizo] *agg* soaked.

*****introdurre** [intro'durre] *v* introduce; (*inserire*) insert; (*far entrare*) show in.

introdotto *agg* (*conosciuto*) well-known, well-established; (*esperto*) well up in.

introduzione *sf* introduction.

introito [in'trɔito] *sm* income; (*incasso*) takings *pl*.

*****intromettersi** [intro'mettersi] *v* meddle, intervene.

intronare [intro'nare] *v* deafen.

introspettivo [introspet'tivo] *agg* introspective.

introvabile [intro'vabile] *agg* unobtainable, not to be found.

introverso [intro'vɛrso], **-a** *s, agg* introvert.

intrusione [intru'zjone] *sf* intrusion.

intruso, -a *sm, sf* intruder.

intuitivo [intui'tivo] *agg* intuitive. **intuire** *v* sense. **intuito** *sm* intuition, instinct, insight.

inumano [inu'mano] *agg* inhuman.

inumidire [inumi'dire] *v* moisten.

inusitato [inuzi'tato] *agg* uncommon.

inutile [i'nutile] *agg* useless; (*non necessario*) unnecessary.

invadente [inva'dɛnte] *agg* intrusive. *s(m+f)* busybody.

*****invadere** [in'vadere] *v* invade, flood.

invalido [in'valido], **-a** *agg* invalid; (*privo di valore*) null and void; (*mutilato*) disabled. *sm, sf* invalid; disabled person.

invalidare *v* (*dir*) invalidate.

invano [in'vano] *avv* in vain. *agg* vain, useless.

invariabile [inva'rjabile] *agg* invariable, even. **invariato** *agg* unchanged.

invasione [inva'zjone] *sf* invasion.

invecchiare [invek'kjare] *v* age. **invecchiamento** *sm* ageing.

invece [in'vetʃe] *avv* instead (of); (*mentre*) whereas, while.

invendibile [inven'dibile] *agg* unsaleable. **invenduto** *agg* unsold.

inventare [inven'tare] *v* invent. **inventore** *sm* inventor. **invenzione** *sf* invention.

inventario [inven'tarjo] *sm* inventory.

inverno [in'vɛrno] *sm* winter. **invernale** *agg* winter, wintry.

inverosimile [invero'simile] *agg* unlikely.

inverso [in'vɛrso] *agg* contrary, opposite; (*mat*) inverse. *sm* contrary, opposite.

inversione *sf* inversion; (*tec*) reversal.

invertebrato [inverte'brato] *sm, agg* invertebrate.

investigare [investi'gare] *v* investigate.

investire [inves'tire] *v* (*comm*) invest; (*scontrare*) collide, hit; (*scontrare persone*) hit, run down. **investimento** *sm* investment; collision, crash.

invetriata [invetri'ata] *sf* (*porta*) glass-door; (*finestra*) window.

invettiva [invet'tiva] *sf* invective.

inviare [invi'are] *v* dispatch, send (off). **inviato, -a** *sm, sf* (*diplomatico*) envoy; (*giornale*) correspondent. **invio** *sm* dispatch.

invidiare [invi'djare] *v* envy. **invidia** *sf* envy. **invidioso** *agg* envious.

invigorire [invigo'rire] *v* invigorate, strengthen.

invincibile [invin'tʃibile] *agg* invincible.

invisibile [invi'zibile] *agg* invisible.

invitare [invi'tare] *v* invite. **invitato, -a** *sm, sf* guest. **invito** *sm* invitation.

invocare [invo'kare] *v* invoke, call for.

invogliare [invo'ʎare] *v* tempt.

*****involgere** [in'vɔldʒere] *v* wrap (up).

involontario [involon'tarjo] *agg* involuntary.

involtino [invol'tino] *sm* (*gastr*) roulade, olive.

involto [in'vɔlto] *sm* bundle, package.

involucro [in'vɔlukro] *sm* covering, wrapper.

invulnerabile [invulne'rabile] *agg* invulnerable.

inzaccherare [indzakke'rare] *v* spatter with mud.

inzuppare [indzup'pare] *v* soak.

io ['io] *pron* I. *sm* self.

iodio ['jɔdjo] *sm* iodine.

ione ['jone] *sm* ion.

iperbole [i'pɛrbole] *sf* hyperbole. **iperbolico** *agg* exaggerated; (*mat*) hyperbolic.

ipertensione [iperten'sjone] *sf* hypertension. **iperteso** *agg* hypertensive.

ipnosi [ip'nɔzi] *sf* hypnosis. **ipnotico** *agg* hypnotic. **ipnotismo** *sm* hypnotism.

ipnotizzare [ipnotid'dzare] *v* hypnotize. **ipnotizzatore, -trice** *sm, sf* hypnotist.

ipocondriaco [ipokon'driako], **-a** *s, agg* hypochondriac. **ipocondria** *sf* hypochondria.

ipocrita [i'pɔkrita] *s(m+f)* hypocrite. *agg* hypocritical. **ipocrisia** *sf* hypocrisy.

ipoteca [ipo'tɛka] *sf* mortgage. **ipotecare** *v* mortgage.

ipotenusa [ipote'nuza] *sf* hypotenuse.

ipotesi [i'pɔtezi] *sf* hypothesis (*pl* -ses). **nella migliore delle ipotesi** at best. **nella peggiore delle ipotesi** if the worst comes to the worst. **ipotetico** *agg* hypothetical.

ippica ['ippika] *sf* horse-racing. **ippico** *agg* horse.

ippocampo [ippo'kampo] *sm* sea-horse.

ippocastano [ippokas'tano] *sm* horse-chestnut.

ippodromo [ip'pɔdromo] *sm* racecourse.

ippopotamo [ippo'pɔtamo] *sm* hippopotamus.

ira ['ira] *sf* rage, anger. **irascibile** *agg* irascible.

iride ['iride] *sf* iris; (*arcobaleno*) rainbow.

Irlanda [ir'landa] *sf* Ireland. **irlandese** *sm, agg* Irish. **gli irlandesi** the Irish.

ironia [iro'nia] *sf* irony. **ironico** *agg* ironic(al).

irradiare [irra'djare] *v* radiate; (*fig*) irradiate.

irraggiungibile [irraddʒun'dʒibile] *agg* unattainable.

irragionevole [irradʒo'nevole] *agg* unreasonable.

irrazionale [irratsjo'nale] *agg* irrational.

irreale [irre'ale] *agg* unreal.

irregolare [irrego'lare] *agg* irregular. **irregolarità** *sf* irregularity.

irreperibile [irrepe'ribile] *agg* that cannot be found.

irrequieto [irre'kwjeto] *agg* restless.

irresistibile [irrezis'tibile] *agg* irresistible.

irresoluto [irrezo'luto] *agg* wavering, undecided. **irresolutezza** *sf* indecision, wavering.

irresponsabile [irrespon'sabile] *agg* irresponsible. **irresponsabilità** *sf* irresponsibility.

irrigare [irri'gare] *v* irrigate. **irrigazione** *sf* irrigation.

irrigidire [irridʒi'dire] *v* stiffen. **irrigidimento** *sm* stiffening; (*fig*) obstinacy.

irrimediabile [irrime'djabile] *agg* irreparable.

irrisorio [irri'zɔrjo] *agg* derisory, ridiculous.

irritare [irri'tare] *v* irritate; (*dar fastidio*) annoy. **irritabile** *agg* irritable. **irritante** *agg* irritating; (*med*) irritant. **irritazione** *sf* irritation.

irriverenza [irrive'rentsa] *sf* disrespect.

***irrompere** [ir'rompere] *v* burst into; (*riversarsi*) pour into.

irsuto [ir'suto] *agg* shaggy, hairy.

irto ['irto] *agg* bristling (with).

***iscrivere** [is'krivere] *v* enrol, register; (*diventar socio*) join. **iscritto** *sm* member. **iscrizione** *sf* registration, enrolment; (*scritta*) inscription.

Islanda [is'landa] *sf* Iceland. **islandese** *sm, agg* Icelandic; *s(m+f)* Icelander.

isola ['izola] *sf* island.

isolare [izo'lare] *v* isolate; (*fis*) insulate. **isolamento** *sm* isolation; insulation.

ispettore [ispet'tore], **-trice** *sm, sf* inspector.

ispezionare [ispetsjo'nare] *v* inspect. **ispezione** *sf* inspection.

ispirare [ispi'rare] *v* inspire.

issare [is'sare] *v* hoist.

istamina [ista'mina] *sf* histamine.

istante [is'tante] *sm* instant, moment. **istantanea** *sf* snapshot. **istantaneo** *agg* instantaneous.

istanza [is'tantsa] *sf* (*domanda*) application, petition.

isterico [is'teriko] *agg* hysterical. **attacco isterico** *sm* hysterics *pl*. **isteria** *sf* hysteria.

istigare [isti'gare] *v* instigate.

istillare [istil'lare] *v* instil.

istinto [is'tinto] *sm* instinct.

istituire [istitu'ire] *v* institute, establish.

istituto [isti'tuto] *sm* institute; (*ente*) institution, organization. **istituzione** *sf* institution.

istrice ['istritʃe] *sm* porcupine; (*persona scontrosa*) touchy person.

***istruire** [istru'ire] *v* instruct, educate. **istruire un processo** (*dir*) prepare a case. **istruttore, -trice** *sm, sf* instructor, -tress, teacher. **giudice istruttore** *sm* examining magistrate. **istruttoria** *sf* (*dir*) examination. **istruttorio** *agg* preliminary. **istruzione** *sf* instruction, education, tuition.

Italia [i'talja] *sf* Italy. **italiano, -a** *s, agg* Italian.

itinerario [itine'rarjo] *sm* itinerary, route.

itterizia [itte'ritsja] *sf* jaundice.

Iugoslavia [jugo'slavja] *sf* Yugoslavia. **iugoslavo, -a** *s, agg* Yugoslav.

iuta ['juta] *sf* jute.

L

la¹ [la] *art* the.

la² [la] *pron* (*cosa, animale*) it; (*persona*) her; (*formula di cortesia*) you.

là [la] *avv* there. **di là** (*nell'altra stanza*) in the other room; (*da quella parte*) that way. **in là** (*oltre*) further. **va là!** come off it!

labbro ['labbro] *sm, pl* -a *f in anat sense* lip; (*orlo*) brim.

labirinto [labi'rinto] *sm* labyrinth, maze.

laboratorio [labora'tɔrjo] *sm* laboratory; (*industria*) workshop.

laborioso [labo'rjozo] *agg* laborious.

laburista [labu'rista] *agg* Labour.

lacca ['lakka] *sf* lacquer.

laccio ['lattʃo] *sm* noose; (*trappola*) snare, trap; (*legame*) tie. **laccio da scarpe** shoe-lace.

lacerare [latʃe'rare] *v* lacerate, tear.

lacrima ['lakrima] *sf* tear.

lacrimogeno [lakri'mɔdʒeno] *agg* **gas lacrimogeno** *sm* tear-gas.

lacuna [la'kuna] *sf* gap.

ladro ['ladro] *sm* thief. **al ladro!** stop thief! **vestito come un ladro** dressed like a tramp.

laggiù [lad'dʒu] *avv* down there.

lagnarsi [la'ɲarsi] *v* complain. **lagna** *sf* bore.

lago ['lago] *sm* lake.

laico ['laiko] *agg* lay. *sm* layman.

lama¹ ['lama] *sf* blade. **lametta** *sf* razor-blade.

lama² ['lama] *sm invar* (*zool*) llama.

lambiccarsi [lambik'karsi] *v* **lambiccarsi il cervello** rack one's brains.

lambire [lam'bire] *v* lick, lap.

lamentare [lamen'tare] *v* lament. **lamentarsi (di)** complain (about). **lamentela** *sf* complaint. **lamentevole** *agg* pitiful. **lamento** *sm* lament. **lamentoso** *agg* plaintive.

lamiera [la'mjɛra] *sf* sheet.

lamina ['lamina] *sf* thin layer; (*metallo*) foil. **laminare** *v* (*ridurre in lamine*) roll; (*coprire con lamine*) laminate. **laminato** *sm* laminate. **laminatoio** *sm* rolling-mill.

lampada ['lampada] *sf* lamp. **lampadario** *sm* chandelier. **lampadina** *sf* (light) bulb. **lampadina tascabile** torch.

lampeggiare [lamped'dʒare] *v* flash.

lampione [lam'pjone] *sm* lamp-post.

lampo ['lampo] *sm* flash; (*temporale*) lightning. **cerniera lampo** *sf* zip.

lampone [lam'pone] *sm* raspberry.

lampreda [lam'prɛda] *sf* lamprey.

lana ['lana] *sf* wool. **di lana** woollen. **industria laniera** *sf* wool industry. **lanificio** *sm* woollen mill.

lancetta [lan'tʃetta] *sf* hand.

lancia¹ ['lantʃa] *sf* (*arma*) lance.

lancia² ['lantʃa] *sf* (*barca*) launch. **lancia di salvataggio** lifeboat.

lanciare [lan'tʃare] *v* throw, fling; (*diffondere*) launch; (*bombe*) drop. **lanciafiamme** *sm invar* flame-thrower. **lanciamissili** *sm invar* rocket-launcher. **lanciare un grido** utter a cry. **lancio** *sm* throw, fling; launching.

languire [lan'gwire] *v* languish; (*diminuire di forza*) flag. **languido** *agg* languid.

lanterna [lan'tɛrna] *sf* lantern.

lanugine [la'nudʒine] *sf* down.

lapide ['lapide] *sf* (*sepolcrale*) tombstone; (*commemorativa*) memorial tablet.

lapis ['lapis] *sm* pencil.

lardo ['lardo] *sm* lard, dripping.

largo ['largo] *agg* wide, broad. **al largo di** away from, off. **far largo a** make room for. **larghezza** *sf* width, breadth; (*fig*) generosity.

larice ['laritʃe] *sm* larch.

laringe [la'rindʒe] *sf* larynx. **laringite** *sf* laryngitis.

larva ['larva] *sf* larva; (*spettro*) shadow.

lasciare [la'ʃare] *v* leave; (*permettere*) let. **lascito** *sm* legacy.

lascivo [la'ʃivo] *agg* lascivious.

laser ['lazer] *sm invar* laser.

lassativo [lassa'tivo] *sm, agg* laxative.

lasso ['lasso] *sm* (*periodo*) lapse. *agg* (*rilassato*) loose.

lassù [las'su] *avv* up there.

lastra ['lastra] *sf* plate; sheet.

lastricare [lastri'kare] *v* pave. **lastrico** *sm* pavement; (*miseria*) poverty.

latente [la'tɛnte] *agg* latent.

laterale [late'rale] *agg* lateral, side.

laterizi [late'ritsi] *sm pl* bricks *pl*, tiles *pl*.

latice [la'titʃe] *sm* latex.

latino [la'tino] *sm, agg* Latin.

latitante [lati'tante] *agg* fugitive. **rendersi latitante** abscond.

latitudine [lati'tudine] *sf* latitude.

lato¹ ['lato] *sm* side. **da un lato ... dall'altro ...** on the one hand ... on the other .... **d'altro lato** on the other hand.
lato² ['lato] *agg* **in senso lato** in a broad sense.
latrare [la'trare] *v* bark.
latrina [la'trina] *sf* latrine.
latta ['latta] *sf* (*lamiera*) tin, tinplate; (*recipiente*) tin, can.
lattaio [lat'tajo] *sm* milkman.
latte ['latte] *sm* milk. **latte magro** skimmed milk. **latteo** *agg* milky. **latteria** *sf* dairy. **lattiera** *sf* milk jug.
lattuga [lat'tuga] *sf* lettuce.
laurea ['laurea] *sf* degree. **laurearsi** *v* graduate. **laureato, -a** *sm, sf* graduate. **essere laureato in ...** have a degree in ....
lauro ['lauro] *sm* laurel.
lauto ['lauto] *agg* generous, sumptuous.
lava ['lava] *sf* lava.
lavabo [la'vabo] *sm* wash-basin.
lavaggio [la'vaddʒo] *sm* washing. **lavaggio a secco** dry-cleaning. **lavaggio del cervello** brain-washing.
lavagna [la'vaɲa] *sf* slate; (*scolastica*) blackboard.
lavanda¹ [la'vanda] *sf* (*bot*) lavender.
lavanda² [la'vanda] *sf* wash(ing).
lavandaia [lavan'daja] *sf* laundress, washer-woman.
lavanderia [lavande'ria] *sf* laundry; (*a gettoni*) launderette.
lavandino [lavan'dino] *sm* sink.
lavapiatti [lava'pjatti] *sm* also **lavastoviglie** *invar* dishwasher.
lavatrice [lava'tritʃe] *sf* washing machine.
lavare [la'vare] *v* wash. **lavare a secco** *v* dry-clean. **lavare il capo a** tell off. **lavarsi** *v* (have a) wash. **lavata di capo** *sf* telling-off. **lavatura** *sf* washing; (*acqua sporca*) dishwater.
lavativo [lava'tivo] *sm* (*fam*) bore, pain in the neck.
lavorare [lavo'rare] *v* work; (*con fatica*) labour; (*aziende, negozi, ecc.*) do business; (*il terreno*) till; (*teatro, ecc.*) act, play. **lavorativo** *agg* working. **lavorato** *agg* finished; (*metallo*) wrought; (*a macchina*) machined.
lavoratore [lavora'tore], **-trice** *sm, sf* worker. **lavoratore a cottimo** piece-worker.
lavorazione [lavora'tsjone] *sf* manufacture; (*fattura*) workmanship; work. **lavorazione in serie** mass-production.

lavoro [la'voro] *sm* work; (*occupazione*) job; (*teatro, ecc.*) play. **lavori di casa** *sm pl* housework *sing*. **lavoro a cottimo** *sm* piece-work. **lavoro straordinario** *sm* overtime.
lazzarone [laddza'rone] *sm* scoundrel.
le¹ [le] *art* the.
le² [le] *pron* (*persona*) (to) her; (*cosa, animale*) (to) it; (*formula di cortesia*) (to) you; (*pl*) them.
leale [le'ale] *agg* sincere; (*onesto*) fair. **lealtà** *sf* loyalty, fairness.
lebbroso [leb'brozo], **-a** *agg* leprous. *sm, sf* leper. **lebbra** *sf* leprosy.
leccare [lek'kare] *v* lick. **leccalecca** *sm invar* (*fam*) lollipop. **leccapiedi** *sm invar* (*fam*) bootlicker. **leccare i piedi a** lick the boots of. **leccornia** *sf* titbit, tasty morsel.
lecito ['letʃito] *agg* (*dir*) lawful; (*permesso*) allowed.
lega ['lega] *sf* league, alliance; (*metalli*) alloy.
legale [le'gale] *agg* legal; (*legittimo*) lawful. **medicina legale** *sf* forensic medicine. **numero legale** *sm* quorum. **ora legale** *sf* summer-time. **legalizzare** *v* legalize, certify.
legame [le'game] *sm* tie, bond; (*fig*) link; (*amoroso*) liaison.
legare [le'gare] *v* tie (up), bind; (*assicurare*) fasten. **matto da legare** crazy, mad as a hatter.
legato [le'gato] *agg* tied (up); (*libro*) bound; (*impacciato*) stiff. *sm* (*papale*) legate; (*testamento*) legacy.
legatura [lega'tura] *sf* binding.
legge ['leddʒe] *sf* law; (*votata dal parlamento*) act (of parliament); (*norma di condotta*) rule. **progetto di legge** *sm* bill. **proposta di legge** *sf* draft bill.
leggenda [led'dʒɛnda] *sf* legend; (*didascalia*) caption. **leggendario** *agg* legendary.
*leggere ['leddʒere] *v* read.
leggero· [led'dʒɛro] *agg* light; (*lieve*) slight. **leggerezza** *sf* lightness; (*frivolezza*) levity; (*sconsideratezza*) thoughtlessness.
leggiadro [led'dʒadro] *agg* graceful, lovely.
leggibile [led'dʒibile] *agg* readable, legible.
leggio [led'dʒio] *sm* music stand; (*chiesa*) lectern.

legione [le'dʒone] *sf* legion.
legislazione [ledʒizla'tsjone] *sf* legislation.
legislatore *sm* legislator.
legittimo [le'dʒittimo] *agg* lawful; (*tale per legge*) legitimate; proper; justifiable.
legna [le'ɲa] *sf invar* firewood. **mettere legna al fuoco** add fuel to the fire.
legname [le'ɲame] *sm* timber; (*in tronchi*) logs *pl*.
legnata [le'ɲata] *sf* blow. **un sacco di legnate** *sm* (*fam*) a good hiding.
legno ['leɲo] *sm* wood. **di legno** wooden, wood. **lavoro in legno** *sm* woodwork; (*edilizia*) timberwork. **legno compensato** plywood. **legno impiallacciato** veneer.
lei ['lɛi] *pron* (*soggetto*) she; (*oggetto*) her; (*formula di cortesia*) you.
lembo ['lembo] *sm* (*orlo*) edge, border; (*striscia*) strip.
lemme lemme ['lɛmme 'lɛmme] *avv* (*fam*) very leisurely.
lena ['lena] *sf* vigour. **lavorare di buona lena** (*fam*) put one's back into it.
lente ['lɛnte] *sf* lens. **lente a contatto** contact lens. **lente d'ingrandimento** magnifying glass. **lenti** *sf pl* glasses *pl*.
lenticchia [len'tikkja] *sf* lentil.
lentiggine [len'tiddʒine] *sf* freckle. **lentigginoso** *agg* freckled.
lento ['lɛnto] *agg* slow; (*allentato*) loose. **lento a capire** slow in the uptake.
lenza ['lɛntsa] *sf* (fishing-)line.
lenzuolo [len'tswɔlo] *sm, pl* -**a** *f when referring to a pair* sheet.
leone [le'one] *sm* lion. **leonessa** *sf* lioness.
leopardo [leo'pardo] *sm* leopard.
lepido ['lepido] *agg* witty.
lepre ['lepre] *sf* hare. **lepre in salmì** jugged hare. **labbro leporino** *sm* hare-lip.
lesbico ['lɛzbiko] *agg* lesbian. **lesbica** *sf* lesbian.
lesina ['lezina] *sf* awl; (*taccagneria*) (*fam*) meanness. **lesinare** *v* skimp.
lesione [le'zjone] *sf* injury; (*med*) lesion; (*danno*) damage. **parte lesa** *sf* injured party.
lessare [les'sare] *v* boil. **lesso** *sm* boiled meat.
lessico ['lɛssiko] *sm* lexicon; vocabulary.
lesto ['lɛsto] *agg* swift, quick. **lesto di lingua** glib. **lesto di mano** light-fingered. **lestofante** *sm* swindler.
letale [le'tale] *agg* lethal, deadly.
letame [le'tame] *sm* manure, dung; (*fig*)

filth. **letamaio** *sm* dung-heap; (*luogo sudicio*) pigsty.
letargico [le'tardʒiko] *agg* lethargic.
letargo *sm* (*zool*) hibernation; (*med, torpore*) lethargy.
letizia [le'titsja] *sf* joy, gladness.
lettera ['lettera] *sf* letter. **alla lettera** literally; verbatim. **lettera d'accompagnamento/raccomandata** covering/registered letter. **lettera di sollecitazione** reminder. **lettera maiuscola/minuscola** capital/small letter.
letterario [lette'rarjo] *agg* literary.
letteratura [lettera'tura] *sf* literature.
lettiga [let'tiga] *sf* litter; (*barella*) stretcher.
letto ['letto] *sm* bed.
lettore [let'tore], -**trice** *sm, sf* reader; (*universitario*) modern language lecturer.
lettura [let'tura] *sf* reading.
leucemia [leutʃe'mia] *sf* leukaemia.
leva¹ ['lɛva] *sf* (*mec*) lever; (*fig*) incentive. **far leva** lever. **far leva su** exploit, play on.
leva² ['lɛva] *sf* call-up; conscripts *pl*.
levante [le'vante] *sm* east.
levare [le'vare] *v* (*alzare*) raise, lift; (*togliere*) take away *or* off; (*estrarre*) pull out. **levare di mezzo** get rid of, remove. **levarsi** *v* (*alzarsi*) rise; (*dal letto*) get up. **levarsi la fame** satisfy one's hunger. **levarsi la sete** quench one's thirst. **levata della posta** *sf* mail collection. **levata del sole** *sf* sunrise.
levatoio [leva'tojo] *agg* **ponte levatoio** *sm* drawbridge.
levatrice [leva'tritʃe] *sf* midwife.
levigare [levi'gare] *v* smooth; polish; (*pomiciare*) rub down; (*con carta vetrata*) sand down.
levriere [le'vrjere] *sm* greyhound.
lezione [le'tsjone] *sf* lesson; class; (*durata*) period; (*universitaria*) lecture.
lezioso [le'tsjozo] *agg* affected, mannered.
lezzo ['lettso] *sm* stench; (*sudiciume*) filth.
li [li] *pron* them.
lì [li] *avv* there. **giù di lì** thereabouts. **lì per lì** (*sul momento*) there and then; (*dapprima*) at first.
libbra ['libbra] *sf* pound.
libellula [li'bellula] *sf* dragonfly.
liberale [libe'rale] *s(m+f)*, *agg* liberal.
liberare [libe'rare] *v* free, liberate; (*salvare*) save, rescue. **liberazione** *sf* liberation; release.

libero ['libero] *agg* free; (*sgombro*) clear; exempt. **aria libera** *sf* open air. **libero pensatore** *sm* freethinker. **tempo libero** *sm* time off.

libertà [liber'ta] *sf* freedom, liberty. **giorno di libertà** *sm* day off. **libertà condizionata** probation. **libertà provvisoria** bail. **mettere in libertà** set free.

Libra ['libra] *sf* Libra.

libraio [li'brajo] *sm* bookseller. **libreria** *sf* (*negozio*) bookshop; (*raccolta di libri*) library; (*casa editrice*) publishers *pl*.

libro ['libro] *sm* book. **a libro** hinged. **libro di cassa** cash register. **libro giallo** thriller. **libro mastro** ledger. **libro nero** blacklist.

licenza [li'tʃɛntsa] *sf* licence, permission; (*scuola*) leaving certificate.

licenziare [litʃen'tsjare] *v* dismiss. **licenziamento** *sm* dismissal.

liceo [li'tʃɛo] *sm* secondary school, high school.

lichene [li'kɛne] *sm* lichen.

lido ['lido] *sm* shore.

lieto ['ljɛto] *agg* glad, happy.

lieve ['ljɛve] *agg* slight, light.

lievito ['ljɛvito] *sm* yeast; (*fig*) ferment.

lignaggio [li'ɲaddʒo] *sm* lineage, pedigree.

ligustro [li'gustro] *sm* privet.

lilla ['lilla] *agg, sm invar* lilac.

lima ['lima] *sf* file. **limare** *v* file. **limatura** *sf* filing; (*polvere*) filings *pl*.

limitare [limi'tare] *v* limit, restrict. **limitazione** *sf* limitation, restraint.

limite ['limite] *sm* limit; (*confine*) boundary. **caso limite** *sm* borderline case. **limitrofo** *agg* bordering.

limo ['limo] *sm* mud, slime.

limone [li'mone] *sm* (*albero*) lemon-tree; (*frutto*) lemon. **limonata** *sf* lemonade.

limpido ['limpido] *agg* clear.

lince ['lintʃe] *sf* lynx.

linciare [lin'tʃare] *v* lynch. **linciaggio** *sm* lynching.

lindo ['lindo] *agg* clean, tidy.

linea ['linea] *sf* line; (*corpo umano*) figure. **lineetta** *sf* dash.

lineamenti [linea'menti] *sm pl* features *pl*; (*elementi essenziali*) outlines *pl*.

lineare [line'are] *agg* linear; coherent; (*di indirizzo stabile*) unswerving.

linfa ['linfa] *sf* lymph; (*bot*) sap.

lingua ['lingwa] *sf* tongue; (*linguaggio*) language. **linguaggio** *sm* language.

linguista *s(m+f)* linguist. **linguistico** *agg* linguistic.

lino ['lino] *sm* (*pianta*) flax; (*tessuto*) linen. **olio di lino** *sm* linseed oil.

liocorno [lio'korno] *sm* unicorn.

liquefare [likwe'fare] *v* liquefy, melt. **liquefazione** *sf* liquefaction.

liquidare [likwi'dare] *v* liquidate; (*conti*) settle; (*merci*) sell off; (*sciogliere*) wind up. **liquidazione** *sf* liquidation, settlement; (*svendita*) clearance sale; winding-up; (*indennità*) leaving bonus. **liquidatore** *sm* receiver.

liquido ['likwido] *sm, agg* liquid, fluid.

liquirizia [likwi'ritsja] *sf* liquorice.

liquore [li'kwore] *sm* liqueur.

lira¹ ['lira] *sf* (*moneta*) lira. **lira sterlina** pound sterling.

lira² ['lira] *sf* (*musica*) lyre.

lirico ['liriko] *agg* lyrical; opera. **cantante lirico** *s(m+f)* opera singer. **dramma lirico** *sm* opera. **teatro lirico** *sm* opera house. **lirica** *sf* lyric poetry.

lisca ['liska] *sf* fish-bone.

lisciare [li'ʃare] *v* smooth. **liscio** *agg* smooth; (*bevanda*) neat. **andar liscio** go smoothly. **passarla liscia** get off scot-free.

liseuse [li'zøz] *sf, pl* -s bed-jacket.

liso ['lizo] *agg* worn.

lista ['lista] *sf* (*striscia*) strip; (*elenco*) list. **lista elettorale** electoral register. **listare** *v* border. **listino** *sm* list.

litania [lita'nia] *sf* litany.

lite ['lite] *sf* quarrel; (*dir*) (law)suit.

litigare [liti'gare] *v* quarrel. **litigio** *sm* quarrel, row. **litigioso** *agg* quarrelsome; (*dir*) contentious.

litorale [lito'rale] *agg* coastal. *sm* shore.

litro ['litro] *sm* litre.

liturgia [litur'dʒia] *sf* liturgy. **liturgico** *agg* liturgical.

liuto [li'uto] *sm* lute.

livellare [livel'lare] *v* level. **livella** *sf* level. **livellatore, -trice** *sm, sf* leveller.

livello [li'vello] *sm* level. **livello del mare** sea-level. **passaggio a livello** *sm* level crossing.

livido ['livido] *agg* livid. *sm* bruise.

Livorno [li'vorno] *sf* Leghorn.

livrea [li'vrɛa] *sf* livery.

lizza ['littsa] *sf* **entrare in lizza** compete.

lo¹ [lo] *art* the.

lo² [lo] *pron* (*persona*) him; (*cosa, animale*) it.

lobo ['lɔbo] *sm* lobe.
locale¹ [lo'kale] *agg* local.
locale² [lo'kale] *sm* room, spot. **locale notturno** night-club. **località** *sf* locality.
localizzare [lokalid'dzare] *v* (*individuare*) locate; (*circoscrivere*) localize.
locanda [lo'kanda] *sf* inn. **locandiere, -a** *sm, sf* innkeeper.
locatario [loka'tarjo] *sm* tenant.
locatore [loka'tore] *sm* landlord.
locazione [loka'tsjone] *sf* lease, tenancy.
locomotiva [lokomo'tiva] *sf* locomotive, engine.
lodare [lo'dare] *v* praise. **lode** *sf* praise. **lodevole** *agg* praiseworthy.
logaritmo [loga'ritmo] *sm* logarithm.
loggia ['lɔddʒa] *sf* loggia; (*massone*) lodge. **loggione** *sm* gallery.
logica ['lɔdʒika] *sf* logic. **logico** *agg* logical.
logistica [lo'dʒistika] *sf* logistics. **logistico** *agg* logistic(al).
logorare [logo'rare] *v* wear out. **logoramento** *sm* wear; (*mentale*) strain. **logorio** *sm* wear and tear. **logoro** *agg* worn out.
Londra ['londra] *sf* London. **londinese** *s(m+f)* Londoner.
longevo [lon'dʒɛvo] *agg* long-lived. **longevità** *sf* longevity.
longitudine [londʒi'tudine] *sf* longitude. **longitudinale** *agg* longitudinal.
lontano [lon'tano] *agg* far, far away; (*assente*) absent; distant; vague. *avv* far. **lontananza** *sf* distance.
lontra ['lontra] *sf* otter.
loquace [lo'kwatʃe] *agg* loquacious.
lordo ['lordo] *agg* (*peso*) gross; (*sporco*) filthy.
loro ['loro] *pron* (*soggetto*) they; (*oggetto*) them; (*formula di cortesia*) you; (*di essi*) theirs. *agg* their.
losco ['losko] *agg* sinister.
loto ['lɔto] *sm* lotus.
lotta ['lɔtta] *sf* struggle, fight; (*sport*) wrestling. **lottare** *v* struggle, fight; wrestle.
lotteria [lotte'ria] *sf* lottery.
lotto ['lɔtto] *sm* portion; (*comm*) lot; lottery.
lozione [lo'tsjone] *sf* lotion.
lubrificante [lubrifi'kante] *agg* lubricating. *sm* lubricant. **lubrificare** *v* lubricate. **lubrificazione** *sf* lubrication.
lucchetto [luk'ketto] *sm* padlock.

luccicare [luttʃi'kare] *v* shine, sparkle.
luccio ['luttʃo] *sm* pike.
lucciola ['luttʃola] *sf* firefly.
luce ['lutʃe] *sf* light.
lucernario [lutʃer'narjo] *sm* skylight.
lucertola [lu'tʃertola] *sf* lizard.
lucidare [lutʃi'dare] *v* polish.
lucido ['lutʃido] *agg* shiny, glossy; (*fig*) lucid. *sm* polish.
luglio ['luʎo] *sm* July.
lugubre ['lugubre] *agg* lugubrious.
lui ['lui] *pron* (*soggetto*) he; (*oggetto*) him.
lumaca [lu'maka] *sf* snail; (*persona*) slowcoach.
lume ['lume] *sm* light; lamp. **far lume su** throw light on.
luminoso [lumi'nozo] *agg* bright, shining.
luna ['luna] *sf* moon. **avere la luna** be in a bad mood. **luna di miele** honeymoon. **luna-park** *sm invar* fun-fair. **lunare** *agg* lunar. **sbarcare il lunario** make ends meet.
lunedì [lune'di] *sm* Monday.
lungo¹ ['lungo] *agg* long; (*alto*) tall; (*lento*) slow; (*diluito*) weak. **alla lunga** in the long run. **a lungo** (for) long. **di gran lunga** by far. **lunghezza** *sf* length.
lungo² ['lungo] *prep* along. **lungomare** *sm* seashore.
luogo ['lwɔgo] *sm* place. **aver luogo** take place. **fuori luogo** out of place. **in luogo di** instead of. **luogotenente** *sm* lieutenant.
lupo ['lupo] *sm* wolf. **lupa** *sf* she-wolf.
luppolo ['luppolo] *sm* hop.
lurido ['lurido] *agg* filthy.
lusingare [luzin'gare] *v* flatter; (*illudere*) delude. **lusinga** *sf* flattery; delusion. **lusinghiero** *agg* flattering, alluring.
Lussemburgo [lussem'burgo] *sm* Luxembourg.
lusso ['lusso] *sm* luxury. **di lusso** luxury, de luxe. **lussuoso** *agg* luxurious.
lustrare [lus'trare] *v* polish. **lustrino** *sm* sequin. **lustro** *sm* polish, sheen; lustre.
lutto ['lutto] *sm* mourning; (*dolore*) grief.

M

ma [ma] *cong* but. **macché!** *inter* (*neanche per sogno*) of course not! not on your life! **ma davvero?** really? **ma no!** of course not! **ma sì!** of course!

macabro ['makabro] *agg* macabre.

maccheroni [makke'roni] *sm pl* macaroni *sing.*

macchia¹ ['makkja] *sf* spot; stain.

macchia² ['makkja] *sf* (*arbusti*) bush.

macchiare [mak'kjare] *v* stain. **caffè macchiato** *sm* coffee with a dash of milk.

macchietta [mak'kjetta] *sf* (*persona*) character.

macchina ['makkina] *sf* machine; (*automobile*) car. **macchina da scrivere** typewriter. **macchina fotografica** camera.

macchinare [makki'nare] *v* plot.

macchinario [makki'narjo] *sm* machinery.

macchinista [makki'nista] *s(m+f)* machinist; (*ferr*) engine driver.

macedonia [matʃe'dɔnja] *sf* fruit salad.

macellare [matʃel'lare] *v* slaughter. **macelleria** *sf* butcher's shop. **macellaio** *sm* butcher. **macello** *sm* slaughterhouse; (*fig*) shambles.

macerare [matʃe'rare] *v* soak; macerate.

macerie [ma'tʃɛrje] *sf pl* ruins *pl.*

macina ['matʃina] *sf* millstone, grindstone. **macinare** *v* grind. **macinino** *sm* (*da caffè*) coffee-mill; (*da pepe*) pepper-mill.

madido ['madido] *agg* soaking wet.

Madonna [ma'dɔnna] *sf* **la Madonna** the Virgin Mary.

madornale [mador'nale] *agg* gross.

madre ['madre] *sf* mother; (*comm*) counterfoil. **madreperla** *sf* mother-of-pearl.

madrigale [madri'gale] *sm* madrigal.

maestà [mae'sta] *sf* majesty. **maestoso** *agg* majestic; imposing.

maestro [ma'ɛstro] *sm* master; teacher. *agg* principal, main. **colpo maestro** *sm* master-stroke. **maestra** *sf* mistress; teacher. **maestranze** *sf pl* work force *sing.*

mafia ['mafja] *sf* mafia. **mafioso, -a** *sm, sf* member of the Mafia.

magagna [ma'gaɲa] *sf* flaw, fault.

magari [ma'gari] *inter* most certainly! (*oh se . . .*) if only . . . . *avv* (*forse*) perhaps; (*perfino*) even.

magazzino [magad'dzino] *sm* store, warehouse. **magazzinaggio** *sm* warehousing. **magazziniere** *sm* warehouseman.

maggio ['maddʒo] *sm* May.

maggiorana [maddʒo'rana] *sf* marjoram.

maggioranza [maddʒo'rantsa] *sf* majority.

maggiore [mad'dʒore] *s(m+f)*, *agg* major; (*più grande*) greater, larger; (*più vecchio*) older; (*di due fratelli*) elder; (*superlativo*) greatest, oldest, eldest. *sm* major. **andare per la maggiore** be a hit.

maggiorenne [maddʒo'rɛnne] *agg* of age. *s(m+f)* major.

maggiormente [maddʒor'mɛnte] *avv* (all the) more; (*di più*) most.

magia [ma'dʒia] *sf* magic. **magico** *agg* magic(al).

magistero [madʒis'tɛro] *sm* teaching (profession). **scuola di magistero** *sf* college of education. **magistrale** *agg* (*di maestro*) magisterial; (*da maestro*) masterly.

magistrato [madʒis'trato] *sm* magistrate.

maglia ['maʎa] *sf* stitch; (*rete*) mesh; (*indumento intimo*) vest; T-shirt; (*maglione*) jersey. **fare la maglia** knit. **lavoro a maglia** *sm* knitting. **maglieria** *sf* knitwear. **maglione** *sm* jersey, pullover.

magnanimo [ma'ɲanimo] *agg* magnanimous.

magnete [ma'ɲɛte] *sm* (*auto*) magneto; (*calamita*) magnet. **magnetismo** *sm* magnetism.

magnetofono [maɲe'tɔfono] *sm* taperecorder.

magnifico [ma'ɲifiko] *agg* magnificent, splendid. **magnificenza** *sf* magnificence.

magnolia [ma'ɲɔlja] *sf* magnolia.

mago ['mago] *sm* (*stregone*) sorcerer; (*illusionista*) magician.

magro ['magro] *agg* thin; (*fig*) meagre; (*povero di grasso*) lean. **magra** *sf* (*fiume*) low level; (*fig*) shortage.

mai ['mai] *avv* never, ever. **caso** *or* **se mai** in case, if ever. **come mai** how (on earth).

maiale [ma'jale] *sm* pig; (*carne*) pork.

maionese [majo'neze] *sf* mayonnaise.

mais ['mais] *sm* maize.

maiuscolo [ma'juskolo] *agg* capital. **maiuscola** *sf* capital (letter).

malaccorto [malak'kɔrto] *agg* ill-advised.

malafede [mala'fede] *sf* bad faith.

malandato [malan'dato] *agg* in bad condition.

malanno [ma'lanno] *sm* misfortune, trouble.

malapena [mala'pena] *sf* **a malapena** scarcely.

malaria [ma'larja] *sf* malaria.

malato [ma'lato], **-a** *agg* sick, ill. *sm, sf* sick person, patient. **malattia** *sf* illness, disease.

malavita [mala'vita] *sf* underworld.

malavoglia [mala'voʎa] *sf* reluctance.

malavveduto [malavve'duto] *agg* unwise.
malconcio [mal'kontʃo] *agg* shabby.
malcontento [malkon'tɛnto] *agg* dissatisfied. *sm* dissatisfaction.
maldestro [mal'dɛstro] *agg* awkward.
maldicente [maldi'tʃɛnte] *agg* slanderous.
male ['male] *avv* (*non bene*) badly; (*in
modo non buono*) ill; (*in modo imperfetto*)
not well; (*indisposto*) unwell. **sentirsi
male** feel unwell *or* ill. *sm* evil; (*dolore*)
pain. **andare a n..ale** go bad. **di male in
peggio** from bad to worse. **far male** hurt.
mal di denti toothache. **mal di gola** sore
throat. **mal di mare** sea-sickness. **mal di
testa** headache.
***maledire** [male'dire] *v* curse, damn.
maledizione *sf* curse.
maleducato [maledu'kato] *agg* ill-mannered, rude.
malefico [ma'lɛfiko] *agg* harmful.
malerba [ma'lɛrba] *sf* weed.
malessere [ma'lɛssere] *sm* malaise.
malevolo [ma'lɛvolo] *agg* hostile.
malfamato [malfa'mato] *agg* ill-famed.
malfatto [mal'fatto] *agg* badly made.
malfattore [malfat'tore] *sm* evil-doer.
malfermo [mal'fermo] *agg* unsteady.
malfido [mal'fido] *agg* unreliable.
malgrado [mal'grado] *prep* notwithstanding, in spite of.
malia [ma'lia] *sf* charm. **maliardo** *agg*
bewitching.
maligno [ma'liɲo] *agg* spiteful; (*med*)
malignant.
malinconia [malinko'nia] *sf* melancholy,
gloom. **malinconico** *agg* gloomy, dismal.
malincuore [malin'kwɔre] *avv* **a
malincuore** reluctantly, half-heartedly.
malinteso [malin'tezo] *agg* misunderstood, mistaken. *sm* misunderstanding.
malizia [ma'litsja] *sf* cunning, malice.
malizioso *agg* malicious, cunning.
mallevadore [malleva'dore] *sm* guarantor,
surety.
malmenare [malme'nare] *v* manhandle.
malnutrito [malnu'trito] *agg* undernourished.
malora [ma'lora] *sf* ruin. **andare in malora**
(*fam*) go to the dogs. **va in malora!** (*al
diavolo*) go to hell!
malsano [mal'sano] *agg* unhealthy.
malsicuro [malsi'kuro] *agg* unsafe.
malta ['malta] *sf* mortar.
maltempo [mal'tempo] *sm* bad weather.
malto ['malto] *sm* malt.

maltrattare [maltrat'tare] *v* ill-treat. **maltrattamento** *sm* ill-treatment.
malumore [malu'more] *sm* bad temper.
malva ['malva] *sm invar* (*colore*) mauve. *sf*
(*bot*) mallow.
malvagio [mal'vadʒo] *agg* wicked.
malversare [malver'sare] *v* embezzle.
malversatore, -trice *sm, sf* embezzler.
malversazione *sf* embezzlement.
malvisto [mal'visto] *agg* unpopular.
malvivente [malvi'vɛnte] *sm* crook.
malvolentieri [malvolen'tjɛri] *avv* reluctantly.
mamma ['mamma] *sf* mother, mum(my).
mamma mia! good gracious!
mammella [mam'mɛlla] *sf* breast.
mammifero [mam'mifero] *sm* mammal.
mammola ['mammola] *sf* violet.
manata [ma'nata] *sf* handful.
mancare [man'kare] *v* (*aver difetto*) lack;
(*essere assente*) be missing; (*fallire, sentire la mancanza*) miss. **ci mancherebbe
altro!** that would be the limit! **mancare
alla parola** not keep one's word. **sentirsi
mancare** feel faint.
mancia ['mantʃa] *sf* tip. **dar la mancia** tip.
mancino [man'tʃino] **-a** *sm, sf* left-hand-
er. *agg* left-handed, left. **colpo mancino**
sm underhand trick.
mandare [man'dare] *v* send. **mandare a
fondo** sink. **mandare avanti** run. **mandar
giù** (*cibo*) swallow. **mandar via** dismiss.
mandarino¹ [manda'rino] *sm* (*cinese*)
mandarin.
mandarino² [manda'rino] *sm* (*albero*)
mandarin tree; (*frutto*) mandarin, tangerine.
mandato [man'dato] *sm* commission;
(*pol*) mandate; (*dir*) warrant.
mandibola [man'dibola] *sf* jaw.
mandolino [mando'lino] *sm* mandolin.
mandorla ['mandorla] *sf* almond.
mandorlo *sm* almond-tree.
mandria ['mandrja] *sf* herd, flock.
mandrino [man'drino] *sm* (*tec*) spindle,
mandrel.
maneggiare [maned'dʒare] *v* handle.
maneggio *sm* handling; (*addestramento
cavalli*) riding-school; (*intrigo*) plot.
manette [ma'nette] *sf pl* handcuffs *pl*.
mangano ['mangano] *sm* mangle.
mangereccio [mandʒe'rɛttʃo] *agg* edible.
mangiare [man'dʒare] *v* eat; (*corrodere*)
eat into; (*dissipare*) squander; (*carte,
scacchi, ecc.*) take. **dar da mangiare a**

feed. **far da mangiare** prepare a meal.
mangiare la foglia smell a rat. **mangiarsi
il fegato** fret. *sm* food.
mangiatoia [mandʒa'toja] *sf* manger.
mangime [man'dʒime] *sm* fodder.
maniaco [ma'niako], **-a** *agg* maniacal. *sm*,
sf maniac. **mania** *sf* mania.
manica ['manika] *sf* sleeve. **senza maniche**
sleeveless.
manichino [mani'kino] *sm* mannequin,
(tailor's) dummy.
manico ['maniko] *sm* handle; (*violino*,
ecc.) neck.
manicomio [mani'kɔmjo] *sm* lunatic asylum.
maniera [ma'njɛra] *sf* manner.
manifattura [manifat'tura] *sf* manufacture.
manifestare [manifes'tare] *v* show;
express; (*pol*) demonstrate. **manifestazione** *sf* display, show; expression; demonstration.
manifesto¹ [mani'festo] *sm* poster, bill;
(*pol*) manifesto. **manifestino** *sm* leaflet.
manifesto² [mani'festo] *agg* clear, manifest.
maniglia [ma'niʎa] *sf* handle.
manipolare [manipo'lare] *v* manipulate.
mano ['mano] *sf*, *pl* **-i** hand; (*strato*) coat.
alla mano ready, to hand. **a portata di
mano** within reach. **dar** *or* **stringere la
mano a** shake hands with. **di
prima/seconda mano** first-/second-hand.
far man bassa make a clean sweep. **fuori
mano** outlying, off the beaten track. **man
mano che** as. **mettere le mani avanti** take
precautions. **sotto mano** handy.
manodopera [mano'dɔpera] *sf invar*
labour, workforce.
*****manomettere** [mano'mettere] *v* tamper
with, violate.
manopola [ma'nɔpola] *sf* (*manubrio*)
hand-grip; (*guanto*) mitten; (*radio*, *ecc.*)
knob.
manoscritto [mano'skritto] *sm* manuscript. *agg* handwritten.
manovale [mano'vale] *sm* labourer.
manovella [mano'vɛlla] *sf* handle, crank.
manovrare [manov'rare] *v* handle,
manoeuvre. **manovra** *sf* manoeuvre.
mansione [man'sjone] *sf* function, duty.
mansueto [mansu'eto] *agg* gentle, meek.
mantello [man'tɛllo] *sm* coat, cloak.
*****mantenere** [mante'nere] *v* maintain,
keep. **mantenimento** *sm* maintenance.

mantice ['mantitʃe] *sm* bellows *pl.*
manto ['manto] *sm* cloak, mantle.
manuale [manu'ale] *agg*, *sm* manual.
manubrio [ma'nubrjo] *sm* handlebar.
manutenzione [manuten'tsjone] *sf* maintenance, upkeep; (*auto*) servicing.
manzo ['mandzo] *sm* (*animale*) steer;
(*carne*) beef.
mappa ['mappa] *sf* map. **mappamondo** *sm*
globe.
maratona [mara'tona] *sf* marathon.
marca ['marka] *sf* brand.
marcare [mar'kare] *v* mark; (*sport*) score;
accentuate.
marchese [mar'keze] *sm* marquis. **marchesa** *sf* marchioness.
marchio ['markjo] *sm* mark; (*comm*)
trade-mark. **marchio depositato** registered trade-mark.
marcia¹ ['martʃa] *sf* march; (*auto*) gear;
(*sport*) walking. **fare marcia indietro**
reverse; (*fig*) back out. **mettere in marcia**
get going, set off.
marcia² ['martʃa] *sf* (*materia*) pus.
marciapiede [martʃa'pjɛde] *sm* pavement.
marciare [mar'tʃare] *v* march; (*sport*)
walk; (*fam*: *funzionare*) work.
marcio ['martʃo] *agg* rotten; (*fig*) corrupt.
sm rottenness; rotten part.
marcire [mar'tʃire] *v* rot, go bad. **marciume** *sm* rot.
marco¹ ['marko] *sm* mark.
mare ['mare] *sm* sea; (*grande quantità*)
host. **alto mare** high sea. **essere in alto
mare** (*fig*) be floundering, be at sea. **mare
agitato** *or* **mosso** rough sea. **maretta** *sf*
choppy sea.
marea [ma'rɛa] *sf* tide.
maresciallo [mare'ʃallo] *sm* (*sottufficiale*)
sergeant major; (*ufficiale*) field-marshal.
margarina [marga'rina] *sf* margarine.
margherita [marge'rita] *sf* daisy.
margine ['mardʒine] *sm* edge, border;
(*fig*) margin.
marina [ma'rina] *sf* navy. **marinaio** *sm*
sailor.
marinare [mari'nare] *v* marinate.
marinare la scuola play truant.
marionetta [marjo'netta] *sf* puppet.
maritare [mari'tare] *v* marry; (*mescolare*)
mix. **maritarsi** *v* get married.
marito [ma'rito] *sm* husband.
marittimo [ma'rittimo] *agg* sea; maritime.

marmaglia [mar'maʎa] *sf* rabble.
marmellata [marmel'lata] *sf* jam; (*di agrumi*) marmalade.
marmo ['marmo] *sm* marble.
marra ['marra] *sf* hoe.
marrone [mar'rone] *sm* chestnut. *agg* brown.
marsupiale [marsu'pjale] *sm, agg* marsupial.
martedì [marte'di] *sm* Tuesday.
martellare [martel'lare] *v* hammer; (*fig*) pound. **martellata** *sf* hammer-blow; (*fig*) heavy blow. **martello** *sm* hammer; (*porta*) knocker; (*orologio*) striker.
martinetto [marti'netto] *sm* jack.
martin pescatore [mar'tin peska'tore] *sm* kingfisher.
martire ['martire] *s(m+f)* martyr. **martirio** *sm* martyrdom. **martoriare** *v* torture.
marxismo [mar'ksizmo] *sm* Marxism. **marxista** *s(m+f), agg* Marxist.
marzapane [martsa'pane] *sm* marzipan.
marziale [mar'tsjale] *agg* martial.
marzo ['martso] *sm* march.
mascalzone [maskal'tsone] *sm* rascal, scoundrel. **mascalzonata** *sf* nasty trick.
mascara [mas'kara] *sm* mascara.
mascella [ma'ʃɛlla] *sf* jaw.
maschera ['maskera] *sf* mask; (*travestimento*) disguise; (*cinema, teatro*) usherette. **mascherare** *v* mask; (*con costumi*) dress up; (*celare*) disguise; (*schermare*) screen; (*mimetizzare*) camouflage.
maschile [mas'kile] *agg* male; (*gramm*) masculine; (*per ragazzi*) boys'; (*per uomini*) men's.
maschio ['maskjo] *sm* male; (*ragazzo*) boy.
masochismo [mazo'kizmo] *sm* masochism. **masochista** *s(m+f)* masochist.
massa ['massa] *sf* mass; (*gran numero*) heap, lot; (*elett*) earth.
massacrare [massa'krare] *v* massacre. **massacro** *sm* massacre.
massaggiare [massad'dʒare] *v* massage. **massaggio** *sm* massage.
massaia [mas'saja] *sf* housewife.
masserizie [masse'ritsje] *sf pl* fixtures and fittings *pl*.
massiccio [mas'sittʃo] *agg* solid.
massima ['massima] *sf* maxim; (*norma*) rule. **di massima** general, informal. **in linea di massima** as a general rule, on the whole.
massimo ['massimo] *agg* greatest;

(*estremo*) utmost; (*il più alto*) highest; (*il migliore*) best; (*fis*) maximum. *sm* maximum; (*tutto ciò che*) most; (*meglio*) best.
massone [mas'sone] *sm* freemason. **massoneria** *sf* freemasonry.
masticare [masti'kare] *v* chew; (*borbottare*) mutter. **gomma da masticare** *sf* chewing gum.
mastice ['mastitʃe] *sm* mastic; (*per vetri*) putty.
mastino [mas'tino] *sm* mastiff.
mastro ['mastro] *sm* ledger.
matassa [ma'tassa] *sf* skein, hank.
matematico [mate'matiko], **-a** *agg* mathematical. *sm, sf* mathematician. *sf* mathematics.
materasso [mate'rasso] *sm* mattress. **materassino (pneumatico)** *sm* air-bed.
materia [ma'tɛrja] *sf* matter; substance; (*argomento, disciplina*) subject; (*fam: marcia*) pus. **entrare in materia** broach a subject. **materia prima** raw material.
materiale [mate'rjale] *sm, agg* material. **materialismo** *sm* materialism. **materialista** *s(m+f)* materialist.
materno [ma'tɛrno] *agg* maternal, motherly. **scuola materna** *sf* nursery school.
maternità *sf* motherhood; (*ospedale*) maternity hospital.
matita [ma'tita] *sf* pencil.
matriarcale [matriar'kale] *agg* matriarchal.
matrice [ma'tritʃe] *sf* matrix; (*modulo*) counterfoil.
matricola [ma'trikola] *sf* register; (*numero*) serial number; (*studente*) freshman. **matricolare** *v* register.
matrigna [ma'triɲa] *sf* stepmother.
matrimonio [matri'mɔnjo] *sm* marriage, matrimony; (*festa nuziale*) wedding. **matrimoniale** *agg* matrimonial. **letto matrimoniale** *sm* double bed.
matta ['matta] *sf* (*carte*) joker.
mattatoio [matta'tɔjo] *sm* slaughterhouse.
matterello [matte'rɛllo] *sm* rolling-pin.
mattina [mat'tina] *sf* morning. **mattinata** *sf* morning; (*teatro*) matinée. **mattiniero** *agg* early rising.
matto ['matto] *agg* mad. **andar matto per** be crazy about. **matto da legare** mad as a hatter. **scacco matto** checkmate.
mattone [mat'tone] *sm* brick; (*fam: noioso*) bore. **mattonella** *sf* tile; (*biliardo*) cushion.

mattutino [mattu'tino] *agg* morning.

maturare [matu'rare] *v* mature, ripen; (*med*) come to a head. **maturazione** *sf* ripening. **maturità** *sf* maturity. **esame di maturità** *sm* school-leaving examination, A level(s). **maturo** *agg* ripe; mature.

mausoleo [mauzo'lɛo] *sm* mausoleum.

mazza ['mattsa] *sf* club; (*martello*) sledge-hammer. **mazzata** *sf* heavy blow.

mazzo ['mattso] *sm* bunch; (*carte*) pack. **fare il mazzo** shuffle the cards *or* pack.

me [me] *pron* me. *V* **mi**.

meccanico [mek'kaniko] *agg* mechanical. *sm* mechanic. **meccanica** *sf* mechanics. **meccanismo** *sm* mechanism, works. **meccanizzare** *v* mechanize. **meccanizzazione** *sf* mechanization.

meccanografico [mekkano'grafiko] *agg* data processing.

medaglia [me'daʎa] *sf* medal. **medaglione** *sm* medallion; (*gioiello*) locket.

medesimo [me'dezimo] *agg* same.

media ['mɛdja] *sf* mean, average; (*scuola*) secondary school. **fare la media di** average.

mediana [me'djana] *sf* median. **mediano** *agg* median, medial.

mediante [me'djante] *prep* through, by (means of).

mediatore [medja'tore], **-trice** *sm*, *sf* intermediary; (*comm*) broker. **mediazione** *sf* mediation; brokerage.

medicare [medi'kare] *v* treat; (*ferita*) dress. **medicina** *sf* medicine.

medicinale [meditʃi'nale] *agg* medicinal. *sm* medicine.

medico ['mɛdiko] *sm* doctor, physician. *agg* medical. **medico chirurgo** surgeon. **medico condotto** medical officer. **medico generico** general practitioner.

medievale [medje'vale] *agg* medieval.

medio ['mɛdjo] *agg* middle; average; (*scuola*) secondary. *sm* middle finger.

mediocre [me'djɔkre] *agg* mediocre, poor.

meditare [medi'tare] *v* meditate, ponder. **meditazione** *sf* meditation.

mediterraneo [mediter'raneo] *sm*, *agg* Mediterranean.

medium ['mɛdjum] *s(m+f)* *invar* medium.

medusa [me'duza] *sf* jelly-fish.

megafono [me'gafono] *sm* loudspeaker.

megera [me'dʒɛra] *sf* harridan.

meglio ['mɛʎo] *agg*, *avv* (*comparativo*) better; (*superlativo*) best. *sm* best. **alla meglio** as well as possible. **tanto meglio!** so much the better!

mela ['mela] *sf* apple. **mela cotogna** quince. **melo** *sm* apple-tree.

melagrana [mela'grana] *sf* pomegranate. **melograno** *sm* pomegranate tree.

melanzana [melan'dzana] *sf* aubergine, egg-plant.

melassa [me'lassa] *sf* treacle, molasses.

melma ['melma] *sf* slime.

melodia [melo'dia] *sf* melody. **melodico** *agg* melodious. **melodioso** *agg* melodious, sweet-sounding.

melodramma [melo'dramma] *sm* melodrama.

melone [me'lone] *sm* melon.

membrana [mem'brana] *sf* membrane; (*acustica*) diaphragm.

membro ['membro] *sm*, *pl* **-a** *f* in collective sense member; (*anat*) limb.

memoria [me'mɔrja] *sf* memory; (*oggetto ricordo*) souvenir; (*scritto*) memoir. **a memoria** by heart. **prendere memoria di** make a note of. **memoriale** *sm* memorial; petition; (*raccolta di documenti*) record. **memorizzare** *v* memorize.

menare [me'nare] *v* lead; (*portare*) take, bring; (*assestare*) strike. **a menadito** at one's fingertips.

mendicare [mendi'kare] *v* beg. **mendicante** *s(m+f)* beggar.

meno ['meno] *avv* (*comparativo*) less; (*superlativo*) least; (*mat*) minus. *agg invar* (*minore*) less; (*in minor numero*) fewer. *prep* (*eccetto*) but (for), except (for). **a meno che** unless. **fare a meno di** do without. **meno male!** thank goodness! **o meno** (*o no*) or not. **tanto meno** let alone. **venir meno** (*svenire*) faint; (*mancare*) fail. **venir meno alla parola** break one's word. *sm invar* (the) least. **i meno** *sm pl* (the) minority *sing*.

menomare [meno'mare] *v* diminish; (*danneggiare*) injure, disable. **menomato, -a** *s*, *agg* disabled.

menopausa [meno'pauza] *sf* menopause.

mensa ['mɛnsa] *sf* table; refectory; (*mil*) mess.

mensile [men'sile] *agg* monthly. *sm* (*giornale*) monthly; (*paga*) monthly pay.

mensola ['mɛnsola] *sf* bracket, shelf; (*caminetto*) mantelpiece.

menta ['menta] *sf* mint; (*peperina*) peppermint; (*romana*) spearmint.

mente ['mente] *sf* mind; intellect. **venire in mente** occur; come to mind. **mentale** *agg* mental. **mentalità** *sf* mentality.
mentire [men'tire] *v* lie. **mentito** *agg* false.
mento ['mento] *sm* chin.
mentre ['mentre] *cong* while, as; (*laddove*) whereas.
menu [mə'ny] *sm* menu.
menzionare [mentsjo'nare] *v* mention. **menzione** *sf* mention.
menzogna [men'dzoɲa] *sf* lie. **menzognero** *agg* lying, false.
meraviglia [mera'viʎa] *sf* wonder, marvel; (*stupore*) surprise. **a meraviglia** wonderfully. **meravigliare** *v* surprise, amaze. **meraviglioso** *agg* marvellous, wonderful.
mercante [mer'kante] *sm* merchant, trader. **mercanteggiare** *v* trade, deal; (*contrattare*) haggle, bargain. **mercantile** *agg* mercantile. **nave mercantile** *sf* merchant ship.
mercanzia [merkan'tsia] *sf* merchandise, goods *pl*.
mercato [mer'kato] *sm* market. **a buon mercato** cheap, inexpensive.
merce ['mertʃe] *sf* merchandise, goods *pl*; (*in magazzino*) stock.
mercenario [mertʃe'narjo] *agg, sm* mercenary.
merciaio [mer'tʃajo], **-a** *sm, sf* haberdasher. **merceria** *sf* haberdashery.
mercoledì [mercole'di] *sm* Wednesday.
mercurio [mer'kurjo] *sm* mercury.
merda ['mɛrda] *sf* (*volg*) shit.
merenda [me'rɛnda] *sf* (afternoon) snack, tea.
meridiano [meri'djano] *sf* (*geog*) meridian. *agg* (*di mezzogiorno*) midday. **meridiana** *sf* (*geog*) meridian line; (*orologio solare*) sundial.
meridionale [meridjo'nale] *agg* southern, south. *s(m+f)* southerner. **meridione** *sm* south.
meringa [me'ringa] *sf* meringue.
meritare [meri'tare] *v* deserve, merit. **meritevole** *agg* deserving, worthy.
merito ['mɛrito] *sm* merit. **a pari merito** equal. **in merito a** regarding, as to, about. **per merito di** thanks to.
merletto [mer'letto] *sm* lace.
merlo ['mɛrlo] *sm* blackbird; (*sempliciotto*) fool.
merluzzo [mer'luttso] *sm* cod; (*nasello*) hake.

mero ['mɛro] *agg* mere.
meschino [mes'kino] *agg* wretched, mean.
mescolare [mesko'lare] *v* mix; (*unire*) blend. **mescolatore, -trice** *sm, sf* mixer.
mese ['meze] *sm* month.
messa¹ ['messa] *sf* (*rel*) Mass. **messale** *sm* missal.
messa² ['messa] *sf* (*il mettere*) placing, putting.
messaggio [mes'saddʒo] *sm* message. **messaggero** *sm* messenger; (*fig*) herald.
messo ['messo] *sm* usher.
mestiere [mes'tjɛre] *sm* job, trade; (*manuale*) craft; profession. **di mestiere** by profession. **essere del mestiere** be an expert. **ferri del mestiere** *sm pl* tools of the trade *pl*.
mesto ['mɛsto] *agg* sad, mournful. **mestizia** *sf* sadness.
mestolo ['mestolo], **-a** *sm, sf* ladle, kitchen spoon.
mestruazione [mestrua'tsjone] *sf* menstruation; (*fam*) period. **mestruale** *agg* menstrual.
meta ['mɛta] *sf* goal, aim; destination; (*rugby*) try.
metà [me'ta] *sf* half; (*centro*) middle. **a metà strada** half-way. **fare a metà** halve; (*fam*) go halves.
metabolismo [metabo'lizmo] *sm* metabolism. **metabolico** *agg* metabolic.
metafisico [meta'fiziko], **-a** *agg* metaphysical. *sm, sf* metaphysician. *sf* metaphysics.
metafora [me'tafora] *sf* metaphor, figure of speech. **metaforico** *agg* metaphorical.
metallo [me'tallo] *sm* metal. **metallico** *agg* metallic. **metallurgia** *sf* metallurgy.
metamorfosi [meta'morfozi] *sf* metamorphosis, transformation.
metano [me'tano] *sm* methane.
meteora [me'tɛora] *sf* meteor. **meteorico** *agg* meteoric.
meteorologia [meteorolo'dʒia] *sf* meteorology. **meteorologico** *agg* meteorological, weather. **bollettino meteorologico** *sm* weather report. **previsioni meteorologiche** *sf pl* weather forecast *sing*.
meticcio [me'tittʃo], **-a** *s, agg* half-caste.
meticoloso [metiko'lozo] *agg* meticulous.
metodista [meto'dista] *s(m+f)*, *agg* methodist.
metodo ['mɛtodo] *sm* method. **metodico** *agg* methodical.

metro ['mɛtro] *sm* metre; (*per misurare*) rule; (*a nastro*) tape-measure. **metrico** *agg* (*misura*) metric; (*poesia*) metrical.

metropoli [me'trɔpoli] *sf* metropolis. **metropolitana** *sf* underground (railway).

***mettere** ['mettere] *v* put; place; lay (down); (*indossare*) put on, wear; (*supporre*) suppose. **mettersi sotto** get down to it.

mezzo [meddzo] *agg* half; (*medio*) middle. **mezzogiorno** *sm* noon, midday; (*geog*) south. *sm* half; (*centro*) middle; (*strumento*) means. **a** or **per mezzo di** by, through. **mezzi** *pl* means *pl*. *avv* half; (*quasi*) nearly. **andarci di mezzo** (*avere la peggio*) suffer for it; (*essere in gioco*) be at stake. **togliere di mezzo** get rid of.

mi [mi], **me** *pron* (to) me; (*riflessivo*) myself.

miagolare [mjago'lare] *v* mew, miaow. **miagolio** *sm* mewing.

mica¹ ['mika] *avv* (*fam*) at all.

mica² ['mika] *sf* mica.

miccia ['mittʃa] *sf* fuse.

microbo ['mikrobo] *sm* microbe.

microcosmo [mikro'kɔzmo] *sm* microcosm.

microfilm ['mikrofilm] *sm invar* microfilm.

microfono [mi'krɔfono] *sm* microphone; (*telefono*) mouthpiece.

microscopio [mikro'skɔpjo] *sm* microscope. **microscopico** *agg* microscopic.

microsolco [mikro'sɔlko] *sm* microgroove; (*disco a 33 giri*) LP; (*disco a 45 giri*) EP.

midollo [mi'dollo] *sm* marrow; (*bot*) pith. **bagnato fino al midollo** soaked to the skin. **fino al midollo** to the core. **midollo spinale** spinal cord.

miele ['mjɛle] *sm* honey.

mietere ['mjɛtere] *v* reap, harvest; (*uccidere*) mow down. **mietitore, -trice** *sm, sf* reaper, harvester. **mietitrebbiatrice** *sf* combine harvester. **mietitura** *sf* reaping, harvesting; (*periodo, messe*) harvest.

migliaio [mi'ʎajo] *sm, pl* **-a** *f* thousand; (*circa mille*) about a thousand.

miglio¹ ['miʎo] *sm, pl* **-a** *f* mile.

miglio² ['miʎo] *sm* (*bot*) millet.

migliore [mi'ʎore] *agg* (*comparativo*) better; (*superlativo*) best. *sm* best.

mignolo ['miɲolo] *sm* (*della mano*) little finger; (*del piede*) little toe.

migrare [mi'grare] *v* migrate. **migratorio** *agg* migratory. **migrazione** *sf* migration.

milione [mi'ljone] *sm* million. **milionesimo** *sm, agg* millionth.

militare [mili'tare] *agg* military. *sm* soldier. *v* militate. **militarismo** *sm* militarism. **militarista** *s(m+f)*, *agg* militarist.

milite ['milite] *sm* soldier, warrior. **milizia** *sf* (*corpo armato*) militia.

millantare [millan'tare] *v* boast. **millantato credito** *sm* false pretences *pl*. **millantatore, -trice** *sm, sf* braggart, show-off. **millanteria** *sf* boasting.

mille ['mille] *agg, sm* thousand. **millennio** *sm* millennium. **millesimo** *agg, sm* thousandth.

milligrammo [milli'grammo] *sm* milligram.

millimetro [mil'limetro] *sm* millimetre.

mimetizzare [mimetid'dzare] *v* camouflage. **mimetizzazione** *sf* camouflage.

mimica ['mimika] *sf* mime. **mimico** *agg* mimic. **mimo** *sm* mime; (*uccello*) mocking-bird.

mina ['mina] *sf* mine; (*di matita*) lead. **minare** *v* mine; (*insidiare*) undermine. **minatore** *sm* miner.

minaccia [mi'nattʃa] *sf* threat. **minacciare** *v* threaten. **minaccioso** *agg* threatening.

minareto [mina'reto] *sm* minaret.

minerale [mine'rale] *agg, sm* mineral. **minerario** [mine'rarjo] *agg* mining.

minestra [mi'nɛstra] *sf* soup.

mingherlino [minger'lino] *agg* skinny.

miniatura [minja'tura] *sf* miniature.

miniera [mi'njɛra] *sf* mine.

minimo ['minimo] *agg* (*il più piccolo*) least, smallest, slightest; (*più basso*) minimum; (*piccolissimo*) very small, very slight; (*molto basso*) very low. *sm* minimum; (*la minima cosa*) least.

ministero [mini'stɛro] *sm* (*pol*) ministry. **pubblico ministero** public prosecutor.

ministro [mi'nistro] *sm* minister.

minore [mi'nore] *s(m+f)*, *agg* (*più piccolo*) less, smaller; (*più basso*) lower; (*più giovane*) younger; (*superlativo*) least, lowest, youngest; (*mat, musica*) minor. **minorità** *sf* minority.

minorenne [mino'rɛnne] *s(m+f)* minor. *agg* under age.

minuetto [minu'etto] *sm* minuet.

minuscolo [mi'nuskolo] *agg* small, diminutive. **minuscola** *sf* small letter.

minuta [mi'nuta] *sf* draft.
minuto[1] [mi'nuto] *agg* small, minute; detailed. **al minuto** retail. **vendere al minuto** retail.
minuto[2] [mi'nuto] *sm* (*primo*) minute. **minuto secondo** second. **spaccare il minuto** be dead on time.
mio ['mio], *m pl* **miei** *agg* my. *pron* mine.
miope ['miope] *agg* short-sighted. **miopia** *sf* short-sightedness.
mira ['mira] *sf* aim.
miracolo [mi'rakolo] *sm* miracle. **miracoloso** *agg* miraculous.
miraggio [mi'raddʒo] *sm* mirage.
mirare [mi'rare] *v* aim; (*prendere mira*) take aim. **mirino** *sm* sight; (*foto*) viewfinder.
mirtillo [mir'tillo] *sm* bilberry. **mirtillo rosso** cranberry.
miscela [mi'ʃɛla] *sf* mixture; (*caffè, tè, tabacco*) blend. **miscelare** *v* mix, blend.
mischia ['miskja] *sf* fray.
mischiare [mis'kjare] *v* mix; (*carte*) shuffle.
miscuglio [mis'kuʎo] *sm* mixture.
miseria [mi'zɛrja] *sm* poverty; (*inezia*) pittance; squalor. **miserabile** *agg* miserable, wretched.
misericordia [mizeri'kɔrdja] *sf* mercy. **senza misericordia** merciless; (*spietato*) ruthless.
misero ['mizero] *agg* poor, wretched.
missile ['missile] *sm* missile.
missione [mis'sjone] *sf* mission. **missionario, -a** *s, agg* missionary.
mistero [mis'tɛro] *sm* mystery. **misterioso** *agg* mysterious.
mistico ['mistiko], **-a** *agg* mystical. *sm, sf* mystic. *sf* mysticism. **misticismo** *sm* mysticism.
misto ['misto] *agg* mixed.
misura [mi'zura] *sf* measure; (*taglia, dimensione*) size; (*atto e modo del misurare*) measurement; moderation. **fatto su misura** made to measure. **prendere delle misure** take steps.
misurare [mizu'rare] *v* measure; limit; (*indumenti*) try on. **misurato** *agg* measured, moderate.
mite ['mite] *agg* mild, moderate.
mito ['mito] *sm* myth. **mitico** *agg* mythical. **mitologia** *sf* mythology. **mitologico** *agg* mythological.
mitra[1] ['mitra] *sf* (*rel*) mitre.

mitra[2] ['mitra] *sm invar* tommy-gun.
mitragliatrice [mitraʎa'tritʃe] *sf* machine-gun. **mitragliamento** *sm* machine-gun fire; (*fig*) bombarding. **mitragliare** *v* machine-gun; (*fig*) bombard.
mittente [mit'tɛnte] *s(m+f)* sender.
mobile ['mɔbile] *agg* mobile, moving; movable. **squadra mobile** *sf* flying squad. *sm* piece of furniture. **mobili** *sm pl* furniture *sing*.
mobilia [mo'bilja] *sf* furnishings *pl*; (*mobili*) furniture.
mobiliare [mobi'ljare] *agg* movable. *v* furnish.
mobilitare [mobili'tare] *v* mobilize. **mobilitazione** *sf* mobilization.
mocassino [mokas'sino] *sm* moccasin.
moccolo ['mɔkkolo] *sm* candle-end. **reggere il moccolo** play gooseberry. **tirare dei moccoli** (*fam*) swear.
moda ['mɔda] *sf* fashion. **di** *or* **alla moda** in fashion, fashionable. **fuori moda** out of fashion. **passare di moda** go out of fashion.
modalità [modali'ta] *sf* procedure, formality.
modellare [model'lare] *v* model. **modella** *sf* model. **modello** *sm* model; (*disegno*) pattern.
moderare [mode'rare] *v* moderate, lower; control. **moderatore** *sm* moderator; (*TV, radio*) chairman. **moderazione** *sf* moderation, restraint.
moderno [mo'dɛrno] *agg* modern; (*al passo coi tempi*) up-to-date. **modernizzare** *v* modernize, bring up-to-date.
modestia [mo'dɛstja] *sf* modesty. **modesto** *agg* modest, unassuming; (*umile*) humble.
modificare [modifi'kare] *v* modify, alter. **modifica** *sf* alteration, modification.
modista [mo'dista] *sf* milliner.
modo ['mɔdo] *sm* manner, way; opportunity; (*gramm*) mood. **ad ogni modo** anyhow, in any case. **di modo che** (*affinche*) so that; (*e così*) and so. **in modo da** so that. **in qualche modo** somehow. **modo di dire** expression, idiom. **modo di fare** manner. **per modo di dire** so to speak.
modulare [modu'lare] *v* modulate.
modulo ['mɔdulo] *sm* form; (*mat, tec*) modulus.
mogano ['mɔgano] *sm* mahogany.
mogio ['mɔdʒo] *agg* downhearted.

moglie ['moʎe] *sf* wife.

moina [mo'ina] *sf* **fare moine** coax.

molare [mo'lare] *v* grind. *agg* molar. **pietra molare** *sf* millstone. **mola** *sf* grinding wheel.

mole ['mɔle] *sf* pile, mass; (*grandezza*) size.

molecola [mo'lɛkola] *sf* molecule.

molesto [mo'lɛsto] *agg* troublesome, annoying. **molestare** *v* trouble, annoy. **molestia** *sf* annoyance, nuisance.

molla ['mɔlla] *sf* spring; (*stimolo*) mainspring. **molle** *sf pl* tongs *pl.* **mollare** *v* (*lasciar andare*) let go; (*allentare*) loosen, slacken. **molleggiato** *agg* sprung. **molletta** *sf* (*biancheria*) (clothes-)peg; (*capelli*) hair-pin.

molle ['mɔlle] *agg* soft; (*bagnato*) wet; (*debole*) weak. **mettere in molle** steep.

mollusco [mol'lusko] *sm* mollusc.

molo ['mɔlo] *sm* jetty; (*banchina*) wharf.

molteplice [mol'teplitʃe] *agg* manifold; varied.

moltiplicare [moltipli'kare] *v* multiply.

moltitudine [molti'tudine] *sm* multitude, host.

molto ['molto] *agg* a lot of, lots of, much; (*pl*) many; (*tempo*) long. *avv* much, a lot; (*con agg e avv positivi*) very. *pron.* a lot, much; (*pl*) many.

momento [mo'mento] *sm* moment. **a momenti** (*tra poco*) shortly; (*quasi*) almost. **al momento d'oggi** nowadays. **dal momento che** since.

monaca ['mɔnaka] *sf* nun. **monaco** *sm* monk.

Monaco ['mɔnako] *sf* (*principato*) Monaco; (*di Baviera*) Munich.

monarca [mo'narka] *sm* monarch, king. **monarchia** *sf* monarchy. **monarchico, -a** *sm, sf* monarchist.

monastero [monas'tɛro] *sm* monastery. **monastico** *agg* monastic.

monco ['monko] *agg* maimed. **essere monco di ...** have ... missing. **moncherino** *sm* stump.

mondezzaio [mondet'tsajo] *sm* rubbish heap; (*ambiente sudicio*) pigsty. **mondare** *v* (*sbucciare*) peel; (*togliere erbacce*) weed.

mondo ['mondo] *sm* world. **mandare all'altro mondo** (*fam*) send to hell. **mettere al mondo** give birth to. **vivere nel mondo della luna** have one's head in the clouds. **mondiale** *agg* world; (*diffuso*) world-wide.

monello [mo'nɛllo] *sm* urchin. **monelleria** *sf* prank.

moneta [mo'neta] *sf* coin; (*denaro*) money; (*spicciola*) (small) change. **monetario** *agg* monetary.

monito ['mɔnito] *sm* warning.

monocolore [monoko'lore] *agg* plain; (*pol*) one-party.

monocromo [mo'nɔkromo] *agg, sm* monochrome.

monogamo [mo'nɔgamo], **-a** *agg* monogamous. *sm, sf* monogamist. **monogamia** *sf* monogamy.

monolitico [mono'litiko] *agg* monolithic.

monologo [mo'nɔlogo] *sm, pl* **-ghi** monologue.

monopolio [mono'pɔljo] *sm* monopoly. **monopolizzare** *v* monopolize.

monoteismo [monote'izmo] *sm* monotheism.

monotono [mo'nɔtono] *agg* monotonous. **monotonia** *sf* monotony.

monsone [mon'sone] *sm* monsoon.

monta ['monta] *sf* (*accoppiamento*) mounting; (*luogo*) stud-farm; (*modo di cavalcare*) riding.

montacarichi [monta'kariki] *sm* goods lift.

montaggio [mon'taddʒo] *sm* assembly; (*cinema*) editing.

montagna [mon'taɲa] *sf* mountain. **montagne russe** switchback *sing.*

montare [mon'tare] *v* (*salire*) climb; (*tec*) assemble; (*incorniciare*) mount; (*film*) edit; (*macchina*) get in(to). **montare a cavallo** get on a horse; (*cavalcare*) ride. **montatura** *sf* assembly; (*occhiali*) frame; (*pubblicitaria*) stunt.

monte ['monte] *sm* mountain; (*davanti a nome*) Mount. **a monte** above, upstream. **andare a monte** fall through. **mandare a monte** upset; (*disdire*) cancel. **monte di pietà** pawnshop. **monte premi** jackpot. **montuoso** *agg* mountainous.

montone [mon'tone] *sm* ram; (*carne*) mutton.

monumento [monu'mento] *sm* monument. **monumentale** *agg* monumental.

mora ['mɔra] *sf* (*gelso*) mulberry; (*rovo*) blackberry.

morale [mo'rale] *agg* moral. *sf* (*dottrina*) ethics *pl*; morality, morals *pl*; (*insegnamento*) moral. *sm* morale. **essere su/giù**

di **morale** be cheerful/depressed. **moralizzare** *v* moralize.

morbido ['mɔrbido] *agg* soft.

morbillo [mor'billo] *sm* measles.

morbo ['mɔrbo] *sm* disease. **morboso** *agg* morbid; pathological.

***mordere** ['mɔrdere] *v* bite; (*afferrare*) grip. **mordere il freno** strain at the leash. **mordace** *agg* biting, caustic.

morfina [mor'fina] *sf* morphine.

morigerato [moridʒe'rato] *agg* sober, clean-living.

***morire** [mo'rire] *v* die. **avere una fame/sete da morire** be terribly hungry/thirsty.

mormorare [mormo'rare] *v* murmur. **mormorio** *sm* murmur.

moro[1] ['mɔro] *agg* dark; (*nero*) black; (*carnagione*) swarthy; (*capelli*) brown.

moro[2] ['mɔro] *sm* (*gelso*) mulberry.

morsa ['mɔrsa] *sf* vice. **morsetto** *sm* clamp; (*elett*) terminal.

morsicare [morsi'kare] *v* gnaw, bite. **morso** *sm* bite; (*fig*) sting; (*cavallo*) bit.

mortaio [mor'tajo] *sm* mortar.

mortale [mor'tale] *agg* mortal; (*implacabile*) deadly. **mortalità** *sf* mortality.

morte ['mɔrte] *sf* death.

morto ['mɔrto] *agg* dead. *sm* dead person; (*carte*) dummy. **fare il morto** float (on one's back).

mosaico [mo'zaiko] *sm* mosaic.

mosca ['moska] *sf* fly; (*barbetta*) goatee. **mosca cieca** blindman's buff. **moscerino** *sm* small fly.

Mosca ['moska] *sf* Moscow.

moscato[1] [mos'kato] *agg* muscat(el). **noce moscata** *sf* nutmeg.

moscato[2] [mos'kato] *agg* (*cavallo*) dappled.

moschea [mos'kɛa] *sf* mosque.

moschetto [mos'ketto] *sm* musket. **moschettiere** *sm* musketeer.

mossa ['mɔssa] *sf* movement; (*fig*) move.

mosso ['mɔsso] *agg* (*mare*) rough; (*capelli*) wavy.

mostarda [mos'tarda] *sf* mustard.

mostrare [mos'trare] *v* show. **mostra** *sf* show, exhibition; ostentation; (*campione*) sample. **mettere in mostra** display.

mostro ['mɔstro] *sm* monster. **mostruosità** *sf* monstrosity. **mostruoso** *agg* monstrous.

motivo [mo'tivo] *sm* ground, reason; (*disegno, musica*) motif. **motivare** *v* motivate. **motivazione** *sf* motivation.

moto[1] ['mɔto] *sm* motion; (*sommossa*) rebellion. **mettere in moto** set in motion, start (up).

moto[2] ['mɔto] *sf* (*fam*) motor-bike.

motocicletta [mototʃik'letta] *sf* motorcycle. **motociclista** *s*(*m*+*f*) motor-cyclist.

motore [mo'tore] *sm* engine. *agg* motor. **albero motore** *sm* crankshaft. **motorino d'avviamento** *sm* starter (motor).

motoscafo [moto'skafo] *sm* motor-boat.

motto ['mɔtto] *sm* motto; (*detto*) saying.

movimento [movi'mento] *sm* movement; activity. **movimentato** *agg* lively, busy.

mozione [mo'tsjone] *sf* motion.

mozzare [mot'tsare] *v* cut off; (*coda*) dock. **mozzare il fiato** take one's breath away.

mozzicone [mottsi'kone] *sm* butt.

mucca ['mukka] *sf* cow.

mucchio ['mukkjo] *sm* heap.

muco ['muko] *sm* mucus. **mucosa** *sf* mucous membrane.

muda ['muda] *sf* moulting.

muffa ['muffa] *sf* mould. **muffoso** *agg* mouldy.

muggire [mud'dʒire] *v also* **mugghiare** bellow; (*mare*) roar; (*vento*) howl.

mughetto [mu'getto] *sm* lily of the valley.

mugnaio [mu'ɲajo] *sm* miller.

mugolare [mugo'lare] *v* howl, whine.

mulattiera [mulat'tjɛra] *sf* (mule-)track.

mulino [mu'lino] *sm* mill; (*a vento*) windmill. **mulinello** *sm* whirlpool; (*pesca*) reel.

mulo ['mulo] *sm* mule.

multa ['multa] *sf* fine.

multicolore [multiko'lore] *agg* multicoloured.

multiplo ['multiplo] *agg*, *sm* multiple.

mummia ['mummja] *sf* mummy. **mummificare** *v* mummify.

***mungere** ['mundʒere] *v* milk.

municipio [muni'tʃipjo] *sm* (*comune*) municipality; (*sede*) town hall. **municipale** *agg* municipal.

munire [mu'nire] *v* supply; fortify.

munizione [muni'tsjone] *sf* munitions *pl*; (military) stores *pl*. **munizioni** *sf pl* ammunition *sing*.

***muovere** ['mwɔvere] *v* move.

muraglia [mu'raʎa] *sf* wall.

muratore [mura'tore] *sm* bricklayer.

muro ['muro] *sm* wall. **mura** *sf pl* city

walls *pl*. **parlare al muro** talk to a brick wall.

musa ['muza] *sf* muse.

muschio[1] ['muskjo] *sm* (*bot*) moss. **muscoso** *agg* mossy.

muschio[2] ['muskjo] *sm* (*odore*) musk.

muscolo ['muskolo] *sm* muscle.

museo [mu'zɛo] *sm* museum.

museruola [muze'rwɔla] *sf* muzzle.

musica ['muzika] *sf* music. **musicale** *agg* musical, music. **musicista** *s(m+f)* musician.

muso ['muzo] *sm* snout; (*spreg*) mug. **mettere il muso lungo** pull a long face.

mussolina [musso'lina] *sf* muslin.

mutande [mu'tande] *sf pl also* **mutandine** (*da donna*) panties *pl*; (*da uomo*) underpants *pl*; (*da bagno*) swimming trunks *pl*.

mutare [mu'tare] *v* change; (*fare la muta*) shed. **mutabile** *or* **mutevole** *agg* changeable; (*fig*) fickle. **mutamento** *sm* change. **mutazione** *sf* mutation.

mutilare [muti'lare] *v* maim, mutilate. **mutilato, -a** *sm, sf* disabled person.

muto ['muto], **-a** *agg* silent; (*affetto da mutismo*) dumb. *sm, sf* mute. **linguaggio dei muti** *sm* deaf-and-dumb language.

mutuo ['mutuo] *agg* mutual. *sm* loan. **mutuo ipotecario** mortgage. **mutua** *sf* insurance.

N

nafta ['nafta] *sf* fuel oil.

nailon ['nailon] *sm invar* nylon.

nanna ['nanna] *sf* **fare la nanna** (*fam*) sleep.

nano ['nano], **-a** *s, agg* dwarf.

Napoli ['napoli] *sf* Naples. **napoletano, -a** *s, agg* Neapolitan.

nappa ['nappa] *sf* tassel; (*fam: naso*) conk; (*pelle*) nappa.

narciso [nar'tʃizo] *sm* narcissus; (*giunchiglia*) daffodil.

narcotico [nar'kɔtiko] *agg, sm* narcotic. **narcosi** *sf* narcosis.

narice [na'ritʃe] *sf* nostril.

narrare [nar'rare] *v* tell. **narrativa** *sf* fiction. **narrazione** *sf* tale.

*****nascere** ['naʃere] *v* be born; (*fig*) (a)rise, start (up). **far nascere** give rise to. **nascita** *sf* birth. **atto di nascita** *sm* birth certificate.

*****nascondere** [nas'kondere] *v* hide. **nascondiglio** *sm* hide-out. **nascondino** *sm* hide-and-seek.

nascosto [nas'kosto] *agg* hidden.

nasello [na'zɛllo] *sm* hake.

naso ['nazo] *sm* nose. **cacciare** *or* **ficcare il naso (in)** poke one's nose (into).

nastro ['nastro] *sm* ribbon; (*tec*) tape. **nastro sonoro** sound-track. **nastro trasportatore** conveyor belt.

nasturzio [nas'turtsjo] *sm* nasturtium.

natale [na'tale] *agg* native. **Natale** *sm* Christmas. **natalizio** *agg* Christmas. **giorno natalizio** *sm* birthday.

natatoia [nata'toja] *sf* flipper, fin.

natica ['natika] *sf* buttock.

nativo [na'tivo] *agg* native.

nato ['nato] *agg* born. **appena nato** newborn. **... nato e sputato** the (spitting) image of .... **nato morto** stillborn.

natura [na'tura] *sf* nature. **naturale** *agg* natural. **naturalezza** *sf* spontaneity; simplicity. **naturalistico** *agg* naturalistic.

naturalizzare [naturalid'dzare] *v* naturalize. **naturalizzazione** *sf* naturalization.

naufragio [nau'fradʒo] *sm* shipwreck; (*fig*) wreck. **naufragare** *v* be shipwrecked; (*fig*) come to grief. **naufrago, -a** *sm, sf* survivor.

nausea ['nauzea] *sf* nausea. **dare la nausea a** make sick. **provar nausea** feel sick. **nauseante** *agg* nauseating, sickening. **nauseato** *agg* nauseated, sickened.

nautico ['nautiko] *agg* nautical. **sport nautici** *sm pl* water sports *pl*.

navata [na'vata] *sf* (*centrale*) nave; (*laterale*) aisle.

nave ['nave] *sf* ship. **nave cisterna** tanker. **nave di salvataggio** lifeboat. **nave traghetto** ferry. **navale** *agg* naval. **navalmeccanica** *sf* shipbuilding. **navalmeccanico** *sm* shipyard worker.

navetta [na'vetta] *sf* shuttle.

navigare [navi'gare] *v* sail, navigate. **navigatore** *sm* navigator. **navigazione** *sf* navigation.

nazionalizzare [natsjonalid'dzare] *v* nationalize. **nazionalizzazione** *sf* nationalization.

nazione [na'tsjone] *sf* nation. **nazionale** *agg* national; (*econ*) domestic. **nazionalismo** *sm* nationalism. **nazionalista** *s(m+f), agg* nationalist. **nazionalità** *sf* nationality.

nazismo [na'dzizmo] *sm* Nazism, National Socialism. **nazista** *s(m+f)*, *agg* Nazi.

ne [ne] *pron* of it *or* them, about it *or* them; (*partitivo*) some, any. *avv* from there.

nè [ne] *cong* neither, nor; (*con altra negazione*) either. **nè ... nè ...** neither ... nor ....

neanche [ne'anke] *avv*, *cong*, also **nemmeno**, **neppure** neither; either; (*rafforzativo*) not even.

nebbia ['nebbja] *sf* fog; (*foschia*) haze, mist. **nebbioso** *agg* foggy.

necessario [netʃes'sarjo] *agg* necessary, needed (for). *sm* necessary. **lo stretto necessario** the bare necessities *pl*.

necessità [netʃessi'ta] *sf* necessity, need. **di prima necessità** essential. **in caso di necessità** if necessary. **trovarsi nella necessità di** be obliged to.

negare [ne'gare] *v* deny. **negato** *agg* denied; (*senza disposizione*) hopeless (at). **negazione** *sf* denial, negation.

negativa [nega'tiva] *sf* negative. **negativo** *agg* negative.

negli ['neʎi] *prep+art* in gli.

negligente [negli'dʒɛnte] *agg* negligent. **negligenza** *sf* negligence.

negoziare [nego'tsjare] *v* negotiate.

negozio [ne'gɔtsjo] *sm* shop; (*affare*) deal. **negoziante** *s(m+f)* shopkeeper; dealer; (*all'ingrosso*) wholesaler; (*al minuto*) retailer.

negro ['negro], -a *agg* Negro, black. *sm*, *sf* Negro, black person. **negriere** *sm* slaver; (*fig*) slave-driver.

nei ['nei] *prep+art* in i.

nel [nel] *prep+art* in il.

nell' [nell] *prep+art* in l'.

nella ['nella] *prep+art* in la.

nelle ['nelle] *prep+art* in le.

nello ['nello] *prep+art* in lo.

nemico [ne'miko], -a *agg* enemy, hostile; (*dannoso*) bad. *sm*, *sf* enemy.

nemmeno [nem'meno] *V* **neanche**.

neo ['nɛo] *sm* mole; (*posticcio*) beauty-spot.

neon ['nɛon] *sm* neon.

neonato [neo'nato], -a *agg* new-born. *sm*, *sf* new-born baby.

neozelandese [neodzelan'deze] *agg* New Zealand. *sm*, *sf* New Zealander.

nepotismo [nepo'tizmo] *sm* nepotism.

neppure [nep'pure] *V* **neanche**.

nerbo ['nɛrbo] *sm* whip; (*fig*) force.

nero ['nero] *agg*, *sm* black. **bestia nera** *sf* bugbear. **borsa nera** *sf* black market. **nerastro** *agg* blackish.

nervo ['nɛrvo] *sm* nerve; (*bot*) rib, vein; (*corda*) string. **avere i nervi** be on edge, be irritable. **dare ai** *or* **sui nervi a qualcuno** get on somebody's nerves. **nervoso** *agg* nervous; irritable; (*eccitabile*) highly strung. **esaurimento nervoso** *sm* nervous breakdown.

nesso ['nɛsso] *sm* connection.

nessuno [nes'suno] *agg* no. *pron* (*persone*) nobody, no-one; (*cose*) none; (*qualcuno*) anybody.

nettare [net'tare] *sm* nectar.

netto ['netto] *agg* clean; (*fig*) clear, sharp; (*peso, comm*) net. **nettezza** *sf* cleanliness; (*precisione*) clarity. **nettezza urbana** *sf* street-cleaning; refuse collection.

neutrale [neu'trale] *s(m+f)*, *agg* neutral. **neutralità** *sf* neutrality. **neutralizzare** *v* neutralize; (*fig*) counteract.

neutro ['nɛutro] *sm*, *agg* neutral; (*gramm, sesso*) neuter. **neutrone** *sm* neutron.

neve ['neve] *sf* snow. **cumulo di neve** *sm* snowdrift. **pupazzo di neve** *sm* snowman. **nevato** *or* **nevoso** *agg* snowy.

nevicare [nevi'kare] *v* snow. **nevicata** *sf* snowfall.

nevischio [ne'viskjo] *sm* sleet.

nevralgia [nevral'dʒia] *sf* neuralgia.

nevrosi [ne'vrɔzi] *sf* neurosis. **nevrotico, -a** *s*, *agg* neurotic.

nibbio ['nibbjo] *sm* kite.

nicchia ['nikkja] *sf* niche, recess.

nichel ['nikel] *sm* nickel. **nichelare** *v* nickel-plate. **nichelatura** *sf* nickel-plating.

nichilismo [niki'lizmo] *sm* nihilism. **nichilista** *s(m+f)* nihilist.

nicotina [niko'tina] *sf* nicotine.

nido ['nido] *sm* nest. **nido d'ape** honeycomb. **nido d'infanzia** crèche, day nursery. **nidiata** *sf* brood.

niente ['njɛnte] *pron* nothing; (*con altra negazione*) anything. *sm* nothing; (*cosa da poco*) slightest thing. **da niente** unimportant. **niente paura!** don't be afraid! **non fa niente** (*non importa*) it doesn't matter.

ninfa ['ninfa] *sf* nymph. **ninfomane** *sf*, *agg* nymphomaniac.

ninfea [nin'fɛa] *sf* water lily.

ninna-nanna [ninna'nanna] *sm* lullaby.

ninnolo ['ninnolo] *sm* (*balocco*) toy; (*gingillo*) knick-knack.

nipote [ni'pote] *sm* (*di nonni*) grandson; (*di zii*) nephew. *sf* (*di nonni*) granddaughter; (*di zii*) niece.

nitido ['nitido] *agg* neat; (*fig*) clear.

nitrire [ni'trire] *v* neigh. **nitrito** *sm* neigh.

no [nɔ] *avv* no. *sm* no; (*rifiuto*) refusal. **come no!** of course! and how! **se no** otherwise, or else. **uno sì e uno no** every other one.

nobile ['nɔbile] *agg* noble. *sm* nobleman. *sf* noblewoman. **nobiltà** *sf* nobility.

nocca ['nɔkka] *sf* knuckle; (*del cavallo*) fetlock.

nocciola [not'tʃɔla] *sf* hazel-nut. *agg, sm invar* (*colore*) hazel. **nocciolina (americana)** *sf* peanut. **nocciolo** *sm* (*pianta*) hazel.

nocciolo ['nottʃɔlo] *sm* (*bot*) stone, kernel; (*fig*) heart, point; (*tec*) core.

noce ['notʃe] *sm* (*albero*) walnut(-tree); (*legno*) walnut. *sf* (*frutto*) walnut. **noce di burro** pat of butter. **noce di cocco** coconut. **noce moscata** nutmeg. **nocepesca** *sf* nectarine.

nocivo [no'tʃivo] *agg* harmful.

nodo ['nɔdo] *sm* knot; (*incrocio*) junction; (*trama*) plot. **avere un nodo alla gola** have a lump in one's throat. **nodo scorsoio** slip-knot. **nodoso** *agg* knotty.

noi ['noi] *pron* (*soggetto*) we; (*oggetto*) us.

noia ['nɔja] *sf* (*tedio*) boredom; (*fastidio*) nuisance; (*fam*) bore. **avere delle noie con** have trouble with. **dare noia (a)** trouble, bother. **noioso** *agg* boring; (*fastidioso*) troublesome.

noleggiare [noled'dʒare] *v* hire, rent. **noleggio** *sm* hire; (*prezzo*) rental. **nolo** *sm* freight. **dare a nolo** hire (out). **prendere a nolo** hire, rent.

nomade ['nɔmade] *agg* nomadic. *s(m+f)* nomad.

nome ['nome] *sm* name; (*gramm*) noun. **a nome di** on behalf of. **conoscere di nome** know by name. **fare il nome di** mention; (*proporre*) propose. **nome di battaglia** pseudonym. **nomignolo** *sm* nickname.

nomina ['nɔmina] *sf* appointment. **nominare** *v* mention; name; (*eleggere*) appoint.

non [non] *avv* not. **non ... affatto** not at all. **non ... mai** never. **non ... nessuno** nobody. **non ... niente** *or* **nulla** nothing. **nonché** *cong* as well as.

noncurante [nonku'rante] *agg* heedless.

nondimeno [nondi'meno] *cong* nevertheless.

nonno ['nɔnno] *sm* grandfather; (*fam*) grand-dad. **nonna** *sf* grandmother; (*fam*) grandma, granny. **nonni** *sm pl* grandparents *pl*.

nono ['nɔno] *sm, agg* ninth.

nonostante [nonos'tante] *prep* notwithstanding, in spite of. *cong* (al)though.

nontiscordardimè [nontiskordardi'mε] *sm* forget-me-not.

nord [nɔrd] *sm* north. **a nord** north. **del nord** north, northern. **nord-est** *sm* northeast. **nord-ovest** *sm* north-west.

norma ['nɔrma] *sf* rule, standard; (*istruzione*) direction; regulation. **a norma di legge** according to (the) law.

normale [nor'male] *agg* normal, regular; standard. *sf* perpendicular. **normalmente** *avv* as a rule.

Norvegia [nor'vedʒa] *sf* Norway. **norvegese** *s(m+f)*, *agg* Norwegian.

nostalgia [nostal'dʒia] *sf* nostalgia; (*della casa*) homesickness. **aver nostalgia di** miss. **nostalgico** *agg* nostalgic, homesick.

nostro ['nɔstro] *agg* our. *pron* ours. **nostrano** *agg* local, home-grown.

nota ['nɔta] *sf* note; list.

notaio [no'tajo] *sm* notary.

notare [no'tare] *v* note; (*osservare*) notice. **far notare** point out.

notificare [notifi'kare] *v* notify; inform. **notificazione** *sf* notification; (*avviso*) notice.

notizia [no'titsja] *sf* news (item), information. **notiziario** *sm* news (bulletin).

noto ['nɔto] *agg* well-known, renowned. **render noto** make known.

notorio [no'tɔrjo] *agg* renowned; (*spreg*) notorious. **notorietà** *sf* renown.

notte ['nɔtte] *sf* night. **buona notte!** goodnight! **dare la buona notte** bid goodnight. **nottata** *sf* night.

notturno [not'turno] *agg* night, nocturnal. *sm* (*musica*) nocturne.

novanta [no'vanta] *sm, agg* ninety. **novantesimo** *sm, agg* ninetieth.

nove ['nɔve] *sm, agg* nine.

novella [no'vɛlla] *sf* short story. **novellista** *s(m+f)* short-story writer.

novello [no'vɛllo] *agg* new.

novembre [no'vɛmbre] *sm* November.

novità [novi'ta] *sf* novelty; (*notizie*) news.

novizio [no'vitsjo] *sm* beginner, novice.

nozione [no'tsjone] *sf* notion, idea.

nozze ['nɔttse] *sf pl* wedding *sing.* **viaggio di nozze** *sm* honeymoon.

nube ['nube] *sf* cloud. **nubifragio** *sm* cloudburst.

nubile ['nubile] *agg* unmarried, single.

nuca ['nuka] *sf* nape of the neck.

nucleo ['nukleo] *sm* nucleus. **nucleo familiare** family. **nucleare** *agg* nuclear.

nudo ['nudo] *agg* bare, naked. *sm* nude. **a piedi nudi** barefoot. **nudismo** *sm* nudism. **nudista** *s(m+f)* nudist. **nudità** *sf* nudity, nakedness.

nulla ['nulla] *pron* nothing; (*con altra negazione*) anything. *sm* nothing; (*cosa da poco*) slightest thing. **da nulla** unimportant. **non fa nulla!** (*non importa*) it doesn't matter!

nullo ['nullo] *agg* null. **dichiarar nullo** annul. **nullaosta** *sm invar* clearance. **nullità** *sf* cipher.

numero ['numero] *sm* number; (*segno*) numeral. **numero chiuso** quota. **numero legale** quorum.

numismatica [numiz'matika] *sf* numismatics. **numismatico, -a** *sm, sf* numismatist.

*****nuocere** ['nwɔtʃere] *v* harm.

nuora ['nwɔra] *sf* daughter-in-law.

nuotare [nwo'tare] *v* swim. **nuotatore, -trice** *sm, sf* swimmer. **nuoto** *sm* swimming.

nuovo ['nwɔvo] *agg* new. **Nuova York** *sf* New York. **Nuova Zelanda** *sf* New Zealand.

nutrire [nu'trire] *v* feed, nourish. **nutrire affetto per** feel affection for. **nutriente** *agg* nourishing. **nutrimento** *sm* nourishment.

nuvola ['nuvola] *sf* cloud. **senza nuvole** cloudless. **nuvoloso** *agg* cloudy; (*cielo*) overcast.

nuziale [nu'tsjale] *agg* wedding.

O

o [o] *cong* or. **o ... o ...** either ... or .... **o l'uno o l'altro** either.

oasi ['ɔazi] *sf* oasis (*pl* -ses).

*****obbedire** [obbe'dire] *v* obey. **obbedienza** *sf* obedience.

obbligare *v* bind, force. **obbligarsi** *v* undertake. **obbligato** *agg* fixed, set; (*riconoscente*) obliged. **obbligatorio** *agg* compulsory. **obbligazione** *sf* (*dir*) obligation; (*comm*) bond, debenture. **obbligo** *sm, pl* -ghi duty, obligation. **essere d'obbligo** be compulsory *or* obligatory.

obbrobrio [ob'brɔbrjo] *sm* disgrace.

obeso [o'bɛzo] *agg* obese. **obesità** *sf* obesity.

obiettare [objet'tare] *v* object. **obiezione** *sf* objection.

obiettivo [objet'tivo] *sm* objective; (*scope*) aim; (*foto, ecc.*) lens. *agg* objective.

obitorio [obi'tɔrjo] *sm* morgue.

oblazione [obla'tsjone] *sf* offering.

oblio [o'blio] *sm* oblivion.

obliquo [o'blikwo] *agg* oblique.

oblò [o'blɔ] *sm* porthole.

oblungo [o'blungo] *agg* oblong.

oboe ['ɔboe] *sm* oboe.

oca ['ɔka] *sf* goose (*pl* geese); (*maschio*) gander.

occasionale [okkazjo'nale] *agg* (*fortuito*) chance; immediate; (*saltuario*) occasional.

occasione [okka'zjone] *sf* chance, opportunity; (*buon affare*) bargain; (*circostanza*) occasion.

occhiali [ok'kjali] *sm pl* glasses *pl*, spectacles *pl*. **occhiali da sole** sun-glasses *pl*. **occhialuto** *agg* bespectacled.

occhio ['ɔkkjo] *sm* eye; (*bot*) bud. **a occhi chiusi** blindly. **a occhio** by sight. **a occhio nudo** with the naked eye. **a quattr'occhi** in private. **costare un occhio della testa** cost the earth. **dare nell'occhio** catch the eye. **tenere d'occhio** keep an eye on.

occidente [ottʃi'dɛnte] *sm* west. **occidentale** *agg* west, western.

*****occorrere** [ok'korrere] *v* be necessary. **all'occorrenza** in case of need.

occulto [ok'kulto] *agg* occult; (*nascosto*) hidden.

occupare [okku'pare] *v* occupy; (*far lavorare*) employ; (*tempo*) spend; (*carica*) hold; (*tener occupato*) keep busy. **occuparsi di** concern oneself with. **occupato** *agg* engaged; (*indaffarato*) busy. **occupazione** *sf* occupation.

oceano [o'tʃeano] *sm* ocean.

ocra ['ɔkra] *sf* ochre.

oculare [oku'lare] *agg* **testimonio oculare** *sm* eye-witness.

oculista [oku'lista] *s(m+f)* oculist.
ode ['ɔde] *sf* ode.
odiare [o'djare] *v* hate, loathe. **odio** *sm* hatred, hate, loathing. **avere in odio** hate, detest. **odioso** *agg* hateful.
odierno [o'djɛrno] *agg* of today; modern.
odissea [odis'sɛa] *sf* odyssey.
odontoiatria [odontoja'tria] *sf* dentistry.
odorare [odo'rare] *v* smell. **odorato** *sm* sense of smell. **odore** *sm* smell, odour. **sentir un odore di** smell. **odoroso** *agg* sweet-smelling.
offendere [of'fɛndere] *v* offend; (*ledere*) injure, hurt. **offendere la legge** break the law. **offendersi** *v* take offence. **offensiva** *sf* offensive. **offensivo** *agg* offensive. **offensore** *sm* attacker; (*dir*) offender.
offerta [of'fɛrta] *sf* offer; (*comm*) bid; (*econ*) supply. **offerente** *s(m+f)* bidder.
offesa [of'feza] *sf* offence; insult; (*danno*) harm.
officina [offi'tʃina] *sf* works, workshop. **capo officina** *sm* (works) foreman.
offrire [of'frire] *v* offer; (*comm*) bid. **offrirsi** *v* offer; present oneself.
offuscare [offus'kare] *v* dim; (*foto, ecc.*) blur; (*fig*) obscure.
oggetto [od'dʒetto] *sm* object; (*argomento*) subject; (*cosa*) thing. **oggettività** *sf* objectivity. **oggettivo** *agg* objective.
oggi ['oddʒi] *avv, sm* today. **al giorno d'oggi** nowadays. **oggi a otto** a week today.
ogni ['oɲi] *agg* every, each. **ad** or **in ogni modo** in any case. **ogni tanto** every so often, now and then.
Ognissanti [oɲis'santi] *sm* All Saints' Day.
ognuno [o'ɲuno] *pron* everybody, everyone; (*ciascuno*) each.
ohimè [oi'mɛ] *inter* alas!
Olanda [o'landa] *sf* Holland. **olandese** *agg* Dutch. **gli olandesi** the Dutch.
oleodotto [oleo'dotto] *sm* (*oil*) pipeline.
oleoso [ole'ozo] *agg* oily.
olfatto [ol'fatto] *sm* sense of smell.
olimpiade [olim'piade] *sf* Olympic games *pl*. **olimpico** *agg* Olympian. **olimpionico** *agg* Olympic.
olio ['ɔljo] *sm* oil. **olio combustibile** (*gasolio*) fuel oil.
oliva [o'liva] *sf* olive. **oliveto** olive grove. **olivo** *sm* olive-tree.
olmo ['olmo] *sm* elm-tree.

olocausto [olo'kausto] *sm* holocaust, sacrifice.
oltraggiare [oltrad'dʒare] *v* outrage. **oltraggio** *sm* outrage. **oltraggio al pudore** indecent behaviour. **oltraggioso** *agg* outrageous.
oltranza [ol'trantsa] *sf* **ad oltranza** to the (bitter) end.
oltre ['oltre] *avv* (*luogo*) further, farther; (*tempo*) beyond. *prep* beyond; (*più di*) more than, over. **oltre a** besides, apart from.
oltremare [oltre'mare] *avv* overseas.
oltremodo [oltre'mɔdo] *avv* exceedingly.
oltrepassare [oltrepas'sare] *v* exceed; surpass.
omaggio [o'maddʒo] *sm* (*dono*) (complimentary) gift. **porgere omaggi a** pay respects to. **rendere omaggio a** pay homage to.
ombelico [ombe'liko] *sm*, *pl* **-chi** navel. **ombelicale** *agg* umbilical.
ombra ['ombra] *sf* shadow; (*opposto di luce*) shade. **ombretto** *sm* eye-shadow.
ombrello [om'brello] *sm* umbrella.
omero ['ɔmero] *sm* humerus.
omettere [o'mettere] *v* omit, leave out.
omicida [omi'tʃida] *agg* murderous. *s(m+f)* murderer, murderess. **omicidio** *sm* homicide, murder. **omicidio colposo** manslaughter.
omissione [omis'sjone] *sf* omission.
omogeneo [omo'dʒɛneo] *agg* homogeneous. **omogeneità** *sf* homogeneity.
omologare [omolo'gare] *v* ratify.
omonimo [o'mɔnimo] *agg* homonymous. *nm* namesake; (*parola*) homonym.
omosessuale [omosessu'ale] *s(m+f)*, *agg* homosexual. **omosessualità** *sf* homosexuality.
oncia ['ontʃa] *sf* ounce.
onda ['onda] *sf* wave. **a onde** wavy. **ondata** *sf* wave, surge.
onde ['onde] *avv* whence. *cong* so that.
ondeggiare [onded'dʒare] *v* wave, sway, roll; (*fig*) waver.
ondulare [ondu'lare] *v* (*capelli*) wave. **ondulato** *agg* wavy; (*lastra, cartone*) corrugated.
onere ['ɔnere] *sm* burden. **oneroso** *agg* burdensome.
onesto [o'nɛsto] *agg* honest; (*prezzo*) fair. **onestà** *sf* honesty, integrity.
onice ['ɔnitʃe] *sm* onyx.

onnipotente [onnipo'tɛnte] *agg* omnipotent.

onnivoro [on'nivoro] *agg* omnivorous.

onomastico [ono'mastiko] *sm* saint's day.

onorare [ono'rare] *v* honour.

onorario [ono'rarjo] *agg* honorary. *sm* fee.

onore [o'nore] *sm* honour. **a onor del vero** to tell the truth. **fare onore a** honour; do credit *or* justice to. **farsi onore** distinguish oneself. **onorevole** *agg* honourable.

onorificenza [onorifi'tʃɛntsa] *sf* honour. **onorifico** *agg* honorary.

onta ['onta] *sf* shame.

ontano [on'tano] *sm* alder.

opaco [o'pako] *agg, m pl* -**chi** opaque, dull.

opale [o'pale] *sm* opal.

opera ['ɔpera] *sf* work; (*teatro*) opera; (*azione*) deed; institution. **mettere in opera** put into practice; instal. **per opera di** thanks to. **operetta** *sf* operetta, light opera. **operoso** *agg* active.

operaio [ope'rajo], -**a** *sm, sf* worker. *agg* working.

operare [ope'rare] *v* function, work; (*med*) operate. **farsi operare** have an operation. **operatore** *sm* (*cinema*) cameraman; (*di borsa*) stockbroker. **operatorio** *agg* operating. **operazione** *sf* operation.

opinione [opi'njone] *sf* opinion.

oppio ['ɔppjo] *sm* opium.

opponente [oppo'nɛnte] *agg* opposing. *s(m+f)* adversary.

*****opporre** [op'porre] *v* oppose. **opporre resistenza** offer resistance. **opporsi a** set oneself against; object to.

opportuno [oppor'tuno] *agg* opportune. **opportunismo** *sm* opportunism. **opportunista** *s(m+f)* opportunist. **opportunità** *sf* opportunity.

opposizione [oppozi'tsjone] *sf* opposition.

opposto [op'posto] *agg, sm* opposite. **all'opposto** on the contrary.

oppressione [oppres'sjone] *sf* oppression. **oppresso** *agg* oppressed. **oppressore** *sm* oppressor.

*****opprimere** [op'primere] *v* oppress, burden.

oppure [op'pure] *cong* or, or else.

opulento [opu'lɛnto] *agg* opulent.

opuscolo [o'puskolo] *sm* pamphlet, booklet.

ora[1] ['ora] *sf* hour; (*tempo*) time. **alla**

buon'ora! at last! **all'ora** (*velocità*) per hour. **di buon'ora** early. **ora di punta** rush-hour. **ora legale** summer-time. **ora straordinaria** overtime.

ora[2] ['ora] *avv* (*adesso*) now; (*appena*) just. **d'ora in poi** from now on, henceforth. **or ora** just (now).

orale [o'rale] *agg* oral. *sm* (*esame*) viva.

orario [o'rarjo] *agg* (*all'ora*) per hour; time. **in senso orario** clockwise. **segnale orario** time-signal. *sm* (*ore*) hours *pl*; (*tabella*) timetable. **in orario** on time.

orazione [ora'tsjone] *sf* speech. **oratore** *sm* orator. **oratorio** *sm* (*chiesa*) oratory; (*musica*) oratorio.

orbene [or'bɛne] *avv* well (now).

orbita ['ɔrbita] *sf* orbit. **orbitare** *v* orbit.

orchestra [or'kɛstra] *sf* orchestra. **orchestrare** *v* orchestrate. **orchestrazione** *sf* orchestration.

orchidea [orki'dɛa] *sf* orchid.

orco ['ɔrko] *sm* ogre.

orda ['ɔrda] *sf* horde.

ordigno [or'diɲo] *sm* device.

ordinare [ordi'nare] *v* order; (*mettere in ordine*) tidy up; (*sistemare*) arrange; (*rel*) ordain. **ordinamento** *sm* order; arrangement; system. **ordinazione** *sf* order; (*rel*) ordination.

ordinario [ordi'narjo] *agg, sm* ordinary.

ordine ['ordine] *sm* order. **ordine del giorno** agenda.

ordire [or'dire] *v* (*tessile*) warp; (*fig*) hatch. **ordito** *sm* warp; (*fig*) plot.

orecchio [o'rekkjo] *sm* ear. **a orecchio** by ear. **a portato d'orecchio** within earshot. **orecchino** *sm* ear-ring. **orecchioni** *sm pl* mumps *sing*.

orefice [o'refitʃe] *sm* goldsmith, jeweller. **oreficeria** *sf* jewellery; (*negozio*) jeweller's (shop).

orfano ['ɔrfano], -**a** *s, agg* orphan. **orfanotrofio** *sm* orphanage.

organico [or'ganiko] *agg* organic. *sm* personnel. **organismo** *sm* organism; (*fig*) body.

organizzare [organid'dzare] *v* organize, arrange. **organizzazione** *sf* organization, body. **organizzatore**, -**trice** *sm, sf* organizer.

organo ['ɔrgano] *sm* organ. **organetto** *sm* barrel-organ.

orgasmo [or'gazmo] *sm* orgasm.

orgia ['ɔrdʒa] *sf* orgy.

orgoglio [or'goʎo] *sm* pride. **orgoglioso** *agg* proud.

orientare [orjen'tare] *v* orient(ate); direct. **orientarsi** *v* find one's bearings; tend. **orientamento** *sm* orientation; (*direzione*) trend. **senso d'orientamento** *sm* sense of direction.

oriente [o'rjɛnte] *sm* East. **orientale** *agg* oriental, eastern, east.

orifizio [ori'fitsjo] *sm* orifice, opening.

origano [o'rigano] *sm* oregano.

originare [oridʒi'nare] *v* (*avere origini*) originate; (*dare origini*) give rise to.

origine [o'ridʒine] *sf* origin; (*inizio*) beginning. **originale** *sm*, *agg* original; eccentric. **originalità** *sf* originality; eccentricity. **originario** *agg* native.

origliare [ori'ʎare] *v* eavesdrop.

orina [o'rina] *sf* urine. **orinare** *v* urinate. **orinatorio** *agg* urinary.

oriundo [o'rjundo] *agg* native.

orizzonte [orid'dzonte] *sm* horizon. **giro d'orizzonte** *sm* general survey. **orizzontale** *agg* horizontal. **orizzontarsi** *v* find one's bearings.

orlo [o'rlo] *sm* edge; (*abisso*) brink; (*bicchiere*) rim; (*tessuto*) hem. **orlare** *v* hem; (*bordare*) trim.

orma ['orma] *sf* footprint; track.

ormai [or'mai] *avv* by now; (*passato*) by then.

ormeggiare [ormed'dʒare] *v* moor. **ormeggio** *sm* mooring.

ormone [or'mone] *sm* hormone.

ornare [or'nare] *v* adorn, decorate. **ornamentale** *agg* ornamental. **ornamento** *sm* ornament, decoration.

ornitologia [ornitolo'dʒia] *sf* ornithology. **ornitologo, -a** *sm*, *sf* ornithologist.

oro ['ɔro] *sm* gold. **d'oro** gold, golden.

orologio [oro'lɔdʒo] *sm* clock; (*da polso o tasca*) watch. **orologeria** *sf* clockwork; (*negozio*) watchmaker's (shop). **bomba ad orologeria** *sf* time-bomb. **orologiaio** *sm* watchmaker.

oroscopo [o'rɔskopo] *sm* horoscope.

orpello [or'pɛllo] *sm* tinsel.

orrendo [or'rɛndo] *agg* hideous, horrifying.

orribile [or'ribile] *agg* horrible, dreadful.

orrore [or'rore] *sm* horror, dread, loathing. **avere orrore di** loathe.

orso ['orso] *sm*, **-a** *sm*, *sf* bear. **orsacchiotto** *sm* bear-cub; (*giocattolo*) teddy-bear.

ortica [or'tika] *sf* nettle. **orticaria** *sf* nettle-rash.

orto ['orto] *sm* kitchen garden. **ortaggi** *sm pl* vegetables *pl*. **orticoltore** *sm* horticulturist. **orticoltura** *sf* horticulture. **ortolano** *sm* greengrocer.

ortodosso [orto'dɔsso] *agg* orthodox. **ortodossia** *sf* orthodoxy.

ortografia [ortogra'fia] *sf* spelling. **errore ortografico** *sm* spelling mistake.

ortopedia [ortope'dia] *sf* orthopaedics. **ortopedico** *agg* orthopaedic.

orzaiolo [ordza'jɔlo] *sm* stye.

orzo ['ɔrdzo] *sm* barley.

osare [o'zare] *v* dare; risk.

osceno [o'ʃɛno] *agg* obscene. **oscenità** *sf* obscenity.

oscillare [oʃil'lare] *v* swing, oscillate.

oscurare [osku'rare] *v* darken; (*fig*) obscure. **oscuramento** *sm* darkening; (*guerra*) black-out. **oscurità** *sf* dark; (*fig*) obscurity.

ospedale [ospe'dale] *sm* hospital. **ospedaliero** *agg* hospital.

ospitare [ospi'tare] *v* offer hospitality (to); (*albergare*) put up. **ospitale** *agg* hospitable.

ospite ['ɔspite] *s(m+f)* (*persona ospitata*) guest; (*oste*) host, hostess.

ospizio [os'pitsjo] *sm* hostel.

ossatura [ossa'tura] *sf* (*arch*) framework; (*anat*) bone structure.

ossequio [os'sɛkwjo] *sm* homage. **ossequi** *sm pl* (*saluti*) regards *pl*. **ossequioso** *agg* respectful.

osservare [osser'vare] *v* obscure; (*notare*) notice. **osservanza** *sf* observance. **osservatore, -trice** *sm*, *sf* observer. **osservatorio** *sm* observatory. **osservazione** *sf* observation; (*nota*) remark. **fare un'osservazione** comment; criticize.

ossessionare [ossessjo'nare] *v* haunt. **ossessionante** *agg* haunting. **ossessione** *sf* obsession. **ossesso** *agg* possessed.

ossia [os'sia] *cong* or rather, in other words.

ossigeno [os'sidʒeno] *sm* oxygen. **ossidare** *v* oxidize. **ossido** *sm* oxide.

osso ['ɔsso] *sm*, *pl* **-a** *f in collective sense* bone. **ossuto** *agg* bony.

ostacolare [ostako'lare] *v* hinder, obstruct. **ostacolo** *sm* obstacle, hindrance; (*atletica*) hurdle. **corsa a ostacolo** *sf* obstacle race; hurdling.

ostaggio [os'taddʒo] *sm* hostage.
oste ['ɔste] *sm* host, innkeeper.
ostello [os'tɛllo] *sm* refuge; (*per la gioventù*) (youth-)hostel.
ostentare [osten'tare] *v* show off.
ostentato *agg* ostentatious.
osteria [oste'ria] *sf* inn.
ostetrico [os'tetriko] *sm* obstetrician.
ostetrica *sf* obstetrician; (*levatrice*) midwife. **ostetricia** *sf* obstetrics; midwifery.
ostia ['ɔstja] *sf* (*rel*) host; (*cialda*) wafer.
ostile [os'tile] *agg* hostile. **ostilità** *sf* hostility.
ostinarsi [osti'narsi] *v* persist. **ostinatezza** *sf* obstinacy, stubbornness. **ostinato** *agg* obstinate, stubborn.
ostrica ['ɔstrika] *sf* oyster.
ostruire [ostru'ire] *v* obstruct, block. **ostruzione** *sf* obstruction.
otite [o'tite] *sf* otitis.
otorinolaringoiatra [otorinolaringo'jatra] *s(m+f)* ear, nose, and throat specialist.
ottagono [ot'tagono] *sm* octagon.
ottano [ot'tano] *sm* octane.
ottanta [ot'tanta] *sm*, *agg* eighty. **ottantesimo** *agg*, *sm* eightieth.
ottava [ot'tava] *sf* octave. **ottavo** *sm*, *agg* eighth.
*ottenere [otte'nere] *v* obtain, get. **ottenibile** *agg* obtainable.
ottico ['ɔttiko] *agg* optic. *sm* optician. **ottica** *sf* (*persona*) optician; (*scienza*) optics.
ottimismo [otti'mizmo] *agg* optimistic.
ottimo ['ɔttimo] *agg* excellent, very good.
otto ['ɔtto] *agg*, *sm* eight.
ottobre [ot'tobre] *sm* October.
ottone [ot'tone] *sm* brass. **ottoni** *sm pl* (*musica*) brass *pl*.
otturare [ottu'rare] *v* plug; (*dente*) fill. **otturatore** *sm* (*foto*) shutter.
ottuso [ot'tuzo] *agg* dull; (*non tagliente*) blunt; (*angolo*) obtuse.
ovaia [o'vaja] *sf* ovary.
ovale [o'vale] *agg*, *sm* oval.
ovatta [o'vatta] *sf* wadding; (*cotone idrofilo*) cotton wool.
ovazione [ova'tsjone] *sf* ovation.
ovest ['ɔvest] *sm* west. **a ovest di** (to the) west of. **dell'ovest** west, western.
ovile [o'vile] *sm* sheepfold.
ovulo ['ɔvulo] *sm* ovum; (*bot*) ovule. **ovulazione** *sf* ovulation.
ovunque [o'vunkwe] *avv* everywhere. *cong* wherever.

ovvero [ov'vero] *cong* or (rather).
ovvio ['ɔvvjo] *agg* obvious.
oziare [o'tsjare] *v* loaf. **ozio** *sm* (*pigrizia*) idleness; (*tempo libero*) leisure, spare time. **ozioso** *agg* idle.

P

pacato [pa'kato] *agg* calm.
pacchia ['pakkja] *sf* godsend.
pacco ['pakko] *sm* parcel. **pacchetto** *sm* packet, small parcel.
pace ['patʃe] *sf* peace.
pacificare [patʃifi'kare] *v* pacify, appease; reconcile. **pacifico** *agg* peaceful; (*ovvio*) self-evident.
pacifismo [patʃi'fizmo] *sm* pacifism. **pacifista** *s(m+f)* pacifist.
padella [pa'dɛlla] *sf* frying pan.
padiglione [padi'ʎone] *sm* pavilion.
Padova ['padova] *sf* Padua.
padre ['padre] *sm* father. **padre adottivo** foster-father. **padrino** *sm* godfather.
padrone [pa'drone], **-a** *sm*, *sf* master, mistress; owner; (*fam*) boss. **padronale** *agg* private; (*non di servizio*) owner's. **padronanza** *sf* mastery. **padroneggiarsi** *v* control oneself.
paesaggio [pae'zaddʒo] *sm* landscape.
paese [pa'eze] *sm* country; village; (*città*) town. **paesano** *agg* rural, country.
paffuto [paf'futo] *agg* plump.
paga ['paga] *sf* pay, wages *pl*.
pagaia [pa'gaja] *sf* paddle.
pagano [pa'gano], **-a** *s*, *agg* pagan, heathen.
pagare [pa'gare] *v* pay. **pagamento** *sm* payment.
pagella [pa'dʒɛlla] *sf* school report.
paggio ['paddʒo] *sm* page(-boy).
pagina ['padʒina] *sf* page.
paglia ['paʎa] *sf* straw. **pagliericcio** *sm* palliasse. **paglietta** *sf* steel wool; (*cappello*) straw hat.
pagliaccio [pa'ʎattʃo] *sm* clown. **pagliacciata** *sf* buffoonery.
pagnotta [pa'ɲɔtta] *sf* loaf (of bread).
pago ['pago] *agg* contented (with).
pagoda [pa'gɔda] *sf* pagoda.
paio ['pajo] *sm*, *pl* **-a** *f* pair; (*due o circa due*) couple.

pala ['pala] *sf* shovel; (*di remo*) blade.
palata *sf* shovel(ful). **soldi a palate** *sm pl*
pots *or* bags of money *pl*.
palato [pa'lato] *sm* palate.
palazzo [pa'lattso] *sm* (*edificio*) building;
(*appartamenti*) block of flats; (*casa di
principe, ecc.*) palace. **palazzina** *sf* villa.
palco ['palko] *sm* platform, stand; (*teatro*)
box. **palcoscenico** *sm* stage.
palese [pa'leze] *agg* obvious, clear.
palesare *v* reveal.
palestra [pa'lɛstra] *sf* gymnasium.
paletto [pa'letto] *sm* bolt.
palio ['paljo] *sm* **mettere in palio** offer as
a prize.
palla ['palla] *sf* ball. **pallacanestro** *sm* basketball. **pallanuoto** *sm* water polo.
palleggiare [palled'dʒare] *v* (*tennis*) knock
up; (*calcio*) dribble. **palleggio** *sm* knock-
up, dribbling.
pallido ['pallido] *agg* pale; (*fig*) faint.
pallino [pal'lino] *sm* (*bocce*) jack; (*fig*)
craze. **a pallini** with polka dots.
pallone [pal'lone] *sm* ball; (*calcio*) football; (*aerostato*) balloon.
pallottola [pal'lɔttola] *sf* pellet; (*rivoltella*)
bullet.
palma[1] ['palma] *sf* (*albero*) palm(-tree).
palma[2] ['palma] *sf* (*anat*) palm. **piede
palmato** *sm* webbed foot.
palmo ['palmo] *sm* palm.
palo ['palo] *sm* pole; (*di porta*) post.
palombaro [palom'baro] *sm* diver.
palpare [pal'pare] *v* feel; pat. **palpabile**
agg palpable.
palpebra ['palpebra] *sf* eyelid. **battere le
palbebre** blink.
palpitare [palpi'tare] *v* throb.
paltò [pal'tɔ] *sm invar* overcoat.
palude [pa'lude] *sf* marsh, swamp. **terreno
paludoso** *sm* marshland.
panca ['panka] *sf* bench. **panchetto** *sm*
(foot)stool. **panchina** *sf* bench, garden
seat. **pancone** *sm* work-bench.
pancetta [pan'tʃetta] *sf* bacon.
pancia ['pantʃa] *sf* belly; (*fam*) tummy.
mal di pancia *sm* (*fam*) tummy-ache.
panciotto *sm* waistcoat. **panciuto** *agg*
(*persona*) pot-bellied; (*cosa*) bulging.
pancreas ['pankreas] *sm invar* pancreas.
panda ['panda] *sm invar* panda.
pandemonio [pande'mɔnjo] *sm* uproar.
pane ['pane] *sm* bread; (*forma*) loaf. **buono come il pane** as good as gold.

guadagnarsi il pane earn one's living. **pan
grattato** breadcrumbs *pl*. **pan tostato**
toast. **panettiere** *sm* baker. **panificio** *sm*
bakery.
panfilo ['panfilo] *sm* yacht.
panico ['paniko] *sm* panic.
paniere [pa'njɛre] *sm* basket.
panino [pa'nino] *sm* roll. **panino imbottito**
sandwich.
panna[1] ['panna] *sf* cream. **panna montata**
whipped cream.
panna[2] ['panna] *sf* (*mec*) breakdown.
pannello [pan'nello] *sm* panel.
panno ['panno] *sm* cloth. **panni** *sm pl* (*vestiti*) clothes *pl*. **pannolino** *sm* nappy.
panorama [pano'rama] *sm* panorama,
view.
pantaloni [panta'loni] *sm pl* trousers *pl*;
(*corti*) shorts *pl*.
pantano [pan'tano] *sm* bog.
pantera [pan'tɛra] *sf* panther.
pantofola [pan'tɔfola] *sf* slipper.
pantomima [panto'mima] *sf* play-acting.
paonazzo [pao'nattso] *agg* purple.
papa ['papa] *sm* pope. **ogni morte di papa**
once in a blue moon. **vivere come un
papa** live like a lord. **papale** *agg* papal.
papà [pa'pa] *sm* (*fam*) dad(dy).
papavero [pa'pavero] *sm* poppy.
papera ['papera] *sf* slip, blunder. **prendere
una papera** slip up.
papero ['papero], **-a** *sm, sf* gosling.
papiro [pa'piro] *sm* papyrus; (*fam*) paper.
pappa ['pappa] *sm* mush. **pappare** *v* gobble up.
pappagallo [pappa'gallo] *sm* parrot.
paprica ['paprika] *sf* paprika.
parabola [pa'rabola] *sf* (*storia*) parable;
(*mat*) parabola.
parabrezza [para'brettsa] *sm invar* windshield.
paracadute [paraka'dute] *sm invar* parachute. **paracadutista** *s(m+f)* parachutist;
(*mil*) paratrooper.
paradiso [para'dizo] *sm* paradise, heaven.
paradosso [para'dɔsso] *sm* paradox.
paradossale *agg* paradoxical.
parafango [para'fango] *sm* mudguard.
paraffina [paraf'fina] *sf* paraffin.
parafrasi [pa'rafrazi] *sf* paraphrase.
parafulmine [para'fulmine] *sm* lightning
conductor.
parafuoco [para'fwɔko] *sm, pl* **-chi**
fireguard, firescreen.

paragonare [parago'nare] *v* compare.
paragonabile *agg* comparable. **paragone** *sm* comparison. **senza paragone** without equal.
paragrafo [pa'ragrafo] *sm* paragraph.
paralisi [pa'ralizi] *sf* paralysis (*pl* -ses).
paralitico, -a *sm, sf* cripple. **paralizzare** *v* paralyse.
parallelo [paral'lɛlo] *agg, sm* parallel.
parallela *sf* parallel (line). **parallelogrammo** *sm* parallelogram.
paralume [para'lume] *sm* lampshade.
paranoia [para'nɔja] *sf* paranoia. **paranoico** *agg* paranoid.
parapetto [para'pɛtto] *sm* parapet.
parare [pa'rare] *v* adorn; (*evitare*) ward off; (*sport*) save.
parasole [para'sole] *sm* sunshade.
parassita [paras'sita] *agg* parasitic. *s(m+f)* parasite.
parata[1] [pa'rata] *sf* (*sfilata*) parade.
parata[2] [pa'rata] *sf* (*scherma*) parry; (*calcio, ecc.*) save.
parato [pa'rato] *sm* **carta da parati** *sf* wallpaper.
paraurti [para'urti] *sm invar* bumper.
paravento [para'vɛnto] *sm* screen.
parcheggiare [parked'dʒare] *v* park.
parcheggio *sm* parking; (*luogo*) car park.
parchimetro [par'kimetro] *sm* parking meter.
parco[1] ['parko] *sm* park; (*industriale*) depot; (*auto*) fleet.
parco[2] ['parko] *agg* frugal, moderate.
parecchio [pa'rekkjo] *agg* quite a lot of, several. **parecchio tempo** quite a long time. *pron* quite a lot, several. *avv* quite a lot.
pareggiare [pared'dʒare] *v* equal; (*sport*) draw; (*comm*) balance. **pareggio** *sm* balance; draw.
parente [pa'rɛnte] *s(m+f)* relative, relation. **parentela** *sf* relationship; (*parenti*) relations *pl.*
parentesi [pa'rɛntezi] *sf* bracket, parenthesis (*pl* -ses). **fra parentesi** incidentally.
*****parere** [pa'rere] *v* seem, appear; (*suono*) sound; (*tatto*) feel. **faccio come mi pare** I do as I like. *sm* opinion.
parete [pa'rete] *sf* wall; (*monte*) face.
pari ['pari] *agg* equal, same; (*non dispari*) even; equivalent. **alla pari** (*in famiglia*) au pair. **essere pari** be quits; (*forze*) be equal *or* level. *s(m+f)* equal, peer.

Parigi [pa'ridʒi] *sf* Paris. **parigino, -a** *s, agg* Parisian.
parità [pari'ta] *sf* parity. **a parità di condizioni** all things being equal.
parlamento [parla'mento] *sm* parliament. **parlamentare** *agg* parliamentary.
parlare [par'lare] *v* speak, talk. **parlar chiaro** speak clearly; (*fig*) speak one's mind. *sm* talk; (*parlata*) way of speaking, dialect.
parmigiano [parmi'dʒano] *agg* Parmesan. *sm* Parmesan cheese.
parodia [paro'dia] *sf* parody.
parola [pa'rɔla] *sf* word. **parola d'ordine** password. **parole crociate** *sf pl* crossword *sing.*
parolacce [paro'lattʃe] *sf pl* bad language *sing.*
parrochia [par'rɔkkja] *sf* parish. **parroco** *sm, pl* -**chi** parish priest.
parrucca [par'rukka] *sf* wig.
parrucchiere [parruk'kjɛre] *sm* hairdresser.
parte ['parte] *sf* part; (*porzione*) share; (*lato*) side; (*dir*) party. **a parte** apart; extra. **dall'altra parte** on the other hand. **da parte** aside. **da parte mia** from me. **da queste parti** round here. **per parte mia** as far as I am concerned.
partecipare [partetʃi'pare] *v* participate, take part; (*condividere*) share; announce. **partecipazione** *sf* sharing; announcement; presence.
partenza [par'tɛntsa] *sf* departure; (*sport*) start.
participio [parti'tʃipjo] *sm* participle.
particolare [partiko'lare] *agg* particular, special. *sm* detail.
partigiano [parti'dʒano], -**a** *s, agg* partisan.
partire [par'tire] *v* leave; go away; start.
partita [par'tita] *sf* game; (*incontro*) match; (*contabilità*) entry; (*merci*) lot.
partito [par'tito] *sm* party; condition; decision. **mal partito** predicament. **per partito preso** having made up one's mind.
partitura [parti'tura] *sf* score.
parto ['parto] *sm* birth; (*umano*) childbirth; (*atto*) delivery. **partorire** *v* give birth (to).
parziale [par'tsjale] *agg* partial; (*predisposto*) biased.
pascere ['paʃere] *v* feed (on). **ben pasciuto** well-fed, plump.

pascolare [pasko'lare] v graze. **pascolo** sm pasture.

Pasqua ['paskwa] sf Easter. **Pasqua degli ebrei** Passover.

passabile [pas'sabile] agg fair.

passaggio [pas'saddʒo] sm passage; (traversata) crossing. **dare un passaggio** give a lift. **diritto di passaggio** sm right of way. **essere di passaggio** be on the way through. **vietato il passaggio** no thoroughfare.

passaporto [passa'pɔrto] sm passport.

passare [pas'sare] v pass; go past; (gastr) strain.

passatempo [passa'tɛmpo] sm pastime.

passato [pas'sato] agg past; (scorso) last. sm past.

passatoia [passa'toja] sf runner.

passeggero [passed'dʒɛro], -a agg passing, transient. sm, sf passenger.

passeggiare [passed'dʒare] v go for a walk or stroll. **passeggiata** sf walk, stroll; (non a piedi) ride.

passerella [passe'rɛlla] sf footbridge.

passero ['passero] sm sparrow.

passibile [pas'sibile] agg liable (to).

passione [pas'sjone] sf passion.

passivo [pas'sivo] agg passive; (comm) debit. sm (gramm) passive; (comm) liability.

passo ['passo] sm step; (andatura) pace; (velocità) rate; (geog) pass; (di vite) thread. **cedere il passo** give way. **fare due passi** go for a stroll. **sbarrare il passo** block the way. **segnare il passo** mark time.

pasta ['pasta] sf dough; (minestra) pasta; (impasto) paste; (dolce) pastry. **pasta frolla** shortcrust pastry. **pasta sfoglia** puff pastry.

pastello [pas'tɛllo] sm pastel.

pasticca [pas'tikka] sf lozenge.

pasticceria [pastittʃe'ria] sf (negozio) confectioner's (shop); (pasticcini) pastries pl. **pasticciere** sm confectioner.

pasticciare [pastit'tʃare] v bungle, mess up. **pasticcio** sm mess; (gastr) pie.

pastiglia [pas'tiʎa] sf tablet.

pasto ['pasto] sm meal. **vino da pasto** sm table wine.

pastore [pas'tore] sm shepherd; (prete) minister. **cane pastore** sm sheepdog. **pastorale** agg pastoral.

pastorizzare [pastorid'dzare] v pasteurize. **pastorizzazione** sf pasteurization.

pastoso [pas'tozo] agg mellow.

pastrano [pas'trano] sm overcoat.

pastura [pas'tura] sf pasture.

patata [pa'tata] sf potato.

patella [pa'tɛlla] sf (anat) knee-cap; (zool) limpet.

patente[1] [pa'tɛnte] agg patent.

patente[2] [pa'tɛnte] sf licence.

paterno [pa'tɛrno] agg paternal. **paternale** sf lecture. **paternità** sf paternity.

patetico [pa'tɛtiko] agg pathetic, moving.

patibolo [pa'tibolo] sm gallows.

patina ['patina] sf coat.

patire [pa'tire] v suffer. **patimento** sm suffering, pain. **patito** sm (fam) fan.

patologico [pato'lɔdʒiko] agg pathological.

patria ['patrja] sf country; home.

patrigno [pa'triɲo] sm stepfather.

patrimonio [patri'mɔnjo] sm estate; fortune. **patrimonio pubblico** public heritage.

patriota [patri'ɔta] s(m+f) patriot. **patriottico** agg patriotic. **patriottismo** sm patriotism.

patrocinio [patro'tʃinjo] sm defence. **patrocinare** v defend.

patrono [pa'trɔno] sm patron. **patronato** sm patronage; institution.

pattinare [patti'nare] v skate. **pattinaggio** sm skating. **pattino** sm skate; (mec) shoe.

patto ['patto] sm pact, agreement; condition, term. **pattuire** v agree.

pattuglia [pat'tuʎa] sf patrol.

pattumiera [pattu'mjɛra] sf dustbin.

paura [pa'ura] sf fear; (spavento) fright. **aver paura di** be afraid of, fear. **far paura** scare. **pauroso** agg (che fa paura) frightening; (che ha paura) timid, afraid.

pausa ['pauza] sf pause, interval.

pavimento [pavi'mento] sm floor.

pavone [pa'vone] sm peacock. **pavonessa** sf peahen.

pavoneggiarsi [pavoned'dʒarsi] v show off.

paziente [pa'tsjɛnte] s(m+f), agg patient. **pazientare** v wait patiently. **pazienza** sf patience.

pazzo ['pattso], -a agg crazy, insane. sm, sf lunatic. **pazzesco** agg mad; incredible. **pazzia** sf madness, folly.

peccare [pek'kare] v sin. **pecca** sf fault. **peccato** sm sin. **che peccato!** what a pity! **peccatore, -trice** sm, sf sinner.

pece ['petʃe] *sf* pitch.

pecora ['pɛkora] *sf* sheep; *(femmina)* ewe.

peculiare [peku'ljare] *agg* peculiar.

pedaggio [pe'daddʒo] *sm* toll.

pedale [pe'dale] *sm* pedal. **pedalare** *v* pedal.

pedana [pe'dana] *sf* platform; *(sport)* springboard.

pedante [pe'dante] *agg* pedantic. *s(m+f)* pedant.

pedata [pe'data] *sf* kick; *(orma)* footprint.

pedestre [pe'dɛstre] *agg* pedestrian.

pediatria [pedja'tria] *sf* paediatrics. **pediatra** *s(m+f)* paediatrician. **pediatrico** *agg* paediatric.

pedicure [pedi'kure] *sf* *(cura)* pedicure. *s(m+f) invar* chiropodist.

pedina [pe'dina] *sf* piece; *(scacchi)* pawn. **muovere una pedina** make a move; *(fig)* pull strings.

pedinare [pedi'nare] *v* shadow.

pedone [pe'done] *s(m+f)* pedestrian. **pedonale** *agg* pedestrian.

peggio ['pɛddʒo] *agg (comparativo)* worse; *(superlativo)* the worst. *sm* the worst. **alla peggio** if the worst comes to the worst.

peggiorare [peddʒo'rare] *v* *(stare)* get worse; *(rendere)* make worse. **peggioramento** *sm* worsening.

peggiore [ped'dʒore] *agg (comparativo)* worse; *(superlativo)* the worst. *s(m+f)* the worst.

pegno ['peɲo] *sm* pledge, pawn.

pelare [pe'lare] *v* peel, skin; *(fig)* fleece. **pelarsi** *v* *(fam)* go bald.

pelle ['pɛlle] *sf* skin; *(cuoio)* hide; *(frutta)* peel; *(carnagione)* complexion. **rimetterci la pelle** lose one's life.

pellegrino [pelle'grino] *sm* pilgrim. **pellegrinaggio** *sm* pilgrimage.

pellicano [pelli'kano] *sm* pelican.

pelliccia [pel'littʃa] *sf* fur; *(mantello)* fur coat. **pelliccaio** *sm* furrier.

pellicola [pel'likola] *sf* film; membrane.

pelo ['pelo] *sm* hair; *(pelame)* coat. **cercare il pelo nell'uovo** split hairs. **contro pelo** against the grain. **per un pelo** by a whisker.

peltro ['peltro] *sm* pewter.

peluria [pe'lurja] *sf* down.

pelvi ['pɛlvi] *sf* pelvis.

pena ['pena] *sf* *(dolore)* pain; *(disturbo)* trouble; punishment. **valere la pena** be worth it, be worthwhile.

penale [pe'nale] *agg* criminal, penal. *sf* fine.

penare [pe'nare] *v* find difficult, be hardly able to.

pendente [pen'dɛnte] *agg* hanging; *(dir, comm)* pending; *(torre)* leaning. *sm* pendant. **pendenza** *sf* slope, incline.

pendere ['pɛndere] *v* hang (down); incline, slope; *(dir)* be pending.

pendio [pen'dio] *sm* slope.

pendolare [pendo'lare] *v* swing. *s(m+f)* commuter. **pendolo** *sm* pendulum.

pene ['pene] *sm* penis.

penetrare [pene'trare] *v* penetrate, pierce. **penetrante** *agg* penetrating, piercing; acute. **penetrazione** *sf* penetration.

penicillina [penitʃil'lina] *sf* penicillin.

penisola [pe'nizola] *sf* peninsula.

penitente [peni'tɛnte] *s(m+f)*, *agg* penitent. **penitenza** *sf* penance; *(gioco)* forfeit. **penitenziario** *sm* jail.

penna ['penna] *sf* feather; *(da scrivere)* pen. **penna a sfera** ball-point pen. **penna stilografica** fountain pen. **pennuto** *agg* feathered.

pennello [pen'nɛllo] *sm* brush.

penombra [pe'nombra] *sf* twilight.

penoso [pe'nozo] *agg* painful.

pensare [pen'sare] *v* think; intend. **pensarci** *v* think about it. **pensarci sopra** think it over. **pensatore, -trice** *sm, sf* thinker.

pensiero [pen'sjɛro] *sm* thought; *(mente, parere)* mind. **essere in pensiero** worry. **pensieroso** *agg* thoughtful; pensive.

pensile [pen'sile] *agg* hanging.

pensionare [pensjo'nare] *v* pension off. **pensionato** *sm* pensioner; *(collegio)* boarding-school. **pensione** *sf* pension. **essere in pensione** be retired. **mezza pensione** half board. **pensione completa** full board.

pentagono [pen'tagono] *sm* pentagon. **pentagonale** *agg* pentagonal.

Pentecoste [pente'kɔste] *sf* Whitsun.

pentirsi [pen'tirsi] *v* regret, be sorry for; *(rel)* repent. **pentimento** *sm* regret; repentance.

pentola ['pentola] *sf* pot.

penultimo [pe'nultimo] *agg* penultimate.

penzolare [pendzo'lare] *v* dangle. **penzoloni** *avv* dangling.

pepe ['pepe] *sm* pepper. **pepare** *v* pepper. **pepato** *agg* peppery, hot. **peperone** *sm* capsicum; (*frutto*) pepper; (*peperoncino*) chili.

pepita [pe'pita] *sf* nugget.

per ['per] *prep* for; (*attraverso*) through; (*mat, entro, tramite*) by. **per caso** by chance. **per cento** per cent. **per di più** in addition. **per lo meno** at least. **per ora** for the present. **per terra** on the floor. **per volta** at a time. **stare per** be about to, be on the point of.

pera ['pera] *sf* pear. **pero** *sm* pear-tree.

perbacco [per'bakko] *inter* by Jove!

perbene [per'bɛne] *agg invar* respectable, nice. *avv* well, nicely.

percentuale [pertʃentu'ale] *agg* per cent. *sf* percentage.

percepire [pertʃe'pire] *v* notice, be aware (of); (*riscuotere*) receive. **percepibile** *agg* noticeable; (*comm*) due. **percettibile** *agg* perceptible. **percezione** *sf* perception.

perché [per'ke] *avv* why. *cong* because, as; (*affinché*) so that. *sm* reason.

perciò [per'tʃo] *cong* so, therefore.

***percorrere** [per'korrere] *v* cover.

percorso [per'korso] *sm* trip, run.

percossa [per'kɔssa] *sf* blow, impact.

***percuotere** [per'kwɔtere] *v* strike, hit.

percussione [perkus'sjone] *sf* percussion.

***perdere** ['pɛrdere] *v* lose; (*colare*) leak; (*sprecare*) waste. **lascia perdere!** skip it! **perdere di vista** lose sight of. **perdersi** *v* get lost. **perdita** *sf* loss; leak; waste.

perdonare [perdo'nare] *v* forgive. **perdono** *sm* forgiveness, pardon.

perenne [pe'rɛnne] *agg* perpetual.

perfetto [per'fɛtto] *agg* perfect.

perfezionare [perfetsjo'nare] *v* (*migliorare*) improve; make perfect. **perfezionarsi** *v* specialize. **perfezionamento** *sm* specialization. **perfezione** *sf* perfection. **perfezionista** *s(m+f)* perfectionist.

perfidia [per'fidja] *sf* treachery, wickedness. **perfido** *agg* treacherous, wicked.

perfino [per'fino] *avv* even.

perforare [perfo'rare] *v* pierce, perforate.

pergamena [perga'mɛna] *sf* parchment.

pericolo [pe'rikolo] *sm* danger; risk. **pericolante** *agg* unsafe. **pericoloso** *agg* dangerous; risky.

periferia [perife'ria] *sf* periphery; (*città*) suburbs *pl*. **periferico** *agg* suburban; peripheral.

perimetro [pe'rimetro] *sm* perimeter.

periodico [peri'ɔdiko] *agg* periodic. *sm* periodical.

periodo [pe'riodo] *sm* period.

peripezia [peripe'tsia] *sf* vicissitude.

perire [pe'rire] *v* perish, die.

periscopio [peri'skɔpjo] *sm* periscope.

perito [pe'rito], **-a** *s, agg* expert. **perizia** *sf* (*bravura*) skill, expertise; (*pratica*) experience; (*valutazione*) examination, expert opinion.

perla ['pɛrla] *sf* pearl.

perlomeno [perlo'meno] *avv* at least.

perlustrare [perlus'trare] *v* patrol; (*mil*) reconnoitre. **perlustrazione** *sf* patrol; reconnaissance.

permaloso [perma'lozo] *agg* touchy.

permanente [perma'nɛnte] *agg* permanent, lasting. *sf* (*fam*) perm. **permanenza** *sf* (*soggiorno*) stay. **in permanenza** permanently. **permanere** *v* remain.

permeare [perme'are] *v* permeate. **permeabile** *agg* permeable.

permesso [per'messo] *sm* permission; licence; (*congedo*) leave, pass. (**con**) **permesso?** may I? (*inter*) allow me!

***permettere** [per'mettere] *v* allow, permit.

pernice [per'nitʃe] *sf* partridge.

perno ['pɛrno] *sm* pivot, pin. **far perno su** hinge on.

pernottare [pernot'tare] *v* spend the night.

pero ['pero] *sm* pear-tree. **pera** *sf* pear.

però [pe'ro] *cong* but; (*tuttavia*) still, yet, however.

perossido [pe'rɔssido] *sm* peroxide.

perpendicolare [perpendiko'lare] *agg, sf* perpendicular.

perpetuo [per'pɛtuo] *agg* perpetual.

perplesso [per'plɛsso] *agg* puzzled; (*incerto*) undecided. **perplessità** *sf* perplexity; indecision.

perquisire [perkwi'zire] *v* search. **perquisizione** *sf* search.

perseguire [perse'gwire] *v* pursue. **perseguimento** *sm* pursuit.

perseguitare [persegwi'tare] *v* persecute. **persecuzione** *sf* persecution.

perseverare [perseve'rare] *v* persevere. **perseveranza** *sf* perseverance.

persiana [per'sjana] *sf* shutter, blind.

persiano [per'sjano] *agg* Persian.

persico ['pɛrsiko] *agg* Persian. (**pesce**) **persico** *sm* perch.

persino [per'sino] *avv* even.

*persistere [per'sistere] *v* persist. **persis-**
tenza *sf* persistence.
perso ['pɛrso] *agg* lost. **a tempo perso** in
one's spare time.
persona [per'sona] *sf* person; (*qualcuno*)
somebody. **di** *or* **in persona** in person,
personally; (*personificato*) personified.
persona di servizio domestic (help).
personaggio [perso'naddʒo] *sm* (*teatro*,
ecc.) character; celebrity.
personale [perso'nale] *agg* personal. *sm*
(*aspetto*) figure; (*dipendenti*) staff. *sf*
(*mostra*) one-man show. **personale di**
direzione management. **personale qualifi-**
cato skilled workers *pl*.
personalità [personali'ta] *sf* personality.
personificare [personifi'kare] *v* personify.
personificazione *sf* personification.
perspicace [perspi'katʃe] *agg* keen,
shrewd.
*persuadere [persua'dere] *v* persuade;
convince. **persuasione** *sf* persuasion;
conviction. **persuasivo** *agg* convincing.
persuaso *agg* convinced.
pertanto [per'tanto] *cong* thus, therefore,
so.
pertica ['pɛrtika] *sf* pole.
pertinace [perti'natʃe] *agg* stubborn;
(*deciso*) determined.
pertinente [perti'nɛnte] *agg* pertaining
(to); (*domanda*) relevant.
pertosse [per'tosse] *sf* whooping cough.
*pervadere [per'vadere] *v* pervade.
*pervenire [perve'nire] *v* arrive (at).
pervertire [perver'tire] *v* corrupt, pervert.
perverso *agg* perverse. **pervertito, -a** *sm*,
sf pervert.
pesare [pe'zare] *v* weigh. **pesa** *sf*
(*pesatura*) weighing; (*basculla*) weighbridge. **pesante** *agg* heavy; (*aria*) stuffy;
(*duro*) rough. **peso** *sm* weight; (*onere*)
burden.
pesca¹ ['peska] *sf* (*bot*) peach. **pesco** *sm*
peach-tree.
pesca² ['peska] *sf* fishing; (*industria*)
fishery; (*quantità*) catch. **pescare** *v* fish;
(*trovare*) pick up, get hold of; (*acciuf-*
fare) catch. **pescatore** *sm* fisherman; (*con*
lenza) angler.
pesce ['peʃe] *sm* fish. **buttarsi a pesce su**
make a dive for. **pesce d'aprile** April
fool. **sano come un pesce** fit as a fiddle.
pescivendolo, -a *sm*, *sf* fishmonger.
pessimismo [pessi'mizmo] *sm* pessimism.

pessimista *s(m+f)* pessimist. **pessimistico**
agg pessimistic.
pessimo ['pɛssimo] *agg* very bad;
(*scadente*, *incapace*) very poor.
pestare [pes'tare] *v* crush; (*fam: picchiare*)
give a (good) hiding. **pestare i piedi a**
qualcuno tread on someone's toes. **pes-**
tello *sm* pestle.
peste ['pɛste] *sf* plague; (*fig*) pest, curse.
pesto ['pesto] *agg* crushed. **essere buio**
pesto be pitch dark.
petalo ['pɛtalo] *sm* petal.
petizione [peti'tsjone] *sf* petition.
petrolifero [petro'lifero] *agg* oil.
petrolio [pe'trɔljo] *sm* oil. **lampada a**
petrolio *sf* paraffin lamp. **petroliera** *sf*
(oil-)tanker.
pettegolo [pet'tegolo], **-a** *sm*, *sf* gossip.
agg gossipy. **pettegolezzo** *sm* gossip.
pettinare [petti'nare] *v* comb. **pettinarsi** *v*
comb one's hair. **pettinato** *sm* (*tessuto*)
worsted. **pettinatura** *sf* combing; (*accon-*
ciatura) hair-style. **pettine** *sm* comb.
petto ['pɛtto] *sm* breast; (*torace*) chest. **a**
doppio/un petto double-/single-breasted.
petulante [petu'lante] *agg* pert.
pezza ['pɛttsa] *sf* rag; (*toppa*) patch; (*pan-*
nolino) napkin. **pezza da piedi** doormat.
pezza di tessuto roll of cloth. **pezzato** *agg*
spotted. **pezzente** *s(m+f)* beggar.
pezzo ['pɛttso] *sm* piece; (*tempo*) period;
(*giornale*) article. **pezzo di ricambio** spare
part. **pezzo di terreno** plot of land. **pezzo**
grosso (*fam*) VIP, big shot.
*piacere [pja'tʃere] *v* please. **mi piace . . .**
I like . . . . *sm* pleasure; favour. **a piacere**
ad lib, freely. **far piacere a** please. **per**
piacere please, if you please. **piacevole**
agg pleasant.
piaga ['pjaga] *sf* sore; (*fig*) wound.
piagnucolare [pjaɲuko'lare] *v* whine,
whimper. **piagnucolio** *sm* whining, whim-
pering. **piagnucolone, -a** *sm*, *sf* (*fam*) cry-
baby.
pialla ['pjalla] *sf* plane. **piallare** *v* plane.
pianella [pja'nɛlla] *sf* (*mattonella*) tile;
(*pantofola*) mule, slipper.
pianerottolo [pjane'rɔttolo] *sm* landing.
pianeta [pja'neta] *sm* planet.
*piangere ['pjandʒere] *v* weep, cry. **far**
piangere *v* move to tears; (*ironico*) be
pathetic.
pianificare [pjanifi'kare] *v* plan. **pianifi-**
catore, -trice *sm*, *sf* planner. **pianifica-**
zione *sf* planning.

pianista [pja'nista] *s(m+f)* pianist.

piano¹ ['pjano] *agg* flat, level; (*chiaro*) clear. *avv* (*adagio*) slow, slowly; (*con cautela*) carefully; (*a voce bassa*) softly. **pian piano** very slowly, very softly; (*poco alla volta*) little by little.

piano² ['pjano] *sm* plane, level; (*casa*) floor, storey; (*autobus*) deck. **primo piano** foreground. **secondo piano** background.

piano³ ['pjano] *sm* (*progetto*) plan. **piano di studi** syllabus. **piano regolatore** town plan.

pianoforte [pjano'forte] *sm* pianoforte; (*fam*) piano. **pianoforte a coda** grand piano.

pianta ['pjanta] *sf* (*bot*) plant; (*disegno*) plan; (*carta di città*) map. **di sana pianta** from scratch. **in pianta stabile** on the permanent staff. **pianta del piede** sole.

piantagione [pjanta'dʒone] *sf* plantation.

piantare [pjan'tare] *v* plant; (*conficcare*) drive; (*tenda*) pitch; (*abbandonare*) quit. **piantare grave** (*fam*) make trouble. **piantare in asso** leave in the lurch.

pianterreno [pjanter'reno] *sm* ground floor.

pianto ['pjanto] *sm* crying; tears *pl*.

pianura [pja'nura] *sf* plain.

piastra ['pjastra] *sf* plate. **piastrella** *sf* tile. **piastrellare** *v* tile.

piattaforma [pjatta'forma] *sf* platform. **piattaforma di lancio** launching pad. **piattaforma girevole** turntable.

piatto ['pjatto] *agg* flat. *sm* plate; (*portata*) dish, course; (*bilancia*) pan. **lavare i piatti** wash up.

piazza ['pjattsa] *sf* square; (*comm*) market; (*posto*) place; (*fam: calvizie*) bald patch. **a due piazze** (*letto, ecc.*) double. **a una piazza** single. **far piazza pulita** make a clean sweep. **scendere in piazza** demonstrate. **piazzaforte** *sf* stronghold. **piazzale** *sm* square. **piazzare** *v* place. **piazzista** *sm* salesman, commercial traveller.

picca ['pikka] *sf* pike. **picche** *sf pl* (*carte*) spades *pl*. **rispondere picche** turn down flat.

piccante [pik'kante] *agg* sharp, spicy; (*arguto*) spirited; (*licenzioso*) racy.

picchiare [pik'kjare] *v* hit, strike; (*colpire*) beat; (*bussare*) knock. **picchiata** *sf* (*aereo*) (nose-)dive.

picchio ['pikkjo] *sm* woodpecker.

piccino [pit'tʃino] *agg* tiny. *sm* child (*pl* -ren).

piccione [pit'tʃone] *sm* pigeon, dove. **piccionaia** *sf* dovecot; (*fam: teatro*) (the) gods.

picco ['pikko] *sm* peak. **a picco** sheer. **colare** *or* **mandare a picco** sink.

piccolo ['pikkolo], **-a** *agg* small, little. *sm, sf* little one, child (*pl* -ren). **da piccolo** as a child. **fin da piccolo** since childhood. **in piccolo** on a small scale. **piccolezza** *sf* (*inezia*) trifle.

piccone ['pikkone] *sm* pick-axe.

pidocchio [pi'dokkjo] *sm* louse (*pl* lice). **pidocchioso** *agg* lousy; (*fig*) mean.

piede ['pjɛde] *sm* foot (*pl* feet). **a piedi** on foot. **a piedi nudi** barefoot. **essere tra i piedi** be in the way. **fatto con i piedi** (*fam*) slipshod. **in piedi** standing. **togliersi dai piedi** get out of the way. **piedistallo** *sm* pedestal.

piega ['pjɛga] *sf* fold; crease; (*ornamento*) pleat. **messa in piega** *sf* set. **mettere in piega** *v* set. **prendere una brutta piega** take a turn for the worse.

piegare [pje'gare] *v* bend; (*foglio, tessuto*) fold.

pieghettare [pjeget'tare] *v* pleat.

pieghevole [pje'gevole] *agg* folding; flexible.

piena ['pjɛna] *sf* flood, spate; (*folla*) crowd.

pieno ['pjɛno] *agg* full. **in pieno** completely; exactly. (*nel mezzo*) in the middle of. **pieno zeppo** full up, chock full. **fare il pieno** (*auto*) fill up.

pietà [pje'ta] *sf* pity, compassion; (*devozione*) piety. **fare pietà** arouse pity. **pietoso** *agg* pitiful.

pietanza [pje'tantsa] *sf* dish, course.

pietra ['pjɛtra] *sf* stone. **pietra dura** semiprecious stone. **pietra di paragone** touchstone. **pietrina** *sf* flint.

piffero ['piffero] *sm* pipe; (*sonatore*) piper.

pigiama [pi'dʒama] *sm* pyjamas *pl*.

pigiare [pi'dʒare] *v* press, squeeze. **pigiatura** *sf* pressing.

pigione [pi'dʒone] *sf* rent.

pigliare [pi'ʎare] (*fam*) *V* **prendere**.

pigmento [pig'mento] *sm* pigment. **pigmentazione** *sf* pigmentation.

pigmeo [pig'mɛo] *sm* pygmy.

pigna ['piɲa] *sf* pine-cone.

pignatta [pi'ɲatta] *sf* pot.

pignolo [pi'ɲɔlo], **-a** *agg* fussy, pedantic. *sm, sf* pedant.

pigolare [pigo'lare] *v* peep, chirp. **pigolio** *sm* peeping, chirping.

pigro ['pigro], **-a** *agg* idle, lazy. *sm, sf* lazy person, loafer. **pigrizia** *sf* laziness, idleness.

pila ['pila] *sf* pile; (*elett*) battery.

pilastro [pi'lastro] *sm* pillar, column.

pillola ['pillola] *sf* pill.

pilone [pi'lone] *sm* pillar; (*ponte*) pier; (*elett*) pylon.

pilotare [pilo'tare] *v* pilot; (*auto*) drive. **pilota** *sm* pilot.

pinacoteca [pinako'tɛka] *sf* picture gallery.

pineta [pi'neta] *sf* pine forest.

pingue ['pingwe] *agg* fat.

pinguino [pin'gwino] *sm* penguin.

pinna ['pinna] *sf* fin.

pinnacolo [pin'nakolo] *sm* pinnacle.

pino ['pino] *sm* pine (tree). **pinolo** *sm* pine-seed.

pinza ['pintsa] *sf* pliers *pl*; (*zool*) pincer. **pinzetta** *sf* tweezers *pl*.

pio ['pio] *agg* pious.

pioggia ['pjoddʒa] *sf* rain. **pioggerella** *sf* *also* **pioggia fine** drizzle.

piolo [pi'ɔlo] *sm* peg; (*scala*) rung.

piombare¹ [pjom'bare] *v* hurtle, plunge; (*avventarsi*) pounce.

piombare² [pjom'bare] *v* (*otturare*) fill; (*sigillare*) seal (with lead). **piombo** *sm* lead; (*piombino*) plummet.

pioniere [pjo'njɛre], **-a** *sm, sf* pioneer.

pioppo ['pjoppo] *sm* poplar.

*****piovere** ['pjɔvere] *v* rain; (*fig*) pour (in). **piovere a catinelle** rain cats and dogs. **piovigginare** *v* drizzle. **piovoso** *agg* rainy.

piovra ['pjɔvra] *sf* (giant) squid; (*persona*) blood-sucker.

pipa ['pipa] *sf* pipe.

pipistrello [pipi'strɛllo] *sm* bat.

pira ['pira] *sf* pyre.

piramide [pi'ramide] *sf* pyramid.

pirata [pi'rata] *sm* pirate. **pirata della strada** hit-and-run driver. **pirateria** *sf* piracy.

piroscafo [pi'rɔskafo] *sm* steamer; (*da carico*) freighter; (*di linea*) liner.

piscia ['piʃa] (*volg*) *sf* piss. **pisciare** *v* piss.

piscina [pi'ʃina] *sf* swimming pool.

pisello [pi'zɛllo] *sm* pea. **pisello odoroso** sweet pea.

pisolino [pizo'lino] *sm* **fare** *or* **schiacciare un pisolino** take a nap.

pista ['pista] *sf* track; (*aero*) runway.

pistola [pis'tɔla] *sf* pistol. **pistola a spruzzo** spray-gun. **pistolettata** *sf* pistol-shot.

pistone [pis'tone] *sm* piston.

pitocco [pi'tɔkko], **-a** *sm, sf* beggar; (*avaro*) miser.

pitone [pi'tone] *sm* python.

pittore [pit'tore] *sm* painter.

pittoresco [pitto'resko] *agg* picturesque.

pittura [pit'tura] *sf* painting; (*descrizione*) picture; (*vernice*) paint. **pitturare** *v* paint.

più [pju] *avv* (*comparativo*) more; (*superlativo*) most. **al più presto** as soon as possible. **il più** the majority. **il più possibile** as much as possible. **più volte** several times. **sempre più ...** more and more .... **tanto più** especially. **tutt'al più** at most.

piuma ['pjuma] *sf* feather. **piumino** *sm* down; (*per cipria*) powder-puff; (*letto*) eiderdown, duvet.

piuttosto [pjut'tosto] *avv* rather.

piviere [pi'vjɛre] *sm* plover.

pizzicare [pittsi'kare] *v* pinch; (*pungere*) sting; (*musica*) pluck. **pizzico** *sm*, *pl* **-chi** pinch, dash. **pizzicore** *sm* itch. **pizzicotto** *sm* pinch.

pizzo ['pittso] *sm* (*merletto*) lace; (*barba*) goatee.

placare [pla'kare] *v* calm down, placate.

placca ['plakka] *sf* plate; (*ornamento*) plaque; (*med*) patch.

placenta [pla'tʃɛnta] *sf* placenta.

placido ['platʃido] *agg* placid.

plagiare [pla'dʒare] *v* plagiarize. **plagiario, -a** *sm, sf* plagiarist.

planare [pla'nare] *v* glide. **planata** *sf* glide.

plasmare [plaz'mare] *v* mould. **plasma** *sm* plasma.

plastica ['plastika] *sf* (*arte*) modelling; (*med*) plastic surgery; (*materia*) plastic. **plasticare** *v* model. **plastico** *agg* plastic.

platano ['platano] *sm* plane-tree.

platea [pla'tɛa] *sf* stalls *pl*.

platino ['platino] *sm* platinum.

platonico [pla'tɔniko] *agg* platonic.

plausibile [plau'zibile] *agg* plausible.

plebe ['plɛbe] *sf* plebs *pl*; (*plebaglia*) mob, riff-raff. **plebeo** *agg* plebeian; common.

plebiscito [plebi'ʃito] *sm* plebiscite.

pleurite [pleu'rite] *sf* pleurisy.

plico ['pliko] *sm* parcel.

plotone [plo'tone] *sm* platoon.
plumbeo ['plumbeo] *agg* leaden.
plurale [plu'rale] *agg, sm* plural.
plutocratico [pluto'kratiko] *agg* plutocratic. **plutocrate** *sm* plutocrat. **plutocrazia** *sf* plutocracy.
pneumatico [pneu'matiko] *sm* tyre. *agg* (*mec*) pneumatic; (*gonfiabile*) inflatable.
po' [po] *V* **poco.**
pochino [po'kino] *agg* not much *or* many. *avv, pron* very little *or* few. *sm* bit.
poco ['poko] *agg* little; (*tempo*) short. *avv* little, not very. *pron* little, not much. **a poco a poco** little by little. **da poco** unimportant. **fra poco** soon. **pochi** *pron, agg* few *pl*. **poco dopo** not long after. **poco fa** a short while ago. **poco male!** never mind! **un poco** *or* **po'** a little.
podere ['podere] *sm* estate.
podestà [podes'ta] *sm* mayor.
podio ['podjo] *sm* platform.
podismo [po'dizmo] *sm* track events *pl*; (*corsa*) running. **podista** *s(m+f)* track athlete; runner.
poema [po'ema] *sm* poem.
poi ['poi] *avv* then; (*più tardi*) later. *sm* future. **da ... in poi** from ... onwards. **il senno di poi** *sm* hindsight.
poiché [poi'ke] *cong* as, since.
polacco [po'lakko], **-a** *agg* Polish. *sm, sf* Pole. *sm* (*lingua*) Polish.
polarizzare [polarid'dzare] *v* polarize. **polare** *agg* polar. **stella polare** *sf* pole star.
polca ['polka] *sf* polka.
polemica [po'lemika] *sf* polemic; controversy. **polemico** *agg* contentious, polemical.
polenta [po'lenta] *sf* (*gastr*) maize porridge; (*fam: persona lenta*) slow-coach.
policlinico [poli'kliniko] *sm* hospital.
poligamo [po'ligamo], **-a** *agg* polygamous. *sm, sf* polygamist. **poligamia** *sf* polygamy.
poligono [po'ligono] *sm* polygon.
polimero [po'limero] *sm* polymer.
polistirolo [polisti'rolo] *sm* polystyrene.
politecnico [poli'tekniko] *sm* polytechnic.
politene [poli'tene] *sm* polythene.
politico [po'litiko] *agg* political. *sm* politician. **politica** *sf* politics; (*linea di condotta*) policy.
polizia [poli'tsia] *sf* police. **poliziesco** *agg* police. **romanzo** *or* **film poliziesco** *sm* thriller. **poliziotto** *sm* policeman.

polizza ['polittsa] *sf* policy; (*ricevuta*) voucher.
pollame [pol'lame] *sm* poultry. **pollaio** *sm* chicken coop. **pollastra** *sf* pullet; (*fam*) lass, chick. **pollastro** cockerel; (*fam*) gullible person, mug.
pollice ['pollitfe] *sm* thumb; (*del piede*) big toe.
polline ['polline] *sm* pollen.
pollo ['pollo] *sm* chicken. **far ridere i polli** be ridiculous.
polmone [pol'mone] *sm* lung. **polmonare** *agg* pulmonary. **polmonite** *sf* pneumonia.
polo ['polo] *sm* pole. **essere ai poli opposti** be poles apart.
Polonia [po'lonja] *sf* Poland.
polpa ['polpa] *sf* flesh; (*carne*) meat; (*fig*) substance. **polpetta** *sf* meatball. **polposo** *agg* fleshy.
polpaccio [pol'pattfo] *sm* (*anat*) calf.
polso ['polso] *sm* wrist; (*med*) pulse; (*polsino*) cuff.
poltiglia [pol'tiʎa] *sf* mush; mixture.
poltrona [pol'trona] *sf* easy chair, armchair; (*teatro*) stall.
poltrone [pol'trone], **-a** *sm, sf* idler, loafer.
polvere ['polvere] *sf* dust; powder. **polveriera** *sf* powder-keg. **polverizzare** *v* pulverize. **polveroso** *agg* dusty.
pomata [po'mata] *sf* ointment.
pomeriggio [pome'riddʒo] *sm* afternoon. **pomeridiano** *agg* afternoon.
pomice ['pomitfe] *sm* pumice-stone.
pomo ['pomo] *sm* (*frutto*) apple; (*albero*) apple-tree.
pomodoro [pomo'doro] *sm* tomato.
pompa¹ ['pompa] *sf* pump. **pompa antincendio** fire-engine. **pompare** *v* pump (up).
pompa² ['pompa] *sf* pomp. **far pompa di** show off. **impresario di pompe funebri** *sm* undertaker. **pomposo** *agg* pompous.
pompelmo [pom'pelmo] *sm* grapefruit.
pompiere [pom'pjere] *sm* fireman.
ponderare [ponde'rare] *v* consider. **ponderato** *agg* careful. **ponderoso** *agg* ponderous.
ponente [po'nente] *sm* west.
ponte ['ponte] *sm* bridge; (*impalcatura*) scaffolding. **ponte aereo** air-lift. **ponte radio** radio link. **ponte sospeso** suspension bridge.

pontefice [pon'tefitʃe] *sm* pontiff. **pontificare** *v* pontificate. **pontificio** *agg* papal.

pontile [pon'tile] *sm* pier; (*da sbarco*) landing stage.

popolare [popo'lare] *agg* popular; working-class; (*tradizionale*) folk. **casa popolare** *sf* council house. *v* populate. **popolarità** *sf* popularity. **popolarizzare** *v* popularize.

popolo ['pɔpolo] *sm* people; common people. **popolazione** *sf* population.

popone [po'pone] *sm* melon.

poppa¹ ['poppa] *sf* (*mar*) stern. **avere il vento in poppa** sail before the wind.

poppa² ['poppa] *sf* (*anat*) breast. **poppare** *v* suck.

porcellana [portʃel'lana] *sf* porcelain, china.

porco ['pɔrko] *sm*, *pl* **-ci** pig. *agg* (*volg*) bloody. **porcaio** *sm* pig-sty. **porcellino d'India** *sm* guinea-pig. **porcheria** *sf* muck, filth; (*cibo*) disgusting stuff; (*cosa malfatta*) rubbish. **porcospino** *sm* porcupine.

*****porgere** ['pɔrdʒere] *v* give, hand. **porgere aiuto** offer help.

pornografia [pornogra'fia] *sf* pornography. **pornografico** *agg* pornographic.

poro ['pɔro] *sm* pore. **poroso** *agg* porous.

porpora ['porpora] *agg invar*, *sf* purple.

*****porre** ['porre] *v* put; set, place. **porre in dubbio** question. **porre in evidenza** stress. **porre rimedio** set right.

porro ['pɔrro] *sm* leek.

porta ['pɔrta] *sf* door. **a porte chiuse** behind closed doors; (*dir*) in camera. **mettere alla porta** (*fig*) throw out. **porta di sicurezza** emergency exit.

portabagagli [portaba'gaʎi] *sm invar* luggage-rack; (*facchino*) porter.

portabile [por'tabile] *agg* portable.

portacenere [porta'tʃenere] *sm invar* ash-tray.

portachiavi [porta'kjavi] *sm invar* key-ring.

portaerei [porta'ɛrei] *sf* aircraft-carrier.

portafinestra [portafi'nɛstra] *sf*, *pl* **portefinestre** French window.

portafoglio [porta'fɔʎʎo] *sm* wallet; (*borsa*) briefcase; (*pol*) portfolio.

portalettere [porta'lettere] *sm invar* postman.

portamonete [portamo'nete] *sm invar* purse.

portare [por'tare] *v* bring; (*prendere*) take; (*trasportare*) carry; (*indossare*) wear; (*addurre*) put forward. **essere portato** have a gift (for). **portatore** *sm* carrier; (*comm*) bearer.

portasapone [portasa'pone] *sm invar* soap-dish.

portasigarette [portasiga'rette] *sm invar* cigarette-case.

portaspilli [porta'spilli] *sm invar* pin-cushion.

portauovo [portauovo] *sm invar* egg-cup.

portavoce [porta'votʃe] *sm invar* spokesman, mouthpiece.

portento [por'tɛnto] *sm* portent; (*persona*) prodigy.

portico ['pɔrtiko] *sm* arcade; (*di casa*) porch.

portinaio [porti'najo], **-a** *sm*, *sf* doorkeeper; caretaker. **portineria** *sf* caretaker's lodge.

porto¹ ['pɔrto] *sm* port, harbour.

porto² ['pɔrto] *sm* (*comm*) carriage. **porto d'armi** gun licence.

porto³ ['pɔrto] *sm* (*vino*) port.

Portogallo [porto'gallo] *sm* Portugal. **portoghese** *agg*, *s(m+f)* Portuguese; *sm* (*lingua*) Portuguese. **fare il portoghese** gate-crash.

portone [por'tone] *sm* front door.

porzione [por'tsjone] *sf* portion, share.

posa ['pɔza] *sf* (*atteggiamento*) pose; (*foto*) exposure.

posare [po'zare] *v* put *or* lay down; rest; (*ritratto*) pose.

poscritto [pos'kritto] *sm* postscript.

positivo [pozi'tivo] *agg* positive; affirmative; practical. **positiva** *sf* (*foto*) positive.

posizione [pozi'tsjone] *sf* position.

*****posporre** [pos'porre] *v* postpone; (*mettere dopo*) place after. **posposizione** *sf* postponement.

*****possedere** [posse'dere] *v* possess, own. **possedimento** *sm also* **possesso** possession. **possessore** *sm* owner.

possibile [pos'sibile] *agg* possible. **fare il possibile** do one's best. **possibilità** *sf* possibility; (*capacità*) means. **possibilmente** *avv* if possible.

posta¹ ['posta] *sf* post, mail; (*ufficio*) post office. **a giro di posta** by return of post. **mettersi alla posta (di)** be on the lookout (for). **posta aerea** air mail. **postale** *agg* postal.

posta² ['posta] *sf* (*gioco*) bet, stake.

post-bellico [post'bɛlliko] *agg* post-war.
posteggiare [posted'dʒare] *v* park. **posteggio** *sm* parking; (*spazio*) parking space.
posteriore [poste'rjore] *agg* back, rear; (*tempo*) later.
posterità [posteri'ta] *sf* posterity.
posticcio [pos'tittʃo] *agg* artificial. *sm* hairpiece.
posticipare [postitʃi'pare] *v* defer.
postino [pos'tino] *sm* postman.
posto ['posto] *sm* (*luogo*) place; (*spazio*) room; (*impiego*) position; (*da sedere*) seat. **essere a posto** be in order; (*star bene*) be well, be content. **mettere a posto** tidy up; repair. **sul posto** on the spot.
postumo ['postumo] *agg* posthumous.
potabile [po'tabile] *agg* (*spreg*) drinkable. **acqua potabile** *sf* drinking water.
potare [po'tare] *v* prune.
potassio [po'tassjo] *sm* potassium. **potassa** *sf* potash.
potente [po'tɛnte] *agg* powerful; (*efficace*) potent; (*valido*) forceful. **potenza** *sf* power; (*forza*) strength; (*efficacia*) potency.
potenziale [poten'tsjale] *agg, sm* potential. **potenzialità** *sf* capacity.
potenziare [poten'tsjare] *v* strengthen, expand. **potenziamento** *sm* strengthening, expansion.
*potere[1] [po'tere] *v* can, be able; (*possibilità, permesso*) may. **non poterne più** (*essere sfinito*) be exhausted; (*essere al limite della sopportazione*) be unable to stand it any longer. **può darsi** maybe.
potere[2] [po'tere] *sm* power.
povero ['povero], **-a** *agg* poor. *sm, sf* poor person. **povero di** lacking in. **povertà** *sf* poverty; (*scarsità*) want, lack.
pozza ['pottsa] *sf* pool. **pozzanghera** *sf* puddle.
pozzo ['pottso] *sm* well; (*cavità*) shaft. **pozzo nero** cesspool.
pranzare [pran'tsare] *v* have dinner; (*a mezzogiorno*) have lunch. **pranzo** *sm* dinner; lunch. **dopo pranzo** (*nel pomeriggio*) in the afternoon. **sala da pranzo** *sf* dining room.
pratica ['pratika] *sf* practice; experience; (*incartamento*) file. **praticante** *s(m+f)* apprentice; (*rel*) churchgoer. **praticare** *v* practise; (*fare*) make; frequent; associate (with).
pratico ['pratiko] *agg* practical; (*esperto*) skilled; (*funzionale*) useful, handy.

all'atto pratico in practice. **essere pratico di** be familiar with.
prato ['prato] *sm* meadow; (*giardino*) lawn. **pratolina** *sf* daisy.
preavvisare [preavvi'zare] *v* also **preavvertire** inform in advance; (*ammonire*) warn. **preavviso** *sm* (advance) notice; warning.
pre-bellico [pre'bɛlliko] *agg* pre-war.
precario [pre'karjo] *agg* precarious.
precauzione [prekau'tsjone] *sf* (*cautela*) caution, care; (*provvedimento*) precaution. **precauzionale** *agg* precautionary.
precedente [pretʃe'dɛnte] *agg* previous, preceding, former. *sm* (*dir*) precedent. **precedenti (penali)** *sm pl* (criminal) record *sing*. **precedentemente** *avv* before. **precedenza** *sf* priority. **in precedenza** previously.
precedere [pre'tʃedere] *v* precede.
precipitare [pretʃipi'tare] *v* hurl (down); (*affrettare*) hasten; (*chim*) precipitate; (*cadere*) crash; (*piombare*) plunge. **precipitoso** *agg* hurried; (*fig*) rash.
precipizio [pretʃi'pitsjo] *sm* precipice.
precisare [pretʃi'zare] *v* specify; (*fam*) spell out. **precisazione** *sf* clarification. **precisione** *sf* precision. **preciso** *agg* precise, exact; identical.
precoce [pre'kɔtʃe] *agg* precocious; premature, untimely.
preconcetto [prekon'tʃɛtto] *sm* preconceived idea, prejudice.
precursore [prekur'sore] *sm* forerunner.
preda ['preda] *sf* prey; (*bottino*) booty. **essere in preda a** be struck by. **in preda alle fiamme** in flames. **predare** *v* plunder.
predecessore [predetʃes'sore] *sm* predecessor.
predestinare [predesti'nare] *v* preordain.
predetto [pre'detto] *agg* aforesaid.
predica ['predika] *sf* sermon; (*ramanzina*) telling-off. **predicare** *v* preach.
prediletto [predi'letto], **-a** *s, agg* favourite.
*predire [pre'dire] *v* predict, foretell.
*predisporre [predis'porre] *v* arrange (in advance); predispose.
predominare [predomi'nare] *v* prevail. **predominio** *sm* sway.
prefabbricato [prefabbri'kato] *agg* prefabricated.
prefazione [prefa'tsjone] *sf* preface, foreword.
preferire [prefe'rire] *v* prefer. **preferenza** *sf* preference. **preferibile** *agg* preferable.

prefetto [pre'fɛtto] *sm* prefect. **prefettura** *sf* prefecture.

*prefiggere [pre'fiddʒere] *v* fix (in advance); (*gramm*) prefix. **prefiggersi** *v* resolve.

prefisso [pre'fisso] *sm* (*gramm*) prefix; (*telefono*) (area) code.

pregare [pre'gare] *v* pray. **prego** *inter* (*per favore*) please! (*risposta*) don't mention it!

pregevole [pre'dʒevole] *agg* valuable.

preghiera [pre'gjɛra] *sf* prayer; (*domanda*) request.

pregiato [pre'dʒato] *agg* valued. **pregio** *sm* regard; merit. **di nessun pregio** worthless.

pregiudicare [predʒudi'kare] *v* prejudice; (*danneggiare*) harm. **pregiudicato** *sm* ex-convict.

pregiudizio [predʒu'ditsjo] *sm* prejudice, bias.

pregustare [pregus'tare] *v* look forward to.

preistorico [preis'tɔriko] *agg* prehistoric.

prelato [pre'lato] *sm* prelate.

prelevare [prele'vare] *v* withdraw.

prelibato [preli'bato] *agg* exquisite.

preliminare [prelimi'nare] *agg* preliminary. *sm* element.

preludio [pre'ludjo] *sm* prelude.

prematuro [prema'turo] *agg* premature.

premeditato [premedi'tato] *agg* premeditated.

premere ['prɛmere] *v* press. **mi preme (di) sapere** I am anxious to know.

premiare [pre'mjare] *v* award a prize to; (*ricompensare*) reward. **premio** *sm* prize; reward; (*comm*) premium.

preminente [premi'nente] *agg* pre-eminent.

premura [pre'mura] *sf* (*fretta*) haste; (*riguardo*) solicitude, attention. **fare premura a** hurry up. **farsi premura** take care. **premuroso** *agg* thoughtful, solicitous.

*prendere ['prɛndere] *v* take; (*cogliere, subire, catturare*) catch; (*ricevere*) receive; (*ritirare*) pick up; (*occupare*) take up; (*assumere*) take on; (*ottenere*) get. **andare a prendere** fetch. **prendere alla lettera** take literally. **prendere per il naso** mock. **prendere qualcuno per il bavero** pull someone's leg. **prendere un**

granchio (*fig*) make a blunder. **prendersela** *v* take it amiss; (*con qualcuno*) get angry with; (*a cuore*) take it to heart.

prenotare [preno'tare] *v* book, reserve. **prenotazione** *sf* booking, reservation.

preoccupare [preokku'pare] *v* worry. **preoccupazione** *sf* worry.

preparare [prepa'rare] *v* prepare; (*tavola*) lay; (*letto*) make. **preparare la strada** pave the way. **preparativo** *sm* arrangement. **preparazione** *sf* preparation.

preposizione [preposi'tsjone] *sf* preposition.

prepotente [prepo'tɛnte] *agg* overbearing. *s*(*m+f*) (*fam*) bully.

prerogativa [preroga'tiva] *sf* privilege.

presa ['preza] *sf* hold; (*stretta*) grasp; (*elett*) socket; (*carte*) trick; (*cattura*) capture. **cane da presa** *sm* retriever. **essere alle prese con** wrestle with. **far presa** set. **macchina da presa** *sf* cine-camera. **presa di posizione** taking sides. **presa in giro** leg-pull. **venire alle prese** come to grips.

presbite ['prɛzbite] *agg* long-sighted.

prescindere [pre'ʃindere] *v* **a prescindere da** apart from.

*prescrivere [pre'skrivere] *v* prescribe. **prescrizione** *sf* ordinance. **prescrizione medica** doctor's orders *pl*; (*ricetta*) prescription.

presentare [prezen'tare] *v* present; (*far conoscere*) introduce; (*mostrare*) show; offer. **presentatore, -trice** *sm, sf* compere, question-master.

presente [pre'zɛnte] *agg* present; in the presence of; (*questo*) this. *sm* present. **i presenti** those present *pl*. **tener presente** keep in mind.

presentimento [presenti'mento] *sm* presentiment, foreboding.

presenza [pre'zentsa] *sf* presence; appearance. **di presenza** personally. **fare atto di presenza** put in an appearance. **presenziare (a)** *v* attend.

preservare [prezer'vare] *v* preserve; protect. **preservativo** *sm* preservative; (*guaina profilattica*) condom. **preservazione** *sf* preservation.

preside ['prɛzide] *sm* headmaster; (*di facoltà*) dean. *sf* headmistress.

presidente [prezi'dɛnte] *sm* president; (*di assemblea*) chairman. **presidente della camera** (*pol*) speaker. **presidente del Consiglio** (*pol*) Prime Minister. **presidenza** *sf*

(*pol*) presidency; chairmanship. **assumere la presidenza** take the chair.
presidio [pre'zidjo] *sm* garrison; (*fig*) protection. **presidiare** *v* garrison; protect.
***presiedere** [pre'sjɛdere] *v* be in charge (of).
pressa ['prɛssa] *sf* press. **pressare** *v* press.
pressappoco [pressap'pɔko] *avv* about, roughly.
pressione [pres'sjone] *sf* pressure.
presso ['prɛsso] *prep* near; (*insieme a, fra*) with; (*accanto a*) by; (*indirizzo*) care of, c/o. *avv* nearby. **pressoché** *avv* almost.
prestabilire [prestabi'lire] *v* prearrange.
prestare [pres'tare] *v* lend. **prestare aiuto** help. **prestar fede** believe. **prestar giuramento** take an oath. **prestazione** *sf* (*rendimento*) performance. **prestazioni** *sf pl* services *pl*.
prestigio [pres'tidʒo] *sm* prestige. **gioco di prestigio** *sm* conjuring trick. **prestigiatore, -trice** *sm, sf* conjurer. **prestigioso** *agg* prestigious.
prestito ['prɛstito] *sm* loan. **dare in prestito** lend. **prendere in prestito** borrow.
presto ['prɛsto] *avv* (*tra poco*) soon; (*in fretta*) quickly; (*di buon'ora*) early. **si fa presto** (*facilmente*) it's easy.
***presumere** [pre'zumere] *v* imagine. **presunto** *agg* presumed; (*erede*) presumptive. **presuntuoso** *agg* presumptuous. **presunzione** *sf* presumption.
***presupporre** [presup'porre] *v* presuppose, assume; (*richiedere*) require. **presupposizione** *sf* assumption.
prete ['prɛte] *sm* priest.
***pretendere** [pre'tendere] *v* (*esigere, presumere*) expect; (*sostenere*) claim. **pretensioso** *agg* pretentious.
pretesa [pre'teza] *sf* claim; (*presunzione*) pretention. **aver poche/molte pretese** be easy/difficult to please.
pretesto [pre'testo] *sm* pretext; (*occasione*) opportunity.
prettamente [pretta'mente] *avv* typically.
***prevalere** [preva'lere] *v* prevail.
***prevedere** [preve'dere] *v* foresee; (*considerare*) provide for. **prevedibile** *agg* foreseeable.
***prevenire** [preve'nire] *v* (*precedere*) arrive before; (*fig*) anticipate; (*evitare*) avert; (*avvertire*) warn. **prevenuto** *agg* (*maldisposto*) biased.

preventivo [preven'tivo] *agg* precautionary; (*dir*) preventive. *sm* estimate. **preventivare** *v* estimate. **prevenzione** *sf* (*ostilità*) bias; (*provvedimento*) prevention.
previdente [previ'dɛnte] *agg* far-sighted, provident. **previdenza** *sf* foresight. **previdenza sociale** social security.
previo ['prɛvjo] *agg* prior.
previsione [previ'zjone] *sf* forecast; (*aspettativa*) anticipation; (*comm*) estimate. **previsto** *agg* foreseen; (*dir*) provided for. **meno/più del previsto** less/more than anticipated.
prezioso [pre'tsjozo] *agg* precious, valuable.
prezzemolo [pret'tsemolo] *sm* parsley.
prezzo ['prettso] *sm* price; (*tariffa*) rate; (*trasporto pubblico*) fare. **a buon prezzo** cheaply.
prigione [pri'dʒone] *sf* prison, jail. **prigionia** *sf* captivity. **prigioniero, -a** *sm, sf* prisoner.
prima ['prima] *avv* (*in anticipo*) first, in advance; (*precedentemente*) before; (*più presto*) earlier; (*una volta*) once; (*in primo luogo*) first. *sf* (*teatro*) première; (*auto*) first gear; (*treno*) first class.
primario [pri'marjo] *agg* primary. *sm* (*med*) consultant.
primato [pri'mato] *sm* supremacy; record.
primavera [prima'vɛra] *sf* spring. **primaverile** *agg* spring.
primitivo [primi'tivo] *agg* primitive; original.
primizia [pri'mitsja] *sf* early produce; (*notizia*) latest news.
primo ['primo] *agg* first; (*precedente*) former; (*principale*) main. **per primo** first.
primula ['primula] *sf* primrose.
principale [printʃi'pale] *agg* principal, main. *sm* principal; (*fam*) boss.
principe ['printʃipe] *sm* prince. **principato** *sm* principality. **principesco** *agg* princely. **principessa** *sf* princess.
principio [prin'tʃipjo] *sm* beginning; (*fondamento*) principle; origin. **da** *or* **in principio** at first. **per principio** on principle.
priorità [priori'ta] *sf* priority.
prisma ['prizma] *sm* prism.
privare [pri'vare] *v* deprive.
privato [pri'vato], **-a** *agg* private; personal. *sm, sf* private citizen. **privatista** *s(m+f)* (*scolaro*) private school pupil;

(*candidato*) external student. **privativa** *sf* monopoly. **privazione** *sf* privation, loss.
privilegio [privi'ledʒo] *sm* privilege. **privilegiato** *agg* privileged.
privo ['privo] *agg* devoid (of), without. **privo di denaro** penniless. **privo di sensi** (*svenuto*) unconscious.
probabile [pro'babile] *agg* probable, likely. **poco probabile** unlikely. **probabilità** *sf* probability, likelihood; (*possibilità*) chance.
problema ['problɛma] *sm* problem. **problematico** *agg* problematic; doubtful.
proboscide [pro'boʃide] *sf* trunk.
procedere [pro'tʃedere] *v* proceed; (*comportarsi*) behave. **procedimento** *sm* (*svolgimento*) course; (*tec*) process; (*dir*) proceedings *pl*.
processione [protʃes'sjone] *sf* procession.
processo [pro'tʃesso] *sm* process; (*dir*) trial, lawsuit. **essere sotto processo** be on trial. **processo verbale** minutes *pl*.
procinto [pro'tʃinto] *sm* **essere in procinto di** be on the point of, be about to.
proclamare [prokla'mare] *v* proclaim. **proclamazione** *sf* proclamation.
proclive [pro'klive] *agg* prone (to).
procreare [prokre'are] *v* procreate. **procreazione** *sf* procreation.
procurare [proku'rare] *v* get; (*dare, causare*) give. **procura** *sf* power of attorney. **per procura** by proxy. **procuratore** *sm* proxy; (*magistrato*) attorney; (*comm*) agent.
proda ['proda] *sf* bank.
prode ['prode] *agg* valiant.
prodigare [prodi'gare] *v* lavish. **prodigo** *agg, m pl* -**ghi** prodigal, lavish.
prodigio [pro'didʒo] *sm* prodigy. **prodigioso** *agg* wonderful, marvellous.
prodotto [pro'dotto] *sm* product; (*alimentare*) foodstuff; (*chimico*) chemical.
*****produrre** [pro'durre] *v* produce; cause; (*mostrare*) show; (*fare*) make. **produrre un testimonio** call a witness. **produttivo** *agg* productive. **produttività** *sf* productivity. **produttore** *sm* producer. **produzione** *sf* production; (*fabbricazione*) manufacture; (*quantità*) output.
profanare [profa'nare] *v* desecrate; (*contaminare*) debase. **profano** *agg* profane; (*empio*) sacrilegious; (*inesperto*) ignorant.
*****proferire** [profe'rire] *v* utter, pronounce.
professare [profes'sare] *v* profess. **professionale** *agg* professional; vocational;

(*connesso alla professione*) occupational. **professione** *sf* profession; (*mestiere*) trade. **di professione** by profession. **professionista** *s(m+f)* professional (person).
professore [profes'sore], -**essa** *sm*, *sf* teacher. **professore titolare/incaricato** university professor/lecturer.
profeta [pro'fɛta] *sm* prophet. **profetico** *agg* prophetic. **profezia** *sf* prophecy.
proficuo [pro'fikuo] *agg* useful.
profilo [pro'filo] *sm* profile; (*contorno*) outline. **profilare** *v* outline; (*mec*) profile. **profilato** *sm* (*mec*) section.
profittare [profit'tare] *v* profit; (*approfittare*) take advantage; (*progredire*) make progress. **profittatore** *sm* profiteer. **profitto** *sm* profit; advantage. **trarre profitto** benefit.
profondo [pro'fondo] *agg* deep; (*radicato*) deep-rooted. *sm* depth. **profondare** *v* sink. **profondità** *sf* depth.
profugo ['profugo], -**a** *sm*, *pl* -**ghi**, *sf* refugee.
profumare [profu'mare] *v* perfume. **profumato** *agg* perfumed; fragrant. **profumeria** *sf* perfumery. **profumo** *sm* fragrance, scent.
profusione [profu'zjone] *sf* profusion.
progettare [prodʒet'tare] *v* plan; (*tec*) design. **progettazione** *sf* planning. **progetto** *sm* project, plan. **progetto di legge** bill. **progetto di massima** preliminary plan.
prognosi ['proɲozi] *sf* prognosis.
programma [pro'gramma] *sm* programme; prospectus; (*scuola*) syllabus. **programmare** *v* programme. **programmatore**, -**trice** *sm*, *sf* programmer. **programmazione** *sf* programming.
progredire [progre'dire] *v* make progress, get on. **progressione** *sf* progression. **progressivo** *agg* progressive. **progresso** *sm* progress. **fare progressi** improve, make progress.
proibire [proi'bire] *v* forbid, prohibit. **proibito** *agg* forbidden. **proibizionismo** *sm* prohibition.
proiettare [projet'tare] *v* project; (*gettar fuori*) eject; (*cine*) screen. **proiettile** *sm* projectile; (*mil*) shell. **a prova di proiettile** bullet-proof. **proiettore** *sm* projector.
prole ['prole] *sf* offspring.
proletario [prole'tarjo], -**a** *s, agg* proletarian. **proletariato** *sm* proletariat.

prolifico [pro'lifiko] *agg* prolific.
prolisso [pro'lisso] *agg* long-winded.
prologo ['prɔlogo] *sm, pl* -ghi prologue.
prolungare [prolun'gare] *v* extend; (*tempo*) prolong; (*spazio*) lengthen. **prolungarsi** *v* (*dilungarsi*) dwell (on). **prolunga** *sf* extension. **prolungamento** *sm* extension.
promemoria [prome'mɔrja] *sm invar* memorandum.
***promettere** [pro'mettere] *v* promise. **promessa** *sf* promise. **promesso** *agg* promised. **promettente** *agg* promising.
prominente [promi'nente] *agg* prominent, jutting (out). **prominenza** *sf* prominence, projection.
promiscuo [pro'miskuo] *agg* mixed; (*scuola*) co-educational; (*relazioni*) promiscuous.
promontorio [promon'tɔrjo] *sm* headland.
promozione [promo'tsjone] *sf* promotion.
***promuovere** [pro'mwɔvere] *v* promote; provoke.
pronome [pro'nome] *sm* pronoun.
pronosticare [pronosti'kare] *v* forecast. **pronostico** *sm* forecast.
pronto ['pronto] *agg* ready; (*rapido*) prompt; (*vivace*) lively. *inter* (*telefono*) hello!
prontuario [prontu'arjo] *sm* handbook.
pronunciare [pronun'tʃare] *v* pronounce. **pronunciarsi a favore di** declare oneself in favour of. **pronuncia** *sf* pronunciation.
propaganda [propa'ganda] *sf* propaganda. **propagandista** *s(m+f)* propagandist.
propagare [propa'gare] *v* propagate.
propenso [pro'penso] *agg* inclined; favourable.
propizio [pro'pitsjo] *agg* propitious; favourable.
proponimento [proponi'mento] *sm* resolution.
***proporre** [pro'porre] *v* propose; intend; suggest.
proporzione [propor'tsjone] *sf* proportion; (*mat*) ratio. **in proporzione a** compared with. **proporzionale** *agg* proportional.
proposito [pro'pɔzito] *sm* purpose; intention; (*scopo*) aim; (*progetto*) plan. **a proposito** (*opportunamente*) at the right time; (*inter*) by the way; (*opportuno*) to the point. **a proposito di** with regard to. **cambiare proposito** change one's mind.

proposizione [propozi'tsjone] *sf* proposition; clause.
proposta [pro'posta] *sf* proposal.
proprietà [proprje'ta] *sf* property; (*precisione, decoro*) propriety; (*possesso*) ownership. **essere di proprietà di** belong to. **proprietà letteraria** copyright.
proprio ['prɔprjo] *agg* one's (own); (*mat, gramm*) proper, characteristic. *avv* exactly, just; (*veramente*) really.
propulsione [propul'sjone] *sf* propulsion.
prora ['prɔra] *sf* prow.
prorogare [proro'gare] *v* (*rinviare*) put off, adjourn; (*prolungare*) extend. **proroga** *sf* adjournment; extension.
***prorompere** [pro'rompere] *v* burst out.
prosa ['prɔza] *sf* prose; theatre. **prosaico** *agg* prosaic.
prosciugare [proʃu'gare] *v* drain.
prosciutto [pro'ʃutto] *sm* ham.
***proscrivere** [pro'skrivere] *v* proscribe.
proseguire [prose'gwire] *v* continue, go on. **proseguimento** *sm* continuation.
prosperare [prospe'rare] *v* prosper, thrive. **prosperità** *sf* prosperity. **prospero** *agg* prosperous, thriving.
prospettiva [prospet'tiva] *sf* (*tec*) perspective; (*previsione*) prospect, outlook. **prospettare** *v* (*esporre*) show; (*guardare*) look out (on). **prospettarsi** *v* (*essere in vista*) be in sight.
prospetto [pros'pɛtto] *sm* (*tabella*) list; (*pubblicità*) prospectus.
prossimo ['prɔssimo] *agg* near; (*seguente*) next; (*vicino nel passato, stretto*) close. **passato/trapassato prossimo** *sm* (*gramm*) present/past perfect. *sm* neighbour. **prossimità** *sf* proximity.
prostituire [prostitu'ire] *v* prostitute. **prostituta** *sf* prostitute. **prostituzione** *sf* prostitution.
protagonista [protago'nista] *s(m+f)* protagonist, chief character.
***proteggere** [pro'teddʒere] *v* protect, shelter; favour.
proteina [prote'ina] *sf* protein.
protesi ['prɔtezi] *sf* prosthesis.
protesta [pro'tɛsta] *sf* protest. **protestare** *v* protest; (*dichiarare*) declare. **protesto** *sm* protest.
protestante [protes'tante] *s(m+f)*, *agg* Protestant.
protetto [pro'tɛtto], **-a** *agg* protected; favourite. *sm, sf* protégé; favourite. **protettorato** *sm* protectorate. **protettore** *sm*

protector, defender. **santo protettore** patron saint.

protezione [prote'tsjone] *sf* protection; (*mecenatismo*) patronage. **protezione antincendio** fireproofing.

protocollo [proto'kɔllo] *sm* protocol; register. **carta protocollo** *sf* foolscap (paper).

protone [pro'tone] *sm* proton.

prototipo [pro'tɔtipo] *sm* prototype.

***protrarre** [pro'trarre] *v* protract; (*prorogare*) put off.

prova ['prɔva] *sf* proof; evidence; (*esame, testimonianza*) test; (*cimento*) trial; (*tentativo*) try; (*sarto*) fitting; (*teatro*) rehearsal. **a prova di acqua** waterproof. **a prova di fuoco** fireproof. **dar buona prova di sè** give a good account of oneself. **reggere alla prova** stand the test.

provare [pro'vare] *v* try (out); (*collaudare*) test; (*spettacolo*) rehearse; (*assaggiare*) taste; (*dimostrare*) prove; (*mettere alla prova*) put to the test; (*abito, ecc.*) try on.

***provenire** [prove'nire] *v* come (from); (*fig*) spring (from), be caused (by). **provenienza** *sf* origin, source.

proverbio [pro'vɛrbjo] *sm* proverb, saying. **proverbiale** *agg* proverbial.

provetta [pro'vetta] *sf* test-tube.

provincia [pro'vintʃa] *sf* province. **di provincia** provincial.

provocare [provo'kare] *v* provoke, cause. **provocatorio** *agg* provocative. **provocazione** *sf* provocation.

***provvedere** [provve'dere] *v* make provision for, provide for; (*prendere provvedimenti*) take steps; (*badare a*) see to; (*procurare*) provide. **provvedimento** *sm* step, measure. **provveditore** *sm* administrator; (*agli studi*) education officer.

provvidenza [provvi'dentsa] *sf* providence; (*fam*) godsend. **provvidenziale** *agg* providential.

provvigione [provvi'dʒone] *sf* commission.

provvisorio [provvi'zɔrjo] *agg* provisional.

provvista [prov'vista] *sf* provisions *pl*, stock. **provvisto** *agg* supplied, provided.

prua ['prua] *sf* prow.

prudente [pru'dɛnte] *agg* prudent, careful, cautious. **prudenza** *sf* care, caution.

***prudere** ['prudere] *v* itch. **prurito** *sm* itch.

prugna ['pruɲa] *sf* plum; (*secca*) prune. **prugno** *sm* plum-tree.

pseudonimo [pseu'dɔnimo] *sm* pseudonym.

psicanalisi [psica'nalizi] *sf* psycho-analysis. **psicanalista** *s(m+f)* psycho-analyst. **psicanalitico** *agg* psycho-analytical.

psichiatra [psi'kjatra] *s(m+f)* psychiatrist. **psichiatria** *sf* psychiatry.

psichico ['psikiko] *agg* psychic.

psicologo [psi'kɔlogo], **-a** *sm, sf* psychologist. **psicologia** *sf* psychology. **psicologico** *agg* psychological.

psicopatico [psiko'patiko], **-a** *agg* psychopathic. *sm, sf* psychopath.

psicosi [psi'kɔzi] *sf* psychosis. **psicotico, -a** *s, agg* psychotic.

psicosomatico [psikoso'matiko] *agg* psychosomatic.

psicoterapia [psikotera'pia] *sf* psychotherapy. **psicoterapista** *s(m+f)* psychotherapist.

pubblicare [pubbli'kare] *v* publish. **pubblicazione** *sf* publication, issue. **pubblicista** *s(m+f)* (freelance) journalist.

pubblicità [pubblitʃi'ta] *sf* publicity; advertising. **fare pubblicità** advertise. **piccola pubblicità** classified advertisements *pl*. **pubblicitario** *agg* advertising, publicity.

pubblico ['pubbliko] *agg* public. *sm* public; (*teatro*) audience.

pubertà [puber'ta] *sf* puberty.

pudico [pu'diko] *agg*, *m pl* **-chi** modest; (*vergognoso*) bashful.

pudore [pu'dore] *sm* modesty; (*vergogna*) shame. **oltraggio al pudore** *sm* indecent behaviour. **senza pudore** shameless.

puerile [pue'rile] *agg* puerile.

pugilato [pudʒi'lato] *sm* boxing. **fare del pugilato** box. **pugile** *sm* boxer. **pugilistico** *agg* boxing.

pugnalare [puɲa'lare] *v* stab. **pugnalata** *sf* stab. **pugnale** *sm* dagger.

pugno ['puɲo] *sm* fist; (*colpo*) punch; (*piccola quantità*) fistful. **essere un pugno in un occhio** be an eyesore. **fare a pugni** fight; (*fig*) clash. **prendere a pugni** punch. **tenere in pugno** clutch; (*fig*) control.

pulce ['pultʃe] *sf* flea. **gioco della pulce** *sm* tiddly-winks.

pulcino [pul'tʃino] *sm* chick. **bagnato come un pulcino** wet through.

puledro [pu'ledro] *sm* colt. **puledra** *sf* filly.

puleggia [pu'leddʒa] *sf* pulley.

pulire [pu'lire] *v* clean; (*lavando*) wash; (*con strofinaccio, ecc.*) wipe (clean); (*con *spazzola*) brush; (*sfregando*) scour; (*lucidare*) polish. **pulirsi il naso** blow one's nose. **pulito** *agg* clean.

pulizia [puli'tsia] *sf* (*il pulire*) cleaning; (*l'essere pulito*) cleanliness. **far le pulizie** do the cleaning. **far pulizia** clean; (*sgombrare*) clear out.

pullman ['pullman] *sm invar* coach.

pullover [pul'lɔver] *sm invar* pullover.

pullulare [pullu'lare] *v* swarm.

pulpito ['pulpito] *sm* pulpit. **montare in pulpito** preach.

pulsare [pul'sare] *v* throb, beat. **pulsante** *sm* button; (*campanello*) buzzer.

***pungere** ['pundʒere] *v* sting; (*morsicare*) bite; (*con spillo*) prick. **pungente** *agg* pungent; (*fig*) sharp; (*ispido*) prickly. **pungiglione** *sm* sting. **pungolo** *sm* goad.

punire [pu'nire] *v* punish. **punibile** *agg* punishable. **punitivo** *agg* punitive. **punizione** *sf* punishment; (*sport*) penalty.

punta ['punta] *sf* point; (*estremità*) tip. **ora di punta** *sf* rush hour. **prendere di punta** clash (with).

puntare [pun'tare] *v* point, direct; (*scommettere*) bet.

puntata [pun'tata] *sf* (*scritto*) instalment, part.

punteggiare [punted'dʒare] *v* punctuate. **punteggiatura** *sf* punctuation.

punteggio [pun'teddʒo] *sm* score.

puntellare [puntel'lare] *v* prop up. **puntello** *sm* prop; (*fig*) support.

puntiglioso [punti'ʎozo] *agg* stubborn. **puntiglio** *sm* stubbornness.

puntina [pun'tina] *sf* (*da disegno*) drawing pin; (*grammofono*) stylus.

punto ['punto] *sm* point; (*segno*) dot; (*med, ricamo, maglia*) stitch. *avv* (*affatto*) at all. **di punto in bianco** point-blank. **due punti** colon. **in punto** (*tempo*) on the dot, sharp. **mettere a punto** put right; (*auto*) tune; (*fig*) clarify. **punto esclamativo/interrogativo** exclamation/question mark. **punto e virgola** semicolon. **punto fermo** full stop.

puntuale [puntu'ale] *agg* punctual, on time.

puntualizzare [puntualid'dzare] *v* define, precisely.

puntura [pun'tura] *sf* sting, bite; (*di spillo, ecc.*) prick; (*med*) injection, puncture; (*dolore*) stitch.

punzecchiare [pundzek'kjare] *v* sting, bite, prick; (*stuzzicare*) tease.

punzonare [puntso'nare] *v* punch. **punzonatrice** *sf* punch. **punzone** *sm* punch, die.

pupa ['pupa] *sf* (*fam*) baby; (*bambola*) doll. **pupattola** *sf* doll. **pupazzo** *sm* puppet. **pupo** (*fam*) baby, little boy.

pupilla [pu'pilla] *sf* pupil.

purché [pur'ke] *cong* provided that, as long as.

pure ['pure] *avv* also, too. *cong* even (though); (*tuttavia*) yet.

purè [pu're] *sm invar* purée. **purè di patate** mashed potatoes *pl*.

purgare [pur'gare] *v* purge; purify. **purga** *sf* purge; (*il purgare*) purging, cleansing; (*purgante*) laxative; (*gastr*) soaking.

purgatorio [purga'tɔrjo] *sm* purgatory.

purificare [purifi'kare] *v* purify.

puritano [puri'tano], **-a** *s, agg* puritan.

puro ['puro] *agg* pure. **purezza** *sf* purity. **purosangue** *agg, sm invar* throughbred.

purpureo [pur'pureo] *agg* purple.

purtroppo [pur'trɔppo] *avv* unfortunately.

pus [pus] *sm invar* pus.

***putrefare** [putre'fare] *v* putrefy, rot. **putrefatto** *or* **putrido** *agg* putrid, rotten.

puttana [put'tana] *sf* whore; (*fam*) tart.

puzzare [put'tsare] *v* stink, smell. **puzzo** *sm* stench, smell. **puzzolente** *agg* stinking.

Q

qua [kwa] *avv* here. (**al**) **di qua di** on this side of. **di qua** (*stato in luogo*) here; (*moto a luogo*) over here; (*da qui*) from here. **fin qua** (*spazio*) up to here; (*tempo*) so far. **per di qua** this way. **qua sopra/sotto/vicino** up/down/near here.

quacchero ['kwakkero], **-a** *sm, sf* Quaker.

quaderno [kwa'dɛrno] *sm* exercise-book.

quadrante [kwa'drante] *sm* (*mat, astron*) quadrant; (*orologio*) dial; (*solare*) sundial.

quadrato [kwa'drato] *agg* square; (*sensibile*) level-headed. *sm* square. **quadrare** *v* square; (*far senso*) make sense; (*garbare*) please.

quadretto [kwa'dretto] *sm* small square; (*fig*) scene. **a quadretti** check(ed), chequered.

quadrifoglio [kwadri'fɔʎʎo] *sm* four-leafed clover; (*autostrada*) clover-leaf.

quadro[1] ['kwadro] *agg* square.

quadro[2] ['kwadro] *sm* (*dipinto*) picture; (*ambito*) scope; (*tabella*) table. **quadri** *sm pl* (*carte*) diamonds *pl*. **a quadri** check(ed), chequered.

quadrupede [kwa'drupede] *agg, sm* quadruped.

quaggiù [kwad'dʒu] *avv* down here.

quaglia ['kwaʎa] *sf* quail.

qualche ['kwalke] *agg* some, any; (*alcuni*) a few. **in qualche luogo** somewhere. **in qualche modo** somehow. **qualcosa** *pron also* **qualche cosa** something, anything. **qualcuno** *pron* somebody, anybody.

quale ['kwale] *agg, pron* what; (*fra numero limitato*) which; (*come*) as. **tale e quale** just like. *inter* what! *avv* as.

qualificare [kwalifi'kare] *v* qualify. **qualifica** *sf* title; position; (*doti professionali*) qualification; (*giudizio*) report. **qualificativo** *agg* qualifying. **qualificato** *agg* skilled.

qualità [kwali'ta] *sf* quality; (*specie*) sort, kind. **qualitativo** *agg* qualitative.

qualora [kwa'lora] *cong* in case.

qualunque [kwa'lunkwe] *agg invar also* **qualsiasi** any; (*ogni*) every; (*non importa quale*) whatever, whichever. **l'uomo qualunque** the man in the street.

quando ['kwando] *avv* when. *cong* when; (*ogniqualvolta*) whenever; (*mentre*) whereas; (*giacché*) since. **da quando** (*dacché*) (ever) since; (*da quanto tempo*) since when. **di quando in quando** from time to time. **fino a quando** until; (*interrogativo*) until when; (*per quanto tempo*) how long.

quantità [kwanti'ta] *sf* quantity. **quantitativo** *sm* amount.

quanto ['kwanto] *agg* how much *or* many; (*esclamativo*) what (a lot of); (*relativo*) as much *or* many ... as. *pron* how much *or* many; as much *or* many; (*quello che*) what. *avv* how (much *or* many); (*tempo*) how long; (*distanza*) how far; (*come*) as; (*nella misura che*) as much as. **da quanto** (*tempo*) how long; (*per ciò che*) as far as. **per quanto** however-er; (*per ciò che*) as far as. **quanto a** as for. **quanto fa?** how much is it? **quanto mai** very much indeed. **quanto prima** soon. **quanto tempo** how long.

quaranta [kwa'ranta] *agg, sm* forty.

quarantena *sf* quarantine. **quarantesimo** *sm, agg* fortieth.

quaresima [kwa'rezima] *sf* Lent.

quarta ['kwarta] *sf* (*auto*) fourth *or* top gear; (*musica*) fourth. **partire in quarta** (*fam*) be off like a shot.

quartetto [kwar'tetto] *sm* quartet.

quartiere [kwar'tjɛre] *sm* district, quarter. **quartieri bassi** slums *pl*.

quarto ['kwarto] *agg* fourth. *sm* quarter. **sono le due e/meno un quarto** it is a quarter past/to two.

quarzo ['kwartso] *sm* quartz.

quasi ['kwazi] *avv* nearly, almost; (*con valore negativo*) hardly. *cong* (*come se*) as if.

quassù [kwas'su] *avv* up here.

quatto quatto ['kwatto 'kwatto] *avv* very quickly.

quattordici [kwat'torditʃi] *agg, sm* fourteen. **quattordicesimo** *agg, sm* fourteenth.

quattrini [kwat'trini] *sm pl* money *sing*; (*fam*) cash *sing*. **quattrini a palate** loads of money *sing*. **senza quattrini** penniless.

quattro ['kwattro] *sm, agg* four. **dirne quattro a qualcuno** give someone a piece of one's mind. **far quattro passi** go for a stroll. **farsi in quattro** go out of one's way.

quegli ['kweʎi] *V* **quello**.

quei ['kwei] *V* **quello**.

quel [kwel] *V* **quello**.

quello ['kwello] *agg* that (*pl* those). *pron* that (one) (*pl* those); (*lo stesso*) the same. **di quello che** than. **quello che** the one who (*pl* those who); (*ciò che*) what.

quercia ['kwertʃa] *sf* oak.

querela [kwe'rela] *sf* lawsuit, action. **presentare** *or* **sporgere querela** bring an action. **querelante** *s(m+f)* plaintiff.

questionario [kwestjo'narjo] *sm* questionnaire.

questione [kwes'tjone] *sf* question; (*affare*) matter; problem; (*disputa*) argument. **fare una questione** make an issue. **mettere in questione** question.

questo ['kwesto] *agg* this (*pl* these). *pron* this (one) (*pl* these). **con questo** (*con queste parole*) with these words; (*ciònonostante*) in spite of this.

questura [kwes'tura] *sf* police station. **questore** *sm* police inspector.

qui ['kwi] *avv* here. **di qui** from here; (*moto a luogo*) here; (*tempo*) from now (on). **fin qui** up to here; (*tempo*) up to now.

quietanza [kwje'tantsa] *sf* receipt.

quietare [kwje'tare] *v* calm. **quiete** *sf* calm; (*assenza di moto*) rest.

quindi ['kwindi] *cong* so. *avv* afterwards.

quindici ['kwinditʃi] *agg, sm* fifteen. **quindici giorni** a fortnight. **quindicesimo** *agg, sm* fifteenth. **quindicinale** *sm* fortnightly.

quinta ['kwinta] *sf* (*teatro*) wing. **dietro le quinte** behind the scenes.

quintessenza [kwintes'sɛntsa] *sf* quintessence.

quintetto [kwin'tetto] *sm* quintet.

quinto ['kwinto] *sm, agg* fifth.

quota ['kwɔta] *sf* (*porzione*) share; (*altitudine*) height; (*livello*) level; (*econ*) quota. **quota zero** square one. **quotare** *v* appreciate; (*borsa*) quote. **quotazione** *sf* quotation.

quotidiano [kwoti'djano] *agg, sm* daily.

quoziente [kwo'tsjɛnte] *sm* quotient.

R

rabarbaro [ra'barbaro] *sm* rhubarb.

rabberciare [rabber'tʃare] *v* patch, mend; (*scritto*) re-hash.

rabbia ['rabbja] *sf* fury, rage; (*idrofobia*) rabies. **che rabbia!** how infuriating! **fare rabbia** a make angry. **rabbioso** *agg* furious; (*idrofobo*) rabid.

rabbino [rab'bino] *sm* rabbi. **rabbinico** *agg* rabbinical.

rabbonire [rabbo'nire] *v* calm down, soothe.

rabbrividire [rabbrivi'dire] *v* shiver; (*fig*) shudder.

rabbuffare [rabbuf'fare] *v* (*scompigliare*) ruffle; (*sgridare*) scold. **rabbuffo** *sm* telling-off, scolding.

rabbuiarsi [rabbu'jarsi] *v* darken.

raccapezzare [rakkapet'tsare] *v* scrape together. **raccapezzarsi** *v* make out.

raccapricciare [rakkaprit'tʃare] *v* be horrified. **raccapricciante** *agg* horrifying.

raccattare [rakkat'tare] *v* pick up, collect.

racchetta [rak'ketta] *sf* racket; (*ping-pong*) bat.

***raccogliere** [rak'kɔʎere] *v* pick; (*riprendere da terra*) pick up; (*riunire*) collect; (*fare il raccolto*) gather, harvest. **raccoglimento** *sm* attention. **raccoglitore** *sm* (*cartella*) binder.

raccolta [rak'kɔlta] *sf* collecting; collection; (*agric*) harvesting. **fare la raccolta** (**di**) collect.

raccolto [rak'kɔlto] *agg* (*concentrato nei pensieri*) deep in thought; (*rannicchiato*) crouching. *sm* harvest, crop.

raccomandare [rakkoman'dare] *v* recommend; (*esortare*) urge. **mi raccomando!** please do! **raccomandarsi a** rely on. (*lettera*) **raccomandata** *sf* registered letter. **raccomandato, -a** *sm, sf* protégé. **raccomandazione** *sf* recommendation.

raccomodare [rakkomo'dare] *v* also **racconciare** repair, mend.

raccontare [rakkon'tare] *v* tell. **racconto** *sm* story, tale; (*resoconto*) account.

raccorciare [rakkor'tʃare] *v* shorten.

raccordare [rakkor'dare] *v* connect. **raccordo** *sm* connection; (*strada, ecc.*) junction.

racimolare [ratʃimo'lare] *v* scrape together.

radar ['radar] *sm invar* radar.

raddolcire [raddol'tʃire] *v* sweeten; (*acqua*) soften.

raddoppiare [raddop'pjare] *v* double; (*fig*) redouble.

raddrizzare [raddrit'tsare] *v* straighten; (*elett*) rectify. **raddrizzatore** *sm* rectifier.

***radere** ['radere] *v* (*sbarbare*) shave; (*sfiorare*) graze. **radere al suolo** raze to the ground.

radiale [ra'djale] *agg* radial.

radiare [ra'djare] *v* expel; (*mil*) cashier; cancel. **radiare dall'albo** strike off the register.

radiatore [radja'tore] *sm* radiator.

radiazione[1] [radja'tsjone] *sf* (*fis*) radiation.

radiazione[2] [radja'tsjone] *sf* expulsion; cancellation.

radica ['radika] *sf* briar.

radicale [radi'kale] *agg* radical. *sm* (*chim*) radical; (*mat*) root.

radicare [radi'kare] *v* (take) root. **radicato** *agg* deep-rooted.

radicchio [ra'dikkjo] *sm* chicory.

radice [ra'ditʃe] *sf* root. **mettere radici** take root. **radice quadrata/cubica** square/cube root.

radio[1] ['radjo] *sm invar* radium.

radio² ['radjo] *sf invar* radio. **giornale radio** *sm* news (broadcast). **segnale radio** *sm* time signal.
radioattivo [radjoat'tivo] *agg* radioactive.
radioattività *sf* radioactivity.
radiocontrollato [radjokontrol'lato] *agg* radio-controlled.
radiodiffusione [radjodiffu'zjone] *sf also* **radiotrasmissione** broadcast. **radiodiffuso** *agg* broadcast.
radiografare [radjogra'fare] *v* X-ray. **radiografia** *sf* (*immagine*) X-ray; (*procedimento*) radiography.
radiologo [ra'djɔlogo], **-a** *sm, pl* **-ghi,** *sf* radiologist.
rado ['rado] *agg* sparse. **di rado** rarely.
radura *sf* clearing.
radunare [radu'nare] *v* gather. **radunarsi** *v* assemble. **radunata** *sf* assembly, meeting.
raduno *sm* meeting.
rafano ['rafano] *sm* radish.
raffica ['raffika] *sf* (*vento*) gust; (*colpi*) volley.
raffigurare [raffigu'rare] *v* represent.
raffinare [raffi'nare] *v* refine. **raffinatezza** *sf* refinement. **raffinazione** *sf* refining. **raffineria** *sf* refinery.
rafforzare [raffor'tsare] *v* reinforce.
raffreddare [raffred'dare] *v* cool. **raffreddarsi** *v* (*diventar freddo*) cool down; (*fam: prendersi un raffreddore*) catch a cold. **raffreddamento** *sm* cooling (down or off). **raffreddore** *sm* cold.
raffrenare [raffre'nare] *v* restrain.
raffrontare [raffron'tare] *v* compare. **raffronto** *sm* comparison.
rafia ['rafia] *sf* raffia.
raganella [raga'nɛlla] *sf* rattle.
ragazza [ra'gattsa] *sf* girl; (*innamorata*) girl-friend. **da ragazza** as a girl. **nome da ragazza** *sm* maiden name. **ragazza madre** unmarried mother.
ragazzo [ra'gattso] *sm* boy, lad; (*fam*) fellow, chap; (*innamorato*) boy-friend. **da ragazzo** as a boy. **fin da ragazzo** since childhood.
raggiare [rad'dʒare] *v* radiate.
raggio ['raddʒo] *sm* ray; (*geom*) radius; (*ambito*) range; (*ruota*) spoke. **raggio d'azione** range; (*fig*) scope. **fare i raggi** X-ray.
raggirare [raddʒi'rare] *v* trick. **raggiro** *sm* trick.
***raggiungere** [rad'dʒundʒere] *v* reach; (*riunirsi*) join; (*allinearsi*) catch up

(with); (*conseguire*) attain. **raggiungibile** *agg* within reach; attainable.
raggiustare [raddʒus'tare] *v* mend; (*fig*) set right.
raggomitolare [raggomito'lare] *v* roll up. **raggomitolarsi** *v* curl up.
raggrinzare [raggrin'tsare] *v also* **raggrinzire** wrinkle, crease.
raggrumare [raggru'mare] *v* clot.
raggruppare [raggrup'pare] *v* group (together). **raggrupparsi** *v* assemble. **raggruppamento** *sm* grouping; (*gruppo*) group; (*mil*) unit.
ragguagliare [raggwa'ʎare] *v* level; (*paragonare*) compare; inform; (*mat*) convert. **ragguaglio** *sm* comparison; information; (*resoconto*) report; conversion.
ragia ['radʒa] *sf* **acqua ragia** *sf* turpentine.
ragionare [radʒo'nare] *v* reason; discuss. **ragionamento** *sm* reasoning; discussion.
ragione [ra'dʒone] *sf* reason; (*diritto*) right; (*rapporto*) rate; (*spiegazione*) account; (*mat*) ratio. **a ragione** rightly. **a ragion veduta** after due consideration. **aver ragione** be right. **dar ragione a qualcuno** admit that someone is right. **rendersi ragione (di)** account (for).
ragioneria [radʒone'ria] *sf* accountancy.
ragionere, -a *sm, sf* accountant.
ragionevole [radʒo'nevole] *agg* reasonable.
ragliare [ra'ʎare] *v* bray. **raglio** *sm* bray.
ragno ['raɲo] *sm* spider. **ragnatela** *sf* cobweb.
ragù [ra'gu] *sm* meat sauce.
raid ['reid] *sm invar* (*mil*) raid; (*sport*) rally.
raion ['rajon] *sm invar* rayon.
rallegrare [rallegʹrare] *v* cheer up. **rallegrarsi** *v* be delighted; congratulate. **rallegramenti** *sm pl* congratulations *pl*.
rallentare [rallen'tare] *v* slacken, slow down. **rallentamento** *sm* slackening, slowing down.
rame ['rame] *sm* copper. **ramaiolo** *sm* ladle.
ramengo [ra'mengo] *sm* **andare a ramengo** (*fam*) go to the dogs.
ramificare [ramifi'kare] *v* ramify. **ramificazione** *sf* ramification.
ramino [ra'mino] *sm* rummy.
rammaricarsi [rammari'karsi] *v* regret; (*lamentarsi*) complain. **rammarico** *sm, pl* **-chi** regret.

rammendare [rammen'dare] v darn. **rammendo** sm (atto) darning; (parte rammendata) darn.

rammentare [rammen'tare] v (ricordare) recall; (richiamare alla memoria) call to mind.

rammollire [rammol'lire] v soften. **rammollito** agg soft; (rimbambito) doddering.

ramo ['ramo] sm branch. **ramoscello** sm twig.

rampa ['rampa] sf ramp; (scala) flight. **rampante** agg rampant.

rampicante [rampi'kante] agg climbing. sm (pianta) creeper.

rampino [ram'pino] sm hook.

rampollo [ram'pɔllo] sm offspring; (pianta) shoot; (acqua) spring.

rampone [ram'pone] sm (pesca) harpoon; (alpinismo) crampon.

rana ['rana] sf frog; (nuoto a rana) breaststroke. **uomo rana** sm frogman.

rancido ['rantʃido] agg rancid.

rancio ['rantʃo] sm meal.

rancore [ran'kore] sm grudge.

randagio [ran'dadʒo] agg stray.

randello [ran'dɛllo] sm club.

rango ['rango] sm rank; (posizione sociale) standing.

rannicchiarsi [rannik'kjarsi] v crouch, huddle.

rannuvolarsi [rannuvo'larsi] v cloud over; (fig) darken.

ranocchio [ra'nokkjo] sm frog.

rantolare [ranto'lare] v wheeze.

ranuncolo [ra'nunkolo] sm buttercup.

rapa ['rapa] sf turnip.

rapace [ra'patʃe] agg rapacious. **uccello rapace** sm bird of prey.

rapare [ra'pare] v crop.

rapido ['rapido] agg quick, rapid. sm express (train).

rapina [ra'pina] sf robbery. **rapinare** v rob.

rapire [ra'pire] v (rapinare) rob; (persone) kidnap, abduct; (estasiare) enrapture. **rapimento** sm kidnapping; (estasi) rapture.

rappezzare [rappet'tsare] v patch.

rapporto [rap'porto] sm (legame) connection; relationship; (resoconto) report; (mec, mat) ratio.

*rapprendersi [rap'prendersi] v coagulate; (latte) curdle.

rappresaglia [rappre'zaʎa] sf reprisal.

rappresentare [rappresen'tare] v represent; (significare) mean; (teatro) show. **rappresentante** s(m+f) representative, agent. **rappresentanza** sf agency. **rappresentativo** agg representative. **rappresentazione** sf representation; description; (teatro, cine) performance.

raro ['raro] agg rare; exceptional. **rarità** sf rarity.

rasare [ra'zare] v shave; (erba, ecc.) cut. **rasoio** sm razor.

raschiare [ras'kjare] v scrape; (cancellare) scratch out. **raschiatura** sf scratching; scratch. **raschietto** sm scraper.

rasentare [razen'tare] v go close (to); (fig) come close (to).

raso ['razo] agg (liscio) smooth; (sbarbato) shaved. sm (tessuto) satin.

raspa ['raspa] sf rasp. **raspare** v rasp.

rassegnare [rasse'ɲare] v **rassegnare le dimissioni** resign. **rassegnarsi** v resign oneself. **rassegna** sf review; inspection; (resoconto) survey.

rasserenarsi [rassere'narsi] v clear up; (fig) cheer up.

rassettare [rasset'tare] v tidy up; (accomodare) repair.

rassicurare [rassiku'rare] v reassure.

rassomigliare [rassomi'ʎare] v resemble. **rassomigliarsi** v look alike.

rastrello [ras'trɛllo] sm rake. **rastrellamento** sm (polizia) round-up. **rastrellare** v rake; (fig) comb. **rastrelliera** sf rack.

rata ['rata] sf instalment.

ratificare [ratifi'kare] v ratify. **ratifica** sf ratification.

ratto[1] ['ratto] sm (zool) rat.

ratto[2] ['ratto] sm (rapimento) rape.

rattoppare [rattop'pare] v patch. **rattoppo** sm (toppa) patch.

rattrappire [rattrap'pire] v make numb.

rattristare [rattris'tare] v sadden. **rattristarsi** v become sad, grieve.

rauco ['rauko] agg hoarse.

ravanello [rava'nello] sm radish.

*ravvedersi [ravve'dersi] v mend one's ways.

ravviare [ravvi'are] v tidy (up).

ravvicinare [ravvitʃi'nare] v bring near; reconcile. **ravvicinamento** sm (pol) rapprochement.

ravvisare [ravvi'zare] v recognize.

ravvivare [ravvi'vare] v revive.

*ravvolgere [rav'vɔldʒere] v wrap (up).

raziocinio [ratsjo'tʃinjo] *sm* reason; common sense.
razionale [ratsjo'nale] *agg* rational.
razionalizzare *v* rationalize. **razionalizzazione** *sf* rationalization.
razionare [ratsjo'nare] *v* ration. **razionamento** *sm* rationing. **razione** *sf* ration.
razza¹ ['rattsa] *sf* race; (*specie*) kind; (*stirpe*) descent; (*animali*) breed. **di ogni razza** of all sorts. **di razza incrociata** crossbred. **di razza (pura)** (*animali*) pedigree, thoroughbred. **razziale** *agg* racial. **razzismo** *sm* racialism, racism. **razzista** *agg*, *s(m+f)* racist, racialist.
razza² ['rattsa] *sf* (*pesce*) ray, skate.
razzia [rat'tsia] *sf* raid.
razzo ['rattso] *sm* rocket.
re [re] *sm* king.
reagire [rea'dʒire] *v* react. **reagente** *sm* reagent.
reale¹ [re'ale] *agg* real. **realismo** *sm* realism. **realista** *s(m+f)* realist. **realistico** *agg* realistic. **realtà** *sf* reality. **in realtà** in (actual) fact.
reale² [re'ale] *agg* (*regale*) royal. **realista** *agg*, *s(m+f)* royalist.
realizzare [realid'dzare] *v* realize; (*effettuare*) put into effect; (*sport*) score. **realizzabile** *agg* feasible. **realizzazione** *sf* realization; (*teatro*, *ecc.*) production. **prezzo di realizzo** cost price.
reato [re'ato] *sm* offence; (*grave*) crime.
reattivo [reat'tivo] *agg* reactive. *sm* (*chim*) reagent; (*psic*) test.
reattore [reat'tore] *sm* reactor; (*aereo*) jet.
reazione [rea'tsjone] *sf* reaction. **motore a reazione** jet engine. **reazionario, -a** *s*, *agg* reactionary.
rebbio ['rebbjo] *sm* prong.
recapito [re'kapito] *sm* (*indirizzo*) address; (*consegna*) delivery. **recapitare** *v* deliver.
recare [re'kare] *v* (*portare*) bear; (*arrecare*) cause.
recensire [retʃen'sire] *v* review. **recensione** *sf* review. **recensore, -a** *sm*, *sf* reviewer.
recente [re'tʃɛnte] *agg* recent. **recentissime** *sf pl* latest news *sing*.
recessione [retʃes'sjone] *sf* recession.
recinto [re'tʃinto] *sm* enclosure; (*per animali*) pen. **recintare** *v* enclose.
recipiente [retʃi'pjɛnte] *sm* container.
reciproco [re'tʃiproko] *agg* reciprocal, mutual. **reciprocare** *v* reciprocate. **reciprocità** *sf* reciprocity.

recitare [retʃi'tare] *v* (*versi, ecc.*) recite; (*una parte*) play; (*sostenere un ruolo*) act; (*fingere*) put on an act. **recita** *sf* performance. **recital** *sm invar* recital. **recitazione** *sf* recitation.
reclamare [rekla'mare] *v* complain; (*richiedere*) demand; protest. **reclamo** *sm* complaint.
reclame [re'klam] *sf invar* advertisement. **fare (della) reclame** advertise.
reclusione [reklu'zjone] *sf* confinement; imprisonment.
reclutare [reklu'tare] *v* recruit. **recluta** *sf* recruit.
record ['rekord] *sm invar* record.
recriminare [rekrimi'nare] *v* recriminate.
redarguire [redargu'ire] *v* rebuke.
redattore [redat'tore], **-trice** *sm*, *sf* editor. **redazione** *sf* editorial staff; (*ufficio*) editor's office; (*atto del redigere*) editing, compiling.
reddito ['reddito] *sm* income; (*statale*) revenue; (*utile*) return. **imposta sul reddito** *sf* income tax. **reddito imponibile** taxable income.
redentore [reden'tore] *agg* redeeming. *sm* redeemer.
***redigere** [re'didʒere] *v* (*compilare*) draw up; (*scrivere*) write; (*giornale*) edit.
***redimere** [re'dimere] *v* redeem. **redimibile** *agg* redeemable.
redini ['redini] *sf pl* reins *pl*.
redivivo [redi'vivo] *agg* (*fig*) another.
reduce ['redutʃe] *agg* returning. *sm* (*mil*) veteran; (*superstite*) survivor.
refe ['refe] *sm* thread.
referendum [refe'rɛndum] *sm invar* referendum.
referenza [refe'rɛntsa] *sf* reference.
refettorio [refet'tɔrjo] *sm* refectory.
refrattario [refrat'tarjo] *agg* refractory; (*fig*) unmoved (by).
refrigerare [refridʒe'rare] *v* refresh, cool.
regalare [rega'lare] *v* give (away). **regalo** *sm* gift, present.
regale [re'gale] *agg* regal.
regata [re'gata] *sf* regatta.
reggente [red'dʒɛnte] *sm* ruler. *agg* ruling.
***reggere** ['rɛddʒere] *v* (*sostenere*) hold; support; (*resistere*) stand; (*dirigere*) run; (*gramm*) govern; (*durare*) last. **reggere al confronto con** bear comparison with. **reggere alla prova** stand the test. **reggersi** *v* stand.

reggia ['rɛddʒa] *sf* royal palace.
reggimento [reddʒi'mento] *sm* regiment.
reggipetto [reddʒi'pɛtto] *sm* bra.
regia [re'dʒia] *sf* (*cinema*) direction; (*teatro*) production.
regime [re'dʒime] *sm* regime. **essere a regime** be on a diet. **regime di vita** way of life.
regina [re'dʒina] *sf* queen.
regio ['rɛdʒo] *agg* royal.
regione [re'dʒone] *sf* region. **regionale** *agg* regional.
regista [re'dʒista] *sf* (*cine*) director; (*teatro, TV*) producer.
registrare [redʒis'trare] *v* record; (*in registro*) register; (*mettere a punto*) adjust. **registratore** *sm* recorder; register.
registrazione *sf* record; registration; adjustment; (*radio, TV*) recording. **registro** *sm* register. **cambiar registro** (*fam*) change one's tune.
regnare [re'ɲare] *v* rule, reign. **regno** *sm* (*territorio*) kingdom, realm; (*periodo, potere*) reign.
regola ['rɛgola] *sm* rule; norm. **di regola** normally. **in regola** in order. **per vostra regola** for your information. **regolamentare** *agg* prescribed. **regolamento** *sm* (*il regolare*) regulation; (*norme*) rules *pl*; (*comm*) settlement.
regolare [rego'lare] *v* regulate; (*mettere a punto*) adjust; (*comm*) settle. **regolarsi** *v* act; control oneself. *agg* regular. **regolarità** *sf* regularity. **regolarizzare** *v* regularize.
regolo ['rɛgolo] *sm* ruler; (*calcolatore*) slide-rule.
reincarnazione [reinkarna'tsjone] *sf* reincarnation.
reintegrare [reinte'grare] *v* reinstate. **reintegrazione** *sf* reinstatement.
relativo [rela'tivo] *agg* relative; concerning; (*corrispondente*) relevant. **relativamente a** regarding. **relatività** *sf* relativity.
relazione [rela'tsjone] *sf* relation(ship), connection; (*resoconto*) report. **essere in buone relazioni** be on good terms. **in relazione a** as regards. **mettere in relazione** relate.
relegare [rele'gare] *v* relegate.
religione [reli'dʒone] *sf* religion. **religiosa** *sf* nun. **religioso** *agg* religious.
reliquia [re'likwja] *sf* relic. **reliquiario** *sf* reliquary.

relitto [re'litto] *sm* wreck; (*rottame*) wreckage.
remare [re'mare] *v* row. **remata** *sf* stroke. **fare una remata** go for a row.
reminiscenza [remini'ʃentsa] *sf* recollection.
remissivo [remis'sivo] *agg* meek.
remoto [re'mɔto] *agg* remote.
***rendere** ['rɛndere] *v* return; (*fruttare*) bring in; (*far diventare*) make; be efficient. **render conto di** account for. **render l'idea** make oneself clear. **rendere omaggio** pay homage. **rendersi conto** (*spiegare*) explain; (*capire*) realize. **rendere un servizio** do a favour.
rendimento [rendi'mento] *sm* (*utile*) yield; (*resa*) output; (*fis, mec*) efficiency.
rendita ['rɛndita] *sf* income; (*econ*) revenue; (*reddito*) yield.
rene ['rɛne] *sm* kidney. **reni** *sf pl* (*fam*) back *sing*.
renna ['rɛnna] *sf* reindeer.
reparto [re'parto] *sm* department; (*mil*) unit. **capo reparto** departmental head; (*maestranza*) foreman; (*negozio*) supervisor.
repellente [repel'lɛnte] *agg* repellent; (*ripugnante*) repulsive.
repentaglio [repen'taʎo] *sm* **mettere a repentaglio** jeopardize.
reperibile [repe'ribile] *agg* to be found; (*disponibile*) available.
repertorio [reper'tɔrjo] *sm* repertoire; (*elenco*) list.
replica ['rɛplika] *sf* repetition; (*risposta*) reply; (*teatro*) performance; objection; copy. **replicare** *v* repeat; reply; perform again; object.
repressione [repres'sjone] *sf* repression. **represso** *agg* repressed.
***reprimere** [re'primere] *v* repress, control.
repubblica [re'pubblika] *sf* republic. **repubblicano** *agg* republican.
reputare [repu'tare] *v* consider. **reputazione** *sf* reputation.
requisire [rekwi'zire] *v* requisition. **requisito** *sm* requirement. **requisitoria** *sf* (*dir*) indictment; (*rimprovero*) reproof.
resa ['reza] *sf* (*l'arrendersi*) surrender; (*restituzione*) return; (*rendimento*) yield. **resa dei conti** statement (of accounts); (*fig*) reckoning.
***rescindere** [re'ʃindere] *v* rescind.

residente [rezi'dɛnte] *s(m+f)*, *agg* resident. **residenza** *sf* residence; (*permanenza*) stay.
residuo [re'ziduo] *agg* residual. *sm* residue; (*fig*) trace. **residuato** *sm* surplus.
resina ['rɛzina] *sf* resin.
resistere [re'zistere] *v* resist; (*sopportare*) bear; (*non essere danneggiato*) be resistant (to). **resistente** *agg* resistant, proof (against). **resistenza** *sf* resistance; (*capacità di resistere*) endurance.
resoconto [rezo'konto] *sm* report.
***respingere** [res'pindʒere] *v* push back, repel; (*rifiutare*) reject; (*bocciare*) fail. **respingente** *sm* buffer.
respirare [respi'rare] *v* breathe. **respiratore** *sm* respirator. **respiratorio** *agg* respiratory. **respirazione** *sf* respiration. **respiro** *sm* breath; (*fig*) breathing space. **sentirsi mancare il respiro** feel breathless.
responsabile [respon'sabile] *agg* responsible. *s(m+f)* person responsible. **responsabilità** *sf* responsibility. **prendersi la responsabilità** take the responsibility.
ressa ['rɛssa] *sf* crowd.
restare [res'tare] *v* remain; (*avanzare*) be left (over). **restarci male** (*delusi*) be disappointed; (*offesi*) be offended. **restare d'accordo** agree. **restante** *sm* remainder.
restaurare [restau'rare] *v* restore. **restauro** *sm* restoration; (*riparazione*) repair.
restio [res'tio] *agg* restive; (*bambini*) fractious.
restituire [restitu'ire] *v* return; (*fig*) restore. **restituzione** *sf* return.
resto ['rɛsto] *sm* remainder; (*di denaro*) change. **del resto** (*d'altronde*) on the other hand; (*inoltre*) besides.
***restringere** [res'trindʒere] *v* (*limitare*) restrict; (*ridurre di larghezza*) narrow; (*vestiario*) take in; (*tessuto*) shrink. **restringimento** *sm* shrinkage, narrowing. **restrizione** *sf* restriction.
rete ['rete] *sf* net; (*sistema, tec*) network; (*calcio*) goal; (*inganno*) trap. **rete metallica** wire netting.
reticente [reti'tʃɛnte] *agg* reticent.
reticolato [retiko'lato] *sm* (*disegno*) grid; (*graticcio*) grating. **reticolo** *sm* lattice, grating.
retina ['rɛtina] *sf* retina.
retorica [re'tɔrika] *sf* rhetoric. **retorico** *agg* rhetorical.

retribuire [retribu'ire] *v* reward. **retribuzione** *sf* reward; (*paga*) payment.
retro ['rɛtro] *sm* back.
retroattivo [retroat'tivo] *agg* retrospective.
***retrocedere** [retro'tʃedere] *v* recede; (*ritirarsi*) retreat; (*mil*) demote; (*sport*) move down.
retrodatare [retroda'tare] *v* back-date.
retrogrado [re'trɔgrado] *agg* retrograde; (*fig*) backward, reactionary.
retroguardia [retro'gwardja] *sf* rearguard.
retromarcia [retro'martʃa] *sf* reverse.
retroscena [retro'ʃena] *sm invar* backstage; (*fig*) background.
retrospettivo [retrospet'tivo] *agg* retrospective.
retrovisore [retrovi'zore] *sm* rear-view mirror.
retta¹ ['rɛtta] *sf* (*geom*) straight line.
retta² ['rɛtta] *sf* **dar retta a** listen to, pay attention to.
retta³ [rɛtta] *sf* fee for board and lodging.
rettangolo [ret'tangolo] *sm* rectangle. **rettangolare** *agg* right-angled, rectangular.
rettificare [rettifi'kare] *v* rectify, correct; (*mec*) grind. **rettifica** *sf* rectification, correction; grinding.
rettile ['rɛttile] *sm* reptile.
rettilineo [retti'lineo] *agg* straight.
retto ['rɛtto] *agg* straight; (*leale*) upright, straightforward; correct; (*geom*) right.
rettore [ret'tore] *sm* rector.
reumatismo [reuma'tizmo] *sm* rheumatism. **reumatico** *agg* rheumatic.
reverendo [reve'rɛndo] *agg* reverend. *sm* (*fam*) priest.
reversibile [rever'sibile] *agg* reversible.
revisione [revi'zjone] *sf* revision; (*tec*) overhaul; (*dei conti*) audit; (*dir*) review. **revisore** *sm* auditor; (*di bozze*) proofreader.
revocare [revo'kare] *v* revoke.
riabbassare [riabbas'sare] *v* lower again.
riabbottonare [riabbotto'nare] *v* button up.
riabbracciare [riabbrat'tʃare] *v* embrace again.
riabilitare [riabili'tare] *v* rehabilitate. **riabilitazione** *sf* rehabilitation.
riaccompagnare [riakkompa'ɲare] *v* take .back.
riacquistare [riakkwis'tare] *v* (*ricomprare*) buy back; (*ricuperare*) recover.

riaddormentarsi [riaddormen'tarsi] *v* fall asleep again.

riaffermare [riaffer'mare] *v* reaffirm.

riallacciare [riallat'tʃare] *v* re-tie; (*fig*) renew.

rialto [ri'alto] *sm* rise.

rialzare [rial'tsare] *v* raise (again). **rialzo** *sm* rise.

*riammettere** [riam'mettere] *v* re-admit. **riammissione** *sf* re-admission.

riammogliarsi [riammo'ʎarsi] *v* remarry.

rianimare [riani'mare] *v* revive; (*fig*) cheer (up).

*riapparire** [riappa'rire] *v* reappear.

*riaprire** [riap'rire] *v* reopen; (*riprendere*) resume. **riapertura** *sf* reopening; resumption.

riarmare [riar'mare] *v* rearm; (*nave*) refit; (*edificio*) reinforce. **riarmamento** *sf* rearmament.

riassestare [riasses'tare] *v* rearrange.

riassettare [riasset'tare] *v* tidy up.

riassicurare [riassiku'rare] *v* reassure; (*dir*) reinsure. **riassicurazione** *sf* reassurance; reinsurance.

*riassumere** [rias'sumere] *v* take on again; (*compendiare*) sum up; (*condensare*) summarize. **riassunto** *sm* summary. **riassunzione** *sf* re-employment; (*dir*) resumption.

riattaccare [riattak'kare] *v* (*con filo*) sew on again; (*con colla*) stick on again; (*riprendere*) resume.

riattivare [riatti'vare] *v* reactivate; put back into service; (*strada*) reopen.

*riavere** [ria'vere] *v* have again; (*ricuperare*) recover.

riavvicinare [riavvitʃi'nare] *v* approach again; (*fig*) reconcile. **riavvicinamento** *sm* (*pol*) rapprochement.

ribadire [riba'dire] *v* rivet; (*fig*) confirm.

ribaldo [ri'baldo] *sm* rogue.

ribaltare [ribal'tare] *v* turn over; (*mandar sottosopra*) overturn. **ribalta** *sf* (*asse*) flap; (*teatro*) proscenium; (*fig*) limelight. **tornare alla ribalta** (*questione*) come up again. **venire alla ribalta** come on to the scene. **ribaltabile** *agg* folding; (*tavolo*) drop-leaf; (*camion*) tip-up.

ribassare [ribas'sare] *v* reduce. **ribasso** *sm* reduction. **essere in ribasso** drop.

ribattere [ri'battere] *v* hit back; (*chiodo*) rivet; (*sport*) return; (*confutare*) refute; (*replicare*) answer back.

ribelle [ri'bɛlle] *agg* rebellious. *s(m+f)*

rebel. **ribellarsi** *v* revolt. **ribellione** *sf* rebellion.

ribes ['ribes] *sm* (red)currant. **ribes nero** blackcurrant.

riboccare [ribok'kare] *v* overflow.

ribollire [ribol'lire] *v* boil (again); ferment; (*fig*) seethe.

ribrezzo [ri'brettso] *sm* disgust. **far ribrezzo** disgust. **provar ribrezzo** be disgusted (by).

ributtare [ribut'tare] *v* throw again; (*buttar fuori*) throw out; vomit; (*rifiutare*) reject.

ricacciare [rikat'tʃare] *v* turn out (again); (*rimettere*) push back.

*ricadere** [rika'dere] *v* fall (back); (*pendere*) hang (down). **ricaduta** *sf* relapse.

ricalcare [rikal'kare] *v* (*disegno*) trace; (*fig*) follow faithfully. **ricalco** *sm* tracing.

ricamare [rika'mare] *v* embroider. **ricamo** *sm* embroidery.

ricambiare [rikam'bjare] *v* (*sostituire*) change; (*scambiare*) exchange; (*di nuovo*) change again. **di ricambio** spare.

ricapitolare [rikapito'lare] *v* sum up.

ricaricare [rikari'kare] *v* recharge; (*armi*) reload; (*orologio*) wind up again; (*pipa*) refill.

ricattare [rikat'tare] *v* blackmail. **ricattatore, -trice** *sm, sf* blackmailer. **ricatto** *sm* blackmail.

ricavare [rika'vare] *v* obtain, get; (*dedurre*) deduce. **ricavato** *or* **ricavo** *sm* proceeds *pl*.

ricchezza [rik'kettsa] *sf* wealth.

riccio[1] ['rittʃo] *agg* curly. *sm* curl; (*voluta*) scroll. **riccioluto** *or* **ricciuto** *agg* curly.

riccio[2] ['rittʃo] *sm* (*zool*) hedgehog; (*castagna*) (chestnut) husk. **riccio di mare** sea-urchin.

ricco ['rikko], **-a** *agg* rich. *sm, sf* rich person.

ricerca [ri'tʃerka] *sf* search; (*scientifica*) research; (*indagine*) investigation. **ricercare** *v* search (for); investigate. **ricercato** *agg* (much-)wanted; in (great) demand; (*affettato*) precious; (*raffinato*) refined. **ricercatezza** *sf* affectation; refinement. **ricercatore, -trice** *sm, sf* (*persona*) research worker; (*apparecchio*) detector.

ricetta [ri'tʃetta] *sf* recipe.

ricettare [ritʃet'tare] *v* receive. **ricettatore** *sm* receiver (of stolen goods).

ricettivo [ritʃet'tivo] *agg* receptive. **ricettività** *sf* receptivity.

***ricevere** [ri'tʃevere] *v* receive; *(accogliere)* welcome. **ricevimento** *sm* reception; *(ricevuta)* receipt. **ricevitore** *sm* receiver; *(impiegato)* collector. **ricevuta** *sf* receipt. **ricezione** *sf* reception.

richiamare [rikja'mare] *v* call back; *(far tornare, ricordare)* recall; *(rimproverare)* rebuke. **richiamare in vita** revive. **richiamo** *sm* call; recall; rebuke. **far da richiamo** act as a decoy.

***richiedere** [ri'kjedere] *v* *(aver bisogno)* require; *(per sapere)* ask; *(per ottenere)* ask for. **richiesta** *sf* request; *(econ)* demand; *(burocratica)* application. **richiesto** *agg* in (great) demand; necessary.

ricino ['ritʃino] *sm* **olio di ricino** *sm* castor-oil.

ricominciare [rikomin'tʃare] *v* start again.

ricompensa [rikom'pɛnsa] *sf* reward. **ricompensare** *v* *(contraccambiare)* repay; *(premiare)* reward.

riconciliare [rikontʃi'ljare] *v* reconcile; *(procurare di nuovo)* win back. **riconciliarsi** *v* make it up.

ricondurre [rikon'durre] *v* take back; *(di nuovo)* take again.

***riconoscere** [riko'noʃere] *v* recognize; *(ammettere)* admit. **riconoscente** *agg* grateful. **riconoscenza** *sf* gratitude. **riconoscibile** *agg* recognizable. **riconoscimento** *sm* recognition; admission; identification.

riconquistare [rikonkwis'tare] *v* win back.

ricopiare [riko'pjare] *v* copy.

***ricoprire** [rikop'rire] *v* cover (again); *(occupare)* hold; *(rivestire)* coat; *(colmare)* smother.

ricordare [rikor'dare] *v* remember; *(richiamare alla memoria)* recall; *(far ricordare)* remind. **ricordo** *sm* recollection; *(oggetto)* souvenir. **ricordo di famiglia** heirloom. **ricordo d'infanzia** childhood memory. **ricordi** *sm pl* *(libro)* memoirs *pl*.

***ricorrere** [ri'korrere] *v* resort; *(dir)* appeal; *(ripetersi)* recur. **ricorso** *sm* resort, recourse; *(dir)* appeal.

ricostituente [rikostitu'ɛnte] *sm* tonic. **ricostituire** *v* reconstitute.

***ricostruire** [rikostru'ire] *v* rebuild; *(fig)* reconstruct. **ricostruzione** *sf* reconstruction.

ricotta [ri'kɔtta] *sf* cottage cheese.

ricoverare [rikove'rare] *v* take in; *(all'ospedale)* send to hospital. **ricoverato, -a** *sm, sf* *(ospedale)* patient; *(ospizio)* inmate. **ricovero** *sm* shelter; *(ospizio)* home; *(in ospedale)* admission to hospital.

ricrearsi [rikre'arsi] *v* amuse oneself. **ricreazione** *sf* recreation; *(scuola)* playtime; *(pausa)* break.

ricredersi [ri'kredersi] *v* change one's mind.

ricuperare [rikupe'rare] *v* recover; *(mar)* salvage. **ricupero** *sm* recovery; salvage.

ricurvo [ri'kurvo] *agg* bent.

ricusare [riku'zare] *v* decline.

***ridare** [ri'dare] *v* *(dare nuovamente)* give again; *(restituire)* give back.

***ridere** ['ridere] *v* laugh. **(cosa) da ridere** *(divertente)* funny; *(inezia)* of no importance. **far ridere** be funny; be ridiculous. *sm* laughter.

ridicolo [ri'dikolo] *agg* ridiculous. *sm* absurdity; *(derisione)* ridicule.

ridimensionare [ridimensjo'nare] *v* reorganize; *(ridurre)* cut down; *(fig)* reappraise.

***ridire** [ri'dire] *v* *(riferire)* tell; *(criticare)* find fault with; *(dire di nuovo)* repeat.

ridosso [ri'dɔsso] *sm* **a ridosso di** close to; *(dietro)* behind.

***ridurre** [ri'durre] *v* reduce; *(trasformare)* turn. **riduzione** *sf* reduction; cut; adaptation.

rielaborare [rielabo'rare] *v* work out again; modify.

***riempire** [riem'pire] *v* fill; *(compilare)* fill in; *(gastr)* stuff. **riempitivo** *sm* filler; *(fig)* stopgap.

rientrare [rien'trare] *v* *(tornare)* return; *(rincasare)* come *or* go home; *(far parte)* come within, form part of; *(entrare nuovamente)* re-enter. **rientro** *sm* return; re-entry; *(rientranza)* recess.

riepilogare [riepilo'gare] *v* summarize. **riepilogo** *sm, pl* -ghi recapitulation.

riesumare [riezu'mare] *v* exhume; *(fig)* unearth.

rievocare [rievo'kare] *v* recall; commemorate.

***rifare** [ri'fare] *v* make *or* do again; *(ricostruire)* rebuild; imitate.

riferire [rife'rire] *v* relate; report. **riferimento** *sm* reference. **punto di riferimento** *sm* landmark.

rifilare [rifi'lare] (*fam*) v palm off; (*dire d'un fiato*) reel off.

rifinire [rifi'nire] v (*dare l'ultima mano*) give the finishing touch; (*ritoccare*) touch up. **rifinitura** *sf* finishing touches *pl*; (*guarnizione*) fittings *pl*.

rifiutare [rifju'tare] v refuse; decline. **rifiuto** *sm* refusal; (*scarto*) refuse, rubbish.

riflessione [rifles'sjone] *sf* reflection; (*osservazione*) remark.

riflessivo [rifles'sivo] *agg* thoughtful; (*gramm*) relexive.

riflesso [ri'flɛsso] *sm* reflection; (*med*) reflex. **di riflesso** indirectly.

*riflettere [ri'flɛttere] v reflect; (*pensarci su*) think (over *or* about). **riflettersi su** (*ripercuotersi*) affect. **riflettore** *sm* reflector; (*cinema, ecc.*) floodlight.

*rifondere [ri'fondere] v recast; (*ricomporre*) recompose; (*risarcire*) refund.

riformare [rifor'mare] v reform; (*formare di nuovo*) re-form. **riforma** *sf* reform.

rifornire [rifor'nire] v supply (with). **rifornirsi di benzina** (*auto*) fill up. **rifornimento** *sm* supply.

rifuggire [rifud'dʒire] v escape (again); (*fig*) shrink (from).

rifugiarsi [rifu'dʒarsi] v (take) shelter. **rifugiato, -a** *sm, sf* refugee.

rifugio [ri'fudʒo] *sm* shelter. **rifugio antiaereo** air-raid shelter. **rifugio fiscale** tax-haven.

*rifulgere [ri'fuldʒere] v glow.

riga ['riga] *sf* line; (*fila*) row; (*righello*) ruler. **a righe** striped. **riga a T** T-square. **rigare** v rule; (*tracciar strisce*) stripe; (*scalfire*) score.

rigaglie [ri'gaʎe] *sf pl* giblets *pl*.

rigettare [ridʒet'tare] v (*buttar fuori*) throw out; (*fig*) reject; vomit; (*gettare indietro*) throw back.

rigido ['ridʒido] *agg* rigid, stiff; (*freddo*) severe. **rigidezza** *or* **rigidità** *sf* rigidity; (*fig*) rigour, severity.

rigirare [ridʒi'rare] v turn round; (*fig*) twist round. **rigiro** *sm* twist. **giri e rigiri** *sm pl* twists and turns *pl*.

rigo ['rigo] *sm* line; (*musica*) stave.

rigoglioso [rigo'ʎozo] *agg* blooming.

rigonfio [ri'gonfjo] *agg* swollen.

rigore [ri'gore] *sm* rigour; (*calcio*) penalty (kick). **a rigor di logica** strictly speaking. **a rigore** in point of fact. **di rigore** compulsory. **rigoroso** *agg* rigorous.

rigovernare [rigover'nare] v (*i piatti*) wash up; (*animali*) tend.

riguardare [rigwar'dare] v regard. **riguardo** *sm* regard; (*cautela*) care; consideration. **di riguardo** of consequence. **riguardo a** regarding. **riguardo a me** as for me. **senza riguardo** inconsiderate. **riguardoso** *agg* thoughtful, respectful.

rilanciare [rilan'tʃare] v launch; (*asta, carte*) raise.

rilasciare [rila'ʃare] v (*liberare*) release; (*consegnare*) issue.

rilassare [rilas'sare] v relax; (*allentare*) slacken. **rilassamento** *sm* relaxation.

rilegare [rile'gare] v bind; (*incastonare*) set. **rilegatura** *sf* binding.

*rileggere [ri'lɛddʒere] v re-read.

rilevare [rile'vare] v (*notare*) notice; (*comm*) take over; (*topografia*) survey.

rilievo [ri'ljɛvo] *sm* relief; importance; (*osservazione*) remark; survey. **mettere in rilievo** stress, emphasize.

riluttante [rilut'tante] *agg* reluctant.

rima ['rima] *sf* rhyme.

rimandare [riman'dare] v send back; (*posporre*) defer.

*rimanere [rima'nere] v remain; (*essere*) be. **rimanere d'accordo** agree. **rimanere in dubbio** be left in doubt. **rimaner male** be put out; (*deluso*) be disappointed; (*offeso*) be hurt.

rimasugli [rima'zuʎi] *sm pl* left-overs *pl*.

rimbalzare [rimbal'tsare] v bounce; (*proiettile*) ricochet.

rimbambire [rimbam'bire] v become childish. **rimbambito** *agg* (*fam*) gaga.

rimbeccare [rimbek'kare] v retort. **di rimbecco** sharply.

rimboccare [rimbok'kare] v turn down. **rimboccarsi le maniche** roll up one's sleeves.

rimbombare [rimbom'bare] v resound.

rimborsare [rimbor'sare] v reimburse. **rimborso** *sm* refund.

rimediare [rime'djare] v remedy; (*fam: racimolare*) scrape together; (*accomodare*) patch; (*provvedere*) take care. **rimedio** *sm* remedy.

rimescolare [rimesko'lare] v stir; (*carte*) shuffle.

rimessa [ri'messa] *sf* (*deposito*) depot; garage; (*trasferimento*) remittance; (*perdita*) loss. **rimessa in gioco** (*calcio*) throw-in.

*rimettere [ri'mettere] *v* put back; *(indossare)* put back on; *(spedire)* send; *(denaro)* remit. **rimetterci** *v* lose. **rimettersi** *v (riaversi)* recover; *(affidarsi)* trust.

rimodernare [rimoder'nare] *v* modernize.

rimontare [rimon'tare] *v (mettere insieme)* reassemble; *(sport)* catch up; *(risalire)* go up; *(a cavallo)* remount; *(auto)* get back in.

rimorchiare [rimor'kjare] *v* (have in) tow. **rimorchio** *sm* trailer. **cavo da rimorchio** *sm* tow-rope.

rimorso [ri'mɔrso] *sm* remorse. **rimorso di coscienza** pangs of conscience *pl.*

rimostrare [rimos'trare] *v* remonstrate.

rimpasto [rim'pasto] *sm (fig)* reshuffle.

rimpatriare [rimpa'trjare] *v* repatriate. **rimpatrio** *sm* repatriation.

*rimpiangere [rim'pjandʒere] *v* regret. **rimpianto** *sm* regret.

rimpiattino [rimpjat'tino] *sm* hide-and-seek.

rimpiazzare [rimpjat'tsare] *v* replace.

rimpiccolire [rimpikko'lire] *v* make smaller.

rimpinzarsi [rimpin'tsarsi] *v* stuff oneself, gorge.

rimproverare [rimprove'rare] *v* reproach; *(sgridare)* scold; *(fam)* tell off; *(biasimare)* blame. **rimprovero** *sm* reproach; blame.

*rimuovere [ri'nɪwɔvere] *v* remove; *(distogliere)* dissuade.

Rinascimento [rinaʃi'mento] *sm* Renaissance.

rinascita [ri'naʃita] *sf* rebirth; *(fig)* revival.

rincagnato [rinka'ɲato] *agg* **naso rincagnato** *sm* pug nose, snub nose.

rincalzare [rinkal'tsare] *v (sorreggere)* prop up; *(lenzuola)* tuck in.

rincarare [rinka'rare] *v (rendere più caro)* raise (the price of); *(essere più caro)* rise, become more expensive.

rincasare [rinka'zare] *v* return home.

*rinchiudere [rin'kjudere] *v* shut in. **rinchiuso** [rin'kjuzo] *agg* shut in; *(aria)* stale, fusty. *sm* enclosure. **saper di rinchiuso** smell fusty or musty.

*rincorrere [rin'korrere] *v* run after, chase. **rincorsa** *sf* run-up.

*rincrescere [rin'kreʃere] *v* cause regret *or* sorrow. **mi rincresce di ...** I'm sorry to .... **ti rincresce ...?** do you mind...? **rincrescimento** *sm* regret.

rinculare [rinku'lare] *v* recoil.

rinforzare [rinfor'tsare] *v* reinforce, strengthen. **rinforzo** *sm* reinforcement.

rinfrescare [rinfres'kare] *v* cool; *(pulire)* freshen up; *(memoria)* refresh; *(ravvivare)* brush up. **rinfrescata** *sf* cooling. **darsi una rinfrescata** freshen up. **rinfreschi** *sm pl* refreshments *pl.* **rinfresco** *sm (ricevimento)* party.

rinfusa [rin'fuza] *sf* **alla rinfusa** higgledy-piggledy.

ringhiare [rin'gjare] *v* growl, snarl.

ringhiera [rin'gjɛra] *sf* railing; *(delle scale)* banister.

ringiovanire [rindʒova'nire] *v* rejuvenate; *(nell'aspetto)* make look younger.

ringraziare [ringra'tsjare] *v* thank. **ringraziamento** *sm* thanks *pl.* **lettera di ringraziamento** *sf* thank-you letter.

rinnegare [rinne'gare] *v* deny. **rinnegato, -a** *s*, *agg* renegade.

rinnovare [rinno'vare] *v* renew. **rinnovamento** *sm* renewal; *(rimodernamento)* renovation. **rinnovazione** *sf* renewal; renovation.

rinoceronte [rinotʃe'ronte] *sm* rhinoceros.

rinomato [rino'mato] *agg* renowned. **rinomanza** *sf* renown.

rinsaldare [rinsal'dare] *v* consolidate; *(inamidare)* starch.

rintoccare [rintok'kare] *v (campana)* toll; *(orologio)* strike. **rintocco** *sm* toll; stroke.

rintracciare [rintrat'tʃare] *v* trace; track down.

rintronare [rintro'nare] *v* thunder; *(assordare)* deafen.

rintuzzare [rintut'tsare] *v (rendere ottuso)* blunt; *(respingere)* repel; *(ribattere)* refute; *(frenare)* check.

rinunciare [rinun'tʃare] *v* give up; *(fare a meno)* forgo; *(dir)* renounce; *(non voler fare)* refrain (from). **rinunce** *sf pl (privazioni)* hardship *sing.* **rinuncia** *sf* abandonment; renunciation.

*rinvenire[1] [rinve'nire] *v (ritrovare)* recover.

*rinvenire[2] [rinve'nire] *v (ritornare in sè)* come to; *(riprendere freschezza)* revive.

rinviare [rinvi'are] *v (mandare indietro)* send back; *(posporre)* put off; *(dir)* adjourn; *(indirizzare)* refer. **rinvio** *sm* postponement; adjournment; *(testo)* (cross-)reference.

rinvigorire [rinvigo'rire] v invigorate; (ritornar vigoroso) regain strength.

rione [ri'one] sm district. rionale agg local.

riordinare [riordi'nare] v rearrange; (comm) reorder.

riorganizzare [riorganid'dzare] v reorganize. riorganizzazione sf reorganization.

ripagare [ripa'gare] v pay back.

riparare [ripa'rare] v (aggiustare) repair; (porre rimedio) make up (for), redress; protect; (esame) repeat. ripararsi v take shelter. riparazione sf repair; redress.

riparo [ri'paro] sm shelter; (protezione) cover; (mec) guard. mettersi al riparo (da) shelter (from).

ripartire¹ [ripar'tire] v (partire di nuovo) leave or start (up) again.

ripartire² [ripar'tire] v (dividere) split up; distribute.

ripassare [ripas'sare] v (tornare) pass again; (visitare) call back; (attraversare) cross again; (rivedere) review; (mec) overhaul. ripassata sf (pittura) fresh coat of paint; revision, overhaul; (stirata) press.

ripensare [ripen'sare] v think (over); (mutare pensiero) reconsider. ripensare a (tornare col pensiero) recall.

ripentirsi [ripen'tirsi] v repent; (cambiar pensiero) have second thoughts.

*ripercuotersi [riper'kwɔtersi] v (suono) reverberate; (fig) have an effect.

ripercussione [riperkus'sjone] sf repercussion.

ripetere [ri'petere] v repeat. ripetizione sf repetition; (studio) coaching.

ripiano [ri'pjano] sm terrace; (scomparto) shelf.

ripido ['ripido] agg steep.

ripiegare [ripje'gare] v fold again; (fig) make do. di ripiego makeshift.

ripieno [ri'pjɛno] agg filled, stuffed. sm filling, stuffing.

*riporre [ri'porre] v put (back).

riportare [ripor'tare] v (portare indietro) bring back; (ricondurre) take again; (riferire) report; (ricevere) get; (mat) carry. riporto sm carrying forward; amount carried forward.

riposare [ripo'zare] v rest. riposarsi v take a rest. riposo sm rest. andare a riposo retire. mettere a riposo pension off. senza riposo without interruption.

ripostiglio [ripos'tiʎo] sm cubby-hole.

*riprendere [ri'prɛndere] v take again; (recuperare) recover; (ricominciare) resume. riprendersi (da) get over.

ripresa [ri'preza] sf resumption; (innovamento) renewal; (calcio) second half; (boxe) round; (auto) acceleration; (cine) shot.

ripristinare [ripristi'nare] v restore. ripristino sm restoration.

*riprodurre [ripro'durre] v reproduce. riproduzione sf reproduction.

riprova [ri'prɔva] sf fresh proof; confirmation. riprovare v blame; (esame) fail.

ripudiare [ripu'djare] v repudiate.

ripugnante [ripu'ɲante] agg repugnant. ripugnare v disgust.

ripulsione [ripul'sjone] sf repulsion.

risaia [ri'zaja] sf rice-field.

risalire [risa'lire] v (andar su) go up (again); (nel tempo) go back.

risaltare [risal'tare] v (distinguersi) stand out; (sporgere) project. far risaltare bring out. risalto sm emphasis; projection.

risanare [risa'nare] v heal; (fig) improve; (bonificare) reclaim.

risaputo [risa'puto] agg well-known.

risarcire [risart'firе] v compensate. risarcimento sm compensation.

risata [ri'zata] sf laugh. fare or farsi una bella risata have a good laugh. scoppiare in una risata burst out laughing.

riscaldare [riskal'dare] v heat, warm up. riscaldamento sm heating; (impianto) heating system.

riscatto [ris'katto] sm ransom; (econ) redemption. riscattare v ransom; redeem.

rischiarare [riskja'rare] v illuminate.

rischiare [ris'kjare] v risk. rischiare di run the risk of. rischio sm risk. rischioso agg risky.

risciacquare [riʃa'kware] v rinse. risciacquatura sf (atto) rinsing; (acqua) dishwater. risciacquo sm mouthwash.

riscontrare [riskon'trare] v (rilevare) find; (confrontare) compare; (controllare) check. riscontro sm finding; comparison; check; (lettera) reply.

riscossa [ris'kɔssa] sf (riconquista) recovery; (insurrezione) revolt.

*riscuotere [ris'kwɔtere] v (ritirare denaro) draw; (riportare) win, earn; (scuotere) shake.

risentire [risen'tire] v (provare) feel; (mostrare) show; (udire di nuovo) hear again; (soffrire) feel the effects of. risentirsi v resent. **risentimento** *sm* resentment; consequence.

riserbo [ri'sɛrbo] *sm* reserve.

riserva [ri'sɛrva] *sf* (*provvista*) supply; (*scorta, sport*) reserve; (*dubbio*) reservation. **riservare** *v* reserve, keep; (*prenotare*) book; (*dimostrare*) show. **riservatezza** *sf* discretion; (*segretezza*) confidential nature; (*carattere*) reserve. **riservato** *agg* reserved; confidential.

risibile [ri'zibile] *agg* laughable.

risiedere [ri'sjɛdere] *v* reside.

risma ['rizma] *sf* (*carta*) ream; (*spreg*) kind.

riso[1] ['rizo] *sm* (*bot*) rice.

riso[2] ['rizo] *sm*, *pl* **-a** *f* laughter; (*risata*) laugh; ridicule.

risoluto [riso'luto] *agg* resolute. **risolutezza** *sf* decisiveness.

risoluzione [risolu'tsjone] *sf* resolution; (*mat*) solution; (*dir*) cancellation.

*risolvere [ri'sɔlvere] *v* resolve; (*mat, indovinello*) solve; (*dir*) cancel; (*scomporre*) break down. **risolversi** *v* (*fig*) turn out; decide.

risonare [riso'nare] *v* also **risuonare** ring; (*echeggiare*) resound.

*risorgere [ri'sɔrdʒere] *v* rise again. **far risorgere** revive. **risorgimento** *sm* revival.

risorsa [ri'sorsa] *sf* resource.

risparmiare [rispar'mjare] *v* spare; (*economizzare, mettere da parte*) save. **risparmiatore, -trice** *sm, sf* saver. **risparmio** *sm* saving; (*denaro*) savings *pl*. **fare risparmio (di)** save.

rispecchiare [rispek'kjare] *v* reflect.

rispettare [rispet'tare] *v* respect; (*mantenere*) keep.

rispettivo [rispet'tivo] *agg* respective.

rispetto [ris'pɛtto] *sm* respect. **rispetto a** (*in relazione a*) with respect to, as to; (*in confronto*) compared to. **rispettoso** *agg* respectful.

risplendere [ris'plɛndere] *v* shine.

*rispondere [ris'pondere] *v* answer; (*rimbeccare*) answer back; (*obbedire*) respond; (*carte*) follow suit. **rispondere di no/sì** say no/yes. **rispondere male** give a wrong answer; (*sgarbatamente*) answer back. **rispondere picche** give a flat refusal.

risposta [ris'posta] *sf* answer, reply. **botta e risposta** tit for tat. **per tutta risposta** merely. **senza risposta** unanswered.

rissa ['rissa] *sf* brawl.

ristabilire [ristabi'lire] *v* restore.

ristagnare [rista'ɲare] *v* stagnate; (*fig*) come to a standstill; (*comm*) be slack. **ristagno** *sm* stagnation; (*econ*) slump.

ristampare [ristam'pare] *v* reprint. **ristampa** *sf* reprint.

ristorante [risto'rante] *sm* restaurant. **vagone ristorante** *sm* dining car.

ristorare [risto'rare] *v* restore. **ristorarsi** *v* refresh oneself. **ristoro** *sm* refreshment.

ristretto [ris'tretto] *agg* (*limitato*) restricted; (*angusto*) narrow; (*caffè*) very strong. **brodo ristretto** *sm* consommé.

risultare [rizul'tare] *v* appear; gather; (*conseguire*) ensue. **mi risulta che ...** I gather that ....

risultato [rizul'tato] *sm* result.

risuonare [riswo'nare] *V* **risonare**.

risurrezione [rizurre'tsjone] *sf* resurrection.

risuscitare [risuʃʃi'tare] *v* revive; (*rel*) resurrect.

risvegliare [rizve'ʎare] *v* wake (up); (*fig*) awaken, revive.

ritaglio [ri'taʎo] *sm* cutting.

ritardare [ritar'dare] *v* be late; (*orologio*) be slow; (*differire*) delay. **ritardatario, -a** *sm, sf* latecomer. **ritardo** *sm* delay. **in ritardo** late.

ritegno [ri'teɲo] *sm* reserve; (*freno*) restraint.

*ritenere [rite'nere] *v* think; consider; (*trattenere*) hold.

ritirare [riti'rare] *v* withdraw; (*ottenere in consegna*) collect. **ritirarsi** *v* withdraw; (*interrompere un'attività*) retire. **ritirata** *sf* retreat. **ritiro** *sm* withdrawal; (*il prendere*) collection; (*luogo appartato*) retreat.

ritmo ['ritmo] *sm* rhythm. **ritmico** *agg* rhythmic(al).

rito ['rito] *sm* rite; (*usanza*) custom. **di rito** customary.

ritoccare [ritok'kare] *v* touch up.

ritornare [ritor'nare] *v* return; (*andare indietro*) go back. **biglietto di andata e ritorno** return ticket. **di ritorno** back. **viaggio di andata e ritorno** round trip. **ritornello** *sm* refrain.

*ritrarre [ri'trarre] *v* (*tirare indietro*) draw back; (*rappresentare*) portray.

ritratto [ri'tratto] *sm* portrait. **ritrattista** *s(m+f)* portrait-painter.

ritroso [ri'trozo] *agg* (*scontroso*) contrary; (*restio*) unwilling. **a ritroso** (*indietro*) backwards; (*controcorrente*) against the stream.

ritrovare [ritro'vare] *v* find (again); (*recuperare*) recover; (*incontrare*) meet again. **ritrovarsi** *v* meet (again); (*orientarsi*) get one's bearings; (*essere a proprio agio*) feel at ease. **ritrovato** *sm* invention; expedient. **ritrovo** *sm* meeting-place; club.

ritto ['ritto] *agg* upright.

rituale [ritu'ale] *agg, sm* ritual.

riunire [riu'nire] *v* gather; (*ricongiungere*) reunite; (*convocare*) call. **riunione** *sf* meeting.

***riuscire** [riu'ʃire] *v* succeed; (*andare a finire*) turn out; (*aver capacità*) be good (at). **mi riesce antipatico/simpatico** I dislike/like him. **riuscita** *sf* result; success.

riva ['riva] *sf* shore; (*fiume*) bank.

rivale [ri'vale] *s(m+f), agg* rival. **rivalità** *sf* rivalry.

rivalutare [rivalu'tare] *v* (*econ*) revalue; (*fig*) reappraise. **rivalutazione** *sf* revaluation; reappraisal.

***rivedere** [rive'dere] *v* see again; (*incontrare*) meet again; (*ripassare*) go over. **rivedere i conti** audit (the accounts).

rivelare [rive'lare] *v* reveal. **rivelatore** *sm* (*tec*) detector. **rivelazione** *sf* revelation.

rivendere [ri'vendere] *v* resell; (*al dettaglio*) retail. **rivendita** *sf* resale; (*negozio*) shop.

rivendicare [rivendi'kare] *v* claim.

riverberare [riverbe'rare] *v* reverberate.

riverire [rive'rire] *v* revere; respect; (*salutare*) pay one's respects (to). **riverenza** *sf* reverence; respect; (*inchino*) bow; (*di donne*) curtsy.

rivestire [rives'tire] *v* cover; (*vernice*) coat; (*fodera*) line. **rivestire una carica** hold an office; (*conferirla*) confer an office. **rivestirsi** *v* dress again, change (clothes). **rivestimento** *sm* covering; coating; lining.

rivetto [ri'vetto] *sm* rivet.

riviera [ri'vjera] *sf* coastal region. **Riviera** *sf* Riviera.

rivincita [ri'vintʃita] *sf* return match. **prendersi la rivincita** take one's revenge.

rivista [ri'vista] *sf* review; (*periodico*) magazine; (*teatro*) revue.

***rivolgere** [ri'voldʒere] *v* turn. **rivolgersi** *v* (*indirizzare*) address; (*ricorrere*) turn to; (*per domandare, ecc.*) apply.

rivolta [ri'volta] *sf* revolt; (*mar, mil*) mutiny.

rivoltare [rivol'tare] *v* turn; (*ripugnare*) revolt; (*insalata*) toss. **rivoltarsi** *v* (*ribellarsi*) revolt.

rivoltella [rivol'tella] *sf* revolver. **rivoltellata** *sf* shot.

rivoluzione [rivolu'tsjone] *sf* revolution. **rivoluzionario, -a** *s, agg* revolutionary.

rivulsione [rivul'sjone] *sf* revulsion.

rizzare [rit'tsare] *v* raise; erect. **far rizzare i capelli** make one's hair stand on end. **rizzare le orecchie** prick up one's ears.

roba ['roba] *sf* stuff, things *pl*. **bella roba!** that's a fine thing! **robaccia** *sf* rubbish.

robusto [ro'busto] *agg* sturdy; solid. **robustezza** *sf* sturdiness; (*fig*) vigour.

rocca[1] ['rokka] *sf* fortress. **cristallo di rocca** *sm* rock-crystal.

rocca[2] ['rokka] *sf* (*conocchia*) distaff; (*bobina*) reel. **rocchetto** *sm* reel; (*elett*) coil.

roccia ['rottʃa] *sf* rock; (*sport*) rock-climbing. **roccioso** *agg* rocky.

rodaggio [ro'daddʒo] *sm* running-in.

***rodere** ['rodere] *v* gnaw. **rodersi il fegato** (*fig*) be eaten up. **roditore** *sm* rodent.

rododendro [rodo'dɛndro] *sm* rhododendron.

rogna ['roɲa] *sf* (*animali*) mange; (*agric*) scab; (*fam*) pain in the neck. **rognoso** *agg* mangy; (*noioso*) boring.

rognone [ro'ɲone] *sm* kidney.

rogo ['rogo] *sm* stake; (*incendio*) fire.

Roma ['roma] *sf* Rome. **romano, -a** *s, agg* Roman. **fare alla romana** go Dutch.

Romania [roma'nia] *sf* Romania. **romeno, -a** *s, agg* Romanian.

romanico [ro'maniko] *agg* Romanesque.

romantico [ro'mantiko] *agg* romantic. **romanticismo** *sm* romanticism; sentimentalism.

romanza [ro'mandza] *sf* romance.

romanzo[1] [ro'mandzo] *sm* novel; (*storia inventata*) fiction. **romanzo a fumetti** comic strip. **romanzo d'appendice** serial story. **romanzo fiume** saga. **romanzesco** *agg* romantic; fantastic.

romanzo[2] [ro'mandzo] *agg* (*lingua*) Romance.

rombo[1] ['rombo] *sm* (*geom*) rhombus; (*pesce*) turbot.

rombo² ['rombo] *sm* roar. **rombare** *v* roar.
***rompere** ['rompere] *v* break; (*spezzare*) break off. **rompere l'anima** (*volg*) pester. **rompicapo** *sm* (*fam*) headache; (*indovinello*) puzzle. **a rompicollo** at breakneck speed. **rompiscatole** *s(m + f)* (*fam*) pain in the neck.
ronda ['ronda] *sf* **fare la ronda** (*mil*) be on watch; (*polizia*) be on the beat.
rondella [ron'dɛlla] *sf* washer.
rondine ['rondine] *sf* swallow.
rondo¹ [ron'do] *sm* (*musica*) rondo.
rondo² [ron'do] *sm* (*incrocio*) roundabout.
rondone [ron'done] *sm* swift.
ronfare [ron'fare] *v* (*fam*) snore.
ronzare [ron'dzare] *v* buzz. **ronzio** *sm* buzz(ing).
ronzino [ron'dzino] *sm* nag.
rosa ['rɔza] *sf* rose. **all'acqua di rose** (*fam*) watered-down. *agg invar* pink. **veder tutto rosa** see everything through rose-coloured spectacles. **rosato** *agg* (*vino*) rosé. **roseo** *agg* rosy. **rosetta** *sf* (*coccarda*) rosette; (*mec*) washer.
rosario [ro'zarjo] *sm* rosary.
rosbif [rɔz'bif] *sm invar* roast beef.
rosicare [rozi'kare] *v also* **rosicchiare** nibble; (*rodere*) gnaw.
rosmarino [rozma'rino] *sm* rosemary.
rosolare [rozo'lare] *v* brown.
rosolia [rozo'lia] *sf* German measles.
rospo ['rɔspo] *sm* toad.
rossetto [ros'setto] *sm* lipstick; (*belletto*) rouge.
rosso ['rosso] *agg* red. *sm* red; (*l'essere rosso*) redness. **rosso d'uovo** egg-yolk. **rossastro** *or* **rossiccio** *agg* reddish. **rossore** *sm* blush.
rosticceria [rostittʃe'ria] *sf* rotisserie.
rostro ['rɔstro] *sm* rostrum.
rotaia [ro'taja] *sf* rail.
rotare [ro'tare] *v* rotate. **rotatorio** *agg* rotatory. **rotazione** *sf* rotation.
roteare [rote'are] *v* wheel; (*occhi*) roll.
rotella [ro'tɛlla] *sf* small wheel; (*mobili*) castor; (*ginocchio*) knee-cap. **gli manca una rotella** (*fam*) he has a screw loose. **pattino a rotelle** *sm* roller-skate.
rotolare [roto'lare] *v* roll. **rotolo** *sm* roll. **andare a rotoli** *or* **rotoloni** go to rack and ruin. **rotoloni** *avv* rolling (over and over).
rotondo [ro'tondo] *agg* round.
rotta¹ ['rotta] *sf* route. **cambiar rotta** change course.
rotta² ['rotta] *sf* (*disfatta*) rout; (*breccia*)

breach. **a rotta di collo** at breakneck speed. **mettere in rotta** (put to) rout.
rotto ['rotto] *agg* broken. **per il rotto della cuffia** by the skin of one's teeth. **rottame** *sm* fragment. **rottami** *sm pl* scrap *sing*. **rottura** *sf* break; (*violazione*) breach; (*interruzione*) breakdown.
rovente [ro'vɛnte] *agg* red-hot.
rovere ['rɔvere] *sm* oak.
rovesciare [rove'ʃare] *v* upset; (*abbattere*) overthrow; (*gettare*) throw (back). **rovesciarsi** *v* overturn; (*barca, ecc.*) capsize; (*affluire*) pour. **rovescio** *sm* shower; (*retro*) back; (*danno*) setback; (*sport*) backhand. **andare a rovescio** go wrong. **a rovescio** the wrong way round; (*capovolto*) upside-down; (*col dentro fuori*) inside out.
rovinare [rovi'nare] *v* ruin. **rovina** *sf* ruin. **andare in rovina** collapse. **mandare in rovina** ruin. **rovinoso** *agg* ruinous.
rovistare [rovis'tare] *v* ransack.
rovo ['rɔvo] *sm* bramble.
rozzo ['roddzo] *agg* rough; (*fig*) coarse.
ruba ['ruba] *sf* **andare a ruba** sell like hot cakes.
rubacchiare [rubak'kjare] *v* pilfer.
rubare [ru'bare] *v* steal. **rubacuori** *s(m + f)* charmer. **rubare il tempo a qualcuno** take up someone's time. **ruberia** *sf* theft.
rubinetto [rubi'netto] *sm* tap. **rubinetto di chiusura** stopcock.
rubino [ru'bino] *sm* ruby.
rubrica [ru'brika] *sf* (*indirizzi*) address-book; (*telefonica*) directory; (*quaderno*) index-book; (*giornale*) feature.
rude ['rude] *agg* rough.
rudere ['rudere] *sm* ruin; (*persona*) wreck.
ruffiano [ruf'fjano] *sm* pimp; (*adulatore*) bootlicker.
ruga ['ruga] *sf* wrinkle. **rugoso** *agg* wrinkled.
ruggine ['ruddʒine] *sf* rust; (*astio*) ill-feeling. **rugginoso** *agg* rusty.
ruggire [rud'dʒire] *v* roar. **ruggito** *sm* roar.
rugiada [ru'dʒada] *sf* dew. **goccia di rugiada** *sf* dewdrop.
rullare [rul'lare] *v* roll; (*aereo*) taxi. **rullio** *sm* rolling. **rullo** *sm* roll; (*tec*) roller.
rum [rum] *sm* rum.
ruminare [rumi'nare] *v* ruminate.
rumore [ru'more] *sm* noise; (*diceria*) rumour; sensation. **rumoreggiare** *v* make a noise; rumble. **rumoroso** *agg* noisy.

ruolo ['rwɔlo] *sm* roll; (*teatro, funzione*) role. **insegnante non di ruolo** supply teacher. **personale di ruolo** permanent staff.

ruota ['rwɔta] *sf* wheel. **andare a ruota libera** free-wheel. **a ruota** circular. **far la ruota** (*pavoneggiarsi*) show off. **seguire a ruota** follow close behind.

rupe ['rupe] *sf* cliff.

rupia [ru'pia] *sf* rupee.

rurale [ru'rale] *agg* rural.

ruscello [ru'ʃɛllo] *sm* stream.

ruspa ['ruspa] *sf* bulldozer. (**pollo**) **ruspante** *sm* free-range chicken.

russare [rus'sare] *v* snore.

Russia ['russja] *sf* Russia. **russo, -a** *s, agg* Russian.

rustico ['rustiko] *agg* rustic; (*contadino*) rural; (*rozzo*) rough.

ruttare [rut'tare] *v* belch. **rutto** *sm* belch.

ruvido ['ruvido] *agg* rough. **ruvidezza** *sf* roughness.

ruzzare [rut'tsare] *v* romp.

ruzzolare [ruttso'lare] *v* tumble; (*rotolare*) roll (down). **ruzzolone** *sm* tumble. **fare un ruzzolone** (*fam*) come a cropper.

S

sabato ['sabato] *sm* Saturday. **il** *or* **di sabato** on Saturdays.

sabbia ['sabbja] *sf* sand. **sabbie mobili** quicksand *sing*. **sabbiare** *v* sand-blast. **sabbioso** *agg* sandy.

sabotaggio [sabo'taddʒo] *sm* sabotage. **sabotare** *v* sabotage. **sabotatore, -trice** *sm, sf* saboteur.

sacca ['sakka] *sf* bag; (*fig*) pocket.

saccarina [sakka'rina] *sf* saccharine.

saccente [sat'tʃɛnte] *s(m+f), agg* know-all.

saccheggiare [sakked'dʒare] *v* sack, loot. **saccheggiatore** *sm* plunderer, looter. **saccheggio** *sm* sacking, looting.

sacco ['sakko] *sm* sack. **cogliere con le mani nel sacco** catch red-handed. **sacco a pelo** sleeping-bag. **sacco da montagna** rucksack. **sacco postale** mail-bag. **un sacco di** lots of.

sacerdote [satʃer'dɔte] *sm* priest. **sacerdozio** *sm* priesthood.

sacramento [sakra'mento] *sm* sacrament.

sacrificare [sakrifi'kare] *v* sacrifice; (*rinunciare*) give up; (*non valorizzare*) waste. **sacrificio** *sm* sacrifice; (*di sè*) self-sacrifice.

sacrilegio [sakri'ledʒo] *sm* sacrilege; (*fig*) crime. **sacrilego** *agg, m pl* **-ghi** sacrilegious; criminal.

sacro ['sakro] *agg* sacred. *sm* (*osso*) sacrum. **sacrosanto** *agg* sacrosanct.

sadico ['sadiko], **-a** *agg* sadistic. *sm, sf* sadist. **sadismo** *sm* sadism.

saetta [sa'etta] *sf* flash (of lightning); (*mec*) bit; (*freccia*) arrow.

sagace [sa'gatʃe] *agg* sagacious. **sagacia** *sf* sagacity.

saggio¹ ['saddʒo], **-a** *agg* wise; (*sapiente*) sage. *sm, sf* sage. **saggezza** *sf* wisdom.

saggio² ['saddʒo] *sm* trial; (*metalli preziosi*) assay; (*prova*) proof; (*dimostrazione pubblica*) display; (*scritto critico*) essay. **saggiare** *v* test; assay. **saggiatura** *sf* assay; (*segno*) hallmark. **saggista** *s(m+f)* essayist.

Sagittario [sadʒit'tarjo] *sm* Sagittarius.

sagoma ['sagoma] *sf* outline; (*forma, modello*) pattern. **sagomare** *v* shape.

sagra ['sagra] *sf* feast.

sagrestano [sagres'tano] *sm* sacristan. **sagrestia** *sf* vestry.

sala ['sala] *sf* room, hall. **sala da pranzo** dining-room. **sala d'aspetto** waiting-room. **sala di lettura/macchine** reading-/engine-room. **sala operatoria** operating theatre.

salace [sa'latʃe] *agg* salacious.

salamandra [sala'mandra] *sf* salamander.

salame [sa'lame] *sm* salami; (*fig*) fool.

salamoia [sala'mɔja] *sf* brine. **mettere in salamoia** pickle.

salare [sa'lare] *v* salt. **salato** *agg* salty; (*conservato*) salted; (*caro*) dear.

salario [sa'larjo] *sm* pay; (*settimanale*) wages *pl*; (*mensile*) salary. **salariale** *agg* pay.

salassare [salas'sare] *v* bleed.

salda ['salda] *sf* size, sizing. **dare la salda a** size; (*inamidare*) starch.

saldare [sal'dare] *v* (*tec*) solder; (*autogeno*) weld; (*econ*) settle, pay. **saldatore** *sm* (*operaio*) solderer, welder; (*utensile*) soldering iron. **saldatrice** *sf* welder. **saldatura** *sf* welding; soldering.

saldo¹ ['saldo] *agg* solid; firm. **saldezza** *sf* solidity; firmness.

saldo² ['saldo] *sm* settlement; (*somma da pagare*) balance. **saldi** *sm pl* (*merce*) remnants *pl.*

sale ['sale] *sm* salt. **non aver sale in zucca** be stupid. **restar di sale** be dumbfounded. **salgemma** *sm* rock-salt. **salino** *agg* saline.

salice ['salitʃe] *sm* willow(-tree). **salice piangente** weeping willow.

saliente [sa'ljɛnte] *agg, sm* salient.

***salire** [sa'lire] *v* climb, go up; (*autobus, treno*) board, get on; (*auto*) get in; (*alzarsi, crescere*) rise. **far salire** send up.

saliscendi *sm invar* (*chiusura*) latch; (*fig*) ups and downs *pl.* **salita** *sf* climb; entrance; (*tratto che sale*) slope. **in salita** uphill; (*che aumenta*) rising.

saliva [sa'liva] *sf* saliva. **salivale** *agg* salivary. **salivare** *v* salivate.

salma ['salma] *sf* corpse.

salmo ['salmo] *sm* psalm.

salmone [sal'mone] *sm* salmon.

salone [sa'lone] *sm* living-room; (*esposizione*) show; (*parrucchiere*) salon.

salotto [sa'lɔtto] *sm* drawing-room, lounge.

salpare [sal'pare] *v* weigh anchor.

salsa ['salsa] *sf* sauce; (*a base di carne*) gravy. **in tutte le salse** in all kinds of ways. **salsiera** *sf* sauce-boat; gravy-boat.

salsiccia [sal'sittʃa] *sf* sausage.

salso ['salso] *agg* salt(y). **salsedine** *sf* saltiness.

saltare [sal'tare] *v* jump; (*balzare*) leap; (*tralasciare*) skip; (*bottone, etc.*) come off; (*gastr*) sauté. **far saltare** destroy, blow up; (*serratura*) force; (*governo*) bring down. **saltare di palo in frasca** switch from one subject to another. **saltare (in aria)** (*esplodere*) blow up. **saltare in bestia** fly into a rage. **saltare in mente** cross one's mind, get into one's head.

saltellare [saltel'lare] *v also* **salterellare** skip *or* hop about.

saltimbanco [saltim'banko] *sm* acrobat; (*spreg*) charlatan.

salto ['salto] *sm* jump, leap; (*omissione*) gap. **in un salto** in a jiffy. **salto con l'asta** pole-vault. **salto in alto/lungo** high-/long-jump. **saltuario** *agg* intermittent, occasional.

salubre ['salubre] *agg* healthy.

salumeria [salume'ria] *sf* delicatessen.

salumi *sm pl* cold meats *pl.* **salumiere, -a** *sm, sf* pork-butcher; grocer.

salutare [salu'tare] *v* greet; (*mil*) salute. **salutami tuo fratello** remember me to your brother. **saluto** *sm* greeting; salute. **cordiali/distinti saluti** yours sincerely/faithfully.

salute [sa'lute] *sf* health; (*benessere*) welfare. *inter* (*a chi starnutisce*) bless you! (*nei brindisi*) cheers!

salvare [sal'vare] *v* save; (*trarre in salvo*) rescue; protect. **salvacondotto** *sm* pass. **salvadanaio** *sm* money-box. **salvagente** *sm* (*ciambella*) lifebelt; (*giacca*) life-jacket; (*strada*) traffic island. **salvaguardare** *v* safeguard. **salvaguardia** *sf* safeguard. **salvataggio** *sm* rescue.

salve ['salve] *inter* hello! (*salute*) bless you!

salvia ['salvja] *sf* sage.

salvietta [sal'vjetta] *sf* (*tovagliolo*) napkin; (*asciugamano*) towel.

salvo ['salvo] *agg* safe. **mettere in salvo** save, put aside. *prep* except (for), bar(ring). **salvo che** except that; (*a meno che*) unless. **salvezza** *sf* salvation; (*sicurezza*) safety.

sambuco [sam'buko] *sm, pl* **-chi** elder.

sanare [sa'nare] *v* heal; (*porre rimedio*) rectify; (*bonificare*) reclaim. **sanatorio** *sm* sanatorium.

sancire [san'tʃire] *v* sanction; ratify.

sandalo¹ ['sandalo] *sm* sandal.

sandalo² ['sandalo] *sm* (*legno*) sandalwood.

sangue ['sangwe] *sm* blood. **al sangue** (*gastr*) rare. **a sangue caldo/freddo** warm-/cold-blooded. **farsi cattivo sangue** get worked up. **puro sangue** thoroughbred. **sangue freddo** sang-froid, composure. **sanguemisto** *sm* half-breed.

sanguigno [san'gwiɲo] *agg* blood; (*colore*) blood-red; (*costituzione*) sanguine.

sanguinare [sangwi'nare] *v* bleed. **sanguinario** *agg* bloodthirsty. **sanguinolento** *agg* bleeding; (*insanguinato*) bloody. **sanguinoso** *agg* bloody.

sanguisuga [sangwi'suga] *sf* leech.

sanità [sani'ta] *sf* health; (*salubrità*) wholesomeness. **sanità mentale** sanity. **sanitario** *agg* sanitary; (*di medicina*) medical.

sano ['sano] *agg* healthy; (*integro*) sound; (*salubre*) wholesome; (*di mente*) sane;

intact. **sano come un pesce** sound as a bell. **sano e salvo** safe and sound.

santo ['santo], **-a** *agg* holy; (*seguito da nome*) Saint; pious; sacred; (*rafforzativo*) blessed. *sm, sf* saint. **santerello, -a** *sm, sf* (*fam*) goody-goody. **santificare** *v* sanctify; (*venerare*) hallow; canonize. **santità** *sf* holiness; (*fig*) sanctity. **santuario** *sm* sanctuary.

sanzione [san'tsjone] *sf* sanction. **sanzionare** *v* sanction.

*****sapere** [sa'pere] *v* know; (*essere capace, aver imparato*) can, know how (to); (*aver odore*) smell (of); (*aver sapore*) taste (of). **buono a sapersi** worth knowing. **far sapere a** let know, inform. **non ne voglio sapere** I don't want to have anything to do with it. **non si sa mai** you never can tell. **per quanto ne sappia** as far as I know. **saperla lunga** know a thing or two. **venire a sapere** learn, gather. *sm* knowledge, learning.

sapienza [sa'pjɛntsa] *sf* wisdom; learning. **sapiente** *agg* wise; learned. **sapientone, -a** *sm, sf* (*fam*) know-all.

sapone [sa'pone] *sm* soap. **sapone in polvere** soap-powder. **saponetta** *sf* bar of soap. **saponiera** *sf* soap-dish. **saponoso** *agg* soapy.

sapore [sa'pore] *sm* taste, flavour. **saporito** *agg* tasty; (*salato*) rather salty; (*arguto*) witty.

saracinesca [saratʃi'nɛska] *sf* roller-blind; (*di chiusa*) floodgate.

sarcasmo [sar'kazmo] *sm* sarcasm. **sarcastico** *agg* sarcastic.

sarchio ['sarkjɔ] *sm* hoe. **sarchiare** *v* hoe.

sarda ['sarda] *sf also* **sardina** pilchard, sardine.

Sardegna [sar'deɲa] *sf* Sardinia. **sardo, -a** *s, agg* Sardinian.

sardonico [sar'dɔniko] *agg* sardonic.

sarta ['sarta] *sf* dressmaker. **sarto** *sm* tailor. **sartoria** *sf* (*laboratorio*) dressmaker's *or* tailor's workshop; (*tecnica*) dressmaking, tailoring.

sasso ['sasso] *sm* stone; (*ciottolo*) pebble; (*roccia*) rock. **prendere a sassate** pelt with stones, stone. **sassoso** *agg* stony.

sassofono [sas'sɔfono] *sm* saxophone. **sassofonista** *s(m+f)* saxophonist.

Satana ['satana] *sm* Satan. **satanico** *agg* satanic.

satellite [sa'tɛllite] *agg, sm* satellite.

satirico [sa'tiriko] *agg* satirical. **satira** *sf* satire. **satireggiare** *v also* **mettere in satira** satirize.

satiro ['satiro] *sm* satyr.

satollo [sa'tollo] *agg* full up.

saturare [satu'rare] *v* saturate; (*fig*) cram. **saturazione** *sf* saturation. **saturo** *agg* saturated; crammed, full.

savio ['savjo] *agg* wise; prudent.

saziare [sa'tsjare] *v* satisfy; (*riempire presto*) be filling. **saziarsi** *v* have one's fill; (*stancarsi*) tire. **sazietà** *sf* surfeit. **a sazietà** more than enough. **mangiare a sazietà** eat *or* have one's fill. **sazio** *agg* satisfied; (*fam*) full up; (*stanco*) tired.

sbadato [zba'dato] *agg* careless, thoughtless. **sbadataggine** *sf* carelessness, thoughtlessness.

sbadigliare [zbadi'ʎare] *v* yawn. **sbadiglio** *sm* yawn.

sbafare [zba'fare] *v* (*scroccare*) scrounge; (*mangiare avidamente*) gobble up. **mangiare/vivere a sbafo** scrounge a meal/living.

sbagliare [zba'ʎare] *v* make a mistake; (*scambiare*) mistake. **sbagliare i calcoli** miscalculate; (*fig*) make a (big) mistake. **sbagliar il passo** stumble; (*mil*) be out of step. **sbagliar numero** get the wrong number. **sbagliar ortografia** spell incorrectly. **sbagliarsi sul conto di** be wrong about. **sbagliato** *agg* wrong, mistaken. **calcolo sbagliato** *sm* miscalculation. **pronuncia sbagliata** *sf* mispronunciation. **sbaglio** *sm* mistake.

sbalestrato [zbales'trato] *agg* unsettled; (*smarrito*) lost.

sballare [zbal'lare] *v* (*merce*) unpack. **sballato** *agg* wild.

sballottare [zballot'tare] *v* toss about. **sballottamento** *sm* tossing.

sbalordire [zbalor'dire] *v* astonish; (*turbare*) bewilder, shock. **sbalordimento** *sm* astonishment; shock, bewilderment. **sbalorditivo** *agg* amazing; (*incredibile*) staggering.

sbalzare[1] [zbal'tsare] *v* throw, fling. **sbalzo** *sm* jerk, jolt; (*fig*) jump. **a sbalzi** jerkily; (*fig*) by fits and starts.

sbalzare[2] [zbal'tsare] *v* (*metallo*) emboss. **lavoro a sbalzo** *sm* embossing.

sbandare [zban'dare] *v* (*auto*) skid; (*mar*) list; (*aero*) bank; (*disperdere*) break *or* split up. **sbandata** *sf* skid. **prendere una sbandata per** have a crush on. **sbandato** *agg* scattered; (*fig*) bewildered.

sbaragliare [zbara'ʎare] v (put to) rout. andare or buttarsi allo sbaraglio risk everything. mettere allo sbaraglio jeopardize.

sbarazzarsi [zbarat'tsarsi] v get rid of.

sbarbare [zbar'bare] v shave. sbarbatello sm novice.

sbarcare [zbar'kare] v land; (merce) unload. sbarco sm landing; unloading.

sbarra ['zbarra] sf bar, barrier; (segno grafico) stroke. sbarramento sm barrage; block(age). sbarrare v bar, block; (porta) bolt; (assegno) cross; (occhi) open wide.

sbatacchiare [zbatak'kjare] v slam; (ali) flap.

sbattere ['zbattere] v (scaraventare) fling; (chiudere violentemente) slam; (urtare) bash; (ali) flap; (gastr) whip, beat. non saper dove sbattere la testa not know which way to turn. sbatter fuori (fam) chuck out.

sbavare [zba'vare] v (emettere bava) dribble; (colore, ecc.) smudge. sbavatura sf dribble; smudge.

sberla ['zbɛrla] sf slap.

sbiadire [zbja'dire] v fade. sbiadito agg faded; (fig) dull.

sbiancare [zbjan'kare] v whiten.

sbianchire [zbian'kire] v whiten; (gastr) blanch.

sbieco ['zbjɛko] agg crooked. guardar di sbieco look askance at. tagliar di sbieco cut on the bias.

sbigottire [zbigot'tire] v astonish; (turbare) dismay. sbigottimento sm astonishment; dismay.

sbilancio [zbi'lantʃo] sm (squilibrio) lack of equilibrium; (econ) deficit. sbilanciare v unbalance.

sbilenco [zbi'lɛnko] agg crooked.

sbloccare [zblok'kare] v free, release; (prezzi) unfreeze.

sboccare [zbok'kare] v come out; (condurre) lead; (fiume) flow (into). sbocco sm outlet.

sbocciare [zbot'tʃare] v bloom, blossom.

sbollentare [zbollen'tare] v blanch.

sbornia [zbɔrnja] sf postumi di una sbornia sm pl hangover sing. prendere una sbornia get drunk.

sborsare [zbor'sare] v pay out, disburse. sborso sm disbursement.

sbottare [zbot'tare] v burst out.

sbottonare [zbotto'nare] v unbutton.

sbozzare [zbot'tsare] v sketch; (fig) outline.

sbracciarsi [zbrat'tʃarsi] v gesticulate; (rimboccarsi le maniche) roll up one's sleeves; (fig) do one's utmost. sbracciato agg (abito) sleeveless.

sbraitare [zbrai'tare] v yell; protest.

sbranare [zbra'nare] v tear to pieces.

sbrattare [zbrat'tare] v tidy up. stanza di sbratto sf lumber-room.

sbriciolare [zbritʃo'lare] v crumble.

sbrigare [zbri'gare] v get done, finish (off); (risolvere) settle. sbrigarsi v (far presto) hurry up; (liberarsi) get rid (of). sbrigativo agg quick; (superficiale) hasty.

sbrigliare [zbri'ʎare] v unbridle, give free rein (to). sbrigliatezza sf unruliness. sbrigliato agg unruly, wild.

sbrindellare [zbrindel'lare] v tear to shreds. sbrindellato agg in rags or tatters.

sbrodolare [zbrodo'lare] v (insudiciare) soil; (fig) spin out; (fam) waffle.

sbrogliare [zbro'ʎare] v disentangle. sbrogliarsi v extricate oneself.

sbronzo ['zbrondzo] agg drunk. prendersi una sbronza get drunk.

sbruffare [zbruf'fare] v spurt; (fig) brag.

sbucare [zbu'kare] v come out, emerge; (fig) spring up.

sbucciare [zbut'tʃare] v peel; (escoriare) scrape. sbucciapatate sm invar potato-peeler. sbucciatura sf scrape, graze.

sbudellare [zbudel'lare] v disembowel; (gastr) gut. sbudellarsi dal ridere split one's sides laughing.

sbuffare [zbuf'fare] v puff, pant; (rabbia) snort.

scabbia ['skabbia] sf scabies. scabbiosa sf (bot) scabious.

scabroso [ska'brozo] agg also scabro rough; (problema) thorny, knotty.

scacciare [skat'tʃare] v drive out or away; (fig) dispel; expel.

scacco ['skakko] sm (quadretto) check; (figurina del gioco) chessman. scacchi sm pl (gioco) chess sing. scacco matto checkmate. subire uno scacco suffer a setback. scacchiera sf chess-board; (per dama) draught-board.

*scadere [ska'dere] v expire; (perdere valore) decline; (econ) fall due. scadente agg poor. scadenza sf expiry; (effetti) maturity. a breve/lunga scadenza short-/long-term. scadimento sm decline.

scafandro [skaˈfandro] *sm* diving-suit; (*astronauta*) space-suit.
scaffale [skafˈfale] *sm* shelf. **scaffalatura** *sf* shelving.
scafo [ˈskafo] *sm* hull.
scagionare [skadʒoˈnare] *v* exonerate.
scaglia [ˈskaʎa] *sf* scale; (*sapone*) flake. **scagliare** *v* flake.
scagliare [skaˈʎare] *v* (*lanciare*) fling, hurl.
scaglione [skaˈʎone] *sm* group; (*mil*) echelon. **scaglionare** *v* stagger; (*mil*) range. **scaglionamento** *sm* staggering.
scala [ˈskala] *sf* stairs *pl*, staircase; (*piano*) level; (*misura, rapporto*) scale; (*apparecchio*) ladder. **far le scale** climb the stairs; (*musica*) practise scales. **scala a chiocciola** spiral staircase. **scala di corda** rope-ladder. **scala portatile** steps *pl*, step-ladder. **scalinata** *sf* flight of stairs.
scalare [skaˈlare] *v* scale. *agg* graduated; (*fis*) scalar. **scalata** *sf* climb. **scalatore, -trice** *sm, sf* climber.
scalcagnato [skalkaˈɲato] *agg* shabby.
scaldare [skalˈdare] *v* warm (up); (*a temperatura più elevata*) heat (up). **scaldabagno** *sm* water-heater.
scalfire [skalˈfire] *v* scratch.
scalmanato [skalmaˈnato] *agg* flustered. *sm, sf* hothead. **scalmana** *sf* chill; (*fig*) craze.
scalo [ˈskalo] *sm* (*banchina*) pier; (*porto d'approdo*) port of call; (*aero*) stopover. **far scalo** (*mar*) call; (*aero*) land, stop. **scalo merci** (*mar*) wharf; (*ferr*) goods yard. **senza scalo** non-stop.
scalogna [skaˈloɲa] *sf* bad luck. **scalognato** *agg* unlucky.
scaloppa [skaˈlɔppa] *sf* cutlet. **scaloppina** *sf* escalope.
scalpello [skalˈpɛllo] *sm* chisel; (*chirurgia*) scalpel. **scalpellare** *v* chisel; cut away.
scalpore [skalˈpore] *sm* sensation.
scaltro [ˈskaltro] *agg* shrewd.
scalzo [ˈskaltso] *agg* barefoot.
scambiare [skamˈbjare] *v* (*dare in cambio*) exchange; (*confondere*) mistake, mix up. **scambievole** *agg* mutual. **scambio** *sm* exchange; (*ferr*) points *pl*. **libero scambio** free trade.
scamosciato [skamoˈʃato] *agg* suede.
scampagnata [skampaˈɲata] *sf* outing.
scampanato [skampaˈnato] *agg* flared.
scampare [skamˈpare] *v* escape; (*evitare*) avoid. **Dio ce ne scampi!** God forbid!

scamparla bella have a narrow escape.
scampato, -a *sm, sf* (*superstite*) survivor. **scampo** *sm* way out.
scampo [ˈskampo] *sm* prawn.
scampolo [ˈskampolo] *sm* remnant.
scanalare [skanaˈlare] *v* groove; (*colonna*) flute. **scanalatura** *sf* groove; flute.
scandagliare [skandaˈʎare] *v* sound (out). **scandaglio** *sm* sounding.
scandalizzare [skandalidˈdzare] *v* shock; (*dar scandalo*) scandalize. **scandalo** *sm* scandal. **scandaloso** *agg* scandalous.
scandire [skanˈdire] *v* (*pronunciare*) articulate; (*versi*) scan.
scanno [ˈskanno] *sm* stall.
scansare [skanˈsare] *v* dodge, shirk; (*spostare*) shift. **scansarsi** *v* get out of the way. **scansafatiche** *s(m + f)* *invar* loafer.
scapaccione [skapatˈtʃone] *sm* slap.
scapestrato [skapesˈtrato], -a *agg* wild, unruly. *sm, sf* madcap, daredevil.
scapigliato [skapiˈʎato] *agg* dishevelled; (*fig*) reckless.
scapitare [skapiˈtare] *sm* loss; (*danno*) injury. **a scapito di** to the detriment of.
scapola [ˈskapola] *sf* shoulder-blade.
scapolo [ˈskapolo] *agg* single. *sm* bachelor.
scappamento [skappaˈmento] *sm* (*auto*) exhaust.
scappare [skapˈpare] *v* run away; escape, flee. **devo scappare** (*ho fretta*) I must rush. **lasciarsi scappar di bocca** blurt out. **scappare di mente** slip one's mind. **scappatella** *sf* escapade. **scappatoia** *sf* way out; (*fig*) loophole.
scappellotto [skapelˈlɔtto] *sm* smack. **passare a scappellotti** (*fam*) scrape through.
scarabocchio [skaraˈbɔkkjo] *sm* (*macchia*) blot; (*sgorbio*) scrawl; (*disegno*) doodle. **scarabocchiare** *v* scrawl; doodle.
scarafaggio [skaraˈfaddʒo] *sm* cockroach.
scaramanzia [skaramanˈtsia] *sf* spell. **per scaramanzia** for luck.
scaramuccia [skaraˈmuttʃa] *sf* skirmish.
scaraventare [skaravenˈtare] *v* hurl, fling.
scarcerare [skartʃeˈrare] *v* release (from prison). **scarceramento** *sm* release.
scardinare [skardiˈnare] *v* unhinge.
scaricare [skariˈkare] *v* discharge; (*deporre un carico*) unload; (*sfogare*) vent; (*liquido*) empty; (*gas*) let out. **scaricare la colpa** shift the blame. **scarica** *sf* discharge; (*raffica*) volley. **scaricalasino** *sm invar* piggy-bank.

scarico ['skariko] *sm, pl* **-chi** discharge; unloading; (*di rifiuti*) dumping; (*i rifiuti stessi*) rubbish; (*deposito di rifiuti*) dump; (*auto*) exhaust. **a mio scarico** in my defence. **a scarico di coscienza** to clear one's conscience. *agg* (*vuoto*) empty; (*batteria*) flat.

scarlattina [skarlat'tina] *sf* scarlet fever.

scarlatto [skar'latto] *agg, sm* scarlet.

scarno ['skarno] *agg* skinny; (*spoglio*) bare; (*povero*) scanty.

scarpa ['skarpa] *sf* shoe. **scarpe da ginnastica** *or* **tennis** plimsolls *pl*. **scarpone** *sm* boot. **scarponi da calciatore/sci** football-/ski-boots *pl*.

scarso ['skarso] *agg* poor; (*manchevole*) lacking (in); (*insufficiente*) short. **un chilo scarso** just under a kilo. **scarseggiare** *v* be scarce; be short (of); (*fig*) lack (in). **scarsezza** *or* **scarsità** *sf* shortage; lack.

scartabellare [skartabel'lare] *v* skim *or* flip through.

scartare[1] [skar'tare] *v* (*togliere dalla carta*) unwrap; (*respingere*) discard, reject. **scarto** *sm* (*cosa scartata*) reject; (*alle carte*) discard. **merci di scarto** *sf pl* inferior goods *pl*, rejects *pl*.

scartare[2] [skar'tare] *v* (*spostarsi lateralmente*) swerve. **scarto** *sm* swerve, skid; difference.

scassare [skas'sare] *v* (*fam: guastare*) smash, bust; (*il terreno*) break up. **furto con scasso** *sm* burglary.

scassinare [skassi'nare] *v* force (open). **scassinatore, -trice** *sm, sf* burglar; (*di banche*) bank-robber.

scatenare [skate'nare] *v* unleash; cause. **scatenarsi** *v* break out.

scatola ['skatola] *sf* box; carton; (*di latta*) can. **averne piene le scatole** (*fam*) be fed up to the back teeth (with). **cibo in scatola** *sm* tinned food. **rompere le scatole** (*fam*) be a nuisance. **scatolame** *sm* tinned goods *pl*.

scattare [skat'tare] *v* spring; (*rilasciarsi*) spring up; (*armi*) go off; (*aprirsi*) spring open; (*chiudersi*) snap shut. **far scattare** release. **scattare a vuoto** misfire. **scatto** *sm* release; (*rumore*) click; (*sport*) spurt; (*accesso*) outburst. **a scatti** jerkily. **di scatto** suddenly.

scaturire [skatu'rire] *v* gush; (*fig*) arise.

scavalcare [skaval'kare] *v* step *or* climb over; (*saltando*) jump over; (*sbalzare di sella*) throw; (*superare*) overtake.

scavare [ska'vare] *v* dig; mine; (*pozzo*) sink; (*trovare*) dig up; (*sartoria*) widen. **scavatore** *sm* digger. **scavatura** *sf* excavation. **scavo** *sm* excavation.

*scegliere ['ʃeʎere] *v* choose. **c'è (molto) da scegliere** there is plenty to choose from. **c'è poco da scegliere** there is little choice.

scellerato [ʃelle'rato], **-a** *agg* wicked. *sm, sf* wicked person. **scelleratezza** *sf* wickedness; (*atto*) misdeed.

scelta ['ʃelta] *sf* choice, selection; quality. **a scelta** according to preference. **non aver possibilità di scelta** have no choice. **scelto** *agg* chosen, picked; (*eccellente*) choice.

scemare [ʃe'mare] *v* diminish.

scemo ['ʃemo], **-a** *agg* stupid, idiotic; (*sciocco*) foolish. *sm, sf* fool, idiot. **scemenza** *sf* (*azione*) idiocy, foolishness; (*parole*) nonsense.

scena ['ʃena] *sf* scene; (*palcoscenico*) stage. **mettere in scena** stage, produce. **scenario** *sm* (*teatro*) set; (*cinema*) scenario, script; (*fig*) setting. **scenata** *sf* scene, row. **sceneggiare** *v* adapt, dramatize. **sceneggiatura** *sf* script. **scenico** *agg* scenic.

*scendere ['ʃendere] *v* (*andar giù*) go down; (*venir giù*) come down; (*autobus, treno*) get off; (*auto*) get out; (*calare*) drop; (*sostare*) stop. **scendere a un accordo** reach an agreement. **scendere dal letto** get up. **scendiletto** *sm invar* (*tappetino*) bedside rug; (*vestaglia*) dressing-gown.

sceriffo [ʃe'riffo] *sm* sheriff.

scervellarsi [ʃervel'larsi] *v* rack one's brains. **scervellato** *agg* hare-brained.

scettico ['ʃettiko], **-a** *agg* sceptical. *sm, sf* sceptic. **scetticismo** *sm* scepticism.

scettro ['ʃettro] *sm* sceptre.

scheda ['skɛda] *sf* card; (*di schedario*) index-card; (*elettorale*) ballot(-paper). **schedare** *v* catalogue; (*archiviare*) file. **schedario** *sm* file; (*mobile*) filing cabinet; (*elenco*) list. **schedina** *sf* coupon.

scheggia ['skeddʒa] *sf* splinter. **scheggiare** *v* splinter, chip.

scheletro ['skɛletro] *sm* skeleton; (*tec*) framework. **scheletrico** *agg* skeletal; (*fig*) bare.

schema ['skɛma] *sm* scheme; (*abbozzo*) outline; (*modello*) pattern. **schema di legge** bill. **schematico** *agg* schematic.

scherma ['skerma] *sf* fencing. **tirare di scherma** fence. **schermaglia** *sf* skirmish. **schermitore, -trice** *sm, sf* fencer.

schermo ['skermo] *sm* screen; (*difesa*) shield. **schermare** *v* screen, shield. **schermire** *v* protect.

schernire [sker'nire] *v* scorn, mock. **schernitore, -trice** *agg* scornful, mocking. **scherno** *sm* mockery, derision; (*oggetto di scherno*) laughing-stock.

scherzare [sker'tsare] *v* joke; (*prendere alla leggera*) trifle (with); (*giocare*) play. **c'è poco da scherzare** it is not a laughing matter. **scherzi!** *inter* you must be joking! **scherzo** *sm* joke; (*tiro*) trick; (*musica*) scherzo. **per scherzo** for fun, as a joke. **scherzoso** *agg* playful; (*giocoso*) jocular.

schettinare [sketti'nare] *v* roller-skate. **schettinaggio** *sm* roller-skating. **schettino** *sm* roller-skate.

schiacciare [skjat'tʃare] *v* (*spiaccicare*) squash; (*frantumare*) crush; (*noci*) crack. **schiacciare un pisolino** have a nap. **schiacciante** *agg* crushing. **schiaccianoci** *sm* nutcrackers *pl*. **schiacciasassi** *sm* steam-roller.

schiaffare [skjaf'fare] *v* (*fam*) chuck. **schiaffo** ['skjaffo] *sm* slap. **schiaffeggiare** *v* slap.

schiamazzare [skjamat'tsare] *v* cackle; (*far baccano*) make a row. **schiamazzo** *sm* cackle; row.

schiantare [skjan'tare] *v* shatter, burst. **schianto** *sm* crash.

schiappa ['skjappa] *sf* (*fam*) washout.

schiarire [skja'rire] *v* clear (up). **schiarimento** *sm* clearing up; (*spiegazione*) explanation; information.

schiavo ['skjavo], **-a** *s, agg* slave. **schiavitù** *sf* slavery.

schiena ['skjɛna] *sf* back. **colpire alla schiena** stab in the back. **mal di schiena** *sm* backache. **schienale** *sm* back.

schiera ['skjɛra] *sf* band; (*moltitudine*) mass, crowd. **schieramento** *sm* formation; line-up. **schierare** *v* line up; (*mil*) deploy. **schierarsi contro** take sides against. **schierarsi dalla parte di** side with.

schietto ['skjetto] *agg* sincere; genuine; frank. **a dirla schietta** (to speak) frankly. **schiettezza** *sf* genuineness; frankness.

schifo ['skifo] *sm* disgust. **avere a schifo** loathe. **far schifo** *v* (*essere disgustoso*) be disgusting; (*disgustare*) (fill with) disgust. **schifare** *v* disgust. **schifezza** *sf* rubbish, muck. **schifiltoso** *agg* fussy; (*esigente*) fastidious. **schifoso** *agg* disgusting.

schioccare [skjok'kare] *v* crack; (*dita*) snap.

schioppo ['skjɔppo] *sm* gun; (*da caccia*) shotgun. **schioppettata** *sf* (gun)shot.

***schiudersi** ['skjudersi] *v* open (up).

schiuma ['skjuma] *sf* foam; (*birra*) froth; (*sapone*) lather; (*feccia*) scum. **aver la schiuma alla bocca** foam at the mouth. **schiumare** *v* skim. **schiumoso** *agg* foamy; frothy; lathery.

schivare [ski'vare] *v* avoid; (*fam*) dodge; (*boxe*) duck.

schizofrenia [skitsofre'nia] *sf* schizophrenia. **schizofrenico, -a** *s, agg* schizophrenic.

schizzare [skit'tsare] *v* (*zampillare*) spurt; (*spruzzare*) squirt; (*sporcare*) splash; (*disegnare*) sketch. **schizzar via** dash off. **schizzetto** *sm* spray; syringe; (*giocattolo*) water-pistol. **schizzo** *sm* spurt; squirt; splash; sketch.

schizzinoso [skittsi'nozo] *agg* fastidious; squeamish.

sci [ʃi] *sm* (*attrezzo*) ski; (*attività*) skiing. **fare dello sci** ski, go skiing. **sci nautico** water-ski; water-skiing. **sciare** *v* ski. **sciatore, -trice** *sm, sf* skier.

scia ['ʃia] *sf* wake; (*traccia*) trail. **seguire la scia di** follow in the footsteps of.

sciabola ['ʃabola] *sf* sabre.

sciacallo [ʃa'kallo] *sm* jackal.

sciacquare [ʃak'kware] *v* rinse (out). **sciacquata** *sf* rinse. **sciacquatura** *sf* (*azione*) rinsing; (*acqua*) dishwater. **sciacquo** *sm* rinsing; (*liquido*) mouthwash.

sciagura [ʃa'gura] *sf* disaster; (*incidente*) accident, crash. **sciagurato** *agg* (*sfortunato*) unlucky, wretched; (*malvagio*) wicked.

scialacquare [ʃalak'kware] *v* squander. **scialacquatore, -trice** *sm, sf* spendthrift.

scialbo ['ʃalbo] *agg* pale; faint; (*fig*) dull.

scialle ['ʃalle] *sm* shawl.

scialo ['ʃalo] *sm* waste.

sciame ['ʃame] *sm* swarm. **sciamare** *v* swarm.

sciancato [ʃan'kato] *agg* lame; (*sedia, ecc.*) shaky, rickety.

sciarada [ʃa'rada] *sf* charade.

sciarpa ['ʃarpa] *sf* scarf.
sciatica ['ʃatika] *sf* sciatica. **sciatico** *agg* sciatic.
sciatto ['ʃatto] *agg* slovenly; (*fam*) sloppy.
scientifico [ʃen'tifiko] *agg* scientific.
scienza ['ʃɛntsa] *sf* science. **scienziato, -a** *sm, sf* scientist; (*studioso*) scholar.
scimmia ['ʃimmja] *sf* monkey; (*senza coda*) ape. **brutto come una scimmia** as ugly as sin. **scimmiottare** *v also* **fare la scimmia a** ape.
scimpanzè [ʃimpan'tse] *sm* chimpanzee.
scimunito [ʃimu'nito], **-a** *agg* foolish. *sm, sf* fool.
***scindere** ['ʃindere] *v* separate; divide.
scintilla [ʃin'tilla] *sf* spark. **dare** *or* **emettere scintille** spark. **scintillare** *v* sparkle; (*lampeggiare*) flash.
sciocco ['ʃɔkko], **-a** *agg* foolish. *sm, sf* fool. **sciocchezza** *sf* foolish thing; (*cosa da niente*) trifle; (*l'essere sciocco*) foolishness. **dire sciocchezze** talk nonsense.
***sciogliere** ['ʃɔʎere] *v* (*fondere*) melt; dissolve; (*porre fine*) break up; (*disfare*) undo; (*allentare*) loosen; (*slegare*) untie; (*società*) wind up. **scioglimento** *sm* dissolution; breaking up; melting.
sciolto ['ʃɔlto] *agg* loose; (*agile*) nimble. **aver la lingua sciolta** have the gift of the gab. **versi sciolti** *sm pl* blank verse *sing.* **scioltezza** *sf* nimbleness; (*fig*) fluency.
scioperare [ʃope'rare] *v* (go on) strike. **scioperante** *s(m+f)* striker. **scioperato** *agg* lazy. **sciopero** *sm* strike. **entrare in sciopero** go on strike. **far sciopero** strike. **sciopero bianco/lampo** sit-down/wildcat strike.
sciorinare [ʃori'nare] *v* (*bucato*) hang out; (*fig*) show off; (*spreg*) dash off. **sciorinare bugie** tell a string of lies.
sciovinismo [ʃovi'nizmo] *sm* chauvinism. **sciovinista** *s(m+f)* chauvinist.
scipito ['ʃipito] *agg* insipid.
scippare [ʃip'pare] *v* snatch. **scippatore, -trice** *sm, sf* bag-snatcher.
scirocco [ʃi'rɔkko] *sm* sirocco.
sciroppo [ʃi'rɔppo] *sm* syrup. **sciroppato** *agg* in syrup. **sciropposo** *agg* syrupy.
scisma ['ʃizma] *sm* schism. **scismatico** *agg* schismatic.
scissione [ʃis'sjone] *sf* split. **scisso** *agg* split.
sciupare [ʃu'pare] *v* (*rovinare*) ruin, spoil; (*perdere*) waste. **sciuparsi** *v* (*salute*) ruin one's health; (*sgualcirsi*) get creased. **sciupato** *agg* ruined; wasted; (*di aspetto*) haggard. **sciupio** *sm* waste. **sciupone, -a** *sm, sf* wastrel.
scivolare [ʃivo'lare] *v* slide; (*sfuggire, sdrucciolare*) slip; (*aero*) glide. **scivolata** *sf* slide; glide. **scivolo** *sm* chute; (*mar*) slipway. **scivolone** *sm* slip; (*caduta*) tumble. **scivoloso** *agg* slippery.
sclerosi [skle'rɔzi] *sf* sclerosis. **sclerotico** *agg* sclerotic.
scoccare [skok'kare] *v* (*orologio*) strike; (*scagliare*) fling.
scocciare [skot'tʃare] *v* bother. **scocciarsi** *v* get bored. **scocciatore, -trice** *sm, sf* bore; (*fam*) pest. **scocciatura** *sf* bore.
scodella [sko'dɛlla] *sf* bowl. **scodellare** *v* serve; (*minestra*) ladle out; (*fig*) come out with.
scoglio ['skɔʎo] *sm* rock; (*fig*) stumbling block. **scogliera** *sf* cliff; (*a fior d'acqua*) reef. **scoglioso** *agg* rocky.
scoiattolo [sko'jattolo] *sm* squirrel.
scolare [sko'lare] *v* drain; (*gastr*) strain. **scolapiatti** *sm invar* draining-board. **scolo** *sm* drainage; (*condotto*) drain.
scolaro [sco'laro], **-a** *sm, sf* pupil; disciple. **scolastico** *agg* (*della scuola*) school; (*spreg*) bookish; (*filosofia*) scholastic.
scollato [skol'lato] *agg* low-necked.
scolorire [skolo'rire] *v also* **scolorare** discolour, fade. **scolorito** *agg* faded.
scolpire [skol'pire] *v* sculpt; (*incidere*) carve; (*fig*) impress.
scombinare [skombi'nare] *v* upset. **scombinato** *agg* (*mal combinato*) badly arranged; confused.
scombro ['skombro] *sm also* **sgombro** mackerel.
scombussolare [skombusso'lare] *v* upset; (*stordire*) stun.
***scommettere** [skom'mettere] *v* bet. **scommessa** *sf* bet. **scommettitore, -trice** *sm, sf* punter.
scomodare [skomo'dare] *v* trouble, inconvenience. **scomodità** *sf* discomfort; (*disagio*) inconvenience. **scomodo** *agg* (*non comodo*) uncomfortable; inconvenient.
scompaginare [skompadʒi'nare] *v* throw into disarray; (*fig*) upset.
***scomparire** [skompa'rire] *v* disappear; (*fig*) look insignificant.
scomparso [skom'parso], **-a** *agg* vanished. *sm, sf* deceased. *sf* disappearance.

scompartimento [skomparti'mento] *sm* compartment. **scomparto** *sm* compartment; (*parete*) partition.

scompigliare [skompi'ʎare] *v* upset; confuse; (*capelli*) ruffle. **scompiglio** *sm* confusion.

*scomporre [skom'porre] *v* take apart; resolve; decompose; (*turbare*) perturb. **senza scomporsi** unperturbed. **scomposto** *agg* broken down; (*in disordine*) untidy; (*indecoroso*) unseemly.

scomunicare [skomuni'kare] *v* excommunicate. **scomunica** *sf* excommunication.

sconcertare [skontʃer'tare] *v* baffle. **sconcertato** *agg* bewildered.

sconcio ['skontʃo] *agg* indecent; obscene. *sm* disgrace. **sconcezza** *sf* obscenity. **dire sconcezze** use foul language. **sconciare** *v* spoil.

sconfessare [skonfes'sare] *v* repudiate.

*sconfiggere [skon'fiddʒere] *v* defeat. **sconfitta** *sf* defeat. **sconfitto** *agg* defeated, beaten. **dichiararsi sconfitto** acknowledge defeat.

sconfortante [skonfor'tante] *agg* disheartening. **sconforto** *sm* discouragement; depression.

scongelare [skondʒe'lare] *v* defrost.

scongiurare [skondʒu'rare] *v* beseech; (*evitare*) avoid; (*rel*) exorcise. **scongiuro** *sm* exorcism.

*sconnettere [skon'nettere] *v* disconnect. **sconnesso** *agg* (*fig*) disjointed.

sconosciuto [skono'ʃuto], -**a** *agg* unknown. *sm*, *sf* stranger.

sconquassare [skonkwas'sare] *v* smash; shake (up). **sconquassato** *agg* shattered.

sconsiderato [skonside'rato] *agg* thoughtless. **sconsideratezza** *sf* thoughtlessness.

sconsigliare [skonsi'ʎare] *v* advise against; dissuade.

sconsolato [skonso'lato] *agg* disconsolate.

scontare [skon'tare] *v* (*detrarre*) deduct; (*econ*) discount; (*debito*) pay off. **sconto** *sm* discount.

scontentare [skonten'tare] *v* dissatisfy; (*lasciare scontento*) disappoint. **scontentezza** *sf* dissatisfaction; disappointment. **scontento** *agg* displeased; disappointed.

scontrarsi [skon'trarsi] *v* meet; (*veicoli*) crash. **scontro** *sm* encounter; (*discussione*) argument; (*violento*) clash; crash.

scontrino [skon'trino] *sm* check.

scontroso [skon'trozo] *agg* surly. **scontrosità** *sf* surliness.

*sconvenire [skonve'nire] *v* be unsuitable; (*non essere decoroso*) be unbecoming. **sconveniente** *agg* unfavourable; unbecoming.

*sconvolgere [skon'vɔldʒere] *v* upset. **sconvolgimento** *sm* upset; confusion. **sconvolto** *agg* upset.

scopa ['skopa] *sf* broom. **scopare** *v* sweep; (*volg*) screw.

scoperchiare [skoper'kjare] *v* take the lid off.

scoperto [sko'pɛrto] *agg* uncovered; (*aperto*) open; (*nudo*) bare. *sm* open; (*conto*) overdraft. **allo scoperto** outdoors, in the open (air). **scoperta** *sf* discovery.

scopo ['skɔpo] *sm* purpose. **a** *or* **allo scopo di** in order to. **senza scopo** pointless.

scoppiare [skop'pjare] *v* burst; explode; (*manifestarsi*) break out. **scoppiettare** *v* crackle. **scoppio** *sm* explosion; outbreak; (*rumore*) bang.

*scoprire [sko'prire] *v* (*fatti, cose nuove*) discover; (*togliere copertura*) uncover, bare; (*esporre*) expose; (*manifestare*) show. **scoprire le (proprie) carte** lay one's cards on the table.

scoraggiare [skorad'dʒare] *v* discourage, dishearten.

scorbuto [skor'buto] *sm* scurvy. **scorbutico** *agg* (*fig*) cantankerous.

scorciare [skor'tʃare] *v* shorten. **scorciatoia** *sf* short cut.

scordare [skor'dare] *v also* **scordarsi** forget.

scordato [skor'dato] *agg* (*musica*) out of tune.

scoreggia [sko'reddʒa] (*volg*) *sf* fart. **scoreggiare** *v* fart.

*scorgere [skɔr'dʒere] *v* notice.

scoria ['skɔrja] *sf* slag; (*fig*) dross.

scorno ['skɔrno] *sm* humiliation.

scorpione [skor'pjone] *sm* scorpion. **Scorpione** *sm* Scorpio.

scorrazzare [skorrat'tsare] *v* run about. **scorrazzata** *sf* trip.

*scorrere ['skorrere] *v* (*liquido*) run, flow; (*tempo*) pass (by); (*scivolare*) glide; (*leggere in fretta*) run through. **scorrevole** *agg* flowing. **scorrevolezza** *sf* fluidity; (*fig*) fluency.

scorretto [skor'retto] *agg* incorrect; (*sgarbato*) impolite; (*non leale*) unfair.

scorrettezza *sf* incorrectness, lack of manners; unfairness.

scorsa ['skɔrsa] *sf* glance.

scorso ['skɔrso] *agg* last. **l'anno scorso** last year.

scorsoio [skor'sɔjo] *agg* **nodo scorsoio** *sm* slip-knot.

scorta ['skɔrta] *sf* escort; (*provvista*) stock, supply; reserve. **di scorta** spare. **fare la scorta a** escort. **fare una scorta (di)** stock up (on). **sotto la scorta di** under the guidance of. **sulla scorta di** on the basis of. **scortare** *v* escort.

scortese [skor'teze] *agg* rude. **scortesia** *sf* rudeness.

scorticare [skorti'kare] *v* skin; (*escoriare*) graze.

scorza ['skɔrtsa] *sf* skin; (*corteccia*) bark.

scosceso [sko'ʃezo] *agg* steep.

scossa ['skɔssa] *sf* shock; (*scatto, sbalzo*) jerk; (*tremore*) shake. **a scosse** jerkily. **scosso** *agg* shaken.

scostare [skos'tare] *v* shift. **scostarsi** *v* move aside; (*deviare*) stray. **scostamento** *sm* shifting; (*mat*) deviation. **scostante** *agg* unpleasant.

scostumato [skostu'mato] *agg* dissolute, licentious. **scostumatezza** *sf* licentiousness.

scotennare [skoten'nare] *v* skin; (*di cuoio capelluto*) scalp.

scottare [skot'tare] *v* burn; (*con liquido bollente*) scald; (*causare bruciatura*) scorch; (*essere caldo*) be hot. **scottatura** *sf* burning; scalding; scorching; (*ustione*) burn, scald.

scovare [sko'vare] *v* (*stanare*) flush out; (*rintracciare*) track down; (*trovare*) find.

Scozia ['skɔtsja] *sf* Scotland. **scozzese** *agg* Scottish, Scotch; *s(m+f)* Scot.

screanzato [skrean'tsato] *agg* rude.

screditare [skredi'tare] *v* discredit.

scremare [skre'mare] *v* skim.

screpolare [skrepo'lare] *v* crack. **screpolatura** *sf* crack.

screziato [skre'tsjato] *agg* variegated.

scribacchiare [skribak'kjare] *v* scribble.

scricchiolare [skrikkjo'lare] *v* creak. **scricchiolio** *sm* creaking noise.

scricciolo ['skrittʃolo] *sm* wren.

scrigno ['skriɲo] *sm* casket.

scriminatura [skrimina'tura] *sf* parting.

scritta ['skritta] *sf* inscription; (*dir*) document.

scritto ['skritto] *agg* written. *sm* writing; letter; document. **scrittoio** *sm* (writing-)desk. **scrittore, -trice** *sm, sf* writer.

scrittura [skrit'tura] *sf* writing; (*contratto*) engagement; (*calligrafia*) handwriting. **(Sacra) Scrittura** (Holy) Scripture. **scritturare** *v* engage.

scrivania [skriva'nia] *sf* (writing-)desk.

*scrivere ['skrivere] *v* write; (*compitando*) spell. **scrivere bene/male** (*calligrafia*) have a good/bad handwriting; (*stile*) write well/badly; (*compitare*) spell correctly/incorrectly.

scroccare [skrok'kare] *v* scrounge. **vivere a scrocco** scrounge a living. **scroccone, -a** *sm, sf* scrounger.

scrocco ['skrɔkko] *sm* **coltello a scrocco** *sm* clasp-knife. **serratura a scrocco** *sf* spring-lock, latch.

scrofa ['skrɔfa] *sf* sow.

scrollare [skrol'lare] *v* shake; (*spalle*) shrug.

scrosciare [skro'ʃare] *v* thunder; (*pioggia*) pelt down. **scroscio** *sm* (*pioggia*) downpour. **scroscio di applausi** thunderous applause. **scroscio di risa** roar of laughter.

scrostare [skros'tare] *v* scrape (off).

scroto ['skrɔto] *sm* scrotum.

scrupolo ['skrupolo] *sm* scruple, qualm. **avere** *or* **farsi scrupoli (di)** have qualms (about). **essere onesto fino allo scrupolo** be scrupulously honest. **senza scrupoli** unscrupulous. **scrupoloso** *agg* scrupulous, meticulous.

scrutare [skru'tare] *v* scan; (*indagare*) delve into. **scrutatore, -trice** *sm, sf* scrutineer. **scrutinare** *v* scrutinize. **scrutinio** *sm* scrutiny; (*elezioni*) poll.

scucire [sku'tʃire] *v* unstitch. **scucitura** *sf* rip.

scudo ['skudo] *sm* shield. **farsi scudo** shield oneself. **scuderia** *sf* (*ricovero*) stable; (*allevamento*) stud; (*auto*) racing team. **scudetto** *sm* (*calcio*) league championship.

scugnizzo [sku'ɲittso] *sm* urchin.

sculacciare [skulat'tʃare] *v* spank. **sculacciata** *sf* spanking.

scultore [skul'tore] *sm* sculptor. **scultrice** *sf* sculptress. **scultura** *sf* sculpture.

scuola ['skwɔla] *sf* school. **scuola dell'obbligo** compulsory schooling. **scuola guida** driving school. **scuola materna** nursery school. **scuola pubblica** state school.

385

*scuotere ['skwɔtere] *v* shake; *(le spalle)* shrug. **scuotersi di dosso** shrug off.
scure ['skure] *sf* axe.
scuro ['skuro] *agg* dark. *sm* dark, darkness. **scuretto** *sm* (window-)shutter.
scurire *v* darken.
scusa ['skuza] *sf* excuse; apology. **chiedere scusa a qualcuno** beg someone's pardon. **scusabile** *agg* excusable; justifiable. **scusante** *sf* excuse; justification. **scusare** *v* excuse; pardon. **scusarsi** *v* apologize; justify oneself. **mi scusi!** (I'm) sorry! I beg your pardon!
sdegnare [zde'ɲare] *v* (*disprezzare*) scorn; irritate. **sdegnato** *agg* indignant; irritated. **sdegno** *sm* indignation. **sdegnoso** *agg* disdainful.
sdoppiare [zdop'pjare] *v* split (in two). **sdoppiamento** *sm* split. **sdoppiamento della personalità** split personality.
sdraiarsi [zdra'jarsi] *v* (*stendersi*) stretch out; (*mettersi a giacere*) lie down. **sdraia** *sf* also **sedia a sdraio** deck-chair.
sdrucciolare [zdruttʃo'lare] *v* slip. **sdrucciolevole** *agg* slippery. **sdrucciolone** *sm* slip.
sdrucire [zdru'tʃire] *v* rip.
se¹ [se] *cong* if; whether; (*se solo*) if only. **come se** as though. **se non altro** if nothing else, at least.
se² [se] *V* si.
sè [se] *pron* one(self); (*lui*) him(self); (*lei*) her(self); (*cosa, animale*) it(self); (*loro*) them(selves). **da sè** on one's own. **di per sè** in itself. **fra sè e sè** to oneself. **va da sè** it goes without saying.
sebbene [seb'bene] *cong* (al)though.
seccare [sek'kare] *v* dry (up); (*importunare*) bother. **seccarsi** *v* (*diventar secco*) dry up; (*annoiarsi*) get bored; (*infastidirsi*) get annoyed. **secca** *sf* shallow; (*fig*) fix. **seccante** boring; annoying. **seccato** *agg* annoyed; (*fam*) fed up. **seccatore, -trice** *sm, sf* nuisance. **seccatura** *sf* nuisance. **secco** *agg* dry; (*essicato*) dried; (*fig*) sharp. **lavare a secco** dry-clean. **rimanere in secco** be left high and dry.
secchia ['sekkja] *sf* bucket. **secchio** *sm* pail; (*per carbone*) coal-scuttle. **secchione** *sm* (*fam: sgobbone*) swot.
*secernere [se'tʃɛrnere] *v* secrete.
secessione [setʃes'sjone] *sf* secession.
secolo ['sɛkolo] *sm* century; (*periodo*) age. **al secolo** alias. **secolare** *agg* centuries old; (*laico*) secular.

secondino [sekon'dino] *sm* warder.
secondo¹ [se'kondo] *sm, agg* second. **in un secondo tempo** on a later occasion. **secondo fine** *sm* ulterior motive.
secondo² [se'kondo] *prep* according to; depending on. *inter* it depends!
secrezione [sekre'tsjone] *sf* secretion.
sedano ['sɛdano] *sm* celery. **sedano rapa** celeriac.
sedare [se'dare] *v* calm; (*reprimere*) quell. **sedativo** *agg, sm* sedative.
sede ['sɛde] *sf* seat; (*comm*) office; residence; (*seduta*) sitting. **in altra sede** (*luogo*) elsewhere; (*tempo*) some other time. **Santa Sede** Holy See. **sede centrale** headquarters. **sede legale** registered office.
*sedere [se'dere] *v* sit (down). **dar da sedere** offer a seat. **sedersi** *v* sit down, take a seat. **tirarsi su a sedere** sit up. *sm* (*deretano*) bottom. **sedentario** *agg* sedentary.
sedia ['sɛdja] *sf* chair.
sedicente [sedi'tʃente] *agg* so-called, would-be.
sedici ['seditʃi] *agg, sm* sixteen. **sedicesimo** *sm, agg* sixteenth.
sedile [se'dile] *sm* seat.
sedimento [sedi'mento] *sm* sediment. **sedimentazione** *sf* sedimentation.
sedizione [sedi'tsjone] *sf* sedition; rebellion. **sedizioso** *agg* seditious.
*sedurre [se'durre] *v* seduce; (*attrarre*) entice. **seducente** *agg* alluring, tempting. **seduttore, -trice** *agg* seductive. **seduzione** *sf* seduction; temptation.
seduta [se'duta] *sf* session; (*pasto, posa*) sitting; (*riunione*) meeting. **seduta spiritica** seance. **seduta stante** forthwith.
sega ['sega] *sf* saw. **a sega** saw-toothed. **sega a catena** chain-saw. **sega da traforo** fretsaw. **segare** *v* saw. **segatrice** *sf* saw. **segatura** *sf* (*azione*) sawing; (*frammenti*) sawdust.
segale ['segale] *sf* rye.
seggio ['sɛddʒo] *sm* seat; (*carica*) chair. **seggiola** *sf* chair. **seggiolino** *sm* seat. **seggiolone** *sm* armchair; (*per bambini*) high chair.
seggiovia [seddʒo'via] *sf* chair-lift.
seghettare [seget'tare] *v* serrate.
segmento [seg'mento] *sm* segment. **segmentare** *v* divide up. **segmentazione** *sf* segmentation; (*fig*) breaking up.

segnalare [seɲa'lare] *v* signal; (*indicare*) point out; (*render noto*) report. **segnalato** *agg* announced, reported; (*straordinario*) outstanding. **segnalatore** *sm* (*persona*) signaller; indicator; alarm. **segnalazione** *sf* signalling; report; notification; (*nota informativa*) notice. **segnalazione stradale** road sign. **segnale** *sm* signal; (*cartello*) sign; (*telefono*) tone. **segnaletica** *sf* road signs *pl*.

segnalibro [seɲa'libro] *sm* bookmark.

segnapunti [seɲa'punti] *sm invar* (*tabellone*) score-board; (*libretto*) score-book.

segnare [se'ɲare] *v* mark; (*marchiare*) brand. **segnare i punti** keep the score. **segnare le ore** tell the time.

segno ['seɲo] *sm* sign; (*traccia*) mark. **come** *or* **in segno di** as a sign of, in token of. **essere segno che** mean. **tiro a segno** *sm* target practice.

sego ['sego] *sm* fallow.

segregare [segre'gare] *v* segregate, set apart. **segregazione** *sf* segregation; isolation. **segregazione cellulare** solitary confinement.

segretario [segre'tarjo], -a *sm, sf* secretary; (*chi redige verbali, ecc.*) clerk. **segretariato** *sm* secretariat. **segreteria** *sf* secretary's office; (*enti pubblici*) secretariat.

segreto [se'greto] *agg* secret. *sm* secret; (*intimità*) depth; (*segretezza*) secrecy. **in segreto** in secret; (*riservatamente*) confidentially. **nel segreto più assoluto** in utmost secrecy. **segreti del mestiere** tricks of the trade *pl*. **segreto di Pulcinella** open secret. **segreta** *sf* dungeon. **segretezza** *sf* secrecy.

seguace [se'gwatʃe] *s(m+f)* follower; disciple.

seguente [se'gwɛnte] *agg* following; (*futuro*) next.

segugio [se'gudʒo] *sm* bloodhound; (*fig*) sleuth.

seguire [se'gwire] *v* follow; (*frequentare*) attend. **segue a tergo** continued overleaf, PTO. **seguitare** *v* continue. **seguito** *sm* following; succession; favour; continuation; consequence. **di seguito** on end, non-stop. **in seguito** later (on). **in seguito a** as a result of, because of.

sei ['sɛi] *agg, sm* six.

selce ['seltʃe] *sf* flint; (*strada*) paving-stone. **selciato** *sm* paving.

selettivo [selet'tivo] *agg* selective. **selettività** *sf* selectivity. **selettore, -trice** *sm, sf* selector.

selezionare [seletsjo'nare] *v* select; grade. **selezionamento** *sm* selection. **selezione** *sf* selection; (*scelta*) choice. **selezione automatica** (*telefono*) automatic dialling, STD.

sella ['sɛlla] *sf* saddle. **sellare** *v* saddle.

seltz ['sɛlts] *sm invar* soda-water.

selva ['selva] *sf* forest. **selvoso** *agg* wooded.

selvaggio [sel'vaddʒo], -a *agg* wild; (*incivile*) savage. *sm, sf* savage. **selvaggina** *sf* game. **selvatico** *agg* wild; (*scontroso*) uncouth.

semaforo [se'maforo] *sm* traffic lights *pl*.

semantica [se'mantika] *sf* semantics. **semantico** *agg* semantic.

sembrare [sem'brare] *v* seem. **cosa te ne sembra?** what do you think of it?

seme ['seme] *sm* seed; (*di mele, pere, ecc.*) pip; (*carte da gioco*) suit. **sementa** *sf* (*operazione*) sowing; (*semente*) seed. **semente** *sf* seed. **semenza** *sf* seed; (*perle*) seed-pearls *pl*.

semestre [se'mɛstre] *sm* half-year. **semestrale** *agg* half-yearly.

semibreve [semi'brɛve] *sf* semibreve.

semicerchio [semi'tʃerkjo] *sm* semicircle.

semicircolare [semitʃirko'lare] *agg* semicircular.

semicroma [semi'krɔma] *sf* semiquaver.

semidio [semi'dio] *sm* demi-god.

semifinale [semifi'nale] *sf* semifinal. **semifinalista** *s(m+f)* semifinalist.

semiminima [semi'minima] *sf* crotchet.

seminare [semi'nare] *v* sow; (*fig*) scatter, strew. **semina** *sf* sowing. **seminale** *agg* seminal. **uscire dal seminato** digress.

seminario [semi'narjo] *sm* (*rel*) seminary; (*università*) seminar. **seminarista** *sm* seminarist.

seminterrato [seminter'rato] *sm* basement.

seminudo [semi'nudo] *agg* half-naked.

semita [se'mita] *s(m+f)* Semite. *agg also* **semitico** Semitic.

semitono [semi'tono] *sm* semitone.

semivivo [semi'vivo] *agg* half-dead.

semola ['semola] *sf* (*crusca*) bran. **semolino** *sm* semolina.

semovente [semo'vɛnte] *agg* self-propelled.

semplice ['semplitʃe] *agg* simple; (*di un solo elemento*) single; (*senza affettazione*) plain. **semplicemente** *avv* simply; (*soltanto*) only. **semplicione** *sm* simpleton. **semplicità** *sf* simplicity. **semplificare** *v* simplify; facilitate. **semplificazione** *sf* simplification.

sempre ['sempre] *avv* always; (*ancora*) still. **da sempre** from the beginning. **per sempre** for ever. **sempre che** (*purché*) as long as, provided that; (*ammesso che*) supposing that. **sempre più** more and more. **sempreverde** *s(m+f)*, *agg* evergreen. **una volta per sempre** once and for all.

senape ['senape] *sf* mustard.

senato [se'nato] *sm* senate. **senatore** *sm* senator.

senile [se'nile] *agg* senile. **senilità** *sf* senility.

senno ['senno] *sm* wits *pl*; (*sensatezza*) (common) sense. **con senno** sensibly. **senno di poi** hindsight. **uscir di senno** go out of one's mind.

seno ['seno] *sm* bosom, breast; (*grembo*) womb; (*anat*) sinus; (*mat*) sine; (*geog*) inlet. **allattare al seno** breast-feed. **in seno a** (*nel mezzo di*) within; (*tra le braccia*) in the arms of.

sensale [sen'sale] *sm* broker.

sensato [sen'sato] *agg* sensible. **sensatezza** *sf* good sense.

sensazione [sensa'tsjone] *sf* feeling, sensation. **sensazionale** *agg* sensational.

sensibile [sen'sibile] *agg* (*che sente*) sensitive; (*notevole*) appreciable; perceptible; susceptible. **sensibilità** *sf* sensitivity. **sensibilizzare** *v* sensitize.

sensitivo [sensi'tivo] *agg* (*funzione*) sensory; (*sensibile*) sensitive. **sensitività** *sf* sensitivity.

senso ['senso] *sm* sense; (*significato*) meaning; (*direzione, modo*) way. **a senso** in one's own words; (*tradurre*) freely. **far senso** (*ripugnare*) disgust. **in senso antiorario** anticlockwise. **in senso orario** clockwise. **non aver senso** not make sense; be pointless. **senso proibito** no entry. **senso unico** one-way. **sensorio** *agg* sensory. **sensuale** *agg* sensual; sensuous. **sensualità** *sf* sensuality; sensuousness.

sentenza [sen'tentsa] *sf* sentence, judgment; (*massima*) saying. **sputare sentenze** be sententious. **sentenziare** *v*

pass judgment *or* sentence; rule; decree. **sentenzioso** *agg* sententious.

sentiero [sen'tjero] *sm* path.

sentimento [senti'mento] *sm* feeling; (*concetto*) sense. **sentimenti** *sm pl* (*modo di sentire*) sentiments *pl*.

sentinella [senti'nella] *sf* sentry.

sentire [sen'tire] *v* feel; (*col gusto*) taste; (*con l'udito*) hear; (*con l'olfatto*) smell; (*dare ascolto*) listen to; (*aver notizia*) gather. **al mio modo di sentire** to my way of thinking. **sentirsela** *v* feel like. **sentirsi** *v* feel.

sentito [sen'tito] *agg* (*udito*) heard; sincere. **per sentito dire** by hearsay.

sentore [sen'tore] *sm* inkling.

senza ['sentsa] *prep* without. **rimanere senza** run out of. **senza contare** apart from; over and above. **senza dire** not to mention. **senza fallo** certainly. **senz'altro** definitely. **senza soldi** penniless. **senzatetto** *s(m+f)* *invar* homeless person.

separare [sepa'rare] *v* separate, divide. **separarsi** *v* part; (*coniugi*) separate. **separazione** *sf* separation, division; parting.

sepolcro [se'polkro] *sm* tomb. **sepolcrale** *agg* sepulchral.

sepolto [se'polto] *agg* buried. **sepoltura** *sf* burial.

*seppellire [seppel'lire] *v* bury.

seppia ['seppja] *sf* (*zool*) cuttlefish. *agg*, *sm invar* (*colore*) sepia.

seppure [sep'pure] *cong* even though, even if.

sequela [se'kwela] *sf* succession.

sequestrare [sekwes'trare] *v* seize, confiscate; (*persona*) imprison unlawfully; (*rapire*) kidnap. **sequestro** *sm* seizure, confiscation; kidnapping; illegal confinement.

sera ['sera] *sf* evening, night. **buona sera!** (*di pomeriggio*) good afternoon! (*di sera*) good evening! **si fa sera** it is getting dark. **serale** *agg* evening, night. **serata** *sf* evening, night; (*ricevimento*) party; (*teatro*) performance.

serbare [ser'bare] *v* (*mantenere*) keep; (*metter da parte*) put aside. **serbare gratitudine verso** be grateful to. **serbatoio** *sm* tank; (*penna*) barrel; (*fucile, ecc.*) magazine.

serbo ['serbo] *sm* **dare in serbo** put into

custody. **mettere in serbo** put by *or*
aside. **tenere in serbo** keep in store.
serenata [sere'nata] *sf* serenade.
serenella [sere'nɛlla] *sf* lilac.
sereno [se'reno] *agg* calm, serene; (*cielo*)
clear; (*senza preoccupazioni*) carefree;
objective. *sm* clear sky; (*aperto*) open air.
serenità *sf* serenity; objectivity.
sergente [ser'dʒɛnte] *sm* sergeant.
serico ['sɛriko] *agg* silk.
serie ['sɛrje] *sf invar* series; (*assortimento*)
set; (*sport*) division. **fuori serie** (*auto*)
custom-built. **modello di serie** *sm* production model. **prodotto in serie** mass-
produced. **produzione in serie** *sf* mass-
production.
serio ['sɛrjo] *agg* serious; (*degno di
fiducia*) trustworthy; (*comm*) reputable.
sm seriousness. **sul serio** (*seriamente*)
seriously; (*davvero*) really. **serietà** *sf* seriousness; (*fidatezza*) reliability.
sermone [ser'mone] *sm* sermon; (*rimprovero*) lecture.
serpeggiare [serped'dʒare] *v* wind.
serpente [ser'pɛnte] *sm* snake, serpent.
serpente a sonagli rattlesnake. **serpentino**
agg snake-like.
serra ['sɛrra] *sf* greenhouse, hothouse.
serraglio [ser'raʎo] *sm* menagerie.
serrare [ser'rare] *v* close; (*a chiave*) lock;
(*stringere*) tighten; (*denti, pugni*) clench.
serrare al cuore embrace. **serramento** *sm*
(*di finestra*) window-frame; (*di porta*)
door-frame. **serrata** *sf* lock-out. **serrato**
agg closed; (*fila*) serried; (*fig*) to the
point.
serratura [serra'tura] *sf* lock. **buco della
serratura** *sm* keyhole. **serratura a cilindro**
Yale lock ®. **serratura a lucchetto**
padlock. **serratura a scatto** latch.
servire [ser'vire] *v* serve; (*fam: occorrere*)
be useful; (*carte da gioco*) deal. **a cosa
serve?** what is the use? **cosa ti serve?**
what do you need? **posso servirti?** can I
help you? **servirsi** *v* use; make use; (*di
cibo*) help oneself. **servile** *agg* servile;
(*fig*) slavish. **servitore** *sm* servant. **servitù**
sf (*schiavitù*) slavery; (*personale di
servizio*) servants *pl*. **ridurre in servitù**
enslave.
servizio [ser'vitsjo] *sm* service; (*lavoro*)
work; favour; (*giornale*) report; (*turno*)
duty. **a mezzo servizio** part-time. **donna
di servizio** *sf* maid. **fare servizio**
(*trasporto*) run; (*negozio*) be open. **fuori**

servizio off duty; (*che non funziona*) out
of order. **in servizio** on duty. **servizievole**
agg obliging.
servo ['sɛrvo], **-a** *sm*, *sf* servant.
sesamo ['sɛzamo] *sm* sesame.
sessanta [ses'santa] *agg*, *sm* sixty. **sessantesimo** *agg*, *sm* sixtieth.
sessione [ses'sjone] *sf* session.
sesso ['sɛsso] *sm* sex. **sessuale** *agg* sexual.
sessualità *sf* sexuality.
sestetto [ses'tetto] *sm* sextet.
sesto¹ ['sɛsto] *sm*, *agg* sixth.
sesto² ['sɛsto] *sm* order; (*di arco*) curve.
mettere in sesto tidy up. **rimettersi in
sesto** get back on one's feet again.
seta ['seta] *sf* silk.
setaccio [se'tattʃo] *sm* sieve. **setacciare** *v
also* **passare al setaccio** sift, sieve.
sete ['sete] *sf* thirst. **aver sete** be thirsty.
mettere la seta a make thirsty.
setola ['setola] *sf* bristle.
setta ['sɛtta] *sf* sect. *agg*, *sm* sectarian.
settanta [set'tanta] *agg*, *sm* seventy. **settantesimo** *agg*, *sm* seventieth.
sette ['sɛtte] *agg*, *sm* seven. **settimo** *agg*,
sm seventh.
settembre [set'tɛmbre] *sm* September.
settentrione [setten'trjone] *sm* north. **settentrionale** *agg* northern, north.
settico ['sɛttiko] *agg* septic. **setticemia** *sf*
blood-poisoning.
settimana [setti'mana] *sf* week; (*pagɔ*)
week's wages. **a metà settimana** mid-
week. **a settimane** by the week; (*una sì e
una no*) every other week. **fine settimana**
sf week-end. **settimanale** *agg*, *sm* weekly.
settore [set'tore] *sm* sector; (*campo*) field.
severo [se'vɛro] *agg* severe, strict; (*grave*)
serious. **severità** *sf* severity.
seviziare [sevi'tsjare] *v* torture;
(*violentare*) rape. **sevizie** *sf pl* torture
sing.
sezione [se'tsjone] *sf* section; (*tribunale*)
division; (*sezionamento*) dissection.
sezionare *v* dissect; (*dividere in sezioni*)
section.
sfaccendato [sfattʃen'dato], **-a** *agg* idle.
sm, *sf* loafer.
sfaccettare [sfattʃet'tare] *v* cut.
sfacchinare [sfakki'nare] *v* slave.
sfacchinata *sf* heavy work.
sfacciato [sfat'tʃato], **-a** *agg* impudent;
(*svergognato*) shameless; (*vistoso*) gaudy.
sm, *sf* impudent *or* shameless person.

sfacciataggine *sf* impudence; shamelessness.

sfacelo [sfa'tʃɛlo] *sm* ruin; (*disfacimento*) decay. andare in sfacelo break up; (*fam*) go to rack and ruin.

sfaldarsi [sfal'darsi] *v* flake; (*sbriciolarsi*) crumble. sfaldatura *sf* flaking; crumbling.

sfalsare [sfal'sare] *v* stagger.

sfamare [sfa'mare] *v* feed. sfamarsi *v* satisfy one's hunger.

sfarfallare [sfarfal'lare] *v* (*svolazzare*) flutter; (*esser vo!ubile*) flit; (*auto*) wobble.

sfarzo ['sfartso] *sm* magnificence, pomp. senza sfarzo simply. sfarzosità *sf* sumptuousness; ostentation. sfarzoso *agg* sumptuous; ostentatious.

sfasciare [sfa'ʃare] *v* (*rompere*) smash.

sfatare [sfa'tare] *v* refute.

sfavillante [sfavil'lante] *agg* glittering, sparkling.

sfavore [sfa'vore] *sm* disfavour, discredit. andare a sfavore di go against. sfavorevole *agg* unfavourable; (*contrario*) adverse.

sfegatato [sfega'tato] *agg* passionate.

sfera ['sfɛra] *sf* sphere; (*ambiente*) circle; (*campo*) field. cuscinetto a sfere *sm* ball-bearing. penna a sfera *sf* ball-point pen. sferico *agg* spherical.

sferrare [sfer'rare] *v* (*attacco*) launch; (*pugno*) deal. sferrare un calcio kick.

sferza ['sfɛrtsa] *sf* whip. sferzare *v* whip; lash.

sfiatato [sfja'tato] *agg* breathless; (*strumento musicale*) cracked; (*fam*) hoarse.

sfibrare [sfi'brare] *v* (*indebolire*) weaken. sfibrante *agg* enervating. sfibrato *agg* exhausted.

sfida ['sfida] *sf* challenge. sfidare *v* challenge; (*invitare*) defy; (*fig*) brave.

sfiducia [sfi'dutʃa] *sf* distrust. avere sfiducia di distrust; lack confidence in. sfiduciarsi *v* lose confidence. sfiduciato *agg* distrustful; (*di sè stesso*) diffident; (*scoraggiato*) disheartened.

sfigurare [sfigu'rare] *v* disfigure; make a bad impression.

sfilacciare [sfilat'tʃare] *v* fray.

sfilare¹ [sfi'lare] *v* (*togliere di dosso*) take off; (*ago*) unthread.

sfilare² [sfi'lare] *v* parade. sfilata *sf* parade; (*lunga fila*) long row.

sfilza ['sfiltsa] *sf* string.

sfinge ['sfindʒe] *sf* sphinx.

sfinire [sfi'nire] *v* wear out. sfinimento *sm* exhaustion.

sfiorare [sfjo'rare] *v* skim (over); (*toccando*) graze, barely touch; (*successo, ecc.*) be on the verge of.

sfiorito [sfjo'rito] *agg* withered.

sfitto ['sfitto] *agg* vacant.

sfocato [sfo'kato] *agg* (*foto*) out of focus; (*fig*) hazy.

sfociare [sfo'tʃare] *v* flow (into); (*fig*) result. sfocio *sm* outlet.

sfogare [sfo'gare] *v* let out; (*fig*) give vent to. sfogarsi *v* (*sfogar l'ira*) give vent to one's anger; (*confidarsi*) pour out one's heart; (*bambino*) run wild. sfogo *sm* outlet; (*sollievo*) relief.

sfoggiare [sfod'dʒare] *v* show off. sfoggio *sm* display; ostentation.

sfogliare¹ [sfo'ʎare] *v also* dare una sfogliata a (*pagine*) leaf or skim through.

sfogliare² [sfo'ʎare] *v* (*levar le foglie*) strip (of leaves). sfoglia *sf* leaf; (*gastr*) puff pastry.

sfolgorare [sfolgo'rare] *v* blaze; (*occhi*) shine.

sfollare [sfol'lare] *v* disperse; evacuate. sfollamento *sm* evacuation. sfollato, -a *sm*, *sf* evacuee.

sfondare [sfon'dare] *v* break through; (*schiantare*) smash; (*logorare*) wear out. sfondato *agg* (*senza fondo*) bottomless; (*logoro*) worn out. ricco sfondato rolling in money. sfondo *sm* background, setting.

sformare [sfor'mare] *v* pull out of shape; (*estrarre dalla forma*) turn out. sformato *sm* (*gastr*) pie.

sfornito [sfor'nito] *agg* sfornito di lacking in, without.

sfortuna [sfor'tuna] *sf* bad luck; (*contrattempo*) misfortune. sfortunato *agg* unlucky; (*senza successo*) unfortunate.

sforzare [sfor'tsare] *v* force, strain. sforzarsi di try hard to. sforzo *sm* effort.

sfottere ['sfottere] *v* (*fam*) take the mickey (out of). sfottimento *sm* teasing, ridicule.

sfracellare [sfratʃel'lare] *v* shatter.

sfrangiato [sfran'dʒato] *agg* fringed.

sfrattare [sfrat'tare] *v* turn out, evict. sfratto *sm* eviction.

sfregare [sfre'gare] *v* rub; (*lucidando*) polish; (*lavando*) scrub. sfregamento *sm* rubbing; polishing; scrubbing.

sfrenare [sfre'nare] *v* let loose. **sfrenatezza** *sf* lack of restraint; wild behaviour. **sfrenato** *agg* unbridled; (*senza ritegno*) immoderate.

*****sfriggere** ['sfridd3ere] *v also* **sfrigolare** sizzle.

sfrondare [sfron'dare] *v* prune.

sfrontato [sfron'tato] *agg* impudent, brazen; (*fam*) cheeky. **sfrontatezza** *sf* effrontery; (*fam*) cheek.

sfruttare [sfrut'tare] *v* exploit. **sfruttamento** *sm* exploitation; utilization. **sfruttatore, -trice** *sm, sf* exploiter.

sfuggire [sfud'd3ire] *v* shun; (*scappare*) escape from. **lasciarsi sfuggire** let slip; (*occasione*) let go by. **sfuggire di mano** slip out of one's hand. **sfuggire di mente** slip one's mind. **sfuggente** *agg* (*mento, fronte*) receding. **di sfuggita** fleetingly.

sfumare [sfu'mare] *v* (*svanire*) disappear; (*colori, suoni*) fade away, tone down. **sfumato** *agg* (*pittura*) shaded; (*fig*) vague. **sfumatura** *sf* nuance.

sfuriata [sfu'rjata] *sf* outburst; (*tempesta*) storm; (*rabbuffo*) telling-off.

sfuso ['sfuzo] *agg* (*sciolto*) loose; (*liquefatto*) melted.

sgabello [zga'bɛllo] *sm* stool.

sgabuzzino [zgabut'tsino] *sm* cubby-hole.

sgambettare [zgambet'tare] *v* (*camminare a piccoli passi*) toddle (along); (*fare lo sgambetto*) trip up.

sganciare [zgan'tʃare] *v* unhook; (*bombe*) release; (*fam: sborsare*) fork out.

sgangherato [zgange'rato] *agg* (*sfasciato*) rickety; (*sconnesso*) incoherent; (*esagerato*) boisterous.

sgarbato [zgar'bato] *agg* rude, discourteous. **sgarbatezza** *sf* rudeness, discourtesy.

sgarbugliare [zgarbu'ʎare] *v* disentangle.

sgargiante [zgar'd3ante] *agg* showy.

sgarrare [zgar'rare] *v* be *or* go wrong.

sgelare [zdʒe'lare] *v* thaw out; (*surgelati*) defrost.

sghembo ['zgembo] *agg* crooked. **di sghembo** askew.

sgherro ['zgɛrro] *sm* thug.

sghignazzare [zgiɲat'tsare] *v* laugh sarcastically, sneer; (*sguaiatamente*) guffaw. **sghignazzata** *sf* sarcastic laughter; guffaw.

sghiribizzo [zgiri'bittso] *sm* whim.

sgobbare [zgob'bare] (*fam*) *v* slave. **sgobbata** *sf* grind. **sgobbone, -a** *sm, sf* slogger; (*studente*) swot.

sgocciolare [zgottʃo'lare] *v* drip; (*vuotare*) drain. **sgocciolatura** *sf* dripping; (*macchie*) drips *pl*. **essere agli sgoccioli** be *or* have nearly finished.

sgolarsi [zgo'larsi] *v* shout oneself hoarse.

sgombrare [zgom'brare] *v also* **sgomberare** clear; (*vuotare*) empty; (*portar via*) clear away; evacuate; (*lasciar libero*) vacate.

sgombro[1] ['zgombro] *sm also* **sgombero** (*trasloco*) move; clearing (away); evacuation. *agg* clear; empty.

sgombro[2] ['zgombro] *V* **scombro**.

sgomentare [zgomen'tare] *v* dismay. **sgomento** *sm* dismay.

sgonfiare [zgon'fjare] *v* deflate; (*fam*) annoy. **sgonfiarsi** *v* go down; (*pneumatico*) go flat; (*fig*) be deflated. **sgonfio** *agg* deflated, flat.

sgorbia ['zgɔrbja] *sf* gouge.

sgorbio ['zgɔrbjo] *sm* (*macchia*) blot; (*scarabocchio*) scrawl.

sgorgare [zgor'gare] *v* gush (out); (*uscire*) spring.

sgradevole [zgra'devole] *agg* disagreeable, unpleasant. **sgradito** *agg* disagreeable; (*non gradito*) unwelcome.

sgrammaticato [zgrammati'kato] *agg* ungrammatical.

sgranare [zgra'nare] *v* shell; (*occhi*) open wide.

sgranchire [zgran'kire] *v* stretch.

sgravare [zgra'vare] *v* relieve; (*partorire*) give birth.

sgraziato [zgra'tsjato] *agg* ungainly, awkward.

sgretolare [zgreto'lare] *v* break up. **sgretolarsi** *v* crumble. **sgretolato** *agg* crumbling.

sgridare [zgri'dare] *v* scold; (*fam*) tell off. **sgridata** *sf* scolding; (*fam*) telling-off.

sguaiato [zgwa'jato] *agg* unseemly; vulgar; (*grossolano*) coarse. **sguaiataggine** *sf* vulgarity; coarseness.

sgualcire [zgwal'tʃire] *v* crease, crumple.

sgualdrina [zgwal'drina] *sf* (*spreg*) tart.

sguardo ['zgwardo] *sm* look; (*occhiata*) glance; (*fisso*) stare; (*prolungato*) gaze. **al primo sguardo** at first sight. **fissare lo sguardo su** stare at. **gettare uno sguardo su** glance at.

sguarnire [zgwar'nire] *v* strip.

sguattero ['zgwattero], **-a** *sm, sf* skivvy.

sguazzare [zgwat'tsare] *v* splash about; (*fig*) wallow.

sguinzagliare [zgwintsa'ʎare] *v* let loose.

sgusciare[1] [zgu'ʃare] *v* (*scivolare*) slip.

sgusciare[2] [zgu'ʃare] *v* shell; (*uova, noci*) crack.

shampoo [ʃam'pu] *sm invar* shampoo.

si [si] *pron* (*lui*) himself; (*lei*) herself; (*cosa, animale*) itself; (*loro*) themselves; (*reciproco*) each other; (*riflessivo*) oneself; (*indefinito*) one.

sì [si] *avv* yes. **credo di sì** I think so. **dire di sì** say yes. **far cenno di sì** nod. **spero di sì** I hope so. **un giorno sì e uno no** every other day.

sia ['sia] *cong* **sia . . . sia . . .** whether . . . or . . . ; (*entrambi*) both.

siamese [sia'meze] *agg, s*(*m*+*f*) Siamese.

sibilare [sibi'lare] *v* hiss. **sibilo** *sm* hiss.

sicario [si'karjo] *sm* hired assassin.

sicché [sik'ke] *cong* (*di modo che*) and so; (*e perciò*) so that.

siccità [sittʃi'ta] *sf* drought.

siccome [sik'kome] *cong* as, since.

Sicilia [si'tʃilja] *sf* Sicily. **siciliano, -a** *s, agg* Sicilian.

sicomoro [siko'mɔro] *sm* sycamore.

sicura [si'kura] *sf* safety catch.

sicurezza [siku'rettsa] *sf* safety; certainty; (*garanzia*) security; (*confidenza*) self-assurance. **di sicurezza** safety. **per maggior sicurezza** to be on the safe side. **pubblica sicurezza** police. **sicurezza sociale** social security; welfare.

sicuro [si'kuro] *agg* safe; (*tranquillo*) secure; certain, sure; (*fidato*) reliable; (*saldo*) steady. *sm* safety; safe place. **andar sul sicuro** take no chances. **dare per sicuro** be certain about. **di sicuro** certainly. **star sicuro** not worry.

sidro ['sidro] *sm* cider.

siepe ['sjɛpe] *sf* hedge.

siero ['sjɛro] *sm* serum.

siesta ['sjɛsta] *sf* siesta; (*fam*) nap. **fare la siesta** take a nap.

sifilide [si'filide] *sf* syphilis.

sifone [si'fone] *sm* siphon.

sigaretta [siga'retta] *sf* cigarette. **sigaro** *sm* cigar.

sigillare [sidʒil'lare] *v* seal. **sigillatura** *sf* sealing, seal. **sigillo** *sm* seal. **anello con sigillo** *sm* signet-ring.

sigla ['sigla] *sf* initials *pl*; (*auto*) registration number. **sigla musicale** signature tune. **siglare** *v* initial.

significare [siɲifi'kare] *v* mean; (*simboleggiare*) stand for. **significativo** *agg* meaningful, significant; important. **significato** *sm* meaning; importance.

signora [si'ɲora] *sf* lady; (*donna*) woman (*pl* women); (*cortesia*) madam; (*seguito dal cognome*) Mrs; (*padrona*) mistress; (*moglie*) wife. **fare la signora** live like a lady.

signore [si'ɲore] *sm* gentleman; (*uomo*) man (*pl* men); (*cortesia*) sir; (*seguito dal cognome*) Mr; (*padrone*) master.

signoreggiare [siɲored'dʒare] *v* rule.

signoria [siɲo'ria] *sf* domination.

signorile [siɲo'rile] *agg* elegant, high-class; (*uomo*) gentlemanly; (*donna*) lady-like. **signorilità** *sf* elegance; refinement.

signorina [siɲo'rina] *sf* young lady *or* woman; (*cortesia*) madam; (*seguito dal cognome*) Miss; (*non sposata*) unmarried woman. **nome da signorina** *sm* maiden name.

silenzio [si'lɛntsjo] *sm* silence. **far silenzio** be quiet. **silenziare** *v* muffle. **silenziatore** *sm* silencer. **silenzioso** *agg* silent, quiet.

silicio [si'litʃo] *sm* silicon. **silice** *sf* silica. **silicone** *sm* silicone. **silicosi** *sf* silicosis.

sillaba ['sillaba] *sf* syllable. **sillabare** *v* (*gramm*) syllabify; (*fig*) spell out. **sillabario** *sm* spelling book.

silo ['silo] *sm* silo.

silofono [si'lɔfono] *sm* xylophone.

silurare [silu'rare] *v* torpedo; (*far fallire*) wreck; (*destituire*) dismiss. **siluramento** *sm* torpedoing; wrecking; dismissal. **siluro** *sm* torpedo.

silvestre [sil'vɛstre] *agg* woody; (*selvaggio*) wild.

silvia ['silvja] *sf* (*bot*) wood anemone; (*zool*) warbler.

simbolo ['simbolo] *sm* symbol; (*rel*) creed. **simboleggiare** *v* symbolize. **simbolico** *agg* symbolic.

simile ['simile] *agg* like, similar; (*predicato*) alike; (*tale*) such. **similitudine** *sf* simile.

simmetria [simme'tria] *sf* symmetry. **simmetrico** *agg* symmetrical.

simpatia [simpa'tia] *sf* (*sentimento di attrazione*) liking; (*qualità*) likeableness; (*affinità*) sympathy. **avere** *or* **provare simpatia per** like, take to. **simpatico** *agg* nice, likeable; (*piacevole*) agreeable; (*anat*) sympathetic. **simpatizzare** *v* sympathize.

simposio [sim'pɔzjo] *sm* symposium.

simulare [simu'lare] *v* feign; (*imitare*) simulate. **simulacro** *sm* image; (*fig*) semblance. **simulazione** *sf* simulation.

simultaneo [simul'taneo] *agg* simultaneous. **simultaneità** *sf* simultaneity.

sinagoga [sina'gɔga] *sf* synagogue.

sincero [sin'tʃero] *agg* sincere, true; (*non artefatto*) genuine. **sincerità** *sf* sincerity.

sincopare [sinko'pare] *v* syncopate. **sincope** *sf* syncope; (*musica*) syncopation.

sincronizzare [sinkronid'dzare] *v* synchronize. **sincronizzatore** *sm* synchronizer. **sincronizzazione** *sf* synchronization.

sindacale [sinda'kale] *agg* (*di sindacato*) (trade) union. **sindacalismo** *sm* trade unionism. **sindacalista** *s(m+f)* trade unionist.

sindacare [sinda'kare] *v* check; (*contabilità*) audit; (*fig*) criticize.

sindacato [sinda'kato] *sm* (*operaio*) trade union; (*padronale, d'impresa*) consortium; (*finanziario*) syndicate.

sindaco ['sindako] *sm* mayor; (*comm*) auditor.

sindrome ['sindrome] *sf* syndrome.

sinfonia [sinfo'nia] *sf* symphony. **sinfonico** *agg* symphonic. **orchestra sinfonica** *sf* symphony orchestra.

singhiozzare [singjot'tsare] *v* (*avere il singhiozzo*) hiccup; (*piangere*) sob. **singhiozzo** *sm* sob; hiccup. **a singhiozzi** by fits and starts.

singolare [singo'lare] *agg* singular; (*strano*) strange. *sm* singular. **singolarità** *sf* singularity; strangeness.

singolo ['singolo] *agg* single, individual. *sm* (*persona*) individual; (*telefono*) private line; (*tennis*) singles; (*canottaggio*) skiff.

sinistra [si'nistra] *sf* left(-hand side); (*mano*) left hand. **a sinistra** on *or* to the left. **tenere la sinistra** keep to the left. **uomo di sinistra** *sm* left-winger.

sinistrare [sinis'trare] *v* damage. **sinistrato, -a** *sm, sf* victim. **zona sinistrata** *sf* disaster area.

sinistro [si'nistro] *agg* left; (*lato*) left-hand; (*fig*) sinister. *sm* accident; (*pugilato*) left.

sino ['sino] *cong* **sino a** (*tempo*) until; (*luogo*) as far as. *avv* (*persino*) even. **sinora** *avv* (*per ora*) so far; (*fino ad ora*) up to now.

sinossi [si'nɔssi] *sf* synopsis (*pl* -ses). **sinottico** *agg* synoptic.

sintassi [sin'tassi] *sf* syntax. **sintattico** *agg* syntactic(al).

sintesi ['sintezi] *sf* synthesis (*pl* -ses). **in sintesi** (*in poche parole*) in short; (*sommariamente*) summing up. **sintetico** *agg* synthetic; (*fig*) concise. **sintetizzare** *v* synthesize; (*riassumere*) summarize.

sintomo ['sintomo] *sm* symptom. **sintomatico** *agg* symptomatic.

sintonizzare [sintonid'dzare] *v* tune in.

sinuoso [sinu'ozo] *agg* sinuous, winding.

sinusite [sinu'zite] *sf* sinusitis.

sipario [si'parjo] *sm* curtain.

sirena [si'rena] *sf* siren; (*creatura*) mermaid.

siringa [si'ringa] *sf* syringe; (*bot*) lilac; catheter. **siringare** *v* syringe; catheterize.

sismico ['sizmiko] *agg* seismic. **sismografo** *sm* seismograph.

sistema [sis'tema] *sm* system; (*modo di fare*) way; method. **sistemare** *v* (*mettere a posto*) arrange; (put in) order; (*risolvere*) settle; organize; (*collocare*) place; install. **sistemarsi** *v* settle (down); (*lavoro*) get a job. **sistematico** *agg* systematic; methodical. **sistemazione** *sf* arrangement; (*composizione*) settlement; (*alloggio*) accommodation; (*lavoro*) job.

situare [situ'are] *v* place; (*collocare*) locate. **situazione** *sf* situation. **situazione di fatto** state of affairs.

slabbrare [zlab'brare] *v* (*vasellame*) chip; (*tessuto*) tear.

slacciare [zlat'tʃare] *v* undo, untie.

slanciare [zlan'tʃare] *v* hurl. **slanciato** *agg* slender, slim. **slancio** *sm* swing; (*di passione, ecc.*) burst. **di slancio** in a rush; (*fig*) on impulse.

slattare [zlat'tare] *v* wean.

slavato [zla'vato] *agg* washed out; (*fig*) dull.

sleale [zle'ale] *agg* disloyal; (*fatto senza lealtà*) unfair. **gioco sleale** *sm* foul play. **slealtà** *sf* disloyalty; unfairness.

slegare [zle'gare] *v* untie. **slegato** *agg* untied; (*non rilegato*) unbound; (*fig*) disjointed.

slip [zlip] *sm invar* (*mutande*) briefs *pl*; (*da bagno*) swimming trunks *pl*.

slitta ['zlitta] *sf* sleigh, sledge; (*tec*) slide. **slittare** *v* slip; (*ruote*) skid; (*scivolare*) slide.

slogan ['zlɔgan] *sm invar* slogan.
slogare [zlo'gare] *v* dislocate. **slogatura** *sf* dislocation.
sloggiare [zlod'dʒare] *v* dislodge.
smacchiare [zmak'kjare] *v* clean. **smacchiatore** *sm* stain-remover. **smacchiatura** *sf* cleaning.
smacco ['zmakko] *sm* defeat.
smagliante [zmaʎ'ʎante] *agg* dazzling.
smagliarsi [zmaʎ'ʎarsi] *v* (*calze*) ladder; (*pelle*) stretch.
smagrire [zma'grire] *v* slim.
smaltare [zmal'tare] *v* enamel; (*unghie*) paint; (*ceramica*) glaze. **smalto** *sm* enamel; glaze; (*per le unghie*) nail-varnish.
smaltire [zmal'tire] *v* digest; (*fig*) swallow; (*comm*) dispose of.
smanceroso [zmantʃe'rozo] *agg* affected; (*smorfioso*) mawkish. **smanceria** *sf* affectation.
smania ['zmanja] *sf* craving; (*agitazione*) frenzy. **aver la smania addosso** fidget.
smaniare *v* (*essere agitato*) fret; (*essere furioso*) rave; (*desiderare*) crave (for).
smantellare [zmantel'lare] *v* dismantle; (*fig*) pull to pieces.
smargiassata [zmardʒas'sata] *sf* brag; bravado. **smargiasso, -a** *sm, sf* braggart. **fare lo smargiasso** brag.
smarrire [zmar'rire] *v* lose; (*non riuscire a trovare*) mislay. **smarrirsi** *v* (*persone*) lose one's way; (*cose*) be mislaid, go astray. **smarrimento** *sm* loss; (*svenimento*) fainting-fit; (*turbamento*) bewilderment.
smascherare [zmaske'rare] *v* unmask, reveal. **smascheramento** *sm* unmasking.
smembrare [zmem'brare] *v* dismember.
smemorato [zmemo'rato], **-a** *agg* forgetful; (*distratto*) absent-minded. *sm, sf* forgetful *or* absent-minded person. **smemorataggine** *sf* forgetfulness; (*dimenticanza*) lapse of memory. **smemoratezza** *sf* forgetfulness; absent-mindedness.
smentire [zmen'tire] *v* deny; (*ritrattare*) retract; (*dimostrare la falsità*) belie. **smentita** *sf* denial.
smeraldo [zme'raldo] *sm* emerald. *agg invar* (*colore*) emerald-green.
smerciare [zmer'tʃare] *v* sell. **smercio** *sf* sale.
smerigliare [zmeri'ʎare] *v* (*mec*) grind; (*vetro*) frost. **carta smerigliata** *sf* (*grossa*) emery paper; (*fine*) sandpaper. **vetro smerigliato** *sm* frosted glass. **smeriglio** *sm* emery.

smerlare [zmer'lare] *v* scallop. **smerlo** *sm* scallop.
*smettere ['zmettere] *v* stop.
smidollato [zmidol'lato] *agg* spineless.
smilitarizzare [zmilitarid'dzare] *v* demilitarize. **smilitarizzazione** *sf* demilitarization.
smilzo ['zmiltso] *agg* lean.
sminuire [zminu'ire] *v* diminish; (*fig*) belittle.
sminuzzare [zminut'tsare] *v* break into small pieces; (*sbriciolare*) crumble.
smistare [zmis'tare] *v* sort (out); (*ferr*) shunt.
smisurato [zmizu'rato] *agg* boundless; enormous.
smobilitare [zmobili'tare] *v* demobilize. **smobilitazione** *sf* demobilization.
smoderato [zmode'rato] *agg also* **smodato** immoderate. **smoderatezza** *sf* lack of moderation; excess.
smoking ['zmɔkiŋ] *sm invar* dinner-jacket.
smontare [zmon'tare] *v* (*scomporre*) dismantle, take apart; (*totalmente*) strip; (*da veicoli*) get out *or* off. **smontaggio** *sm* dismantling; stripping.
smorfia ['zmɔrfja] *sf* wry face. **fare una smorfia** pull a face; (*di dolore*) wince with pain. **smorfioso** *agg* simpering.
smorto ['zmɔrto] *agg* pale, wan; (*fig*) colourless.
smorzare [zmor'tsare] *v* (*colori*) tone down; (*suoni*) muffle; (*luce*) dim; (*fig*) dampen. **smorzata** *sf* (*tennis*) drop-shot.
smunto ['zmunto] *agg* emaciated.
*smuovere ['zmwɔvere] *v* shift; (*commuovere*) touch; dissuade.
smussare [zmus'sare] *v* smooth; (*angolo*) round off; (*fig*) soften. **smussarsi** *v* become blunt.
snaturare [znatu'rare] *v* distort. **snaturato** *agg* unnatural; degenerate.
snazionalizzare [znatsjonalid'dzare] *v* denationalize. **snazionalizzazione** *sf* denationalization.
snellire [znel'lire] *v* slim (down); simplify; speed up. **snellezza** *sf* slimness. **snello** *agg* slim; (*agile*) nimble; simple, easy.
snervare [zner'vare] *v* exhaust.
snidare [zni'dare] *v* drive out.
snob ['znɔb] *agg, s(m+f) invar* snob. **snobbare** *v* snub. **snobismo** *sm* snobbery.
snocciolare [znottʃo'lare] *v* stone; (*fam: spendere*) shell out; (*fam: spiattellare*) rattle off.

snodare [zno'dare] v unknot; (articolare meglio) loosen (up); (piegare) bend. **snodabile** agg (tec) articulated. **snodato** agg flexible, loose.

soave [so'ave] agg delicate, sweet. **soavità** sf sweetness, delicacy.

sobbalzare [sobbal'tsare] v jolt; (trasalire) jump. **di sobbalzo** with a start.

sobbarcarsi [sobbar'karsi] v undertake.

sobbollire [sobbol'lire] v simmer.

sobborgo [sob'borgo] sm suburb.

sobillare [sobil'lare] v incite, stir up. **sobillatore, -trice** sm, sf trouble-maker.

sobrio ['sɔbrjo] agg sober. **sobrietà** sf sobriety.

***socchiudere** [sok'kjudere] v half-close. **socchiuso** agg half-closed; (porta) ajar.

soccombere [sok'kombere] v succumb.

***soccorrere** [sok'korrere] v assist; come to the aid of; (salvare) rescue.

soccorritore [sokkorri'tore], **-trice** agg helping. sm, sf helper.

soccorso [sok'korso] sm help, assistance; rescue. **pronto soccorso** first aid; (all'ospedale) casualty ward. **soccorsi** sm pl (rinforzi) reinforcements pl; (rifornimenti) supplies pl.

socialdemocratico [sotʃaldemo'kratiko], **-a** sm, sf social democrat. **socialdemocrazia** sf social democracy.

sociale [so'tʃale] agg social; (benessere) welfare; (comm) relating to a firm, company. **assistente sociale** s(m+f) welfare officer, social worker. **assistenza sociale** sf welfare. **tessera sociale** sf membership card.

socialismo [sotʃa'lizmo] sm socialism. **socialista** agg, s(m+f) socialist.

società [sotʃe'ta] sf society; (comm) company, partnership; association. **gioco di società** sm parlour game. **mettersi in società** go into partnership. **società anonima** limited company. **società dei consumi** consumer society. **società per azioni** limited company.

socievole [so'tʃevole] agg social; (persona) sociable. **socievolezza** sf sociability.

socio ['sɔtʃo], **-a** sm, sf partner; member.

sociologia [sotʃolo'dʒia] sf sociology. **sociologico** agg sociological. **sociologo, -a** sm, sf sociologist.

soda ['sɔda] sf soda.

sodalizio [soda'litsjo] sm brotherhood; (amicizia) fellowship.

***soddisfare** [soddis'fare] v satisfy; (appagare) gratify; (riparare) make amends for. **soddisfacente** agg satisfactory; satisfying. **soddisfatto** agg satisfied; (contento) pleased. **soddisfazione** sf satisfaction. **bella satisfazione!** big deal!

sodio ['sɔdjo] sm sodium.

sodo ['sɔdo] agg firm; (fig) sound. **uovo sodo** sm hard-boiled egg. avv hard; (profondamente) soundly.

sofà [so'fa] sf sofa, settee.

sofferente [soffe'rɛnte] agg suffering. **sofferenza** sf suffering.

soffermarsi [soffer'marsi] v linger (over).

soffiare [sof'fjare] v blow; (sbuffare) puff; (dama, scacchi) huff. **soffiare di rabbia** fume (with rage). **soffio** sm puff; (med) murmur. **in un soffio** in a flash. **per un soffio** by a whisker.

soffice ['sɔffitʃe] agg soft.

soffietto [sof'fjetto] sm bellows pl; (fam: articoletto) plug. **a soffietto** folding. **lavorar di soffietto** (fam) tell tales.

soffitta [sof'fitta] sf attic.

soffitto [sof'fitto] sm ceiling.

soffocare [soffo'kare] v suffocate, choke; (reprimere) suppress, stifle. **soffocamento** sm suffocation.

***soffriggere** [sof'friddʒere] v brown.

***soffrire** [sof'frire] v suffer (from); (sopportare) bear, stand; (consentire) allow. **soffrire la fame** go hungry. **soffrir di (mal di) cuore** have heart trouble.

sofisma [so'fizma] sm sophistry. **sofisticare** v (sottilizzare) quibble; (fam) split hairs; (adulterare) doctor.

soggetto [sod'dʒetto] sm subject; (argomento) topic; person. **recitare a soggetto** improvise. agg subject, liable; (sottomesso) subjected; (predisposto) prone. **soggettivo** agg subjective. **soggezione** sf subjection; embarrassment; (timore) awe. **aver soggezione di** (sentirsi imbarrazzato) feel uneasy in the presence of; (averne timore) be overawed by. **ispirare soggezione a** make uneasy; overawe.

sogghignare [soggi'nare] v sneer.

***soggiacere** [soddʒa'tʃere] v be subjected; succumb.

soggiorno [sod'dʒorno] sm stay; (luogo) resort; (stanza) living room. **permesso di soggiorno** sm residence permit. **soggiornare** v stay.

***soggiungere** [sod'dʒundʒere] v add.

soglia ['sɔʎa] *sf* threshold.
sogliola ['sɔʎola] *sf* sole.
sognare [so'ɲare] *v* dream; (*ad occhi aperti*) daydream. **sognatore, -trice** *sm, sf* dreamer. **sogno** *sm* dream. **fare un sogno** have a dream. **neanche per sogno!** not likely!
soia ['sɔja] *sf* soya (bean).
solaio [so'lajo] *sm* (*soffitta*) loft; (*piano di edificio*) floor.
solare [so'lare] *agg* solar. **luce solare** *sf* sunlight.
solco ['solko] *sm* (*agric*) furrow; (*traccia*) track; (*lampo*) streak; (*disco*) groove.
soldato [sol'dato] *sm* soldier. **andare soldato** join up. **fare il soldato** be in the army.
soldo ['sɔldo] *sm* penny. **soldi** *sm pl* (*denaro*) money *sing*. **essere al soldo di** be in the pay of. **essere senza soldi** be penniless.
sole ['sole] *sm* sun. **al sole** in the sun. **chiaro come il sole** clear as daylight. **fare un bagno di sole** sunbathe. **occhiali da sole** *sm pl* sun-glasses *pl*. **soleggiato** *agg* sunny.
solenne [so'lɛnne] *agg* solemn; (*fig*) tremendous. **solennità** *sf* solemnity; (*festa*) holiday. **solennizzare** *v* solemnize.
*****solere** [so'lere] *v* be in the habit of.
soletta [so'letta] *sf* sole; (*suola interna*) insole.
solfato [sol'fato] *sm* sulphate. **solforico** *agg* sulphuric. **solfuro** *sm* sulphide.
solidale [soli'dale] *agg* (*tec*) integral; (*d'accordo*) in agreement (with); (*dir*) joint. **solidarietà** *sf* solidarity.
solidificare [solidifi'kare] *v* harden. **solidificarsi** *v* set. **solidificazione** *sf* hardening; setting.
solido ['sɔlido] *agg* solid; stable; (*robusto, valido*) sound; (*colori*) fast. *sm* solid. **solidità** *sf* solidity; stability; soundness; fastness.
soliloquio [soli'lɔkwjo] *sm* soliloquy.
solista [so'lista] *s(m + f)* soloist.
solitario [soli'tarjo], **-a** *agg* solitary. *sm, sf* loner. *sm* (*brillante, gioco*) solitaire.
solito ['sɔlito], **-a** *agg* usual. *pron* same. *sm* (*abitudine*) habit; (*cosa*) usual. **come al solito** as usual. **di solito** usually, as a rule. **essere solito a fare** be used to doing.
solitudine [soli'tudine] *sf* solitude.
sollazzare [sollat'tsare] *v* amuse.

sollecitare [solletʃi'tare] *v* press for; (*affrettare*) speed up; (*mec*) stress; (*chiedere con insistenza*) solicit. **sollecitazione** *sf* solicitation, entreaty; (*mec*) stress. **lettera di sollecitazione** *sf* reminder.
sollecito [sol'letʃito] *agg* (*fatto con premura*) prompt; (*premuroso*) solicitous. **sollecitudine** *sm* (*prontezza*) dispatch; (*preoccupazione*) solicitude.
solleticare [solleti'kare] *v* tickle; (*fig*) arouse. **solletico** *sm* tickle. **fare il solletico** tickle. **sentire** *or* **soffrire il solletico** be ticklish.
sollevare [solle'vare] *v* raise; (*tirar su*) lift (up). **sollevarsi** *v* rise; (*riprendersi*) recover.
sollievo [sol'ljɛvo] *sm* relief.
solo ['solo] *agg* alone; by oneself; (*unico*) only, sole; (*semplice*) mere; (*musica*) unaccompanied. *avv* (*soltanto*) only; (*ma*) but. **da solo** alone, by oneself. **solo che** only. **solo soletto** quite alone. **una sola volta** once only. **un solo** just one, only one.
solstizio [sol'stitsjo] *sm* solstice.
soltanto [sol'tanto] *avv* only.
solubile [so'lubile] *agg* soluble. **solubilità** *sf* solubility. **soluzione** *sf* solution.
solvente [sol'vɛnte] *agg, sm* solvent. **solvibile** *agg* (*comm*) solvent. **solvibilità** *sm* (*comm*) solvency.
soma ['sɔma] *sf* burden.
somaro [so'maro] *sm* donkey.
somigliare [somi'ʎare] *v* resemble, be like. **somigliante** *agg* similar. **somiglianza** *sf* resemblance.
somma ['somma] *sf* sum. **fare la somma** add up. **tirare le somme** sum up. **sommare** *v* add *or* sum up. **tutto sommato** all things considered.
sommario [som'marjo] *agg* brief; (*dir*) summary. *sm* summary, outline.
*****sommergere** [som'mɛrdʒere] *v* submerge. **sommergibile** *sm* submarine.
sommesso [som'messo] *agg* meek.
somministrare [somminis'trare] *v* administer.
sommità [sommi'ta] *sf* peak, summit.
sommo ['sommo] *agg* highest; (*fig*) supreme. *sm* peak.
sommossa [som'mɔssa] *sf* riot.
sommozzatore [sommottsa'tore] *sm* skin-diver; (*mil*) frogman.

sonaglio [sc'naʎo] *sm* bell. **serpente a sonagli** *sm* rattlesnake.

sonare [so'nare] *v also* **suonare** sound; (*campanello*) ring; (*musica*) play; (*orologio*) strike; (*fam: imbrogliare*) cheat.

sonata *sf* (*musica*) sonata; (*fam: bastonatura*) caning; (*fam: fregatura*) swindle. **prendersi una sonata** be taken in.

sonato *agg* (*compiuto*) past; (*rimbambito*) gaga.

sonda ['sonda] *sf* probe. **sondaggio** *sm* probing, sounding; (*indagine*) poll.

sondare *v* sound, probe.

sonnambulo [son'nambulo], **-a** *sm, sf* sleep-walker.

sonnecchiare [sonnek'kjare] *v* doze.

sonnifero [son'nifero] *agg* soporific. *sm* sleeping pill.

sonno ['sonno] *sm* sleep; (*senso di torpore*) drowsiness. **aver sonno** be sleepy. **fare un bel sonno** have a good sleep. **sonnolento** *agg* sleepy, drowsy.

sonnolenza *sf* drowsiness.

sonoro [so'nɔro] *agg* sound; (*che risona*) resonant; (*consonanti*) voiced. **sonorità** *sf* resonance; (*fis*) acoustics *pl*.

sontuoso [sontu'ozo] *agg* sumptuous. **sontuosità** *sf* sumptuousness.

soporifero [sopo'rifero] *agg, sm* soporific.

sopperire [soppe'rire] *v* provide for.

soppesare [soppe'zare] *v* weigh up.

soppiantare [soppjan'tare] *v* supplant.

soppiatto [sop'pjatto] *agg* **di soppiatto** stealthily. **entrare/uscire di soppiatto** steal in/away.

sopportare [soppor'tare] *v* (*reggere*) support; (*fig*) bear, stand. **sopportabile** *agg* bearable. **sopportazione** *sf* endurance.

*****sopprimere** [sop'primere] *v* suppress; abolish. **soppressione** *sf* suppression; abolition.

sopra ['sopra] *prep* on, upon; (*senza contatto diretto*) over, above. **al di sopra di** above; (*oltre*) beyond. *avv* on; (*più in su*) above; (*al piano superiore*) upstairs. **come/vedi sopra** (*nei rinvii*) as/see above.

soprabito [so'prabito] *sm* overcoat.

sopracciglio [soprat'tʃiʎo] *sm* eyebrow.

sopraccitato [soprattʃi'tato] *agg* above-mentioned.

sopraccoperta [soprakko'pɛrta] *sf* (*letto*) counterpane; (*libro*) dust-jacket.

*****sopraffare** [sopraf'fare] *v* overcome; dominate.

sopraffino [sopraf'fino] *agg* excellent; highly refined.

sopraggiungere [soprad'dʒundʒere] *v* turn up; (*accadere improvvisamente*) happen, arise.

sopralluogo [sopral'lwɔgo] *sm, pl* **-ghi** (on the spot) inspection; (*statistica*) poll.

sopralzo [so'praltso] *sm* extension.

soprammobile [sopram'mɔbile] *sm* knick-knack.

soprannaturale [soprannatu'rale] *agg, sm* supernatural.

soprannome [sopran'nome] *sm* nickname. **soprannominare** *v* call.

soprannumero [sopran'numero] *sm* excess.

soprano [so'prano], **-a** *sm, sf* soprano.

soprappensiero [soprappen'sjɛro] *avv* lost in thought.

soprappiù [soprap'pju] *sm* surplus; (*aggiunta*) addition. **di** *or* **per soprappiù** in addition, besides.

soprapprezzo [soprap'prettso] *sm* (*econ*) premium; (*maggiorazione*) increase in price.

soprassalto [sopras'salto] *sm* sudden start. **di soprassalto** suddenly.

soprassedere [soprasse'dere] *v* put off.

soprattassa [soprat'tassa] *sf* additional charge.

soprattutto [soprat'tutto] *avv* above all; (*per la maggior parte*) mainly.

sopravanzare [sopravan'tsare] *v* be left over.

sopravvalutare [sopravvalu'tare] *v* overrate. **sopravvalutazione** *sf* overestimate.

*****sopravvenire** [sopravve'nire] *v* turn up; (*accadere d'improvviso*) happen, arise.

sopravvento [soprav'vɛnto] *agg, avv* windward. *sm* (*fig*) upper hand.

*****sopravvivere** [soprav'vivere] *v* survive. **sopravvissuto, -a** *sm, sf* survivor. **sopravvivenza** *sf* survival.

soprelevare [soprele'vare] *v* raise.

*****soprintendere** [soprin'tendere] *v* supervise; be in charge of. **soprintendente** *s(m+f)* superintendent. **soprintendenza** *sf* (*atto*) supervision; (*ufficio*) superintendence.

sopruso [so'pruzo] *sm* outrage.

soqquadro [sok'kwadro] *sm* **mettere a soqquadro** turn upside down.

sorbetto [sor'betto] *sm* sorbet, water ice.

sorbire [sor'bire] *v* sip. **sorbirsi** *v* (*sopportare*) put up with.

sorcio ['sortʃo] *sm* mouse (*pl* mice).

sordido ['sordido] *agg* sordid. **sordidezza** *sf* sordidness.

sordina [sor'dina] *sf* (*musica*) mute. **in sordina** (*fig*) on the quiet.

sordo ['sordo], **-a** *agg* deaf; (*smorzato*) dull; (*fig*) hidden. **sordo come una campana** deaf as a post. *sm, sf* deaf person. **fare il sordo** feign deafness. **sordità** *sf* deafness.

sordomuto [sordo'muto], **-a** *agg* deaf and dumb. *sm, sf* deaf-mute.

sorella [so'rella] *sf* sister. **sorellastra** *sf* step-sister, half-sister.

*sorgere ['sordʒere] *v* rise; (*aver origine*) arise. **sorgente** *sf* source. **acqua sorgiva** *sf* spring water.

soriano [so'rjano] *sm, agg* tabby.

sormontare [sormon'tare] *v* surmount; (*stoffa*) overlap.

sornione [sor'njone] *agg* sly.

sorpassare [sorpas'sare] *v* (*oltrepassare*) overtake; (*eccedere*) exceed. **sorpassare in altezza/lunghezza** be higher/longer. **sorpassato** *agg* (*non più attuale*) out of date. **sorpasso** *sm* overtaking. **divieto di sorpasso** *sm* no overtaking.

*sorprendere [sor'prendere] *v* surprise; (*cogliere all'improvviso*) catch. **sorprendente** *agg* surprising. **sorpresa** *sf* surprise.

*sorreggere [sor'reddʒere] *v* hold up; sustain. **sorreggersi** *v* stand upright.

*sorridere [sor'ridere] *v* smile; (*destar piacere*) appeal. **sorridente** *agg* smiling. **sorriso** *sm* smile.

sorso ['sorso] *sm* (*sorsata*) sip; (*d'un fiato*) gulp; (*piccola quantità*) drop. **sorseggiare** *v also* **bere a piccoli sorsi** sip.

sorta ['sorta] *sf* kind, sort. **di sorta** (*di nessun tipo*) whatever.

sorte ['sorte] *sf* fate; fortune; (*condizione propria*) lot. **sorteggiare** *v also* **tirare a sorte** draw lots. **sorteggio** *sm* draw.

sortilegio [sorti'ledʒo] *sm* spell.

sorvegliare [sorve'ʎare] *v* watch; (*sovrintendere*) oversee; (*vigilare*) keep an eye on. **sorvegliante** *s*(*m+f*) overseer; (*custode*) caretaker; (*guardiano*) watchman. **sorveglianza** *sf* surveillance, watch.

sorvolare [sorvo'lare] *v* fly over; (*fig*) skip.

sosia ['sozja] *sm invar* double.

*sospendere [sos'pendere] *v* suspend; (*attaccare in alto*) hang; interrupt; (*seduta*) adjourn; defer. **sospendere il lavoro** stop work. **sospensione** *sf* suspension; interruption; (*cessazione*) stoppage. **sospeso** *agg* hanging; (*non definito*) outstanding. **col fiato sospeso** with bated breath. **in sospeso** in suspense; (*non risolto*) pending.

sospettare [sospet'tare] *v* suspect; (*diffidare*) distrust, be suspicious (of). **sospetto** [sos'petto] *agg* suspect, suspicious. **persona sospetta** *sf* suspect. *sm* suspicion. **sospettoso** *agg* distrustful.

*sospingere [sos'pindʒere] *v* push; (*fig*) drive. **a ogni piè sospinto** at every step.

sospirare [sospi'rare] *v* sigh; (*aspettare con ansia*) long *or* yearn for. **sospiro** *sm* sigh.

sosta ['sosta] *sf* stop; pause; (*riposo*) rest; (*aspettare*) wait. **divieto di sosta** no waiting. **senza sosta** ceaselessly; without stopping. **sostare** *v* stop; pause; wait; rest.

sostantivo [sostan'tivo] *agg* substantive. *sm* noun.

sostanza [sos'tantsa] *sf* matter; (*parte utile*) substance; (*parte nutritiva*) nourishment; (*patrimonio*) property. **cibo di sostanza** nourishing food. **in sostanza** essentially; **sostanza alimentare** foodstuff. **sostanziale** *agg* substantial; essential. **sostanzioso** *agg* nourishing.

sostegno [sos'teɲo] *sm* support.

*sostenere [soste'nere] *v* support; (*asserire*) maintain; (*tenere alto*) keep up; (*tollerare*) stand. **sostenere una carica** hold an office. **sostenere una parte** act a part. **sostenersi** *v* (*star su*) hold oneself up, stand up; (*fig*) hold water. **sostenibile** *agg* tenable.

sostenitore [sosteni'tore], **-trice** *agg* supporting. *sm, sf* supporter.

*sostentare [sosten'tare] *v* support; maintain. **sostentamento** *sm* support; maintenance.

sostenuto [soste'nuto] *agg* (*contegnoso*) reserved; (*musica*) sostenuto. **sostenutezza** *sf* reserve.

sostituire [sostitu'ire] *v* substitute; (*rimpiazzare*) replace. **sostituto, -a** *sm, sf* deputy, substitute. **sostituzione** *sf* substitution; replacement.

sottaceto [sotta'tʃeto] *avv* **mettere sottaceto** pickle. **sottaceti** *sm pl* pickles *pl*.

sottalimentazione [sottalimenta'tsjone] *sf* undernourishment.

sottana [sot'tana] *sf* skirt; (*sottoveste*) slip, underskirt; (*rel*) cassock.

sottecchi [sot'tekki] *avv* **di sottecchi** stealthily.

sottentrare [sotten'trare] *v* replace.

sotterfugio [sotter'fudʒo] *sm* subterfuge.

sotterraneo [sotter'raneo] *agg* underground. *sm* basement. **sotterranea** *sf* underground (railway); (*fam*) tube.

sotterrare [sotter'rare] *v* bury. **sotterra** *avv* underground.

sottile [sot'tile] *agg* thin; fine; (*acuto*) sharp. **sottigliezza** *sf* thinness; sharpness; (*sofisticheria*) nicety.

sottinsù [sottin'su] *avv* **di sottinsù** from below.

***sottintendere** [sottin'tɛndere] *v* imply, infer; (*non esprimere*) leave out. **sottinteso** *agg* implied; (*chiaro da sè*) understood. *sm* allusion. **senza sottintesi** plainly.

sotto ['sotto] *prep* under; (*al di sotto di*) below, beneath; (*in cambio di*) on. *avv* underneath, below; (*al piano di sotto*) downstairs. **andar sotto le armi** join up. **metter sotto** (*investire*) run down. **mettersi sotto** get down to. **sotto la pioggia** in the rain. **sotto questo punto di vista** from this point of view. **sotto questo riguardo** in this respect. **sotto sotto** deep down.

sottobanco [sotto'banko] *avv* under the counter.

sottobicchiere [sottobik'kjɛre] *sm* mat, coaster.

sottobraccio [sotto'brattʃo] *avv* arm-in-arm. **prendere sottobraccio qualcuno** take someone's arm.

sottocchio [sot'tɔkkjo] *avv* **tenere sottocchio** keep an eye on.

sottocommissione [sottokommis'sjone] *sf* subcommittee; subcommission.

sottocoppa [sotto'kɔppa] *sm invar* mat; (*piattino*) saucer.

***sottoesporre** [sottoes'porre] *v* underexpose.

sottofondo [sotto'fondo] *sm* foundation; (*suono*) background noise. **musica in sottofondo** *sf* background music.

sottolineare [sottoline'are] *v* underline; (*fig*) stress.

sottomano [sotto'mano] *avv* (*a portata di mano*) within (easy) reach, on hand; (*di nascosto*) on the quiet; (*sport*) underhand.

***sottomettere** [sotto'mettere] *v* (*assoggettare*) subject; (*costringere a sottostare*) subdue; subordinate. **sottomettersi** *v* submit. **sottomesso** *agg* subdued; (*obbediente*) submissive.

sottopassaggio [sottopas'saddʒo] *sm* underpass.

***sottoporre** [sotto'porre] *v* (*presentare*) submit; (*costringere*) subject, expose. **sottoporsi a un'operazione** undergo an operation. **sottoposto, -a** *sm, sf* subordinate.

sottoprodotto [sottopro'dotto] *sm* by-product.

sottordine [sot'tordine] *sm* suborder. **in sottordine** of minor importance.

***sottoscrivere** [sotto'skrivere] *v* sign; (*fig*) support; (*econ*) underwrite, subscribe. **sottoscritto, -a** *sm, sf* undersigned; (*fam*) yours truly. **sottoscrizione** *sf* subscription.

sottosopra [sotto'sopra] *avv* upside down.

***sottostare** [sotto'stare] *v* be under; (*sottomettersi*) give in. **sottostante** *agg* (down) below.

sottosuolo [sotto'swɔlo] *sm* subsoil.

sottoterra [sotto'tɛrra] *avv* underground.

sottotitolo [sotto'titolo] *sm* subtitle.

sottovalutare [sottovalu'tare] *v* underestimate.

sottoveste [sotto'vɛste] *sf* slip.

sottovoce [sotto'votʃe] *avv* in a low voice, softly.

***sottrarre** [sot'trarre] *v* remove; (*mat*) subtract; (*salvare*) save (from). **sottrarsi a** escape; (*evitare*) avoid. **sottrazione** *sf* subtraction; removal.

sottufficiale [sottuffi'tʃale] *sm* non-commissioned officer; (*mar*) petty officer.

sovente [so'vɛnte] *avv* also **di sovente** frequently.

soverchio [so'vɛrkjo] *agg* excessive. **soverchieria** *sf* bullying; (*sopruso*) outrage.

sovietico [so'vjɛtiko], **-a** *s, agg* Soviet.

sovrabbondante [sovrabbon'dante] *agg* plentiful; excessive. **sovrabbondanza** *sf* plenty; excess.

sovraccaricare [sovrakkari'kare] *v* overburden; (*tec*) overload. **sovraccarica** *sf* overcharge. **sovraccarico** *agg, m pl* **-chi** overloaded.

*sovr(a)esporre [sovr(a)es'porre] *v* over-expose. **sovresposizione** *sf* over-exposure.
sovraffollato [sovraffol'lato] *agg* over-crowded.
sovrano [so'vrano], **-a** *agg* sovereign, supreme. *sm, sf* sovereign. **sovranità** *sf* sovereignty; (*fig*) supremacy.
sovrappopolato [sovrappopo'lato] *agg* overpopulated.
*sovrapporre [sovrap'porre] *v* superimpose; (*fig*) set over; (*accavallare*) overlap.
sovrastante [sovra'stante] *agg* towering; (*imminente*) impending.
sovreccitare [sovrettʃi'tare] *v* over-excite. **sovreccitarsi** *v* become over-excited. **sovreccitazione** *sf* over-excitement.
sovrumano [sovru'mano] *agg* superhuman.
sovvenzione [sovven'tsjone] *sf* subsidy. **sovvenzionare** *v* subsidize.
sovversione [sovver'sjone] *sf* subversion. **sovversivo, -a** *s, agg* subversive. **sovvertire** *v* subvert.
sozzo ['sottso] *agg* filthy; (*fig*) loathsome. **sozzura** *sf* filth; loathsomeness.
spaccare ['spakkare] *v* (*fendere*) split; (*rompere*) break; (*legna*) chop. **spaccarsi** *v* split (open); break (up). **spaccare il minuto** be dead on time. **fare la spaccata** do the splits. **spacco** *sm* split; (*strappo*) tear; (*giacca*) vent.
spacciare ['spattʃare] *v* (*vendere*) sell off; (*mettere in circolazione*) peddle; (*dichiarar inguaribile*) give up. **spacciato** *agg* (*fam: rovinato*) done for. **spacciatore, -trice** *sm, sf* pedlar; (*di droghe*) pusher; (*di notizie false*) rumour-monger. **spaccio** *sm* sale; (*negozio*) shop; (*mil, fabbrica*) canteen.
spaccone [spak'kone] *sm* braggart. **fare lo spaccone** brag.
spada ['spada] *sf* sword; (*sport*) épée. **a spada tratta** vigorously. **pesce spada** *sm* sword-fish. **tirar di spada** fence. **spadaccino** *sm* swordsman. **spadista** *s(m+f)* fencer.
spadroneggiare [spadroned'dʒare] *v* be bossy.
spaesato [spae'zato] *agg* lost.
Spagna ['spaɲa] *sf* Spain. **spagnolo, -a** *agg, sm* Spanish; *sm, sf* (*abitante*) Spaniard.
spago ['spago] *sm* string, twine.
spalancare [spalan'kare] *v* open wide.

spalancare gli orecchi prick up one's ears. **spalancato** *agg* wide open.
spalare [spa'lare] *v* shovel.
spalla ['spalla] *sf* shoulder; (*dorso*) back. **alle spalle di** (*stato*) behind; (*moto*) from behind. **aver le spalle grosse** be broad-shouldered. **aver sulle spalle** (*fig*) be responsible for. **alzar le spalle** shrug one's shoulders. **ridere alle spalle di qualcuno** laugh behind someone's back. **vivere alle spalle di** live off. **spallata** *sf* (*spinta*) push with the shoulder; (*alzata di spalle*) shrug. **spalletta** *sf* parapet.
spalmare [spal'mare] *v* spread.
spanare [spa'nare] *v* strip.
spanciare [span'tʃare] *v* bulge. **spanciarsi dalle risa** split one's sides laughing.
*spandere ['spandere] *v* (*versare*) shed; (*involontariamente*) spill; (*stendere, divulgare*) spread.
spanna ['spanna] *sf* span.
spappolare [spappo'lare] *v* crush.
sparare [spa'rare] *v* fire; (*tirare*) shoot. **sparare grosse** (*fam*) shoot a line; tell tall stories. **sparata** *sf* volley. **sparo** *sm* shot.
sparecchiare [sparek'kjare] *v* clear (away).
spareggio [spa'reddʒo] *sm* (*sport*) decider.
*spargere ['spardʒere] *v* scatter; (*versare*) shed; (*involontariamente*) spill; (*sale, pepe, ecc.*) sprinkle; (*diffondere*) spread.
*sparire [spa'rire] *v* disappear. **far sparire** (*nascondere*) hide; (*fam: rubare*) pinch.
sparlare [spar'lare] *v* speak ill (of).
sparo ['sparo] *sm* shot.
sparpagliare [sparpa'ʎare] *v* scatter.
spartire [spar'tire] *v* divide; (*in parti*) share out; (*musica*) score. **spartiacque** *sm invar* watershed. **spartineve** *sm invar* snow-plough. **spartitraffico** *sm* traffic island. **spartito** *sm* score.
sparuto [spa'ruto] *agg* gaunt; (*esiguo*) scanty.
sparviere [spar'vjɛre] *sm* sparrow-hawk.
spasimare [spazi'mare] *v* suffer agonies; (*fig*) crave, long (for). **spasimo** *sm* pang; (*med*) spasm. **spasmodico** *agg* spasmodic.
spassarsela [spas'sarsela] *v* enjoy oneself.
spassionato [spassjo'nato] *agg* dispassionate.
spasso ['spasso] *sm* fun. **andare a spasso** go for a walk. **mandare a spasso** (*fam: licenziare*) sack; (*fam: liberarsene*) get rid of. **portare a spasso** take for a walk. **quel**

ragazzo è uno spasso! that boy is a
scream! spassoso agg amusing.
spastico ['spastiko], -a s, agg spastic.
spasticità sf spasticity.
spatola ['spatola] sf spatula; (di pittore)
palette-knife; (zool) spoonbill.
spatriare [spatri'are] v expatriate.
spaurire [spau'rire] v scare. spauracchio
sm scarecrow.
spavaldo [spa'valdo] agg defiant;
(baldanzoso) bold; (arrogante) cocky.
spavalderia sf defiance; boldness; cocki-
ness.
spaventare [spaven'tare] v frighten, scare.
spaventarsi v get frightened, get scared.
spaventapasseri sm scarecrow.
spaventevole agg terrifying. spavento sm
fright. fare spavento frighten, scare.
prendersi uno spavento have a fright.
spaventoso agg frightful; (terribile)
dreadful; (enorme) tremendous.
spazientirsi [spatsjen'tirsi] v lose one's
patience.
spazio ['spatsjo] sm space; (estensione
limitata) room; distance. spaziale agg
space, spatial. spaziare v space; (fig)
range. spazioso agg roomy.
spazzare [spat'tsare] v sweep; (spazzar
via) sweep away. spazzacamino sm chimney-sweep. spazzaneve sm invar snow-
plough. spazzatura sf cleaning; sweeping; (rifiuti) rubbish. spazzaturaio sm
dustman. spazzino sm road sweeper.
spazzola ['spattsola] sf brush. capelli a
spazzola crew-cut. spazzola per capelli
hairbrush. spazzolare v brush. spazzolino
da denti/unghie sm tooth-/nail-brush.
spazzolone (per lavare) scrubbing brush.
specchio ['spekkjo] sm mirror; model;
(prospetto) table; summary. specchio
d'acqua sheet of water. specchio
retrovisore driving mirror. specchiarsi v
(guardarsi) look at oneself in the mirror;
(riflettersi) be reflected. specchiato agg
(fig) exemplary. specchiera sf large mirror; (toletta) dressing-table. specchietto
sm small mirror; (tavola) table, summary.
speciale [spe'tʃale] agg special; particular; (fuori del solito) peculiar. specialista
s(m+f) specialist. specialità sf speciality;
(prodotto speciale) specialty; (farmaceuti-
ca) proprietary medicine. specializzarsi v
specialize. specializzato agg specialized;

(operaio) skilled; (medico) specialist.
specializzazione sf specialization.
specie ['spetʃe] sf invar kind, sort; (bot,
zool) species; surprise. mi fa specie it
surprises me. sotto specie di in the form
of.
specificare [spetʃifi'kare] v specify.
specifica sf detailed list. specificazione sf
specification. specifico agg specific.
speculare [speku'lare] v speculate. speculativo agg speculative. speculatore, -trice
sm, sf speculator; (di borsa) stockbroker.
speculazione sf speculation.
spedalità [spedali'ta] sf hospitalization.
spedire [spe'dire] v send; post; (inoltrare)
forward. spedire all'altro mondo (fam)
bump off. spedito agg (veloce) quick;
(corrente) fluent. speditore, -trice sm, sf
sender; (comm) shipper. spedizione sf
dispatch; (trasporto) shipment; (cosa
spedita) consignment. casa di spedizione
forwarding or shipping agents pl. fare
una spedizione send a consignment.
spedizioniere sm shipping or forwarding
agent.
*spegnere ['speɲere] v extinguish, put
out; (con interruttore) switch or turn off;
(sete) quench. spegnersi v go out;
(motore) stall.
spelacchiato [spelak'kjato] agg (con pochi
peli) mangy; (logoro) threadbare.
spellare [spel'lare] v skin; (escoriare)
graze. spellarsi v peel. spellatura sf skin-
ning; grazing; peeling.
spelonca [spe'lonka] sf hovel.
*spendere ['spendere] v spend. senza
spender fatica effortlessly. spendere
bene/male use one's money wise-
ly/unwisely. spendereccio agg extravagant.
spennacchiare [spennak'kjare] v also
spennare pluck; (fig) fleece.
spensierato [spensje'rato] agg carefree.
spensierataggine sf thoughtlessness; irresponsibility. spensieratezza sf light-
heartedness.
spento ['spento] agg out, off; (fig) dull.
spenzolare [spendzo'lare] v dangle.
speranza [spe'rantsa] sf hope. avere
buone speranze have high hopes. avere
una speranza have a chance. filo di speranza sm glimmer of hope. senza speranza
hopeless.
sperare [spe'rare] v hope; (aspettarsi)
expect. sperare (in) bene hope for the

best. **sperare in Dio** trust in God. **spero di no/sì** I hope not/so.

*sperdersi ['spɛrdersi] *v* get lost. **sperduto** *agg* lost; (*fuori mano*) out-of-the-way; (*solo*) lonely.

spergiurare [sperdʒu'rare] *v* commit perjury, perjure oneself. **spergiuro** *sm* perjury; (*persona*) perjurer.

spericolato [speriko'lato] *agg* reckless.

sperimentare [sperimen'tare] *v* experiment (with); (*mettere alla prova*) try out, test; (*farne esperienza*) experience. **sperimentale** *agg* experimental.

sperma ['sperma] *sm* sperm.

sperone [spe'rone] *sm* spur; (*mar*) ram. **sperone di cavaliere** larkspur. **speronare** *v* ram.

sperperare [sperpe'rare] *v* squander. **sperpero** *sm* waste.

sperticato [sperti'kato] *agg* (*fig*) excessive.

spesa ['speza] *sf* expenditure; (*costo*) expense; (*acquisto*) purchase; (*compra*) shopping. **a spese di** at the expense of. **con poca spesa** cheaply; (*fig*) easily. **conto spese** *sm* expense account. **far la spesa** go shopping. **non badare a spese** spare no expense. **senza spesa** free. **spese** *sf pl* cost *sing*, charges *pl*. **spese generali** overheads *pl*. **essere spesato** have one's expenses paid.

spesso ['spesso] *agg* thick. *avv* often, frequently. **spesse volte** very often, frequently. **spessore** *sm* thickness.

spettacolo [spet'takolo] *sm* show; (*rappresentazione*) performance; (*vista*) sight. **dare spettacolo di sè** make an exhibition of oneself. **spettacolo pomeridiano** matinée. **spettacoloso** *agg* spectacular.

spettare [spet'tare] *v* (*competere per dovere*) be up (to); (*appartenere per diritto*) be due (to); (*essere di pertinenza*) be the concern (of).

spettatore [spetta'tore], **-trice** *sm*, *sf* spectator; (*testimone*) witness. **spettatori** *sm pl* audience *sing*.

spettinare [spetti'nare] *v* ruffle the hair of. **spettinato** *agg* unkempt, dishevelled.

spettro ['spettro] *sm* ghost; (*fig*) spectrum.

spezie ['spɛtsje] *sf pl* spices *pl*.

spezzare [spet'tsare] *v* break; (*staccando*) break off; (*fare a pezzi*) break up; (*gastr*) cut up. **spezzatino** *sm* stew. **spezzettare** *v* chop (up). **spezzone incendiario** *sm* incendiary bomb.

spia ['spia] *sf* spy, informer; (*indizio*) sign; (*apertura*) spy-hole; (*tec*) warning light. **fare la spia** be a spy; (*polizia*) inform; (*riportare*) tell tales.

spiaccicare [spjattʃi'kare] *v* squash.

*spiacere [spja'tʃere] *v* displease. **mi spiace ...** I dislike .... **mi spiace di ...** (*rammarico*) I'm sorry .... **se non ti spiace** if you don't mind. **spiacevole** *agg* unpleasant, disagreeable; (*increscioso*) regrettable.

spiaggia ['spjaddʒa] *sf* (sea-)shore, beach.

spianare [spja'nare] *v* level-; (*render liscio*) smooth; (*radere al suolo*) flatten, raze (to the ground); (*fig*) iron out. **spianato** *agg* smooth. **spianatoia** *sf* pastry board. **spianatoio** *sm* rolling-pin. **a tutto spiano** flat out.

spiantare [spjan'tare] *v* uproot; (*rovinare*) ruin.

spiare [spi'are] *v* spy (on); (*aspettare*) look out for; explore.

spiazzo ['spjattso] *sm* open space; (*radura*) clearing.

spiccare [spik'kare] *v* pick; (*pronunciare distintamente*) spell out; (*dir*) issue; (*comm*) draw; (*risaltare*) stand out. **spiccare il volo** take off. **spiccato** *agg* distinct, marked; (*notevole*) striking. **spicco** *sm* prominence. **far spicco** catch the eye.

spicchio ['spikkjo] *sm* segment; (*aglio*) clove.

spicciare [spit'tʃare] *v* dispatch. **spicciarsi** *v* hurry up. **spicciativo** *agg* quick; (*brusco*) abrupt. **spiccio** *agg* swift. **alla spicciolata** in dribs and drabs. **spiccioli** *sm pl* (small) change *sing*. **spicciolo** *agg* small.

spiedo ['spjɛdo] *sm* spit. **spiedino** *sm* skewer.

spiegare [spje'gare] *v* (*distendere*) unfold; (*ali*) spread; (*vele*) unfurl; (*render chiaro*) explain. **spiegarsi** *v* (*capire*) understand; (*diventar comprensibile*) explain oneself, make oneself understood. **spieghiamoci!** let's get it straight! **spiegabile** *agg* explicable.

spiegazione [spjega'tsjone] *sf* explanation; (*ragione*) reason.

spiegazzare [spjegat'tsare] *v* crumple (up), crease.

spietato [spje'tato] *agg* (*senza pietà*) pitiless; (*accanito*) relentless.

spifferare [spiffe'rare] *v* blab, blurt out. **spiffero** *sm* (*fam*) draught.

spiga ['spiga] *sf* ear. **disegno a spiga** *sm* herringbone pattern.
spigliato [spi'ʎato] *agg* (free and) easy; (*padrone di sè*) self-possessed. **spigliatezza** *sf* ease.
spigola ['spigola] *sf* bass.
spigolare [spigo'lare] *v* glean. **spigolature** *sf pl* tit-bits *pl*.
spigolo ['spigolo] *sm* corner; edge.
spilla ['spilla] *sf* brooch. **spilla da cravatta** tie-pin.
spillare [spil'lare] *v* tap; (*attingere*) draw.
spillo ['spillo] *sm* pin. **spillo di sicurezza** safety-pin.
spilluzzicare [spilluttsi'kare] *v* nibble.
spilorcio [spi'lortʃo], **-a** *agg* stingy. *sm, sf* miser. **spilorceria** *sf* meanness.
spina ['spina] *sf* (*bot*) thorn; (*aculeo*) sting; (*riccio*) quill; (*elett*) plug. **birra alla spina** *sf* draught beer. **spina di pesce** fishbone. **spina dorsale** backbone. **star sulle spine** be on tenterhooks. **spinare** *v* bone. **spinato** *agg* (*pesce*) filleted; (*filo*) barbed.
spinacio [spi'natʃo] *sm* (*bot*) spinach. **spinaci** *sm pl* (*gastr*) spinach *sing*.
*spingere ['spindʒere] *v* push, drive; (*stimolare*) urge; (*premere*) press.
spino ['spino] *sm* (*bot*) blackthorn, bramble. **spineto** *sm* bramble bush. **spinoso** *agg* prickly, thorny.
spinta ['spinta] *sf* push; pressure; (*aiuto*) (helping) hand; (*stimolo*) boost; (*fis*) thrust. **spinto** *agg* pushed; disposed; (*fam*) extremist. **spintone** *sm* hard push, shove; (*raccomandazione*) good word.
spionaggio [spio'naddʒo] *sm* espionage. **spione** *sm* (*fam*) tell-tale.
spiovente [spjo'vɛnte] *agg* (*baffi*) drooping; (*spalle*) stooping; (*tetto*) sloping.
spira ['spira] *sf* coil. **spirale** *agg, sf* spiral.
spiraglio [spi'raʎo] *sm* chink; (*di luce, speranza*) glimmer; (*aria*) breath (of air).
spirare[1] [spi'rare] *v* (*soffiare*) blow; (*emettere*) give off *or* out; (*emanare*) be given off *or* out.
spirare[2] [spi'rare] *v* (*morire*) expire.
spirito ['spirito] *sm* spirit; (*animo*) mind; sense of humour. **bello spirito** wit. **condizioni di spirito** *sm pl* mood *sing*. **con spirito** wittily. **pieno di spirito** (*vivace*) lively; (*arguto*) witty.
spiritosaggine [spirito'zaddʒine] *sf* witticism.
spiritoso [spiri'tozo], **-a** *agg* witty. *sm, sf* funny person.

spirituale [spiritu'ale] *agg* spiritual. **spiritualismo** *sm* spiritualism. **spiritualista** *s(m+f)* spiritualist.
spiumare [spju'mare] *v* pluck.
spizzicare [spittsi'kare] *v* nibble. **a spizzico** *or* **spizzichi** in dribs and drabs.
*splendere ['splɛndere] *v* shine. **splendido** *agg* brilliant; (*meraviglioso*) splendid. **splendore** *sm* brilliance; splendour.
spodestare [spodes'tare] *v* (*cacciare*) oust; (*privare di beni*) dispossess.
spogliare [spo'ʎare] *v* strip; (*svestire*) undress; (*esaminare*) go through; sort out. **spogliarsi** *v* undress. **spogliarello** *sm* strip-tease. **spogliatoio** *sm* changing-room. **spoglie** *sf pl* (*bottino*) spoils *pl*; (*mortali*) (mortal) remains *pl*. **spoglio** *agg* (*nudo*) bare; (*privo*) devoid (of); (*libero*) free (from). **fare lo spoglio** (*corrispondenza*) sort out; (*dati*) extract; (*voti*) scrutinize.
spola ['spola] *sf* shuttle; (*macchina da cucire*) spool, bobbin. **far la spola** shuttle, ply. **spoletta** *sf* bobbin; (*tec, mil*) fuse.
spolmonarsi [spolmo'narsi] *v* shout oneself hoarse.
spolverare [spolve'rare] *v* dust. **spolverat(ur)a** *sf* dusting.
sponda ['sponda] *sf* (*mare, lago*) shore; (*fiume*) bank; (*bordo*) edge; (*biliardo*) cushion.
spontaneo [spon'taneo] *agg* spontaneous. **di mia spontanea volontà** of my own free will. **spontaneità** *sf* spontaneity.
spopolare [spopo'lare] *v* depopulate; (*vuotare*) empty; (*aver successo*) be a hit.
spora ['spora] *sf* spore.
sporadico [spo'radiko] *agg* sporadic.
sporco ['sporko] *agg* dirty; dishonest. **aver la coscienza sporca** have a guilty conscience. **sporcizia** *sf* dirt, filth; (*fam*) muck.
*sporgere ['spordʒere] *v* stick out, project, protrude. **sporgersi** *v* lean out. **sporgere querela contro** sue. **sporgente** *agg* jutting out; (*dente*) protruding; (*occhio*) bulging. **sporgenza** *sf* projection.
sport [sport] *sm invar* sport. **fare per sport** do for fun.
sporta ['sporta] *sf* (*sacca*) shopping-bag; (*quantità*) bagful. **una sporta di legnate** a good hiding. **un sacco e una sporta** a lot.
sportello [spor'tɛllo] *sm* counter; (*per biglietti*) ticket office; (*porta*) door.

sportivo [spor'tivo] *agg* sports; (*interessato*) sporty, sporting; (*leale*) sportsmanlike, sporting. *sm* sportsman. **sportiva** *sf* sportswoman.

sposa ['spɔza] *sf* bride. **sposalizio** *sm* wedding. **sposare** *v* marry; (*fig*) wed. **sposarsi** *v* get married. **sposata** *sf* married woman. **sposato** *sm* married man. **sposino, -a** *sm*, *sf* newly-wed. **sposo** *sm* bridegroom.

spossare [spos'sare] *v* exhaust. **spossatezza** *sf* exhaustion; (*stanchezza*) weariness. **spossato** *agg* worn out, weary.

spossessare [sposses'sare] *v* dispossess.

spostare [spos'tare] *v* shift; (*rimuovere*) displace; (*turbare*) upset; transfer. **spostamento** *sm* shift; displacement; transfer. **spostato** [spos'tato], **-a** *agg* (*fuori posto*) out of place; (*fig*) unsettled. *sm*, *sf* misfit.

spranga ['spranga] *sf* crossbar; (*chiavistello*) bolt. **sprangare** *v* bolt.

sprazzo ['sprattso] *sm* flash.

sprecare [spre'kare] *v* waste. **è tempo/fiato sprecato** it is a waste of breath/time. **spreco** *sm* waste. **sprecone, -a** *sm*, *sf* spendthrift.

spregevole [spre'dʒevole] *agg* despicable. **spregiare** *v* despise, spurn. **spregiativo** *agg* disparaging; (*gramm*) pejorative.

spregiudicato [spredʒudi'kato], **-a** *agg* (*senza pregiudizi*) open-minded; (*senza scrupoli*) unscrupulous. *sm*, *sf* unscrupulous person. **spregiudicatezza** *sf* open-mindedness; unscrupulousness.

spremere ['spremere] *v* squeeze. **spremersi il cervello** rack one's brains. **spremilimoni** *sm* lemon squeezer. **spremuta** *sf* (*bevanda*) juice.

sprezzare [spret'tsare] *v* despise. **sprezzante** *agg* contemptuous. **sprezzo** *sm* scorn.

sprigionare [spridʒo'nare] *v* give off.

sprint [sprint] *sm invar* (*sport*) sprint; (*auto*) pick-up. *sf* sports car.

sprizzare [sprit'tsare] *v* (*acqua*) squirt; (*sangue*) spurt; (*fig*) burst with.

sprofondare [sprofon'dare] *v* collapse; (*affondare*) sink; (*lasciarsi sopraffare*) be overwhelmed (by). **sprofondarsi** *v* sink; (*fig*) immerse oneself. **sprofondamento** *sm* collapse. **sprofondato** *agg* (*fig*) immersed, engrossed.

spronare [spro'nare] *v* spur (on). **spronata** *sf* spur. **sprone** *sm* spur.

sproporzionato [sproportsjo'nato] *agg* out of proportion; disproportionate. **sproporzione** *sf* lack of proportion.

sproposito [spro'pɔzito] *sm* blunder; (*strafalcione*) howler. **a sproposito** (*inopportunamente*) at the wrong time; (*fuori luogo*) in the wrong place. **commettere uno sproposito** do something silly. **costare uno sproposito** cost the earth. **spropositato** *agg* excessive.

sprovvisto [sprov'visto] *agg also* **sprovveduto** short (of); (*privo*) lacking (in). **alla sprovvista** unawares.

spruzzare [sprut'tsare] *v* spray; (*senza intenderlo*) splash. **spruzzata** *sf* sprinkling. **spruzzatore** *sm* sprinkler; (*profumi*) atomizer. **spruzzo** *sm* spray; (*schizzo*) spurt; splash.

spudorato [spudo'rato] *agg* shameless. **spudoratezza** *sf* shamelessness.

spugna ['spuɲa] *sf* sponge; (*tessuto*) towelling; (*fam*) boozer. **bere come una spugna** drink like a fish. **spugnatura** *sf* sponging down. **spugnoso** *agg* spongy.

spuma ['spuma] *sf* froth. **spumante** *sm* sparkling wine. **spumare** *v* (*bevande gassate*) fizz; (*vino*) sparkle. **spumare dalla rabbia** (*fam*) foam at the mouth. **spumeggiare** *v* froth. **spumoso** *agg* frothy.

spuntare [spun'tare] *v* (*germogliare*) sprout; (*apparire improvvisamente*) emerge; (*sorgere*) rise; (*fig*) overcome; (*capelli, ecc.*) trim. **spuntato** *agg* (*matita*) blunt; (*vino*) sour.

spuntino [spun'tino] *sm* snack.

spunto ['spunto] *sm* cue; idea; (*sport*) spurt. **prendere lo spunto da** start (off) from.

spuntone [spun'tone] *sm* spike.

spurgare [spur'gare] *v* clear out. **spurgarsi** *v* clear one's throat.

spurio ['spurjo] *agg* spurious.

sputacchiare [sputak'kjare] *v* splutter. **sputacchiera** *sf* spitoon.

sputare [spu'tare] *v* spit. **sputa fuori!** spit it out! **sputar sentenze** lecture. **sputar veleno** speak spitefully. **sputo** *sm* spit(tle), saliva; (*espettorato*) sputum.

squadernare [skwader'nare] *v* leaf through.

squadra¹ ['skwadra] *sf* (*strumento*) square. **a squadra** at right angles. **fuori squadra** crooked; (*fuori posto*) out of place; (*disordinato*) disorderly. **squadrare** *v* square; (*fig*) eye.

squadra² ['skwadra] *sf* (*mil*) section, squad; (*aero*) squadron; (*gruppo*) gang; (*sport*) team. **squadra mobile** flying squad. **squadriglia** *sf* band; (*mar, aero*) squadron.
squadro ['skwadro] *sm* angel-fish.
squagliarsi [skwa'ʎarsi] *v* melt. **squagliarsela** *v* sneak off.
squalificare [skwalifi'kare] *v* disqualify. **squalifica** *sf* disqualification.
squallido ['skwallido] *agg* dismal; (*fig*) squalid. **squallore** *sm* dreariness, squalor.
squalo ['skwalo] *sm* dog-fish; (*pescecane*) shark.
squama ['skwama] *sf* scale. **squamare** *v* scale. **squamoso** *agg* scaly.
squarciare [skwar'tʃare] *v* tear (to pieces), rend. **a squarciagola** at the top of one's voice. **squarcio** *sm* (*stoffa*) tear; (*ferita*) gash; (*fig*) passage.
squartare [skwar'tare] *v* quarter. **squartatoio** *sm* cleaver.
squassare [skwas'sare] *v* shake violently.
squattrinato [skwattri'nato] *agg* penniless.
squilibrare [skwili'brare] *v* unbalance. **squilibrarsi** *v* lose one's balance. **squilibrato** *agg* (mentally) unbalanced. **squilibrio** *sm* lack of equilibrium; (*econ*) imbalance; disproportion; (*mentale*) derangement.
squillare [skwil'lare] *v* ring; (*tromba*) sound; (*voce*) be shrill. **squillo** *sm* ring; (*suono*) squeal; (*tromba*) sound. **ragazza squillo** *sf* call-girl.
squinternare [skwinter'nare] *v* take to pieces; (*fig*) upset.
squisito [skwi'zito] *agg* excellent; delicious; (*raffinato*) exquisite. **squisitezza** *sf* deliciousness; delicacy.
squittire [skwit'tire] *v* (*uccelli*) chirp; (*topi*) squeak.
sradicare [sradi'kare] *v* (*divellere*) uproot; (*fig*) root out, eradicate.
sregolato [srego'lato] *agg* (*smodato*) immoderate; (*scapestrato*) wild.
stabbio ['stabbjo] *sm* pen; (*porcile*) pigsty; (*letame*) dung.
stabile ['stabile] *agg* stable; (*che non oscilla*) steady; permanent; (*durevole*) lasting.
stabilimento [stabili'mento] *sm* establishment; (*fabbrica*) factory, works; (*edificio*) building.
stabilire [stabi'lire] *v* establish; decide. **stabilirsi** *v* settle. **stabilità** *sf* stability.

stabilito *agg* (*istituito*) established; (*fissato*) fixed; (*convenuto*) agreed. **stabilizzare** *v* stabilize. **stabilizzarsi** *v* settle. **stabilizzazione** *sf* stabilization.
staccare [stak'kare] *v* (*togliere*) take off; (*separare*) detach; (*tagliando*) cut off; (*strappando*) pluck; (*sganciare*) unhook; (*risaltare*) stand out. **staccare il lavoro** (*fam*) knock off work. **staccarsi** *v* move away; (*venir via*) come off; separate. **staccato** *agg* detached; separate; (*musica*) staccato.
stadio ['stadjo] *sm* (*sport*) stadium; (*tec, fase*) stage.
staffa ['staffa] *sf* stirrup; (*mec*) bracket; (*calza*) heel. **perdere le staffe** (*fig*) lose one's temper. **staffetta** *sf* courier; (*sport*) relay(-race).
staffilare [staffi'lare] *v* lash; (*fig*) lash out (at). **staffilata** *sf* lash; (*fig*) lashing criticism. **staffile** *sm* stirrup-strap; (*sferza*) lash.
stagione [sta'dʒone] *sf* season; (*condizioni atmosferiche*) weather. **fuori stagione** out of season; (*fig*) untimely. **stagionale** *agg* seasonal. **stagionare** *v* season; (*invecchiare*) age; mature. **stagionatura** *sf* ageing; maturing; seasoning.
stagno¹ ['staɲo] *sm* (*metallo*) tin. **stagnare** *v* tin; (*saldare*) solder; (*chiudere*) seal. **stagnola** *sf* tin foil.
stagno² ['staɲo] *sm* (*bacino d'acqua*) pool. *agg* (*a tenuta d'acqua*) watertight. **stagnare** *v* stagnate; (*sangue*) stanch; (*fermare*) stop.
stalagmite [stalag'mite] *sf* stalagmite.
stalattite [stalat'tite] *sf* stalactite.
stalla ['stalla] *sf* stable; (*bovini*) cow-shed; (*fig*) pigsty. **stallaggio** *sm* stabling. **stallone** *sm* stallion.
stallo ['stallo] *sm* seat; (*scacchi*) stalemate. **andare in stallo** (*aero*) stall.
stamattina [stamat'tina] *avv* also **stamani** this morning.
stamberga [stam'berga] *sf* hovel.
stambugio [stam'budʒo] *sm* cubby-hole.
stame ['stame] *sm* (*bot*) stamen; (*tessile*) fine yarn.
stamigna [sta'miɲa] *sf* bunting.
stampa ['stampa] *sf* printing; (*giornali*) press; (*immagine, foto*) print. **errore di stampa** *sm* misprint. **stampe** *sf pl* (*posta*) printed matter *sing*. **stampaggio** (*foto*) printing; (*metallo*) forging; (*plastici*) moulding. **stampare** *v* print; publish;

(con pressa) press; forge; mould.
stampatello sm block letters pl. **stampato** sm printed matter; (modulo) form; (disegno) print. **stampatore, -trice** sm, sf printer.
stampella [stam'pɛlla] sf crutch.
stampiglia [stam'piʎa] sf stamp. **stampigliare** v stamp.
stampino [stam'pino] sm stencil; (punzone) punch.
stampo ['stampo] sm mould; (matrice) die; (fig) kind, sort.
stanare [sta'nare] v drive out.
stancare [stan'kare] v tire; (annoiare) bore. **stancarsi** v get tired, tire. **stanchezza** sf tiredness; (fiacchezza) fatigue. **stanco** agg tired; bored.
standard ['standard] sm invar standard. **standardizzare** v standardize. **standardizzazione** sf standardization.
stanga ['stanga] sf bar. **stangare** v (colpire) thrash; (bocciare) fail; (scuola) give a bad mark; (far pagare troppo) rob. **stangata** sf blow.
stanotte [sta'nɔtte] avv tonight.
stante ['stante] agg a sè stante apart. **seduta stante** straight away. prep (a causa di) on account of.
stantio [stan'tio] agg stale.
stantuffo [stan'tuffo] sm piston; (di pressa idraulica) plunger.
stanza ['stantsa] sf room; (poesia) stanza. **stanza da bagno** bathroom. **stanza da pranzo** dining-room.
stanziare [stan'tsjare] v allocate; deliberate.
stappare [stap'pare] v uncork.
***stare** ['stare] v stay, remain; (abitare) live; (essere) be; (vestiario) suit; (spettare) be up to. **come stai?** how are you? **lasciar stare** leave alone. **non poter stare senza** be unable to do without. **stare a dieta** be on a diet. **stare in guardia** be on one's guard. **stare per** be about to. **sto bene** I am well. **sto male** I am not well.
starna ['starna] sf partridge.
starnutire [starnu'tire] v sneeze. **starnuto** sm sneeze.
stasera [sta'sera] avv this evening.
stasi ['stazi] sf standstill.
statale [sta'tale] agg state. **strada statale** sf trunk road. s(m+f) civil servant.
statica ['statika] sf statics. **statico** agg static; (senza movimento) motionless.
statista [sta'tista] sm statesman.

statistica [sta'tistika] sf statistics. **statistico** agg statistical.
stato ['stato] sm state; condition; (posizione sociale) status. **colpo di stato** sm coup d'état. **Stati Uniti** sm pl United States pl. **stato d'animo** mood. **ufficio di stato civile** sm register office. **statunitense** s(m+f), agg American.
statua ['statua] sf statue. **statuario** agg statuary.
statura [sta'tura] sf (altezza) height; (fig) stature.
statuto [sta'tuto] sm statute; constitution. **statutario** statutory.
stavolta [sta'vɔlta] avv this time.
stazione [sta'tsjone] sf station; (località di soggiorno) resort. **stazionamento** sm parking. **stazionare** v stop; park. **stazionario** agg stationary.
stecca ['stekka] sf small stick; (biliardo) cue; (persiane) slat; (sigarette) carton; (hockey) stick. **steccare** v fence (in); (sonare) play a wrong note. **steccato** sm fence. **a stecchetto** (senza soldi) hard up; (senza cibo) on short rations. **stecchito** agg (rinsecchito) dried up; (magrissimo) skinny. **morto stecchito** stone dead. **stecco** sm dry twig. **steccone** sm post.
stella ['stella] sf star. **alle stelle** (prezzi) sky-high. **stella alpina** edelweiss. **stella cadente** or **filante** shooting star; (di carta) streamer. **stella di mare** starfish. **stellare** agg (astron) stellar; (forma) star-shaped; (bot) stellate. **stellato** agg starry; (fig) studded. **stelletta** (mil) star; (fam) pip.
stelo ['stɛlo] sm stem; (fiore) stalk; (gambo di utensile) shank.
stemma ['stɛmma] sm coat of arms.
stemp(e)rare [stemp(e)'rare] v dissolve.
stendardo [sten'dardo] sm standard.
***stendere** ['stɛndere] v (allungare) stretch (out); (distendere) spread (out); (bucato) hang out; (contratto) draw up. **stendersi** v stretch out.
stenodattilografia [stenodattilogra'fia] sf shorthand typing. **stenodattilografo, -a** sm, sf shorthand typist. **stenografare** v take down in shorthand. **stenografia** sf shorthand. **stenografo, -a** sm, sf stenographer.
stentare [sten'tare] v find it hard, have difficulty. **stentatezza** sf difficulty. **stentato** agg laboured; (di crescita arrestata) stunted; (pieno di stenti) hard.

stento *sm* hardship; difficulty. **a stento** barely.

steppa ['steppa] *sf* steppe.

sterco ['sterko] *sm* excrement; (*letame*) dung.

stereo ['stereo] *agg, sm* stereo.

stereofonico [stereo'fɔniko] *agg* stereophonic; (*fam*) stereo.

stereotipato [stereoti'pato] *agg* stereotyped; (*fisso*) frozen. **concezione stereotipata** *sf* stereotype.

sterile ['sterile] *agg* sterile; (*fig*) vain. **sterilire** *v* sterilize. **sterilità** *sf* sterility; (*fig*) uselessness. **sterilizzare** *v* sterilize. **sterilizzatore** *sm* sterilizer. **sterilizzazione** *sf* sterilization.

sterlina [ster'lina] *sf* pound (sterling).

sterminare [stermi'nare] *v* exterminate. **sterminato** *agg* boundless. **sterminio** *sm* extermination.

sterna ['sterna] *sf* tern.

sterno ['sterno] *sm* breastbone.

sterzo ['stertso] *sm* (*auto*) steering; (*bicicletta*) handlebars *pl*. **sterzare** *v* (*auto*) steer; (*fig*) swerve. **sterzata** *sf* steering; swerve. **fare una sterzata** make a sharp turn.

stesso ['stesso] *agg* same; (*proprio*) very; (*personificato*) itself; (*in persona*) personally; (*rafforzativo, riflessivo*) myself, yourself, etc.

stesura [ste'zura] *sf* drafting; draft.

stetoscopio [stetos'kɔpjo] *sm* stethoscope.

stia ['stia] *sf* chicken coop. **essere (pigiati) come in una stia** be cooped up.

stigma ['stigma] *sm* stigma. **stigmatizzare** *v* stigmatize.

stilare [sti'lare] *v* draw up.

stile ['stile] *sm* style; (*eleganza*) stylishness. **di stile** stylish. **in grande stile** in style. **stilista** *s(m+f)* stylist. **stilistico** *agg* stylistic. **stilizzare** *v* stylize.

stilla ['stilla] *sf* drop. **a stilla a stilla** drop by drop. **stillare** *v* (*trasudare*) ooze, exude; (*gocciolare*) drip. **stillarsi il cervello** rack one's brains. **stillicidio** *sm* constant trickle.

stilo ['stilo] *sm* (*per scrivere*) stylus; (*stadera*) beam. **stilografica** *sf* fountainpen.

stima ['stima] *sf* (*buona opinione*) esteem, regard; (*giudizio*) estimation; (*valutazione*) estimate. **a mia stima** in my estimation. **aver stima di** hold in high esteem. **con (la massima) stima** (*in lettere*) yours faithfully.

stimare [sti'mare] *v* estimate; (*apprezzare*) value, esteem; consider. **stimatore, -trice** *sm, sf* (*perito*) valuer; (*ammiratore*) admirer.

stimolare [stimo'lare] *v* stimulate; (*fig*) arouse; (*appetito*) whet. **stimolante** *sm* stimulant. **stimolatore cardiaco** *sm* pacemaker. **stimolazione** *sf* (*med*) stimulation; (*fig*) arousal. **stimolo** *sm* stimulus (*pl* -li).

stinco ['stinko] *sm* shin. **stincata** *sf* blow on the shin.

***stingere** ['stindʒere] *v* (*macchiare*) run; (*sbiadire*) fade.

stipare [sti'pare] *v* pack, cram.

stipendio [sti'pendjo] *sm* salary. **stipendio arretrato** back pay.

stipite ['stipite] *sm* doorpost.

stipulare [stipu'lare] *v* stipulate. **stipulazione** *sf* stipulation.

stiracchiare [stirak'kjare] *v* stretch; (*lesinare*) skimp. **stiracchiare sul prezzo** haggle. **stiracchiamento** *sm* stretching; haggling. **stiracchiatura** *sf* distortion.

stirare [sti'rare] *v* (*col ferro*) iron, press. **stirarsi** *v* stretch. **stiro** *sm* ironing; pressing. **ferro da stiro** *sm* iron. **tavolo da stiro** *sm* ironing-board.

stirpe ['stirpe] *sf* (*origine*) descent, extraction; (*razza*) race; family; (*discendenti*) offspring.

stitico ['stitiko] *agg* constipated; (*fig*) stingy. **stitichezza** *sf* constipation.

stiva ['stiva] *sf* hold. **stivaggio** *sm* stowage.

stivale [sti'vale] *sm* boot. **lustrar gli stivali a** (*fig*) lick the boots of. **rompere gli stivali a** (*fig*) pester.

stivaletto [stiva'letto] *sm* bootee.

stizza ['stittsa] *sf* anger. **avere *or* provare stizza per** be angry about. **stizzire** *v* anger. **stizzirsi** *v* get angry. **stizzito** *agg* angry. **stizzoso** *agg* irritable.

stoccafisso [stokka'fisso] *sm* dried cod.

stoccata [stok'kata] *sf* stab; (*scherma*) thrust; (*battuta*) gibe. **stocco** *sm* rapier.

Stoccolma [stok'kolma] *sf* Stockholm.

stoffa ['stɔffa] *sf* fabric, material; (*dote*) makings *pl*. **ha della stoffa** he has what it takes.

stoico ['stɔiko], **-a** *agg* stoical. *sm, sf* stoic.

stoino [sto'ino] *sm* doormat.

stola ['stɔla] *sf* stole.

stolto ['stolto], **-a** *agg* foolish. *sm*, *sf* fool. **stoltezza** *sf* foolishness; (*azione*) foolish action; (*parole*) nonsense.

stomaco ['stɔmako] *sm* stomach; (*fam*) tummy; (*fam: coraggio*) guts. **mal di stomaco** *sm* stomach-ache. ... **mi sta** *or* **rimane sullo stomaco** I cannot stomach .... **stomacare** *v* nauseate. **stomachevole** *agg* revolting.

stonare [sto'nare] *v* (*cantare*) sing out of tune; (*sonare*) play out of tune; (*contrastare*) clash. **stonata** *sf* wrong note. **stonato** *agg* out of tune; clashing; (*turbato*) upset.

stoppa ['stoppa] *sf* tow. **stoppare** *v* (*otturare*) block; (*sport*) stop. **stoppaccio** *sm* wad. **stoppie** *sf pl* stubble *sing*. **stoppino** *sm* wick.

***storcere** ['stortʃere] *v* twist; (*piegare*) bend. **storcersi il naso** turn up one's nose. **storcersi la bocca** make a wry face. **storcersi per il dolore** writhe in pain. **storcimento** *sm* twisting; wrench.

stordire [stor'dire] *v* stun; (*rumore*) deafen. **stordimento** *sm* (*stato d'animo*) bewilderment. **stordito** *agg* stunned; bewildered; (*distratto*) scatter-brained.

storia ['stɔrja] *sf* history; (*racconto*) story, tale; (*frottola*) fib, lie; (*faccenda*) business. **la solita storia** the same old story. **libro di storia** history book. **storie** *sf pl* (*trambusto*) fuss *sing*. **storiella** *sf* little story; (*barzelletta*) joke; (*fandonia*) fib.

storico ['stɔriko], **-a** *agg* (*della storia*) historical; (*famoso*) historic. *sm*, *sf* historian.

storione [sto'rjone] *sm* sturgeon.

stormo ['stormo] *sm* (*uccelli*) flock; (*cani*) pack; (*persone*) crowd; (*fig*) mess. **sonare a stormo** sound the alarm.

stornare [stor'nare] *v* (*allontanare*) avert; dissuade; transfer; annul. **storno** *sm* transfer.

stornello [stor'nɛllo] *sm* *also* **storno** (*uccello*) starling.

storno ['storno] *agg* dapple-grey.

storpio ['stɔrpjo], **-a** *agg* crippled. *sm*, *sf* cripple. **storpiare** *v* cripple; mispronounce.

storto ['stɔrto] *agg* crooked; (*sbagliato*) wrong. **aver gli occhi storti** squint. **aver le gambe storte** be bandy-legged. **storta** *sf* twist, sprain; (*recipiente*) retort. **prendersi una storta alla caviglia** twist one's ankle.

stoviglie [sto'viʎe] *sf pl* crockery *sing*. **lavar le stoviglie** wash the dishes, wash up.

strabico ['strabiko] *agg* cross-eyed. **strabismo** *sm* squint. **essere affetto da strabismo** have a squint.

strabiliante [strabi'ʎante] *agg* amazing.

straboccare [strabok'kare] *v* overflow. **strabocchevole** *agg* excessive.

stracarico [stra'kariko] *agg*, *m pl* **-chi** overloaded; (*fig*) overburdened.

stracciare [strat'tʃare] *v* tear; (*facendo a pezzi*) tear up. **straccio** ['strattʃo] *sm* rag. *agg* waste. **straccione, -a** *sm*, *sf* ragamuffin; beggar.

stracco ['strakko] (*fam*) *agg* worn out, done in. **stracco morto** dead beat.

stracotto [stra'kɔtto] *agg* overcooked. **cotto e stracotto** overdone. *sm* (*gastr*) stew, casserole.

strada ['strada] *sf* road, street; (*percorso*) way; (*itinerario*) route; (*cammino*) journey; (*varco*) path. **a mezza strada** halfway. **che strada fai?** which way are you going? **far strada a qualcuno** show someone the way. **farsi strada** (*aprirsi un passaggio*) clear a way for oneself; (*ottener successo*) do well for oneself. **fuori strada** off the road; (*fig*) on the wrong track. **lungo** *or* **per la strada** on the way. **strada facendo** on the way. **stradale** *agg* road. **codice stradale** *sm* highway code. **lavori stradali** *sm pl* roadworks *pl*.

strafalcione [strafal'tʃone] *sm* blunder.

***strafare** [stra'fare] *v* overdo it.

straforo [stra'foro] *sm* **di straforo** indirectly; (*di nascosto*) on the quiet; (*di sfuggita*) in passing.

strage ['stradʒe] *sf* slaughter; (*distruzione*) havoc; (*fam*) mass.

stragrande [stra'grande] *agg* huge. **stragrande maggioranza** *sf* great majority.

stralciare [stral'tʃare] *v* take out; (*dedurre*) deduct; (*mettere in liquidazione*) wind up. **stralcio** *sm* removal; extract; liquidation. **vendere a stralcio** sell off.

stralunare [stralu'nare] *v* roll one's eyes. **stralunato** *agg* (*fig*) distraught.

stramazzare [stramat'tsare] *v* fall to the ground.

strambo ['strambo] *agg* odd; eccentric. **stramberia** *sf* oddity; eccentricity.

strampalato [strampa'lato] *agg* weird.

strangolare [strango'lare] *v* strangle. strangolarsi *v* choke. strangolamento *sm* strangulation.

straniero [stra'njɛro], -a *agg* foreign. *sm, sf* foreigner; (*termine burocratico*) alien.

strano ['strano] *agg* strange, odd. *sm* strange *or* odd thing. strano a dirsi oddly enough. stranezza *sf* peculiarity; (*atteggiamento*) odd behaviour.

straordinario [straordi'narjo] *agg* extraordinary; (*insolito*) unusual; special. lavoro straordinario *sm* overtime. *sm* unusual thing; overtime.

strapagare [strapa'gare] *v* (*fam*) pay through the nose.

strapazzare [strapat'tsare] *v* wear out; (*trattar male*) ill-treat. uova strapazzate *sf pl* scrambled eggs *pl*. strapazzata *sf* (*sgridata*) dressing-down; (*faticata*) strain. strapazzo *sm* strain; ill-treatment. vestiti da strapazzo *sm pl* working clothes *pl*.

strapieno [stra'pjɛno] *agg* full up.

strapiombare [strapjom'bare] *v* overhang, jut out. a strapiombo sheer, overhanging.

strappare [strap'pare] *v* snatch; (*portar via*) pull off *or* out; (*rompendo*) tear (off *or* out); (*in più pezzi*) tear up. strappata *sf* tug. strappo *sm* pull, tug; (*strattone*) jerk; tear. strappo muscolare pulled *or* torn muscle.

straripare [strari'pare] *v* overflow. straripamento *sm* overflowing.

strascicare [straʃi'kare] *v* trail; (*con fatica*) drag; (*fig*) drag out; (*pronuncia*) drawl. strascico *sm, pl* -chi (*fig*) after-effect; (*vestito*) train.

strascinare [straʃi'nare] *v* drag along.

stratagemma [strata'dʒɛmma] *sm* stragem; (*fig*) trick.

strategia [strate'dʒia] *sf* strategy. strategico *agg* strategic. stratego, -a *sm, sf* strategist.

strato ['strato] *sm* layer; (*vernice*) coat; (*geol, classe*) stratum (*pl* -a). stratificato *agg* stratified.

strattone [strat'tone] *sm* pull, jerk. a strattoni jerkily.

stravagante [strava'gante] *agg* extravagant. stravaganza *sf* extravagance.

stravecchio [stra'vɛkkjo] *agg* very old.

*stravincere [stra'vintʃere] *v* win hands down; (*battere*) beat hollow.

straviziare [stravi'tsjare] *v* over-indulge. stravizio *sm* over-indulgence.

*stravolgere [stra'vɔldʒere] *v* twist; (*fig*) affect deeply. stravolgere gli occhi roll one's eyes. stravolgimento *sm* twisting; contortion. stravolto *agg* twisted; (*fig*) deeply upset.

straziare [stra'tsjare] *v* torture, torment. straziare il cuore a qualcuno break someone's heart. cuore straziato *sm* broken heart. strazio *sm* torment, agony. far strazio di (*fig*) play havoc with.

strega ['strega] *sf* witch. stregare *v* bewitch. stregone *sm* wizard; (*mago*) sorcerer; (*popoli primitivi*) witch-doctor. stregoneria *sf* witchcraft; sorcery. fare stregonerie cast spells.

stregua ['stregwa] *sf* alla stregua di in the same way as. a questa stregua at this rate.

stremato [stre'mato] *agg* exhausted.

stremo ['strɛmo] *sm* limit.

strenna ['strɛnna] *sf* gift.

strenuo ['strɛnuo] *agg* valiant; (*fig*) untiring.

strepitare [strepi'tare] *v* make a din; (*gridando*) shout. strepito *sm* clamour, uproar. fare strepito cause a stir. strepitoso *agg* noisy; (*fragoroso*) resounding; (*fig*) tremendous.

streptococco [strepto'kɔkko] *sm* streptococcus. streptomicina *sf* streptomycin.

stretta ['stretta] *sf* hold; (*abbraccio*) embrace; (*presa*) grip; critical point; (*situazione difficile*) predicament. essere *or* trovarsi alle strette be in a tight corner. stretta alla gola lump in the throat. stretta di mano handshake.

stretto ['stretto] *agg* narrow; (*vestiario*) tight; (*rigoroso*) strict; (*denti, pugni*) clenched. *sm* strait. strettoia *sf* (*strada*) narrowing of the road; (*fig*) tight spot.

striato [stri'ato] *agg* striped.

stricnina [strik'nina] *sf* strychnine.

stridere ['stridere] *v* (*strillare*) shriek, screech; (*insetti*) chirp; (*cigolare*) squeak; (*fig*) clash. stridente *agg* strident; clashing. strido *sm, pl* -a *f* shriek, screech; squeak; chirp.

strigliata [stri'ʎata] *sf* dressing-down.

strillare [stril'lare] *v* scream; (*parlare ad alta voce*) shout. strillo *sm* scream. strillone *sm* news-vendor.

striminzito [strimin'tsito] *agg* skimpy; (*magro*) skinny.

strimpellàre [strimpel'lare] v strum.

strinare [stri'nare] v scorch.

stringa ['stringa] sf lace. stringare v lace (up); (fig) condense.

*stringere ['strindʒere] v (avvicinare) squeeze or press (together); (serrare) clasp, clutch; (vestiario) pinch; (concludere) make; (denti, pugni) clench. il tempo stringe time is getting short. stringere i tempi speed things up; (musica) quicken the tempo. stringere la cinghia (fig) tighten one's belt. stringere la mano a shake hands with. stringere un'amicizia strike up a friendship. stringi stringi when all is said and done.

striscia ['striʃa] sf strip; (riga larga) stripe; (traccia) streak. a strisce striped. strisce pedonali sf pl zebra crossing sing. strisciare v creep, crawl; (sfiorando) slide; (sfiorare) graze. strisciare i piedi drag one's feet. colpire di striscio graze. striscione sm banner.

stritolare [strito'lare] v crush.

strizzare [strit'tsare] v wring out; (spremere) squeeze. strizzar l'occhio wink. strizzata sf squeeze; wink.

strofinare [strofi'nare] v rub. strofinaccio sm rag. strofinata sf quick rub. strofinio sm prolonged rubbing.

strombazzare [strombat'tsare] v shout from the roof-tops. strombazzare i propri meriti blow one's own trumpet.

strombettare [strombet'tare] v blare; (auto) blow the horn.

stroncare [stron'kare] v break off; (tagliando) cut off; (fig) cut short; (criticare) slate. stroncatura sf slating.

stronzo ['strontso] sm (volg) turd; (fig) idiot.

stropicciare [stropit'tʃare] v rub. stropicciarsene v (fam) not care a damn.

strozzare [strot'tsare] v strangle, choke; (med) strangulate. strozzatura sf narrowing; (occlusione) bottle-neck; strangling. strozzino, -a sm, sf usurer.

*struggere ['struddʒere] v melt; (fig) eat up. struggersi v be consumed.

strumento [stru'mento] sm instrument; (arnese) tool. strumento ad arco stringed instrument. strumento a fiato woodwind instrument. strumentale agg instrumental. strumentare v orchestrate.

strusciare [stru'ʃare] v scrape.

strutto ['strutto] sm lard.

struttura [strut'tura] sf structure. strutturale agg structural. strutturare v structure. strutturazione sf organization.

struzzo ['struttso] sm ostrich. fare lo struzzo bury one's head in the sand.

stuccare[1] [stuk'kare] v plaster; (decorare) stucco. stuccatore sm plasterer; stuccoworker. stucco sm plaster; (per finestre) putty; (arte) stucco. rimaner di stucco be dumbfounded.

stuccare[2] [stuk'kare] v (nauseare) make sick; (annoiare) bore. stucchevole agg sickly; boring. stucco agg sick (of).

studente [stu'dente], -essa sm, sf student. studentesco agg (di scuola) school; university.

studiare [stu'djare] v study; (cercar di trovare) try and find. studiare a memoria learn by heart. studiato agg studied; affected.

studio ['studjo] sm study; (progetto) plan; (di avvocato) office; (di medico) surgery; (di artista, fotografo, ecc.) studio. allo studio under consideration. fare gli studi study.

studioso [stu'djozo], -a agg studious. sm, sf scholar.

stufa ['stufa] sf stove, heater. stufare v (gastr) stew; (fam: annoiare) bore. stufarsi di get sick and tired of. stufato sm stew. stufo agg fed up (with).

stuoia ['stwɔja] sf mat. stuoino sm doormat.

stuolo ['stwɔlo] sm crowd.

*stupefare [stupe'fare] v astound. stupefacente sm drug, narcotic. stupefatto agg astonished, amazed.

stupendo [stu'pendo] agg stupendous.

stupido ['stupido] agg stupid; (sciocco) foolish. stupidaggine sf stupidity; (atto) foolish thing; (parole) nonsense; (inezia) trifle. dir stupidaggini talk nonsense. stupidità sf stupidity.

stupire [stu'pire] v amaze, astonish. stupirsi v be amazed or astonished (at). stupore sm astonishment, amazement; (med) stupor.

stuprare [stu'prare] v rape. stupro sm rape.

sturare [stu'rare] v uncork. sturabottiglie sm invar corkscrew. sturalavandini sm invar plunger.

stuzzicare [stuttsi'kare] *v* prod; (*molestare*) annoy; (*punzecchiare*) tease; (*stimolare*) excite. **stuzzicadenti** *sm invar* toothpick. **stuzzicar l'appetito** whet the appetite. **stuzzicante** *agg* exciting; appetizing.
su [su] *prep* on; (*senza contatto*) over; (*più in alto di*) above; (*vicino*) by; (*verso*) towards; (*intorno a, circa*) about; (*oltre*) after. **dare su** look out over. **novanta volte su cento** (*fig*) nine times out of ten. *avv* (*in alto*) up; (*indosso*) on; (*al piano superiore*) upstairs. **avercela su con** (*fam*) be cross with. **in su** up; (*età, numero*) upwards. **su per giù** roughly. *inter* come on!
subacqueo [su'bakkweo] *agg* underwater.
subaffittare [subaffit'tare] *v* sublet. **dare in subaffitto** sublet.
subalterno [subal'tɛrno], **-a** *s, agg* subordinate.
subappaltare [subappal'tare] *v* subcontract. **subappalto** *sm* subcontract.
subbia ['subbja] *sf* chisel.
subbio ['subbjo] *sm* beam.
subbuglio [sub'buʎo] *sm* turmoil; confusion.
subconscio [sub'kɔnʃo] *sm, agg* subconscious.
subdolo ['subdolo] *agg* underhand.
subentrare [suben'trare] *v* take the place of; succeed.
subire [su'bire] *v* suffer; (*sottoporsi a*) undergo.
subissare [subis'sare] *v* (*fig*) overwhelm.
subisso *sm* (*fam*) load; (*rovina*) ruin.
subito ['subito] *avv* at once, immediately. **subito prima** just before. **subitaneità** *sf* suddenness. **subitaneo** *agg* sudden.
sublimare [subli'mare] *v* sublimate. **sublimato** *sm* sublimate. **sublimazione** *sf* sublimation.
sublime [sub'lime] *agg, sm* sublime.
subnormale [subnor'male] *agg, sm* subnormal.
subodorare [subodo'rare] *v* **subodorare un inganno** smell a rat.
subordinare [subordi'nare] *v* subordinate. **subordinato, -a** *agg, s* subordinate. **subordinazione** *sf* subordination.
subornare [subor'nare] *v* suborn. **subornazione** *sf* subornation.
suburbano [subur'bano] *agg* suburban.

*****succedere** [sut'tʃedere] *v* follow; succeed; (*capitare*) happen. **cosa sta succedendo?** what is happening? **cosa ti succede?** what is the matter with you? **sono cose che succedono** these things will happen.
successione [suttʃes'sjone] *sf* succession. **successione delle colture** crop rotation. **tasse di successione** *sf pl* death duties *pl*. **successivamente** *avv* subsequently. **successivo** *agg* (*seguente*) following; (*uno dopo l'altro*) consecutive. **successore** *sm* successor.
successo [sut'tʃɛsso] *sm* success. **aver cattivo successo** be unsuccessful. **aver successo** be successful.
succhiare [suk'kjare] *v* suck. **succhietto** *or* **succhiotto** *sm* dummy. **succhione** *sm* sucker.
succhiello [suk'kjɛllo] *sm* gimlet.
succinto [sut'tʃinto] *agg* scanty; (*fig*) succinct.
succitato [suttʃi'tato] *agg* above-mentioned.
succo ['sukko] *sm* juice; (*fig*) essence, gist. **succoso** *agg* juicy; (*fig*) meaty. **succulento** *agg* succulent, juicy; (*pasto*) tasty.
succube ['sukkube] *s(m+f)* slave.
succursale [sukkur'sale] *sf* branch.
sud [sud] *sm* south. **abitante del sud** *s(m+f)* southerner. **al sud** (*stato*) in the south; (*moto*) to the south. **del sud** south, southern. **Sudafrica** *sf* South Africa. **sudafricano, -a** *s, agg* South African. **Sudamerica** *sf* South America. **sudamericano, -a** *s, agg* South American.
sudare [su'dare] *v* sweat, perspire; (*lavorar molto*) toil. **sudar freddo** be in a cold sweat. **sudata** *sf* sweat. **sudaticcio** *agg* sweaty.
suddetto [sud'detto] *agg* above-mentioned.
suddito ['suddito], **-a** *sm, sf* subject.
*****suddividere** [suddi'videre] *v* subdivide, divide. **suddivisione** *sf* division, subdivision.
sud-est [sud'ɛst] *sm* south-east. **del sud-est** south-east(ern).
sudicio ['suditʃo] *agg* dirty; (*molto sporco*) filthy. *sm invar* filth. **sudiciume** *sm* filth.
sudore [su'dore] *sm* sweat, perspiration.
sud-ovest [sud'ɔvest] *sm* south-west. **del sud-ovest** south-west(ern).
sufficiente [suffi'tʃɛnte] *agg* enough;

(*adeguato*) sufficient; presumptuous. **sufficiente a se stesso** self-sufficient. *sm* enough. **avere il sufficiente per vivere** have enough to live on. **sufficienza** *sf* sufficiency. **a sufficienza** more than enough.

suffisso [suf'fisso] *sm* suffix.

suffragio [suf'fradʒo] *sm* suffrage. **suffragetta** *sf* suffragette.

suffumicare [suffumi'kare] *v* fumigate. **suffumicazione** *sf* fumigation.

suga ['suga] *agg* **carta suga** *or* **sugante** *sf* blotting paper.

suggello [sud'dʒɛllo] *sm* seal. **suggellare** *v* seal.

suggerire [suddʒe'rire] *v* suggest; (*consigliare*) advise; (*richiamare*) bring to mind; (*teatro*) prompt. **suggerimento** *sm* suggestion; piece of advice. **suggeritore, -trice** *sm, sf* prompter.

suggestione [suddʒes'tjone] *sf* suggestion; impression; (*fascino*) charm. **suggestionabile** *agg* easily influenced, impressionable. **suggestionabilità** *sf* suggestibility. **suggestionare** *v* influence; (*persuadere*) induce. **suggestivo** *agg* suggestive; evocative. **domanda suggestiva** *sf* leading question.

sughero ['sugero] *sm* cork.

sugli ['suʎi] *prep* + *art* su gli.

sugna ['suɲa] *sf* pork fat.

sugo ['sugo] *sm* (*succo*) juice; (*salsa*) sauce; (*fig*) main point. **senza sugo** (*fig*) pointless. **sugoso** *agg* juicy; (*fig*) meaty.

sui ['sui] *prep* + *art* su i.

suicida [sui'tʃida] *agg* suicidal. *s(m+f)* suicide. **suicidarsi** *v* commit suicide. **suicidio** *sm* suicide.

suino [su'ino] *sm* pig, swine. *agg* pig. **carne suina** *sf* pork.

sul [sul] *prep* + *art* su il.

sulfureo [sul'fureo] *agg* sulphurous.

sull' [sull] *prep* + *art* su l'.

sulla ['sulla] *prep* + *art* su la.

sulle ['sulle] *prep* + *art* su le.

sullo ['sullo] *prep* + *art* su lo.

sultano [sul'tano] *sm* sultan. (**uva**) **sultanina** *sf* sultana.

sunto ['sunto] *sm* summary. **sunteggiare** *v* also **fare il sunto** sum up, summarize.

suo ['suo], *m pl* **suoi** *agg* (*uomo*) his; (*donna*) her; (*cosa, animale*) its; (*riflessivo*) one's. *pron* his; hers. **a ciascuno il suo** to each his own.

suocera ['swɔtʃera] *sf* mother-in-law;

(*spreg*) battle-axe. **suocero** *sm* father-in-law.

suola ['swɔla] *sf* sole. **suolare** *v* (*mettere la suola*) sole.

suolo ['swɔlo] *sm* ground; (*terreno*) soil.

suonare [swo'nare] *V* **sonare**.

suono ['swɔno] *sm* sound; tone. **suono falso** discord; (*fig*) false ring.

suora ['swɔra] *sf* nun, sister.

super ['super] *agg* (*benzina*) four-star.

superare [supe'rare] *v* (*dimensione, quantità*) exceed; (*oltrepassare*) go beyond, surpass; (*di passaggio*) pass, overtake; (*sostenere*) get over *or* through. **superato** *agg* (*antiquato*) old-fashioned; (*non più valido*) obsolete.

superbo [su'pɛrbo] *agg* haughty; (*fiero*) proud; (*fig*) magnificent, superb. **superbia** *sf* haughtiness. **senza superbia** modestly.

supercongelato [superkondʒe'lato] *agg* deep-frozen.

superficie [super'fitʃe] *sf* surface; area. **alla superficie** on the surface. **superficiale** *agg* superficial; (*geom*) plane. **tensione superficiale** *sf* surface tension.

superfluo [su'pɛrfluo] *agg* (*eccessivo*) superfluous; (*inutile*) unnecessary. *sm* surplus.

superiore [supe'rjore] *agg* (*più in alto*) upper; (*maggiore*) higher; (*fig*) superior; (*di grado*) senior; advanced. **superiore alla media** above average. **superiorità** *sf* superiority.

superlativo [superla'tivo] *sm, agg* superlative.

supermercato [supermer'kato] *sm* supermarket.

supero ['supero] *sm* surplus.

supersonico [super'sɔniko] *agg* supersonic.

superstite [su'pɛrstite] *agg* surviving. *s(m+f)* survivor.

superstizione [supersti'tsjone] *sf* superstition. **superstizioso** *agg* superstitious.

superuomo [supe'rwɔmo] *sm* superman.

supervisione [supervi'zjone] *sf* supervision. **supervisore** *sm* supervisor.

supino [su'pino] *agg* supine. **giacere supino** lie on one's back.

suppellettili [suppel'lɛttili] *sf pl* furnishings *pl*; (*di casa*) household goods *pl*.

suppergiù [supper'dʒu] *avv* roughly, more or less.

supplemento [supple'mento] *sm* supplement; (*prezzo*) additional charge; (*biglietto*) excess fare. **supplementare** *agg* additional, extra; (*econ, mat*) supplementary.

supplicare [suppli'kare] *v* implore. **supplica** *sf* plea. **in atto di supplica** imploringly. **supplicante** *s(m+f)* supplicant. **supplichevole** *agg* imploring.

supplire [sup'plire] *v* make up for; (*fare le veci*) stand in for. **supplente** *s(m+f)* supply teacher.

supplizio [sup'plitsjo] *sm* torture; (*pena di morte*) capital punishment. **suppliziare** *v* torture.

***supporre** [sup'porre] *v* suppose; imagine. **supposizione** *sf* supposition. **supposto che** assuming that, supposing.

supporto [sup'pɔrto] *sm* support; (*mec*) bearing; (*sostegno*) stand.

supposta [sup'posta] *sf* suppository.

suppurare [suppu'rare] *v* fester. **suppurazione** *sf* festering.

supremo [su'prɛmo] *agg* supreme; (*massimo*) highest. **supremazia** *sf* supremacy.

surgelare [surdʒe'lare] *v* freeze. **surgelato** *sm* frozen food.

surreale [surre'ale] *agg* unreal. **surrealismo** *sm* surrealism. **surrealista** *s(m+f)*, *agg* surrealist.

surriscaldare [surriskal'dare] *v* overheat. **surriscaldamento** *sm* overheating.

surrogare [surro'gare] *v* substitute. **surrogato** *sm, agg* substitute. **surrogazione** *sf* surrogation.

suscettibile [suʃet'tibile] *agg* capable (of), susceptible; (*facile a risentirsi*) touchy. **suscettibilità** *sf* susceptibility. **offendere la suscettibilità di qualcuno** hurt someone's feelings.

suscitare [suʃi'tare] *v* provoke, give rise to.

susina [su'zina] *sf* plum, damson. **susino** *sm* plum-tree, damson-tree.

susseguirsi [susse'gwirsi] *v* follow (each other). **susseguente** *agg* following, subsequent.

sussidiare [sussi'djare] *v* subsidize. **sussidiario** *agg* subsidiary. **sussidio** *sm* aid; (*di denaro*) subsidy.

sussistere [sus'sistere] *v* exist; (*esser fondato*) subsist. **sussistenza** *sf* subsistence; (*mil*) catering.

sussultare [sussul'tare] *v* (give a) start. **far sussultare** startle. **sussulto** *sm* start.

sussurrare [sussur'rare] *v* murmur; (*dire a bassa voce*) whisper. **sussurro** *sm* murmur; whisper.

sutura [su'tura] *sf* suture. **suturare** *v* suture.

suvvia [suv'via] *inter* come on!

svago ['zvago] *sm* diversion; (*divertimento*) amusement. **svagare** *v* distract. **svagarsi** *v* amuse oneself. **svagatezza** *sf* absent-mindedness. **svagato** *agg* absent-minded.

svaligiare [zvali'dʒare] *v* ransack. **svaligiatore, -trice** *sm, sf* burglar.

svalutare [zvalu'tare] *v* devalue. **svalutazione** *sf* devaluation.

svanire [zva'nire] *v* vanish; (*fig*) fade away; (*esaurirsi*) lose strength. **svanito** *agg* (*odore*) evaporated; (*mente*) feeble-minded.

svantaggio [zvan'taddʒo] *sm* disadvantage; (*pregiudizio*) drawback; (*danno*) detriment. **svantaggiato** *agg* handicapped. **svantaggioso** *agg* disadvantageous; detrimental.

svariare [zva'rjare] *v* vary; diversify. **svariato** *agg* various.

svasato [zva'zato] *v* flared. **svasatura** *sf* flare.

svastica ['zvastika] *sf* swastika.

svecchiare [zvek'kjare] *v* renew.

svedese [zve'deze] *agg* Swedish. *sm* (*lingua*) Swedish; (*fiammifero*) safety match. *s(m+f)* (*persona*) Swede.

svegliare [zve'ʎare] *v* wake up; (*fig*) arouse. **svegliarsi** *v* wake up. **sveglia** *sf* call; (*mil*) reveille; (*orologio*) alarm-clock. **sveglio** *agg* awake; (*fig*) quick (-witted).

svelare [zve'lare] *v* reveal.

svelto ['zvɛlto] *agg* quick; intelligent; (*slanciato*) slim. **svelto di mano** light-fingered. **sveltezza** *sf* quickness; (*rapidità*) speed; slimness. **sveltire** *v* quicken; (*render disinvolto*) smarten *or* liven up; make (more) slender.

svendere ['zvendere] *v* sell off. **svendita** *sf* sale.

***svenire** [zve'nire] *v* faint. **svenevole** *agg* mawkish. **svenimento** *sm* fainting fit.

sventare [zven'tare] *v* foil. **sventatezza** *sf* thoughtlessness. **sventato** *agg* thoughtless.

sventola ['zvɛntola] *sf* fan; (*pugilato*) hook; (*schiaffo*) slap. **sventolare** *v* flutter; (*arieggiare*) air.

T

sventrare [zven'trare] *v* rip open; (*animale*) disembowel; (*fig*) demolish. **sventramento** *sm* demolition.

sventura [zven'tura] *sf* misfortune; (*mala sorte*) bad luck. **per colmo di sventura** to crown it all. **per mia sventura** unluckily for me. **sventurato** *agg* unlucky.

svergognare [zvergo'ɲare] *v* (put to) shame. **svergognatezza** *sf* impudence. **svergognato, -a** *sm, sf* shameless *or* impudent person.

svernare [zver'nare] *v* winter.

sverza ['zvɛrtsa] *sf* splinter. **sverzare** *v* splinter.

svestire [zves'tire] *v* undress.

Svezia ['zvetsja] *sf* Sweden.

svezzare [zvet'tsare] *v* wean. **svezzamento** *sm* weaning.

sviare [zvi'are] *v* divert; (*fig*) lead astray. **sviare il discorso** change the subject. **sviamento** *sm* diversion. **sviato** *agg* misguided.

svignarsela [zvi'ɲarsela] *v* sneak away.

svigorire [zvigo'rire] *v* weaken.

sviluppo [zvi'luppo] *sm* development; (*crescita*) growth. **età dello sviluppo** *sf* puberty. **sviluppare** *v* develop; (*produrre*) generate; (*estendersi*) grow.

svincolare [zvinko'lare] *v* release; (*riscattare*) redeem. **svincolarsi** *v* free oneself (from). **svincolo** *sm* release; (*comm*) clearance; (*autostrada*) exit.

svisare [zvi'zare] *v* twist.

sviscerare [zviʃe'rare] *v* disembowel; (*fig*) exhaust. **sviscerarsi per** dote on. **sviscerato** *agg* passionate; (*spreg*) obsequious.

svista ['zvista] *sf* oversight.

svitare [zvi'tare] *v* unscrew. **svitato, -a** *sm, sf* (*fam*) nut.

Svizzera ['zvittsera] *sf* Switzerland. **svizzero, -a** *s, agg* Swiss.

svogliato [zvo'ʎato] *agg* listless; unenthusiastic; (*indolente*) slack. **svogliatezza** *sf* listlessness.

svolazzare [zvolat'tsare] *v* flutter. **svolazzo** *sm* flourish.

*svolgere ['zvɔldʒere] *v* develop. **svolgersi** *v* proceed, go; (*distendersi*) unfold; (*voltarsi*) turn. **svolgimento** *sm* development. **svolta** *sf* turning; (*fig*) turning point; curve.

svuotare [zvwo'tare] *v* empty.

tabacco [ta'bakko] *sm* tobacco. **tabaccaio, -a** *sm, sf* tobacconist. **tabaccheria** *sf* tobacconist's (shop).

tabella [ta'bella] *sf* table; list. **tabellone** *sm* notice-board; (*per affissioni murali*) hoarding; (*sport*) score-board.

tabù [ta'bu] *agg, sm* taboo.

tabulatore [tabula'tore], **-trice** *sm, sf* tabulator.

tacca ['takka] *sf* nick; (*macchia*) blotch; (*qualità*) kind; (*difetto*) fault.

taccagno [tak'kaɲo] *agg* stingy. **taccagneria** *sf* stinginess.

taccheggiatore [takkeddʒa'tore], **-trice** *sm, sf* shop-lifter. **taccheggio** *sm* shop-lifting.

tacchino [tak'kino] *sm* turkey.

taccia ['tattʃa] *sf* (bad) reputation. **tacciare** *v* accuse.

tacco ['takko] *sm* heel. **battere i tacchi** click one's heels.

taccuino [takku'ino] *sm* note-book.

*tacere [ta'tʃere] *v* be *or* keep quiet; (*fam*) shut up; (*non dir nulla*) say nothing. **far tacere** hush.

tachimetro [ta'kimetro] *sm* speedometer.

tacito ['tatʃito] *agg* tacit; (*silenzioso*) silent. **taciturno** *agg* taciturn.

tafano ['tafano] *sm* horsefly.

tafferuglio [taffe'ruʎo] *sm* brawl.

taglia ['taʎa] *sf* (*premio*) reward; (*statura*) size.

tagliando [ta'ʎando] *sm* coupon; (*scontrino*) voucher.

tagliare [ta'ʎare] *v* cut; (*staccare, interrompere*) cut off; (*trinciare*) carve; (*in più parti*) cut up; (*vino*) blend. **tagliaboschi** *sm invar* woodcutter. **tagliacarte** *sm invar* paper-knife. **tagliapietre** *sm invar* stonemason. **tagliare la testa al toro** settle a matter once and for all.

tagliente [ta'ʎente] *agg* cutting.

tagliere [ta'ʎere] *sm* chopping board.

taglio ['taʎo] *sm* cut; (*parte staccata*) piece; (*parte tagliente*) (cutting) edge; (*importo*) denomination.

tagliola [ta'ʎola] *sf* trap.

tagliuzzare [taʎut'tsare] *v* chop up; (*a strisce*) cut to shreds.

tailleur [ta'jœr] *sm* suit.

talco ['talko] *sm* talc.

tale ['tale] *agg* such; certain. **tal dei tali** so-and-so. **tale quale** exactly like. **tale ...** **tale ... like ... like ....** **un (certo) tale** a certain person.

talento [ta'lento] *sm* talent.

talismano [taliz'mano] *sm* talisman, charm.

talloncino [tallon'tʃino] *sm* counterfoil.

tallone [tal'lone] *sm* heel. **tallonare** *v* shadow; (*sport*) mark.

talora [ta'lora] *avv* at times.

talpa ['talpa] *sf* mole.

taluni [ta'luni] *pron, agg* some.

talvolta [tal'vɔlta] *avv* sometimes.

tamburo [tam'buro] *sm* drum; (*sonatore*) drummer; (*mec*) barrel, drum. **tamburellare** *v* drum. **tamburello** *sm* tambourine.

Tamigi [ta'midʒi] *sm* Thames.

tamponare [tampo'nare] *v* plug; (*auto*) bump into. **tamponare una falla** stop a leak. **tampone** *sm* plug; tampon.

tana ['tana] *sf* den.

tanfo ['tanfo] *sm* musty smell.

tangente [tan'dʒente] *sf* tangent. **tangenziale** *sf* (*strada*) ring road.

tangibile [tan'dʒibile] *agg* tangible.

tango ['tango] *sm* tango.

tanto ['tanto] *agg* (so) much *or* many; (*altrettanto*) as much *or* many; (*molto*) a lot (of). **tanto ... quanto ...** as much ... as .... *pron* a lot; much *or* many. **tanti** *pron* (*persone*) so many (people). **tanto per** so much for. *avv* so (much); (*soltanto*) just. **da tanto** (*tempo*) for such a long time. **di tanto in tanto** from time to time. **ogni tanto** from time to time. **tanti auguri!** best wishes! congratulations! **tanto meglio** so much the better. **tanto più che** especially as.

tappa ['tappa] *sf* stage; (*sosta*) stop.

tappare [tap'pare] *v* shut; (*con tappo*) bung (up). **tapparsi il naso** hold one's nose. **tapparsi le orecchie** close one's ears.

tapparella [tappa'rɛlla] *sf* blind.

tappeto [tap'peto] *sm* carpet; (*piccolo*) rug; (*sport, tec*) mat. **mettere al tappeto** knock down.

tappezzare [tappet'tsare] *v* (*di carta*) paper; (*di legno*) panel; (*di stoffa*) cover, upholster. **tappezzeria** *sf* (*carta*) wallpaper; (*stoffa*) tapestry; (*legno*) panelling; (*mobili*) upholstery. **tappezziere** *sm* decorator; upholsterer.

tappo ['tappo] *sm* stopper, plug; (*sughero*) cork; (*a vite*) screw-cap.

tara ['tara] *sf* tare; defect. **tarato** *agg* (*tec*) calibrated; (*difettoso*) tainted.

tarantola [ta'rantola] *sf* tarantula.

tarchiato [tar'kjato] *agg* sturdy.

tardare [tar'dare] *v* be late. **tardi** *avv* late. **tardivo** *agg* late; retarded. **tardo** *agg* (*lento*) slow; (*tempo*) late; (*età*) ripe old.

targa ['targa] *sf* plate; (*auto*) number-plate. **targare** *v* (*auto*) register.

tariffa [ta'riffa] *sf* rate; (*trasporto pubblico*) fare; (*dogana*) tariff.

tarlo ['tarlo] *sm* woodworm. **tarlo del dubbio** gnawing doubt. **tarlato** *agg* worm-eaten.

tarma ['tarma] *sf* moth.

tarpare [tar'pare] *v* **tarpare le ali a** clip the wings of.

tartagliare [tarta'ʎare] *v* stammer.

tartaro ['tartaro] *sm* tartar.

tartaruga [tarta'ruga] *sf* tortoise.

tartassare [tartas'sare] *v* ill-treat.

tartina [tar'tina] *sf* canapé.

tartufo [tar'tufo] *sm* truffle.

tasca ['taska] *sf* pocket. **avere le tasche piene (di)** (*fam*) be sick and tired (of). **conoscere come le proprie tasche** know like the back of one's hand. **tascabile** *agg* pocket.

tassa ['tassa] *sf* tax; (*imposta*) duty; (*giudiziaria, scolastica*) fee. **tassametro** *sm* meter.

tassare [tas'sare] *v* tax. **tassare troppo** (*fig*) overtax. **tassabile** *agg* taxable; subject to duty. **tassativo** *agg* express; definite.

tassello [tas'sɛllo] *sm* dowel; (*prelievo*) wedge; (*indumento*) gusset.

tassi [tas'si] *sm* taxi. **tassista** *sm* taxi-driver.

tasso¹ ['tasso] *sm* (*zool*) badger.

tasso² ['tasso] *sm* (*bot*) yew(-tree).

tasso³ ['tasso] *sm* (*rapporto*) rate.

tastare [tas'tare] *v* feel. **tastare il terreno** (*fig*) see how the land lies. **tastiera** *sf* keyboard. **tasto** *sm* key; (*argomento*) subject; (*tatto*) touch. **a tastoni** feeling one's way.

tattica ['tattika] *sf* tactics *pl*. **tattico** *agg* tactical.

tatto ['tatto] *sm* touch; (*fig*) tact. **con tatto** tactfully. **mancare di tatto** be tactless. **senza tatto** tactlessly.

tatuaggio [tatu'addʒo] *sm* tattoo. **tatuare** *v* tattoo.

tautologia [tautolo'dʒia] *sf* tautology. **tautologico** *agg* tautological.

taverna [ta'vɛrna] *sf* inn, pub.

tavola ['tavola] *sf* table; (*asse*) board. **tavola calda** snack-bar. **tavola da disegno/stiro** drawing/ironing board. **tavola di comando** console. **tavola nera** blackboard. **tavola reale** (*gioco*) backgammon.

tavolato [tavo'lato] *sm* (*pavimento*) flooring; (*assito*) partition; (*geog*) plateau.

tavolo ['tavolo] *sm* table; (*ufficio, studio*) desk.

tavolozza [tavo'lɔttsa] *sf* palette.

tazza ['tattsa] *sf* cup; (*gabinetto*) lavatory pan; (*fontana*) basin.

te [te] *pron* you. *V* **ti.**

tè [te] *sm* tea.

teatro [te'atro] *sm* theatre; (*attività professionale*) stage; (*complesso di opere*) plays *pl*. **teatro lirico** (*edificio*) opera house; (*genere*) opera. **teatrale** *agg* theatrical.

tecnica ['tɛknika] *sf* technique; technology.

tecnico ['tɛkniko], **-a** *agg* technical. *sm, sf* technician, engineer; expert. **tecnicismo** *sm* technicality.

tecnologia [teknolo'dʒia] *sf* technology. **tecnologico** *agg* technological.

tedesco [te'desko], **-a** *s, agg* German.

tedio ['tɛdjo] *sm* tediousness. **tedioso** *agg* tedious.

tegame [te'game] *sm* (frying-)pan. **uova al tegame** *sf pl* fried eggs *pl*.

teglia ['teʎa] *sf* baking tin.

tegola ['tegola] *sf* (roofing-)tile. **coprire di tegole** tile. **tetto di tegole** *sm* tiled roof.

tela ['tela] *sf* cloth; (*pittura*) canvas; (*teatro*) curtain. **tela cerata** oilcloth. **tela da lenzuola** sheeting. **tela di lino** linen.

telaio [te'lajo] *sm* loom; (*auto*) chassis; (*tec*) frame.

telecabina [teleka'bina] *sf* cable-car.

telecomando [teleko'mando] *sm* remote control. **telecomandare** *v* operate by remote control.

telecronaca [tele'krɔnaka] *sf* news bulletin. **telecronista** *s(m+f)* television commentator.

telefonare [telefo'nare] *v* telephone; (*fam*) phone. **telefonata** *sf* telephone call. **telefonata urbana/interurbana/con preavviso** local/trunk/personal call. **telefonico**

agg telephone. **telefonista** *s(m+f)* telephonist. **telefono** *sm* telephone.

telegiornale [teledʒor'nale] *sm* television news.

telegrafare [telegra'fare] *v* telegraph. **telegrafico** *agg* telegraph; (*conciso*) telegraphic. **telegrafista** *s(m+f)* telegraph operator.

telegramma [tele'gramma] *sm* telegram.

telepatia [telepa'tia] *sf* telepathy. **telepatico** *agg* telepathic.

teleschermo [tele'skɛrmo] *sm* television screen.

telescopio [tele'skɔpjo] *sm* telescope.

telespettatore [telespetta'tore], **-trice** *sm, sf* viewer.

teletrasmissione [teletrazmis'sjone] *sf* television programme.

televisione [televi'zjone] *sf* televison; (*fam*) TV. **televisore** *sm* television set.

telone [te'lone] *sm* tarpaulin.

tema ['tɛma] *sm* theme, subject; (*scolastico*) essay. **fuori tema** off the point.

temerario [teme'rarjo] *agg* reckless; (*avventato*) rash. **temerità** *sf* temerity.

temere [te'mere] *v* fear, be afraid. **non temere!** don't worry!

temperamento [tempera'mento] *sm* temperament.

temperare [tempe'rare] *v* temper; (*matita*) sharpen. **temperato** *agg* temperate. **temperino** *sm* pen-knife.

temperatura [tempera'tura] *sf* temperature.

tempesta [tem'pɛsta] *sf* storm. **tempestare** *v* storm; (*ornare*) stud; (*importunare*) bombard. **tempestoso** *agg* stormy.

tempestivo [tempes'tivo] *agg* timely. **tempestività** *sf* timeliness.

tempia ['tɛmpja] *sf* temple.

tempio ['tɛmpjo] *sm* temple.

tempista [tem'pista] *s(m+f)* opportunist.

tempo ['tɛmpo] *sm* time; (*atmosferico*) weather; (*gramm*) tense; (*musica*) tempo, movement. **a suo tempo** (*passato*) originally; (*futuro*) in due course; (*al momento giusto*) at the right time. **a tempo debito** in due course. **a tempo perso** in one's spare time. **da tempo** for some time. **in un primo tempo** at first. **tempo da cani** foul weather.

temporale¹ [tempo'rale] *agg* temporal.

temporale² [tempo'rale] *sm* (thunder)storm. **temporalesco** *agg* stormy.

temporaneo [tempo'raneo] *sm* temporary.
temporeggiare [tempored'dʒare] *v* mark time, temporize.
temprare [tem'prare] *v* temper. **tempra** *sf* (*tec*) tempering, temper; (*fig*) fibre; (*voce*) timbre.
tenace [te'natʃe] *agg* firm; (*fig*) tenacious. **tenacia** *sf* tenacity. **tenacità** *sf* tenacity, firmness.
tenaglie [te'naʎe] *sf pl* pincers *pl*; (*pinze*) pliers *pl*; (*molle*) tongs *pl*.
tenda ['tɛnda] *sf* (*drappo*) curtain; (*da campo*) tent; (*tendone da sole*) awning. **tenda alla veneziana** Venetian blind. **tendina** *sf* net curtain.
tendenza [ten'dentsa] *sf* tendency; (*attitudine*) bent; (*orientamento, econ*) trend. **tendenziale** *agg* potential. **tendenzioso** *agg* tendentious.
*****tendere** ['tɛndere] *v* (*mettere in tensione*) stretch; (*porgere*) hold out; (*reti*) cast. **tendere a** (*mirare*) aim at; be inclined to; (*volgersi verso*) tend towards. **tendere un tranello** set a trap.
tendine ['tɛndine] *sm* tendon.
tenebre ['tɛnebre] *sf pl* darkness *sing*. **tenebroso** *agg* dark; (*fig*) mysterious.
tenente [te'nɛnte] *sm* lieutenant.
*****tenere** [te'nere] *v* hold; (*mantenere, trattenere*) keep; (*seguire una direzione*) keep to. **tenerci a** attach great importance to. **tenere a** (*volere*) want. **tener d'occhio** keep an eye on. **tener presente** bear in mind.
tenero ['tɛnero] *agg* tender. **tenerezza** *sf* tenderness.
tenia ['tɛnja] *sf* tapeworm.
tennis ['tɛnnis] *sm* tennis. **tennista** *s(m+f)* tennis player.
tenore [te'nore] *sm* tenor; content. **a tenore di** in accordance with. **tenore di vita** living standard.
tensione [ten'sjone] *sf* tension.
tentacolo [ten'takolo] *sm* tentacle.
tentare [ten'tare] *v* (*cercare*) try; (*sperimentare*) try out; (*cercare di fare*) attempt; (*invogliare*) tempt. **tentativo** *sm* attempt. **tentatore** *sm* tempter. **tentatrice** *sf* temptress. **tentazione** *sf* temptation. **aver la tentazione** (di) be tempted (to).
tentennare [tenten'nare] *v* wobble; hesitate.
tentoni [ten'toni] *avv* **a tentoni** groping one's way.

tenue ['tɛnue] *agg* slender; (*debole*) faint; (*fig*) slight.
tenuta [te'nuta] *sf* (*divisa*) uniform; (*possedimento fondiario*) estate; capacity; (*auto*) road-holding; (*tec*) seal. **a tenuta d'acqua** water-tight. **a tenuta d'aria** airtight.
teologia [teolo'dʒia] *sf* theology. **teologico** theological. **teologo, -a** *sm, sf* theologist.
teorema [teo'rɛma] *sm* theorem.
teoria [teo'ria] *sf* theory. **in teoria** theoretically.
teorico [te'ɔriko], **-a** *agg* theoretical. *sm, sf* theorist.
tepore [te'pore] *sm* warmth.
teppa ['teppa] *sf* also **teppaglia** rabble. **teppismo** *sm* hooliganism. **teppista** *s(m+f)* hooligan.
terapia [tera'pia] *sf* therapy. **terapeutico** *agg* therapeutic. **terapista** *s(m+f)* therapist.
tergicristallo [terdʒikris'tallo] *sm* windshield-wiper.
tergiversare [terdʒiver'sare] *v* prevaricate.
tergo ['tɛrgo] *sm* **a tergo** (*di dietro*) behind. **vedi a tergo** (*nei rinvii*) please turn over, PTO.
terme ['tɛrme] *sf pl* (thermal) baths *pl*. **termale** or **termico** *agg* thermal.
terminare [termi'nare] *v* end. **terminazione** *sf* ending. **termine** *sm* term; limit; (*punto estremo*) end; (*comm*) expiry (date). **a breve/lungo termine** short-/long-term. **ai termini di legge** by law. **a rigor di termini** strictly speaking. **terminologia** *sf* terminology.
termodinamica [termodi'namika] *sf* thermodynamics.
termometro [ter'mɔmetro] *sm* thermometer.
termonucleare [termonukle'are] *agg* thermonuclear.
termos *V* **thermos.**
termosifone [termosi'fone] *sm* radiator.
termostato [ter'mɔstato] *sm* thermostat. **termostatico** *agg* thermostatic.
terra ['tɛrra] *sf* earth; (*estensione di terreno, paese*) land; (*suolo*) soil. **a terra** (*senza soldi*) broke; (*depresso*) in low spirits; (*gomma*) flat. **collegare** or **mettere a terra** (*elett*) earth. **raso terra** close to the ground.
terraglia [ter'raʎa] *sf* earthenware. **terraglie** *sf pl* (*vasellame*) crockery *sing*.

terrapieno [terra'pjɛno] *sm* embankment.
terrazza [ter'rattsa] *sf* terrace. **terrazzo** *sm* terrace; (*alpinismo*) ledge.
terremoto [terre'mɔto] *sm* earthquake. **terremotato, -a** *sm*, *sf* earthquake victim.
terreno¹ [ter'reno] *agg* earthly, worldly. **piano terreno** ground floor.
terreno² [ter'reno] *sm* land; (*suolo*) ground; (*podere*) plot (of land); (*fig*) field.
terreo ['tɛrreo] *agg* earthy; (*colorito*) deathly pale.
terrestre [ter'rɛstre] *agg* terrestrial.
terribile [ter'ribile] *agg* terrible.
territorio [terri'tɔrjo] *sm* territory. **territoriale** *agg* territorial.
terrore [ter'rore] *sm* terror. **aver terrore (di)** be terrified (of). **terrorismo** *sm* terrorism. **terrorista** *s(m+f)* terrorist. **terroristico** *agg* terrorist. **terrorizzare** *v* terrorize.
terzo ['tɛrtso] *agg*, *sm* third. **terzi** *sm pl* (*comm, dir*) third party *sing*. **terzina** *sf* triplet.
tesa ['teza] *sf* (*cappello*) brim; (*reti*) spreading.
teschio ['tɛskjo] *sm* skull.
tesi ['tɛzi] *sf* thesis (*pl* -ses).
teso ['tezo] *agg* taut; (*nervoso*) tense. **stare con le orecchie tese** prick up one's ears.
tesoro [te'zɔro] *sm* treasure; (*tesoreria, pol*) treasury. **far tesoro (di)** treasure. **tesoriere** *sm* treasurer.
tessera ['tɛssera] *sf* card; (*lasciapassare*) pass; (*ferr*) season-ticket. **tesseramento** *sm* rationing. **tesserare** *v* give a membership card; ration.
tessere ['tɛssere] *v* weave. **tessitura** *sf* weaving; (*stabilimento*) (weaving) mill; (*trama*) plot. **tessuto** *sm* fabric; (*bot, zool, fig*) tissue.
tessile ['tɛssile] *agg* textile. *sm* textile; (*operaio*) textile worker.
testa ['tɛsta] *sf* head. **a testa** (*ciascuno*) each, per head. **colpo di testa** *sm* (*sport*) header; (*fig*) whim. **essere in testa** be in the lead. **fare a testa e croce** toss up. **passare in testa** take the lead. **rompersi la testa** rack one's brains.
testamento [testa'mento] *sm* will; (*bibbia*) testament.
testardo [tes'tardo] *agg* stubborn. **testardaggine** *sf* stubbornness.
testata [tes'tata] *sf* (*intestazione*) heading;

(*colpo di testa*) butt; (*auto*) cylinder head; (*parte anteriore*) head.
testicolo [tes'tikolo] *sm* testicle.
testimone [testi'mone] *s(m+f)* witness. **testimoniale** *sm* evidence. **testimonianza** *sf* testimony; (*prova*) evidence. **testimoniare** *v* testify; (*deporre in giudizio*) (bear) witness.
testo ['tɛsto] *sm* text; (*libro*) text-book. **far testo** be an authority. **testuale** *agg* exact.
testone [tes'tone] *sm* (*stupido*) blockhead; (*testardo*) pig-headed person.
testuggine [tes'tuddʒine] *sf* tortoise; (*di mare*) turtle.
tetano ['tɛtano] *sm* tetanus.
tetro ['tɛtro] *agg* gloomy.
tetta ['tetta] *sf* (*fam*) breast. **tettarella** *sf* dummy.
tetto ['tetto] *sm* roof (*pl* -s). **essere senza tetto** be homeless. **tettoia** *sf* roofing, canopy.
Tevere ['tevere] *sm* Tiber.
thermos ® *or* **termos** ['tɛrmos] *sm invar* thermos (flask) ®.
ti [ti], **te** *pron* (to) you; (*riflessivo*) yourself.
tiara ['tjara] *sf* tiara.
tic [tik] *sm invar* tic.
ticchettare [tikket'tare] *v* click; (*pioggia*) patter; (*orologio*) tick.
ticchio ['tikkjo] *sm* whim.
tictac [tik'tak] *sm* tick.
tiepido ['tjɛpido] *agg* lukewarm.
tifo ['tifo] *sm* (*med*) typhus; (*fam: sport*) fanaticism. **fare il tifo per** be a fan of. (**febbre**) **tifoide** *sf* typhoid (fever).
tifone [ti'fone] *sm* typhoon.
tifoso [ti'fozo], **-a** *sm*, *sf* fan.
tiglio ['tiʎo] *sm* lime(-tree); (*fibra*) bast.
tigna ['tiɲa] *sf* ringworm.
tignola [ti'ɲola] *sf* moth.
tigre ['tigre] *sf* tiger.
timbrare [tim'brare] *v* stamp; (*posta*) postmark. **timbro** *sm* stamp; postmark; (*suono*) timbre.
timido ['timido] *agg* shy; (*timoroso*) timid.
timo ['timo] *sm* (*bot*) thyme.
timone [ti'mone] *sm* rudder; (*fig*) helm. **timoniere** *sm* helmsman; (*canottaggio*) cox.
timore [ti'more] *sm* fear. **senza timore** fearless. **timoroso** *agg* fearful; (*preoccupato*) anxious.
timpano ['timpano] *sm* (*anat*) ear-drum;

(*musica*) kettle-drum. **timpani** *sm pl* timpani *pl.*

tinca ['tinka] *sf* tench.

*tingere ['tindʒere] *v* dye; (*macchiare*) spot.

tino ['tino] *sm* tub, vat.

tinta ['tinta] *sf* colour; (*sfumatura*) shade. **tintarella** *sf* tan. **tinto** *agg* dyed; (*macchiato*) tinged. **tintore** *sm* dyer. **tintoria** *sf* cleaners. **tintura** *sf* dyeing; (*med*) tincture.

tipo ['tipo] *sm* type; (*genere*) sort, kind. **tipico** *agg* typical.

tipografia [tipogra'fia] *sf* typography; (*stamperia*) press. **tipografico** *agg* typographical. **tipografo, -a** *sm, sf* printer.

tiranneggiare [tiranned'dʒare] *v* tyrannize. **tirannia** *sf* tyranny. **tirannico** *agg* tyrannical. **tiranno** *sm* tyrant.

tirante [ti'rante] *sm* (connecting) rod; brace.

tirapiedi [tira'pjɛdi] *sm invar* hanger-on.

tirare [ti'rare] *v* pull, draw; (*lanciare*) throw; (*sparare*) shoot. **tirare avanti** keep going. **tirar fuori** pull out; (*estrarre*) take out. **tirare in lungo** draw out. **tirarsi indietro** draw back. **tirarsi su** draw oneself up; (*fam*) get back on one's feet. **tirata** *sf* pull; (*discorso*) tirade. **tiratura** *sf* printing; (*numero*) run.

tirchio ['tirkjo] *agg* stingy.

tiritera [tiri'tɛra] *sf* rigmarole.

tiro ['tiro] *sm* (*lancio*) throw; (*arma*) shot. **fuori tiro** out of range.

tirocinio [tiro'tʃinjo] *sm* apprenticeship.

tiroide [ti'rɔide] *sf* thyroid.

titolare [tito'lare] *agg* titular, regular. *s(m+f)* proprietor.

titolo ['titolo] *sm* title; (*comm*) share; (*obbligazione*) bond; (*filato*) count. **a titolo di** out of.

titubare [titu'bare] *v* hesitate.

tizio ['titsjo] *sm* fellow. **Tizio, Caio, e Sempronio** Tom, Dick, and Harry.

tizzo ['tittso] *sm* ember.

toboga [to'bɔga] *sm invar* toboggan.

toccare [tok'kare] *v* touch; (*riguardare*) concern. **tocca a me** it is my turn; (*spettare di diritto*) I am entitled; (*spettare di dovere*) it is up to me. **toccasana** *sm invar* panacea.

tocco¹ ['tokko] *sm* touch; (*campana*) stroke; (*l'una*) one o'clock.

tocco² ['tɔkko] *sm* (*pezzo*) hunk.

toga ['tɔga] *sf* toga.

*togliere ['tɔʎere] *v* take away; (*indumenti*) take off. **ciò non toglie che** it does not alter the fact that. **togliere di mezzo** get out of the way. **togliersi** *v* (*levarsi*) take off; (*soddisfare*) satisfy.

toletta [to'letta] *sf also* **toilette** toilet; (*mobile*) dressing table; (*acconciatura*) toilette; (*abito*) outfit.

tollerare [tolle'rare] *v* tolerate, stand; (*permettere*) allow. **tollerabile** *agg* bearable. **tollerante** *agg* tolerant. **tolleranza** *sf* tolerance.

tomaia [to'maja] *sf* upper.

tomba ['tomba] *sf* tomb.

tombola¹ ['tombola] *sf* (*gioco*) tombola; bingo.

tombola² ['tombola] *sf* (*caduta*) fall.

tomo ['tɔmo] *sm* tome; (*tipo strano*) odd type.

tonaca ['tɔnaka] *sf* (*frati, monache*) habit; (*preti*) cassock.

tonalità [tonali'ta] *sf* tonality; (*colore*) shade.

tonare [to'nare] *v* thunder.

tonchio ['tonkjo] *sm* weevil.

tondo ['tondo] *agg* round. *sm* round plate; (*forma*) circle. **parlar chiaro ɜ tondo** speak bluntly.

tonfo ['tonfo] *sm* thud; (*nell'acqua*) splash.

tonico ['tɔniko] *agg* tonic. **tonica** *sf* (*musica*) tonic.

tonnellata [tonnel'lata] *sf* ton. **tonnellaggio** *sm* tonnage.

tonno ['tonno] *sm* tuna, tunny.

tono ['tɔno] *sm* tone. **cambiar tono** change (one's) tune. **fuori tono** out of tune. **giù di tono** out of sorts. **in tono** in tune; (*fisicamente*) fit.

tonsilla [ton'silla] *sf* tonsil. **tonsillite** *sf* tonsillitis.

tonto ['tonto], **-a** *agg* silly. *sm, sf* fool.

topazio [to'patsjo] *sm* topaz.

topico ['tɔpiko] *agg* local; (*fig*) topical.

topo ['tɔpo] *sm* mouse (*pl* mice); (*campagnolo*) fieldmouse. **topo di biblioteca** bookworm.

topografia [topogra'fia] *sf* topography. **topografico** *agg* topographical.

toporagno [topo'raɲo] *sm* shrew.

toppa ['tɔppa] *sf* patch; (*serratura*) keyhole.

torace [to'ratʃe] *sm* chest.

torba ['tɔrba] *sf* peat.
torbido ['tɔrbido] *agg* turbid, muddy. **c'è del torbido** there's something fishy going on.
***torcere** ['tɔrtʃere] *v* twist; (*strizzare*) wring out. **torcere il collo a qualcuno** wring someone's neck. **torcere il naso** turn up one's nose. **torcersi il collo** crane one's neck. **torcicollo** *sm* crick in the neck.
torchio ['tɔrkjo] *sm* press. **torchiare** *v* press.
torcia ['tɔrtʃa] *sf* torch.
tordo ['tordo] *sm* thrush.
Torino [to'rino] *sf* Turin.
torma ['torma] *sf* herd; (*persone*) throng.
tormentare [tormen'tare] *v* torment. **tormento** *sm* torment; (*infastidire*) plague.
tornaconto [torna'konto] *sm* advantage.
tornante [tor'nante] *sm* hairpin bend.
tornare [tor'nare] *v* return; (*andare di nuovo*) go back; (*venire di nuovo*) come back; (*ricominciare*) start again. **ben tornato!** welcome back! **qualcosa non torna** something is not quite right.
torneo [tor'nɛo] *sm* tournament.
tornio ['tɔrnjo] *sm* lathe. **tornire** *v* turn. **tornitore** *sm* (*tec*) lathe operator; (*di legno*) wood turner.
toro ['tɔro] *sm* bull. **Toro** *sm* Taurus.
torpedine [tor'pedine] *sf* torpedo.
torpedone [torpe'done] *sm* coach.
torpido ['tɔrpido] *agg* sluggish. **torpore** *sm* sluggishness.
torre ['torre] *sf* tower; (*scacchi*) rook, castle. **torretta** *sf* turret.
torrefare [torre'fare] *v* roast. **torrefazione** *sf* roasting.
torrente [tor'rɛnte] *sm* torrent. **torrenziale** *agg* torrential.
torrido ['tɔrrido] *agg* torrid.
torrone [tor'rone] *sm* nougat.
torso ['tɔrso] *sm* stalk; (*frutta*) core; (*anat*) torso. **a torso nudo** bare-chested.
torsolo ['tɔrsolo] *sm* stalk; (*frutta*) core.
torta ['tɔrta] *sf* cake; (*di frutta*) tart; (*pasticcio*) pie.
tortiglione [torti'ʎone] *sm* spiral. **a tortiglione** spiral.
torto¹ ['tɔrto] *sm* wrong; (*colpa*) fault. **a torta** wrongfully. **aver torto** be wrong. **dar torto a** prove wrong.
torto² ['tɔrto] *agg* twisted.
tortora ['tɔrtora] *sf* turtle-dove.
tortuoso [tortu'ozo] *agg* tortuous.

torturare [tortu'rare] *v* torture. **tortura** *sf* torture.
torvo ['torvo] *agg* surly.
tosare [to'zare] *v* shear; (*cani*) clip; (*fig*) fleece. **tosatrice** *sf* (*capelli*) hair-clippers *pl*; (*erba*) lawn-mower. **tosatura** *sf* shearing; clipping.
Toscana [tos'kana] *sf* Tuscany. **toscano, -a** *s*, *agg* Tuscan.
tosse ['tosse] *sf* cough. **tossire** *v* cough.
tossico ['tossiko] *agg* poisonous. *sm* poison. **tossicità** *sf* toxicity. **tossicomane** *s(m+f)* drug addict. **tossicomania** *sf* drug addiction. **tossina** *sf* toxin.
tostare [tos'tare] *v* roast; (*pane*) toast. **tostapane** *sm invar* toaster.
tosto ['tɔsto] *agg* **faccia tosta** *sf* (*fam*) cheek.
totale [to'tale] *agg*, *sm* total. **totalità** *sf* entirety.
totalitario [totali'tarjo] *agg* (*pol*) totalitarian.
totano ['tɔtano] *sm* squid.
totocalcio [toto'kaltʃo] *sm* football pools *pl*.
tovaglia [to'vaʎa] *sf* table-cloth. **tovagliolo** *sm* napkin, serviette.
tozzo¹ ['tottso] *agg* squat; (*persone*) stocky.
tozzo² ['tottso] *sm* piece.
tra [tra] *prep* among(st); (*tra due*) between; (*nel mezzo*) in the midst of; (*tempo*) in. **tra breve** *or* **poco** soon. **tra l'altro** among other things; (*inoltre*) besides.
traballare [trabal'lare] *v* wobble; (*persone, fig*) totter.
traboccare [trabok'kare] *v* overflow. **trabocchetto** *sm* trap.
tracannare [trakan'nare] *v* gulp down.
traccia ['trattʃa] *sf* track, trail; (*orma*) footprint; (*indizio*) trace. **tracciare** *v* trace; (*abbozzare*) sketch (out); (*a grandi linee*) outline. **tracciato** *sm* layout.
trachea [tra'kɛa] *sf* windpipe.
tracolla [tra'kɔlla] *sf* shoulder-strap. **a tracolla** over one's shoulder. **borsetta a tracolla** *sf* shoulder-bag.
tradire [tra'dire] *v* betray; (*coniugi*) be unfaithful (to). **tradimento** *sm* treachery; (*dir*) treason. **a tradimento** by surprise. **traditore** *sm* traitor. **traditrice** *sf* traitress.
tradizione [tradi'tsjone] *sf* tradition. **tradizionale** *agg* traditional.

*tradurre [tra'durre] v translate; (condurre) convey. traduttore, -trice sm, sf translator. traduzione sf translation.
trafelato [trafe'lato] agg out of breath.
trafficare [traffi'kare] v (commerciare) trade, deal; (spreg) traffic; (darsi da fare) busy oneself. traffico sm traffic.
*trafiggere [tra'fiddʒere] v pierce.
trafila [tra'fila] sf (operazione) (lengthy) procedure. trafilare v draw. trafiletto sm paragraph.
traforare [trafo'rare] v bore, drill; (legno) cut with a fretsaw. traforatrice sf drill; (sega) fretsaw. traforo sm tunnel; fretsaw.
tragedia [tra'dʒɛdja] sf tragedy.
traghetto [tra'getto] sm ferry. traghettare v ferry (across).
tragico ['tradʒiko] agg tragic. sm tragedy; (autore) tragedian; (attore) tragic actor. prendere sul tragico dramatize.
tragitto [tra'dʒitto] sm journey; (traversata) crossing.
traguardo [tra'gwardo] sm finish; (sport) winning-post; (fig) goal.
traiettoria [trajet'tɔrja] sf trajectory; (di volo) flight-path.
trainare [trai'nare] v pull or haul along; (rimorchiare) tow. traino sm haulage; (rimorchio) trailer; (con pattini) sledge.
tralasciare [trala'ʃare] v leave out; interrupt; (trascurare) neglect.
tralcio ['traltʃo] sm shoot.
traliccio [tra'littʃo] sm (tessuto) ticking; (struttura) truss; (graticcio) trellis.
tram [tram] sm invar tram.
trama ['trama] sf (tessile) weft; (fig) plot. tramare v plot.
tramandare [traman'dare] v hand down.
trambusto [tram'busto] sm turmoil.
tramezzare [tramed'dzare] v interpose; (dividere un locale) partition (off). tramezzo sm partition.
tramite ['tramite] sm means pl; intermediary. prep (per mezzo di) through.
tramontana [tramon'tana] sf (nord) north; (vento) north wind.
tramontare [tramon'tare] v set; (aver fine) come to an end; (dileguarsi) wane. tramonto sm sunset; (fig) decline.
tramortire [tramor'tire] v stun.
trampolino [trampo'lino] sm springboard; (piscina) diving-board; (palestra) trampoline; (sci) ski-jump.
trampolo ['trampolo] sm stilt.

tramutare [tramu'tare] v transform.
trancia ['trantʃa] sf (taglierina) cutter; (gastr) slice.
tranello [tra'nɛllo] sm trap; (fig) catch.
trangugiare [trangu'dʒare] v gulp down; (fig) swallow.
tranne ['tranne] prep except or but (for).
tranquillo [tran'kwillo] agg quiet, calm. stare tranquillo keep quiet or calm; (non turbarsi) not worry. tranquillità sf calm. tranquillante sm tranquillizer.
transatlantico [transat'lantiko] agg transatlantic. sm ocean liner.
transazione [transa'tsjone] sf (comm) transaction; (dir) settlement.
transistor [tran'sistor] sm invar transistor.
transitivo [transi'tivo] agg transitive.
transito ['transito] sm transit. transito interrotto road closed. transitabile agg practicable. transitorio agg transitory; (fis) transient.
transizione [transi'tsjone] sf transition.
tranvai [tran'vaj] sm tram. tranvia sf tramway.
trapanare [trapa'nare] v drill. trapanatrice sf drill. trapanatura sf drilling. trapano sm drill.
trapassare [trapas'sare] v run through; pass. trapassato sm past perfect. trapasso sm passing; transition; (dir) transfer.
trapelare [trape'lare] v leak out.
trapezio [tra'pɛtsjo] sm (geom) trapezium; (sport) trapeze. trapezista s(m+f) trapeze artist.
trapiantare [trapjan'tare] v transplant. trapianto sm transplant; (agric) transplantation.
trappola ['trappola] sf trap, snare.
trapuntare [trapun'tare] v quilt; (ricamare) embroider. trapunta sf quilt.
*trarre ['trarre] v draw. trarre in inganno deceive. trarre in tentazione lead into temptation.
trasalire [trasa'lire] v jump.
trasandato [trazan'dato] agg untidy.
*trascendere [tra'ʃɛndere] v transcend.
trascinare [traʃi'nare] v drag; (fig) carry away.
*trascorrere [tras'korrere] v spend; (tempo) pass.
*trascrivere [tras'krivere] v transcribe. trascrizione sf transcription.
trascurare [trasku'rare] v neglect; (omettere) fail. trascurato agg neglected; (noncurante) careless; (sciatto) slovenly.

trasferire [trasfe'rire] *v* transfer. **trasferirsi** *v* (*traslocare*) move. **trasferibile** *agg* transferable. **trasferimento** *sm* transfer. **trasferta** *sf* (*sport*) away match; (*viaggio*) business trip; (*indennità*) travelling expenses *pl*.

trasformare [trasfor'mare] *v* transform; (*cambiare*) change. **trasformare in** turn into. **trasformatore** *sm* transformer. **trasformazione** *sf* transformation.

trasfusione [trasfu'ːjone] *sf* (*med*) transfusion.

trasgredire [trazgre'dire] *v* disobey; (*legge*) infringe. **trasgressione** *sf* infringement.

traslocare [trazlo'kare] *v* move; (*impiegato*) transfer. **trasloco** *sm*, *pl* -chi move; transfer.

*****trasmettere** [traz'mettere] *v* transmit; (*communicare, dir*) convey; (*radio*) broadcast. **trasmettitore** *sm* transmitter; (*malattia*) carrier. **trasmissione** *sf* transmission; broadcast. **trasmittente** *sf* transmitter.

trasmodato [trazmo'dato] *agg* excessive.

trasognato [traso'ɲato] *agg* dreamy.

trasparente [traspa'rɛnte] *agg* transparent. *sm* transparency. **trasparenza** *sf* transparency.

trasparire [traspa'rire] *v* show through; (*alla luce*) shine through; (*palesarsi*) appear.

traspirare [traspi'rare] *v* transpire.

trasportare [traspor'tare] *v* carry; (*trascinare*) transport, carry away. **trasportatore** *sm* carrier; (*tec*) conveyor. **trasporto** *sm* transport; (*comm*) carriage; (*inoltro*) forwarding; (*per nave*) shipping.

trastullare [trastul'lare] *v* amuse. **trastullo** *sm* amusement; (*fig*) plaything.

trasudare [trasu'dare] *v* ooze.

trasversale [trazver'sale] *agg* transverse.

trasvolare [trazvo'lare] *v* fly across; (*fig*) barely touch.

tratta ['tratta] *sf* (*comm*) draft; (*traffico illecito*) trade.

trattare [trat'tare] *v* treat, deal with, handle. **si tratta di** ... it is about ..., it is a question of ... . **trattabile** *agg* negotiable; (*persona*) tractable. **trattamento** *sm* treatment. **trattativa** *sf* negotiation. **trattato** *sm* (*opera*) treatise; (*dir*) treaty.

tratteggiare [tratted'dʒare] *v* hatch; (*abbozzare*) outline.

*****trattenere** [tratte'nere] *v* (*far rimanere*)

keep (back); (*frenare*) restrain, hold back; (*detrarre*) withhold. **trattenersi** *v* (*restare*) stay; restrain oneself. **trattenimento** *sm* reception; (*spettacolo*) show.

tratto ['tratto] *agg* drawn. *sm* stroke; (*elemento caratteristico*) feature; (*frazione*) stretch; (*brano*) passage. **a tratti** at times. **di tratto in tratto** every now and then. **d'un tratto** all of a sudden.

trattore [trat'tore] *sm* tractor.

trattoria [tratto'ria] *sf* restaurant.

traudire [trau'dire] *v* mishear.

trauma ['trauma] *sm* trauma. **traumatico** *agg* traumatic.

travagliare [trava'ʎare] *v* torment. **travaglio** *sm* torment; (*angoscia*) distress **travaglio di parto** labour.

travasare [trava'zare] *v* decant.

trave ['trave] *sf* beam; (*di tetto*) rafter; (*di soffitto*) joist. **fare una trave di ogni fuscello** make a mountain out of a molehill.

traversare [traver'sare] *v* cross; (*da parte a parte*) go through. **traversata** *sf* crossing. **traversina** *sf* sleeper.

traverso [tra'vɛrso] *agg* cross, transverse. *sm* breadth, width. **andare di traverso** (*cibo*) go down the wrong way. **a traverso** sideways on. **guardare di traverso** look askance at. **prendere di traverso** take the wrong way.

travestire [traves'tire] *v* disguise. **travestito, -a** *sm*, *sf* (*psic*) transvestite.

traviare [travi'are] *v* lead astray. **traviamento** *sm* straying; corruption.

travisare [travi'zare] *v* distort. **travisamento** *sm* distortion.

*****travolgere** [tra'vɔldʒere] *v* sweep away; (*investire*) knock down; (*fig*) overwhelm. **travolgente** *agg* sweeping; overwhelming.

trazione [tra'tsjone] *sf* traction; (*auto*) drive.

tre [tre] *agg, sm* three.

trebbiare [treb'bjare] *v* thresh. **trebbia** *or* **trebbiatrice** *sf* threshing machine. **trebbiatura** *sf* threshing.

treccia ['trettʃa] *sf* braid, plait. **farsi le trecce** plait one's hair.

tredici ['treditʃi] *agg, sm* thirteen. **tredicesimo, -a** *agg* thirteenth.

tregua ['trɛgwa] *sf* truce; (*riposo*) rest. **senza tregua** unremitting; without respite; (*senza sosta*) non-stop.

tremare [tre'mare] *v* tremble; (*di freddo*) shiver; (*per emozioni*) shudder. **la tremarella** *sf* (*fam*) the shivers *pl*.

tremendo [tre'mɛndo] *agg* terrible, dreadful.

trementina [tremen'tina] *sf* turpentine.

tremito ['trɛmito] *sm* shaking, shudder(ing).

tremolare [tremo'lare] *v* quiver; (*stelle*) twinkle; (*luce*) flicker.

tremore [tre'more] *sm* tremor; (*agitazione*) trembling.

treno ['trɛno] *sm* train. **treno accelerato/diretto/direttissimo/rapido** slow/fast/through/express train. **treno di gomme/ruote** set of tyres/wheels.

trenta ['trenta] *sm*, *agg* thirty. **trentesimo** *sm*, *agg* thirtieth.

trepidare [trepi'dare] *v* be anxious.

trespolo ['trespolo] *sm* trestle; (*sgabello*) stool.

triangolo [tri'angolo] *sm* triangle. **triangolare** *agg* triangular.

tribolare [tribo'lare] *v* suffer; (*far soffrire*) torment. **vita tribolata** *sf* hard life.

tribordo [tri'bordo] *sm* starboard.

tribù [tri'bu] *sf* tribe. **membro di tribù** *sm* tribesman.

tribuna [tri'buna] *sf* platform; (*palco riservato*) gallery; (*campo sportivo*) stand; (*coperta*) grandstand.

tribunale [tribu'nale] *sm* court.

tributo [tri'buto] *sm* tribute. **tributare** *v* render. **tributario** *agg* (*tributi*) tax; (*fiume*) tributary.

tricheco [tri'kɛko] *sm* walrus.

triciclo [tri'tʃiklo] *sm* tricycle.

tricolore [triko'lore] *sm*, *agg* tricolour.

tric-trac ['tric'trac] *sm invar* backgammon.

tridimensionale [tridimensjo'nale] *agg* three-dimensional.

trifoglio [tri'fɔʎʎo] *sm* clover.

triglia ['triʎa] *sf* red mullet. **far l'occhio di triglia** (*fam*) make sheep's eyes.

trigonometria [trigonome'tria] *sf* trigonometry.

trillare [tril'lare] *v* trill. **trillo** *sm* trill.

trilogia [trilo'dʒia] *sf* trilogy.

trimestre [tri'mɛstre] *sm* quarter; (*scolastico*) term. **trimestrale** *agg* quarterly.

trina ['trina] *sf* lace.

trincare [trin'kare] *v* drink.

trincea [trin'tʃɛa] *sf* (*mil*) trench; (*ferr*) cutting. **trincerare** *v* entrench. **trinceramento** *sm* entrenchment.

trinciare [trin'tʃare] *v* cut up; (*pollo, ecc.*)

carve; (*in strisce sottili*) shred. **trinciato** *sm* (*tabacco*) shag.

trinità [trini'ta] *sf* trinity.

trio ['trio] *sm* trio.

trionfare [trion'fare] *v* triumph. **trionfale** *agg* triumphal. **trionfante** *agg* triumphant. **trionfo** *sm* triumph; success.

triplice ['triplitʃe] *agg* threefold. **in triplice copia** in triplicate. **triplo** *agg* treble, triple; (*di tre parti*) threefold. **il triplo** *sm* three times as much.

tripode ['tripode] *sm* tripod.

trippa ['trippa] *sf* tripe.

tripudiare [tripu'djare] *v* rejoice. **tripudio** *sm* jubilation.

triste ['triste] *agg* sad. **tristezza** *sf* sadness.

tristo ['tristo] *agg* (*malvagio*) wicked; (*meschino*) mean.

tritare [tri'tare] *v* grind; (*carne*) mince. **carne tritata** *sf* mince. **tritacarne** *sm invar* mincer. **trito** *agg* chopped, ground, minced; (*fig*) trite.

trittico ['trittiko] *sm* triptych.

trivellare [trivel'lare] *v* drill, bore. **trivella** *sf* auger; (*succhiello*) gimlet; (*miniera*) drill. **trivellazione** *sf* drilling, boring.

triviale [tri'vjale] *agg* vulgar; (*banale*) trivial. **trivialità** *sf* vulgarity; triviality.

trofeo [tro'fɛo] *sm* trophy.

trogolo ['trɔgolo] *sm* trough.

troia ['trɔja] (*volg*) *sf* (*scrofa*) sow; (*prostituta*) whore. **troiaio** *sm* pigsty. **troiata** *sf* (*lavoro mal fatto*) awful mess; (*azione sudicia*) dirty trick.

tromba ['tromba] *sf* trumpet; (*mil*) bugle; (*auto*) horn; (*ascensore, scale*) well; (*anat*) tube. **tromba d'aria** tornado. **trombetta** *sm* trumpeter; (*trombettiere*) bugler. **trombone** *sm* trombone. **trombonista** *s(m+f)* trombonist.

trombosi [trom'bɔzi] *sf* thrombosis.

troncare [tron'kare] *v* cut off; (*spezzare, fig*) break off.

tronco[1] ['tronko] *agg* cut off, broken off; (*mat, parole*) truncated.

tronco[2] ['tronko] *sm* trunk; (*tratto*) section; (*arch*) shaft.

tronfio ['tronfjo] *agg* puffed up, pompous.

trono ['trɔno] *sm* throne.

tropico ['trɔpiko] *sm* tropic. **tropicale** *agg* tropical.

troppo ['trɔppo] *agg* too much; (*pl*) too many. *avv* too much; (*con agg e avv*) too.

trota ['trɔta] *sf* trout.

trottare [trot'tare] *v* trot. **trotto** *sm* trot; (*andatura svelta*) brisk pace. **andare al piccolo trotto** jog-trot. **rompere il trotto** break into a gallop. **trotterellare** *v* jog (along); (*bambini*) toddle (along).

trottola ['trɔttola] *sf* (spinning) top.

trovare [tro'vare] *v* find. **andare a trovare** go to see, call on. **trovare in fallo** catch red-handed. **trovarsi** *v* (*essere*) be; (*per caso*) happen to be; (*sentirsi*) get on; (*incontrarsi*) meet; (*pensare*) think. **trovata** *sf* good idea; expedient. **trovata pubblicitaria** publicity stunt. **trovatello, -a** *sm, sf* foundling.

truccare [truk'kare] *v* make up; (*falsificare*) doctor; (*auto*) soup up; (*sport*) fix. **truccarsi** *v* disguise oneself; (*imbellettarsi*) put make-up on. **truccatore, -trice** *sm, sf* make-up artist. **truccatura** *sf* (*teatro*) making-up; (*belletto, ecc.*) make-up. **trucco** *sm* make-up; (*inganno*) trick.

truce ['trutʃe] *agg* grim.

truciolo ['trutʃolo] *sm* (wood) chip, shaving.

truffare [truf'fare] *v* cheat, swindle; (*dir*) defraud. **truffa** *sf* swindle; (*dir*) fraud. **truffatore, -trice** *sm, sf* swindler, cheat.

truppa ['truppa] *sf* troop; (*fig*) horde.

tu [tu] *pron* you. **a tu per tu** face to face.

tuba ['tuba] *sf* (*musica*) tuba; (*cappello*) top-hat; (*anat*) tube.

tubare [tu'bare] *v* coo.

tubercolosi [tuberko'lɔzi] *sf* tuberculosis.

tubo ['tubo] *sm* pipe, tube; (*flessibile*) hose(-pipe); (*anat*) canal. **tubazione** *sf* piping. **tubetto** *sm* tube. **tubolare** *agg* tubular.

tuffare [tuf'fare] *v* plunge, dip. **tuffarsi** *v* plunge; (*fare un tuffo*) dive. **tuffo** *sm* dive.

tulipano [tuli'pano] *sm* tulip.

tumefatto [tume'fatto] *agg* swollen.

tumore [tu'more] *sm* tumour.

tumulto [tu'multo] *sm* uproar; (*sommossa*) riot. **tumultuoso** *agg* tumultuous; (*chiassoso*) rowdy.

tunica ['tunika] *sf* tunic.

tuo ['tuo], *m pl* **tuoi** *agg* your. *pron* yours.

tuono ['twɔno] *sm* thunder. **tuonare** *v* thunder.

tuorlo ['twɔrlo] *sm* yolk.

turare [tu'rare] *v* plug; (*con sughero*) cork. **turarsi il naso** hold one's nose. **turacciolo** *sm* stopper; (*di sughero*) cork; (*botte*) bung.

turba ['turba] *sf* mob.

turbante [tur'bante] *sm* turban.

turbare [tur'bare] *v* trouble; disturb; (*sconvolgere*) upset. **turbarsi** *v* get upset. **turbamento** *sm* disturbance, anxiety.

turbina [tur'bina] *sf* turbine.

turbine ['turbine] *sm* whirl; (*neve, sabbia*) storm; (*fig*) (seething) horde. **turbine di vento** whirlwind. **turbolento** *agg* turbulent; (*inquieto*) unruly.

turchese [tur'keze] *s(m+f)*, *agg* turquoise.

Turchia [tur'kia] *sf* Turkey. **turco, -a** *sm, agg* Turkish; *sm, sf* (*persona*) Turk. **bestemmiare come un turco** swear like a trooper. **fumare come un turco** smoke like a chimney. **parlare (in) turco** (*fam*) talk double Dutch.

turchino [tur'kino] *agg, sm* deep blue.

turismo [tu'rizmo] *sm* tourism; (*culturale*) sight-seeing. **fare del turismo** tour, travel. **turista** *s(m+f)* tourist; sightseer.

turlupinare [turlupi'nare] *v* swindle; (*fam*) take in.

turno ['turno] *sm* (*volta*) turn; (*lavoro*) shift; (*mil*) guard. **essere di turno** be on duty. **fare a turno** take turns. **lavoro a turni** *sm* shift-work.

turpe ['turpe] *agg* foul. **turpiloquio** *sm* foul language.

tuta ['tuta] *sf* overalls *pl*; (*sport*) tracksuit.

tutela [tu'tɛla] *sf* defence; (*dir*) guardianship, protection. **tutelare** *v* protect; (*salvaguardare*) safeguard.

tuttavia [tutta'via] *cong* nevertheless.

tutto ['tutto] *agg* all; (*intero*) the whole (of); (*pl*) every. *pron* everything; (*pl*) everybody *sing*. *avv* completely. **a tutta velocità** at full speed. **il tutto** the whole (thing), everything. **innanzi tutto** first of all. **in tutti i modi** anyhow. **noi tutti** all of us. **tutt'ad un tratto** all of a sudden. **tutt'altro** anything but. **tutti e due** both (of them). **tutti i giorni** every day. **una volta per tutte** once and for all.

tuttora [tut'tora] *avv* still.

U

ubbia [ub'bia] *sf* silly idea; prejudice.

ubbidire [ubbi'dire] *v* obey; (*essere ubbidiente*) be obedient; (*dar retta*) listen (to). **ubbidiente** *agg* obedient. **ubbidienza** *sf* obedience.

ubriacare [ubria'kare] *v* make drunk, intoxicate. **ubriacarsi** *v* get drunk. **ubriachezza** *sf* drunkenness. **ubriaco, -a** *s*, *agg*, *m pl* **-chi** drunk. **ubriaco fradicio** dead drunk.

uccello [ut'tʃɛllo] *sm* bird.

***uccidere** [ut'tʃidere] *v* kill; (*assassinare*) murder. **uccisione** *sf* killing; murder. **ucciso** *agg* killed; murdered. **uccisore** *sm* killer; murderer.

***udire** [u'dire] *v* hear. **udibile** *agg* audible. **udienza** *sf* hearing; (*formale*) audience. **uditivo** *agg* (*fis*) audible; (*med*) auditory. **udito** *sm* hearing. **uditore, -trice** *sm*, *sf* listener. **uditorio** *sm* audience.

uffa ['uffa] *inter* **uffa, che noia!** what a bore!

ufficiale [uffi'tʃale] *agg* official. *sm* officer. **ufficiale di stato civile** registrar.

ufficio [uf'fitʃo] *sm* office; (*dovere, compito*) duty. **d'ufficio** official; (*ufficialmente*) officially; (*in veste ufficiale*) ex officio. **ufficio di collocamento** employment exchange. **ufficioso** *agg* unofficial.

ufo ['ufo] *avv* **a ufo** for nothing. **mangiare a ufo** scrounge a meal.

uggia ['uddʒa] *sf* boredom. **avere in uggia** dislike. **prendere in uggia** take a dislike to. **uggioso** *agg* boring.

uggiolare [uddʒo'lare] *v* whine.

ugola ['ugola] *sf* (*anat*) uvula; (*fig*) voice.

uguagliare [ugwa'ʎare] *v* (*essere uguale*) equal; (*rendere uguale*) equalize, even out; (*livellare*) level. **uguaglianza** *sf* equality.

uguale [u'gwale] *agg also* **eguale** the same; uniform; (*mat*) equal. *sm* equal. **ugualmente** *avv* equally; uniformly; (*tuttavia*) just *or* all the same.

ulcera ['ultʃera] *sf* ulcer.

uliva [u'liva] *V* **oliva**.

ulteriore [ulte'rjore] *agg* further. **ulteriormente** *avv* further; (*più avanti*) farther on; (*in seguito*) subsequently.

ultimo ['ultimo], **-a** *agg* last; (*più recente*) latest; (*fondamentale*) ultimate. *sm*, *sf* last. **all'ultimo** at the end; (*in fine*) finally. **fino all'ultimo** to the very end. **ultimamente** *avv also* **negli ultimi tempi** lately.

ultimare *v* finish. **ultimatum** *sm invar* ultimatum. **ultimazione** *sf* completion.

ultrasensibile [ultrasen'sibile] *agg* hypersensitive.

ultrasonico [ultra'sɔniko] *agg* supersonic.

ultravioletto [ultravio'letto] *agg* ultraviolet.

ululare [ulu'lare] *v* howl. **ululato** *sm* howling; (*urlo*) howl.

umanesimo [uma'nɛzimo] *sm* humanism. **umanista** *s(m+f)* humanist. **umanistico** *agg* humanist.

umano [u'mano] *agg* human; (*compassionevole*) humane; (*comprensivo*) understanding. **umanità** *sf* humanity. **umanitario** *agg* humanitarian.

umettare [umet'tare] *v* moisten.

umido ['umido] *agg* damp; (*clima*) humid. *sm* dampness; humidity; (*gastr*) stew. **cucire in umido** stew. **umidità** *sf* dampness; humidity.

umile ['umile] *agg* humble. **umiltà** *sf* (*virtù, sentimento*) humility; (*qualità*) humbleness.

umiliare [umi'ljare] *v* humiliate, humble. **umiliazione** *sf* humiliation.

umore [u'more] *sm* (*disposizione*) mood; (*indole*) temperament; (*liquido*) humour. **essere di buon/cattivo umore** be in a good/bad mood; (*abitualmente*) be good-/bad-tempered. **umorismo** *sm* humour. **umorista** *s(m+f)* humorist. **umoristico** *agg* humorous; (*spiritoso*) witty.

un [un] *V* **uno**.

unanime [u'nanime] *agg* unanimous. **unanimità** *sf* unanimity. **all'unanimità** unanimously.

uncino [un'tʃino] *sm* hook. **uncinare** *v* hook. **croce uncinata** *sf* swastika. **uncinetto** *sm* crochet-hook. **lavorare all'uncinetto** crochet.

undici ['unditʃi] *agg*, *sm* eleven. **undicesimo** *sm*, *agg* eleventh.

***ungere** ['undʒere] *v* grease; (*rel*) anoint. **Ungheria** [unge'ria] *sf* Hungary. **ungherese** *s(m+f)*, *agg* Hungarian.

unghia ['ungja] *sf* nail; (*artiglio*) claw; (*minima distanza*) hair's breadth. **unghie** *sf pl* (*fig*) clutches *pl*. **unghiata** *sf* scratch; (*temperino*) indentation.

unguento [un'gwɛnto] *sm* ointment.

unico ['uniko] *agg* only; (*esclusivo*) sole; (*senza pari*) unique; (*enfatico*) one and only. **unicamente** *avv* only.

unicorno [uni'kɔrno] *sm* unicorn.
unificare [unifi'kare] *v* unify; (*fondere*) merge; standardize. **unificazione** *sf* union; merger; standardization.
uniforme [uni'forme] *sf*, *agg* uniform.
uniformare *v* (*adattare*) bring into line (with); (*render piano*) level out; standardize. **uniformarsi** *v* comply (with); adapt (to). **uniformità** *sf* uniformity; (*di superficie*) evenness; (*accordo*) agreement.
unione [u'njone] *sf* union; (*concordia*) unity.
unire [u'nire] *v* join; (*fig*) unite. **unirsi** *v* join; (*insieme con altri*) join up with.
unità [uni'ta] *sf* unity; (*misura*, *mil*) unit. **unità di misura** measure.
unito [u'nito] *agg* united; (*tinta*) plain. **unitamente a** together with.
università [universi'ta] *sf* university.
universitario, -a *sm*, *sf* university student.
universo [uni'vɛrso] *sm* universe. **universale** *agg* universal.
uno ['uno] *agg* one, a. *art* a, an. *pron* one; (*qualcuno*) someone. **fare un po' per uno** share equally. **nè l'uno nè l'altro** neither. **non me ne va bene una!** I can't get one thing right! **tutt'uno** the same thing. **uno a uno** one by one.
unto ['unto] *agg* (*cosparso di grasso*) greasy, oily; (*spalmato*) greased, oiled; (*sporco*) dirty. *sm* grease; (*gastr*) fat. **untuoso** *agg* greasy; (*fig*) unctuous.
uomo ['wɔmo] *sm*, *pl* **uomini** man (*pl* men). **l'uomo qualunque** the man in the street. **uomo d'affari** businessman. **uomo di fiducia** right-hand man. **uomo di spirito** wit.
uopo ['wɔpo] *sm* **all'uopo** (*a tale scopo*) for this purpose; (*al momento opportuno*) at the right moment. **essere d'uopo** be necessary.
uovo ['wɔvo] *sm*, *pl* **-a** *f* egg. **uovo al burro** *or* **tegame** fried egg. **uovo alla coque** boiled egg. **uovo in camicia** poached egg. **uovo sodo/strapazzato** hardboiled/scrambled egg.
uragano [ura'gano] *sm* hurricane; (*tempesta*) storm.
uranio [u'ranjo] *sm* uranium.
urbano [ur'bano] *agg* (*di città*) town, urban; (*cortese*) urbane. **nettezza urbana** refuse collection. **urbanistica** *sf* town-planning. **urbanista** *s(m+f)* town-planner.

urgente [ur'dʒɛnte] *agg* urgent. **urgenza** *sf* urgency. **aver urgenza di** need urgently. **chiamata d'urgenza** *sf* emergency call.
urgere ['urdʒere] *v* (*sollecitare*) urge; (*abbisognare*) be required urgently.
urina [u'rina] *sf* urine. **urinare** *v* urinate. **urinario** *agg* urinary.
urlare [ur'lare] *v* scream; (*animali*) howl; (*dire ad alta voce*) shout. **urlo** *sm*, *pl* **-a** *f* shout; howl; scream.
urna ['urna] *sf* urn. **andare alle urne** go to the polls.
urrà [ur'ra] *inter* hurrah!
urtare [ur'tare] *v* knock *or* bump (into); (*dare uno spintone*) jostle; (*fig*) annoy. **urtarsi** *v* (*scontrarsi*) clash; (*auto*) collide; (*fig*) get irritated. **urto** *sm* (*spinta*) push; (*scontro*) clash, collision.
usare [u'zare] *v* use; (*essere solito a*) be accustomed to; (*essere di moda*) be fashionable; (*servirsi di*) make use of; (*fig*) exercise. **usanza** *sf* custom; habit.
uscio ['uʃo] *sm* door. **mettere fuori dell'uscio** turn out (of the house). **uscio di casa** front door.
***uscire** [u'ʃire] *v* leave; (*andar fuori*) go out; (*venir fuori*) come out; (*scendere*) get off; (*sboccare*) lead. **uscir di mente** slip one's mind. **uscir di strada** go off the road. **uscire in macchina** go for a drive.
uscita *sf* (*passaggio*) exit, way out; (*sbocco*) outlet; (*motto di spirito*) witty remark; (*spesa*) outlay; (*a carte*) lead. **essere in libera uscita** be off duty. **giorno di libera uscita** *sm* day off. **uscita di sicurezza** emergency exit.
usignolo [uzi'ɲɔlo] *sm* nightingale.
uso ['uzo] *sm* use; (*usanza*) custom; (*voga*) fashion. **c'è l'uso** it is customary. **uso e consumo** wear and tear. **usuale** *agg* usual; customary; common.
ustionare [ustjo'nare] *v* scald. **ustione** *sf* scald.
usufruire [uzufru'ire] *v* benefit (from).
usura[1] [u'zura] *sf* usury. **a usura** with interest. **usuraio, -a** *sm*, *sf* usurer.
usura[2] [u'zura] *sf* (*tec*) wear. **resistente all'usura** hard-wearing.
usurpare [uzur'pare] *v* usurp. **usurpatore, -trice** *sm*, *sf* usurper.
utensile [u'tɛnsile] *sm* tool, utensil. **macchina utensile** *sf* machine tool.
utente [u'tɛnte] *s(m+f)* user.

utero ['utero] *sm* womb.
utile ['utile] *agg* useful; (*persona di aiuto*) helpful. **in tempo utile** in good time. **tornar utile** come in handy. *sm* profit. **utili** *sm pl* (*reddito*) income *sing*. **utilità** *sf* usefulness, use; profit. **utilizzare** *v* utilize. **utilizzazione** *sf* utilization.
utopia [uto'pia] *sf* utopia.
uva ['uva] *sf* grapes *pl*. **acino d'uva** *sm* grape. **uva secca** *or* **passa** raisins *pl*. **uva spina** gooseberry.

V

vacanza [va'kantsa] *sf* holiday; (*l'essere vacante*) vacancy. **vacante** *agg* vacant.
vacca ['vakka] *sf* cow. **vaccata** *sf* (*volg*) rubbish. **vacchetta** *sf* (*cuoio*) cowhide.
vaccinare [vattʃi'nare] *v* vaccinate. **vaccinazione** *sf* vaccination. **vaccino** *sm* vaccine.
vacillare [vatʃil'lare] *v* totter; (*essere incerto*) waver.
vagabondo [vaga'bondo] **-a** *agg* roving. *sm*, *sf* vagrant; (*spreg*) loafer. **vagabondare** *v* wander (about).
vagare [va'gare] *v* stray.
vagina [va'dʒina] *sf* vagina.
vagire [va'dʒire] *v* wail. **vagito** *sm* wail(ing).
vaglia¹ ['vaʎa] *sm invar* money order. **vaglia postale** postal order.
vaglia² ['vaʎa] *sf* **di vaglia** of note.
vagliare [va'ʎare] *v* sift; (*argomenti, ecc.*) weigh (up). **vagliatura** *sf* sifting; (*esame attento*) careful consideration. **vaglio** *sm* sieve; close examination.
vago ['vago] *agg* vague. **vaghezza** *sf* vagueness.
vagone [va'gone] *sm* (*per passeggeri*) carriage; (*per merci*) wagon. **vagone letto/ristorante** sleeping-/dining-car.
vaiolo [va'jɔlo] *sm* smallpox.
valanga [va'langa] *sf* avalanche; (*fig*) shower.
valente [va'lɛnte] *agg* skilled, clever.
*****valere** [va'lere] *v* (*aver valore*) be worth; (*aver merito*) be good; (*aver forza legale*) apply; (*esser regolare*) be valid; (*contare*) count; (*essere utile*) be of use; (*importare*) matter. **far valere** assert. **farsi valere** demand respect; (*imporsi*) assert

oneself. **vale a dire** that is to say. **tanto vale** one might as well. **valere la pena** be worth it. **valere un occhio della testa** be worth a fortune.
valevole [va'levole] *agg* valid.
valicare [vali'kare] *v* cross. **valico** *sm*, *pl* **-chi** pass; crossing.
valido ['valido] *agg* valid; (*efficace*) effective; (*forte*) strong. **validità** *sf* validity.
valigia [va'lidʒa] *sf* suitcase. **far le valigie** pack. **valigeria** *sf* (*merce*) travel goods *pl*.
valle ['valle] *sf also* **vallata** valley. **a valle di** below. **scendere a valle** go downhill.
vallone *sm* deep valley; (*depressione*) gorge.
valletto [val'letto] *sm* page; assistant.
valore [va'lore] *sm* value; (*pregio*) worth; validity; (*significato*) meaning; (*coraggio*) valour. **aver valore di** amount to. **carte valori** *sf pl* securities *pl*. **di valore** of value, valuable; (*professionista*) leading. **imposta di valore aggiunto (IVA)** valued added tax (VAT). **privo di valore** worthless; of no value. **valori** *sm pl* valuables *pl*.
valorizzare [valorid'dzare] *v* exploit; (*mettere in evidenza*) make the most of. **valorizzazione** *sf* exploitation.
valuta [va'luta] *sf* currency.
valutare [valu'tare] *v* value; (*calcolare*) estimate; (*tenere in considerazione*) rate; (*vagliare*) weigh. **valutazione** *sf* evaluation; estimation; (*calcolo approssimativo*) estimate.
valvola ['valvola] *sf* valve; (*elett*) fuse. **valvola di sicurezza** safety-valve.
valzer ['valtser] *sm invar* waltz.
vampa ['vampa] *sf* blaze; (*arrossamento*) flush. **vampata** *sf* blaze; (*fig*) burst; flush; (*al viso*) blush.
vampiro [vam'piro] *sm* vampire.
vandalo ['vandalo] *sm* vandal. **vandalismo** *sm* vandalism.
vaneggiare [vaned'dʒare] *v* rave.
vanesio [va'nɛzjo] *agg* fatuous, vain.
vangare [van'gare] *v* dig (over). **vanga** *sf* spade.
vangelo [van'dʒɛlo] *sm* gospel.
vaniglia [va'niʎa] *sf* vanilla.
vanità [vani'ta] *sf* vanity. **vanitoso** *agg* vain.
vano ['vano] *agg* vain. *sm* (*locale*) room; (*spazio*) space. **rendere vano** make useless. **riuscir vano** be unsuccessful.

vantaggio [van'taddʒo] *sm* advantage; (*sport*) lead, handicap; profit. **vantaggiare** *v* favour. **vantaggioso** *agg* advantageous.
vantare [van'tare] *v* boast (of). **vantarsi** *v* boast, brag. **vantatore, -trice** *sm*, *sf* boaster, braggart. **vanteria** *sf* boasting, bragging. **vanto** *sm* (*vanteria*) boasting, bragging; (*atto*) boast.
vanvera ['vanvera] *sf* **a vanvera** (*senza riflettere*) without thinking; (*a casaccio*) at random.
vapore [va'pore] *sm* steam; (*nave*) steamer. **a tutto vapore** full steam ahead.
vaporizzare *v* vaporize. **vaporizzatore** *sm* vaporizer; (*profumi*) atomizer.
varare [va'rare] *v* launch. **varo** *sm* launch(ing).
varcare [var'kare] *v* cross; (*eccedere*) go beyond. **varco** *sm* opening. **aspettare al varco** lie in wait (for).
variare [va'rjare] *v* change; (*esser diverso*) vary. **(tanto) per variare** (just) for a change. **variare d'aspetto** look different. **variabile** *sf*, *agg* variable. **variabilità** *sf* variability. **variante** *sf* variant. **variato** *agg* varied. **variazione** *sf* variation.
varicella [vari'tʃɛlla] *sf* chicken-pox.
varicoso [vari'kozo] *agg* varicose.
varietà [varje'ta] *sf* variety. *sm* (*teatro*) variety.
vario ['varjo] *agg* (*variato*) varied; (*diverso*) various, different; (*non regolare*) variable. **variopinto** *agg* multicoloured. **vari** *pron pl* various people *pl*, several people *pl*.
vasca ['vaska] *sf* basin; (*da bagno*) bathtub; (*tino*) vat; (*piscina*) (swimming-) pool. **fare una vasca** (*sport*) swim a length.
vascello [va'ʃɛllo] *sm* vessel, warship. **ufficiale di vascello** *sm* naval officer.
vasellame [vazel'lame] *sm* crockery; (*di metallo prezioso*) plate; (*di porcellana*) china; (*di vetro*) glassware.
vaso ['vazo] *sm* pot; (*per fiori recisi*) vase; (*anat*) vessel. **vaso da fiori** flower-pot. **vaso da notte** chamber-pot. **vasaio, -a** *sm*, *sf* potter.
vassoio [vas'sojo] *sm* tray; (*del muratore*) mortar-board.
vasto ['vasto] *agg* wide, vast. **vastità** *sf* vastness.
Vaticano [vati'kano] *sm* Vatican. **città del Vaticano** *sf* Vatican City.

vaticinio [vati'tʃinjo] *sm* prediction. **vaticinare** *v* predict.
ve [ve] *V* vi.
vecchio ['vekkjo] *agg* old. *sm* old man. **vecchia** *sf* old woman. **vecchiaia** *sf* old age. **vecchiotto** *agg* oldish, fairly old; (*fuori moda*) out-of-date.
vece ['vetʃe] *sf* **fare le veci di** take the place of. **in mia vece** in my place.
*vedere [ve'dere] *v* see. **avere a che vedere con** have to do with. **dare a vedere** let it be understood. **far vedere** show. **non vederci più** (*fam*) be furious. **non veder l'ora di** look forward to. **stare a vedere** (*attendere*) see; (*guardare*) watch; (*scommettere*) bet. **vedere di buon occhio** approve (of). **vediamo un po'** let's see *sm*. **a mio vedere** in my opinion.
vedetta [ve'detta] *sf* look-out.
vedova ['vedova] *sf* widow. **vedovo** *sm* widower. **rimaner vedova** *or* **vedovo** be widowed. **vedovanza** *sf* widowhood.
veemente [vee'mɛnte] *agg* vehement.
vegetale [vedʒe'tale] *agg*, *sm* vegetable. **vegetariano, -a** *s*, *agg* vegetarian. **vegetativo** *agg* vegetative. **vegetazione** *sf* vegetation.
vegetare [vedʒe'tare] *v* vegetate. **vegeto** *agg* flourishing. **vivo e vegeto** alive and kicking.
vegliare [ve'ʎare] *v* (*vigilare*) watch; (*fare la veglia*) keep watch; (*star sveglio*) stay up. **veglia** *sf* watch, vigil; (*lo star desto*) wakefulness; (*festa*) party; (*funebre*) wake. **veglione** *sm* ball, party.
veicolo [ve'ikolo] *sm* vehicle; (*malattia*) carrier.
vela ['vela] *sf* sail; (*sport*) sailing. **a gonfie vele** booming. **barca a vela** *sf* sailing-boat. **volo a vela** *sm* gliding. **veleggiare** *v* sail; (*velivolo*) glide. **veliero** *sm* sailing-ship.
velare [ve'lare] *v* veil; cover; (*offuscare*) cloud, dim; (*suono*) muffle.
veleno [ve'leno] *sm* poison. **avere il veleno in corpo** (*fam*) have a chip on one's shoulder. **sputare veleno** (*fig*) vent one's spleen. **velenoso** *agg* poisonous; (*fig*) venomous.
velino [ve'lino] *agg* **carta velina** *sf* flimsy (paper). **velina** *sf* (*copia*) carbon copy.
velivolo [ve'livolo] *sm* aircraft; (*aliante*) glider.
velleità [vellei'ta] *sf* vain ambition.

vellicare [velli'kare] *v* titillate.
vello ['vɛllo] *sm* fleece.
velluto [vel'luto] *sm* velvet. **di velluto** velvet. **vellutato** *agg* velvety.
veloce [ve'lotʃe] *agg* quick, fast. **velocista** *s(m+f)* sprinter. **velocità** *sf* speed; (*fis*) velocity. **eccedere la velocità** (*auto*) speed.
velodromo [ve'lɔdromo] *sm* cycle-track.
veltro ['veltro] *sm* greyhound.
vena ['vena] *sf* vein; (*fig*) talent; inspiration. **essere in vena** be in the mood.
venale [ve'nale] *agg* saleable; (*spreg*) mercenary.
vendemmiare [vendem'mjare] *v* harvest (grapes). **vendemmia** *sf* grape harvest.
vendere ['vendere] *v* sell. **aver ... da vendere** have ... to spare; have plenty of .... **vendere a contanti** sell for cash. **vendere al dettaglio** *or* **minuto** retail. **vendere all'asta** auction. **vendere all'ingrosso** sell wholesale. **vendere fumo** bluff. **vendibile** *agg* saleable; (*messo in vendita*) for sale.
vendetta [ven'detta] *sf* revenge; (*castigo meritato*) vengeance.
vendicare [vendi'kare] *v* avenge. **vendicarsi** take revenge. **vendicativo** *agg* vindictive.
vendita ['vendita] *sf* sale. **vendita a rate** hire-purchase. **venditore, -trice** *sm, sf* vendor; (*negoziante*) shopkeeper.
venerare [vene'rare] *v* revere; (*rel*) worship. **venerabile** *agg* venerable. **venerazione** *sf* veneration.
venerdì [vener'di] *sm* Friday. **Venerdì Santo** Good Friday.
venereo [ve'nɛreo] *agg* venereal.
Venezia [ve'netsja] *sf* Venice. **veneziana** *sf* Venetian blind. **veneziano, -a** *s, agg* Venetian.
veniale [ve'njale] *agg* venial.
*venire [ve'nire] *v* come; (*riuscire*) come out; (*essere*) be. **far venire** (*mandare a chiamare*) call, send for. **mi viene da ...** I feel like .... **venire alle mani** come to blows. **venire incontro** come towards; (*incontrare*) meet; (*fig*) meet halfway. **venir meno** (*mancare*) be lacking; (*svenire*) pass out.
ventaglio [ven'taʎo] *sm* fan.
venti ['venti] *agg, sm* twenty. **ventesimo** *agg, sm* twentieth.

ventilare [venti'lare] *v* air; (*agric*) winnow. **ventilato** *agg* airy, ventilated. **ventilazione** *sf* ventilation.
vento ['vɛnto] *sm* wind.
ventosa [ven'toza] *sf* sucker.
ventre ['vɛntre] *sm* stomach; abdomen; (*forma*) belly; (*grembo materno*) womb. **ventrale** *agg* ventral.
ventricolo [ven'trikolo] *sm* ventricle.
ventriloquo [ven'trilokwo], **-a** *sm, sf* ventriloquist.
ventura [ven'tura] *sf* fortune. **alla ventura** at random. **andare** *or* **mettersi alla ventura** trust to luck; take a chance. **soldato di ventura** *sm* mercenary.
venturo [ven'turo] *agg* next.
vera ['vera] *sf* wedding ring.
verace [ve'ratʃe] *agg* (*veritiero*) truthful; (*vero*) true, real. **veracità** *sf* truthfulness.
veranda [ve'randa] *sf* veranda.
verbale [ver'bale] *sm* record, minutes *pl*. **mettere a verbale** put on record. *agg* verbal.
verbo ['vɛrbo] *sm* verb; (*parola*) word. **verboso** *agg* verbose, long-winded.
verde ['verde] *agg* green. *sm* green; (*natura*) greenery; (*zona*) green belt. **essere** *or* **trovarsi al verde** be broke. **verdastro** *agg* greenish. **verdeggiare** *v* be verdant; (*diventar verde*) turn green.
verdetto [ver'detto] *sm* verdict.
verdura [ver'dura] *sf* greens *pl*, vegetables *pl*.
verga ['verga] *sf* rod. **verga magica** magic wand. **vergare** *v* line; (*scrivere*) write.
vergine ['verdʒine] *sf, agg* virgin. **Vergine** *sf* Virgo. **verginale** *agg* virginal. **verginità** *sf* virginity.
vergogna [ver'goɲa] *sf* shame; (*disonore*) disgrace. **fare vergogna** shame. *inter* shame on you! **vergognarsi** *v* be *or* feel ashamed (of); (*non osare*) be too shy (to). **vergognoso** *agg* shameful; shy.
verificare [verifi'kare] *v* check. **verificarsi** *v* (*avvenire*) occur; (*avverarsi*) come true. **verifica** *sf* control; verification; (*dei conti*) audit. **verificabile** *agg* verifiable. **verificazione** *sf* verification, check; audit.
verità [veri'ta] *sf* truth; (*giustezza*) truthfulness. **veritiero** *agg* truthful.
verme ['vɛrme] *sm* worm; (*larva di insetto*) maggot.
vermiglio [ver'miʎo] *agg, sm* vermilion.
vermut ['vɛrmut] *sm invar* vermouth.

verniciare [verni'tʃare] v paint; (con vernice trasparente) varnish; (a smalto) enamel. **vernice** sf varnish, lacquer; (apparenza) veneer; (strato sottile) film. **verniciata** sf coat of paint. **verniciatura** sf painting; varnishing.

vero ['vero] agg true; real. sm truth. **a onor del vero** to tell the truth. **di vero cuore** from the bottom of one's heart. **vero e proprio** out and out.

verosimile [vero'simile] agg likely. **aver del verosimile** be likely.

verricello [verri'tʃello] sm winch.

verro ['vɛrro] sm boar.

verruca [ver'ruka] sf wart.

versare [ver'sare] v pour (out); (rovesciare) spill; (spargere) shed; (pagare) pay; (trovarsi) find oneself. **versamento** sm payment, deposit. **versante** sm side. **versato** agg paid (up); (pratico) skilled.

versatile [ver'satile] agg versatile. **versatilità** sf versatility.

versione [ver'sjone] sf version; (traduzione) translation.

verso[1] ['vɛrso] prep towards; (circa) about. **verso il basso** down(wards). **verso l'alto** up(wards).

verso[2] ['vɛrso] sm (metrica) verse; (suono particolare) sound; gesture; direction; (modo) means. **in verso antiorario** anticlockwise. **in verso orario** clockwise. **per un verso o per un altro** in one way or another.

vertebra ['vɛrtebra] sf vertebra (pl -brae). **vertebrato** agg, sm vertebrate.

vertenza [ver'tentsa] sf dispute; (dir) lawsuit.

verticale [verti'kale] agg, sf vertical.

vertice ['vɛrtitʃe] sm summit; (mat) vertex.

vertigini [ver'tidʒini] sf pl dizziness sing; (attacco) dizzy spell sing; (med) vertigo sing. **aver le vertigini** feel dizzy or giddy. **vertiginoso** agg dizzy.

vescica [ve'ʃika] sf bladder; (bolla cutanea) blister.

vescovo ['veskovo] sm bishop. **vescovado** sm (dignità) bishopric; (territorio) diocese; (palazzo) bishop's palace. **vescovile** agg episcopal.

vespa ['vɛspa] sf wasp. **vespaio** sm wasps' nest.

vestaglia [ves'taʎa] sf dressing-gown; (vestaglietta) housecoat.

veste ['vɛste] sf dress; (rel) vestment; (fig) capacity. **in veste di amico** as a friend. **in veste ufficiale** in an official capacity. **vestiario** sm wardrobe; (indumenti) clothes pl. **capo di vestiario** sm item of clothing.

vestibolo [ves'tibolo] sm vestibule, lobby.

vestigio [ves'tidʒo] sm trace.

vestire [ves'tire] v dress; (indossare) wear; (detto di abiti) fit. **vestirsi** v dress. **vestito** sm dress.

veterano [vete'rano], **-a** s, agg veteran.

veterinario [veteri'narjo] agg veterinary. sm veterinary surgeon, vet. **veterinaria** sf veterinary science.

veto ['vɛto] sm invar veto.

vetro ['vetro] sm glass; (di finestra) pane. **vetro smerigliato** frosted glass. **vetraio** sm glazier. **vetrata** sf (porta) glass door; (finestra) stained-glass window.

vetta ['vetta] sf top.

vettore [vet'tore] sm vector; (comm) carrier.

vettovaglie [vetto'vaʎe] sf pl provisions pl.

vettura [vet'tura] sf carriage; (auto) car. **biglietto di vettura** sm (comm) bill of lading.

vezzeggiare [veddzed'dʒare] v fondle.

vi [vi], **ve** pron (to) you; (riflessivo) yourselves; (reciproco) each other. avv (qui) here; (lì) there.

via[1] ['via] sf way; (strada) street; (sentiero) path. **in via di costruzione** under construction. **in via eccezionale** exceptionally. **per via aerea** by air. **per via di** (a causa di) because of. **via mare/terra** by sea/land.

via[2] ['via] avv away; (suvvia) come on. sm invar starting signal. **e così via** and so on. **va via!** go on! **via le mani!** hands off! **via via** gradually; (a mano a mano) as.

viabilità [viabili'ta] sf road conditions pl.

viadotto [via'dotto] sm viaduct.

viaggiare [viad'dʒare] v travel; (veicoli) run; (essere trasportato) be carried. **viaggiatore, -trice** sm, sf traveller; passenger. **piccione viaggiatore** sm carrier pigeon.

viaggio [vi'addʒo] sm journey, trip. **mettersi in viaggio** set out or off. **viaggio d'andata/di ritorno** outward/return journey. **viaggio d'andata e ritorno** round trip. **viaggio di nozze** honeymoon.

viale [vi'ale] sm avenue.

viandante [vian'dante] s(m+f) wayfarer.

viavai [via'vaj] *sm* coming and going.
vibrare [vib'rare] *v* vibrate; (*fig*) quiver; (*assestare*) hurl. **vibrare un colpo** deal a blow. **vibrazione** *sf* vibration; (*fremito*) quiver.
vicario [vi'karjo] *sm* vicar.
viceconsole [vitʃe'kɔnsole] *s(m+f)* vice-consul.
vicedirettore [vitʃediret'tore], **-trice** *sm*, *sf* assistant manager; (*scuola*) deputy head.
vicenda [vi'tʃɛnda] *sf* event; succession. **vicendevolmente** *avv* also **a vicenda** (*a turno*) in turns; (*scambievolmente*) each other, one another.
vicepresidente [vitʃeprezi'dɛnte], **-essa** *sm*, *sf* vice-president, vice-chairman.
viceversa [vitʃe'vɛrsa] *avv* vice versa; (*invece*) but.
vicinanza [vitʃi'nantsa] *sf* vicinity.
vicinato [vitʃi'nato] *sm* neighbourhood.
vicino [vi'tʃino], **-a** *agg* near; (*accanto*) next; (*confinante*) neighbouring; (*fig*) close. *avv* close (by); near (by); (*accanto a*) beside, by. **da vicino** at close quarters. *sm*, *sf* neighbour. **vicino di casa** next-door neighbour.
vicolo ['vikolo] *sm* alley.
video ['video] *sm invar* (television) screen.
vidimare [vidi'mare] *v* certify. **vidimazione** *sf* certification.
vietare [vje'tare] *v* prohibit; (*impedire*) prevent. **vietato** *agg* forbidden. **ingresso vietato** no admission. **sosta vietata** no parking.
vigente [vi'dʒɛnte] *agg* current; (*dir*) in force.
vigilare [vidʒi'lare] *v* watch (over); keep a watch (on). **vigilante** *agg* watchful. **vigilanza** *sf* vigilance; (*controllo*) supervision; (*urbana*) police.
vigile ['vidʒile] *agg* watchful. *sm* policeman. **vigile del fuoco** fireman.
vigilia [vi'dʒilja] *sf* eve; (*rel*) vigil. **vigilia di Natale/Capodanno** Christmas/New Year's Eve.
vigliacco [vi'ʎakko] *agg* cowardly. *sm*, *sf* coward. **vigliaccheria** *sf* cowardice; cowardly action.
vigna ['viɲa] *sf* vineyard.
vignetta [vi'ɲetta] *sf* sketch; (*umoristica*) cartoon.
vigore [vi'gore] *sm* force; (*forza vitale*) vigour. **entrare in vigore** (*dir*) come into force. **vigoria** *sf* energy.

vile ['vile] *agg* (*vigliacco*) cowardly; (*basso*) base, low. *s(m+f)* coward. **vilipendio** *sm* contempt.
villa ['villa] *sf* villa. **villa di campagna** country house.
villaggio [vil'laddʒo] *sm* village.
villano [vil'lano], **-a** *agg* rude; (*rozzo*) uncouth; offensive. *sm*, *sf* lout, boor. **villania** *sf* rudeness.
villeggiare [villed'dʒare] *v* spend a holiday. **villeggiatura** *sf* holidays *pl*.
viltà [vil'ta] *sf* cowardice; cowardly action.
viluppo [vi'luppo] *sm* tangle.
vimini ['vimini] *sm pl* wicker *sing*. **di vimini** wicker. **lavoro in vimini** *sm* wickerwork.
*****vincere** ['vintʃere] *v* win; (*battere*) beat; (*sopraffare*) overcome; (*sconfiggere*) defeat. **lasciarsi vincere (da)** yield (to). **vincita** *sf* win.
vincitore [vintʃi'tore], **-trice** *sm*, *sf* winner; (*di battaglia*) victor. *agg* winning, victorious.
vincolare [vinko'lare] *v* bind; (*comm*) tie up. **vincolo** *sm* tie.
vino ['vino] *sm* wine. **vino di mele** cider. **vinicolo** *agg* wine.
viola¹ [vi'ɔla] *sf* (*bot*) violet. *agg*, *sm invar* (*colore*) violet. **viola del pensiero** pansy. **violacciocca** *sf* stock; (*gialla*) wallflower. **violaceo** *agg* violet.
viola² [vi'ɔla] *sf* (*musica*) viola.
violare [vio'lare] *v* violate; (*una donna*) rape; (*domicilio*) break into. **violare l'ordine pubblico** cause a breach of the peace. **violazione** *sf* violation. **violazione carnale** rape. **violazione della pace** breach of the peace. **violazione di domicilio** house-breaking.
violentare [violen'tare] *v* force; (*una donna*) rape. **violentatore** *sm* rapist. **violento** *agg* violent. **violenza** *sf* violence.
violetta [vio'letta] *sf* violet. **violetto** *agg*, *sm invar* violet.
violino [vio'lino] *sm* violin. **violinista** *s(m+f)* violinist.
violoncello [violon'tʃɛllo] *sm* (violon)cello. **violoncellista** *s(m+f)* (violon)cellist.
viottolo [vi'ɔttolo] *sm* path.
vipera ['vipera] *sf* viper.
virale [vi'rale] *agg* viral.
virare [vi'rare] *v* (*alare*) haul (in); (*mutar*

direzione) veer, change course; (*aero*) turn.

virgola ['virgola] *sf* comma; (*mat*) point. **tra virgolette** in inverted commas.

virile [vi'rile] *agg* virile; masculine; (*fig*) manly. **virilità** *sf* virility.

virtù [vir'tu] *sf* virtue; faculty. **in virtù di** by virtue of, in accordance with. **virtuale** *agg* virtual.

virtuoso [virtu'ozo], **-a** *agg* virtuous. *sm*, *sf* virtuoso.

virulento [viru'lɛnto] *agg* virulent.

virus ['virus] *sm invar* virus.

viscere ['viʃere] *sm* internal organ. *sf pl* intestines *pl*; (*di animali*) entrails *pl*. **le viscere della terra** the bowels of the earth *pl*.

vischio ['viskjo] *sm* mistletoe; (*estratto*) bird-lime; (*fig*) snare. **viscido** *agg* slimy.

visconte [vis'konte] *sm* viscount.

viscoso [vis'kozo] *agg* viscous. **viscosa** *sf* viscose. **viscosità** *sf* viscosity.

visibile [vi'zibile] *agg* visible. **andare/mandare in visibilio** go/send into raptures. **visibilità** *sf* visibility.

visiera [vi'zjera] *sf* visor; (*berretto*) peak; (*scherma*) mask.

visione [vi'zjone] *sf* sight; (*apparizione*) vision; idea; (*cinema*) showing. **prendere in visione** inspect. **ricevere in visione** receive on approval. **visionario, -a** *sm, sf* visionary.

visita ['vizita] *sf* visit; (*persona*) visitor; (*esame*) examination. **visita domiciliare** domiciliary visit; (*perquisizione*) house search. **visitare** *v* visit; (*andare a trovare*) call on; (*med*) examine. **visitatore, -trice** *sm, sf* visitor.

visivo [vi'zivo] *agg* visual. **campo visivo** *sm* field of vision.

viso ['vizo] *sm* face. **a viso aperto** openly. **far buon viso a cattiva sorte** make the best of it. **fare il viso lungo** sulk.

visone [vi'zone] *sm* mink.

vispo ['vispo] *agg* lively; (*svelto*) brisk.

vista ['vista] *sf* sight; (*spettacolo*) view. **avere in vista** have in mind. **a vista** on sight. **a vista d'occhio** before one's very eyes. **conoscere di vista** know by sight. **perdere di vista** lose sight (of).

visto ['visto] *sm* visa. **visto di soggiorno** tourist visa.

vistoso [vis'tozo] *agg* showy; (*notevole*) considerable.

visuale [vizu'ale] *agg* visual. *sf* view; line of vision. **visualizzare** *v* visualize.

vita[1] ['vita] *sf* life; (*durata*) lifetime. **a vita** for life. **condanna a vita** *sf* life sentence. **essere in fin di vita** be at death's door. **guadagnarsi la vita** earn one's living.

vita[2] ['vita] *sf* (*corpo*) waist.

vitale [vi'tale] *agg* vital. **vitalità** *sf* vitality.

vitalizio [vita'litsjo] *agg* life(long). *sm* (*rendita*) annuity.

vitamina [vita'mina] *sf* vitamin.

vite[1] ['vite] *sf* (*bot*) vine. **viticcio** *sm* tendril. **viticoltura** *sf* viticulture.

vite[2] ['vite] *sf* (*mec*) screw. **cadere in vite** (*aero*) go into a spin.

vitello [vi'tɛllo] *sm* calf; (*gastr*) veal. **vitellone** *sm* bullock; (*fig*) loafer.

vitreo ['vitreo] *agg* glassy, vitreous.

vittima ['vittima] *sf* victim; (*chi subisce danni*) casualty. **essere vittima di un incidente** be involved in an accident. **fare la vittima** (*fig*) be a martyr.

vitto ['vitto] *sm* food; (*nutrimento giornaliero*) board. **vitto e alloggio** board and lodging.

vittoria [vit'tɔrja] *sf* victory; (*sport*) win. **vittorioso** *agg* victorious.

vituperare [vitupe'rare] *v* berate. **vituperio** *sm* insult; (*causa*) disgrace.

viva ['viva] *inter* hurrah! **viva ... !** long live ... !

vivacchiare [vivak'kjare] *v* manage.

vivace [vi'vatʒe] *agg* lively; (*intenso*) bright. **vivacità** *sf* liveliness; brightness.

vivaio [vi'vajo] *sm* nursery; (*pesci*) fishpond.

vivanda [vi'vanda] *sf* food; (*piatto*) dish.

***vivere** ['vivere] *v* live; (*trascorrere*) spend. **avere di che vivere** have enough to live on. **lasciar vivere** leave in peace. **vivere alla giornata** live from hand to mouth. *sm* life; (*modo di vivere*) living.

viveri ['viveri] *sm pl* provisions *pl*.

vivido ['vivido] *agg* vivid.

vivisezione [vivise'tsjone] *sf* vivisection.

vivo ['vivo] *agg* living; (*vivace*) lively; (*intenso*) bright. **a viva forza** by force. **farsi vivo** show up; (*mettersi in contatto*) get in touch. *sm* living person; (*fig*) heart. **ferire nel vivo** wound to the quick.

viziare [vi'tsjare] *v* spoil; (*dir*) vitiate.

vizio ['vitsjo] *sm* vice; bad habit; defect; (*peccato*) sin. **vizio parziale (di mente)** diminished responsibility. **vizioso** *agg* depraved.

vizzo ['vittso] *agg* withered.
vocabolo [vo'kabolo] *sm* word. **vocabolario** *sm* vocabulary; dictionary.
vocale [vo'kale] *agg* vocal. *sf* vowel.
vocazione [voka'tsjone] *sf* vocation; (*inclinazione naturale*) leaning. **vocazionale** *agg* vocational.
voce ['votʃe] *sf* voice; expression; (*elemento di elenco*) heading; opinion. **a bassa voce** softly. **ad alta voce** out loud. **aver voce in capitolo** have a say in the matter. **corre voce** rumour has it. **dire a (viva) voce** tell personally. **sotto voce** in an undertone.
vociare [vo'tʃare] *v* bawl.
vociferare [votʃife'rare] *v* talk at the top of one's voice; (*fig*) rumour.
vodka ['vɔdka] *sf* vodka.
vogare [vo'gare] *v* row **vogatore** *sm* oarsman.
voglia ['voʎa] *sf* wish; (*disposizione*) will; (*capriccio*) fancy; (*med*) birthmark. **avere una gran voglia di** be dying to. **aver voglia di (fare)** feel like (doing), want to (do). **di buona voglia** willingly. **di cattiva** *or* **mala voglia** unwillingly.
voi ['voi] *pron* you.
volano [vo'lano] *sm* (*mec*) flywheel; (*sport*) shuttlecock.
volare [vo'lare] *v* fly. **volar giù** hurtle down. **volata** *sf* (*sport*) sprint; (*corsa rapida*) dash. **di volata** in a rush. **fare una volata** make a dash.
volatile [vo'latile] *agg* volatile.
volentieri [volen'tjɛri] *avv* willingly; with pleasure. **fare volentieri** like doing.
***volere** [vo'lere] *v* want; (*desiderare*) wish; (*comando*) will; (*intendere*) mean; (*cortesia*) like. **l'hai voluto tu!** you've asked for it! **neanche a volere** not even if you try. **non vuol dire** (*non ha importanza*) it doesn't matter. **se Dio vuole** God willing. **senza volere** without meaning to. **volerci** *v* take. **voler bene a** (*aver affetto*) be fond of; (*amare*) love. **voler dire** mean.
volgare [vol'gare] *agg* vulgar; common. *sm* (*lingua*) vernacular. **volgarità** *sf* vulgarity. **volgarizzare** *v* popularize.
***volgere** ['vɔldʒere] *v* turn. **col volgere degli anni** with the passing of time. **volgere alla fina** near the end. **volgere la parola a** address.
volgo ['volgo] *sm* common people *pl*.

volo ['volo] *sm* flight. **cogliere al volo** seize. **volo a vela** gliding. **volo in picchiata** nose-dive.
volontà [volon'ta] *sf* will. **di mia spontanea** *or* **propria volontà** of my own free will.
volontario [volon'tarjo], -a voluntary. *sm*, *sf* volunteer. **volontario del sangue** blood donor. **volontariato** *sm* voluntary service.
volonteroso [volonte'rozo] *agg* willing.
volpe ['volpe] *sf* fox; (*femmina*) vixen.
volta[1] ['vɔlta] *sf* time; turn. **alla volta** at a time. **alla volta di** towards. **a volte** sometimes. **spesse volte** often. **una buona volta** once and for all. **una volta** once; (*nelle fiabe*) once upon a time.
volta[2] ['vɔlta] *sf* (*arch*) vault.
voltare [vol'tare] *v* turn. **voltagabbana** *s(m+f)* *invar* fickle person.
volto ['volto] *sm* face.
volubile [vo'lubile] *agg* fickle.
volume [vo'lume] *sm* volume; (*mole*) size. **voluminoso** *agg* voluminous; (*ingombrante*) bulky.
voluta [vo'luta] *sf* scroll.
voluttuoso [voluttu'ozo] *agg* voluptuous. **voluttà** *sf* voluptuousness.
vomitare [vomi'tare] *v* vomit, be sick. **aver voglia di vomitare** feel sick. **vomito** *sm* (*atto*) vomiting; (*materia*) vomit. **mi viene il vomito** I feel sick.
vongola ['vongola] *sf* clam.
vorace [vo'ratʃe] *agg* greedy.
voragine [vo'radʒine] *sf* chasm, gulf.
vortice ['vɔrtitʃe] *sm* vortex; (*gorgo*) whirlpool; (*fig*) whirl.
vostro ['vɔstro] *agg* your. *pron* yours.
votare [vo'tare] *v* vote; (*approvare*) pass; put to the vote; (*dedicare*) devote. **votazione** *sf* voting; (*scrutinio*) ballot; (*scuola*) marks *pl*. **voto** *sm* vote; (*promessa*) vow; (*scuola*) mark. **a pieni voti** with full marks. **pronunciare i voti** take one's vows.
vulcano [vul'kano] *sm* volcano. **vulcanico** *agg* volcanic; (*fig*) brilliant.
vulnerabile [vulne'rabile] *agg* vulnerable. **vulnerabilità** *sf* vulnerability.
vuotare [vwo'tare] *v* empty. **vuotare il sacco** (*fig*) spill the beans.
vuoto ['vwɔto] *agg* empty. *sm* void; (*fis*) vacuum; (*fig*) emptiness, gap. **andare a vuoto** fail. **a vuoto** in vain. **girare a vuoto** (*mec*) idle.

X

xenofobo [kse'nɔfobo], **-a** *agg* xenophobic. *sm, sf* xenophobe. **xenofobia** *sf* xenophobia.
xerocopiare [kseroko'pjare] *v* Xerox ®
xilofono [ksi'lɔfono] *sm* xylophone.

Y

yoga ['jɔga] *sm invar* yoga.
yoghurt ['jɔgurt] *sm invar* yoghurt.

Z

zacchera ['dzakkera] *sf* splash (of mud).
zaffata [dzaf'fata] *sf* whiff; (*getto di liquido*) splash.
zafferano [dzaffe'rano] *sm* saffron.
zaffiro [dzaf'firo] *sm* sapphire.
zaino ['dzajno] *sm* kit-bag; (*alpinisti*) rucksack.
zampa ['dzampa] *sf* leg; (*con unghie*) paw; (*maiale*) trotter. **a quattro zampe** on all fours. **zampe di gallina** *sf pl* (*rughe*) crow's-feet *pl*; (*scrittura*) scrawl *sing*. **zampare** *v* paw (the ground). **aver lo zampino in** have a hand in. **mettere lo zampino** interfere.
zampillare [dzampil'lare] *v* spurt, gush. **zampillo** *sm* spurt.
zampogna [dzam'poɲa] *sf* bagpipes *pl*.
zangola ['dzangola] *sf* churn. **zangolare** *v* churn.
zanna ['dzanna] *sf* fang; (*di elefante, cinghiale*) tusk.
zanzara [dzan'dzara] *sf* mosquito. **zanzariera** *sf* mosquito-net.
zappare [dzap'pare] *v* hoe. **zappa** *sf* hoe.
zattera ['dzattera] *sf* raft.
zazzera ['dzaddzera] *sf* mop of hair.
zebra ['dzɛbra] *sf* zebra. **zebre** *sf pl* (*passaggio*) zebra crossing *sing*. **zebrato** *agg* striped.
zecca¹ ['dzekka] *sf* mint. **nuovo di zecca** brand-new. **zecchino** *sm* gold coin.
zecca² ['dzekka] *sf* (*zool*) tick.
zelo ['dzelo] *sm* zeal. **zelante** *agg* keen, zealous.
zenzero ['dzendzero] *sm* ginger.
zeppa ['dzeppa] *sf* wedge. **zeppare** *v*

wedge.
zeppo ['dzeppo] *agg* (**pieno**) **zeppo** packed, cram-full.
zerbino [dzer'bino] *sm* (door-)mat.
zero ['dzɛro] *sm* nought; (*fig, mat*) zero; (*sport*) nil; (*tennis*) love.
zia ['dzia] *sf* aunt.
zibellino [dzibel'lino] *sm* sable.
zibetto [dzi'betto] *sm* civet.
zigzag [dzig'dzag] *sm* zigzag. **andare a zigzag** zigzag.
zimbello [dzim'bello] *sm* decoy; (*oggetto di scherno*) laughing-stock. **zimbellare** *v* lure.
zinco ['dzinko] *sm* zinc.
zingaro ['dzingaro], **-a** *s, agg* gipsy.
zio ['dzio] *sm* uncle.
zirlare [dzir'lare] *v* chirp.
zitella [dzi'tɛlla] *sf* spinster. **vecchia zitella** (*spreg*) old maid.
zittire [dzit'tire] *v* (*far tacere*) hush; (*disapprovazione*) hiss.
zitto ['dzitto] *agg* quiet. **star zitto** keep quiet; (*fam*) shut up.
zoccolo ['dzɔkkolo] *sm* clog; (*zool*) hoof; base; (*parete*) skirting-board.
zodiaco [dzo'diako] *sm* zodiac.
zolfo ['dzolfo] *sm* sulphur.
zolla ['dzolla] *sf* clod.
zona ['dzɔna] *sf* zone; area. **zona pedonale** pedestrian precinct. **zona verde** (*periferica*) green belt.
zonzo ['dzondzo] *avv* **andare a zonzo** wander about.
zoo [dzo] *sm invar* zoo.
zoologia [dzoolo'dʒia] *sf* zoology. **zoologico** *agg* zoological. **zoologo, -a** *sm, sf* zoologist.
zoppicare [dzoppi'kare] *v* limp; (*tavolo, ecc.*) be rickety; (*fig*) be shaky. **zoppo** *agg* lame; rickety; shaky.
zotico ['dzɔtiko], **-a** *agg* boorish. *sm, sf* boor.
zucca ['dzukka] *sf* pumpkin; (*fam: testa*) nut. **zuccone** *sm* (*fam*) blockhead.
zucchero ['dzukkero] *sm* sugar. **zucchero a velo** icing sugar. **zucchero semolato** castor sugar. **zuccherare** *v* sweeten.
zucchino [dzuk'kino], **-a** *sm, sf* courgette.
zuffa ['dzuffa] *sf* scuffle, brawl.
zuppa ['dzuppa] *sf* soup. **zuppa inglese** trifle. **zuppiera** *sf* tureen. **zuppo** *agg* drenched.

Other Italian Interest Titles from Hippocrene...

ITALIAN HANDY DICTIONARY
120 pp • 5 x 7 ¾ • 0-7818-0011-0 • USA • $8.95 • (196)

SICILIAN-ENGLISH/ENGLISH-SICILIAN
CONCISE DICTIONARY
210 pp • 4 x 6 • 0-7818-0457-4 • W • $11.95pb • (422)

MASTERING ITALIAN
360 pp • 5 ½ x 8 ½ • 0-87052-057-1 • USA • $11.95pb • (517)
2 Cassettes: 0-87052-066-0 • USA • $12.95 • (521)

MASTERING ADVANCED ITALIAN
278 pp • 5 ½ x 8 ½ • 0-7818-0333-0 • W • $14.95pb • (160)
2 Cassettes: 0-7818-0334-9 • W • $12.95 • (161)

BEGINNER'S SICILIAN
158 pp • 5 ½ x 8 ½ • 0-7818-0640-2 • W • $11.95pb • (716)

TREASURY OF ITALIAN LOVE
128 pp • 5 x 7 • 0-7818-0352-7 • W • $11.95hc • (587)
Audio Cassettes: 0-7818-0366-7 •$12.95 • (581)

DICTIONARY OF 1,000 ITALIAN PROVERBS
131 pp • 5 ½ x 8 ½ • 0-7818-0458-2 • W • $11.95pb • (370)

A TREASURY OF ITALIAN CUISINE
Recipes, Sayings and Proverbs in Italian and English
Joseph F. Privitera, Illustrated by Sharon Privitera
Don Peppino (a.k.a Joseph) Privitera outlines the basics of hearty and delicious
Italian cooking in this appealing bilingual cookbook. Among the 60 recipes in
Italian and English are such staples as *Cozze alla Parmigiana* (Baked Mussels),
Minestrone, Salsa di Pomodoro (Basic Tomato Sauce), *Ossobuco al Marsala* (Veal
Shanks in Marsala), and *Cannoli Siciliani* (Sicilian Cannoli), all adapted for the
modern cook and the North American kitchen. Chapters include: Antipasti,
Soups, Pasta and Sauces, Meat, Fish and Fowl, Side Dishes, Salads, and Fruits
and Desserts. Line drawings, proverbs and bits of folk wisdom add to the
volume's charm. This book is the perfect gift for students of the Italian culinary
tradition, culture and language.
146 pp • 5 x 7 • line drawings • 0-7818-0740-9 • $11.95hc • W • (149)

THE HIPPOCRENE MASTERING SERIES

These imaginative courses, designed for both individual and classroom use, assume no previous knowledge of the language. The unique combination of practical exercises and step-by-step grammar emphasizes a functional approach to new scripts and their vocabularies. Everyday situations and local customs are explored variously through dialogues, newspaper extracts, drawings and photos. Cassettes are available for each language.

MASTERING FRENCH
288 pp • 5 ½ x 8 ½ • 0-87052-055-5 • $14.95pb • (511)
2 Cassettes: • 0-87052-060-1 USA • $12.95 • (512)

MASTERING ADVANCED FRENCH
348 pp • 5 ½ x 8 ½ • 0-7818-0312-8 • W • $14.95pb • (41)
2 Cassettes: • 0-7818-0313-6 • W • $12.95 • (54)

MASTERING GERMAN
340 pp • 5 ½ x 8 ½ • 0-87052-056-3 • $11.95pb • (514)
2 Cassettes: • 0-87052-061-X USA • $12.95 • (515)

MASTERING JAPANESE
368 pp • 5 ½ x 8 ½ • 0-87052-923-4 • USA • $14.95pb • (523)
2 Cassettes: • 0-87052-983-8 • USA • $12.95 • (524)

MASTERING NORWEGIAN
183 pp • 5 ½ x 8 ½ • 0-7818-0320-9 • W • $14.95pb • (472)

MASTERING POLISH
288 pp • 5 ½ x 8 ½ • 0-7818-0015-3 • W • $14.95pb • (381)
2 Cassettes: • 0-7818-0016-1 • W • $12.95 • (389)

MASTERING RUSSIAN
278 pp • 5 ½ x 8 ½ • 0-7818-0270-9 • W • $14.95pb • (11)
2 Cassettes: • 0-7818-0271-7 • W • $12.95 • (13)

MASTERING SPANISH
338 pp • 5 ½ x 8 ½ • 0-87052-059-8 USA • $11.95 • (527)
2 Cassettes: • 0-87052-067-9 USA • $12.95 • (528)

MASTERING ADVANCED SPANISH
326 pp • 5 ½ x 8 ½ • 0-7818-0081-1 • W • $14.95pb • (413)
2 Cassettes: • 0-7818-0089-7 • W • $12.95 • (426)

HIPPOCRENE'S BEGINNER'S SERIES

Do you know what it takes to make a phone call in Russia? Or how to get through customs in Japan? This new language instruction series shows how to handle oneself in typical situations by introducing the business person or traveler not only to the vocabulary, grammar, and phrases of a new language, but also the history, customs, and daily practices of a foreign country.

The Beginner's Series consists of basic language instruction, which also includes vocabulary, grammar, and common phrases and review questions, along with cultural insights, interesting historical background, the country's basic facts and hints about everyday living-driving, shopping, eating out, and more.

BEGINNER'S ASSYRIAN
185 pp • 5 x 9 • 0-7818-0677-1 • $11.95pb • (763)

BEGINNER'S CHINESE
150 pp • 5 ½ x 8 • 0-7818-0566-x • $14.95pb • (690)

BEGINNER'S BULGARIAN
207 pp • 5 ½ x 8 ½ • 0-7818-0300-4 • $9.95pb • (76)

BEGINNER'S CZECH
200 pp • 5 ½ x 8 ½ • 0-7818-0231-8 • $9.95pb • (74)

BEGINNER'S ESPERANTO
400 pp • 5 ½ x 8 ½ • 0-7818-0230-x • $14.95pb • (51)

BEGINNER'S HUNGARIAN
200 pp • 5 ½ x 7 • 0-7818-0209-1 • $7.95pb • (68)

BEGINNER'S JAPANESE
200 pp • 5 ½ x 8 ½ • 0-7818-0234-2 • $11.95pb • (53)

BEGINNER'S LITHUANIAN
230 pp • 6 x 9 • 0-7818-0678-X • $19.95pb • (764)

BEGINNER'S MAORI
121 pp • 5 ½ x 8 ½ • 0-7818-0605-4 • $8.95pb • (703)

BEGINNER'S PERSIAN
150 pp • 5 ½ x 8 • 0-7818-0567-8 • $14.95pb • (696)

BEGINNER'S POLISH
200 pp • 5 ½ x 8 ½ • 0-7818-0299-7 • $9.95pb • (82)

BEGINNER'S ROMANIAN
200 pp • 5 ½ x 81/2 • 0-7818-0208-3 • $7.95pb • (79)

BEGINNER'S RUSSIAN
200 pp • 5 ½ x 8 ½ • 0-7818-0232-6 • $9.95pb • (61)

BEGINNER'S SWAHILI
200 pp • 5 ½ x 8 ½ • 0-7818-0335-7 • $9.95pb • (52)

BEGINNER'S UKRAINIAN
130 pp • 5 ½ x 8 ½ • 0-7818-0443-4 • $11.95pb • (88)

BEGINNER'S VIETNAMESE
517 pp • 7 x 10 • 30 lessons • 0-7818-0411-6 • $19.95pb • (253)

BEGINNER'S WELSH
210 pp • 5 ½ x 8 ½ • 0-7818-0589-9 • $9.95pb • (712)

All prices are subject to change without prior notice. To order Hippocrene Books, contact your local bookstore, call (718) 454-2366, or write to: Hippocrene Books, 171 Madison Ave. New York, NY 10016. Please enclose check or money order adding $5.00 shipping (UPS) for the first book and $.50 for each additional title.